Lecture Notes in Computer Science 9936

Commenced Publication in 1973
Founding and Former Series Editors:
Gerhard Goos, Juris Hartmanis, and Jan van Leeuwen

Services Science

Subline of Lectures Notes in Computer Science

Subline Editors-in-Chief

Subline Editorial Board

More information about this series at http://www.springer.com/series/7408

Quan Z. Sheng · Eleni Stroulia
Samir Tata · Sami Bhiri (Eds.)

Service-Oriented Computing

14th International Conference, ICSOC 2016
Banff, AB, Canada, October 10–13, 2016
Proceedings

 Springer

Editors
Quan Z. Sheng
The University of Adelaide
Adelaide, SA
Australia

Eleni Stroulia
Department of Computing Science
University of Alberta
Edmonton, AB
Canada

Samir Tata
Telecom SudParis
University of Paris-Saclay
Evry Cedex
France

Sami Bhiri
ISIMM
University of Monastir
Monastir
Tunisia

ISSN 0302-9743 ISSN 1611-3349 (electronic)
Lecture Notes in Computer Science
ISBN 978-3-319-46294-3 ISBN 978-3-319-46295-0 (eBook)
DOI 10.1007/978-3-319-46295-0

Library of Congress Control Number: 2016950880

LNCS Sublibrary: SL2 – Programming and Software Engineering

Printed on acid-free paper

This Springer imprint is published by Springer Nature
The registered company is Springer International Publishing AG Switzerland

Preface

The service-oriented computing (SOC) paradigm has evolved over the years to be a comprehensive, interdisciplinary methodology for modern software development. Indeed, it has gone beyond just a "software componentization" technology to embody and express the software manifestation of a trend that transforms our society from an industrial, production-centric economy into a digital, service-centric economy. Since the first edition of the International Conference on Service-Oriented Computing (ICSOC) in 2003, the conference has grown to become the top international forum for academics, industry researchers, developers, and practitioners to report and share latest research results and innovation in service-oriented computing.

This volume contains the conference proceedings of ICSOC 2016, the 14th International Conference on Service-Oriented Computing, which took place at Banff, Alberta, Canada, October 10–13, 2016. ICSOC 2016 built upon the tradition of 13 previous successful editions that were held in Goa, India (2015), Paris, France (2014), Berlin, Germany (2013), Shanghai, China (2012), Paphos, Cyprus (2011), San Francisco, USA (2010), Stockholm, Sweden (2009), Sydney, Australia (2008), Vienna, Austria (2007), Chicago, USA (2006), Amsterdam, The Netherlands (2005), New York, USA (2004), and Trento, Italy (2003).

As with previous editions, this year's call for papers generated substantial interest from the community. A total of 137 full research and industry submissions were received from 23 countries across six continents. Each paper submission was carefully reviewed by at least three members of the Program Committee (PC), followed by a rebuttal from its authors, and then discussions moderated by a senior PC member who made a recommendation in the form of a meta-review. The PC consisted of 180 world-class experts in service-oriented computing and related areas (158 PC members and 22 senior PC members) from 28 different countries. The ICSOC 2016 program featured 30 full papers (acceptance rate of 21 %) and 18 short papers in the research track. It also featured eight papers in the industry track. The selected papers covered a wide variety of important topics in the area of service-oriented computing, including foundational issues on service discovery and service-systems design, business process modelling and management, economics of service-systems engineering, as well as services on the cloud, social networks, the Internet of Things (IoT), and data analytics. The conference program was complemented by three outstanding keynotes given by Elisa Bertino (Purdue University, USA), Valérie Issarny (Inria, France), and Richard Hull (IBM Research, USA), demonstrations, a PhD symposium, a panel discussion, as well as a collection of seven workshops.

We would like to express our gratitude to all individuals, institutions, and sponsors that supported ICSOC 2016. This high-quality program would not have been possible without the expertise and dedication of our PC members and in particular our senior PC members. We are grateful for the guidance of the general chairs (Barbara Pernici and Munindar P. Singh), the untiring efforts of external reviewers, the workshop chairs

(Khalil Drira, Hongbing Wang, and Qi Yu), the PhD symposium chairs (François Charoy, Yan Wang, and Yuhong Yan), the demonstration chairs (Jan Mendling, Mohamed Mohamed, and Zhongjie Wang), the panel chairs (Boualem Benatallah, Heiko Ludwig, and Jianwu Su), the publicity chairs (Naouel Moha, Mohamed Sellami, Lucinéia Heloisa Thom, and Lina Yao), the publication chair (Sami Bhiri), the finance chair (Bernd J. Krämer), the Web chairs (Nguyen Khoi Tran and Wei Emma Zhang), and the local organization chair (Ying Zou). We also would like to acknowledge the support of the members of the conference Steering Committee. All of them helped make ICSOC 2016 a success. Finally, we would like to thank all researchers, practitioners, and students who contributed with their work and participation in the conference. We hope that you find the papers in the proceedings interesting and stimulating.

October 2016

Quan Z. Sheng
Eleni Stroulia
Samir Tata

Organization

General Chairs

Barbara Pernici — Polytechnic University of Milan, Italy
Munindar P. Singh — North Carolina State University, USA

Program Chairs

Quan Z. Sheng — University of Adelaide, Australia
Eleni Stroulia — University of Alberta, Canada
Samir Tata — Institute of Mines-Telecom, France and
IBM Research-Almaden, USA

Steering Committee

Boualem Benatallah — University of New South Wales, Australia
Fabio Casati — University of Trento, Italy
Bernd J. Krämer — University of Hagen, Germany
Winfried Lamersdorf — University of Hamburg, Germany
Heiko Ludwig — IBM Research-Almaden, USA
Mike Papazoglou — Tilburg University, The Netherlands
Jian Yang — Macquarie University, Australia
Liang Zhang — Fudan University, China

Publication Chair

Sami Bhiri — University of Monastir, Tunisia

Workshop Chairs

Khalil Drira — University of Toulouse, France
Hongbing Wang — Southeast University, China
Qi Yu — Rochester Institute of Technology, USA

Panel Chairs

Boualem Benatallah — University of New South Wales, Australia
Heiko Ludwig — IBM Research-Almaden, USA
Jianwen Su — UC Santa Barbara, USA

Finance Chair

Bernd J. Krämer   University of Hagen, Germany

Demonstration Track Chairs

Jan Mendling   Vienna University of Economics and Business, Austria
Mohamed Mohamed   IBM Research-Almaden, USA
Zhongjie Wang   Harbin Institute of Technology, China

PhD Symposium Chairs

Yan Wang   Macquarie University, Australia
Yuhong Yan   Concordia University, Canada
François Charoy   University of Lorraine, France

Publicity Chairs

Naouel Moha   University of Québec in Montréal, Canada
Mohamed Sellami   ISEP, France
Lucinéia Heloisa Thom Federal University of Rio Grande do Sul, Brazil
Lina Yao   University of New South Wales, Australia

Local Organization Chair

Ying Zou   Queen's University, Canada

Web Chairs

Nguyen Khoi Tran   University of Adelaide, Australia
Wei Emma Zhang   University of Adelaide, Australia

Senior Program Committee

Boualem Benatallah   University of New South Wales, Australia
Athman Bouguettaya   RMIT University, Australia
Fabio Casati   University of Trento, Italy
Flavio De Paoli   University of Milano-Bicocca, Italy
Marlon Dumas   University of Tartu, Estonia
Schahram Dustdar   Technical University of Vienna, Austria
Xavier Franch   Polytechnic University of Catalonia, Spain
Aditya Ghose   University of Wollongong, Australia
Mohand-Said Hacid   University of Lyon, France
Grace Lewis   Carnegie Mellon Software Engineering Institute, USA
Heiko Ludwig   IBM Research - Almaden, USA
Michael Maximilien   IBM Cloud Labs, USA

Cesare Pautasso	University of Lugano, Switzerland
Barbara Pernici	Polytechnic University of Milan, Italy
Gustavo Rossi	National University of La Plata, Argentina
Michael Sheng	Adelaide University, Australia
Jianwen Su	University of California at Santa Barbara, USA
Stefan Tai	Technical University of Berlin, Germany
Zahir Tari	RMIT University, Australia
Mathias Weske	HPI/University of Potsdam, Germany
Jian Yang	Macquarie University, Australia
Liang Zhang	Fudan University, China

Program Committee

Rama Akkiraju	IBM, USA
Vasilios Andrikopoulos	University of Stuttgart, Germany
Alvaro Arenas	Instituto de Empresa Business School, Spain
Ebrahim Bagheri	Athabasca University, Canada
Luciano Baresi	Polytechnic University of Milan, Italy
Alistair Barros	Queensland University of Technology, Australia
N. Md. Jubair Basha	Muffakham Jah College of Engineering and Technology, India
Nejib Ben Hadj-Alouane	National Engineering School of Tunis (ENIT), Tunisia
Moez Ben Haj Hmida	National Engineering School of Tunis (ENIT), Tunisia
Salima Benbernou	University of Paris Descartes, France
Reda Bendraou	University of Pierre and Marie Curie, France
Djamal Benslimane	University of Lyon, France
Sami Bhiri	Télécom SudParis, France
Domenico Bianculli	University of Luxembourg, Luxembourg
Frederique Biennier	INSA of Lyon, France
Walter Binder	University of Lugano, Switzerland
M. Brian Blake	University of Miami, USA
Omar Boucelma	University of Aix-Marseille, France
Christoph Bussler	Oracle Corporation, USA
Cristina Cabanillas	Vienna University of Economics and Business, Austria
Manuel Carro	IMDEA Software Institute and Technical University of Madrid, Spain
Wing-Kwong Chan	City University of Hong Kong, Hong Kong, SAR China
François Charoy	University of Lorraine, France
Faouzi Ben Charrada	University of Tunis El Manar, Tunisia
Sanjay Chaudhary	Ahmedabad University, India
Liang Chen	RMIT University, Australia
Shiping Chen	CSIRO ICT, Australia
Lawrence Chung	University of Texas at Dallas, USA
Edward Curry	Insight Centre, Ireland
Hoa Khanh Dam	University of Wollongong, Australia

Florian Daniel	University of Trento, Italy
Bruno Defude	Télécom Sud Paris, France
Shuiguang Deng	Zhejiang University, China
Nirmit Desai	IBM T.J. Watson Research Center, USA
Hai Dong	RMIT University, Australia
Khalil Drira	LAAS-CNRS, France
Yucong Duan	Hainan University, China
Joyce El Haddad	University of Paris Dauphine, France
Abdelkarim Erradi	Qatar University, Qatar
Rik Eshuis	Eindhoven University of Technology, The Netherlands
Onyeka Ezenwoye	Georgia Regents University, USA
Noura Faci	University of Lyon 1, CNRS, France
Marcelo Fantinato	University of Sao Paulo, Brazil
Marie-Christine Fauvet	University of Joseph Fourier, France
Joao E. Ferreira	University of Sao Paulo, Brazil
Marios-Eleftherios Fokaefs	York University, Canada
Xiang Fu	Hofstra University, USA
Walid Gaaloul	Télécom SudParis, France
N.D. Gangadhar	MS Ramaiah University of Applied Sciences, India
G.R. Gangadharan	IDRBT, India
Paolo Giorgini	University of Trento, Italy
Claude Godart	University of Lorraine, France
Mohamed Graiet	University of Monastir, Tunisia
Sven Graupner	Hewlett-Packard, USA
Daniela Grigori	University of Paris Dauphine, France
Georg Grossmann	University of South Australia, Australia
Armin Haller	Australian National University, Australia
Jun Han	Swinburne University of Technology, Australia
Peng Han	Chongqing Academy of Science and Technology, China
Chihab Hanachi	IRIT Laboratory - Toulouse University, France
Qiang He	Swinburne University of Technology, Australia
Bernhard Holtkamp	Fraunhofer ISST, Germany
Richard Hull	IBM Research, USA
Fuyuki Ishikawa	National Institute of Informatics, Japan
Hai Jin	Huazhong University of Science and Technology, China
Ejub Kajan	State University of Novi Pazar, Serbia
Dimka Karastoyanova	University of Stuttgart, Germany
Raman Kazhamiakin	Fondazione Bruno Kessler, Italy
Hamamache Kheddouci	University of Lyon, France
Kais Klai	University of Paris 13, France
Ryan Ko	University of Waikato, New Zealand
Gerald Kotonya	Lancaster University, UK
Peep Kungas	University of Tartu, Estonia
Philippe Lalanda	Joseph Fourier University, France

Philipp Leitner	University of Zurich, Switzerland
Henrik Leopold	VU University Amsterdam, The Netherlands
Huma Mehadisa Lepakshi	Infosys, India
Frank Leymann	University of Stuttgart, Germany
Xitong Li	HEC Paris, France
Ying Li	Zhejiang University, China
Xuanzhe Liu	Peking University, China
Xumin Liu	Rochester Institute of Technology, USA
Alessio Lomuscio	Imperial College London, UK
Jiangang Ma	Victoria University, Australia
Zakaria Maamar	Zayed University, United Arab Emirates
Javam Machado	UFC, Brazil
Zaki Malik	Wayne State University, USA
Maude Manouvrier	University of Paris Dauphine, France
Jordi Marco	Polytechnic University of Catalonia, Spain
Patrick Martin	Queen's University, Canada
Massimo Mecella	Sapienza University of Rome, Italy
Brahim Medjahed	University of Michigan - Dearborn, USA
Lars Moench	University of Hagen, Germany
Mohamed Mohamed	IBM Almaden Research Center, USA
Hamid Reza Motahari-Nezhad	IBM Research, USA
Michael Mrissa	University of Lyon, France
Nanjangud C. Narendra	Cognizant Technology Solutions, India
Surya Nepal	Commonwealth Scientific and Industrial Research Organisation, Australia
Anne Ngu	Texas State University, USA
Talal H. Noor	Taibah University, Saudi Arabia
Alex Norta	Tallinn University of Technology, Estonia
Srinivas Padmanabhuni	Infosys Labs, India
Helen Paik	University of New South Wales, Australia
Olivier Perrin	University of Lorraine, France
Marco Pistore	Fondazione Bruno Kessler, Italy
Pierluigi Plebani	Polytechnic University of Milan, Italy
Pascal Poizat	LIP6/Paris Ouest University, France
Artem Polyvyanyy	Queensland University of Technology, Australia
Karthikeyan Ponnalagu	IBM Research, India
Mu Qiao	IBM Almaden Research Center, USA
Xiaoqiang Qiao	Huawei Technologies, China
Lakshmish Ramaswamy	University of Georgia, USA
Manfred Reichert	Ulm University, Germany
Wolfgang Reisig	Humboldt University of Berlin, Germany
Stefanie Rinderle-Ma	University of Vienna, Austria
Colette Roland	Paris 1 University, France
Antonio Ruiz-Cortés	University of Seville, Spain
Sherif Sakr	University of New South Wales, Australia

Demonstration Program Committee

Florian Daniel	University of Trento, Italy
Zhiyong Feng	Tianjin University, China
Marios Fokaefs	York University, Canada
Adnene Guabtni	NICTA, Australia
Armin Haller	CSIRO, Australia
Raman Kazhamiakin	Fondazione Bruno Kessler, Trento, Italy
Philippe Lalanda	Joseph Fourier University, France
Philipp Leitner	University of Zurich, Switzerland
Xumin Liu	Rochester Institute of Technology, USA
Helen Paik	University of New South Wales, Australia
Pierluigi Plebani	Polytechnic University of Milan, Italy
Mohammad Sadoghi	IBM Research, USA
Mark Shtern	York University, Canada
Bradley Simmons	York University, Canada
Mike Smit	Dalhousie University, Canada
Wei Tan	IBM Research, USA
Jianwei Yin	Zhejiang University
Uwe Zdun	University of Vienna, Austria

External Reviewers

Husain Aljafer	Wayne State University, USA
Mohammad Amiri	UC Santa Barbara, USA
José Antonio Parejo	University of Seville, Spain
Nour Assy	Eindhoven University of Technology, The Netherlands
Farah Bellaaj	University of Sfax, Tunisia
Rania Ben Halima	University of Sfax, Tunisia
Kristof Böhmer	University of Vienna, Austria
Souha Boubaker	Télécom SudParis, France
Hayet Brabra	University of Sfax, Tunisia
Antonio Bucchiarone	Fondazione Bruno Kessler, Italy
Jürgen Cito	University of Zurich, Switzerland
Martina De Sanctis	Fondazione Bruno Kessler, Italy
Paul De Vrieze	Bournemouth University, UK
Wenxiu Ding	Xidian University, China
Boris Duedder	Technical University of Dortmund, Germany
Michael Esktrand	Texas State University, USA
Walid Fdhila	University of Vienna, Austria
Wei Feng	Xidian University, China
Pablo Fernández	University of Seville, Spain
Manuel Gall	University of Vienna, Austria
José María García	University of Seville, Spain
SimonPierre Genot	IBM Almaden Research Center, USA
Leopoldo Gomez-Barba	Univesity of Guadalajara Mexico
Emna Hachicha	Télécom SudParis, France
Conrad Indiono	University of Vienna, Austria

Security and Privacy in the IoT (Keynote)

Department of Computer Science, Purdue University, West Lafayette, USA
bertino@purdue.edu

Abstract. The Internet of Things (IoT) paradigm refers to the network of physical objects or "things" embedded with electronics, software, sensors, and connectivity to enable objects to exchange data with servers, centralized systems, and/or other connected devices based on a variety of communication infrastructures. IoT makes it possible to sense and control objects creating opportunities for more direct integration between the physical world and computer-based systems. IoT will usher automation in a large number of application domains, ranging from manufacturing and energy management (e.g. SmartGrid), to healthcare management and urban life (e.g. SmartCity). However, because of its fine-grained, continuous and pervasive data acquisition and control capabilities, IoT raises concerns about the security and privacy of data. Deploying existing data security solutions to IoT is not straightforward because of device heterogeneity, highly dynamic and possibly unprotected environments, and large scale. In this talk, after outlining key challenges in data security and privacy, we present initial approaches to techniques and services for securing IoT data, including efficient and scalable encryption protocols, software protection techniques for small devices, and fine-grained data packet loss analysis for sensor networks.

Bio: Elisa Bertino is professor of computer science at Purdue University, and serves as Director of Purdue Cyber Center and Research Director of the Center for Information and Research in Information Assurance and Security (CERIAS). She is also an adjunct professor of Computer Science & Info Tech at RMIT. Prior to joining Purdue in 2004, she was a professor and department head at the Department of Computer Science and Communication of the University of Milan. She has been a visiting researcher at the IBM Research Laboratory (now Almaden) in San Jose, at the Microelectronics and Computer Technology Corporation, at Rutgers University, at Telcordia Technologies. Her recent research focuses on data security and privacy, digital identity management, policy systems, and security for drones and embedded systems. She is a Fellow of ACM and of IEEE. She received the IEEE Computer Society 2002 Technical Achievement Award, the IEEE Computer Society 2005 Kanai Award and the 2014 ACM SIGSAC outstanding contributions award. She is currently serving as EiC of IEEE Transactions on Dependable and Secure Computing.

Contents

Service Analytics

Service Economy

Service Management

Service Recommandation

Service UIs, APIs and Mashup

Service/Process Foundation

Service Management (Short Papers)

Service Recommendation (Short Papers)

Service Uis, APIs and Mashup (Short Papers)

Service/Process Foundation (Short Papers)

Social Services (Short Papers)

Keynotes

Revisiting Service-Oriented Architecture for the IoT: A Middleware Perspective

Valérie Issarny[(✉)], Georgios Bouloukakis[(✉)],
Nikolaos Georgantas, and Benjamin Billet

MiMove Team, Inria Paris, Paris, France
{valerie.issarny,georgios.bouloukakis,
nikolaos.georgantas,benjamin.billet}@inria.fr

Abstract. By bridging the physical and the virtual worlds, the Internet of Things (IoT) impacts a multitude of application domains, among which smart cities, smart factories, resource management, intelligent transportation, health and well-being to name a few. However, leveraging the IoT within software applications raises tremendous challenges from the networking up to the application layers, in particular due to the ultra-large scale, the extreme heterogeneity and the dynamics of the IoT. This paper more specifically explores how the service-oriented architecture paradigm may be revisited to address challenges posed by the IoT for the development of distributed applications. Drawing from our past and ongoing work within the MiMove team at Inria Paris, the paper discusses the evolution of the supporting middleware solutions spanning the introduction of: probabilistic protocols to face scale, cross-paradigm interactions to face heterogeneity, and streaming-based interactions to support the inherent sensing functionality brought in by the IoT.

Keywords: Internet of things · Interoperability · Middleware · Service-oriented architecture · Scalability

1 Introduction

The Internet of Things promises the easy integration of the physical world into computer-based systems. In effect, real-world objects become connected to the virtual world, which allows for the remote sensing of as well as the remote acting upon the physical world by computing systems. Improved efficiency and accuracy are expected from this paradigm shift. However, although the vision emerged about 2 decades ago, enacting IoT based systems is still raising tremendous challenges for the supporting infrastructure from the networking up to the programming abstractions. Key challenges relate to [26]: *scale* as we are dealing with systems that may have to coordinate millions of devices; *deep heterogeneity*

The work is supported by the Inria Project Lab CityLab (citylab.inria.fr) and the EU-funded H2020 projects CHOReVOLUTION (chorevolution.eu) and Fiesta-IoT (fiesta-iot.eu).

© Springer International Publishing Switzerland 2016
Q.Z. Sheng et al. (Eds.): ICSOC 2016, LNCS 9936, pp. 3–17, 2016.
DOI: 10.1007/978-3-319-46295-0_1

since the IoT brings together sensor and actuator networks with cloud-based systems and thus the very small and the very large; *high dynamics* in relation with the unknown topology of the network and further presence of mobile things as well as uncertainty about the features of the networked things.

The challenges that the IoT is raising in the development of computing systems along with perspectives on how to address them have been the focus of numerous papers over the last decade, such as in: [3,12,23,26]. Among the software architecture paradigms envisioned for IoT-based systems, the literature suggests that service-orientation is promising due to its inherent support for interoperability and composability [13]. A large number of Service-oriented Middleware (SOM) platforms have then been proposed for the IoT, which subsumes revisiting the core elements of the service-oriented architecture paradigm starting with the service abstraction itself.

Towards building a SOM platform for the IoT, the starting point is to abstract Things or their measurements as services [1,7–9,19,22]. Compared to the classical *Business services*, *Thing-based services* must encompass highly heterogeneous software entities among which resource-constrained ones [2]. An early attempt in that direction is illustrated by the SenseWrap middleware, which features virtual sensors that deal with the transparent discovery of the supporting resources using ZeroConf protocols [19]. The discovery of resource-constrained resources is also the main focus of Hydra [8], *aka* LinkSmart (https://linksmart. eu). Hydra further provides interoperability at a semantic level by leveraging semantic Web services technologies for the description of the capabilities of thing-based services. SOCRADES is another one of the early IoT-based SOMs [13], which aims at easing the integration of physical devices into existing enterprise information systems. SOCRADES builds upon the DPWS (Devices Profile for Web Services) standard so that physical Things may expose their resources and may communicate through the Internet as standardized Web services. *EQoSystem* (Emergent QoS System) [20] goes one step further by dealing with the quality of the services delivered by resource-constrained Things. EQoSystem monitors the resources of the underlying devices and triggers resource management strategies (e.g., adapting the service workflow) at runtime for providing acceptable QoS. Similarly in [18], authors investigate a heuristic task allocation algorithm, named *SACHSEN*, which constitutes the core component of their SOM. The algorithm aims to distribute WSN applications to sensor nodes by dealing with the applications' performance requirements and the nodes' energy resources.

In addition to coping with the abstraction of resource-constrained Things as services, the access to the related services also requires special care in IoT-based SOA. We identify two approaches to access a resource-constrained node (typically a sensor or actuator): either *(i)* using a proxy/gateway; or *(ii)* deploying the middleware component on the sensor/actuator node itself. The former approach was initially favored. However, with the technological evolution of sensor nodes and of SOM, the latter approach is now deserving much attention. Indeed, it provides greater flexibility for managing the physical network infrastructure.

The authors in [17] undertake this approach by deploying SOAP-based Web services (DPWS) directly on the nodes without using gateways. Nevertheless, deploying the middleware component directly on the device might cause several issues, such as message delays, limited supported interactions, limited computational capacity, high energy consumption, etc. Taking into account these problems, the authors in [25] leverage the lightweight CoAP protocol (Constrained Application Protocol, http://coap.technology/) on sensor devices and evaluate the trade-off between response times and delivery success rates. Despite the fact that CoAP supports extremely low-resource interactions, it is more suitable for synchronous interactions. Several other protocols have been developed to address the above issues, along with standardization efforts that will guarantee interoperability. The authors in [10] compare the most promising IoT protocols: DPWS for large-scale enterprise deployments, CoAP for lightweight interactions, and MQTT for high reliability. Therefore, it is essential to combine one or more protocols in a WSN application to better exploit the physical network infrastructure.

As briefly outlined above, revisiting SOA and the supporting SOM for the IoT has undergone various steps, as a direct consequence of the technological evolution of the IoT. Obviously, the fact that a growing a number of application domains sees the benefits of leveraging the IoT has also encouraged the development of the enabling hardware and software technologies. This is for instance illustrated by the large literature on middleware solutions for the IoT, as surveyed in [23]. The present paper focuses on the complementary SOM solutions that we have been developing within the MiMove team at Inria Paris to face the scale, dynamics and heterogeneity of the IoT with a special emphasis on enabling resource-constrained Things to become first-class service providers. The next section then outlines our vision of a Thing-based SOA, and is followed by an overview of the supporting SOM solutions in Sects. 3 to 5. Section 6 concludes with our perspective for future work.

2   Thing-Based SOA

Traditional SOA involves three main actors that interact directly with one another: a Service Provider, a Service Consumer, and a Registry for services. Any service-oriented middleware adopting this architecture supports three core functionalities: *Discovery*, *Composition* of, and *Access* to services. More specifically, *Discovery* is used to publish (register) services in registries that hold service metadata and to look up services that can satisfy a specific request. *Composition* of services is used when discovered services are unable to individually fulfill the request. In such case, existing services are combined to provide a new convenient functionality. The composed services can further be used for more complex compositions. Finally, *Access* enables interaction with the discovered services. This basic SOA architecture is shown in Fig. 1.

The IoT brings new requirements and calls for substantially different approaches to the above traditional SOA. Regarding discovery, the principal new challenge is scale when having to deal with millions of Things that produce data

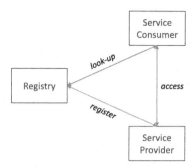

Fig. 1. Traditional Service-Oriented Architecture (SOA).

of interest, typically sensors that provide real-world measurements. In traditional SOA, even if millions of services are registered, one (or few for backup) is finally selected to fulfill a specific request. On the other hand, discovery in the IoT means selecting from a potentially very big number of Things a sufficient subset that will provide, in combination, quality data for a pending query, while limiting unnecessary redundancy for the sake of the scarce resources. Furthermore, a considerable portion of the networked Things that connect with the physical world are endowed with the ability to change their location either autonomously or, for instance, with human involvement (e.g., mobile phones, vehicles, etc.). These mobile Things are now within everyone's reach. For instance, all mobile phones nowadays host at least two sensors, a camera and a microphone. As of 2011, there were 5.3 billion phones users, of whom more than 1 billion owned a smartphone[1] with additional sensors, such as gyroscopes and barometers. Another example is the increasing integration of sensors and actuators in vehicles. We look into the problem of scalable discovery of Things – both fixed and mobile – in Sect. 3 and report on our related research results.

Concerning composition, the key challenge is resource saving, especially when it comes to dealing with continuous complex processing of data streams produced by numerous Things that are resource constrained. While, in traditional SOA, a composite service typically involves an exchange (direct or indirect) of a few discrete messages between the constituent services, in IoT data streaming, big volumes of data need to be collected from sensors, processed, composed and finally stored or delivered to actuators. Even if relying on the cloud is a widely adopted solution to this challenge, this incurs high communication and energy cost for Things and networks. We discuss this issue along with our in-network solution approach in Sect. 4.

Finally, access is essential for any IoT deployment, whether there is direct communication among Things or through the cloud. The hard challenge here is heterogeneity, which is particularly acute in the highly fragmented IoT world and concerns all hardware and software aspects of Things. In traditional SOA, standardization has been particularly effective, with WS-* and REST web

---

[1] US Strategy Analytics: www.strategyanalytics.com.

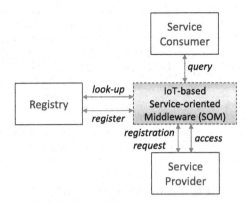

Fig. 2. Thing-based SOA.

services being the two dominant technologies. Regarding the same aspect in the IoT, i.e., public service description and middleware-level service access, where we assume Things sufficiently powerful to support IP protocol stacks, there is much bigger diversity. Message-, event- and data-based interaction styles are all widely used in the IoT with various protocol realizations. We analyze this issue and provide an overview of our current related research in Sect. 5.

3   Discovery in the Ultra-Large Scale IoT

Real-world measurements in the IoT require a large number of Things, since it is unlikely for a single or even a few Things to be sufficient. Applying the proposed traditional approaches of SOA to discover Things (i.e., discover all the appropriate devices that are reachable), will return a large set of accessible Things, many of which provide redundant functionalities. Moreover, mobility in the IoT constitutes an additional challenge regarding the discovery of sensors embedded in mobile devices.

More specifically, the application of SOA to the IoT results in some apparent problems. On the one hand, all the tasks in SOA revolve around some business logic that can be satisfied by one or several services. On the other hand, in the IoT, all the tasks and interactions revolve around what we refer to as a Thing-based query that senses/actuates some real world phenomenon. An example of a Thing-based query would be "What is the air pollution level on highways in Paris?". Thus, with such queries it is unlikely to have only one or just a few services that can provide accurate answers to represent a real-world feature. Hence, expecting the service consumer to interact with the numerous relevant service providers individually to access their services and acquire their measurements, then know how to treat each and every value (with different possible formats, types, units, etc.), in addition to the aggregation logic to apply, requires high communication and computation capabilities that the consumer will most likely not possess.

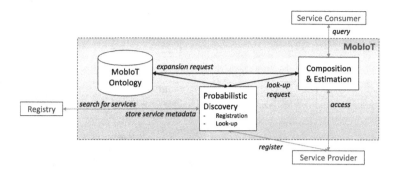

Fig. 3. MobIoT architecture.

As an alternative, our approach revisits the SOA and renders most interactions and heavy computations transparent to the consumer, who is only expected to know the sought after measurements. Figure 2 depicts the Thing-based SOA that is to be contrasted with the traditional SOA of Fig. 1. This has further led us to introduce the supporting *MobIoT* service-oriented middleware [16]. As depicted in Fig. 3, MobIoT supports the core functionalities of SOA (discovery, composition and access), while enabling Thing-based queries. In particular, MobIoT features a novel probabilistic discovery protocol. In MobIoT, the Discovery component wraps *Registration* and *Look-up* functionalities as follows:

– *Probabilistic Registration:* the registration of a provider's service is probabilistic. The goal is to allow only a subset of willing providers to register their services, depending on whether the already registered ones are sufficient. More precisely, in MobIoT, the *Registration component* generates the decision to allow or prevent a Thing from registering its services. The component estimates whether or not the mobility path to be followed by this Thing can be covered by other, already registered, mobile Things with similar sensing/actuating services. To that end, the component computes the probability that any of the latter Things be present at each of the future locations on the path of the former Thing when the former Thing crosses them. Then, the component compares the resulting probability value to a required sensing coverage. We consider that the coverage requirement (threshold) depends on the sensor and can be specified in its metadata. Only if the resulting probability is lower than the threshold, the Thing registers its service. We use the *Truncated Lévy Walk* mobility model [24] to estimate the mobility of registered Things and compute the probabilities above. The Registration component can use any other mobility model as long as the corresponding mathematical formulas to compute the probabilities are provided. As shown in [15], our registration solution successfully limits the registration of redundant services.

– *Probabilistic Look-up:* the look-up is also probabilistic and returns only a subset of sensing services based on the total area coverage they can provide [14]. We adopt the same logic as in intrusion detection solutions [27], where the spatial distribution of sensors has a major effect on the performance of the sensing system. Based on those solutions, when measuring a feature over some area (e.g., Air quality level), we sample sensors from a Uniform distribution in space, so that sensors from all over that area have the same likelihood of being selected. However, when the concept of interest is at a specific point in space, a better distribution would be Normal, as it selects more sensors around that point and less as we move farther. More specifically, in MobIoT, the *Look-up component* is in charge of returning a subset of services to access that can satisfy the Thing-based query. Based on the requested measurement and the location of interest, the component determines the most adequate probability distribution and the number of needed services. This number is computed based on the coverage requirement, expressed as a percentage of the area of interest to be sensed/acted upon by the selected subset. The result is then forwarded to the Registry to determine the actual Things to sample.

4   Composition in the Dynamic Resource-Constrained IoT

A major feature of a SOA is supporting the composition of the operations of existing services in order to create composite services [21]. Contracts describe the inputs and the outputs of service operations and enable the specification of a workflow of service invocations that represents the logic of a new more complex operation. In practice, composite services execute in a centralized or a distributed fashion. The former approach, called *service orchestration*, introduces an orchestrator to manage the invocations of the underlying services. The latter approach, called *service choreography*, leverages negotiation and routing mechanisms to let the service providers manage the composite services autonomously.

Applying a similar approach in the IoT is not a trivial procedure. We are, in particular, interested in the composition of Things that collaboratively produce, process and consume IoT data streams. Our emphasis is on in-network continuous processing of sensed data streams, as opposed to delegating all of the computation to the cloud, aiming to reduce the energy cost of communication over computation incurred by the massive scale of the IoT. Additionally, the IoT is characterized by a network topology that may be unknown and highly dynamic, due to the mobility of Things or their short life span. As a consequence, services required by an IoT application may suddenly become unavailable, because the host ran out of battery or just changed its location abruptly. To deal with all the above issues, the traditional composition of SOA must be extended in order to infer which service providers have to be used for executing the services, according to a set of scenario-dependent properties (e.g., throughput, energy consumption). This problem is a variation of the *task mapping problem*, where a set of communicating tasks with several properties (constraints, resource consumption, etc.) must be mapped to a set of connected nodes given their characteristics (location, hardware capabilities, etc.).

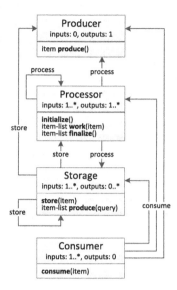

Fig. 4. The four-roles model.

Both centralized and distributed approaches have been studied to solve the above problem. The centralized approach computes and executes an allocation plan on a single machine (similar to service orchestration). The distributed approach lets the nodes compute parts of the allocation plan based on the knowledge they have about their peers (similar to service choreography). In MiMove, we have studied this problem and have introduced *Dioptase*, a distributed data streaming middleware for the Web of Things [4]. Dioptase makes it possible to: *(i)* integrate the Things with today's Web by exposing sensors and actuators as Web services, *(ii)* manage physical data as streams, and *(iii)* use any Thing as a generic pool of resources that can process streams by running tasks that are provided by developers over time.

More concretely, we introduce in [5] a dedicated centralized solver (Dioptase component) to allocate tasks on resource-constrained Things that produce data as streams. Depending on the available resources, each Thing may play one (or more in combination) of the identified four high-level roles (Fig. 4): *(i)* a production role where the Thing presents sensor data as streams, *(ii)* a processing role where the Thing continuously processes streams, *(iii)* a consumption role where the Thing acquires streams and drives actuators, and *(iv)* a storage role where the Thing saves data extracted from streams (in its memory, or persistently).

Subsequently, a *Dioptase mashup* is composed of distributed components, called *atomic components*, derived from the above roles. These components interact (are connected) by continuously exchanging data as streams. Each component defines *input ports* for the consumption of streams, depending on the component type, and *output ports* where new stream items are produced. Provided the data types specified for the input and output streams match, any output port

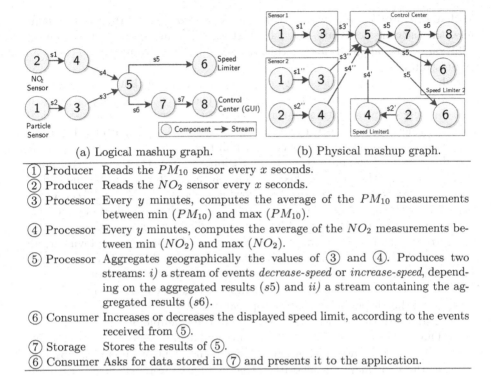

(a) Logical mashup graph.   (b) Physical mashup graph.

① Producer Reads the PM_{10} sensor every x seconds.
② Producer Reads the NO_2 sensor every x seconds.
③ Processor Every y minutes, computes the average of the PM_{10} measurements between min (PM_{10}) and max (PM_{10}).
④ Processor Every y minutes, computes the average of the NO_2 measurements between min (NO_2) and max (NO_2).
⑤ Processor Aggregates geographically the values of ③ and ④. Produces two streams: *i)* a stream of events *decrease-speed* or *increase-speed*, depending on the aggregated results ($s5$) and *ii)* a stream containing the aggregated results ($s6$).
⑥ Consumer Increases or decreases the displayed speed limit, according to the events received from ⑤.
⑦ Storage Stores the results of ⑤.
⑥ Consumer Asks for data stored in ⑦ and presents it to the application.

Fig. 5. Logical and physical mashup graphs for air control pollution.

can be connected to any input port through a one-to-one connection. We represent the above components as services of SOA. The ports provided by a service define its *interface*, while the *contract* specifies the schemas of *(i)* the streams readable by each input port and *(ii)* the streams produced by each output port. Given a contract, the service consumer can reason about the operations of the service and the streams that each operation processes and produces.

The *mashup* can then be easily described as an acyclic directed graph where the nodes are producers (sources), processors, consumers (sinks) and storages, and the edges of the graph, are streams that link services together through the input and output ports. We call this graph a *logical mashup graph* because it describes the tasks that the network has to perform. This graph is provided by the developer either directly or expressed as a query that is translated into a mashup graph. As an illustration, Fig. 5a presents an example of a simple mashup that analyzes air pollution based on the level of nitrogen dioxide (NO_2) and particulate matter (PM_{10}), in order to control the digital speed limiters located along city highways. In this mashup, two producers (① and ②) read the PM_{10} and NO_2 values from available sensors. Those data are acquired by two processors (③ and ④) that aggregate the values on a 10 min basis (time window). Processors ③ and ④ send these aggregated results to the processor

⑤ that will produce an event stream for the speed limiters ⑥. At the same time, the measurements are saved by a storage ⑦ and consumed by the air pollution control application ⑧, which presents historical values or alerts to an administrator.

Subsequently, the *logical mashup graph* is executed through its conversion into a *physical mashup graph*, as depicted in Fig. 5b. The execution of a logical graph is done through: *(i)* instantiating the services (i.e., maps a service onto a host device) and *(ii)* connecting their ports according to the graph edges. Regarding the latter, the data exchanged between two services is pull-based (where a consumer requests a producer to send the data stream), and Dioptase connects the services' ports (input or output) that are specified in each contract. After executing the logical graph, the services are hosted on the following devices (Fig. 5b): a PM_{10} sensor (Sensor 1), a $PM_{10} + NO_2$ sensor (Sensor 2), a speed limiter embedding an NO_2 sensor (Speed Limiter 1), a speed limiter embedding no sensors (Speed Limiter 2), and the control center computer. According to this physical deployment, an instance of Processor ③ will execute on the same device that hosts Producer ①, thus reducing network traffic. Moreover, processor ⑤, which controls the speed limiters, will run on the control center computer together with the history database ⑦ and the air pollution control application ⑧.

To instantiate the services as illustrated in the example, we use information about Things' locations and available resources. Then, depending on its capabilities, a Thing can be assigned either a single component or an entire subgraph by using the task mapping algorithm that we have proposed in [5]. In brief, we formalize therein the task mapping problem in the specific context of the IoT, which results in a binary programming problem. We provide a heuristic algorithm to solve it and demonstrate experimentally the efficiency, sufficient optimality, and reasonable resource requirement of our solution. Consequently, the mapping can be performed directly within the network, without requiring any centralized infrastructure.

5   Access in the Heterogeneous IoT

The *access* mechanism of traditional SOA enables the interaction between service consumers and service providers. In particular, services interact in a unified way following specific data formats on top of common overlay infrastructures across different system platforms. Web services constitute the dominant technology in SOA, with well known protocols such as SOAP or REST as the overlay infrastructure. The research community and many businesses have adopted these protocols and their standards in order to describe and implement their services (i.e., the supported operations, data formats, etc.). Also regarding the interconnection of these protocols, the existence of standards facilitates the development of frameworks for interoperability.

On the other hand, the (mobile) IoT comprises sensors and actuators that are heterogeneous with different operating (e.g., operating platforms) and hardware (e.g., sensor chip types) characteristics, hosted on diverse Things (e.g., mobile phones, vehicles, clothing, etc.). To support the deployment of such devices, major tech industry actors have introduced their own APIs and protocols, which deal with: *(i)* the limited energy resources of Things; *(ii)* several data formats found in the IoT; *(iii)* specific guarantees regarding response times and data delivery success rates; *(iv)* the efficient transfer of small data payloads which are common in the IoT; etc. The resulting APIs and pro(tocols are highly heterogeneous. In particular, protocols differ significantly in terms of interaction styles and data formats. For instance, protocols such as CoAP relying on *client-service* interactions, MQTT based on the *publish-subscribe* interaction paradigm, Semi-Space offering a lightweight shared *tuple space*, or Websockets based on *streaming* interactions, are among the most widely employed ones.

Hence, providing *access* to Things establishes a new challenge with respect to traditional SOA. To deal with this challenge, we have introduced the *eVolution Service Bus (VSB)*. VSB is a development and runtime environment dedicated to complex distributed applications. Its objective is to seamlessly interconnect, Things that employ heterogeneous interaction protocols at the middleware level (e.g., DPWS, CoAP, MQTT, Dioptase, etc.). This is based on runtime conversions between such protocols, with respect to their primitives and data type systems, while properly mapping between their semantics. This also includes mapping between the public service interfaces of Things, regarding their operations and data, from the viewpoint of the middleware: the latter means that operations and data are converted based on their middleware-level semantics, while their business semantics remains transparent to the conversion. VSB follows the well-known Enterprise Service Bus (ESB) paradigm [6]. In this paradigm, a *common intermediate bus protocol* is used to facilitate interconnection between multiple heterogeneous middleware protocols: instead of implementing all possible conversions between the protocols, we only need to implement the conversion of each protocol to the common bus protocol, thus considerably reducing the development effort. This conversion is done by a component associated to the Thing in question and its middleware, called a *Binding Component (BC)*, as it enables the interaction between the Thing and the common bus protocol. VSB follows a fully distributed architecture implemented by a number of Binding Components (BCs) that interact among themselves through the VSB common bus protocol.

A view of the VSB architecture is depicted in Fig. 6, showing the interconnection of *Sensor 2* and the *Control Center* of the physical mashup in Fig. 5b. Within every mashup, there are streams of data exchanged using the Dioptase middleware. However, Sensor 2 publishes data through an MQTT middleware component and the Control Center accepts data through a CoAP component. Thus, using VSB we enable the interconnection of heterogeneous protocols. Particularly, *BC 1* is associated to *Sensor 2*, while *BC 2* is associated to the *Control Center*. Implementation-wise, a BC employs the same (or symmetric, e.g., client vs. server) middleware protocol library as its associated Thing, and all BCs use a library implementing the bus protocol, which in our case is the Dioptase middleware. MQTT, CoAP and Dioptase are treated in the same way within the

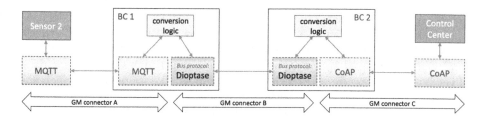

Fig. 6. VSB architecture.

VSB architecture. More specifically, each end-to-end interaction using the same middleware-layer protocol is modeled and abstracted by the *Generic Middleware (GM) connector*, as indicated in Fig. 6.

The GM connector abstracts interactions among peer components that employ the same middleware protocol in a unifying fashion for any middleware protocol. We propose an API (application programming interface) for GM and a related interface description, which we call *GIDL (Generic Interface Description Language)*, for application components that (abstractly) employ GM. Concrete middleware protocols and related interface descriptions of application components that employ these middleware protocols can be mapped to GM API and GIDL, respectively. Based on these abstractions, we elaborate a generic architecture for BCs (which we call *Generic BC*), an *Implementations' Pool*, which contains implementations of the GM API for concrete middleware or bus protocols, as well as a related method for *BC Synthesis*.

We provide more details concerning the *GM connector*, *GIDL*, and *BC synthesis* in the following:

- *Generic Middleware (GM) Connector*: based on our experience with middleware protocols/paradigms and their modeling in [11], we introduce a detailed API for GM. The GM API identifies and supports basic interaction styles found in most middleware protocols: *one-way interaction, two-way asynchronous interaction, two-way synchronous interaction*, and *stream interaction*. It also distinguishes between the two roles involved in an interaction, such as: *provider* and *consumer*. Essentially, the API relies on two main actions: a *post* action for sending a piece of data and a *get* action for receiving a piece of data.
- *Generic Interface Description Language (GIDL)*: by relying on the GM API, we elicit a generic interface description (GIDL) for a Thing that employs a middleware protocol abstracted by GM. *GIDL* enables the definition of operations provided or required by a Thing and that follow the interaction styles and roles identified in the GM API. Besides an operation's type, the names and data types of its parameters are also specified. The description is complemented by the physical address of the Thing.
- *BC Synthesis*: the functioning of *BC Synthesis* for the generation of a BC intended to serve a specific Thing is illustrated in Fig. 7, which depicts VSB's development and runtime environments. *BC synthesis* receives as input the GIDL description of the Thing and the information of the bus protocol in use.

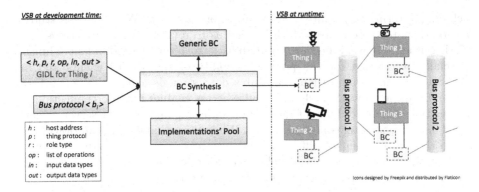

Fig. 7. VSB development and runtime environments.

Based on this input, *BC synthesis* refines the Generic BC in two steps: *(1)* by selecting appropriate GM API implementations from the Implementation's Pool that correspond to the Thing's middleware protocol and bus protocol; and *(2)* by inserting specific information about the Thing's operations and data from its GIDL description. The outcome of *BC synthesis* is a BC that will be deployed to serve the Thing.

VSB enables *access* to heterogeneous Things, while taking into account the current diversity but also the future evolution of IoT protocols. Hence, as shown in Fig. 7, a Thing may participate in more than one runtime topologies, which can be readily supported by multiple BCs and buses. Additionally, depending on the constraints found in an application scenario (e.g., devices with limited energy resources), any new protocol can be introduced as the VSB's common bus protocol. Accordingly, BCs are built and deployed as necessary: no BC is needed when a Thing employs the same middleware protocol as the bus protocol. Finally, there is no need for relying on and/or providing a full-fledged ESB platform (e.g., a cloud-based platform), which makes the VSB solution particularly flexible and lightweight.

6   Conclusion

IoT-based SOA holds the promise of easing the development of rich applications integrating the physical with the virtual worlds in a multitude of domains. This paper has presented our perspective on the definition of a supporting Service-oriented Middleware, which primarily revolves around enabling the provision of services by resource-constrained Things, typically sensors and actuators. Challenges then relate to: dealing with the ultra-large number of Things that are expected to be deployed in most environments, composing the services offered by the Things while coping with their inherent resource limitations and dynamics, and accessing the various networked things despite their high heterogeneity, including in terms of supported communication protocols. We have been studying solutions to these issues, which has led us to revisit the core functions of a SOM: service discovery becomes probabilistic to filter out redundant Things, especially accounting for the possible mobility of the service clients and/or providers; service composition aggregates data streams *within* the network so as to reduce the network load; and service access enables the interconnection of Things that adhere to different interaction styles (spanning client-server, event-based and data sharing communication). While those middleware solutions have led to the development of different SOM instances, we are now studying their integration so as to support the development of application toward smarter cities, in particular in the area of urban pollution monitoring.

References

1. Aberer, K., Hauswirth, M., Salehi, A.: Infrastructure for data processing in large-scale interconnected sensor networks. In: 2007 International Conference on Mobile Data Management, pp. 198–205. IEEE (2007)
2. Athanasopoulos, D., Autili, M., Georgantas, N., Issarny, V., Tivoli, M., Zarras, A.: An architectural style for the development of choreographies in the future internet. Glob. J. Adv. Softw. Eng. **1**(1), 14–28 (2014). https://hal.inria.fr/hal-01110502
3. Atzori, L., Iera, A., Morabito, G.: The internet of things: a survey. Comput. Netw. **54**(15), 2787–2805 (2010)
4. Billet, B., Issarny, V.: Dioptase: a distributed data streaming middleware for the future web of things. J. Internet Serv. Appl. **5**(1), 28 (2014)
5. Billet, B., Issarny, V.: From task graphs to concrete actions: a new task mapping algorithm for the future internet of things. In: 2014 IEEE 11th International Conference on Mobile Ad Hoc and Sensor Systems, pp. 470–478. IEEE (2014)
6. Chappell, D.A.: Enterprise Service Bus. O'Reilly Media, Sebastopol (2004)
7. Corredor, I., Martínez, J.F., Familiar, M.S., López, L.: Knowledge-aware and service-oriented middleware for deploying pervasive services. J. Netw. Comput. Appl. **35**(2), 562–576 (2012)
8. Eisenhauer, M., Rosengren, P., Antolin, P.: Hydra: a development platform for integrating wireless devices and sensors into ambient intelligence systems. In: Giusto, D., Iera, A., Morabito, G., Atzori, L. (eds.) The Internet of Things, pp. 367–373. Springer, Heidelberg (2010)
9. Fok, C.L., Roman, G.C., Lu, C.: Servilla: a flexible service provisioning middleware for heterogeneous sensor networks. Sci. Comput. Program. **77**(6), 663–684 (2012)
10. Fysarakis, K., Askoxylakis, I., Manifavas, C., Soultatos, O., Papaefstathiou, I., Katos, V.: Which IoT protocol? Comparing standardized approaches over a common M2M application. IEEE Global Communications Conference (2016)
11. Georgantas, N., Bouloukakis, G., Beauche, S., Issarny, V.: Service-oriented distributed applications in the future internet: the case for interaction paradigm interoperability. In: European Conference on Service-Oriented and CloudComputing (2013)
12. Gubbi, J., Buyya, R., Marusic, S., Palaniswami, M.: Internet of things (IoT): a vision, architectural elements, and future directions. Future Gener. Comput. Syst. **29**(7), 1645–1660 (2013). http://dx.doi.org/10.1016/j.future.2013.01.010

13. Guinard, D., Trifa, V., Karnouskos, S., Spiess, P., Savio, D.: Interacting with the SOA-based internet of things: discovery, query, selection, and on-demand provisioning of web services. IEEE Trans. Serv. Comput. **3**(3), 223–235 (2010)
14. Hachem, S.: Service-oriented middleware for the large-scale mobile internet of things. Ph.D. thesis, Université de Versailles-Saint Quentin en Yvelines (2014)
15. Hachem, S., Pathak, A., Issarny, V.: Probabilistic registration for large-scale mobile participatory sensing. In: 2013 IEEE International Conference on Pervasive Computing and Communications (PerCom), pp. 132–140. IEEE (2013)
16. Hachem, S., Pathak, A., Issarny, V.: Service-oriented middleware for large-scale mobile participatory sensing. Pervasive Mob. Comput. **10**, 66–82 (2014)
17. Kyusakov, R., Eliasson, J., Delsing, J., van Deventer, J., Gustafsson, J.: Integration of wireless sensor and actuator nodes with it infrastructure using service-oriented architecture. IEEE Trans. Ind. Inform. **9**(1), 43–51 (2013)
18. Li, W., Delicato, F.C., Pires, P.F., Lee, Y.C., Zomaya, A.Y., Miceli, C., Pirmez, L.: Efficient allocation of resources in multiple heterogeneous wireless sensor networks. J. Parallel Distrib. Comput. **74**(1), 1775–1788 (2014)
19. Meling, H., et al.: Sensewrap: a service oriented middleware with sensor virtualization and self-configuration. In: 2009 5th International Conference on Intelligent Sensors, Sensor Networks and Information Processing (ISSNIP), pp. 261–266. IEEE (2009)
20. Newman, P., Kotonya, G.: A resource-aware framework for resource-constrained service-oriented systems. Future Gener. Comput. Syst. **47**, 161–175 (2015)
21. Papazoglou, M.P.: Service-oriented computing: concepts, characteristics and directions. In: 2003 Proceedings of the Fourth International Conference on Web Information Systems Engineering WISE 2003, pp. 3–12. IEEE (2003)
22. Perera, C., Jayaraman, P.P., Zaslavsky, A., Christen, P., Georgakopoulos, D.: Mosden: an internet of things middleware for resource constrained mobile devices. In: 2014 47th Hawaii International Conference on System Sciences, pp. 1053–1062. IEEE (2014)
23. Razzaque, M.A., Milojevic-Jevric, M., Palade, A., Clarke, S.: Middleware for internet of things: a survey. IEEE Internet Things J. **3**(1), 70–95 (2016)
24. Rhee, I., Shin, M., Hong, S., Lee, K., Kim, S.J., Chong, S.: On the levy-walk nature of human mobility. IEEE/ACM Trans. Netw. (TON) **19**(3), 630–643 (2011)
25. Sheng, Z., Wang, H., Yin, C., Hu, X., Yang, S., Leung, V.C.: Lightweight management of resource-constrained sensor devices in internet of things. IEEE Internet Things J. **2**(5), 402–411 (2015)
26. Teixeira, T., Hachem, S., Issarny, V., Georgantas, N.: Service oriented middleware for the internet of things: a perspective. In: ServiceWave 2011 Proceedings of the 4th European Conference on Towards a Service-Based Internet, pp. 220–229. Springer-Verlag, Berlin, Heidelberg (2011)
27. Wang, Y., Fu, W., Agrawal, D.P.: Gaussian versus uniform distribution for intrusion detection in wireless sensor networks. IEEE Trans. Parallel Distrib. Syst. **24**(2), 342–355 (2013)

Towards a Shared Ledger Business Collaboration Language Based on Data-Aware Processes

Richard Hull[1]([✉]), Vishal S. Batra[2], Yi-Min Chen[1], Alin Deutsch[3],
Fenno F. Terry Heath III[1], and Victor Vianu[3]

[1] IBM T.J. Watson Research Center, Yorktown Heights, NY, USA
{hull,ymchee,theath}@us.ibm.com
[2] IBM India Research Lab, New Delhi, DL, India
vibatra1@in.ibm.com
[3] University of California, La Jolla, San Diego, CA, USA
{deutsch,vianu}@cs.ucsd.edu

Abstract. Shared ledger technologies, as exemplified by Blockchain, provide a new framework for supporting business collaborations that is based on having a high-reliability, shared, trusted, privacy-preserving, nonrepudiable data repository that includes programmable logic in the form of "smart contracts". The framework has the potential to dramatically transform business collaboration across numerous industry sectors, including finance, supply chain, food production, pharmaceuticals, and healthcare. Widespread adoption of this technology will be accelerated by the development of business-level languages for specifying smart contracts. This paper proposes that data-aware business processes, and in particular the Business Artifact paradigm, can provide a robust basis for a shared ledger Business Collaboration Language (BCL). The fundamental rationale for adopting data-aware processes is that shared ledgers focus on both data and process in equal measure. The paper examines potential advantages of the artifact-based approach from two perspectives: conceptual modeling, and opportunities for formal reasoning (verification). Broad research challenges for the development, understanding, and usage of a shared ledger BCL are highlighted.

1 Introduction

The shared ledger paradigm, as exemplified by Blockchain, was first introduced in Bitcoin [39] to enable a cryptocurrency, but a number of industries are seeing strong potential for generalizations that will dramatically increase the efficiency of many different kinds of business collaboration. A leading initiative towards diverse applications of Blockchain is Hyperledger, a consortium led by the Linux Foundation that includes a global family of partners from finance, banking, Internet of Things, supply chains, manufacturing and Technology [31]; other initiatives include Etherium, R3, and Digital Asset. Widespread adoption of this technology will be accelerated by the development of business-level languages for specifying *smart contracts*, i.e., the programs that run on shared

© Springer International Publishing Switzerland 2016
Q.Z. Sheng et al. (Eds.): ICSOC 2016, LNCS 9936, pp. 18–36, 2016.
DOI: 10.1007/978-3-319-46295-0_2

ledgers. This paper proposes that data-aware business processes [29], and in particular the Business Artifact paradigm [32,41], can provide a robust basis for a shared ledger *Business Collaboration Language* (BCL).

The core value of Blockchain for business collaboration is that it provides *high-reliability, shared, trusted, privacy-preserving, non-repudiable data repositories*. This is achieved through families of clever, intricate algorithms relating to encryption, distributed computing, and consensus. Data updates to Blockchains obey the "ACID" transactional properties of classical database systems. Furthermore, updates to a blockchain can trigger execution of smart contracts, so blockchains are reminiscent of active databases. Using a blockchain a group of businesses can share data and invoke agreed upon processing in connection with a collaboration in a secure and selective manner. In the absence of Blockchain technology, most multi-party business collaborations are implemented in the form of multiple binary relationships. This leads to more intricate modeling and programming, and increased cost of tracking down the root causes of issues and disagreements. In contrast, blockchains hold the promise of supporting a much more holistic view of business collaborations, and can give immediate transparency to all relevant stakeholders if conflicts arise. They can also simplify the use of analytics to understand collaborations in the aggregate.

We recall the principle of "logical separation" from relational databases, which helps to insulate relational database design and query langauges such as SQL from the physical storage of data on disk. By analogy, we believe that a shared ledger BCL can be designed based on abstractions suitable for business leaders and analysts, and can be largely insulated from Blockchain implementation details. There is early evidence that this is quite feasible: reference [48] shows how the business process language BPMN can be mapped into executable smart contracts on the Ethereum Blockchain. This suggests that a BCL based on various other abstractions can also be successfully mapped onto Blockchain.

A Business Collaboration Language will be a form of *domain specific language*. As such, we expect that developing and maintaining smart contracts with a BCL will be substantially faster and cheaper than using the base smart contract languages on blockchains, e.g., Turing complete languages such as Go or Java. Other domain specific languages for Blockchain include R3's Corda [10] and Digital Asset's DAML [21], which focus on financial transactions, and Ethereum's Solidity [45], whose focus is more general.

Conceptually speaking, the data stored in a blockchain can provide a logical "anchor" for a collaboration between businesses. Indeed, in typical blockchain-enabled collaborations it is assumed that all business-relevant data shared between two or more of the participants will be placed onto and persisted in the blockchain (or an auxiliary data store). This brings a fundamental focus on data that is not traditionally part of process-centric BPM paradigms, such as the BPMN standard including the BPMN constructs for conversations and choreography [9].

The data-centricity of Blockchain suggests that we should base a Business Collaboration Language on the field of *data-aware business processes* [29], that is, business processes or workflows that incorporate data as a first-class citizen along with process. This data-aware approach was introduced in 2003 by the Business Artifact model [32,41] (see also [8,11,14,18,30]), and is also found in modern case management [2,37], and in Business Objects [33,43,44]). The core construct for these approaches focuses on key conceptual entities that progress through business operations. Called *business artifacts* (or *cases* or *business objects*), these entities are modeled using both an *information model* and a *lifecycle model*. A classical example of a business artifact type is the concept of Fedex delivery, not the package itself, but the overall phenomenon, starting with a customer request to ship something, details about the shipping and delivery, and also details about payment. For each such delivery, the corresponding business artifact will hold a growing data set, and the progression of the artifact will follow one of the possible paths in the lifecycle model. When modeling a typical scope of business operations, a handful of interacting business artifact types will be used.

From the perspective of Business Process Management (BPM) and the field of services interoperation (including orchestration and choreography), Blockchain brings unique characteristics. It is logically similar to an orchestrator, in that it can serve as a hub that communicates with each participant in a collaboration. But while orchestrators are typically pro-active and controlling, collaborations might use a blockchain in a more re-active manner. That is, the blockchain might be relatively passive and wait for new updates from participants before producing more data and perhaps alerting other participants of changes. In this sense, a blockchain may act more as a facilitator, similar to the loosely coupled style of choreographies. The Artifact-Centric Services Interoperation (ACSI) approach of [7,8,27,34], developed before the emergence of Blockchain, enables this style of collaboration and provides mechanisms for fine-grained control of data privacy and sharing, and of permissions to make updates or invoke services.

The goal of this paper is to examine the suitability of constructs from business artifacts and ACSI as the foundation for a shared ledger BCL. We focus on the core conceptual abstractions of business artifacts, rather than detailed language design. We consider the viability of using business artifacts as the basis for a BCL from two perspectives: conceptual modeling (Sect. 4) and support for informal and formal reasoning (Sect. 5). A brief overview of Blockchain is presented in Sect. 2 and some research challenges are outlined in Sect. 6.

2   Short Overview of Blockchain: The Logical Level

There are several introductions to Blockchain and shared ledger technology available (e.g., [22,31,48]). We provide here a brief overview that focuses on the logical level rather than on, e.g., encryption and consensus. This logical level provides the basis upon which a BCL will be designed, implemented, and used.

While there are variations, a common set of core elements is shared across most blockchain implementations. There are two classes of logical computational actors that perform processing: *peers* that form a blockchain *network* (i.e., set of computational actors working together to support a given blockchain deployment), and *participants* that are executing on behalf of the businesses (or other organizations) that are collaborating by using the network. Each participant connects to a single peer, that serves as the connection point between the participant and the network.

In traditional blockchain networks it is assumed that the organizations running the peers have no trust relationship established between them. The encryption, consensus, and other algorithms of blockchain guarantee trusted outcomes in this context. Some recent blockchain initiatives, including Hyperledger [31], are constructed to also enable contexts where groups of businesses have trust relationships that exist outside of the blockchain network (e.g., a consortium of banks, or a large retailer and all of its suppliers and transporters). In such contexts the consensus algorithm may work with a subset of the peers, rather than with all of the peers.

For this paper we are primarily concerned with the *application-level data and processing* in a blockchain network, and largely ignore the additional data and processing used to support encryption, consensus, and the like. At the application level the basic unit of executable code on a blockchain is called a *smart contract* (or a *chaincode*). In the context of business collaborations, it is typical that a smart contract is focused on progressing some type of collaboration (or a part of one) towards completion. A service invocation corresponds to recording a particular step of a collaboration onto the blockchain and potentially computing some additional values and/or generating alerts for interested participants. For example, a smart contract might manage various activities associated with fulfilling a Purchase Order, and one service invocation might focus on an update that says, intuitively, that one line item of the Order has been succefully received.

The basic unit of application-level work on a blockchain is a *transaction*. A transaction is *initiated* by a single participant that sends a service invocation to an identified smart contract running in the blockchain. (Technically, the invocation might be against an already running smart contract instance, or might deploy a new instance.) The service invocation is digitally *signed* by the requestor, which allows tracing of who invoked which transactions. Speaking intuitively, in workflow terms a transaction includes automated processing that results from the service invocation; it will not include inputs or activity by any participant except for the initial service invocation. (Actually, techniques are emerging to enable secure, trusted queries to external sources [49], but this is not considered here.) Once the service invocation is made the blockchain network undergoes a significant amount of processing. The service invocation results in one of two outcomes: (a) the associated transaction becomes *committed*, in which case it is recorded on all (or some pre-determined subset) of the peers, or (b) it is *rejected*, in which case it is essentially removed from all of the peers. Transactions in blockchain follow the "ACID" properties of database transactions.

The processing for a service invocation involves distribution of the invocation to all (or a subset) of the peers, checking for validity of the signature, execution of the code invoked by the service invocation, and reaching consensus amongst the peers. Depending in part on the number of peers, this can take seconds, 10's of seconds, or in some contexts up to a minute [22].

If the transaction associated with a service invocation is committed then the blockchain may return an *output* to the initiating participant. The transaction may be a *query* that does not modify the application data on the blockchain. Or, the transaction may be an *update* that potentially does modify the data. In the case of updates, the blockchain may also generate *alerts* (with payloads) to other participants about the transaction and/or about values in the blockchain that are related to the transaction.

Traditional blockchain networks incorporate a notion of cryptocurrency payments for participation in the blockchain. For example, Bitcoin and Ethereum have constructs relating to the *transaction fee* to be paid for transaction processing. Other approaches, such as Hyperledger, do not have built-in cryptocurrency, and optionally enable payment for participation through a separate mechanism that is essentially outside of the application-level processing on the blockchain.

In a typical setup, a blockchain network works on multiple initiated transactions in a group. A specific sequencing of the transactions in this group is determined as part of the consensus building process. Once it is determined which of the transactions in the group are to be committed or rejected, and in which order, the application-level data relating to the results of executing the committed transactions is recorded as a *block*. (In some cases, some of the transaction data is recorded into an auxiliary data store rather than in the block itself; see next paragraph.) No semantic relationship is implied about the transactions that are combined into a block. The blockchain itself is essentially a sequential linked list of these blocks. All peers hold an identical copy of this list. (A variation is used for networks in which subsets of peers perform consensus building.)

A blockchain network may maintain a persistent, replicated data store that is referred to by transactions and is updated according to the committed transactions. As one example, Hyperledger maintains a store organized around key-value pairs. In some networks the cost or time involved in storing large volumes of data may be prohibitive. In this case auxiliary stores might be maintained to hold selected data that is encrypted but not widely replicated (see [48]).

In most networks one smart contract can invoke another one. In typical setups, at the logical level the call to the second smart contract is *synchronous*, i.e., the first smart contract will wait until the second smart contract finishes its work and returns a value or a handshake. There may be a family of smart contract invocations stemming from a single service invocation by a participant. All of these invocations are considered to be part of a single transaction; if it is successful at the consensus level then the combined result of the invocations are committed to the blockchain.

It is common to use a "factory" paradigm when working with smart contracts. That is, most smart contracts are written to be used to support numerous instances of collaborations (e.g., financial trades, importing contracts, etc.), where each instance may involve a different set of participants. As the industry's ability to work with blockchains grows, we anticipate that eco-systems of smart contracts and executing instances of them will emerge. For example, a large manufacturer might maintain two levels of smart contract: "umbrella" contracts that focus on establishing shipping costs, etc., for a year-long period, and "shipping" contracts that focus on supporting individual shipments. Also, different development or standards organizations might create smart contracts for different aspects of large-scale business collaborations (e.g., one might focus on import/export and another on trucking within a country); and a single collaboration might rely on instances of smart contracts that were developed by the different organizations.

While many use cases today involve one or several smart contracts that interact within a single blockchain network, we also anticipate a future with interacting smart contracts that run on different blockchain networks [31]. The messaging between such smart contracts will most likely be asynchronous, because of the time it takes for single blockchain transactions to commit, and the fact that the block commit cycles on different networks will not be aligned.

Blockchain technologies are still evolving, and new features and capabilities will continue to emerge. As such, the selection of abstractions for a BCL should not depend too closely on the capabilities of one blockchain technology. Also, the needs of a BCL may imply the desirability of certain capabilities in the underlying networks, and help to guide how the core blockchain technologies evolve.

3   Overview of Business Artifacts and ACSI Approach

This section overviews the business artifact approach for modeling business operations, including the notion of Artifact-Centric Services Interoperation (ACSI). The presentation here is informal and by example; the reader is referred to the numerous articles about business artifacts, including the surveys [11,14,18,30]. We illustrate some of the core notions of business artifacts with an example that could be executed on a shared ledger. The illustration is based on the use of Finite State Machines (FSM's) for the artifact lifecycles, but quite different styles of lifecycle meta-models can also be used (see below).

The modeling focus in business artifacts is on key business-relevant entities that progress through a business, or through a collaboration amongst businesses. Some of the literature uses the phrases *Business Entities* or *Business Entities with Lifecycles* to refer to business artifacts. Typical examples are a Purchase Order or a Financial Transaction; each of these might go through various stages of activity, achieve various business objectives along the way, and access and create data values. In a typical business modeling context there will be a handful of relevant kinds of business entity, that interact in specified ways.

A (*business*) *artifact type* (or schema) consists primarily in an *information model* and a *lifecycle model*. There are numerous options for the meta-model used for the information models, we focus here on nested relations that satisfy the natural property that for each relation (top-level or nested) the scalar columns form a key (see [3,26]). There are also several options for the meta-model used for the lifecycle models. Our running example uses FSM's; other options are

discussed below. Various mechanisms have been studied for specifying the interaction between business artifacts, including messages [46], service invocations
[13], and the ability for conditional triggering to refer to multiple artifacts [28].
In the running example we use service invocations, which parallels the typical
style of communication between smart contracts on blockchains.

We now introduce a simplified example that uses business artifacts to support
business collaborations in the space of manufacturing commerce. This example
loosely follows the running example of [48], and is focused on the management of
orders for industrial equipment (e.g., freeze driers for large-scale pharmaceutical
packaging), including management of ordering and shipping of the component
parts to the manufacturer. In the example there are five kinds of participants:
Buyers (who issue Purchase Orders for machines), Manufacturers (who build
them), Middlemen (who facilitate purchases and shipments of component parts
for the Manufacturers), Suppliers (of component parts), and Shippers.

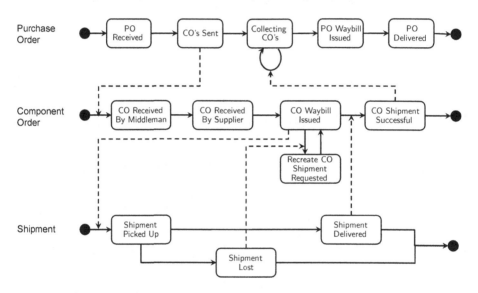

Fig. 1. Sketch of the lifecycle schemas of three interacting business artifact types,
including interactions between them (simplified)

Figures 1 and 2 together provide a high-level, simplified illustration of three
business artifact types that can support this collaboration. The three artifact
types are *Purchase Order* (*PO*), *Component Order* (*CO*), and *Shipment*. The
first figure shows sketches of their FSM-based lifecycles (many details have been
omitted), and the second one shows a snapshot of the data that might be held
by an instance of PO at one point in its progression. Importantly, the artifact
types are focused on data and processing that are relevant to the collaboration
itself; the tasks performed individually by the respective participants are out of
scope for the model supported on the blockchain.

In a typical execution of artifacts based on these artifact types, a Buyer would issue a purchase order for a machine, leading to the creation of a PO artifact. After analyzing the order, the Manufacturer would determine which component parts are needed and order them from one or more Middlemen. A new CO artifact instance is created for each component part. Focusing on the lifecycle for CO, each FSM state can be viewed intuitively as a *milestone*, i.e., a key business objective that the collaboration around the CO may achieve. The CO's would progress through a lifecycle involving receipt by the Middleman, posting onto the blockchain by the Middleman of a Supplier Order, posting onto the blockchain of a Waybill by the Supplier (e.g., after the Supplier has created the component and chosen a Shipper), and (hopefully) reaching the state where the component has been shipped to the Manufacturer. In this simplified example most exception handling is not included, except for the case of lost shipments. In particular, if a Shipment moves into the Shipment Lost state this will invoke a service to the CO that another shipment should be created.

PO ID	PO State	Price	Mfr.	Component	CO ID	Middleman	Received Date
				Vacuum Pump	CO111	AllPro Solutions	10 July 2016
PO123	Collecting CO's	$1,500,000	JLH Inc.	Condenser	CO222	Central Logistics	24 June 2016
				Shelving	CO333	AllPro Solutions	–

Fig. 2. Representative snapshot of data held by the information model in an instance of the Purchase Order artifact type (simplified)

Figure 2 shows a simplifed example of the information held by a PO artifact instance. In practice, a PO will typically hold a wealth of information about a PO that is business-relevant to the progression of the collaboration, including dates, contract signatories, relevant history of exceptions and how they were handled, etc. It would also be natural to include a history of service invocations and FSM states visited. The artifact information model provides a conceptually convenient place for storing any information of interest, in business-digestable form. This contrasts with typical BPMN-based solutions, where a lot of business-relevant data may become buried in message bodies and system logs.

The solid lines in Fig. 1 correspond to state transitions of the FSM's that result from service invocations. The dashed edges indicate synchronous service invocations that are made between artifact instances. (The synchronous call will result in one state transition in the called FSM, after which control will return to the calling FSM.) Solid edges without incoming dashed edges correspond to services that are invoked from outside the blockchain, i.e., by participants to the collaboration. Some dashed edges have the effect of launching new artifact instances, while others in this simplifed example have the effect of causing state transitions in the called artifact. (In the diagram each dashed line points to a transition; in practice, a service invocation might cause different transitions depending on the payload of the service invocation and the data held by the called artifact.)

The approach to supporting business collaboration illustrated in this example follows the basic form of Artifact-Centric Services Interoperation (ACSI) hubs as introduced in [27] in 2009. That paper developed access control constructs that seem especially well-suited for use in the shared ledger context. Three forms of access control are defined there. First, a *view* over an artifact type includes restrictions on both the data and the lifecycle. The data portion of a view is essentially a projection of the data (i.e., subset of the columns). For the lifecycle, a view specifies a *condensation* of the FSM, that is, a mapping of the FSM to a new FSM, where multiple states of the source FSM might get mapped to a single state of the target FSM (certain well-formedness restrictions must be followed). This has the effect of hiding from some participants the possible steps that other participants might be involved in. The second form of access control is *window*, which is essentially a selection condition on what artifact instances a participant can see. For example, we would expect that a Shipper can see only the Shipment instances that he is directly involved in supporting. Finally, [27] supports the specification of Create-Read-Update-Delete-Append-Execute (*CRUDAE*) access controls, to limit the ways that participants can modify artifact instances. The BizArtifact system [7,8,34] supports variations of the view, window, and CRUDAE constructs of [27] for two artifact lifecycle meta-models. These abstractions are important for a BCL, because they provide intuitive mechanisms for specifying confidentiality constraints in a business-oriented framework. These constructs will also be useful for understanding compatibility of smart contracts for interoperation.

Essentially any process-oriented meta-model can be used for the lifecycle models of business artifacts, including, e.g., Petri nets, BPMN [9], or state charts. For example, the proclets meta-model [1] uses Petri nets to specify a family of interacting processes; similar to business artifacts they provide a top-down way to factor business operations into coherent chunks, although data is not explicitly modeled. Business Objects (e.g., [33,43,44]) use FSMs for the lifecycle models and messages for communication between objects. The Guard-Stage-Milestone (GSM) variant of business artifacts [15,28] provides a declarative, rules-based lifecycle meta-model in which condition-based milestones are supported, and where tasks are hierarchically grouped into *stages* that are launched if certain conditions are met. GSM was used as a basis for the OMG Case Management Model and Notation (CMMN) standard [37]. As discussed in Sect. 4, the modularity, hierarchy, and declarative characteristics of GSM and CMMN may prove useful when specifying intricate smart contracts at the business level.

4   The Case for Business Artifacts: Conceptual Modeling

Business artifacts were developed to reduce the conceptual distance between (i) how business leaders and analysts think about the processes supporting business operations, and (ii) how those processes are implemented in practice [14,41]. This section reviews this and other benefits of the business artifacts and ACSI approaches in the context of supporting business collaborations on shared ledgers. The section includes comparison with process-centric approaches to model collaborations and choreographies.

Holistic, top-down factoring based on business-relevant concepts. The central tenet of business artifacts modeling of business operations is to focus on the key business entities, including milestones they may achieve and the data needed and/or produced to achieve them. These business entities are often the conceptual building blocks used by business leaders to think about their operations, and the milestones provide the basis for many of the Key Performance Indicators (KPI's) that the operations are measured by [35]. Additional information that naturally fits into a business artifact information model, such as the price paid, production cost, time taken, etc., provides the basis for additional KPI's, some of which relate directly to a business's financial performance.

An effective business modeling method. The Business Entity Lifecycle Analysis (BELA) method [46] was developed at IBM to support business operations modeling using business artifacts. The approach follows a five-stage process (with some back-and-forth) as follows: (1) Identify the key business artifact types in the business scope; (2) Identify key milesteons for these artifact types and place these into a sequencing diagram (e.g., an FSM or something more declarative); (3) Identify the data needed and/or produced to achieve these milestones; (4) Identify the tasks needed to achieve the milestones; and (5) Identify interactions between the artifacts. The BELA method has been applied in numerous application areas (e.g., [5]), and is supported in the IBM Service-Oriented Method and Architecture (SOMA) tool suite [40].

In multiple situations the BELA method (and its precursors) solved business modeling and deployment challenges that the Lean Six Sigma approach was unable to effectively resolve [5,12]. The BELA method was found most effective in two kinds of contexts: (a) where the targeted business operations spanned across multiple business silos, and (b) where multiple organizations (e.g., obtained through acquisitions) were performing essentially the same function for different geographic areas. Context (a) is of course very relevant to Blockchain-enabled collaborations.

Modeling flexible processes. Business artifacts information models provide a unified store of business-relevant data, which enables natural, declarative, rules-based approaches such as GSM and CMMN for specifying process. This in turn enables artifacts to model rich flexibility in processes. Consider for example the use case of mortgage origination, that is, the processing involved in obtaining a mortgage loan for a house. In this process a broad variety of documents and data is gathered from numerous stakeholders, and then evaluated in various ways by a small set of stakeholders (e.g., bank, underwriter, insurance company). The documents and data arrive in various orders, processing can be done on subsets of the incoming data, and sometimes new versions of the documents or data are needed. A rules-based lifecycle specification enables flexible response to the data as it arrives. Combining a rules-based style with hierarchy further increases modeling flexibility. For example, it makes it easier to support variation as might arise when working on a given use case across differently-sized contracts, with various partners, and involving different countries.

Another kind of flexibility relates to distribution of responsibilities between participants. Business artifacts enable a separation of concerns, with business-relevant data and milestones at one level, and distribution across participants at a second level. This enables the use of a single family of business artifact types to support instances of business collaboration where responsibilities are divided among participants in differing ways.

Support for evolution. It has been argued that the business artifact [5, 46] and Business Objects [33, 43, 44] approaches enable evolution of process models in ways that are both intuitively natural and relatively inexpensive. This again stems from the top-down factoring of models created using these approaches. This flexibility will be useful as business needs change and new variations on existing smart contracts are created.

Comparison with process-centric approaches. It is informative to compare and contrast the use of business artifacts and ACSI to support business collaboration vis-a-vis process-centric approaches. We focus here on the embodiment found in the BPMN version 2.0 [9] frameworks for *collaboration* and *choreography*. Reference [48] mentioned above provides an illustration of a BPMN collaboration and the corresponding BPMN choreography.

BPMN *collaboration* focuses on the parties in a collaboration, where the internal process of each party is represented in a separate BPMN pool (that is, a specification of a BPMN process, possibly spread across swimlanes that are performed by different participants and/or roles). Messages between those pools (in particular, between *send tasks* and *receive tasks*) guide the collaborative process. BPMN *choreography* enables a complimentary view. The primary building block is the *choreography activity*, which in turn may be a *choreography task*, a subchoreography, or a "call choreography" which acts as a placeholder for a choreography. A choreography task corresponds to an interaction between two or more partipants, where one of these is the initiator. Choreography activities are strung together using flow constructs (including gateways for conditionals, joins, etc.)

In both BMPN collaboration and choreography the information shared between businesses is modeled using a family of individual messages that go between susbsets of participants. The ACSI approach provides a paradigm shift, because the information shared between businesses is modeled in a single, logically coherent data store. This data store is organized around business artifacts that can hold all business-relevant information about the collaboration, regardless of which participants create or use it. Data privacy is layered on top. This paradigm shift, from modeling shared information in messages to modeling it in a top-down unified way, can provide substantial benefits in design, implementation, maintenance, reporting on progress, and tracking of disputes and exceptions. As noted above, the use of a unified data model permits the use of rules-based lifecycle models, which in turn enables intuitive specification of highly flexible kinds of collaborations.

The artifact-centric approach provides a natural, flexible way to represent 1-many relationships between the conceptual entites. The example of Sect. 3 illustrates a 1-many relationship between PO's and CO's; more complex 1-many relationships can arise in shipping scenarios where shipments and invoices may refer to overlapping sets of line items, or in financial applications where, e.g., mortgage loans are bundled into mortgage-backed securities, grouped into tranches (e.g., groupings based on differing risk levels), and then divided amongst multiple buyers. BPMN processes support *multi-instance* tasks and sub-processes, BPM collaborations support *multi-instance* pools, and BPMN collaborations support *multi-instance* choreography activities. All of these use constructs that essentially package the multi-instance aspect into a sub-process of the parent instance. As a result, it may be very cumbersome in BPMN to faithfully represent some styles of business artifact interactions, e.g., where a parent artifact progresses through several states, and in parallel the child artifacts progress through their states, with interleaved interactions between parent and children. In contrast, rules-based artifact lifecycle models can support such interactions in an intuitive and succinct manner.

Potential for community adoption. Case management has emerged as an important style of Business Process Management, especially in connection with knowledge-worker intensive processes. The number of case management deployments continues to grow, and so does the number of case management savvy business analysts and developers. The underlying paradigms of case management and business artifacts are very close [37]. Business analysts and developers will be able to bring their experiences and knowledge of case management to the creation of artifact-centric smart contracts.

Turning now to FSM-based artifacts in particular, we mention a report from the U.S. Office of Financial Research [23], that argues that many financial contracts can and should be represented using FSM's. The paper encourages workers in the financial field, who have had little or no exposure to programming or Computer Science abstractions, to make the effort to understand how FSM's can bring value and systematic, repeatable approaches to financial exchanges.

Academic foundations. The business artifact and related approaches have spawned a broad and growing body of academic and industrial research since the first publications in 2003, as indicated in the surveys [11,30].

5   The Case for Business Artifacts: Formal Reasoning

The ability to reason about smart contracts, including their interaction with each other and with external business processes, will be a crucial enabler in the success and wide-spread adoption of the shared ledger approach. Both informal and formal styles of reasoning will be significant. By "informal reasoning" we mean the kind of reasoning that developers and others often carry out to convince themselves that programs will operate as desired. By "formal reaoning" we mean both mathematical styles of reasoning (such as a proof of that two-phase locking ensures serializability of transactions) and automated reasoning (as in automatic verification by tools such as SPIN [25] or WAVE [16]). Smart contracts involve both data and process at fundamental levels, and so reasoning about process, reasoning about data, and reasoning about process together with data will all bring important value.

Effective support of informal reasoning will rely in part on conceptual models that are natural and intuitive for both business analysts and developers, and that enable focus on critical aspects of the processing, including achievement of key business goals, smart contract interactions, and privacy guarantees. The discussion in Sect. 4 suggests several reasons why the business artifact approach can provide an appropriate basis for this informal reasoning.

The use of FSM's for artifact lifecycles can bring strong advantages, because of their intuitive simplicity and the wealth of widely known informal intuitions and formal algorithms and results about them. However, reasoning about data will be essential, given the importance of ensuring data privacy across different participants. Data can be incorporated in varying degrees, e.g., as follows.

(a) Ignore data, and furthermore focus on situations where there is a bounded number of artifact instances (e.g., at most 10 CO's per PO).

(b) Include modeling of 1-many relationships between artifact instances, e.g., between a PO and its CO's. In one variation, the number of CO's may be unbounded and essentially unrestricted. In another variation, the number of CO's might be unbounded in general, but for each PO there might be a bound on the number of CO's based on the initial input.

(c) Ability to specify structural properties on the data held by one or more artifact instances. This might include referential constraints, e.g., for each instance of Shipment there must be a CO that refers to it, and in turn the ID of that CO is held in the PO data. It might also include key and functional dependencies, perhaps extended to the nested relation context, e.g., that across all CO instances, each shipper can be associated with only one middleman.

(d) It might include arithmetic properties, e.g., that the price of a PO must be below \$5M. The arithmetic properties might cut across artifact instances and rely on aggregation, e.g., that the total price of all CO's is below some percentage of the overall price of the PO.

(e) Finally, these might include *privacy ensuring* constraints. An informal example is that no middleman can see the price associated with any CO that he is not handling.

We now turn more specifically to automatic verification. This relies on precisely defined abstractions that capture key elements of a framework. This sometimes brings a loss of completeness in the model being studied (e.g., by ignoring data, or arithmetical relationships between data values). In the context of automatic verification, achieving decidability and relatively low complexity in the presence of data can require carefully designed restrictions on the model studied. It is typical for verifiers to support algorithms that are *sound* (they are never wrong when they claims correctness of a specification) but not necessarily *complete* (they may produce false negatives, i.e., candidate counter-examples to the desired property, which need to be validated by the user). Importantly, the perspectives and tools developed from the formal perspective may also be helpful for the informal reasoning. As just one example, formal languages developed to specify integrity constraints (both static and temporal) may help in the formulation of targets for informal reasoning, and also lead to design principles. The theory of relational database integrity constraints illustrates how these kinds of mathematical models can have far-reaching practical impact.

A primary goal of formal reasoning about smart contracts is to ensure that during operation they will achieve certain goals, and they will avoid various conditions. The conditions to avoid may be specified in terms of *static constraints*. In the running example, e.g., we may want to avoid any situation where there is a CO and a corresponding Shipment, where the CO is in the state Shipment Delivered and the Shipment is in state Recreate Shipment Requested. This can be thought of as a constraint on a cross-product of all the FSM's of the relevant artifact instances. Richer static constraints involving data might be considered, e.g., relating to structural properties and (aggregate) arithmetic properties.

For such constraints, formal reasoning will typically focus on *reachability*, that is, given (i) a static constraint and (ii) a class of possible input sequences, determine if there is any input sequence that leads to a family of artifact instances that violates the constraint. If data is ignored (and the number of artifact instances is bounded) this reduces essentially to reachability in FSMs. In some contexts this has complexity NLOGSPACE-complete and is tractable. In more general settings, e.g., if the FSM's have non-determinism (as might arise when data is abstracted away), or with the richer kinds of temporal constraints discussed below, verification is PSPACE-complete. Approaches have been developed (e.g., state vector models [24]) to enable practical algorithms for such verification problems. The modeling approach of Petri Nets provides another broad family of verification results to draw upon for contexts where data is ignored [20].

Reachability of states violating a static constraint is in fact a form of *temporal constraint*. More broadly, it is common to reason about the behaviors of a system by using temporal operators, such as those from Linear Temporal Logic (LTL) [42]: **G** (always), **F** (eventually), **X** (next), and **U** (until). For example, $\mathbf{G}p$ (where p is a propositional variable) says that p holds at all times in the run, $\mathbf{F}p$ says that p will eventually hold, and $\mathbf{G}(p \rightarrow \mathbf{F}q)$ says that whenever p holds, q must hold sometime in the future. While LTL (and its variants) are useful for FSM's and other models without data, an extension is needed to include data-aware properties, such as items (b) through (e) in the list given above. To this end an extension of LTL is used, called here LTL-FO [36], in which First-Order (FO) logic formulas are used in place of propositional variables in LTL formulas.

Verification problems for smart contracts with data can be formulated along the lines originally developed in [6,17] for business artifacts. In that setting, each (parameterized) invocable action (a.k.a., "service") is associated with (parameterized) pre- and post-conditions expressed in FO. A common restriction is that the pre- and post-conditions be expressed in existential FO (that is, only existential quantifiers). Suppose now that we are given a system SC with one or more smart contracts, which includes a family $\mathcal{A}$ of invocable actions. Suppose further that φ is an LTL-FO formula. The basic verification problem for SC and φ can be stated as follows: Does every run of SC satisfy φ?

There is already a rich family of results for automatic verification of data-aware processes [11,18]. Several restricted classes of artifact systems have been studied, along with temporal properties expressed in restricted variants of LTL-FO. This includes classes that impose restrictions on how the actions (services) manipulate set-valued attributes, and classes that permit orderings on domain elements, permit arithmetic operators, etc. In most cases the verification problem for the restricted family has worst-case complexity of PSPACE-complete, which is reasonable given that the classical propositional model-checking problem is PSPACE-complete. Further, the WAVE verification tool [16] provides evidence that verification for data-aware processes can be practical. Also, recent theoretical work leverages hierarchy in GSM artifact specifications to enable optimizations in verification algorithms [19].

6   Conclusions

This paper has discussed the merit of using abstractions from business artifacts and its relatives as the basis for a shared ledger Business Collaboration Language (BCL). The use of these abstractions for Blockchain brings several research challenges, some of which are highlighted below.

Modeling abstractions. There are several variations on the basic theme of business artifacts, based mainly a spectrum of possible lifecycle meta-models, ranging from the fully procedural to the fully declarative. A key challenge is choosing the right mix of abstractions that cover the use cases from multiple industry sectors. Designing a coherent BCL that supports the more procedural style of, e.g., FSM's, and also the more declarative style of, e.g., GSM and CMMN, is a particular challenge.

Views. An important aspect of the meta-model underlying a BCL will be support for intuitive ways to specify access rights, that is, to ensure privacy of data and processing steps. Another important area concerns specifying interfaces for how business artifacts from one smart contract will interact with business artifacts from smart contracts. Some notion of business artifact *view* and related constructs (e.g., [27]) will be central in helping to make progress in these areas; see also [4,38].

"On-ramps" to Blockchain: If Blockchain is successful in providing a new level of efficiency for business collaborations, then many businesses will need to convert existing collaborating business processes into blockchain-enabled ones. Adapting legacy business processes will bring many challenges, including the impedance mismatch between the data-aware style of coordination enabled by Blockchain vs. the process-centric style of most legacy processes. The BELA method [46] for business process design can be adapted to help with the conversions, and [47] may provide a useful starting point for managing linkages between data on a blockchain and data maintained by collaboration participants.

Reasoning and Validation. A variety of tools are needed to give strong confidence in the smart contracts that people deploy and mix together. This will include well thought out testing strategies and frameworks, and also succinct representations to simplify human reasoning about the contracts. As suggested in Sect. 5, automatic verification techniques and results for business artifacts can be extended to the Blockchain context. This brings new questions to the forefront, including how to obtain practical verification results in connection with 1-many relationships between business artifacts.

Implementation. Realizing the vision of Blockchain, including scalability and reasonable running speeds, is an on-going work. Finding accurate and efficient ways to support a BCL on top of Blockchain adds another dimension to the engineering challenges. The use of a BCL may permit certain optimizations, analogous to optimizations of database query languages. It remains open whether it will be better to implement a BCL using auto code generation, i.e., mapping a BCL program into, e.g., a Go or Java smart contract, or to create a BCL interpreter that can run on top of blockchains.

Smart Contract Eco-systems. In the coming years we anticipate large libraries of smart contracts that are designed to interact. In a BCL each smart contract might be based on one or several business artifact types. Tools are needed for discovering smart contracts based on artifact types and their milestones, for quickly checking compatibility between them, and for reasoning about and testing behaviors resulting from their interactions.

References

1. van der Aalst, W.M.P., Barthelmess, P., Ellis, C., Wainer, J.: Proclets: a framework for lightweight interacting workflow processes. Int. J. Coop. Inf. Syst. **10**(4), 443–481 (2001)
2. van der Aalst, W., Weske, M., Grünbauer, D.: Case handling: a new paradigm for business process support. Data Knowl. Eng. **53**(2), 129–162 (2005)
3. Abiteboul, S., Bidoit, N.: Non first normal form relations: an algebra allowing data restructuring. J. Comput. Syst. Sci. **33**(3), 361–393 (1986)
4. Abiteboul, S., Vianu, V.: Collaborative data-driven workflows: think global, act local. In: International Symposyum on Principles of Database Systems (PODS) (2013)
5. Bhattacharya, K., Caswell, N.S., Kumaran, S., Nigam, A., Wu, F.Y.: Artifact-centered operational modeling: lessons from customer engagements. IBM Syst. J. **46**(4), 703–721 (2007)
6. Bhattacharya, K., Gerede, C.E., Hull, R., Liu, R., Su, J.: Towards formal analysis of artifact-centric business process models. In: Alonso, G., Dadam, P., Rosemann, M. (eds.) BPM 2007. LNCS, vol. 4714, pp. 288–304. Springer, Heidelberg (2007)

7. Boaz, D., Limonad, L., Gupta, M.: BizArtifact: Artifact-centric Business Process Management (open-source code base), June 2013. http://sourceforge.net/projects/bizartifact/. Accessed 20 July 2016

8. Boaz, D., Heath, T., Gupta, M., Limonad, L., Sun, Y., Hull, R., Vaculín, R.: The ACSI hub: a data-centric environment for service interoperation. In: Proceedings of BPM Demo Sessions (2014)

9. Business Process Model and Notation (BPMN), version 2.0, 3 January 2011. http://www.omg.org/spec/BPMN/2.0. Accessed 10 July 2016

10. Brown, R.G.: Introducing R3 Corda^{TM}: A Distributed Ledger Designed for Financial Services. http://r3cev.com/blog/2016/4/4/introducing-r3-corda-a-distributed-ledger-designed-for-financial-services. Accessed 20 July 2016

11. Calvanese, D., De Giacomo, G., Montali, M.: Foundations of data-aware process analysis: a database theory perspective. In: International Symposyum Principles of Database Systems (PODS) (2013)

12. Chao, T., Cohn, D., Flatgard, A., Hahn, S., Linehan, M., Nandi, P., Nigam, A., Pinel, F., Vergo, J., Wu, F.: Artifact-based transformation of IBM global financing. In: Dayal, U., Eder, J., Koehler, J., Reijers, H.A. (eds.) BPM 2009. LNCS, vol. 5701, pp. 261–277. Springer, Heidelberg (2009)

13. Cohn, D., Dhoolia, P., Heath III, F., Pinel, F., Vergo, J.: Siena: from powerpoint to web app in 5 minutes. In: Bouguettaya, A., Krueger, I., Margaria, T. (eds.) ICSOC 2008. LNCS, vol. 5364, pp. 722–723. Springer, Heidelberg (2008)

14. Cohn, D., Hull, R.: Business artifacts: a data-centric approach to modeling business operations and processes. IEEE Data Eng. Bull. **32**, 3–9 (2009)

15. Damaggio, E., Hull, R., Vaculín, R.: On the equivalence of incremental and fixpoint semantics for business artifacts with guard-stage-milestone lifecycles. Inf. Syst. **38**, 561–584 (2013)

16. Deutsch, A., Vianu, V.: WAVE: automatic verification of data-driven web services. IEEE Data Eng. Bull. **31**(3), 35–39 (2008)

17. Deutsch, A., Hull, R., Patrizi, F., Vianu, V.: Automatic verification of data-centric business processes. In: International Conference on Database Theory (ICDT) (2009)

18. Deutsch, A., Hull, R., Vianu, V.: Automatic verification of database-centric systems. SIGMOD Rec. **43**(3), 5–17 (2014)

19. Deutsch, A., Li, Y., Vianu, V.: Verification of hierarchical artifact systems. In: International Symposyum on Principles of Database Systems (PODS) (2016)

20. Diaz, M. (ed.): Petri Nets: Fundamental Models, Verification and Applications. Wiley, Jersey City (2009)

21. Introducing the Digital Asset Modeling Language. https://digitalasset.com/press/introducing-daml.html. Accessed 20 July 2016

22. A Next-Generation Smart Contract and Decentralized ApplicationPlatform (2016). https://github.com/ethereum/wiki/wiki/White-Paper. Accessed 20 July 2016

23. Flood, M.D., Goodenough, O.R.: Contract as automaton: the computational representation of financial agreements, 26 March 2015. https://financialresearch.gov/working-papers/files/OFRwp-2015-04_Contract-as-Automaton-The-Computational-Representation-of-Financial-Agreements.pdf. Accessed 16 July 2016

24. Holzmann, G.J.: An improved protocol reachability analysis technique. Softw. Pract. Exper. **18**(2), 137–161 (1988)

25. Holzmann, G.J., Bosnacki, D.: Multi-core model checking with SPIN. In: International Parallel and Distributed Processing Symposium (IPDPS) (2007)

26. Hulin, G.: On restructuring nested relations in partitioned normal form. In: International Conference on Very Large Data Bases (VLDB) (1990)
27. Hull, R., Narendra, N.C., Nigam, A.: Facilitating workflow interoperation using artifact-centric hubs. In: Baresi, L., Chi, C.-H., Suzuki, J. (eds.) ICSOC-ServiceWave 2009. LNCS, vol. 5900, pp. 1–18. Springer, Heidelberg (2009)
28. Hull, R., et al.: Business artifacts with guard-stage-milestone lifecycles: Managing artifact interactions with conditions and events. In: ACM International Conference on Distributed Event-based Systems (DEBS) (2011)
29. Hull, R., Su, J.: Report on NSF Workshop on Data-CentricWorkflows (2012). http://dcw2009.cs.ucsb.edu/report.pdf
30. Hull, R., Su, J., Vaculín, R.: Data management perspectives on business process management: tutorial overview. In: International Conference on Management of Data (SIGMOD) (2013)
31. Hyperledger white paper (2015). www.the-blockchain.com/docs/Hyperledger%20Whitepaper.pdf. Accessed 16 July 2016
32. Kumaran, S., Nandi, P., Heath III., F.T., Bhaskaran, K., Das, R.: ADoc-oriented programming. In: Symposyum on Applications and the Internet (SAINT) (2003)
33. Künzle, V., Reichert, M.: PHILharmonicflows: towards a framework for object-aware process management. J. Softw. Maint. **23**(4), 205–244 (2011)
34. Limonad, L., Boaz, D., Hull, R., Vaculín, R., Heath III., F.T.: A generic business artifacts based authorization framework for cross-enterprise collaboration. In: SRII Global Conference (2012)
35. Liu, R., Vaculín, R., Shan, Z., Nigam, A., Wu, F.: Business artifact-centric modeling for real-time performance monitoring. In: Rinderle-Ma, S., Toumani, F., Wolf, K. (eds.) BPM 2011. LNCS, vol. 6896, pp. 265–280. Springer, Heidelberg (2011)
36. Manna, Z., Pnueli, A.: Verification of concurrent programs, part i: the temporal framework. Technical Report STAN-CS-81-836, Stanford University (1981)
37. Marin, M., Hull, R., Vaculín, R.: Data-centric BPM and the emerging Case Management standard: a short survey. In: Business Process Management, Workshops (2012)
38. Moffitt, V.Z., Stoyanovich, J., Abiteboul, S., Miklau, G.: Collaborative access control in webdamlog. In: ACM International Conference on Management of Data (SIGMOD) (2015)
39. Nakamoto, S.: Bitcoin: A Peer-to-Peer Electronic Cash System (2009). https://bitcoin.org/bitcoin.pdf. Accessed 16 July 2016
40. Nguyen, T., Fiammante, M.: Match processes to business needs: ApplyBELA to case management, October, 2011. http://www-01.ibm.com/software/solutions/soa/newsletter/october11/bela_case_management.html. Accessed 20 July 2016
41. Nigam, A., Caswell, N.S.: Business artifacts: an approach to operational specification. IBM Syst. J. **42**(3), 428–445 (2003)
42. Pnueli, A.: The temporal logic of programs. In: Symposium on Foundations of Computer Science (FOCS) (1977)
43. Redding, G., et al.: A flexible, object-centric approach for business process modelling. SOCA **4**(3), 191–201 (2010)
44. Redding, G., Dumas, M., ter Hofstede, A.H.M., Iordachescu, A.: Transforming object-oriented models to process-oriented models. In: ter Hofstede, A.H.M., Benatallah, B., Paik, H.-Y. (eds.) BPM Workshops 2007. LNCS, vol. 4928, pp. 132–143. Springer, Heidelberg (2008)
45. Solidity. https://solidity.readthedocs.io/en/latest/. Accessed 20 July 2016
46. Strosnider, J., Nandi, P., Kumaran, S., Ghosh, S., Arsanjani, A.: Model-driven synthesis of SOA solutions. IBM Syst. J. **47**(3), 415–432 (2008)

47. Sun, Y., Su, J., Yang, J.: Universal artifacts: a new approach to business process management (BPM) systems. ACM Trans. Manag. Inf. Syst. **7**(1) (2016). Article id. 7
48. Weber, I., Xu, X.S., Riveret, R., Governatori, G., Ponomarev, A., Mendling, J.: Untrusted business process monitoring and execution using blockchain. In: International Conference Business Process Management (BPM), Rio de Janeiro, Brazil, September 2016
49. Zhang, F., Cecchetti, E., Croman, K., Juels, A., Shi, E.: Towncrier: an authenticated data feed for smart contracts. IACR Cryptology ePrint Archive 2016 (2016). http://eprint.iacr.org/2016/168. Accessed 20 July 2016

Business Process Management

Optimizing Process Model Redesign

Akhil Kumar[1]([⊠]) and Paronkasom Indradat[2]

[1] Smeal College of Business, Penn State University,
University Park, PA 16802, USA
akhil@psu.edu
[2] Department of Industrial Engineering, Penn State University,
University Park, PA 16802, USA
pxi5005@psu.edu

Abstract. In recent years there has been considerable interest in business process redesign. A process model may be redesigned by combining various tasks and services according to best practices so as to satisfy predefined business rules and constraints to achieve a specific purpose. This purpose may be stated in terms of functional goals (such as desired or acceptable process behavior) and non-functional goals like cost, time and quality of service. There are many ways to redesign a process instance by applying improvements such as: making a task optional, replacing a task by another faster task (or service), task postponement, task combination, task splitting, task restructuring, etc. Given many such alternatives, there is no systematic way of evaluating their costs and benefits, and the tradeoffs among them. We describe a novel approach based on a formal model to optimize the "benefits" or net effects of a redesign with respect to a baseline design and show how it can be used to evaluate and compare alternative models at both design and run time.

1 Introduction

Organizations are constantly trying to improve their business processes to make them more efficient in terms of time, cost, quality and flexibility [6, 11, 13], and also to deal with exigencies. Thus, under higher workload conditions an Australian insurance service company may decide to escalate its claim handling by collecting less information than they normally do, e.g. during the storm season when the call volume doubles [18]. Escalation may involve changing the routing of work, the work distribution, or the requirements with respect to available data. Such temporary or periodic redesign measures are necessary to maintain the service quality during a busy season, while other redesigns may be permanent. In a similar vein, a car rental company may decide to make the car wash task before renting out a car optional or replace it by an express wash when the demand is too high or there is a resource shortage. Clearly, this can save on the cost and time of a car wash but it may hurt customer service.

A bank that normally requires two officers to approve a mortgage application may instead have only one officer approve them when the workload is very high. In this situation, it is possible that the quality of the customer service will not suffer but the likelihood of making a bad loan may go up and may impact profitability. Sometimes there are alternative designs for the same process. For example, the bank may choose to

© Springer International Publishing Switzerland 2016
Q.Z. Sheng et al. (Eds.): ICSOC 2016, LNCS 9936, pp. 39–54, 2016.
DOI: 10.1007/978-3-319-46295-0_3

use a faster credit appraisal service that does appraisals in 3 days instead of the normal 6 days but at a higher cost than the normal cost. Thus, there is a tradeoff between the two scenarios that has both cost and time implications. The bank must decide whether to pursue scenario 1, scenario 2 or both scenarios. In a medical context, there may be a tradeoff between a normal test that takes 5 days and costs $100, and an expedited test that takes 3 days and costs $300. In such a situation, deciding whether to select the normal test or the expedited test is also an optimization issue.

Our goal in this paper is to develop a way to model such process design scenarios and find the optimal design in view of business constraints. Hence, the ideal design will depend on the actual realities of a dynamic situation. In the literature there have already been efforts to develop best practices and heuristics to improve processes, notably by Mansar and Reijers [11]. Our work is in part inspired by these ideas, and we wish to apply them in the context of a formal model that can help us determine and recommend the best design that satisfies cost and time constraints. We also build upon our previous work on approaches for modeling and optimizing temporal workflows [8] by extending that model to add support for redesign. In particular we show how to add support in our model for 6 different types of process improvements: *optional tasks*; *task replacement*; *task restructuring* (from sequence to parallel); *task combination*; *task splitting*; and *task postponement*.

In qualitative terms we can see that each alternative scenario in the situations described above represents a clear tradeoff with other scenarios. But it is also important to have a mechanism to evaluate and compare them systematically. We will show how such tradeoffs can be evaluated and optimized using metrics like cost, time, quality and flexibility. To the best of our knowledge this paper is a first effort towards a formal approach for evaluating alternative options for redesign.

The main contributions of this paper are as follows: First, we develop a new approach to model process improvement alternatives correctly. Second, we show how these different scenarios can be evaluated in terms of key metrics like cost, quality, time and flexibility. Third, we show how the scenarios and the metrics can be combined into an optimization model. Fourth, we present results of analysis using a realistic case study. Finally, we also describe an implementation approach for our proposal.

This paper is organized as follows. In Sect. 2 we discuss a basic model for describing temporal constraints and show how it can be translated into structural and temporal constraint equations. Then, in Sect. 3, we describe common improvement scenarios based on best practices. Next, Sect. 4 develops an optimal redesign model using evaluation metrics. Section 5 illustrates our approach with a detailed case study. Later, Sect. 6 discusses the main features and limitations of our approach, and Sect. 7 concludes the paper with some thoughts for future work.

2 Preliminaries

To be able to evaluate redesign alternatives the first step is to have a formal method to describe the control flow of a model and the temporal constraints for each task. In this section we describe a simple temporal model and show how structural and temporal constraints are represented.

2.1   A Simple Temporal Model

A temporal model of a process is made by combining two types of constraints: (1) structural constraints, and (2) temporal constraints. The structural constraints capture the control flow of the process to coordinate the proper sequence in which the tasks occur. The temporal flow model considers the permitted durations of each activity and the minimum or maximum gaps between them.

Definition 1. A general temporal process model TP can be represented as:

$$TP = (T, A, X, E, TD, TI)$$

Where

T: set of task nodes, T_1, T_2, ...

A: set of AND control nodes, A_1, A_2, ...

X: set of XOR control nodes, X_1, X_2, ...

E: set of edges among the nodes in $\{T, A, X\}$

TD: set of task duration ranges: $\{(T_i, D_{i\_min}, D_{i\_max}), ...\}$, where D_{i_min}, $D_{i\_max} \in R+$

TI: set of additional inter-task constraints: $\{(T_i, T_j, S|F, S|F, TI_{i\_min}, TI_{i\_max}), ...\}$, TI_{i_min}, $TI_{i\_max} \in R+$

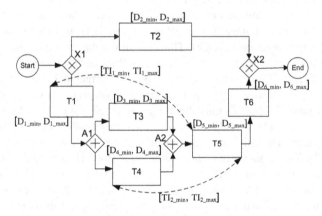

Fig. 1. A basic temporal model with XOR and AND connectors

Figure 1 is an example of a simple temporal model. It shows the control flow, along with [min, max] durations of each task and inter-task constraints. It is expressed as:

T : $\{T_1, T_2, ..., T_6\}$

A : $\{A_1, A_2\}$

X : $\{X_1, X_2, X_3, X_4\}$

$E : \{(\text{start}, X_1), (X_1, T_1), (X_1, T_2), (T_1, A_1), (A_1, T_3), (A_1, T_4), (T_3, A_2), (T_4, A_2), \ldots\}$

$TD : \{(T_1, D_{1\_min}, D_{1\_max}), (T_2, D_{2\_min}, D_{2\_max}), (T_3, D_{3\_min}, D_{3\_max}), \ldots\}$

$TI : \{(T_1, T_5, S, S, TI_{1\_min}, TI_{1\_max}), (T_4, T_5, S, F, TI_{2\_min}, TI_{2\_max})\}$

In addition to the time intervals of each task, an inter-task constraint (TI) can also be represented by a dashed line connecting the start or end of a task to the start or end of another task. For example, in Fig. 1, the inter-task constraint TI_2 between T_4 and T_5 requires that the elapsed time from the start of T_4 until the end of T_5 must lie in the $[TI_{2\_min}, TI_{2\_max}]$ interval. Also note that while we only consider task and inter-task durations, fixed time activities can also be modeled by setting their relative time with respect to the start of a process and converting them into delays with respect to the start activity.

2.2   Structural and Temporal Constraints

Next we show how to map the above model into structural and temporal constraint equations that can be solved using a constraint satisfaction approach. The flow constraints capture the coordination sequence among tasks, while the temporal constraints specify the task and inter-task durations.

Structural Constraints (SC). Structural constraints are represented by structural equations to capture the flow of a process. In doing so, each task, and also the start and end tasks, are treated as binary 0–1 variables (where 1(0) denotes the presence (absence) of a task in a process instance). The structural balance equations for sequence, choice and parallel patterns expressed in terms of their corresponding variable names are shown in Fig. 2. These equations describe the correct behavior of a workflow consisting of various structures. A sequence structure (see row 1 of Fig. 2) requires that two sequential tasks T_1 and T_2 must have the same value, i.e. $T_1 = T_2 = 0$; or $T_1 = T_2 = 1$. Further, at a choice-split node, the balance equation ensures that when a choice-split is activated, only one outgoing branch becomes active but not both (see row 2 of Fig. 2). The behavior at a choice-join node (row 3) forces $X2 = 1$ only when exactly one but not both of T_1 and T_2 are 1. Note that in row 3, M is a very large number (say, 10000), and Y is an auxiliary variable used to hold a temporary binary value that in turn is used to determine $X2$. Rows 4 and 5 capture the correct behavior at an AND-split or-join node.

Similarly one could describe mandatory, prohibited, co-existing, exclusive and constrained choice patterns. As discussed in [8] a complete structural process model is one that includes: (a) one equation that captures the link of each task T_i (or connector X_i, A_i) to its preceding task(s) and/or connector(s) unless T_i is the first task in the process; and (b) one equation that captures the link of each task T_i (or connector X_i, A_i) to its succeeding task(s) and/or connector(s) unless T_i is the last task in the process. By solving the system of equations simultaneously for a sound process model a solution for an instance of the process is found with values for T_i, X_i, and A_i variables.

Temporal constraints (TC). The temporal constraints express a variety of temporal relationships. Here we consider three types of constraints: flow, task duration and inter-task gap constraints. Temporal Flow (TF) constraints are derived from the edge set E. For every node n_i and successive node pair (n_i, n_j) in E, we add two constraints as:

$TS_i \leq TF_i$

$TF_i \leq TS_j$

where

TS_i: start time of node i relative to the start time of the workflow instance

TF_i: finish time of node i relative to the start time of the workflow instance

	Structure	Representation	Constraint equation
1.	Sequence	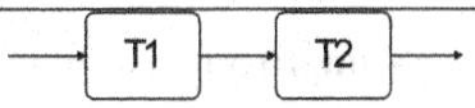 T1 — T2	$T2 = T1;$
2.	Choice-Split	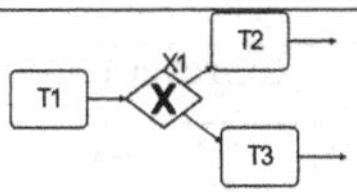 T1 — X — T2 / T3	$X1 = T2 + T3;$
3.	Choice-Join	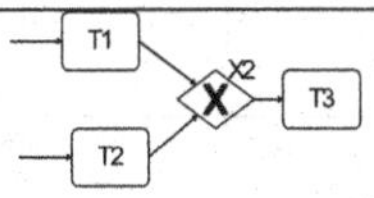 T1 / T2 — X2 — T3	$T1 + T2 - 1 \leq M(1 - Y);$ $2 - T1 - T2 \leq M*Y;$ $X2 \leq T1 + T2; X2 \leq Y$ $X2 \geq T1 - T2; X2 \geq T2 - T1;$
4.	Parallel-Split	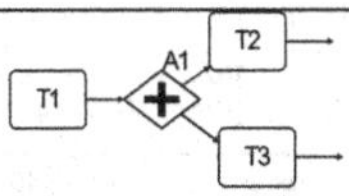 T1 — A1 — T2 / T3	$T2 = A1; T3 = A1;$
5.	Parallel-Join	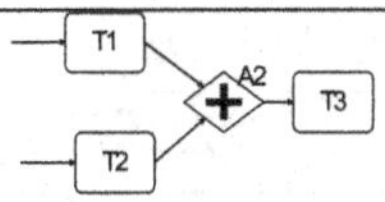 T1 / T2 — A2 — T3	$A2 \geq T1 + T2 - 1;$ $A2 \leq T1; A2 \leq T2;$

Fig. 2. Structural balance equations for process modeling structures

The Task duration (TD) constraints ensure that the duration of a task T_i lies between the permitted range $[D_{i\_min}, D_{i\_max}]$. They are specified as: $D_{i\_min} \leq TF_i - TS_i \leq D_{i\_max}$. The Inter-task (TI) constraints ensure that the gap or delay between the start (end) of an activity pair (i, j) lies in the permitted $[G_{ij\_min}, G_{ij\_max}]$ range. They are specified as: $G_{ij\_min} \leq TF_j (TS_j) - TS_i (TF_i) \leq G_{ij\_max}$. Finally, duration constraints for X and A-split connectors are: $XF_i - XS_i = 0$; and $AF_i - AS_i = 0$, respectively. For A-join connectors, $AF_j = Max(TF_i)$, $\forall TF_i$ s.t. $(TF_i, AF_j) \in E$. A solution of a (combined structural and temporal process model) is of the form:

$\forall T_i, (T_i, TS_i, TF_i), T_i = 0$ or $1, TS_i, TF_i \in R+$

$\forall X_i, (X_i, XS_i, XF_i), X_i = 0$ or $1, XS_i, XF_i \in R+$

$\forall A_i, (A_i, AS_i, AF_i), A_i = 0$ or $1, AS_i, AF_i \in R+$

if $T_i (X_i$ or $A_i) = 0$ then $TS_i (XS_i$ or $AS_i)$ and $TF_i (AS_i$ or $AF_i)$ are not valid.

It has been shown previously [8] that a process model is consistent if for every valid and complete execution path (from start to end) there exists a solution that satisfies the duration and inter-task constraints.

3 Process Redesign Strategies

In [11] various process improvement strategies to redesign a process are discussed. After analysis, we identified six important strategies that are amenable to our formal approach as shown in Table 1. The first row shows a baseline, existing process and subsequent rows show the effect of applying various strategies to it.

Table 1. Process improvement strategies

Improvement	Representation	T	C	Q
0.Normal process (default or baseline)				
1.Optional task (if $O_2 = 1$, duration of $T_2 = 0$)		+	+	-
2.Task Replacement (if $R_2 = 1$, duration of $T_2 = [R_{2min}, R_{2max}]$)		+	+	-
3.Task Combination (if $C_{12} = 1$, revise durations of T_1, T_2)		+	+	-
4.Task Splitting (if $S_2 = 1$, split T_2 into T_2 and $T_{2'}$)		-	-	+
5.Parallelism (if $P_{23} = 1$, restructure T_2 and T_3 into a parallel structure)		+	+	-
6. Task postponement (delay T_1 until after T_2 and T_3)		+	+	-

Strategy 1 is to make a task optional so at run time it may be skipped (e.g. skip the car wash task when work load is high). Strategy 2 replaces a normal task with an alternative task (e.g. replace a regular car wash with an express wash). Strategies 3 and 4 combine two (or more) small tasks into one, and split a large task into multiple tasks, respectively. Strategy 5 aims to take two tasks in sequence and run them in parallel to save time. Finally strategy 6 would reorder the tasks in a process such that one task is postponed from its normal position and performed later. Along with the strategy we describe how it can be modeled by modifying the temporal model discussed above. The last three columns show whether the effect of the improvement on time, cost and quality metrics is positive or negative.

Table 2. Modifying constraints to capture redesign alternatives in the model:

Improvement	Benefit	Cost	Modified/New constraints
1. Make T_i optional (Variable $O_i = 1$)	Save time by skipping one approval	Quality may suffer from higher risk of error or poor service	Duration of T_i = $[D_{imin} - O_i * D_{imin}, D_{imax} - O_i * D_{imax}]$
2. Replace Ti with task R_i (Variable $R_i = 1$)	R_i takes Δ_r less time than T_i	R_i may cost more than T_i. It may also not be as reliable	Duration of T_i = $[D_{imin} - R_i * \Delta\_r, D_{imax} - R_i * \Delta\_r]$
3. Combine T_i, T_j into one task T_{ij} (variable $C_{ij} = 1$)	Finish early and save cost of resource for T_j	Quality may improve if two tasks are closely related. It may also suffer since one point of control is removed	Duration of T_i = $[D_{imin} + C_{ij} * \Delta_c, D_{imax} + C_{ij} * \Delta_c]$; Duration of $T_j = 0$
4. Split T_i into two tasks, T_i and $T_{i'}$ (variable $S_i = 1$)	Break difficult task into two tasks for better results	Extra cost of handoff between tasks is incurred	Duration of T_i = $[D_{2min} - \Delta_{s1}, D_{2max} - \Delta_{s1}]$. Duration of $T_{i'}$ = $[D_{2min} - \Delta_{s2}, D_{2max} - \Delta_{s2}]$
5. Change T_i and T_j from sequence to parallel (variable $P_{ij} = 1$)	Finish early since 2 tasks occur in parallel	Possible drop in quality since the two approvals are not in sequence	$TS_j \geq TF_i - M * P_{ij}$ $TS_j \geq TS_{i\_pred} - (1-P_{ij}) * M$ $TS_i \leq TF_{j\_succ} - (1-P_{ij}) * M$
6. Task Postponement (variable $PO_i = 1$)	Do task T_i later out of order. May be able to skip it.	Possible loss of information or accuracy from changing the order of a task	$TS_j \geq TF_i - M * PO_i$ [M is a very large number]

Next we show how these strategies can be captured into the modeling framework developed in the previous section. The modeling approach for each strategy is described in Table 2. The last three columns show the positive or negative effect of applying each strategy on time (T), cost (C) and quality (Q) on the base model. To make task T_i optional, we introduce another task variable O_i. In addition we make the duration of T_i a function of variable O_i such that it will be 0 when $O_i = 1$. This is equivalent to skipping T_i. Similarly, we introduce a variable R_i to allow replacement of T_i. If $R_i = 1$, then the duration of T_i is adjusted by Δ_r to be the same as the duration of R_i. For task combination, two tasks T_i and T_j are combined into a new task T_i (with a duration $[D_{imin} + C_{ij} * \Delta_c, D_{imax} + C_{ij} * \Delta_c])$ and T_j with a duration of 0. In a task split $(S_i = 1)$, we replace task T_i with two tasks T_i and $T_{i'}$ and change their durations. If a variable $P_{ij} = 1$ then tasks T_i and T_j are restructured into a parallel structure. To do so the sequential constraint $TS_j \geq TF_i$ between T_i and T_j is relaxed to $TS_j \geq TF_i - M * P_{ij}$, where M is a very large number (say, 10000). Two more constraints are added to maintain the ordering relationship of T_i and T_j with their preceding (TS_{i_pred}) and succeeding (TS_{i_succ}) tasks. The effect of M in these constraints is to activate them only when $P_{ij} = 1$, and disable them when $P_{ij} = 0$.

For task postponement the ordering of tasks may be changed in a similar way. Thus, $T_1-T_2-T_3$ may be reordered as $T_2-T_3-T_1$ or as $T_1-T_3-T_2$. This requires relaxing the temporal relationship between a postponed task T_i and its successor task T_j. Table 2 summarizes the benefits and costs of each improvement discussed and also shows the modified or additional constraints. We will discuss the correctness of our approach later in the paper.

4   Building and Solving a General Optimal Redesign Model

Above we have described a general framework for incorporating various model improvements into a formal model. In this way a model can be designed by simply setting parameter values for O_i, R_i, C_{ij}, P_{ij}, S_i, PO_i, etc. suitably. However, in general we would like the model to give us an optimal solution that tells us which design to select particularly when several improvements are possible and they cannot be applied at the same time. This means that we need a metric to evaluate each design. In quantitative terms we wish to study the effect of key metrics like cost, time and quality (where a positive effect is good and a negative effect is bad). Thus, we could have an objective function to express the total benefit (or net effect) of a design as the weighted sum of the redesign variables:

$$\textbf{max } \textit{Obj} = \sum_i BO_i * O_i + BR_i * R_i + BS_i * S_i + \sum_{i,j} BC_{ij} * C_{ij} + BP_{ij} * P_{ij}$$

Where

BO_i = Benefit coefficient of parameter O_i

BR_i = Benefit coefficient of parameter R_i

BP_{ij} = Benefit coefficient of parameter P_{ij}

BC_{ij} = Benefit coefficient of parameter C_{ij}

BS_i = Benefit coefficient of parameter S_i

BPO_i = Benefit coefficient of parameter PO_i

Each BX_i or BX_{ij} term in the objective function above represents a net benefit of making the design change. Thus, each term captures the main factors of cost and quality. The time factor is reflected in the model separately as we have seen above. Cost is already in dollar terms and would represent the savings if an optional task i is skipped or the increase/decrease if a task j is replaced by another task and would be a component of coefficient BO_i and BR_j, respectively. Another consideration in these coefficients is the quality factor. Skipping an optional task may hurt the quality of the process and lead to extra cost in repairs or loss because a task was skipped. This would be a second component of the BO_i and BR_j coefficients.

$$
\begin{array}{|l|}
\hline
\text{Min } \mathbf{Obj} = W1{*}\text{Cost} + W2 * \text{Time} + W3 * \text{Quality} \\
\text{S.T.} \\
\text{1) Structural constraints} \\
\text{2) Temporal constraints} \\
\text{3) Design improvement constraints} \\
\text{4) Design integrity constraints} \\
\text{5) Constraints on metrics, e.g.} \\
\qquad \text{Total time} < T_{max}; \\
\qquad \text{Total Cost} < C_{max}; \\
\qquad \text{Quality} > Q_{min}; \\
\hline
\end{array}
$$

Fig. 3. An optimization model for selecting the best redesign

The net effect of these two components would produce a value that may be negative or positive. A negative value of BO_i or BR_j may be compensated by a reduction in the throughput time of the process. For example, consider the effect of skipping task T_2 ('check credit report and appraisal') in the process of Fig. 4. This will clearly have a positive effect on cost (since a resource does not have to work on this task) but negative effect on quality (as it may raise the chances of making a bad loan). Say the imputed effect on cost is a savings of $50. However, the negative effect on quality has an imputed value of $100 based on the higher risk of a bad loan. Thus, $BO_2 = 50 - 100 = -50$. Similarly, say, task T_2 can be outsourced to another service that is faster by 5 h but costs more. In this case the quality does not suffer but there is an additional cost of $25 in using this service. Hence, $BR_2 = -25$.

As we shall illustrate in the next section, the general problem can be framed in different ways by modifying the objective function and the set of constraints. The objective function can be a weighted sum (using weights W1, W2, ...) of cost, time, quality, and flexibility terms. The constraints may be modified to impose various limits on these metrics as well. Then we can frame the problem in terms of a generic mixed integer linear programming (MILP) model as shown in Fig. 3.

5   A Case Study

In this section we discuss a realistic case to illustrate how our redesign optimization approach works. We first describe an example of a mortgage loan approval process, then show how it is modeled using our approach and finally, solve the model to create alternative redesign scenarios.

Consider the example in Fig. 4 of a loan approval process. In this process an application is received (T_1), then a credit report for the applicant and an appraisal report for the property are obtained (T_2) from an external service provider. Depending upon the contents of the reports, some applicants are automatically rejected and in these cases the instance follows the lower path at the XOR node. Along this path, a manager approves the rejection (T_4), an assistant prepares the rejection notice (T_5) and then the applicant is notified (T_{10}). If the reports are 'OK', then the instance follows the upper path at the XOR node. Along this path a financial officer makes a recommendation (T_3) and this is followed by two approvals $(T_6$ and T_7 - by a manager and a VP) in the next two steps. An assistant then prepares the notification (T_8) and it is sent to the applicant (T_{10}).

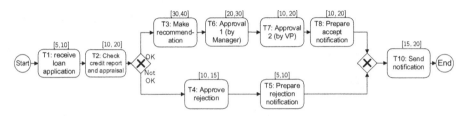

Fig. 4. An example base process model

There are several redesign possibilities in this process model as follows:

- Task T_2 may be replaced by another task R_2 that takes 5 time units less
- Tasks T_6 and T_7 are each optional (but not both together)
- Tasks T_6 and T_7 may be performed in parallel if they are not skipped
- Tasks T_6 and T_7 are combined into a new task T_{67} that takes 5 units more than T_6

Now in this situation, we are interested in creating scenarios that help us to answer the following kinds of questions by solving the optimization model at design/run time:

1. Find the design in which a process instance can finish in the fastest time?
2. Find the design in which a process instance gives the maximum benefit?
3. Find the maximum benefit design subject to an instance finish time limit?

Next we will show how the process of Fig. 4 can be modeled for redesign. Figure 5 (a) shows the original (partial) model and Fig. 5(b) shows the corresponding changes made to the constraint set to ensure that the above design constraints are satisfied. There are three important observations with respect to Fig. 5(b). First we modify the temporal flow constraints to model the effect of a change in the structure of T_i and T_j from sequence to parallel. This is achieved by relaxing the strict $TS_j \geq TF_i$ requirement by adding $-1000 * P_{ij}$ term to the right hand side. Thus, if P_{ij} is 1 then the sequential requirement is relaxed. Moreover, two other constraints are needed to ensure that the sequential relationships of T_i with the successor of T_j, and T_j with the predecessor of T_i, are maintained.

Minimize Obj.
s.t.
//Structural constraints (SC)
Start. Start = 1;
End. End = 1;
SF0. T_1 = Start;
SF1. $T_2 = T_1$;
SF2. $X_1 = T_2$;
SF3. $T_3 + T_4 = X_1$;
SF4. $T_6 = T_3$; $T_7 = T_6$; $T_8 = T_7$;
...
//Temporal flow constraints (TF)
TF1. $TS_7 \geq TF_6$;
TF2. $TS_8 \geq TF_7$;
...
//Temporal duration constraints (TD)
TD1. $10 \leq TF_2 - TS_2 \leq 20$;
TD2. $20 \leq TF_6 - TS_6 \leq 30$;
TD3. $10 \leq TF_7 - TS_7 \leq 20$;

(a) Original model

Minimize Obj.
s.t.
//Modified temporal flow constraints (TF)
TF1'. $TS_7 \geq TF_6 - 1000 * P_{67}$;
TF2'. $TS_7 \geq TF_3 - 1000 * (1 - P_{67})$;
TF2''. $TS_8 \geq TF_6 - 1000 * (1 - P_{67})$;
...
//Modified duration constraints (TD)
TD1'. $TF_2 - TS_2 \leq 20 - 5 * R_2 - 20 * O_2$;
TD2'. $TF_6 - TS_6 \leq 30 + 5 * C_{67} - 30 * O_6$;
TD3'. $TF_7 - TS_7 \leq 20 - 20 * C_{67} - 20 * O_7$;
...
// Add design integrity constraints
C0. $TS_i \leq TF_i$; (for i = 2, 6, 7)
C1. $P_{67} = 1 \rightarrow O_6 + O_7 == 0$;
C2. $C_{67} = 1 \rightarrow O_6 + O_7 == 0$;
C3. $P_{67} + C_{67} \leq 1$;
C4. $O_2 + R_2 \leq 1$;
C5. $C_{67} + O_6 \leq 1$; $C_{67} + O_7 \leq 1$;

(b) Modified model

Fig. 5. Original model and modifications needed to incorporate improvements

Second, we modify the duration of an optional task T_i based on whether it is skipped ($O_i = 1$), replaced by task R_i ($R_i = 1$), or combined with task T_j ($C_{ij} = 1$). Thus,

$$TF_i - TS_i \geq D_{i\_min} - O_i * D_{i\_min} - R_i * \Delta_{r1} + C_{ij} * \Delta_{c1}$$
$$TF_i - TS_i \leq D_{i\_max} - O_i * D_{i\_max} - R_i * \Delta_{r2} + C_{ij} * \Delta_{c2}$$
$$TF_i \geq TS_i$$

Third, additional constraints are needed to ensure the integrity of the design: The duration of a constraint must be non-negative (C_0). Also, if $P_{ij} = 1$ or $C_{ij} = 1$, then T_i and T_j should not be optional tasks (constraints C_1, C_2). Moreover, P_{ij} and C_{ij} are mutually exclusive (C_3). O_i and R_i are also exclusive as a task cannot be optional and be replaced by another task at the same time (C_4).

It is important to note that our formulation will revert to the original "baseline" model if the O_i, R_i, C_{ij} and P_{ij} variables are all set to 0. Now we discuss the scenarios that were introduced above. In each case we modify the **Obj** function. Also note that in these solutions we focus on the upper path in the process of Fig. 4 that corresponds to the credit report and proposal being 'OK' since this is the more interesting case.

Scenario 1: *Shortest finish time redesign.* Here we set **Obj** = TF_{10}. On solving the model we get $TF_{10} = 70$. The solution for this model using CPlex [2] is:

- $T_1 = T_2 = T_3 = T_6 = T_7 = T_8 = T_{10} = 1$; $O_2 = O_6 = 1$.

All other variables are 0. The interpretation of this solution is that tasks T_2 and T_6 are skipped since O_2 and O_6 are 1. In doing so we obtain the solution that takes the least time. Note that in the way we construct the model, the values of variables T_2 and T_6 are still 1, but their durations are 0, i.e. they are skipped.

Scenario 2: *Max benefit redesign.* Now we modify the objective Obj to a benefit function by aggregating the effect of various redesign options as follows:

Obj = Maximize

$BO_2 * O_2 + BR_2 * R_2 + BO_6 * O_6 + BO_7 * O_7 + BP_{67} * P_{67} + BC_{67} * C_{67} - 0.01 * TF_{10}$;

Where

BO_2: net benefit from skipping optional task $T_2 = -50$

BR_2: net benefit from replacing task T_2 with task $R_2 = -25$

BO_6: net benefit from skipping optional task $T_6 = 25$

BO_7: net benefit from skipping optional task $T_7 = -50$

BP_{67}: net benefit from doing T_6 and T_7 in parallel $= -10$

BC_{67}: net benefit from combining T_6 and T_7 into one task $= 50$

The objective function consists of the sum of the individual benefit from each *design* option. The last term in the objective function includes the finish time of the last task TF_{10} so that among solutions of equal benefit one with the smallest finish time is found. The solution for this model is:

$T_1 = T_2 = T_3 = T_6 = T_7 = T_8 = T_{10} = 1$.

$C_{67} = 1$.

$TF_{10} = 95$.

Obj = 50. (neglecting the effect of $0.01*TF_{10}$ in the objective function)

In this design tasks T_6 and T_7 are combined. One can see that this design finishes in a time of 95 which is more than for the design in scenario 1.

Scenario 3: *Maximum benefit within a time limit.* In this scenario, we keep the same objective function as in scenario 2 but add a new constraint: $TF_{10} \leq 75$ to impose a finish time limit. We know from scenario 1 that a solution exists with a finish time of 70. Now we get a solution that is similar to the one in scenario 2 with two changes:

$O_6 = 1$.

$R_2 = 1$.

$TF_{10} = 75$.

Obj = -50.

This means that a solution does exist within a time limit of 75 by skipping the optional task T_6 and replacing task T_2 with a faster task. However, now the Obj value drops to -50 because a negative benefit of 50 occurs from each adjustment.

Scenario 4: *Maximum benefit within a relaxed time limit.* Now we modify scenario 2 slightly by relaxing the time limit from 75 to 80. In this case we get a new solution:

$O_6 = 1$.

$TF_{10} = 80$.

Obj = -25.

This shows that by accepting an increase of 5 in the time limit, we have a new design with a benefit of -25, a gain of 25 over scenario 3. In this case task T_6 is optional in the optimal solution.

Table 3 summarizes the four scenarios above and two more scenarios (5,6) by showing the finish time, net benefit and the values of the various design variables. By considering these alternatives a decision can be made on the most suitable design. Row 1 shows that the minimum flow time for an instance is 70 which is an improvement of 30 over the base case, but at a net benefit of –75. However, optimizing the maximum benefit (Row 2) shows that the baseline case is dominated by a design ($C_{67} = 1$) where the flow time is 95 and the benefit is 50. The remaining rows (3-6) show tradeoffs between time and benefit by imposing a different time constraint and finding the design with the maximum benefit. It is interesting to note how the design changes in each setting. In fact, no two designs are the same. Most of the design options are selected in some design or another except for the one with the parallel structure. On trying to force a solution by setting $P_{67} = 1$ in the model we get a design with a finish time of 90 and benefit of -10 which is dominated by scenario 6.

Table 3. Understanding tradeoffs among redesign scenarios

Scenario	Finish time	Benefit	O_2	R_2	O_6	O_7	C_{67}	P_{67}
0. Baseline	100	0	0	0	0	0	0	0
1. Least time	70	−75	1	0	1	0	0	0
2. Max benefit	95	50	0	0	0	0	1	0
3. Max benefit with time limit 75	75	−50	0	1	1	0	0	0
4. Time limit is relaxed to 80	80	−25	0	0	1	0	0	0
5. Time limit is relaxed to 85	85	0	1	0	0	0	1	0
6. Time limit is relaxed to 90	90	25	0	1	0	0	1	0

Of course, other scenarios may also be created by a user on demand. The results above suggest that as the various parameters of the model change (e.g. resource cost, service cost, time constraints, etc.) the choice of the best design can change. Hence, it is necessary to revisit the baseline model periodically. Moreover, the ability to change the design of a process instance in response to constraints adds flexibility as illustrated in Table 3. An organization can price its time sensitive services based on the benefit calculations and adjust its process model for each instance accordingly.

6   Discussion and Related Work

We did not model flexibility explicitly. It needs deeper exploration along the lines suggested in [14] based on mix, labor, routing, volume and process flexibility. We also did not consider interactive effects. So, the cost of skipping task T_2 is BO_2 and that of skipping T_6 is BO_6. However, the cost of skipping both could be a function $f(BO_2, BO_6)$. It is also possible to make the values of benefit coefficients a function of case data. Thus, consider:

If (Loan_amount $\leq$ 100 K) then $BO_2 = -50$;
If (100 K < Loan_amount $\leq$ 200 K) then $BO_2 = -75$;
If (200 K < Loan_amount $\leq$ 300 K) then $BO_2 = -100$;

Here Loan_amount is a case variable whose value is provided by the user at run time to determine BO_2. Other parameter values can also be functions of case variables. In practice the values of these parameters have to be determined by the end users based on an understanding of the time required to perform a task (from process logs), wage rate of an employee (from payroll), and other internal records of a company.

The modeling power of our approach is comparable to that of first order logic. To informally argue correctness of our approach we first note that the basic structural and temporal model has been shown to be correct elsewhere [8]. In this paper we extend this formulation by allowing certain tasks to be optional (case 1) or replaceable (case 2). We also allow a pair of tasks to combine into a single task (case 3) or restructure into parallel (case 4). In cases 1–3 there is no structural change in the formulation; only the task duration expressions are changed by introducing new variables like O_i, R_i and C_{ij} respectively as explained in Sect. 5. In case 4, the structure of two tasks, say, T_i and T_j, is changed from sequence to parallel. This requires relaxing the sequence constraint between T_i and T_j by adding a $M * (1 - P_{ij})$ term and modifying the successor and predecessor relationships of T_i and T_j. In all four cases existing relationships are modified to satisfy the alternative designs by introducing new variables. But this does not affect correctness. The split and postponement cases can also be explained with similar reasoning.

Flexibility and the need for managing change, customization and adaptation are important issues in BPM research (see e.g. [15, 17, 18, 20, 21]. . One aspect of change is the need for systematic business process redesign. In [4, 11], many different best practices and heuristics for redesign have been proposed. In a related work [6], performance measures like cost, time, quality and flexibility for evaluating a new design are discussed at length. An evolutionary approach for generating redesign alternatives by applying best practices to an existing process is proposed in [13, 14]. While their goals are similar to ours their evaluation method is mostly based on simulation or enumeration. In contrast our approach is novel in that if offers an optimal solution and also the ability to add/modify constraints. Other work on redesign relates to identifying process improvement patterns [22], applying them effectively to processes [10] and detecting weaknesses in models [1]. Approaches based on goal models expressed in KAOS or Tropos/i* notations can offer guidance for process (re)design strategies [12]. Since the same goal model can be converted into multiple process designs it is possible to select the optimal one based on considerations of time, cost, quality and flexibility.

Our work also relates closely with research on configurable processes [3, 5]. Configurable processes are designed for flexibility using constructs like hidden and blocked tasks, and flexible gateways. Some early work on configurable processes was done in the context of EPC diagrams [3] and reference models [16]. A fine survey of business process modeling for variability that covers many configuration approaches appears in [9]. An approach for modeling flexible processes using templates and rules is discussed in [7]. Basically, a configurable model allows for the various kinds of improvements we have discussed here as configuration possibilities. Hence, each configurable node or gateway can be modeled as a redesign option in our framework and optimized with our approach.

7 Conclusions

In this paper we presented a novel approach for optimizing the redesign of process models. It is based on capturing process improvement strategies as constraints in a structural-temporal model. Each improvement strategy is represented by a binary variable. An objective function that represents a net benefit function of cost and quality is then maximized subject to these constraints to find the best combination of process improvements that can be made to maximize the objective. The strategy variable values in the solution to this MILP formulation show the optimal strategies. We tested this model with a realistic case study and showed that it is possible to generate multiple redesign solutions by modifying the objective function and constraints.

In future work we would like to explore ways to model flexibility and resources in more depth. It will also be useful to extend the current approach to more patterns like knock out, numerical involvement, contact reduction, case types, etc. [11, 13, 19]. There is also a need to study ways to determine the parameters of the objective function more accurately and to analyze the sensitivity of the objective function to them. Further, in our current model a user must identify all valid strategies and include them in the model. However, it would be nice to investigate a recommendation system that will suggest the Top-3 or Top-5 process redesign scenarios to a user by systematically considering the application of all valid improvement strategies. To do so more semantic information about the process model may be needed by the system.

Acknowledgment. This work was initiated while the first author was visiting the BPM group at QUT, Brisbane. He thanks the BPM group, and especially Marcello La Rosa and Chun Ouyang for their inputs and suggestions.

References

1. Bergener, P., Delfmann, P., Weiss, B., Winkelmann, A.: Detecting potential weaknesses in business processes – an exploration of semantic pattern matching in process models. Bus. Process Manag. J. **21**(1), 25–54 (2015)
2. CPLEX: Reference manual. IBM corporation (2009)
3. Dreiling, A., Rosemann, M., Alast, W., van der Heuser, L., Schulz, K.: Model-based software configuration: patterns and languages. Eur. J. Inf. Syst. **15**(6), 583–600 (2006)
4. Dumas, M., Rosa, L.M., Mendling, J., Reijers, H.A.: Fundamentals of Business Process Management. Springer, Heidelberg (2013)
5. Gottschalk, F., van der Aalst, W.M.P., Jansen-Vullers, M.H., la Rosa, M.: Configurable workflow models. Int. J. Coop. Inf. Syst. **17**(2), 177–221 (2008)
6. Jansen-Vullers, M.H., Kleingeld, P.A.M., Mariska, N.: Quantifying the performance of workflows. IS Manage. **25**(4), 332–343 (2008). http://dblp.uni-trier.de/db/journals/ism/ism25.html#Jansen-VullersKN08
7. Kumar, A., Yao, W.: Design and management of flexible process variants using templates and rules. Comput. Ind. **63**(2), 112–130 (2012)
8. Kumar, A., Sabbella, S., Barton, R.: Managing controlled violation of temporal process constraints. In: Motahari-Nezhad, H.R., Recker, J., Weidlich, M. (eds.) BPM 2015. LNCS, vol. 9253, pp. 280–296. Springer, Switzerland (2015)
9. La Rosa, M., van der Aalst, W.M., Dumas, M., Milani, F.P.: Business Process Variability Modeling : A Survey. QUT Reprint (2013)
10. Lohrmann, M., Reichert, M.: Effective application of process improvement patterns to business processes. Softw. Syst. Model. **15**(2), 1–23 (2014)

11. Mansar, L., Reijers, H.A.: Best practices in business process redesign: use and impact. Bus. Process Manage. J. **13**(2), 193–213 (2007)
12. Nagel, B., Gerth, C., Post, J., Engels, G.: Kaos4SOA - extending KAOS models with temporal and logical dependencies. In: Proceedings of CAiSE Forum, pp. 9–16 (2013)
13. Netjes, M., Mansar, S.L., Reijers, H.A., van der Aalst, W.M.P.: Performing business process redesign with best practices: an evolutionary approach. In: Filipe, J., Cordeiro, J., Cardoso, J. (eds.) ICEIS 2007. LNBIP, vol. 12, pp. 199–211. Springer, Heidelberg (2008)
14. Netjes, M., Mansar, S.L., Reijers, H.A., van der Aalst, W.M.P.: An evolutionary approach for business process redesign - towards an intelligent system. ICEIS **3**, 47–54 (2007). http://dblp.uni-trier.de/db/conf/iceis/iceis2007-3.html#NetjesMRA07
15. Reichert, M., Weber, B.: Enabling Flexibility in Process-aware Information Systems: Challenges, Methods, Technologies. Springer, Heidelberg (2012)
16. Rosemann, M., van der Aalst, W.M.P.: A configurable reference modelling language. Inf. Syst. **32**(1), 1–23 (2007)
17. Sadiq, S.W., Marjanovic, O., Orlowska, M.E.: Managing change and time in dynamic workflow processes. Int. J. Coop. Inf. Syst. **9**(1–2), 93–116 (2000)
18. van der Aalst, W.M., Rosemann, M., Dumas, M.: Deadline-based escalation in process-aware information systems. Decis. Support Syst. **43**(2), 492–511 (2007)
19. van der Aalst, W.M., Ter Hofstede, A.H., Kiepuszewski, B., Barros, A.P.: Workflow patterns. Distrib. Parallel Databases **14**(1), 5–51 (2003)
20. Weber, B., Reichert, M., Mendling, J., Reijers, H.A.: Refactoring large process model repositories. Comput. Ind. **62**, 467–486 (2011)
21. Weber, B., Reichert, M., Rinderle-Ma, S.: Change patterns and change support features - enhancing flexibility in process-aware information systems. Data Knowl. Eng. **66**(3), 438–466 (2008)
22. Zellner, G.: Towards a framework for identifying business process redesign patterns. Bus. Process Manage. J. **19**(4), 600–623 (2013)

QoS-Driven Management of Business Process Variants in Cloud Based Execution Environments

Rahul Ghosh[1]([✉]), Aditya Ghose[2], Aditya Hegde[1], Tridib Mukherjee[1], and Adrian Mos[3]

[1] Xerox Research Center India, Bangalore, India
{rahul.ghosh,aditya.hegde,tridib.mukherjee}@xerox.com
[2] University of Wollongong, Wollongong, NSW 2522, Australia
aditya@uow.edu.au
[3] Xerox Research Center Europe, Grenoble, France
adrian.mos@xrce.xerox.com

Abstract. Economy of scale is a key driver behind the Cloud based adoption of a business process. Typically, the management of business process variants focuses on design variants, which permit (ideally small) variations in design (and hence, functionality) for achieving the same (functional) goal, under different functional constraints (such as the compliance obligations that have to be met in different jurisdictions). Little attention has been paid to: (a) variations in process design driven by non-functional considerations (e.g., performance, reliability and cost of operation) and (b) variations in process provisioning in Cloud. This paper seeks to develop means for identifying the correlation between both design and provisioning alternatives and the QoS of business processes deployed in the Cloud. Additionally, we explore the role of the context in determining the performance of a process. We use a set of data mining techniques (specifically decision tree learning, support vector machine and the k-nearest neighbour technique) to mine insights about these correlations. Proposed approaches are evaluated using a synthetic dataset as well as a real dataset.

Keywords: Cloud · Process adaptation · Resource · QoS · Context

1 Introduction

Cloud-based deployment of business processes raises several important challenges. Organizations that deploy business processes in a variety of heterogeneous settings have to manage *process variants*, which modify the original (or *reference*) process design to accommodate the compliance requirements of different jurisdictions or varying client requirements but which still achieve the intended goals of the process [17].

Much of the current literature on the management of business process variants focuses on design variants, which permit (ideally small) variations in design

© Springer International Publishing Switzerland 2016
Q.Z. Sheng et al. (Eds.): ICSOC 2016, LNCS 9936, pp. 55–69, 2016.
DOI: 10.1007/978-3-319-46295-0_4

(and hence, functionality) for achieving the same (functional) goal, under different functional constraints (such as the compliance obligations that have to be met in different jurisdictions). Little attention has been paid to variations in process design driven by non-functional considerations (such as the improvement of processing time or the reduction of cost - factors that we shall henceforth informally describe using the term *QoS*). Little attention has also been paid to variations in process provisioning. Sometimes, the same process design can exhibit very different QoS profiles under different resourcing modes.

Thus, both the design of a process and the resources provided for its execution determine its performance under various QoS measures. The broader research program within which this paper is situated seeks to develop means for identifying and leveraging the correlation between both design and provisioning alternatives and the QoS of business processes deployed in the Cloud. This paper focuses on the provisioning aspect of this question.

This paper additionally explores the role of the context in determining the QoS of a process. We view the context as consisting of exogeneous knowledge about the operating environment of a process that is neither consumed by a process nor generated by it (and hence sitting outside the ambit of what is traditionally described as *process data*). The role of the context in determining the QoS of a process is often mediated by the impact the context has on the resources allocated to a process. For instance, we might find that a process with a significant proportion of human-mediated steps (such as customer complaint handling) leads to positive outcomes (as evidenced by a higher proportion of satisfied customers) when executed earlier in the day. The underlying contextual phenomenon that manifests in this behaviour could be the higher efficiency of the customer contact centre workers at the start of the working day. Sometimes, the context influences process performance in other ways. There is some anecdotal evidence that insurance claims processes progress to completion faster during periods when the economic climate is positive (and take longer to complete when this is not the case). Of particular interest for the purposes of this study is the *load* on hardware and software resources that provision a business process deployed in the Cloud.

There are a number of use cases for the techniques we develop in this paper. Given a description of a context, we are interested in identifying (or *prescribing*) the alternate set of resources with which to provision a process in order to achieve a set of thresholds on the applicable QoS factors e.g., cost, processing time, reliability etc. Given a context, and the set of resources being allocated to a process, we are interested in *predicting* its QoS. We are interested in answering these questions both at the start of the execution of a process (where a process design provides approximate guidance on what tasks are to be executed - the specific task sequence being determined at run-time) and during the execution of a process (where we have, in addition to a process design, a sequence of tasks already executed).

These questions are best answered by using a causal theory that relates aspects of the context, the process and the resources to the QoS of a process. Such a theory does not exist at this time (although preliminary attempts have been made to use queueing theory to address part of the problem [8]). We therefore propose to adopt a data-driven approach, by using a history of past process executions as a proxy for this theory. We make the (realistic) assumption that we have access to an execution history that records for each executed process instance: (1) the context (consisting of the load, and potentially other contextual factors), (2) the process design, (3) the process instance, (4) the resource set deployed for that instance, and (5) the QoS (in terms of values for a set of QoS factors).

We use a set of data mining techniques (specifically decision tree, support vector machines and the k-nearest neighbour technique) to mine insights about these correlations. The overall strategy is to mine correlations between the context, the process, the resource set and the QoS, and use these correlations to support the *prescriptive* and *predictive analytics* use cases discussed above. We also leverage an ontology of resource types to describe the resource sets with which process instances are provisioned. In addition to providing a vocabulary, this *resource ontology* also forms the basis for a *resource set ontology*. We leverage the latter to obtain insights about superclasess (of classes of resource sets that are well-represented in the available datasets) which can then support prescriptive, predictive and diagnostic analytics for other classes of resource sets (potentially under-represented in the available data).

We evaluate our proposal in the context of two datasets: a synthetic dataset and real-life dataset drawn from the Business Process Intelligence (BPI) Challenge [2].

The literature directly related to our proposal is quite sparse. A substantial body of work addresses business process flexibility, but the focus of these approaches is primarily on the generation of design variants (as opposed to the generation of variations in resourcing that we focus on). Some recent work addresses the role of the context in process execution, but not in the kinds of analytics we have outlined above.

2 The Proposed Framework

We present the conceptual basis for our proposal in this section. Our overall strategy is to view an execution history as a proxy, or an alternative, for a causal theory that might inform resource allocation decisions in the given context. We might view the causal theory of interest providing the functions described below. These functions will refer to a *process* P, a *resource set* R, a context C and the QoS of a process, denoted by QoS. The first function of interest is the following:

$$f_{QoS} : C \times P \times R \mapsto QoS \tag{1}$$

This function helps us predict the QoS of a process, given a characterization of the context, the process and the resources allocated to the process. In much of our evaluation, we will focus on the *load* in Cloud-based deployment as the context C, but it is useful to note that our overall framework is far more general, and could be leveraged in settings with a richer description of the context. We encode a characterization of the process in P. In parts of our evaluation, we use a fairly coarse-grained characterization of a process (in terms of number of tasks, in settings where it is reasonable to assume that the resource requirements of the tasks in a process are fairly uniform). We also consider a more finer-grained characterization in other parts of our evaluation, where we take cognisance of the identities (i.e., task types) of the tasks executed in a process (this characterization is useful in settings where tasks have heterogeneous resource requirements). More generally, we could characterize a process by referring to the actual process instance (which describes the sequence, and not just the set of tasks executed. We could make the characterization even richer by referring to the process design. We use a *resource ontology* to help characterize the resource sets that are used to provision each process instance.

Another function of interest is:

$$f_R : C \times P \times QoS \mapsto R \qquad (2)$$

This function helps us predict the resource sets that must be provided to a process instance, in a given context C, in order to ensure that certain thresholds on the QoS, given by QoS are met (note that we have over-used the term QoS, which was used to denote actual QoS measures in the case of function f_{QoS}). C and P would be characterized as per the discussion above.

Our focus in this paper is to mine execution histories to obtain approximations of these two functions. We assume a general schema for the execution history, given by the tuple $\langle C, P, R, QoS \rangle$ (with the provision that C, P, R and QoS might be differently instantiated, as discussed above). Our overall strategy is to use classification techniques such as decision tree learning and support vector machine (SVM) to learn an approximation of function f_{QoS} and to use the k-nearest neighbour technique to learn an approximation of function f_R (which would support the prescriptive analytics discussed in the previous section). The remainder of this paper illustrates the feasibility of our approach via experimental evaluation using both synthetic and real-life datasets.

3   Evaluation

We evaluate the proposed approach using two types of datasets: (a) simulated process execution logs and (b) real process execution logs. Using both simulated and real execution logs, we answer interesting questions around the resource allocation and QoS.

3.1   Insights from Simulated Process Execution Logs

Simulated process logs are generated in the domain of Infrastructure-as-a-Service (IaaS) Cloud and contains a rich variety of Cloud resources. We first describe the resource ontology considered in this context.

Resource Ontology. As shown in Fig. 1, infrastructure resources in the Cloud can be divided into three classes: physical machines (PM), virtual machine (VM), operating system containers (OC). For each of the above classes, there are three sub-classes - large, medium and small, which denote the amount of computing capacity given to a resource instance. For example, a large PM can have 32 CPU cores, 16 GB of memory and 1 TB of disk, while a small PM can have 4 CPU cores, 4 GB of memory and 256 GB disk. Further, using the resource types (r_t) shown in the *primary ontology* R_p in Fig. 1, we create a *derived ontology* R_d. A derived ontology consists of a number of *resource sets* R_s. Let c_t denotes the cardinality of resource type (r_t). The resource set can then be given as:

$$R_s = \{(x, y) : x = r_t, y = c_t\} \tag{3}$$

Examples of R_s are: (i) {3 large PMs}, (ii) {1 large PM, 2 medium VMs}, (iii) {2 large VMs, 1 large OC} and so on. For tractability of the dataset, we vary the value of c_t from 1 to 10. A singular element of R_s is called an *atomic resource unit* r_a. Examples of r_a are: 1 large PM, 1 small VM, 1 medium OC and so on. The universal resource set R_u is the power set of R_s.

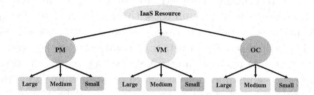

Fig. 1. Primary resource ontology for IaaS Cloud.

Generation of Synthetic Logs. Figure 2 shows the conceptual process of synthetic log generation. For a given sequential Cloud based BP, we randomly generate n tasks which constitute a BP instance. For each task, we randomly generate the total number of resources needed (r_{total}). The values of n and r_{total} are generated by drawing samples from uniform distributions $U(3, 10)$ and $U(18, 45)$ respectively. Once the value of r_{total} is generated, we draw a resource set R_s from R_u such that the cardinality of R_s is same as r_{total}. For instance, when the value r_{total} is 3, possible resource sets could be: (a) 3 large PMs, (b) 3 small OCs, (c) 1 PM, 1 VM, 1 OC etc.

The next step is to generate the task level QoS. To keep things realistic, we adopt a statistical model to compute QoS from resources as described in [10]. Given an atomic resource unit, a value of load (λ), it can be shown that there is a linear relationship between the throughput and the atomic resource unit. Response time can then be computed as the inverse of throughput. Note that, while we adopt a linear model for QoS computation, we randomly vary the values of slope and y-axis intercept for an atomic resource unit. Let T_i and S_i denote

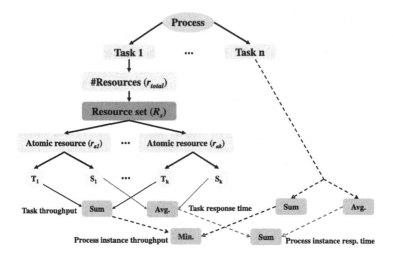

Fig. 2. Conceptual process showing the generation of synthetic dataset.

the throughput and response time of i-th atomic resource unit. The throughput of a task is then computed as the sum total throughput of each atomic resource unit. This is intuitive as we put more resources onto a task, overall task throughput increases. The response time of a task is computed as the average response time of individual atomic resource units. Next, we aggregate the task level data to compute the process instance level QoS. Since we assume that the tasks are sequential in nature, overall throughput is determined by the *slowest* (bottleneck) task. Thus, process instance level throughput is computed by the minimum of individual task throughputs. Overall response time is computed as the sum of individual task level response times. In total, 25000 process instances are simulated and the generated data is used to provide the following insights. We use the `scikit-learn` [3] package in `Python` for all the data mining approaches used in this paper.

Classification Based Approaches for QoS Prediction. We use two classification approaches: (1) decision tree based learning and (2) SVM based learning for answering the two questions related to QoS prediction.
Q1. Given a QoS threshold and a process that is about to start, can we predict if the process will meet its QoS?

Considering response time as the QoS, we first replace the QoS value in our dataset to binary variable *isQoSsatisfied*. For a given process instance, if the value of QoS is less than or equal to the value of QoS threshold, we set the value of *isQoSsatisfied* as *True*, otherwise, we set it to *False*. Thus, given *isQoSsatisfied* as the target (or dependent) variable, the dataset contains the following independent variables (predictor): load (λ), #tasks (n), #total resources (r_{total}), #small PMs, #medium PMs, #large PMs, #small VMs, #medium VMs, #large VMs, #small OCs, #medium OCs, #large OCs. Table 1 shows the feature importance

Table 1. Predictor importance in synthetic data when QoS is predicted for a process that is about to start.

Predictor	Importance (decision tree)	Importance (SVM)
Load (λ)	0.591	4.236
#tasks (n)	0.226	-3.132
#resources (r_{total})	0.013	0.002
#small PMs (PM-small)	0.010	0.345
#medium PMs (PM-medium)	0.010	0.392
#large PMs (PM-large)	0.013	0.441
#small VMs (VM-small)	0.073	-1.256
#medium VMs (VM-medium)	0.027	-0.429
#large VMs (VM-large)	0.013	-0.099
#small OCs (OC-small)	0.007	0.107
#medium OCs (OC-medium)	0.006	0.217
#large OCs (OC-large)	0.009	0.288

for both decision tree and SVM based approaches. The weights of a linear SVM can have both positive and negative values because the result of a linear SVM is a hyperplane that separates the classes as best as possible. The weights form the coordinates of a vector which is orthogonal to the hyperplane. The values of the weights/coefficients relative to the other ones give an indication of how important the feature was for the separation.

The accuracy of decision tree and SVM based approach is 94.52 % and 97.32 % respectively.

Q2. Given a QoS threshold and a partially executed process log, can we predict if the QoS will be met at the end of process execution?

For answering this question we have a similar data set as used for *Q1*. Instead of using aggregated resource set, we have introduced task level resource sets. So the independent variables are: load (λ), #tasks (n), #total resources (r_{total}), resources required for a task, i.e., #small PMs, #medium PMs, #large PMs, #small VMs, #medium VMs, #large VMs, #small OCs, #medium OCs, #large OCs and task response time. To construct the target (dependent) variable, we transform the process level QoS (i.e., process response time) to a binary variable *isQoSsatisfied* indicating a response time threshold. For an instance of the dataset, *isQoSsatisfied* is set to *True* if the underlying process met its QoS else it is set to *False*. The training dataset consists of the history of complete executions of process instance along with the task related information. The test dataset consists of partial executions of the process instance, i.e., a set of tasks. The developed model (decision tree or SVM) predicts if the underlying process can meet its QoS or not when the tasks are submitted to the model. Since the process model consists of sequential tasks, the test tasks are fed to the model one after another. If the prediction is *False*, subsequent tasks for the test process

Table 2. Predictor importance for synthetic data when QoS is predicted for a partially executed process.

Feature	Importance (decision tree)	Importance (SVM)
Load (λ)	0.679	1.649
#tasks (n)	0.183	-1.196
#resources (r_{total})	0.041	0.019
#small PMs for a task	0.005	0.016
#medium PMs for a task	0.004	0.021
#large PMs for a task	0.003	0.007
#small VMs for a task	0.002	-0.046
#medium VMs for a task	0.004	$-0.0.013$
#large VMs for a task	0.004	0.002
#small OCs for a task	0.004	0.006
#medium OCs for a task	0.005	0.008
#large OCs for a task	0.005	0.016
Task response time	0.056	-0.481

are no longer fed to the model. Table 2 shows the predictor performance for both decision tree and SVM based approaches. The accuracy of decision tree and SVM based approach is 88.44 % and 92.46 % respectively.

Clustering Based Approach for Resource Prediction. Using kNN, we answer the three questions related to resource prediction. For all the questions, we replace the QoS value in our dataset to binary variable *isQoSsatisfied*. The value of *isQoSsatisfied* is set to be 1 in case the QoS is met w.r.t. a given threshold, otherwise it is set to 0.

Q3. Given a process instance that met its QoS, can we predict an alternate resource set such that it meets the QoS?

There are several motivations behind such a question including reducing the cost of resource procurement [9], lack of availability of certain types of resources etc. Using response time as the QoS, we leverage the full process logs from the historical data to answer this question. The attributes of the dataset are in the following order: (load, #tasks, #total resources, #small PMs, #medium PMs, #large PMs, #small OCs, #medium OCs, #large OCs, #small VMs, #medium VMs, #large VMs, *isQoSsatisfied*). We use the given process instance as a test data, where *isQoSsatisfied* is set to 1 (as the process instance met the QoS). From historical data, we then determine the process instances that are closest to the test process and for which *isQoSsatisfied* is set to 1. For example, consider the test process instance z:

$$z = (537, 4, 11, 1, 1, 0, 2, 0, 2, 1, 3, 1, 1) \tag{4}$$

This instance has 4 tasks which got executed on 2 PMs (1 small, 1 medium), 4 OCs (2 small, 2 large), and 5 VMs (1 small, 3 medium, 1 large). Using kNN approach, the top 2 closest process instances which meet the QoS are given by:

$$z_1 = (535, 3, 10, 1, 1, 0, 2, 0, 1, 2, 3, 0, 1), z_2 = (535, 4, 12, 0, 3, 0, 1, 0, 2, 1, 3, 2, 1)$$

Without compromising the QoS target, these resource sets of these alternate process instances can then be opportunistically used by a Cloud provider.

We also study another variant of this question when different types of tasks are considered within a process. In this case, the dataset has an additional attribute: #tasks for a given type. We re-generate our synthetic dataset considering 5 types of tasks. The attributes are then given by: (load, #tasks, #tasks for type 1, #tasks for type 2, #tasks for type 3, #tasks for type 4, #tasks for type 5, #total resources, #small PMs, #medium PMs, #large PMs, #small OCs, #medium OCs, #large OCs, #small VMs, #medium VMs, #large VMs, isQoSsatisfied). For example, consider the test process instance y:

$$y = (986, 12, 3, 3, 3, 1, 2, 34, 1, 2, 7, 4, 4, 2, 3, 7, 4, 1) \tag{5}$$

This instance has 3 tasks for type 1, 2, and 3 each, 1 task for type 4, 2 tasks for type 5. Using kNN approach, the top 2 closest process instances which meet the QoS are given by:

$$y_1 = (989, 11, 3, 2, 1, 3, 2, 34, 1, 3, 5, 3, 6, 4, 5, 2, 5, 1),$$
$$y_2 = (986, 10, 3, 2, 1, 1, 3, 30, 4, 3, 6, 1, 2, 4, 2, 4, 4, 1)$$

Q4. Given a process instance that did not meet its QoS, can we predict alternate resource set such that it meets the QoS?

The analysis carried out for this question is similar to that of Q3. The main difference is that, when a process instance is considered as a test data, *isQoS-satisfied* is set to 0 (as the process instance did not meet QoS). From historical data, we then determine the process instances that are closest to the test process and for which *isQoSsatisfied* is set to 1. For example, consider the test process instance t:

$$t = (343, 6, 21, 3, 3, 1, 2, 3, 2, 1, 4, 2, 0) \tag{6}$$

This instance has 6 tasks which got executed on 7 PMs (3 small, 3 medium, 1 large), 7 OCs (2 small, 3 medium, 2 large), and 7 VMs (1 small, 4 medium, 2 large). Using kNN approach, the top 2 closest process instances which meet the QoS are given by:

$$t_1 = (348, 5, 17, 2, 1, 2, 1, 5, 2, 0, 2, 2, 1), t_2 = (342, 5, 15, 1, 1, 4, 2, 3, 4, 0, 0, 0, 1)$$

The resource allocation in any of these neighboring process instances can be used as an alternate resource set for the test process instance to meet the QoS.

When different types of tasks are involved within a process instance we run an analysis similar to the variant described in *Q3*. Consider the test process instance w:

$$w = (397, 13, 3, 3, 2, 2, 3, 40, 7, 4, 3, 1, 1, 7, 6, 4, 7, 0) \tag{7}$$

This instance missed its QoS target and has 3 tasks for type 1, 2, and 5 each, 2 tasks for type 3 and 4 each. Using kNN approach, the top 2 closest process instances which meet the QoS are given by:

$$w_1 = (399, 11, 2, 2, 1, 3, 3, 37, 5, 3, 8, 3, 3, 3, 3, 2, 7, 1),$$
$$w_2 = (396, 11, 2, 2, 2, 2, 3, 34, 3, 3, 7, 4, 2, 5, 1, 6, 3, 1)$$

Q5. Given a partially executed process instance, can we predict an alternate resource set such that it can meet the QoS at the end of entire process execution?

To answer this question, instead of using aggregated resource set, we have introduced task level resource sets. So the features are: load, #tasks, #total resources (r_{total}), resources required for a task, i.e., #small PMs, #medium PMs, #large PMs, #small OCs, #medium OCs, #large OCs, #small VMs, #medium VMs, #large VMs, task response time, value of *isQoSsatisfied*. In this case, a sequence of tasks belonging to the same process are considered as the test data. The goal is to determine the *similar* tasks with alternate resource allocations that can meet the QoS. Consider the following two test tasks:

$$v_1 = (259, 6, 18, 0, 0, 0, 1, 1, 0, 0, 0, 0, 0.504, 0),$$
$$v_2 = (259, 6, 18, 0, 1, 0, 0, 0, 1, 0, 0, 0, 0.300, 0)$$

Both tasks belong to a process instance for which load is 259 requests/sec, #tasks is 6, #total resources is 18 and the QoS is not met (i.e., *isQoSsatisfied* = 0). Task v_1 requires 1 small and medium OCs and has a response time of 0.504 ms. Task v_2 requires 1 medium PM and 1 large OC and has a response time of 0.300 ms. Using kNN approach, the top 2 closest process instances v_1 which meet the QoS are given by:

$$v_{11} = (261, 6, 17, 1, 0, 1, 1, 0, 0, 0, 0, 0, 0.357, 1),$$
$$v_{12} = (261, 6, 17, 0, 0, 1, 0, 0, 0, 0, 1, 0, 0.555, 1)$$

Similarly, the top 2 closest process instances v_2 which meet the QoS are given by:

$$v_{21} = (259, 6, 18, 0, 1, 0, 0, 0, 1, 0, 0, 0, 0.300, 1),$$
$$v_{22} = (261, 6, 17, 1, 1, 1, 0, 0, 1, 0, 0, 0, 0.293, 1)$$

3.2   Insights from Real Process Execution Logs

The real dataset comes from Dutch financial institute provided as part of BPI challenge 2012 [2]. The event logs are for an application process for a personal loan or overdraft within a global financial organization. The log contains 2,62,200 events in 13,087 cases. Every process instance starts from a specific event and ends up in any one of the 13 different end events. Based on this observation we divide the process instances into 13 different instance types (*itype*). We calculate the response time of the process instance as the time difference between the end event and the start event. We define a threshold for the response time. The target (dependent) variable *isQoSsatisfied* is created using the defined threshold. If the response time is below the threshold we set *isQoSsatisfied* to *True* otherwise it is set to *False*. Unlike the synthetic data, this dataset does not have the richness around resource information. Individual resources are identified by a unique resource ID. For every resource ID we mark the instance with *True* if the corresponding resource participates in the instance. There are 68 unique resources who work on this process across various instances. We extract the following predictors from this event log: loan amount, instance type (*itype*), #tasks (n), #total resources (r_{total}), resource ID.

Q1. Given a QoS threshold and a process that is about to start, can we predict if the process will meet its QoS?

Following a similar approach taken for the synthetic logs, we use decision tree and SVM to answer this question. Table 3 shows the predictor performance for both decision tree and SVM based approaches. As the predictor space for resource ids is large we show the importance of only a subset of resource ids. The accuracy of decision tree and SVM based approach is 94.32 % and 96.32 % respectively.

Table 3. Predictor importance for real data when QoS is predicted for a process that is about to start.

Predictor	Importance (decision tree)	Importance (SVM)
Loan amount	0.025	0.045
Instance type	0.027	−0.621
#tasks	0.866	−1.317
#resources	0.022	−0.194
Resource ID 11180	0.002	−0.092
Resource ID 11181	0.001	−0.048
Resource ID 10929	0.000	−0.022

Q2. Given a process instance that met its QoS, can we predict an alternate resource set such that it meets the QoS?

The analysis carried out for this question is similar to that of Q3 of Sect. 3.1. From historical data, we determine the process instances that are closest to the test process and have met their QoS. For example, consider the test process instance t (the semicolon separated items are resource Ids):

$$t = (5862, 3, 6, 2, 112; 11019, 1) \tag{8}$$

The loan amount and instance type for process instance t are 5862 and 3 respectively. In total, 6 tasks are performed by 2 resources with ids 112 and 11339. Using kNN approach, the top 2 closest process instances which meet the QoS are given by:

$$t_1 = (5867, 4, 16, 4, 112; 11119; 10982; 11202, 1), t_2 = (5900, 3, 6, 2, 112; 10881, 1)$$

Q3. Given a process instance that did not meet its QoS, can we predict alternate resource set such that it meets the QoS?

Here, when a process instance is considered as a test data, *isQoSsatisfied* is set to 0. From historical data, we then determine the process instances that are closest to the test process and for which *isQoSsatisfied* is set to 1. For example, consider the test process instance t:

$$t = (5000, 2, 23, 4, 10609; 10899; 112; 11201, 0) \tag{9}$$

This type 2 instance has the loan amount of 5000 and has 23 tasks which are performed by 4 resources with ids 10609, 10899, 112 and 11201. Using kNN approach, the top 2 closest process instances which meet the QoS are given by

$$t_1 = (5000, 2, 22, 2, 112; 10629, 1), t_2 = (5000, 2, 25, 2, 112; 10629, 1)$$

4   Related Research

The field of software performance modelling and prediction is vast. A comprehensive survey of modelling approaches for performance prediction is presented in [4]. Important contributions have been presented in [1, 18, 20, 21] reporting significant results in the improvement of the software development process, specifically the use of Software Performance Engineering methods aided by related tools such as SPE-ED [18]. The techniques and the supporting tools require developers to create software and/or system models of the application under development. These models must have performance parameters such as I/O utilisation, CPU cycles or network characteristics, specified by the developers in order for the performance predictions to generate meaningful results. It has been proved that such techniques and tools like SPE-ED help in achieving performance goals and reducing performance related risks for general object-oriented systems and even for distributed systems. However, BPM environments exhibit an inherent complexity, which analysts find hard if not impossible to quantify even in simple models. Complex contextual and provisioning details such as resource allocation, design options, underlying engine requirements, virtualisation and many others contribute to an improved and at the same time highly unpredictable run-time environment. It is therefore impractical for the various stakeholders involved in building and maintaining process based applications to create performance models where they manually specify the mapping of methods to processes or instances to processors, I/O characteristics or CPU utilisation. A related approach to modelling systems in UML is presented in [11]. OAT is a tool that implements a framework for performance modelling of distributed systems using UML. It consists of a method for decomposition of models and performance modelling techniques. UML models, created at different development stages can be mapped to queuing networks and solved to predict application performance. UML diagrams, in particular sequence diagrams, can be seen as similar to process description in BPMN so the approach could provide starting points for process performance analysis and prediction. However, users must create and maintain the models and augment them with performance annotations leading to a similar disadvantage with that of the SPE-ED [18] approach. In addition, it is not clear how this approach can be used for large systems, as it does not address issues such as large-scale model management. Since BPM environments embed complex server software they share similarities with traditional middleware systems. Predicting the performance of middleware-based systems has been approached in the past. Among the most common techniques are Petri-Nets [7] and Layered Queuing Network (LQN) [16,20] models. Similarly to the generic software performance prediction approaches, such work may not scale particularly well to the complexities of process environments with the rich contextual and provisioning variability.

Closer to the BPM space there has been a lot of work in monitoring processes for performance understanding and analysis, while not particularly targeting QoS correlation with provisioning and design. In [6], authors present potential openings driven by associating semantics with traditional BPM, which could potentially be used as further input in the context descriptions; as done in the approach presented here. Related work that leverages semantic descriptions to boost process understanding and monitoring includes [15] and the associated COBRA terminology is presented in [14]. Other monitoring and analysis work targeting complex and large scale process and service environments is presented in [13]. These approaches, while comprehensive in the analysis scope in particular with regard to service dependencies and process structure, do not particularly target Cloud-based provisioning aspects, nor do they propose QoS oriented performance prediction.

Specifically, in process performance prediction, existing work [19] has looked at using forecasting techniques to generate dynamic predictive models. The contribution is certainly useful but does not take into account the correlation between design, complex contextual data, provisioning and performance in a unified way that would allow the understanding of the reasons for performance results, in contrast to the work presented in this paper. In contrast, the authors in [5] propose a mechanism based on LQN to predict performance of processes at design time based on an extended BPMN profile called PyBPMN. Such predictions can be used to quickly simulate overall performance based on expected characteristics, but it does not take into account runtime information from previous executions nor does it combine them with provisioning and contextual data.

While not Cloud-specific, previous work in correlative process monitoring presented in [12] uses domain-specific information to aggregate non-functional properties extracted from process execution at various levels including BPM engine and enterprise service bus platforms. This provides an important capability for better understanding previous executions in terms that are easier to understand by business stakeholders. As such, this work could provide an additional layer of interpretation when correlated with the predictive work presented in this paper. This would allow specification of QoS requirements and matching of predictive results using a consistent terminology related to the business domain, rendering such data easier to use in practice.

5 Conclusions and Future Work

In this paper, we develop an approach for identifying the correlation between both design and provisioning alternatives and the QoS of business processes deployed in the Cloud. Specifically, we view an execution history as a proxy for a causal theory that might inform resource allocation decisions in the given context of a Cloud based business process. Data mining techniques, specifically, decision tree, SVM and kNN are used to provide an approximation of the underlying causal theory that helps predicting the QoS or resource requirements in Cloud. Classification techniques such as decision tree learning and SVM are used to approximate the function that leads to QoS prediction. For both synthetic as well as real dataset, one interesting insight that comes out from our analysis is that, among the classification based approaches, SVM performs better than decision tree in terms of accuracy of prediction. While this paper focuses on QoS and resource prediction problems, in future, we plan on developing similar approach for predicting alternate process variants as well. We believe that similar approximation model for predicting process variants can significantly improve the design of business processes from non-functional aspect.

References

1. Performance Solutions: A Practical Guide to Creating Responsive, Scalable Software. Addison Wesley Longman Publishing Co., Inc., Redwood City (2002)
2. BPI Challenge 2012 (2016). https://www.win.tue.nl/bpi/doku.php?id=2012: challenge
3. Scikit-learn: Machine Learning in Python (2016). http://scikit-learn.org/stable/index.html
4. Balsamo, S., Di Marco, A., Inverardi, P., Simeoni, M.: Model-based performance prediction in software development: a survey. IEEE Trans. Softw. Eng. **30**(5), 295–310 (2004). http://dx.doi.org/10.1109/TSE.2004.9
5. Bocciarelli, P., D'Ambrogio, A.: A model-driven method for enacting the design-time QoS analysis of business processes. Softw. Syst. Model. **13**(2), 573–598 (2014)
6. de Medeiros, A.K.A., Pedrinaci, C., van der Aalst, W.M.P., Domingue, J., Song, M., Rozinat, A., Norton, B., Cabral, L.: An outlook on semantic business process mining and monitoring. In: Meersman, R., Tari, Z. (eds.) OTM-WS 2007, Part II. LNCS, vol. 4806, pp. 1244–1255. Springer, Heidelberg (2007)
7. Dimitrov, E., Schmietendorf, A., Dumhe, R.: Uml-based performance engineering possibilities and techniques. IEEE Softw. **19**(1), 74–83 (2002)
8. Ghosh, R.: Scalable stochastic models for cloud services. Ph.D. thesis, Duke University (2012)
9. Ghosh, R., Longo, F., Xia, R., Naik, V., Trivedi, K.: Stochastic model driven capacity planning for an infrastructure-as-a-service cloud. IEEE Trans. Serv. Comput. **7**(4), 667–680 (2014)
10. Jung, G., Sharma, N., Goetz, F., Mukherjee, T.: Cloud capability estimation and recommendation in black-box environments using benchmark-based approximation. In: IEEE CLOUD (2013)

11. Kähkipuro, P.: UML based performance modeling framework for object-oriented distributed systems. In: France, R.B. (ed.) UML 1999. LNCS, vol. 1723, pp. 356–371. Springer, Heidelberg (1999)

12. Mos, A.: Domain specific monitoring of business processes using concept probes. In: Toumani, F., et al. (eds.) ICSOC 2014 Workshops. LNCS, vol. 8954, pp. 213–224. Springer, Berlin (2015)

13. Mos, A., Pedrinaci, C., Rey, G.A., Gomez, J.M., Liu, D., Vaudaux-Ruth, G., Quaireau, S.: Multi-level monitoring and analysis of web-scale service based applications. In: Dan, A., Gittler, F., Toumani, F. (eds.) ICSOC/ServiceWave 2009. LNCS, vol. 6275, pp. 269–282. Springer, Heidelberg (2010)

14. Pedrinaci, C., Domingue, J., Alves de Medeiros, A.K.: A core ontology for business process analysis. In: Bechhofer, S., Hauswirth, M., Hoffmann, J., Koubarakis, M. (eds.) ESWC 2008. LNCS, vol. 5021, pp. 49–64. Springer, Heidelberg (2008)

15. Pedrinaci, C., Lambert, D., Wetzstein, B., Van Lessen, T., Cekov, L., Dimitrov, M.: Sentinel: a semantic business process monitoring tool. In: Proceedings of 1st International Workshop on Ontology-Supported Business Intelligence, p. 1. ACM (2008)

16. Petriu, D.C., Shen, H.: Applying the UML performance profile: graph grammar-based derivation of LQN models from UML specifications. In: Field, T., Harrison, P.G., Bradley, J., Harder, U. (eds.) TOOLS 2002. LNCS, vol. 2324, pp. 159–177. Springer, Heidelberg (2002)

17. Ponnalagu, K., Ghose, A.K., Narendra, N.C., Dam, H.: Cloud capability estimation and recommendation in black-box environments using benchmark-based approximation. In: BPM (2015)

18. Smith, C.U., Williams, L.G.: Performance and scalability of distributed software architectures: an SPE approach. Parallel Distrib. Comput. Pract. 3(4), 74106–80700 (2002)

19. Solomon, A., Litoiu, M.: Business process performance prediction ONA tracked simulation model. In: Proceedings of 3rd International Workshop on Principles of Engineering Service-Oriented Systems, PESOS 2011, pp. 50–56. ACM, New York (2011). http://doi.acm.org/10.1145/1985394.1985402

20. Williams, L.G., Smith, C.U.: Performance evaluation of software architectures. In: Proceedings of 1st International Workshop on Software and Performance, WOSP 1998, pp. 164–177. ACM, New York (1998). http://doi.acm.org/10.1145/287318.287353

21. Woodside, M., Petriu, D.C., Merseguer, J., Petriu, D.B., Alhaj, M.: Transformation challenges: from software models to performance models. Softw. Syst. Model. 13(4), 1529–1552 (2014). http://dx.doi.org/10.1007/s10270-013-0385-x

Propagation of Event Content Modification in Business Processes

John Wondoh$^{(\boxtimes)}$, Georg Grossmann, and Markus Stumptner

University of South Australia, Adelaide, Australia
john.wondoh@mymail.unisa.edu.au, {georg.grossmann,mst}@cs.unisa.edu.au

Abstract. Business processes are composed mainly of activities and events. The latter has gained much focus recently which has resulted in the drift towards *Event-Driven Business Process Management* (EDBPM). Events are used in both monitoring and controlling the execution of business processes. They are considered to be instantaneous and their content cannot be modified after they occur. However, this is not always the case in the real world. An event's content can be modified at runtime under circumstances such as: earlier event information containing errors, or new information being obtained about the event. In such cases, the content modification for that event must be taken into consideration in the execution of the process. Additionally, the modified event's content may affect other events within the process resulting in altering the content of those events as well. Therefore, it is important to determine the propagation of event content modification in an event network within a business process. In this work, we determine the types of event content modifications that can occur within processes, how content modification of one event affects other events within the process, and how the modification affects the process as a whole.

Keywords: Business processes · Event content modification (ECM) · Modification propagation

1 Introduction

Events are important in business process management (BPM) as they provide flexible and effective means of monitoring and controlling the execution of business processes. Events and activities are the main components of business processes with the focus drifting from activities to events in recent years [1]. In fact, the adoption of event processing techniques into BPM has resulted in rigorous research in areas including [9]: event-driven business activity monitoring (EDBAM) [12,17], event-driven process control (EDPC) [8,14], and event-driven predictive analysis (EDPA) [11,20]. In general, all these fall under a single broad area termed event-driven business process management (EDBPM). However, approaches developed in these areas do not consider the possibility of modifying an event's content (attributes), although this occurs in the real world [6,19]. In this work, we develop an approach to improve monitoring and control of

© Springer International Publishing Switzerland 2016
Q.Z. Sheng et al. (Eds.): ICSOC 2016, LNCS 9936, pp. 70–84, 2016.
DOI: 10.1007/978-3-319-46295-0_5

activities within business processes by taking into consideration the possibility of event content modification (ECM).

An ECM may occur as a result of two factors: (i) new information about an event is obtained [6,19], or (ii) errors are detected within the event's information that require correction [16]. In both cases, the content of the original event must be modified to correctly represent the real world or information system. Consider the following example:

Example 1. Some patients discharged from a hospital may require home care services. This responsibility is passed on to a homecare organisation. To provide the services on time, the hospital must assess the patient's health condition and inform the homecare organisation of the planned discharge time of the patient. Based on this information, the homecare organisation will plan scheduled home care visits to the patient to provide the required services. In an EDBPM system, interactions between the homecare organisation and the hospital are driven by events. Figure 1 illustrates a simplified version of the homecare process interacting with a hospital process (not shown) via a service request event. However, this may not happen as planned due to changes that may occur in the business environment. For example, the planned discharge time of the patient may be modified to an earlier time than expected. This leads to the modification of the content of the earlier service request event. Once the ECM becomes known by the homecare organisation, they must take into consideration the modified event's content in their process.

The homecare process consist of several events with a complex network and dependency. To be able to handle an ECM on the fly, two main problems need to be solved:

1. Identifying event dependency within a business process as well as identifying the relationships between attributes of different events. We use the term *event attribute dependency* to describe the latter.
2. Identifying the impact of the ECM of one event on the content of other events within the business process with the aim of identifying how much the business process has been affected by one ECM. For example, modifying the discharge date of a patient should lead to modifying the service delivery date. This is done by utilising identified event dependencies and event attribute dependencies.

Currently, these problems remind unsolved as most event driven approaches in BPM consider either events to be immutable [2,18], or ECM to be limited to a single event [6,16]. In our approach, we capture an event's content modification, and propagate it to other events by utilising event attribute dependencies. We adopt event processing networks (EPNs) [5] for realising event dependencies with the aim of developing an event dependency graph for a given process. The purpose of the event dependency graph is for propagating ECM within the event network. This is important as it helps in identifying how the process can be altered to accommodate certain changes. The main contributions of our work are as follows:

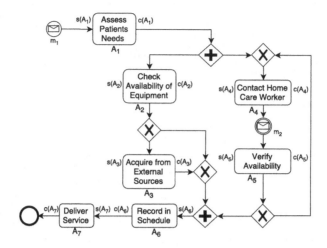

Fig. 1. A homecare process [19]

1. We introduce and formalise the concept of event content modification and event attribute dependencies.
2. We introduce an event dependency graph capable of capturing both event dependencies and event attribute dependencies within business processes.
3. We introduce propagation of event content modification in a business process instance based on our event dependency graph.

The remainder of this paper is organised as follows: Sect. 2 provides a general discussion of events in business processes, followed by Sect. 3 which deals with different types of event dependencies in business processes. Sections 4 and 5 covers event content modification and its propagation. A brief discussion of the usability of the presented approach is given in Sect. 6, followed by a review of related work in Sect. 7. We conclude the paper and discuss future work in Sect. 8.

2 Events in Business Processes

An event is basically a happening within a domain and it may be instantaneous or have a duration. There are three main types of events in business processes [3]: *activity invocation* or *start event* which initiates an instance of an activity type, *activity termination* or *end event* which terminates the execution of an activity instance, and *message* or *request event*. The latter can further be classified as either a *send event* or a *receive event* [7] with respect to the system under consideration, where a send event represents an outgoing message and the receive event represents an incoming message.

The properties of an event include [13] an *event name* (a name describing the type of event), and a *timestamp* (indicating when the event occurred). These properties may vary based on the type of event under consideration as shown in Table 1. In this table, the column S/H represents a simpler representation of an event. The attributes of an event may be categorised as either mutable (attributes that can be changed) or immutable (attributes that must remain constant). From Table 1, immutable properties of events include: event identification number (id) and activity name. Immutable properties are utilised in event identification. On the other hand, mutable properties include time, additional information (addInfo), role, and payload.

Table 1. Event Structure

Event type	Attributes	Structure	S/H
start event	id, activityName, role, addInfo, time	start{id, activityName, role, addInfo, time}	$s(A)$
end event	id, activityName, role, addInfo, time	end{ id, activityName, role, addInfo, time }	$c(A)$
send event	id, payload, time	send{ id, payload, time }	m
send event	id, payload, time	receive{ id, payload, time }	m

The time attribute captures the time at which an event occurs. Other important temporal attributes not represented in this table include, the detection time of an event, i.e., the time an event becomes known in a system, and its processing time. The latter captures the time an event is utilised in a process, which is application dependent. Hence, it is not captured in the event structure, but is known internally within the business process. The relationship between occurrence time ot_e, detection time dt_e, and processing time pt_e of an event e is such that, $ot_e \leq dt_e \leq pt_e$, except for the case of a future (planned) event where its occurrence is in the future. Temporal constraints of a business process can be expressed in terms of events, and this can prove to be useful in monitoring business processes for constraint violation [4,10,12]. For instance, the start and end events of an activity can be used to determine the duration of the activity. Similarly, the end event of an activity and the start event of a succeeding activity can be used to determine the delay between the two activities.

In Table 1, the payload attribute of a message event represents the information that can be used by the business process in decision making. The addInfo attribute of the start and end events also captures information that will be useful in the execution of the activity. For example, it may provide contextual information required to improve on the quality of the resulting service.

Example 2. Figure 1 shows the different types of events in the process described in Example 1. The start event of an activity is represented by $s(A_i)$ and its end event is represented by $c(A_i)$. Other attributes of each event are ignored for simplicity. 'Receive events', m_1 and m_2, are shown as well. 'Send events' are ignored as they have an external effect but not necessarily on the process.

In the above example, event attributes may be modified after they occur, leading to a possible alteration of the effect of the event. Since the business process interacts with partners such as the hospital, patient, and nurse[1], changes that occur from these systems propagate to the home care process. An example is the change in the proposed discharge date by the hospital (contained in the message event m_1). Other changes may include: nurses changing their availability, and the service requirement of a patient changing. These modifications need to be incorporated into the business process and its impact evaluated.

In the next section we shall discuss event processing networks and how they capture the relationship between events. This is a first step in capturing dependency between events and propagating modification of an event's content to other events within the event network.

3   Event Dependencies in Business Processes

The main concept utilised here is the event processing network (EPN) which captures the relationship between event producers, consumers, event processing agents, and channels. The definition of an EPN as presented in [15] is given as follows:

Definition 1 (Event Processing Network). *An EPN is a graph $G = (V, E)$ where $V = C \cup P \cup A \cup EC$. V is a set of nodes of four types, with C denoting an event consumer, P denoting an event producer, A denoting an EPA, and EC denoting an event channel.*
$E = \{(u, v) | (u \in (P \vee A) \to v \in EC) \wedge (u \in EC \to v \in (C \vee A))\},$

where E is a set of ordered pairs of nodes representing directed edges. These edges are either between an event producer and an event channel, an event channel and an event consumer, an EPA and an event channel, or an event channel and an EPA.

An event producer introduces an instance of an event into a business process, whereas an event consumer receives and utilises an event [5]. Business activities are first class event producers and consumers as they utilise events for instance activation and produce an event when completed (or cancelled). Other event producers and consumers may be external to the system. A receive event is produced externally and utilised by the process. Similarly, a send event is produced internal but utilised by an external system.

An event processing agent (EPA) processes a set of input events and produces a set of output events [5,15]. EPAs are different from event producers and consumers as they only perform computations on the event without necessarily consuming or producing them. In this work, we limit ourselves to two types of EPAs, compose EPAs which composes a new event from at least two different events, and translate EPAs which translates an event of one type into an event

---

[1] The nurse may be an external partner, i.e., a firm that outsources to a casual nurse or an internal partner (an employed worker).

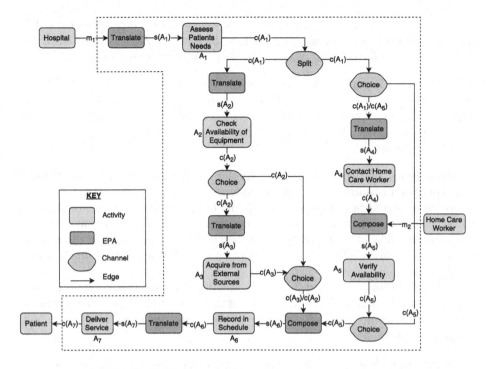

Fig. 2. EPN representation of a homecare process

of another type. An event channel, unlike an EPA, receives a set of input events, makes routing decisions, and sends out the input events unchanged to one or more target processing elements in accordance with these routing decisions [5]. In an EPN representation of a business process, the event channels replace the control flow elements such as the BPMN gateways.

Figure 2 shows the EPN corresponding to the business process of Fig. 1. We have two main types of event producers here, activities within the process as well as external systems that send events to the business process. Note that a key of the various EPN components is provided in Fig. 2.

3.1 Event Dependencies

As shown in Fig. 2, an EPN representation of a business process puts the focus on the steps and components involved in processing events. It is therefore capable of capturing dependencies among events in a process. For instance, it is possible to identify that the occurrence of one event relies on the occurrence of another event. These dependencies can be categorised as either *in/out dependencies* or *temporal dependencies* as defined below.

Definition 2 (In/Out Dependency). *Let A be an EPA or an activity, and let E_i be a set of input events and E_j be a set of output events to A such that*

$E_i \neq \emptyset$, $E_j \neq \emptyset$, $E_i \cap E_j = \emptyset$. We say E_j is dependent on E_i, denoted as $E_i \rightarrow E_j$. The statement $e_i \rightarrow e_j$ is true of events $e_i \in E_i$ and $e_j \in E_j$ if e_i must occur for e_j to occur, i.e., for e_j to be produced by A, e_i must be consumed by A.

Definition 3 (Temporal Dependency). *There exists a temporal dependency between two events e_i and e_j if the occurrence time of e_j, denoted as ot_{e_j}, is dependent on the occurrence time ot_{e_i} of e_i, i.e., $ot_{e_i} \rightarrow ot_{e_j}$. Temporal dependencies may include: $(ot_{e_j} = ot_{e_i}) \vee (ot_{e_j} > ot_{e_i}) \vee (ot_{e_j} < ot_{e_i}) \vee (ot_{e_j} \leq ot_{e_i}) \vee (ot_{e_j} \geq ot_{e_i})$.*

Both types of dependencies are similar and are therefore best utilised together. For instance, an in/out dependency between e_1 and e_2 may have a temporal dependencies of $ot_{e_2} > ot_{e_1}$. While temporal dependencies deal solely with the time of occurrences of events, they do not take into consideration EPAs and activities. Therefore, temporal dependencies facilitate identifying the general ordering of events while in/out dependencies identify the relationship between input and output events.

Utilising Definitions 2 and 3, we can identify dependencies between events. We can further utilise these identified dependencies to realise other types of dependencies within the business process. We break this down into direct and indirect dependencies.

1. Direct Dependencies: In this type of dependency, one event's occurrence is a direct result of another event occurrence. Given two events e_j and e_i, e_j is directly dependent on e_i if (i) $ot_{e_i} \rightarrow ot_{e_j}$ and (ii) $e_i \rightarrow e_j$. For instance, in Fig. 2, $s(A_1)$ is directly dependent on m_1 since m_1 occurs before $s(A_1)$ and $s(A_1)$ is derived from m_1 by translation.
2. Indirect Dependencies: These capture transitive dependencies between events. For instance, in Fig. 2, $s(A_2)$ is directly dependant on $c(A_1)$, while $c(A_2)$ directly depends on $s(A_2)$, therefore, $c(A_2)$ indirectly depends on $c(A_1)$.

Identifying event dependencies are a necessary step to identifying event attribute dependency. This is because attribute dependencies only exist within events that have some form of dependency. Thus, attribute dependency does not exist between unrelated events. We now proceed to discuss event attribute dependencies.

3.2 Event Attribute Dependency

An event's attributes, also referred to as the event's content, may be derived from attributes of other events. The value of these attributes is a function of the other event's attributes. We use the term event attribute dependency to describe some relationship that exists between attributes of different events. A formal definition is given as follows:

Definition 4 (Event Attribute Dependency). *Let a_i and a_j be attributes of event e_i and e_j such that $a_i \in e_i$ and $a_j \in e_j$. a_j is dependent on a_i if*

- *there exists a dependency between e_i and e_j such that $e_i \to e_j$*
- *there exists a relationship r such that a_j is a function of a_i, i.e., $e_j.a_j = r(e_i.a_i)$.*

If $e_i = e_j$, then the attributes under consideration are attributes of the same event; that is, a self attribute dependency exists within the event. However, an inter-event attribute dependency results when we consider the attribute relationship of two different events, i.e., $e_i \neq e_j$.

Temporal dependency (Definition 3) discussed in Sect. 3.1 is a type of attribute dependency as it compares the occurrence time of events. However, we focus on attributes that are functions of other attributes here, such that modifying one attribute results in the modification of the other. Therefore, we utilise temporal dependencies here to capture general ordering of events relative to each other. In this way, we can capture the relative positions of events in our proposed event dependency graph.

Determining event attribute dependency is important since it aids in determining the attributes of other events that are prone to modification due to an attribute modification of an event. We now proceed to discuss event dependency graphs where we capture both event and event attributes dependencies.

3.3 Event Dependency Graphs

An EPN is important for capturing the relationship between different components in processing an event, i.e., producers, consumers, EPAs and channels. While general event dependencies can be in such a network, the focus is not on capturing event dependencies as well as event attribute dependencies. We propose the use of an event dependency graph (EDG) for this purpose. A dedicated EDG puts the focus on event dependencies as well as capturing inter-event attribute dependency. An EDG is defined as follows:

Definition 5 (Event Dependency Graph). *An EDG is a graph $D = (E, R)$ where $E \neq \emptyset$ is a set of nodes representing events such that $e_i \in E$, and $R \neq \emptyset$ is a set of directed arcs $R \subseteq (E \times E)$ representing dependencies. We distinguish between event dependencies R_e and event attribute dependencies R_a such that for any given EDG, $R_e \cup R_a \in R$ and $R_e \cap R_a \neq \emptyset$.*

Event attribute dependencies (R_a) are represented in an EDG by dashed lines with labels representing the dependency relationship between the two events under consideration. On the other hand, R_e (event dependencies) is represented by solid lines with optional labels representing the type of relationship.

Example 3. Consider the example of an EDG shown in Fig. 3. Event dependencies are captured from m_1 to $c(A_7)$. The attribute discharge date is part of the payload of m_1, while the attribute delivery date of $s(A_7)$ is a function

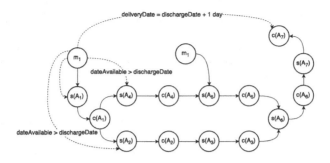

Fig. 3. Event dependency graph for a homecare process

of discharge date, expressed as: $deliveryDate = dischargeDate + 1$, i.e., service delivery should begin a day after the patient has been discharged. These attribute relationships are captured by labels on the arcs. The EDG captures all related events within a particular process and determines dependencies between the attributes of the events. This forms the basics for the propagations of content modification of events. We deal with the latter in the following section.

4   Event Content Modification

Mutable attributes of events are prone to modification or revision, which leads to what we term event content modification. The latter can happen after an event has occurred, has been detected or has been processed. Other literature refers to ECM as event information update [6,19] or revision [16]. Event modification is essential for ensuring that event instances correspond correctly to the real world. Meaning, an event should be able to adapt to changes. The main reasons for ECM is correcting erroneous event information and introducing new event content (resulting from changes in the real world or information system).

There are two main approaches to modifying the content of an event as shown in Fig. 4: (a) utilising a *modification event* e_m that revises the content of the original event, (b) directly updating the event by considering changes in a database. We prefer the modification event approach as it avoids the direct reliance on database systems which may result in additional complexities. A modification event is an event that occurs to modify the content of an existing event. In both cases, a specialised EPA termed as a modification EPA is utilised in modifying the event which we discuss later in this section.

The modified event is considered to be the same as the original event after modification as given in Definition 6. This is because the immutable properties used in event identification are not modified during the modification process. The immutable properties of an event can also be referred to as the event's key.

Definition 6 (Event Equivalence). *Two events e and e' are considered equivalent if the set of immutable event properties, termed key of e is the same as the set of immutable properties key' of e', i.e., $e \equiv e' \Leftrightarrow key = key'$.*

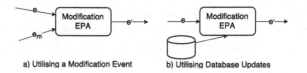

a) Utilising a Modification Event   b) Utilising Database Updates

Fig. 4. Event content modification approaches

Since for any given point in time there may exist a set of events with the same key in a system, we utilised the detection time of each event to determine the ordering (Definition 7). This is to enable us determine the latest modified version of the event that should be utilised by the process.

Definition 7 (Event Ordering). *Let e and e′ be two events that have occurred in a business process such that e ≡ e′ and let dt_e be the detection time of e and $dt_{e'}$ be the detection time of e′. If e′ is a modified version of e, then $dt_{e'} > dt_e$.*

Definition 8 (Modification EPA). *Let e and e_m be events within a business process such that e_m is a modification event to e. A modification EPA utilises as inputs e and e_m and produces an output e′ such that e′ ≡ e and $dt_{e'} > dt_e$.*

A modification EPA may further be categorised into two specialised EPAs based on the type of event modification: *correction EPA* which revise erroneous event attributes with correct information provided by e_m, and *addition EPA* which adds additional content to the existing content of an event.

5   Propagation of Event Content Modification

Modifying the content of one event instance at runtime may affect other events in the business process resulting in ECMs of other events in the process. The notion of propagation of ECM is used here to describe a series of ECMs in an event network resulting from modifying a single event's content. Propagation of ECM is achieved by using the event dependency graph (EDG) and the dependencies that can be derived from it. Propagating modification in an EDG of a business process is essential in ensuring that each event in the network correctly represents the real world. Since the real world is not ideal, changes do occur and these changes must be captured and resolved in the business process. We argue that events being the drivers of processes in an EDBPM should as well be the drivers of change in the process.

In order to determine if an event's content should be modified based on the modification of another event's content, we need to take two important aspects into consideration: event dependency (Definitions 2 and 3) and event attribute dependency (Definition 4). Event dependencies are generic in determining both direct and indirect dependencies between events in the process. Conversely, event attribute dependency is a more specific form of dependency as it specifies dependency between attributes of different events. However, there is a link between both types of dependency, i.e., event attribute dependency will not exist between attributes of two different events unless one event is dependent on the other. Therefore, to establish attribute dependency, we need to first verify if there exist some generic dependency between the events.

Figure 5 shows a flow chart for identifying events that will be affected by modifying another event's content. It first establishes the need for event dependencies to exist before evaluating for attribute dependency. Event dependencies are either direct or indirect. For direct dependencies, we simply evaluate for attribute dependency between the events. On the other hand, for indirectly dependent events, we need to evaluate for transitive attribute dependency between the events if there exist no direct attribute dependency. In both cases, one of two conclusions are arrived: a) $e_j.a_j$ is modified by modifying $e_i.a_i$, and b) modifying $e_i.a_i$ does not result in the modification of $e_j.a_j$. Making use of such an approach, we can determine all ECMs resulting from a single ECM in a dependency graph for a given business process.

ECM propagation can be represented formally as follows: ECM of event e_i will propagate to event e_j, denoted $e_i' \rightarrow e_j'$ if

1. Direct event and attribute dependency exist: $(a_j \in e_j) \wedge (a_i \in e_i) \wedge (e_j \rightarrow e_i) \wedge (a_j = r(a_i))$.
2. Direct event dependency exist but attribute dependencies must be inferred. We use an event e_k that has an attribute a_k with dependency relationships r_1 with a_i and r_2 with a_j for inference: $(a_j \in e_j) \wedge (a_i \in e_i) \wedge (a_k \in e_k) \wedge (e_k \rightarrow e_j) \wedge (e_i \rightarrow e_k) \wedge (e_i \rightarrow e_j) \wedge (a_j \neq r(a_i)) \wedge (a_k = r_1(a_i)) \wedge (a_j = r_2(a_k))$.
3. Indirect event dependency and direct event attribute dependency exist: $(a_j \in e_j) \wedge (a_i \in e_i) \wedge \neg(e_j \rightarrow e_i) \wedge (e_k \rightarrow e_j) \wedge (e_i \rightarrow e_k) \wedge (a_j = r(a_i))$.
4. Indirect event dependencies and indirect event attribute dependency exist: $(a_j \in e_j) \wedge (a_i \in e_i) \wedge (a_k \in e_k) \wedge \neg(e_i \rightarrow e_j) \wedge (a_j \neq r(a_i)) \wedge (e_k \rightarrow e_j) \wedge (e_i \rightarrow e_k) \wedge (a_k = r_1(a_i)) \wedge (a_j = r_2(a_k))$.

The new value of a_j of event e_j is determined by its relation $r_a \in R_a$ with a_i of event e_i. Given a relation $e_j.a_j = r_a(e_i.a_i)$, modifying the value of a_i must be accompanied by modifying a_j as well. This is to ensure that the attribute relation is not violated. The important aspect of determining a new value of a_j such that the attribute dependency is satisfied is to determine the relation r between a_i and a_j. r is either known during design time and it may be discovered by adopting mining techniques. However, discovering the value r is not in the scope of this paper as we assume that we already have access to this value.

Example 4. Event m_1 which is the message event from the hospital responsible for initiating the homecare process has some attribute dependencies with other events including $s(A_7)$ and $s(A_2)$ in the EDG shown in Fig. 3. The attribute relations are provided in the figure as well: $s(A_7).deliveryDate = m_1.dischargeDate + 1$ (service delivery should begin a day after the patient has been discharged) and $s(A_2).dataAvailable > m_1.dischargeDate$ (equipment must be made available after discharge date). To maintain consistency as well as satisfy the attribute relations, a change in discharge date of m_1 must result in

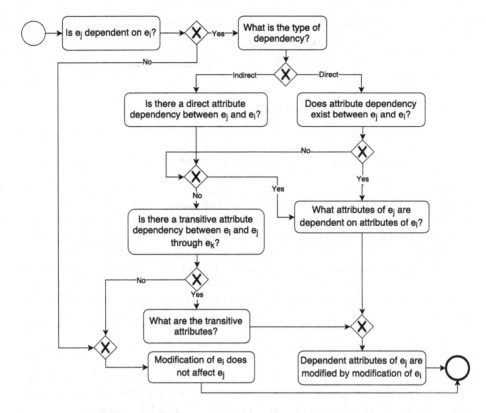

Fig. 5. ECM propagation approach

a change in delivery date of $s(A_7)$, i.e., new deliver date = new discharge date + one day, and a change in availability date of $s(A_2)$ such that new availability data > new discharge date. Using the approach presented in Fig. 5, we can come to this conclusion. First, we realise that there is no direct dependency between m_1 and $s(A_2)$ (or $s(A_7)$); however, a transitive relationship exist between the events. Next we can determine the attribute dependency from the EDG in Fig. 3. Finally, the dependent attributes of $s(A_2)$ and $s(A_7)$ are modified based on the modification of the determinant attribute of m_1.

Identifying and propagating ECM is important as it facilitates process adaptations to changes (especially external changes). The propagation of these changes is driven by events which have become the main drivers of business processes management [1]. The application of the discussed approach in a running business process is given in the discussion in the next section.

6   Discussion

Propagation of ECM in business process presents a less complex approach where the impact of a change in event attributes on a process can easily be determined.

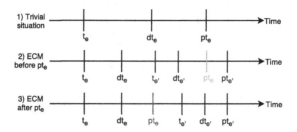

Fig. 6. Processing time relationships

Modification of an event may occur at different times within the lifecycle of a business process or activity. This results in the modified event having different effects on the business process. The processing time of the original event is essential in determining how the modified event affects the business process. Three potential situations may arise when we consider the processing time of an event to the time a modification occurs. Figure 6 shows these three situations. ot_e, dt_e, and pt_e are the occurrence, detection, and processing time of an event e and $ot_{e'}$, $dt_{e'}$, and $pt_{e'}$ are the equivalent time of e' such that $e \equiv e'$.

1. Trivial situation: In this situation the content of the event is not modified, i.e., e' does not occur.
2. ECM before pt_e: In this case, e' occurs and is detected before e is utilised by the process, i.e., $ot_{e'} \leq dt_{e'} < pt_e$. ECM may have no effect on the process instance as the original event's content can be completely ignored.
3. ECM after pt_e: In this case, e' occurs and is detected after the unmodified event is utilised by the process, i.e., $pt_e < ot_{e'} \leq dt_{e'}$. This calls for a modification of the process instance to accommodate for the ECM.

The propagation of ECM improves process adaptability and flexibility by providing information about the potential impact of changes in event attributes. Therefore, an improved approach for handling external contingency can easily be developed. This is beneficial not only to business processes, but also to any event-driven domains, including distributed event-based systems and web services.

7   Related Work

Most work in BPM [1,3,8,12] consider events to be first class citizens and the main driving component of business processes. However, events are only considered to be immutable once they occur, i.e., the event's content cannot be modified after the event has occurred. Therefore, these approaches lean towards the ideal world scenario and are not equipped to handle situations where revision of an events content is required. To handle such a situation, a new event with different identifications are used to represent modification. Therefore, these events must be anticipated during design time and contingency plans put in place to handle them when they occur. However, this is unachievable in the real world as it is difficult to identify all cases at design time. This is because content modification can happen unexpectedly during runtime of a business process. Determining the impact on the fly by using the approach presented here will ensure improvement in runtime contingency management in business processes.

There is some work outside the domain of business processes that consider event content modification. In Furche et al. [6], they provide an approach for web event information update with the aim of improving decisions that are consistent with the real world. However, they do not consider propagation of the update in an event network as they considered only single composite web events. A similar approach is presented in Sripada [16] where they provide an approach for revising erroneous event information. Similarly, they do not provide an approach to determine other events that may be affected by the change.

In our earlier work [19], we considered propagation of temporal modification of an event in a business process. This approach determines an update to an events temporal attribute and determines its propagation by utilising activity lifecycles and the underlying data model of the process. This approach does not make use of other events that may exist within the business process. Compared to the approach presented in this work (which utilises only events), it is complex and tedious as it considers data model dependencies as well as activity lifecycles. In addition, it focuses only on temporal attributes while ignoring other potentially mutable attributes.

8 Conclusion

In this work, we provide an approach that captures modification in an event's content and propagates this modification to other events within a business process by utilising an event dependency graph. We exploit dependencies that exist between event attributes and we capture these in an event dependency graph. The extent to which a single event's content modification can affect a process at a point in the time can be determined by using this approach. There-fore, a suitable contingency plan can easily be adopted to manage the impact. In our future work, we shall develop and implement an intervention approach for contingency management that utilises the proposed techniques in this work for identifying and determining the impact of contingencies on a business process.

Acknowledgements. This research was partially funded by the Data to Decisions Cooperative Research Centre (D2D CRC).

References

1. Buchmann, A., Appel, S., Freudenreich, T., Frischbier, S., Guerrero, P.E.: From calls to events: architecting future BPM systems. In: Barros, A., Gal, A., Kindler, E. (eds.) BPM 2012. LNCS, vol. 7481, pp. 17–32. Springer, Heidelberg (2012)
2. Chakravarthy, S., Mishra, D.: Snoop: an expressive event specification language for active databases. Data Knowl. Eng. **14**(1), 1–26 (1994)

3. Damaggio, E., Hull, R., Vaculín, R.: On the equivalence of incremental and fixpoint semantics for business artifacts with guard-stage-milestone lifecycles. Inf. Syst. **38**(4), 561–584 (2013)
4. Eder, J., Panagos, E., Rabinovich, M.I.: Time constraints in workflow systems. In: Jarke, M., Oberweis, A. (eds.) CAiSE 1999. LNCS, vol. 1626, pp. 286–300. Springer, Heidelberg (1999)
5. Etzion, O., Niblett, P.: Event Processing in Action. Manning Publications Company, London (2010)
6. Furche, T., Grasso, G., Huemer, M., Schallhart, C., Schrefl, M.: Bitemporal complex event processing of web event advertisements. In: Lin, X., Manolopoulos, Y., Srivastava, D., Huang, G. (eds.) WISE 2013, Part II. LNCS, vol. 8181, pp. 333–346. Springer, Heidelberg (2013)
7. Knuplesch, D., Reichert, M., Kumar, A.: Visually monitoring multiple perspectives of business process compliance. In: Proceedings of BPM, pp. 263–279 (2015)
8. Koetter, F., Kochanowski, M., Kintz, M.: Leveraging model-driven monitoring for event-driven business process control. In: Proceedings of EMoV, pp. 21–33 (2014)
9. Krumeich, J., Weis, B., Werth, D., Loos, P.: Event-driven business process management: where are we now? A comprehensive synthesis and analysis of literature. Bus. Process Manag. J. **20**(4), 615–633 (2014)
10. Lanz, A., Weber, B., Reichert, M.: Time patterns for process-aware information systems. Requir. Eng. **19**(2), 113–141 (2014)
11. Leitner, P., Michlmayr, A., Rosenberg, F., Dustdar, S.: Monitoring, prediction and prevention of SLA violations in composite services. In: Proceedings of ICWS, pp. 369–376 (2010)
12. Montali, M., Maggi, F.M., Chesani, F., Mello, P., van der Aalst, W.M.P.: Monitoring business constraints with the event calculus. ACM TIST **5**, 17:1–17:30 (2013)
13. Patri, O.P., Sorathia, V.S., Panangadan, A.V., Prasanna, V.K.: The process-oriented event model (poem): a conceptual model for industrial events. In: Proceedings of DEBS, pp. 154–165. ACM (2014)
14. Scheer, A.W., Thomas, O., Adam, O.: Process modeling using event-driven process chains. In: Process-Aware Information Systems, pp. 119–146 (2005)
15. Sharon, G., Etzion, O.: Event-processing network model and implementation. IBM Syst. J. **47**(2), 321–334 (2008)
16. Sripada, S.M.: A logical framework for temporal deductive databases. In: Proceedings of VLDB, pp. 171–182 (1988)
17. Weidlich, M., Ziekow, H., Mendling, J., Günther, O., Weske, M., Desai, N.: Event-based monitoring of process execution violations. In: Rinderle-Ma, S., Toumani, F., Wolf, K. (eds.) BPM 2011. LNCS, vol. 6896, pp. 182–198. Springer, Heidelberg (2011)
18. Wieringa, R.J.: Design Methods for Reactive Systems: Yourdon, Statemate, and the UML. Elsevier, Amsterdam (2003)
19. Wondoh, J., Grossmann, G., Stumptner, M.: Utilising bitemporal information for business process contingency management. In: Proceedings of APCCM, pp. 45:1–45:10. ACM (2016)
20. Zeng, L., Lingenfelder, C., Lei, H., Chang, H.: Event-driven quality of service prediction. In: Bouguettaya, A., Krueger, I., Margaria, T. (eds.) ICSOC 2008. LNCS, vol. 5364, pp. 147–161. Springer, Heidelberg (2008)

Business Process Modeling

Discovery of Multi-perspective Declarative Process Models

Stefan Schönig[1]([envelope]), Claudio Di Ciccio[1], Fabrizio M. Maggi[2],
and Jan Mendling[1]

[1] Vienna University of Economics and Business, Vienna, Austria
{stefan.schoenig,claudio.di.ciccio,jan.mendling}@wu.ac.at
[2] University of Tartu, Tartu, Estonia
f.m.maggi@ut.ee

Abstract. Process discovery is one of the main branches of process mining that allows the user to build a process model representing the process behavior as recorded in the logs. Standard process discovery techniques produce as output a procedural process model (e.g., a Petri net). Recently, several approaches have been developed to derive declarative process models from logs and have been proven to be more suitable to analyze processes working in environments that are less stable and predictable. However, a large part of these techniques are focused on the analysis of the control flow perspective of a business process. Therefore, one of the challenges still open in this field is the development of techniques for the analysis of business processes also from other perspectives, like data, time, and resources. In this paper, we present a full-fledged approach for the discovery of multi-perspective declarative process models from event logs that allows the user to discover declarative models taking into consideration all the information an event log can provide. The approach has been implemented and experimented in real-life case studies.

Keywords: Process mining · Process discovery · Multi-perspective process model · Declarative process model · Declare

1 Introduction

Process mining, and specifically process discovery, is driven by the ambition to understand how a process is truly executed, why certain activities are executed and under which circumstances. It aims at constructing a process model from an event log consisting of traces, such that each trace corresponds to one execution of the process. Each event in a trace consists as a minimum of an event class (i.e., the activity to which the event corresponds) and generally a timestamp. In some cases, other information may be available such as the originator of the event (i.e., the performer of the activity) as well as data produced by the event in the form of attribute-value pairs. Discovery is of particular value for processes that offer various options to execute them. Those processes are often referred to as flexible,

© Springer International Publishing Switzerland 2016
Q.Z. Sheng et al. (Eds.): ICSOC 2016, LNCS 9936, pp. 87–103, 2016.
DOI: 10.1007/978-3-319-46295-0_6

adaptive, unstructured or knowledge-intense. Often, procedural process models resulting from discovery are colloquially called Spaghetti models due to their complex structure [1]. Therefore, discovered process models can be represented as a set of declarative constraints for directly representing the causality of the behavior [25].

The benefits of declarative languages such as Declare [24], DPIL [32] or DCR Graphs [12] have been emphasized in the literature. It is also well known that behavior is typically intertwined with dependencies upon value ranges of data parameters and resource characteristics [15,27]. Therefore, Declare has been extended towards Multi-Perspective Declare (MP-Declare) [5]. However, state-of-the-art mining tools such as MINERful [8,9] and DeclareMiner [16,19] do not support MP-Declare at this moment.

In this paper, we address this problem by proposing a mining technique for discovering MP-Declare models. We show that the discovery of MP-Declare allows for the acquisition of knowledge that goes beyond the classical declarative mining, which is focused only on the behavioral perspective in the vast majority of cases. Furthermore, we present the first foundational categorization of the conditions that are posed on declarative constraints with a special focus on how these categories are reflected into discovery metrics. We implemented our approach starting from the SQL-based process mining approach described in [29], relying on RXES, a standardized architecture for storing event log data in relational databases [11]. The approach has been validated with several real-life event logs provided by a large academic hospital, by five Dutch municipalities and by an Italian local police office for managing fines for road traffic violations.

The paper is structured as follows. Section 2 presents a typical discovery problem that we tackle with our research, and the notions both of Declare and MP-Declare modeling. Section 3 defines the framework we propose to delineate the boundaries of the process discovery task. Section 4 describes the approach developed on top of SQL. Section 5 presents the evaluation of our technique with 3 real-life cases. Section 6 discusses related work before Sect. 7 that concludes the paper.

2   Research Background

In this section, we first illustrate the research problem that we are addressing. We then summarize concepts of Declare and MP-Declare.

2.1   Research Problem

Declarative constraints are strong in representing the permissible behavior of business processes. Modeling languages like Declare [2] describe a set of *constraints* that must be satisfied throughout the process execution. Constraints, in turn, are based on *templates*. Templates are patterns that define parameterized classes of properties, and constraints are their concrete instantiations. Their semantics can be formalized using formal logics such as Linear Temporal Logic over finite traces (LTL_f) [23].

Table 1. Semantics for declare templates in LTL_f.

Template	LTL_f semantics	Activation activity	Target activity
Existence	$\top \rightarrow \mathbf{F}(A) \vee \mathbf{O}(A)$	–	A
Responded existence	$\mathbf{G}(A \rightarrow (\mathbf{O}B \vee \mathbf{F}B))$	A	B
Response	$\mathbf{G}(A \rightarrow \mathbf{F}B)$	A	B
Alternate response	$\mathbf{G}(A \rightarrow \mathbf{X}(\neg A \mathbf{U} B))$	A	B
Chain response	$\mathbf{G}(A \rightarrow \mathbf{X}B)$	A	B
Precedence	$\mathbf{G}(B \rightarrow \mathbf{O}A)$	B	A
Alternate precedence	$\mathbf{G}(B \rightarrow \mathbf{Y}(\neg B \mathbf{S} A))$	B	A
Chain precedence	$\mathbf{G}(B \rightarrow \mathbf{Y}A)$	B	A
Not responded existence	$\mathbf{G}(A \rightarrow \neg(\mathbf{O}B \vee \mathbf{F}B))$	A	B
Not response	$\mathbf{G}(A \rightarrow \neg\mathbf{F}B)$	A	B
Not precedence	$\mathbf{G}(B \rightarrow \neg\mathbf{O}A)$	B	A
Not chain response	$\mathbf{G}(A \rightarrow \neg\mathbf{X}B)$	A	B
Not chain precedence	$\mathbf{G}(B \rightarrow \neg\mathbf{Y}A)$	B	A

A central shortcoming of languages like Declare is the fact that templates are not directly capable of expressing the connection between the behavior and other perspectives of the process. Consider the example of a loan application process. The process analyst would be interested to learn about constraints such as the following:

1. Activation conditions: When a loan was requested and *account balance* > 4, 000 *EUR*, the loan was subsequently granted in 95 % of the cases.
2. Correlation conditions: When a loan was requested, the loan was subsequently granted and *amount requested = amount granted* in 95 % of the cases.
3. Target conditions: When a loan was requested, the loan was subsequently granted in 95 % of the cases by a specific member of the financial board.
4. Temporal conditions: When a loan was requested, the loan was subsequently granted *within the next 30 days* in 95 % of the cases.

Standard Declare only supports constraints like the ones shown in Table 1. Here, the $\mathbf{F}$, $\mathbf{X}$, $\mathbf{G}$, and $\mathbf{U}$ LTL_f future operators have the following meanings: formula $\mathbf{F}\psi_1$ means that ψ_1 holds sometime in the future, $\mathbf{X}\psi_1$ means that ψ_1 holds in the next position, $\mathbf{G}\psi_1$ says that ψ_1 holds forever in the future, and, lastly, $\psi_1 \mathbf{U} \psi_2$ means that sometime in the future ψ_2 will hold and until that moment ψ_1 holds (with ψ_1 and ψ_2 LTL_f formulas). The $\mathbf{O}$, $\mathbf{Y}$ and $\mathbf{S}$ LTL_f past operators have the following meaning: $\mathbf{O}\psi_1$ means that ψ_1 holds sometime in the past, $\mathbf{Y}\psi_1$ means that ψ_1 holds in the previous position, and $\psi_1 \mathbf{S} \psi_2$ means that ψ_1 has held sometime in the past and since that moment ψ_2 holds. Consider, for example, the *response* constraint $\mathbf{G}(A \rightarrow \mathbf{F}B)$. It indicates that if A *occurs*, B must eventually *follow*. Therefore, this constraint is fully satisfied in traces such as $\mathbf{t}_1 = \langle A, A, B, C \rangle$, $\mathbf{t}_2 = \langle B, B, C, D \rangle$, and $\mathbf{t}_3 = \langle A, B, C, B \rangle$, but not for

$\mathbf{t}_4 = \langle A, B, A, C \rangle$ because, in this case, the second occurrence of A is not followed by a B. In $\mathbf{t}_2$, it is *vacuously satisfied* [4,13], i.e., in a trivial way, because A never occurs.

An *activation activity* of a constraint in a trace is an activity whose execution imposes, because of that constraint, some obligations on the execution of other activities (target activities) in the same trace (see Table 1). For example, A is an activation activity for the *response* constraint $\mathbf{G}(A \rightarrow \mathbf{F}B)$ and B is a target, because the execution of A forces B to be executed, eventually. An activation of a constraint leads to a *fulfillment* or to a *violation*. Consider, again, $\mathbf{G}(A \rightarrow \mathbf{F}B)$. In trace $\mathbf{t}_1$, the constraint is activated and fulfilled twice, whereas, in trace $\mathbf{t}_3$, it is activated and fulfilled only once. In trace $\mathbf{t}_4$, it is activated twice and the second activation leads to a violation (B does not occur subsequently).

2.2   Multi-perspective Declare

The importance of more complex constraints that integrate activation, correlation, target and temporal dependencies has been emphasized by prior research and has led to the definition of a multi-perspective version of Declare [5]. Table 2 shows the semantics of Multi-Perspective Declare (MP-Declare) formally defined using LTL$_f$.

This semantics build on the notion of *payload* of an event. Consider again the loan request example. Henceforth, we write $e(credit\,check)$ to identify the occurrence of an event, in order to distinguish it from the activity name (*credit check*) when it is not clear from the context. At the time of *credit check*, i.e., when the timestamp $\tau^e_{credit\,check}$ elapses, the attributes *Req.ID*, *Resource*, *Applicant*, *AgeOfApplicant*, and *Debt* have the values *20160202*, *FinancialBoardU001*, *John*, *40*, and *10,000*, respectively. We refer to $p^e_{credit\,check} = (20160202,\ Financial$-$cialBoardU001,\ John,\ 40,\ 10,000)$ as its payload. To denote the projection of

Table 2. Semantics for MP-Declare constraints in LTL$_f$.

Template	LTL$_f$ semantics
Existence	$\top \rightarrow \mathbf{F}(e(A) \wedge \varphi_a(x)) \vee \mathbf{O}(e(A) \wedge \varphi_a(x))$
Responded existence	$\mathbf{G}((A \wedge \varphi_a(x)) \rightarrow (\mathbf{O}(B \wedge \varphi_c(x,y) \wedge \varphi_t(y)) \vee \mathbf{F}(B \wedge \varphi_c(x,y) \wedge \varphi_t(y))))$
Response	$\mathbf{G}((A \wedge \varphi_a(x)) \rightarrow \mathbf{F}(B \wedge \varphi_c(x,y) \wedge \varphi_t(y)))$
Alternate response	$\mathbf{G}((A \wedge \varphi_a(x)) \rightarrow \mathbf{X}(\neg(A \wedge \varphi_a(x))\mathbf{U}(B \wedge \varphi_c(x,y) \wedge \varphi_t(y)))$
Chain response	$\mathbf{G}((A \wedge \varphi_a(x)) \rightarrow \mathbf{X}(B \wedge \varphi_c(x,y) \wedge \varphi_t(y)))$
Precedence	$\mathbf{G}((B \wedge \varphi_a(x)) \rightarrow \mathbf{O}(A \wedge \varphi_c(x,y) \wedge \varphi_t(y)))$
Alternate precedence	$\mathbf{G}((B \wedge \varphi_a(x)) \rightarrow \mathbf{Y}(\neg(B \wedge \varphi_a(x))\mathbf{S}(A \wedge \varphi_c(x,y) \wedge \varphi_t(y)))$
Chain precedence	$\mathbf{G}((B \wedge \varphi_a(x)) \rightarrow \mathbf{Y}(A \wedge \varphi_c(x,y) \wedge \varphi_t(y)))$
Not responded existence	$\mathbf{G}((A \wedge \varphi_a(x)) \rightarrow \neg(\mathbf{O}(B \wedge \varphi_c(x,y) \wedge \varphi_t(y)) \vee \mathbf{F}(B \wedge \varphi_c(x,y) \wedge \varphi_t(y))))$
Not response	$\mathbf{G}((A \wedge \varphi_a(x)) \rightarrow \neg\mathbf{F}(B \wedge \varphi_c(x,y) \wedge \varphi_t(y)))$
Not precedence	$\mathbf{G}((B \wedge \varphi_a(x)) \rightarrow \neg\mathbf{O}(A \wedge \varphi_c(x,y) \wedge \varphi_t(y)))$
Not chain response	$\mathbf{G}((A \wedge \varphi_a(x)) \rightarrow \neg\mathbf{X}(B \wedge \varphi_c(x,y) \wedge \varphi_t(y)))$
Not chain precedence	$\mathbf{G}((B \wedge \varphi_a(x)) \rightarrow \neg\mathbf{Y}(A \wedge \varphi_c(x,y) \wedge \varphi_t(y)))$

the payload $p_A^e = (x_1, \ldots, x_n)$ over attributes $x_1, \ldots, x_m$ with $m \leqslant n$, we use the shorthand notation $p_A^e[x_1, \ldots, x_m]$. In the example, $p_{\text{credit check}}^e[Req.ID]$ is (20160202), and $p_{\text{credit check}}^e[Applicant, AgeOfApplicant]$ is $(John,\ 40)$.

In Table 2, we use a shorthand notation for n-ples of attributes x_i, namely $\boldsymbol{x}$. Referring to the formal specification of constraints in LTL_f (cf. Tables 1 and 2), we call *activation* ϕ_a the sub-formula that lies on the left-hand side of the implication $\rightarrow$ operator, whereas the *target* ϕ_t is the formula that lies on its right-hand side. Templates in MP-Declare extend standard Declare with additional conditions on attributes: given events $e(A)$ and $e(B)$ with payloads $p_A^e = (x_1, \ldots, x_n)$ and $p_B^e = (y_1, \ldots, y_n)$, we define the *activation condition* φ_a, the *correlation condition* φ_c, and the *target condition* φ_t. The activation condition is part of the activation ϕ_a, whilst the correlation and target conditions are part of the target ϕ_t, according to their respective time of evaluation.

The *activation* condition is a statement that must be valid when the activation occurs. In the case of the response template, the activation condition has the form $\varphi_a(x_1, \ldots, x_n)$, meaning that the proposition φ_a over $(x_1, \ldots, x_n)$ must hold true. For example, to express that whenever *credit check* is executed and *Debt* is $< 20,000$, then eventually *grant* follows, we write: $\mathbf{G}((e(credit\ check) \wedge p_{\text{credit check}}^e[Debt] < 20,000) \rightarrow \mathbf{F}(e(grant)))$. In this example, activation ϕ_a consists of a statement about the occurrence of an event $(e(credit\ check))$ and of a condition over an attribute of such event $(\varphi_a = p_{\text{credit check}}^e[Debt] < 20,000)$. In case *credit check* is executed but *Debt* is $\geqslant 20,000$, the constraint is not activated. Target ϕ_t remains in the form of a standard Declare definition, because it specifies only the occurrence of the target event $(e(grant))$.

The *correlation* condition is a statement that must be valid when the target occurs, and relates the values of the attributes in the payloads both of the activation and the target event. It has the form $\varphi_c(x_1, \ldots, x_m, y_1, \ldots, y_m)$ with $m \leqslant n$, where φ_c is a propositional formula on the variables both of the payload of $e(A)$ and the payload of $e(B)$. For instance, whenever *credit check* is executed, then eventually *grant* must follow and the *Req.ID* attribute value associated with $e(credit\ check)$ must be the same as for $e(grant)$. We write: $\mathbf{G}((e(credit\ check) \rightarrow \mathbf{F}(e(grant) \wedge p_{\text{credit check}}^e[Req.ID] = p_{\text{grant}}^e[Req.ID]))$. In the example, target ϕ_t is the conjunction of $e(grant)$, specifying the occurrence of the event, and $p_{\text{credit check}}^e[Req.ID] = p_{\text{grant}}^e[Req.ID]$, correlating the attribute values of activation and target events. The activation remains defined as in the form of a standard Declare constraint.

Target conditions exert limitations on the values of the attributes that are registered at the moment wherein the target activity occurs. It has the form $\varphi_t(y_1, \ldots, y_m)$ with $m \leqslant n$, where φ_t is a propositional formula involving variables in the payload of $e(B)$. As an example, when activity *credit check* is performed, then eventually *grant* is executed and the *Resource* associated with $e(grant)$ must be *FinancialBoardU001*. We write $\mathbf{G}((e(credit\ check) \rightarrow \mathbf{F}(e(grant) \wedge p_{\text{grant}}^e[Resource] = FinancialBoardU001))$. As before, activation ϕ_a only consists of a statement about the occurrence of an event ($e(credit\ check)$), as for standard Declare. Target ϕ_t specifies what the value of an attribute of the target event ($p^e_{grant}[Resource] = FinancialBoardU001$) is, when it occurs ($e(grant)$). As shown in Table 2, declarative templates like *existence* have an activation which is meant to be always satisfied ($\phi_a = \top$). Therefore, only the target is meant to be enriched with target conditions.

In MP-Declare, also a *temporal* condition can be specified through an interval ($I = [\tau_0, \tau_1)$) indicating the minimum and the maximum temporal distance allowed between the occurrence of the activation and the occurrence of the corresponding target. It plays a fundamental role process modeling through constraints, thus we consider it as a first-class citizen in the categorization of conditions in MP-Declare. However, it falls in the category of correlation conditions, as it is based on the comparison of values associated to both activation and target events. In the light of Table 2, for example, the *response* constraint with a temporal condition indicates that, if the *credit check* occurs at time $\tau^e_{credit\ check}$, *grant* must occur at some point $\tau^e_{grant} \in [\tau^e_A + 1\text{day}, \tau^e_A + 7\text{days})$, hence $\mathbf{G}((e(credit\ check) \rightarrow \mathbf{F}(e(grant) \wedge \tau^e_{credit\ check} + 1\text{day} \leqslant \tau^e_{grant} < \tau^e_{credit\ check} + 7\text{days}))$.

Until now, no mining approach that can fully support MP-Declare is available.

3   Multi-perspective Declare Discovery Framework

In this section, we describe our proposed framework for the discovery of MP-Declare models. In particular, we introduce the requirements and discuss how constraints are distinguished between the ones that are fulfilled and the ones that are not fulfilled throughout the log. An implementation of the framework is described in Sect. 4.

3.1   Requirements for the Discovery of Multi-perspective Declare Constraints

The requirements presented in this paper concern the discovery of MP-Declare constraints like the ones introduced in Sect. 2.2. In particular, the requirements describe different types of multi-perspective conditions that can be discovered from a log and used to specify valid MP-Declare constraints. In line with the semantics introduced in Sect. 2.2, the conditions that can be discovered are activation, correlation, target, and time conditions.

Activation Conditions. An activation condition can be used for two different purposes, i.e., to build *discriminative constraints* or to build *descriptive constraints*. Suppose that, for a given standard Declare constraint, in an event log, there are both activations corresponding to fulfillments and activations corresponding to violations. The payloads of fulfillments and violations can be used as positive and negative examples to train a classifier that solves the following classification problem: "What is the (activation) condition to be specified on the payload of an activation of a constraint to guarantee that activation corresponds to a fulfillment for that constraint?". In this case, the activation condition is a condition that is only valid in the positive cases and not in the negative cases (or vice versa) and is used to *discriminate* between fulfillments and violations for a given constraint. For example, consider the response constraint between *loan request* and *grant*. Suppose that when attribute *Amount* associated to *e(loan request)* is lower than *100,000*, *e(loan request)* is eventually followed by *e(grant)*, and when attribute *Amount* associated to *e(loan request)* is greater than or equal to *100,000 e(loan request)* is not eventually followed by *e(grant)*. In such a case, the activation condition $p^e_{grant}[Amount] < 100,000$ discriminates between fulfillments and violations for the given response constraint. This is the type of constraints that is possible to discover with the approach presented in [18].

Nevertheless, activation conditions can also be *descriptive*. For example, it is possible to find the distribution (or the average) of the values of each attribute connected to the fulfillments of a constraint, regardless of their values when the constraint is violated. Notice that in all the examples mentioned so far, activation conditions consist of a binary proposition between a variable and a constant. These are the conditions we deal with in this paper. However, in general, these conditions can be more complex, because they can involve 2 or more variables.

Target and Correlation Conditions. Positive constraints, corresponding to the templates in rows 2–8 in Tables 1 and 2, are characterized by the fact that a fulfillment has always a correlated target and a violation never has a correlated target. In contrast, for negative constraints, a fulfillment never has a correlated target and a violation has always a correlated target. Therefore, target and correlation conditions can only be defined for positive constraints in case of fulfillment, whereas for negative constraints a correlation/target condition can only be defined in case of violation. For this reason, target and correlation conditions cannot discriminate between fulfillments and violations and can only be descriptive. Note that, for negative constraints, we talk about "negative correlations," i.e., conditions that should disconnect a forbidden target from a possible corresponding activation.

Complex correlation conditions can be discovered from an event log, i.e., every relation involving variables belonging to the payload of the activation and the target of a constraint. Here, we focus on relations between homologous attributes of activations and targets. For example, in the precedence constraint specifying that activity *check report* must be preceded by *write report*, it can be the case that the resource associated to *e(check report)* is in 95 % of the cases different from the one associated to *e(write report)* and in 5 % of the cases is the same. Note that we are here connecting homologous attributes, i.e., the resource associated to the activation and the same attribute associated to the target of the precedence constraint.

Time Conditions. Finally, time conditions relate to the time distance between the activation and corresponding targets. For example, for the response constraint between *make diagnosis* and *surgery*, the time distance between these two activities can be between 7 days and 14 days in 30 % of the cases, between 15 days and 30 days in 60 % of the cases, and higher than 30 days in 10 % of the cases.

To summarize, the requirements we identify for the discovery of MP-Declare are:

1. discovering discriminative activation conditions;
2. discovering descriptive activation conditions;
3. discovering (descriptive) target and correlation conditions;
4. discovering time conditions.

3.2   Support and Confidence

In this subsection, we describe the metrics that we use to discriminate those constraints that are fulfilled in the majority of cases, from those that are rarely satisfied, namely support and confidence. We consider two notions of support already defined in the literature, namely the event-based support [9] and the trace-based support [19]. The former is meant to be used for all constraints wherein both activation and target do not correspond to $\top$. For all the others, we use the second notion of support.

We denote the set of *events* in a *trace* $\mathbf{t}$ of an event log L that fulfill an LTL_f formula[1] ψ as $\models_{\mathbf{t}}^{e}(\psi)$. The set of all the *events* in *log* L that fulfill ψ are denoted as $\models_{L}^{e}(\psi)$. All the *traces* in *log* L consisting only of events that fulfill ψ are indicated as $\models_{L}^{\mathbf{t}}(\psi)$. Given a constraint $\varXi$ comprising activation ϕ_a and target ϕ_t, we formally define the event-based support $\mathcal{S}_L^e$ and the trace-based support $\mathcal{S}_L^{\mathbf{t}}$ as follows:

$$\mathcal{S}_L^e = \frac{\sum_{i=1}^{|L|} \left| \models_{\mathbf{t}_i}^{e}(\varXi) \right|}{\left| \models_{L}^{e}(\phi_a) \right|} \qquad (1) \qquad\qquad \mathcal{S}_L^{\mathbf{t}} = \frac{\left| \models_{L}^{\mathbf{t}}(\varXi) \right|}{|L|} \qquad (2)$$

The confidence metric scales the support by the fraction of traces in the log wherein the activation condition is satisfied. According to the adopted notion of support, we have that:

(i) $\mathcal{C}_L^e = \mathcal{S}_L^e \times \left| \models_{L}^{e}(\phi_a) \right| / |L|$, and *(ii)* $\mathcal{C}_L^{\mathbf{t}} = \mathcal{S}_L^{\mathbf{t}} \times \left| \models_{L}^{e}(\phi_a) \right| / |L|$.

$\mathcal{S}_L^{\mathbf{t}}$ counts the number of events that fulfill the constraint in every trace and sums such numbers up along the log. In the example of Sect. 2.1, the four occurrences of A fulfill *response*(A, B), out of which 2 occur in $\mathbf{t}_1$, 1 in $\mathbf{t}_3$ and 1 in $\mathbf{t}_4$. Thereupon, it scales the number of events fulfilling the constraint by the number of events

---

[1] We recall that a propositional formula is an LTL_f formula.

that fulfill the activation only. In the example, the five occurrences of A satisfy the activation. Therefore, the event-based support of $response(A, B)$ is equal to $4/5$, namely 0.8. Its confidence amounts to $4/5 \times 3/4 = 0.6$, because A occurs in 3 traces over 4. $\mathcal{S}_L^t$ counts instead the number of traces that fulfill the constraint. In the example, $\mathbf{t}_1$, $\mathbf{t}_3$ and $\mathbf{t}_3$ fulfill $existence(A)$. Thereafter, such quantity is scaled by the number of traces in the log, which are four in the example. Thus, the trace-based support of $existence(A)$ is $3/4$, i.e., 0.75. In the next section, we show how these notions apply to MP-Declare.

4   Multi-perspective Declare Discovery with SQL

Our proposed discovery framework has been implemented using the SQL-based process discovery approach described in [29] because of its versatility towards customization. The approach has been adopted for the realization of a proof-of-concept software module and relies on the use of RXES. RXES is a standardized architecture for storing event log data in relational databases introduced in [11]. The RXES architecture uses a database to store the event log where traces and events are represented by tables with identifiers. RXES provides a full implementation of all OpenXES interfaces using the database as a backend. In [29], it has been shown that it is possible to discover commonly used process constraints by means of conventional SQL queries. Queries can be tailored to arbitrary aspects of a process, e.g., control flow, data attributes, and organizational issues.

4.1   Declarative Process Discovery with SQL

First, we describe the general functionality of SQL-based process discovery. The following query represents the basic structure of an SQL-query that discovers all constraints instantiation of the standard template $Response$ with two thresholds $minSupp$ and $minConf$. Here, subqueries are marked with brackets.

```
SELECT  'Response', A, B, [Support], [Confidence]
FROM Log 11, Log 12, [ActivityCombinations] c
WHERE 11.Activity = c.A AND 12.Activity = c.B AND
        12.ID IN(SELECT TOP 1 ID
                FROM [Log] 12
                WHERE b.Activity = c.B AND 12.case = 11.Trace AND
                      12.Time > 11.Time
                ORDER BY Time ASC)

GROUP BY c.A, c.B
HAVING [Support] > minSupp AND [Confidence] > minConf
```

The SQL expression for calculating the $support$ of $response$ constraints is given as:

```
COUNT(*) / (SELECT COUNT(ID) FROM Log WHERE Activity = A)
```

The query tests if at least one occurrence of activity B exists that follows the currently observed occurrence of A. In case the logical EXISTS term in the WHERE clause evaluates to true, the currently observed tuple corresponds to a fulfillment of the constraint. The resulting set of tuples represents all the fulfillments of the $response$ template.

Table 3. Event log excerpt stored in a denormalized relational database table.

Event ID	Case ID	Activity name	Timestamp	x_1	x_2	...	x_n
1	1	a	2015-11-06 15:31:00	id_1	3	...	5
2	1	b	2015-11-06 15:35:00	id_1	2	...	4
3	1	c	2015-11-06 15:37:00	id_2	3	...	4
4	2	b	2015-11-06 16:22:00	id_2	4	...	4
5	2	c	2015-11-06 16:45:00	id_2	3	...	4
...							

4.2   The Multi-perspective Case

Consider the event log excerpt given in Table 3. In addition to the columns for
Event ID, *Case ID*, *Activity Name* and *Timestamp* the table contains n columns
for different data attributes x_1, x_2,..., x_n. SQL queries like the *response* query can
be enhanced to comprise data attributes as well. For example, the *MP-Response*
query below discovers all the *response* constraints for each value combination of
the involved data attributes x_1, x_2,..., x_n. Therefore, the GROUP BY and the
SELECT clause additionally contain the list of event parameters. Each query can
be adjusted to the analyst's needs, i.e., additional constraint activation, target
or correlation conditions like $l1.x_1 = l2.x_1$ or $l1.x_2 > l2.x_2$ can be added to
the WHERE clause of the query. Note, that $l1$ and $l2$ respectively refer to the
events assigned to the first and the second parameter of the *response* template.
Consequently, the result set provides a fine-grained resolution of the constraints
that hold for certain activities specifying information about the data perspective,
e.g., by providing the distribution or the average of the values of the considered
data attributes when a fulfillment of the constraint occurs.

```
SELECT 'MP-Response', A, B, l1.x1, ..., l1.xn, [Support], [Confidence]
FROM Log l1, Log l2, [ActivityCombinations] c
WHERE l1.Activity = c.A AND l2.Activity = c.B AND
      l2.ID IN(SELECT TOP 1 ID
               FROM [Log] l2
               WHERE b.Activity = c.B AND l2.Trace = l1.Trace AND
                     l2.Time > l1.Time
               ORDER BY Time ASC)

GROUP BY c.A, c.B, l1.x1, ..., l1.xn
HAVING [Support] > minSupp AND [Confidence] > minConf
```

The subquery to compute the *support* value implements the event-based *support* definition in Eq. 1 as described in Sect. 3. The subquery is given by:

```
COUNT(*) / (SELECT COUNT(ID)
            FROM Log
            WHERE Activity = A AND Log.x1 = l1.x1 AND ... AND Log.xn = l1.xn)
```

Similar to the *MP-Response* query also other templates can be discovered
with SQL queries considering the data perspective. The following *MP-Existence*
query, e.g., discovers the values of the data attributes when a certain activity is
performed.

```
SELECT 'MP-Existence', A, l1.x1, ..., l1.xn, [Support], [Confidence]
FROM Log l1, [ActivityCombinations] c
WHERE l1.Activity = c.A
GROUP BY c.A, c.B, l1.x1, ..., l1.xn
HAVING [Support] > minSupp AND [Confidence] > minConf
```

Here, the *support* value is computed with the subquery below. SQL queries for other MP-Declare constraints can be formulated in a similar way.

```
COUNT(Distinct Instance) /
(SELECT COUNT(*) FROM (SELECT Trace FROM Log GROUP BY Trace))
```

5   Evaluation

In order to assess our approach, we have applied it on several well-known benchmarks in the process mining field. The evaluation shows that important information would be most likely neglected if perspectives other than the pure behavioral one were not taken into account.

5.1   Activation Conditions: Road Traffic Fine Management Log

We first evaluated our approach for the discovery of activation conditions using the publicly available real-life event log of a Road Traffic Fine Management Process.[2] The event log records executions of the process enacted in an Italian local police office for managing fines for road traffic violations. It contains 150,370 traces and 561,470 events for 11 different activities. We first queried the event log for standard *response* constraints without considering data attributes. Using the thresholds *minSupp=0.7* and *minConf=0.3* we extracted five constraints. In order to discover data conditions, we exemplarily focus on the constraint $C = response(add\ penalty, send\ for\ credit\ collection)$. After the discovery phase, it was found $\mathcal{S}_L^e(C) = 0.74$ and $\mathcal{C}_L^e(C) = 0.39$, i.e., in 74 % of the cases where a penalty was given, the case was sent for credit collection.

We then discovered *MP-Existence* and *MP-Response* constraints. In particular, we incorporate data in the form of the data attribute *Amount* that indicates the amount of money an accused person has to pay as a penalty. First, we mined the event log for *MP-Existence* constraints on the activity *add penalty*. The results (Fig. 1a) show the support of the existence of the activity in correlation with the occurring values of the penalty amount. The distribution reveals that, in most of the cases, when *add penalty* was performed, the penalty amount had a value between 470 and 795. Furthermore, we discovered the influence of the penalty amount on the probability that the case is sent for credit collection by applying an *MP-Response* query for discovering activation conditions over the data attribute *Amount*. Figure 1b shows that the support of *MP-Response* constraints between *add penalty* and *send for credit collection* on average increases with an increasing amount of the penalty, i.e., the higher the penalty amount is, the lower the probability that the fine is paid is.

---

[2] DOI: 10.4121/uuid:270fd440-1057-4fb9-89a9-b699b47990f5.

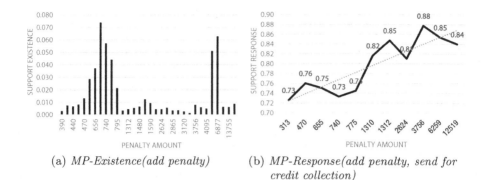

(a) *MP-Existence(add penalty)*

(b) *MP-Response(add penalty, send for credit collection)*

Fig. 1. Support values of *MP-Existence* and *MP-Response* constraints.

Table 4. *MP-Response* constraints discovered with average time differences.

	Activity A	Activity B	TimeDiff [d]	Support	Confidence
MunA	Assessment Completed	Generating Decision	8	1	0.06
	Register Date Request	Phase Appl. Received	5	0.92	0.92
MunB	Assessment Completed	Generating Decision	18	1	0.90
	Register Date Request	Phase Appl. Received	25	1	1
MunC	Assessment Completed	Generating Decision	5	0.97	0.78
	Register Date Request	Phase Appl. Received	15	1	1
MunD	Assessment Completed	Generating Decision	6	1	0.06
	Register Date Request	Phase Appl. Received	3	0.8	0.82
MunE	Assessment Completed	Generating Decision	12	0.98	0.34
	Register Date Request	Phase Appl. Received	6	0.95	0.95

5.2   Time Conditions: Building Permit Process in Municipalities

Next, we applied our approach to the event logs pertaining to an administrative process in five Dutch municipalities for evaluating the time differences between activations and correlated targets of a constraint. The different event log files[3] contain all building permit applications over a period of approximately four years. The processes in the five municipalities are almost identical. The event log *MunA* contains 1,199 cases, *MunB* 832 cases, *MunC* 1,409 cases, *MunD* 1,053 cases and *MunE* 1,156 cases. For each event log, we executed an *MP-Response* query that discovers response constraints considering the time perspective and evaluating the time difference (with the granularity of days) between activation and target activities. Table 4 shows an excerpt of the results for each log, i.e., the constraints over activity pairs (*assessment of content completed, generating decision environmental permit*) and (*register submission date request, phase application received*). There are two conclusions that can be drawn from these results:

---

[3] DOI: 10.4121/uuid:31a308ef-c844-48da-948c-305d167a0ec1.

(i) The time between activation and target activities in the different event logs is significantly different. While for *MunA* and *MunD* the average time from the completion of the content assessment to the generation of the permit decision is only 8 and 6 days respectively, for *MunB* the difference is 18 days on average. A similar observation can be made for the time between the registration of the request date and the notice of application received. Here, the difference is on average even bigger between *MunB* (25 days) and *MunA* (5 days), *MunD* (3 days) and *MunE* (6 days).

(ii) There is a clear discrepancy between the constraint fulfillment (support) in case of big and small time differences between activation and target activities. Consider the response constraints between the registration of the request date and the notice of application received. In those municipalities where the time difference between activation and target activity is high, i.e., *MunB* (25 days) and *MunC* (15 days), the constraint has been fulfilled in every case (*support* = *1*). For *MunA* (5 days, support = 0.92), *MunD* (3 days, 0.8) and *MunE* (6 days, 0.95) on the other hand, the time differences are lower and the constraint has only been fulfilled in a considerably smaller amount of cases. A potential conclusion might be that a more thorough and systematic way of work leads to a higher degree of constraint satisfaction, i.e., more compliant process executions.

Table 5. Standard *response* constraints for selected activities.

Activity A	Activity B	Support	Confidence
Calcium Speed Test	Receiving Laboratory Analysis	0.95	0.13
Chloride Speed Test	Receiving Laboratory Analysis	0.96	0.06
Bicarbonat Test	Receiving Laboratory Analysis	0.96	0.22
Phosphate Speed Test	Receiving Laboratory Analysis	0.96	0.03

Table 6. Target resource conditions extracted with *MP-Response*.

Activity A	Activity B	Resource(B)	Support	Confidence
Calcium Speed Test	Rec. Lab Analysis	Gen. Lab	0.91	0.12
Chloride Speed Test	Rec. Lab Analysis	Gen. Lab	0.96	0.06
Bicarbonat Test	Rec. Lab Analysis	Gen. Lab	0.96	0.22
Phosphate Speed Test	Rec. Lab Analysis	Gen. Lab	0.96	0.03

5.3   Target and Correlation Conditions: Hospital Log

Finally, we validated the approach with an event log[4] that records the treatment of patients diagnosed with cancer from a large Dutch hospital. The event log contains 1,143 cases and 150,291 events distributed across 623 activities.

---

[4] DOI: 10.4121/uuid:d9769f3d-0ab0-4fb8-803b-0d1120ffcf54.

We first queried the event log for standard *response* constraints without considering the data perspective. Then, we discovered conditions considering the *Resource* attribute of the target activity (denoted as *Resource(B)*) using an *MP-Response* query. Finally, we discovered correlation conditions taking into consideration the resources of both activation (denoted as *Resource(A)*) and target activities by querying the log with an *MP-Response* query. All queries have been specified with the following thresholds: *minSupp = 0.9* and *minConf = 0.02*. We explain the results by means of four constraints referring to different blood test activities and the activity *receiving laboratory analysis*. Table 5 shows the results for standard *response*. After tests for *chloride, bicarbonate* and *phosphate* the *laboratory analysis results* have been received in 96 % of all cases, while for *calcium* they have been received in 95 % of the cases. Note, that these constraints do not consider the data perspective.

Let us now take into account the resources performing activities. Table 6 shows the target conditions for these constraints. The results reveal that after most of the considered blood tests the receipt of the analysis results has always been performed by *General Lab Clinical Chemistry*. This is highlighted by the fact that the support values of the *MP-Response* constraints are identical to the standard *response* constraints, i.e., *support = 0.96*. Only in case of *calcium* the support decreased to 0.91, which indicates that in this case also other resources performed the target activity. An even more specific result set is given in Table 7 that shows the correlation conditions for the constraints, i.e., the support values in case of identical resources for both activities. The results for the *MP-Response* query highlight that in most of the cases wherein the analysis results have been received after the blood tests, the performing resources of the two corresponding activities are identical and equal to *General Lab Clinical Chemistry*. For *calcium*, again, this fact only applies to 91 % of the cases. In order to get an insight into the set of resources involved in activity *receiving laboratory analysis*,

Table 7. Correlation resource conditions extracted with *MP-Response*.

Activity A	Activity B	Res(A)	Res(B)	Support	Confidence
Calcium Speed Test	Rec. Lab Analysis	Gen. Lab.	Gen. Lab.	0.91	0.12
Chloride Speed Test	Rec. Lab Analysis	Gen. Lab	Gen. Lab	0.96	0.06
Bicarbonat Test	Rec. Lab Analysis	Gen. Lab	Gen. Lab	0.96	0.22
Phosphate Speed Test	Rec. Lab Analysis	Gen. Lab	Gen. Lab	0.96	0.03

Table 8. Resource-based *MP-Existence* constr. for *Receiving Laboratory Analysis*.

Activity	Resource	Cases	Support	Confidence
Receiving Laboratory Analysis	General Lab Clinical Chemistry	797	0.697	0.697
	Medical Microbiology	315	0.276	0.276
	Pharmacy Laboratory	5	0.004	0.004
	Special Lab Radiology	3	0.002	0.002
	Special Lab Nurosensory	2	0.001	0.001

we applied an *MP-Existence* query. The results in Table 8 show a diverse set of resources performing this activity, which explains why the support is lower in case of *calcium*. The evaluation reported hitherto shows the range of disclosing previously unknown relationships between behavioral constraints and all the additional perspectives that can be analyzed using the information contained in an event log.

6 Related Work

Several approaches have been proposed in the literature for the discovery of declarative process models. In [19], the authors present an approach that allows the user to select from a set of predefined Declare templates the ones to be used for the discovery. Maggi et al. propose an evolution of this approach in [20] to improve performances. Other approaches to improve the performances of the discovery task are presented in [10,31]. Additionally, there are post-processing approaches that aim at simplifying the resulting Declare models in terms of redundancy elimination [7,9,21] and disambiguation [3].

The approaches proposed in [6,14] allow for the specification of rules that go beyond the traditional Declare templates. An approach similar to the SQL-based one used in this paper is presented in [26] and is based on temporal logic query checking. In [30], the authors define *Timed Declare*, an extension of Declare that relies on timed automata. In [17], an approach for analyzing event logs with Timed Declare is proposed. The *DPILMiner* [28] exploits a discovery approach to incorporate the resource perspective and to mine for a set of predefined resource assignment constraints. In [22], the authors introduce for the first time a data-aware semantics for Declare and [18] first covered the data perspective in declarative process discovery, although this approach only allows for the discovery of *discriminative* activation conditions.

7 Conclusions

In this paper, we proposed a framework for the discovery of MP-Declare models. We implemented our approach using SQL queries tailored to analyze a process from different perspectives, e.g., control flow, data attributes as well as organizational and time perspectives. The approach has been validated with several real-life event logs provided by a large academic hospital, by five Dutch municipalities and by an Italian local police office for managing fines for road traffic violations. The application of our technique to these real-life process event logs revealed dependencies and correlations with additional parameters such as data values, time conditions and resource specifications.

The approach at hand serves as a building block for a variety of extensions in future work. For example, we plan to ease the interpretation of multi-perspective mining results by applying preprocessing methods to event logs and postprocessing methods to the discovered multi-perspective models. Furthermore, the full specification of a new, domain-independent and user-customizable SQL-based framework for mining MP-Declare constraints is in our plans for future research.

References

1. van der Aalst, W.: Process Mining: Discovery, Conformance and Enhancement of Business Processes. Springer, Heidelberg (2011)
2. van der Aalst, W., Pesic, M., Schonenberg, H.: Declarative workflows: balancing between flexibility and support. Comput. Sci. - R&D **23**, 99–113 (2009)
3. Bose, R.P.J.C., Maggi, F.M., van der Aalst, W.M.P.: Enhancing declare maps based on event correlations. In: Daniel, F., Wang, J., Weber, B. (eds.) BPM 2013. LNCS, vol. 8094, pp. 97–112. Springer, Heidelberg (2013)
4. Burattin, A., Maggi, F.M., van der Aalst, W.M., Sperduti, A.: Techniques for a posteriori analysis of declarative processes. In: EDOC, pp. 41–50. IEEE, Beijing, September 2012
5. Burattin, A., Maggi, F.M., Sperduti, A.: Conformance checking based on multi-perspective declarative process models (2015). CoRR arxiv:1503.04957
6. Chesani, F., Lamma, E., Mello, P., Montali, M., Riguzzi, F., Storari, S.: Exploiting inductive logic programming techniques for declarative process mining. In: Jensen, K., Aalst, W.M.P. (eds.) Transactions on Petri Nets and Other Models of Concurrency II. LNCS, vol. 5460, pp. 278–295. Springer, Heidelberg (2009)
7. Di Ciccio, C., Maggi, F.M., Montali, M., Mendling, J.: Ensuring model consistency in declarative process discovery. In: Motahari-Nezhad, H.R., Recker, J., Weidlich, M. (eds.) BPM 2015. LNCS, vol. 9253, pp. 144–159. Springer, Berlin (2015)
8. Di Ciccio, C., Mecella, M.: A two-step fast algorithm for the automated discovery of declarative workflows. In: CIDM, pp. 135–142. IEEE, April 2013
9. Di Ciccio, C., Mecella, M.: On the discovery of declarative control flows for artful processes. ACM TMIS **5**(4), 24:1–24:37 (2015)
10. Di Ciccio, C., Schouten, M.H.M., de Leoni, M., Mendling, J.: Declarative process discovery with MINERful in ProM. In: BPM Demos, pp. 60–64 (2015)
11. van Dongen, B.F., Shabani, S.: Relational XES: data management for process mining. In: CAiSE Forum 2015, pp. 169–176 (2015)
12. Hildebrandt, T.T., Mukkamala, R.R., Slaats, T., Zanitti, F.: Contracts for cross-organizational workflows as timed dynamic condition response graphs. J. Log. Algebr. Program. **82**(5–7), 164–185 (2013)
13. Kupferman, O., Vardi, M.Y.: Vacuity detection in temporal model checking. Int. J. Softw. Tools Technol. Transf. **4**, 224–233 (2003)
14. Lamma, E., Mello, P., Riguzzi, F., Storari, S.: Applying inductive logic programming to process mining. In: Blockeel, H., Ramon, J., Shavlik, J., Tadepalli, P. (eds.) ILP 2007. LNCS (LNAI), vol. 4894, pp. 132–146. Springer, Heidelberg (2008)
15. de Leoni, M., van der Aalst, W.M.P., Dees, M.: A general process mining framework for correlating, predicting and clustering dynamic behavior based on event logs. Inf. Syst. **56**, 235–257 (2016)
16. Maggi, F.M.: Declarative process mining with the declare component of ProM. In: BPM Demo Sessions 2013, pp. 26–30 (2013)
17. Maggi, F.M.: Discovering metric temporal business constraints from event logs. In: Johansson, B., Andersson, B., Holmberg, N. (eds.) BIR 2014. LNBIP, vol. 194, pp. 261–275. Springer, Heidelberg (2014)
18. Maggi, F.M., Dumas, M., García-Bañuelos, L., Montali, M.: Discovering data-aware declarative process models from event logs. In: Daniel, F., Wang, J., Weber, B. (eds.) BPM 2013. LNCS, vol. 8094, pp. 81–96. Springer, Heidelberg (2013)
19. Maggi, F.M., Mooij, A., van der Aalst, W.: User-guided discovery of declarative process models. In: CIDM, pp. 192–199 (2011)

20. Maggi, F.M., Bose, R.P.J.C., van der Aalst, W.M.P.: Efficient discovery of understandable declarative process models from event logs. In: Ralyté, J., Franch, X., Brinkkemper, S., Wrycza, S. (eds.) CAiSE 2012. LNCS, vol. 7328, pp. 270–285. Springer, Heidelberg (2012)
21. Maggi, F.M., Bose, R.P.J.C., van der Aalst, W.M.P.: A knowledge-based integrated approach for discovering and repairing declare maps. In: Salinesi, C., Norrie, M.C., Pastor, Ó. (eds.) CAiSE 2013. LNCS, vol. 7908, pp. 433–448. Springer, Heidelberg (2013)
22. Montali, M., Chesani, F., Mello, P., Maggi, F.M.: Towards data-aware constraints in declare. In: SAC, pp. 1391–1396. ACM (2013)
23. Montali, M., Pesic, M., van der Aalst, W.M.P., Chesani, F., Mello, P., Storari, S.: Declarative specification and verification of service choreographies. ACM Trans. Web 4(1), 3 (2010)
24. Pesic, M., Schonenberg, H., van der Aalst, W.M.P.: Declare: full support for loosely-structured processes. In: IEEE International EDOC Conference 2007, pp. 287–300 (2007)
25. Pichler, P., Weber, B., Zugal, S., Pinggera, J., Mendling, J., Reijers, H.A.: Imperative versus declarative process modeling languages: an empirical investigation. In: Daniel, F., Barkaoui, K., Dustdar, S. (eds.) BPM Workshops 2011, Part I. LNBIP, vol. 99, pp. 383–394. Springer, Heidelberg (2012)
26. Räim, M., Di Ciccio, C., Maggi, F.M., Mecella, M., Mendling, J.: Log-based understanding of business processes through temporal logic query checking. In: Meersman, R., Panetto, H., Dillon, T., Missikoff, M., Liu, L., Pastor, O., Cuzzocrea, A., Sellis, T. (eds.) OTM 2014. LNCS, vol. 8841, pp. 75–92. Springer, Heidelberg (2014)
27. Rozinat, A., Mans, R.S., Song, M., van der Aalst, W.M.P.: Discovering simulation models. Inf. Syst. 34(3), 305–327 (2009)
28. Schönig, S., Cabanillas, C., Jablonski, S., Mendling, J.: A framework for efficiently mining the organisational perspective of business processes. Decis. Support Syst. 89, 87–97 (2016)
29. Schönig, S., Rogge-Solti, A., Cabanillas, C., Jablonski, S., Mendling, J.: Efficient and customisable declarative process mining with SQL. In: Nurcan, S., Soffer, P., Bajec, M., Eder, J. (eds.) CAiSE 2016. LNCS, vol. 9694, pp. 290–305. Springer, Heidelberg (2016). doi:10.1007/978-3-319-39696-5_18
30. Westergaard, M., Maggi, F.M.: Looking into the future. In: Meersman, R., et al. (eds.) OTM 2012, Part I. LNCS, vol. 7565, pp. 250–267. Springer, Heidelberg (2012)
31. Westergaard, M., Stahl, C., Reijers, H.: UnconstrainedMiner: efficient discovery of generalized declarative process models. In: BPM CR, No. BPM-13-28 (2013)
32. Zeising, M., Schönig, S., Jablonski, S.: Towards a common platform for the support of routine and agile business processes. In: Collaborative Computing: Networking, Applications and Worksharing (2014)

Declarative Process Models: Different Ways to Be Hierarchical

Riccardo De Masellis[1], Chiara Di Francescomarino[1], Chiara Ghidini[1], and Fabrizio M. Maggi[2(✉)]

[1] FBK-IRST, Trento, Italy
{r.demasellis,dfmchiara,ghidini}@fbk.eu
[2] University of Tartu, Tartu, Estonia
f.m.maggi@ut.ee

Abstract. In the literature, hierarchical dimensions for *procedural* process models have been widely investigated as they provide different ways to relate, organize and classify models. Such a categorization is based on the dimensions of *inheritance*, behavioral *equivalence*, and *modularization* and can be used to better understand and modify models as well as handle their complexity. Unfortunately, in the context of *declarative* process models hierarchical dimensions have been sparsely investigated. This paper addresses such a research gap. More specifically, we study a formal semantics for the dimensions above and show how they naturally induce hierarchies on a declarative process language based on DECLARE.

Keywords: Hierarchical process model · Linear temporal logic · Declare

1 Introduction

Hierarchical relations have been widely investigated and adopted in practice in the context of business process modeling as a key mechanism to handle complexity, organization and categorization. Concepts such as *modularization, decomposition, refinement, inheritance, reduction* and so on have been introduced, not infrequently with conflicting meanings, to hierarchically structure and relate business processes along different dimensions. Despite the terminological differences, we follow the analysis of [15] and identify three different dimensions along which processes can be arranged in a hierarchy.

The first dimension aims at achieving *inheritance* among process models. Inheritance is often interpreted with a behavioral connotation, wherein a child model enables a restrictive set (i.e., a subset) of its parents behaviors (see Fig. 1a). This can also be achieved, in some special cases, through syntactical inheritance, where parts of the parent model are borrowed by the child. However, this dimension cannot be characterized from a syntactic viewpoint, e.g., through specific constructs. We adopt the UML terminology, and use *specialization* and *generalization* to indicate the top-down and bottom-up directions of the inheritance relation. The second dimension can be seen as a special case of the first one, as it categorizes equivalent process models, that is, those that differ from the syntactic point of view but accept the same set of behaviors.

© Springer International Publishing Switzerland 2016
Q.Z. Sheng et al. (Eds.): ICSOC 2016, LNCS 9936, pp. 104–119, 2016.
DOI: 10.1007/978-3-319-46295-0_7

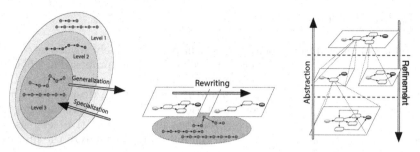

(a) (behavioral) Inheritance. (b) Rewriting processes. (c) Decomposable modules.

Fig. 1. Three ways to be hierarchical.

However, it differs from the inheritance dimension by being "horizontal" and, as such, it is not characterized by bottom-up and top-down directions but rather realized through *rewriting* of the processes, as depicted in Fig. 1b. Finally, the third hierarchical dimension involves the process-subprocess decomposition, and its graphical representation is provided in Fig. 1c, where increasing levels specify more and more process details. This dimension is essential to obtain *modularization* through decomposable modules, or subsystems, as observed in [13,15], and is usually achieved, in a procedural process specification, by means of ad hoc syntactic constructs, e.g., the BPMN subprocess construct. In this paper, we adopt the terminology from [13] and use *refinement* and *abstraction* to indicate the top-down and bottom-up directions of modular decomposition.

While the notion of hierarchy is well investigated and supported in procedural approaches to business process modeling, it is less understood and used in the context of declarative models. This can be ascribed to the intrinsic difficulty of characterizing and supporting these dimensions in declarative process models. In this work, we aim at addressing such a gap by investigating, in a precise and logic-based manner, the formalization and the effects of *inheritance, rewriting,* and *modularization* in the context of the DECLARE modeling language [14]. We chose DECLARE as it is the most popular declarative language for modeling business processes, and because it grounds on a formal, logic-based, semantics. This latter fact enables us to embed the conceptual understanding of the three hierarchical relations into the modeling language in a precise manner and to characterize them by means of logical properties holding between the hierarchically related processes. This formal investigation highlights the following: first, DECLARE, in its current form, fails to support hierarchies in full. Thus, Sect. 5 introduces HIDEC, a DECLARE extension which fills this gap. Second, each dimension is indeed represented by means of a hierarchy, i.e., a computationally decidable (partial) order among HIDEC processes (Sect. 6). The formal analysis provided Sects. 5 and 6 is grounded in a literature review (Sect. 2) and in a conceptual investigation of how to interpret the three dimensions above in a declarative setting (Sect. 4).

2   Related Work

Hierarchies of procedural process models have been widely investigated. The classification provided in this paper is inspired by the work proposed in [15] where the research on procedural process model hierarchies is recognized to provide contributions to *inheritance, rewriting* and *modularization*. Most of the work in the literature on hierarchical procedural models fall in one of these categories and even if there are much less contributions in the declarative settings, the same concepts/categories also apply. In the following, we analyze the literature according to its contribution to each dimension.

In [1], the authors study inheritance of behavior in a simple process-algebraic setting as well as in a Petri-net framework. The approach in [11] groups together similar process models where similarity measures are (also) based on the concept of inheritance borrowed by object-oriented programming. Inheritance is also used in the context of process configuration to customize generic process model "templates" instead of building one from scratch. From a template, several process variants can be derived by means of a restricted set of change operations [23]. In the last decade, configurability of procedural process models has been widely investigated [16], while for declarative ones the approach in [21] has been recently proposed.

Concerning rewriting, several works provide reduction rules to support the analysis of procedural process models. In [24], reduction rules translating reset-nets to much smaller ones (whilst preserving the original properties) are shown. Analogously, [25] presents reduction rules for YAWL workflows with cancelation regions and OR-joins. Also, [17] introduces a set of graph reduction rules as a verification mechanism to identify structural conflicts in a procedural process model. In the context of declarative process models, reduction rules to remove redundancies in DECLARE models obtained from process discovery are investigated in [10].

Coming to modularization, in [2], the authors provide guidelines to select parts of procedural process models, represented as meta-graphs, for modularization purposes. Good candidates for subprocesses are fragments with a single input and a single output control flow arc. Other work [9,22] provide recommendations regarding the size of a subprocess in a process model. To assess which modularization should be preferred starting from the characteristics of a complex process model, quality metrics are proposed in [12]. In [23], the ability to extract a subprocess from a process model has been described as a change pattern for process-aware information systems. In the context of declarative process models, in [27] the understandability of hierarchical declarative models is discussed and how subprocesses enhance the expressiveness of declarative modeling languages is shown. Differently form what we propose, this paper discusses a cognitive-psychology-based framework to assess the impact of hierarchy on the understandability of declarative models, rather than formally studying its properties. A different approach to modularization for declarative process models has been presented in [5], where a definition of hierarchical declarative process models based on Dynamic Condition Response (DCR) graphs is given, and can be used for incremental refinement, adaptation, and dynamic creation of subprocesses.

However, besides being based on a semantics different from LTL, the focus of the paper is providing constructs that support modularization, rather than studying the different dimensions of hierarchy. Lastly, also the recently-introduced Declarative Process Intermediate Language (DPIL) [26] allows for modeling subprocesses, and it focuses not only on the model behavioral dimension, i.e., the traditional control-flow, but also on other perspectives such as the organizational perspective (tasks may be assigned/performed by specific roles/groups) and the informational perspective (resources/entities accessed by activities). Given the expressivity of DPIL, several hierarchies can be defined by considering the different perspectives, e.g., hierarchies between roles [18]. Our analysis focus on the core traditional control-flow perspective only so as to first have a formal basis on top of which possibly many other constructs/extensions can be considered.

Table 1. Aspects of hierarchical dimensions.

Aspect	Inheritance	Rewriting	Modularization
Understandability		[10, 24]	[9, 12, 15, 22, 27]
Reusability	[11, 16, 21]		[15, 23]
Scalability		[17, 25]	[15]
Analysis		[17, 25]	

The importance of these dimensions in the context of hierarchical declarative process models is also demonstrated by the number of properties and aspects that they affect. Table 1 maps the three dimensions of hierarchical models (columns) to the corresponding affected aspects (rows). The table shows that for instance, *understandability* is affected by both modularization and equivalence. As shown in several studies, indeed, understandability is affected by modularization, because smaller modules are usually easier to understand for humans (see, e.g., [12]). On the other hand, also different representations of the same set of behaviors (equivalence) impact on understandability [10]. *Reusability* is affected by both inheritance and modularization. Inheritance, for example, enables the reuse of (process) variants [21] while modularization the reuse of (process) modules [23]. Rewriting and modularization, enabling respectively the optimized [17, 25] and distributed [15] execution of process models impact on *scalability*. Finally, rewriting also supports formal *analysis* of models [17, 25], as conflict detection.

From the above literature review, we can conclude that contributions on hierarchical declarative process models have been sparse, often ad hoc, and, in the vast majority of cases ([5] is a notable exception) the proposed semantics is not formally grounded. In addition, they usually deal with a subset of dimensions thus not providing a comprehensive interpretation/semantics for all of them, which we tackle in this work.

3 Preliminaries

Our choice of using DECLARE [14] grounds on the fact that it adopts the semantics of a well-known and well-studied temporal logics. This not only paves the way

Table 2. Graphical notation and LTL formalization of some DECLARE templates.

TEMPLATE	FORMALIZATION	NOTATION	DESCRIPTION
existence(A)	$\Diamond A$	$\begin{smallmatrix}1..*\\ \boxed{A}\end{smallmatrix}$	A has to occur at least once
absence(A)	$\neg \Diamond A$	$\begin{smallmatrix}0\\ \boxed{A}\end{smallmatrix}$	A has to never occur
exactly1(A)	$\Diamond A \wedge \neg(A \wedge \bigcirc(\Diamond A))$	$\begin{smallmatrix}1\\ \boxed{A}\end{smallmatrix}$	A has to occur exactly once
coexistence(A,B)	$(\Diamond A \rightarrow \Diamond B) \wedge \neg(\Diamond B \rightarrow \Diamond A)$	$\boxed{A} \bullet\!\!-\!\!\bullet \boxed{B}$	If A occurs, B must occur and viceversa
not coexistence(A,B)	$(\Diamond A \rightarrow \neg \Diamond B)$	$\boxed{A} \bullet\!\!-\!\!\Vert\!\!-\!\!\bullet \boxed{B}$	If A occurs, B must not occur and viceversa
response(A,B)	$\Box(A \rightarrow \Diamond B)$	$\boxed{A} \bullet\!\!-\!\!\rightarrow \boxed{B}$	If A occurs, B must eventually follow
chain response(A,B)	$\Box(A \rightarrow \bigcirc B)$	$\boxed{A} \blacktriangleright\!\!-\!\!\blacktriangleright \boxed{B}$	If A occurs, B must occur next

for a mathematical characterization of dimensions and hierarchy, but also allows us to borrow some of the theoretical results originally developed for that logics.

A DECLARE model is a set of constraints that must hold in conjunction during the process execution, declaratively setting the boundaries that process instances must not overcome. Each constraint is chosen among a set of predefined "templates" that express different (partial) orders on the activities the process is intended to perform.

Definition 1 (DECLARE). *Given a finite alphabet of activities Σ, a DECLARE process Φ is a set of constraints, intended to be in conjunction, inductively defined as follows:*

$$\varphi :: = \text{DECUN}(A) \mid \text{DECBIN}(A_1, A_2)$$
$$\Phi :: = \{\varphi\} \mid \Phi_1 \cup \Phi_2$$

where $A, A_1, A_2 \in \Sigma$, $\text{DECUN}(\cdot)$ *is a unary DECLARE template and* $\text{DECBIN}(\cdot, \cdot)$ *is a binary DECLARE template. We denote with $\mathcal{D}$ the set of DECLARE processes and with $\Sigma(\Phi)$ the set of activities occurring in Φ.*

Together with a mnemonic name for specific LTL formulas, DECLARE also offers a graphical representation for each template. Table 2 reports the graphical notation, the formalization and a brief description of the DECLARE templates that we use in this paper. As examples, the binary $response(A, B)$ template says that each occurrence of activity A must be eventually followed by activity B, and it indeed represents the LTL formula $\Box(A \rightarrow \Diamond B)$, where $\Box$ is the LTL "always" temporal operator and $\Diamond$ is the "eventually" temporal operator, while the unary template $existence(A)$ (resp., $absence(A)$) says that activity A must be eventually performed (resp., never be performed), and its LTL formula is $\Diamond A$ (resp., $\neg\Diamond A$).

Given a DECLARE process Φ, its semantics is given in terms of *finite* sequences of activities, also called traces, satisfying Φ, which we denote by $\mathcal{L}(\Phi)$, where only one activity is performed at a time. This is formally achieved by taking the finite-trace semantics of LTL [3,4] and by adding an (implicit) global constraint in each process expressing the mutual exclusion among activities. From a practical viewpoint, the reasoning tasks on processes Φ, $\Psi \in \mathcal{D}$, namely, satisfiability (is $\mathcal{L}(\Phi) \neq \emptyset$?), validity (is every trace in $\mathcal{L}(\Phi)$?) and logical implication (is $\mathcal{L}(\Phi) \in \mathcal{L}(\Psi)$?), reduce to each other and can be solved by building the so-called *automaton* for Φ (and Ψ) [3], which we denote by $A(\Phi)$. We observe that when adopting the LTL finite-trace semantics, automata for formulas are actually *finite-state machines* and as such, they can be manipulated by using well-known and optimized algorithms (we exploit some of them in Sect. 6). In the remainder, we refer to LTL by implicitly meaning LTL with finite-trace semantics, which allows for using the term *automata* and *finite-state machine* as synonyms. We stress that the result presented here *do not* carry to traditional (infinite-trace semantics) LTL (see [4] for a dissertation on the difference between finite- and infinite-trace semantics).

4 Conceptual Investigation

In this section, we provide a conceptual investigation of *inheritance, rewriting* and *modularization* with the help of a running example inspired by [7].

In a typical *loan application* (LA) scenario, after a customer has requested a loan (Request Loan (RL)), the customer application is assessed (Assess Application (AA)) and, once assessed, a decision about the loan (Decide on Loan (DL)) is taken. This is modeled in DECLARE with the two *response* constraints (see Sect. 3): $response(\mathsf{RL}, \mathsf{AA})$ and $response(\mathsf{AA}, \mathsf{DL})$, whose graphical representation is:

The first dimension we study is process *inheritance*, whose bottom-up and top-down directions are defined as *specialization* and *generalization*, respectively. Intuitively, a process model *specializes* another (parent) process model if the behaviors allowed by the specialization are a subset of the behaviors allowed by the parent. Generalization is defined symmetrically. For instance, let us consider the *mortgage loan* (ML) specializing the behavior of LA in that it restricts the behaviors of the latter (i.e., those satisfying the two *response* constraints) to those containing exactly one occurrence of the activity Send Home Insurance Quote (SHIQ), i.e., those focusing on house loans.

As the above graphical representation of the DECLARE constraints shows, in this case, we have not only a behavioral inheritance between the two process models but also a syntactical one, as the specialized process model is obtained by adding constraints (e.g., the $exactly1(\mathsf{SHIQ})$ in the example) to the set of constraints of the parent.

A slightly different example of specialization of the LA process is the loan application process for fidelity customers FCL which restricts the behaviors allowed by the general LA process by imposing that fidelity customers are served immediately after the loan request is presented:

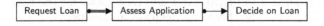

As the above constraints shows, FCL does not inherit the syntactical description of LA, as the *response*(RL, AA) is replaced by a *chain_response*(RL, AA), indicating that Assess Application has to be executed immediately after Request Loan. Nonetheless, it accepts a subset of the parent's behaviors. In general, we can have several layers of inheritance. We can think for instance at the process for the mortgage loan for fidelity customers:

which is (*i*) a specialization of the mortgage loan process, restricting its behaviors to those dedicated to fidelity customers, (*ii*) a specialization of the fidelity customers loan, restricting its behaviors to those related to the mortgage, and (*iii*) a specialization of the loan process, restricting its behaviors to mortgage processes and fidelity customers.

A second hierarchical dimension relates to *rewriting*. Intuitively, rewriting refers to the case in which two (declarative) process models describe exactly the same set of behaviors although their representation is different and, in particular, one is more compact than the other. In other terms, the process models are only semantically but not syntactically equivalent. Let us consider again the DECLARE model of the fidelity customer loan FCL and the one below (called FCLRed):

Although the two DECLARE descriptions are different (FCLRed contains an extra-constraint with respect to the FCL) the behaviors they allow are exactly the same ones since according to the DECLARE order relationships [20], the *chain response* is stronger than the *response* constraint. We can conclude that original FCL is more compact, and indeed is also the *minimal* one, i.e., it cannot be further reduced.

The third dimension of hierarchical models identified in Sect. 2 is *modularization*, whose top-down direction is called *refinement*, and represents the process-subprocess relation, whilst the bottom-up direction, called *abstraction*, is the vice versa. Let us consider the LA model presented before: the behavior of the Decide on Loan activity can be *refined*, by detailing that the loan decision consists of either a loan request approval or a loan request rejection. The following figure shows the refinement of the Decide on Loan activity, imposing a *not coexistence* between the Approve Loan and the Reject Loan activities.

We notice that, while inheritance can easily be defined in DECLARE, modularization, although being very common and well-investigated in procedural languages, cannot. In order to overcome this limitation, we extend the traditional DECLARE language by defining and investigating the properties of the different hierarchical dimensions it enables.

5   HiDec: Hierarchical Declarative Processes

We introduce HiDec, a DECLARE extension that allows for the formal definition and implementation of the three hierarchical dimensions.

Definition 2 (HiDec). *Given a finite set of activities Σ, a HiDec process Φ is a set of constraints, intended to be in conjunction, inductively defined as follows:*

$$\varphi :: = \text{DECUN}(A) \mid \text{DECUN}(\varphi) \mid$$
$$\text{DECBIN}(A_1, A_2) \mid \text{DECBIN}(\varphi_1, \varphi_2) \mid \text{DECBIN}(A, \varphi) \mid \text{DECBIN}(\varphi, A)$$
$$\Phi :: = \{\varphi\} \mid \{A \leftrightarrow \varphi\} \mid \Phi_1 \cup \Phi_2$$

Where $A, A_1, A_2 \in \Sigma$, $\text{DECUN}(\cdot)$ is a unary DECLARE template and $\text{DECBIN}(\cdot, \cdot)$ is a binary DECLARE template. We denote with C the set of HiDec constraints, i.e., the φ formulas of the above grammar, with $\mathcal{H}$ the set of HiDec processes, i.e., the Φ formulas, and with $\Sigma(\Phi)$ the set of activities occurring in Φ.

HiDec allows us to represent all the three different types of hierarchies, included modularization, which we would not have been able to represent with traditional DECLARE. Theorem 1 shows indeed that HiDec is more expressive than DECLARE.

Theorem 1. HiDec *is more expressive than* DECLARE.

Proof (Sketch). Since Σ is finite, the number of different DECLARE constraints is finite, and, as a consequence, the number of (syntactically) different processes of $\mathcal{D}$ is finite as well. This in turn implies that the number of semantically different processes is finite (some syntactically different processes may, in fact, be equivalent). Conversely, the number of HiDec syntactically different processes is (countably) infinite, given that an arbitrary nesting of sub-processes is allowed. Also, the capability of having an arbitrary nesting of temporal operators allows us to express a (countably) infinite number of semantically different processes. As an example, for each $n \in \mathbb{N}$, it is possible to express a formula Υ_n saying: "Activity A occurs at least n times", and for each $i, j \in \mathbb{N}$, $\mathcal{L}(\Upsilon_i) \neq \mathcal{L}(\Upsilon_j)$.

By means of such an extended language, we are able to represent also process RefLA, a refinement of LA described in Sect. 4, where activity Decide on Loan is defined as the subprocess Decide on Loan $\leftrightarrow$ ($\Diamond$Accept Loan $\rightarrow$ $\neg$($\Diamond$Reject Loan)). The Figure below shows a graphical representation of the above constraint.

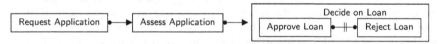

6 Hierarchies in Declarative Models

In this section, we provide a precise mathematical structure to concepts introduced before. Such a formalization is naturally originated by the definition of *hierarchy*: an *arrangement* or classification of things according to some dimension. In what follows, indeed, the previous ideas take shape into formal relations between processes which we prove to be (partial) orderings. We recall that a partial order is a set equipped with a binary relation R among its elements which satisfies the property of reflexivity ($R(a, a)$), antisymmetry ($R(a, b)$ and $R(b, a)$ entails $a = b$) and transitivity ($R(a, b)$ and $R(b, c)$ entails $R(a, c)$). Our goal is therefore to define such relations so that they reflect the informal intuitions as well as provide fine properties on the set of HiDec formulas.

6.1 The Inheritance Hierarchy

The inheritance dimension we explore is purely semantic. We say that process Ψ specializes Φ if the set of traces accepted by Ψ is a subset of those accepted by Φ, or, equivalently, if Ψ logically implies Φ.

Definition 3. *Let Σ be a set of activities, $\mathcal{H}$ the HiDec language over Σ and $\Phi \in \mathcal{H}$. Process $\Psi \in \mathcal{H}$ is a* specialization *of Φ, if $\mathcal{L}(\Psi) \subseteq \mathcal{L}(\Phi)$.*

Generalization is defined symmetrically: a process generalizes another one if the former is logically implied by the latter. Being semantic, such a definition applies to traditional DECLARE as well. However, since HiDec subsumes DECLARE, we stick to HiDec to be consistent with the definitions of the other hierarchical dimensions.

Unfortunately, relation $\subseteq$ on the set of traces does not order the set $\mathcal{H}$. Specifically, the antisymmetry fails, as there are formulas Φ, Ψ for which $\mathcal{L}(\Phi) \subseteq \mathcal{L}(\Psi)$ and $\mathcal{L}(\Psi) \subseteq \mathcal{L}(\Phi)$ holds, i.e., $\mathcal{L}(\Phi) = \mathcal{L}(\Psi)$ but $\Phi \neq \Psi$. Intuitively, logical languages contain *synonyms*, i.e., syntactically different formulas semantically describing the same set of accepted traces. Next section formalizes this concept and provides a way out.

6.2 The Rewriting Hierarchy

Definition 4. *Let Σ be a set of activities, $\mathcal{H}$ the HiDec language over Σ and Φ, $\Psi \in \mathcal{H}$. Processes Φ and Ψ are* equivalent, *written $\Phi \sim \Psi$,if $\mathcal{L}(\Psi) = \mathcal{L}(\Phi)$.*

It is immediate to verify that relation $\sim \subseteq \mathcal{H} \times \mathcal{H}$ is an equivalence relation, i.e., it is reflexive, transitive and symmetric and as such, it partitions the set $\mathcal{H}$ into *equivalence classes*. The equivalence class of an element $\Phi \in \mathcal{H}$ is denoted by $[\Phi]$, and contains all synonyms of Φ: this formally underpins the intuitive notion of "horizontal" hierarchy among processes that can be obtained by rewriting a model into an equivalent one. The set of all equivalence classes of $\mathcal{H}$ by $\sim$ is called the quotient set, and denoted by $\mathcal{H}/\sim$. Since formulas in an equivalence class are satisfied by the same traces, i.e., they are semantically indistinguishable, they all behave the same with respect to the specialization relation: if Ψ is a specialization of Φ, then for any other $\Psi' \in [\Psi]$ and $\Phi' \in [\Phi]$ we have that Ψ' is a specialization of Φ'. This motivates the extension of the specialization definition to the set $\mathcal{H}/\sim$.

Definition 5. *Let Σ, $\mathcal{H}$, Φ and Ψ as before. We define relation $\sqsubseteq \subseteq \mathcal{H}/\sim \times \mathcal{H}/\sim$ as follows: $[\Psi] \sqsubseteq [\Phi]$ if Ψ is a specialization of Φ.*

Theorem 2. *Relation $\sqsubseteq$ is a partial order.*

Proof (Sketch). The definition of $\sqsubseteq$ grounds on the language inclusion $\subseteq$ relation, hence its reflexivity, antisymmetry and transitivity properties trivially follow from those of $\subseteq$, which is a partial order for any set.

This result establishes that $\sqsubseteq$ induces a hierarchy among equivalence classes, which can be used to order HiDec processes, from the more "permissive" ones, i.e., those that allow for more behaviors, to the "stricter" ones, which accept only few traces.

We notice that equivalence classes are countably infinite and that there is always a *least element* Ψ_ℓ, i.e., the most specialized process which does not allow for any behavior $(\mathcal{L}(\Psi_\ell) = \emptyset)$. Also, for any two processes Φ and Ψ one of the following holds:

1. $[\Psi] \sqsubseteq [\Phi]$ meaning that Ψ is more restrictive than Φ (or, equivalently, Φ is more permissive than Ψ);
2. the other way around;
3. both $[\Phi] \sqsubseteq [\Psi]$ and $[\Psi] \sqsubseteq [\Phi]$ meaning that $\Phi \sim \Psi$ (or, equivalently $[\Phi] = [\Psi]$), i.e., they belong to same equivalence class; y
4. they are incomparable, because neither $[\Phi] \sqsubseteq [\Psi]$ nor $[\Psi] \sqsubseteq [\Phi]$ hold.

Example 1. The LA process in Sect. 4 is parent of both ML and FCL process, namely, $[ML] \sqsubseteq [LA]$ and $[FCL] \sqsubseteq [LA]$, and ML and FCL are incomparable. Also, FCL and FCLRed belongs to the same equivalence class, i.e., $[FCL] = [FCLRed]$.

Notice that in HiDec we can express unsatisfiable processes, which all belong to the most restrictive $[\bot]$ equivalence class (no trace is accepted), but the $[\top]$ class is missed, as there is no way to describe processes accepting all traces.

We conclude the section by remarking that relation $\sqsubseteq$ is decidable. Indeed, checking whether $[\Psi] \sqsubseteq [\Phi]$ amounts to checking if Ψ logically implies Φ, which is known to be a PSPACE-complete problem [3].

On Process Rewriting. Once the equivalence relation $\sim$ on $\mathcal{H}$ has been defined, one is typically interested in electing a *representative* of each equivalence class, i.e., a formula which has the same semantic properties of any other in the same class, but that is different in other aspects. One interesting metric can be the "compactness" of the formula (which can be simply defined as its length) or the "understandability" of the process. As pointed out in Sect. 2, the literature usually considers these two aspects related.

Unfortunately, it is very hard to find a procedure to transform a process into an equivalent one that is, e.g., more compact, for at least two reasons. The first one is that there is no effective way to syntactically reduce an LTL formula by being sure it keeps the same semantic properties (apart from the trivial well-known equivalences, such as $\Box\Box\Phi \sim \Box\Phi$). Existing works in the literature address the problem specifically for DECLARE formulas either by dropping redundant constraints [6] or finding ad-hoc "reduction rules" for DECLARE patterns [10]. These works cannot therefore be used for HiDec. Moreover, there is no guarantee, in general, to find the *minimal* formula. The second motivation concerns the intrinsic difficulty of the problem, as each equivalence class of HiDec (as well as LTL), has in general (countably) infinite cardinality, thus ruling out any brute-force approach.

Our motivation is foundational: do we really need to transform the *syntactic* model? DECLARE, HiDec and LTL formulas are just the "front-end" of a process/dynamic system, and, as such, they are used for modeling purposes only.

The whole reasoning machinery behind, which is highly affected, performance-wise, by unnecessary redundancies, actually uses *automata*. We therefore move to the semantic level and, as representative of each class, we find the *minimal* and *unique* automaton accepting all and only the traces of that class, and use it for the actual reasoning tasks. In this way we decouple the representation layer from the semantic layer and leave the modeler free of choosing the representation he prefers. We believe that the process' representation, i.e., the HiDEC (or DECLARE, or LTL) constraints can possibly be redundant, as long as the reasoning services are guaranteed to be efficient.

By notational abuse, let $\mathcal{L}(\mathcal{H})$ be the set of all possible traces that can be represented by using formulas in $\mathcal{H}$, $\mathcal{A}$ the set of all possible automata (we stress again, on *finite* traces), A an automaton in $\mathcal{A}$ and $\mathcal{L}(A)$ the set of traces recognized by A.

Definition 6. *Let A, $A' \in \mathcal{A}$ two automata. We say that A and A' are* equivalent, *written $A \approx A'$ if $\mathcal{L}(A) = \mathcal{L}(A')$.*

Trivially, $\approx$ is an equivalence relation, partitioning the set $\mathcal{A}$ into equivalence classes. The quotient set of $\mathcal{A}$ by $\approx$ is $\mathcal{A}/\approx$. Notice that we can actually consider the automaton A for a formula $\Phi \in \mathcal{H}$ as a function $A : \mathcal{H} \to \mathcal{A}$ transforming formulas into automata.

Theorem 3. *Let Φ, $\Psi \in \mathcal{H}$. Function $A : \mathcal{H} \to \mathcal{A}$ is an* equivalence-preserving *function, i.e., if $\Phi \sim \Psi$ then $A(\Phi) \approx A(\Psi)$. Moreover, for each $A' \in [A(\Phi)]$, we have that $\mathcal{L}(A') = \mathcal{L}(\Phi)$.*

Proof. If $\Phi \sim \Psi$, then, by Definition 4, $\mathcal{L}(\Phi) = \mathcal{L}(\Psi)$. By the correctness of automata construction in [3], it follows that $\mathcal{L}(A(\Psi)) = \mathcal{L}(A(\Phi))$, and hence $A(\Psi) \approx A(\Phi)$. By Definition 6 and from $\approx$ being an equivalence relation, it also follows that $\mathcal{L}(A') = \mathcal{L}(\Phi)$.

This result allows us to use, as a representative of a class $[\Phi]$, the minimum automaton $min(A(\Phi))$ recognizing the language $\mathcal{L}(\Phi)$, that can be obtained by using any automata minimizing algorithm on $A(\Phi)$ based on the Myhill-Nerode Theorem (see, e.g., [8]), which guarantees $min(A(\Phi))$ to be:

- *sound*, i.e., $\mathcal{L}(min(A(\Phi))) = \mathcal{L}(\Phi)$;
- the *smallest* automaton for $\mathcal{L}(\Phi)$, i.e., for each $A' \in [A(\Phi)]$, $|min(A(\Phi))| \leq |A'|$ (where $|A|$ measures number of states and transitions) and
- *unique*, i.e., for each $A' \in [A(\Phi)]$, $min(A') = min(A(\Phi))$ (modulo isomorphisms, namely, renaming of states).

Example 2. The (non-trimmed) automaton for the redundant process FCLRed in Sect. 4 obtained with the algorithm[1] in [3], has 14 states and 85 transitions, while after the minimization, it has 6 states and 24 transitions.

---

[1] An ongoing implementation is available at: https://github.com/RiccardoDeMasellis/FLLOAT.

6.3   The Modularization Hierarchy

The last dimension we study is syntactical, and covers the intuitive process/sub-process relation. We propose a step-by-step methodology to *refine* a HIDEC process model by specifying its subprocesses, which notably defines a (partial) order.

Definition 7. *Let Σ be an alphabet of activities, and let $\Phi \in \mathcal{H}$. Process $\Psi \in \mathcal{H}$ is a* refinement *of Φ, written $\Psi \preceq \Phi$, if Ψ can be obtained from Φ by applying $n \geq 0$ refinement steps $\Phi_0 \Rightarrow \ldots \Rightarrow \Phi_n$ where:*

- *$\Phi_0 = \Phi$ and*
- *$\Phi_n = \Psi$ and*
- *each Φ_i $i \in \{1, \ldots n - 1\}$ is such that either:*
  - *$\Phi_i = \Phi_{i-1} \cup \{A \leftrightarrow \varphi\}$ with $A \in \Sigma(\Phi_{i-1})$ and $\varphi \in \mathcal{C}$ (recall $\mathcal{C}$ is the set of HIDEC constraints as in Definition 2) or*
  - *Φ_i can be obtained from Φ_{i-1} by applying a partial function r_i : $\Sigma(\Phi_{i-1}) \to \mathcal{C}$ which intuitively substitutes (some) activities occurring in Φ_{i-1} with a constraint in $\mathcal{C}$.*

Abstraction can be defined analogously, with an abstraction step consisting in either removing a $A \leftrightarrow \varphi$ constraint or applying function $r_i^{-1} : \mathcal{C} \to \Sigma$ which substitutes a HIDEC constraint with an activity. Intuitively, a process is refined when a single activity, say A, is "expanded" in a complex subprocess φ. Such an expansion can take place either by adding a constraint $A \leftrightarrow \varphi$[2] or by substituting all occurrences of A with φ. This two variants are worth to be discussed. First of all, we observe that the two procedures are semantically different, as the following example illustrate.

Example 3. Let $\Phi = \{\neg\Diamond A\}$, and let us assume we want to refine A with sub-process $\neg\Diamond A$. By adding the (unsatisfiable) constraint $A \leftrightarrow \neg\Diamond A$, the whole process Φ becomes unsatisfiable. Conversely, by using the substitution $r(A) = \neg\Diamond A$, the refined process $\Psi = \{\Box\Diamond A\}$ is still satisfiable.

Furthermore, the two choices covers different practical needs. The first option is more suitable for refining a process with a bottom-up approach, as it follows the natural human procedure of specifying a process from a more abstract level to a more specific one, still allowing a comprehensive view of all levels, being "conservative". The second one is instead a more "destructive" option for refinement, as, after few steps, the structure of the original process is lost. However, it is more appropriate for abstraction, as when a complex process contains no $A \leftrightarrow \varphi$ constraints, it can only be abstracted by applying the r^{-1} function.

The notion of refinement (and abstraction) naturally defines an ordering $\preceq$ on set $\mathcal{H}$.

Theorem 4. *Relation $\preceq \subseteq \mathcal{H} \times \mathcal{H}$ is a partial order.*

---

[2] To match the intended semantics of the "$\leftrightarrow$" used for expanding a process, we relax the assumption of one activity true at the time by leaving out activities occurring in the left-hand part of double implication constraints, which, after the refinement, do not intuitively represent activities anymore, but rather "placeholders" or syntactic "shortcuts" for sub-processes.

Proof (Sketch). Reflexivity is trivial, given that every process is a refinement of itself (by applying 0 steps). Transitivity is also immediate since the composition of refinement steps is a refinement. Antisymmetry is proven by noticing that each step increases the length of the process. Since processes of different lengths are necessarily syntactically different, the only way to have $\Phi \preceq \Psi$ and $\Psi \preceq \Phi$ is when both refinements consists of 0 steps, thus entailing $\Phi = \Psi$.

Relation $\preceq$ therefore induces a hierarchy among HiDec processes, from the more "abstract" ones, i.e., those providing a high-level view of the process, to the more "refined" ones, i.e., those showing the details. We notice that HiDec allows for expressing countably many syntactically different processes and that $\preceq$ does not define a greatest nor least element. However, given Φ and Ψ one of the following holds:

1. $\Psi \preceq \Phi$, that is, Ψ is more refined than Φ (equivalent., Φ more abstract than Ψ);
2. $\Phi \preceq \Psi$;
3. both $\Phi \preceq \Psi$ and $\Psi \preceq \Phi$ hold, hence $\Phi = \Psi$;
4. they are incomparable, because neither $\Phi \preceq \Psi$ nor $\Psi \preceq \Phi$ hold.

Example 4. Process RefLA in Sect. 5, obtained from LA by adding the constraint Decide on Loan $\leftrightarrow$ ($\Diamond$Accept Loan $\rightarrow \neg$($\Diamond$Reject Loan)), is therefore a child of LA according to the modularization hierarchy, i.e., RefLA $\preceq$ LA.

Given a set of processes, a refinement/abstraction hierarchy can be built in practice: given Φ and $\Psi \in \mathcal{H}$, checking whether $\Psi \preceq \Phi$ is decidable. Refinement steps can be indeed seen as grammar production rules which never decrease the length of the process. Since Σ is finite, to check whether $\Psi \preceq \Phi$ we start from Φ, we apply the production rules in all possible ways and we stop when the current process exceeds the length of Ψ.

On the Satisfiability of the Refined Process. The refinement relation is syntactical. As such, it is of interest to study syntactical restrictions on refinements which guarantee semantic properties of the refined processes. One of such semantic properties may be inheritance itself (see [19] for a similar analysis in the context of object-oriented systems). Given the lack of space, here we focus on a more basic yet useful semantic property: satisfiability. Given $\Psi \preceq \Phi$, are there straightforward restrictions on refinements that guarantee the (semantic) satisfiability of Ψ? We provide a negative answer.

Definition 8. *Let $\Phi, \Psi \in \mathcal{H}$ and let Ψ be a refinement of Φ, i.e., $\Phi_0 \Rightarrow \ldots \Rightarrow \Phi_n$, with $\Phi_0 = \Phi$ and $\Phi_n = \Psi$. We define the set of constraints introduced by the refinement as the set $\Delta = \bigcup_{i \in 0,\ldots n} \Delta_i$ where $\Delta_0 = \emptyset$ and each Δ_i with $i \in 1 \ldots n$ is the set of constraints (in $\mathcal{C}$) introduced by the $i - th$ refinement step, namely:*

- $\Delta_i = \varphi$ *if the step added a formula* A $\leftrightarrow \varphi$ *to Φ_i or*
- $\Delta_i = \Im(r_i)$, *where $\Im(r_i)$ is the image of r_i, otherwise.*

As a first remark, we observe that the satisfiability of both Φ and Δ is not a sufficient condition to establish the satisfiability of Ψ, as the following counterexample shows.

Example 5. Let $\Phi = \{\neg\Diamond A, \Diamond B\}$ and $\Psi = \{\neg\Diamond A, \Diamond(\Diamond A))\}$ obtained from Φ by applying one refinement step with $r(B) = \Diamond A$. Clearly, Φ is satisfiable, as well as $\Delta = \{\Diamond A\}$, but Ψ is not.

This is not surprising, as, intuitively, new constraints in Δ may generate inconsistencies with other constraints in the original process Φ. It is also interesting that the unsatisfiability of some constraints in Δ does not entail the unsatisfiability of Ψ.

Example 6. Let $\Phi = \{\Diamond A, \neg\Diamond B\}$ and $\Psi = \{\Diamond A, \neg\Diamond B, B \leftrightarrow (\Diamond C \wedge \neg\Diamond C)\}$. Set $\Delta = \{\Diamond C \wedge \neg\Diamond C\}$ is unsatisfiable, but Ψ is not, as it is satisfied by every trace that eventually contains A but never contains B (which would imply the inconsistency).

Given the above results, we investigate a reasonable restrictions on refinements. The intuition suggests that inconsistencies are typically generated by adding constraints which include activities that are already mentioned in other, existing, constraints. We follow this idea and study special refinements in which each refinement step talk about "fresh" activities only, i.e., activities not that do not appear where else in the process, in order to understand if this is a sufficient condition to guarantee the satisfiability of the refined process. Unfortunately, this is not the case, as the following Theorem prove.

Theorem 5. *Let Φ and Ψ as in Definition 8. Let Φ and each Δ_i be satisfiable and such that for each $i \neq j$ we have $\Sigma(\Delta_i) \cap \Sigma(\Phi) = \emptyset$ and $\Sigma(\Delta_i) \cap \Sigma(\Delta_j) = \emptyset$. Then Ψ can be unsatisfiable.*

Proof. By using the r function is easy to nest temporal operators to generate a formula that can only be satisfied by a trace where two (or more) activities must be true at the same time, which clashes with the assumption of only one activity performed at the time (see Sect. 3). An example follows. Let $\Phi = \{\neg\Diamond A, \neg\Diamond B\}$ and let $\Psi = \{\neg\Diamond(\neg\Diamond C), \neg\Diamond(\neg\Diamond D)\}$ obtained from Φ by using the refinement function $r(A) = \neg\Diamond C$ and $r(B) = \neg\Diamond D$. Using the well-known equivalence rules we get $\Psi = \{\Box\Diamond C, \Box\Diamond D\}$, which is true only if in the last instant both C and D are true.

7   Concluding Remarks

The formal investigation about declarative hierarchies carried out in this work allows us to provide a number of interesting results. First of all, the inheritance, rewriting and modularization dimensions, widely investigated for procedural models, are tailored to fit the declarative setting, thus providing a comprehensive perspective on hierarchical dimensions on declarative processes. We concretize such a conceptual view in HIDEC, a language extending DECLARE that, beyond the formalization of inheritance, rewriting and modularization, supports the following results. The mathematical definition of the inheritance dimension based on logical implication allows us to carry any formal property entailed by a specialized process to all its parents, and provide a concrete way for optimizing reasoning tasks on redundant models while preserving the representation designed by the modeler. Finally, the definition of refinement (and abstraction) offers an actual methodology to refine (abstract) any HIDEC model, which is an essential feature when dealing with complex processes.

As future work, we plan to empirically investigate a suitable graphical notation for specifying modular HIDEC processes, which is only sketched here, as well as to develop a tool for supporting modelers in defining reduction/abstraction steps.

References

1. Basten, T., van der Aalst, W.M.P.: Inheritance of behavior. J. Log. Algebr. Program. **47**(2), 47–145 (2001)
2. Basu, A., Blanning, R.W.: Synthesis and decomposition of processes in organizations. Inf. Syst. Res. **14**(4), 337–355 (2003)
3. De Giacomo, G., De Masellis, R., Grasso, M., Maggi, F.M., Montali, M.: Monitoring business metaconstraints based on LTL and LDL for finite traces. In: Sadiq, S., Soffer, P., Völzer, H. (eds.) BPM 2014. LNCS, vol. 8659, pp. 1–17. Springer, Heidelberg (2014)
4. De Giacomo, G., De Masellis, R., Montali, M.: Reasoning on LTL on finite traces: Insensitivity to infiniteness. In: Proceedings of the AAAI 2014, pp. 1027–1033 (2014)
5. Burattin, A., Maggi, F.M. Sperduti, A.: Conformance checking based on multi-perspective declarative process models. Expert Syst. Appl. (2016). http://www.sciencedirect.com/science/article/pii/S0957417416304390, http://dx.doi.org/10.1016/j.eswa.2016.08.040
6. Di Ciccio, C., Maggi, F.M., Montali, M., Mendling, J.: Ensuring model consistency in declarative process discovery. In: Motahari-Nezhad, H.R., Recker, J., Weidlich, M. (eds.) BPM 2015. Lecture Notes in Computer Science, vol. 9253, pp. 144–159. Springer, Heidelberg (2015)
7. Dumas, M., La Rosa, M., Mendling, J., Reijers, H.A.: Fundamentals of Business Process Management. Springer, Heidelberg (2013)
8. Hopcroft, J.E., Motwani, R., Ullman, J.D.: Introduction to Automata Theory, Languages, and Computation. Addison-Wesley Longman Publishing Co. Inc., Boston (2006)
9. Kock Jr., N.F., McQueen, R.J.: Product flow, breadth and complexity of business processes: an empirical study of 15 business processes in three organizations. Bus. Process Re-eng. Manag. J. **2**(2), 8–22 (1996)
10. Maggi, F.M., Bose, R.P.J.C., van der Aalst, W.M.P.: A knowledge-based integrated approach for discovering and repairing declare maps. In: Salinesi, C., Norrie, M.C., Pastor, Ó. (eds.) CAiSE 2013. LNCS, vol. 7908, pp. 433–448. Springer, Heidelberg (2013)
11. Malone, T.W., Crowston, K., Lee, J., Pentland, B., Dellarocas, C., Wyner, G., Quimby, J., Osborn, C.S., Bernstein, A., Herman, G., Klein, M., O'Donnell, E.: Tools for inventing organizations: Toward a handbook of organizational processes. Manage. Sci. **45**(3), 425–443 (1999)
12. Mendling, J., Reijers, H.A., Cardoso, J.: What makes process models understandable? In: Alonso, G., Dadam, P., Rosemann, M. (eds.) BPM 2007. LNCS, vol. 4714, pp. 48–63. Springer, Heidelberg (2007)
13. Moody, D.L.: The "Physics" of notations: toward a scientific basis for constructing visual notations in software engineering. IEEE TSE **35**(6), 756–779 (2009)
14. Pesic, M., van der Aalst, W.M.P.: A declarative approach for flexible business processes management. In: Eder, J., Dustdar, S. (eds.) BPM Workshops 2006. LNCS, vol. 4103, pp. 169–180. Springer, Heidelberg (2006)

15. Reijers, H.A., Mendling, J.: Modularity in process models: review and effects. In: Dumas, M., Reichert, M., Shan, M.-C. (eds.) BPM 2008. LNCS, vol. 5240, pp. 20–35. Springer, Heidelberg (2008)
16. La Rosa, M., van der Aalst, W.M., Dumas, M., Milani, F.P.: Business process variability modeling: a survey. Technical report (2013). http://eprints.qut.edu.au/61842/
17. Sadiq, W., Orlowska, M.E.: Analyzing process models using graph reduction techniques. Inf. Syst. **25**(2), 117–134 (2000)
18. Schönig, S., Cabanillas, C., Jablonski, S., Mendling, J.: A framework for efficiently mining the organisational perspective of business processes. Decis. Support Syst. **89**, 87–97 (2016)
19. Schrefl, M., Stumptner, M.: Behavior-consistent specialization of object life cycles. ACM Trans. Softw. Eng. Methodol. **11**(1), 92–148 (2002)
20. Schunselaar, D.M.M., Maggi, F.M., Sidorova, N.: Patterns for a log-based strengthening of declarative compliance models. In: Derrick, J., Gnesi, S., Latella, D., Treharne, H. (eds.) IFM 2012. LNCS, vol. 7321, pp. 327–342. Springer, Heidelberg (2012)
21. Schunselaar, D.M.M., Maggi, F.M., Sidorova, N., van der Aalst, W.M.P.: Configurable declare: designing customisable flexible process models. In: Meersman, R., et al. (eds.) OTM 2012, Part I. LNCS, vol. 7565, pp. 20–37. Springer, Heidelberg (2012)
22. Sharp, A., McDermott, P.: Workflow Modeling: Tools for Process Improvement and Application Development, 1st edn. Artech House Inc., Norwood (2001)
23. Weber, B., Reichert, M., Rinderle-Ma, S.: Change patterns and change support features - enhancing flexibility in process-aware information systems. Data Knowl. Eng. **66**(3), 438–466 (2008)
24. Wynn, M.T., Verbeek, H.M.W., van der Aalst, W.M.P., ter Hofstede, A.H.M., Edmond, D.: Soundness-preserving reduction rules for reset workflow nets. Inf. Sci. **179**(6), 769–790 (2009)
25. Wynn, M.T., Verbeek, H.M.W.E., van der Aalst, W.M.P., ter Hofstede, A.H.M., Edmond, D.: Reduction rules for YAWL workflows with cancellation regions and or-joins. Inf. Softw. Technol. **51**(6), 1010–1020 (2009)
26. Zeising, M., Schönig, S.S., Jablonski, S.: Towards a common platform for the support of routine and agile business processes. In: CollaborateCom 2014, 94–103 (2014)
27. Zugal, S., Soffer, P., Haisjackl, C., Pinggera, J., Reichert, M., Weber, B.: Investigating expressiveness and understandability of hierarchy in declarative business process models. Softw. Syst. Model. **14**(3), 1081–1103 (2015)

Cloud and Internet of Services/Things

FitScale: Scalability of Legacy Applications Through Migration to Cloud

Jinho Hwang[✉], Maja Vukovic, and Nikos Anerousis

IBM T.J. Watson Research Center, New York, USA
{jinho,maja,nikos}@us.ibm.com

Abstract. One of the key benefits of Cloud computing is elasticity, the ability of the system infrastructure to adapt to the workload changes by automatically adjusting the resources on-demand. Horizontal scaling refers to the method of adding or removing resources from the resource pool. As such it is appealing to enterprises who seek to migrate their legacy systems as it requires no application rewrite or refactoring. Vertical scaling approach offers a mechanism to maintain continuous performance while reducing resource cost through reconfiguration of the resource. The challenge is, however, in being able to automatically identify the right size of the target resource such as a VM or a container. Moreover, choice of scalability policies is not intuitive due to application complexity, topology and variability in system performance parameters that need to be considered.

This paper presents a transformation model, FitScale, which provides scalability with minimum price of resources. The paper describes the framework that employs the application functional and operational properties to recommend the target sizing and scalability policies. We evaluate proposed approach in an on-premise and cloud environments, with a dataset of 2023 servers hosting 6737 applications. The experimental results show about 5 times cost reduction with minimum performance impact.

Keywords: Cloud · Migration · Elasticity · Scalability

1 Introduction

Application development in the cloud typically follows the micro-services style, an approach where applications are built from the composition of smaller atomic services, each one running independently in the cloud and communicating through REST APIs. Microservices [15] are designed to represent distinct business functions, and are deployed independently[1].

A question that often comes up is how existing applications, developed in the "traditional" style, and running on previous generation systems can take advantage of cloud platforms, or even become native to the cloud themselves.

---

[1] http://martinfowler.com/articles/microservices.html.

© Springer International Publishing Switzerland 2016
Q.Z. Sheng et al. (Eds.): ICSOC 2016, LNCS 9936, pp. 123–139, 2016.
DOI: 10.1007/978-3-319-46295-0_8

The latter would imply a significant transformation of the application architecture, including a breakdown of many application sub-components into independently running micro-services. The benefits are many and significant: agility for development and deployment; reduced cost in OS/middleware management, ability for applications to leverage cloud native services.

When considering transformation of legacy applications to Cloud environments there are a number of choices available. On one end of the spectrum is the plain migration (the so called "lift and shift"), which moves the application into one functional entity such as, a server [9] or a container [16] to mimic a micro-service architecture. On the other end of the spectrum is the full transformation to a micro-services architecture (by refactoring and rewriting the application). Given that the latter is both a time and resource-consuming task, a more reasonable approach is to perform a like-to-like migration first (the application is moved in its entirety to one or more virtual machines in the cloud in a way that resembles its original topology). After the migration is completed, the more involved transformation to a micro-services architecture can be performed in increments over a period of time.

As legacy applications are often not built to be scalable in themselves, setting the right scalability after migrating into clouds is still a delicate, time-consuming process. There are a number of challenges in ensuring the scalability of legacy applications during migration to Cloud:

- The root cause of why scalability is required is often unclear. For example, is that due to cpu, memory, or network? If one of them is a bottleneck all the time, then we may buy more of that resource and achieve both horizontal and vertical scalability.
- Auto scaling policies should be defined well to meet performance expectation based on the usage patterns at the source. For example, AWS has its own policy syntax.
- "Like-to-like migration" to Cloud does not take advantage of the benefits provided by Cloud such as elastic scalability.
- In most cases, it is hard to decide whether or not applications should be put in a scaling group.
- It is hard to estimate the properties of initial resources.
- It is challenging to identify the right scaling policy.

In this paper we discuss an approach to migrating applications to the cloud to meet scalability requirements using elastic compute services in the cloud. Elasticity can be achieved through carefully selected policies to meet application demands.

There are three key objectives that drive design of our approach to policy-based scalability: (a) minimize the cost of the resources during scalability, (b) ensure high-performance is maintained, with low-to-no degradation impact and (c) maintain stability of the application through correctly chosen right initial size (thus avoiding the slow-downs during scaling). This in itself is a challenging endeavor as policies are automatically selected and fixed, and any subsequent changes require reconfiguration.

This paper makes the following three contributions:

- TheFitScale framework for application transformation to Cloud with consideration for scaling requirements
- Method for pattern discovery for application topology and performance
- Method for target sizing and scaling policy assignment

2   Background and Motivation

Scaling horizontally (or scaling out/in) means adding more compute nodes to (or removing nodes from) a system. As an example a Web server may be scaled out from one compute node to three. As compute prices have dropped and performance continues to increase, high-performance computing applications such as seismic analysis and biotechnology workloads have adopted low-cost "commodity" systems for tasks that once would have required supercomputers. System architects may configure hundreds of small computers in a cluster to obtain aggregate computing power that often exceeds that of computers based on a single traditional processor. The development of high-performance interconnects such as Gigabit Ethernet, InfiniBand and Myrinet further fueled this model. Such growth has led to demand for software that allows efficient management and maintenance of multiple nodes, as well as hardware such as shared data storage with much higher I/O performance. Size scalability is the maximum number of processors that a system can accommodate [5]. To scale vertically (or scale up/down) means to add resources to (or remove resources from) a single node in a system, typically involving the addition of CPUs or memory to a single computer. Such vertical scaling of existing systems enables them to use virtualization technology more effectively, as it provides more resources for the hosted set of operating system and application modules to share. Taking advantage of such resources is also referred to as "scaling up", such as expanding the number of Apache daemon processes currently running. Application scalability refers to the improved performance of running applications on a scaled-up version of the system.

There are tradeoffs between these two models. A larger numbers of computers implies increased management complexity, as well as a more complex programming model and issues such as throughput and latency between nodes; also, some applications do not lend themselves to a distributed model. In the past, the price difference between the two models has favored "scale up" computing for those applications that fit its paradigm, but recent advances in virtualization technology have blurred that advantage, since deploying a new virtual system over a hypervisor (where possible) is often less expensive than actually buying and installing a physical one. Configuring an existing idle system has always been less expensive than buying, installing, and configuring a new one, regardless of the model.

Still, reconfiguration is challenging for a number of reasons: unknown or inaccurate information about source environment, ability to reason and make

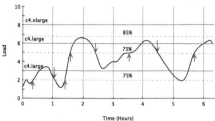

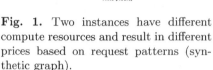

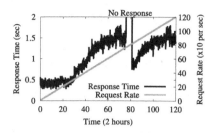

Fig. 1. Two instances have different compute resources and result in different prices based on request patterns (synthetic graph).

Fig. 2. Scaling up has a provisioning delay while adding an additional application (i.e., virtual machine).

decisions about scalability for multi-tier applications, lack of automatic rule and policy generation.

Figure 1 is a simple experiment that depicts cost benefits of allocating applications with the right size of compute resources. Given the request pattern for 6 h, we show two different deployment cases. An application is deployed to *c4.xlarge* virtual machine capable of 8 loads with 85 % threshold, and *c4.large* virtual machine capable of 3 loads with 75 % threshold. We use AWS prices in the graph for the sake of reader's familarity, but the same scenario can be applied for other cloud providers. *c4.xlarge* costs $0.209 per hour, and *c4.large* costs $0.105 per hour. Note that a partial hour of usage is also considered as a full hour. Upward arrows mean scaling up applications on demand (adding an instance), whereas downward arrows mean scaling down applications.

The reactive horizontal scaling is used, so when loads pass the threshold, a new instance is added. The total number of hours used is 16 for *c4.large*, and 6 for *c4.xlarge*. Thus, the total cost of *c4.large* is $0.105 × 16 = $1.68, whereas the total cost of *c4.xlarge* is $0.209 × 6 = $1.254. *c4.xlarge* provides 33 % less operational cost in this case. Therefore, this corroborates determining the right size is an important factor.

Figure 2 illustrates a simple web server response time with a linear increase of the request rate. "No response" around 70 min incurs because of the provisioning delay, and zeroed memory without cached data when adding an additional application. Therefore, not only minimizing cost, but also choosing the right thresholds is critical to avoid a service level agreement (SLA) violation.

3   FitScale Framework

The FitScale framework integrates multiple, independent, workflow processes that rely on a common data set. With access to source infrastructure or compiled data, FitScale discovers the necessary data and converts unstructured data into structured data such as matrices or comma separated values. Especially graphs with large data points are summarized to help identify moving patterns in the analysis step. Once the data is converted into structured data, FitScale seeks usage trends of critical resources which are performance bottlenecks, and creates resource plans such as an initial virtual machine size and number of virtual machines in a pool, and defines scaling policies that are appropriate to the target clouds.

Figure 3 depicts the FitScale architecture for end-to-end migration automation. In Step ① a user needs to collect information such as a server list with credentials, infrastructure API key from on-premise data centers, or to install agents depending on the infrastructure discovery tool[2]. At Step ② a user inserts the collected information to FitScale. Step ③ FitScale launches a discovery process with the provided information. This may take a couple of days or weeks depending on the application usage patterns. If the usage patterns are stationary over a short period of time, the discovery process stops and moves on to the next step. Otherwise, it keeps watching the source infrastructure to find the stable application usage patterns. The information collected in this stage are performance (resource usage), application configurations, running processes, and network connectivity. Step ④ in the analysis step, FitScale seeks metrics such as request patterns, resource usage patterns, variability (a rate of scaling up and down), and dependency that are used in the modeling step. At Step ⑤ together with the target information, FitScale optimizes the scalability with the objective to minimize the cost. At step ⑥ the final outputs are resource plans that decide on the size of instances and scaling policies that define the timing of scalability.

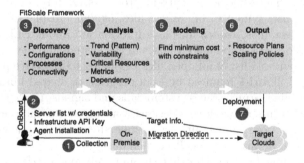

Fig. 3. A FitScale framework concatenates multiple workflow processes to automatically generate scalability plans.

4 Understanding Applications

The first step to understanding application configuration is to define what needs to be discovered. Understanding applications is a complex process, as they run on operating systems with various library dependencies, and operate across multiple network-connected servers. The process of inferencing how applications will

---

[2] There are agent-based discovery tools [17] and agentless discovery tools (i.e., using scripts) [1].

operate in target Cloud environment relies on information about vertical (local) and horizontal (remote) dependencies, and how resources such as, cpu, memory, disk and network are utilized. In short, to be able to reason about applications we require dependencies and resource usage data. The discovery and analysis phases of the FitScale framework provide these insights about applications.

4.1 Discovery

The discovered data about the source environment needs to be mapped into what are the scalability requirements of the target Cloud. Following are the key data items required:

- resource allocation: cpu, memory, disk, network bandwidth
- resource usage: cpu (%), memory read/write (bytes), disk read/write (bytes), network in/out (bytes)
- network connectivity
- operating system and application configurations

There are number of agent and agent-less tools for system information discovery. In the FitScale framework, we use a script-based approach (agentless) to uncover the necessary configuration and operational data. The shell is the easiest and the most convenient way to program and run. For example, on Linux based systems ./proc directory contains system attributes including process information and system information. Many standardized tools can provide us with key data. *ps* reports a snapshot of the current processes, *df* reports filesystem disk space usage, *nm* lists symbols from object files, *objdump* displays detailed information from object files, *readelf* displays information about ELF object files, *lspci* displays information about PCI buses in the system and devices connected to them, *lsof* provides a list of all open files belonging to all active processes, *ldd* prints the shared libraries required by each program or shared library specified on the command line, *strace* traces system calls and signals, *ltrace* traces library call, and *netstat* prints network connections, routing tables, interface statistics, masquerade connections, and multicast memberships. On Windows-based systems vbscripts can be utilized to collect such data [8].

Servers are connected to each other through network interfaces. A web service may need web applications, databases, file systems, or memory cache servers in the backend. This distributed (micro-service) architecture needs to be taken into consideration to capture the propagation of application processes. The inter-server attributes can help make decisions on simultaneous scalability. To collect the inter-server data, we can look at the network statistics derived from *netstat* information, gather network ports used for communication, and infer performance propagation impact between servers [12].

4.2 Pattern Analysis

Using the data about source infrastructure FitScale provides the following insights:

1. Which resources are bottlenecks? (this helps find key metrics that impact on performance).
2. How variable the processing (request) trend (pattern) is? (the answer helps decide the size of virtual machines).
3. How fast the processing trend increases or decreases? (the answer helps determine the increasing or decreasing rate and timing of virtual machines).
4. Where are request sources from (geographical analysis based on the connections)? (the answer helps decide how/where global scalability is requred).
5. How is a multi-tier application distributed? (the answer helps find how much load propagation impacts when loads increase).

In addition, we can easily derive simple insights. For example, the questions like how many (virtual) CPU cores/memory/disk/network bandwidth are assigned or how many virtual machines are used in the source are rather straightforward computations.

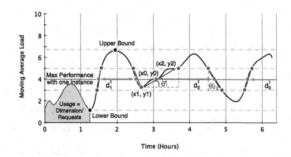

Fig. 4. Sample CPU usage graph (synthetic) to illustrate how to analyze data in FitScale.

The answers are quantified, and translated into scalability decisions to create scalability policies or determine the size of target resources. Figure 4 illustrates a sample graph $y = f(x)$ that shows a certain trend (pattern) along the x-axis and y-axis to explain how the answers to the questions can be made from the data (resource usage) observation. Note that we do not use this graph to formulate an optimization problem, but use its properties to draw useful information. Since the usage graph fluctuates in a very short time period, we use the moving average, a form of average which has been adjusted to allow for smoothing of a time series. Moving average smoothing is a smoothing technique used to make the long term trends of a time series clearer [3]. We use a simple moving average technique denoted as $\frac{1}{n} \sum_{i=0}^{n-1} x_{M-i}$, where n is the averaging window size, and M is current time. The following numbers correspond to the questions earlier.

1. To find which resources are bottlenecks, we look at the overall resource usage of CPU, memory, disk, and network when user requests arrive in applications. Given a fixed period of time T with the number of requests per second r_i, each resource usage is calculated as $u(t) = \frac{\sum_{i=0}^{T} m_i}{\sum_{i=0}^{T} r_i}$, where m is a resource

usage (%) per second (i.e., measurement unit), and t is a resource type. In other words, $u(t)$ is an average resource usage (%) per request, and this is a metric to decide which resources are potential bottlenecks.

2. The variability can be interpreted as a rate of scaling up and down, so the high variability means there are more adding/removing servers. The variability of the graph does not need to be statistically analyzed since we only need to know how much the graph is fluctuating based on the maximum performance line of a target virtual machine [4]. The variablity of this graph f is

$v(f,t) = \frac{|\{x|f(x) \overset{+}{=} l(t)\}|}{H}$, where $l(t)$ is the maximum load of the instance type t, an

operator $\overset{+}{=}$ represents an increasing intersection when load increases, H is the total number of monitoring hours. In Fig. 4, the middle line (at load 4) represents the maximum performance line with one instance type, and the total time H is 6. Therefore, $v(f,t) = \frac{3}{6}$, meaning that in a time unit (1 h), the resource usage surpasses the maximum performance line 0.5 times.

3. The speed of increasing or descreasing load decides the change rate of the number of virtual machines and also the timing of when to scale up or down. We measure the moving speed by calculating the slope of the change between critical ranges. The critical ranges mean the lines above/below of the maximum performance line and left/right of the crossing-point. In Fig. 4, the critical ranges are defined as 25 % above (load 5) and below (load 3) of the maximum performance line (load 4), and 0.5 h left/right. The slope of slope triangles (red line with θ) shows the speed of increasing loads. Therefore, the average speed is $s(f,t) = \frac{\sum_{i=0}^{n} sin(\theta)}{v(f,t)}$, where n is the number of crossings with

$|\{x|f(x) \overset{+}{=} l(t)\}|$, and $sin(\theta) = \frac{opposite}{hypotenuse} = \frac{y_2-y_1}{\sqrt{(x_2-x_1)^2+(y_2-y_1)^2}}$. Likewise, the

decreasing loads can be calculated the same way.

4. The geographical distribution of request sources provides a useful information on how/where the scalability should happen. For example, some vendors allow to scale up the number of virtual machines across multiple data centers based on the geographical requirements. In this case, we can locate additional servers close to where requests are generated. The source network addresses of requests provide geographical distribution.

5. A multi-tier (distributed) application consists of applications that communicate each other to process a request and generate a response. For example, a web server talks to a database server to retrieve information. This directional dependency is important because the scalability is done in just one tier, meaning the scaling up of the web server does not necessarily lead to the scaling up of the database. Therefore, we have to consider the impact of other tiers when we design scalability policies. The application dependency is the same as the network dependency, thus the network connectivity between applications is captured.

Note that FitScale takes heed of dependency among connected servers because often the connected servers need to scale together and the backend server (not scaling elastically) should be able to accommodate maximum loads from the frontend servers (scaling elastically). While the most of applications are formed in a multi-tier architecture (for example, service oriented architecture, and micro-services architecture), considering request flows in a scaling group should not be obviated in order not to countervail the scalability configurations.

5   Understanding Clouds

Cloud providers offer different ways to scale applications elastically, and therefore it is important to understand the differences in scalability models. This section describes scalability offerings by major cloud providers and how users are charged.

5.1   Scalability

The first step towards elastic scalability is to monitor instances at the platform level. Most cloud providers provide average metrics for every 5 min, and optionally more fine-grained monitoring with additional charges. CloudWatch, AzureWatch, and Nimsoft are examples. The monitored metrics are checked against policies in every monitoring period. Once one of user-defined policies is triggered from the monitoring engine, the actions defined by the policies initiate scalability processes (add or remove instances). When adding instances, cloud providers automatically attach the new instances to a load balancer to forward requests to them.

Table 1 shows some scalability examples of major cloud providers. There are two ways to provision instances when thresholds are surpassed: on-demand and pool-based. The on-demand provisioning adds instances by replicating a running instance when needed. This approach is cost efficient and does not have (state) synchronization problem, but is expected to be slow. On the other hand, the pool-based provisioning pre-previsions instances and uses them when needed (usually keep them in stopped mode). This approach expects fast addition of instances, but renders waste of resources and may result in synchronization problem because it is replicated when an application is initially created.

5.2   Scalability Cost

Cloud providers charge users either hourly or monthly for running instances, called the pay-as-you-go model. Prices for the scalability are varied. In fact, users are not charged by the scalability function itself, but by the number of used instances. A unit of charging a running instance for scalability is only per-hour, and a partial hour of usage is also charged the same as a full hour. Intuitively, frequent scaling up and down can charge more than just running more instances without elastic scalability for the same period of time. Therefore, it is imperative to find an optimal scaling model that can provide a minimum price and sustain performance.

Table 1. Cloud providers have different scalability metrics and provisioning strategy. The queue length metric scales based on how many messages are waiting in the queue.

Cloud provider	Scaling metrics	Actions	Provisioning strategy
SoftLayer (IBM)	CPU percentage, Private network incoming/outgoing (Mbps), Public network incoming/outgoing (Mbps)	Add/remove/set scale group by quantity/percentage	On-demand
AWS (Amazon)	CPU utilization (%), Disk reads (Bytes), Disk read operations (Operations), Disk writes (Bytes), Disk write operations (Operations), Network in/out (Bytes)	Add/remove/set scale group by quantity/percentage	On-demand
GCP (Google)	CPU utilization (%), HTTP(S) load balancing serving capacity (%), Cloud Monitoring metrics (80 metrics in https://cloud.google.com/ monitoring/api/metrics) also network load balancing (for other protocols such as SMTP) is applicable preprovisioned managed instance group	Add/remove/set scale group by quantity/percentage	Pool-based
Azure (Microsoft)	CPU (%), Queue length	Add/remove/set scale group by quantity/percentage	Pool-based

6 Scaling Model

The two main objectives are (1) finding the right resource size that minimizes cost and guarantees performance and (2) creating policies based on the observation from the discovery and pattern analysis in order to scale at the right moment with the right size. Specifically, the outputs of the model are:

- Instance size: using an auto scaling function usually does not involve any pricing unless augmenting monitoring capabilities, but the instance (resource) size is directly related to the final cost, so it is important to define the right size.
- Maximum number of instances: instances are either pre-provisioned in the resource pool or provisioning on the fly with the maximum capacity definition.
- Scaling policy: depending on the performance (cpu, memory, disk, network), we need to scale up/down the service. The properties that need to be found are threshold (%), watching time (minutes) above the threshold, and scaling size unit (# of instances or % of the scaling group).

We have input information from the discovery and the pattern analysis from Sect. 4: bottleneck resources, upper-bound/lower-bound loads, load variability, the speed of increasing/descreasing, geographical distribution, and dependency.

To achieve the two main goals mentioned earlier, we need to find the minimum cost while guaranteeing performance, which can be translated into the question of how we set up a scalability configuration at the target cloud because the size of instance and the scalability policies directly affect the operational expenditure. First of all, we need to define how we calculate the cost. The cost function is

$$C(f,t) = \sum_{i=0}^{M(f,t)} \sum_{j=0}^{|d^i|} p(t) * d_j^i(t) + p(t) * H, \tag{1}$$

where f is the observed function for a particular bottlenek resource type (for example, cpu, memory, disk, or network) with the number of data points D, t is the target instance type (for example, c4.large with cpu, memory, disk, network), $M(f,t)$ is the maximum number of instances of type t used in the function f, $|d^i|$ is the number of segments for d^i, $p(t)$ is the price of the type t, and H is the total number of monitoring hours. The time complexity to find the cost for each instance type is bounded by the data points of the graph because it goes through all data points to find crossing points. Thus, the time complexity is $O(D)$. The objective function to minimize cost for scalability is:

$$\operatorname*{argmin}_{t \in T} C(f,t)$$

$$\text{s.t } f \in F, \text{ and} \tag{2}$$

$$M(f,t) \times L(t) \geq U(f),$$

where the cost function $C(f,t)$ is defined in Eq. (1), T is the list of all instance types, F is the list of observed functions with resource types, $L(t)$ is the load of the instance type t, and $U(f)$ is the uppper bound. The time complexity to find the best t is $O(|T| \cdot D)$.

Now that we know the size of the target instance with the type t from Eq. (2), and the maximum number of instances, we need to define policies. As shown in Table 1, scalability policies need threshold (%), watching time (minutes) above the threshold, and scaling size unit (# of instances or % of the scaling group). Furthermore, we can configure the availability zone for geographical distribution. The threshold determines when we start triggering the resource usage alarm to further make decisions on scaling up and down. It is often defined as a percentage of the total resource capacity. For example, if CPU utilization goes over 80 %, we can count down to see whether the load sustains for pre-defined sustaining time.

We derive the threshold according to how fast loads reach the maximum capacity of the instance and how long it takes to provision an instance. While the increasing speed is defined in Sect. 4.2 with a parameter θ, the average (increasing) time to reach the maximum performance line from the threshold is noted as $\tau^+ = \frac{\sum_{i=0}^{|\theta^+|} hypotenus \times cos(\theta_i^+)}{|\theta^+|}$, where $|\theta^+|$ is the total number of increasing loads, and $hypotenus$ is the slope of the slope triangle, $\sqrt{(x_0 - x_1)^2 + (y_0 - y_1)^2}$. Therefore, the average (increasing) time should be within boundary of the provisioning time. The condition is noted as

$$\tau^+ > B(t), \tag{3}$$

where $B(t)$ is provisioning time (or booting time for the pool-based provisioning strategy) of the instance type t. However, since in reality, some workloads may increase too fast to meet this condition, we predictively provision instances even when small increase incurs. This means that FitScale sets a very low threshold and a short watching time. There are prior arts that use the predictive and autonomous scalability [6,11], so we do not focus on the predictive methods in this paper.

When the threshold is set, we need to configure the watching time starting when loads cross upward the threshold. The watching time is reset when loads cross downward the threshold. The watching time should also satisfy Eq. (3) in order to trigger to spin up more instances for increasing loads.

To scale up/down, we define a scaling size as either the number of instances or the percentage of the scaling group. We use the average number of expected instances from the pattern analysis. We count the added number of instances appended to the scaling group every time loads increase, then find the expected (average) number of instances added each time, and use that number as a scaling size.

If users are international, data centers distributed across globe can help serve requests better when applications are deployed close to users. Availability zones can be used to define geographical locations where the scalability is required. FitScale simply recommends potential data centers that can be included in the availability zones based on the network address of users.

7 Evaluation

Note that we do not intend to compare cloud platform performance of cloud providers since there are many prior arts to compare performance [10,13]. Instead, we focus on how transformation with appropriate scalability can help applications make use of scalability provided by clouds. We first case study applications of a real enterprise (on-premise) data center to analyze discovered data (Sect. 7.1). Then, we run experiments on the real cloud provider with the outcome from FitScale (Sect. 7.2). Lastly, we perform cost and performance analysis (Sect. 7.3).

7.1 Case Study: Legacy Data Center

We study a real (on-premise) data center with 2023 servers (physical and virtual), running 6737 applications to see some of pointers made in previous sections. Figure 5 depicts a cumulative density function of normalized resource usage to show how resources are used. CPU seems to be the most under-utilized resource and only about average 6 % is used. This is mainly because the CPU is a time sharing resource, which can go down to 0 % when it is not used. We have observed that CPU is heavily used in a certain period of time during day and night (up to 100 %). Disk is also under-utilized because users often reserve space for future uses. However, memory is well utilized because lots of cache data are stored both from applications and from operating systems.

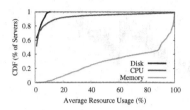

Fig. 5. CDF with resource usage shows CPU/disk is under-utilized, but memory is well utilized.

Table 2. 5 min average resource usage statistics of a machine (AVG = average, STD = standard deviation).

Resource	AVG	STD	MIN	MAX
CPU (%)	6.598	17.653	0	100
Network in (KB)	111851	172954	0	869880
Network out (KB)	89543	166628	0	829791
Disk read (KB)	53814	2149716	0	502722620
Disk write (KB)	53209	895461	0	395700840

Additionally, Table 2 shows some resource metrics (used in scalability policies) and some statistical results. As mentioned, CPU has low average number, but maximum usage shows that CPU is used heavily in a certain time period. Network and disk are also consistently used (average), and saturated in a certain period of time (maximum).

As previously shown in Table 1, cloud providers have different scaling metrics that can be used as a monitoring/triggering metric. It is worthwhile to identify what resource type is the most bottlenecked in the real data center. Figure 6(a) illustrates ratios of bottleneck resource types. Even though average CPU is unterutilized as depicted in Fig. 5, more than 43 % of servers have CPU as a bottleneck. The next highest bottleneck is the network as 17 %, and only 9 % of servers have disk as a bottleneck. The combination of resource types show some insights that C+N (CPU+Net) has high correlation, meaning when the network traffic increases, CPU load increases together. The rest of servers (about 30 %) not shown in any of bottleneck do not have any load changes.

While global companies maintain on-premise data centers across continents, it is important to decide how to scale out across geo-distributed locations. The geo-locations can be configured with scalability policies, and it is important to see where requests come from. Geographical distributions show where requests originate, which can determine the need for geographical scalability. Figure 6(b) depicts the datasets have most of requests from European countries (Italy, German), and some US.

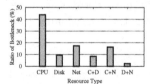

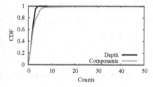

(a) Ratios of bottlenecked resource.

(b) Geographical distributions.

(c) Multi-tier apps with components with depth.

Fig. 6. Experimental results from legacy data center.

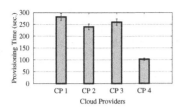
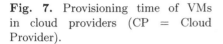
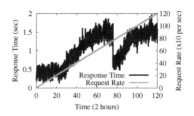

Fig. 7. Provisioning time of VMs in cloud providers (CP = Cloud Provider).

Fig. 8. Scaling experiment in the real cloud.

Business applications run as a multi-tier application spanning multiple servers with functional separation. In this multi-tier application, the high load may be propagated along server dependencies, thus it is important to figure out topological dependencies among servers. Figure 6(c) shows a statistical summary with CDF to show the number of components (instances) and depths (layers) of multi-tier applications. 98 % of multi-tier applications have less than 10 servers, and its depth is less than 7. The average number of components is 3, and the maximum is 105 with depth 1 (this was a monitoring server). The average number of depth is 2 and the maximum was 8.

7.2 Study in the Wild

As explained in Sect. 4, provisioning time may countervail benefits of elastic scalability due to slow responsiveness, and this is shown in Fig. 2. Therefore, FitScale takes into consideration the provisioning time when making policies. Figure 7 shows provisioning time of cloud providers, which spins up a small virtual machine with 2 CPUs, 4 GB memory, and 25 GB local disk. This corroborates the provisioning time is an important factor to consider in order to avoid any performance violation.

We repeat the same experiment as in Fig. 2 to see whether FitScale creates a good scalability policy for increasing loads. A simple web server with a database access in the backend is deployed in the cloud, and httperf is used to generate HTTP requests [14]. Figure 8 illustrates how well FitScale can create a scalability policy based on the source observation. The main difference between the two experiments is the level of threshold, which differentiates the provisioning time of each case.

7.3 Study in Laboratory

To expand the experiments to more diverse topologies than just two nodes, we take common topologies from the observation of the on-premise data center. Since 85 % of multi-tier applications consists of less than 5 servers as shown in Fig. 6(c), we consider up to 5 servers in each multi-tier application.

Figure 9 shows 5 common topologies observed from the on-premise data center. Black circles are able to scale horizontally and white circles are only able to scale vertically, meaning only resource size (# of CPUs, memory, etc.) can be adjusted due to application limitations.

We take multi-tier applications' patterns (topology, resource allocation/usage) from the on-premise data center dataset (Sect. 7.1) to simulate the scalability. The experiment is done in the Xen hypervisor in the local machine with 24 cores (Xeon CPU X5650 2.67 GHz) and 32 GB memory. The sample

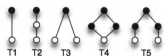

Fig. 9. Five common topologies of multi-tier applications.

request pattern (12 h) in Fig. 10(a) is from the dataset, and it is already smoothed with 5 min moving average. We compare FitScale with like-to-like (LTL) case, and aim to validate cost benefits and performance violation.

FitScale picks virtual machines based on the minimum cost as shown in Eq. (1). Figure 10(b) shows a relative cost of each topology that sets FitScale as a baseline. In all cases, LTL needs 5 times more operational expenditure and this continues to increase over time (note that we only look at 12 h). Reducing instance costs could result in a performance violation, but as shown in Fig. 10(c), the violation is minimum. We observe that performance violations occur because of initial memory caching (application behavior), not because of scalability policies.

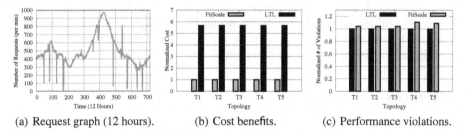

(a) Request graph (12 hours).   (b) Cost benefits.   (c) Performance violations.

Fig. 10. Performance evaluation with sample traffic by comparing with like-to-like (LTL) migration.

8   Related Works

Gallant et al. [5] survey relate work on scalability and propose a classification of elasticity methods based on four characteristics: scope (infrastructure or application), policy (manual or automatic, reactive or predictive), purpose (performance, cost, energy, capacity) and method (replication, redimensioning or migration). In the context of application scalability they note PaaS platforms, such as Aneka [2], where new container instances are executed to handle increase in the demand. In contrast, in Microsoft Azure, user defines resources used by applications. Hasan et al. [7] reasons that the current autoscaling policies consider resources from three separate domains, compute, storage and network, are acquired or released on-demand without regard to each other. Moreover, network resources are typically not auto-scaled. They propose a mechanism for an integrated auto-scaling system overcoming the above mentioned limitations. Vaquero et al. [18] present the survey of scalability techniques from PaaS and IaaS perspective. They observe that the Cloud benefits are centered around scalability of resources, and this is chiefly achieved by employing a set of service provider defined rules (that may be customized). Most of the prior art focuses on auto-scaling mechanisms, and our work addresses the gap in transforming the application to a scalable functional unit (such as container).

9   Conclusion

We looked at the problem of workload migration from a legacy environment to the cloud, and specifically the challenge of automatically identifying the right level of scalability, while at the same time minimizing the operational expenditure. This paper introduces the FitScale framework, develops a method for pattern discovery in application topologies and performance, and develops a method for target sizing and scaling policy assignment. FitScale reasons about functional and operational properties of applications, and derives the target sizing recommendation, coupled with the scalability policies. We evaluated FitScale in an on-premise data center with a dataset of 2023 servers/6737 applications. The experimental results show about 5 times cost reduction with minimum performance impact. As the scalability needs to continue to adapt to changing demands, our future work will focus on identifying how to predict future demands and deliver adequate recommendations.

References

1. Bai, K., Ge, N., Jamjoom, H., Jan, E., Renganarayana, L., Zhang, X.: What to discover before migrating to the cloud. In: 2013 IFIP/IEEE International Symposium on Integrated Network Management (IM 2013), Ghent, Belgium, May 27–31, 2013, pp. 320–327 (2013)
2. Calheiros, R.N., Vecchiola, C., Karunamoorthy, D., Buyya, R.: The aneka platform and qos-driven resource provisioning for elastic applications on hybrid clouds. Future Gener. Comput. Syst. **28**(6), 861–870 (2012). http://dx.doi.org/10.1016/j.future.2011.07.005
3. Casella, G., Berger, R.L.: Statistical Inference, vol. 2. Duxbury Press, Pacific Grove (2002)
4. Chiang, R.C., Hwang, J., Huang, H.H., Wood, T.: Matrix: achieving predictable virtual machine performance in the clouds. In: 11th International Conference on Autonomic Computing (ICAC 14), USENIX Association, Philadelphia, PA, pp. 45–56 (2014). https://www.usenix.org/conference/icac14/technical-sessions/presentation/chiang

5. Galante, G., de Bona, L.C.E.: A survey on cloud computing elasticity. In: Proceedings of the 2012 IEEE/ACM Fifth International Conference on Utility and Cloud Computing, UCC 2012, pp. 263–270 (2012). http://dx.doi.org/10.1109/UCC.2012.30
6. Gandhi, A., Dube, P., Karve, A., Kochut, A., Zhang, L.: Adaptive, model-driven autoscaling for cloud applications. In: 11th International Conference on Autonomic Computing (ICAC 14), USENIX Association, Philadelphia, PA, pp. 57–64 (2014). https://www.usenix.org/conference/icac14/technical-sessions/presentation/gandhi
7. Hasan, M.Z., Magana, E., Clemm, A., Tucker, L., Gudreddi, S.L.D.: Integrated and autonomic cloud resource scaling. In: 2012 IEEE Network Operations and Management Symposium (NOMS), pp. 1327–1334. IEEE (2012)
8. Hwang, J.: Towards beneficial transformation of enterprise workloads to hybrid clouds. IEEE Trans. Netw. Serv. Manag. **PP**(99), 1 (2016)
9. Hwang, J., Huang, Y.W., Vukovic, M., Anerousis, N.: Enterprise-scale cloud migration orchestrator. In: 2015 IFIP/IEEE International Symposium on Integrated Network Management (IM), pp. 1002–1007, May 2015
10. Hwang, J., Zeng, S., Wu, F., Wood, T.: A component-based performance comparison of four hypervisors. In: 2013 IFIP/IEEE International Symposium on Integrated Network Management (IM 2013), pp. 269–276, May 2013
11. Hwang, J., Wood, T.: Adaptive performance-aware distributed memory caching. In: Proceedings of the 10th International Conference on Autonomic Computing (ICAC 13), USENIX, San Jose, CA, pp. 33–43 (2013). https://www.usenix.org/conference/icac13/technical-sessions/presentation/hwang
12. Jermyn, J., Hwang, J., Bai, K., Vukovic, M., Anerousis, N., Stolfo, S.: Improving readiness for enterprise migration to the cloud. In: Proceedings of the Middleware Industry Track, pp. 5:1–5:7. Industry papers, ACM, New York (2014). http://doi.acm.org/10.1145/2676727.2676732
13. Li, A., Yang, X., Kandula, S., Zhang, M.: Cloudcmp: comparing public cloud providers. In: Proceedings of the 10th ACM SIGCOMM Conference on Internet Measurement, pp. 1–14. ACM (2010)
14. Mosberger, D., Jin, T.: httperfa tool for measuring web server performance. ACM SIGMETRICS Perform. Eval. Rev. **26**(3), 31–37 (1998)
15. Newman, S.: Building Microservices. O'Reilly Media Inc., Sebastopol (2015)
16. Slominski, A., Muthusamy, V., Khalaf, R.: Building a multi-tenant cloud service from legacy code with docker containers. In: 2015 IEEE International Conference on Cloud Engineering (IC2E), pp. 394–396, March 2015
17. Tivoli-Application-Dependency-Discovery-Manager (2016). http://www-03.ibm.com/software/products/en/tivoliapplicationdependencydiscoverymanager
18. Vaquero, L.M., Rodero-Merino, L., Buyya, R.: Dynamically scaling applications in the cloud. ACM SIGCOMM Comput. Commun. Rev. **41**(1), 45–52 (2011)

Monitoring-Based Task Scheduling in Large-Scale SaaS Cloud

Puheng Zhang$^{(\boxtimes)}$, Chuang Lin, Xiao Ma, Fengyuan Ren, and Wenzhuo Li

Tsinghua National Laboratory for Information Science and Technology,
Department of Computer Science and Technology,
Tsinghua University, Beijing 100084, China
zhangph14@mails.tsinghua.edu.cn, chlin@tsinghua.edu.cn

Abstract. With the increasing scale of SaaS and the continuous growth in server failures, task scheduling problems become more intricate, and both scheduling quality and scheduling speed raise further concerns. In this paper, we first propose a virtualized and monitoring SaaS model with predictive maintenance to minimize the costs of fault tolerance. Then with the monitored and predicted available states of servers, we focus on dynamic real-time task scheduling in large-scale heterogeneous SaaS, targeting at jointly optimizing the long-term performance benefits and energy costs in order to improve scheduling quality. We formulate a dynamic programming problem, where both the state and action spaces are too large to be solved by simple iterations. To address these issues, we take advantage of Machine Learning theory, and put forward an approximate dynamic programming algorithm. We utilize value function approximation and candidate-heuristic method to separately solve state and action explosions. Thus, computation complexity is significantly reduced and scheduling speed is greatly enhanced. Finally, we conduct experiments with both random simulation data and Google cloud trace-logs. Qos evaluations and comparisons demonstrate that our approach is effective and efficient under bursty requests and high throughputs.

Keywords: Multi-objective optimization · SaaS cloud · Data center · Task scheduling · Approximate dynamic programming

1 Introduction

Currently, services and businesses of SOFTWARE-AS-A-SERVICE (SaaS) cloud are exponentially growing, and one cloud data center is often built with thousands of servers, equipped with complex networking and power apparatuses [2]. SaaS brings vast opportunities and enormous benefits, but introduces many new requirements and challenges.

For one thing, a more efficient scheduling algorithm is in urgent need to cope with server failures. Due to inexpensive commodity hardware equipments, cloud service providers are faced with high hardware and software failures [19]. Thus, the maintenance culture is on the move [13]. In the era of "Internet of Things", all manner of equipments are embedded with intelligent sensors, and sophisticated

© Springer International Publishing Switzerland 2016
Q.Z. Sheng et al. (Eds.): ICSOC 2016, LNCS 9936, pp. 140–156, 2016.
DOI: 10.1007/978-3-319-46295-0_9

analysis can then be applied to describe the health status of servers and predict the needs for repairs in advance. Therefore, predictive maintenance, which means identifying problems and executing maintenance procedures beforehand, is strongly recommended and advocated recently [8]. It can effectively minimize unplanned asset downtime, make full use of resources, and reduce maintenance costs. With predictive maintenance, health states of servers can be real-time monitored and predicted, and scheduling a request to an unhealthy server can be avoided maximally. Otherwise, if unhealthy servers break down half way, unfinished tasks should be redone. No matter "Check pointing/Restart" or other reactive fault-resilient mechanisms will lead to huge waste of time and resources.

For another, two targets, scheduling quality and speed, deserve equal attentions. In order to maximize resistance to failures, provide good performance, save energy, and cut costs, careful placement of tasks is needed but it is always ignored by sampling methods. Meanwhile, fast scheduling is also important to guarantee user experience, especially for real-time tasks, but many complex multi-objective scheduling algorithms last long. Therefore, the two targets should be reconciled, and a new approach is required.

Besides, virtual machine (VM) migrations ought to be avoided as possible, for they are time consuming and energy intensive. In most cases, there are two motives of VM migrations, one for fault tolerance and the other for energy consolidation. If under the scheme of predictive maintenance, only VMs on healthy servers can be allocated with tasks to avoid faults. At the same time, if tasks are first distributed to VMs on the busy servers for energy consolidation purposes, VM migration incidents can be minimized. What is more, servers with all their VMs switched off can then hibernate, thus auto-scaling can be realized.

In theory, multi-objective task scheduling problem for large-scale cloud data centers is rather complicated. Not only should we arbitrate the tradeoff of multi factors such as performance and power, but also we need to solve the problems of state and decision explosions. Consider the real-time queue of each VM. Each queue length can take continuous values. The number of states for one server is uncountable and infinite, let alone the combination states of a huge number of servers. When tasks or requests arrive, they should be allocated to some of the massive available servers. The static distribution problem for thousands of servers itself is NP-hard, let alone the dynamic scheduling for various types of tasks. If we pursue long-term overall rewards, the method of Markov Decision Processes (MDP) is often used. However, it does not work in this scenario due to curses of dimensionality [15]. When the number of servers is very large, many classical algorithms may also not work well within an acceptable time limit.

Tasks scheduling is a classical problem in cloud data centers, and there have already been many algorithms to address this issue. Liu et al. [10] built an analytical framework to do the task scheduling in SaaS clouds, and Alahmadi et al. [1] developed a new, energy-aware task scheduling framework. However, they are both under the assumption of homogenous servers, and do not take into account failures of servers and deadlines of tasks. Hosseinimotlagh et al. [7] proposed a cooperative two-tier approach for scheduling real-time tasks to benefit both cloud providers and their customers. Mao et al. [11] put forward a task scheduling algorithm concerning the delay of the associated tasks in cloud computing systems. Zhu et al. [21] developed an energy-aware scheduling algorithm in cloud for real-time, periodic, independent tasks in virtualized clouds. Nevertheless, they do not consider metrics of throughput, and energy consolidation for various types of tasks. Cheng et al. [3] proposed an energy-saving task scheduling algorithm based on the queuing theory. Yet, it relied on the assumption that the coming tasks must conform to an established distribution. Moreover, most limited the number of servers, for multi-objective scheduling in large-scale commercial SaaS can not be efficiently conducted by their algorithms.

Consequently, all previous studies cannot simultaneously address all the requirements and challenges mentioned above. Motivated by the need of high efficient real-time tasks scheduling algorithms in large-scale heterogeneous SaaS cloud, we put forward a heuristic approximate dynamic programming (H-ADP) algorithm to jointly optimize the performance and power with predictive maintenance. The main contributions of this work are as follows:

(1) We put forward a virtualized and monitoring model of SaaS cloud with predictive maintenance, based on which we constitute a scheduling rule to minimize the costs and overheads caused by fault tolerance.
(2) We introduce popular Machine Learning theory into solving traditional stochastic dynamic programming (SDP) problems, and propose a novel task scheduling algorithm, simultaneously considering scheduling speed and quality. Both random synthetic data and real trace-logs are used in experiments to demonstrate the applicability and superiority of our approach under bursty requests and high throughputs.
(3) We solve the problems of both state and action explosions in task scheduling problems. Firstly, we carefully design the basis function with the method of value function approximation (VFA), by which state values can be parameterized and recursively estimated step by step. And in this way, we effectively solve the optimization problems of infinite states. Secondly, we develop a candidate-selection heuristic algorithm in the procedure of policy search, and effectively solve the optimization problems that contain massive decision variables. Henceforth, we make it possible to conduct time-effective multi-objective optimizations for SDP problems with extremely large state and action spaces.

The remainder of this paper is organized as follows. In Sect. 2, we demonstrate the model of a heterogeneous SaaS cloud, and formulate the scheduling problem as an SDP problem. Section 3 proposes the Heuristic ADP algorithm. Simulations and experiments are conducted to make Qos evaluations in Sect. 4. Section 5 concludes the paper.

2   Problem Formulation

In this section, we illustrate models and notions used in this paper, introduce predictive maintenance strategy, and formulate an SDP problem for task scheduling issues in SaaS.

2.1 System Model

A virtualized and monitoring model for SaaS cloud can be described in Fig. 1 [10]. A cloud data center is comprised of J heterogeneous servers, each of which is virtualized as I types of VMs to process the corresponding I different types of tasks. We set C_j as the processing capacity of the jth server, which is measured in (Million Instructions Per Second) MIPS. Without loss of generality, we assume a server's processing capacity is fairly distributed among its I hosted VMs in this work [10]. Then the processing capacity of each VM is $1/I$ of the total processing capacity of its hosting server. Each VM is equipped with a buffer queue, and we define the queue length of type-i VM on Server j, $Q_{i,j}$, as the total volume of tasks waiting to be processed, and it is measured in Million Instructions (MI). $R = \{R_1, \ldots, R_k, \ldots, R_K\}$ characterizes K independent and non-preemptive requests. Each coming task can be marked as a

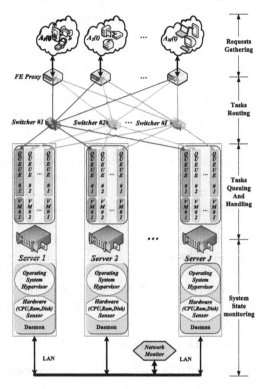

Fig. 1. A virtualized and monitoring SaaS model under predictive maintenance

four tuple, and $R_k = (ArrTime, Type, Size, Deadline)^T$. $ArrTime$ means the arriving time of a task, and $Type$ represents the service type. $Size$ denotes the length of instructions measured in Million Instructions, and $Deadline$ indicates the point of time before which the task must be completed.

When no hardware and software failures happen, the normal serving flow is as follows. Customer requests or tasks are first collected by adjacent front-end proxies, and then distributed to the relative type of request routing switchers. A switcher is responsible for distributing a specified type of requests to proper servers. Then the corresponding type of VM-queues on each server, buffer and pool the tasks. Corresponding VMs handle the tasks and return results. The serving flows for each type of tasks are marked with different colors in Fig. 1. If a task cannot be finished within its deadline, it will be abandoned and result into a penalty.

2.2   Scheduling with Predictive Maintenance Strategy

In practice, we ought to consider probabilities of various kinds of failures in SaaS. Currently, modern processors are equipped with sensors that can be used to monitor CPU temperature, fan speeds, and other parameters [9]. One of the most commonly used examples is "Lm-sensors" [20]. Operating systems and VM software can also be monitored by hypervisors [18]. Additionally, many sophisticated patents and products have involved into the network monitoring [12]. These sensors can be equipped as described in Fig. 1. So the overall health states of servers can be real-time monitored and predicted by virtue of the comprehensive analysis of hardware, software and network sensor feedbacks. Specific calculation procedure for predicting health states of servers is illustrated in [4]. We define $Sa = (Sa_1, Sa_2, \cdots, Sa_J)^T$ as the predicted result of server available states, and each element can be "1" or "0", respectively denoting a server is available or not to receive tasks.

Scheduling with predictive maintenance strategy can be summarized in one phrase: only assigning applications to the servers that are "healthy" enough to handle and finish the tasks. In other words, after predictions, if one server is imminent to break down because of hardware, software or network reasons, and whatever the reason, new tasks are not permitted to be allocated to that server and it must receive repairs or treatment right away. When the server is fixed out and all states return to normal, it can receive tasks as before.

2.3   An SDP Problem

A standard SDP problem is usually comprised of 5 ingredients as follows.

Decision Time Epochs. Decisions are executed at the end of each time slot, i.e., at $t = \tau, 2\tau, 3\tau \cdots$, and τ is the decision time interval.

States. State S_t can be categorized as two components: endogenous states matrix Q_t, which change with different actions, and exogenous states tuple $EX_t = (R_t, Sa_t, C)$, which are only determined by external factors, irrelevant to specific actions. Endogenous state matrix Q_t characterizes the queue length of all VMs on all servers at time t, and it is a matrix comprised of elements $Q_{t,i,j}$, which means the type-i VM queue length on server j. $Q_{t,i,j}$ varies over time due to the arriving tasks and serving rates. Exogenous state R_t denotes the coming tasks during one time slot. Vector $Sa_t = (Sa_{t1}, Sa_{t2}, \ldots, Sa_{tJ})^T$ captures the available state of each server at each time slot. Vector C represents the processing capacity of servers mentioned in Sect. 2.1, and it does not change with time.

Suppose that a data center is comprised of 10000 nodes, each node is in possession of a buffer queue, and the length of each queue is separated into 1000 discrete values. Suppose there are totally 8 types of requests, and a VM can be in a binary state of available or not. Then the total number of states would be $(1000 \times 2)^{10000 \times 8}$, absolutely an astronomical number! Moreover, the queue length of each VM can take continuous values, so the number of states is uncountable and infinite.

Actions. At each system state S_t, there is a corresponding control action $x_t(S_t)$. At each time epoch t, considering n_t tasks ($n_{t,i}$ tasks of type-i) are coming, and then the decision (action) is to assign each task to the proper VM among huge number of nodes. The actions at each time slot comprise a set of n_t-dimensional vector, i.e. $(100, 2098, 298, \ldots, 3980)$, and the lth element represents a server index for assigning the lth task. Under the same assumption of a cloud data center with 10000 servers, then one task may have 10000 choices, and let $n_t = 5000$. Therefore, for only a time period of 100 time slots, the size of action spaces would become 100×10000^{5000}, an astronomical number again!

Transition Function. Genetic transition function can be described as $S_{t+1} = S^M(S_t, x_t, Ex_{t+1})$ and the superscript M stands for "model" [15]. In this work, we focus on the transitions of endogenous state matrix Q_t. The dynamic forward transition function of each element in Q_t can be written as in Eq. (1). If the lth type-i task is allocated to server j at time t, $R_{t,i,l,j}$ equals the size of that task, otherwise, $R_{t,i,l,j} = 0$. Equation (1) shows that the queue length at time $t+1$ is associated with both the coming tasks and the processing capacity of each VM during time t.

$$Q_{t+1,i,j} = max \left\{ \left(Q_{t,i,j} + \sum_{l=1}^{n_{t,i}} R_{t,i,l,j} - \frac{C_{t,j}}{I} \right), 0 \right\} \tag{1}$$

Rewards and Value Function. Rewards of S_t means the income or cost when choosing an action in a given state at time t. Value function of S_t denotes the supremum over all policies of the expected total rewards from decision epoch t onwards [16].

Rewards. The rewards gained by the SaaS cloud can be defined in many ways in accordance with the engineering requirements in business. Whatever the reward formula, they all can be applied into our algorithm. In this work, we focus on the performance benefit, energy consumption, as well as penalty for unfinished tasks.

The performance benefit is in proportion to throughputs and has an inverse relationship with the response time [14]. At each time epoch, if task l of type i is handled, throughput equals the size of the task, measured in MIPS. Response time T can be calculated as Eq. (2). The performance benefit is in proportion to throughput and in inverse proportion to response time. Performance benefit of n_t tasks in the period of time $[t, t+\tau]$ can be expressed as Eq. (3), where $n_{t,i}$ means the number of type-i tasks, and σ is a constant coefficient.

$$T_{t,i,l,j} = \frac{Q_{t,i,j} + R_{t,i,l,j}}{C_{i,j}/I} \tag{2}$$

$$BR_t = \sum_{i=1}^{I} \sum_{j=1}^{J} \sum_{l=1}^{n_{t,i}} \sigma \left(\frac{R_{t,i,l,j}}{T_{t,i,l,j}} \right) \tag{3}$$

$$P = P_{idle} + \mu \left(P_{busy} - P_{idle} \right) \tag{4}$$

In addition, power consumption of a server grows linearly with the growth of the CPU utilization from the idle to fully utilized state, as is found in [5]. It can be expressed in Eq. (4), where P is the estimated power consumption of one node. P_{idle} and P_{busy} respectively represent the power consumed when the server is idle and fully utilized. μ is a parameter in proportion to the CPU utilization. Worth to mention, there may be some other forms of expressions for the assessment of power consumption, and they all can be applied to this algorithm after slight alterations to VFA. In SaaS, when all VM queues of a server are empty, the server may sleep or hibernate, and then P_{idle} of this server equals 0. Otherwise, P_{idle} is a fixed value and does not change with the number of VMs at work in the server. As a result, VM consolidation, which refers to aggregating VMs on minimal physical nodes, provides a good way to save energy. Power consumption of the jth server at time t, $P_{t,j}$ can be calculated by Eq. (4). μ can be indirectly but easily deduced from matrix Q_t. The overall energy consumption during the period of time $[t, t + \tau]$ can be calculated as $EC_t = \sum_{j=1}^{J} P_{t,j}\tau$.

Finally, the penalty of tasks, which cannot be handled within their deadlines, should be subtracted. Assume there are $n_{t,fail}$ tasks unfinished during the period of epoch t, then the relative penalty can be denoted as Eq. (5), where δ can be both a constant or a function changing with time or throughput.

$$PE_t = n_{t,fail} \cdot \delta \tag{5}$$

To sum up, the overall rewards in the period of $[t, t + \tau]$ can be calculated as $R_t = BR_t - EC_t - PE_t$.

Objective Value Function. Let $x_t^\pi(S_t)$ denotes the decision made in state S_t under policy π. $\pi = (x_0, x_1, x_2, \dots)$ specifies a series of decisions made at one time slot. Then our objective is to find the best policy $\pi^* \in \Pi$ with the largest expected total discounted rewards over the infinite horizon [16]:

$$V^{\pi^*} = \max \mathbb{E}^\pi \left\{ \lim_{N \to \infty} \sum_{t=1}^{T} \gamma^{t-1} R_t(S_t, x_t^\pi(S_t)) \right\}. \tag{6}$$

$\gamma \in [0, 1)$ is a discount factor, which measures the value at time t of one unit reward received at time $t+\tau$ [16]. Therefore, one unit of reward received t periods later, only has the present value of γ^t and it is discounted. Equation (6) can also be expressed by the recursive Bellman Equations:

$$V_t(S_t) = \max_{x_t \in X_t} \left\{ R_t(S_t, x_t) + \gamma \mathbb{E}\{V_{t+1}(S_{t+1}) | S_t\} \right\}. \tag{7}$$

Altogether, if different types of tasks are assigned to as least number of servers as possible, there would be more servers that can hibernate, and then the overall P_{idle} will be low. However, in that case, the queue length of each VM at work will be long, which leads to high response delay and low profit of performance.

Algorithm 1. Outline of H-ADP algorithm

INPUT: Sample path ω, server available states Sa, CPU processing capacity of servers C, an iteration number T, feature basis functions $\phi_f(S)$, a discounted factor λ.
OUTPUT: Recursively estimated parameter θ_T.

1: Initialize θ_1, $\overline{V}(S)$ and$\phi_f(S)$ for all states.
2: Choose an initial state S_1.
3: **for** $t = 1, 2, \ldots, T$ **do**
4:    **if** $t > 1$ **then**
5:       Derive $\phi_f(S)$ from Q_t.
6:       Calculate $\overline{V}_t^x(S_{t-1}^x|\theta_{t-1})$ by Eq. (9).
7:    **end if**
8:    Solve Eq. (8), and let x_t' the value of x_t that solve the maximization problem.
9:    Change PDSV S_t^x by substituting x_t' into $S_t^x = S_{t+1} = S^M(S_t, x_t, Ex_{t+1})$.
10:   Compute $\hat{v}_t(S_t)$ using Eq. (8).
11:   Update θ_t using Eq. (11).
12:   Choose ω_{t+1} and update S_{t+1} with Eq. (1).
13: **end for**
14: return θ_T.

Accordingly, to jointly arbitrate the tradeoff between performance and energy efficiency is a daunting and arduous work especially when the number of servers is large. Besides, exogenous probability distributions of state R_t and Sa_t may not be known beforehand in practice, so the expectation in Eq. (7) cannot be calculated directly. Thus, we put forward H-ADP algorithm in the next section.

3 Heuristic ADP Algorithm

In this section, we first introduce the framework of H-ADP, as is shown in Algorithm 1. Then the VFA approach by virtue of basis functions is illustrated. At last, we elaborate the candidate heuristic (C-H) method.

3.1 Outline of the Algorithm

Firstly, in order to take advantage the time-sequenced sample data path ω_t, which represents exogenous values at time t, the algorithm should step forward in time. In classical dynamic programming, it proceeds by stepping backward in time, and Eq. (7) has to be solved for each state S_t, such as in MDP. But the states are infinite in this paper, and an exhaustive algorithm does not work. Thus, we first extract features (a term widely used in the field of artificial intelligence), and construct an approximate value function to appraise the value of all states. We then propose a heuristic method to find the global optimal action in line 8 of Algorithm 1 under each sample. These are the two important steps to simplify the computation, which are separately illustrated in Sects. 3.2 and 3.3.

Secondly, to conveniently compute the expectation in Eq. (7), we introduce concepts of post-decision states variables (PDSVs) S_t^x. S_t^x means the system state at time t immediately after making decision x, but before time $t+1$. After a decision is made in line 8, then PDSV is equivalent to the state value at the next time slot, $S_t^x = S_{t+1}$. With PDSVs, the hard-to-calculate expectation in Eq. (7) can be eliminated, and Bellman equations can be rewritten as Eq. (8).

$\hat{v}_t(S_t)$ represents the sample values at time t, and $\overline{V}_{t+1}^x(S_t^x)$ denotes approximate post-decision value which equals the state value at the next time epoch. $\overline{V}_{t+1}^x(S_t^x)$ might be captured in the parameter form using the basis functions $\phi_f(S)$. $f \in F$, where f is a feature, and $\phi_f(S)$ is a vector of feature values that can be calculated by extracting feature information from the state Q_t. The approximate value function $\overline{V}_t^x(S_{t-1}^x)$ might be rewritten as Eq. (9), where θ is an $|F|$ dimensional vector. Specific definitions of $\phi_f(S)$ in SaaS cloud are described in Sect. 3.2.

$$\hat{v}_t(S_t) = \max_{x_t \in X_t} \{R_t(S_t, x_t) + \gamma \overline{V}_{t+1}^x(S_t^x)\} \tag{8}$$

$$\overline{V}_t^x(S_{t-1}^x|\theta) = \sum_{f \in F} \theta_t \phi_f(S_{t-1}^x) \tag{9}$$

Thirdly, we use a stochastic gradient updating strategy, which stems from Machine Learning theory, to progressively train vector θ following ω_t. Vector θ represents parameters for estimating feature values. We aim at finding the most suitable θ^* that produces the minimum expected squared error (MESE) between $\hat{v}_t(S_t)$ and $\overline{V}_t^x(S_{t-1}^x|\theta)$, as is illustrated in Eq. (10). And θ can be updated step by step to approach θ^*, as is shown in Eq. (11). α_{t-1} means step size, and ∇ denotes the Nabla Operator for gradient calculation.

$$\theta^* = \arg\min_{\theta} \mathbb{E}\left\{ \frac{(\hat{v}_t - \overline{V}_t^x(S_{t-1}^x|\theta))^2}{2} \right\} \tag{10}$$

$$\begin{aligned} \theta_t &= \theta_{t-1} - \alpha_{t-1}\big(\hat{v}_t(S_t) - \overline{V}_t^x(S_{t-1}^x|\theta_{t-1})\big)\nabla_\theta \overline{V}_t^x(S_{t-1}^x|\theta_{t-1}) \\ &= \theta_{t-1} - \alpha_{t-1}\big(\hat{v}_t(S_t) - \overline{V}_t^x(S_{t-1}^x|\theta_{t-1})\big)\phi(S_{t-1}^x) \end{aligned} \tag{11}$$

Fourthly, we should care more about the step size α_{t-1}. To choose the proper step size is really an art form which is based on experience and specific problem structures. A step size that is too large can produce unstable behaviors. However, if it is small, the procedure of regression may be too slow. In general, it should satisfy the constraints in Eq. (12) [15]. Several ways of setting the step sizes may be possible, and we will carefully design it in Sect. 4.

$$\begin{cases} \displaystyle\sum_{t=1}^{\infty} \alpha_{t-1} = \infty \\[2ex] \displaystyle\sum_{t=1}^{\infty} (\alpha_{t-1})^2 < \infty \\[2ex] \alpha_{t-1} \geq 0 \\[1ex] t = 1, 2, \ldots \end{cases} \tag{12}$$

Algorithm 2. Candidate-Heuristic algorithm

INPUT: A request Runit, estimated parameter θ, queue state of VMs Q, CPU processing capacity C, number of candidate Nc, server available states Sa, a discounted factor λ.
OUTPUT: The optimal server index p of the target VM.

1: $i = Runit.Type$.
2: Create and derive a J-dimensional vector Nen, and Nen_j represents the number of VM engagement excluding type i on server j.
3: In server comparisons, set the weighting orders from high to low as C_j, Nen_j and $Q_{t,i,j}$.
4: Find the indexes of top Nc healthy nodes giving priority to severs with the highest C_j.
5: In server comparisons, set the weighting orders from high to low as $Q_{t,i,j}$, C_j and Nen_j.
6: Find the indexes of top Nc healthy nodes giving priority to VMs with the least $Q_{t,i,j}$.
7: In server comparisons, set the weighting orders from high to low as Nen_j, $Q_{t,i,j}$ and C_j.
8: Find the indexes of top Nc healthy nodes giving priority to servers that more VMs are engaged (with the highest Nen_j).
9: Merge the indexes of $3Nc$ candidates by removing duplication items.
10: Rank the rewards of these candidates with Eq. (8) and (9), and choose the best indexed by p.
11: Return p.

3.2 Value Function Approximation

As is illustrated in Eq. (9), approximated value function of each state can be derived with live updated θ_t and $\phi_f(S)$, which are tailored for specific scenarios. In the task scheduling scenario, rewards during one time epoch, are mainly comprised of two parts, performance and energy. Performance benefit for the type-i tasks is in proportion to the sum of available CPU processing capacity on all type-i VMs ($Avai\_CPU(i)$), and is in negative proportion to the average queue length of type-i ($Ave\_Q(i)$). Energy consumption for the type-i tasks is also in proportion to $Avai\_CPU(i)$, and in proportion to the number of all physical machines that are at work (N_PM_on). So if there are I type of tasks, $2I + 1$ features are needed. Thus $\phi_f(S)$ can be expressed as Eq. (13). Each element in $\phi_f(S)$ at each time t can be easily derived from endogenous state Q_t.

$$
\phi_f(S) = \begin{pmatrix} Avai\_CPU(1) \\ Avai\_CPU(2) \\ \dots \\ Avai\_CPU(I) \\ Ave\_Q(1) \\ Ave\_Q(2) \\ \dots \\ Ave\_Q(I) \\ N\_PM\_on \end{pmatrix}
\tag{13}
$$

3.3 Candidate Heuristic Algorithm

Generally, there are two ways of finding the optimum decision in line 8 of Algorithm 1. First, we can compute the complicated rewards of all actions, and then rank and find the best. However, the action space is extremely large, so this method is too intricate to implement in practice. The other method is to equivalently transform it into classical resource allocation problems, using linear programming (LP) approach. The number of variables is equal to that of servers, and there are thousands of servers in a large-scale SaaS cloud. Thus, it is also infeasible to solve this LP in an acceptable time. Accordingly, an elegant and ingenious method tailored for the task scheduling problem is in urgent need.

After analyzing the optimal choices of servers for tasks, target VMs usually possess three characteristics: (1) with high processing capacity to diminish response time and increase profits, (2) with low queue length for the same reason, (3) on servers where more different type of VMs are at work. Here are illustrations for (3): If three types of requests are assigned to VMs on three distinct servers, all servers will be on. Yet, if they are allocated to VMs on only one server, the other two can hibernate. It is similar to the reason of VM consolidations.

Therefore, in order to find the optimal nodes, there are mainly three strategies, each focusing on one characteristic mentioned above. In each strategy, we can choose Nc candidates for comparisons. Then we merge the indexes of $3Nc$ candidates by removing duplication items. Nc should be set according to specific circumstances. If Nc is large, there will be more chances of finding the best candidate, but higher computation complexity, and vice versa. Usually, $Nc = 5$ is enough. At last, we compute and rank the rewards of all these candidates in order to choose the best. In this approach, for every task, we reduce calculating the complex rewards of thousands of nodes into computing rewards of only a few candidates. As the number of requests accumulates with time, the computation complexity can be greatly reduced. We compute the state values with Eqs. (8) and (9), simultaneously considering current and future circumstances.

The whole algorithm is demonstrated in Algorithm 2. It is worth noting that, in line 4, 6 and 8, only "healthy" nodes (indicated by $Sa_{t,j} = 1$), can be listed and selected. Besides, we do the task scheduling in consideration of the deadline of each request, and if all VMs are unable to finish a task before its deadline, the request will be marked and rejected. Of course, unhandled tasks will bring additional losses, which can be calculated in Eq. (5).

4   Qos Evaluation

In this section, we conduct simulations in Matlab 2012a, on a PC with i5 processor at 3.5 GHz and memory size of 4GB. After steps of approximations in Sect. 3, complicated scheduling procedure of each task is simplified into comparing metrics of only a few candidates with elementary operations. Computation complexity is reduced from $O(J^2)$ to $O(3Nc)$, and $J = 10000, Nc = 5$ in this work. It is obvious that scheduling speed is no more a problem with modern computers. Due to space limit, demonstration for scheduling speed is omitted here. We focus on evaluating scheduling quality of the "oversimplified" H-ADP. We make evaluations based on both random synthetic workloads and Google trace-logs of real-world data. Due to the large scale of servers, many classical multi-objective algorithms are unavailable. Thus, we conduct comparisons of our approach with two commonly used algorithms in task scheduling of data centers, and they are load-balancing (L-B) and randomized-selection (R-S) algorithms.

4.1   Simulations on Random Workloads

In order to testify the generality and versatility of H-ADP algorithm, we conduct simulations under various input parameters in high throughputs.

Rules of Generating Main Input Parameters.

Number of servers: Due to characteristics of large-scale SaaS cloud, we set the number of nodes $J = 10000$ throughout this paper.

Task type: In most cases, the task type I is an integer not more than 10.

Task count: The number of coming tasks per unit of time is assumed to conform to Poisson distribution with a mathematical expectation $\lambda \in [10^3, 5 \times 10^3]$. Then the total number of tasks arriving during time t is λt.

Task size: The task sizes of all types are assumed to conform to exponential distribution, each with the expectation $ER \in [5 \times 10^4, 10^5]$ MI.

Task deadline: The deadline of all types of tasks is designated as $d = fb + v$ [19], where fb is a fixed base value, and v conforms to exponential or uniform distribution. We may set $fb = 15$, and set $E(v) = 20$.

Server available state: According to [17], we assume that the mean time to failure (MTTF) of each server conforms to Weibull distribution. We set the shape parameter as 0.8, and scale parameter as 500. In [17], it also argues that repair time is better modeled by a lognormal distribution. Thus, in this simulation, we assume the mean and standard deviation of the variable's natural logarithm respectively equal 4 and 0.9. Thus, as time goes by, the available state of each server may alternatively change along with its MTTF and repair time.

Server capacity: In this work, as in most data centers, we assume that servers are divided into several categories of servers, and servers of the same category possess the same processing capacity. Then the capacity of each server can be chosen from a set of configurations.

Step size: Three methods [15] of setting the step size are used in this paper. (1) In a constant rule, α_{t-1} takes a fixed value all the time. (2) In a harmonic way, α_{t-1} is large at the beginning, but gets smaller with the increase of t. Step size $\alpha_{t-1} = b/(b + t)$ at time t, where b is a fixed base value. (3) In a search-then-converge (STC) learning rule, it produces delayed learning compared with harmonic step size. Step size can be calculated as $\alpha_{t-1} = \alpha_0(\frac{a}{t} + b))/(\frac{a}{t} + b + t^\varphi)$. Under the constant rule, we set the step size as 0.01, simultaneously ensuring the convergence rate and stability of the algorithm. Under the last two rules, we can adjust parameters along with arriving tasks, and if we get divergent results, it demonstrates that the step size is so large that we should adjust parameters to diminish the step size, and vice versa.

A Typical Simulation and Analysis. In our first experiment, we set $\lambda = 3 \times 10^3$, $I = 6$ and $ER = 8 \times 10^3$ MI. The corresponding step sizes changing with iterations under three rules are depicted in Fig. 2. Under each rule of step sizes, we can recursively get the convergence of all the 13 elements in vector θ. Random examples, $\theta(Ave\_CPU(1))$, $\theta(Ave\_Q(2))$ and $\theta(N\_PM\_on)$, are separately plotted in Figs. 3, 4 and 5. In the constant step-size rule, as the step size

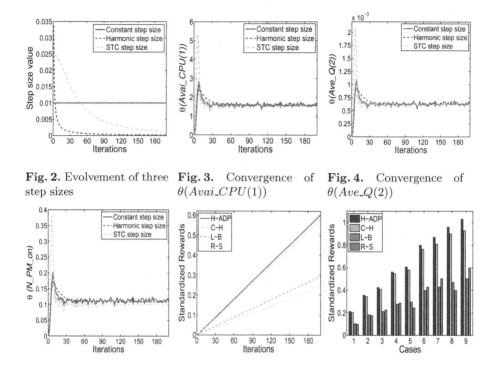

Fig. 2. Evolvement of three step sizes

Fig. 3. Convergence of $\theta(Avai\_CPU(1))$

Fig. 4. Convergence of $\theta(Ave\_Q(2))$

Fig. 5. Convergence of θ (N_PM_on)

Fig. 6. Rewards changing with iterations

Fig. 7. Overall rewards in all cases

does not diminish with iterations, all the curves may slightly oscillate in the end. Meanwhile, in the harmonic and STC step-size rules, the curves are steep at the beginning and the peaks are pretty high especially under the STC step size, but both curves are relatively flat in the end.

What can be summarized from these figures are as follows: (1) All parameters (elements) in vector θ experience similar evolving processes; (2) Our approach can quickly extract information from raw data, and only after 30 iterations, all the curves oscillate around relatively fixed values; (3) Each parameter in θ respectively converges into consistent values, despite of the different processes under three different step sizes; (4) The convergence results of each parameter under three step sizes are slightly different.

Under different step-size rules, each element converges into similar results, which demonstrates the validity and correctness of our algorithm. Besides, due to the different convergent values under three step-size rules, we always set the final result of $\overline{\theta}$ as the average value in practice. In this simulation, $\overline{\theta}$ is a 13-dimentional vector expressed in Eq. (14). All elements are different due to various incoming workloads of each task type.

$$\overline{\theta} = (1.54292, 1.65964, 1.76832, 1.64586, 1.45819, 1.69651,$$
$$0.00057, 0.00062, 0.00066, 0.00059, 0.00058, 0.00046, 0.10530)^T \quad (14)$$

Utilizing the trained vector $\bar{\theta}$, we can conduct H-ADP algorithm for task scheduling. Meanwhile, the C-H algorithm can be used standalone in scheduling tasks as a kind of myopic or greedy algorithm. There are also two commonly used algorithms, load-balancing and randomized-selection. For the same incoming workloads, we simultaneously run four algorithms. Four overall rewards changing with iterations are respectively depicted in Fig. 6.

We can clearly see that all rewards are approximately in linear growth over time but with different slopes. Rewards of H-ADP and C-H are remarkably higher than L-B and R-S at each time epoch. H-ADP is in pursuit of long-term profits, and it takes into consideration of outcomes for both current and future decisions. Meanwhile, the C-H algorithm makes decisions only in accordance with immediate circumstances. Therefore, the overall reward of H-ADP in the long term is superior to that of C-H, and the gap between them cumulates with time. For a SaaS cloud that is in service day after night, the incremental benefit of H-ADP over the other three approaches will be quite substantial.

Comparative Experiments and Analysis.
Next, we do simulations under different λ that increases from 1000 to 5000 with steps of 500. Meanwhile, we randomly set the number of task types and expected size of requests in their respective ranges mentioned above in this section. Thus, there are 9 cases altogether, and the main parameters are depicted in Table 1.

In each case, we conduct H-ADP algorithm under three step sizes, and get similar convergence curves of all elements in θ as Figs. 3, 4 and 5. Besides, all the four algorithms possess similar reward changing curves that increase with iterations as in Fig. 6. As space is limited, both θ and reward curves changing with iterations are omitted here. We only care about the total rewards after 200 iterations. Figure 7 shows that the overall rewards of the four approaches keep an ascending trend with the increase of λ (task count per unit of time). The comparison results and the causes are in accordance with the previous experiment analyzed above. A group of experiments demonstrates that our approach is superior in all circumstances. We can also discover that with the increase of λ, the gaps between the rewards of H-ADP and C-H are becoming more apparent. Meanwhile, the rewards of L-B and the rewards of R-S are alternately higher than each other, and which is higher depends on specific random data of R_t and Sa_t in each case.

Table 1. Workload parameters in all cases

Case	λ	I	ER (MI)
1	10^3	5	10^4
2	1.5×10^3	3	8×10^3
3	2×10^3	4	8×10^3
4	2.5×10^3	10	9×10^3
5	3×10^3	6	7×10^3
6	3.5×10^3	7	7.5×10^3
7	4×10^3	5	6.5×10^3
8	4.5×10^3	9	8.5×10^3
9	5×10^3	4	5.5×10^3

4.2 Evaluation Based on Google Trace-Logs

The group of simulations above demonstrates the Qos improvement and strong applicability of our approach in random synthetic workloads. In order to verify the feasibility of H-ADP in practical use, we further conduct experiments

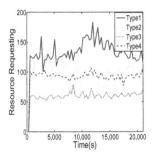 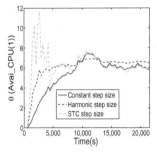 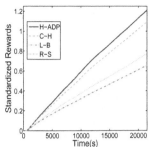

Fig. 8. Resource requesting statistics for Google trace-logs

Fig. 9. Convergence of $\theta(Ave\_CPU(1))$ with Google trace-logs

Fig. 10. Rewards changing with time with Google trace-logs

with Google cloud trace-logs [6]. The trace-logs describe workload information of 25 million tasks that span 29 days. It is particularly difficult and not essential to utilize all the log data, so we select the data set of *Trace Version1*, which recorded a 7-h period of traces containing 4 type of 3,535,031 tasks. Each task is marked with arriving time, type, normalized resource consuming and so on. Total standardized resource requesting of each type of tasks at each time epoch are depicted in Fig. 8. We can see clearly that the coming tasks of each type are not evenly distributed and accompanied with bursty requests. Therefore, it is hard to discover any distribution law of the trace-logs, and we need to take advantage of Machine Learning theory.

With H-ADP, we can also recursively get the convergence curves of all the 9 ($2 \times 4 + 1 = 9$) elements in vector θ under three rules of step sizes. As real workloads are disordered and unpredictable, the curves fluctuate more acutely but they all converge in the end. Convergence for $\theta(Ave\_CPU(1))$ with three step sizes is plotted as an example in Fig. 9. We can then calculate the average $\bar{\theta}$ for H-ADP and do algorithm comparisons.

Our approach does not rely on pre-knowing the probability distribution function (PDF) of requests, and H-ADP can learn recursively from unpredictable and bursty requests, but myopic algorithms can not. Therefore, H-ADP is remarkably superior to C-H in terms of rewards as time accumulates, as is demonstrated in Fig. 10. Again, these two approaches significantly outperform L-B and R-S.

5   Conclusions

In this paper, we tackle the real-time task scheduling problems in SaaS cloud. We first construct an SDP problem and analyze the ingredients. With reference to Machine Learning theory, we put forward an ADP algorithm combined with candidate-heuristic method. Comprehensive experiments and comparisons are conducted to evaluate the algorithm. Results demonstrate that the proposed work provides an elegant and effective approach to handle complex scheduling problems in large-scale heterogeneous SaaS.

Acknowledgments. This work is supported by the National Natural Science Foundation of China (No. 61472199 and No. 61370132).

References

1. Alahmadi, A., Che, D., Khaleel, M., Zhu, M.M., Ghodous, P.: An innovative energy-aware cloud task scheduling framework. In: 2015 IEEE 8th International Conference on Cloud Computing, pp. 493–500. IEEE (2015)
2. Barroso, L.A., Clidaras, J., Hölzle, U.: The datacenter as a computer: an introduction to the design of warehouse-scale machines. Synth. Lect. Comput. Archit. **8**(3), 1–154 (2013)
3. Cheng, C., Li, J., Wang, Y.: An energy-saving task scheduling strategy based on vacation queuing theory in cloud computing. Tsinghua Sci. Technol. **20**(1), 28–39 (2015)
4. Egwutuoha, I.P., Cheny, S., Levy, D., Selic, B., Calvo, R.: Energy efficient fault tolerance for high performance computing (HPC) in the cloud. In: 2013 IEEE Sixth International Conference on Cloud Computing, pp. 762–769. IEEE (2013)
5. Fan, X., Weber, W.D., Barroso, L.A.: Power provisioning for a warehouse-sized computer. In: ACM SIGARCH Computer Architecture News, vol. 35, pp. 13–23. ACM (2007)
6. Google: Cloud trace-logs. code.google.com/p/googleclusterdata/wiki
7. Hosseinimotlagh, S., Khunjush, F., Hosseinimotlagh, S.: A cooperative two-tier energy-aware scheduling for real-time tasks in computing clouds. In: 2014 22nd Euromicro International Conference on Parallel, Distributed, and Network-Based Processing, pp. 178–182. IEEE (2014)
8. IBM: Predictive maintenance (2015). www-01.ibm.com/software/analytics/solutions/operational-analytics/predictive-maintenance/
9. Kumar, A., Shang, L., Peh, L.S., Jha, N.K.: System-level dynamic thermal management for high-performance microprocessors. IEEE Trans. Comput. Aided Des. Integr. Circuits Syst. **27**(1), 96–108 (2008)
10. Liu, F., Zhou, Z., Jin, H., Li, B., Li, B., Jiang, H.: On arbitrating the power-performance tradeoff in saas clouds. IEEE Trans. Parallel Distrib. Syst. **25**(10), 2648–2658 (2014)
11. Mao, Y., Xu, Z., Ping, P., Wang, L.: Delay-aware associate tasks scheduling in the cloud computing. In: 2015 IEEE Fifth International Conference on Big Data and Cloud Computing (BDCloud), pp. 104–109. IEEE (2015)
12. Nakamura, H., Matsuda, H., Akazawa, F., Shiraga, M.: U.S. Patent No. 8,195,985. U.S. Patent and Trademark Office, Washington, DC (2012)
13. O'Brien, J.: Datacenter facilities maintenance (2014). www.datacenterjournal.com/datacenter-facilities-maintenance-time-change-culture
14. Peterson, L.L., Davie, B.S.: Computer Networks: A Systems Approach. Elsevier, Amsterdam (2007)
15. Powell, W.B.: Approximate Dynamic Programming: Solving the Curses of Dimensionality, vol. 703. Wiley, Hoboken (2007)
16. Puterman, M.L.: Markov Decision Processes: Discrete Stochastic Dynamic Programming. Wiley, Hoboken (2014)
17. Schroeder, B., Gibson, G.: A large-scale study of failures in high-performance computing systems. IEEE Trans. Dependable Secure Comput. **7**(4), 337–350 (2010)

18. Tchana, A., Broto, L., Hagimont, D.: Approaches to cloud computing fault toler-
    ance. In: 2012 International Conference on Computer, Information and Telecom-
    munication Systems (CITS), pp. 1–6. IEEE (2012)
19. Wang, J., Bao, W., Zhu, X., Yang, L.T., Xiang, Y.: Festal: fault-tolerant elastic
    scheduling algorithm for real-time tasks in virtualized clouds. IEEE Trans. Com-
    put. **64**(9), 2545–2558 (2015)
20. Wikipedia: Lm-sensors. en.wikipedia.org/wiki/Lm_sensors
21. Zhu, X., Yang, L.T., Chen, H., Wang, J., Yin, S., Liu, X.: Real-time tasks oriented
    energy-aware scheduling in virtualized clouds. IEEE Trans. Cloud Comput. **2**(2),
    168–180 (2014)

Are REST APIs for Cloud Computing Well-Designed? An Exploratory Study

Fabio Petrillo[1,3,4(✉)], Philippe Merle[2], Naouel Moha[1],
and Yann-Gaël Guéhéneuc[3]

[1] Département d'informatique, Université du Québec à Montréal, Montreal, Canada
fabio@petrillo.com, moha.naouel@uqam.ca
[2] Equipe Spirals, Inria Lille - Nord Europe, Villeneuve d'Ascq, France
philippe.merle@inria.fr
[3] DGIGL, École Polytechnique, Montréal, Montreal, Canada
yann-gael.gueheneuc@polymtl.ca
[4] PPGC, Federal University of Rio Grande do Sul, Porto Alegre, Brazil

Abstract. Cloud computing is currently the most popular model to offer and access computational resources and services. Many cloud providers use the REST architectural style (Representational State Transfer) for offering such computational resources. However, these cloud providers face challenges when designing and exposing REST APIs that are easy to handle by end-users and/or developers. Yet, they benefit from best practices to help them design understandable and reusable REST APIs.

However, these best practices are scattered in the literature and they have not be studied systematically on real-world APIs. Consequently, we propose two contributions. In our first contribution, we survey the literature and compile a catalog of 73 best practices in the design of REST APIs making APIs more understandable and reusable. In our second contribution, we perform a study of three different and well-known REST APIs from three cloud providers to investigate how their APIs are offered and accessed. These cloud providers are Google Cloud Platform, OpenStack, and Open Cloud Computing Interface (OCCI). In particular, we evaluate the coverage of the features provided by the REST APIs of these cloud providers and their conformance with the best practices for REST APIs design.

Our results show that Google Cloud follows 66 % (48/73), OpenStack follows 62 % (45/73), and OCCI 1.2 follows 56 % (41/73) of the best practices. Second, although these numbers are not necessarily high, partly because of the strict and precise specification of best practices, we showed that cloud APIs reach an acceptable level of maturity.

1 Introduction

Cloud computing has transformed the Information Technology (IT) industry [1] by hosting applications and providing resources (e.g., CPU and storage) as services on-demand over the Internet [15]. Cloud providers, such as Google Cloud

© Springer International Publishing Switzerland 2016
Q.Z. Sheng et al. (Eds.): ICSOC 2016, LNCS 9936, pp. 157–170, 2016.
DOI: 10.1007/978-3-319-46295-0_10

Platform and OpenStack, usually offer these services in the form of REST (REpresentational State Transfer) [4] APIs, the *de facto* standard adopted by many software organisations for publishing their services.

However, although cloud computing offers huge opportunities for the IT industry and has gained maturity, there are still many issues that must be addressed [15]. In particular, we observe that cloud providers, such as Google Cloud Platform, present their own proprietary APIs. Other cloud APIs, although proprietary such as OpenStack, provide open implementations of cloud services. Conversely, open and standard cloud APIs have been proposed, such as the Open Cloud Computing Interface (OCCI) [7], which is a neutral-vendor cloud standard.

Consequently, there exists a wide variety of cloud APIs that might be difficult to understand and use by developers, especially within a complex and technical context as cloud computing. Moreover, well-designed REST APIs may attract client developers to use them more than poorly designed ones, particularly in the current open market, where Web services are competing against one another [6]. Indeed, client developers must understand the providers' APIs while designing and developing their systems that use these APIs. Therefore, in the design and development of REST APIs, their understandability and reusability are two major quality characteristics, which are reachable when best practices for REST APIs design [6] are followed.

Several practices were proposed or identified in the literature [2,6,8,9,12] as *CRUD function names should not be used in URIs* or *Lowercase letters should be preferred in URI paths*. In particular, a valuable contribution is the one of Massé [6], who compiles several design practices about REST APIs. Yet, despite proposing a large list of 65 practices, Massé [6] did not propose a complete list.

Consequently, we propose two contributions. For our first contribution, we review the literature extensively and compile a catalog of 73 best practices in the design of REST APIs making APIs more understandable and reusable.

For our second contribution, we evaluate and compare the design of the cloud computing REST APIs using best practices of this catalog. Compared to previous works, including some of ours [2,8,9], we study the conformance with best practices of REST APIs from the perspective of cloud providers.

After identifying and analysing 73 best practices, our results show that Google Cloud Platform follows 66 % (48/73), OpenStack follows 62 % (45/73), and OCCI 1.2 follows 56 % (41/73) of the best practices. Second, although these numbers are not necessarily high, partly because of the strict and precise specification of best practices, we showed that cloud APIs reach an acceptable level of maturity.

The reminder of the paper is organised as follows. Section 2 presents a survey about best practices on REST APIs to support our evaluation. Section 3 describes the study performed on the three cloud computing REST APIs. Section 4 presents and discusses our results and the threats to their validity. Section 5 presents some related work. Finally, Sect. 6 concludes the paper with future work.

2   Best Practices on REST API Design

REST APIs are hard to design [6] because they are not often based on precise and documented specifications but only on an architectural style [4]. Thus, we now present a catalog of REST API best practices, pertaining to understandability and reusability, extracted from the literature and organised to support our analysis on cloud REST APIs.

To build our catalog, we surveyed several studies of REST APIs elaborated by Massé [6], Rodrigues et al. [2], Palma et al. [8,9], Vinoski [13], Stowe [12], and Richardson and Ruby [11]. In particular, Massé [6] provides a concise catalog of practices organised by categories. We analysed all the cited studies to identify good practices and organise them by categories inspired from Massé's work.

Table 1. Numbers of practices by category

Category	Number of practices
URI	20
Request methods	8
Error handling	16
HTTP headers	10
Others	19
Total	73

Our literature review produced a catalog of 73 best practices to design understandable and reusable REST APIs, grouped into five categories. Table 1 lists the categories and the numbers of practices per category. Tables 2, 3, 4, 5 and 6 describe the identified practices in each category with a short description, relevant references, and the results of our analysis on the three Cloud REST APIs. The analysis of each API is further discussed in Sect. 4.

The first category, URI practices, describes how URIs are exposed by services (Table 2). The second category, Request Methods, describes how HTTP methods must be used by REST APIs (Table 3). Error Handling practices specify how HTTP messages must be used as a response of a HTTP request method (Table 4). HTTP Header practices describe how must be used HTTP headers to complete requests with metadata or complementary data (Table 5). Finally, Others is the category for grouping different and various practices as Media Types, Message Body Format, Versioning, Security, Response Representation Composition, Documentation and Hypermedia Representation (Table 6).

Table 2. URI design best practices

	Practices	References	Google	OpenStack	OCCI
1	Forward slash separator (/) must be used to indicate a hierarchical relationship	[6,9,11]	✓	✓	✓
2	A trailing forward slash (/) should not be included in URIs	[2,6,9]	✓	✓	✓
3	Hyphens (-) should be used to improve the readability of URIs	[6,9]	-	-	-
4	Underscores (_) should not be used in URIs	[2,6,9]	✓	✓	-
5	Lowercase letters should be preferred in URI paths	[2,6,9]	✓	✓	-
6	File extensions should not be included in URIs	[6]	✓	✓	-
7	Consistent subdomain names should be used for your APIs	[6,9,11]	✓	✓	✓
8	A singular noun should be used for document names	[6,9]	✓	✓	-
9	A plural noun should be used for collection names	[6,9]	✓	✓	-
10	A plural noun should be used for store names	[6,9]	✓	✓	-
11	A verb or verb phrase should be used for controller names	[6,9]	✓	✓	-
12	CRUD function names should not be used in URIs	[2,6,9]	✓	✓	-
13	Use path variables to separate elements of a hierarchy, or a path through a directed graph	[11]	✓	✓	-
14	Avoiding version number in the path	[2]	-	-	-
15	API as part of the subdomain	[2]	✓	-	-
16	The query component of a URI may be used to filter collections or stores	[6]	✓	✓	✓
17	The query component of a URI should be used to paginate collection or store results	[6]	✓	✓	✓
18	Keeping as much information as possible in the URI, and as little as possible in request metadata	[11]	✓	✓	-
19	Avoiding version number in the query params	[2]	✓	✓	✓
20	Avoiding CRUD actions in query params	[2]	✓	✓	✓

Table 3. Request methods best practices

	Practices	References	Google	OpenStack	OCCI
1	GET and POST must not be used to tunnel other request methods	[2,6,8,12]	✓	✓	✓
2	GET must be used to retrieve a representation of a resource	[6,11–13]	✓	✓	✓
3	HEAD should be used to retrieve response headers	[6,11–13]	✓	✓	-
4	PUT must be used to both insert and update a stored resource	[6,11–13]	-	-	✓
5	PUT must be used to update mutable resources	[6,11–13]	✓	✓	✓
6	POST must be used to create a new resource in a collection	[6,11–13]	✓	✓	✓
7	POST must be used to execute controllers	[6,12]	✓	✓	✓
8	DELETE must be used to remove a resource from its parent	[6,11–13]	✓	✓	✓

Table 4. Error handling best practices

	Practices	References	Google	OpenStack	OCCI
1	200 ("OK") should be used to indicate nonspecific success	[6, 12]	✓	✓	✓
2	200 ("OK") must not be used to communicate errors in the response body	[6, 12]	✓	✓	✓
3	201 ("Created") must be used to indicate successful resource creation	[6, 12]	-	-	✓
4	202 ("Accepted") must be used to indicate successful start of an asynchronous action	[6, 12]	-	-	-
5	204 ("No Content") should be used when the response body is intentionally empty	[6, 12]	-	-	✓
6	302 ("Found") should not be used	[6, 12]	-	-	✓
7	304 ("Not Modified") should be used to preserve bandwidth	[6, 12, 13]	-	-	-
8	400 ("Bad Request") may be used to indicate nonspecific failure	[6, 12]	✓	✓	✓
9	401 ("Unauthorized") must be used when there is a problem with the client's credentials	[6, 12]	-	✓	✓
10	403 ("Forbidden") should be used to forbid access regardless of authorization state	[6, 12]	-	-	✓
11	404 ("Not Found") must be used when a client's URI cannot be mapped to a resource	[6, 12]	✓	-	✓
12	405 ("Method Not Allowed") must be used when the HTTP method is not supported	[6, 12]	-	-	✓
13	406 ("Not Acceptable") must be used when the requested media type cannot be served	[6, 12]	-	-	✓
14	409 ("Conflict") should be used to indicate a violation of resource state	[6, 12]	-	✓	✓
15	500 ("Internal Server Error") should be used to indicate API malfunction	[6, 12]	✓	-	✓
16	Use JSON as error message response	[6, 12]	✓	✓	-

Table 5. HTTP header best practices

	Practices	Ref.	Google	OS	OCCI
1	Content-type must be used	[6, 12, 13]	✓	✓	-
2	Content-length should be used	[6]	✓	✓	-
3	Last-modified should be used in responses	[6]	-	✓	-
4	ETag should be used in responses	[6, 13]	✓	✓	-
5	Stores must support conditional PUT requests	[6]	-	-	-
6	Location must be used to specify the URI of a newly created resource	[6]	-	-	-
7	Cache-control, expires, and date response headers should be used to encourage caching	[6]	✓	✓	-
8	Cache-control, expires, and pragma response headers may be used to discourage caching	[6]	-	-	-
9	Caching should be encouraged	[6]	✓	✓	-
10	Custom HTTP headers must not be used to change the behavior of HTTP methods	[6]	✓	✓	✓

Table 6. Other best practices

	Practices	Ref.	Google	OS	OCCI
1	Application-specific media types should be used	[6]	-	-	✓
2	Media type negotiation should be supported when multiple representations are available	[6]	-	-	✓
3	Media type selection using a query parameter may be supported	[6]	-	-	-
4	JSON should be supported for resource representation	[6]	✓	✓	✓
5	XML and other formats may optionally be used for resource representation	[6]	-	-	✓
6	Additional envelopes must not be created	[6]	✓	✓	✓
7	New URIs should be used to introduce new concepts	[6]	✓	✓	✓
8	Schemas should be used to manage representational form versions	[6]	✓	-	✓
9	Entity tags should be used to manage representational state versions	[6]	-	-	✓
10	OAuth may be used to protect resources	[6, 12]	✓	✓	-
11	The query component of a URI should be used to support partial responses	[6]	-	-	✓
12	The query component of a URI should be used to embed linked resources	[6, 11]	-	-	-
13	Consistent subdomain names should be used for your client developer portal	[6]	-	-	-
14	Accompanying human-readable documentation	[6, 12]	✓	✓	✓
15	Interactive experiences to try/test API calls	[12]	✓	-	-
16	Code examples for multiple languages	[12]	✓	-	-
17	A consistent form should be used to represent links	[6, 8]	✓	✓	✓
18	A consistent form should be used to advertise links	[6, 8]	✓	✓	✓
19	A self link should be included in response message body representations	[6, 8]	✓	✓	✓

3   Study Design

This section presents the design of our study, which aims to address the following four research questions:

RQ1 What are the main services provided by cloud REST APIs?
RQ2 How many best practices are followed by cloud REST APIs?
RQ3 What best practices are adopted by all APIs?
RQ4 What best practices are adopted by none of the APIs?

3.1   Objects

The objects of our study are three different cloud REST APIs including the proprietary cloud API of Google Cloud Platform, the open source API of Open-Stack, and the standard OCCI. We specifically target these APIs because they represent the range of the different types of cloud APIs available: commercial offer, open source implementation, and open standard.

Here is a short description of each of the three studied APIs:

Google Cloud Platform is a proprietary cloud platform that consists of a set of physical assets (e.g., computers and hard disk drives) and virtual resources (e.g., virtual machines, a.k.a. VMs) hosted in Google's data centers around the globe. Google Cloud documentation is available at https://cloud.google.com/docs.

OpenStack is an open source cloud platform that controls large pools of compute, storage, and networking resources throughout a datacenter. OpenStack documentation is available at http://docs.openstack.org.

Open Cloud Computing Interface (OCCI) is a cloud computing standard that comprises a set of open community-lead specifications delivered through the Open Grid Forum. OCCI is a protocol and API for all kinds of management tasks. OCCI 1.2 documentation is available at http://occi-wg.org/about/specification.

3.2   Procedure

We investigated and analysed manually in details the documentation of each of the three APIs studied. More precisely, we identified the services provided by each API and extracted the list of URIs. Then, we compared them with each best practice as defined in our compiled catalog of best practices. The analysis of OCCI has been cross-validated by two contributors of the standard. We performed an analysis of the three APIs and reported the results of this analysis in several tables given in the next section dedicated to the results.

4   Results

We now report the results of our analysis to answer our four research questions.

4.1   RQ1 What Are the Main Services Provided by Cloud REST APIs?

We performed a manual analysis on each REST API documentation to identify the services provided. This first analysis allows us to identify 11 services as listed in Table 7. Our results show that Google Cloud Platform and OpenStack provide all identified services (11/11) while OCCI describes only four services in its specifications (4/11). We conclude that **Google and OpenStack API have a good support for several services while OCCI has yet some lacks**.

Indeed, current OCCI 1.2 official specifications only cover 4 of the 11 services listed in Table 7: VM Managing, Storage, Networking, and Tagging. However, OCCI-based services were proposed for Container Managing [10] and Monitoring [3]. Image Managing, Scaling, Access Control, Data Processing and Machine Learning would be addressed in future as there are key services for building open standard cloud platforms.

Table 7. Service analysis comparing Google Cloud, OpenStack, and OCCI

Main services	Google	OpenStack	OCCI
VM managing	✓	✓	✓
Container managing	✓	✓	✗
Image managing	✓	✓	✗
Storage	✓	✓	✓
Networking	✓	✓	✓
Scaling	✓	✓	✗
Access control	✓	✓	✗
Monitoring	✓	✓	✗
Tagging	✓	✓	✓
Data processing	✓	✓	✗
Machine learning	✓	✓	✗

4.2 RQ2 How Many Best Practices Are Followed by Cloud REST APIs?

For each practice, we analysed the documentation of the corresponding API to assess whether this provider follows or not the practice. Tables 2-6 present the detailed results of this assessment for each API and the 73 best practices by category. Table 8 presents a summary of this assessment by category of practices and shows that **on average 61 % (44/73) of the practices are followed by the three APIs.** Google Cloud Platform follows 66 % (48/73), OpenStack follows 62 % (45/73), and OCCI follows 56 % (41/73) of the best practices.

Moreover, OCCI follows only 35 % (7/20) of URI practices, while Google Cloud Platform and OpenStack follow URI practices in 90 % (18/20) and 85 % (17/20), respectively. OCCI 1.2 fails to support URI design best practices, but future OCCI releases could improve this as the OCCI REST API is automatically synthetised from a metamodel instead of designed by hand as in Google Cloud Platform and OpenStack.

All APIs strongly apply Request Methods best practices listed in Table 3 with 87 % on average. Each API requires just one improvement on PUT method for Google Cloud Platform and OpenStack, and on HEAD method for OCCI. For the latter, OCCI implementations such as erocci[1] and rOCCI[2] already support HEAD method best practice, so a consensus in the OCCI community should be easily attainable to include this best practice into OCCI specifications.

Finally, Error Handling, HTTP Headers, and the other categories are the less followed with only 52 %, 46 %, and 56 %.

---

[1] http://erocci.ow2.org.

[2] http://gwdg.github.io/rOCCI/.

Error handling in Google Cloud Platform and OpenStack (6/16 or 37,5 % in Table 8) requires to be strongly improved with a better documentation in the error messages.

Regarding HTTP header best practices, all the three cloud REST APIs can be improved but especially OCCI 1.2, which only supports 1 practice, i.e., 10 % in Table 5. Here the OCCI 1.2 HTTP Protocol specification must be extended to support more HTTP header best practices. For instance, this specification must explicitly state that *Content-Type must be used, Content-Length should be used, Last-Modified should be used in responses, ETag should be used in responses, Cache-Control, Expires, and Date response headers should be used to encourage caching, Cache-Control, Expires, and Pragma response headers may be used to discourage caching,* and *Caching should be encouraged*. Let's note that OCCI implementations such as erocci and rOCCI already implement most of these best practices, so the consensus into the OCCI community should be reasonably attainable. In contrast, both *stores must support conditional PUT requests* and *location must be used to specify the URI of a newly created resource* are best practices that no API seems to want to support.

Table 8. Followed practices by category and API

Category	Total	Google	OpenStack	OCCI	Average	Avg/Total
URI	20	18	17	7	14	70 %
Request methods	8	7	7	7	7	87 %
Error handling	16	6	6	13	8	52 %
HTTP headers	10	6	7	1	4	46 %
Others	19	11	8	13	10	56 %
Total	73	48	45	41	44	61 %

4.3   RQ3 What Best Practices Are Adopted by All APIs?

In Table 9, we identified from our results the set of practices that **all APIs follow**, forming a "consensus". We found that only 32 % (24/73) of practices were followed by all APIs. This means that the cloud API providers are not yet in agreement on the main good practices to prioritise and might be guided by technical decisions. However, it should be pointed out that the practices are strict and detailed. This explains why this number is very low. Moreover, we could identify that the majority of practices are adopted at least by one API. Overall, the APIs, even if do not follow strictly all best practices, implement relatively well all practices and are thus well-designed.

4.4   RQ4 What Best Practices Are Adopted by None of the APIs?

An opposite analysis allows us to identify the set of practices that **none API follows**, forming a negative "consensus". We found that only ten best practices

Table 9. Practices followed by All APIs

Practices	Categories
Forward slash separator (/) must be used to indicate a hierarchical relationship	URI format
A trailing forward slash (/) should not be included in URIs	URI format
Consistent subdomain names should be used for your APIs	URI authority
The query component of a URI may be used to filter collections or stores	URI query
The query component of a URI should be used to paginate collection or store results	URI query
Avoiding version number in the query params	URI query
Avoiding CRUD actions in query params	URI query
GET and POST must not be used to tunnel other request methods	Request methods
GET must be used to retrieve a representation of a resource	Request methods
PUT must be used to update mutable resources	Request methods
POST must be used to create a new resource in a collection	Request methods
POST must be used to execute controllers	Request methods
DELETE must be used to remove a resource from its parent	Request methods
200 ("OK") should be used to indicate nonspecific success	Error handling
200 ("OK") must not be used to communicate errors in the response body	Error handling
400 ("Bad Request") may be used to indicate nonspecific failure	Error handling
Custom HTTP headers must not be used to change the behavior of HTTP methods	HTTP headers
JSON should be supported for resource representation	Message body
Additional envelopes must not be created	Message body
New URIs should be used to introduce new concepts	URI
Accompanying human-readable documentation	Documentation
A consistent form should be used to represent links	Hypermedia
A consistent form should be used to advertise links	Hypermedia
A self link should be included in response message body representations	Hypermedia

(14 %) are applied by none of the three APIs analysed. Table 10 lists the practices followed by no API. This list could be analysed to understand why these practices are not followed by more APIs. For example, as any cloud API provider performs long running actions, e.g. starting a virtual machine takes some minutes, then all cloud APIs must return *202 ("Accepted")* HTTP status to indicate successful start of an asynchronous action. Another example is that *304 ("Not Modified")* should be used by all cloud APIs to preserve network bandwidth.

4.5   Threats to Validity

As with any such empirical study, threats exist that reduce its validity, which we attempted to mitigate or had to accept. We now discuss these threats and the measures that we took with respect to them.

Threats to the construct validity of our study concern the relationship between theory and observations. We assumed (1) that good practices can be codified and

Table 10. Practices followed by No API

Practices	Categories
Hyphens (-) should be used to improve the readability of URIs	URI format
Avoiding version number in the path	URI path
202 ("Accepted") must be used to indicate successful start of an asynchronous action	Error handling
304 ("Not Modified") should be used to preserve bandwidth	Error handling
Stores must support conditional PUT requests	HTTP request
Location must be used to specify the URI of a newly created resource	HTTP request
Cache-Control, Expires, and Pragma response headers may be used to discourage caching	HTTP request
Media type selection using a query parameter may be supported	URI format
The query component of a URI should be used to embed linked resources	URI format
Consistent subdomain names should be used for your client developer portal	URI authority

shared among developers and (2) that these good practices improve the quality of the REST APIs of the cloud providers that follow them [15]. Although these assumptions are legitimate and have been withheld by many researchers and works before for example that of Zhang and Budgen [14], future work should study whether these good practices apply universally to all cloud services.

Threats to internal validity concern confounding factors that can affect our dependent variables. Although we did not carry any statistical analysis on the characteristics of the studied REST APIs, we assumed that the good practices were representative characteristics of the REST APIs. However, there may be other characteristics that describe more accurately these REST APIs, in particular their understandability and reusability. Future work include analysing and contrasting more APIs with more practices to uncover possible other characteristics. We also related the APIs and the practices manually thanks to the information provided in the literature and by the APIs documentations. Yet, other researchers should perform similar analysis to confirm/infirm ours.

Threats to conclusion validity deal with the relation between the treatment and the outcome. Again, we did not carry any statistical analysis between the REST APIs and the identified good practices and the characteristics of understandability and reusability. Yet, we argued that comparing these REST APIs according to their use of the practices is sensible because they belong to the same design space. We also accepted that external characteristics could influence their design and, hence, their quality. We accepted this threat and future work could uncover more novel characteristics and measures of REST APIs.

Threats to external validity concern the generalisability of our results. Although we presented, to the best of our knowledge, the largest study on the design of REST APIs based on an catalog of good practices from the literature, we cannot generalise our results to all REST APIs. Future work is necessary to analyse more REST APIs, from other cloud providers, to confirm and–or infirm our observations on their design quality characteristics.

5   Related Work

To the best of our knowledge, few work studied the evaluation of REST APIs.

Rodríguez et al. [2] evaluated the conformance of good and bad practices in REST APIs from the perspective of mobile applications. They analysed large data logs of HTTP calls collected from the Internet traffic of mobile applications, identified usage patterns from logs, and compared these patterns with design best practices. Zhou et al. [16] showed how to fix design problems related to the use of REST services in existing Northbound networking APIs in a Software Defined Network and how to design a REST Northbound API in the context of OpenStack. Both of these two previous work made contributions to the design evaluation of REST APIs for two specific domains, mobile and networking, while we consider the domain of cloud services.

Maleshkova et al. [5] analysed a set of 220 publicly-available Web APIs, including RPC, REST, and hybrid (a mix of RPC and REST) styles. They investigated six characteristics of the APIs: general information, types of Web APIs, input parameters, output formats, invocation details, and complementary documentation. This work provides a view on how Web APIs are developed and exposed. In particular, it shows that Web APIs are not necessarily REST and that they suffer from under-specification because important information such as data-type and HTTP methods are missing. This work supports our paper on the need to study the design of REST APIs.

In our previous works [8,9], we evaluated the design of several REST APIs based on REST patterns and antipatterns, which correspond to good and bad practices in the design of REST services. However, the APIs evaluated were selected from different and general domains. They included Facebook, Twitter, Dropbox, and Bestbuy. So, it was not possible to compare and discuss the results among the APIs. Moreover, the list of patterns and antipatterns was really limited compared to the catalog of best practices presented in this paper.

6   Conclusion and Future Work

In this paper, we claimed that well designing REST APIs is difficult for cloud providers although there exist best practices pertaining to understandability and reusability. We supported our claim by performing, to the best of our knowledge, the first study evaluating and comparing the designs of the REST APIS of several cloud providers. We included in our study the REST APIs provided by Google Cloud Platform, OpenStack, and OCCI. We presented thus two contributions, a catalog of best practices from the literature and an evaluation of the use of these practices in three sets of APIs.

For our first contribution, we reviewed the literature extensively and compiled a catalog of 73 best practices in the design of REST APIs making APIs more understandable and reusable. We believe that our catalog is exhaustive at the time of writing. We hope that this catalog can be used by other researchers to study some quality characteristics of REST APIs as well as practitioners when designing, implementing, and assessing their own REST APIs.

For our second contribution, we evaluated and compared the design of the REST APIs using best practices from the literature and showed that Google Cloud follows 66 % (48/73), OpenStack follows 62 % (45/73), and OCCI 1.2 follows 56 % (41/73) of the best practices.

Thus, we showed that best practices can help evaluate REST APIs and design better REST APIs in terms of understandability and reusability. Moreover, in opposition of a recent assessment [2], we also showed that cloud APIs reach an acceptable level of maturity when considering good practices pertaining to understandability and reusability.

Future work includes studying whether these good practices apply universally to all cloud APIs. In particular, we planned to analyse and contrast more APIs, especially other commercial offers like Amazon Web Services and other open source cloud stacks like Apache's CloudStack, with more practices to uncover possible other characteristics. Finally according to the results of this study, we will contribute to the improvement of OCCI specifications in order to make them more visible as OCCI is the only open standard addressing the management of any cloud computing resource.

Acknowledgment. Thank to Boris Parak from CESNET and Jean Parpaillon from Inria for their helps in evaluating the support by OCCI of our catalog of best practices. This work is partially supported by the OCCIware research and development project (http://www.occiware.org) funded by French Programme d'Investissements d'Avenir (PIA).

References

1. Armbrust, M., Stoica, I., Zaharia, M., Fox, A., Griffith, R., Joseph, A.D., Katz, R., Konwinski, A., Lee, G., Patterson, D., Rabkin, A.: A view of cloud computing. Commun. ACM **53**(4), 50 (2010). http://portal.acm.org/citation.cfm?doid=1721654.1721672

2. Rodríguez, C., Baez, M., Daniel, F., Casati, F., Trabucco, J.C., Canali, L., Percannella, G.: REST APIs: a large-scale analysis of compliance with principles and best practices. In: Bozzon, A., Cudré-Mauroux, P., Pautasso, C. (eds.) ICWE 2016. LNCS, vol. 9671, pp. 21–39. Springer, Heidelberg (2016). doi:10.1007/978-3-319-38791-8_2

3. Ciuffoletti, A.: Application level interface for a cloud monitoring service. Comput. Stand. Interfaces **46**, 15–22 (2016). http://www.sciencedirect.com/science/article/pii/S0920548916000027

4. Fielding, R.T.: Architectural styles and the design of network-based software architectures. Ph.D. thesis, University of California, Irvine (2000). http://www.ics.uci.edu/fielding/pubs/dissertation/top.htm

5. Maleshkova, M., Pedrinaci, C., Domingue, J.: Investigating web APIs on the world wide web. In: 2010 Eighth IEEE European Conference on Web Services, pp. 107–114. IEEE (2010). http://ieeexplore.ieee.org/lpdocs/epic03/wrapper.htm?arnumber=5693251

6. Masse, M.: REST API Design Rulebook, vol. 53. O'Reilly Media, Sebastopol (2011)

7. Merle, P., Barais, O., Parpaillon, J., Plouzeau, N., Tata, S.: A precise metamodel for open cloud computing interface. In: 2015 IEEE 8th International Conference on Cloud Computing, pp. 852–859, June 2015

8. Palma, F., Dubois, J., Moha, N.: Service-Oriented Computing. Lecture Notes in Computer Science, vol. 8831. Springer, Berlin, Heidelberg (2014). http://link.springer.com/10.1007/978-3-662-45391-9

9. Palma, F., Gonzalez-Huerta, J., Moha, N., Guéhéneuc, Y.G., Tremblay, G.: Are RESTful APIs well-designed? Detection of their linguistic (anti)patterns. In: Toumani, F., et al. (eds.) ICSOC 2014. LNCS, vol. 8954. Springer, Heidelberg (2015). http://link.springer.com/10.1007/978-3-319-22885-3, http://link.springer.com/10.1007/978-3-662-48616-0_11

10. Paraiso, F., Challita, S., Al-Dhuraibi, Y., Merle, P.: Model-driven management of docker containers. In: Proceedings of 9th IEEE International Conference on Cloud Computing (CLOUD) (2016, to appear)

11. Richardson, L., Ruby, S.: RESTful Web Services. O'Reilly Media Inc., Sebastopol (2007)

12. Stowe, M.: Undisturbed REST: A Guide to Designing the Perfect API. MuleSoft, San Francisco (2015)

13. Vinoski, S.: RESTful web services development checklist. IEEE Internet Comput. **12**(6), 95–96 (2008). http://ieeexplore.ieee.org/lpdocs/epic03/wrapper.htm?arnumber=4670126

14. Zhang, C., Budgen, D.: What do we know about the effectiveness of software design patterns? IEEE Trans. Softw. Eng. **38**(5), 1213–1231 (2012)

15. Zhang, Q., Cheng, L., Boutaba, R.: Cloud computing: state-of-the-art and research challenges. J. Internet Serv. Appl. **1**(1), 7–18 (2010). http://www.springerlink.com/index/10.1007/s13174-010-0007-6

16. Zhou, W., Li, L., Luo, M., Chou, W.: REST API design patterns for SDN northbound API. In: 2014 28th International Conference on Advanced Information Networking and Applications Workshops, pp. 358–365. IEEE (2014). http://ieeexplore.ieee.org/lpdocs/epic03/wrapper.htm?arnumber=6844664

Cross-Device Integration of Android Apps

Dennis Wolters[1(⊠)], Jonas Kirchhoff[1], Christian Gerth[2], and Gregor Engels[1]

[1] Department of Computer Science, Paderborn University, Paderborn, Germany
{dennis.wolters,engels}@uni-paderborn.de, jonaskir@mail.uni-paderborn.de
[2] Faculty of Business Management and Social Sciences,
Osnabrück University of Applied Sciences, Osnabrück, Germany
c.gerth@hs-osnabrueck.de

Abstract. Integrating apps on mobile devices into applications running on other devices is usually difficult. For instance, using a messenger on a smartphone to share a text written on a desktop computer often ends up in a cumbersome solution to transfer the text, because many applications are not designed for such scenarios. In this paper, we present an approach enabling the integration of apps running on Android devices into applications running on other devices and even other platforms. This is achieved by specifying adapters for Android apps, which map their services to a platform-independent service interface. For this purpose, we have developed a domain-specific language to ease the specification of such mappings. Our approach is applicable without the need to modify the existing Android apps providing the service. We analyzed its feasibility by implementing our approach and by specifying mappings for several popular Android apps, e.g., phone book, camera, and file explorer.

Keywords: Cross-Device · Integration · Android · Adapter · DSL

1 Introduction

Android devices like smartphones or tablets incorporate a high degree of interaction between apps. For instance, users usually have two choices when changing the profile picture in a messenger app: they can either select an existing picture from the gallery app or capture and insert a new picture with the help of the camera app. In this service-oriented interaction the messaging app is acting as the service requestor and the gallery/camera app is acting as service provider, who provides a service returning a picture. Furthermore, it is very easy for the user to add new integrable services by simply installing additional apps using an app store. However, this integration of another app's services is only available to apps on the same Android device. An integration of apps running on different devices is usually not supported, forcing users to find workarounds in order to integrate these apps to some extent [16]. For example, when users want to update their profile picture using their desktop computer with a picture taken on their smartphone, they have to transfer the picture somehow, e.g., manually or by using file synchronization tools like DropBox.

© Springer International Publishing Switzerland 2016
Q.Z. Sheng et al. (Eds.): ICSOC 2016, LNCS 9936, pp. 171–185, 2016.
DOI: 10.1007/978-3-319-46295-0_11

It would be highly beneficial from a user's perspective if functionality provided by apps running on mobile devices could be integrated and accessed by applications on devices like desktop computers as well. However, these apps usually do not provide a public interface that is accessible by applications on other devices, e.g., via the internet. Therefore, application developers wanting to integrate apps running on other devices are missing both integrable services and an infrastructure to access these services from their applications. But as we have described earlier, apps on Android devices already provide services that can be integrated by other apps on the same device. In fact, the Android platform encourages app developers to program their apps in a way such that they can be integrated by other apps. Thus, integrable services already exist but until now they cannot be accessed from other devices. Hence, a solution is required that enables developers to integrate those services into their application, providing users a seamless cross-device experience as envisioned by Satyanarayanan [17].

In this paper, we present an approach that enables the cross-device integration of Android apps into applications running on different devices. In order to realize this without requiring any changes to the implementation of the Android apps providing the services, our approach allows the specification of adapters which map these services to platform-independent service interfaces, e.g., a RESTful interface. Thereby, services can be integrated by applications running on other devices and on other platforms. To ease the specification of such adapters, we present an extensible domain-specific language (DSL). Using this DSL it is possible to develop adapters for existing apps with only a fraction of the complexity that native code would require.

Additionally, we have implemented a prototype of our approach, which allows to find and integrate services provided by apps on Android devices. Along with our prototype we specified adapters using our DSL for several standard Android apps like the camera, phone book, or the file explorer. Thereby, we demonstrate the capabilities of our approach as well as the expressiveness of our DSL, and enable developers to integrate these services into their own applications.

The remainder of this paper is structured as follows: In Sect. 2, we explain fundamental concepts of the Android platform needed to understand our approach. Section 3 gives an overview of our approach and in Sect. 4 we present our DSL to specify adapters, followed by Sect. 5 describing our implementation. In Sect. 6, we discuss the feasibility of our approach and its limitations. Related work is presented in Sect. 7. Finally, Sect. 8 concludes the paper and gives an outlook on future work.

2   Fundamentals of the Android Platform

Since our approach focuses on the Android platform, some basic knowledge of the Android platform is needed. In particular, we explain how Android apps can provide services for other apps on the same device.

We first have a look at the internal structure of Android apps. Android apps are written in Java and are divided into several components, where each component is an instance of the following component types: *Activity*, *Background*

Service[1], *Broadcast Receiver*, or *Content Provider*. An app may contain arbitrary many instances of each component type. An Activity represents one screen of an app, e.g., a phone book app would contain an Activity for the contact list as well as one for displaying the details of a single contact. Activities are used to interact with the user. In contrast, Background Services are used in the background, usually invisible for the user, to perform certain long-running operations like downloading a file. Broadcast Receivers can react on events, e.g., when the device is plugged into a docking station, and invoke corresponding logic, mostly by starting an Activity or a Background Service. Content Providers encapsulate access to data stores like relational databases. For instance, Android's phone book app has a Content Provider storing all contacts.

In order to start components of type Activity, Background Service, or Broadcast Receiver, Android uses a message data structure called *Intent*. Such Intents can be sent by the Android system or by app components. In case of Activities and Background Services, an Intent can explicitly specify which Activity or Background Service should be started. In addition, an Intent can contain data which is passed to the started component. For Activities, it is also possible to implicitly define which Activity should be started by specifying only the action to be performed, e.g., "Take Picture". At runtime the Android system resolves these implicit Intents by offering the user a list of apps capable of performing this action. For this purpose, developers have to declare at design time which Activities can handle certain actions. By only implicitly defining the providing app, a loose coupling between the requesting and providing app can be realized.

In addition to this unidirectional style of communication, where only one Intent is sent to the providing app, the Intent-based communication with Activities can also be bidirectional. For instance, if an Intent is used to start an Activity in order to get a certain result, e.g., a phone number from the phone book, the result is encapsulated in a second Intent and sent back to the component from where the request originated. Additionally, Intents can be used to broadcast events, which are received by Broadcast Receivers that subscribed to receive those events.

In contrast to other component types, Content Providers cannot be accessed via Intents. Instead, apps have access to predefined system functions in order to query or manipulate data items encapsulated in a Content Provider. Even though Content Providers can be used as front ends for other kinds of data stores, their whole interface is inspired by interfaces of relational databases. Furthermore, some parts of RESTful interfaces are adopted as well, like using Uniform Resource Identifiers (URIs) to identify Content Providers as well as every single data item being stored in those providers.

By default, interaction between components is limited to components within an app. However, apps can declare their components as public. By doing so, these public components become entry points into the app and other apps on the device

---

[1] A Background Service component is actually just called Service but it is not necessarily a service being provided for other apps. To avoid confusion, we call this component Background Service.

can integrate these components. For instance, a public Content Provider can be queried or manipulated by other apps. In the case of Activities, Background Services, or Broadcast Receivers, it means that they accept Intents sent by other apps. From a requesting app's perspective, public components are distinct units of logic, and therefore, they can be seen as services provided by the corresponding app. In this sense, Intents can be seen as Android-specific service request. Since Intents are also used to encapsulate the result that is sent back to the service requestor, it is also the Android-specific response format.

3   Cross-Device Integration of Android Apps

As explained in the previous section, services offered by Android apps can be integrated by other apps on the same device. In this section, we introduce our approach that enables the integration of apps running on Android devices into applications running on other devices. First, we present requirements for such an approach, and subsequently, we provide a general overview of our approach.

3.1   Requirements

We have identified the following requirements for an approach to enable the cross-device integration of Android apps:

- **R1 Applicable on existing apps**: The approach shall enable the cross-device integration of existing Android apps without having to alter them in any form. Thereby, it enables the reuse of a huge number of existing services, provided by currently available apps.
- **R2 Usage of platform-independent service technologies**: Intents are an Android-specific concept which is barely used outside of the Android domain. Hence, it must be possible for requestors running on different platforms to use platform-independent standards like RESTful or SOAP-based web services to access the services provided by apps on Android devices.
- **R3 Service registry and device management**: It must be possible to find and select devices offering certain services.

3.2   Overview of Our Approach

In this section, we provide an overview of our approach and explain how it addresses requirements R1 to R3. A visualization of our approach is given in Fig. 1. As stated in Requirement R1, the approach shall be applicable on existing apps and services offered by those apps shall be provided in a platform-independent manner (see Requirement R2) to requesting applications on other devices. Consequently, we chose to build adapters for existing Android apps, similar to using adapters to integrate legacy systems into service-oriented architectures [14]. In particular, we use adapter apps installed on the same device as the app providing the service. Adapter apps utilize Android's inter-app communication and map services provided by Android apps to platform-independent service technologies. For the remainder of this paper, we call the services provided by apps on Android devices *internal services*, because they are only available for apps on the same device and have an Android-specific interface. Adapter apps convert these internal services to *external services*, which have a platform-independent service interface and can therefore be integrated by applications running on other device/platforms.

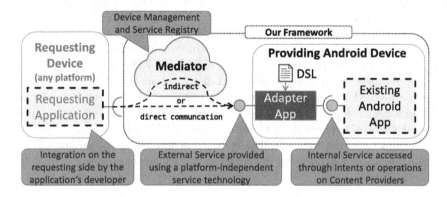

Fig. 1. General overview of our approach

Integrating the external services into the requesting application is not part of our approach. However, since we support the provisioning of external services using well-known service technologies like RESTful web services, developers of requesting applications can use well-supported, mature client implementations of those technologies to integrate these services. Additionally, if a requesting application already supports the integration of other applications via an import interface, an external service can be defined in such a way that it is directly usable by the requesting application. Alternatively, existing adapter-based approaches, as discussed in Sect. 7, can be utilized to deal with interface mismatches on the requesting side.

In addition to adapter apps, our approach includes a central entity called mediator, which addresses Requirement R3. A mediator serves as a service registry [14] and as a registry for devices. Moreover, when dealing with heterogeneous communication technologies, e.g., when a requestor wants to use HTTP and a provider is only reachable via push notification, the mediator can bridge between these different technologies. In order to deal with connectivity problems, the mediator can be used for indirect communication between requestor and provider, which includes buffering of requests and responses if either side is temporarily not available, which is common when using mobile devices.

To find devices and services, users must first register them at the mediator. If this has been done, we provide several ways to find devices providing a certain service: (i) select the provider from a list of accessible devices on the requesting device, (ii) send a broadcast to all accessible devices and claim the request on the providing device, or (iii) perform an indirect binding based on a PIN or QR code. By default, users can only see and access services offered by their own devices. However, the indirect binding also allows to use services offered by devices owned by other users.

Figure 2 visualizes how an adapter app converts an internal to an external service. Applications on other devices send a service request to an external service interface (see ❶). Details on the representation of external requests/responses are discussed in Sect. 5. An external request is received by an adapter which delegates the service request to internal services by converting the request to an equivalent Intent (see ❷). Subsequently, this Intent is sent explicitly or implicitly to an existing app on the Android device. In order to use our approach for existing apps, we must provide the data as expected by the existing app. Hence, if the app requires input data to be stored in a Content Provider, we must copy the data provided in the request to the corresponding Content Provider and must add a data reference to the Intent (see ❸). We must proceed in the similar manner if the app expects data to be provided within files. Mapping external requests to internal requests is sufficient to allow unidirectional communication with existing apps, e.g., sharing information via a messenger app.

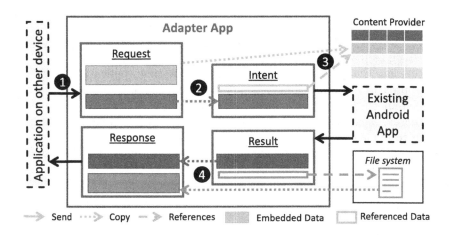

Fig. 2. Internal view of an adapter app

If the communication is bidirectional, we must map the internal result returned by the existing app to an external service response that is understood by the requestor on the other device. Thus, if the result references data in a Content Provider or as a local file, we must resolve these references and include the data in the service response (see ❹), or alternatively, create external services granting access to the corresponding Content Provider or the file system. While the former is privacy preserving since only necessary data is exchanged, the latter exposes more data than needed and is not advisable if privacy is a concern.

4   A DSL to Specify Adapter Apps

Initially, we implemented adapter apps for various common services offered by Android apps, e.g., selecting a file, taking a picture, and sharing text or images. Even though these adapters work, their source code is not easily understandable, because a lot of boiler plate code is needed, e.g., for error handling. Additionally, the Android API as well as the asynchronism of certain actions lead to the distribution of coherent code fragments across various methods and classes. Furthermore, extensive knowledge about the Android platform is needed to build these adapters. To ease the applicability of our approach, we decided to develop a DSL to specify adapters.

In the following, we present requirements as well as the definition of our DSL, which includes a discussion of the metamodel, the concrete syntax, the interpretation of our DSL, and an example mapping.

4.1   Requirements for a DSL to Specify Adapter Apps

Based on prototypical implementations of adapters for various internal services, we have identified the most common steps an adapter performs and defined them as requirements for a DSL to specify mappings performed by adapter apps:

- **D1 Specification of Intents**: The DSL must allow to specify Intents, which are sent explicitly or implicitly to other apps. This includes the specification of data embedded into an Intent.
- **D2 Specification of CRUD[2] operations on files and Content Providers**: In order to provide the data as needed for the providing app and abstract from local data stores for external requesting applications, the DSL must provide means to specify CRUD operations on the local file system and on Content Providers.
- **D3 Specification of a response**: The DSL must allow the specification of a response, which is sent back to the requestor (see Fig. 2).
- **D4 Value passing**: Data being received in a request or as part of a result shall be usable as input for other operations. For instance, a service provided by an Activity might return a reference to a data item being stored in a Content Provider. To resolve this reference, we need to use it as an input for a read operation on this Content Provider. The return value of the read operation might again be included into the response sent to the requesting application.

4.2   Language Definition

Based on the Requirements D1 to D4, we developed the DSL presented in this subsection. We start by explaining the metamodel and how mappings are being interpreted, followed by an explanation of the concrete syntax.

---

[2] Create, Read, Update, and Delete.

Metamodel. Figure 3 shows the metamodel of our DSL as an UML class diagram. A mapping document can describe multiple external services by defining mappings to one or more internal services offered by existing Android apps. Each external service specified in the mapping document has a unique name. A mapping from an external to an internal service consists of an ordered sequence of instructions. Based on the requirements D1 to D3 we have defined instructions for the most common steps which need to be performed during a mapping. The attributes of these instructions can be set to values provided with the request or values created by other instructions, e.g., the result of a bidirectional Intent. Additionally, constant values can be used.

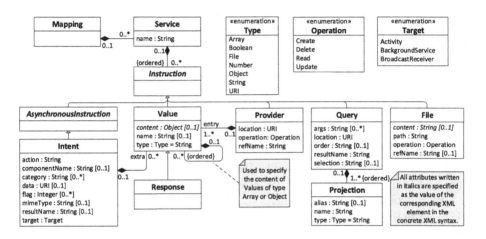

Fig. 3. Metamodel of our DSL

In order to work with values provided in the request or by other instructions (Requirement D4), we allow to define variables. Each variable is a `Value`. A `Value` is a key-value object structure. The `type` attribute of a `Value` specifies the type of the `content` attribute. For instance, if the type is `String`, the `content` attribute is interpreted as a string. If the type is `Object` or `Array`, the `content` attribute is not used, instead the `Value` has further `Values` as children. For items of an array `Value`, consecutive ordinal indices are used as names of the respective items. A variable starts with the $ sign followed by the name of the variable. To access members of a variable, we use the operators commonly known from Java. In particular, accessing a subproperty is done using the dot operator and accessing a specified array item is done via an index enclosed by square brackets. For instance, if a request from an external application contains a property `items` with an array of strings, the variable reference for the first item would be `$request.items[0]`. The `$request` variable always holds the information being passed in the service request. In addition to serving as a data structure for variables, a `Value` can also be used as an instruction to specify complex objects inside a mapping. In this case, the described object is available as a variable with the name specified in the **name** attribute.

The `Intent` instruction is used to create and send an Intent within the Android system (see Requirement D1). The **target** attribute specifies whether the Intent is directed towards an Activity, a Broadcast Receiver, or a Background Service. If the target is an Activity, the presence of the attribute **resultName** indicates whether a result Intent is expected. The result Intent is stored in a variable with the name specified in the **resultName** attribute. The recipient is either defined explicitly using the **componentName** attribute or implicitly using the attributes **action** and **category**. The payload of an Intent can be specified using the attributes **data**, **type**, and **flag**. Additional payload can be specified in a key-value-map called **extras**. A detailed description of these fields is given in the documentation of the Intent data structure in [7]. Using the `Intent` instruction, we are already able to specify simple mappings which only rely on a single Intent and unidirectional communication.

The `File` instruction provides CRUD operations on files (see Requirement D2). The affected file is specified by the attribute **path**. A reference to the affected file is available as a variable with the name specified in the **refName** attribute. The instruction can be used to create blank files and to create or update existing files using static content or values provided by variables. This content has to be specified using the **content** attribute. Furthermore, the instruction can be used to delete files and to read the content of a file into a variable.

CRUD operations on Content Providers (see Requirement D2) are realized using the **Provider** and **Query** instruction. The former instruction is used for create, update, and delete operations on Content Providers. The data items being manipulated are specified as entries, e.g., an entry might specify the content "555-1234" with the name "phonenumber". Such an entry could be inserted into a Content Provider, similar to adding a row to a table of a relational database, where "555-1234" would be the value of the cell of the "phonenumber" column. The URI of an inserted item is stored in a variable with the name specified in **refName** attribute. The **Query** instruction is used to perform queries on Content Providers. The result of the **Query** instruction is an array stored under a variable with the name specified in the **resultName** attribute. A **Projection** specifies which fields are retrieved. The **type** attribute of the **Projection** instruction specifies the type of the retrieved data field. The content of the field is available under the field's name in the corresponding list item. If the **alias** attribute is set, the field's content is available under the alias. Selection criteria are specified using the **selection** and **args** attribute. The result list sortation can be changed using the **order** attribute.

The **Response** instruction addresses Requirement D3 and allows to specify a **Value** being sent as a response to the requestor. Since it is a specialized form of the **Value** instruction, it can be used to create complex types as well. We allow only one **Response** instruction per mapping.

Based on our experience in developing adapter apps, the instructions which are already part of our DSL allow to describe mappings for most services offered by Android apps (see Sect. 6). However, there will be cases where the mapping is more complex and current instructions do not suffice. To address this issue, we provide means to add new instructions to our language. More information on the extensibility of our DSL is given in the Sect. 5.

Interpretation. Figure 4 visualizes the interpretation of a mapping in terms of a UML activity diagram. Upon receiving a request for a certain service, the corresponding mapping is loaded and the instructions are executed in the order they are listed in the mapping-document. Most instructions represent synchronous actions and after they have been processed, we continue with the next instruction. However, for asynchronous instructions like the `Intent` instruction, the processing of the next instruction is postponed until the result has been received and processed. Thereby, we can define mappings in sequential manner even if asynchronous instructions are used (see Sect. 4.3).

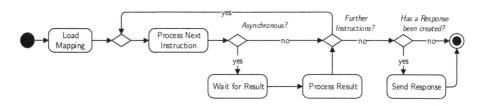

Fig. 4. Interpretation of a mapping visualized as a UML activity diagram

Since there might be additional instructions after a `Response` instruction, e.g., instructions to remove temporarily created files or Content Provider items, the response is sent after all instructions have been processed. Thereby, we can add error messages to the response if those operations fail or discard the response completely.

Concrete Syntax. To formulate instances of our language, we defined a concrete XML syntax. The mapping between the metamodel and the concrete XML syntax is rather straightforward: Every class represents an XML element. Compositions describe parent-child relations. For instance, a `<query>` element can have `<projection>` elements as children. If role names are specified, these are used as element names instead of the name of the class, e.g., extras of an Intent are specified using `<extra>` instead of `<value>`. Attributes of classes are specified as attributes of the XML element but there are two exceptions from this rule: First, those attributes in the metamodel which are written in italics are specified between the opening and closing tag of the corresponding XML element, e.g., `<value>foobar</value>`. Second, attributes with an upper bound greater than 1 are specified as children of the corresponding XML element. For example, categories are specified as XML elements and not as attributes. If an attribute is omitted, the default value specified in the metamodel is assumed.

4.3   Example

This subsection presents a concrete example for an external service, which allows to pick a contact from a smartphone's phone book. The corresponding mapping in shown in Listing 1. In Line 1, the name of the service is specified. To select a contact from the phone book, a bidirectional Intent is sent with the action ACTION_PICK and a reference to the Content Provider storing the contacts (Lines 2–3). Once the Intent has been sent, the phone book is being started on the Android device and the user has to select a contact. The user's selection is returned as an Intent stored under the variable name *$contact* (Line 3) and the data attribute contains an URI referencing a concrete contact in the phone book's Content Provider. Further contact information like the contact's name and phone number are retrieved by querying the Content Provider on the referenced item (Lines 4–7). Thereby, we resolve the local data references and are able to build a response containing the selected contact information (Lines 8–11), which is sent back to the requestor.

Listing 1. Mapping for a service to pick a contact from the user's phone book

```
 1 <service name="pickContact">
 2  <intent target="Activity" action="ACTION_PICK"
 3    data="content://contacts/data/phones" resultName="contact"/>
 4  <query location="$contact.data" resultName="result">
 5   <projection alias="name" name="display_name"/>
 6   <projection alias="no" name="data1"/>
 7  </query>
 8  <response name="contact" type="object">
 9   <value name="name">$result[0].name</value>
10   <value name="number">$result[0].no</value>
11  </response>
12 </service>
```

5   Implementation

We have built a framework implementing the approach described in the previous sections. Figure 5 gives an overview of our framework, which includes an implementation of the mediator as a node.js web server as well as a generic adapter app that can be specialized through mappings defined using our DSL. We outsourced the provisioning of the platform-independent interface into separate interface apps to enable different interfaces for the external services. Thereby, we are able to reuse our adapter for different kinds of external service interfaces, e.g., a RESTful interface or one using XML-RPC.

Interface and adapter apps use the `Value` data structure (see Fig. 3) as an intermediate format to exchange requests and responses. Interface apps have to perform a bidirectional transformation between the `Value` data structure and the actual representation format. We implemented such a transformation for JSON and XML and are confident that we can support other formats as well.

Currently, we have implemented an interface app providing a RESTful interface via the mediator. The mediator uses push notifications or, if available, a web socket connection to contact the device providing the service. Other interface apps, e.g., one providing an XML-RPC interface, are possible but have not yet been implemented. Also, services do not necessarily need be offered via the mediator, interface apps could directly provide access to the service, e.g., over a socket connection.

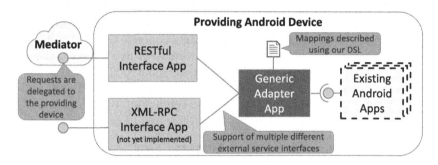

Fig. 5. Overview of our implementation

We implemented a generic adapter app that includes an interpreter for our DSL. This app can be specialized by defining a mapping document using our DSL and by requesting the necessary permissions to perform these mappings. Specialized versions of this generic adapter app can be deployed on devices which shall offer the services defined by the mapping document.

The generic adapter app allows to extend our DSL by introducing further instructions. For this purpose, one must define a new instruction handler, which is a Java class that interprets the XML code for a single instruction and has access to the variable scope. Hence, it is possible to access existing variables from an instruction handler and to make results available for other instructions by defining them as variables.

6   Feasibility Study and Limitations

Based on our implementation, we tested the feasibility of integrating apps running on Android devices into applications running on other devices. For this purpose, we identified relevant services offered by current Android apps and converted them to external services by specifying mappings using our DSL. In addition, we implemented a demo web application that allows to invoke all of the defined external services from another device[3].

---

[3] A demo video can be found at http://xdai.dwolt.de.

We mainly focused on services offered by Activities, since we are interested in services which contain user interaction on the Android device. As mentioned in Sect. 2, Activity-based services are accessed by sending and receiving Intents. The Android documentation lists over 20 *Common Intents*[4], which are supported by Activities of various apps, and we were able to define mappings for all of these Common Intents. An example is the mapping discussed in Sect. 4.3.

With regard to services accessible through Common Intents, there are limitations we need to mention: If the input data items for a service are already stored on the device providing the service, we need to know the URIs referencing these data items. There are two options to handle those situations: (i) the requestor has to know the appropriate URIs from previous requests, e.g., from insert actions, and has to include them in the request, or (ii) the user has to choose the data item before the respective service can be used. This can be realized by orchestrating multiple Intents, e.g., the URI that was returned as the result of a pick Intent can be used as an input for a second Intent.

Intents can include objects of self-defined data types as payload. Even though our approach supports the definition complex key-value object structures with the `Value` instruction, we do not support the usage of self-defined data types. However, this is not a problem regarding the before mentioned Common Intents as none of them require any self-defined data types. Additionally, most Intents do not use any other data types than those supported by our language, since using custom data types often results in a tight coupling between the requesting and providing app as both have to know this data type. Nevertheless, to support such scenarios, our language can simply be extended by specifying a new instruction to construct objects of the respective data type (see Sect. 5).

In addition to defining mappings for Activity services, we also defined mappings for services offered by Content Providers and Broadcast Receivers. In particular, we defined external services to query the phone book and the calendar without user interaction on the Android device, e.g., to enable the browsing of the phone book on another device. Furthermore, we created a service to control the media playback on Android devices.

Our language allows to define mappings aggregating multiple internal services offered by apps on the same Android device into a single external service. As an example for such an aggregation, we defined a service that utilizes the camera app to take a picture, which is then passed to a second app, where the user can crop this picture before it is sent back to the requestor. All mappings created during our feasibility study can be used out-of-the-box with our implementation. Furthermore, they show that the current instructions suffice to define external services based on the most common services offered by Android apps.

7 Related Work

Languages to deal with interface mismatches are presented in [4,5] and Autili et al. developed an approach to synthesize mediators for heterogeneous

---

[4] http://developer.android.com/guide/components/intents-common.html.

networked systems [2]. All of these approaches assume that the existence of an external interface on the providing side, which is not the case in our scenario. For the same reason, the approach presented in [12] is not applicable, since it uses adapters on the requestor's side. Nonetheless, this can be beneficial to integrate external services created with our approach.

Conductor [8] is framework to enable cross-device integration between Android apps running on different devices. In contrast to our approach, Conductor is an invasive framework requiring that both providing and requesting app use this framework. For the Android platform, Iyer et al. [10] build the counter part for our approach. If an existing Android app is loosely coupled to services of other Android apps, their approach allows to substitute these services with web services like external services created using our approach. Thus, combining these two approaches enables cross-device interaction between two Android apps without having to alter any of them. Lee et al. [11] developed an approach to wrap Android activities into OSGi bundles. Thereby, they enable that these activities are composed along with other services by an extended BPEL engine. With our approach, any kind of Android component can directly be exposed as a SOAP-based web service and be composed by standard BPEL engines.

Non-intrusive approaches exist that enable the cross-device usage of single web applications [6] and for mashups which combine multiple web applications [9]. Those approaches leverage the fact that web applications can be channeled through a proxy and that the user interface is interpreted by a browser. Both is not the case for Android apps.

The feasibility of providing web services on mobile devices is analyzed in [1,13], but none of these approaches mention the reuse of existing applications, and thereby, offer their services beyond the device boundaries. Web Intents [3] was an approach trying to expand the idea of Android Intents to a mechanism to integrate any kind of application. It would have been logical to transform Android Intents to Web Intents, but the development has been ceased. Therefore, we decided to abstract completely from Intents and support the usage of widespread technologies for the external interface.

Paulheim [15] developed an approach for UI level integration, but only for applications running on the same device. We also enable cross-device UI level integration since we allow to define external service for Activity-based services, which involve user interaction on the Android device providing the service.

8   Conclusion and Future Work

In this paper, we present an approach to enable the integration of services offered by existing Android apps into applications running on other devices/platforms. Our approach is non-intrusive with regard to existing apps, since we use adapter apps to map the existing Android-specific interfaces to platform-independent service interfaces. We introduced a DSL to specify such mappings and described an architecture supporting the cross-device integration of existing Android apps. We implemented a framework demonstrating the feasibility of our approach.

Along with our framework we already created mappings for various common services offered by standard Android apps.

As part of this paper, we analyzed which current Android services are supported by our approach. In the future, we want to analyze the impact on the user's performance by comparing cross-device interactions using our automated approach vs. manually coordinated cross-device interactions in a user study. Additionally, we are exploring how we can extend the ideas presented in this paper to cover further platforms like iOS or Windows.

References

1. AlShahwan, F., Moessner, K.: Providing SOAP web services and RESTful web services from mobile hosts. In: ICIW 2010, pp. 174–179. IEEE (2010)
2. Autili, M., Inverardi, P., Mignosi, F., Spalazzese, R., Tivoli, M.: Automated synthesis of application-layer connectors from automata-based specifications. In: Dediu, A.-H., Formenti, E., Martín-Vide, C., Truthe, B. (eds.) LATA 2015. LNCS, vol. 8977, pp. 3–24. Springer, Heidelberg (2015)
3. Billock, G., Hawkins, J., Kinlan, P.: Web Intents (2013). http://www.w3.org/TR/web-intents/
4. Cavallaro, L., Di Nitto, E.: An approach to adapt service requests to actual service interfaces. In: SEAMS 2008, pp. 129–136. ACM (2008)
5. Dumas, M., Spork, M., Wang, K.: Adapt or perish: algebra and visual notation for service interface adaptation. In: Dustdar, S., Fiadeiro, J.L., Sheth, A.P. (eds.) BPM 2006. LNCS, vol. 4102, pp. 65–80. Springer, Heidelberg (2006)
6. Ghiani, G., Paternò, F., Santoro, C.: Push and pull of web user interfaces in multi-device environments. In: AVI 2012, pp. 10–17. ACM (2012)
7. Google Inc.: Android Developers (2016). http://developer.android.com/
8. Hamilton, P., Wigdor, D.: Conductor: enabling and understanding cross-device interaction. In: CHI 2014, pp. 2773–2782. ACM (2014)
9. Husmann, M., Nebeling, M., Pongelli, S., Norrie, M.C.: MultiMasher: providing architectural support and visual tools for multi-device mashups. In: Benatallah, B., Bestavros, A., Manolopoulos, Y., Vakali, A., Zhang, Y. (eds.) WISE 2014, Part II. LNCS, vol. 8787, pp. 199–214. Springer, Heidelberg (2014)
10. Iyer, A., Roopa, T.: Extending android application programming framework for seamless cloud integration. In: MS 2012, pp. 96–104. IEEE (2012)
11. Lee, J., Lee, S.J., Wang, P.F.: A framework for composing SOAP, non-SOAP and non-Web services. IEEE Trans. Serv. Comput. **8**(2), 240–250 (2015)
12. Lin, B., Gu, N., Li, Q.: A requester-based mediation framework for dynamic invocation of web services. In: SCC 2006, pp. 445–454. IEEE (2006)
13. Mohamed, K., Wijesekera, D.: A lightweight framework for web services implementations on mobile devices. In: MS 2012, pp. 64–71. IEEE (2012)
14. Papazoglou, M.P., van den Heuvel, W.J.: Service oriented architectures: approaches, technologies and research issues. VLDB J. **16**(3), 389–415 (2007)
15. Paulheim, H.: Ontology-Based System Integration. Springer, Heidelberg (2011)
16. Santosa, S., Wigdor, D.: A field study of multi-device workflows in distributed workspaces. In: UbiComp 2013, pp. 63–72. ACM (2013)
17. Satyanarayanan, M.: Pervasive computing: vision and challenges. IEEE Pers. Commun. **8**(4), 10–17 (2001)

A Model-Driven Framework for Interoperable Cloud Resources Management

Denis Weerasiri[1]([⊠]), Moshe Chai Barukh[1], Boualem Benatallah[1],
and Jian Cao[2]

[1] University of New South Wales, Sydney, Australia
{denisw,mosheb,boualem}@cse.unsw.edu.au
[2] Shanghai Jiaotong University, Shanghai, China
cao-jian@cs.sjtu.edu.cn

Abstract. The proliferation of cloud computing has enabled powerful virtualization capabilities and outsourcing strategies. Suitably, a vast variety of cloud resource configuration and management tools have emerged to meet this needs, whereby DevOps are empowered to design end-to-end and automated cloud management tasks that span across a selection of best-of-breed tools. However, inherent heterogeneities among resource description models and management capabilities of such tools pose fundamental limitations when managing complex and dynamic cloud resources. In this paper we thus propose the notion of "Domain-specific Models" – a higher-level model-driven approach for describing elementary and federated cloud resources as reusable knowledge artifacts over existing tools. We also propose a pluggable architecture to translate these artifacts into lower-level resource descriptions and management rules. This paper describes concepts, techniques and a prototypical implementation. Experiments on real-world federated cloud resources display significant improvements in productivity. As well as notably enhanced usability achieved by our approach in comparison to traditional techniques.

Keywords: DevOps · Cloud resource management · Interoperability

1 Introduction

Cloud computing is evolving in both public and private cloud networks [14]. A third option involves a *hybrid* or *federated* cloud [2,16], drawing resources from both public and/or private clouds. The benefits include virtualization capabilities and outsourcing strategies. It is estimated that by 2016 the growth in cloud computing will consume the bulk of IT spend, whereby nearly half of all large enterprises will comprise hybrid cloud service deployments by end of 2017 [6].

However, exploiting cloud services poses great complexity. As development becomes increasingly distributed across multiple heterogeneous and evolving networks, it proves increasingly difficult to manage interoperable and portable

Q.Z. Sheng et al. (Eds.): ICSOC 2016, LNCS 9936, pp. 186–201, 2016.
DOI: 10.1007/978-3-319-46295-0_12

cloud resource solutions. Moreover, cloud applications inherently possess varying resource requirements during different phases of their life-cycle [9,14]. Consequently, designing effective cloud management solutions that cope with both heterogeneous and dynamic environments remains a deeply challenging problem.

Existing cloud management solutions typically rely on procedural programming (general-purpose or low-level scripting) languages [9,10,13,14,20]. Prominent examples include: *Puppet, Juju, Docker* and *Amazon OpsWorks*, [5]. This implies even DevOps (i.e. software and/or system engineers who design, develop, deploy and manage cloud applications) are forced to understand the different low-level cloud service APIs, command line syntax, Web interfaces, and procedural programming constructs - in order to create and maintain complex cloud configurations. Moreover, the problem intensifies with the increasing variety of cloud services, together with different resource requirements and constraints for each application. This inevitably leads to an inflexible and costly environment which adds considerable complexity, demands extensive programming effort, requires multiple and continuous patches, and perpetuates closed cloud solutions.

Drawing analogies from service representation (e.g. Web Service Description Language (WSDL)), and composition techniques (e.g. Business Process Execution Language (BPEL)), we are inspired to likewise support the abstract *representation* and *orchestration* of cloud resource by devising rich abstractions to reason about cloud resource requirements and their constraints. In this paper we therefore investigate how to effectively represent, organize and manipulate otherwise low-level, complex, cross-layer cloud resource descriptions into meaningful and higher-level segments. We believe this would greatly simplify the representation, manipulation as well as reuse of heterogeneous cloud resources. To enable this, we propose a methodology to support the automated translation of high-level resource requirements to underlying provider-specific resource and service calls. More specifically, this paper makes the following main contributions:

Domain-Specific Models to effectively *represent, manage* and *share* Cloud Resources. The ability to share and reuse cloud artifacts offer a powerful enhancement to DevOps' productivity. However, as these artifacts are inherently low-level and heterogenous between different cloud platforms, sharing such artifacts are almost useless in practice. To address this, we propose *Domain-specific Models* (DSMs) for representing cloud resources and their management strategies as high-level entities. Based on the Entity-Relationship (ER) model, our proposed model features: a vocabulary and set of constructs for describing or representing both elementary (e.g. VMs, DBs, load balancers), and federated cloud resources (e.g. packaged virtual appliances); and their relationships (e.g. dependencies, configuration parameters, resource constraints). We architect this layer over existing cloud management platforms to harness interoperability capabilities. This means cloud resources could be easily combined to create higher-level virtual entities, called *Federated cloud resources*, thereby masking the complexity and heterogeneity from the underlying cloud services. For instance, by identifying common concepts among different tools, we can seamlessly merge those features for end-to-end configuration. For example, a VM deployed by *Vagrant* can be modified by another tool, such as *Puppet* with fine-grained configuration tasks (e.g., installing software within the VM) that are not supported by the initial tool. We assume one particular DevOps who is an expert of a particular cloud tool would specify the associated *Domain-specific Model* at the onset.

Connectors for *automated translation* of DSM-based models into native resource artifacts. Connectors accomplish the magic behind the scenes. As mentioned, there are a large variety of resource representation *languages* (e.g. procedural, activity based and declarative); as well as several different types of *tools/APIs* to manage/orchestrate these resources; that all may need to adapt to different *environments* (i.e., public, private and federated). This three-fold level of heterogeneity make cloud resource management a tedious task. We therefore propose the notion of *Connectors*, which provide a high-level interface (i.e. API) for DevOps to deploy, configure and manage cloud resources. As mentioned, the proposed Domain-Specific Model could be used to represent resource configuration using high-level entities and relationships. Behind the scenes, connectors are thereby able to: (a) translate these high-level descriptions into their native format (e.g., files, shell code snippets); and (b) interpret what are the required management operations and transform them into low-level API calls. For example, to create an Image using *Docker's Remote API*, traditionally DevOps would need to be skilled in the tool's communication protocol[1]. This is alleviated using our proposed approach. In addition, *Connectors* may include basic events that are to be monitored by periodically querying for data using low-level APIs. DevOps are thus empowered to write automated management processes such as Event-Condition-Action (ECA) rules and workflows over the operations exposed by the *Connectors*. We assume *Connectors* are implemented by DevOps, who have expertise in programming and knowledge on the particular cloud tool.

The rest of this paper is organized as follows: In Sect. 2, we investigate in the context of example scenarios, specific limitations amongst existing cloud management techniques. In Sect. 3, we present our proposed system architecture. In Sect. 4, we elucidate our domain-specific model, with a case-study on *Docker*. In Sect. 5, we discuss our implementation, while in Sect. 6 we present our implementation and evaluation. In Sect. 7, we examine related work, and conclude with remarks and a discussion of future work.

2   Limitations in Current Cloud Management Solutions

As mentioned, current cloud management solutions rely on low-level script-based languages. For example, Ubuntu Juju employs *Charms*[2]; and similarly Docker employs *Dockerfiles*[3]). Charms and Dockerfiles are a collection of configuration attributes and executable scripts that configure, install and start an application. Inevitably constructs of these scripts typically include basic commands

---

[1] http://docs.docker.com/reference/api/docker_remote_api/.

[2] https://jujucharms.com/.

[3] https://docs.docker.com/reference/builder/.

(e.g., RUN, COPY, CMD), which provide little or no abstraction for DevOps to identify the main attributes and relationships of the constituent cloud resources.

Scenario 1. Consider describing composite cloud resources: A Web Application stack, with a *Node.js* application engine and *MySQL* database. DevOps could describe attributes (e.g. memory, size) of these resources, as well as their relationship (e.g. app engine stores data in database), using *Dockerfiles*. Docker provides either a RESTful or CLI interface to interpret *Dockerfiles* in order to build, deploy, monitor and control necessary resources known as *Containers* on a given Virtual Machine (VM) (refer to Fig. 1(a)). However, as Docker does not support configuring and deploying VMs[4], another cloud management tool would be needed, such as *AWS-EC2 CLI* or *Rackspace CLI*. This therefore forces DevOps to employ multiple tools to automate end-to-end management tasks.

Moreover, considering that every cloud management tool employs their own resource description models, management capabilities and interfaces – the challenges described above only increases several-fold. For example, Fig. 1(b) lists the variety of heterogeneous configuration and management interfaces exposed by different tools. Consequently, these ad-hoc scripts introduce hard-coded dependencies among resources that are orchestrated by different tools. Reusing knowledge artifacts, which include such ad-hoc scripts is not scalable as DevOps are required to manually analyze those knowledge artifacts in order to apply cross-domain relationships among resources within a composite cloud solution.

Scenario 2. This time consider the case of federated cloud resource management. For example, VMs deployed and managed amongst two different cloud services, such as AWS and Backspace. If additional VMs would want to be added (in order to improve reliability and handle increasing demands of the Web application), DevOps would need to implement additional orchestration scripts that monitor the application load and deploy the Web application in either AWS or Rackspace based on a certain load-balancing algorithm. However, both AWS and Rackspace employ different formats of access credentials and management interfaces to deploy VMs.

Overall the level of heterogeneity amongst current cloud solutions entails great complexity when exploiting cloud services. More specifically, with existing cloud delivery models, developing a new cloud-based solution generally leads

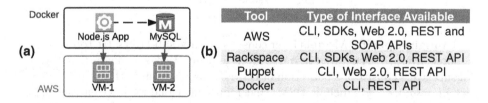

Fig. 1. (a) Components and Relationships of a *Node.js* Web application Stack; (b) List of available cloud Configuration and Management Interfaces

---

[4] This feature was only later introduced by Docker (the principle remains the same).

to uncontrollable fragmentation across the use of different cloud languages and tools (e.g., Puppet, Chef, Juju, Docker, SmartFrog, AWS OpsWorks) [4,5,7,8]. This makes it very difficult to develop interoperable and portable cloud solutions. It also degrades performance as applications cannot be partitioned or migrated easily into another cloud platform when demand cycles increase.

3   Next-Generation Cloud Resource Management: Architecture Overview

The next-generation in cloud resource management with require ease of inter-operability - enhanced productivity with a viable opportunity for reuse. The limitations mentioned above is an immense setback. To overcome this, we pro-pose a layered architecture (see Fig. 2) that enables: (a) *Domain-Specific Models (DSM)* (for high-level representation and management models of cloud resources; and (b) *Connectors* (to automate translation of these high-level DSMs into low level resource descriptions and management scrips.

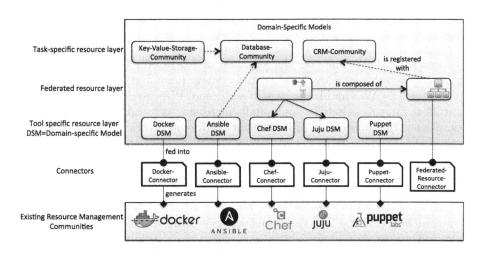

Fig. 2. System Overview

Domain-Specific Models layer consists of three sub-layers: (i) Tool-specific resource layer; (ii) Federated resource layer; and (iii) Task-specific resource layer. All sub-layers consist of a collection of DSMs. Starting from bottom-up, the *tool-specific resource layer* include DSMs that represents cloud resource entities (e.g., resource descriptions, management rules) and relationships among those entities of a 'particular' cloud tool. For example, *Docker DSM* describe linked entities that are provided specifically by the Docker engine. Tool-specific *Domain-specific Models* can also be combined to create higher-level DSMs that represent *federated cloud resources*, which may be managed by two or more existing cloud tools.

For example, a customer relationship management application of an organization, which is deployed in a public cloud service (e.g., AWS), may access a client information database server, which is managed within the organization's private cloud infrastructure (e.g., VMWare). Finally, the *task-specific resource layer* represent "splices" of the fundamental DSM that are reformulated to specific types of categories. For example, DSMs for the *Database Community* may include models that facilitate key-value storages, relational databases and graph databases. The extended goals of DSMs are also to abstract unwanted heterogeneous notations in order to simplify for the end-developer. DSMs can thus be customized to further accommodate this.

Connectors layer, are essentially the glue between the high-level DSM model and underlying cloud tool – it serves to abstract an otherwise complex and heterogenous interface into a simplistic and interoperable one. Connectors assume a DSM has been defined for a particular cloud tool. As we will describe in the next section, a particular DSM has both a *description model* and actionable *management model*. Connectors utilize both these models to auto translate high-level calls into low-level actions. We have observed every cloud tool supports three basic operations: *deploy*, *control* (or *reconfigure*) and *undeploy*. Accordingly, we have built Connectors to function with the following interface:

`init(resource_model)`: Translates a high-level resource DSM-based "description model" into its native script, (e.g. files, shell code) and returns a `unique-ID`.

`deploy(resource_model)`: The runtime selects a particular connector implementation that can deploy the inputted resource configuration model. The connector implements runs the tool-specific `deploy` command.

`control(resource_ID, actions)`: Actions are also described using the high-level DSM-based "management model". The connector implementation maps this into low-level API calls to apply over the inputted `resource_ID`.

`undeploy(resource_ID)`: The runtime detects the appropriate Connector and calls the `undeploy` operation over the specified resource.

Additionally, connectors are also vital for enabling dynamic control. As we will describe in the next section, our "management model" also support events (e.g., connection failure to VM), and DevOps may annotate resource configurations with simple rules that trigger actions upon particular events.

4 Extracting Domain-Specific Models

As mentioned, we have adopted the *Entity-Relationship (ER)* notation to represent *Domain-Specific Models*. The process of building DSMs for a particular tool involves analyzing existing knowledge sources (e.g. language specifications, user documentations, forums and resource description repositories) to understand key entities for describing resources. We assume at least one domain expert would contribute this for a particular, which may then be reused multiple times by other DevOps. Next, we extracted relationships between the entities by understanding how entities are associated when describing composite cloud resources.

Similarly, we extracted what *actions* and *events* are provided by these tools, such as for manipulating the given resource. These events and actions allow DevOps to annotate resource descriptions with ECA rules.

In essence, our embryonic data-model consists of the following elements:

1. **Resource Description Model:** It describes cloud resources in terms of relevant entities (and their attributes), as well as their interconnection of relationships. For example, a VM entity may include CPU, memory and storage as attributes.
2. **Resource Management Model:** It allows to specify cloud management operations, particularly to configure, deploy, monitor and control cloud resources. This model consists of two sub-models:
   (a) *Action Model:* It specifies available actions (e.g., deploy, configure, migrate) to manage cloud resources. It is expressed a set of entities with relevant attributes that express required input and output parameters.
   (b) *Event Model:* It expresses events related to the lifecycle of cloud resources in terms of entities with necessary attributes that describe events [14]. It should be noted that, the issues of event detection while important, are complementary to the research issues addressed in our work and thus outside the scope of this paper.

The benefit of the model, as stated earlier, is that DSMs enables DevOps to work with a high-level design that captures cloud resources as entities and relationships. Concrete cloud configurations can be described based on the DSM. Additionally, DSMs provide a lightweight documentation approach. In contrast with existing script-based approaches, complex resource configurations are often only documented separately in form of ad-hoc Wikis that quickly gets outdates unless continuously maintained. Additionally, our ER-based model inherently supports machine-readable syntax, which can be consumed by software like Connectors to automatically generate cloud resource descriptions, deployment and management scripts.

4.1 *Docker* Case-Study

We built DSMs for a diverse range of tools and languages, including: *Docker*, *Juju* and *TOSCA*. Due to space constraints, we have chosen Docker as a case-study to illustrate in this paper (see Fig. 3). *Docker* is an open-source and emerging industry standard. (Example of other models have been published online[5]

By analyzing the provided specifications[6,7], we identified six key resource description entity types: (1) Container, (2) Image, (3) Application, (4) Registry, (5) Hosting-Machine and (6) Cluster (refer to Fig. 3).

---

[5] http://mosheb.web.cse.unsw.edu.au/DSM/appendix.html

(Appendix of this paper has been published online for readers' further interest).

[6] https://docs.docker.com/reference/builder/.

[7] https://docs.docker.com/compose/reference/.

The central entity: **Container** represents a virtualized software container where DevOps may deploy an application. Deployment knowledge of the application and its dependencies is represented via the entity, **Image**. Such knowledge is either represented using one monolithic **Image** instance or a set of **Image** instances. In other words, the **Image** possesses deployment knowledge required to instantiate a **Container**. An **Application** represents a logical entity that includes a collection of related **Containers**. Each **Container** constitutes a component of the **Application**. The entity **Registry** represents a repository of **Images** where DevOps organize, curate and share resource deployment knowledge. The entity **Hosting-Machine** represents the location where a Container is hosted (e.g., VM or physical machine). A **Cluster** represents a set of **Hosting Machines**. This reduces the overhead of dynamically managing multiple machines. For example, the **Cluster** may automatically decide which **Hosting Machine** will be chosen to deploy the given container based on an optimization algorithm [15].

We then derive the *attributes* that characterize each entity; and the *relationships* amongst them. For example, the relationship between **Hosting-Machine** and **Container** is **Deployment**. The **Containment** relationship defines the hierarchical organization of entities. For example, a **Containment** relationships exist between a **Container** and its related **Application**; and between a

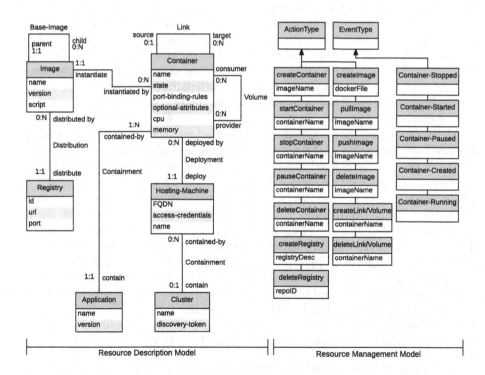

Fig. 3. *Domain-specific Model* for Docker

Hosting-Machine and its related Cluster. Similarly, we derive all other relevant relationships.

Next we extract *actions*. For example, create, start, stop, pause and delete to manipulate Containers. As well as all other actions that Docker offers.

We then extract basic *events* that are supported[8]. Such as: @Created, @Started, @Stopped, @Paused, @Running and @Killed, to detect the runtime state of Containers.

We then specify additional events that are not directly supported by the tool, but are required by the *Connector* for resource management. For example, we may specify a periodic event that includes memory usage data of a particular Container. In addition, we may specify composite events based on previously extracted events using an existing event-pattern specification language (e.g., Esper EPL). For example, we may specify a composite event, which gets triggered if the memory usage of a Container exceeds 95 % and then the Container is killed, to identify Containers that get crashed due to the shortage of available memory.

5   Implementation

Curating DSMs and Connectors. Our design is based on crowd-driven incremental contributions, whereby domain experts of a particular tool collectively participate in curating (i.e. creating and/or updating) DSMs. In our current implementation, we serialize *entities* and *relationships* using *JSON-Schema*. DSMs therefore produce high-level cloud resource schemas that enforce constraints over entity attributes (e.g. datatype, optionality); and relationships (e.g. cardinality). Additionally, actions and events of DSMs may also be defined. Complex or customizable events are also supported using *Esper EPL*[9].

Similarly, experts may also contribute *Connectors*, by providing the necessary business logic for each specified operations that make up the connector interface. Earlier at Sect. 3, we defined a generic programmable interface for DevOps to implement connectors, this include four mandatory operations. Additionally, a Connector may have any number of operations that implement the actions specified in the relevant DSM. For example, Docker defines a createContainer method, which: (i) accepts the name of an Image; (ii) prepare the Hosting-Machine to deploy a Container; and (iii) invoke docker run command in the Docker CLI[10] along with an Image. A snippet of a connector interface is shown at Fig. 4.

Once both the *DSM* and *Connector/s* are registered, DevOps are then able to create cloud resources and moreover, implement management processes/rules based on the simplicity offered by the high-level DSM.

User-Interface. Our current implementation provides a *Command-Line Interface (CLI)*, as well as a prototypical *Graphical User Interface (GUI)*. Our GUI

---

[8] https://docs.docker.com/engine/reference/commandline/events/.

[9] http://rsper.codehaus.org.

[10] https://docs.docker.com/reference/commandline/cli/.

includes *DSM Editor* that enables curators to *graphically* specify the structure of entities, relationships, actions and events when describing a DSM. We reuse Java-script library named *JSON Schema Based Editor*[11] for the generation and verification of JSON schemas.

The CLI can also accomplish DSM specifications albeit programmatically. In addition, the CLI enables DevOp to invoke operations. For example, calling the `init` and `deployContainer` actions in order to deploy a Container within the Docker runtime (refer to Code 1.1). Behind the scenes an appropriate connector is selected, which fires the action call. DevOps are required to first locate the DSM, as shown at Listing 1.1.

Code 1.1. CLI command to deploy a container in Docker

```
1  cd ~/base-git-repo/node-app-1   #location of the JSON-based
                resource description
2  cloudbase docker.rest -action=init
3  cloudbase docker.rest -action=deployContainer
4                  -input={"resource":"node-engine.json"}
```

Automated Translation into Native Artifacts. Figure 4 provides an illustrative overview. The *translation logic* utilizes both the preregistered DSM and Connector/s. A DevOp may then describe a resource configuration: in this example, a `MySQL` and `Node.js` Web application (based on *Scenario 1* we described in Sect. 2). Subsequently, a `Dockerfile` and `build.sh` file is automatically generated for each resource. Note: The files shown in Fig. 4 are for illustrative purposes only. For larger print, readers are directed to our online appendix (See footnote 5).

Similarly, the *build.sh* file is generated based on a sequence of commands, which: (a) reads the *Dockerfile*; (b) generates a concrete Image; (c) uploads the generated Image to a specified `Registry` (i.e., *Registry-1*); and (d) creates a concrete Container from the concrete Image in a specified `Hosting-Machine` (i.e., *HostingMachine-1*). The *build.sh* file may also include commands to instantiate relationships (e.g. `Links` and `Volumes`) between dependent concrete Containers. The transformation logic extracts the required input data for these commands from attributes that were defined in Docker's DSM.

In addition, management scripts such as event/action rules are also auto-translated into low-level API calls. For example, a management rule, that creates new `Containers` to handle increasing load is depicted at the bottom of Fig. 4. The generated file depicts a sequence of API calls which: (a) logs-in to a particular `Hosting-Machine`; (b) creates an `Image` (if it doesn't already exist); and (c) creates and starts a `Container`.

Storage. We utilize a *JSON Object Store*; a Git[12] repository to store and share *DSMs* and their objects as JSON files. Related cloud resource descriptions are organized into separate folders within the repository. The *JSON Object Store*

---

[11] https://github.com/jdorn/json-editor.
[12] https://git-scm.com/.

allows keeping multiple versions of JSON files and trigger events when certain modifications (e.g., store, update, delete cloud resource descriptions) occur. These features are very useful to dynamically reconfigure cloud resources and roll-back to a previous stable configuration if an error occurs.

Event Management System. We detect and process lower-level monitoring events (e.g., (re)starting, CPU and memory usage) from different cloud services (e.g., Docker, AWS), and thereby generate higher-level events for DevOps. Events to be collected are defined as part of the DSM. We support both *Pull* and

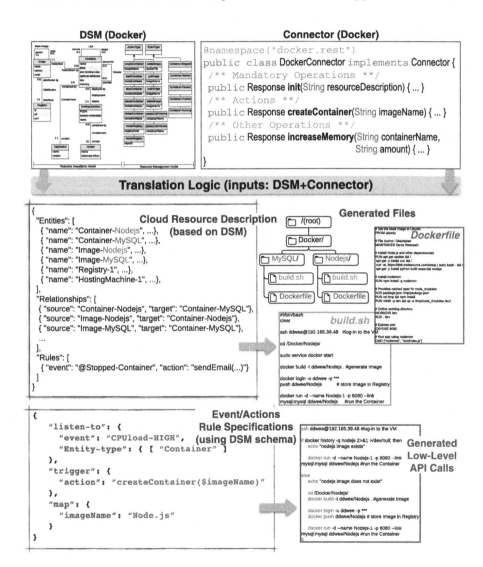

Fig. 4. Automated translation of high-level models into native artifacts

PuSH -based detection. We use *Fluentd*[13] to perform *polling* and extract JSON-based events. For example, events related to state changes of `Containers` as per Docker's DSM. For extracting *PuSH*-based events, we leverage Apache Camel[14]. For specifying, processing and generating high-level events we use *Esper EPL*. High-level events enable defining events based on a series of low-level events. For example, *Esper* may trigger an event named `CPULoad-High` for a particular Application in Docker if the CPU usage of each Container of the Application is over 95 %, (as illustrated in Fig. 4). We also implement a Java-based event publishing channel for consumers (such as the *Rule Processor*) to subscribe.

Rule Processor. We also support automation capabilities via simple reactive rules. For example, DevOps may specify *if* `@Stopped` *then* `#notify`, which implies if some resource has stopped, perform some notification action. We greatly simplify the definition of by reusing our previous work [3], where we adopted a *"knowledge-based"* approach, which means APIs and their constituents (i.e. operations, input/output types) of the orchestration tools are loaded in a knowledge-base. This makes it possible to write high-level rule definitions and translate into concrete actions. At Fig. 4, we showed a simple rule. The `listen-to` construct specifies events to detect; the `trigger` construct specifies what *actions* to invoke; and the `map` construct describes the required input parameters for the invocation.

6   Evaluation

We conducted a user-study to evaluate the following hypotheses: **H**, the *Domain-Specific Model* approach is more *efficient* to *accurately* configure and deploy cloud resources. We measured efficiency as the time taken to complete the tasks and the number of lines-of-code excluding whitespace; whereas accuracy was determined by deploying each cloud resource description and checking whether the resultant deployment complied with the initial deployment specification.

Participant Selection and Grouping. Participants were sourced with diverse levels of technical expertise. For the sake of analysis, we classified a total of 14 participants into 2 main groups: (I) Experts (8 participants) with sophisticated understanding of cloud orchestration tools with 2–8 years of experience. And (II) Generalists (6 participants) who have average knowledge of cloud orchestration tool for day-to-day requirements, with around 1–5 years of experience.

Use-Case. We asked participants to configure and deploy the following scenario: A platform that requires an AWS-EC2 VM where a Docker Container resides within. The container includes Redmine[15], a project management service, and a Git client[16]. The Redmine service is intended to: (i) extract commits from a

---

[13] http://www.fluentd.org/.

[14] http://camel.apache.org/.

[15] http://www.redmine.org/.

[16] http://git-scm.com/.

specified source repository in GitHub via the Git client; and (ii) link them with relevant bug reports. In addition an AWS-S3 bucket (i.e. key-value store), which acts as a software distribution repository, is required.

Experimental Setup. Prior to the experiment, participants attended an individual training session, where our tool was explained via a hands-on presentation. We also explained them the use-case scenario. For quantitative comparison purposes, we conducted the same experiment against two third-party tools: *Docker* and *Juju*. Only a total of 8 and 5 out of 14 DevOps participated in the *Docker* and *Juju* based experiments respectively. This was due to some DevOps not having expertise and confidence to use those tools. In addition, a total of 7 participants implemented the same deployment specification using Shell scripts to estimate an upper bound of the test results.

6.1   Experiment Results and Analysis

Evaluation of H. The hypothesis H was evaluated based on the time taken and number of lines-of-code. Alternatively, we sought to disprove the null hypothesis H_0. The hypothesis was examined by conducting a t-test with a probability threshold of 5 %, and assuming unequal variance.

As shown in Fig. 5, it was pleasantly surprising that even generalists demonstrated a significant increase in efficiency (i.e. reduction in time and lines-of-code). More specifically, the time taken to complete the task was reduced by 31 % in comparison to there other approaches. Similarly, the number of lines-of-code was reduced by 37.2 %. Participants reported that they much rather preferred an *entity-relationship (ER)* based abstraction for describing resources, as opposed to script-based languages that are provided by otherwise widely adopted cloud management tools, such as *Docker* and *JuJu*. DevOps confirmed this greatly helped improve their configuration and deployment time.

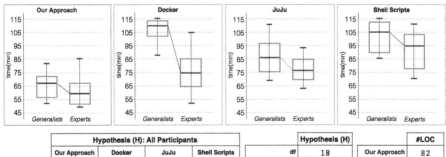

Fig. 5. Results (Time, grouped by expertise); *t-test* Results; and *Lines-of-Code*

On the other hand, our approach assumes that appropriate *Domain-Specific Models* and *Connectors* have been defined and registered. This does incur additional costs to implement, however we argue this is typically a one-off for the benefit of many. Once registered, countless DevOps would benefit over many occasions. Moreover, our *knowledge-driven* approach implies knowledge (such as high-level representations of cloud resource configurations) can be incrementally shared and collectively reused, which significantly improve productivity to implement federated management spanning across multiple cloud services.

Due to the vast number of alternative tools, and project-based constraints, a more exhaustive comparative experiment was outside the scope. However, given the notable differences in times (mean of 63, against 93, 72 and 101 min), we postulate it is unlikely to observe fundamental differences when comparing with any other tools similar to Docker or Juju. Accordingly, given our observations the likelihood of H_0 (equal mean modeling time) was around 5 %. Therefore, we could safely reject these null hypotheses, and imply the truth of H.

7   Related Work and Concluding Remarks

Tools such as, *Puppet, Chef, Juju, Docker, SmartFrog* and *AWS OpsWorks*, as well as various research initiatives [4,5,7,8,19], all provide domain specific languages to represent and manage resources in a cloud environment. These languages are either template-based or model-driven [11].

Cloud Resource Representation and Management Languages. Template-based approaches (e.g., Open Virtualization Format) aggregate resources from a lower-level of the cloud stack and expose the package, along with some configurability options, to a higher-layer. Model-driven approaches (e.g., TOSCA [12]) define various models of the application at different levels of the cloud stack, and aim to automate the deployment of abstract pre-defined composite solutions on cloud infrastructure [9,14]. Our approach proposes *Domain-specific Models* – a methodology to extract cloud resource management entities from such model-driven and template-based languages. In contrast, our approach invites an interoperable vocabulary to build elementary and federated cloud resources, as an *abstract*-layer over these "multiple and diverse languages".

Enabling Federated Cloud Management. Federation of cloud resources implies building cross-provider solutions. For example, `Hosting-Machine` in *Docker* represents a VM where `Containers` are deployed, albeit the *Docker* run-time itself cannot provision VMs. *JuJu* on the other hand focuses on managing a set of VMs, and can provision these VMs. To support this, we require a middleware that either: (i) defines a unified cloud resource language; or (ii) provide a pluggable architecture that accepts and interprets different resource models. The former is clearly not feasible, would be costly and require existing tools to undergo major architectural changes or complex model transformations to conform to a new language provided by the middleware. We thus believe the latter approach provides a more pragmatic and adaptive solution that can be integrated amongst a set of already existing and prevalent tools. To solve this gap, we thus precisely propose the notion of Domain-specific models, to automate end-to-end deployment (e.g. Docker Containers on VMs which are provisioned by Juju).

Model-Driven Approach and Combating Heterogeneity. *TOSCA* is an open-standard for unified representation and orchestration of cloud resources [12]. Wettinger et al. proposes a model transformation technique that generates TOSCA-based descriptions from resource descriptions in *Chef* and *Juju* [18]. *MODAClouds* [1] is another approach to design and manage multi-cloud applications. It proposes four layers that incrementally transform functional and non-functional requirements of applications into tool-specific resource tasks. Konstantinous et al. [8] presents a description and deployment model that first models a resource as a provider-independent resource configuration, called "Virtual Solution Model", and then another party can transform the provider-independent model to a provider-specific model called, "Virtual Deployment Model". However, this approach only allows users to compose federated resource configurations from a single provider for a single deployment. In contrast, our approach considers the resource federation from multiple providers as a first class citizen.

Summary. The "cloud" plays an increasingly vital role in modern-computing technology. Accordingly, a vast variety of configuration and management tools have been proposed, albeit they differ with respect to representation language, as well as user-interface. Overall they assume a low-level and sophisticated programmatic approach. The paper provides an innovative approach for dealing with this: Firstly, in stead of competing with existing approaches, we embrace them by providing a "higher-level" and "interoperable" layer via the notion of Domain-specific Models. Such models can recompose to even higher-level models, in order to capture a particular use-case. Moreover, we encourage a knowledge-sharing paradigm unlike any other existing approach. We realized our approach via a pluggable architecture (i.e., *Connectors*) – a programmable interface that allows DevOps to deploy and manage high-level cloud resource representations. Behind the scenes, *Connectors* translate high-level models into native scripts. We evaluated our work with a user-study that yielded significantly promising results. We are therefore confident our work provides an innovative approach to a new way of cloud management. As future work, we plan to integrate a recommender system, and visual notations based on our previous work [17].

References

1. Ardagna, D., et al.: Modaclouds: a model-driven approach for the design and execution of applications on multiple clouds. In: MISE, pp. 50–56, June 2012
2. Bahga, A., Madisetti, V.K.: Rapid prototyping of multitier cloud-based services and systems. Computer **46**(11), 76–83 (2013)
3. Barukh, M.C., Benatallah, B.: *ProcessBase*: a hybrid process management platform. In: Franch, X., Ghose, A.K., Lewis, G.A., Bhiri, S. (eds.) ICSOC 2014. LNCS, vol. 8831, pp. 16–31. Springer, Heidelberg (2014)

4. Chieu, T.C., et al.: Solution-based deployment of complex application services on a cloud. In: SOLI, pp. 282–287. IEEE (2010)
5. Delaet, T., Joosen, W., Vanbrabant, B.: A survey of system configuration tools. In: 24th International Conference on LISA, pp. 1–8. USENIX Association (2010)
6. Gartner says cloud computing will become the bulk of new it spend by 2016. http://www.gartner.com/newsroom/id/2613015. Accessed 07 Dec 2014
7. Goldsack, P., et al.: The smartfrog configuration management framework. ACM SIGOPS Oper. Syst. Rev. **43**(1), 16–25 (2009)
8. Konstantinou, A.V., et al.: An architecture for virtual solution composition and deployment in infrastructure clouds. In: VTDC, pp. 9–18. ACM (2009)
9. Liu, C., Loo, B.T., Mao, Y.: Declarative automated cloud resource orchestration. In: Proceedings of the SOCC 2011, pp. 1–8. ACM (2011)
10. Lu, H., et al.: Pattern-based deployment service for next generation clouds. In: 2013 IEEE Ninth World Congress on SERVICES, pp. 464–471, June 2013
11. Misic, V., et al.: Guest editors' introduction: special issue on cloud computing. IEEE Trans. Parallel Distrib. Syst. **24**(6), 1062–1065 (2013)
12. OASIS: Topology and Orchestration Specification for Cloud Applications (TOSCA), Version 1.0 (2013)
13. Ponge, J., Benatallah, B., Casati, F., Toumani, F.: Analysis and applications of timed service protocols. ACM Softw. Eng. Methodol. **19**(4), 11:1–11:38 (2010)
14. Ranjan, R., Benatallah, B.: Programming cloud resource orchestration framework: operations and research challenges. CoRR abs/1204.2204 (2012)
15. Schulte, S., Janiesch, C., Venugopal, S., Weber, I., Hoenisch, P.: Elastic business process management: state of the art and open challenges for BPM in the cloud. Future Gener. Comput. Syst. **46**, 36–50 (2015)
16. Veeravalli, B., Parashar, M.: Guest editors' introduction: special issue on cloud of clouds. IEEE Trans. Comput. **63**(1), 1–2 (2014)
17. Weerasiri, D., Barukh, M.C., Benatallah, B., Jian, C.: *Cloudmap*: a visual notation for representing and managing cloud resources. In: Nurcan, S., Soffer, P., Bajec, M., Eder, J. (eds.) CAiSE 2016. LNCS, vol. 9694, pp. 427–443. Springer, Heidelberg (2016)
18. Wettinger, J., Breitenbucher, U., Leymann, F.: Standards-based devOps automation and integration using TOSCA. In: 2014 IEEE/ACM 7th International Conference on Utility and Cloud Computing (UCC), pp. 59–68, December 2014
19. Wilson, M.S.: Constructing and managing appliances for cloud deployments from repositories of reusable components. In: Proceedings of the 2009 Conference on HotCloud 2009. USENIX Association (2009)
20. Zeng, L., et al.: QoS-aware middleware for web services composition. IEEE Trans. Softw. Eng. **30**(5), 311–327 (2004)

Detecting Cloud (Anti)Patterns: OCCI Perspective

Hayet Brabra[1,4(✉)], Achraf Mtibaa[2], Layth Sliman[3], Walid Gaaloul[4], Boualem Benatallah[5], and Faiez Gargouri[1]

[1] ISIMS Sfax, Miracl Laboratory, Sfax, Tunisia
brabra.hayeet@gmail.com, faiez.gargouri@gmail.com
[2] ENETCOM Sfax, Miracl Laboratory, Sfax, Tunisia
achrafmtibaa@gmail.com
[3] Efrei, Paris, France
layth.sliman@efrei.fr
[4] TELECOM SudParis, CNRS UMR Samovar, Évry, France
walid.gaaloul@mines-telecom.fr
[5] UNSW, Sydney, Australia
boualem.benatallah@gmail.com

Abstract. Open Cloud Computing Interface (OCCI) follows a set of guidelines (i.e. best practices) to create interoperable APIs over Cloud resources. In this paper, we identify a set of patterns that must be followed and anti-patterns that should be avoided to comply with the OCCI guidelines. To automatically detect (anti)patterns, we propose a Semantic-based approach, relying on SWRL (Semantic Web Rule Language) rules and in SQWRL (Semantic Query-Enhanced Web Rule Language) queries to describe the (anti)patterns symptoms. An evaluation, conducted on real world Cloud service APIs, shows the feasibility of the proposed approach by assessing their compliance to OCCI standard.

Keywords: OCCI · Pattern · Anti-pattern · Ontology · SWRL · SQWRL

1 Introduction

Cloud Computing has emerged as a new technological paradigm that aims to offer a novel vision to deliver computing resources with significant cost reduction. However, its rapid evolution has reached a level of complexity due mainly to the vast and heterogeneous amount of services and resources. More precisely, the management of a potentially large number of Cloud services with heterogeneous interfaces is a challenge [13]. The lack of interoperability solutions may hinder the widespread adoption of Cloud Computing because organization fear of vendor lock-in [6,12]. The latter refers to a situation in which once an organization has selected a Cloud provider changing to another provider can be only very costly.

A common way for avoiding these issues is the use of open standards [6,9,12]. Actually, many Cloud projects are developing standards for the Cloud.

© Springer International Publishing Switzerland 2016
Q.Z. Sheng et al. (Eds.): ICSOC 2016, LNCS 9936, pp. 202–218, 2016.
DOI: 10.1007/978-3-319-46295-0_13

However, the most popular one is Open Cloud Computing Interface (OCCI) [1]. OCCI is an open standard defining a meta-model for Cloud resources and a RESTful API for management tasks. A well-designed management API hides the heterogeneity and evolution of the managed resources across various providers, while providing unified and efficient access to them. Among the OCCI specifications, OCCI HTTP Protocol [16] provides a set of guidelines (i.e. recommended best practices) to create unified APIs for managing Cloud resources. These best practices represent together a minimal set to achieve the interoperability and provide a uniform way to discover and manage Cloud resources across various providers. The non-compliance or poor adoption of such practices in current Cloud resource management APIs may negatively impact the interoperation of Cloud services. Currently, OCCI members provide a textual description of suggested guidelines in [16] as well as a compliance test tool [2] that does not provide a clear and detailed description. This tool can be used to show the presence of best practices, but never to show the absence of one of them. In this paper, we aim at providing developer both good and poor practices in Cloud RESTful APIs according to OCCI perspective and thus increasing its understandability. Some efforts have been realized in the past to deal with RESTful APIs. For example, Francis et al. [8] proposed a heuristic-based approach to detect (anti)patterns in RESTful systems to enhance their understandability and reusability. Such approach is tailored to deal with REST APIs like facebook and Twitter as it only focuses on REST aspects. Therefore, they cannot be applied to RESTful APIs developped for cloud services or ressources. Along with REST aspects, OCCI provides guidelines that relate to the structure and definition of Cloud resources that have not been so far considered in existing research work.

In this paper, we define non-compliance (respectively, compliance) to OCCI RESTful API guidelines as OCCI REST Anti-patterns (respectively, OCCI REST Patterns). We propose semantic-based detection of OCCI REST Patterns and Anti-patterns in Cloud RESTful APIs. More specifically, we propose (1) a semantic specification of 28 common OCCI REST(anti)patterns for Cloud RESTful APIs; (2) SWRL rules[1] in conjunction with SQWRL queries[2] for automatic detection of OCCI REST(anti)patterns (3) and a validation of our approach by analyzing the 28 OCCI REST (anti)patterns on real world Cloud RESTful APIs, including Openstack, COAPS, OpenNebula, Amazon S3, Microsoft Azure and Rackspace. The remainder of the paper is structured as follows: in Sect. 2 we discuss the related work. Section 3 presents the proposed approach. Section 4 presents a validation of our solution. Finally, we conclude the paper and provide insight for future works.

2   Related Work

Over the last years, several researches used patterns and anti-patterns to express architectural concerns and solutions in Object Oriented Systems (OO systems),

---

[1] https://www.w3.org/Submission/SWRL/.

[2] http://protege.cim3.net/cgi-bin/wiki.pl?SQWRL.

Service Oriented Architectures (SOAs) and recently in RESTful APIs. In the context of OO systems, Kessentini et al. [11] proposed an automated approach to detect various types of design defects in the source code. The proposed approach is based on detection rules that are defined as combinations of metrics and thresholds that better conform to known instances of design defects. Fourati et al. [7] proposed an approach that identifies anti-patterns in UML designs through the use of existing and newly defined quality metrics. The proposed approach examines the structural and behavioral information through the class and sequence diagrams. Another interesting effort has been done in [20] which proposed SPARSE, an OWL ontology based knowledge system that aims at assessing software project managers in the anti-pattern detection process.

Other related works have focused on the detection of anti-patterns and patterns in SOA. Dudney et al. [4] have defined a catalog of 53 anti-patterns related to the architecture, design, and implementation of J2EE-based systems. In [15], Moha et al. addressed the lack of methods and techniques for detecting SOA anti-patterns in service-based systems (SBSs). The aim is to provide an approach based on BNF grammar to detect the anti-patterns that may occur under SBSs in order to help the software engineer in assessing the design and QoS. This approach is also adapted to detect anti-patterns in Web Services [19].

However, we noted that both OO and SOA detection methods cannot be directly applied to RESTful APIs because OO focuses only on classes and SOA focuses on services and WSDL descriptions. In consequence, Francis et al. in [8] proposed a heuristics-based approach to detect (anti)patterns in RESTful systems. Additionally, the same authors have proposed DOLAR approach which applies syntactic and semantic analyses for the detection of linguistic (anti)patterns in RESTful APIs [18]. Both approaches only define a set of (anti)patterns focusing on properties related to REST architecture. Thus, they cannot be applied to RESTful APIs developped for cloud services or ressources. Motivated by these considerations, in this paper, we will focus on (anti)patterns that relate to the structure and definition of Cloud resources that have not been so far considered in previous research works. These (anti)patterns will be then used to assess the compliance of current Cloud RESTful APIs to OCCI guidelines.

3   Approach Overview

Our approach is based on semantics solutions to formally define (anti)patterns and ensure their automatic detection. The first reason to have such choice is the need for a technique that deals with the structure and semantic relations among resources, services, and parameters and able to resolve the ambiguity in terminologies used by developer to describe a cloud RESTful API. The second is to provide an automatic support to detect (anti)patterns through applying a reasoning process to draw inferences from details in a Cloud RESTful API with the assurance that the provided new knowledge is sound. In this section, we present an overall overview of our proposed approach. As shown in Fig. 1, our approach proceeds in three steps:

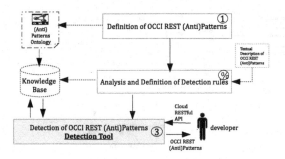

Fig. 1. Approach overview

Step 1. Definition of OCCI REST (Anti)Patterns: This step allows to define the core ontology that we call *(Anti)Patterns Ontology*. The proposed ontology contains the relevant and necessary concepts for the detection purpose.

Step 2. Analysis and Definition of Detection Rules: This step consists of analyzing the textual description of OCCI REST(anti)patterns from the OCCI RESTful Protocol [16] to identify their relevant features. We use these relevant features to define semantic rules required for the detection of (anti)patterns. Both rules and (Anti)Patterns Ontology are then stored in a knowledge base which can be later interrogated with SQWRL queries for analysing the detection results.

Step 3. Detection of OCCI REST (Anti)Patterns: This step deals with the automatic application of detection rules defined in Step 2 using our detection tool to detect each (anti)pattern. This tool will return to the developer a set of detecting OCCI REST (anti)patterns in a given RESTful API.

3.1   Definition of OCCI REST (Anti)Patterns

In this step, we perform a domain analysis on both OCCI descriptions for Cloud resources and documentations of the RESTful API existing in the literature in order to build (Anti)Patterns Ontology, a model that provides a semantic definition of OCCI REST (anti)patterns using OWL 2 (OWL 2 Web Ontology Language) [3]. (Anti)Patterns Ontology is specified as a set of interrelated ontologies viz. *Pattern Ontology, Anti-Pattern Ontology, REST API Ontology* and *OCCI Ontology*.

Pattern Ontology: The Pattern Ontology, as depicted in Fig. 2, captures the necessary information defining an OCCI REST pattern in term of attributes that are linked to its main concept *Ptt:Pattern*. Those attributes (i.e. equivalent to data type properties in OWL language) are *Ptt:name, Ptt:description* and *Ptt:required* its value is a boolean that depicts whether the pattern is required or no. In addition, the *Ptt:Pattern* concept has two relationships which are *Ptt:Disjoint* and *Ptt:Concerns* and represents a range of *Rest:hasPattern*, which denotes that it can be an occurrence of the pattern either for a given API or its elements. The *Ptt:Disjoint* relationship shows the corresponding anti-pattern for

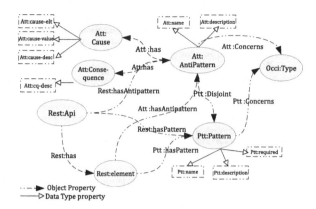

Fig. 2. (Anti)patterns ontology

a given pattern. The Ptt:Concerns relationship indicates that a pattern concerns a given OCCI Type (i.e. Resource, Mixin, etc.).

Anti-Pattern Ontology: As depicted in Fig. 2, the definition of Anti-Pattern Ontology is similar to the Pattern Ontology. However, as opposed to OCCI REST pattern, we use OCCI REST anti-pattern to capture a bad practice of such OCCI RESTful API guidelines. For that reason, we add along with the provided definition for a pattern except the attribute *Ptt:required*, the *Att:Cause* and *Att:Consequence* as concepts defining respectively the cause of OCCI RESTful anti-pattern and the consequence that may result from its occurrence. *Att:has* relationships links respectively the *Att:AntiPattern* concept with *Att:Cause* and *Att:Consequence* concepts. In that way, we provide developer enough knowledge overviewing the detected anti-pattern. *Rest:hasAntipattern* denotes that the given API or one of its elements can have an anti-pattern.

REST API Ontology: The REST API ontology aims at providing a semantic-based description of the structural and functional characteristics of the OCCI RESTful API. OCCI RESTful API follows a RESTful API design, meaning that applications use standard HTTP methods to retrieve and manipulate OCCI resources. To define this ontology, we exploit the various documentations of the RESTful API while taking OCCI RESTful API specificities into account. The main concept is *Rest:API* (a REST API) which is linked, as shown in Fig. 3(b), to the following three concepts: *Rest:AuthorizationProtocol* (an authorization protocol used to access the API), *Rest:Element* (an abstract type describing through its subclasses the possible components that we can find in a REST API, including request header, response header, code status, operation, URL, request, response, etc.) and *Rest:Operation* (a REST operation such as *Create a Server*)

OCCI Ontology: All RESTful API operations are applied on OCCI types (i.e. Category, Resource, etc.) that are already defined both in OCCI Core [17] and OCCI infrastructure [14]. To allow such capability, we define OCCI ontology

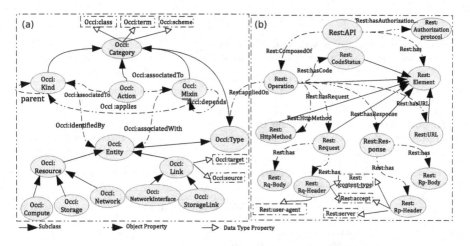

Fig. 3. (a) OCCI ontology; (b) REST API ontology

that provides a semantic description of the real-world resources abstraction provided in these two specifications while taking the OCCI rendering syntax of those resources [5] into account. The Fig. 3(a) gives an overview of the OCCI Ontology. The heart of the OCCI Ontology is the *Occi:Resource* concept which has three sub-concepts *Occi:Storage*, *Occi:Compute* and *Occi:Network*. In such way, a Resource can be a virtual machine, a virtual switch, etc. *Occi:Resource* is complemented by the *Occi:Link* concept which associates one resource instance with another. The Link type can be a *Storage Link* or *Network Interface* and contains a number of common attributes (e.g. *Occi:source*, *Occi:target*). Both *Occi:Resource* and *Occi:Link* inherit the *Occi:Entity* concept. The *Occi:Kind* is the core of the classification system built into the OCCI Core Model. *Occi:Kind* is a specialization of *Occi:Category* and introduces additional capabilities in terms of actions. Occi:Action identifies an invocable operation applicable to an entity instance. The last type defined by the OCCI Core Model is the Occi:Mixin type. An instance of Mixin can be associated with an entity instance to mix-in additional capabilities at run-time [17].

3.2   Analysis and Definition of Detection Rules

In this step, we analyses the textual definitions of the (anti)patterns listed in Tables 1, 2, and 3 to identify their relevant features. These features will then be used to define the semantic rules required to detect (anti)patterns. We rely on SWRL language to properly define these rules. A SWRL rule consists of two parts which are called the *Antecedent* and *Consequent*. An *Antecedent* represents a conjunction of one or more atom aiming together to define the conditions that must be met. Whereas, *the Consequent* specifies the fact that may be resulted in case of fulfillment of the conditions defined in *Antecedent*. SWRL rules can contain also SWRL built-ins (e.g. swrlb:matches) or SQWRL queries

Table 1. Management related (anti)patterns.

1.Query Interface Support vs Missing Query Interface
Description: To be compliant with OCCI, Query interface must be implemented. It allows the client to discover all capabilities he refers to [16]. It represents three operations applied on Actions, Kind, and Mixin, including retrieval of all registered Kinds, Actions and Mixins (HTTP verb GET must be used), adding (HTTP verb POST must be used) and removing a Mixin(HTTP verb DELETE must be used). It must be found at the path /-/ on the root of the implementation. The poor practice of query interface or the no support of it leads to the *Missing query interface anti-pattern*
2. Compliant Create vs. Non-Compliant Create
Description: The Create operation that can be applied to whatever entity (i.e. Mixin, Resource) should be compliant with the OCCI RESTful Protocol. This compliance requires the respect of the creation guidelines regarding the type of the entity that may be created. These constraints are summarized as follows:
- To create a Mixin definition, the HTTP verb POST must be used and HTTP Category term, scheme and location must be supported in this definition
- To create a Resource instance, the HTTP verb POST or PUT must be used and the request must contain one and only one HTTP Category rendering which refers to a specific Kind instance defining the type of a resource instance
The poor practice of one of those guidelines leads to *the Non-Compliant Create anti-pattern*
3. Compliant Update vs. Non-Compliant Update
Description: The Update operation, which can be applied to entities (i.e. Mixin, Resource) should be compliant with the OCCI RESTful Protocol. This compliance requires the respect of the update guidelines regarding the type of the entity that may be updated. These guidelines are summarized as follows:
- To full update a Mixin, HTTP verb PUT must be used and all URIs which are part of the collection must be provided along with the request
- To partial update a Resource, HTTP verb POST must be used and the information which are updated must be provided along with the request
- To full update a Resource, HTTP verb Put must be used in the request
The poor practice of one of those guidelines leads to *the Non-Compliant Update anti-pattern.*
4. Compliant Delete vs. Non-Compliant Delete
Description: The Delete (or Remove) operation that can be applied either to Mixin or Resource, should be compliant with the OCCI RESTful Protocol. This compliance requires the respect of the Delete guidelines regarding the type of the entity that may be deleted. These guidelines are summarized as follows:
- To remove a Mixin definition, HTTP verb DELETE must be used and the information about which Mixin should be deleted must be provided
- To delete all Resources below a given path or only one, i.e. The HTTP verb DELETE must be used and no other information should be added to the request
The poor practice of one of those guidelines leads to *the Non-Compliant Delete anti-pattern*
5. Compliant Retrieve vs. Non-Compliant Retrieve
Description: The Retrieve operation, which can be applied to Resource or Link, should be compliant with the OCCI RESTful Protocol. This compliance requires the respect of the Retrieve guidelines regarding the type of the entity that may be retrieved [16]. These guidelines are summarized as follows:
- To Retrieve a Resource or Link instance, the HTTP verb GET must be used in the request and the server response must return at least the HTTP Category which defines the Kind of the Resource or Link and associated attributes
- To Retrieve all Resources belonging to Mixin or Kind, HTTP verb GET must be used and a list containing all resource instances which belong to the requested Mixin or Kind must be returned
The poor practice of one of those guidelines leads to *the Non-Compliant Retrieve anti-pattern*
6. Compliant Trigger Action vs. Non-Compliant Trigger Action
Description: The Trigger action that can be applied to a Resource should be compliant with the OCCI RESTful Protocol, i.e. HTTP verb POST must be used and a query exposing the term of the Action must be added to the URI. Additionally, the HTTP Category defining the Action must be also provided [16]. The poor practice of one of those guidelines leads to the *Non-Compliant Trigger Action anti-pattern*

(e.g. sqwrl:select). SWRL built-ins are user-defined predicates, including basic mathematical operators and functions for string manipulations. SQWRL queries define a set of operators that can be seen as SQL-like operations used to exploit the knowledge inferred by SWRL rules.

Table 2. Cloud structure (anti)patterns.

---

1. Compliant Link between Resources vs. Non-Compliant Link between Resources

Description: To create a Link between two resources, the HTTP POST verb must be used and its kind as well as a "source" and "target" attributes must be provided. The non existence of one of them leads to the *Non-Compliant Link between Resources anti-pattern*

---

2. Compliant Association of resource(s) with Mixin vs. Non-compliant Association of resource(s) with Mixin

Description: Association of resource(s) with a Mixin should be compliant, i.e. HTTP POST verb must be used and the URIs which uniquely define the resources must be provided in the request. The poor practice of one of those guidelines leads to *the Non-compliant Association of resource(s) with Mixin anti-pattern*

---

3. Compliant Dissociation of resource(s) From Mixin vs. Non-compliant dissociation of resource(s) From Mixin

Description: Dissociation of resource(s) from a Mixin should be compliant, i.e. HTTP DELETE verb must be used and the URIs which uniquely define the resources must be provided in the request. The poor practice of one of those guidelines leads to *the Non-compliant Dissociation of resource(s) From Mixin anti-pattern*

Table 3. REST related (anti)patterns

---

1. Compliant URL vs. Non-Compliant URL

Description: A URL Path should be Compliant, i.e. Whenever the URL Path is rendered it must be either a String or as defined in RFC6570 [10]. The *non-Compliant URL anti-pattern* occurs as the consequence of the poor practice of such guidelines

---

2. Compliant Request Header vs. Non-Compliant Request Header

Description: A Request Header can be considered compliant, i.e. client (e.g. OCCI client) should specify the media types its implementation data formats (e.g. OCCI Data formats) support in the Accept header and the implementation (e.g. OCCI version) version number in the User-Agent header and must specify the media type its implementation data format (e.g. OCCI data format) support in the Content-type header [16]. The poor practices of those guidelines leads to the *Non-Compliant Request Header anti-patern*

---

3. Compliant Response Header vs. Non- Compliant Response Header

Description: A Response Header can be considered compliant, i.e. a server (e.g. OCCI server) should specify the media types its implementation data formats (e.g. OCCI Data formats) support in the Accept header, and must specify the media type its implementation data format (e.g. OCCI data format) used in an HTTP response in Content-type header and the implementation (e.g. OCCI version) version number in the Server header [16]. The poor practices of all guidelines leads to the *Non-Compliant Response Header anti-patern*

We distinguish three categories of (anti)patterns, two mainly focus on the Cloud service aspects and one addresses general aspects of the REST services according to OCCI perspective: Management Related (Anti)Patterns, Cloud Structure Related (Aanti)Patterns, and REST Related (Anti)Patterns. In the following, we define these categories, while explaining SWRL rules for detecting an example of (anti)pattern under each one.

Management Related (Anti)Patterns: They represent the poor and best practices in the main management operations applied on Cloud resources and services, with respect to OCCI perspective (see Table 1). We identify 6 patterns and its opposite anti-patterns respectively in Query interface, Create, Retrieve, Update, Delete operations and in Trigger actions. Figure 4 illustrates the SWRL rules we define for the *Query interface support pattern* and the *Missing query interface anti-pattern*. The SWRL rule for *Query interface support Pattern* aims to evaluate for each operation both the value of an URL and the used verb of an HTTP Method. We report that the API has this pattern if we find at least an URL value match "\- \" path and the verb of HTTP method is one of the common HTTP verbs. swrlb:matches(?urlval, "\-\") consists to check whether the URL value equal to "\-\". detection: matches (?verb, "POST", "PUT", "GET", "DELETE") is our custom built-in we create in order to check whether the verb of the HTTP method (i.e. ?verb) contains one of the common HTTP verb. The mechanism to extend the SWRL language in order to define new built-ins is detailed in our project site (http://www-inf.it-sudparis.eu/SIMBAD/tools/ORAP-DT/).

Figure 5 illustrates a partial instantiation of the (Anti)Pattern Ontology with knowledge extracted from the REST operation (GET /-/ HTTP/1.1: that is means what a Cloud provider can be provisioned) existing in an OpenStack RESTful API. After executing the above SWRL rule, the object property "*Rest: hasPattern*" in red color was added between the *Rest:OS-Query* (an instance of REST:Operation concept) and *Ptt:Query-interface-support* (an instance of Ptt:Pattern concept). Conversely, we report an occurrence of *Missing query interface Anti-pattern* if we haven't found the "\- \" path among all possible URLs existing in an API. This is carried out through sqwrl:makeSet(?s1,?urlset) that makes any URL its value equal to "\- \" in a set ?urlset and the built-in sqwrl:isEmpty(?urlset) that ensures that the resulted set is empty.

1.Rest:API(?ap) ∧ Rest:ComposedOf(?ap,?operation) ∧ Rest:hasURL(?operation, ?url) ∧ Rest:value(?url, ?urlval) ∧ swrlb:matches(?urlval,"\-\") ∧ Rest:hasHttpMethod(? operation, ?httpmethod) ∧ Rest:verb(?httpmethod, ?verb) ∧ detection:matches(?verb, "POST", "PUT", "GET", "DELETE")->Rest:hasPattern(?ap, Ptt:Query_interface_support)	1.Rest:API(?ap) ∧ Rest:ComposedOf(?ap, ?operation) ∧ Rest:hasURL(?operation,?url) ∧ Rest:value(?url, "\-*) ∧ sqwrl:makeSet(?s1, ?url) ∧ sqwrl:isEmpty(?s1) -> Rest:hasAntiPattern(?ap, Att:Missing_query_interface)
(a) Query interface support Pattern	**(b) Missing query interface Anti-pattern**

Fig. 4. SWRL rule for query interface (anti)pattern

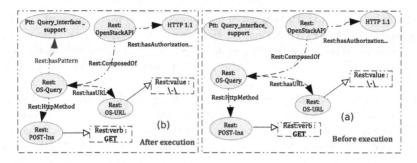

Fig. 5. SWRL rule for *Query interface support Pattern* (a) before execution and (b) after execution (Color figure online)

Cloud Structure Related (Anti)Patterns: They represent the poor and best practices to link Cloud resources between each others as well as to create a collection of resources using a Mixin, with respect to OCCI perspective (see Table 2). We identify 3 patterns and their opposite anti-patterns respectively in the creation of the Link between two Cloud resources, Association of resource(s) with a Mixin and Dissociation of resource(s) from a Mixin.

Figure 6 illustrates the SWRL rule that we define for the *Compliant Link between Resources Pattern*. The latter aims to evaluate for each operation applied on the link type Occi:Link(?link) the used verb in the HTTP Method, the Kind that identifies the link type and whether the link type contains both the source and target attributes. We report that the given operation Rest:Operation(?op) has the *Compliant Link between Resources Pattern* if we ensure firstly, that the verb of the HTTP method is "POST" using (swrlb:matches(?verb, "POST")), secondly the kind type (?kind) has ethier "Network Interface" or "Storage Link" as value for its attribute *?term* using (detetion:matches(?term, "Storage link", "Network Interface"), non-empty value for its attribute ?Occi:scheme(?kind, ?scheme) and a "kind" value for its attribute ?class and finally if the link type contains non-empty values for both source and target attributes. Conversely, we report an occurrence of *Non-Compliant Link between Resources Anti-pattern* if we detect poor practice of one of those constraints. The SWRL rules for this anti-pattern as well as an instantiation of the (Anti)Pattern Ontology showing the usefulness of those rules are available on our project Web site.

---

1. Rest:Operation(?op) ∧ Rest:hasHttpMethod(?op, ?httpmd) ∧ Rest:verb(?httpmd, ?verb) ∧ swrlb:matches(?verb, "POST") ∧ Rest:hasRequest(?op,?req)∧ Rest:has(?req,?reqbody) ∧ Rest:hasParameterDefinition(?reqbody, ?pradef) ∧ Occi:Link(?link) ∧ Rest:isComposedOf(?pradef, ? link) ∧ Occi:identifiedBy(?link, ?kind) ∧ Occi:term(?kind, ?term) ∧ detetion:matches(?term, "Storage link", "Network Interface")∧ Occi:scheme(?kind, ?schee) ∧ Occi:class(?kind, "kind") ∧ Occi:source(? link, ?source) ∧ Occi:target(?link, ?target) -> Rest:hasPattern(?op, Ptt:Compliant_Link)
Compliant Link between Resources Pattern

Fig. 6. SWRL Rule for Compliant Link between Resources Pattern

REST Related (Anti)Patterns: They represent the poor and best practices in the main REST API components. Here, we note that some of the existing REST (anti)Patterns already defined in [8,18], can be used, particularly, Verbless URIs (respectively, CRUDy URIs) and Ignoring Status Code (respectively, Supported Status Code). Additionally, according to OCCI perspective, we identify 3 new REST (anti)patterns relating respectively to the URL, request header and response header (see Table 3). Like management related (anti)patterns and Cloud Structure (anti)patterns, the detection rules for the REST (anti)patterns are also specified through SWRL language in conjunction with SQWRL queries.

3.3   Detection of OCCI REST (Anti)Patterns

This step consists of applying the detection rules defined in step 2 to detect the possible OCCI (anti)patterns in Cloud RSTTful APIs. To do so, we have implemented a detection tool to verify those APIs and automatically detect the (anti)patterns may be occurred into them. The detection of (anti)patterns in a given Cloud RESTful API requires firstly the instantiation of the different proposed ontologies with the knowledge extracted from this API. The instantiated ontologies as well as the defined SWRL rules construct together the knowledge base that we apply in the reasoning process to detect such (anti)pattern.

4   Validation

This section discusses the validation of our approach. We have developed a proof of concept implementation detailed on our project site[3]. Then we have used real world Cloud REST APIs to conduct this evaluation. Our objective is twofold. Firstly, we aim to show the effectiveness of our approach in terms of accuracy (i.e. precision, recall and F-measure values). Then, we aim to explore whether the selected Cloud providers respect OCCI REST patterns. In the following subsections, we firstly describe our proof of concept and the used datasets. Secondly, we discuss and analyze the experiment results.

4.1   Proof of Concept and Experiment Setting

Proof of Concept. We evaluate our approach through a proof of concept which is a web-based application developed using J2EE integrating with a query and a reasoning engine developed using OWLAPI and SWRLAPI. These APIs are used to deal with SWRL rules and SQWRL queries. Our tool takes into account the semantic base knowledge provided in order to detect the possible OCCI REST (Anti)patterns. It is based on 65 SWRL rules, including 28 SWRL rules for the patterns and 37 for the anti-patterns.

---

[3] Description: http://www-inf.it-sudparis.eu/SIMBAD/tools/ORAP-DT/.

Experiment Setting. We built the experimental datasets by performing an analysis in the Cloud RESTful APIs of Cloud services. We choose only 6 candidates, including OpenStack, COAPS, OpenNebula, Amazon S3, Microsoft Azure and Rackspace, since its underlying REST operations are well explained. From those operations, we have collected the required knowledge in order to semantically describe each API. Then, we have involved an expert manually evaluated the REST operations in order to identify the true positives and false negatives required to compute precision, recall and F1-measure values. Precision is the ratio between the true detected (anti)patterns and all detected (anti)patterns [18]. Recall is the ratio between the true detected (anti)patterns and all existing true (anti)patterns [18]. Finally, the F1-measure represents the weighted harmonic mean of the precision and recall values.

4.2   Experiment Results Analysis

Herein, we present the detection results in all selected Cloud REST APIs, the validation of our development tool in terms of precision, recall, and F1-measure values and show whether Cloud providers respect the OCCI REST patterns by computing their compliance degrees to those patterns.

Table 4 shows detailed detection results for the 28 OCCI REST (anti)patterns on 6 Cloud RESTful APIs. The first column lists the identified (anti)patterns. The remaining columns present the analysed Cloud RESTful APIs. For each (anti)pattern in each Cloud RESTful API, we report the total number of its occurrences derived from our detection tool. The last column indicates the occurrence percentage (OP) of each (anti)pattern compared to the total number of operations that may contain such kind of (anti)pattern (i.e. the percentage of Query interface support is computed compared to all existing query operations in the selected API). As specified in Table 4, in the management related (anti)patterns category, the most frequent patterns are *Compliant Delete* and *Compliant Update* Patterns. This means that the majority of the analyzed APIs follows either explicitly or implicitly the OCCI guidelines in deleting and updating of a given Cloud resource. In contrast, the most frequent anti-patterns are *Non-Compliant Trigger Action* and *Non-Compliant Create*. A clear majority of Cloud RESTful APIs does not include the category rendering which refers to a specific Kind instance defining the type of resource instance that will be created. Likewise, for triggering an action on a resource, neither the query exposing the term of the action, nor the HTTP Category defines the action were included in the REST operation. With regard to Cloud Structure (Anti)Patterns, the most frequent pattern is the *Compliant Link between Resources*. However, this pattern is tested using a low number of operations related to a link type due to its lack in the selected Cloud RESTful APIs. Additionally, we do not report any occurrence of (anti)patterns related both to the association and dissociation of resources from Mixin. Finally, with regard to REST Related (Anti)patterns, the most frequent patterns are *Compliant URL* and *Verbless URIs*. The majority of the analysed APIs did not include any CRUDy terms or any of their synonyms and all used URIs were either string or follow the structure as defined in [10].

Table 4. Detection results of the 28 OCCI REST (anti)patterns

Cloud REST API	Open-Stack (28)	COAPS (18)	Open-Nebula (20)	Amazon S3 (56)	Microsoft Azure (119)	Rack-space (62)	O.P %
Management Related (Anti)patterns							
Query interface support (3/8)	3	0	0	0	0	0	3 %
Missing query interface (5/8)	0	1	1	1	1	1	60 %
Compliant Create (9/44)	5	1	0	1	2	0	20 %
Non-Compliant Create (35/44)	0	1	3	8	13	10	80 %
Compliant Update(34/50)	3	2	3	6	14	6	68 %
Non-Compliant Update(16/50)	0	0	0	0	16	0	32 %
Compliant Delete(41/44)	3	2	3	8	16	9	93 %
Non-Compliant Delete (3/44)	0	0	0	1	2	0	7 %
Compliant Retrieve(69/130)	10	5	5	19	30	0	54 %
Non-Compliant Retrieve(61/130)	0	0	6	2	31	22	46 %
Compliant Trigger Action(4/39)	4	0	0	0	0	0	10 %
Non-Compliant Trigger Action(35/39)	0	7	0	6	14	8	90 %
Cloud Structure (Anti)patterns							
Compliant Link between Resources(4/4)	2	0	2	0	0	0	100 %
Non-Compliant Link between Resources (0/4)	0	0	0	0	0	0	0 %
Compliant Association of resource(s) with Mixin	0	0	0	0	0	0	-
Non-Compliant Association of resource(s) with Mixin	0	0	0	0	0	0	-
Compliant Dissociation of resource(s) from Mixin	0	0	0	0	0	0	-
Non-Compliant Dissociation of resource(s) from Mixin	0	0	0	0	0	0	-
REST Related (Anti)patterns							
Compliant URL(303/303)	28	18	20	56	119	62	100 %
Non-Compliant URL (0/303)	0	0	0	0	0	0	0 %
Compliant Request Header(62/303)	0	0	0	0	0	62	20 %
Non-Compliant Request Header(241/303)	28	18	20	56	119	0	80 %
Compliant Response Header (118/303)	0	0	0	56	0	62	39 %
Non-Compliant Response Header(185/303)	28	18	20	0	119	0	61 %
Supported Status Code(303/303)	28	18	20	56	119	62	100 %
Ignoring Status Code(0/303)	0	0	0	0	0	0	0 %
Verbless URIs(297/303)	28	15	20	54	119	62	98 %
CRUDy URIs(6/303)	0	3	0	2	1	0	2 %

Table 5 shows the validation results of our detection tool on OpenStack, Microsoft and Rackspace RESTful APIs. The first column lists the identified (anti)patterns. The remaining columns list the three selected APIs for the validation followed by precision, recall and F1-measure values. For each (anti)pattern in each Cloud RESTful API, we report precision, recall and F1-measure values for the detection results. The last two rows show the average and total average

Table 5. Complete validation results on Openstack, Microsoft and Rackspace REST APIs

(Anti)Patterns	OpenStack			Microsoft Azure			Rackspace		
	P	R	F1	P	R	F1	P	R	F1
Query interface support	100 %	100 %	100 %	-	-	-	-	-	-
Missing query interface	-	-	-	100 %	100 %	100 %	100 %	100 %	100 %
Compliant Create	100 %	100 %	100 %	-	-	-	-	-	-
Non-Compliant Create	-	-	-	86 %	100 %	92 %	100 %	100 %	100 %
Compliant Update	100 %	100 %	100 %	87 %	100 %	93 %	100 %	100 %	100 %
Non-Compliant Update	-	-	-	94 %	100 %	96 %	-	-	-
Compliant Delete	100 %	100 %	100 %	100 %	100 %	100 %	100 %	100 %	100 %
Non-Compliant Delete	-	-	-	66 %	100	79 %	-	-	-
Compliant Retrieve	100 %	100 %	100 %	96 %	100	98 %	-	-	-
Non-Compliant Retrieve	-	-	-	100 %	100 %	100 %	100 %	100 %	100 %
Compliant Trigger Action	100 %	100 %	100 %	-	-	-	-	-	-
Non-Compliant Trigger Action	-	-	-	100 %	100 %	100 %	100 %	100 %	100 %
Compliant Link between Resources	100 %	100 %	100 %	-	-	-	-	-	-
Non-Compliant Link between Resources	-	-	-	-	-	-	-	-	-
Compliant Association of resource(s) with Mixin	-	-	-	-	-	-	-	-	-
Non-Compliant Association of resource(s) with Mixin	-	-	-	-	-	-	-	-	-
Compliant dissociation of resource(s) from Mixin	-	-	-	-	-	-	-	-	-
Non-Compliant dissociation of resource(s) from Mixin	-	-	-	-	-	-	-	-	-
Compliant URL	100 %	100 %	100 %	100 %	100 %	100 %	100 %	100 %	100 %
Non-Compliant URL	-	-	-	-	-	-	-	-	-
Compliant Request Header	-	-	-	-	-	-	100 %	100 %	100 %
Non-Compliant Request Header	100 %	100 %	100 %	100 %	100 %	100 %	-	-	-
Compliant Response Header	-	-	-	-	-	-	100 %	100 %	100 %
Non-Compliant Response Header	100 %	100 %	100 %	100 %	100 %	100 %	-	-	-
Supported Status Code	100 %	100 %	100 %	100 %	100 %	100 %	100 %	100 %	100 %
Ignoring Status Code	-	-	-	-	-	-	-	-	-
Verbless URIs	100 %	100 %	100 %	100 %	100 %	100 %	100 %	100 %	100 %
CRUDy URIs	-	-	-	100 %	100 %	100 %	-	-	-
Average	**100 %**	**100 %**	**100 %**	**95 %**	**100 %**	**97 %**	**100 %**	**100 %**	**100 %**
Total Average	Precision = 98 %			Recall = 100 %			F1-measure = 99 %		

results of those values respectively. For the Openstack RESTful API which is an OCCI-based API, we obtained the best results of the detection with a precision of 100 %, signifying that all the detected (anti)patterns are in the list that the expert determined manually. The recall in this sample is 100 %, signifying that all (anti)patterns, that may occur, have been successfully detected by our tool. The average of these values obtained for this API is 100 % for the precision, 100 % for the recall and 100 % for the F1-measure. We report the same values for the Rackspace RESFful API. However, we obtain the detection results for

Microsoft API with average values that are lower than the previous ones, viz. a precision of 95 %, a recall of 100 %, and an F1-measure of 97 %.

Finally, we aim at showing whether the Cloud providers respect the OCCI REST patterns. To do so, we have computed for each Cloud RESTful API its compliance degree. The compliance degree indicates the percentage of OCCI REST patterns that each API has over all its operations. The compliance degree is defined as follows:

$$\textbf{Compliance degree} = \frac{1}{14} * \sum\nolimits_{i=1}^{14} \left(\frac{\sum P_i}{\sum OP_Pi} \right)$$

where P_i is a pattern (e.g. P_1 denotes the Query interface support pattern), 14 is the number of patterns, $\sum OP_Pi$ is the total number of operations that may contain the pattern P_i (e.g. three operations that may contain the Query interface support pattern in OpenStack RESTful API). As shows in Fig. 7, Openstack RESTful API represents the most compliant API with OCCI patterns. This is not surprisingly because this API is already based on OCCI standard. Additionally, Rackspace as well as Amason S3 has acceptable compliance degrees, this signifying that over 47 % of operations in those APIs follow implicitly the OCCI standard. In contrast, although OpenNebula and COAPS RESTful APIs had already based on OCCI, it seems that they did not carefully follow all OCCI guidelines. Microsoft Azure RESTful API uses its own model to describe Cloud resources, thus explaining the poor compliance degree it has.

Summarizing up, our detection approach performs better when dealing with Cloud RESTful APIs have based on OCCI standard than with non OCCI-based APIs. This is mainly due to the fact that our ontology defines the RESTful API based on OCCI descriptions. However, we can resolve this limitation by adding some semantic equivalence relations between the terminologies used to describe Cloud resources according to OCCI perspective and those according to a specific Cloud provider. Our detection tool has achieved a total average precision value of 98 %, a recall value of 100 % and an F1-measure of 99 % in detecting of 28 (anti)patterns on three Cloud RESTful APIs. Moreover, the obtained compliance degrees for the selected Cloud RESTful API shows their handful support of the OCCI REST patterns.

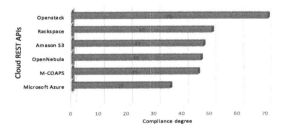

Fig. 7. OCCI Compliance degrees of Cloud RESTful APIs

5   Conclusion and Future Work

This paper identifies from OCCI Standard a set of (anti)patterns related to Cloud management APIs. It proposes a Semantic-based detection approach of OCCI REST (Anti)patterns in Cloud RESTful APIs. To validate this approach, we conducted an evaluation by analyzing 28 OCCI REST (anti)patterns on a real world Cloud RESTful APIs that invoking 303 operations. We showed that the proposed approach allows the detection of the OCCI REST (anti)patterns with good results in terms of precision, recall and F1-measure. We observed also through the obtained compliance degrees that there is no widespread adoption of the OCCI patterns in the selected Cloud RESTful APIs.

At short term, we want to apply our approach on other Cloud RESTful APIs for better understanding the OCCI REST patterns in the Cloud and their applications. At long term, we will propose our management API based on those identified patterns while avoiding their anti-patterns in order to resolve the heterogeneity and evolution problem of the managed Cloud resources.

References

1. Open Cloud Computing Interface. http://occi-wg.org/
2. OCCI Compliance Testing Tool (2011). http://occi-wg.org/2011/01/18/occi-compliance-testing-tool/
3. OWL 2 Web Ontology Language Document Overview, 2nd edn. (2012). https://www.w3.org/TR/owl2-overview/
4. Dudney, B., Asbury, S., Krozak, J.K., Wittkopf, K.: J2EE An-tiPatterns. Wiley, Hoboken (2003)
5. Edmonds, A., Metsch, T.: Open cloud computing interface - text rendering. Technical report, Open Grid Forum (2016)
6. Edmonds, A., Metsch, T., Papaspyrou, A., Richardson, A.: Toward an open cloud standard. IEEE Internet Comput. **16**(4), 15–25 (2012)
7. Fourati, R., Bouassida, N., Abdallah, H.B.: A metric-based approach for anti-pattern detection in UML designs. In: Lee, R. (ed.) Computer and Information Science 2011. Studies in Computational Intelligence, vol. 364, pp. 17–33. Springer, Heidelberg (2011)
8. Palma, F., Dubois, J., Moha, N., Guéhéneuc, Y.-G.: Detection of REST patterns and antipatterns: a heuristics-based approach. In: Franch, X., Ghose, A.K., Lewis, G.A., Bhiri, S. (eds.) ICSOC 2014. LNCS, vol. 8831, pp. 230–244. Springer, Heidelberg (2014)
9. Garcia, A.L., del Castillo, E.F., Fernandez, P.O.: ooi: Openstack occi interface. SoftwareX (2016, in press)
10. Gregorio, J., Fielding, R., Hadley, M., Nottingham, M., Orchard, D.: URI Template. RFC 6570,423 Internet Engineering Task Force (2012). http://www.ietf.org/rfc/rfc6570.txt
11. Kessentini, M., Vaucher, S., Sahraoui, H.: Deviance from perfection is a better criterion than closeness to evil when identifying risky code. In: Proceedings of the IEEE/ACM International Conference on Automated Software Engineering, ASE 2010, pp. 113–122 (2010)

12. Lewis, G.A.: The role of standards in cloud-computing interoperability. Technical report, Software Engineering Institute, Carnegie Mellon University (2012)
13. Martino, B.D., Esposito, A., Cretella, G.: Semantic representation of cloud patterns and services with automated reasoning to support cloud application portability. IEEE Trans. Cloud Comput. **PP**(99), 1 (2015). doi:10.1109/TCC.2015.2433259
14. Metsch, T., Edmonds, A.: Open cloud computing interface - infrastructure. Technical report, Open Grid Forum (2016)
15. Moha, N., Palma, F., Nayrolles, M., Conseil, B.J., Guéhéneuc, Y.-G., Baudry, B., Jézéquel, J.-M.: Specification and detection of SOA antipatterns. In: Liu, C., Ludwig, H., Toumani, F., Yu, Q. (eds.) Service Oriented Computing. LNCS, vol. 7636, pp. 1–16. Springer, Heidelberg (2012)
16. Nyren, R., Edmonds, A., Metsch, T., Parak, B.: Open cloud computing interface - http protocol. Technical report, Open Grid Forum (2016)
17. Nyren, R., Papaspyrou, A., Metsch, T., Parak, B.: Open cloud computing interface -core. Technical report, Open Grid Forum (2016)
18. Palma, F., Gonzalez-Huerta, J., Moha, N., Gueheneuc, Y.G., Guy, T.: Are RESTful APIs well-designed? Detection of their linguistic (anti)patterns. In: Barros, A., Grigori, D., Narendra, N.C., Dam, H.K. (eds.) Service-Oriented Computing. Lecture Notes in Computer Science, pp. 171–187. Springer, Heidelberg (2015)
19. Palma, F., Moha, N., Tremblay, G., Guéhéneuc, Y.-G.: Specification and detection of SOA antipatterns in web services. In: Avgeriou, P., Zdun, U. (eds.) ECSA 2014. LNCS, vol. 8627, pp. 58–73. Springer, Heidelberg (2014)
20. Settas, D.L., Meditskos, G., Stamelos, I.G., Bassiliades, N.: SPARSE: a symptom-based antipattern retrieval knowledge-based system using semantic web technologies. Expert Syst. Appl. **38**(6), 7633–7646 (2011)

Service Analytics

Automated Quality Assessment of Unstructured Resolution Text in IT Service Systems

Shivali Agarwal$^{(\boxtimes)}$, Giriprasad Sridhara, and Gargi Dasgupta

IBM Research, Bengaluru, India
{shivaaga,girisrid,gaargidasgupta}@in.ibm.com

Abstract. In customer-care service centers, upon remediation of customer issues, the human agents are expected to record their resolution summary in a clear, concise and understandable manner. These resolution summaries create a rich untapped source of unstructured information. In this work, we have addressed the problem of how to enable human agents to write better quality resolution text. This helps curate data artifacts which can reduce problem diagnosis time and create repeatable resolution recipes by a cognitive system. The problem is addressed through a two pronged approach: (i) On the fly automated scoring of the agent's resolution summary and (ii) identifying concrete areas of improvement in the summary and offering appropriate recommendations. The model for automatic scoring is derived from a feature set that encodes all significant and relevant aspects of the domain and text. The model is trained using annotated data and achieves an accuracy of 88.2 % which is a significant improvement over naive method of text based classification (68.5 %).

1 Introduction

Customer care service centers for IT service providers have human agents who resolve large number of infrastructure and application issues [7] on a daily basis. The issues are very diverse in terms of complexity and impact to customer. Not surprisingly the percentage of automated remediation tools for the IT domain has remained low (10–15 %). Generating automation cookbooks for these IT issues is of primary interest to service management. IT manuals typically written for troubleshooting the stand-alone product of interest often fall short of providing adequate guidelines for automation in wake of complex inter-dependencies among components. Blogs and open forums like stack overflow where human agents pose questions and provide answers act as a better data source with rich content. However in these uncontrolled environments, a lot of data cleaning and vetting needs to be done before they can turn into reliable data sources for automation. The good news is that the actual resolution work is often recorded along with the problem ticket logged for the IT issue; an example of one such recorded resolutions is "Took Remote; Configured Lotus Notes; She was able to load mails; Issue Resolved". If curated, this resolution history in the IT environments can turn into a very valuable data source for a provider looking for automated remediation tools. The resolution actions taken to solve customer

© Springer International Publishing Switzerland 2016
Q.Z. Sheng et al. (Eds.): ICSOC 2016, LNCS 9936, pp. 221–235, 2016.
DOI: 10.1007/978-3-319-46295-0_14

issues in the face of service level agreements also has higher credibility than the open source forums.

Currently most service providers mandate some remediation steps to be manually entered by human agents and this resolution data entered by the human agents resides within the service providers' ticket management systems. However, the written text suffers from quality problems. As a true characteristic of any human generated data source, every agent tends to write their low level resolution notes differently from the other. Some humans seem to be naturally less inclined towards adequately recording their actions than others e.g. their resolution summaries may often contain text like "problem closed" or "action taken". Often there are distinct styles of writing, manifested through language, tone, usage of grammar and certain words. It is extremely challenging to extract relevant content out of many different styles. Manual analysis also confirmed that grammatically well written text does not always indicate a good content. Given this context, and the over-arching need to be a step closer towards automation of IT issues, the community is faced with two immediate research challenges: (i) design efficient techniques to tap into the resolution notes data source; mine and extract relevant resolution knowledge from it and (ii) encourage/recommend agents to improve their summaries that enable curation of high quality resolution text and enhance its usefulness for mining and analytics. While there is active research happening for mining information from the resolution text, there has been very little in-depth work in the context of IT services that actively persuades human agents to write better quality resolutions by providing them run-time recommendations.

In this paper we propose a system that addresses the curation problem with help of specially designed automated data analysis techniques. The system focuses on how to help the human agents write better quality resolution text. As the agent enters the resolution text, the goal of the system is to (i) analyze the resolution text and assign it a score from the quality perspective and (ii) provide a real time feedback that identifies concrete areas of improvement in the resolution summary being created by the agent with appropriate recommendations. This timely recommendation helps agents write better quality resolution text, which in turn will help curate better content for automation. The main contributions of the paper are: (i) Comprehensive set of linguistic and non-linguistic features that capture goodness of resolution text, (ii) Method for building domain catalog (vocabulary) automatically, (iii) Prediction model for computing text quality scores on the fly and model's in-depth analysis, and (iv) Recommendation model that gives pointed recommendations to agents on how to improve text. We have developed a multinomial logistic regression based prediction model that uses the specially designed feature set and achieved an accuracy of 88.2 % which is significantly higher than accuracy of a naive text based classification model (68.5 %).

Rest of the paper is organized as follows: Sect. 2 motivates the need for a specialized scoring model. Section 3 describes the system that has been designed to help the agents in data curation. Section 4 describes features considered for

Table 1. Correlation: existing readability measures and resolution text quality

Readability metric	Smog	FK	FR	GF
Pearson	0.45	0.27	−0.0.4	0.1
Spearman	0.46	0.38	−0.21	0.27

Table 2. Correlation: attributes and resolution quality

Attribute	Severity	Type	Words	Sentence
Pearson	−0.13	0.13	0.24	0.18
Spearman	−0.08	0.13	0.66	0.3

good quality text and their extraction and Sects. 5 and 6 present the prediction and recommendation model respectively. The system is evaluated in Sect. 7.

2 Motivation for Specialized Text Quality Scoring Model

As a first step to address the problem of assessing resolution text quality, we started by trying to map the text quality to a standard readability metric like Flesch-Kincaid, Gunning Fog and some others [2]. In order to carry out this experiment, the first task was to create reliable annotated data. We gathered 1000 random incident resolution texts from a repository of 60000 incident resolutions for a client account. These resolution texts were then independently annotated by two domain experts. For each resolution, each annotator gave a score from 1 to 5 (with 1 denoting poor quality and 5 denoting high quality). While assessing quality score manually, aspects like re-usability, well formedness, self sufficiency (or completeness), relevant information only, clarity of exposition, appropriate cross referencing were considered for goodness. We obtained value of 0.57 as inter-annotator agreement using Cohen's Kappa [6], which indicates that there is good agreement. The distribution of the score is: 12.6 % resolution texts had score 1, 13.1 % had score 2, 27.3 % had score 3, 21.6 % had score 4 and 25.4 % had score 5.

The correlation scores between these standard readability measures and resolution quality scores are shown in Table 1 where the abbreviation are: FK = Flesch-Kincaid, FR = Flech Reading and GF = Gunning Fog. As can be seen from the table, all measures show either no correlation or little correlation. This can be attributed to the fact that these readability metrics were created for typical English text and a well written English sentence need not form a valid resolution text at all.

Having ruled out use of any off the shelf readability measures, we studied if resolution quality score has any correlation with other ticket attributes like severity, incident type etc. The ticket attributes for studying correlation were selected based on (i) attribute type, (ii) significance and (iii) presence. The attributes of type timestamp were not considered. The unstructured text type attributes were represented as count of words and sentences in order to study correlation with quality. The significance of attributes was determined by their role in aiding the resolution process e.g. resolver agents. Presence implies that the attribute is non-null in at least 90 % data points. Table 2 shows the results obtained for correlation study on the four main attributes of interest.

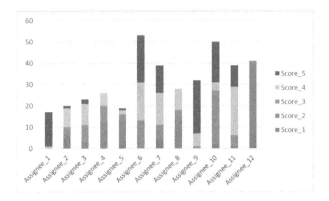

Fig. 1. Score variations by assignees

There appears to be no correlation of score with severity and type. However, there is a positive correlation of quality with number of words in the resolution text as suggested by the Spearman score. The number of sentences in the text did not show correlation. Finally, we studied if scores have any correlation with resolvers who write resolution text. Agents (resolvers) with atleast 15 ticket resolutions were picked and variations in their quality scores was plotted as shown in Fig. 1. Though the amount of variations rule out agent driven prediction, we observed that agents who write good quality continue to do so for majority times while mediocre quality writing oscillate between good and bad. This indicates that there is a good scope for helping agents write good quality text so that their writing quality can stabilize eventually.

With no obvious correlation predictors for the resolution quality, a machine learning approach on the unstructured resolution text was tried. The annotated resolution text was used to train a SVM based text classification model. The words in the resolution text became the features and each resolution text was represented as a vector using tf*idf score of the word-term. The ten-fold cross validation accuracy was found to be 68.5 % which leaves lot of room for improvement. This provided us the motivation to develop a specialized quality assessment system for resolution text, that uses specialized features extracted from text to learn logistic regression based prediction model and provide recommendations.

3   Automated Quality Assessment System

The automated scoring and recommendation system for data curation is shown in Fig. 2. The system takes as input a resolution text once an agent completely enters it and passes it to a quality assessment model. The block called 'Quality Assessment Model' in the figure shows that the input text is processed to get the features of the text (explained in Sect. 4) and then these features are used to predict the score using multinomial logistic regression model, as will be explained in Sect. 5. The multinomial logistic regression based model for predicting scores

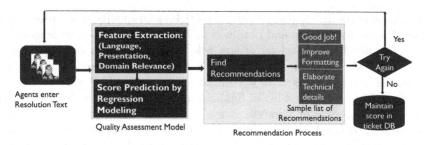

Fig. 2. Automated quality assessment system

uses carefully chosen feature set such that the features meet the criteria of (i) being quantitative or categorical and (ii) being computable automatically from the input text. The model has been trained on the feature set apriori and can be re-trained as per requirement. The predicted score along with the feature information is fed into the recommendation process which uses rule based model to gives pointed areas of improvement to the agent. The system provides a real time feedback to the agent on how to improve the text. Upon receiving the recommendations, the agent can decide to improve the text by incorporating the feedback or if the score is above a threshold, the agent has an option to continue with storing it in the ticket database. The value of threshold is more of a business decision and we do not put any restrictions by design.

Next, we explain the first step in design of quality assessment system which is to identify and extract the features indicative of a good resolution text. These features are then used to learn the prediction and recommendation models.

4   Identified Features and Their Extraction

Feature identification is key to quality assessment model. It is important to ensure that the features in the model capture the aspects that have gone into manual evaluation of resolution text for quality scores. In order to achieve this, feature identification was done using two step process. In the first step, we went through thousands of random samples of resolution texts and came up with a set of features that could potentially play a role in quality scoring model. This step was guided by two considerations: (i) It should be possible to algorithmically extract the feature without any manual intervention. (ii) The features should be an eclectic mix of linguistic and non-linguistic features. This is because, not all linguistic features are relevant or amenable in the domain; e.g. resolution text is usually terse making it non-amenable to linguistic cohesion or coherence and many good to have domain based features are not linguistic in conventional sense. The linguistic feature categories like syntactic structure, vocabulary, coherence and discourse relations as prescribed in [15] provided a starting point to identify the feature set suitable for linguistic features. For non-linguistic features, we used the features described in [5,8,20] as a starting point. In the second step, the domain experts who had annotated 1000 tickets for quality score were shown the list of features that we had obtained in the first step. They were asked to pick the features that played significant role in at least 20 annotations. Based on their combined input, we finalized the feature set to be used for regression based model. The features that were marked significant by both the experts were picked. The categorized list of finalized features is presented in Table 3. All features are categorical or numeric. Some of the features require learning over historical data in which case the learned model is stored in the memory which can be accessed efficiently real time. The feature extraction is described next for each category.

Table 3. Features grouped by categories

Language	Number of Words, Number of Lines, %age Misspelled words, %age Abbreviation, Well formed sentences,
Presentation	Well formatted, Supporting emails or Shell commands
Domain relevance	Entity/Operation Density, Action phrases density

4.1 Language

This category contains features that capture desired use of language. Most of these features are domain adaptations of standard linguistic features.

Verbosity - The resolution summary should not be too verbose. At the same time being too terse does not capture enough information. Verbosity is captured using (i) *Number of words* - This is extracted by simply splitting the input text on spaces, and (ii) *Number of Lines* - This again is extracted by splitting the input text on the newline character.

Percentage of misspelled words - We use an English dictionary and determine the number of words which are not present in the dictionary.

Percentage of abbreviated words - Any abbreviations and acronyms that are colloquial and not standard are best avoided. For example, usage of HK instead of Housekeeping is bad for readability. This is found using the heuristics such as a word in all capital letters is an acronym and a word with alphanumeric characters is likely to be a server name.

Has well formed sentences - Good quality resolution text typically uses sentences to describe the resolution. We have often seen poor resolution text which contains single words such as "resolved", "reran" and so on. Good resolution text should adhere to the desired linguistic syntactic structure. We use the confidence score output of natural language processing parsers to determine if the resolution text has well formed sentences.

4.2 Presentation

This category contains features that capture quality of presentation. Formatting the text appropriately is important to improve readability. As an example, an instruction list is much more easy to follow if written in bulletted style compared to a paragraph style of presentation.

Has Cause-Action-Prevention Information - We have observed the good quality resolution text often contains contingency discourse relation by explicitly stating the "cause" of the problem, the "action" taken to resolve the problem and the way to "prevent" the problem from occurring in future. We analyze the text for the presence of these words or their abbreviations like (C:, A:, P:) to determine if the text has Cause-Action-Prevention Information.

Has Bulleted-List - Good quality resolution text is often written in a nice bulleted list format using ASCII delimiters such as "*" and "-". We search the text for a minimum of 3 such occurrences of these ASCII delimiters to determine if the resolution text has Bulleted-List.

Uses EMail/Commands To Aid Description - The copy-pasting of email conversations or low level shell commands often enhance the descriptiveness of the resolution text. This maps to domain specific expansion discourse relation. We analyze the text for common email headers such as "From:", "To:", "Subject:" to determine if the resolution text uses emails to aid description.

4.3   Domain Relevance

Use of proper language and well formatted presentation does not guarantee that the text is indeed relevant to the domain. The presence of relevant domain information builds confidence that the text is indeed useful. In the following, we present the proposed domain relevance features that capture domain information. They are all numeric and use domain vocabulary learned from historical data. Domain vocabulary (knowledge) is cataloged in form of entities, operations and phrases by mining historical data. The domain features and their extraction is presented first. The automatic construction of domain vocabulary referred to as catalog is explained thereafter.

Entity/Operation Density - Entities in IT domain are typically hardware objects or softwares on which some operation is done for e.g. server, filesystem, database etc. Some examples of operations from the domain are copy, move, restart etc. A good resolution text should contain such entities and operations from IT domain. The operations and entities are extracted from an input text by finding the verbs and nouns respectively in dependency parse tree relations of type *dobj, nsubj, nsubjpass or nn* generated by NLP parsers [13] for the text. For example, in input text *sent mail to the user*, one of the dependency parse relations output is `sent-VBD mail-NN dobj`; being of type dobj, the verb *sent* is extracted as operation and noun *mail* as entity. The extracted operations and entities in the dependency parse relations are searched for in the domain catalog. The total number of matches is the value of the feature.

Action Phrases Density - Action phrases are a combination of operation and entities eg. *server rebooted, backup completed*. Action phrases provide a better confidence compared to just entities or operations. The phrases that have the dependency parse tree relation of type 'dobj', 'nsubj' or 'nsubjpass' as generated by NLP parsers for an input text are marked as Action phrases.

For example, in input text *sent mail to the user*, the phrases generated that match the desired type are: sent mail, sent user. These phrases are then searched in the domain action phrase catalog. The feature is present if there is a match. The total matches are counted to come up with phrase density number.

Table 4. Learning the domain - entities, operations

Input: Resolution text for a large set of historical tickets
Method 1:
1. Parts of Speech (POS) tagging of resolution text is done without removing stop words. The retention of stop words ensures a more precise tagging.
2. Extract n-grams, n ranges from 2 to 5, of POS tags from the tagged text after removing stop words. Select the set of relevant n-grams, called POS patterns, using measures of generality, reliability and diversity [9]
3. Selected POS patterns are used as regular expressions to extract matching text from resolution text.
Output: POS tag patterns list and matching phrases from resolution text. Sample illustrations below

Table 5. Sample output of learnt relevant POS patterns

POS pattern	Matching phrases from resolution text
Noun Verb (past tense) Verb (past participle) NN VBD VBN:	Backup was reran
Noun Verb (past tense) Noun: NN VBD NN	Client rebooted printer

Table 6. Domain knowledge catalogue sample (with frequencies for entities and operations)

Entities	[email, mails]: 181, [password, passwrd]: 160, [file(s)]: 114, [job(s)]: 110, [server(s)]: 89
Operations	resolve: 226, reset: 161, change: 135, check: 104, fix: 78, update: 64, delete: 59, ran: 42
Action phrases	ran job, upgrade os, checked server, increase disk space, change password, submit job

Learning the Domain Catalog. The domain vocabulary is built at mainly two levels, (a) operation and the entity keywords, (b) action phrases that denote the actions that have been taken historically.

(a) Entity and Operation Catalog: First, identification of text fragments from historical resolution text that are likely to represent actions is done using two

Table 7. Model fitting information

Model	Chi-Square	df	Sig
Intercept only			
Final	1841.725	573	.001

Table 8. Statistically Significant Features

Effect	Chi-Square	p-value
Intercept	.000	
Entity/Operation Density	11.739	0.008
Action PhraseDensity	11.004	0.012
numWords	762.264	0.001
hasCAPInfo	17.353	0.001
hasBulletedList	41.587	0.001
usesEmail/Commands	11.181	0.011

methods: (i) using the POS patterns obtained using the method 1 shown in Table 4, illustrated samples shown in Table 5, (ii) using phrases from text that are of type 'dobj', 'nsubj', 'nsubjpass', or 'nn' as given by dependency parse trees generated by NLP parsers.

Then, deduction of domain vocabulary in terms of operations and entities from the extracted fragments is done. Verbs are marked as operations and Nouns are marked as entities; for example, server reboot has server as entity and reboot as operation. These form the domain catalog for entities and operations. Table 6 shows examples of catalog entries for entities, operations that we got from the sample of 1000 tickets.

(b) Action Phrase Catalog: The phrases of type 'dobj', 'nsubj' or 'nsubjpass' as generated by dependency parse tree relations are added to the catalog of actions phrases. We also use the entity and operation catalog to create succinct action phrases. This is done by associating operations with suitable entities based on proximity in resolution text. Proximity rule relates entities and operations if they co-occurr within a n-gram window (n ranged from 2 to 6) in the raw resolution text. In case of multiple operations/entities in a n-gram window, the first operation in the window is usually the most relevant and in case of entity, the last one is usually the most meaningful. The phrases thus obtained are much refined and less noisy. Table 6 shows sample of action phrases catalogue entries obtained using this method.

The domain catalog is stored in a data store to enable scoring and recommendation of text.

5   Quality Score Prediction Model

The prediction model for quality scoring is learnt using multinomial logistic regression. The extracted features as described in Sect. 4 are the predictor (independent) variables and quality score is the dependent variable. We chose multinomial logistic regression because the independent variables are nominal or numeric and the dependent variable (score) is multi-level nominal with mutually exclusive and exhaustive categories. Multinomial logistic regression does not make any assumptions of normality, linearity, and homogeneity of variance for the

Table 9. Recommendation rules

If score==1	"Specify what steps were taken for resolution with details. Bulleted List is recommended"
If score==2	"Provide more details on how the resolution actions were performed"
If score<=4	if "!hasBulletedList" or "!hasCAPInformation" then
	"Format the text using bullets or CAP format"
	if "hasAbbreviationOrAcronyms" then "Expand the acronyms for
	better readability"
	if "numWords/numLines< 4" then "Sentences too short."
	if "numWords/numLines> 10" then "Sentences too long."
	if "action phrases density==0" then "Use standard terminology for
	IT infrastructure components and actions"
	if "no hasEmail/Commands" then "Add supporting evidence like
	commands or emails for actions"
	if "no affirmative Evidence" then "Did the action solve the issue?
	Please specify"
If score==5	"Good Job!"

independent variables. The dependent variable is a score and intuitively ordinal regression model should be used, but the assumption in ordinal regression
that the effect of the predictors on the odds of an event occurring in every subsequent category is the same for every category does not hold here. So, it was ruled
out. The annotated data as prepared in Sect. 7 was used to learn multinomial
logistic regression model. All the features that were identified in Sect. 4 were
computed for the training dataset. The model was built incrementally with the
starting point as three independent variables, namely, number of words, domain
keywords and bulleted text. Then we incrementally included all the features
as independent variables. As can be seen from Table 7, the "Final" row presents
information on whether the variables we added statistically significantly improve
the model compared to the intercept alone (i.e., with no variables added). The
"Sig." column shows that p = .001, which means that the full model statistically significantly predicts the dependent variable better than the intercept-only
model alone. The McFadden pseudo R-Square value was 0.742 and Cox and Snell
pseudo R-Square value was 0.842. As can be seen from Table 8, the features that
helped are fairly generic in nature and the model is not subject to overfitting.

6   Recommendation Model for Improving Quality

The recommendations for improving resolution text quality is an important component of the proposed system for data curation. The recommendations are
subjective to the predicted quality scores. The quality scores have the following
interpretation: 1 - Poor, 2 - Below Average, 3 - Average, 4 - Good, 5 - Very Good.
For each score, there are set of recommendations that are provided to improve
the text quality. Table 9 provides the rules for coming up with recommendations. For score levels 1 and 2, the recommendations are at an overall level and a
detailed level that capture specific areas of improvement, while level 3 onwards
the recommendations are more specific to the areas which need improvement.

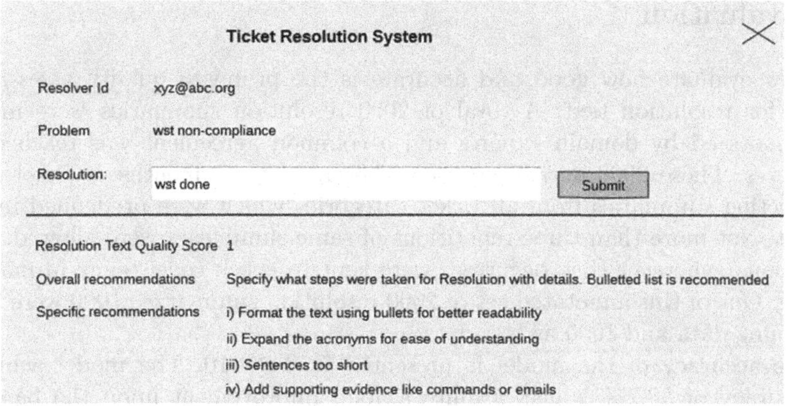

Fig. 3. Service demonstration

The specific areas of improvement are determined by the feature values as computed for predicting quality score. If the feature does not have the desired value, then that is flagged as an area of improvement as can be seen in the table. The agent who has entered the text gets all the recommendations corresponding to if-condition statements that are true. In addition to the features that were identified in Sect. 4, there is one more feature, namely, *Affirmative Evidence* that is used in recommendation rules. This feature was added after getting feedback from agents who were asked to evaluate recommendations[1]. This non-linguistic feature answers the question if the text really indicates resolving the problem? There are some texts that describe only the problem and there is no conclusive evidence of problem resolution. We have tackled this problem by casting it as a sentiment analysis problem. The idea is that if a text contains only symptom descriptions, then the sentiment of such text is usually negative because of presence of words like 'fail', 'not working', 'error' etc. When a text has a significant focus on actions and possibly outcomes, then the sentiment shifts to being neutral or positive. For sentiment analysis, we have used AlchemyAPI [1] service. The output is in the form of 'positive','negative' or 'neutral'.

We have developed a prototype service for scoring and recommendation of resolution text. The screenshot of the user interface is shown in Fig. 3. An agent enters the resolution text and submits it for evaluation. The service returns with the score predicted from the learned model and provides recommendations using the rule based model as described above. The usefulness of recommendations is evaluated next.

---

[1] Affirmative evidence feature is used only for recommendation model. It did not come up as statistically significant in the score prediction model; hence it was not included in prediction model.

7 Evaluation

We now evaluate how good and accurate is the proposed quality assessment model for resolution text. A total of 2000 resolution summaries were manually annotated by domain experts and a common agreement was reached on the scores. These 2000 datapoints were chosen from six months of ticket data by selecting summaries from all ticket categories which were predefined in the dataset. Not more than three repetitions of same summaries were allowed. The repetitions, wherever they occurred, were kept to check consistency in manual scoring. Out of this annotated set of 2000 resolution summaries, 1000 were used as training data and 1000 as test data.

The accuracy of the model is presented in Table 10. The model achieves an accuracy of 88.2 % which is quite a good improvement upon the baseline accuracy of 68.5 % based on SVM based classification on unstructured text as mentioned in Sect. 2. The accuracy for score value of 2 is low at 65.6 % which can be attributed to comparatively smaller set of training samples.

Table 10. Classification accuracy

Observed	Predicted					%Correct
	1	2	3	4	5	
1	124	2	0	0	0	98.4
2	20	86	25	0	0	65.6
3	2	4	225	39	3	82.4
4	0	0	21	195	0	90.3
5	0	0	2	0	251	99.2
Overall%	14.6	9.2	27.3	23.4	25.4	88.2

The individual effects of the features as extracted in Sect. 4 were studied and not all were found to contribute in statistically significant manner for the prediction of dependent variable. Table 8 provides the list of the features that were significant with p-value of 0.05 as the threshold. The model interestingly showed that quality scores for resolution texts are not so much a function of grammatical wellformedness as other features, which is the reason that state of art for readability measures did not work well. Though affirmative evidence feature did not play an important role in prediction with $p = 0.334$, it was found useful in recommendations.

We also compared the performance of our model against an existing method for computing quality scores in IT domain [12]. In [12], a score is arrived at using weighted linear combination of proportion of actual technical content with desired technical content and the total content. The paper also suggests values for the co-efficients used in the formula. We implemented this and used the technical content as determined by our domain dictionary for phrases. The objective of this experiment was to see if the formula can be re-used in our system setting.

The accuracy obtained was 51 % (rounded off). Last but not the least, we compared with SVM model obtained using the extracted features as proposed in the Sect. 4 and the accuracy obtained was 78.3 %.

7.1 How Good Are the Recommendations?

The recommendation model is based on predicted scores and specific feature values as seen in Table 9. The goodness of recommendations is therefore judged on two parameters: (i) Accuracy of score prediction model which is 88.2 % as evaluated earlier, (ii) Accuracy of automated feature values which is discussed next. We found that the features in *Language, Presentation* and *Domain relevance* categories had fairly good accuracy of 89.0 % and above. The accuracy of *Affirmative evidence* feature was found to be 81.2 %. On deeper analysis, we found that positive sentiment accuracy was 91.6 % and negative sentiment accuracy was 43.5 %. Though the text having negative sentiment formed a small percentage of 21.6 %, this is an area for improvement. Evaluating goodness based on accuracy is only one dimension. We also performed controlled experiments to determine the usefulness of recommendations for the agents. Two agents were asked to provide 30 random samples of resolutions written by them. We used the recommendation service shown in Fig. 3 to generate recommendations and asked agents to rate their usefulness. In 67 % of the cases, the recommendations were rated very useful and in the remaining cases, they were rated as partially useful. We conclude that recommendations are good for purpose of helping agents in improving text quality.

8 Related Work

Readability Scores for evaluating complexity of English text [2,14] have received lot of attention in computational linguistics. Feature based readability assessment [8,15] has found vocabulary and discourse based features very useful. We used this insight to design IT domain specific features. There has also been a fair body of work on recommending and evaluating quality of technical content for online forums, posts and blogs [5,18]. They have emphasized on author specific interactions and link navigations that do not have a meaningful mapping in resolution text. For domain based document readability measures, [20] proposes document *scope* and *cohesion* using *manually* predefined concept ontology which got ruled out because we wanted a technique that could discover domain knowledge automatically. Some of the notable works that are specifically focused for IT domain are [12,17]. The comparison with [12] has been done in the evaluation section already. The work in [17] describes a method to compute the quality score of ticket data as a whole. The quality score is a function of number of populated structured fields that are marked important, size of the problem description and number of domain specific keywords present in the description. The domain dictionary is created manually. In order to try the effectiveness of this method, we applied this formula for resolution summary text and mapped their grading to our scores. Different variations of the grade mapping were tried and the best accuracy obtained was 36 % (rounded off). The low accuracy can be attributed to the mapping being not perfect and the coefficients being not suitable for the dataset. Nonetheless, this work provided us a good direction in terms of feature selection. Technical readability has been explored in [10] in context of ranking. The method used is latent semantic indexing. We tried this technique but due to terse text, the term cohesion could not be captured well in latent space. The work in [11] uses the NLP techniques to identify actions in tasks in the context of commitment for service engagements. Sentiment analysis of text for affirmative evidence is something that we have not come across yet in any of quality score analysis. In a somewhat related work, there has been some work on defining good quality code using NLP techniques [3]. In the space of resolution text mining, there have been efforts as seen in [4,16,19,21]. These efforts rely heavily on good quality data and have been shown to be useful in context of IT automation.

9   Conclusion

We presented a solution to automatically assess the quality of resolution text entered by humans and offer recommendations to improve the same. Our solution had an accuracy of 88.2 % in assessing the resolution quality (when compared with a gold standard created by human experts). We conclude that a good quality resolution text encompasses aspects of text layout, discourse relations (contingency and expansion) and domain vocabulary and these aspects can be used to learn an accurate score prediction model. As future work, we plan to extend the system to other types of manual data like incident description, change plans.

References

1. Alchemy (2014). http://www.alchemyapi.com/products/alchemylanguage
2. AUSSIE: a beginner's guide to text complexity. In: New York City Department of Education, Secondary Literacy Pilot (2013)
3. Buse, R.P.L., Weimer, W.R.: Learning a metric for code readability. IEEE Trans. Softw. Eng. **36**(4), 546–558 (2010)
4. Catherine, R., Gangadharaiah, R., Visweswariah, K., Raghu, D.: Semi-supervised answer extraction from discussion forums. In: Sixth International Joint Conference on Natural Language Processing, IJCNLP 2013, Nagoya, Japan, 14–18 October 2013, pp. 1–9 (2013)
5. Catherine, R., Singh, A., Gangadharaiah, R., Raghu, D., Visweswariah, K.: Does similarity matter? The case of answer extraction from technical discussion forums. In: COLING 2012, 24th International Conference on Computational Linguistics, Proceedings of the Conference, Mumbai, India, pp. 175–184 (2012)
6. Cohen, J.: A coefficient of agreement for nominal scales. Educ. Psychol. Meas. **20**(1), 37 (1960)
7. Dasgupta, G.B., Nayak, T.K., Akula, A.R., Agarwal, S., Nadgowda, S.J.: Towards auto-remediation in services delivery: context-based classification of noisy and unstructured tickets. In: Barros, A., Grigori, D., Narendra, N.C., Dam, H.K. (eds.) ICSOC 2015. LNCS, vol. 9435, pp. 478–485. Springer, Heidelberg (2014). doi:10. 1007/978-3-662-45391-9_39

8. Feng, L., Jansche, M., Huenerfauth, M., Elhadad, N.: A comparison of features for automatic readability assessment. In: Proceedings of the 23rd International Conference on Computational Linguistics: Posters, COLING 2010, pp. 276–284 (2010)

9. Geng, L., Hamilton, H.J.: Interestingness measures for data mining: a survey. ACM Comput. Surv. **38**(3) (2006)

10. Jameel, S., Qian, X.: An unsupervised technical readability ranking model by building a conceptual terrain in LSI. In: Proceedings of the 2012 Eighth International Conference on Semantics, Knowledge and Grids, SKG 2012, pp. 39–46 (2012)

11. Kalia, A.K., Nezhad, H.R.M., Bartolini, C., Singh, M.P.: Monitoring commitments in people-driven service engagements. In: 2013 IEEE International Conference on Services Computing, Santa Clara, CA, USA, June 28–July 3 2013, pp. 160–167 (2013)

12. Majumdar, D., Catherine, R., Ikbal, S., Visweswariah, K.: Privacy protected knowledge management in services with emphasis on quality data. In: Proceedings of the 20th ACM International Conference on Information and Knowledge Management, CIKM 2011, pp. 1889–1894 (2011)

13. Manning, C.D., Surdeanu, M., Bauer, J., Finkel, J., Bethard, S.J., McClosky, D.: The Stanford CoreNLP natural language processing toolkit. In: Proceedings of 52nd Annual Meeting of the Association for Computational Linguistics: System Demonstrations, pp. 55–60 (2014)

14. Mhlenbock, K.H., Kokkinakis, S.J., Liberg, C., af Geijerstam, A.: A multivariate model for classifying texts readability. In: Proceedings of the 20th Nordic Conference of Computational Linguistics, pp. 257–261 (2015)

15. Pitler, E., Nenkova, A.: Revisiting readability: a unified framework for predicting text quality. In: Proceedings of the Conference on Empirical Methods in Natural Language Processing, EMNLP 2008, pp. 186–195 (2008)

16. Raghavan, P., Catherine, R., Ikbal, S., Kambhatla, N., Majumdar, D.: Extracting problem and resolution information from online discussion forums. In: Proceedings of the 16th International Conference on Management of Data 2010, Nagpur, India, p. 77 (2010)

17. Vukovic, M., Laredo, J., Salapura, V.: h-IQ: human intelligence for quality of service delivery data. In: 2012 IEEE Ninth International Conference on Services Computing (SCC), pp. 586–593. IEEE (2012)

18. Wanas, N., El-Saban, M., Ashour, H., Ammar, W.: Automatic scoring of online discussion posts. In: Proceedings of the 2nd ACM Workshop on Information Credibility on the Web, WICOW 2008, pp. 19–26 (2008)

19. Wei, X., Sailer, A., Mahindru, R., Kar, G.: Automatic structuring of IT problem ticket data for enhanced problem resolution. In: Integrated Network Management, IM 2007, 10th IFIP/IEEE International Symposium on Integrated Network Management, Munich, Germany, 21–25 May 2007, pp. 852–855 (2007)

20. Yan, X., Song, D., Li, X.: Concept-based document readability in domain specific information retrieval. In: Proceedings of the 15th ACM International Conference on Information and Knowledge Management, CIKM 2006, pp. 540–549 (2006)

21. Zhou, W., Tang, L., Li, T., Shwartz, L., Grabarnik, G.: Resolution recommendation for event tickets in service management. In: IFIP/IEEE International Symposium on Integrated Network Management, IM 2015, Ottawa, ON, Canada, 11–15 May 2015, pp. 287–295 (2015)

Time-Aware Customer Preference Sensing and Satisfaction Prediction in a Dynamic Service Market

Haifang Wang, Zhongjie Wang, and Xiaofei Xu[✉]

Harbin Institute of Technology,
Harbin, Heilongjiang, People's Republic of China
{wanghaifang, rainy, xiaofei}@hit.edu.cn

Abstract. In the dynamic service market, massive services and variations of their Quality of Services (QoS) and service contract make it difficult for customers to acquire the information of all the services comprehensively and timely. As a result, customers cannot raise accurte expectations. A customer has to choose services in terms of the incomplete information of the dynamic service market to achieve higher Satisfaction Degree (SD) as much as possible. Besides, because a customer's preferences vary over time, his SD is also time-aware. Therefore, for service providers, to accurately recommend services to customers, it is necessary to sense the customer preferences varying against time and predict personalized customers' satisfaction. To address this challenge, we propose a time-aware customer preference sensing and satisfaction prediction method based on customer's service usage history and change history of services. Firstly, the customer satisfaction model on contract-based services is proposed to measure customers' satisfaction for services. Then, we adopt the box-plot method and the frequency histogram to sense time-aware customer preferences. In addition, a time-aware personalized SD prediction algorithm called SDPred is presented to predict the missing values due to information asymmetry. Meanwhile, several experiments have been conducted based on a released data set, which verify the effectiveness of our methods. Besides, the impact of parameter settings in the SDPred algorithm is further studied, which provides more evidences to illustrate the superiority of our method.

Keywords: Customer satisfaction · Customer preference · Time-aware · Satisfaction degree prediction

1 Introduction

The increasingly diverse services have been deployed on the Internet, however, facing massive services with the same or similar functionalities, customers usually feel vacant while selecting one. Since these services are variable over time in the dynamic service market, it is impossible for customers to know all the information of services comprehensively and propose their expectation clearly. However, customers usually choose services that approximate to their preferences based on the known information of services, which makes it difficult to identify the customer requirement for the Quality of

© Springer International Publishing Switzerland 2016
Q.Z. Sheng et al. (Eds.): ICSOC 2016, LNCS 9936, pp. 236–251, 2016.
DOI: 10.1007/978-3-319-46295-0_15

Services (QoS) and to satisfy their preferences only by reducing overhead blindly. Therefore, it is becoming vital to confirm the personalized selection rules based on their preferences. In addition, in real life, our experience tells us that customer preferences to goods vary against time, for instance, customer *A* preferred to *Air China* last year, nevertheless, he enjoy *China Southern Airlines* today, which is called customer preference drift [8, 16]. Besides, the time-aware customer preferences play an important role in selecting services from a large pool of services with same or similar functionalities. Therefore, a novel issue can be summarized as **RQ1** shown in Fig. 1, which takes a customer as an example: **How can we acquire the time-aware customer preference sensing based on customers' service usage history?** For instance, for customer *A*, his time-aware preferences to airline companies can be sensed based on his service usage history, which will affect his future selection.

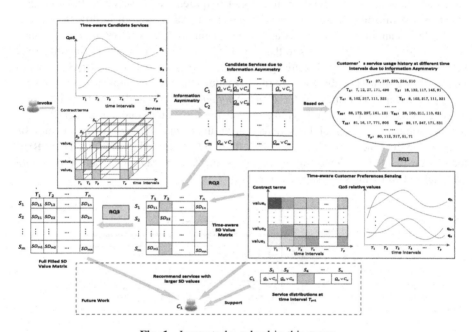

Fig. 1. Issues to be solved in this paper

While depicting customer preferences, it is easy to discover that conventional functional properties and QoS are not enough to describe the individual customer requirements as well as the characteristics of the services offered by the broker, e.g. payment method, etc. Therefore, service contract [1] is introduced into services in this paper to describe the individual customer requirements and the characteristics of services. Service contract is the agreement between providers and customers while invoking a specific service in given conditions [15], which may meet the actual demands. However, the traditional customer satisfaction measurement methods based on QoS cannot satisfy the demand. Thus, **RQ2** presented in Fig. 1 is identified as following: **How do we measure the customer satisfaction degree for contract-based services?** For customer *A*, he focused on QoS preferences before, e.g. the response time of the app or website to reserve plane tickets should be no more than 20 s. However, today he raises another preference that the payment method should be *Alipay*, which cannot be described by QoS and measured by the conventional methods.

In addition, customer preferences affect their Satisfaction Degree (SD) for goods, which means that the SD values change over time. Similarly, the SD values of customers for services vary against with time as well. Given a set of services with same or similar functionalities, Fig. 2 illustrates a toy example of the SD changes we study in this paper. In this figure, customer C_1 has invoked several services S_1, S_2, etc. in the past. C_1 has different preferences to them with specific invocation time, which means these services correspond to the distinct SD values during different time intervals. Likewise, other customers keep diverse preferences to various services with corresponding SD values called time-aware personalized SD values. The premise of the issues above is that customers can make their requirements clearly and they are provided all the information of services. However, in reality, due to information asymmetry, they cannot raise their requirements distinctly for services in the dynamic service market, which also leads to the loss of parts of the time-aware personalized SD values. As a result, a critical challenge is formed, which is defined as **RQ3** shown in Fig. 1: **How can we predict the missing SD values?** For the example above, customer *A* keeps different SD values for the *China Southern Airlines* at diverse time intervals, however, due to information asymmetry that the QoS and contracts of services are fuzzy at some a time interval, his satisfaction for the *China Southern Airlines* cannot be measured at the time interval, e.g. T_1: 0.71, T_2: 0.69, T_3: null, T_4: 0.75, etc. Then, **RQ3** focuses on the SD prediction at T_3 based on the known SD values and time-aware personalized SD values of other customers.

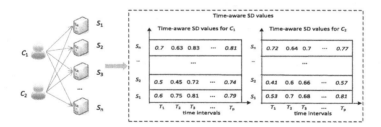

Fig. 2. SD values changes for customers with various services at different time intervals

Based on the customer preferences analyzed and the full filled SD value matrix, we can recommend the more valuable services to customers precisely, which will be focused on in our future work.

To answer **RQ1**, we have sensed time-aware customer preferences by the box-plot method and colorful frequency histogram according to their service usage history to show the customer preference distributions. Then, the Customer Satisfaction Model on Contract-based Services called CMS and the SDCalculation algorithm are proposed based on the paper [11, 17] to answer **RQ2**. The SD values are calculated based on the QoS and contract terms. To predict the missing time-aware personalized SD values, the

SDPred algorithm has been proposed, which has answered **RQ3**. This method collects SD values of different customers for various services at individual time intervals to build a customer-service-time tensor. By performing tensor factorization technique, the unknown SD values will be predicted by the feature matrices.

To verify our methods, several experiments have been conducted based on the data set WR-Dream released by [19]. Firstly, we extract 1000 services with similar functionalities from the data set. Then, we randomly assign two contract term values to each customer-specific and time-specific service. Afterwards, according to the generation customers' service usage history, time-aware customer preference distributions can be sensed by our methods. Besides, a customer-service-time tensor can be built by the SDCalculation algorithm. Then, the missing SD values can be predicted by the SDPred algorithm. Eventually, several comparison experiments have been conducted, which adequately illustrate the effectiveness of our algorithm. In addition, the impact of three parameters in the SDPred algorithm is studied, which provides more evidences to prove the superiority of our methods.

In summary, this paper makes the following contributions:

- We formally identify the time-aware customer preference sensing issue in the dynamic service market and adopt statistical method to answer the question.
- We propose a novel customer satisfaction model, which considers service contract and presents the SDCalculation algorithm to measure the customer satisfaction.
- We define the time-aware personalized SD prediction issue formally, and propose a novel algorithm SDPred to predict the missing values, which outweighs another three methods demonstrated by our experiments.

The remainder of the paper is organized as follows. Section 2 presents the customer satisfaction model on contract-based services. Section 3 introduces the time-aware customer preference sensing methods. Section 4 presents the time-aware satisfaction degree prediction. Section 5 discusses the experimental setting and results. Section 6 gives a review on the related work. Finally, Sect. 7 offers some concluding remarks and overviews the future work.

2 Customer Satisfaction Model on Contract-Based Services

Based on the introduction above, it is clear that service contract focuses on the non-functional properties and consists of several contract terms. The paper [9] divided contract terms into five types, namely Provider Obligations, Usage of Information, Warranties and Liabilities, Delivery Time, Price and Payment terms. However, we distinguish QoS from contract and describe them respectively. QoS are quantitative with numeric values associated with specific measurement units, e.g., price = 21\$. Nevertheless, contract terms are qualitative where the values are assumed to be defined by concepts, e.g., payment method = credit card. According to the research, QoS mainly includes price, response time, etc. Meanwhile, several terms have been summarized, including payment method, right of privacy, service coverage, etc.

The paper [11] tells us that each service has its own contract. By introducing contracts to services, we build a novel service moedel $S = (FP, QoS, Contract)$, where

FP represents the functional properties, and *Contract* stands for a group of non-numerical contract terms difined as *Contract* = <$term_1$, $term_2$, ..., $term_a$ >. In addition, each term can be described as $term_i$ = (< *name, operator, value* >), where *name* says its identifier, e.g. payment method, and *operator* mainly includes set operators, e.g. "*all*", "*exactlyOne*", etc., and *value* represents specific values of $term_i$. Meanwhile, *QoS* may contain several indicators, which can be expressed as *QoS* = <q_1, q_2,.., q_b >. And q_i = (<*name, operator, value unit* >), where *name* also stands for identifier, e.g. price, however, *operator* represents the numeric operators, e.g. <, >, =, etc., and *value* means the numeric values, e.g. 200, *unit* says the measurement unit, e.g. dollar.

$$SD = \begin{cases} 1, & if \quad QoS_1 \wedge Contract_1 \\ \cdots & \cdots \\ SD\_Value_i, & if \quad QoS_i \wedge Contract_i \\ \cdots & \cdots \\ 0, & if \quad QoS_w \wedge Contract_w \end{cases} \tag{1}$$

Provided that a stack of services has the same or similar functionalities, in the novel service model above, how to measure the level that a service may satisfy the customer preferences is becoming a critical challenge. Therefore, a new customer satisfaction model called CSM is proposed in our paper, which can be defined as Formula (1).

In the formula, SD stands for the satisfaction degree of a service satisfying customer requirements. Each set of $QoS_i \wedge Contract_i$ represents the customer expectation on QoS and contracts. If $QoS_i \wedge Contract_i$ is satisfied, then $SD = SD\_Value_i$. In addition, $\forall i > j$, $SD\_Value_i < SD\_Value_j$, and $SD\_Value_1 = 1$, $SD\_Value_w = 0$. $\forall 1 < i < w$, $SD\_Value_i \in (0, 1)$. Typically, QoS_i and $Contract_i$ in each set can be defined as follows respectively, $QoS_i = <q_{1,i} \wedge q_{2,i} \wedge \ldots \wedge q_{a,i} >$, $Contract_i = <terms_{1,i} \wedge terms_{2,i} \wedge \ldots \wedge terms_{b,i} >$.

Usually, the SD_value_i in the Formula (1) is provided by customers, however, due to the information asymmetry, customers cannot raise their requirements preferences clearly. Therefore, a novel approach called SDCalculation is proposed to calculate the SD value based on the corresponding QoS and contract values. For a service, this method calculates the satisfaction degree defined as SD_Q that its QoS satisfies the QoS constraints offered by the customer and the satisfaction degree called SD_C that its contract terms satisfy the contract preferences provided by the customer. Then, it is clear that $SD = SD_Q \times SD_C$. The method is presented in the algorithm 1, where *Num* (t_i) is the function that count all the values of the term t_i, and Q and C represent the QoS values and the contract term values of the service, and W stands for the different preference weights to the indicators of QoS, besides, Q_i^{max} is the maximum value of ith indicator of QoS in the whole candidate service set. QC and CP represent the QoS Constraints and the Contract preferences offered by the customer, respectively.

Algorithm 1. The SDCalculation Algorithm
Input: QC, CP, Q, C, W
Output: SD

```
1 Initialize SDꝴ=0, SDᴄ=0;
2 if each qi in QC is satisfied by Q then SDꝴ=1;
3 else
4    for (i=0;i<QC.size;i++)
5
```

$$SD_Q += W[i] \cdot \frac{|Q_i - QC_i|}{Q_i^{max}};$$

```
6 while ti in CP do
7    if ti=C.ti     then SDᴄ =1;
8    else if the value of ti is enumeration type
9        if
```

$$t_i \cap C.t_i \neq \varnothing \text{, then } SD_C = \frac{Num(t_i \cap C.t_i)}{Num(t_i)}$$

```
10       else SDᴄ=0;
11 else if ti is contained by C.ti then SDᴄ=1;
12       else SDᴄ=0;
13 SD= SDꝴ × SDᴄ;
14 output SD;
```

3   Time-Aware Customer Preference Sensing

In this section, we try to sense the time-aware customer preferences based on customers' service usage history at different time intervals. For a customer whose requirement is unclear, we analyze his selection standards or preferences in turn at each time interval, which reveals his requirements partly, and the process is shown in Fig. 3.

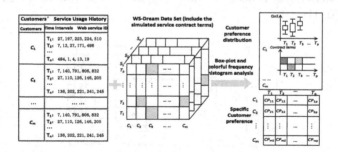

Fig. 3. Time-aware customer preference sensing process

To observe customer preferences for QoS or numerical contract terms, the box-plot method from mathematical statistics is adopted. Thus, the values of Q_1, Q_2, Q_3, the Whisker upper limit and the Whisker lower limit need to be calculated respectively. Before this, the QoS values of services in the service usage history should be unified by Formula (2), which may reflect the actual preferences at individual time intervals.

$$P = \frac{s_{QoS_i} - QoS_{imin}}{QoS_{imax} - QoS_{imin}} \qquad (2)$$

Here, QoS_{imax}, QoS_{imin} represent the maximum and minimum values of the ith indicator of QoS respectively. And s_{QoS_i} stands for the ith indicator value of the current service.

In terms of non-numerical contract terms, we employ the colorful frequency histogram to show the customer preference distributions. For a term value, we count the times of it appearing in the service usage history at each time interval, which will contribute to draw the histogram, where the deeper the color, the greater its frequency in the service usage history is, which will be illustrated by the Figures in Sect. 5.2.

Based on the analysis methods above, we can know the general distribution of the customer preferences against with time as well as the specific customer preferences at individual time interval. Here, to acquire the specific customer preferences, we adopt the Q_2 value as the QoS preferences at different time intervals, besides, we utilize the term with highest frequencies as the contract term preferences at each time interval.

4   Time-Aware Satisfaction Degree Prediction

4.1   Problem Formulation

Based on the introduction above, through integrating all the SD information from other customers, a three-dimensional customer-service-time tensor can be formed motivated by [19], which is shown in Fig. 4. The tensor can be split into massive slices with each one representing a time interval. Within a slice, each entry denotes a SD value of a service from a customer during the specific time interval. In this paper, we pay more attention to the study how to efficiently and precisely predict the missing entries in the tensor based on the existing entries. Thus, the problem of SD prediction for various users and services can be defined as follows. Typically, all the SD values are unified to the interval [0, 1].

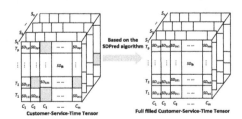

Fig. 4. Time-aware satisfaction degree prediction process

Definition: Suppose that the group of m customers, the set of n services and the set of p time intervals can be defined as C, S and T respectively, then a SD element is a quartet (i,j,k, SD_{ijk}) representing the SD value of service S_j for customer C_i at time interval t_k, where $i \in \{1,\ldots,m\}, j \in \{1,\ldots,n\}, k \in \{1,\ldots,p\}$, and $SD_{ijk} \in \mathbb{R}$.

Besides, we regard the set of all triads (i,j,k) as Σ and define the set of all known triads (i,j,k) in Σ as Δ. If we consider a tensor $Z \in \mathbb{R}^{m \times n \times p}$ with each entry Z_{ijk} representing the SD value of S_j for C_i at time interval t_k, then the missing entries $\{Z_{ijk}|(i,j,k) \in \Sigma - \Delta\}$ should be predicted based on the existing entries $\{Z_{ijk}|(i,j,k) \in \Delta\}$.

4.2   Feature Matrix Learning

To acquire the feature matrices of customers, services and time, tensor factorization technique is adopted to fit a factor model to the customer-service-time tensor. The factorized customer-specific, service-specific and time-specific matrices are utilized to further predict missing entries, which is shown in Fig. 4. Therefore, a high-quality low-dimensional feature representation of customers, services and time can be derived by analyzing the customer-service-time tensor. The premise is that only a small number of factors influence the various SD values. In this paper, we consider a $m \times n \times p$ SD tensor consisting of m customers, n services and p time intervals. A low-rank tensor factorization approach is adopted to seek to approximate the SD tensor Z by a multiplication of r-rank factors [14], which is expressed as Formula (3).

$$Z \approx M \times_u C \times_s S \times_t T \tag{3}$$

Where $M \in \mathbb{R}^{r \times r \times r}, C \in \mathbb{R}^{m \times r}, S \in \mathbb{R}^{n \times r}$ and $T \in \mathbb{R}^{p \times r}$ are feature matrices. r is the number of features. Each column in C, S and T represents a customer, a service and a time interval, respectively. $\times_u$, $\times_s$ and $\times_t$ are tensor-matrix multiplication operators, e.g. $M \times_u C = \sum_{i=1}^{r} M_{ijk} C_{ij}$. M is set to the diagonal tensor. If $i = j = k$ then $M = 1$, otherwise $M = 0$.

Typically, in reality, each customer has invoked only a small portion of services and massive customers had not evaluated the services they had invoked, thus, $r \ll m, n, p$. Besides, customers cannot clearly raise expectations due to information asymmetry. Therefore, Z is usually very sparse. From the definition above, it is clear that the low-dimensional matrices C, S and T are unknown and need to be estimated.

$$\min_{C,S,T} F(Z,C,S,T) = \sum_{i=1}^{m}\sum_{j=1}^{n}\sum_{k=1}^{p} D_{ijk}(Z_{ijk} - \hat{Z}_{ijk})^2 + \alpha \sum_{i=1}^{m}\sum_{j=1}^{r} |C_{ij}|^2 + \beta \sum_{i=1}^{n}\sum_{j=1}^{r} |S_{ij}|^2 + \gamma \sum_{i=1}^{p}\sum_{j=1}^{r} |T_{ij}|^2 \tag{4}$$

To access the quality of tensor approximation, a loss function for evaluating the residue between the estimated tensor and the original tensor needs to be constructed. We define the optimization problem as Formula (4), which avoids the over fitting issue. Here, D_{ijk} is the indicator function that equals to 1 if customer C_i invoked and evaluated service S_j at the time interval t_k and equals to 0 otherwise.

In Formula (4), where $\alpha, \beta, \gamma > 0$ minimizes the objective function defined as the sum-of-squared-residue with quadratic regularization terms. Therefore, a local minimum of the objective function given by Formula (4) can be found by performing incremental gradient descent in feature vectors C_i, S_j, and T_k. And the corresponding formulas during performing incremental gradient descent are presented in Formula (5).

$$\frac{\partial F_A}{\partial C_{iy}} = 2\sum_{j=1}^{n}\sum_{k=1}^{p} D_{ijk}(\widehat{Z}_{ijk} - Z_{ijk})S_j^T T_k + 2\alpha C_{iy},$$

$$\frac{\partial F_A}{\partial S_{jy}} = 2\sum_{i=1}^{m}\sum_{k=1}^{p} D_{ijk}(\widehat{Z}_{ijk} - Z_{ijk})C_i^T T_k + 2\beta S_{jy}, \qquad (5)$$

$$\frac{\partial F_A}{\partial T_{ky}} = 2\sum_{i=1}^{m}\sum_{j=1}^{n} D_{ijk}(\widehat{Z}_{ijk} - Z_{ijk})C_i^T S_j + 2\gamma T_{ky}.$$

$$\widehat{Z}_{ijk} = D_{ijk}\sum_{y=1}^{r} C_{iy}S_{jy}T_{ky} \qquad (6)$$

Based on the formulas above, the customer-specific, service-specific and time-specific feature matrices C, S and T can be learned. Hence, for the missing entry Z_{ijk} in the tensor, the SD value can be predicted by Formula (6).

Based on the analysis above, the algorithm name SDPred is summarized, which is presented in Algorithm 2. It also shows the iterative process for feature metrics learning. Firstly, matrices C, S and T are initialized with small random non-negative values. According to the update rules derived from Formula (5), the updating process is iterated until the algorithm converges to a local minimum of the objective function given in Formula (4). After the iteration, the matrices C, S and T can be acquired eventually. Then, the missing SD values can be predicted by Formula (6).

```
Algorithm 2.the SDPred algorithm
Input: Z,r,α,β,γ
Output: Ẑ
1 Initialize C∈ℝ^{m×r},S∈ℝ^{n×r},T∈ℝ^{p×r} with small random numbers;
2 repeat
3    while (i,j,k)∈Δ do
4        Ẑ_ijk = D_ijk Σ_{y=1}^{r} C_iy S_jy T_ky ;
5    while (i,j,k)∈Δ do
6       for (q=1;q<=r;q++)
7           C_iq ← C_iq −[(Ẑ_ijk − Z_ijk)S_j^T T_k +αC_iq];
8           S_jq ← S_jq −[(Ẑ_ijk − Z_ijk)C_i^T T_k +βS_jq];
9           T_kq ← T_kq −[(Ẑ_ijk − Z_ijk)C_i^T S_j +γT_kq];
10 until the converge;
11 while (i,j,k)∈Σ−Δ do
12     Ẑ_ijk = D_ijk Σ_{y=1}^{r} C_iy S_jy T_ky ;
13 output Ẑ ;
```

5 Experiments and Comparisons

5.1 Experimental Setting

(1) Candidate Services. We adopt a released QoS data set http://www.wsdream.net/ called WS-Dream. Firstly, 1000 Web services with same or similar functionalities have been extracted. Then, we collect the QoS information of these services invoked by 142 customers at 64 time intervals, including response time and throughput. Based on the data extracted, we simulate the contract term values of each Web service for each customer at each time interval, including payment method and right of privacy with the corresponding values {*Credit card*, *Applypay*, *Alipay*}, {true, false} respectively.

(2) Customer's Service Usage History. Based on the reconstructed WS-Dream above, we simulate service usage histories of 142 customers during different time intervals with the format < customerID, timeIntervalID, wsID list, amount >, where the four dimensions stand for the customer ID, time interval ID, all the service IDs selected by the customer at the corresponding time interval and the invocation times, respectively.

5.2 Time-Aware Customer Preference Sensing

Based on the customers' service usage history generated above, we adopt the methods presented in Sect. 3 to analyze the time-aware preference distributions of each customer. Here, we take it an example where customerID = 0 and customerID = 1. The analysis results are shown in Figs. 5 and 6.

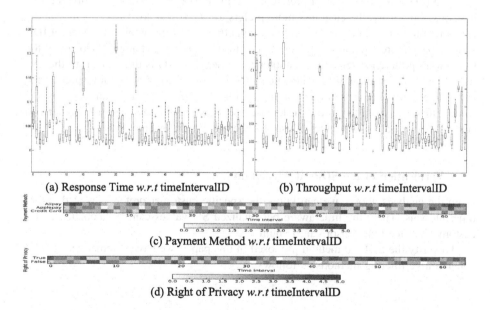

(a) Response Time *w.r.t* timeIntervalID

(b) Throughput *w.r.t* timeIntervalID

(c) Payment Method *w.r.t* timeIntervalID

(d) Right of Privacy *w.r.t* timeIntervalID

Fig. 5. Customer preference distributions based on customerID = 0

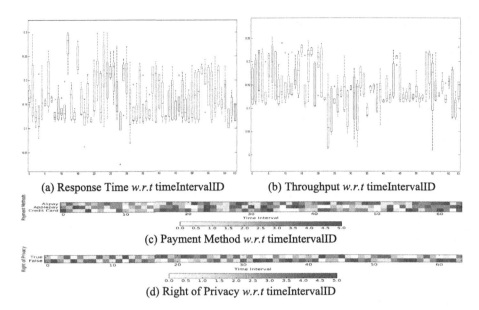

(a) Response Time *w.r.t* timeIntervalID   (b) Throughput *w.r.t* timeIntervalID

(c) Payment Method *w.r.t* timeIntervalID

(d) Right of Privacy *w.r.t* timeIntervalID

Fig. 6. Customer preference distributions based on customerID = 1

According to Fig. 5 (a), (b), it is clear that the preferences to QoS of the customer (ID = 0) have not changed significantly during the 64 time intervals, except for several cases, which may reflect the actual customer preference, e.g. the customer's location changed, as a result, his preferences to response time and throughput varied as well. Figure 5 (c) shows the customer preferences to three payment methods at different time intervals. Obviously, the customer more prefers to *Alipay*. Figure 5 (d) tells us that the customer only takes notice of his privacy sometimes with the small time interval IDs. And he pays more attention to his privacy with time intervals changing. However, the time-aware preference sensing of another customer (ID = 1) is different from the former, which is shown in Fig. 6, where he had less rigorous constraints for response time and stricter constraints for throughput in general. His preferences to contract terms had some differences from the former. Likewise, the time-aware preferences of another 140 customers can be sensed, which illustrates the validity of our methods.

5.3   Verification of the SDPred Algorithm

From the analysis above, we can know the specific customer preferences at different time intervals. Then, the time-aware personalized SD values can be calculated and a customer-service-time tensor can be built.

To verify the SDPred method proposed in this paper, we have summarized several collaborative filtering methods as follows:

(1) **MSU**(Most similar user): For a specific time interval t, if user U_i does not evaluate the service S_j, then MSU takes the corresponding SD value the most similar user of U_i keeps for S_j as the prediction of the missing SD value.

(2) **KMSU**(Top-k most similar user): Similar to MSU, it identifies top-k most similar users and regards the average SD value of them at a time interval as the prediction.

(3) **TSR**(Time-aware similar requirement): For a single user U_i, if he has not accessed the service S_j at a specific time interval t_x, then TSR tries to distinguish the most similar time interval t_y when the user requirement is similar to that of t_x. Afterwards, TSR takes the SD value corresponding to t_y as the prediction of the missing value at t_x.

In addition, in order to compare these methods with SDPred, two metrics have been proposed, including the Mean Residue (*MR*) defined as Formula (7) and the Root Mean Squared Residue (*RMSR*) expressed in Formula (8).

$$MR = \frac{1}{N} \sum_{i=1}^{m} \sum_{j=1}^{n} \sum_{k=1}^{p} |\widehat{Z}_{ijk} - Z_{ijk}| \tag{7}$$

$$RMSR = \sqrt{\frac{1}{N} \sum_{i=1}^{m} \sum_{j=1}^{n} \sum_{k=1}^{p} (\widehat{Z}_{ijk} - Z_{ijk})^2} \tag{8}$$

Besides, to evaluate the performance of different approaches above, some entries have been removed from the tensors, which will be compared with the prediction values. The tensors with missing SD values are in different densities, which are defined as the removal density. For instance, 20 % means that 20 % entries have been removed from the original tensor and will apply the remaining 80 % entries to predict the removed ones. The values of α, β, γ are tuned by performing cross-validation on the existing SD values. By massive attempts, we confirm that $r = 30, \alpha = \beta = \gamma = 0.002$. And in the KMSU method, $k = 5$. With different removal densities, these methods are compared with each other by the values of *MR* and *RMSR*, which are presented in Fig. 7.

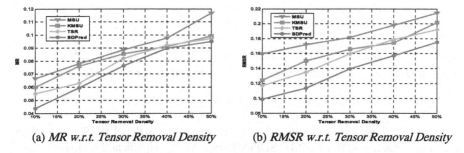

(a) *MR w.r.t. Tensor Removal Density*   (b) *RMSR w.r.t. Tensor Removal Density*

Fig. 7. Performance comparisons based on *Tensor Removal Density*

From Fig. 7, it is clear that the SDPred algorithm outperforms another three methods (lower *MR* and *RMSR* values) under different tensor removal densities. With the *Tensor Removal Density* growing up, both *MR* and *RMSR* of these methods increase gradually, which means that the more missing SD values exist, the less accurate the predictions of the four methods are. In general, the SDPred method has the best performance, then the followings are TSR, KMSU, MSU respectively, which adequately illustrate the effectiveness of our method. However, sometimes the KMSU method performs better than the TSR method. Therefore, if the tensor is much sparse, the SDPred will be recommended to acquire more precise predictions.

5.4   Impact of Three Parameters in the SDPred Algorithm

Here, we further focus on the impact of three parameters in the SDPred algorithm, including m, n and p representing the amount of customers, the number of services and the amount of time intervals individually. Suppose that *Tensor Removal Density* = 50 %, three experiments are set $n = 1000$, $p = 64$; $m = 142$, $p = 64$; $m = 142$, $n = 1000$, respectively. Then, the comparison results are shown in Figs. 8, 9 and 10.

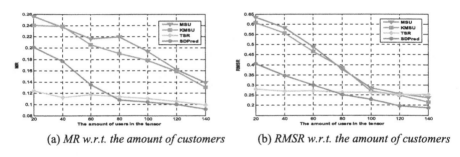

(a) *MR w.r.t. the amount of customers*   (b) *RMSR w.r.t. the amount of customers*

Fig. 8. Performance comparisons based on *the amount of customers in the tensor*

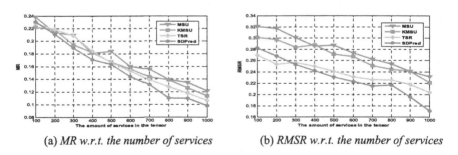

(a) *MR w.r.t. the number of services*   (b) *RMSR w.r.t. the number of services*

Fig. 9. Performance comparisons based on *the number of services in the tensor*

From Fig. 8, we can know that with the increase of m, *MR* and *RMSR* of the three methods (including MSU, KMSU, SDPred) both decline significantly. However, *MR* and *RMSR* of TSR go down slowly. Although TSR performs best with smaller values of m, SDPred can achieve higher prediction accuracy while m increasing. Figure 8 tells

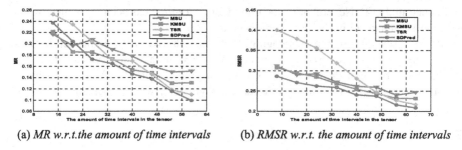

(a) *MR w.r.t.the amount of time intervals*   (b) *RMSR w.r.t. the amount of time intervals*

Fig. 10. Performance comparisons based on the amount of time intervals in the tensor

us that the amount of customers has greater impact on MSU, KMSU and SDPred along with smaller influence on TSR, which are consistent with their mechanisms.

Figure 9 clearly presents that the *MR* and *RMSR* corresponding to these methods also fall down while *n* increases. In addition, the former declines significantly shown in Fig. 9 (a), while the latter goes down gradually presented in Fig. 9 (b). It is convinced that SDPred has best performance basically followed by TSR, which is followed closely after by KMSU and MSU. However, they have fewer differences, which mean that the amount of services has little impact on these methods.

Based on Fig. 10, it is easy to know that in terms of these methods, both the *MR* and *RMSR* decline while *p* grows up. Besides, TSR has a remarkable decline and another three methods drop down non-significantly. Therefore, it clearly illustrates that the amount of time intervals has larger impact on TSR. However, SDPred can achieve higher prediction accuracy on the whole, which can prove its superiority.

Combined with Figs. 8, 9 and 10, it is obvious that regardless of various assignments of the three parameters (*m*, *n* and *p*), overall, the SDPred method performs best, which provides more evidences to illustrate the effectiveness of our method.

6 Related Work

Service contract has been widely studied from different perspective to describe a service comprehensively. A policy centered meta-model was presented in [4] to describe service contracts, which unified the policy [7], service level agreements [10], etc. In this model, each term corresponded to one non-functional property.

In addition, several methods to calculate the customer satisfaction degree had been proposed, including the method based on QoS [18] and the method based on QoS and contract [3]. However, [13] only considered the QoS, which cannot reflect the reality adequately. And the method in [17] may not be applied actually, since the SD values were provided by customers, which were difficult to be collected. In [3], a novel model to calculate customer satisfaction in the cloud was presented, which took the service level agreements into account. However, these methods have not considered the actual factor that SD values have varied with various time intervals changing.

Customer preference analysis has aroused wide attentions, including modeling user preference by mutual information in a statistical framework [6], the context-aware user preference study [2]. Nevertheless, the important factor time has been weakened, which needs to be enhanced in the user preference analysis.

Besides, several researchers recognized information asymmetry in the service field [12]. Then, trust was proposed as the important source of value in service relationships characterized by high degrees of information asymmetry in [5]. And two types of trust-based approach for reducing information asymmetry ware presented in [13].

7 Conclusions and Future Work

This paper proposes the customer satisfaction model on contract-based services. In the model, a novel SD calculation method is presented. Besides, we adopt the box-plot method and colorful frequency histogram to sense the time-aware customer preferences. Then, time-aware personalized SD values can be calculated, including several missing values due to information asymmetry. To predict the missing values, the SDPred algorithm is proposed, which is the first to research time-aware personalized satisfaction. Based on WS-Dream and the customers' service usage history, the verification and comparison experiments are conducted, which verify the effectiveness of our methods. And we further research the impact of parameter settings in the SDPred algorithm, which provides more evidence to illustrate the superiority of our method.

Some future work is summarized shown in Fig. 1, including (1) to research the changing trends of services over the time; (2) to further focus on the time-aware customer preferences; (3) to recommend services for customers based on the work (1), (2).

Acknowledgments. This work is supported by the Natural Science Foundation of China (No. 61272187, 61472106).

References

1. Alrifai, M., Risse, T., Nejdl, W.: A hybrid approach for effcient web service composition with end-to-end qos constraints. ACM Trans. Web **6**(2), 1–29 (2012)
2. Campos, P.G., Díez, F., Cantador, I.: Time-aware recommender systems: a comprehensive survey and analysis of existing evaluation protocols. User Model. User-Adap. Inter. **24**(1–2), 67–119 (2014)
3. Chen, J., Wang, C., Zhou, B.B., Sun, L., Lee, Y.C., Zomaya, A.Y.: Tradeoffs between profit and customer satisfaction for service provisioning in the cloud. In: Proceedings of the 20th International Symposium on High Performance Distributed Computing, pp. 229–238. ACM (2011)
4. De Paoli, F., Palmonari, M., Comerio, M., Maurino, A.: A meta-model for non-functional property descriptions of web services. In: Proceedings of IEEE International Conference on Web Services, pp. 393–400 (2008)
5. Gallouj, C.: Asymmetry of information and the service relationship: selection and evaluation of the service provider. Int. J. Serv. Ind. Manage. **8**(1), 42–64 (1997)
6. Jung, S.Y., Hong, J.H., Kim, T.S.: A statistical model for user preference. IEEE Trans. Knowl. Data Eng. **17**(6), 834–843 (2005)

7. Kamoda, H., Yamaoka, M., Matsuda, S., Broda, K., Sloman, M.: Policy conflict analysis using free variable tableaux foraccess control in web services environments. In: Proceedings of the Policy Management for the Web Workshop at the 14th International World Wide Web Conference, pp. 121–126 (2005)
8. Koychev, I., Schwab, I.: Adaptation to drifting user's interests. In: Proceedings of ECML Workshop: Machine Learning in New Information Age, pp. 39–45 (2000)
9. Lamparter, S., Luckner, S., Mutschler, S.: Semi-automated management of web service contracts. Int. J. Ser. Sci. 1(3–4), 288–314 (2008)
10. Lewis, L., Ray, P.: Service level management definition, architecture and research chal-lenges. In: Proceedings of the Global Telecommunications Conference, pp. 1974–1978 (1999)
11. Liu, P.F., Ma, C., Wang, Z.J., Comerio, M., Xu, X., Batini, C.: Generating global contract for composite services. In: Proceeding of IEEE International Conference on Service Science, pp. 9–16 (2015)
12. Nayyar, P.R.: Information asymmetries: a source of competitive advantage for diversified service firms. Strateg. Manag. J. 11(1), 513–519 (1990)
13. Rajeswary, C.: A survey on efficient evolutionary algorithms for web service selection. Int. J. Manage., IT Eng. 2(9), 177–191 (2012)
14. Rendle, S., Schmidt-Thieme, L.: Pairwise interaction tensor factorization for personalized tag recommendation. In: Proceedings of WSDM 2010, pp. 81–90 (2010)
15. Tian, C.H., Ray, B.K., Lee, J., Cao, R., Ding, W.: BEAM: a framework for business eco-system analysis and modeling. IBM Syst. J. 47(1), 101–114 (2008)
16. Wai, L., Javed, M.: Modeling user interest shift using a bayesian approach. J. Am. Soc. Inform. Sci. Technol. 52(5), 416–429 (2001)
17. Wang, Z.J., Wu, Q., Xu, X.F.: Value-added analysis of bi-lateral e-business services. In: Proceedings of International Conference on e-Business Engineering, pp. 185–192 (2012)
18. Zeng, L., Benatallah, B., Ngu, A.H., Dumas, M., Kalagnanam, J., Chang, H.: Qos-aware middleware for web services composition. IEEE Trans. Software Eng. 30(5), 311–327 (2004)
19. Zhang, Y., Zheng, Z., Lyu, M.R.: WSPred: a time-aware personalized QoS prediction framework for Web services. In: IEEE 22nd International Symposium on Software Relia-bility Engineering, pp. 210–219 (2011)

A Skewness-Based Framework for Mobile App Permission Recommendation and Risk Evaluation

Keman Huang[1,2], Jinjing Han[1,2], Shizhan Chen[1,2,3(✉)],
and Zhiyong Feng[1,2,3(✉)]

[1] Tianjin Key Laboratory of Cognitive Computing and Application,
Tianjin, China
{keman.huang,hanjinjing,shizhan,zyfeng}@tju.edu.cn
[2] School of Computer Science and Technology,
Tianjin University, Tianjin, China
[3] School of Computer Software, Tianjin University, Tianjin, China

Abstract. Mobile ecosystem has penetrated into people's daily life over these years and most web services are now using mobile application for service consumption. Permission system has been developed to protect the sensitive and valuable information stored in mobile. However, due to the complexity of permission framework, the *permission over-privilege problem* has become a serious problem bringing huge risk for the mobile ecosystem. Therefore, in this paper, we present a skewness-based framework for permission recommendation and risk evaluation, intending to facilitate the permission configuration and identify the risk applications. Specially, the topic model Latent Dirichlet Allocation is presented to build the mapping between app's functionality and permission. Then a two-phase skewness-based filtering strategy is developed and combined with the collaborative filtering framework to remove the abnormal applications and permissions. Finally, the high risk permissions for each application are identified based on the difference between the malicious applications and popular applications. The experiments based on the Apps from Google Play shows that comparing with the state-of-the-art; our approach can effectively remove the abnormal applications and permissions, identify the unexpected and risk permissions, as well as generate the recommended permission configurations with better performance to reduce the permission over-privilege problem.

Keywords: Permission over-privilege · Skewness-based filtering · Unexpected permissions · Risk permissions · Permission recommendation

1 Introduction

With the rapid development of mobile internet technology, mobile terminals and mobile applications have penetrated into people's daily life. The rise of the mobile app ecosystem has drastically changed the way software and services are produced and consumed [1]. More and more web services are now used by end-users through mobile

© Springer International Publishing Switzerland 2016
Q.Z. Sheng et al. (Eds.): ICSOC 2016, LNCS 9936, pp. 252–266, 2016.
DOI: 10.1007/978-3-319-46295-0_16

apps. As a new and widely accepted approach for service delivery and consumption, it is important and necessary to carry out related researches in the mobile service domain. Actually, by the end of December 2015, the number of available applications on Google Play has been more than 1.87 million. Since more and more sensitive and valuable information are stored in the mobile phone, attacking mobile system to get potential benefits is becoming more and more attractive [2]. In order to protect the mobile system, the permission system has been developed to implement security mechanism. If the application needs to use some protected resources, it must request the relevant permissions. However, due to the complexity of the permission framework, the dialogs based permission framework for end users have been proved invalid [3, 4]: most users just touch the accept button to approve permission request, no matter at installation or during runtime because of risk underestimate [5] while many apps will request unnecessary permissions which brings risk for the use of the apps [6]. Consequently, the *permission over-privilege problem* becomes an important concern for both academia and industry.

Many efforts have been strived to improve the performance of the permission dialogs [7, 8] but fail to lead to the desired effect [4]. Some approaches [6, 9] turn to use the source code analysis to identify the precise set of permissions, while the technology used by malware such as repackaging, and update attack causes obvious delay for the permission detection methods [10]. Therefore, many efforts are shifting towards to a more promising track which uses the machine learning to automatically recommend the required permissions and identify the risk ones from the functionality such as category and description, or similarity with other apps [11–14]. Most of these approaches are based on the assumption that *permissions are well-configured for the popular apps so that they can be used for permission recommendation*. However, conversely, not only the malware applications but also many popular applications are suffering from the permission over privilege problem [6, 15]. H*ow to identify the abnormal permissions and remove the negative-effect* becomes important for permissions recommendations and risk evaluation.

In this paper, we present a framework based on collaborative filtering to help developers and users to configure the permissions. The basic hypothesis here is that *"applications with similar functions should request similar permissions"* [16]. Therefore, we combine the Latent Dirichlet Allocation and collaborative filtering framework to build the mapping between the functionality and the corresponding permissions. Note that, even the popular applications also request some unexpected permissions [6]. Good news is that *if an application request significantly different permissions from other similar ones, then the permissions configuration is abnormal and the application is risky*. Hence, we develop a two-phase skewness-based methodology to identify the abnormal candidate applications and permissions to guarantee the performance of the recommendation. Finally, *malicious applications request not only necessary permissions to enable the functionally, but also risk permissions for attack*. So we use the gap between the popular applications and malicious applications to further identify the risk permissions to evaluate the risk of the application.

Therefore, the main contribution of this paper is the skewness-based collaborative filtering framework for permission recommendation and risk evaluation, consisting of the following folds:

- A two-phase skewness-based strategy is developed to identify and remove the abnormal applications and permissions.
- A methodology based on the permission request difference between malicious and popular applications is proposed to evaluate the risk permissions and applications.
- The experiments based on Apps from Google Plays Store shows the effectiveness of our proposed framework: comparing with the state-of-the-art [17], 83.43 % and 61.61 % improvement in identify unexpected and risk permissions for malicious applications; 188.49 % and 99.13 % MAP improvement of permission recommendation for popular and malicious applications; as well 26.00 % and 53.47 % permissions reductions for and malicious popular applications.

The remainder of this paper is organized as follows. Section 2 defines the problem and presents the framework's overview. Section 3 details the permission recommendation and risk evaluation. Section 4 reports the experiments. Section 5 discusses the related work and Sect. 6 draws the conclusion.

2 Framework Overview

2.1 Problem Definition

As we are focusing on the relations between the requested permissions and the application's functionality, we can formally define each mobile application as:

$$a_i = <F_i, P_i > = \{ <tf_{i,1}, \ldots tf_{i,K} > , <p_{i,1}, \ldots p_{i,n_i} > \} \tag{1}$$

Where $F_i = <tf_{i,1}, \ldots tf_{i,K} >$ refers to the functionality, K is the total number of different functional domains for all the applications; $0 \le tf_{i,j} \le 1$ represents the probability that an application is relevant to a certain functional domain. $P_i = <p_{i,1}, \ldots p_{i,n_i} >$ refers to the requested permissions, n_i is the permissions' number.

Therefore, the *permission recommendation* problem can be defined as:

Q1: *given the application a_i and its functionality F_i, how to recommend its permissions RP_i?*

The *risk evaluation* problem can be defined as:

Q2: *given the application a_i, its functionality F_i and its requested permission P_i, how to evaluate its risk?*

2.2 Framework Overview

In order to solve these two problems, as shown in Fig. 1, we present the overview of our collaborative filtering variant which combines the collaborative filtering framework and Latent Dirichlet Allocation to build the mapping between functionality and permission. It consists of the following five processes:

- **Functionality Topic Detection:** The goal for this process is to identify the functionality for all the applications based on their functional descriptions, such as description, title and category. Here we follow the methodology using in [12], using

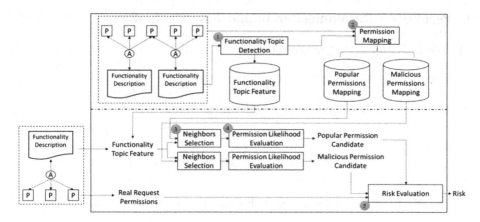

Fig. 1. Overview of Skewness-based Framework (SF)

the Latent Dirichlet Allocation (LDA) on the functional description to cluster applications into different functionality topics so that we can get the probability that an application is relevant to the certain functionality. Note that the summation of all the elements for each topic feature vector equals to 1.

- **Permission Mapping:** For each application, we extract its binary APK file with Apktool[1] and obtain the requested permission features from its manifest file in the APK file. As we will use the difference between popular and malicious applications' permission configurations for risk evaluation, we build the relations between permissions, applications and functionality topics for both the popular applications and the malicious applications separately.

- **Neighbors Selection:** Given an application a_i, based on the functionality topic feature, it is easy for us to get its functionality topic feature $F_i = <tf_{i,1}, \ldots tf_{i,K}>$. Then we can identify its neighbor applications with similar functionality based on the popular and malicious permissions mapping. We will discuss the detail for the neighbor selection in Sect. 3.1.

- **Permission Likelihood Evaluation:** Based on the selected neighbor applications, similar to the user-based collaborative filtering recommendation, we can calculate the permission's likelihood for the given application to generate the recommended permission candidates. Detail will be discussed in Sect. 3.2.

- **Risk Evaluation:** Given the recommended permission candidates, including the popular permission candidates and the malicious permission candidates, we can calculate the difference between them and the real request permissions to evaluate the risk of the given application. Detail will be discussed in Sect. 3.3.

---

[1] http://ibotpeaches.github.io/Apktool.

3 Permission Recommendation and Risk Evaluation

3.1 *Skewness-Based* Neighbors Selection

As we use LDA to map the applications into the functionality space, each application is represented as a topic feature vector. Therefore, we can calculate the correlation distance between two applications a_i, a_j as follow:

$$Dist(a_i, a_j) = \sqrt{\sum_{k=1}^{K} (fp_{i,k} - fp_{j,k})^2} \tag{2}$$

Then, we can calculate the similarity between two applications a_i, a_j as follows:

$$Sim(a_i, a_j) = \frac{1}{1 + Dist(a_i, a_j)} \tag{3}$$

Therefore, we can get a list of related applications with similarity to the given applications. It is well known that *using a subset of applications for recommendation can gain a better performance in the collaborative filtering framework because of the noise in the dataset.* Therefore, we use the threshold method which obtains a subset of appropriate applications with similarity larger than the given threshold θ_{sim}.

Further, just as we discuss above, the permission over-privilege problem is common for the applications, no matter for the malicious apps or the popular ones. Therefore, we need to remove the abnormal applications to reduce the negative effect of the permission over privilege. In fact, if an application request unusually large or small number of permissions comparing with the majority, then it can be considered as **abnormal application** that we should remove it in further processes.

The metric "*Skewness*" is a measure to evaluate the symmetry of a given distribution. If the distribution is symmetric, which means the left side is exactly the same to the right side of the center point, the skewness will be 0. A negative skewness indicates that there is a long tail on the left side that some data are very small while a positive skewness means that some data are very large comparing with the others. Therefore, we can use skewness to identify the abnormal candidate applications for the given application.

Given the candidate applications with similarity larger than the given threshold θ_{sim}, we sort these applications based on its requested permission number and get the permission distribution, $NP(a_i) = \ <np(a_{i,1}), \ldots np(a_{i,n_i})>$ where $F(a_i) = \ <a_{i,1}, \ldots a_{i,n_i}>$ are the candidate application list, $Sim(a_i, a_{i,k}) \geq \theta_{sim}, 1 \leq k \leq n_i$; $np(a_{i,k})$ refers to the number of request permissions for application $a_{i,k}$, $np(a_{i,k}) \leq np(a_{i,l}), 1 \leq k < l \leq n_i$. Its skewness is computed as follows:

$$sk(F(a_i)) = \frac{\frac{1}{n_i}\sum_{k=1}^{n_i}(np(a_{i,k}) - \mu)^3}{(\frac{1}{n_i-1}\sum_{k=1}^{n_i}(np(a_{i,k}) - \mu)^2)^{3/2}} \tag{4}$$

Where $\mu = \frac{1}{n_i}\sum_{k=1}^{n_i}np(a_{i,k})$ refers to the average number of the request permissions.

If $sk(F(a_i)) = 0$ then no abnormal applications are included in $F(a_i)$ that we use it as the final candidate applications $F^*(a_i)$. Otherwise, if $sk(F(a_i)) > 0$ which means $F(a_i)$ contains the abnormal application with too many request permissions, then we remove the applications with the largest number of permissions in $F(a_i)$; if $sk(F(a_i)) < 0$ which means $F(a_i)$ contains the abnormal application with too few request permissions, then we remove the applications with the smallest number of permissions in $F(a_i)$. This filtering process will be continue until it reaches symmetry that $sk(F(a_i)) = 0$, or only a given percent of neighbors θ_{NA} are retained. In this paper, we set $\theta_{NA} = 80\%$.

3.2 Skewness-Based Permission Likelihood Evaluation

Given the selected neighbor applications after the skewness-based filtering $F^*(a_i)$, we can calculate the recommend permissions based on the combination of their request permissions. The likelihood that application a_i need permission p_j is calculated as follow:

$$l(a_i, p_j) = \frac{\sum_{a_k \in F^*(a_i)} Sim(a_i, a_k)I(a_k, p_j)}{\sum_{a_k \in F^*(a_i)} Sim(a_i, a_k)} \tag{5}$$

$I(a_k, p_j) = 1$ if application a_k requests permission p_j, otherwise $I(a_k, p_j) = 0$.

Therefore we can get the likelihood vector for the given applications $L(a_i) = <l(a_i, p_{i1}), \ldots l(a_i, p_{iM}) >$ where $l(a_i, p_{ij}) \geq l(a_i, p_{ik}) \geq \theta_{NP}, 1 \leq j < k \leq M$, θ_{NP} is the likelihood threshold. Similarly, we can calculate its skewness as:

$$sk(L(a_i)) = \frac{\frac{1}{M}\sum_{k=i1}^{iM}(l(a_i, p_k) - \overline{\mu})^3}{(\frac{1}{M-1}\sum_{k=i1}^{iM}(l(a_i, p_k) - \overline{\mu})^2)^{3/2}} \tag{6}$$

Where $\overline{\mu} = \frac{1}{M}\sum_{k=1}^{iM}l(a_i, p_k)$ is the average of the likelihood for each permission.

Note that, if $sk(L(a_i)) \leq 0$, then all the permissions have a relative small likelihood value that these permissions should not be considered as the recommended permissions. Additionally, the larger the likelihood value is the higher possibility that the permission is needed for the application. Therefore as detailed in Algorithm 1, when

$sk(L(a_i)) > 0$, we get the permission p_{ij} with the largest likelihood value from $L(a_i)$ and add it into the recommended list, then we revise its likelihood value as $\overline{\mu}$. This process will be ended until the skewness value equals to or smaller than 0.

Algorithm 1. Skewness-based Permission Filtering
Input: $L(a_i)$: likelihood vector of permissions for a_i
Output: $R(a_i)$: recommend permission list for a_i
Procedure:
01. $R(a_i) \leftarrow \phi$
02. **FOR** $1 \le j \le M$
03.   **IF** $L(a_i) \ne \phi$ **AND** $sk(L(a_i)) > 0$
04. $R(a_i) \leftarrow R(a_i) \cup p_{ij}$
05. $l(a_i, p_{ij}) \leftarrow \overline{\mu} = \dfrac{1}{M} \sum\limits_{k=1}^{iM} l(a_i, p_k)$
06.   **ELSE**
07.   **BREAK**;
08.   **ENDIF**
09. **ENDFOR**

3.3 Gap-Based Risk Evaluation

The candidate permissions based on the framework represent the expected permissions considering the similar applications' functionality. Then the real request permissions which are not included in the candidates can be considered as the *unexpected permissions* for the given training dataset. Therefore, given the applications a_i, its request permissions $P_i = <p_{i,1}, \ldots p_{i,np(a_i)}>$ and the candidate permissions $RP^*(a_i) = <p_{i,r1}, \ldots p_{i,n_r}>$, the unexpected permissions $UP(a_i)$ can be formally defined as:

$$p_i \in UP^*(a_i) \leftrightarrow p_i \in P(a_i) - RP^*(a_i) \cap P(a_i) \tag{7}$$

Where $* \in \{P, M\}$ refers to the training datasets to get the candidate permissions. P means the candidates are generated based on the popular applications while M means the malicious applications.

Note that the candidate permissions $RP^M(a_i)$ will contain not only the necessary permissions but also the high risk permissions. On the other hand, most of the candidate permissions $RP^P(a_i)$ are supposed to be necessary. Then, the permissions belong to the gap $RP^M(a_i) - RP^M(a_i) \cap RP^P(a_i)$ between the malicious candidates and the good candidates can be considered as the *risk permissions* $RiP(a_i)$ for the given application:

$$p_i \in RiP(a_i) \leftrightarrow p_i \in RP^M(a_i) - RP^M(a_i) \cap RP^P(a_i) \qquad (8)$$

Therefore, if an application contains an unexpected permission which also belongs to the risk permissions, then we can consider the application is in risk.

$$a_i \in Risk \leftarrow \exists p_j \in P(a_i),\ s.t.\ p_j \in UP^P(a_i) \cap RiP(a_i) \qquad (9)$$

Finally we can calculate its risk as follow:

$$Risk(a_i) = \sum\nolimits_{p_j \in (UP^P(a_i) \cap RiP(a_i))} r(p_j) \qquad (10)$$

Here $r(p_j)$ refers to the risk of the permission based on its protection level. The android platform defines four protection levels: *normal, dangerous, signature, signatureOrsystem* and we assign their risk as 1, 2, 3, 4 respectively. For example, if an unexpected permission belongs to dangerous level, then its risk will be 2. Obviously, the more risky permissions requested by the application, the more risk the application will be, so that the user should not install it.

4 Experiment and Discussion

4.1 Data Set

Since Android ecosystem is no doubt the mainstream in the mobile ecosystem and Google Play Store is the most well-known Android application platform, we use the "*app market*" dataset from [18] which consists of 1,402,894 unique .apk files and the metadata such as name, description, version, category, user ratings or downloads. Then we choose the 22,907 applications with more than 100 downloads and five stars in Google play store, forming the "*Popular*" dataset. Furthermore, in order to study the permissions requested by the malware applications, we get the malware dataset from VirusShare[2] which consists of 24,317 malicious applications. Unfortunately, all of these malicious applications don't offer functionality information such as title or description. Therefore we map them into the "*app market*" dataset based on the package identifier and get the "*Malicious*" dataset consisting of 524 applications.

For the permissions in the Android ecosystem, there exist two kinds of permissions: *system permissions* defined by the Android platform and *custom permissions* defined by developers themselves. As the custom permissions are only used by the application itself, we only take the system permissions into account. Furthermore, as the Android platform has grown into different versions, we consider all the permissions which are ever defined, no matter deleted in new version or not, for applications, resulting into 285 unique permissions (see Table 1).

---

[2] http://virusshare.com.

Table 1. Ovewview of datasets

DataSet	Number of applications
Popular (P)	22,907
Malicious (M)	524
Permissions	Number of permissions
System permissions	285

4.2   Evaluation Metrics

In this paper, we use the following metrics to evaluate the performance:

Mean Average Precision (MAP). Mean Average Precision (MAP) is widely used to evaluate the performance of accuracy for recommendation algorithm which can take the relative order into account. It can be formally defined as follow:

$$MAP = \frac{1}{T}\sum_{k=1}^{T}\frac{1}{N_k}\sum_{j=1}^{N_k}\frac{H_j}{j}I_j \qquad (11)$$

Where T refers to the number of applications in testing dataset, N_k refers to the number of the recommended permissions for kth application a_k, H_j refers to the number of actually used permissions in the top j recommended permissions, $I_j = 1$ indicates the permission at jth ranking position is actually used while $I_j = 0$ means it is not used.

Difference Between Recommendations Based on Different Dataset. Note that given an application, the recommended permissions based on different dataset are different. Therefore, we can define the following two metrics to represent this gap: *DMG* refers to the average difference in recommended permission number while *RMG* refers to the average number of the risk permissions:

$$DMG = \frac{1}{T}\sum_{i=1}^{T}(|RP^M(a_i)| - |RP^P(a_i)|) \qquad (12)$$

$$RMG = \frac{1}{T}\sum_{i=1}^{T}|RiP(a_i)| = \frac{1}{T}\sum_{i=1}^{T}(|RP^M(a_i)| - |RP^P(a_i) \cap RP^M(a_i)|) \qquad (13)$$

Obviously, $DMG \leq RMG$. The larger the gap between DMG and RMG is, the more permissions recommended based on the malicious dataset are not included in the recommended permissions based on the popular dataset.

Ratio of Applications with Unexpected Permissions (AUPR). Here we consider the percent of applications which have unexpected permissions in the testing dataset, formally defined as *AUPR*:

$$AUPR = \frac{1}{T}\sum_{i=1}^{T} I(UP^P(a_i)) \tag{14}$$

Where $I(UP^P(a_i)) = 1$, if $|UP^P(a_i)| > 0$. Otherwise $I(UP^P(a_i)) = 0$.

Risk Application Ratio (RAR). As discussed above, our approach can identify whether an application is risk or not. Therefore, we can define the ratio of applications which are considered as risky (RAR) in the datasets as follows:

$$RAR = \frac{1}{T}\sum_{i=1}^{T} I(a_i, Risk) \tag{15}$$

Where $I(a_i, Risk) = 1$ if $a_i \in Risk$; otherwise $I(a_i, Risk) = 0$.

In this paper, we don't consider the time cost as an evaluation metric. Actually, we are using 20-threads for parallel computing, sorting the apps based on the functionality similarity and only considering the related apps, for average, it takes about 0.04 s to generate the permission recommendations for an app, which is definitely acceptable.

4.3   Parameter Selection for Similiarity Threshold θ_{sim}

In our framework, we use the similarity threshold θ_{sim} to select the neighbor applications with reasonal similarity for the given application. Therefore, in order to evaluate its influence, we randomly select 20 % applications from the popular dataset as the testing dataset and the consider the four experiments reported in Table 2.

Table 2. Experiments for similarity threshold

		Training data base	
		Rest 80 % popular applications	Malicious applications
Skewness-filtering for abnormal application	Yes	Popular-Skewness filtering	Malicious-Skewness filtering
	NO	Popular	Malicious

Finally, we vary θ_{sim} from 0 to 1 to generate different permission recommendations. The MAP of the recommendation is reported in Fig. 2. As shown in Fig. 2, it can be seen that for the popular dataset, if $\theta_{sim} > 0.6$, the MAP is decreasing; similarly, if $\theta_{sim} > 0.4$, the MAP for the malicious dataset is decreasing. This is because that with a too larger similarity threshold, most of applications can not have enough neighbor applications to generate a valid recommendation. Therefore, in the rest of this paper, we will set $\theta_{sim} = 0.6$ for the popular permission mapping, and $\theta_{sim} = 0.4$ for the malicious permission mapping.

Additionally, it can be seen that given the selected threshold, using the skewness to filter the permissions with low likelihood can gain a relative better performance. Actually, for the recommendation based on popular applications, it can gain a 14.7 % improvement in MAP.

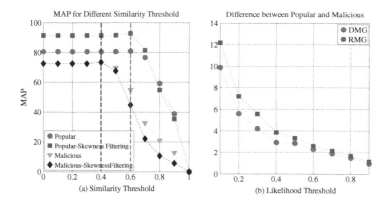

(a) Similarity Threshold

(b) Likelihood Threshold

Fig. 2. Similarity threshold selection and gaps between popular and malicious

4.4 Difference Between Popular Applications and Malicious Applications

From Fig. 2 (a), we can see that RP^P gains a better performance than RP^M. This is because that we use the 20 % popular applications as the testing dataset and the malicious applications have a different pattern in permission configuration.

Furthermore, in order to understand the differences between the popular applications and the malicious applications, based on the given θ_{sim}, we can calculate the *DMG* and *RMG* for different threshold of the permission likelihood value. As shown in Fig. 2 (b), it can be seen that DMA and RMG are always larger than 0, which means that *the malicious applications request more permissions than the popular applications*. Additionally, with the increasing of the permission likelihood threshold, these two metrics are both decreasing while the gap bettwen DMG and RMG is also decreasing, representing that *the permissions with high likelihood value are requested by both the popular and malicious applications*. These permissions are the neccessary requirements to support the functionality of the applications.

4.5 Performance Comparison

In order to prove the effectiveness of our approach, we consider the state-of-the-art methodology which has been partially deployed in Chrome Web Store and Google Play Store:

- Peer-group Model (PGM) [17]: In PGM, given the permission used by the candidate application, the applications in the same category, named *peer group*, are used to calculate the ratio of applications using the given permission; if the ratio is smaller than a given threshold, then the permission is considered as the unexpected permissions. The threshold is set as 0.05.

Then we randomly selected 80 % of the popular applications to train the popular permission mapping, 80 % of the malicious applications to train the malicious permission mapping. The rest of the popular and malicious applications are used as the training data. The similarity threshold is set as $\theta_{sim}^{P} = 0.6, \theta_{sim}^{M} = 0.4$. The likelihood threshold is set as $\theta_{NP} = 0.1$. Table 3 summarizes the improvement of our framework comparing with PGM. Here *ARISK* refers to the average of the risk value for the testing applications, *AP* refers to the average number of the real requested permissions, *ARP* refers to the average number of the recommended permissions.

Table 3. Performance comparing with State-of-the-art

DataSet/Approach		AUPR	RAR	ARISK	MAP	AP	ARP
Popular (P)	SF	0.732	0.191	0.701	0.877	6.77	5.01 (−26.00 %)
	PGM	0.258	0.105	0.293	0.304		20.20 (+198.38 %)
		/	/	/	188.49 %		/
Malicious (M)	SF	0.908	0.543	2.536	0.914	8.94	4.16 (−53.47 %)
	PGM	0.495	0.336	1.460	0.459		17.20 (+92.39 %)
		83.43 %	61.61 %	73.70 %	99.13 %		/

As shown in Table 3, comparing with PGM, it can be seen that for malicious detections, our approach shows that for the malicious applications, 90.8 % request unexpected permissions and 54.3 % contain risk permissions. However, PGM only finds 49.5 % malicious applications with unexpected permission, and 33.6 % malicious applications use risk permission. Additionally, our approach can assign a 73.7 % higher risk value for the malicious applications, as well as a 99.13 % improvement in MAP. For the popular applications, we get a 188.49 % improvement in MAP.

Note that our approach also shows that even the popular applications will request the unexpected and risk permissions, though the RAR is not as high as the malicious ones. This result is consistent with the observation in [6, 15]. Furthermore, from Table 3, it can be seen that our approach will recommend a fewer number of permissions for both the popular applications and the malicious applications which can help to reduce the over-privilidge problem. Actually, we get a 26.00 % reductions for popular applications and 53.47 % for malicious applications, while PGM even recommends more permissions.

Therefore, comparing with PGM, we can draw the conclusion that our approach can effectively identify the abnormal usage of permission, generate a better recommended permission configuration to reduce the permission over-privilidge.

5 Related Work

Permission system is one of the most important mechanisms to protect the mobile ecosystem. Due to the fact that permission dialogs fail to lead to the desired effect [4], some approaches are turning to identify the risky of the permissions requested by an application [19]. However, as the application's functionality is ignored that it often results into spurious warnings. In order to solve this problem, many efforts are shifting towards to a more promising track which uses the machine learning to automatically recommend the required permissions from the functionality such as category and description, or similarity with other apps [11–14]. Peng et al. [20] uses the similarity with other applications to evaluate the risk of a given application. Pandita et al. [14] and Qu et al. [13] build a permission semantic model to determine which sentences in the description indicate the use of permissions. By comparing the result with the requested permissions, they can detect gap between the description and requested permissions. Wang et al. [11] further identifies the minimum set of permissions an app needs by tailored the requested permissions that are not listed in the semantic permissions in the app descriptions. Gorla et al. [12] develops a tool called CHABADA that uses Latent Dirichlet Allocation (LDA) on app descriptions to cluster Android applications with similar textual descriptions together. The most similar approach to our framework is the peer-group model (PMG) introduced by Jana et al. [17], which has been partially deployed in Chrome Web Store and Google Play Store. In PMG, the software peer group analysis is developed to identify least privilege violation by the proportions of permissions requested by applications from peer group. Peer groups are generated by different information, ranging from pre-defined static categories, list of other related applications, textual descriptions.

Most of these approaches are based on the assumption that permissions are well-configured for good applications or the applications developers are all malicious. By contrast, most of the careless and lazy developers are not actively malicious [17]. Additionally, due to the complexity of the permission system, most of the popular applications also break the least-privileged principle. Therefore, unlike these approaches, based on the assumptions that *the malicious applications will request different permissions with the good applications* and *the application with similar functionality should request similar permissions*, we develops a collaborative filtering variant framework which employs the skewness-based filtering strategy to recommend permissions and uses the difference between good applications and malicious applications to identify the risk permissions.

6 Conclusions

Mobile ecosystem has penetrated into people's every aspect of life recently. More and more web services are turning to offer mobile application for users to consume the services. As the security of the mobile ecosystem becomes an important issue for the web service community, while permission system is designed to protect the mobile ecosystem, how to help the developers and consumers to use the permission system is attracting attentions both from academia and industry. In this paper, based on the collaborative filter framework using LDA to identify applications' functionality topics, we develop a two-phase skewness-based filtering strategy to remove the abnormal application candidates and the low-likelihood permissions to generate recommended permissions. Furthermore, based on the recommended permissions from popular applications and malicious applications, we identify the unexpected and risk permissions for each application so that we can evaluate their risk just based on the permission configurations. The experiment based on the dataset from Google Play Store shows that comparing with the state-of-the-art:

- For the malicious applications, our approach gains a 83.43 % and 61.61 % improvement in unexpected permission and risk permission identification;
- We gain a 188.49 % improvement for popular applications and 99.13 % for malicious applications;
- More importantly, comparing with the real request permissions, we can cut 26.00 % permissions for popular applications and 53.47 % for malicious ones, which is helpful for reduce the permission over-privilege problem.

In the future, we will further extend our framework to effectively identify the least privilege permissions to help the developers and users for permission configuration. Also we will mitigate the approach to Apache Mahout to guarantee the scalability of the framework.

Acknowledgment. This work is supported by the National Natural Science Foundation of China grants 61373035, 61502333, 61572350 and the Tianjin Research Program of Application Foundation and Advanced Technology grant 14JCYBJC15600.

References

1. Petsas, T., Papadogiannakis, A., Polychronakis, M., Markatos, E.P., Karagiannis, T.: Rise of the planet of the apps. In: Proceedings of the 2013 Conference on Internet Measurement Conference - IMC 2013, pp. 277–290 (2013)
2. Leavitt, N.: Mobile security: finally a serious problem? Computer **44**, 11–14 (2011)
3. Wijesekera, P., Columbia, B., Baokar, A., Hosseini, A., Egelman, S., Wagner, D.: Android permissions remystified: a field study on contextual integrity. In: 24th USENIX Security Symposium (USENIX Security 15), pp. 499–514 (2015)
4. Acar, Y., Backes, M., Bugiel, S., Fahl, S., Mcdaniel, P., Smith, M.: SoK: lessons learned from android security research for appified software platforms. In: 37th IEEE Symposium on Security and Privacy, pp. 1–19 (2016)
5. Felt, A.P., Ha, E., Egelman, S., Haney, A., Chin, E., Wagner, D.: Android permissions: user attention, comprehension, and behavior. In: Proceedings of the Eighth Symposium on Usable Privacy and Security, pp. 3:1–14 (2012)
6. Felt, A.P., Chin, E., Hanna, S., Song, D., Wagner, D.: Android permissions demystified. In: Proceedings of the 18th ACM Conference on Computer and Communications Security - CCS 2011, p. 627 (2011)
7. Liu, B., Lin, J., Sadeh, N.: Reconciling mobile app privacy and usability on smartphones: could user privacy profiles help? In: Proceedings of the 23rd International Conference on World Wide Web, pp. 201–212 (2014)

8. Kelley, P.G., Cranor, L.F., Sadeh, N.: Privacy as part of the app decision-making process. In: Proceedings of the SIGCHI Conference on Human Factors in Computing Systems, p. 11 (2013)

9. Au Kathy Wain Yee, Zhou, Y.F., Huang, Z., Lie, D.: PScout: analyzing the android permission specification. In: Proceedings of the 2012 ACM Conference on Computer and Communications Security, pp. 217–228 (2012)

10. Zhou, Y., Jiang, X.: Dissecting Android malware: characterization and evolution. In: Proceedings - IEEE Symposium on Security and Privacy, pp. 95–109 (2012)

11. Wang, J., Chen, Q.: ASPG: generating android semantic permissions. In: Proceedings - 17th IEEE International Conference on Computational Science and Engineering, CSE 2014, pp. 591–598 (2014)

12. Gorla, A., Tavecchia, I., Gross, F., Zeller, A.: Checking app behavior against app descriptions. In: Proceedings of the 36th International Conference on Software Engineering, pp. 1025–1035. ACM (2014)

13. Qu, Z., Rastogi, V., Zhang, X., Chen, Y., Zhu, T., Chen, Z.: AutoCog: measuring the description-to-permission fidelity in Android applications. In: Proceedings of the 2014 ACM SIGSAC Conference on Computer and Communications Security - CCS 2014, pp. 1354–1365 (2014)

14. Pandita, R., Xiao, X., Yang, W., Enck, W., Xie, T.: Whyper: towards automating risk assessment of mobile applications. In: 22nd USENIX Security Symposium (USENIX Security 13), pp. 527–542 (2013)

15. Wei, X., Gomez, L., Neamtiu, I., Faloutsos, M.: Permission evolution in the Android ecosystem. In: Proceedings of the 28th Annual Computer Security Applications Conference, pp. 31–40 (2012)

16. Liu, R., Cao, J., VanSyckel, S., Gao, W.: PriMe: human-centric privacy measurement based on user preferences towards data sharing in mobile participatory sensing systems. In: 2016 IEEE International Conference on Pervasive Computing and Communications (PerCom), pp. 1–8. IEEE (2016)

17. Jana, S., Erlingsson, Ú., Ion, I.: Apples and Oranges: Detecting Least-Privilege Violators with Peer Group Analysis, pp. 1–11 (2015). arXiv:1510.07308

18. Viennot, N., Garcia, E., Nieh, J.: A measurement study of google play. In: Measurement and Modeling of Computer Systems – SIGMETRICS, pp. 221–233 (2014)

19. Enck, W., Ongtang, M., McDaniel, P.: On lightweight mobile phone application certification. In: Proceedings of the 16th ACM Conference on Computer and Communications Security - CCS 2009, pp. 235–245 (2009)

20. Peng, H., Gates, C., Sarma, B., Li, N., Qi, Y., Potharaju, R., Nita-Rotaru, C., Molloy, I.: Using probabilistic generative models for ranking risks of Android apps. In: Proceedings of the 2012 ACM Conference on Computer and Communications Security, pp. 241–252 (2012)

On Engineering Analytics
for Elastic IoT Cloud Platforms

Hong-Linh Truong$^{(\boxtimes)}$, Georgiana Copil, Schahram Dustdar, Duc-Hung Le,
Daniel Moldovan, and Stefan Nastic

Distributed Systems Group, TU Wien, Vienna, Austria
{truong,e.copil,dustdar,d.le,d.moldovan,s.nastic}@dsg.tuwien.ac.at

Abstract. Developing IoT cloud platforms is very challenging, as IoT
cloud platforms consist of a mix of cloud services and IoT elements, e.g.,
for sensor management, near-realtime events handling, and data analytics. Developers need several tools for deployment, control, governance
and analytics actions to test and evaluate designs of software components and optimize the operation of different design configurations. In
this paper, we describe requirements and our techniques on supporting the development and testing of IoT cloud platforms. We present our
choices of tools and engineering actions that help the developer to design,
test and evaluate IoT cloud platforms in multi-cloud environments.

1 Introduction

Recent complex business and societal requirements, e.g., in smart cities, cyber-
physical systems, building information management, and logistics [7,16], have
fostered the integration between the Internet of Things (IoT) and cloud services.
Generally speaking, an IoT cloud platform includes several "Things" connected
to cloud services in data centers using various software and layered protocols, as
intensively discussed in [5–7,15]. Technically, such platforms are realized by having sensors and actuators interfacing 'Things"; these sensors and actuators are
used to monitor and control "Things" (sensors/actuators can also be "Things").
These sensors and actuators are connected to and/or accessible from cloud services via gateways or intermediate nodes. Inside IoT gateways, different software
components are used to relay sensing data to data centers, to (pre)process
sensing data, or to execute commands from data centers to Things. There are
various forms of integration of the IoT part (sensors and gateways at the edge)
and the cloud part (cloud services in data centers), such as shown in [5,7,16],
creating so-called IoT cloud platforms. Such IoT cloud platforms include mixed
functionalities from typical cloud services and IoT elements that require novel
engineering techniques [20]. Clearly, development and testing of such IoT cloud
platforms are very challenging due to several reasons. First, it is not easy to

This work was partially supported by the European Commission in terms of the
CELAR FP7 project (FP7-ICT-2011-8 #317790) and the U-Test H2020 project
(H2020-ICT-2014-1 #645463).

Q.Z. Sheng et al. (Eds.): ICSOC 2016, LNCS 9936, pp. 267–281, 2016.
DOI: 10.1007/978-3-319-46295-0_17

specify and control complex topologies of sensors and gateways in the IoT side that emulate a real-world deployment, e.g., for equipment management in a city. Second, when storing and/or processing IoT data in the cloud, cloud services have to be designed in such a way that they support elasticity/change in the IoT side, enabling efficient operation of the whole IoT cloud platform in an end-to-end manner. However, it is challenging to monitor and control software components and services spanning across multiple clouds, including those at the edge of the clouds, in order to adapt the varying load, cost and performance. Therefore, it would take a long time to design IoT cloud platforms, as it is still hard to test configurations and features as early as possible, especially when we need to combine all running pay-per-use services in the cloud with IoT elements.

As integrating cloud software services and IoT in complex, large-scale scenarios is very challenging, various works have been focused on cloud engineering techniques for IoT cloud platforms [2,7,9]. Nevertheless, we still face great engineering difficulties due to the lack of suitable tools to test and evaluate complex designs of IoT cloud platforms. In our previous work, we have presented a demo of the iCOMOT framework [19] as a toolset for simplifying the management of IoT cloud systems. In this paper, we detail requirement analysis, designs, and engineering actions for iCOMOT which can help accelerating the development of IoT cloud platforms. Relying on fundamental concepts of virtualization and elasticity for both IoT and cloud resources, we utilize different tools to speed up the development of IoT cloud platforms. With our solutions we help reduce complexity and effort of IoT cloud platforms development by leveraging (i) suitable elasticity engineering techniques for cloud services, which already offer several common features for executions, data, computation and networks, (ii) open data sets, which can be used to emulate sensor behaviors, and (iii) appropriate integrated engineering tools for performing deployment, control and analytics tasks for IoT cloud platforms. In this paper, we also illustrate the usefulness of our techniques through a case study for predictive maintenance.

The rest of this paper is organized as follows. Section 2 presents our motivation. Section 3 describes our iCOMOT toolset. We present requirements and our design and engineering actions in Sect. 4. We present a case study in Sect. 5. Related work is discussed in Sect. 6. We conclude the paper and outline our future work in Sect. 7.

2   Motivation – IoT and Cloud Integration Support

2.1   IoT and Cloud Integration Models

Developers of IoT cloud platforms can have varying goals:

- *Goal 1:* developers might need only to develop IoT elements (e.g., sensors, actuators and gateways) for a specific customer and to connect these IoT elements to existing cloud services. In this case, they might just want to develop and test a set of sensors that can be deployed into certain gateways sending the data to public cloud services.

– *Goal 2:* developers focus on only cloud services at data centers that serve IoT elements. Typically they focus on a set of complex cloud services, e.g., for data storage, complex event processing, and data analytics.
– *Goal 3:* developers want to design and test a complete IoT cloud platform for a specific customer. They, therefore, focus on both IoT elements and cloud services and on how to coordinate them in a unified view for the customer.

Numerous works support the development of either the IoT part or the cloud services for IoT [2,12,21]. However, there is a lack of tools and discussions for the development and operations of the last goal– *Goal 3*. We focus on supporting developers to concentrate on *Goal 3*, which is complex but of paramount importance for several customers, e.g., predictive maintenance of equipment, on-demand crowd sensing for safe cities [1], and sports events [3]. For such platforms, we must deal with different engineering principles outlined in [20].

2.2   Development in Distributed IoT and Cloud Systems

As the IoT cloud platform is complex, it is expected that during the development, components of the platform must be deployed in multiple IoT and cloud systems. For this, we must have a set of connectors allowing the developer access to clouds and IoT specific systems so that the developer can deploy testing infrastructures and run tests across clouds and IoT specific systems. We also need to deal with different mechanisms of controlling virtual resources and different performance settings (e.g., expected time for allocating a resource, expected performance for each resource). As discussed in the related work (Sect. 6), most tools either enable IoT deployment or cloud deployment; even many industrial systems support IoT and cloud services, and enable their integration, these systems support *Goal 1* and *Goal 2* separately.

Moreover, at runtime, both IoT elements and cloud services need to be controlled, monitored, and analyzed in a coordinated manner. While throughout the development lifecycle the developer would need mechanisms to emulate sensors and gateways in the heterogeneity of different clouds, in a production environment we have to do an end-to-end control of cloud services and gateways deployed across IoT networks and clouds. This has to be done in a uniform manner, as most of the times control on one end of the IoT cloud platform would affect the control on the other end (e.g., deploying new data processing services on the gateway would change the characteristics of the load on cloud software services). As discussed in the related work, this feature is missing in most toolsets.

3   Overview of iCOMOT

To support *Goal 3* in multi-IoT and -cloud environments, we design, develop and experience different tools and engineering actions to address two different main issues: (i) to provide main software components which are software-defined, deployable and configurable, and (ii) to support easy configuration, deployment, control, and monitoring in a unified manner. To achieve the first point, we base on two main emerging research directions:

- software-defined IoT units: sensor and gateway components are considered as units that can be composed and controlled via software-defined APIs.
- cloud-based elastic services: they are common cloud services offered by different providers. To enable the elasticity, some services will be associated with elasticity capabilities.

To achieve the second point, we build a toolset to enable elasticity control developments. Figure 1 describes how we leverage our existing tools and our engineering actions to develop IoT cloud platforms. Cloud providers and third-party developers can design and provide several components and services that will available through PaaS/IaaS and public repositories/marketplaces. A developer will utilize these services and components and to develop her/his own services and components. Then s/he can utilize various tools to support service deployment, configuration, analytics and control to test and evaluate her/his designs.

To this end, we have demonstrated the iCOMOT framework to support the developer to develop and test different configurations and runtime behaviors of IoT cloud systems. iCOMOT (http://tuwiendsg.github.io/iCOMOT/) includes several individual research tools for configuring, deploying, monitoring and controlling IoT cloud platforms, such as SYBL, SALSA, MELA and GovOps [19]. We connect several common repositories and together with these tools to support automation of IoT cloud platform configurations deployment. Furthermore, several sensors with data sets are also provided. The following sections, we will explain main insightful engineering actions, designs and experiences.

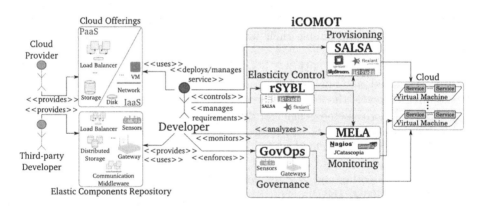

Fig. 1. Engineering tools and actions

4   Design and Engineering Actions

4.1   Software Components for IoT Cloud Platforms

IoT Units and Cloud Services Repository. *Requirements:* Existing cloud APIs already allow us to invoke suitable cloud services at data centers and to emulate execution environments (e.g., lightweight virtual machines for emulated IoT gateways). However, they do not support the IoT side well, such as, modeling, configuring, deploying and testing different types of sensors, gateway software components, and libraries for cloud connectivity.

Solutions: To model and capture IoT unit capabilities and configuration with software artifact, we leverage the concept of IoT cloud units [14] to successfully model suitable IoT resources and enable some useful behaviors, such as dynamically changing communication protocols between IoT gateways and cloud services at runtime. As IoT units can be provided by different developers and providers, we support access to different component repositories for existing IoT units, such as gateways execution environment, virtual network routers and communication protocols for cloud connectivity. These repositories can be leveraged by well-developed technologies, such as Docker Hub, Git-based repositories and Maven, and IoT marketplaces, such as [2, 4, 21].

Software Sensors. *Requirements:* One important type of IoT software units are sensors. For development and testing, it is crucial to have emulated sensors whose behavior is similar to real sensors but with advanced features to allow us to easily control the sensors. An emulated sensor just takes time series datasets, e.g., obtained from industrial real systems, and replays/simulates events by sending them to gateways. By leveraging different real datasets, we can instantiate different sensors by configuring these instances with different sample data and behavior models. With this way, we can emulate GPS, temperature sensors, and chiller's operation sensors, etc., for different types of IoT cloud platforms.

Solutions: In our framework, the developer can develop her/his real sensors or emulated sensors and then deposit the sensors into the repository from which they can be deployed into IoT cloud platforms. To support rapid development of the IoT side, one important issue is to have emulated sensors as executable code that can be deployed at a very large-scale in multi-cloud environments to emulate real situations, e.g., monitoring chillers in a city, in IoT cloud platforms. We also enable the users to modify configurations while the sensors are running, for simulating different workloads or for testing their application under various out-of-the ordinary circumstances (e.g., fire at a location). The developer can also design topologies of different sensors for better management and reuse. In production scenarios of an IoT cloud platform, sensors will be physically distributed at different places, while, in simulations and tests, sensors are deployed in different VMs, OS containers, lightweight machines like Raspberry Pi, or cloud data centers. To enhance interoperability and reusability of possible sensor architectures, we present the topologies of sensors by well-known description languages, such as TOSCA (https://www.oasis-open.org/committees/tosca/), for the deployment and control process.

Software-Defined Gateways. *Requirements:* In certain IoT cloud platforms, sensors can directly connect to cloud services. However, in our experience, very often gateways are needed as intermediate nodes for handling different types of sensing data and connectivities. We consider and support gateways as another type of IoT software/hardware units. Gateways are much more complex than sensors. For example, gateways can store information and execute some lightweight components to process sensing data in the cloudlets model [18].

Solutions: From the architecture design perspective, we develop and provision gateways functionality by using our concept of software-defined IoT units [14]. Generally, a software-defined gateway consists of a set of dependent IoT units deployed in a virtualized environment, e.g. CentOS or Docker. These IoT units are responsible for managing data streams, controls of actuators, cloud connectivity and lightweight data storage and processing. The key point of a software-defined gateway is that it enables dynamic deployment and configuration of IoT units to handle data, control and connectivity, allowing the developer to implement IoT-side distributed data processing, such as pre-processing data in gateways and splitting streams, i.e., sending events to multiple cloud services.

Cloud Services for IoT. *Requirements:* At data centers, both cloud-offered services and custom-built software components can be used for building the IoT cloud platform. Main cloud providers, such as Amazon EC2 (http://aws.amazon. com), Rackspace (http://www.rackspace.com), Windows Azure (http://azure. microsoft.com/en-us/) or Flexiant (http://www.flexiant.com/), offer diverse types of cloud services, from infrastructure (e.g., VMs, networking, virtual storage), to platform (e.g., load balancer, message queue), to management (e.g., monitoring, backup, auto scaling), and data analysis applications (e.g., stream data processing services). However, it is challenging to combine and use such services in a coordinated mode with IoT elements, for example, to enable the elasticity coordination between IoT sensors and cloud services.

Solutions: Focusing on elastic software components, we enable developers to employ a series of off-the-shelf software components in building their elastic platforms. The most commonly used software components are load balancers (e.g., HTTP load balancer – HAProxy http://www.haproxy.org/), which enable elasticity of web servers serving platform clients. Next, distributed data storage frameworks (e.g., Cassandra – http://cassandra.apache.org/ – and MongoDB – http://www.mongodb.org/) are crucial in building elastic data ends, but must be configured and managed accordingly, as scaling a data end is usually a complex operation, implying data moving and copying. Another class of software components used for enabling elasticity is message oriented middleware, (e.g., Apache ActiveMQ – http://activemq.apache.org/), which, by decoupling the communication between components, enable seamless addition and removal of component's instances. In general, while we are not developing such common software, we focus on how to glue them using elasticity techniques for elastic IoT cloud platforms.

4.2   Deployment, Control, and Monitoring Actions

Deployment. _Requirements:_ The developer has to deploy components of IoT cloud platforms very often in order to study and test them. Generally, a deployment service will have to deal with both IoT and cloud service sides. We need to deploy different types of services and to manage from single components to the entire platform configuration at runtime. Therefore, the developer has to prepare at set of deployment artifacts in the repository including the dataset, configuration script, software artifacts. The APIs and information for accessing IoT and cloud infrastructures must also be prepared. We witnessed that these complex tasks cannot be done by a single tool, but multiple tools and connectors to different clouds, orchestrated by a centralized service.

Solutions: Currently we can describe deployment descriptions using various format such as TOSCA, HEAT (https://wiki.openstack.org/wiki/Heat) or AWS CloudFormation (http://aws.amazon.com/cloudformation/), Juju (https://juju. ubuntu.com), Cloud Foundry build packs (http://docs.cloudfoundry.org/ buildpacks/custom.html). We use TOSCA intensively as it provides a generic model to define cloud services and support loose-coupling relationships between multiple component types, which makes the description independent from cloud providers and deployment tools. However, we experienced that TOSCA description is complex to create, maintain and process, so it requires comprehensive and easy-to-use tools for users and developers, especially for deploying IoT units into gateways. For the application provider who just wants to deploy the services or sensors, a description tool with GUI that hides the low-level information is more convenient. With an end-to-end aspect, our deployment tool copes with different levels of deployment, including requesting cloud provider resources, configuring virtual machines, middleware and dependencies, and deploying artifacts.

Elasticity Analytics. _Requirements:_ For analyzing the elasticity change of the IoT cloud platform (e.g., scaling in/out cloud services and sensor instances), elasticity analytics will be deployed at different parts of the platform to provide different performance and elasticity metrics. An elastic IoT cloud platform would have elasticity requirements defined over its components, based on which intelligent controllers can analyze its behavior and take appropriate actions. Due to the potential complexity of IoT cloud platforms, the developer might not know such requirements for all platform components, especially reflecting the dependencies between the IoT part and the cloud part. For example, a developer might not understand the cloud storage performance required to fulfill the requirement of activating more sensors.

Solutions: To custom IoT cloud platform-specific analytics, we follow two different approaches: (i) bottom-up: common built-in metrics are structured and analyzed automatically, providing an overview over the platform's elasticity, and (ii) top-down: the platform developer can define custom, potentially domain-specific, metrics and analytics functions. Thus, we provide a complete end-to-end view over behavioral limits of the platform to enable the developer to refine the platform, and improve its control strategies. Especially, it is crucial to define an analytics function, which, based on supplied requirements, records encountered bounds on the monitored metrics not targeted by user requirements, in which the developer requirements were respected.

Elasticity Control. *Requirements:* We need to enable elasticity for various parts of the IoT cloud platforms, such as sensors, gateways and cloud services, during the development and operation. This means that elasticity control mechanisms and tools must work across sub-platforms for design, test and operation purposes and must interface various protocols (e.g., REST, MQTT, ssh + bash execution) used to change software components. Moreover, most developers would be interested in specifying abstract, high-level requirements (e.g., not focused on system-level metrics, controlling the software service as a whole).

Solutions: For sensors, developers could control the behavior of sensors (e.g., data reading frequency), to which gateway a sensor connects as well as the protocols between by gateways and sensors. At gateways, developers could control the number of sensor connections, the amount of data which is stored locally considering various constraints (e.g., the gateway has very limited computational power, memory and space). Moreover, we can add/remove various components for locally processing information, or change their sensitivity. For cloud services in an IoT cloud platform, we can support various known control mechanisms: (i) virtual infrastructure capabilities (e.g., add/remove virtual machines, network interfaces, disks), (ii) platform specific capabilities (e.g., start/stop web server, deploy/undeploy service in existing web server), or (iii) application-specific capabilities (e.g., using API offered by cloud services developers). Each of these can be enforced separately or grouped into complex control processes. However, elasticity setup cannot be completely automated, and completely application-independent. When developers need more advanced elasticity controls, they can encapsulate them into their application-specific control mechanisms (e.g., use a web server deployed together with a new configuration to result into other performance/cost characteristics). For controlling elasticity, we enable interaction-based control to empower the developers with refining their control strategies, considering the evolution of the service at runtime.

5   Experiments

5.1   Case Studies

Let us consider a scenario in which a predictive maintenance company would like to focus on predictive analytics for chillers in a city. The company wants to reuse/rent as much as possible IoT cloud infrastructures so that the company will focus on deploying its sensors, gateways, and cloud services. These sensors, gateways and cloud services establish the company's IoT cloud platform. The IoT cloud platform includes gateways at the IoT part and cloud services at the data center. All of them are virtualized services, meaning that they can be deployed, configured and used on-the-fly. The predictive maintenance company will need features from the IoT cloud platform provider, which provides the right configuration of the IoT cloud platform for the predictive maintenance company. The IoT cloud platform can offer features for a predictive maintenance company which monitors chillers and performs data analytics and maintenance tasks. In this case study, we will focus on the case that the predictive maintenance company wants to buy services from an IoT cloud platform provider to create a configuration of its own elastic IoT cloud platform. Then the company develops and tests different sensors which connect to its elastic cloud services to have a complete IoT cloud system for gathering data to support data analytics[1].

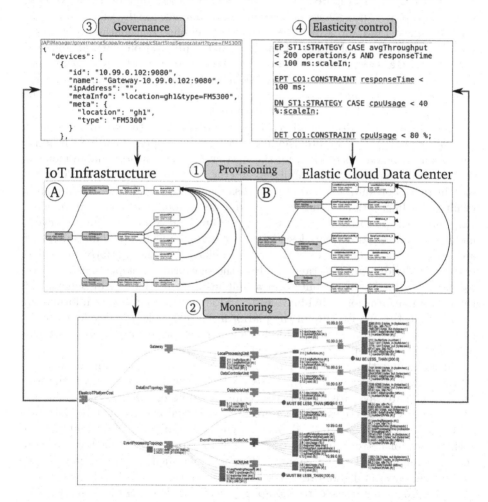

Fig. 2. Toolset for developing and testing elastic IoT cloud platforms

---

[1] See https://github.com/tuwiendsg/DaaSM2M and https://github.com/tuwiendsg/SDM.

5.2   Development and Deployment

First all of all, to make the (re)configuration of the IoT cloud platform flexible, using our toolset (Fig. 2), the predictive maintenance company can deploy two separate configurations: a configuration of the IoT sensors and gateways (Part Ⓐ), and another of the cloud data center (Part Ⓑ). This enables them to play with different sensors easily regarding data and topology, communication protocols, bursting workload, while the cloud services might be stable. For both configurations, IoT units and cloud services are provided from different providers from various repositories. The configurations will be specified in TOSCA and we *Provision* (①) them. Figure 2 – Part Ⓐ – shows an example of TOSCA-based sensor topology, which allows the developer to manage single sensors and sensor topologies[2] (and VM which hosts sensors in emulated scenarios). Figure 2 – Part Ⓑ – shows the deployment of an elastic IoT configuration platform – named `ElasticIoTPlatform` – at the data center to reflect real cloud services and emulated gateways. With our techniques, such configurations (for sensors and for gateways/services) can be also programmed using Java code, enabling different ways to program and test IoT cloud platforms.

Having the entire IoT cloud platform is provisioned, the company focuses on *Monitoring*(①). Before provisioning, platform developers must have in mind what monitoring data is relevant for the elasticity of the platform, and implement the necessary monitoring capabilities. A crucial factor in elastic platforms is that instances of units tend to appear/disappear dynamically at run-time as a result of scaling actions being enforced due to various elasticity requirements (e.g., platform performance, quality, cost). Thus, the company wants to avoid monitoring information being lost due to scaling in/out of individual units, and also to have and overview over the overall behavior of the platform units and not only individual unit instances. Thus, the platform developer must use our tool for deciding the contribution of a unit instance to the overall behavior of the entire platform, or individual units, and structure monitoring information according to the architecture of the platform. For example, the developer could decide that CPU usage of all unit instances must be averaged, and that the network data transfer must be summed.

After having the platform deployed and monitored, the company focuses on the various *Governance*(③) processes which must be enforced over the IoT sensors and gateways, arising from the company's different security, geo-political, or performance objectives. For example, an abnormal event might be detected by the IoT platform, such as dangerous gas detected in a smart building. In such a case, for better analyzing the cause of the event, the frequency and data collected might need to be changed. For enabling such dynamic changes, we can invoke sensor and gateway capabilities through their APIs for changing data collection frequency, or execute a complex process for changing the security levels and protocols used to send data. Leveraging these capabilities, we can enable processes for governing the gateways and sensors in different situations.

---

[2] See https://github.com/tuwiendsg/DaaSM2M/tree/master/Configurations/sensors for samples of TOSCA.

Governance processes might change the frequency, size, and mechanisms in which sensor data is collected, processed and sent to the cloud data center. Thus, an *Elasticity control*(④) mechanism is crucial for ensuring the performance and quality of the overall IoT cloud platform, especially during and after the execution of governance processes, through elasticity. To enable elasticity control, the platform developers must design and develop elasticity capabilities for the individual platform units, w.r.t, their type and purpose. Any capability that enables dynamic reconfiguration of any aspect or property of the platform units qualifies as an elasticity capability, and must be designed and implemented in the platform units, and enforced at run-time. For example, if a governance process increases the data collection frequency, the elasticity control mechanism should scale the cloud services in the platform to handle the load increase.

One lesson learned is that from architectural design, development and operation, we need to decide if all of these complex services, gateways and sensors should be specified and deployed in a single software configuration or not. It is possible but it is not flexible and it is hard to manage. On the other hand, from an IoT cloud platform provider perspective, it is typical to provide a platform that includes gateways (at the edge) connecting to cloud services (in the data center) and let the customer to deploy possible sensors and configure these gateways and services to fit into the customer need.

5.3   Elasticity Analytics and Control

After developing the `ElasticIoTPlatform` configuration, the developer can use our toolset for deploying and running it. At runtime, the developer is able to follow the behavior of the application using our monitoring features, in order to refine the elasticity and governance requirements and respectively policies. For such a complex use-case, which encompasses both IoT and cloud environments, there are two main control perspectives: (i) controlling the services deployed in the cloud which manage data processing and storing, (ii) controlling the IoT parts for addressing the governance policies.

In a critical situation, the entire `ElasticIoTPlatform` needs to react in order to localize or to better analyze the cause of the critical situation. For this, further data needs to be collected, for avoiding errors and miss-predictions. Figure 3 shows a process described by the developer for addressing such case, in which the **sensor push rate** is increased (i.e., due to governance policy), and the cloud services are allowed to scale to higher cost levels. The latter is intended to address the issue of cost limit in the elasticity requirements, as normally the developer specifies a cloud service cost limit, for urgency reasons. In a day-to-day case, with an increasing workload the cloud service would employ more and more virtual resources up to the cost limit, while in the critical situation, the cloud service can exceed the respective limit. From our experiences, we learned that, in our architectural designs, controlling elasticity of cloud software services should give sufficient powers to developers (e.g., controlling multiple software services at a time, different software stacks, both system and application level metrics), while maintaining a simple mechanism of elasticity control specification. Moreover, this

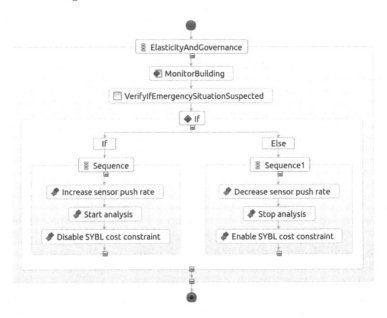

Fig. 3. Elasticity and governance process for the `ElasticIoTPlatform` configuration

control of gateways or of sensors, should interface with a variety of tools (e.g., different cloud providers, using different protocols, different gateway vendor-specific tools), for providing an end-to-end control of IoT cloud platforms.

5.4 Deployment and Failures

Let us consider some aspects related to the use of tools to evaluate IoT cloud platform deployment. We use our private DSG OpenStack, Stratuslab LAL public cloud (http://www.stratuslab.eu) and Flexiant public cloud. We run our deployment engine in our private OpenStack with m1.medium VM (2 CPU and 3,750 MB RAM) in the DSG cloud in order to test deployment issues for sensors and a configuration of an elastic IoT cloud platform – `ElasticIotPlatform`. While we deploy `ElasticIoTPlatform` in our DSG cloud, we want to emulate several sensors by deploying them in both clouds where on each m1.small VM (1 CPU, 2 GB RAM)[3], we deploy 30 sensors. We tested our studied configuration of an IoT cloud platform by deploying and activating from 100 to 350 sensors (when we use both clouds we deploy sensors equally in each cloud). Figure 4 show an increasing and varying trend of deployment failure rates. We can see that Flexiant has higher software failure rate by looking the deviation of failure percent of sensors and VMs, and VM failures are caused by the high number of concurrent requests on clouds. Our examples here are *not* about the performance issue of

---

[3] A CPU on DSG is T7700 @2.40 GHz, on Stratus is a QEMU CPU @2.20 GHz, and on Flexiant is QEMU CPU @3.10 GHz.

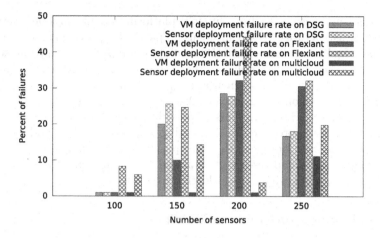

Fig. 4. Deployment failure rate for testing sensors in a multicloud environment

underlying clouds or deployment tools but show that by using a rich toolset, one can understand uncertain performance of clouds to utilize elasticity control and analytics features not only to deal with these performance and failure issues but to coordinate actions carried out at the IoT side.

6   Related Work

Several challenges of IoT and cloud integration are discussed intensively [5,7]. Many IoT platforms have been developed [2,21] based on which different services can be added. Our work is not about developing a particular IoT cloud platform, but focusing on techniques accelerating the development of such platforms. Although experiences have been shared, we have not seen similar experiences discussing rapid end-to-end development of elastic IoT cloud platforms.

Several frameworks support the development of IoT, such as [8,10,17]. Industrial tools, such as Predix (http://www.predix.io) and Microsoft Azure IoT (https://azure.microsoft.com/en-us/documentation/suites/iot-suite), also allow us to write IoT sensors and connect the sensors to cloud services. But they do not support elasticity controls. In our work, we do not focus on programming IoT sensors but recombine existing units and deploy them cross-issue spanning both IoT and clouds. The IBM experimental Internet of Thing Workbench   (console.ng.bluemix.net/catalog/services/internet-of-things-workbench) offers capabilities to design and simulate end-to-end IoT cloud systems, but it does not support end-to-end monitoring and elasticity control.

In [11] experiences and evaluations of cloud application portability have been provided. Such evaluations are useful for us to decide the infrastructure used for the cloud service part of the IoT PaaS. However, they have not focused on IoT clouds in general. Zarko et al. [22] describe the CUPUS middleware, part of the OpenIoT platform [23], which provides a functionality for dynamically adding/removing sensors to/from an IoT platform spanning mobile networks and cloud infrastructures. We do not focus on particular platforms but we enable such a functionality. Mazhelis et al. [13] conduct a comparative study on existing IoT platforms. The authors emphasize the need of having complex IoT platforms and supporting design and implementation phase and operation phase, although none of the compared ones (e.g., Xively, Axeda, Etherios) fully supports the end-to-end requirements. Our work aims at providing tools for such need.

There are some approaches on supporting simulation of IoT and IoT cloud systems, such as [24]. However, they are purely simulation systems, while we support configuration and testing of emulated sensors and gateways running in the cloud that interact with real-world cloud systems.

7   Conclusions and Future Work

In this paper, we described requirements, toolsets and engineering analytics for elastic IoT cloud platforms that simplify and accelerate the development of IoT cloud platforms, based on our development of the iCOMOT. Given the complexity of IoT cloud platform development requirements, it is hard to find any single, even powerful, toolset that will meet all the requirements. Therefore, we have to carry out appropriate engineering actions and also integrating different tools into our iCOMOT toolset. We show how utilizing such an integrated toolset we can simplify the development and and testing of IoT cloud platforms.

Currently, we focus on building a common knowledge of components, topologies and artifacts for supporting testing and evaluation of uncertainties in elastic IoT cloud platforms, in particular, and cyber-physical systems, in general.

References

1. Crowd analytics archives. http://www.dfrc.ch/tag/crowd-analytics/
2. The pacific controls galaxy. http://pacificcontrols.net/products/galaxy.html. Accessed 17 May 2016
3. U-test geo sports case study. http://www.u-test.eu/use-cases/#tab-1429727705-1-5
4. Akpinar, K., Hua, K.A., Li, K.: ThingStore: a platform for internet-of-things application development and deployment. In: Eliassen, F., Vitenberg, R. (eds.) Proceedings of the 9th ACM International Conference on Distributed Event-Based Systems, DEBS 2015, Oslo, Norway, 29 June - 3 July, 2015, pp. 162–173. ACM (2015)
5. Alamri, A., Ansari, W.S., Hassan, M.M., Hossain, M.S., Alelaiwi, A., Hossain, M.A.: A survey on sensor-cloud: architecture, applications, and approaches. IJDSN 2013 (2013). http://dx.doi.org/10.1155/2013/917923
6. Bonomi, F., Milito, R., Zhu, J., Addepalli, S.: Fog computing and its role in the internet of things. In: Proceedings of the 1st Edition of the MCC Workshop on Mobile Cloud Computing. MCC 2012, pp. 13–16. ACM, New York (2012)
7. Botta, A., de Donato, W., Persico, V., Pescape, A.: On the integration of cloud computing and internet of things. In: 2014 International Conference on Future Internet of Things and Cloud (FiCloud), pp. 23–30, August 2014

8. Chauhan, S., Patel, P., Sureka, A., Delicato, F.C., Chaudhary, S.: IoTSuite: a framework to design, implement, and deploy IoT applications: demonstration abstract. In: Proceedings of the 15th International Conference on Information Processing in Sensor Networks, pp. 37:1–37:2. IEEE Press, Piscataway (2016)

9. He, W., Yan, G., Xu, L.D.: Developing vehicular data cloud services in the IoT environment. IEEE Trans. Ind. Inf. 10(2), 1587–1595 (2014)

10. Hong, K., Lillethun, D., Ramachandran, U., Ottenwälder, B., Koldehofe, B.: Mobile fog: a programming model for large-scale applications on the internet of things. In: Proceedings of the Second ACM SIGCOMM Workshop on Mobile Cloud Computing. MCC 2013, pp. 15–20. ACM, New York (2013)

11. Katsaros, G., Menzel, M., Lenk, A., Rake-Revelant, J., Skipp, R., Eberhardt, J.: Cloud application portability with TOSCA, chef and openstack. In: 2014 IEEE International Conference on Cloud Engineering, Boston, MA, USA, 11–14 March 2014, pp. 295–302. IEEE (2014). http://dx.doi.org/10.1109/IC2E.2014.27

12. Li, T., Liu, Y., Tian, Y., Shen, S., Mao, W.: A storage solution for massive IoT data based on NoSQL. In: GreenCom, pp. 50–57. IEEE (2012)

13. Mazhelis, O., Tyrvainen, P.: A framework for evaluating internet-of-things platforms: application provider viewpoint. In: 2014 IEEE World Forum on Internet of Things (WF-IoT), pp. 147–152, March 2014

14. Nastic, S., Sehic, S., Le, D.H., Truong, H.L., Dustdar, S.: Provisioning software-defined IoT systems in the cloud. In: FiCloud (2014)

15. Pereira, P.P., Eliasson, J., Kyusakov, R., Delsing, J., Raayatinezhad, A., Johansson, M.: Enabling cloud connectivity for mobile internet of things applications. In: Proceedings of the 2013 IEEE Seventh International Symposium on Service-Oriented System Engineering. SOSE 2013, pp. 518–526 (2013). http://dx.doi.org/10.1109/SOSE.2013.33

16. Petrolo, R., Loscrí, V., Mitton, N.: Towards a smart city based on cloud of things. In: Proceedings of the 2014 ACM International Workshop on Wireless and Mobile Technologies for Smart Cities. WiMobCity 2014, pp. 61–66. ACM, New York (2014)

17. Riliskis, L., Hong, J., Levis, P.: Ravel: programming IoT applications as distributed models, views, and controllers. In: Proceedings of the 2015 International Workshop on Internet of Things Towards Applications. IoT-App. 2015, pp. 1–6. ACM, New York (2015). http://doi.acm.org/10.1145/2820975.2820977

18. Satyanarayanan, M., Lewis, G.A., Morris, E.J., Simanta, S., Boleng, J., Ha, K.: The role of cloudlets in hostile environments. IEEE Pervasive Comput. 12(4), 40–49 (2013). http://dx.doi.org/10.1109/MPRV.2013.77

19. Truong, H.L., Copil, G., Dustdar, S., Le, D., Moldovan, D., Nastic, S.: ICOMOT - a toolset for managing iot cloud systems. In: 16th IEEE International Conference on Mobile Data Management, MDM 2015, Pittsburgh, PA, USA, 15–18 June 2015, vol. 1, pp. 299–302. IEEE Computer Society (2015)

20. Truong, H.L., Dustdar, S.: Principles for engineering IoT cloud systems. IEEE Cloud Comput. 2(2), 68–76 (2015)

21. Xively. https://xively.com/. Accessed 17 May 2016

22. Zarko, I., Pripuzic, K., Serrano, M., Hauswirth, M.: IoT data management methods and optimisation algorithms for mobile publish/subscribe services in cloud environments. In: 2014 European Conference on Networks and Communications (EuCNC), pp. 1–5, June 2014

23. Zaslavsky, A.B., Perera, C., Georgakopoulos, D.: Sensing as a service and big data. CoRR abs/1301.0159 (2013). http://arxiv.org/abs/1301.0159

24. Zeng, X., Garg, S.K., Strazdins, P.E., Jayaraman, P.P., Georgakopoulos, D., Ranjan, R.: IOTSim: a cloud based simulator for analysing iot applications. CoRR abs/1602.06488 (2016). http://arxiv.org/abs/1602.06488

Prediction of Web Services Evolution

Hanzhang Wang[1], Marouane Kessentini[1(✉)], and Ali Ouni[2]

[1] Computer and Information Science Department, University of Michigan, Ann Arbor, USA
{hanzhang,marouane}@umich.edu
[2] Graduate School of Information Science and Technology, Osaka University, Suita, Japan
ali@ist.osaka-u.ac.jp

Abstract. Web service interfaces are considered as one of the critical components of a Service-Oriented Architecture (SOA) and they represent contracts between web service providers and clients (subscribers). These interfaces are frequently modified to meet new requirements. However, these changes in a web service interface typically affect the systems of its subscribers. Thus, it is important for subscribers to estimate the risk of using a specific service and to compare its evolution to other services offering the same features in order to reduce the effort of adapting their applications in the next releases. In addition, the prediction of interface changes may help web service providers to better manage available resources (e.g. programmers' availability, hard deadlines, etc.) and efficiently schedule required maintenance activities to improve the quality. In this paper, we propose to use machine learning, based on Artificial Neuronal Networks, for the prediction of the evolution of Web services interface design. To this end, we collected training data from quality metrics of previous releases from 6 Web services. The validation of our prediction techniques shows that the predicted metrics value, such as number of operations, on the different releases of the 6 Web services were similar to the expected ones with a very low deviation rate. In addition, most of the quality issues of the studied Web service interfaces were accurately predicted, for the next releases, with an average precision and recall higher than 82 %. The survey conducted with active developers also shows the relevance of prediction technique for both service providers and subscribers.

Keywords: Web services evolution · Prediction · Quality of services

1 Introduction

Service-based systems heavily depend on the interface of selected services used to implement specific features. However, service providers do not know, in general, the impact of their changes, during the evolution Web services, on the applications of subscribers. The subscribers are reluctant, in general, to use Web services that are risky and not stable [10]. Thus, analyzing and predicting Web service changes is critical but also challenging because of the distributed and dynamic nature of services. As a consequence, recent studies were proposed to understand the evolution of Web services especially at the interface level [9, 10, 19].

© Springer International Publishing Switzerland 2016
Q.Z. Sheng et al. (Eds.): ICSOC 2016, LNCS 9936, pp. 282–297, 2016.
DOI: 10.1007/978-3-319-46295-0_18

The few existing work studying the evolution of Web services are limited to the detection of changes between different releases [9] or the analysis of the types of change introduced to the service interfaces. Romano et al. [10] proposed a tool called *WSDLDiff* to detect changes between different versions of a Web service interface based on structural and textual similarities measure. Fokaefs et al. [9] suggested another tool, called *VTracker*, which uses *XML* differencing techniques, to detect changes in *WSDL* documents. However, both tools are just limited to the detection of changes between different Web service releases and did not target the problem of predicting future changes or providing recommendations to the service providers or subscribers about the quality of services interface based on the collected data.

We use, in this paper, the changes collected from previous Web service releases to address the following problems. Most of the changes in a web service interface typically affect the systems of its subscribers. Thus, it is important for subscribers to estimate the risk of using a specific service and compare its evolution to other services offering the same features in order to reduce the effort of adapting their applications in the next releases. Subscribers prefer to use, in general, Web services that are stable with a low risk to include bugs and introduce major revisions in the future. In addition, the prediction of interface changes may help web service providers to better manage available resources (e.g. programmers' availability) and efficiently schedule required maintenance activities to improve the quality of developed services. In fact, the prediction of Web service changes can be used to identify potential quality issues that may occur in the future releases. Thus, it is easier to fix these quality issues as early as possible before that they become more complex.

In this work, we propose a machine learning approach based on Artificial Neural Networks (ANN) [5] to predict the evolution of Web services interface from the history of previous releases' metrics. The predicted interface metrics value are used to predict and estimate the risk and the quality of the studied Web services. We evaluated our approach on a set of 6 popular Web services including more than 90 releases. We report the results on the efficiency and effectiveness of our approach to predict the evolution of Web services interfaces and provide useful recommendations for both service providers and subscribers. The results indicate that the prediction results of several Web service metrics, on the different releases of the 6 Web services, were similar to the expected ones with very low deviation rate. Furthermore, most of the quality issues of Web service interfaces were accurately predicted, for the next releases, with an average precision and recall higher than 82 %. The survey conducted with a set of developers also shows the relevance of prediction technique for both service providers and subscribers.

The remainder of this paper is as follows: Sect. 2 presents the related work; Sect. 3 gives an overview about the proposed predictive modelling technique; Sect. 4 discusses the obtained evaluation results and possible threats of validity of our experiments. Finally, Sect. 5 concludes and proposes future research directions.

2   Related Work

We summarize, in this section, the existing work that focus on studying the evolution of Web services.

Fokaefs *et al.* [9] used the *VTracker* tool to calculate the minimum edit distance between two trees representing two WSDL files. The outcome of the tool is the percentage of interface changes such as added, changed and removed elements among the XML models of two WSDL interfaces. Romano *et al.* [10] proposed a similar tool called *WSDLDiff* that can identify fewer types of change than *VTracker* that may help to analyze the evolution of a WSDL interface without manually inspecting the XML changes. Aversano *et al.* [11] analyzed the relationships between sets of services change during the service evolution based on formal concept analysis. The main focus of the study is to extract relationships among services.

Several studies have been proposed to measure the similarity between different Web services to search for relevant ones or classify them but not to analyze their evolution. Xing *et al.* [12] suggested a tool, called *UMLDiff* to detect differences between different UML diagram versions to understand their evolution. Zarras *et al.* [13] detected evolution patterns and regularities by adapting Lehman's laws of software evolution. The study was focused only on Amazon Web Services (AWS).

Based on this overview of existing work in the area of Web services evolution, the problem of predicting the evolution of Web services was not addressed before. In addition, the use of machine learning algorithms in Web services was limited to the classification of Web Services and their messages into ontologies [22]. These existing machine learning-based studies are not concerned with the analysis of the releases within the same Web service but more about mining different Web services (one release per service) to classify them in order to help the composition of services process for the subscribers based on their requirements.

Another category of related work focus on detecting and specifying antipatterns in SOA and Web services which is a relatively new area. Rotem-Gal-Oz described the symptoms of a range of SOA antipatterns [15]. Kral et al. [18] listed seven "popular" SOA antipatterns that violate accepted SOA principles. A number of research works have addressed the detection of such antipatterns. Recently, Moha et al. [20] have proposed a rule-based approach called SODA for SCA systems (Service Component Architecture). Later, Palma et al. [19] extended this work for Web service antipatterns in SODA-W using declarative rule specification based a domain-specific language (DSL) to specify/identify the key symptoms that characterize an antipattern using a set of WSDL metrics. Rodriguez et al. [14, 15] and Mateos et al. [16] provided a set of guidelines for service providers to avoid bad practices while writing WSDLs based on eight bad practices in the writing of WSDL for Web services. Recently, Ouni et al. [7] proposed a search-based approach based on standard GP to find regularities, from examples of Web service antipatterns, to be translated into detection rules.

In the next section, we describe the adaptation of the ANN algorithm to the prediction of the evolution of Web services.

3 Prediction of Web Services Evolution Using Artificial Neural Networks

As described in Fig. 1, our technique takes as input the previous releases of the Web service interfaces to predict its evolution, an exhaustive list of metrics to predict, and a list of detection rules to detect potential future quality issues, called Web service anti-patterns, based on the predicted metrics. Ou approach generates as output the set of predicted evolution metrics values and possible future quality issues for the next release.

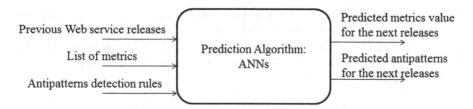

Fig. 1. Prediction approach: overview

Our prediction model is based on machine learning algorithm using Aritificial Neural Network (ANN) model. In the following we describe the ANN adaptation to our Web services evolution prediction problem.

Artificial Neural Network (ANN): ANN models are mathematical models inspired by the functioning of nervous systems [2–5], which are composed by a number of inter-connected entities, the artificial neurons. ANNs are based on learning which is a characteristic of adaptive systems which are capable of improving their performance on a problem as a function of previous experience [1]. An ANN builds a map between a set of inputs and the corresponding outputs. This model can deal with non-linear regression analysis with noisy signals and also incomplete data. In this work, we used a Multi-Layer Perception ANN (MLP-ANN) [2]. It is well-known that MLP-ANNs are universal approximators, which makes them attractive for modeling black-box functions for which little information about their form is known. The output of each neuron is expressed as follows:

$$y = \phi\left(\sum_{i=1}^{n} w_i a_i + b \right)$$

where w denotes the weight vector, a is the input vector, b is the bias, ϕ is the activation function, and n is the number of neurons in the hidden layer. A hidden neuron influences the network outputs only for those inputs that are near to its center, therefore requiring an exponential number of hidden neurons to cover entirely the input space. For this reason, it is suggested that MLP-ANN are suitable for problems with a small number of inputs like our prediction of Web services evolution problem.

We applied the ANN as being among the most reliable predictive models, especially, in the case of noisy and incomplete data. Its architecture is chosen to be a multilayered architecture in which all neurons are fully connected; weights of connections have been, randomly, set at the beginning of the training. Regarding the activation function, the sigmoid function is applied [5] as being adequate in the case of continuous data. The network is composed of three layers: the first layer is composed of p input neurons. Each neuron is assigned the value x_{kt}. The hidden layer is composed of a set of hidden neurons. The learning algorithm is an iterative algorithm that allows the training of the network. Its performance is controlled by two parameters. The first parameter is the momentum factor that tries to avoid local minima by stabilizing weights. The second factor is the learning rate which is responsible of the rapidity of the adjustment of weights.

Learning process. Before the learning process, the data used in the training set should be normalized. In our case, we choose to apply the *min-max* technique since it is among the most accurate techniques according to [8]. In our adapation, we used the following list of metrics from the literature [7] to predict for the next Web service releases, as described in Table 1.

Table 1. Web service interface metrics used.

Metric name	Definition
NPT	Number of port types
NOD	Number of operations declared
NAOD	Number of accessor operations declared
NOPT	Average number of operations in port types
ANIPO	Average number of input parameters in operations
ANOPO	Average number of output parameters in operations
NOM	Number of messages
NBE	number of elements of the schemas
NCT	Number of complex types
NST	Number of primitive types
NBB	Number of bindings
NBS	Number of services
NPM	Number of parts per message
NIPT	Number of identical port types
NIOP	Number of identical operations
COH	Cohesion
COU	Coupling
AMTO	Average meaningful terms in operation names
AMTM	Average meaningful terms in message names
AMTMP	Average meaningful terms in message parts
AMTP	Average meaningful terms in port-type names
ALOS	Average length of operations signature
ALPS	Average length of port-types signature
ALMS	Average length of message signature

During the learning process, our ANN solutions are represented as follows: let us denote by O the matrix that includes numerical values related to the set of metrics to predict. O is composed of n lines and p columns where n is equal to the number of metrics to predict and p is equal to the number of steps (releases).

$$O = \begin{bmatrix} x_{11} & x_{12} & \cdots & x_{1p} \\ x_{21} & x_{22} & \cdots & x_{2p} \\ \cdot & \cdot & \cdot & \cdot \\ \cdot & \cdot & \cdot & \cdot \\ \cdot & \cdot & \cdot & \cdot \\ x_{n1} & x_{n2} & \cdots & x_{np} \end{bmatrix}$$

Learning technique. There are several learning algorithms, depending on whether the ANN model is linear or non-linear. Our MLP model utilizes a supervised learning technique called back-propagation (BP) for training the network. MLP is a modification of the standard linear perceptron and can distinguish data that are not linearly separable. BP is one of the most popular and common training procedures used, that is described in depth in the literature [5]. Our BP neural network has been trained with moderate values for the learning rate (α) and momentum (μ). The weights are recalculated every time a training vector is presented to the network. The exit strategy or the termination condition for the network is based on the sum square error until it reaches a certain threshold assigned prior to running the network. Our implementation is based on the Weka[1] framework with it default configuration.

4 Experiments

In order to evaluate the ability of our prediction framework to efficiently predict the evolution trends of Web services, we conducted a set of experiments based on six widely used Web services. In this section, we first present our research questions, the experiments setup and then describe and discuss the obtained results. Finally, we discuss some threats related to our experiments.

4.1 Research Questions and Evaluation Metrics

We defined the following three research questions that address the applicability, performance, and the usefulness of our Web services prediction approach. The three research questions are as follows:

RQ1: To what extent can our approach predict correctly the evolution of Web services?

RQ2: To what extent can our approach predict Web service quality issues?

RQ3: Can our prediction results be useful for developers?

---

[1] http://www.cs.waikato.ac.nz/ml/weka.

To answer RQ1, we calculated the deviation between the actual expected metrics value and the predicted ones using our ANNs algorithm on different Web service relases. To this end, we considered the list of metrics described in the previous section. The error rate is defined as follows:

$$e\_rate(M_i, S) = |PM_i - EM_i|,$$

where PM is the predicted metric value using ANNs and EM is the expected value. We calculated the error rate for one and many steps (releases) over time for every of the considered Web services.

To answer RQ2, we calculated precision and recall scores to compare between the predicted Web services antipatterns and the expected ones:

$$RCrecall = \frac{\text{predicted antipatterns} \cap \text{expected antipatterns}}{\text{expected antipatterns}} \in [0, 1]$$

$$PR_{precision} = \frac{\text{predicted antipatterns} \cap \text{expected antipatterns}}{\text{predicted antipatterns}} \in [0, 1]$$

We considered five types of antipatterns from the literature [20]: Multi-service (MS: a service implementing many operations), Nano-service (NS: too-fine grained service), Chatty-service (CS: a service including many fine-grained operations), Data-service (DS: a service including only data access operations) and Ambigous service (AS: a service including ambiguous names of operations). More details about existing Web service antipatterns can be found in the following references [19, 20]. We used the manually defined rules in [7] to detect the predicted and actual Web service antipatterns.

To answer RQ3, we used a post-study questionnaire that collects the opinions of developers on our prediction results. We also wished to assess how these results may help developers working on services-based applications. To this end, we asked 24 software developers, including 11 developers working in a Web development startup and providing some Web services for customers from the automotive industry sector. The remaining participants are 13 graduate students (8 MSc and 5 PhD students) in Software Engineering at the University of Michigan-Dearborn. 9 out the 13 students are working either full-time or part-time programmers in Software industry. All the participants are volunteers and have a minimum of 2 years experience as a developer. The participants were first asked to fill out a pre-study questionnaire containing five questions. The questionnaire helped to collect background information such as their role within the company, their programming experience, their familiarity with Web services and service-based applications. In addition, all the participants attended one lecture about Web service antipatterns and passed five tests to evaluate their performance to evaluate the desing of Web services using quality metrics.

4.2   Studied Web Services

We selected these 6 Web services for our validation because different releases of their WSDL interface are publicly available and belong to different categories. Table 2 provides some descriptive statistics about these six Web services:

- Amazon EC2: Amazon Elastic Compute Cloud is a web service that offers resizable compute capacity in the cloud. In this study we have considered a total of 44 releases from 2006 until 2014.
- Amazon Simple Queue Service (Amazon SQS) offers reliable hosted queues for storing messages exchanged between computers. We considered in our study a total of 6 releases.
- Fedex Track service offers accurate update of the status of shipments. We used 10 releases from this Web service.
- FedEx Ship Service: the Ship Service provides functionalities for managing package shipments and their options. A total of 17 releases are considered in our experiments from this Web service.
- FedEx Rate Service: the Rate Service provides the shipping rate quote for a specific service combination depending on the origin and destination information supplied in the request. We used 18 releases for our prediction algorithm.
- Amazon Mechanical Turk Requester: it is a web service that provides an on-demand, scalable, human workforce to complete jobs that humans can do better than computers such as recognizing objects in photos. We used 15 releases developed between 2005 until 2012.

Table 2. Web service statistics

Web service name	# Releases	Average number of antipatterns
Amazon EC2	44	134
Amazon Mechanical Turk	15	61
Amazon Simple Queue	6	21
FedEx Rate Service	18	17
FedEx Ship Service	17	82
FedEx Track Service	10	44

4.3   Results

Results for RQ1. Figures 2, 3 and 4 summarize the outcome for the first research question. Most of the Web service metrics were predicted accurately on the different Web services with an average error rate lower than 2.8 as described in Fig. 3. For Fedex Track service and Fedex Rate service, the average error rate is the highest. This could be related to the lower training set comparing to the other services. For Amazon EC2, the metrics were predicted with a minimum deviation score of 2.1 due to the large training set available for this service. However, Amazon Simple Queue has one of the lowest deviation score of 1.8. This confirms that our prediction results are independent from the size of the Web services to evaluate and the training data.

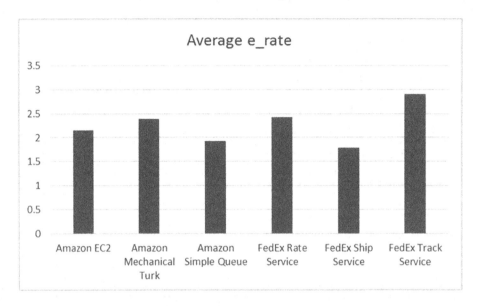

Fig. 2. Average error rate (e_rate) on the different Web services

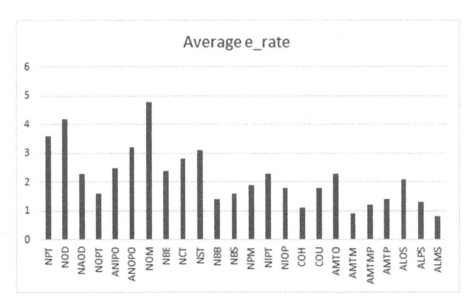

Fig. 3. Average error rate (e_rate) per metric on the different Web services

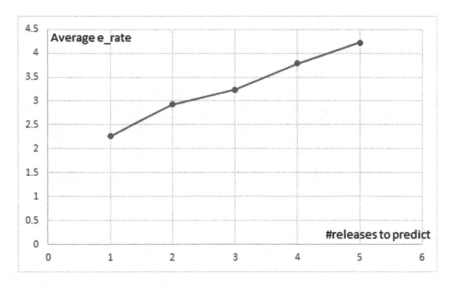

Fig. 4. Average error rate (e_rate) of the different metrics on the Web services (except Amazon Simple Queue) per prediction step

Figure 3 shows more detailed results of the average error rate by metric. The results clearly support the claim that our results are independent from the type of metric to predict. However, the error rate depends on the range of every metric. For example, it is expected that the number of operations per service may get the highest error rate since the variation of this metric is high and its range is larger than the other metrics.

Figure 4 describes the ability of our algorithm to predict the metrics value not only for the next release but for up-to the next 5 releases. In fact, the obtained results on the different Web services (except Amazon Simple Queue, not considered due to the limited number of releases) clearly show that the error rate for the 5th upcoming release is minimal with a score less than 4.5.

To answer the first research question, our approach is able to predict the evolution of Web service metrics with a high accuracy.

Results for RQ2. Figures 5, 6 and 7 summarize our findings. Overall, most of the expected quality issues (Web service antipatterns) for the next release were identified as described in Fig. 5. Our prediction algorithm were able to detect Web service anti-patterns on the different services with an average precision and recall respectively higher than 84 % and 86 %. For Fedex Ship service and Amazon Mechanical Turk, the precision is higher than for the other systems with more than 88 %. This can be explained by the fact that these systems are smaller than others and contain a lower number of antipatterns to predict. For FedEx Rate Service, the precision is also high (around 82 %), *i.e.*, most of the predicted antipatterns are correct. This confirms that our precision results are independent from the size of the Web services to evaluate. For Amazon EC2, the precision is one of the lowest (81 %) but still acceptable. Amazon EC2 contains a high number of ambiguous services that are difficult to detect using metrics.

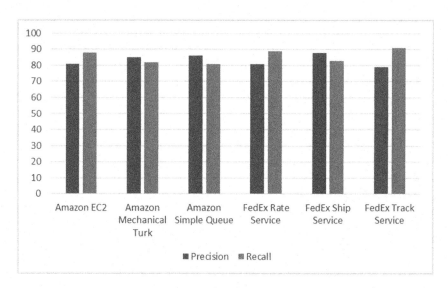

Fig. 5. Average precision and recall of the predicted antipatterns on the different Web services

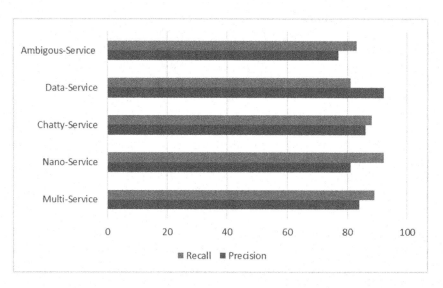

Fig. 6. Figure 5. Average precision and recall per antipattern type on the different Web services

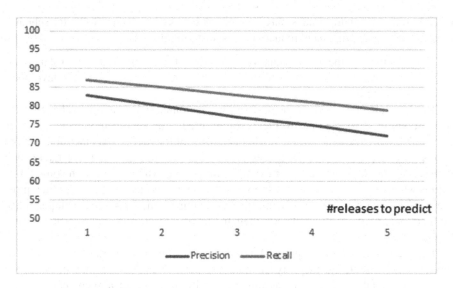

Fig. 7. Average precision and recall on the Web services (except Amazon Simple Queue) per prediction step

The same observations are valid for the recall. The average recall on the six Web services was higher than 86 %. For Fedex Track service and Amazon EC2, the precision is higher than for the other systems with more than 90 %. This can be explained by the fact that these systems are using more training data than others. For FedEx Ship Service, the precision is also high (around 81 %), thus the impact of the size of the training data was not high on the quality of the prediction results. An interesting observation is that the obtained precision and recall scores are conflicting since the services with the highest precision scores received the lowest recall. However, both scores are acceptable for all the Web services.

One key strength of our technique is the ability to predict quality issues not only for the next release but for up-to the next 5 releases as described in Fig. 7. In fact, the obtained results clearly show that both precision and recall are still high for all the Web services when predicting quality issues for the 5th upcoming release with an average higher than 73 %. We did not consider in our evaluation the Amazon Simple Queue due to the limited number of available releases.

To summarize, it is clear based on the obtained results that our approach predict Web service quality issues with a high accuracy.

Results for RQ3. To answer RQ3, we used a post-study questionnaire to the opinions of the participants about their experience in using our prediction tool and results. The questionnaire asked participants to rate their agreement on a Likert scale from 1 (complete disagreement) to 5 (complete agreement) with the following statements:

- The predicted metrics value are useful to estimate the risk and cost of using a specific Web service and may help the developer to select the best service based on his preferences.

- The predicted quality issues may help developers and managers to better schedule maintenance activities and reduce the cost of fixing these issues.

The agreement of the participants was 4.6 and 4.8 for the first and second statements respectively. This confirms the usefulness of our prediction results for the developers considered in our experiments.

The remaining questions of the post-study questionnaire were about the benefits and also limitations (possible improvements) of our prediction approach. We summarize in the following the feedback of the developers. Most of the participants mention that our results may help developers of the service providers to decide when to refactor their Web service implementations. For example, they can consider to perform some refactorings when the prediction results show that the quality issue may become much more severe after few releases such as a multi-service antipattern. Thus, the developers liked the functionality of our tool that helps them to identify refactoring opportunities as early as possible.

The participants found our tool helpful for also the developers of Service-based applications. In fact, the majority of the participants mention that they consider the stability and quality of services as important critieria to select a Web service when several options are available. The non-stability of a service may negatively impact their systems in the future and it is maybe an indication that the used service includes many bugs explaining several new releases. Furthermore, the subject liked the prediction of antipatterns feature since it is easier for them to evaluate the quality of Web services in next releases based on the number of antipatterns rather than analyzing a set of metrics.

The participants also suggested some possible improvements to our prediction approach. Some participants believe that it will be very helpful to extend the tool by adding a new feature to automatically calculate the risk, cost and benefits of using different possible Web services. Another possibly suggested improvement is to use some visualization techniques to evaluate the evolution of the We services to easily estimate their stability.

4.4   Threats to Validity

There are four types of threats that can affect the validity of our experiments. We consider each of these in the following paragraphs.

Conclusion validity is concerned with the statistical relationship between the treatment and the outcome. The parameter tuning of the ANNs used in our experiments creates a threat that we need to evaluate in our future work. The parameters' values used in our experiments are found by trial-and-error. However, it would be an interesting perspective to design an adaptive parameter tuning strategy for our approach so that parameters are updated during the execution in order to provide the best possible performance.

Internal validity is concerned with the causal relationship between the treatment and the outcome. We used a set of manually defined rules for the detection of possible future quality issues in the next releases [19]. However, the obtained results depends on the used rules and some of the predicted quality issues may not be important antipatterns to fix by the service provider's developers.

Construct validity is concerned with the relationship between theory and what is observed. To evaluate the relevance of our prediction results, we interviewed a group of developers. For the selection threat, the participant diversity in terms of experience could affect the results of our study. We addressed the selection threat by making sure that all the participants have almost the same experience in web development and familiarity with Web services. For the fatigue threat, we did not limit the time to fill the questionnaire and we also sent the questionnaires to the participants by email and gave them the required time to complete each of the required tasks.

External validity refers to the generalizability of our findings. In this study, we performed our experiments on six widely used Web services belonging to different domains and having different sizes. However, we cannot assert that our results can be generalized to other Web services, and to other practitioners. Future replications of this study are necessary to confirm our findings. In addition, our study was limited to the use of specific metrics. Future replications of this study are necessary to confirm our findings.

5   Conclusion and Future Work

We proposed, in this paper, an approach to predict the evolution of Web services. In fact, it is maybe important for subscribers to estimate the risk of using a selected service and compare its evolution to other possible services offering the same features. Furthermore, the prediction of future changes may help web service providers to better manage available resources and efficiently schedule required maintenance activities to improve the quality. In this paper, we propose to use machine learning, based on Artificial Neuronal Networks, for the prediction of the evolution of Web services interface design. To validate the proposed approach, we collected training data from quality metrics of previous releases from 6 Web services. The validation of our prediction techniques shows that the predicted metrics value, such as number of operations, on the different releases of the 6 Web services were similar to the expected ones with a very low deviation rate. In addition, most of the quality issues of the studied Web service interfaces were accurately predicted, for the next releases, with an average precision and recall higher than 82 %. The survey conducted with developers also shows the relevance of prediction technique for both service providers and subscribers.

Future work involves validate our prediction technique with additional metrics, Web services and developers to conclude about the general applicability of our methodology. Furthermore, in this paper we only focused on the prediction of Web services evolution. We plan to extend the approach by defining new risk measures based on the predicted metrics value. In addition, we will study of the impact of predicted quality issues on the usability and popularity of Web services over time.

References

1. Simon, H.A.: Why should machines learn? (Chap. 2). In: Michalski, R.S., Carbonell, J.G., Mitchell, T.M. (eds.) Machine Learning. Tioga, Palo Alto (1983)
2. Gardner, M.W., Dorling, S.R.: Artificial neural networks (the multilayer perceptron). Atmos. Environ. **32**, 2627–2636 (1998)
3. Cobourn, W., Dolcine, L., French, M., Hubbard, M.: A comparison of nonlinear regression and neural network models for ground-level ozone forecasting. J. Air Waste Manag. Assoc. **4**, 19–68 (2001)
4. Agirre-Basurko, E., Ibarra-Berastegi, G., Madariaga, I.: Regression and multilayer perceptron-based models to forecast hourly O_3 and NO_2 levels in the Bilbao area. Environ. Model Softw. **21**, 430–446 (2006)
5. Haykin, S.: Neural Networks: A Comprehensive Foundation. Macmillan College Publishing Company, New York (1994)
6. Ouni, A., Kessentini, M., Inoue, K.: Search-based web service antipatterns detection. In: IEEE Transactions on Services Computing, pp. 1–21. IEEE (2016, to appear)
7. Ouni, A., Gaikovina, K.R., Kessentini, M., Inoue, K.: Web service antipatterns detection using genetic programming. In: 24th ACM Genetic and Evolutionary Computation Conference (GECCO), pp. 1351–1358 (2015)
8. Al Shalabi, L., Shaaban, Z., Kasasbeh, B.: Data mining: a preprocessing engine. J. Comput. Sci. **2**(9), 735–739 (2006)
9. Fokaefs, M., Mikhaiel, R., Tsantalis, N., Stroulia, E., Lau, A.: An empirical study on web service evolution. IEEE International Conference on Web Services (ICWS11), pp. 261–269. IEEE (2011)
10. Romano, D., Pinzger, M.: Analyzing the evolution of web services using fine-grained changes. In: 19th IEEE International Conference on Web Services, ICWS, Honolulu, pp. 392–399 (2012)
11. Aversano, L., Di Penta, M., Falanga, A., Scognamiglio, R.: Visualizing the evolution of web services using formal concept analysis. In: Eighth International Workshop on Principles of Software Evolution, pp. 57–60 (2005)
12. Xing, Z., Stroulia, E.: UMLDiff: an algorithm for object-oriented design differencing. In: Proceedings of the 20th IEEE/ACM International Conference on Automated Software Engineering (ASE 2005), pp. 54–65. ACM, New York (2005)
13. Zarras, A.V., Vassiliadis, P., Dinos, I.: Keep calm and wait for the spike! Insights on the evolution of amazon services. In: Proceedings of the 28th International Conference on Advanced Information Systems Engineering (CAiSE), (2016, to appear)
14. Rodriguez, J.M., Crasso, M., Mateos, C., Zunino, A.: Best practices for describing, consuming, and discovering web services: a comprehensive toolset. Softw. Pract. Experience **43**(6), 613–639 (2013)
15. Rodriguez, J.M., Crasso, M., Zunino, A., Campo, M.: Automatically detecting opportunities for web service descriptions improvement. In: Cellary, W., Estevez, E. (eds.) Software Services for e-World. IFIP AICT, vol. 341, pp. 139–150. Springer, Heidelberg (2010)
16. Mateos, C., Rodriguez, J.M., Zunino, A.: A tool to improve code-first web services discoverability through text mining techniques. Softw. Pract. Experience **45**(7), 925–948 (2015)
17. Rotem-Gal-Oz, A., Bruno, E., Dahan, U.: SOA Patterns, pp. 38–62. Manning Publications, Greenwich (2012)
18. Kral, J., Zemlicka, M.: Popular SOA antipatterns. In: Future Computing, Service Computation, Cognitive, Adaptive, Content, Patterns, pp. 271–276. IEEE (2009)

19. Palma, F., Moha, N., Tremblay, G., Guéhéneuc, Y.-G.: Specification and detection of SOA antipatterns in web services. In: Avgeriou, P., Zdun, U. (eds.) ECSA 2014. LNCS, vol. 8627, pp. 58–73. Springer, Heidelberg (2014)

20. Moha, N., Palma, F., Nayrolles, M., Conseil, B.J., Guéhéneuc, Y.-G., Baudry, B., Jézéquel, J.-M.: Specification and detection of SOA antipatterns. In: Liu, C., Ludwig, H., Toumani, F., Yu, Q. (eds.) Service Oriented Computing. LNCS, vol. 7636, pp. 1–16. Springer, Heidelberg (2012)

21. Oldham, N., Thomas, C., Sheth, A.P., Verma, K.: METEOR-S web service annotation framework with machine learning classification. In: Cardoso, J., Sheth, A.P. (eds.) SWSWPC 2004. LNCS, vol. 3387, pp. 137–146. Springer, Heidelberg (2005)

22. Klusch, M., Kapahnke, P., Zinnikus, I.: SAWSDL-MX2: a machine-learning approach for integrating semantic web service matchmaking variants. IEEE International Conference on Web Services, ICWS 2009, pp. 275–288. IEEE (2009)

Service Economy

Features of IT Service Markets:
A Systematic Literature Review

Bahar Jazayeri[1]([✉]), Marie C. Platenius[2], Gregor Engels[1],
and Dennis Kundisch[3]

[1] Database and Information Systems Research Group, Paderborn University,
Paderborn, Germany
{bahar.jazayeri,gregor.engels}@upb.de
[2] Software Engineering Group, Paderborn University, Paderborn, Germany
marie.c.platenius@upb.de
[3] Chair of Information Management and E-Finance, Paderborn University,
Paderborn, Germany
dennis.kundisch@upb.de
http://is.uni-paderborn.de

Abstract. The provision of IT solutions over electronic marketplaces became prominent in recent years. We call such marketplaces *IT service markets*. IT service markets have some core architectural building blocks that impact the quality attributes of these markets. However, these building blocks and their impacts are not well-known. Thus, design choices for IT service markets have been made ad-hoc until now. Furthermore, only single aspects of such markets have been investigated until now, but a comprehensive view is missing. In this paper, we identify common features and their interrelations on the basis of a systematic literature review of 60 publications using grounded theory. This knowledge provides an empirical evidence on the interdisciplinary design choices of IT service markets and it serves as a basis to support market providers and developers to integrate market features. Thereby, we make a first step towards the creation of a reference model for IT service markets that provides a holistic integrated view that can be used to create and maintain successful markets in the future.

Keywords: Systematic literature review · Market architecture · Service marketplaces · Grounded theory · Service-oriented computing

1 Introduction

The business model of App stores became drastically popular by the introduction of Apple App Store and Google Play providing mobile applications in 2008 [53]. Nowadays, the range of IT solutions provided by electronic marketplaces goes beyond mobile applications. There are *API marketplaces* (e.g., ProgrammableWeb[1]) that allow trading APIs among programmers. *Cloud markets*

---

[1] programmableweb.com. Accessed May 2016.

© Springer International Publishing Switzerland 2016
Q.Z. Sheng et al. (Eds.): ICSOC 2016, LNCS 9936, pp. 301–316, 2016.
DOI: 10.1007/978-3-319-46295-0_19

(e.g., AWS marketplace[2] and Salesforce AppExchange[3]) support enterprise application developers with cloud services. Furthermore, *software repositories* [42] (e.g., Binpress[4]) facilitate the exchange of source codes [31]. We call such electronic marketplaces providing IT solutions *IT service markets*.

Until now, all these markets have been developed ad-hoc and without any systematic process or reference model. Furthermore, only single aspects of such markets have been investigated, but a complete view is missing. As a consequence, IT enterprises and entrepreneurs that also wish to grow their businesses by employing marketplace models encounter unforeseen challenges, which make them go out of budget and fail to deliver a successfully running IT service market. Reported failures mainly show that they miss to include core functionalities of IT service markets, e.g., application discovery, rating and reviewing, or application categorization [1,2,50]. Another problem that arises is that many market functionalities are not applied although they have been investigated and implemented in academia for many years. For example, there are masses of tools and concepts for service matchers [52] or for composition engines [15] that have never been integrated into IT service markets because the developers of such functionalities do not have much knowledge about market models.

One main reason for such deficiencies is the lack of any reference model for IT service markets. A reference model provides a comprehensive set of building blocks of a concept and their important relationships. This allows the communication of shared knowledge among the community and enables reusing well-established solutions [43]. According to this, a reference model for IT service markets is beneficial to the research community as well as to practitioners regarding two different perspectives: (a) Providers of such markets, like enterprises or individuals, gain a benefit because they can use the comprehensive insight into the design choices of IT service markets in order to develop and integrate new market features and, thereby, improve their market's success. (b) Developers of market functionalities like matchers, composition engines, reputation systems, etc. benefit from the possibility to take into account how their components can (and have to) interact with the market or with specific market features, in order to become applicable in practice.

A first step towards a reference model for IT service markets is to gain a comprehensive view on their interdisciplinary building blocks. Such a comprehensive view is still missing in the literature. Schmid and Lindemann [60] developed a generic reference model for electronic markets that mostly considers elements of business architecture. However, infrastructure and application aspects, e.g., service orchestration for software services, are overlooked. Moreover, some work provides a detailed perspective on IT aspects, e.g., high performance service recommendation mechanisms [24]. Furthermore, other work that considers both business and IT aspects is limited to certain instances of IT service markets, for instance, a comparison of Apple App Store and Nokia Ovi Store [65].

---

[2] aws.amazon.com/marketplace. Accessed May 2016.

[3] appexchange.salesforce.com. Accessed May 2016.

[4] binpress.com. Accessed May 2016.

In this paper, we provide a first step towards a holistic integrated view on IT service markets by identifying their business and IT building blocks (*features*) that are addressed in literature. Accordingly, our research question is:

RQ What are the primary features of IT service markets and how are they related to each other?

In order to answer this question, we performed a systematic literature review (SLR) [35], aiming at capturing as many publications as possible related to our research question. The SLR filtering process resulted in the identification of 60 (out of 333) publications that focus on certain aspects of IT service markets or that propose an instance of an IT service market. We developed an extraction scheme using grounded theory (GT) [61] to interpret the data and extract a primary set of features from the final set of the publications. The results of our survey reveal a categorization of the mostly addressed functional features of IT service markets and the relation between those features.

In the following, Sect. 2 describes the survey procedure including the filtering process of the literature. Section 3 presents the process of literature analysis and the extraction scheme of the features. Section 4 discusses the extracted features and their interrelations. In Sect. 5, we discuss how our work is distinguished from the other works. Section 6 presents concluding remarks and future work.

2   Survey Procedure

The objective of our investigation is to extract the primary features of IT service markets, which are discussed in literature. We follow Kitchenham's guidelines [35] in performing a systematic literature review (SLR) to ensure reproducibility and minimizing biases regarding our results. The literature search is performed between February 2016 and May 2016. We chose **Google Scholar** as the search database, as suggested by Kitchenham [36]. Google Scholar is a meta-search engine that performs searches through several digital libraries.

Initially, a review protocol is specified, which is driven from the **RQ** and our fundamental context (IT service markets). The review protocol defines the step by step actions that are undertaken in the SLR. In this section, we describe how the publications are filtered at each stage using precise criteria (search phrases and in-/exclusion criteria). In addition, we applied snowballing [68] by inspecting the outgoing references cited by the sources, aiming at identifying more relevant sources related to our context.

1. Initial Set of Sources: To find the initial set of sources, we defined a set of search terms. The ideas of the search terms are inspired from the **RQ** and our observation of the existing IT service markets as discussed in Sect. 1. Our main search terms are *service* and *market*. We specified alternative terms to detect as many of the relevant sources as possible. *Software, App, application, third-party, plug-in,* and *component* are the alternatives to the term *service*. Furthermore, the alternatives to the term *market* are defined as *marketplace, store, "App store",* *repository*, *"archive network"*, and *catalog*. Lastly, we determined our search phrase as a combination of the search terms and boolean operators. During the search, a source is selected if at least one of the terms from each set appears in the title. This process resulted in finding 329 sources. Supplementary material including the complete lists can be found in our technical report [31].

2. Final Set of Sources: We filtered the initial set of sources using the in-/exclusion criteria. We included a source if: (a) it deals with the definition of IT service markets, (b) it deals with one of the functional or the non-functional aspects of IT service markets, (c) it introduces a new instance of IT service markets, or (d) it considers architecture of IT service markets. Furthermore, the source must be available through the most prominent digital libraries, e.g., Springer Link, ACM Digital Library, IEEE Xplore, Citeseer library, and Science Direct. We excluded a source from our survey if: (a) the service discussed by the source is not an IT solution and (b) the marketplace, provided by the source, provides other services/products than IT solutions. We evaluated the sources firstly based on their abstracts and conclusions. Secondly, if we still could not decide about the relevance of a source, we read the whole source. After applying in-/exclusion criteria, the set of results consists of 142 sources. We added two additional exclusion criteria:

- the source should not be in the form of a preface, tutorial, book review, or presented slide. This allows us to focus on the high quality research, e.g., by excluding the publications, which have not been peer reviewed.
- the source should not be published earlier than 2008. The reasons for choosing this specific year are the introduction of the concept of cloud market by BUYYA et al. [7] and the launch of the first mobile App stores ever, Apple App Store and Google Play in 2008 [30]. Using this exclusion criterion, we focus on the most recent work. We expect the most prominent research achievements, which were published before 2008, are reflected by the recent work.

At this stage of filtering, the final set of results includes 60 sources that objectively address the concept of IT service markets.

3   Extraction Scheme of Features

This section presents the extraction process of primary features from the final set of sources. The challenge regarding IT service markets is that firstly, unlike other paradigms like cloud computing [47] and service-oriented computing [27], there is no reference model or comprehensive definition. Consequently, the publications do not usually address IT service markets directly. Secondly, when addressing IT service markets, the publications use inconsistent terminologies according to the underlying technologies. For instance, we encounter alternative words for "service", e.g., "application", "App", "SaaS", "API", etc. As a result, we cannot directly identify a set of features from the sources using keyword-based data search. Instead, an interpretation of the information provided by the sources is needed.

We developed an extraction scheme for primary features of IT service markets based on an adoption of grounded theory (GT). GLASER AND STRAUSS [20] originally proposed GT to support researchers to elaborate a theory or a theoretical report of the general features of a topic by performing a bottom-up conceptualization of the data. Such data is collected based on empirical observations. We follow the guidelines provided by WOLFSWINKEL et al. [69] for rigorously reviewing and analyzing literature using GT.

The literature analysis consists of an initial excerpting and three stages of codings (open, axial, and selective codings). Initially, research focus of the sources is excerpted according to an initial research question. Open coding is the process of grouping a set of excerpts into a concept and building categories from a set of concepts. Each category is an abstract interpretation of its concepts. Axial coding is the process of defining sub-categories and specifying the relation between categories and sub-categories. By selective coding, main categories and the relation between them are identified [69].

To extract primary features of IT service markets from the final set of sources, in the first step, we inspected the sources carefully, while having the **RQ** in mind. During reading, we looked for possible answers to our **RQ**. Specially, we considered *what* the sources deal with. We highlighted and made notes of the data, where a building block, component, or architectural element of IT service markets is discussed. After extracting the important information, we applied the open coding, which resulted in 41 codes in total. In the second step, we performed axial coding. In comparison with the open codes, the axial codes capture less specific architectural concepts. We also considered *what interrelations* the research results discover regarding the concepts. Finally, we developed six main categories by performing selective coding: reputation system, business model, recommendation system, mediating electronic product catalog (MEPC), security, and service level agreement (SLA). We terminated the process of coding, when, so called, *theoretical saturation* happened. This means no new category, concepts, or interesting relations could be found [61].

The result of our extraction scheme is shown in Fig. 1. The tables within demonstrate the research focus of the sources regarding the main categories. A table is dedicated to each main category. Each table represents the sub-categories of each category. A cell marked with X denotes that a sub-category is discussed by the source. In addition, some sources studied the relation between a main category with other categories. In this case, the tables demonstrate such relations by the columns with border lines at the right side of the tables. A cell marked with O denotes that such a relation exists between the main category and another category that is discussed by the source.

As an example, we explain how the coding technique resulted in generating the main category reputation system (cf. Fig. 1(a)). After reading the sources and extracting excerpts, we started to perform open coding from [39], which resulted in the identification of two concepts: ranking chart and download rank. Afterwards, [25] shared the concept download rank with [39] and generated a new concept App mining. This process proceeds with [9,24,32,38,64], which resulted

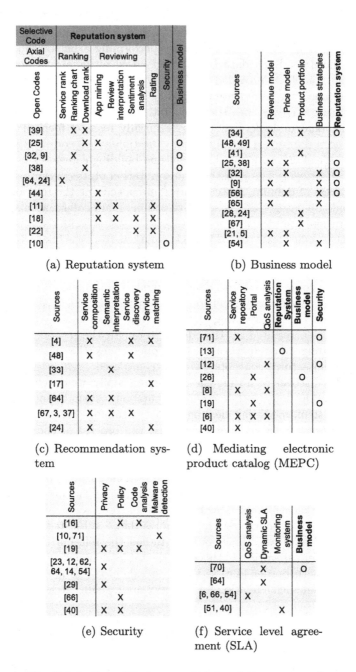

(a) Reputation system

(b) Business model

(c) Recommendation system

(d) Mediating electronic product catalog (MEPC)

(e) Security

(f) Service level agreement (SLA)

Fig. 1. The distribution of features and their relations among the sources

in sharing two concepts ranking chart and download rank with the previous sources and in generating a new concept service rank. Later, by performing axial coding, we grouped service rank, ranking chart and download rank into one category: ranking. Furthermore, the open coding of [11, 18, 44], and [22] shared App mining with previously coded sources and generated two new concepts: review interpretation and sentiment analysis. These two concepts are categorized as reviewing through the axial coding. Moreover, the open coding of [11, 18, 22] generated the category of rating. Finally, we grouped three categories of ranking, reviewing, and rating into a main category of reputation system. In addition, the coding process reveals links (sharing codes) between reputation system and two other main categories, which we have identified later (security and business model). More details about the coding results can be found in [31].

4   Discussion

In this section, we report the results of the literature analysis. The results are the identification of six main categories and their sub-categories related to our **RQ** as shown in Fig. 1. The main categories represent the most abstract architectural elements of IT service markets. We call them *primary features*. We also call the sub-categories *sub-features*. While reporting the information regarding each feature, we answer three questions: (a) What is the feature? (b) What are its sub-features? (c) What are the relations between the feature and other features? In the following, Sect. 4.1 discusses the questions (a) and (b). Section 4.2 answers the question c). In addition, Sect. 4.3 offers analytic data regarding the results.

4.1   Primary Features of IT Service Markets

Reputation system is responsible for collecting and aggregating users' ratings and generating rankings. A well-functioning reputation system builds trust among market participants [55]. The main sub-features, identified by our literature analysis, are rating, reviewing, and ranking (cf. Fig. 1(a)). Reviewing consists of the possibility that users can insert their comments and then the interpretation of such comments. While interpreting the reviews, IT service markets need to support opinion analysis, an informative interpretation of a mass amount of user reviews, and detecting inconsistencies between user comments and ratings [18]. Furthermore, rankings are associated to services, market participants, and reviews. Service ranking algorithms highly rely on the download rank as a valid indicator to generate ranking charts [39].

    Business model outlines the elements that make a business successfully generate and deliver value to its stakeholders including customers [63]. The most important sub-features are revenue model, price model, product portfolio, and business strategies (cf. Fig. 1(b)). Revenue model includes market providers' strategies to choose revenue sources, revenue sharing for service compositions, and generated revenue for developers [48, 49]. Price model includes the strategies to choose pricing schemes by market providers for developers to grant access to the market platform and by developers for service consumers [56]. Furthermore, product portfolio represents the strategies regarding characteristics of a service, e.g., product diversification, which is the support for multi-homing [28] (i.e., a company's strategy to support multiple platforms with one software product). Further examples are covering several service categories, and targeting different groups of users. Business strategies [63] are analytic plan-makings regarding the competitive environment of markets, e.g., service providers' decisions on licensing greatly influence their survival in the market.

Recommendation system handles the discovery and delivery of a desired service using existing knowledge and statistics in the markets [57]. Our results show that recommendation systems in IT service markets involve service discovery, service matching, semantic interpretation, and service composition (cf. Fig. 1(c)). Service discovery includes techniques, like comprehensive service specifications or SLA-based service selection, to optimize the discovery of a service in the pool of services. Service matching is a decision-making function that evaluates an approximate matching of a request to a service specification or a software service to an execution resource. Service composition enables the dynamic provisioning of individually composed services, each provided by different providers. The outcome of a recommendation system can be enhanced by taking the advantages of semantic interpretation, for instance, by employing ontologies to improve the service discovery [4,34,48].

Mediating electronic product catalog (MEPC) acts as an intermediary between requesters and providers of services by linking several service catalogs to each other and allowing requesters to search through those catalogs in electronic marketplaces [60]. In this paper, we take the concept of MEPC in electronic marketplaces for IT service markets. As shown in Fig. 1(d), the concept of MEPC in IT service markets is mainly discussed as portal, service repository, and QoS analysis. A portal is where service providers make services and their specification available to requesters. Furthermore, a service repository hosts back-box services, source codes, or catalogs of service specifications that are published on the portal. In addition, MECPs demand assuring Quality of Service (QoS) by including QoS analysis. Examples of QoS are multi-tenancy, elasticity, and scalability of service repositories [12,26].

Security is another important feature within IT service markets. The subfeatures are privacy, policy, code analysis, and malware detection (cf. Fig. 1(e)). IT service markets need to protect the integrity of users' sensitive data, which can be misused by third-party applications. Moreover, source code analysis, intrusion detection and malware detection algorithms need to be employed to avoid malicious applications in the markets. Market providers may consider such security techniques as market regulations and laws [71].

SLA is a contract between service providers and requesters to ensure a certain degree of quality. This is directly related to the on-time and scalable fulfillment of QoS expectations, which implies using QoS analysis and monitoring system. In addition, dynamic SLAs support frequent changes in service requesters and the heterogeneity of execution resources (cf. Fig. 1(f)) [51,70].

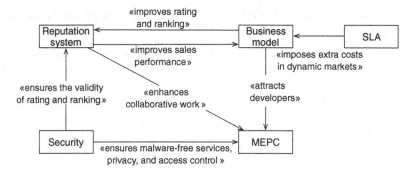

Fig. 2. Outline of the interrelations between the primary features

4.2 Primary Features Interrelations

The literature analysis reveals the significant interrelations between the primary features (see the cells marked with O in Fig. 1). Figure 2 summarizes these interrelations. An arrow from feature A to feature B shows that A influences B in a certain way that is shown as an arrow label.

Business Model – Reputation System: Both business model and reputation system significantly affect each other. On one hand, strategic decisions taken regarding price model and product portfolio mainly influence rating and ranking. A suitable pricing scheme improves users' ratings, service rank, and customer loyalty. For instance, IT services with a combination of free and paid price models receive a better download rank in the market [38]. Furthermore, strategies regarding product portfolio like diversifying service categories improve rating and service rank [33,38]. On the other hand, rating and ranking affect sales performance and users' willingness to pay. Consequently, they influence business model and revenue model of the market [9,25].

SLA – Business Model: Execution of software services demands execution resources. Service providers normally purchase such resources from external resource providers. In dynamic markets, requesters of a service change frequently, which implies changes in requirements and the corresponding SLAs. Service providers, who would like to support a wider range of requesters, need to be able to cope with such heterogeneous SLAs. To avoid SLA violations, the service providers have to take care of heterogeneous execution resources needed by different SLAs. This situation continuously imposes extra cost on the service providers. Such trade-offs between cost and the fulfillment of SLAs need to be foreseen in a business model by choosing suitable resource allocation algorithms that handles dynamic SLAs with minimum costs [70].

MEPC – Reputation System: IT service markets that enable collaborative service development among developers need to motivate developers by providing transparency of activities. This makes the developers interested in self-promotion and improving their reputation. In this case, a reputation system facilitates rating and ranking for developers. This is additionally supported by providing incentives to developers [13].

MEPC – Security: Service repositories as a sub-feature of MEPCs need to detect new samples of known malware families in order to ensure malware-free services [71]. Other security concerns of service repositories are privacy and access control, which demand encrypted queries on repositories [12]. Furthermore, centralized portals improve the policy enforcement by market providers. For instance, the market providers may apply such policies to third-party applications before granting access to the markets. An example of such policies is security validation to avoid misusing users' privacy-sensitive data [19,26].

MEPC – Business Model: Business strategies taken regarding MEPCs greatly impact on attracting developers to the market. However, such strategies usually come with trade-offs. For instance, centralized portal makes developers' businesses centralized and more accessible to their customers. In addition, it reduces the distribution costs imposed on the developers. Such costs include the maintenance costs of updating services and registration fees of the market entrance. However, centralized portals restrict developers' freedom, because they have to conform to a centralized market policy. Once they cannot conform to the centralized policies, they leave the market [26].

Reputation System – Security: Generating valid rankings demands a high degree of security in preventing and detecting manipulated ratings and spam reviews. In addition, such manipulated ratings and rankings unjustly persuade service consumers. The consequences are disturbing trust and decreasing the QoS delivered by the market [10].

4.3 Result Analysis

Figure 3 shows the popularity of features determined on the basis of the literature from 2008 to May 2016. One interesting finding is that the *business model*, as well as *security*, and *reputation system* have been identified as important features ranging from 19 % to 22 %. The reason for the first might be that both computer scientists and economics are interested in business models of such markets. In contrast, *SLAs* have only been mentioned in 11 % of the publications. One reason could be that this is a concept well known from cloud computing, but not within marketplaces for mobile apps, where more simple contracts are needed in order to target a large mass of end users.

Furthermore, Fig. 4 presents the distribution of the sources of the survey per year. The number of publications increased significantly from 2008 to 2012. This explains the attention that IT service markets as an emerging technology received from the research communities due to the introduction of the mobile App stores (Apple App Store and Google Play) in 2008. However, the decreasing number of publications in the following years shows a decline in research interests, probably due to remained open questions that make further spread of IT service markets challenging in other domains rather than mobile applications,

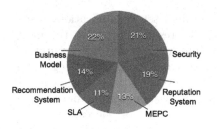
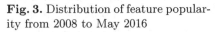
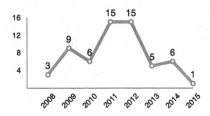

Fig. 3. Distribution of feature popularity from 2008 to May 2016

Fig. 4. Distribution of the total number of sources per year

e.g., barriers of establishing in-house marketplaces for enterprise applications. Moreover, the survey captures no sources, which are published in the year 2016. This can be for the reason that the time frame of this survey covers only less than half of this year.

5 Related Work

Until now, there is no survey or work that studies IT service markets independent of their underlying technologies while covering both business and IT building blocks. [59] analyses deficiencies in business strategies of existing IT service markets and suggests a set of design choices to be considered by market providers to achieve market's success. [49] makes a deeper discussion on the business model of mobile App stores by considering the impact of aspects like platform differentiation and quality assurance on market's success. [30] aims at identifying the common features of marketplaces in software ecosystems by observing the existing App stores on the web. [58] specifies a business model for software companies that covers technological aspects, however, core aspects of IT service markets, e.g., reputation, are not considered. [46] discusses business and marketing considerations in developing Apps for mobile App stores.

Moreover, [26] presents technical design choices concerning providers of mobile App markets, e.g., platform integration alternatives, and the impact of these choices on developers' work. There are already works in the literature that consider business and IT aspects of IT service markets, however, the comparisons are limited to certain instances of IT service markets: [65] compares Nokia Ovi and Apple App Store based on organizational, technological, and market innovation factors. [45] performs an analysis of Google Play and Windows Phone Store to identify the most common analysis topics.

6 Conclusion and Future Work

We performed a systematic literature review of the publications that address the concept of IT service markets. In particular, we extracted the architectural building blocks of IT service markets from the final set of publications using the guidelines provided by grounded theory. The results show that the most prominent architectural building blocks are business models, security, reputation systems, recommendation systems, mediating electronic product catalogs, and service level agreements. Furthermore, the results reveal that the design choices of the features are not independent, but rather, they influence the outcome of each other. Such effects ultimately contribute to the markets' success.

This knowledge gives market operators, IT enterprises, and service providers an insight into IT service markets and their design choices regarding an enhanced market development and feature integration. However, there is still a need for an investigation of benefits and risks of IT service market model for enterprises. In the future, our results will serve as a conceptual basis that we will use in developing a reference model for IT service markets. In addition, such a reference model will include interface definitions and interaction protocols between different market participants and components. Furthermore, processes of market development and technology realization can be an interesting future research direction. As a benefit, new IT service markets can be developed much more efficiently and existing IT service markets can be improved so that they satisfy stakeholders as well as customers.

Acknowledgments. This work was supported by the German Research Foundation (DFG) within the Collaborative Research Center "On-The-Fly Computing" (CRC 901).

References

1. Build an in-house enterprise app store without breaking the budget. http://searchcloudapplications.techtarget.com/answer/Build-an-in-house-enterprise-app-store-without-breaking-the-budget. Accessed May 2016
2. Challenges in Creating a Great Cloud App Store. http://info.appdirect.com/uploads/channel/Resources/Articles/AppDirect-Top_Ten-Challenges_in_Creating_a_Great_Cloud_App_Store_(12-14-2011).pdf. Accessed May 2016
3. Abramowicz, W., Haniewicz, K., Kaczmarek, M., Zyskowski, D.: E-marketplace for semantic web services. In: Bouguettaya, A., Krueger, I., Margaria, T. (eds.) ICSOC 2008. LNCS, pp. 271–285. Springer, Heidelberg (2008). doi:10.1007/978-3-540-89652-4_22
4. Arifulina, S., Platenius, M.C., Becker, S., Gerth, C., Engels, G., Schäfer, W.: Market-optimized service specification and matching. In: Franch, X., Ghose, A.K., Lewis, G.A., Bhiri, S. (eds.) ICSOC 2014. LNCS, pp. 543–550. Springer, Heidelberg (2014). doi:10.1007/978-3-662-45391-9_47
5. Bacon, D.F., Chen, Y., Parkes, D., Rao, M.: A market-based approach to software evolution. In: 24th ACM SIGPLAN Conference on Companion on Object Oriented Programming Systems Languages and Applications, pp. 973–980. ACM (2009)
6. Buyya, R., Ranjan, R., Calheiros, R.N.: InterCloud: utility-oriented federation of cloud computing environments for scaling of application services. In: Hsu, C.-H., Yang, L.T., Park, J.H., Yeo, S.-S. (eds.) ICA3PP 2010. LNCS, pp. 13–31. Springer, Heidelberg (2010). doi:10.1007/978-3-642-13119-6_2

7. Buyya, R., Yeo, C.S., Venugopal, S.: Market-oriented cloud computing: vision, hype, and reality for delivering it services as computing utilities. In: 10th IEEE International Conference on High Performance Computing and Communications, pp. 5–13. IEEE (2008)
8. Calder, B., Wang, J., Ogus, A., Nilakantan, N., Skjolsvold, A., McKelvie, S., Xu, Y., Srivastav, S., Wu, J., Simitci, H., et al.: Windows Azure storage: a highly available cloud storage service with strong consistency. In: 23rd Symposium on Operating Systems Principles, pp. 143–157. ACM (2011)
9. Carare, O.: The impact of bestseller rank on demand: evidence from the app market. Int. Econ. Rev. **53**(3), 717–742 (2012)
10. Chandy, R., Gu, H.: Identifying spam in the iOS app store. In: 2nd Joint WICOW/AIRWeb Workshop on Web Quality, pp. 56–59. ACM (2012)
11. Chen, N., Lin, J., Hoi, S.C., Xiao, X., Zhang, B.: AR-Miner: mining informative reviews for developers from mobile app marketplace. In: 36th International Conference on Software Engineering, pp. 767–778. ACM (2014)
12. Curino, C., Jones, E.P., Popa, R.A., Malviya, N., Wu, E., Madden, S., Balakrishnan, H., Zeldovich, N.: Relational cloud: a database-as-a-service for the cloud. In: 5th Biennial Conference on Innovative Data Systems Research, pp. 235–241 (2011)
13. Dabbish, L., Stuart, C., Tsay, J., Herbsleb, J.: Social coding in GitHub: transparency and collaboration in an open software repository. In: The Conference on Computer Supported Cooperative Work, pp. 1277–1286. ACM (2012)
14. Dixon, C., Mahajan, R., Agarwal, S., Brush, A.J., Lee, B., Saroiu, S., Bahl, V.: The home needs an operating system (and an app store). In: 9th ACM SIGCOMM Workshop on Hot Topics in Networks, p. 18. ACM (2010)
15. Dustdar, S., Schreiner, W.: A survey on web services composition. Int. J. Web Grid Serv. **1**(1), 1–30 (2005)
16. Ernst, M.D., Just, R., Millstein, S., Dietl, W., Pernsteiner, S., Roesner, F., Koscher, K., Barros, P.B., Bhoraskar, R., Han, S., et al.: Collaborative verification of information flow for a high-assurance app store. In: 21st ACM SIGSAC Conference on Computer and Communications Security, pp. 1092–1104. ACM (2014)
17. Ferrer, A.J., Hernández, F., Tordsson, J., Elmroth, E., Ali-Eldin, A., Zsigri, C., Sirvent, R., Guitart, J., Badia, R.M., Djemame, K., et al.: OPTIMIS: a holistic approach to cloud service provisioning. Future Gener. Comput. Syst. **28**(1), 66–77 (2012)
18. Fu, B., Lin, J., Li, L., Faloutsos, C., Hong, J., Sadeh, N.: Why people hate your app: making sense of user feedback in a mobile app store. In: 19th ACM SIGKDD International Conference on Knowledge Discovery and Data Mining, pp. 1276–1284. ACM (2013)
19. Gilbert, P., Chun, B.G., Cox, L.P., Jung, J.: Vision: automated security validation of mobile apps at app markets. In: 2nd International Workshop on Mobile Cloud Computing and Services, pp. 21–26. ACM (2011)
20. Glaser, B.G., Strauss, A.L.: The Discovery of Grounded Theory. Aldine, Chicago (1967)
21. Goncalves, V., Walravens, N., Ballon, P.: "How about an app store?" enablers and constraints in platform strategies for mobile network operators. In: 9th International Conference on Mobile Business and Global Mobility Roundtable, pp. 66–73. IEEE (2010)
22. Goul, M., Marjanovic, O., Baxley, S., Vizecky, K.: Managing the enterprise business intelligence app store: sentiment analysis supported requirements engineering. In: 45th Hawaii International Conference on System Science (HICSS), pp. 4168–4177. IEEE (2012)

23. Hamad, H., Al-Hoby, M.: Managing intrusion detection as a service in cloud networks. Int. J. Comput. Appl. **41**(1), 35–40 (2012)
24. Han, S.M., Hassan, M.M., Yoon, C.W., Huh, E.N.: Efficient service recommendation system for cloud computing market. In: 2nd International Conference on Interaction Sciences: Information Technology, Culture and Human, pp. 839–845. ACM (2009)
25. Harman, M., Jia, Y., Zhang, Y.: App store mining and analysis: MSR for app stores. In: 9th IEEE Working Conference on Mining Software Repositories, pp. 108–111. IEEE (2012)
26. Holzer, A., Ondrus, J.: Mobile application market: a developer's perspective. Telematics Inform. **28**(1), 22–31 (2011)
27. Huhns, M.N., Singh, M.P.: Service-oriented computing: key concepts and principles. IEEE Internet Comput. **9**(1), 75–81 (2005)
28. Idu, A., van de Zande, T., Jansen, S.: Multi-homing in the apple ecosystem: why and how developers target multiple apple app stores. In: International Conference on Management of Emergent Digital EcoSystems, pp. 122–128. ACM (2011)
29. Itani, W., Kayssi, A., Chehab, A.: Privacy as a service: privacy-aware data storage and processing in cloud computing architectures. In: International Conference on Dependable, Autonomic and Secure Computing, pp. 711–716. IEEE (2009)
30. Jansen, S., Bloemendal, E.: Defining app stores: the role of curated marketplaces in software ecosystems. In: Herzwurm, G., Margaria, T. (eds.) ICSOB 2013. LNBIP, pp. 195–206. Springer, Heidelberg (2013). doi:10.1007/978-3-642-39336-5_19
31. Jazayeri, B., Platenius, M.C., Engels, G., Kundisch, D.: IT service markets: a systematic literature review - supplementary material. Techical report tr-ri-16-350, Heinz Nixdorf Institute, University of Paderborn (2016). https://www.hni.uni-paderborn.de/pub/9342
32. Jung, E.Y., Baek, C., Lee, J.D.: Product survival analysis for the app Store. Mark. Lett. **23**(4), 929–941 (2012)
33. Kim, J., Park, Y., Kim, C., Lee, H.: Mobile application service networks: Apple's app store. Serv. Bus. **8**(1), 1–27 (2014)
34. Kim, J., Kang, S., Lim, Y., Kim, H.M.: Recommendation algorithm of the app store by using semantic relations between apps. J. Supercomputing **65**(1), 16–26 (2013)
35. Kitchenham, B., Brereton, O.P., Budgen, D., Turner, M., Bailey, J., Linkman, S.: Systematic literature reviews in software engineering–a systematic literature review. Inf. Softw. Technol. **51**(1), 7–15 (2009)
36. Kitchenham, B., Charters, S.: Guidelines for performing systematic literature reviews in software engineering. Keele University and Durham University, Technical report (2007)
37. Kuropka, D., Weske, M.: Implementing a semantic service provision platform. Wirtschaftsinformatik J. **1**, 16–24 (2008)
38. Lee, G., Raghu, T.S.: Product portfolio and mobile apps success: evidence from app store market. In: 17th Americas Conference on Information Systems (2011)
39. Lim, S.L., Bentley, P.J.: Investigating app store ranking algorithms using a simulation of mobile app. ecosystems. In: Congress on Evolutionary Computation (CEC), pp. 2672–2679. IEEE (2013)
40. Lin, G., Fu, D., Zhu, J., Dasmalchi, G.: Cloud computing: IT as a service. IT Prof. **11**(2), 10 (2009)
41. Lotia, S., Montojo, J., Dong, Y., Bader, G.D., Pico, A.R.: Cytoscape app store. Bioinformatics, btt138 (2013). Oxford University Press

42. Lucredio, D., do Prado, A.F., De Almeida, E.S.: A survey on software components search and retrieval. In: 30th Euromicro Conference, pp. 152–159. IEEE (2004)
43. MacKenzie, C.M., Laskey, K., McCabe, F., Brown, P.F., Metz, R., Hamilton, B.A.: Reference model for service oriented architecture 1.0. OASIS Committee Specification (2006)
44. Martin, W., Harman, M., Jia, Y., Sarro, F., Zhang, Y.: The app sampling problem for app store mining. In: 12th IEEE Working Conference on Mining Software Repositories (MSR), pp. 123–133. IEEE (2015)
45. Martin, W., Sarro, F., Jia, Y., Zhang, Y., Harman, M.: A survey of app store analysis for software engineering. University College London, Technical report (2016)
46. McCann, T.: The Art of the App Store: The Business of Apple Development. Wiley, Hoboken (2011)
47. Mell, P., Grance, T.: The NIST definition of cloud computing. NIST Spec. Publ. **145**(6), 7 (2011)
48. Menychtas, A., Vogel, J., Giessmann, A., Gatzioura, A., Gomez, S.G., Moulos, V., Junker, F., Müller, M., Kyriazis, D., Stanoevska-Slabeva, K., et al.: 4caast marketplace: an advanced business environment for trading cloud services. Future Gener. Comput. Syst. **41**, 104–120 (2014)
49. Müller, R.M., Kijl, B., Martens, J.K.: A comparison of inter-organizational business models of mobile app stores: there is more than open vs. closed. J. Theoret. Appl. Electron. Commer. Res. **6**(2), 63–76 (2011)
50. O'Neill, S.: 5 Mistakes to Avoid When Deploying an Enterprise App Store. http://www.cio.com/article/2394413/mobile/5-mistakes-to-avoid-when-deploying-an-enterprise-app-store.html. Accessed May 2015
51. Patel, P., Ranabahu, A.H., Sheth, A.P.: Service level agreement in cloud computing. In: Cloud Workshops at OOPSLA (2009)
52. Platenius, M.C., von Detten, M., Becker, S., Schäfer, W., Engels, G.: A survey of Fuzzy service matching approaches in the context of on-the-fly computing. In: 16th International ACM Sigsoft Symposium on Component-Based Software Engineering, pp. 143–152. ACM (2013)
53. President, S.V., BCG: Number of apps available in leading app stores 2015—Statistic (2015). http://www.statista.com/statistics/276623/number-of-apps-available-in-leading-app-stores/
54. Prodan, R., Ostermann, S.: A survey and taxonomy of infrastructure as a service and web hosting cloud providers. In: 10th IEEE/ACM International Conference on Grid Computing, pp. 17–25. IEEE (2009)
55. Resnick, P., Kuwabara, K., Zeckhauser, R., Friedman, E.: Reputation systems. Commun. ACM **43**(12), 45–48 (2000)
56. Rohitratana, J., Altmann, J.: Impact of pricing schemes on a market for software-as-a-service and perpetual software. Future Gener. Comput. Syst. **28**(8), 1328–1339 (2012)
57. Sarwar, B., Karypis, G., Konstan, J., Riedl, J.: Analysis of recommendation algorithms for e-commerce. In: 2nd ACM Conference on Electronic Commerce, pp. 158–167. ACM (2000)
58. Schief, M., Buxmann, P.: Business models in the software industry. In: 45th Hawaii Internationl Conference on System Science (HICSS), pp. 3328–3337. IEEE (2012)
59. Schlauderer, S., Overhage, S.: How perfect are markets for software services? an economic perspective on market deficiencies and desirable market features. In: 19th European Conference on Information Systems (2011)

60. Schmid, B.F., Lindemann, M.A.: Elements of a reference model for electronic markets. In: 31st Hawaii International Conference on System Sciences, vol. 4, pp. 193–201. IEEE (1998)
61. Strauss, A., Corbin, J.: Grounded theory methodology. In: Handbook of Qualitative Research, pp. 273–285 (1994)
62. Subashini, S., Kavitha, V.: A survey on security issues in service delivery models of cloud computing. J. Netw. Comput. Appl. **34**(1), 1–11 (2011)
63. Teece, D.J.: Business models, business strategy and innovation. Long Range Plan. **43**(2), 172–194 (2010)
64. Tsai, W.T., Sun, X., Balasooriya, J.: Service-oriented cloud computing architecture. In: 7th International Conference on Information Technology: New Generations, pp. 684–689. IEEE (2010)
65. Tuunainen, V.K., Tuunanen, T., Piispanen, J.: Mobile service platforms: comparing Nokia OVI and Apple app store with the iisin model. In: 10th International Conference on Mobile Business (ICMB), pp. 74–83. IEEE (2011)
66. Vecchiola, C., Pandey, S., Buyya, R.: High-performance cloud computing: a view of scientific applications. In: 10th International Symposium on Pervasive Systems, Algorithms, and Networks, pp. 4–16. IEEE (2009)
67. Wei, Y., Blake, M.B.: Service-oriented computing and cloud computing: challenges and opportunities. IEEE Internet Comput. **14**(6), 72 (2010)
68. Wohlin, C.: Guidelines for snowballing in systematic literature studies and a replication in software engineering. In: 18th International Conference on Evaluation and Assessment in Software Engineering, p. 38. ACM (2014)
69. Wolfswinkel, J.F., Furtmueller, E., Wilderom, C.P.: Using grounded theory as a method for rigorously reviewing literature. Eur. J. Inf. Syst. **22**(1), 45–55 (2013)
70. Wu, L., Garg, S.K., Buyya, R.: SLA-based resource allocation for software as a service provider (SaaS) in cloud computing environments. In: 11th IEEE/ACM International Symposium on Cluster, Cloud and Grid Computing, pp. 195–204. IEEE (2011)
71. Zhou, Y., Wang, Z., Zhou, W., Jiang, X.: Hey, you, get off of my market: detecting malicious apps in official and alternative Android markets. In: 19th Network and Distributed System Security Symposium (2012)

Qualitative Economic Model for Long-Term IaaS Composition

Sajib Mistry[1], Athman Bouguettaya[1], Hai Dong[1]([✉]), and Abdelkarim Erradi[2]

[1] School of Science, RMIT University, Melbourne, Australia
{sajib.mistry,athman.bouguettaya,hai.dong}@rmit.edu.au
[2] Department of Computer Science and Engineering,
Qatar University, Doha, Qatar
erradi@qu.edu.qa

Abstract. We propose a new qualitative economic model based optimization approach to compose an optimal set of infrastructure service requests over a long-term period. The economic model is represented as a temporal CP-Net to capture the provider's dynamic business strategies in qualitative service provisions. The multidimensional qualitative preferences are indexed in a k-d tree to compute the preference ranking of a set of incoming requests. We propose a heuristic based sequential optimization process to select the most preferred composition without the knowledge of historical request patterns. Experimental results prove the feasibility of the proposed approach.

1 Introduction

An Infrastructure-as-a-Service (IaaS) provider offers Virtual Machines (VMs) as services in a cloud market [2]. An IaaS service (VM) is a configuration of functional or resource attributes, such as CPU, memory, and network units, and Quality of Services (QoSs) attributes, such as availability, throughput, response time and price [2]. Typical IaaS providers, such as Amazon, Windows Azure and Rackspace preconfigure their services and set the prices of those services [2]. However, there exists a different IaaS model where consumers are allowed to create custom IaaS requests (custom configurations of the functional and non-functional attributes) [6]. The prices of the services are either set by the provider [2] or the consumers are allowed to quote their own prices for the services [18].

The long-term IaaS composition is defined as to select an optimal set of custom consumer requests that maximizes the profit of the provider [10]. In our previous research, the prices of each unit of resource and QoS attributes are advertised by the provider. Hence, two identical requests generate the same level of revenue. However, they can be distinguished from their usage behaviors, such as under-utilization and over-utilization [11]. We have proposed an quantitative economic model for the IaaS provider that predicts consumers' service usage behaviours and calculates the operation costs of the requests [10].

According to [18], the functional and QoS attributes in a long-term consumer request are variable over a time period, qualitative in nature and closely related

Q.Z. Sheng et al. (Eds.): ICSOC 2016, LNCS 9936, pp. 317–332, 2016.
DOI: 10.1007/978-3-319-46295-0_20

with the price. For example, a consumer may prefer an IaaS service that has less response time in the first year. While in the second year, the consumer may find response time is less important and quote lower price to save the cost as much as possible. The proposed quantitative economic models [10] fail to capture the business strategies of the provider to evaluate such long-term requests.

A qualitative IaaS economic model should capture the long-term business strategies of the provider. For example, the mobile carrier companies normally create different plans for different types of consumers [9]. Sometimes they offer mobile phones in low prices as a business strategy. Similarly in the cloud market, if a provider finds its CPU units are more fault-tolerant than the hard disks, it may prefer CPU-intensive service requests more than the space-intensive requests to avoid probable Service Level Agreement (SLA) violations. The acceptance or rejection of an incoming request should follow an strategy as accepted requests are committed for the whole period. Partial service provisioning is treated as a SLA violation. We assume the provider operates with fixed amount of resources [5]. We focus on the deterministic arrivals of the incoming requests, i.e., all the requests are known at the start of the composition.

Existing qualitative economic models represent the consumers' qualitative preferences [13,15,18]. They do not consider the following issues related to the long-term composition from the provider's perspective:

- **Dynamic temporal semantic preferences:** In a typical short-term composition, the qualitative preferences remain static during the composition time [13,15,18]. The relative ordering of the provider's preferences may vary in the long-term period. For example, a provider may prefer providing CPU based services over Network based services in the first year and prefer the opposite in the second year. It creates a set of temporal segments of preferences in the economic model. The semantics of preferences may not be static during the whole period of composition. It is relative to the competitions in the market [5,9]. For example, 10ms response time is treated as a high QoS in this year, but it may become a moderate QoS in the next year because of an upgrade of the hardware in the market.
- **Temporal mismatch between the service request and the provider's preferences:** The long-term service requests may not have exact temporal match with the temporal segments of the economic model. For example, the provider has a preference on provisioning CPU intensive services in January and Network intensive services in February. If a service request spans from the middle of January to the middle of February, any economic model could not be applied directly for evaluating the merit of the requests.

We propose a novel approach to compose requests using the provider's long-term qualitative economic model. We represent the economic model as Temporal CP-Nets (TempCP-Net), which is a collection of dynamic CP-nets [4] spanning over the composition time segments. CP-Nets [4] is a compact and intuitive formalism for representing and reasoning with conditional preferences under the ceteris paribus ("all else being equal") semantics. The dynamic semantics of the preferences are indicated using a Conditional Preference Table (CPT) [4] of the TempCP-Net. The temporal mismatch between the service request and the provider's preferences is solved through the semantic temporal segmentation of the requests which preserves the inherent dependencies among the attributes in the original long-term request. Moreover, the induced preference graph [15] from TempCP-Net is indexed in a multidimensional k-d tree [3] to effectively match with the multidimensional attributes of the consumer requests. We transform the TempCP-net into a k-d tree as nodes in the preference graph could be considered as points and k-d tree is widely used for multidimensional point query in different applications [1]. The k-d tree is treated as an objective function to compute the global preference ranking of a composition. Hence, we transform the IaaS composition as a preference maximization optimization problem.

We consider both the global and local optimization approaches to select the optimal composition considering k-d tree represented TempCP-net as the objective function. A typical Dynamic Programming (DP) [8] based global approach considers all the requests at the time of optimization. This may pose a scalability issue in the runtime due to comparisons among a large number of candidate solutions. We devise a heuristic based local optimization approach to accept or reject requests in each segment so that local decisions are collectively converged to an acceptable approximate global optimal composition.

2   Related Work

An economic model for profit maximization of cloud service providers is proposed in [10]. The profit maximization based IaaS composition in stochastic arrival of requests is proposed in [10]. An economic model of federated clouds is described in [5]. The model evaluates the cost of using resources from a cloud federation and develops a resource management core for the profit maximization. A CP-Net based economic model is proposed for the service composition from the consumers' perspective in [18]. The consumer preferences are fine grained using Weighted CP-Net (WCP-Net) in [16]. Service selection from incomplete user preferences are proposed in [15]. Such models do not consider temporal changes in the providers' preferences for a long-term period.

An integer programming formulation for IaaS composition is proposed in [11]. Heuristic algorithms are proposed to determine whether a new request can be admitted without impacting accepted requests in [17]. Meta-heuristic optimization is proposed for stochastic incoming requests in [10]. In operations research, the restaurant reservation problem is solved using Dynamic Programming techniques (DP) [8]. The DP is used to optimize the IaaS service scheduling in [5]. Markovian Decision Process (MDP) is used as a machine learning technique to solve sequential iterative optimization in [14]. As we do not have the history of previous incoming requests, we devise a heuristic based sequential optimization technique using only the current set of incoming requests.

3   Motivation: A Qualitative IaaS Economic Model

Let us assume, a new IaaS provider starts offering virtual CPU services associated with QoS of availability for simplicity. It can provide maximum 100 CPU units and 100 % availability. The provider's qualitative preferences on CPU, availability, and price can be interpreted into three semantic levels - high, moderate, and low, as shown in Fig. 1(a). The provider now has different preference ranks based on its annual goals in a three-year period. For the first year, the provider prefers to provide high quality services with relatively lower prices, to build its reputation in the market. Hence, the provider decides that "availability" of a service is the most important attribute, followed by "CPU" and "price". For the second year, the provider expects to provide services with higher prices and relatively lower resources and QoS to maximize the profit. Thus "price" decides "CPU" and "availability". For the third year, the provider considers that the ageing infrastructure may cause problematic CPUs and lower availability. Therefore the provider's preference is that providing relatively lower "CPU" has a higher priority than relatively higher "price" and lower "availability". The interpretation of the semantic levels remains static in the three years for simplicity.

The CP-Net can elegantly represent these qualitative preferences. For example, an arc from "CPU" to "availability" means the preference of "availability" depends on the preference of "CPU" units. The provider's economic preferences are captured in a Temporal CP-Net denoted as TempCP-Net, which is a collection of time-period based CP-Nets. As the provider has annual preferences, the three-year TempCP-Net is a set {(CP1, Year 1),(CP2, Year 2) (CP3, Year 3)}, in which each subcomponent corresponds to an annual preference (Fig. 1(b)). CP1 captures the first-year reputation building strategy in Fig. 1(b). Hence, the "high" availability has a higher priority than the "moderate" availability, i.e., $A1 \succ A2$. Note that, the "low" availability ($A3$) is not in the provider's preference in CP1. The choice of availability dictates the choice of CPU units. If the "high" availability ($A1$) is chosen, the provider prefers to provide the "high" CPU units than the "moderate" CPU units ($C1 \succ C2$). However, if the "moderate" availability ($A2$) is chosen, the provider prefers to provide the "moderate" CPU units than the "high" CPU units ($C2 \succ C1$). This is because a moderate QoS may not increase the reputation as expected, thus packaging it with lower CPU units may increase the probability to reduce SLA violations than packaging with higher CPU units. Finally, the price of the service is chosen based on the selection of the levels of availability and CPU units. As this is a reputation building phase, the provider will not charge "high" price ($P1$) while providing "moderate" CPU units ($C2 : P2 \succ P3$). In CP1, the most preferred service provision is ($A1, C1, P1$) and the least preferred choice is ($A2, C1, P3$). Similarly, CP2 and CP3 capture the profit maximization and risk management strategies in the second and third years respectively. In CP2, the most preferred service provision is ($P1, C3, A3$) and the least preferred service is ($P2, C2, A2$) expressing the preference on the higher price. In the third year, the most preferred service provision is ($C3, P1, A3$) and the least preferred service is ($C2, P3, A3$).

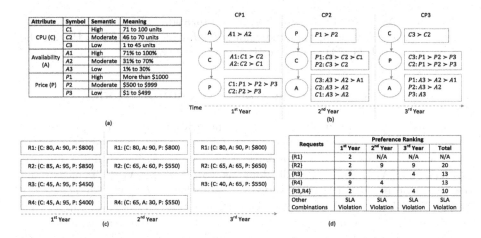

Fig. 1. (a) Semantic representation of preferred service attributes, (b) A TempCP-Net, (c) Incoming requests, (d) The preference ranking table

Let us assume, four different requests, $\{R1\}, \{R2\}, \{R3\}$, and $\{R4\}$ arrive at the beginning of the composition (Fig. 1(c)). For simplicity, a request is specified in annual segments. In Fig. 1(c), $(C:80, A:90, P:\$800)$ is the first year segment of $\{R1\}$, which means that the consumer requires a VM with 80 CPU units and 90 % availability and is able to pay $800 for this service in the first year. The annual requirements of $\{R2\}, \{R3\}$ and $\{R4\}$ are described in the same way. As there are four requests, the optimal composition will be selected from $2^4 = 16$ combinations of the requests in the brute-force approach. The TempCP-net (Fig. 1(b)) provides the objective function for the optimal IaaS composition selection. The preference ranking (lower values indicate higher preference ranks) of the combinations of the requests is retrieved through the matching between the TempCP-net and the combinations of the requests. For example, the first year segment of $\{R1\}$ falls into the "high" CPU units, "high" availability, and "moderate" price in Fig. 1(a). It is the 2nd ranked preference in the first year. However, the second year segment of $\{R1\}$ requires the "high" availability in the "moderate" cost, which is out of the preference (N/A) in CP2. The total preference rank of each request is tabulated under "Total" in Fig. 1(d). As two segments of $\{R1\}$ are out of the preference ranking, its total rank is N/A. $\{R3\}$ and $\{R4\}$ are combined into a request $\{R3, R4\}$. We cannot consider the other combinations due to the constraint of maximum 100 CPU units. According to the total qualitative ranks, $\{R3, R4\}$ is the optimal composition.

A heuristic based sequential optimization process may produce the global solution in fewer number of comparisons. Let us assume, the sequential optimization operates in the right to left year sequence (3rd, 2nd and 1st). In the 3rd year $2^3 = 8$ comparisons are performed and only the highest ranked R3 is accepted. The 9th ranked R2 violates the constraint of maximum 100 CPU units when it is combined with R3. As R1 (N/A ranking) and R2 are already rejected, they are not considered in the subsequent optimization. The local optimizations in the 2nd and 1st year accepts the remaining $R4$ in the solution. Hence, the optimal solution $\{R3, R4\}$ is produced in 10 comparisons.

4   The Temporal CP-Net Based Economic Model

We require not only an intuitive tool for structuring the provider's preferences, but also a support for an efficient optimization process. We assume a set of functional and non-functional attributes $V = \{X_1, ..., X_n\}$ with finite domains $\{D(X_1), ..., D(X_n)\}$ and semantic domains $\{S(X_1), ..., S(X_n)\}$. Typical functional attributes are CPU (C), Network bandwidth (NB), and Memory (M), and QoS attributes are Availability (A), Response time (RT), Throughput (TP) and Price (P). The numerical value x_n in $D(X_n)$ is mapped into a semantic value s_n in $S(X_n)$ using a mapping table, $s_n = Sem\_Table(X_n, x_n)$. Figure 1(a) is such a semantic table that maps 70–100 units of CPU as a "high" CPU value. In the long-term, the preference order and related semantics of V remain constant for a time period, but they may get changed in the next period. Let us assume, the total composition time, T is divided into m intervals $\{I_1, I_2, ..., I_m\}$ where, $T = \sum_{i=1}^{m} I_i$. In an interval I_k, the IaaS provider can specify a preference ranking of service configurations over complete assignments on V with the semantic domain $Sem\_D^{I_k}(V)$. The set of all service configurations is denoted as O^{I_k} for the interval I_k. A preference ranking is a total order $(\succeq)$ over the set of service configurations: $o_1 \succeq o_2$ means that a configuration o_1 is equally or more preferred than o_2. We use $o_1 \succ o_2$ to denote the fact that provisioning service o_1 is more preferred than o_2 (i.e., $o_1 \succeq o_2$ and $o_2 \not\succeq o_1$), while $o_1 \sim o_2$ denotes that the provider's preference is indifferent, i.e., $o_1 \not\succeq o_2$ and $o_2 \not\succeq o_1$.

Direct assessment of a long-term preference relation is generally infeasible due to the exponential size of $O^{I_k} \mid \forall k \in [1, m]$. We represent the long-term economic model in a Temporal CP-Net (TempCP-Net), which is a set of CP-Nets and semantic mapping tables over different intervals defined as TempCP-Net $= \{(CP^{I_k}, Sem\_Table^{I_k}, I_k) \mid \forall k \in [1, m]\}$. A CP-Net can concisely specify a preference relation in a graphical structure. A CP-net in the interval I_k, CP^{I_k} is a directed graph G over V whose nodes are annotated with conditional preference tables $CPT(X_i)$ for each $X_i \in V$. In this paper, we focus on only acyclic CP-Nets. Each conditional preference table $CPT(X_i)$ associates a total order $\succ_u^i$ with each instantiation u of X_i's parents $Pa(X_i) = U$ [13]. For example, in $CP1$, $A = Pa(C)$ and the $CPT(C)$ contains $\{A1, A2\}$ while preferences are made over $\{C1, C2\}$ (Fig. 1(b)). The preference $o \succ ó$ is a *consequence* of TempCP-Net, iff $o \succ ó$ holds in all preference orderings consistent with the *ceteris paribus* preference statements ("all else being equal") encoded by the CPTs of the TempCP-Net [16]. The set of consequences $o \succ ó$ of an acyclic TempCP-Net constitutes a partial order over the service configuration. This partial order can be represented by an acyclic directed graph, referred to as the *induced preference graph*. The nodes of the induced preference graph correspond to the complete assignments to the variables of the network. There is

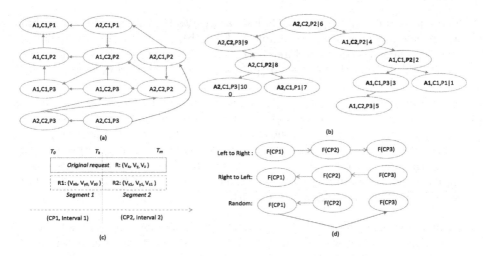

Fig. 2. (a) The induced preference graph of CP1, (b) The k-d tree representation, (c) Temporal semantic segmentation of a request, (d) Some sequential orders for local optimization

an edge from node $ó$ to node o iff the assignments at $ó$ and o differ only in the value of a single variable X. Given the values assigned by $ó$ and o to $Pa(X)$, the value assigned by o to X is preferred to the value assigned by $ó$ to X. Figure 2 depicts the induced preference graph of $CP1$. There is no outgoing edge from $(A1, C1, P1)$ as it is the most preferred request configuration. Similarly, there is no incoming edge to $(A2, C1, P3)$ as it is the least preferred configuration. As the $CPT(CP1)$ states $A1 \succ A2$, there is an edge from $(A2, C1, P1)$ to $(A1, C1, P1)$ considering the *ceteris paribus* preference statements. The induced preference graph (total ordering) of all the configurations is created using pair wise comparison (ordering queries) of the configurations [13]. If n is the number of attributes in the TempCP-net and q is the number of output configurations in an interval, the time complexity for ordering queries in an interval is $O(nq^2)$.

4.1   The k-d Tree Indexing of the Induced Preference Graph

Given a semantic request configuration $Sem\_Req = (s_1, ..., s_n) \mid$ where $s_i \in S(X_i)$, and $X_i \in V$, the induced preference graph enables searching the preference ranking of $(s_1, ..., s_n)$. Such a graph based searching approach requires linearly traversing over the graph (time complexity $O(n)$) [13]. Considering the tuple $(s_1, ..., s_n)$ as a multidimensional vector, we improve the search process using the k-d tree [1]. The k-d tree is a binary tree in which every node is a k-dimensional point (Fig. 2(b)). Every non-leaf node can be thought of as implicitly generating a splitting hyperplane that divides the space into two parts, known as half-spaces. Points on the left and right sides of this hyperplane are represented by the left and right subtree of that node respectively. We use the canonical method to construct the k-d tree [3]:

- The selection of splitting planes follows a cycle as the construction algorithm moves down on the tree. For example, in Fig. 2(b), the root is an "Availability-aligned" plane, the root's children both have "CPU-aligned planes", the root's grandchildren have "Price-aligned" planes, the root's great-grandchildren have again "Availability-aligned" planes, and so on.
- As all the n points are available from the induced preference graph, we insert points by selecting the median of the points being put into the subtree, with respect to their coordinates in the axis being used to create the splitting plane. This would result in a balanced k-d tree construction in $O(n \, log(n))$ times [3]. Each node in the k-d tree is annotated with its respective preference order from the induced graph. For example, the root node $(A2, C2, P2)$ is annotated with the preference ranking 6 in Fig. 2(b).

Starting with the root node, the searching algorithm moves down on the tree recursively, in the same way that it would if the search point was being inserted. If the search point is matched with a node, it returns the annotated ranking value. For example, the search for the request $(A2, C1, P3)$ returns rank 10 using only 4 comparisons. A non-matched search point is discarded in the composition. The time complexity in k-d tree searching of an interval is $O(log(n))$.

4.2   Ranking of the Consumers' Requests Using the TempCP-Net

Let us assume, a consumer divides its service usage time in n intervals and service requirements in the intervals vary from each other. We define the request of consumer u over the composition time T as $R_u = \{(x_i, I_j) \mid x_i \in D(X_i), X_i \in V,$ and $T = \sum_{j=1}^{m} I_j\}$. A set of N requests is represented as $\bar{R} = \{R_1, ..., R_N\}$. We combine the requests in $\bar{R}$ using the composition rules [10]:

$$\text{Summation rule: } \bar{x}_i = \sum_{i=1}^{N} x_i, \text{where } X_i \in \{C, M, NB, RT, P\} \qquad (1)$$

$$\text{Maximization rule: } \bar{y}_i = max(y_i), \forall i \in [1, N] \text{ where } Y_i \in \{A, TP\}$$

For example, the combined first year request $\{R1 : (C : 80, A : 90, P : \$800), R2 : (C : 85, A : 95, P : \$850)\}$ in Fig. 1(c) is $(C : 165, A : 95, P : 1650)$.

Note that, the intervals in consumer requests may be different from the intervals in the provider's TempCP-Net. In the first case, the starting time and the ending time of an *inclusive* request segment are from the same temporal segment of the TempCP-Net. For example, if a CP-Net in TempCP-net operates between 1st January and 31st January, a request spanning from 4th January to 25th January is an inclusive segment. As a single CP-Net is operating over the request, the request could be directly matched with the induced k-d tree from Sect. 4.1. In the second case, the starting time and the ending time of a *overlapping* request segment are from different temporal segments of the TempCP-Net. As more than one CP-Nets are operating over the request, we divide an overlapping request, R (interval $[T_0, T_m]$) into smaller inclusive segments. In Fig. 2(c), a request R is divided into R_1 and R_2 to match with corresponding $CP1$ and $CP2$. Note that, only attributes with *temporal semantics* require such a segmentation. For example, "Price" has *temporal semantics* in the consumer requests. If the consumer requires 100 units of CPU in 12 months for \$120, it still requires 100 units of CPU in every month but the monthly cost will be \$10. If the attribute X in R has *temporal semantics* and the segmentation is applied in $[T_j, T_k]$, the new value for X is calculated as follows:

$$x_i^{[T_j, T_k]} = x_i^{[T_0, T_m]} \times \frac{|T_k - T_j|}{|T_m - T_0|} \tag{2}$$

We define $Pref(\text{TempCP-Net}, \bar{R}) : V \to [1, n]$ as the ranking function that finds the preference order of $\bar{R}$ in the k-d trees of the TempCP-Net. As the TempCP-Net is constructed in semantic domains, we transform $\bar{R}$ into the semantic $\overset{s}{\bar{R}} = \{(s_i, I_j) \mid s_i \in S(X_i), X_i \in V, \text{and } T = \sum_{j=1}^m I_j\}$ using the *Sem_Table* in the TempCP-Net. Each temporal segments in $\overset{s}{\bar{R}}$ is matched with the corresponding temporal k-d tree using the matching process in Sect. 4.1. We denote the matching process in interval i as $M^i(s_i)$. Hence, ranking function can be defined as follows:

$$Pref(\text{TempCP-Net}, \bar{R}) = M^1(s_1) + \ldots + M^i(s_i) + \ldots + M^m(s_n) \tag{3}$$

5   Optimization Algorithm for IaaS Requests Composition

Given a set of N long-term requests $\bar{R}$ and the IaaS provider's TempCP-Net, the IaaS composition is to find an optimal set $\bar{r} \subseteq \bar{R}$ that minimizes the ranking output $Pref(\text{TempCP-Net}, \bar{r})$ in Eq. 3 (a lower value means a higher rank). There are two approaches to solve the temporal optimization problems: (a) global optimization, (b) sequential local optimization [8]. The global approach considers the entire time period and the input set at the time of composition. A common way of global optimization is the brute-force approach, that attempts all the combinations of requests over the entire composition period and finds the minimum one. The time complexity of this approach is exponential (2^N) which is not applicable in realtime applications. We formulate a dynamic programming (DP) approach that solves the optimization in super-polynomial time ($N^{O(N)}$) [8]. As the size of the input requests is in proportion to the length of the composition time, the global DP approach may not be feasible for a long-term composition. We propose a sequential local approach that divides the total time into segments according to the corresponding time intervals and each segment optimizes the requests that only operates in that interval [14]. This approach has a sequential effect for overlapping requests. Two local optimizations in different intervals may have different accept or reject opinion for the same overlapping request. As the quality of the final composition is dependent on the sequence order, we devise a heuristic based approach to approximate the optimal solution.

5.1   Dynamic Programming Based IaaS Composition

We propose a dynamic programming framework to weigh the benefits of accepting versus rejecting a request. Accepting a request will lead to immediate revenue, but it is possible that this acceptance will diminish future resource utilization for other requests. Dynamic Programming (DP) is an algorithmic paradigm that solves a given complex problem by breaking it into sub-problems (overlapping sub-problems) and stores the results of sub-problems to avoid repeated computation (optimal substructure) [8]. We denote $\bar{R}(N)$ as a set of N requests and $i \in [1, N]$ as the i_{th} request. If $C(\bar{R}(N), k)$ returns the optimal subset of requests of size k, it either accepts the N_{th} request (the k_{th} place is already filled) or rejects it (reduces $\bar{R}(N)$ to $\bar{R}(N-1)$). We formulate the DP as follows:

$$\bar{R}_1 = \{N \cup C(\bar{R}(N-1), k-1)\} \qquad (4)$$
$$\bar{R}_2 = C(\bar{R}(N-1), k)$$

$$C(\bar{R}(N), k) = \begin{cases} \bar{R}_1, \text{ if } Pref(\text{TempCP-Net}, \bar{R}_1) < Pref(\text{TempCP-Net}, \bar{R}_2) \\ \bar{R}_2, \text{ if } Pref(\text{TempCP-Net}, \bar{R}_1) \geq Pref(\text{TempCP-Net}, \bar{R}_2) \\ \{i\} \text{ if } k = 1 \text{ and } Pref(\text{TempCP-Net}, \{i\}) \text{ is minimum} \\ \emptyset \text{ if } k = 0 \end{cases}$$

In Eq. 4, $\bar{R}_1$ refers to the set that accepts the N_{th} request and $\bar{R}_2$ refers to the set that rejects the N_{th} request. The base case is defined on $K = 1$ (only one request output) that performs a linear search to find the highest ranked request i. The DP can reduce the re-computations of same sub-problems by constructing a temporary array in the bottom-up manner [8]. The complexity of finding $C(\bar{R}(N), k)$ is $O(N^k)$. The final optimal subset can have at most N requests. Hence, we can find the optimal solution (Sol) through the iterative operation in Eq. 5. The final complexity of the DP based solution is $O(N^{O(N)})$.

$$Sol = C(\bar{R}(N), i), \text{where } Pref(\text{TempCP-Net}, C(\bar{R}(N), i)) \text{ is minimum} \qquad (5)$$

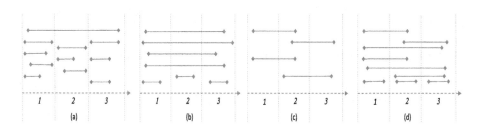

Fig. 3. The key composition scenarios (a) Almost Disjoint (b) Almost Overlapping (c) Chain, (d) Hybrid patterns

5.2 Heuristic Based Sequential Optimization

We use a heuristic based sequential aggregation of local optimizations to approximate the global optimization in reduced time complexity. Each interval in TempCP-Net only considers the request segments within its range and performs DP based optimization by using its own CP-Net as TempCP-Net (TempCP-Net = CP_i) in Eq. 4. These local optimizations in the intervals can run in parallel if there is no overlapping requests. However acceptance or rejection decision of overlapping requests can not be taken in parallel. Hence, different sequences of optimization order are performed to produce the optimal composition. For example, the left to right sequence first carries out optimization from the left intervals to the right intervals in Fig. 2(d). Finding the best sequence in sequential optimization is NP-Complete [8]. We build our heuristics by exploring several key composition scenarios:

- Almost Disjoint Pattern: In this pattern, the requests in an interval are mostly disjoint and evenly cover that interval (Fig. 3(a)). An interval that contains such a pattern can be assumed that rejecting an overlapping request may not affect the global ranking, as the overlapped request can be replaced by one or more disjoint requests with high possibility.
- Almost Overlapping Pattern: The requests in an interval are mostly long-overlapping in this pattern (Fig. 3(b)). The local optimization at a certain interval of a sequence may not be changed in other sequences as the acceptance and rejection of most of requests are decided in the first interval.
- Chain Pattern: In this pattern, the requests are short-overlapped and almost evenly distributed over the intervals (Fig. 3(c)). Several sequences of local optimization need to be applied to achieve the optimal result.
- Hybrid Pattern: Both the long-overlapping and short-overlapping requests are almost evenly distributed in this pattern (Fig. 3(d)). The final result should also maintain the ratio of different types of requests.

We formulate the following generic heuristics to find out the optimal sequences of local optimizations for different patterns. We define the overlapping ratio of a request N as follows:

$$O\_Ratio(N) = \frac{\text{Number of operating intervals of } N}{\text{Total number of intervals}} \tag{6}$$

- **Heuristic 1:** If most of the local optimizations reject a long-overlapping request independently, the final output should also reject it. If most of the local optimizations accept the request independently, the final output should also accept it. This heuristic is common in collective decision processes.
- **Heuristic 2:** If two set of requests $\{1, 2, ..., i, .., n\}$ and $\{1, 2, ..., j, ..., n\}$ produce the final ranking x and y respectively in an interval, a local optimization prefers accepting the request i than the request j if $O\_Ratio(j) < O\_Ratio(i)$ and $|x - y| < \tau$. τ is the highest acceptable difference in the ranking set by the provider. The heuristic prefers disjoint requests to the overlapping requests

---

Algorithm 1. The heuristic based sequential optimization

Input: The Request set($\bar{R}$), Acceptance window(l) and Maximum additive ranking (p)

Output: The optimal composition

1: final solution $= \emptyset$
2: Run local dynamic programming based optimization in each of the n intervals in parallel. Store the cumulative appearance frequency of a request in the first l ranking (the acceptance window will be set by the provider). For example, if $l = 5$ and A appears in both 1st rank and 3rd rank, the frequency of A is 2. By default the frequency is 0. Rank the requests based on their frequencies.
3: Add the rankings of a request from each interval. Accept the request and add to the final solution if its additive ranking is less than p (set by the provider).
4: temporary solution $=$ final solution
5: Generate the left to right sequence of intervals $(I_1, I_2, ..., I_m)$.
6: Start dynamic programming based optimization in the first interval. Add new requests in the temporary solution by following heuristic 2. Only add requests if there are available resources. After finishing optimization in an interval, continue adding new requests in the following intervals of the sequence. If the ranking of the temporary solution is greater than the final solution, set final solution = initial solution (update operation).
7: Generate the right to left sequence of intervals $(I_m, I_{n-1}, ...I_1)$ and try to update the final solution by following step 6.
8: Generate a new random sequence of intervals $(I_k, I_{n-1}, ...I_l)$ and try to update the final solution by following step 6. If the ranking of the final solution is improved, start step 8 again. Otherwise, return the final solution.

---

when optimizing an interval. It reduces the effect of sequencing by replacing overlapping requests with disjoint requests without affecting the ranking in individual optimization.

We devise a two-phase based approach (Algorithm 1) to incorporate these heuristics. In the first phase, we filter long-overlapping requests for the acceptance or the rejection (heuristic 1). The first phase is described in step 1 to 3 in Algorithm 1. It sets the final solution with a set of long-overlapping requests which are voted by the intervals independently. In the second phase, we add new requests in the final using heuristic 2 (step 4 to 8). At least three different sequences are generated and the final solution is updated only when the ranking of the solution is improved. The random generation of sequences are stopped when no improvements are made in the final ranking in Algorithm 1.

6   Experiments and Results

A set of experiments are conducted to evaluate the efficiency of the proposed approach. At first we compare the ranking of the sequential optimized composition with the global dynamic programming based composition. Next we compare the time complexity between the two approaches. All the experiments are conducted on computers with Intel Core i7 CPU (2.13 GHz and 4 GB RAM). Java is used to implement the algorithms.

6.1 Simulation Setup

As it is difficult to find a real world IaaS provider's business strategies, we synthetically create 10 different yearly temporal CP-Nets with 12 intervals in each TempCP-Net. Each TempCP-Net has 5 attributes (CPU, Memory Availability, Response time, Throughput and Price) and dependencies among the attributes are randomly generated. The values of an attribute are divided into 10 semantic levels (from high to low). Each CPT is filled with random conditional preferences, each of which is a random order of the attribute semantic values. We

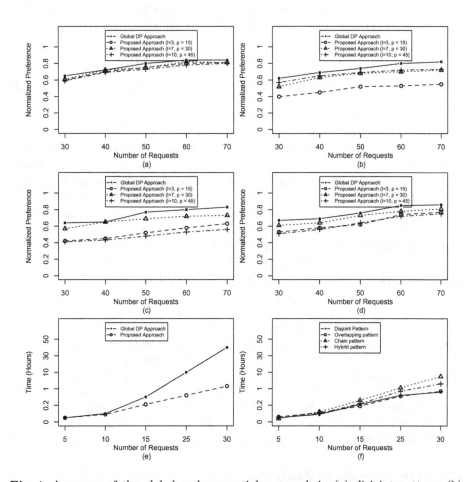

Fig. 4. Accuracy of the global and sequential approach in (a) disjoint pattern, (b) overlapping pattern, (c) chain pattern, (d) hybrid pattern, (e) The global vs sequential time complexity, (f) Time complexity of the sequential approach

create the user requests as a mixture of Google Cluster resource utilization [12], real world cloud QoS performance [7], and randomly generated availability and prices. Google Cluster data include CPU and Memory utilization and allocation time series of 70 jobs over a 1-month period. Real world QoS data [7] include two time series (i.e., response time and throughput) for 100 cloud services over a 6-month period. We randomly pick 70 Google Cluster jobs and make one-to-one mapping with the 100 sets of QoS data. A 6-month request is extended to a 12-month request using random duplication of segments. We create 4 different patterns of the input requests: (a) disjoint pattern: 80 % of the request set is segmented into requests of 1 to 2 month period. (b) overlapping pattern: 80 % of the request set is segmented into requests of 8–12 month period. (c) chain pattern: 80 % of the request set is segmented into requests of 2–8 month period. (d) hybrid pattern: It is a collection of 35 % disjoint requests, 35 % overlapping requests and 30 % of requests which spans in 2 to 8 month period. In each of the patterns, other types of requests are randomly distributed into different intervals.

6.2   Efficiency of the Heuristic Based Sequential Optimization

In the first experiment, we analyse the efficiency of the proposed heuristic based sequential optimization. As the proposed Algorithm 1 needs an acceptance window (l) and additive ranking (p) in its first phase (accepting long-overlapping requests), we use 3 different configurations of acceptance window: (a) conservative ($l = 3, p = 15$), (b) moderate ($l = 7, p = 30$) and liberal ($l = 10, p = 45$). Each of the request patterns (disjoint, overlapping, chain and hybrid) is filled with different numbers of requests ranging from 30 to 70. A request pattern filled with a certain number of requests is executed in 10 different TempCP-Nets using the proposed heuristic approach (with 3 different acceptance windows) and the global DP approach. The outputs are averaged and normalized as ($\frac{1}{ranking}$) (higher values mean top rankings, lower values mean low rankings). Figure 4(a),(b),(c) and (d) depict the performance of the approaches in the disjoint, overlapping, chain and hybrid patterns respectively. In all of the figures, the quality of the output is increased when the number of requests is increased. At least one of the acceptance windows produces close outputs to the DP based approach in higher number of requests. All three acceptance window configurations of the heuristic based approach perform close to the DP based approach in the disjoint and hybrid patterns (Fig. 4(a) and (d)). Among the three, only the output of conservative ($l = 3, p = 15$) configuration is not performing close to the DP based approach in the overlapping pattern (Fig. 4(b)). It may refuse too many possible overlapping requests in the final output composition. In Fig. 4(c), only the output of the moderate ($l = 7, p = 30$) configuration is acceptable and close to the DP approach in higher numbers of requests (Fig. 4(c)).

6.3   Time Complexity Analysis

Although the global DP based approach produces better results than proposed approach, it is not applicable in runtime. The convergence time of the global approach and the proposed approach are close for the smaller numbers of requests in Fig. 4(e). However, the convergence time of the proposed approach is significantly lower than the global approach for a high number of requests (Fig. 4(e)). Figure 4(f) depicts the time complexity of the proposed approach in different patterns. It takes relatively higher time to converge in the chain pattern than the other patterns in Fig. 4(f).

7 Conclusion

We propose the TempCP-Net framework to represent the long-term economic model of an IaaS provider. The proposed model allows a provider to apply qualitative business strategies in composing consumer requests. It is a more natural and simplified composition process than the quantitative approach which focuses the composition on complex resource levels, i.e., operation cost calculation and scheduling. We propose a heuristic based sequential optimization algorithm that does not require the history of different input patterns and corresponding composition decisions. Hence, it will be mostly helpful to start-up IaaS providers. Experimental results show that the proposed approach is applicable in runtime and significantly faster than global DP based approaches. The accuracy of the solution is also acceptable in different input patterns. In the future work, we want to explore the TempCP-Net with the root causes of their different business strategies. We will find correlations between the TempCP-Net and different market factors, such as peer competitions, the supply and demand of the services, and the reputation.

Acknowledgements. This research was made possible by NPRP 7-481-1-088 grant from the Qatar National Research Fund (a member of The Qatar Foundation). The statements made herein are solely the responsibility of the authors.

References

1. Andoni, A., Indyk, P.: Near-optimal hashing algorithms for approximate nearest neighbor in high dimensions. In: Proceedings of FOCS, pp. 459–468. IEEE (2006)
2. Armbrust, M., Fox, A., Griffith, R.: Above the clouds: a berkeley view of cloud computing. Technical report, University of California, Berkeley (2009)
3. Bentley, J.L.: Multidimensional binary search trees used for associative searching. Commun. ACM **18**(9), 509–517 (1975)
4. Boutilier, C., Brafman, R.I., Domshlak, C., Hoos, H.H., Poole, D.: Cp-nets: a tool for representing and reasoning with conditional ceteris paribus preference statements. J. Artif. Intell. Res. **21**, 135–191 (2004)
5. Goiri, Í., Guitart, J., Torres, J.: Economic model of a cloud provider operating in a federated cloud. Inf. Syst. Front. **14**, 827–843 (2012)
6. Inc, G.: Compute engine features (2015). https://cloud.google.com
7. Jiang, W., Lee, D., Hu, S.: Large-scale longitudinal analysis of soap-based and restful web services. In: Proceedings of ICWS, pp. 218–225 (2012)
8. Kimes, S.E., Thompson, G.M.: Restaurant revenue management: determining the best table mix. Decis. Sci. **35**(3), 371–392 (2004)

9. Lim, H., Widdows, R., Park, J.: M-loyalty: winning strategies for mobile carriers. J. Consum. Mark. **23**(4), 208–218 (2006)
10. Mistry, S., Bouguettaya, A., Dong, H., Qin, A.K.: Metaheuristic optimization for long-term iaas service composition. IEEE Trans. Serv. Comput. **PP**(99), 1 (2016)
11. Mistry, S., Bouguettaya, A., Dong, H., Qin, A.K.: Predicting dynamic requests behavior in long-term iaas service composition. In: Proceedings of ICWS. IEEE (2015)
12. Reiss, C., Wilkes, J., Hellerstein, J.L.: Google cluster-usage traces: format + schema. Google Inc., Mountain View, CA, USA, Technical report (2011)
13. Santhanam, G.R., Basu, S., Honavar, V.: Web service substitution based on preferences over non-functional attributes. In: Proceedings of SCC, pp. 210–217 (2009)
14. Vien, N.A., Toussaint, M.: Hierarchical monte-carlo planning. In: Proceedings of AAAI, pp. 3613–3619 (2015)
15. Wang, H., Shao, S., Zhou, X., Wan, C., Bouguettaya, A.: Preference recommendation for personalized search. Knowl.-Based Syst. **100**, 124–136 (2016)
16. Wang, H., Zhang, J., Sun, W., Song, H., Guo, G., Zhou, X.: WCP-Nets: a weighted extension to CP-Nets for web service selection. In: Liu, C., Ludwig, H., Toumani, F., Yu, Q. (eds.) ICSOC 2012. LNCS, pp. 298–312. Springer, Heidelberg (2012). doi:10.1007/978-3-642-34321-6_20
17. Wu, L., Kumar Garg, S., Buyya, R.: Sla-based admission control for a software-as-a-service provider in cloud computing environments. J. Comput. Syst. Sci. **78**(5), 1280–1299 (2012)
18. Ye, Z., Bouguettaya, A., Zhou, X.: QoS-aware cloud service composition based on economic models. In: Proceedings of ICSOC, pp. 111–126 (2012)

Service Management

An Uncertain Assessment Compatible Incentive Mechanism for Eliciting Continual and Truthful Assessments of Cloud Services

Lie Qu, Yan Wang$^{(\boxtimes)}$, and Mehmet Orgun

Macquarie University, Sydney, Australia
{lie.qu,yan.wang,mehmet.orgun}@mq.edu.au

Abstract. The evaluation of dynamic performance of cloud services relies on continual assessments from cloud users, e.g., ordinary consumers and testing parties. In order to elicit continual and truthful assessments, an effective incentive mechanism in cloud environments should allow users to provide uncertain assessments when they are not sure about the real performance of cloud services, e.g., when users do not access cloud services on time, rather than providing untruthful or arbitrary assessments. Different from all prior works, we propose a novel uncertain assessment compatible incentive mechanism. Under this mechanism, a user not only has sufficient incentives to continually provide truthful assessments, but also would prefer providing uncertain assessments over untruthful or arbitrary assessments since uncertain assessments can bring more benefits than untruthful or arbitrary assessments. We theoretically analyze the proposed incentive mechanism and evaluate it through simulations under different circumstances. The theoretical analysis demonstrates the effectiveness of our approach. Moreover, the experimental results based on simulations strongly support the results from the theoretical analysis.

1 Introduction

As cloud services have become increasingly popular, reliable service evaluation is quite important for cloud consumers. Cloud service evaluation is usually based on cloud users' assessments, which can be either subjective (e.g., user ratings) or objective (e.g., QoS monitoring or testing). No matter what types of assessments are used, the trustworthiness of users' assessments has a great impact on the reliability of cloud service evaluation. For avoiding ambiguity, all the parties which provide cloud assessments are called *cloud users* in this paper, e.g., ordinary consumers or testing organizations.

In cloud environments, service performance may vary substantially and frequently due to the dynamic nature of cloud services. Thus, continual assessments over time are needed to effectively reflect the dynamic performance of services. Recent studies [18,25] point out that continual assessments are vital for not only evaluating cloud users' trustworthiness of providing assessments, but also predicting the dynamic performance of cloud services. However, eliciting continual

© Springer International Publishing Switzerland 2016
Q.Z. Sheng et al. (Eds.): ICSOC 2016, LNCS 9936, pp. 335–351, 2016.
DOI: 10.1007/978-3-319-46295-0_21

and truthful assessments in cloud environments is still a challenging problem since it is usually hard to make self-interested users behave cooperatively in an online community [1]. A cloud user usually does not have sufficient incentives to regularly provide assessments of cloud services on time. To motivate users, an effective incentive mechanism should be designed. A common solution is that a cloud user can be paid if it provides assessments on scheduled time. The monetary rewards[1] could be provided by some professional cloud evaluation organizations, such as CloudReviews[2], the aim of which is to provide cloud selection services to potential cloud consumers based on cloud users' assessments and thus earn profits from the potential consumers. Nevertheless, such a simple mechanism cannot prevent a user from "free-riding" (i.e., providing arbitrary assessments) [10,24]. Moreover, sometimes an honest user may also provide arbitrary assessments in order to obtain monetary rewards when it does not really know the real performance of cloud services (e.g., a user does not consume services on the scheduled time while a user is required to provide an assessment). Such arbitrary assessments may be erroneous and misleading, and therefore greatly affect the effectiveness of service evaluations. To avoid the submission of arbitrary assessments, an effective incentive mechanism should motivate users to always tell the truth, i.e., motivating users to provide truthful assessments, and allowing users to provide uncertain assessments to express their uncertainty about service performance when necessary. However, there are no such incentive mechanisms in the literature, which considers uncertain assessments.

In our prior work [16], we proposed a basic framework supporting our incentive mechanism, which can take uncertain assessments into account. Based on this framework, the proposed incentive mechanism in this paper makes a further step, i.e., presenting the theoretical analysis of the effective incentive design and the optimal incentive design in our framework as well as discussing the whitewashing problem (See Sect. 3.6). The features and contributions of our work are summarized as follows:

(1) Under our proposed mechanism, a user is considered *honest* if it gives truthful assessments most of the time, but may give a small proportion of uncertain assessments once it is not sure about the real performance of a service. The word "honest" indicates such a user always tells the truth. Thus, a UAC (*uncertain-assessment-compatible*) assessment scheme is first proposed. In particular, the new scheme can be extended from any type of ordinary (subjective or objective) assessment systems, but includes an extra uncertain state (see Sect. 3.1). Then the behaviors of users providing assessments are modeled using a repeated game framework (see Sect. 3.2).

(2) A user can receive monetary rewards from a professional organization (called a *broker*) mentioned above for regularly providing assessments on schedule for the cloud services it consumes. In order to control the monetary

---

[1] The rewards can be paid in any form, e.g., points, discount and privileges, each of which can be taken as monetary rewards.

[2] www.cloudreviews.com.

rewards for the incentive mechanism design, we propose an assessment scoring scheme (see Sect. 3.3). In a nutshell, *truthful assessments* would bring the most rewards; *uncertain assessments* would bring less rewards; *untruthful* or *arbitrary assessments* would bring the very least rewards. Through our proposed mechanism, a rational user would choose its best option, i.e., providing truthful assessments. Once it is not sure about service performance, there still exists a second-best option, i.e., providing uncertain assessments.

(3) In order to build an effective incentive mechanism, we present the theoretical analysis (see Sects. 3.4) of the scoring scheme according to the different strategies of users (i.e., providing truthful/uncertain/untruthful/arbitrary assessments). Moreover, we discuss how to build an optimal incentive mechanism in our framework (see Sect. 3.5) and the feasibility of solving the *whitewashing* problem [4] based on our proposed mechanism (see Sect. 3.6).

(4) The results from the theoretical analysis show that our approach is effective in most circumstances (see Sect. 4.1). Furthermore, in order to evaluate the feasibility of our approach, we carry out simulation experiments under different situations. The results from the simulation strongly support the results from the theoretic analysis (see Sect. 4.2).

2   Related Work

In the literature, incentive mechanisms for eliciting truthful information are usually modeled in a seller-buyer scenario, where speaking the truth is an equilibrium for buyers. According to the applied techniques, those mechanisms can generally be classified into two groups: peer-prediction based approaches and reputation-based approaches. In addition to these approaches, some recent studies of incentive mechanisms in crowdsourcing environments are proposed for eliciting effective contributions of workers. In general, all these approaches are proposed for eliciting the cooperation of users, and thus are related to our work.

Peer-Prediction Based Approaches: Miller *et al.* [13] propose the pioneering "Peer-Prediction" method for eliciting truthful feedback. In their work, every user can obtain monetary payment from an authorized center. The amount of payment depends on how well a user can predict the signal from some other user (called a reference user) based on its own signal. Their work is feasible based on several common knowledge assumptions, e.g., product type distributions and conditional distributions of signals. However, there is a drawback in Miller *et al.*'s work, i.e., there may exist lying equilibria that can bring higher expected payoffs than the truthful equilibrium [13]. To overcome this drawback, Jurca and Faltings [7,8] propose a collusion-resistant feedback payment approach, in which several reference reports are applied in the scoring rules instead of the one-reference-report scheme in the prior work. They prove that speaking the truth is the unique equilibrium if at least three reports are used.

In later studies, Witkowski [19] point out that the quality of goods or services provided by sellers is assumed fixed in prior works. However, in many real-world situations, the quality is inherently dynamic. Thus, he proposes a payment mechanism based on the hidden Markov setting to deal with such dynamics. It is worth noting that all these peer-prediction-based incentive mechanisms make strong common knowledge assumptions. To lift these assumptions, Witkowski and Parkes [20] propose peer prediction without a common prior. Their mechanism allows participants to adopt subjective and private priors instead of a common prior by asking a participant to offer two reports (one before the transaction and one afterwards), and their approach is proved to provide strict incentives for truthful reports. Compared to the peer-prediction-based approaches, our work needs fewer knowledge assumptions and no extra belief report submission.

Reputation Based Approaches: some incentive mechanisms focus on evaluating participants' reputations on how truthfully they provide assessments or do something they have committed to. And the reputation would influence a participant's future opportunities of obtaining profits. Jurca and Faltings [6] propose an incentive-compatible reputation mechanism, which allows sellers to "confess" when they did not provide the goods or services as those they have committed. Due to such a confession, a seller can prevent further losses for his/her cheating, which give sellers incentives to speak the truth. Papaioannou and Stamoulis [14], propose a reputation-based incentive mechanism in a peer-to-peer system to motivate peers for truthful reporting. In their work, a non-credibility metric is designed for controlling a peer's punishment of having disagreed transaction feedback with other peers. Zhang *et al.* [22] propose a trust-based incentive mechanism, which is an extension of their prior work [21], in a reverse auction scenario. In this mechanism, a seller whose reputation is below a threshold is forbidden to participate in future auctions and therefore suffers a loss.

Incentive Mechanism Studies for Crowdsourcing: incentive mechanisms are employed in crowdsourcing environments for motivating users' effective contributions. Mason and Watts [12] study the relationship between financial incentives and working performance, and argue that increasing financial incentives could only bring more workers, but not a working quality improvement as expected. A similar conclusion can be found in DiPalantino and Vojnovic's work [2]. They argue that worker participation rates logarithmically increase with monetary rewards. Zhang and van der Schaar [24] focus on solving workers' "free-riding" problem and requesters' false-report problem. They designed optimal and sustainable incentive protocols based on social norms [9]. After that, they propose a generic rating protocol for online communities [23].

In our prior work [16], a basic framework for uncertain-assessment-compatible incentive mechanism is proposed without theoretical analysis. Different from all the above works, in this paper, we propose a novel incentive mechanism which is compatible with users' uncertain assessments, and present the theoretical proofs of our work as well as the illustrative results, both of which demonstrate the feasibility of our work.

3   The Proposed Approach

The basic idea behind our approach is as follows: cloud users can get paid by selling their assessments for cloud services to a *broker* via a user agent system. Cloud users are allowed to provide uncertain assessments for the services when they are not sure about the real performance of the services. The cloud performance evaluation is carried out by the broker based on cloud users' assessments, and the broker pays monetary rewards to the current cloud users for their assessments and obtains profits from potential cloud consumers by offering cloud selection services.

A user's incentive is represented through its expected long-term payment. The long-term payment is composed of the payments obtained in the continual time windows, e.g., 9 am–10 am every day. Through an assessment scoring scheme, users' participation of selling their assessments are controlled. In a nutshell, if a user is considered to submit a truthful assessment in a time window, it can keep on selling assessments until it is considered to have submitted an uncertain or untruthful assessment in a subsequent time window. Due to the submitted uncertain or untruthful assessment, the user would be isolated from selling assessments for a period of time, so that its long-term payment would suffer a loss because of such isolation. This is like fixed-term imprisonment. After the "imprisonment", the user can still be involved in the subsequent assessment transactions. Hence, in a time window, the user would believe that truthful reporting can maximize its long-term payoff and an uncertain assessment would bring a larger payoff than an untruthful or arbitrary one, if the broker can correctly judge the truthfulness of an assessment with an overwhelming probability.

3.1   The UAC Assessment Schemes

A cloud user can give its own assessments for different performance aspects of the cloud services it consumes. For each aspect, such assessments can be expressed in any reasonable form including subjective or objective assessments. Taking service response time as an example, a cloud user can give its numerical ratings (e.g., "1", "2" or "3") or linguistic ratings (e.g., "poor", "fair" or "good") to express its subjective assessments. On the other hand, a user can also provide objective assessments according to QoS testing (e.g., 200 ms for response time). For any type of an assessment system, an uncertain state can be added into the system to express users' uncertainty about service performance. For example, if a rating scheme consists of three states: "good", "fair" and "poor". The UAC assessment scheme, which can be applied in our incentive mechanism, is composed of four states, i.e., "good", "fair", "poor" and "uncertain", where the first three are considered as *certain* assessments.

3.2   Game Setup

Broker and Payment Settings: the broker requires cloud users to provide continual assessments for services at regular time intervals. A user can get paid by providing an assessment in a scheduled time window. In each time window, only the latest assessment can be paid for by the broker. If the user misses a time window, it cannot give assessments until the next time window. In addition, we assume that the cloud users are long-lived, and care about their long-term payoffs of providing assessments.

In each time window, the broker must pay each user no matter what type of an assessment the user gives. The amount of payment has two levels. If a user gives a certain assessment, it would get a payment P regardless of the value of the assessment. Conversely, if a user gives an uncertain assessment, it would get a discounted payment λP for $\lambda \in [0, 1]$. The reason for why a user can get such a discounted payment is that uncertain assessments cannot benefit the broker but the user still tells the truth without giving untruthful or arbitrary assessments which may even make the broker suffer losses by falsely evaluating the performance of cloud services. If a user does not provide any assessment in a time window, an uncertain assessment would be automatically submitted by a user agent instead.

The compulsory payment setting in our work aims to prevent the broker from "false-reporting" [3]. If the broker can afterwards decide whether to pay according to the quality of assessments, it would always have incentives to refuse to pay to users by cheating about the real quality of assessments. Thus, the payment from the broker in our framework can be considered "*ex-ante*" [24] with two amount levels. The compulsory payment and the judgement of certain or uncertain assessments can be supervised by a *third-party authority* (e.g., a payment management center). The authority can keep both levels of payment (for a/an certain or uncertain assessment) before each time window, and then transfers one level of payment to a user according to the certainty of its assessment, and returns the other level of payment to the broker. Therefore, the broker cannot deny that an assessment is certain or uncertain.

User Strategies: based on our framework, the payoff matrix between the broker and a user in a time window can be specified in Table 1. We follow the common assumption of incentive mechanisms made in the literature: a user is rational and self-interested, i.e., every user is motivated to maximize its own payoffs. A user would have three strategies of "*cooperation*", "*semi-cooperation*" or "*non-cooperation*". In our framework, cooperation for a user means giving a truthful assessment; semi-cooperation means giving an uncertain assessment; non-cooperation means giving an untruthful or arbitrary assessment (these two situations will be further discussed separately). B is the benefit a truthful assessment can create for the broker in a time window. P is the full payoff a user can obtain by giving a certain assessment. C is the cost of the effort for a user providing a truthful assessment. In the situations of semi-cooperation and non-cooperation, we consider that a user does not have any cost since it does not try to provide a truthful assessment. We follow the common assumption in the literature of incentive mechanisms, i.e., $B > P > C$. Here, we consider that all users are identical in terms of their knowledge and preference, thus B and C are constant, but P is adjustable. Note that, our work can be easily extended

Table 1. Payoff matrix in a time window

	User		
Broker	Cooperation	Semi-cooperation	Non-cooperation
	$B-P, P-C$	$-\lambda P, \lambda P$	$-P, P$

to a situation where there are different types of users by setting suitable system parameters for different users. Table 1 indicates that a user's dominant strategy is to always behave non-cooperatively, which is not expected by the broker and cause quite negative effects in cloud performance evaluations.

3.3 The Assessment Scoring Scheme

In order to make a user's dominant strategy cooperation, we propose an assessment scoring scheme to control users' participation in the transactions of selling their assessments. In our framework, a user has an assessment score to determine if it can sell its assessments to the broker in a time window. At the end of each time window, a new assessment score will be assigned to each user according to its current score and the submitted assessment. An assessment score θ is a positive integer from a nonempty finite set Θ ($\theta \in \Theta = \{0, 1, 2, \cdots, L\}$), where L is the largest score.

At the end of each time window, the broker can judge whether an assessment is truthful or untruthful through some approaches (e.g., majority opinions). Then it reports its judgement for every user to the authority. According to the broker's reports and users' current assessment scores, the authority updates a new score for every user. Note that, the broker would always report the truth about a user's assessments since the payment is ex-ante and the broker cannot lie about the certainty of an assessment in our framework. However, there may exist an error probability α of the broker falsely reporting without intention, e.g., a truthful assessment is reported as an untruthful one, and vice versa. And α should be smaller than the probability of random guessing, i.e., $\alpha \in [0, 0.5]$.

Let $\tau(\theta, b)$ denote the assessment scoring scheme, and the new score of a user at the end of a time window is computed as follows:

$$\tau(\theta, b) = \begin{cases} L, & \text{if } \theta = L \text{ and } b = T, \\ h_U, & \text{if } \theta = L \text{ and } b = U, \\ 0, & \text{if } \theta = L \text{ and } b = UT, \\ \theta + 1, & \text{if } \theta < L, \end{cases} \tag{1}$$

where θ is a user's current score and b is its reported behavior. h_U can be considered as a punishment level for users providing uncertain assessments. A user can be reported as having three types of behaviors, i.e., providing *truthful* (*T*), *uncertain* (*U*) or *untruthful* (*UT*) assessments. Figure 1 shows the scoring scheme. If a user having the largest score L is considered to have submitted a/an truthful/uncertain/untruthful assessment, its new score will be maintained

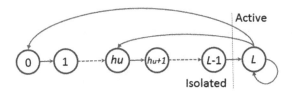

Fig. 1. The assessment scoring scheme

at L, or become h_U or 0 respectively, where $0 < h_U < L$. If a user has a score less than L, its score will always increase by 1. Furthermore, the authority requires that only the users having the score L are allowed to submit and sell their assessments to the broker. This means that all users can be classified into two groups: active users and isolated users. If a user is considered to give a/an uncertain or untruthful assessment, it would be punished by being prohibited from selling assessments for a period of time. Thus it will suffer a loss in its future incomes. If a user is not be able to behave cooperatively for some reason, it has a second-best option, i.e., giving uncertain assessments. That is because giving uncertain assessments would cause a shorter period of isolation due to the requirement of $0 < h_U < L$.

3.4 Effective Incentive Mechanism Design

In order to build an effective incentive mechanism based on the proposed assessment scoring scheme, we need to analyze the long-term expected payoffs that an "honest" user can obtain and find out what values of L and h_U are necessary for an effective incentive mechanism.

An *honest user* refers to a user who gives truthful assessments most of the time, but may give a small part of uncertain assessments. We apply the infinite-horizon discounted sum criterion to analyze an honest user's long-term expected payoffs. Let $p(\theta'|\theta)$ denote the transition probability of an honest user's assessment scores between two adjacent time windows, which is shown as follows:

$$
p(\theta'|\theta) = \begin{cases} (1-\alpha)(1-\beta), & \text{if } \theta = L \text{ and } \theta' = L, \\ \beta, & \text{if } \theta = L \text{ and } \theta' = h_U, \\ \alpha(1-\beta), & \text{if } \theta = L \text{ and } \theta' = 0, \\ 1, & \text{if } \theta < L \text{ and } \theta' = \theta + 1, \\ 0, & \text{otherwise,} \end{cases} \tag{2}
$$

where θ represents the user's current score and θ' is the user's new score. α is the error probability of the broker making a false judgement about the user's assessment. β is the probability of the user giving an uncertain assessment in a time window. For an identical type of users and a broker, α and β should be fixed in all time windows. Hence, an honest user's long-term expected payoff in a time window can be computed by solving the following recursive equation:

$$
v^\infty(\theta) = v(\theta) + \delta \sum_{\theta'} p(\theta'|\theta) v^\infty(\theta'), \text{for all } \theta \in \Theta, \tag{3}
$$

where $v^\infty(\theta)$ denotes a user's long-term payoff when it has the assessment score θ in a time window. And $v(\theta)$ denotes the user's instant payoff after giving its assessment in the current time window. $\delta \in (0,1)$ represents a user's patience about its future payoffs. A larger δ means that the user cares more about its future payoffs, and vice versa. Equation (3) indicates that an honest user's long-term expected payoff consists of two parts, i.e., the instant payoff and the expected future payoff based on the score transition probability shown in Eq. (2). The notations of our approach are summarized in Table 2.

Theorem 1 (Existence of Long-term Expected Payoffs): Given the transition probabilities specified in Eq. (2), for any $\alpha \in [0, 0.5]$, $\beta \in [0,1]$, $\sigma \in (0,1)$, $\lambda \in [0,1]$ and $P > C$, the recursive equation Eq. (3) has a unique positive solution.

Proof. All proofs in this paper are omitted due to the space limitation, and presented in [15]. □

Based on Theorem 1, we have the following property:

Table 2. The parameters of the incentive mechanism

Notations	Explanations
α	The probability for falsely judging an assessment
β	The probability of giving uncertain assessments
γ	The probability for a user guessing correctly
δ	A user's patient for future payoffs
B	The benefit for the broker from a truthful assessment
C	The cost of effort of giving a truthful assessment
P	The ex-ante price for an assessment
λ	The payment discounted factor
L	The largest assessment score
h_U	The assessment score for giving an uncertain assessment

Property 1: The long-term expected payoffs defined in Eq. (3) satisfy the following conditions:

(1) $v^\infty(\theta + 1) > v^\infty(\theta)$, for $\forall \theta \in \Theta - \{L\}$;

(2) $v^\infty(\theta + 1) - v^\infty(\theta) > v^\infty(\theta) - v^\infty(\theta - 1)$, for $\forall \theta \in \Theta - \{0, L\}$. □

In Property 1, the statement (1) indicates that the higher the assessment score of a user, the more the long-term expected payoff. The statement (2) shows that the increase of the long-term expected payoff between two adjacent assessments scores becomes larger with the increase of users' assessment scores. Property 1 demonstrates that an honest user always has incentives to pursue a higher score for obtaining a higher long-term payoff.

In our framework, there should be a dominant strategy for a user, and a second-best strategy if it cannot choose the dominant strategy for some reason. We expect the dominant strategy is to provide truthful assessments, and the second-best strategy is to provide uncertain assessments. As a user's long-term expected payoffs can be computed in a recursive form, its strategy can be determined based on the *one-shot deviation principle* [5], i.e., if a user cannot increase its long-term expected payoff by choosing a strategy other than the dominant one in a time window, the user would not be able to increase the payoff by choosing any strategy other than the dominant one. The one-shot deviation principle can also be applied for the second-best strategy. Hence, we study an active (its assessment score is L) user's long-term expected payoff[3]. If a user provides a *truthful* (T) assessment in a time window, and then its long-term expected payoff can be computed according to Eq. (3) as follows:

$$v_T^\infty(L) = P - C + \delta[(1 - \alpha)v^\infty(L) + \alpha v^\infty(0)]. \tag{4}$$

And if a user provides an *uncertain* (U) assessment, its payoff can be computed as follows:

$$v_U^\infty(L) = \lambda P + \delta[v^\infty(h_U)]. \tag{5}$$

At last, if a user provides an *untruthful* (UT) assessment, its payoff can be computed as follows:

$$v_{UT}^\infty(L) = P + \delta[\alpha v^\infty(L) + (1 - \alpha)v^\infty(0)]. \tag{6}$$

In order to determine the unique dominant strategy and the second-best strategy, a user's long-term expected payoff should satisfy the constraints: $v_T^\infty(L) > v_U^\infty(L) > v_{UT}^\infty(L)$, i.e.,

$$\delta[(1 - \alpha)v^\infty(L) + \alpha v^\infty(0) - v^\infty(h_U)] + (1 - \lambda)P - C > 0,$$
$$\delta[v^\infty(h_U) - \alpha v^\infty(L) - (1 - \alpha)v^\infty(0)] + (\lambda - 1)P > 0. \tag{7}$$

An assessment scoring scheme satisfying Eq. (7) indicates that a user can obtain the most long-term expected payoffs when giving a truthful assessment, and the second-best expected payoffs when giving an uncertain assessment.

Strategic Users: In Eq. (7), we consider that a user only has three kinds of behaviors: providing truthful, uncertain or untruthful assessments. However, there may be *strategic users* who believe that they can guess the real performance of cloud services without actually knowing it. Even for the users who provide *arbitrary* assessments, there should be a small probability that they can guess the right results, so that they would not be punished for "free-riding".

---

[3] Isolated users are not considered here since such users cannot participate in the transactions of selling assessments until they become active users (their scores increase to L).

The free-riders can be considered as a kind of strategic users. To solve the strategic user problem, we need to reconsider the constraints in Eq. (7) for an effective incentive mechanism in our framework.

For strategic users, the computations of the long-term expected payoff of giving a/an truthful or uncertain assessment in a time window are the same as Eqs. (4) and (5). Let γ denote the probability that a strategic user (S) guesses the right result of cloud performance. The long-term payoff the user can obtain by giving a strategic assessment in a time window is computed as follows:

$$v_S^\infty(L) = P + \delta\{\gamma[(1-\alpha)v^\infty(L) + \alpha v^\infty(0)] + \\ (1-\gamma)[\alpha v^\infty(L) + (1-\alpha)v^\infty(0)]\}. \tag{8}$$

Note that, we only consider the most beneficial case for a strategic user, i.e., a strategic assessment would not incur any cost of effort. Hence, without the consideration of the broker's payoffs, an incentive mechanism is said to be effective if it satisfies all the following constraints:

$$v_T^\infty(L) > v_U^\infty(L), v_U^\infty(L) > v_S^\infty(L) \text{ and } v_U^\infty(L) > v_{UT}^\infty(L). \tag{9}$$

Through straightforward calculations, $v_S^\infty(L) > v_{UT}^\infty(L)$ if and only if $\gamma\alpha < \frac{1}{2}$. In practice, α should usually be in the range of $(0, 0.5)$ (0.5 for random guessing), thus the third constraint in Eq. (9) can be omitted in most cases.

3.5 Optimal Incentive Mechanism

For a type of users and a broker, there may be many assessment scoring schemes with different parameters L and h_U to satisfy the constraints in Eq. (9). In order to find out which parameters are optimal, the total payoffs obtained by both the broker and a user should be analyzed. As only the users having the assessment score L can participate in the transactions of assessments, the total payoffs depend on the proportion of the active users in all users. Let $\eta(\theta)$ denote the proportion of the users having the score θ. Because a user's score is updated at the end of each time window, $\eta(\theta)$ would vary over time. As we assume that users care about their long-term payoffs, we analyze the stationary distribution of $\eta(\theta)$ for $\forall \theta \in \Theta$ if all users are honest. Hence, the stationary distribution can be defined according to the score transition probability in Eq. (2) as follows:

$$\begin{aligned}
\eta(L) &= \eta(L-1) + (1-\alpha)(1-\beta)\eta(L), \\
\eta(\theta) &= \eta(\theta-1), \text{ if } h_U < \theta < L, \\
\eta(h_U) &= \eta(h_U-1) + \beta\eta(L), \\
\eta(\theta) &= \eta(\theta-1), \text{ if } 0 < \theta < h_U, \\
\eta(0) &= \alpha(1-\beta)\eta(L), \\
\sum_\theta \eta(\theta) &= 1 \text{ and } \eta(\theta) \geqslant 0, \text{ for } \forall \theta.
\end{aligned} \tag{10}$$

Theorem 2 (Existence of a Stationary Distribution): Given the transition probabilities specified in Eq. (2), for any $\alpha \in [0, 0.5]$, $\beta \in [0, 1]$ and $L > h_U > 0$, there exists a unique stationary distribution satisfying Eq. (10). $\square$

Based on Theorem 2, we have the following property:

Property 2: Given the stationary distribution specified in Eq. (10), $\eta(L)$ monotonically increases with h_U and monotonically decreases with L. $\square$

Property 2 indicates that adjusting L and h_U can change the proportion of active users. The proportion can affect the broker and users' total benefits.

The expected total payoffs obtained by the broker and an honest user in a time window can be computed as follows:

$$\begin{aligned} U^* &= \eta(L) \times [(1 - \beta)(B - P + P - C) + \beta(-\lambda P + \lambda P)] \\ &= \eta(L) \times (1 - \beta)(B - C). \end{aligned} \tag{11}$$

Equation (11) illustrates that U monotonically increases with $\eta(L)$ and decreases with β. In addition, the expected payoff the broker can obtain from an honest user in a time window can be computed as follows:

$$U = \eta(L) \times [(1 - \beta)(B - P) - \beta\lambda P]. \tag{12}$$

Hence, an effective incentive mechanism in our framework should satisfy the constraints specified in Eq. (9) and ensure that the broker can obtain a positive expected payoff in a time window, which is defined as follows:

Definition 1 (Effective Incentive Mechanism): An incentive mechanism with the adjustable parameters L, h_U, λ and P is considered effective if it satisfies the following constraints:

$$v_T^\infty(L) > v_U^\infty(L), v_U^\infty(L) > v_S^\infty(L), v_U^\infty(L) > v_{UT}^\infty(L) \\ \text{and } U > 0. \tag{13}$$

In this paper, we consider maximizing the total payoffs U^* for an optimal incentive mechanism. Thus, we have the following definition:

Definition 2 (Optimal Incentive Mechanism): An effective incentive mechanism is considered optimal if U^* is the maximum for some L, h_U, λ and P.

Note that our work can be simply adjusted for satisfying other targets in any situation, e.g., maximizing the broker's payoff U.

3.6   Whitewashing

Whitewashing is a common problem for the reputation or score based incentive mechanisms [4, 23], which refers to the situation where a user can reset its reputation or score by repeatedly re-participating in the activity with new identities. In our scenario, if a user having a score less than L is isolated from assessment transactions, it may try to create a new identity for transactions and expect to come back sooner from the isolation. Here, we assume that a user cannot hold multiple identities at the same time.

By finding out suitable mechanism parameters (i.e., L, h_U and λ), our approach can prevent users from whitewashing. In order to solve this problem, a new user should not enter the assessment transactions instantly. It needs to wait for a period of time as an initializing period, and therefore cannot obtain any benefits. For a new user, an initial assessment score I is assigned. In order to prevent whitewashing, the initial score should satisfy the following constraint:

$$v^\infty(I) - v^\infty(\theta) \leqslant c_w, \text{ for } \forall \theta \in \Theta \text{ and } I \in \Theta, \tag{14}$$

where $c_w \geqslant 0$ is the cost of a user whitewashing, e.g., the cost of creating a new identity. The expression $v^\infty(I) - v^\infty(\theta)$ indicates the expected long-term gain of a user with the assessment score θ whitewashing. If the gain is no larger than the cost, a user would have no motivation to reset its score. Considering the worst case for preventing whitewashing, i.e., $c_w = 0$, as $v^\infty(0)$ is the smallest long-term expected payoff according to the statement (1) of Property 1, $I = 0$ (lowest) is always a solution of Eq. (14). Assigning the lowest score to a new user means it can only enter assessment transactions after an initializing period. That means a user with any assessment score cannot gain more payoffs by carrying out whitewashing.

4   Illustrative Results and Simulation Results

4.1   Parameter Analysis

In our framework, the parameters of an incentive mechanism (see Table 2) can be grouped into two classes. The first class includes the intrinsic parameters α, β, γ, δ, B and C. For a type of users and a broker, the intrinsic parameters should be fixed. Thus, an incentive mechanism designer cannot adjust these parameters for an optimal incentive mechanism. The second class includes the adjustable parameters P, λ, L and h_U, where P and λ may need to be conditionally adjusted according to the broker's requirement since they can affect the broker's payoffs. Due to space limitations, we only illustrate several main results.

Figure 2 illustrates the impact caused by α. The vertical axis of the left subfigure represents the percentage of effective incentive mechanisms in the total number of solutions. Here, we set that L is adjusted from 2 to 10 and λ increases from 0 to 1 by steps of 0.05. The vertical axis of the right sub-figure represents the stationary percentage of active users in the corresponding optimal incentive mechanism. Figure 2 shows that the number of effective incentive mechanisms and active users decrease with α. When α approaches nearly 0.4, there would not be any possible assessment scoring scheme which can be applied to building an effective incentive mechanism, thus the optimal total payoffs (U^*) would be 0. In addition, a larger β would bring a smaller number of active users since an honest user would more often be punished for giving more uncertain assessments. Note that, the maximum possible value of α should only be 0.5 (random guessing) and be much smaller in most of practical cases. In the literature, many approaches are proposed to improve the accuracy of judging assessments for service evaluation, e.g., [11,17]. Thus, the assumption of the error probability α in our approach is reasonable, so that our work can be applied in most circumstances.

Likewise, Fig. 3 shows that the number of effective incentive mechanisms decreases as γ increases. Even if γ reaches a very large value near 0.8, there still exist effective incentive mechanisms, but in those situations, U^* would become very low since the punishment for a strategic user with a high correctness probability should be more serious to prevent its guessing.

Figure 4 demonstrates the results when the price P is adjusted between C and B. When P is near C, the constraints specified in Eq. (9) can be hardly satisfied. Conversely, U would be negative when P reaches close to B. Thus, the number of active users would reach the maximum when $\frac{P-C}{B-C}$ is between 0.4 and 0.7 since more effective incentive mechanisms can be built based on such P.

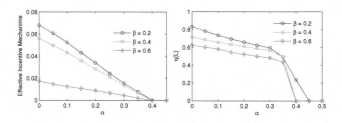

Fig. 2. Incentive mechanisms affected by α

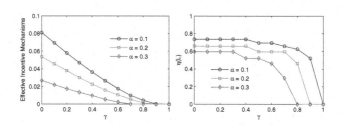

Fig. 3. Incentive mechanisms affected by γ

4.2 Simulation Experiments

Setting: since there are no suitable real environments supporting our framework, we have carried out simulation experiments and compared the simulation results with our theoretical results. We have simulated a cloud service environment containing many users, in which a user has its own strategies to provide assessments. Then, we set the same intrinsic parameters for both the simulation environment and the theoretical analysis, and compared the similarity

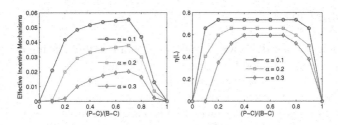

Fig. 4. Incentive mechanisms affected by P

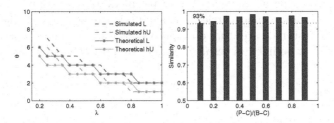

Fig. 5. Comparison between simulated results and theoretical results

between the two kinds of results. In the simulation experiments, a setting of the adjustable parameters is considered to build an effective incentive mechanism if, after a number of transactions of selling assessments, a user providing a smaller number of uncertain assessments would get a higher long-term payoff, and a user providing a proportion of uncertain assessments would get a higher long-term payoff than another user providing the same proportion of untruthful or strategic assessments.

Results and Analysis: the left sub-figure of Fig. 5 illustrates that the optimal L and h_U between the two kinds of results are very similar when adjusting λ. In some cases, L and h_U in these two kinds of results are not exactly equal since there are unavoidable computational errors in the simulation experiments when taking an action according to a specific probability. If some values of the constraints in Definition 1 are very small but still positive in some assessment scoring schemes, such schemes may be evaluated not to be able to make an effective incentive mechanism in the simulation experiments. Thus, the number of effective incentive mechanisms in the theoretical analysis is usually larger than that in the simulation experiments. According to the experimental results, the average rate between the latter number and the former one is approximately 75 %. Likewise, if the values of the constraints are negative but very near 0, such a scheme may be considered to be effective for an incentive mechanism. Even so, the experimental results show that at least 93 % of the effective incentive mechanisms in the simulation experiments are the same as those from the theoretical analysis. The right sub-figure of Fig. 5 shows such results when P is adjusted between C and B.

5 Conclusion

This paper has proposed a novel incentive mechanism for eliciting continual and truthful assessments in cloud environments. The main novelty is that, different from prior works, our incentive mechanism is compatible with uncertain assessments. Hence, it can protect a user's honesty by allowing it to give uncertain assessments in unavoidable situations. Through a suitable assessment scoring scheme, a user would have a dominant strategy (giving truthful assessments) and a second-best strategy (giving uncertain assessments). Meanwhile, the total payoffs of transacting assessments would be maximized. We have theoretically analyzed our approach and carried out simulation experiments. The proposed theoretical analysis indicates that our approach is feasible in most circumstances. The simulation experimental results strongly support the theoretical analysis.

References

1. Awerbuch, B., Patt-Shamir, B., Peleg, D., Tuttle, M.R.: Collaboration of untrusting peers with changing interests. In: ACM Conference on Electronic Commerce, pp. 112–119 (2004)
2. DiPalantino, D., Vojnovic, M.: Crowdsourcing and all-pay auctions. In: ACM Conference on Electronic Commerce, pp. 119–128 (2009)
3. Feldman, M., Papadimitriou, C.H., Chuang, J., Stoica, I.: Free-riding and white-washing in peer-to-peer systems. IEEE J. Sel. Areas Commun. **24**(5), 1010–1019 (2006)
4. Friedman, E.J., Resnick, P.: The social cost of cheap pseudonyms. J. Econ. Manage. Strategy **10**, 173–199 (2000)
5. Fudenberg, D., Tirole, J.: Game Theory. MIT Press, Cambridge (1991)
6. Jurca, R., Faltings, B.: Confess - an incentive compatible reputation mechanism for the online hotel booking industry. In: IEEE Conference on E-Commerce, pp. 205–212 (2004)
7. Jurca, R., Faltings, B.: Collusion-resistant, incentive-compatible feedback payments. In: ACM Conference on Electronic Commerce, pp. 200–209 (2007)
8. Jurca, R., Faltings, B.: Mechanisms for making crowds truthful. J. Artif. Intell. Res. (JAIR) **34**, 209–253 (2009)
9. Kandori, M.: Social norms and community enforcement. Rev. Econ. Stud. **59**(1), 63–80 (1992)
10. Lopez-Pintado, D.: The spread of free-riding behavior in a social network. East. Econ. J. **34**(4), 464–479 (2008)
11. Malik, Z., Bouguettaya, A.: RATEWeb: reputation assessment for trust establishment among web services. VLDB J. **18**(4), 885–911 (2009)
12. Mason, W.A., Watts, D.J.: Financial incentives and the "performance of crowds". SIGKDD Explor. **11**(2), 100–108 (2009)
13. Miller, N., Resnick, P., Zeckhauser, R.: Eliciting informative feedback: the peer-prediction method. Manage. Sci. **51**(9), 1359–1373 (2005)
14. Papaioannou, T.G., Stamoulis, G.D.: An incentives' mechanism promoting truthful feedback in peer-to-peer systems. In: 5th International Symposium on Cluster Computing and the Grid (CCGrid 2005), 9–12 May 2005, Cardiff, UK, pp. 275–283 (2005)

15. Qu, L., Wang, Y., Orgun, M.: Appendix: Proofs (2016). www.dropbox.com/s/yxpr7f1ot9zujam/appendix.pdf?dl=0
16. Qu, L., Wang, Y., Orgun, M.: A novel incentive mechanism for truthful performance assessments of cloud services. In: AAMAS, pp. 1325–1326 (2016)
17. Qu, L., Wang, Y., Orgun, M.A., Liu, L., Bouguettaya, A.: Cloud service selection based on contextual subjective assessment and objective assessment. In: AAMAS, pp. 1483–1484 (2014)
18. Qu, L., Wang, Y., Orgun, M.A., Liu, L., Liu, H., Bouguettaya, A.: CCCloud: context-aware and credible cloud service selection based on subjective assessment and objective assessment. IEEE T. Serv. Comput. 8(3), 369–383 (2015)
19. Witkowski, J.: Eliciting honest reputation feedback in a markov setting. In: IJCAI, pp. 330–335 (2009)
20. Witkowski, J., Parkes, D.C.: Peer prediction without a common prior. In: ACM Conference on Electronic Commerce, pp. 964–981 (2012)
21. Zhang, J., Cohen, R.: Design of a mechanism for promoting honesty in e-marketplaces. In: AAAI, pp. 1495–1500 (2007)
22. Zhang, J., Cohen, R., Larson, K.: A trust-based incentive mechanism for e-marketplaces. In: AAMAS-TRUST, pp. 135–161 (2008)
23. Zhang, Y., Park, J., van der Schaar, M.: Rating protocols in online communities. ACM Trans. Econ. Comput. 2(1), 4 (2014)
24. Zhang, Y., van der Schaar, M.: Reputation-based incentive protocols in crowd-sourcing applications. In: IEEE INFOCOM, pp. 2140–2148 (2012)
25. Zheng, Z., Wu, X., Zhang, Y., Lyu, M.R., Wang, J.: QoS ranking prediction for cloud services. IEEE Trans. Parallel Distrib. Syst. 24(6), 1213–1222 (2013)

Bi-level Identification of Web Service Defects

Hanzhang Wang[1], Marouane Kessentini[1(✉)], and Ali Ouni[2]

[1] Computer and Information Science Department, University of Michigan, Ann Arbor, USA
{hanzhang,marouane}@umich.edu
[2] Graduate School of Information Science and Technology, Osaka University, Suita, Japan
ali@ist.osaka-u.ac.jp

Abstract. Successful Web services must evolve to remain relevant (e.g. requirements update, bugs fix, etc.), but this process of evolution increases complexity and can cause the Web service interface design to decay and lead to significantly reduced usability and popularity of the services. Maintaining a high level of design quality is extremely expensive due to monetary and time pressures that force programmers to neglect improving the quality of their interfaces. A more fundamental reason is that there is little support to automatically identify design defects at the Web service interface level and reduce the high calibration effort to determine manually the threshold value for each quality metric to identify design defects. In this paper, we propose to treat the generation of interface design defects detection rules as a bi-level optimization problem. To this end, the upper level problem generates a set of detection rules, as combination of quality metrics, which maximizes the coverage of a base of defects examples extracted from several Web services and artificial defects generated by the lower level. The lower level maximizes the number of generated artificial defects that cannot be detected by the rules produced by the upper level. The statistical analysis of our experiments over 30 runs on a benchmark of 415 Web services shows that 8 types of Web service defects were detected with an average of more than 93 % of precision and 98 % recall. The results confirm the outperformance of our bi-level proposal compared to state-of-art Web service design defects detection techniques and the survey performed by potential users and programmers also shows the relevance of the detected defects.

Keywords: Web service interface · Design defects · Quality of services

1 Introduction

Web services have been emerging in recent years to become one of the most popular techniques for building service-based systems (SBSs) [1]. The implementation of these systems is highly relying on the operations selected from the interface of the employed Web services that are provided by several companies such as Fedex, eBay, Google, FedEx and PayPal [5]. Like any software project, the evolution of Web services may increase the complexity of the Web service interface design. However, maintaining a high level of Web service design quality is extremely expensive due to monetary and time pressures that force programmers to neglect improving the quality of their interfaces

© Springer International Publishing Switzerland 2016
Q.Z. Sheng et al. (Eds.): ICSOC 2016, LNCS 9936, pp. 352–368, 2016.
DOI: 10.1007/978-3-319-46295-0_22

that may leads to significantly reduced usability and popularity of the services. Thus, investigating quality of Web services is becoming more and more important. An example of well-known interface design defect is *God object Web service* (GOWS) [8] which implements a multitude of operations related to different business and technical abstractions in a single service leading to low cohesion of its methods and unavailability to end users because it is overloaded.

Unlike the area of object oriented design, there has been recently few studies focusing on the study of bad design practices for web services interface [3–5, 8]. The vast majority of these work relies on declarative rule specification. In these settings, rules are manually defined to identify the key symptoms that characterize an interface design defect using combinations of mainly quantitative metrics. For each possible interface design defect, rules that are expressed in terms of metric combinations need high calibration efforts to find the right threshold value for each metric. Another important issue is that translating symptoms into rules is not obvious because there is no consensual symptom-based definition of design defects [3]. These difficulties explain a large portion of the high false-positive rates reported in existing research [5]. Recently, a heuristic-based approach based on genetic programming [8] is used to generate design defects detection. However, such approaches require a high number of interface design defect examples (data) to provide efficient detection rules solutions. In fact, design defects are not usually documented by developers. In addition, it is challenging to ensure the diversity of the examples to cover most of the possible bad-practices.

In this work, we start from the hypothesis that the generation of efficient Web service defects detection rules heavily depends on the coverage and the diversity of the used defect examples. In fact, both mechanisms for the generation of detection rules and the generation of defect examples are dependent. Thus, the intuition behind this work is to generate examples of defects that cannot be detected by some possible detection solutions then adapting these rules-based solutions to be able to detect the generated defect examples. These two steps are repeated until reaching a termination criterion (e.g. number of iterations). To this end, we propose, for the first time, to consider the Web services defects detection problem as a bi-level one [6]. Bi-Level Optimization Problems (BLOPs) are a class of challenging optimization problems, which contain two levels of optimization tasks. The optimal solutions to the lower level problem become possible feasible candidates to the upper level problem.

In our adaptation, the upper level generates a set of detection rules, combination of quality metrics, which maximizes the coverage of the base of defect examples; and artificial defects are generated by the lower level. The lower level maximizes the number of generated "artificial" interface defects that cannot be detected by the rules produced by the upper level. The overall problem appears as a BLOP task, where for each generated detection rule, the upper level observes how the lower-level acts by generating artificial Web service interface defects that cannot be detected by the upper level rule, and then chooses the best detection rule which suits it the most, taking the actions of the defects generation process (lower level or follower) into account. The main advantage of our bi-level formulation is that the generation of detection rules is not limited to some interface defect examples identified manually that are difficult to collect but it allows the prediction of new interface defect behaviours that are different from those in the base of examples.

The primary contributions of this paper can be summarized as follows:

(1) The paper introduces a novel formulation of the Web services design defects detection as a bi-level problem.
(2) The paper reports the results of an empirical study with an implementation of our bi-level approach. The statistical analysis of our experiments over 30 runs on a benchmark of 415 Web services shows that 8 types of interface design defects were detected with an average of more than 93 % of precision and 98 % recall. The results confirm the outperformance of our bi-level proposal compared to state-of-art Web service design defects detection techniques [5, 8] and the survey performed by potential users and programmers also shows the relevance of detected defects.

The remainder of this paper is as follows: Sect. 2 presents the relevant background and the motivation for the presented work; Sect. 3 describes the search algorithm; an evaluation of the algorithm is explained and its results are discussed in Sect. 4; Sect. 5 is dedicated to related work. Finally, concluding remarks and future work are provided in Sect. 6.

2   Background

2.1   Web Service Interface Defects

Web service interface defects are defined as bad design choices that can have a negative impact on the interface quality such as maintainability, changeability and comprehensibility which may impacts the usability and popularity of services [1, 3]. They can be also considered as structural characteristics of the interface that may indicate a design problem that makes the service hard to evolve and maintain, and trigger refactoring [2]. In fact, most of these defects can emerge during the evolution of a service and represent patterns or aspects of interface design that may cause problems in the further development of the service. In general, they make a service difficult to change, which may in turn introduce bugs. It is easier to interpret and evaluate the quality of the interface design by identifying different defects definition than the use of traditional quality metrics. To this end, recent studies defined different types of Web services design defects [1–3]. In our experiments, we focus on the eight following Web service defect types:

– *God object Web service (GOWS):* implements a high number of operations related to different business and technical abstractions in a single service.
– *Fine grained Web service (FGWS):* is a too fine-grained service whose overhead (communications, maintenance, and so on) outweighs its utility.
– *Chatty Web service (CWS):* represents an antipattern where a high number of operations are required to complete one abstraction.
– *Data Web service (DWS):* contains typically accessor operations, i.e., getters and setters. In a distributed environment, some Web services may only perform some simple information retrieval or data access operations.

- *Ambiguous Web service (AWS):* is an antipattern where developers use ambiguous or meaningless names for denoting the main elements of interface elements (e.g., port types, operations, messages).
- *Redundant PortTypes (RPT):* is an antipattern where multiple portTypes are duplicated with the similar set of operations.
- *CRUDy Interface (CI):* is an antipattern where the design encourages services the RPC-like behavior by declaring create, read, update, and delete (CRUD) operations, e.g., createX(), readY(), etc.
- *Maybe It is Not RPC (MNR):* is an antipattern where the Web service mainly provides *CRUD*-type operations for significant business entities.

We choose these defect types in our experiments because they are the most frequent and hard to detect [4, 5, 8], cover different maintainability factors, due to the availability of defect examples and to compare the performance of our detection technique to existing studies [5, 8]. However, the proposed approach in this paper is generic and can be applied to any type of defects.

Table 1. List of metrics

Metric name	Definition
NPT	Number of port types
NOD	Number of operations declared
NAOD	Number of accessor operations declared
NOPT	Average number of operations in port types
ANIPO	Average number of input parameters in operations
ANOPO	Average number of output parameters in operations
NOM	Number of messages
NBE	number of elements of the schemas
NCT	Number of complex types
NST	Number of primitive types
NBB	Number of bindings
NBS	Number of services
NPM	Number of parts per message
NIPT	Number of identical port types
NIOP	Number of identical operations
COH	Cohesion
COU	Coupling
AMTO	Average meaningful terms in operation names
AMTM	Average meaningful terms in message names
AMTMP	Average meaningful terms in message parts
AMTP	Average meaningful terms in port-type names
ALOS	Average length of operations signature
ALPS	Average length of port-types signature
ALMS	Average length of message signature

The defects detection process consists in finding interface design fragments that violate structural or semantic properties such as the ones related to coupling and complexity. In this setting, internal attributes used to define these properties, are captured through several metrics, and properties are expressed in terms of valid values for these metrics. The list of metrics is described in Table 1.

In the following, we introduce some issues and challenges related to the detection of the Web service defects. Overall, there is no general consensus on how to decide if a particular design violates a quality heuristic. In fact, there is a difference between detecting symptoms and asserting that the detected situation is an actual design defect. Another issue is related to the definition of thresholds when dealing with quantitative information. For example, the *GOWS* defect detection involves information such as the interface size as illustrated in Fig. 1. Although we can measure the size of an interface, an appropriate threshold value is not trivial to define. An interface considered large in a given service/community of users could be considered average in another. The generation of detection rules requires a large defect example set to cover most of the possible bad-practice behaviors. Defects are not usually documented by developers (unlike bugs report and object oriented design). Thus, it is time-consuming and difficult to collect defects and inspect manually large Web services. In addition, it is challenging to ensure the diversity of the defect examples to cover most of the possible bad-practices then using these examples to generate good quality of detection rules.

Fig. 1. God object Web service (*GOWS*) example

To address the above-mentioned challenges, we propose to consider the Web service defects detection problem as a bi-level optimization problem.

2.2 Bi-level Optimization

Most studied real-world and academic optimization problems involve a single level of optimization. However, in practice, several problems are naturally described in two levels. These latter are called BLOPs [6]. In such problems, we find a nested optimization problem within the constraints of the outer optimization one. The outer optimization task is usually referred as the *upper level problem* or the *leader problem*. The nested inner optimization task is referred as the *lower level problem* or the *follower problem*, thereby referring the bi-level problem as a leader-follower problem or as a Stackelberg game. The follower problem appears as a constraint to the upper level, such that only an optimal solution to the follower optimization problem is a possible feasible candidate to the leader one.

BLOPs are intrinsically more difficult to solve than single-level problems, it is not surprising that most of existing studies to date has tackled the simplest cases of BLOPs, i.e., problems having nice properties such as linear, quadratic or convex objective and/ or constraint functions. In particular, the most studied instance of BLOPs has been for a long time is the linear case in which all objective functions and constraints are linear with respect to the decision variables.

3   Bi-level Identification of Web Services Design Defects

3.1   Approach Overview

As described in Fig. 2, Our bi-level formulation includes two levels as described in the previous section. At the upper level, the detection rules generation process has a main objective which is the generation of detection rules that can cover as much as possible the Web service defects in the base of examples. The defects generation process has one objective that is maximizing the number of generated artificial defects that cannot be

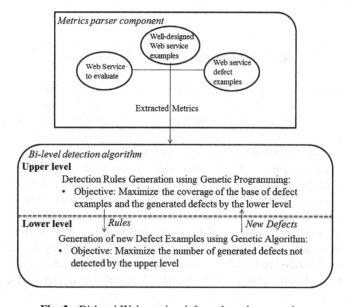

Fig. 2. Bi-level Web service defects detection overview

detected by the detection rules. The generated defects are dissimilar from the base of well-designed Web services design based on a defined distance using the different metrics. There is a hierarchy in the problem, which arises from the manner in which the two entities operate. The detection rules generation process has higher control of the situation and decides which detection rules for the defects generation process to operate in. It should be noted that in spite of different objectives appearing in the problem, it is not possible to handle such a problem as a simple multi-objective optimization task. The reason for this is that the leader cannot evaluate any of its own strategies without knowing the strategy of the follower, which it obtains only by solving a nested optimization problem.

The leader (upper level) takes as inputs a base (i.e. a set) of Web service defect examples, and takes, as controlling parameters, a set of metrics as described in Table 1 and generates as output a set of detection rules. The rule generation process selects randomly, from the list of possible metrics, a combination of quality metrics (and their threshold values) to detect a specific defect types. Consequently, the ideal solution is a set of rules that best detect the defects of the base of examples and those generated by the lower level. For example, the following rule of Fig. 3 states that a Web service s satisfying the following combination of metrics and thresholds is considered as a *GOWS* defect:

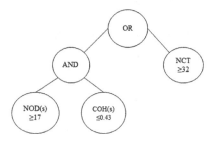

Fig. 3. Solution representation at the upper level

R1: **IF** *(NOD(s) ≥ 17 AND COH(s) ≤ 0.43) OR NCT ≥ 32,* **THEN** s = *GOWS*.

An upper-level detection rules solution is evaluated based on the coverage of the base of defect examples (input) and also the coverage of generated "artificial" Web service design defects by the lower-level problem. These two measures are used to be maximized by the population of detection rules solutions. The follower (lower level) uses a set of well-designed Web service examples to generate "artificial" defects based on the notion of deviation from a reference (well-designed) set of Web services. The generation process of artificial defect examples is performed using a heuristic search that maximizes on one hand, the distance between generated defects examples and reference code examples using the list of considered metrics and, on the other hand, maximizes the number of generated examples that are not detected by the leader (detection rules). As described in Fig. 4, the generated structure of defects are represented as a vector where each element is a (metric, threshold) pair that characterises the generated Web service.

NOD= 34	NCT= 64	NPT=104

Fig. 4. Solution representation at the lower level

There is no parallelism in our bi-level formulation. The upper level is executed for number iterations then the lower level for another number of iterations. After that the best solution found in the lower level will be used by the upper level to evaluate the associated solution (detection rules), and then this process in repeated several times until reaching a termination criterion (e.g. number of iterations). Thus, there is no parallelism since both levels are dependent.

Next, we describe our adaptation of bi-level optimization to the Web service defects detection problem in more details.

3.2 Bi-level Adaptation

At the upper level, the objective function is formulated to maximize the coverage of Web services defect examples (input) and also maximize the coverage of the generated artificial Web service defects at the lower level (best solution found in the lower level). Thus, the objective function at the upper level is defined as follows:

$$Maximize\ f_{upper} = \frac{\dfrac{Precision(SR,\ WSDefectExamples) + Recall(SR,\ WSDefectExamples)}{2} + \dfrac{\#detectedArtificialWSDefects}{\#artificialWSDefects}}{2}$$

It is clear that the evaluation of solutions (detection rules) at the upper level depends on the best solutions generated by the lower level (artificial Web service defects). Thus, the fitness function of solutions at the upper level is calculated after the execution of the optimization algorithm in the lower level at each iteration.

At the lower level, for each solution (detection rule) of the upper level an optimization algorithm is executed to generate the best set of artificial Web service defects that cannot be detected by the detection rules at the upper level. An objective function is formulated at the lower level to maximize the number of un-detected artificial defects that are generated and also maximize the distance with well-designed Web services. Formally,

$$Maximize\ f_{lower} = u + Min\left(\sum_{j=1}^{ms} \left| M_j(ArtificialDefect) - M_j(ReferenceExamples) \right| \right)$$

where ms is the number of structural metrics used to compare between artificial defects and the well-designed web services, M is a structural metric (such as the number of operations, etc.) and u is the number of artificial defects uncovered by the detection rule solution defined at the upper level.

For the GP algorithm (upper-level), the mutation operator can be applied to a function node (metric), or to a terminal node (logical operator) in our tree representation. It starts by randomly selecting a node in the tree. Then, if the selected node is a terminal (metric), it is replaced by another terminal (metric or another threshold value); if it is a function (AND-OR), it is replaced by a new function; and if tree mutation is to be carried out, the node and its sub-tree are replaced by a new randomly generated sub-tree. For the GA (lower-level), the mutation operator consists of randomly changing a metric in one of the vector dimension.

Regarding the crossover, two parent individuals are selected at the upper level, and a sub-tree is picked on each one. Then crossover swaps the nodes and their relative sub-trees from one parent to the other. This operator must ensure the respect of the depth limits. The crossover operator can be applied with only parents having the same rule category (defect type to detect). Each child, thus combines information from both parents. For the GA (lower-level), the crossover operator allows to create two offspring o_1 and o_2 from the two selected parents p_1 and p_2, where the first k elements of p_1 become the first k elements of o_1. Similarly, the first k elements of p_2 become the first k elements of o_2.

4 Experiments

4.1 Research Questions

In order to evaluate the feasibility and the performance of our bi-level (BLOP) approach comparing to existing Web service defects detection approaches, we addressed the following research questions:

RQ1: How does BLOP perform to detect different types of Web service defects? The goal of this research question is to quantitatively assess the completeness and correctness of our approach.

RQ2: How do BLOP perform compared to existing mono-level Web service defects detection algorithms? The goal is to evaluate the benefits of the use of a bi-level approach in the context of Web service defects detection.

RQ3: How does BLOP perform compared to the existing Web service defects detection approaches not based on the use of metaheuristic search?

RQ4: Can our approach be useful for developers during the development of software systems?

4.2 Experimental Setup

To evaluate the performance of our approach, we used an existing benchmark [5, 8] that includes a set of Web services from different categories as described in Table 2.

We considered the different antipattern types described in Sect. 2. We used a 10-fold cross validation procedure. We split our data into training data and evaluation data. For each fold, one category of services is evaluated by using the remaining nine categories as training examples. We use the two measures of precision and recall to evaluate the accuracy of our approach and to compare it with existing techniques [5, 8]. Precision denotes the ratio of true antipatterns detected to the total number of detected antipatterns, while recall indicates the ratio of true antipatterns detected to the total number of existing antipatterns.

Table 2. Used Web services in our experiments

Category	# services	# defects
Financial	94	67
Science	34	3
Search	37	13
Shipping	38	10
Travel	65	28
Weather	42	15
Media	19	14
Education	26	20
Messaging	29	22
Location	31	136

To answer RQ1, we use both recall and precision to evaluate the efficiency of our approach in identifying antipatterns. We also investigated the Web service defect types that were detected to find out whether there is a bias towards the detection of specific Web service defect types.

To answer RQ2, we investigate and report on the effectiveness of BLOP comparing to existing approaches. We implemented random search (RS) with the same used fitness functions used at the two levels. If an intelligent search method fails to outperform random search, then the proposed formulation is not adequate. In addition, we compared our bi-level algorithm to an existing mono-level and mono-objective approach where only examples of defects were considered [8] without the use of the lower level.

To answer RQ3, we compared our approach with the SODA-W approach of Palma et al. [5]. SODA-W manually translates Web services defect symptoms into detection rules based on a literature review of Web service design. All three approaches are tested on the same benchmark described in Table 2.

To answer RQ4, we used a post-study questionnaire that collects the opinions of developers on our detection tool and Web service defects. To this end, we asked 31 software developers, including 17 professional developers working on the development of services-based application and 14 graduate students form the University of Michigan. The experience of these subjects on web development and Web services ranged from 2 to 16 years. All the graduate students have an industrial experience of at least 2 years with large-scale systems especially in automotive industry.

4.3 Parameters Tuning

We performed a set of experiments using several population sizes: 30, 40 and 50. The stopping criterion was set to 500,000 fitness evaluations. We used a high number of evaluations as a stopping criterion since our bi-level approach requires involves two levels of optimization. Each algorithm was executed 30 times with each configuration and then comparison between the configurations was performed based on precision and recall using the Wilcoxon test with a 95 % confidence level ($\alpha = 5$ %). The other parameters setting were fixed by trial and error and are as follows: (1) crossover probability = 0.6; mutation probability = 0.4 where the probability of gene modification is 0.2. Both lower-level and upper-level are run each with a population of 40 individuals and 50 generations.

4.4 Results

The results for the first research question RQ1 are presented in Table 3. The obtained results show that we were able to detect most of the expected antipatterns in the different categories with a median precision higher than 96 %. The highest precision value for *Science* (100 %) can be explained by the fact that these Web services contain the lowest number of Web service defects. For the Web service *Location*, the precision is the lowest one (89 %), but is still an acceptable score. It could be explained by the nature of the antipatterns involved which are typically data or chatty Web services. These antipatterns are likely to be difficult to detect using metrics alone. Similar observations are valid for the recall. The obtained results indicate that our approach is able to achieve an average recall of more 93 %. The highest values (after the Science category) were recorded for *Location* services with 98 % where most of the expected defects are detected but with the lowest precision. The lowest recall score was achieved the *Financial* services (92 %). Indeed, these Web services contain the highest number of expected defects to be detected. Figures 5 and 6 confirm that our detection rules can detect different types of Web service defects with almost similar scores of precision and recall. Thus, the quality of the detection rules are good for almost all the defect types considered in our experiments. Overall, all the 8 antipattern types are detected with good precision and recall scores (more than 89 %). This could be explained by the diverse set of generated defects by the lower level leading to a better coverage of possible defects to detect. This ability to identify different types of Web service defects underlines a key strength to our approach. Most other existing detection techniques rely heavily on the notion of size to

Table 3. Median precision and recall results based on 30 runs

Category	Precision	Recall
Financial	96	92
Science	100	100
Search	97	94
Shipping	98	96
Travel	94	96
Weather	93	97
Media	98	94
Education	96	96
Messaging	94	97
Location	89	98

detect defects. This is reasonable considering that some Web service defects like the *GOWS* are associated with the notion of size. For defects like *AWS*, however, the notion of size is less important, and this makes this type of defect hard to detect using structural information. Thus, we can conclude that our BLOP approach detects well all the types of considered antipatterns (RQ1).

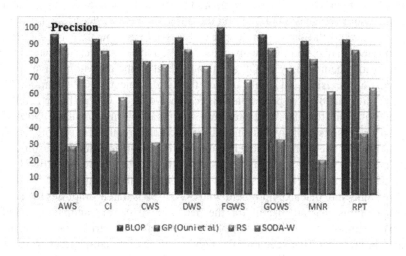

Fig. 5. Median precision value over 30 runs on all the 10 Web service categories using the different detection techniques with a 95 % confidence level ($\alpha < 5$ %)

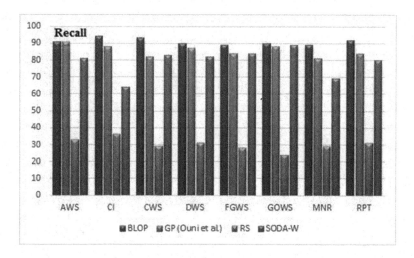

Fig. 6. Median recall value over 30 runs on all the 10 Web service categories using the different detection techniques with a 95 % confidence level ($\alpha < 5$ %)

The goal of research questions RQ2 and RQ3 is to investigate how well BLOP performs against random search (RS), an existing mono-level and single-objective approach (GP) [8] where only defect examples are used (without the consideration of the lower-level algorithm), and an existing detection tool (SODA-W) [5] not based on computational search. Figures 5 and 6 report the average comparative results. Over 30 runs, RS did not perform well when compared to BLOP both in terms of precision and recall achieving average around 30 % on the different Web services. The main reason could be related to the large search-space of possible combinations of metrics and threshold values to explore, and the diverse set of Web service defects to detect. Furthermore, the results achieved by BLOP are also better than the mono-objective approach [8] in terms of precision and recall. In fact, the single-objective GP technique has an average of 86 % and 87 % of precision and recall however BLOP has better scores with an average of more than 93 % of precision and recall on most of the different Web services. These results confirm that an intelligent search is required to explore the search space and that the use of the two levels improved the obtained detection results.

While SODA-W shows promising results with an average precision of 71 % and recall of 83 % (Figs. 5 and 6), it is still less than BLOP in all the eight considered defect types. We conjecture that a key problem with SODA-W is that it simplifies the different notions/symptoms that are useful for the detection of certain antipatterns. Indeed, SODA-W is limited to a smaller set of WSDL interface metrics comparing to our approach. In an exhaustive scenario, the number of possible antipatterns to manually characterize with rules can be large, and rules that are expressed in terms of metric combinations need substantial calibration efforts to find the suitable threshold value for each metric. However, our approach needs only some examples of defects to generate detection rules.

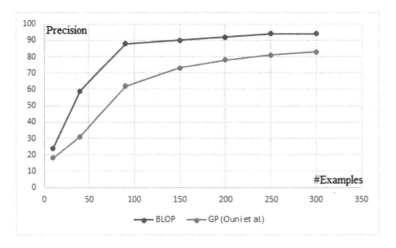

Fig. 7. The impact of the number of Web service defect examples on the quality of the results (Precision on the *Financial* Web services).

One of the advantages of using our BLOP adaptation is that the developers do not need to provide a large set of examples to generate the detection rules. In fact, the lower-level optimization can generate examples of Web service defects that are used to evaluate the detection rules at the upper level. Figure 7 shows that BLOP requires a low number of manually identified defects to provide good detection rules with reasonable precision scores. The existing mono-level work of Ouni et al. [8] (GP) require a higher number of defect examples than BLOP to generate good quality of detection rules. We can conclude, based on the obtained results that our BLOP approach outperforms, in average, an existing mono-level search technique [8] and an approach not based on heuristic search [5] (response to RQ2 and RQ3).

To answer RQ4, subjects were first asked to fill out a pre-study questionnaire containing five questions. The questionnaire helped to collect background information such as their role within the company, their programming experience, their familiarity with Web services and web-based applications. The first part of the questionnaire includes questions to evaluate the relevance of some detected Web service defects using the following scale: 1. Not at all relevant; 2. Slightly relevant; 3. Moderately relevant; and 4. Extremely relevant. If a detected Web service defect is considered relevant then this is mean that the developer considers that it is important to fix it. The second part of the questionnaire includes questions for those defects that are considered at least "moderately relevant", we asked the subjects to specify their usefulness based on the following list: 1. Refactoring guidance; 2. Quality assurance; 3. Bug prediction; 4. Web service stability; and 4. Web service selection. During the entire process, subjects were encouraged to think aloud and to share their opinions, issues, detailed explanations and ideas with the organizers of the study and not only answering the questions.

Figure 8 illustrates that only less than 16 % of detected Web service defects are considered not at all relevant by the developers. Around 67 % of the defects are considered as moderately or extremely relevant by the developers. This confirms the importance of the detected Web service defects for developers that they need to fix them for a better quality of their systems. It is also important to evaluate the usefulness of the detected Web service defects for the users. Figure 9 shows that the main usefulness is

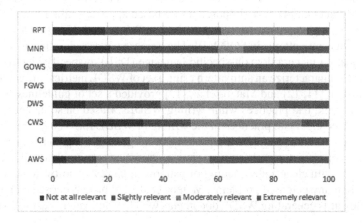

Fig. 8. The relevance of detected Web service defects evaluated by the subjects.

related to the Web services selection. In fact, most of the developers of service-based systems that we interviewed found that the detected defects give relevant advices about which service to select when several options are available. The users prefer, in general, to select services that are stable and have lower risk to include quality issues or bugs. However, we believe that we cannot generalize the results of our survey due to the limited number of participants.

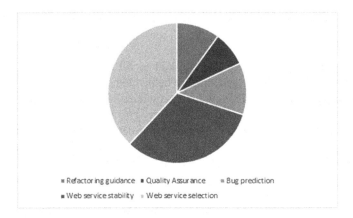

Fig. 9. The usefulness of detected Web service defects evaluated by the subjects.

5   Related Work

Detecting and specifying antipatterns in SOA and Web services is a relatively new area. The first book in the literature was written by Dudney et al. [1] and provides informal definitions of a set of Web service antipatterns. More recently, Rotem-Gal-Oz described the symptoms of a range of SOA antipatterns [2]. Furthermore, Král and Žemlicka [3] listed seven "popular" SOA antipatterns that violate accepted SOA principles. In addition, a number of research works have addressed the detection of such antipatterns. Recently, Moha et al. [4] have proposed a rule-based approach called SODA for SCA systems (Service Component Architecture). Later, Palma et al. [5] extended this work for Web service antipatterns in SODA-W. The proposed approach relies on declarative rule specification using a domain-specific language (DSL) to specify/identify the key symptoms that characterize an antipattern using a set of WSDL metrics. In another study, Rodriguez et al. [11, 12] and Mateos et al. [13] provided a set of guidelines for service providers to avoid bad practices while writing WSDLs. Based on some heuristics, the authors detected eight bad practices in the writing of WSDL for Web services. In other work [14], the authors presented a repository of 45 general antipatterns in SOA. The goal of this work is a comprehensive review of these antipatterns that will help developers to work with clear understanding of patterns in phases of software development and so avoid many potential problems. Mateos et al. [15] have proposed an interesting approach towards generating WSDL documents with less antipatterns using text mining techniques.

Recently, Ouni et al. [6, 8] proposed a search-based approach based on standard GP to find regularities, from examples of Web service antipatterns, to be translated into detection rules. However, the proposed approach can deal only with Web service interface metrics and cannot consider all Web service antipattern symptoms. Similar to [5], the latter did not consider the deviation from common design practices which leads to several false positives.

6   Conclusion and Future Work

In this paper, we have proposed a bi-level evolutionary optimization approach for the problem of Web service defects detection. The upper-level optimization produces a set of detection rules, which are combinations of quality metrics, with the goal to maximize the coverage of not only a defect examples base but also a lower-level population of artificial defects. The lower-level optimization tries to generate artificial Web service defects that cannot be detected by the upper-level detection rules, thereby emphasizing the generation of broad-based and fitter rules. The statistical analysis of the obtained results over an existing benchmark have shown the competitiveness and the outperformance of our proposal in terms of precision and recall over a single-level genetic programming [8] and a non-search-based approach [5]. As part of our future work, we are planning to extend the current work by proposing a bi-level approach for the correction of Web service defects. Furthermore, owe will propose several new measures that can be used to rank the detected Web service defects by our rules. Finally, we will extend our experiments by considering a larger set of subjects, defects and Web services.

References

1. Dudney, B., Krozak, J.K., Asbury, S., Osborne, D.: J2EE Antipatterns, 1st edn. Wiley, Hoboken (2003)
2. Rotem-Gal-Oz, A., Bruno, E., Dahan, U.: SOA Patterns, pp. 38–62. Manning Publications, Greenwich (2012)
3. Král, J., Žemlicka, M., Popular SOA antipatterns. In: Future Computing, Service Computation, Cognitive, Adaptive, Content, Patterns, pp. 271–276. IEEE (2009)
4. Moha, N., Palma, F., Nayrolles, M., Conseil, B.J., Guéhéneuc, Y.-G., Baudry, B., Jézéquel, J.-M.: Specification and detection of SOA antipatterns. In: Liu, C., Ludwig, H., Toumani, F., Yu, Q. (eds.) Service Oriented Computing. LNCS, vol. 7636, pp. 1–16. Springer, Heidelberg (2012)
5. Palma, F., Moha, N., Tremblay, G., Guéhéneuc, Y.-G.: Specification and detection of SOA antipatterns in web services. In: Avgeriou, P., Zdun, U. (eds.) ECSA 2014. LNCS, vol. 8627, pp. 58–73. Springer, Heidelberg (2014)
6. Bard, J.: Practical Bilevel Optimization: Algorithms and Applications, vol. 30. Kluwer, Dordrecht (1998)
7. Giri, B.K., Hakanen, J., Miettinen, K., Chakraborti, N.: Genetic programming through bi-objective genetic algorithms with a study of a simulated moving bed process involving multiple objectives. Appl. Soft Comput. 13(5), 2613–2623 (2013)
8. Ouni, A., Kessentini, M., Inoue, K.: Search-based web service antipatterns detection. In: IEEE Transactions on Services Computing, pp. 1–21. IEEE (2016, to appear)

9. Frakes, W.B., Baeza-Yates, R. (eds.): Information Retrieval: Data Structures and Algorithms. Prentice-Hall, Inc., Upper Saddle River (1992)
10. Rodriguez, J.M., Crasso, M., Mateos, C., Zunino, A.: Best practices for describing, consuming, and discovering web services: a comprehensive toolset. Softw. Pract. Experience **43**(6), 613–639 (2013)
11. Rodriguez, J.M., Crasso, M., Zunino, A., Campo, M.: Automatically detecting opportunities for web service descriptions improvement. In: Cellary, W., Estevez, E. (eds.) Software Services for e-World. IFIP AICT, vol. 341, pp. 139–150. Springer, Heidelberg (2010)
12. Ankur, S., Pekka, M., Anton, F., Kalyanmoy, D.: Multi-objective Stackelberg game between a regulating authority and a mining company: a case study in environmental economics. In: IEEE Congress on Evolutionary Computation, Cancun, Mexico, pp. 478–485 (2013)
13. Mateos, C., Zunino, A., Coscia, J.L.O.: Avoiding WSDL bad practices in code-first web services. SADIO Electron. J. Inf. Oper. Res. **11**(1), 31–48 (2012)
14. Torkamani, M.A., Bagheri, H.: A systematic method for identification of anti-patterns in service oriented system development. Int. J. Electr. Comput. Eng. **4**(1), 16–23 (2014)
15. Mateos, C., Rodriguez, J.M., Zunino, A.: A tool to improve code-first web services discoverability through text mining techniques. Softw. Pract. Experience **45**(7), 925–948 (2015)

Service Recommandation

Meta-Path Based Service Recommendation in Heterogeneous Information Networks

Tingting Liang[1(✉)], Liang Chen[2], Jian Wu[1], Hai Dong[2],
and Athman Bouguettaya[2]

[1] College of Computer Science and Technology, Zhejiang University,
Hangzhou, China
{liangtt,wujian2000}@zju.edu.cn
[2] School of Computer Science and Information Technology, RMIT,
Melbourne, Australia
{liang.chen,Hai.dong,athman.bouguettaya}@rmit.edu.au

Abstract. In the scenario of service recommendation, there are multiple object types (e.g. services, mashups, categories, contents and providers) and rich relationships among these objects, which naturally constitute a heterogeneous information network (HIN). In this paper, we propose to recommend services for mashup creation by exploiting different types of relationships in service related HIN. Specifically, we first introduce meta-path based measure for similarity estimation between mashups along different types of paths in HIN. We then design a recommendation model based on collaborative filtering and meta-path based similarities, and employ Bayesian ranking based optimization algorithm for model learning. Comprehensive experiments based on real data demonstrate the effectiveness of the HIN based service recommendation approach.

1 Introduction

The increasing adoption of Service-Oriented Architecture (SOA) leads to a surge of services in forms of Web services, cloud services, APIs, mashups, etc. As a consequence, several service repositories, such as ProgrammableWeb (PW)[1] and Mashape[2], have emerged to incessantly accumulate services and their compositions in recent years. As a web application generated through service composition, mashup has become a popular technique for integrating applications and data over the Web. However, creating a mashup may be difficult and time consuming for inexperienced developer due to the increasing presence and adoption of services on the Internet. Therefore, how to effectively recommend and select services for mashup creation is becoming an urgent problem.

Previous studies for service recommendation and selection can be mainly classified into several categories which are respectively based on semantic similarity [5,7], collaborative filtering (CF) technique [4,14], and quality of services

---

[1] ProgrammableWeb: http://www.programmableweb.com.
[2] Mashape: https://www.mashape.com.

© Springer International Publishing Switzerland 2016
Q.Z. Sheng et al. (Eds.): ICSOC 2016, LNCS 9936, pp. 371–386, 2016.
DOI: 10.1007/978-3-319-46295-0_23

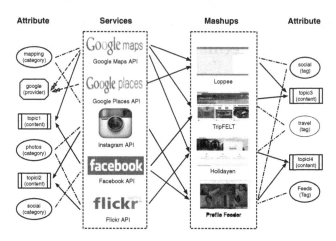

Fig. 1. A heterogeneous information network organized by objects and relationships in the scenario of service recommendation for mashup creation

(QoS) [6,19]. The limitation of semantics-based and CF-based methods is mainly caused by the singleness of employed data. The drawback of QoS-based recommendation approach is that the QoS information is not always available, which limits its generalization ability [17]. Recently, some studies try to recommend services by exploiting information network analysis [3,9]. However, most of information network-based methods only utilize a single type of relationship, e.g., composition relationship between services and mashups.

In reality, service recommender system generally includes multiple object types (e.g. services, mashups, and related attributes) and rich relationships among those objects, which naturally constitute a HIN. An illustration of a HIN in the scenario of service recommendation can be seen in Fig. 1. In this example, except for services, mashups, and the service-mashup interaction relationships, there exist many other object types (e.g. categories, contents, providers, and tags) and kinds of relationships among objects. For instance, *Instagram* and *flickr* are connected as they belong to the same category (*photos*); both of *TripFELT* and *Holidayen* are tagged by *travel*. Moreover, the paths composed by multiple relationships in the HIN have different semantics, based on which similarities with different meanings between objects can be evaluated. For example, *Google maps* and *Google places* can be considered similar as they belong to the same category (*mapping*), from another perspective, they are similar because of the same service provider. Refer to the traditional CF idea, service recommendation based on the similarity between mashups is workable because the recommended service meets the need of target mashup which has the similar demand with mashups having interactions with the service. The more detailed discovery of different semantics of paths can be found in Sect. 3.1. The combination of objects similarities with different semantics can improve the recommendation quality since allround demands of mashups for services are considered.

In this paper, we propose a meta-path based service recommendation approach called PaSRec for mashup creation. PaSRec effectively combines the heterogeneous relationship information to generate a service recommendation model and provides high-quality recommendation results with model learning algorithm. Specifically, we first introduce the meta-path based similarity measurement, based on which the similarities between objects along different paths in HIN are calculated. Considering the fact that the services employed by a mashup should be complementary but not similar with each other, we compute the similarities between mashups. By setting multiple meta-paths, a recommendation model is proposed to combine heterogeneous information referring to the idea of collaborative filtering. We adopt a Bayesian ranking based optimization algorithm [12] to learn the model with implicit feedback data. Note that the feedback in service recommendation is implicit since mashups employ services without expressing their tastes explicitly (e.g. ratings). Experiments on a real world dataset crawled from PW are implemented for the demonstration of the effectiveness of PaSRec.

In particular, the main contributions of our paper are summarized as follows:

1. We propose a service recommendation approach called PaSRec for mashup creation by exploiting service related heterogeneous information network, which is first proposed in the field of service recommendation.
2. We introduce a meta-path based similarity measurement to build a service recommendation model, and adopt a Bayesian ranking based optimization algorithm to learn it with implicit feedback data.
3. Empirical studies based on a real world dataset crawled from PW demonstrate the power of the proposed PaSRec.

The remainder of paper is structured as follows. Section 2 introduces the background and preliminaries of this work. The the meta-path based recommendation model and model learning algorithm are described in Sect. 3. Section 4 illustrates the concrete evaluation process and performance analysis. Finally, we discuss related work in Sect. 5 and make a conclusion in Sect. 6.

2   Background and Preliminaries

In this section, we present the background and some preliminary knowledge of this study.

2.1   Heterogeneous Information Network

An information network represents an abstraction of the real world, focusing on the objects and the interactions among these objects. Refer to [15], an information network is defined as follows.

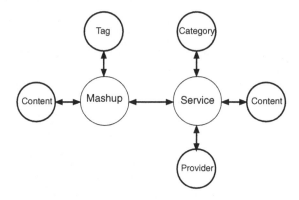

Fig. 2. Network schema of service network

Definition 1 *(Information Network). An information network is defined as a directed graph $G = (\mathcal{V}, \mathcal{E})$ with an object type mapping function $\varphi : \mathcal{V} \to \mathcal{A}$ and a relationship type mapping function $\psi : \mathcal{E} \to \mathcal{R}$, where each object $v \in \mathcal{V}$ belongs to one particular object type $\varphi(v) \in \mathcal{A}$, each link $e \in \mathcal{E}$ belongs to a particular relationship type $\psi(e) \in \mathcal{R}$. If two links belong to the same relationship type, the two links share the same starting object type as well as the ending object type.*

Different from the traditional network definition, we explicitly distinguish object types and relationship types in the network. The information network is called **heterogeneous information network** if the types of objects $|\mathcal{A}| > 1$ or the types of relationships $|\mathcal{R}| > 1$; otherwise, it is a **homogeneous information network**. As mentioned in Sect. 1, Fig. 1 shows an example of heterogeneous information network in service recommender system.

For better understanding the object types and relationship types in a complex heterogeneous information network, it is essential to provide the meta-level (schema-level) description of the network. Therefore, the concept of network schema is proposed as follows to describe the meta structure of a network.

Definition 2 *(Network Schema). The network schema, denoted as $T_G = (\mathcal{A}, \mathcal{R})$, is a meta template for a heterogeneous network $G = (\mathcal{V}, \mathcal{E})$ with the object type mapping $\varphi : \mathcal{V} \to \mathcal{A}$ and the link type mapping $\psi : \mathcal{E} \to \mathcal{R}$, which is a directed graph defined over object types $\mathcal{A}$, with edges as relationships from $\mathcal{R}$.*

Network schema identifies how many types of objects there are in the heterogeneous information network and where the links exist.

For the network in service recommender system described in Sect. 1, the network schema is shown as Fig. 2. Links exist between services and mashups denoting the composing or composed-by relationships, between contents and mashups denoting describing or described-by relationships, between providers and services denoting providing or provided-by relationships, etc. In addition, two objects in a network can be connected via different paths and these paths have different meanings. For instance, mashups can be connected via "Mashup-Service-Mashup" (M-S-M) path, "Mashup-Tag-Mashup" (M-T-M) path, "Mashup-Service-Category-Service-Mahsup" (M-S-Ca-S-M) path and so on. These paths are called meta-paths that are the combinations of a sequence of relations between object types.

2.2   Meta-Path Based Similarity

Refer to [16], the meta-path based similarity is defined as follows.

Definition 3 *(Meta-Path based Similarity). Given a symmetric meta path $\mathcal{P}$, the meta-path based similarity between two objects of the same type x and y is:*

$$s(x, y) = \frac{2 \times |\{p_{x \to y} : p_{x \to y} \in \mathcal{P}\}|}{|\{p_{x \to x} : p_{x \to x} \in \mathcal{P}\}| + |\{p_{y \to y} : p_{y \to y} \in \mathcal{P}\}|} \tag{1}$$

where $p_{x \to y}$ is a path instance between object x and y.

The similarity $s(x, y)$ is defined in terms of two parts: (1) their connectivity is defined by the number of paths between them following $\mathcal{P}$; (2) the balance of their visibility which is defined as the number of paths between themselves.

3   Services Recommendation Method PaSRec

In this section, we illustrate the proposed service recommendation method for mashup creation called PaSRec. PaSRec includes a meta-path based recommendation model and a model learning algorithm with implicit feedback data, which are described in Sects. 3.1 and 3.2, respectively.

3.1   Meta-Path Based Recommendation Model

This subsection proposes a meta-path based services recommendation model for mashup creation. Considering the fact that the services employed for a mashup should be complementary but not similar with each other, we compute the similarity between mashups for our recommendation model. Specifically, the model first evaluates the meta-path based similarity of mashups, and infers the predicted scores of candidate services according to the similar mashups of the target mashup. It should be noted that the meta-paths between mashups have different semantics. For example, "Mashup-Service-Mashup" (M-S-M) means mashups that are composed by the same services with the target mashup. Following that path, it will recommend services used for mashups having the similar composition with the target mashup. Another example is that "Mashup-Service-Category-Service-Mashup" (M-S-Ca-S-M) means mashups that are composed by the services belonging to the same category with that of the target mashup. According to M-S-Ca-S-M, it will recommend services that are classified to the same categories with components of the target mashup. Table 1 demonstrates the other representative paths and their semantic meanings. Note that for M-Co-M and

Table 1. The meanings of representative meta paths

No.	Meta-Path	Semantic meaning
1	M-S-M	mashups that are composed by the same services with the target mashup
2	M-T-M	mashups that are labeled by the same tags with the target mashup
3	M-Co-M	mashups that have the same topics extracted from contents with the target mashup
4	M-S-Ca-S-M	mashups that are composed by the services belonging to the same categories with that of the target mashup
5	M-S-Co-S-M	mashups that are composed by the services having the same topics extracted from contents with that of the target mashup
6	M-S-P-S-M	mashups that are composed by the services offered by the same providers with that of the target mashup

M-S-Co-S-M, "Co" represents the content (description) of services (mashups). As content of each service (mashup) is unique, we try to extract topics from content by Latent Dirichlet Allocation (LDA) model [1] and connect two services (mashups) through those topics. Based on different meta-paths, the mashups can receive quite different recommended service lists. How to effectively integrate these recommendation results generated by different meta-paths is a critical problem.

By measuring the meta-path based similarity of mashups, we can find the similar mashups to a target mashup with a given path. Refer to the idea of collaborative filtering, the rating of the target mashup on a service can be inferred depending on the ratings of its similar mashups on the service. Under a meta-path $\mathcal{P}_l$, the predicted rating of a mashup m on a service i, denoted as $r^{(l)}(m, i)$ can be calculated as follows,

$$r^{(l)}(m, i) = \sum_{n \in D(m,K) \cap N(i)} s^{(l)}(m, n) r(n, i), \qquad (2)$$

where $D(m, K)$ is a set of K mashups that are most similar with mashup m, $N(i)$ denotes a set of mashups having been composed by service i, $s^{(l)}(m, n)$ is the similarity of mashup m and n under meta-path $\mathcal{P}_l$, and $r(n, i)$ denotes the rating score of mashup n on service i. Note that feedback in the scenario of service recommendation is not explicit but implicit and $r(n, i) = 1$.

By repeating the process formulated as Eq. (2) under all L meta-paths, we can obtain L predicted ratings of a mashup m on a service i. The different predicted ratings under diverse meta-paths may have different importance. For example, services may be more likely to be used for mashup creation because of their topics rather than their providers. With this intuition, the final predicted rating under all meta-paths, denoted as $r(m, i)$, can be generated by the weighted sum of predicted ratings under L meta-paths,

$$r(m, i) = \sum_{l=1}^{L} \theta^{(l)} \cdot r^{(l)}(m, i), \tag{3}$$

where $\theta^{(l)}$ denotes the weight for the predicted rating of a mashup on a service under meta-path $\mathcal{P}_l$.

With the recommendation model as shown in Eq. (3), we can predict recommendation scores of all services and accordingly rank these services for a given mashup. The estimation of the parameters in the recommendation model would be presented in the next subsection.

3.2   Learning Model with Implicit Feedback

In this subsection, we introduce a learning algorithm for the proposed meta-path based recommendation model. The recommendation model takes advantage of the heterogeneous relationships in information network. Specifically, we intend to integrate meta-path based similarities with parameters indicating the importance of the corresponding paths in a HIN.

Since the feedback generated by mashups in the scenario of service recommendation is not explicit, we use these implicit feedbacks as training data. Inspired by [18], we introduce BPR method [12] which is widely accepted in implicit feedback recommendation to learn the proposed model. We set value 1 for positive (observed) feedback (mashups have been composed by services) in implicit feedback data while set the value 0 for a mixture of negative feedback (services are not appropriate for the composition of mashups) and unobserved potential interactions (mashups are not aware of such services). Then an objective function is defined to rank mashups with 1 values higher than those with 0 values for each service. The assumption is that services are more likely to be used for the mashups with value 1 in training data than the rest of the mashups.

Bayesian Ranking Based Optimization. Let M be the set of all mashups and S be the set of all services. We use $>_i \subset M^2$ to denote a total ranking of all mashups for service i. $m >_i n$ certainly represents service i is more appropriate for the creation of mashup m than that of n. The Bayesian formulation of finding the optimal ranking for all mashups is to maximize the posterior probability as follows,

$$p(\theta| >_i) \propto p(>_i |\theta)p(\theta), \tag{4}$$

where $\theta = \{\theta_1, ..., \theta_L\}$ denotes the model parameters, and $p(>_i |\theta)$ represents the probability that all mashup pairs can be ranked correctly.

We assume the services are chosen independently by mashups and the ordering of each pair of mashups (m, n) for a specific service is independent. Thus, the likelihood function $p(>_i |\theta)$ can be represented as a product of single densities and then be combined for all service $i \in S$ as follows,

$$\prod_{i \in S} p(>_i |\theta) = \prod_{(i,m,n) \in Z} p(m >_i n|\theta), \tag{5}$$

where $Z \subset S \times M \times M$ denotes the set of triples (i, m, n) where feedback of mashup m on service i is positive and value of mashup n on i is 0.

We formulate $p(m >_i n|\theta)$ as:

$$p(m >_i n|\theta) = \sigma(r(m, i) - r(n, i)), \tag{6}$$

where σ is the logistic sigmoid function $\sigma(x) = \frac{1}{1+e^{-x}}$.

We introduce normal distribution with zero mean and variance-covariance matrix $\Sigma_\theta = \lambda I$ as the prior density $p(\theta)$. Based on the likelihood and probability discussed above, the objective function can be derived as follows,

$$
\begin{aligned}
OPT &= -\mathrm{ln}p(\theta| >_i) = -\mathrm{ln}p(>_i |\theta)p(\theta) \\
&= -\mathrm{ln} \prod_{(i,m,n) \in Z} p(m >_i n|\theta)p(\theta) \\
&= - \sum_{(i,m,n) \in Z} \mathrm{ln}p(m >_i n|\theta) + \lambda \|\theta\|_2^2 \\
&= - \sum_{(i,m,n) \in Z} \mathrm{ln}\sigma(r(m, i) - r(n, i)) + \lambda \|\theta\|_2^2,
\end{aligned}
\tag{7}
$$

where λ is a model specific regularization parameter.

With the minimization of objective function OPT, the recommendation parameter θ can be learned from the implicit feedback data.

Learning Algorithm. As Eq. (7) is differentiable, gradient descent based algorithms are obvious choices to estimate parameter θ. In this paper, we employ the stochastic gradient descent (SGD) method [2] to learn the parameters for evaluation. The gradient of Eq. (7) with respect to θ is:

$$
\begin{aligned}
\frac{\partial OPT}{\partial \theta} &= - \sum_{(i,m,n) \in Z} \frac{\partial}{\partial \theta}\mathrm{ln}\sigma(r_{mn,i}) + \frac{\lambda}{2}\frac{\partial}{\partial \theta}\|\theta\|_2^2 \\
&= - \sum_{(i,m,n) \in Z} \frac{e^{-r_{mn,i}}}{1 + e^{-r_{mn,i}}}\frac{\partial}{\partial \theta}r_{mn,i} + \lambda\theta,
\end{aligned}
\tag{8}
$$

where $r_{mn,i} = r(m, i) - r(n, i)$.

The whole process of service recommendation PaSRec can be found in Algorithm 1. The time complexity of PaSRec is analyzed as follows. PaSRec contains two main parts as shown in Algorithm 1. The first part described in lines 1–5 is the computation of similarities and predicted ratings along with different meta-paths. The main time-consuming component is the calculation

Algorithm 1. Heterogeneous Information based Service Recommendation

Input:
    Information network and implicit feedback data
Output:
    Recommended list $RecList$
 1: Decide L meta-paths
 2: **for** $\mathcal{P}_l \in \mathcal{P}$ **do**
 3:    Evaluate mashup similarity s^l with Eq. (1)
 4:    Calculate predicted rating r^l with Eq. (2)
 5: **end for**
 6: Initialize θ
 7: **repeat**
 8:    Draw (m, n, i) from Z
 9:    Calculate $\frac{\partial OPT}{\partial \theta}$ with Eq. (8)
10:    $\theta \leftarrow \theta - \alpha \frac{\partial \hat{O}PT}{\partial \theta}$
11: **until** convergence
12: Rank predicted ratings calculated with Eq. (3)
13: **return** $RecList$

of similarity which can be completed offline. Another part in lines 6–11 is the model learning process, and its time complexity is $O(|M|^2|S||\mathcal{P}|)$ where $|M|$ is the number of mashups, $|S|$ is the number of services, and $|\mathcal{P}|$ denotes the number of decided meta-paths.

4 Empirical Study

In this section, we present the empirical studies of the proposed service recommendation approach. We implement PaSRec along with several general or state-of-the-art recommendation methods to demonstrate the effectiveness of the proposed approach.

4.1 Data

We evaluate the proposed service recommendation approach PaSRec on the dataset crawled from PW. The dataset includes 6,340 mashups and 1,399 API services with 13,685 composition relationships, and the sparsity of the interaction matrix is about 99.8 %. The dataset includes the attribute information of APIs and mashups. The detailed description of this dataset can be found in Table 2, and their network schema is shown as Fig. 2. The average degree of a object related a relationship is calculated by dividing the number of relationship instances by the number of object instances.

For overall comparison, we use 60 % of the composition records as training set to predict the remaining 40 %. Besides, we assign different training data settings (10 %–90 %) to show the comparison results in different data sparseness.

4.2 Evaluation Metrics

We employ three widely used metrics, precision, recall and mean reciprocal rank (MRR), to measure the performance of PaSRec.

$$\text{Precision} = \frac{1}{|M|} \sum_{m \in M} \frac{|rec(m) \cap test(m)|}{|rec(m)|}, \qquad (9)$$

$$\text{Recall} = \frac{1}{|M|} \sum_{m \in M} \frac{|rec(m) \cap test(m)|}{|test(m)|}, \qquad (10)$$

where $rec(m)$ is a recommended list for mashup m, and $test(m)$ is a set of services that have interactions with m in test set.

$$\text{MRR} = \frac{1}{|M|} \sum_{m \in M} (\sum_{i \in test(m)} \frac{1}{rank(m,i)}), \qquad (11)$$

where $rank(m,i)$ represents the position of service i in the recommended list for mashup m.

Table 2. Statistics of ProgrammableWeb dataset

Relations (X-Y)	Number of X	Number of Y	Number of (X-Y)	Ave. degrees of A/B
Mashup-API	6340	1399	13685	2.16/9.78
Mashup-Tag	6300	393	19013	3.02/48.38
Mashup-Content	6340	50	28267	4.46/565.34
API-Category	1367	323	3540	2.59/10.96
API-Content	1399	50	6652	4.75/133.04
API-Provider	1100	952	1100	1.00/1.16

4.3 Methods for Comparison

To demonstrate the effectiveness of the proposed service recommendation approach, we compare PaSRec with other four recommendation methods described as follows.

- **SVD**: This method is a traditional matrix factorization technique in recommender systems [11].
- **CF**: Collaborative filtering is a classical and widely used technique in recommender systems [13].
- **BPR-SVD**: This method learns SVD model using implicit feedback data with Bayesian Personalized Ranking (BPR) method proposed in [12].
- **BPR-kNN**: This method learns k-Nearest Neighbor (kNN) model using implicit feedback data with BPR method.

In the implement of our PaSRec, we select 6 meaningful meta-paths as shown in Table 1 for experiments. The parameter α in PaSRec is 0.001 and λ is set as 0.001 for the best performance. The parameters in those comparison methods are set with the best performances.

4.4 Learning Rate Decision

The learning rate constant α in the model learning algorithm is a key parameter, which can be determined experimentally. Given the training set, we fix the regularization parameter $\lambda = 0.001$ and set the number of iterations as 15. Then we run the learning algorithm with different values of $\alpha \in \{0.1, 0.01, 0.001, 0.0001\}$. Figure 4 records the change of loss values with the increasing number of iterations. It can be observed that the middle values of α (i.e., 0.01 and 0.001) are the relatively satisfactory selections, which is judged according to (i) the slow convergence of $\alpha = 0.0001$; and (ii) the big fluctuation of curve caused by $\alpha = 0.1$. Between 0.01 and 0.001, we choose $\alpha = 0.001$ in this paper, since its loss curve shown in Fig. 4 is more smooth, which can enhance the robustness of the learning algorithm.

Table 3. Performance comparison

Method	Precision@k			Recall@k			MRR@k		
	$k = 3$	$k = 5$	$k = 10$	$k = 3$	$k = 5$	$k = 10$	$k = 3$	$k = 5$	$k = 10$
SVD	0.0747	0.0832	0.0585	0.1404	0.2659	0.3802	0.1217	0.1655	0.1880
BPR-SVD	0.1082	0.0944	0.0622	0.2148	0.2983	0.3988	0.2311	0.2637	0.2839
BPR-kNN	0.0737	0.0646	0.0497	0.1472	0.2053	0.3026	0.1245	0.1474	0.1707
CF	0.1648	0.1338	0.0915	0.2953	0.3975	0.5276	0.3609	0.4012	0.4334
PaSRec	**0.3421**	**0.2371**	**0.1338**	**0.6946**	**0.7704**	**0.8281**	**0.7051**	**0.7417**	**0.7625**
Improvement	51.83 %	43.57 %	31.61 %	57.49 %	48.40 %	36.29 %	48.82 %	45.91 %	43.16 %

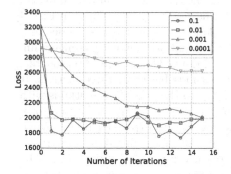

Fig. 3. Loss of PaSRec as a function of the number of iterations

Fig. 4. Loss of PaSRec with the change of percentage of training data

4.5 Performance Comparison

We evaluate and compare all the methods listed in Sect. 4.3. Table 3 shows the performances of all 5 methods in the dataset crawled from PW, from which we can draw some observations (Fig. 3).

SVD, BPR-SVD and BPR-kNN achieve worse performance among all the baselines. SVD model is more appropriate for recommendation problem with explicit rating data since it is a matrix factorization based method. BPR-SVD introduces the idea of pairwise based ranking and combines the basic SVD model with BPR learning algorithm for implicit feedback. The improvements made by BPR-SVD compared to SVD respectively reach up to 30.96 %, 34.64 % and 47.34 % in terms of three metrics (precision@3 = 0.1082, recall@3 = 0.2148, MRR@3 = 0.2311). BPR-kNN achieves the worst performance due to the lack of extra information such as content and network information.

CF method outperforms other baseline methods overall. Essentially, this method leverages the relationships between mashups and services to measure the similarity. CF achieves precision@5 = 0.1388 (compared to 0.0832 with SVD, 0.0944 with BPR-SVD, and 0.0646 with BPR-kNN), and the similar results are shown in terms of other two metrics. The performance of CF method proves the usefulness of the information network constructed with mashups and services.

Our proposed service recommendation model PaSRec, which sufficiently leverages heterogeneous information network and the implicit feedback data, overwhelmingly beats all baseline methods. From Table 3, we can find that PaSRec improves precision@5, recall@5 and MRR@5 by 43.57 %, 48.40 % and 45.91 % compared to CF method. The obvious improvement demonstrates the effectiveness of the related heterogeneous information network and our proposed PaSRec approach can significantly improve the recommendation quality.

Moreover, we compare the proposed service recommendation approach PaS-Rec with all the baseline methods with respect to different amounts of training data. Specifically, we select first 10 %–90 % of the dataset as training data and assign the last 10 % for testing at each run. The results are presented in Figs. 4 and 5. Figure 4 shows the loss of PaSRec along with the change of percentage of training data. We can find that the loss obtained when the algorithm converges reduces with the increase of training data, which is quite reasonable. Figure 5 illustrates the performances of all methods based on three metrics. It is obvious that our PaSRec approach is superior to the other four methods with any percentage of training data. In addition, PaSRec makes significant improvements when the training data increases, which can be explained by following: more triple samples can be generated with the raise of training data proportion, which can improve the quality of parameters learning. In addition, it can be easily observed that SVD and BPR-SVD make nearly no improvement when the percentage of training data changes. We infer it is caused by the sparsity of the training data, which reaches 99.8 % in the whole dataset as mentioned above. It indicates that our proposed PaSRec can alleviate the data sparsity issue to a certain extent.

Overall, the proposed recommendation approach outperforms all comparison methods in the dataset crawled from PW. The empirical studies verify that exploiting heterogeneous information network can bring positive influences for service recommendation.

5   Related Work

In recent years, there is a surge of research works of service discovery and recommendation. Previous work can be mainly classified into several types, semantics-based, CF-based, QoS-based, and information network-based. The semantics-based approaches generally consider the semantic similarity of services which have been frequently introduced, and here we discuss the rest three types of service recommendation methods.

Inspired by the techniques used in recommender systems, many works started to introduce the widely employed collaborative filtering into service recommendation. Cao et al. [4] handled service recommendation problem with a cube model, based on which a standard deviation based hybrid collaborative Filtering approach is proposed. Sun et al. [14] designed a new similarity measure to compute similarity between services and proposed a normal recovery collaborative filtering method to recommend services for consumers. In [20], Zhong et al. provided a

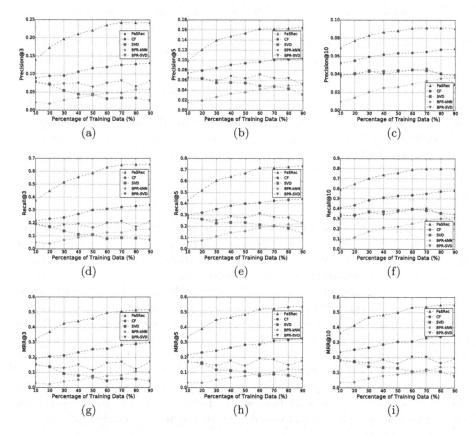

Fig. 5. Performance comparison in terms of precision, recall and MRR based on different percentages of training data.

time-aware service recommendation approach for mashup creation with the combination of service evolution, collaborative filtering and contend matching.

Furthermore, a number of works focus on QoS-based service recommendation. Zheng et al. [19] proposed a QoS prediction approach by combining traditional user-based and item-based collaborative filtering methods, and employ the predicted QoS for service recommendation. Chen et al. [6] designed a large-scale web service recommendation approach by employing the characteristic of QoS and achieved considerable improvement on the recommendation performance. However, QoS information is not always available.

Another direction in service recommendation is introducing information network analysis. In [3], Cao et al. proposed an framework to recommend mashup services, which considered users' interests mined from their usage history and the information network based on relations among mashup services, APIs and tags. Huang et al. [9] built a service network prediction method based on rank aggregation, and presented how to recommend potential compositions, top services and service chains by using this network prediction model. Maaradji et al. [10] introduced a framework named SoCo to provide dynamic recommendations for services discovery by using users' interactions and a social network built from interactions between users and services. Gao et al. [8] recommended services using manifold ranking algorithm which incorporate relationships between services and mashups.

However, most information network-based approaches only consider homogeneous relations between objects in the constructed service network. In this paper, we propose a service recommendation approach for mashup creation by sufficiently utilize heterogeneous information in the network including services, mashups, and their attributes.

6   Conclusion

In this paper, we propose a service recommendation approach for mashup creation called PaSRec, which exploits heterogeneous relationships in service related HIN. PaSRec takes advantages of different types of relationships between objects for the similarity computation under different semantic meanings. We design a recommendation model based on collaborative filtering and meta-path based similarities. A Bayesian ranking based optimization algorithm is applied to learn the model parameters with implicit feedback data. In the part of evaluation, we compare the proposed approach with several widely employed recommendation techniques, and the results show the superiority of our approach PaSRec. We also study the impact of learning rate in the process of model learning.

In our future work, we plan to use an online version of PaSRec to improve the efficiency of service recommendation, which makes it available for the approach to scale to a massive number of services, mashups, and the related attributes.

Acknowledgment. This research was partially supported by the Natural Science Foundation of China under grant of No. 61379119, National Science and Technology Supporting Program of China under grant of No. 2015BAH18F02, the Fundamental Research Funds for the Central Universities under grant of No. ZH2016007.

References

1. Blei, D.M., Ng, A.Y., Jordan, M.I.: Latent dirichlet allocation. J. Mach. Learn. Res. **3**, 993–1022 (2003)
2. Bottou, L.: Large-scale machine learning with stochastic gradient descent. In: Lechevallier, Y., Saporta, G. (eds.) Proceedings of COMPSTAT 2010, pp. 177–186. Springer, Heidelberg (2010)
3. Cao, B., Liu, J., Tang, M., Zheng, Z., Wang, G.: Mashup service recommendation based on user interest and social network. In: 2013 IEEE 20th International Conference on Web Services (ICWS), pp. 99–106. IEEE (2013)
4. Cao, J., Wu, Z., Wang, Y., Zhuang, Y.: Hybrid collaborative filtering algorithm for bidirectional web service recommendation. Knowl. Inf. Syst. **36**(3), 607–627 (2013)
5. Chen, L., Wu, J., Zheng, Z., Lyu, M.R., Wu, Z.: Modeling and exploiting tag relevance for web service mining. Knowl. Inf. Syst. **39**(1), 153–173 (2014)
6. Chen, X., Zheng, Z., Liu, X., Huang, Z., Sun, H.: Personalized qos-aware web service recommendation and visualization. IEEE Trans. Serv. Comput. **6**(1), 35–47 (2013)
7. Dojchinovski, M., Kuchar, J., Vitvar, T., Zaremba, M.: Personalised graph-based selection of web APIs. In: Cudré-Mauroux, P., et al. (eds.) ISWC 2012. LNCS, vol. 7649, pp. 34–48. Springer, Heidelberg (2012). doi:10.1007/978-3-642-35176-1_3
8. Gao, W., Chen, L., Wu, J., Gao, H.: Manifold-learning based api recommendation for mashup creation. In: Proceedings of the 22nd IEEE International Conference on Web Services, pp. 432–439. IEEE (2015)
9. Huang, K., Fan, Y., Tan, W.: Recommendation in an evolving service ecosystem based on network prediction. IEEE Trans. Autom. Sci. Eng. **11**(3), 906–920 (2014)
10. Maaradji, A., Hacid, H., Daigremont, J., Crespi, N.: Towards a social network based approach for services composition. In: 2010 IEEE International Conference on Communications (ICC), pp. 1–5. IEEE (2010)
11. Paterek, A.: Improving regularized singular value decomposition for collaborative filtering. In: Proceedings of the KDD Cup Workshop, vol. 2007, pp. 5–8 (2007)
12. Rendle, S., Freudenthaler, C., Gantner, Z., Schmidt-Thieme, L.: Bpr: bayesian personalized ranking from implicit feedback. In: Proceedings of the Twenty-Fifth Conference on Uncertainty in Artificial Intelligence, pp. 452–461. AUAI Press (2009)
13. Sarwar, B., Karypis, G., Konstan, J., Riedl, J.: Item-based collaborative filtering recommendation algorithms. In: Proceedings of the 10th International Conference on World Wide Web, pp. 285–295. ACM (2001)
14. Sun, H., Zheng, Z., Chen, J., Lyu, M.R.: Personalized web service recommendation via normal recovery collaborative filtering. IEEE Trans. Serv. Comput. **6**(4), 573–579 (2013)
15. Sun, Y., Han, J.: Mining heterogeneous information networks: a structural analysis approach. ACM SIGKDD Explor. Newsl. **14**(2), 20–28 (2013)
16. Sun, Y., Han, J., Yan, X., Yu, P.S., Wu, T.: Pathsim: meta path-based top-k similarity search in heterogeneous information networks. Proc. VLDB Endowment **4**(11), 992–1003 (2011)

17. Wu, J., Chen, L., Feng, Y., Zheng, Z., Zhou, M.C., Wu, Z.: Predicting quality of service for selection by neighborhood-based collaborative filtering. IEEE Trans. Syst. Man Cybern. Syst. **43**(2), 428–439 (2013)

18. Yu, X., Ren, X., Sun, Y., Sturt, B., Khandelwal, U., Gu, Q., Norick, B., Han, J.: Recommendation in heterogeneous information networks with implicit user feedback. In: Proceedings of the 7th ACM Conference on Recommender Systems, pp. 347–350. ACM (2013)

19. Zheng, Z., Ma, H., Lyu, M.R., King, I.: Qos-aware web service recommendation by collaborative filtering. IEEE Trans. Serv. Comput. **4**(2), 140–152 (2011)

20. Zhong, Y., Fan, Y., Huang, K., Tan, W., Zhang, J.: Time-aware service recommendation for mashup creation in an evolving service ecosystem. In: Proceedings of the 21st IEEE International Conference on Web Services (ICWS), pp. 25–32. IEEE (2014)

A Robust Approach to Finding Trustworthy Influencer in Trust-Oriented E-Commerce Environments

Feng Zhu[1,2], Guanfeng Liu[1,2(✉)], Yan Wang[3], Mehmet A. Orgun[3], An Liu[1,2], Zhixu Li[1,2], and Kai Zheng[1,2]

[1] School of Computer Science, Soochow University, 215006 Suzhou, China
{gfliu,anliu,zhixuli,zhengkai}@suda.edu.cn
[2] Collaborative Innovation Center of Novel Software Technology
and Industrialization, Nanjing, Jiangsu, China
[3] Department of Computing, Macquarie University, Sydney, NSW 2102, Australia
{yan.wang,mehmet.orgun}@mq.edu.au

Abstract. With the recognition of the significance of OSNs (Online Social Networks) in the recommendation of services in e-commerce, there are more and more e-commerce platform being combined with OSNs, forming *social e-commerce*, where a participant could recommend a product to his/her friends based on the participant's corresponding purchasing experience. For example, at Epinions, a buyer could share product reviews with his/her friends. In such platforms, a buyer providing lots of high quality reviews is very likely to influence many potential buyers' purchase behaviours. Such a buyer is believed to have *strong* social influence. However, dishonest participants in OSNs can deceive the existing social influence evaluation models, by mounting attacks, such as *Constant* (Dishonest advisors constantly provide unfairly positive/negative ratings to sellers.) and *Camouflage* (Dishonest advisors camouflage themselves as honest advisors by providing fair ratings to build up their trustworthiness first and then gives unfair ratings.), to obtain fake strong social influence. Therefore, it is crucial to devise a robust social influence evaluation model that can defend against attacks and deliver more accurate social influence evaluation results. In this paper, we propose a novel robust Trust-Aware Social Influencer Finding, *TrustINF*, method that considers the evolutionary trust relationship and the variations of historical social influences of participants, which can help deliver more accurate social influence evaluation results in social e-commerce. Our experiments conducted on four real social network datasets validate the effectiveness and robustness of our proposed method, which is greatly superior to the state-of-the-art method.

1 Introduction

1.1 Background

On trust-oriented e-commerce platforms, like Epinions (epinions.com), after a transaction, a buyer can provide a review to introduce the quality of the

Q.Z. Sheng et al. (Eds.): ICSOC 2016, LNCS 9936, pp. 387–401, 2016.
DOI: 10.1007/978-3-319-46295-0_24

purchased product and the experience of the transaction. This review is visible to other buyers, and is much valuable to their decision-making of purchasing. In addition, a buyer can rate the existing reviews given by others as *Not Helpful*, *Somewhat Helpful*, *Helpful*, or *Very Helpful* based on his/her own experiences [1]. If a buyer usually provides *Very Helpful* product reviews in a specific domain, like Digital Cameras, his/her recommendation is believed to be trustworthy in that domain. As indicated in the studies of *Social Psychology* [2] and *Computer Science* [3–5], a buyer is very likely to make a purchase decision following the recommendations (product reviews) given by trustworthy buyers. Such trustworthy buyers posses strong influences and can impact many buyers' purchase behaviours in a specific domain. These trustworthy buyers are called the *advisors* of those participants who trust their product reviews.

1.2   The Problem

In e-commerce environments, a buyer can write product reviews and rate others' reviews freely, and thus the product review scheme is highly vulnerable to some typical attacks [1]. For example, in order to obtain a strong influence, a dishonest advisor can cheat the product review system via some typical attacks, such as *Constant*[1] and *Camouflage*[2] [6], by (1) recommending a low quality product, and/or (2) providing an unfair review to a high quality product, each of which severely harms the benefits of both potential buyers and sellers. The problem of unfair rating becomes more and more concerned by not only industrial circles but also academic circles in this filed. Plenty of unfair ratings exist in the reviews of products, which significantly affect the decision-making of buyers [7,8].

In the literature, the existing influence evaluation methods mainly focus on studying the influence maximization under the popular linear threshold (LT) model and independent cascade (IC) model [9], and evaluating social influence through the process of information diffusion [10]. However, they do not apply any strategies to defend against the afore-mentioned typical attacks, and thus the existing models might recommend a participant as an advisor who has obtained the fake strong social influence by cheating the review systems via the above mentioned typical attacks. Some methods have been proposed to defend against collusive [11] or spamming rating attacks [12], which however cannot be directly applied in defending against the typical *Camouflage* and *Constant* attacks in trust-oriented e-commerce environment. The following *Example* 1 illustrates the process of the typical Camouflage attack in e-commerce platforms.

Example 1. *Fig. 1 depicts a trust-oriented e-commerce environment, which contains two sellers S_1 and S_2 and three buyers B_1 to B_3. Firstly, B_1 and B_3 bought the same product (such as digital camera) from S_1, so there exist the transaction relationships between B_1 and S_1, and between B_3 and S_1, respectively (represented by arrows with dashed lines in Fig. 1). Next, suppose both B_1*

---

[1] Dishonest advisors constantly provide unfairly positive/negative ratings to sellers.

[2] Dishonest advisors camouflage themselves as honest advisors by providing fair ratings to build up their trustworthiness first and then gives unfair ratings.

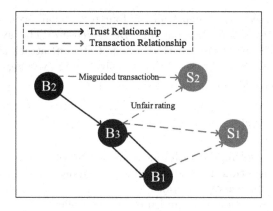

Fig. 1. The camouflage attack

and B_3 wrote a review for the camera sold by S_1, and they find that their purchase experiences are similar with each other. Then B_1 and B_3 trust each other, and thus there exist trust *relationships between B_1 and B_3 (represented by arrows with solid lines in Fig. 1). Finally, B_2 regards the review of B_3 is Very Helpful, then a trust relationship is established between them. In such a situation, if B_2 wants to buy a new camera, B_3's review has a strong influence on B_2's decision making. But suppose B_3 wrote an unfair positive review to the camera sold by S_2, whose camera has a low quality. If B_2 wants to buy a new digital camera, naturally B_2 would choose the camera sold by S_2 because B_2 trusts B_3. Then B_2 makes a wrong decision misled by B_3's dishonest action. In such a scenario, B_3 is a* Camouflage *attacker who establishes fake trustworthiness first and then misleads other buyers.*

The above discussed typical attacks widely exist in trust-oriented e-commerce, which leads to severe deviation of the reliability of the recommendations [6]. This motivates us to develop a robust influence evaluation method to accurately find the participants who have real strong influence under the typical attacks mounted by dishonest buyers in e-commerce environments.

1.3   Contributions

The main contributions of this paper are summarized as follows:

- We propose a novel Trustworthy Influencer Finding method *TrustINF* based on the evolutionary trust model [6] and the variations of historical influences of participants, which can measure the attack probability for each buyer, and defend against the typical attacks, *Constant* and *Camouflage*.
- To the best of our knowledge, this is the first work that defends *Camouflage* and *Constant* attacks in influence evaluation. The proposed *TrustINF* approach is based on *Skyline* [13] and its time complexity achieves $\mathcal{O}(n^2)$, where n is the number of buyers in e-commerce environments.

– We have conducted experiments on the four real social e-commerce datasets, i.e., *Epinions*, *Slashdot*, *Amazon* and *BeerAdvocate*. The average *Attacker Identification Ratios* of our TrustINF under *Constant* attack and *Camouflage* attack achieve 66.33 % and 81.33 % respectively. On average, our *Trust-IMM* can improve the robustness of *IMM* by 85.82 %.

2   Related Work

In the literature, according to different influence problems, we categorize them as influence maximization, individual influence evaluation and the unfair rating identification in influence evaluation.

Influence maximization is to find important applications in viral marketing [14], where a product provider selects K influencers in an OSN and provides them with incentives (e.g., free samples) to accept a new product, excepting the social influence of these influencers can work and attract more potential users. [15] propose an algorithm that has a simple tunable parameter, for users to control the balance between the running time and the influence spread. [16] propose an algorithm IRIE that integrates the advantages of influence ranking (IR) and influence estimation (IE) methods. [17] provide a scalable influence approximation algorithm, Independent Path Algorithm (IPA). [18] investigate a *novelty decay* phenomenon where the influence of a participant decays with the increase of the number of sending the same message to others in OSNs. Then they [19] investigate the effect of the novelty decay in the influence maximization in OSNs. Recently, [20] proposed an algorithm which is based on martingales, a classic statistical tool, to support a larger class of information diffusion model over the existing methods. Moreover, [21] propose a local influence maximization problem. This problem is to find a group of nodes that have the maximal impact on a specified participant. In addition, [22] propose a probabilistic model to discover the latent influence between participants in OSNs.

In individual social influence evaluation, [23] propose an approach, called SoCap, to find influencers in OSNs by using the social capital value. They model the problem of finding influencers in OSNs as a value-allocation problem, where the allocated value denotes the individual social capital. In addition, [24] propose a method to identify influential agents in open multi-agent systems without centralised control and individuals have equal authority. The above existing methods in influence evaluation did not consider any strategies defending against attacks, and thus are vulnerable to the attacks, like *Camouflage* and *Constant*, from dishonest participants.

In order to identify the unfair ratings and improve the robustness of influence evaluation models, some approaches [11,12] have been proposed to defend against the collusive and the spamming rating attacks respectively in trust-oriented e-commerce environments. However, their methods cannot be used directly to defend against the Camouflage and Constant attacks that widely exist in e-commerce environments.

3 Preliminary

3.1 Trust Relationship

In e-commerce environments, a *Trust Relationship* is a relationship between a buyer and an advisor, which illustrate the probability of a buyer who will make the purchase decision based on the reviews of the advisor. This type of trust relationship widely exist in trust-oriented e-commerce, like Epionions, Amazon, FilmTrust, etc. Let $T_{i,j}$ to denote the trust relationship between B_i and B_j.

3.2 Transaction Relationship

In trust-oriented e-commerce environment, a *Transaction Relationship* is a relationship between a buyer and a seller when they have at least one transaction. Let $R_{i,j}$ denote the transaction relationship between B_i and S_j. If B_i have bought m items from S_j, and the rating values to those m items are $r_{i,j} = \{r_{i,j}^1, ..., r_{i,j}^m\}$, $m > 0$, then

$$R_{i,j} = \frac{1}{m} \sum_{k=1}^{m} r_{i,j}^k. \tag{1}$$

3.3 Evolutionary Trust Model

The Evolutionary Trust Model [6] is usually used to cope with unfair rating attacks from dishonest advisors. By using this model, if a buyer finds the real transactional experience is different with the reviews given by an advisor, the buyer could evolve his/her trust relationships to absorb the advisors whose reviews better match the buyer's purchase experience and distrust the previous advisor whose review is not recognized by the buyer. The following Example 2 illustrates the evolutionary process.

Example 2. *In Fig. 2, suppose there is a low rating given by B_2 to S_2 (i.e., $R_{2,2} = 0.2$), which is quite different with B_3's review with $R_{3,2} = 1.0$. Then B_2 evolves his/her trust relationships to form a new trust relationship $T_{2,1} = 1.0$ with B_1 as B_1's review with $R_{1,1} = 0.2$ matches B_2's purchase experience. Meanwhile B_2 removes the trust relationship with B_3. Finally, B_1 becomes a new advisor of B_2. This process is called the* Trust Evolution.

The below fitness function in Eq. (2) is used for buyers to measure the quality of their trust networks by comparing the two types of derived reputation values of sellers [6].

$$f(VT_i) = \frac{1}{m} \sum_{j=1}^{m} |R_{i,j} - \widetilde{R}_{i,j}| \tag{2}$$

where m is the number of sellers who have been rated by both B_i and B_i's advisors. $\widetilde{R}_{i,j} = \frac{1}{|A(B_i)|} \sum_{k=1}^{|A(B_i)|} R_{k,j}$ denotes the average rating value given

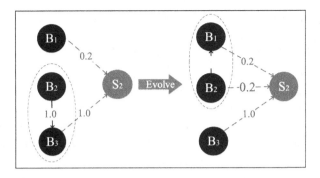

Fig. 2. Evolutionary process

by B_i's advisors to seller S_j. $f(VT_i)$ means that the little difference of ratings given by a buyer and his/her advisors illustrating the high quality of their trust relationship.

The following Eq. (3) is used to measure the difference of trust relationships between two buyers B_i and B_j.

$$\text{diff}(VT_i, VT_j) = \frac{1}{m'} \sum_{k=1}^{m'} |T_{i,k} - T_{j,k}| \tag{3}$$

where m' is the number of both B_i's and B_j's advisors; it reflects the difference between the trust relationships of B_i and B_j. The less the value of $\text{diff}(VT_i, VT_j)$ the less the difference of the trust value from B_i and B_j to their common advisors.

Equation (4) is used to measure the difference of fitness.

$$\text{diff}(f(VT_i), f(VT_j)) = |f(VT_i) - f(VT_j)| \tag{4}$$

In evolutionary process, a function $\delta(\cdot)$ is used to judge the compatibility of new trust relationship resource and calculated as follows:

$$\begin{aligned} \delta(VT_i, VT_j) =& (\text{diff}(VT_i, VT_j) - 0.5) \\ & \times (\text{diff}(f(VT_i), f(VT_j)) - 0.5) \end{aligned} \tag{5}$$

Here, we set threshold as 0, only when two buyers B_i and B_j satisfy $\delta(VT_i, VT_j) > 0$.

4   Impact Factors of Influence

With adopting the *Evolutionary Trust Model*, we propose two impact factors which have significant impact on real influence evaluation of participants in e-commerce.

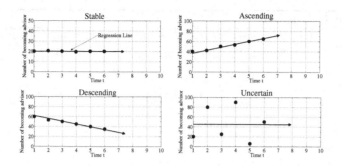

Fig. 3. Four typical cases of FTBA

4.1   Fluctuant Trend of Becoming Advisor (FTBA)

Observing the trend of buyers' trust can largely recognize their reputations [1]. Here, we use the historical data of trust relationships to regress the trend of trust for each buyer, i.e., Fluctuant Trend of Becoming Advisor (FTBA), which illustrates the fluctuant trend of a buyer to become an advisor of a buyer in a certain period. The typical cases of FTBA are depicted in Fig. 3, i.e., "stable", "ascending", "descending" and "uncertain". "stable" means no more other buyers trust the buyer in this period; "ascending" means more and more buyers trust the buyer; "descending" means less and less buyers trust the buyer based on his/her reviews; "uncertain" means the trend of becoming an advisor of the buyer is unclear. We utilize a regression line to model FTBA, whose gradient (denoted as *grad*) and mean distance (denoted as *md*) can measure FTBA well [25].

Let x_i^j denote the number of becoming advisors of B_i at time t_j, and let $(t_s, x_i^s), (t_2, x_i^2), ..., (t_e, x_i^e)$ denote the given data points of B_i from t_s to t_e. In this paper, t_s denotes the start time of the historical transactions and t_e denotes the end time of transactions. Then FTBA can be computed by Eq. (6):

$$y = kt + b \qquad (6)$$

where k and b are constants to be determined, and k represents the *grad* value.

Then the shortest distance from point (t_j, x_i^j) to the regression line can be computed by Eq. (7):

$$d_i^j = \frac{x_i^j - b - kt_j}{\sqrt{1 + k^2}}. \qquad (7)$$

Based on the theory of least squares [26], the sum of squares of the distance can be calculated:

$$S_i^p = \sum_{j=1}^{p} (d_i^j)^2 = \sum_{j=1}^{p} \frac{(x_i^j - b - kt_j)^2}{1 + k^2}. \qquad (8)$$

Next we minimise the sum of squares of the distance S_i^p with respect to the parameters k and b, with the method of undetermined coefficients. Since the

Algorithm 1. TrustINF

Input: Buyer set B, the parameter sets of all buyers X, the number of buyer set n;
Output: The set of probability of attack of all buyers $P = \{P_i\}$;
1: $P \longleftarrow \emptyset$;
2: $N \longleftarrow \emptyset$ /* The dominating numbers of buyers */
3: $N' \longleftarrow \emptyset$ /* The numbers dominated by other buyers for all buyers */
4: **for** each X_i in X **do**
5:    **for** each X_j in X, $j \neq i$ **do**
6:       /* Confirming whether X_i dominates X_j, which is based on Definition 1 */
7:       $m = 0$;
8:       $flag = false$;
9:       **for** $k = 1$ to 4 **do**
10:          **if** $(X_i^k > X_j^k)$ **then**
11:             $m++$;
12:             $flag = true$;
13:          **end if**
14:          **if** $(X_i^k == X_j^k)$ **then**
15:             $m++$;
16:          **end if**
17:       **end for**
18:       **if** $(m == 4$ and $flag)$ **then**
19:          N_i++;
20:          $N_j'++$;   /* B_j is dominated by B_i */
21:       **end if**
22:    **end for**
23: **end for**
24: **for** each B_i in B **do**
25:    $P_i = (N_i' - N_i)/(n-1)$
26: **end for**
27: Return P;

---

function S_i^p is continuous and differentiable, as we know, based on the method of two variables' function extremum, the minimization point of S_i^p makes the first derivative of function S_i^p be zero, and the second derivative positive, which could be easily proved by Taylor formula for function of two variables [26]. For this purpose, we differentiate S_i^p with respect to k and b, and set the results to zero. Then we can obtain:

$$k = grad_i = (-u - \sqrt{u^2 + 4})/2 \tag{9}$$

and

$$b = \frac{S_f - kS_t}{n}, \tag{10}$$

where $u = \frac{pS_{f2} - S_f^2 + S_t^2 - pS_{t2}}{S_f S_t - pS_{ft}}$, $S_{f2} = \sum_{j=1}^{p}(x_i^j)^2$, $S_f = \sum_{j=1}^{p} x_i^j$, $S_t = \sum_{j=1}^{p} t_j$, $S_{t2} = \sum_{j=1}^{p} t_j^2$ and $S_{ft} = \sum_{j=1}^{p} x_i^j \cdot t_j$.

According to above results, the equation of mean distance can be computed by Eq. (11):

$$md_i = \frac{\sum_{j=1}^{p} |x_i^j - b - kt_j|}{p\sqrt{1 + k^2}}. \tag{11}$$

4.2 Fluctuant Trend of Total Trustworthiness (FTT)

Here, we propose another impact factor of influence evaluation, Fluctuant Trend of Total Trustworthiness (FTT), together with FTBA to measure the probability of attack for each buyer. FTT illustrates the fluctuant trend of total trustworthiness which is the total value of trust given by buyers to an advisor from t_s to t_e. We use a regression line to model FTT, which is based on the theory of least squares [26]. The gradient and mean distance of the regression line are denoted as $grad'$ and md' respectively. Let $x_i'^j$ denote the total trust value at time t_j, and $(t_s, x_i'^s), (t_2, x_i'^2), (t_3, x_i'^3),...,(t_e, x_i'^e)$ denote the given data points of B_i from t_s to t_e.

$$x'_i = \sum_{k=1}^{m} T_{k,i} \tag{12}$$

where m is the number of buyers who have trust relationship with B_i.

Then FTT can be computed by using the theory of least squares [26] (i.e., replace (t_j, x_i^j) with $(t_j, x_i'^j)$ in Eqs. (9–11)).

Intuitively, these trends are conducive to indicate the changing process of trust of a buyer and detect the behaviors of the typical attacks. FTT reflects the changing trend of the quality of trust, but FTBA reflects the changing trend of the amount of trust.

Thus, in order to indicate the trust of a buyer more completely, both FTBA and FTT are needed to be combined to in the measurement of trust for a buyer in trust-oriented e-commerce environments.

5   Trust-Aware Influencer Finding Algorithm

In this section, we propose a Trust-Aware Influencer Finding method, *TrustINF*, that considers four parameters, i.e., FTBA's gradient, FTBA's mean distance, FTT's gradient and FTT's mean distance which have significant impact on trust-oriented influence evaluation. Finding influencers with multi-attributes is a typical multi-criteria optimal decision making problem [27]. Let P denote the parameter sets of all buyers, and let $X_i = \{X_i^k | k = 1, ..., 4\}$ denote FTBA's gradient, FTBA's mean distance, FTT's gradient and FTT's mean distance respectively. Intuitively, a buyer with lower gradients and higher mean distances will have a higher probability to be an attacker. Without loss of generality, we equally treat four parameters by setting X_2 as the negative value of FTBA's mean distance and X_4 as the negative value of FTT's mean distance in our algorithm.

A *skyline query* retrieves all points that are not dominated by any other point, which is an import method to solve the multi-criteria optimal decision

Table 1. The details of datasets

Data set	Epinions	Slashdot	Amazon	BeerAdvocate
Nodes	4,553	5,155	782	7,116
Links	16,939	9,674	2,385	103,690
Average In-degree	3.72	1.877	3.05	14.571

making problem [13]. In order to accurately identify attackers, we adopt a Skyline method to evaluate the probability of an advisor to be an attacker, and propose the concept of *Influencer Domination* based on the definitions in [28] as follows.

Definition 1 *Influencer Domination: A buyer B_i dominates another buyer B_j on an trust-oriented e-commerce platform if and only if for all $k \in \{1, ..., 4\}$, $X_i^k \geq X_j^k$ and $\exists\ t \in \{1, ..., 4\}$, $X_i^t > X_j^t$.*

Based on *Definition* 1, we use $N = \{N_i\}$ and $N' = \{N_i'\}$ to denote the dominating number of buyer B_i and the number dominated by other buyers respectively. If N_i' has a large value and N_i has a small value, the trust trend of B_i is downward, causing by the drastic change of ratings to sellers, which is a representative feature of *Camouflage* attack [6]. Thus, we define a function to measure the probability of B_i to be an attacker as Eq. (13).

$$P_i = (N_i' - N_i)/(n - 1), \tag{13}$$

where n is the number of buyers and $P_i \in [-1, 1]$.

The pseudo-code of the *TrustINF* algorithm is given in Algorithm 1. As the impact factors have been pre-calculated and pre-stored, Algorithm 1 only needs to calculate $N = \{N_i\}$ and $N' = \{N_i'\}$ by iteratively scanning the set of impact factors n times. Thus, the time complexity of *TrustINF* is $\mathcal{O}(n^2)$, where n is the number of buyers.

Summary: In our TrustINF, firstly, we improves evolutionary trust model and adopt it to evolve trust network after every transaction to obtain the trustworthy historical ratings. Secondly, we calculate every buyer's FTBA and FTT based on these historical ratings to indicate the trust trend of each buyer. Finally, as the social influence evaluation with defending against attacks is a typical multi-criteria optimal decision making problem, and the Skyline method is an important method to solve such a problem, we adopt the skyline method in our TrustINF.

6 Experiments

6.1 Experimental Setting

Dataset. In our experiments, we collect four real trust oriented e-commerce datasets, i.e., *Epinions, Slashdot, Amazon* and *BeerAdvocate* from snap.stanford.edu/data/, to investigate the performance of our *TrustINF* algorithm. These datasets have been widely used in the literature for the studies trust-oriented e-commerce [6]. The details of these datasets are listed Table 1.

The Setting of Attacks. In our experiments, we consider two typical attacks, i.e., *Constant* and *Camouflage*. We randomly choose α buyers from each of the dataset as attackers, $\alpha \in [5\,\%, 10\,\%, 15\,\%, 20\,\%, 25\,\%]$. Then, we investigate the *attacker identification ratio* of our *TrustINF*, and investigate the performance of our *Trust-IMM* and *IMM* [20]. Based on the definitions of the two types of attacks [6], we define the typical attackers in our experiments as below:

Constant Attacker: Dishonest buyers constantly provide unfairly positive/negative ratings to sellers [6].

For an attacker B_i, we set the ratings of B_i to give all products which B_i will buy from different sellers as extremely positive ([0.9,1]) or extremely negative ([0,0.1]) values. In our experiments, we randomly select $\alpha/2$ negative attackers and $\alpha/2$ positive attackers. The rating of product p_k can be calculated as below:

$$r_{i,k} = \begin{cases} \text{rand}(0.1) & \text{if } B_i \text{ is negative}, \\ 1 - \text{rand}(0.1) & \text{otherwise}. \end{cases} \tag{14}$$

Camouflage Attacker: Dishonest buyers camouflage themselves as honest buyers by providing fair ratings to build up their trustworthiness first and then gives unfair ratings [6].

For an attacker B_i, if B_i rated product p_k, then

$$r_{i,k} = (r_{i,k} + 0.5) \bmod 1. \tag{15}$$

After updating all ratings of B_i based on Eq. (19), B_i becomes a *Camouflage* attacker in our experiments. In

We define the *Identified Attacker* and *Attacker Identification Ratio* to measure the performance of our method:

Definition 2 *Identified Attacker*: *Attacker B_i is an Identified Attacker if and only if B_i is an attacker and the probability of attack P_i for B_i is ranked in Top-α, where α is the ratio of attackers included in trust-oriented e-commerce environments. This means that these attackers can be identified by influencer finding approaches.*

Definition 3 *Attacker Identification Ratio*: *Attacker Identification Ratio is the ratio of identified attackers to the all attackers, which is to measure the scale of identifying attackers delivered by influencer finding approaches.*

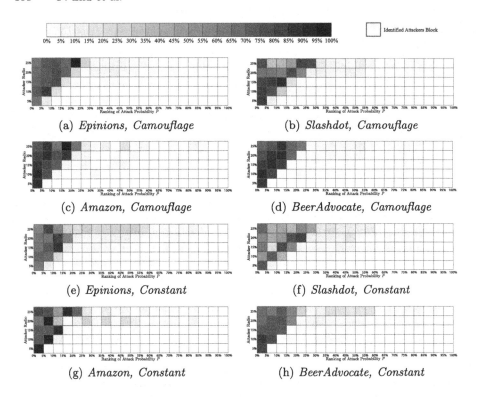

Fig. 4. The Attacker Identification on the four datasets. The color of each block reflects the proportion of the attackers in different ranges of ranking. (Color figure online)

Parameters in IMM and Diffusion Models. In this paper, we adopt two typical diffusion models, i.e., *Linear Threshold (LT)* model [29] and *Independent Cascade (IC)* model [9] to investigate the performance of *Trust-IMM*.

- **IMM:** *IMM* [20] is an influence maximization algorithm which adopts sampling method to return an approximate solution under the triggering model. In this experiments, we consider two kinds of triggering models, i.e., *LT* and *IC*. For *IMM*, we set $\varepsilon = 0.5$, $\ell = 1$, and $K \in [10, 20, 30, 40, 50]$.
- **Linear Threshold (LT) Model:** *LT* model is the first model to imitate the diffusion process of information. The approach is based on the node-specific thresholds [29]. In the model, at time step t, all buyers that were influenced in step $t-1$ remain being influenced. A buyer B_i is influenced based on a monotonic function of its influenced neighbors $f(In(i,t)) \in [0,1]$ (see Eq. (16)) and a threshold $\theta_i \in [0,1]$, i.e., B_i is influenced at time t if $f(In(i,t)) \geq \theta_i$.

$$f(In(i,t)) = \sum_{B_j \in In(i,t)} b_{i,j} \qquad (16)$$

where $In(i,t)$ is the influenced neighbors of B_i at time step t. Here, we set $b_{i,j} = T_{i,j} / \sum_{B_k \in Ad_i} T_{i,k}$; Ad_i is the advisor of B_i and $\sum_{B_j \in Ad_i} b_{i,j} \leq 1$.

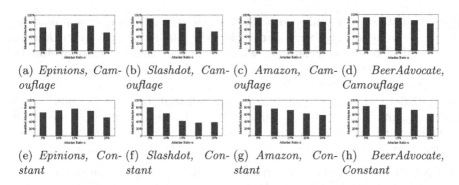

(a) *Epinions, Camouflage*   (b) *Slashdot, Camouflage*   (c) *Amazon, Camouflage*   (d) *BeerAdvocate, Camouflage*

(e) *Epinions, Constant*   (f) *Slashdot, Constant*   (g) *Amazon, Constant*   (h) *BeerAdvocate, Constant*

Fig. 5. The attacker identification ratio on the four datasets.

In our experiments, in order to investigate the effectiveness of our method based on different thresholds, for each B_i, we set $\theta_i = rand()$.

- **Independent Cascade (IC) Model:** *IC* model is a dynamic cascade model for the diffusion process. The model is based on the interacting particle system from probability theory [9]. At each time step t, each buyer is either influenced or susceptible. A buyer B_j that was influenced at time step $t-1$ has a single chance to influence each of its incoming neighbors B_i. The influence succeeds with probability $P_{i,j}$ (see Eq. (17)). Therefore, for buyer B_i, if at least one of its influenced advisors succeeds, B_i gets influenced. The probability of buyer B_i getting influence at time step t is:

$$f(i,t) = 1 - \prod_{B_j \in In(i,t-1)} (1 - P_{i,j}) \tag{17}$$

where $In(i,t-1)$ is the influenced neighbors of B_i at time step $t-1$. Here, we set $P_{i,j} = T_{i,j}$, i.e., the trust value from B_i to B_j.

Experimental Environment. All experiments were run on a machine powered by two Intel Core i5-3470 CPU 3.20 GHz processors with 8 GB RAM, using Windows 7 operating system. The code was implemented using Java 8 and the experimental data was managed by MySQL Server 5.6.

6.2   Experimental Results and Analysis

Figure 4 plots the probabilities of the identified attackers who are ranked in Top-α delivered by *TrustINF* model on four datasets. From the Fig. 4, we can see that our *TrustINF* method can identify the attackers who have been ranked in the top of the e-commerce (the dark color of blocks). Namely, our *TrustINF* method can help identify those influencers who have fake strong influence. In addition, with the increase of α, $\alpha \in [5\,\%, 10\,\%, 15\,\%, 20\,\%, 25\,\%]$, our *TrustINF* can always identify the attackers with the corresponding Top-α ranking (the triangle area of the dark blocks). This is because our *TrustINF* has considered the historical data of trust and regress the trend of trust to measure the probability of a buyer to be an attacker. Figure 5 plots the *Attacker Identification Ratio* of our *TrustINF* on the four datasets, where we can see that the range of *Attacker Identification Ratio* delivered by *TrustINF* is [36.02 %, 86.64 %] under the *Constant* attack, and is [53.67 %, 92.41 %] under the *Camouflage* attack. Based on the statistics, on average, the *Attacker Identification Ratio* of *Constant* attack is 66.33 %; and 81.33 % for *Camouflage* attack. This is because when an advisor providing unfair ratings to sellers, the buyers will no longer trust them based on the trust evolutionary model, and *FTBA* and *FTT* of the advisor will descend.

Summary: From the above experimental results, we can see that our *TrustINF* method can effectively identify the attackers who involve in the *Camouflage* attack and the *Constant* attack. In addition, *TrustINF* can effectively identify the attackers who have fake strong influence, which can greatly help buyers and sellers in the transactions in trust-oriented e-commerce environments.

7   Conclusion and Future Work

In this paper, we have proposed a novel Trust-Aware Influencer Finding (TrustINF) method which can defend against the *Camouflage* and the *Constant* attacks in trust-oriented e-commerce environments. The experiments conducted on four real e-commerce datasets have demonstrated our proposed *TrustINF* method can greatly help identify the attackers in the influencer finding, and can greatly improve the robustness of the influence maximization in trust-oriented e-commerce environments.

In future work, we plan to incorporate our *TrustINF* method into some influence evaluation methods in real e-commerce systems to further investigate the effectiveness of our model in defending against attacks.

Acknowledgement. This work was partially supported by Natural Science Foundation of China (Grant Nos. 61303019, 61572336, 61532018, 61402313, 61502324), Doctoral Fund of Ministry of Education of China (20133201120012), Postdoctoral Science Foundation of China (2015M571805, 2015M581859), Open Project Program of the Key Laboratory of Intelligent Information, Institute of Computing Technology, Chinese Academy of Science, and Collaborative Innovation Center of Novel Software Technology and Industrialization, Jiangsu, China.

References

1. Jøsang, A., Ismail, R., Boyd, C.: A survey of trust and reputation systems for online service provision. Decis. Support Syst. **43**(2), 618–644 (2007)
2. Fiske, S.T.: Social Beings: Core Motives in Social Psychology. Wiley, New York (2009)
3. Bedi, P., Kaur, H., Marwaha, S.: Trust based recommender system for semantic web. In: IJCAI, pp. 2677–2682 (2007)
4. Liu, G., Wang, Y., Orgun, M.A.: Optimal social trust path selection in complex social networks. In: AAAI, pp. 1391–1398, July 2010

5. Liu, G., Wang, Y., Orgun, M.A.: Social context-aware trust network discovery in complex contextual social networks. In: AAAI, pp. 101–107 (2012)
6. Jiang, S., Zhang, J., Ong, Y.S.: An evolutionary model for constructing robust trust networks. In: AAMAS, pp. 813–820 (2013)
7. Liu, A., Zheng, K., Li, L., Liu, G., Zhao, L., Zhou, X.: Efficient secure similarity computation on encrypted trajectory data. In: ICDE 2015, pp. 66–77 (2015)
8. Liu, A., Li, Q., Huang, L., Xiao, M.: Tolerant composition of transactional web services. IEEE Trans. Serv. Comput. 3(1), 46–59 (2010)
9. Kempe, D., Kleinberg, J., Tardos, É.: Maximizing the spread of influence through a social network. In: KDD, pp. 137–146 (2003)
10. Kimura, M., Saito, K.: Tractable models for information diffusion in social networks. In: PKDD, pp. 259–271 (2006)
11. Wang, D., Muller, T., Zhang, J., Liu, Y.: Quantifying robustness of trust systems against collusive unfair rating attacks using information theory. In: IJCAI, pp. 111–117 (2015)
12. Gao, J., Dong, Y., Shang, M., Cai, S., Zhou, T.: Group-based ranking method for online rating systems with spamming attacks. Europhys. Lett. (2015)
13. Borzsonyi, S., Kossmann, D., Stocker, K.: The skyline operator. In: ICDE, pp. 421–430 (2001)
14. Domingos, P., Richardson, M.: Mining the network value of customers. In: KDD, pp. 57–66. ACM (2001)
15. Chen, W., Wang, C., Wang, Y.: Scalable influence maximization for prevalent viral marketing in large-scale social networks. In: KDD, pp. 1029–1038 (2010)
16. Jung, K., Heo, W., Chen, W.: IRIE: Scalable and robust influence maximization in social networks. In: ICDM, pp. 918–923 (2012)
17. Kim, J., Kim, S.K., Yu, H.: Scalable and parallelizable processing of influence maximization for large-scale social networks? In: ICDE, pp. 266–277 (2013)
18. Ver Steeg, G., Ghosh, R., Lerman, K.: What stops social epidemics? In: ICWSM (2011)
19. Feng, S., Chen, X., Cong, G., Zeng, Y., Chee, Y.M., Xiang, Y.: Influence maximization with novelty decay in social networks. In: AAAI, pp. 37–43 (2014)
20. Tang, Y., Shi, Y., Xiao, X.: Influence maximization in near-linear time: a martingale approach. In: SIGMOD, pp. 75–86. ACM (2015)
21. Guo, J., Zhang, P., Zhou, C., Cao, Y., Guo, L.: Personalized influence maximization on social networks. In: CIKM, pp. 199–208 (2013)
22. Iwata, T., Shah, A., Ghahramani, Z.: Discovering latent influence in online social activities via shared cascade Poisson processes. In: KDD, pp. 266–274 (2013)
23. Subbian, K., Sharma, D., Wen, Z., Srivastava, J.: Finding influencers in networks using social capital. In: ASONAM, pp. 592–599 (2013)
24. Franks, H., Griffiths, N., Anand, S.S.: Learning influence in complex social networks. In: AAMAS, pp. 447–454 (2013)
25. Li, L., Wang, Y.: A trust vector approach to service-oriented applications. In: ICWS, pp. 270–277 (2008)
26. Okelo, B., Boston, S., Minchev, D.: Advanced Mathematics The Differential Calculus for Multi-variable Functions. LAP Lambert Academic, Saarbrücken (2012)
27. Velichenko, V.V.: Sufficient conditions for absolute minimum of the maximal functional in the multi-criterial problem of optimal control. In: Marchuk, G.I. (ed.) Optimization Techniques 1974. LNCS, vol. 27, pp. 220–225. Springer, Heidelberg (1975)
28. Chan, C.Y., Jagadish, H., Tan, K.L., Tung, A.K., Zhang, Z.: Finding k-dominant skylines in high dimensional space. In: SIGMOD, pp. 503–514 (2006)
29. Granovetter, M.: Threshold models of collective behavior. Am. J. Soci. 83(6), 1420–1443 (1978)

Context-Aware Recommendation of Task Allocations in Service Systems

Renuka Sindhgatta[1]([✉]), Aditya Ghose[2], and Hoa Khanh Dam[2]

[1] IBM Research-India, Bangalore, India
renuka.sr@in.ibm.com
[2] University of Wollongong, New South Wales, Australia
{aditya.ghose,hoa}@uow.edu.au

Abstract. In a service system comprising of knowledge intensive tasks, a pull-based allocation strategy (where knowledge workers decide on tasks to commit to, as opposed to having these commitments decided for them) can often be quite effective. Such a scenario is characterized by different types of tasks and workers with varying efficiencies. As workers and tasks change with time, a key challenge faced by knowledge workers is in deciding the most suitable tasks to commit to. Organizational roles of workers provide them the privilege of working on the tasks that the role is authorized to perform, but the suitability of a worker to perform a task varies because workers could have varying operational performance on different types of tasks. Past allocations, when correlated with execution histories annotated with quality of service (or performance) measures, can provide insights on the suitability of a task for a worker. It has been recognized that the effectiveness of a resource in performing a task often depends on the context in which the task is executed. In this work, we present a context-aware collaborative filtering recommender system that predicts a worker's suitability for a task, in different contexts or situations. The context-aware recommender uses information on the performance of similar resources in similar contexts to predict a resource's suitability for a task. Experiments performed on real-world execution logs demonstrate the effectiveness of the proposed approach.

Keywords: Task allocation · Context-aware recommender systems · Collaborative filtering

1 Introduction

A service system [15] is an organization of resources and processes that support and drive service interactions such that the outcomes meet customer expectations. Given that the underlying business processes in a service system are typically knowledge-intensive, the most critical resources in such systems are, arguably, the human resources or knowledge workers. It is common for service systems with knowledge intensive processes to use a pull-based dispatch policy [20]. In such a scenario, workers or resources commit to tasks as compared to

© Springer International Publishing Switzerland 2016
Q.Z. Sheng et al. (Eds.): ICSOC 2016, LNCS 9936, pp. 402–416, 2016.
DOI: 10.1007/978-3-319-46295-0_25

push-based dispatch where tasks are assigned to workers dynamically by the system or manually by a team leader. Pull-based dispatch is preferred because resources tend to multi-task and completion times of these tasks are not *a priori* known. A resource (or service/knowledge worker - we will use the two terms interchangeably in the remainder of this paper) evaluates the task based on available task attributes (description, urgency, customer), and decides on her suitability to commit to the task. The decision making is non-trivial and often knowledge workers, especially novice workers, find it hard to identify tasks that they are most suitable for. An added challenge is the fact that operational efficiencies of workers does not depend on the task alone, but also depends on the context or situation when executing a task. For example, a worker may be very efficient when processing a single task but may do poorly when catering to multiple tasks. Some workers may be effective in teams while other not. Clearly, the context of the task is as important a determinant of task performance as the attributes of the task itself. Hence, the notion of *context* plays a key role in the decision making. Dourish [5] presents some key characteristics of a context: (1) that it is a body of information and (2) that it is separable from the activity. The context is a body of information that can be specified using a set of attributes that can be observed and collected. The values of these attributes do not change and are clearly distinguishable from features describing the underlying activity of the user within the context. In line with Dourish's characterization, we define the context to be that body of *exogenous knowledge potentially relevant to the execution of the task that is available at the start of the execution of the task, and that is not impacted/modified via the execution of the task.* In our work, we use a fine-grained notion of context - i.e., we focus on the context of a task rather than the context of a process. Our proposed approach involves recommendation of tasks to resources taking into consideration the context of the resource and the task. To this end, we build a context-aware recommender system (CARS). The input to the system is data from historical executions of tasks by resources annotated with contextual information (some of which are inferred) and the outcome of the execution (a set of performance indicators or non-functional attributes defined for the task). The recommender predicts the suitability of a task for a resource, by providing a rating indicative of the resources' operational performance on that task. Prediction is based on the assumption that resources who have similar ratings on similar tasks, under similar context, are likely to be rated similarly on other similar tasks. The approach that we propose is of considerable practical value. Conventionally, the decision taken by a resource (in many practical service system settings) is based on human judgment, experience and on her implicit understanding of the context. Consequently, task allocation activity is subjective and relies on the experience of a resource. Automated, data-driven support can potentially serve as a game-changer in these settings. The paper is organized as follows. Section 2 presents overview of concepts used in our work. Model elements of CARS are outlined in Sect. 3, and a detailed empirical evaluation is presented in Sect. 4. Related work is presented in Sect. 5, followed by conclusions and future work in Sect. 6.

2 Overview

This section presents an overview of the approach and discusses pull-based dispatch policy commonly used in a service system, collaborative filtering and context awareness in recommender systems.

2.1 Pull-Based Dispatching in Service Systems

When a service system adopts a pull-based dispatching policy, a work request or task instantiated in the system enters a common queue and remains there till a knowledge worker or resource commits to the task. Every knowledge worker is able to peek into the common queue and view the tasks they are authorized to work on, based on their roles and organizational positions. Workers evaluate the type of task, their suitability to execute the task and other factors to decide if they should commit to a task or not. Once a task is committed to, performance measures associated to the task need to be met (target completion time, degree of customer satisfaction and so on). While experienced workers in the system, learn to identify tasks that they are best suited for, novice workers need help in identifying suitable tasks. Incorrect decision making results in a worker placing work back into the queue or leads to a longer completion time or poor degree of customer satisfaction. A recommender system prioritizing tasks suitable for a worker, would reduce erroneous dispatching decisions.

2.2 Collaborative Filtering Based Recommender System

Collaborative Filtering (CF) is a technology that has been widely used in e-commerce applications to produce personalized recommendations for users [8]. Functionally, CF builds a database of preferences or ratings done by distinct users on specific items. As indicated by Sarwar et al. [23], given a list of m users $U = \{u_1, u_2 \ldots u_m\}$ and a list of n items $I = \{i_1, i_2, \ldots, i_n\}$, each user u_i has a list of items I_{ui}, which are already rated. Here, *rating* is a totally ordered set. A CF algorithm provides recommendations in following ways:

- Prediction, a numeric value, expressing the predicted preference or rating of an item for a user. This predicted value is within the same scale as the rating values provided by user.
- Recommendation, a list of items, that a user will like. The recommended list is on items that have not been already rated by the user.

The key in CF is to locate other users with similar profiles to that of the user for which the recommendations need to be provided (or the active user). These similar users are commonly referred to as 'neighbors'. The similarity weight $w_{a,u}$ between the active user a and neighbor u, is defined by a similarity measure (e.g., Pearson correlation coefficient). The prediction of user a, rating on item i is done by computing a weighted average of the ratings, using the similarity weight as given in [8] is:

$$p_{a,i} = \bar{r_a} + k \sum_{u=1}^{n} (r_{u,i} - \bar{r_u}) * w_{a,u} \qquad (1)$$

where n is the number of best neighbors chosen and k is a normalizing factor such that the sum of absolute values of the weights is 1. $r_{u,i}$ is the rating of user u for item i. $\bar{r_u}, \bar{r_a}$ are average ratings of user u and a respectively. Hence, with users representing resources, items representing the tasks and rating representing performance outcomes (such as completion times of tasks), CF can be used to recommend tasks to a resource based on ratings of neighbors.

2.3   Context-Aware Recommendation System

Importance of contextual information has been recognized in many disciplines, including e-commerce personalization, ubiquitous and mobile computing. It is important to incorporate contextual information into the recommendation process in order to recommend tasks to resources in certain circumstances. For example, recommending a complex and time consuming task at the start of the work-shift could result in a different performance outcome as compared to recommending the same task, when close the completion of the work-shift. Context-aware recommender systems (CARS) address this gap and use contextual information for providing better recommendations [1]. CARS deals with modeling and predicting user preferences or ratings by incorporating available contextual information into the recommendation as explicit additional data. The ratings, hence are modeled as the function of not only items and users, but also of the context. The input data for traditional recommender systems is based on data records of the form $\langle user; item; rating \rangle$. In contrast, context-aware recommender systems are built based on the knowledge of contextual information, with data records of the form $\langle user; item; context; rating \rangle$, where each specific record includes not only the rating of a user on a specific item, but also the contextual information in which the item was rated by this user. In this work, we use contextual characteristics defined for a business process [22] to model context and incorporate it into our context-aware task recommender.

3   Modeling CARS for Service System

The elements of a context-aware recommender system are users, items, rating of users to items, context and the similarity measure to identify neighbors. In this section we model resource, task, context and define similar resources for a service system to build a context-aware recommender for task allocation.

3.1   Resource

We use the resource model described by Muehlen et al. [16] to model resources (user). In Muehlen's resource model, each resource owns some *roles* that represents capabilities and privileges to perform tasks, occupies *positions* in organization units, that further provide privileges to perform task. Model of a resource is essential to ensure that the recommender does not recommend tasks that are out of a resource's capacity or privilege. A resource is represented by a set of attributes D_R representing role, position, organization and other relevant information. These attributes characterize the resource and are static - they do not change during the execution of a task. Hence, a resource r is represented by attribute-value pairs $v_r = (v_r^1, v_r^2 \ldots v_r^{D_R})$.

3.2   Task

Item is a task that needs to be completed by a resource. Task is an executing instance of an activity in a process. Task is characterized by attributes of the process instance it belongs to, and the attributes specific to the task. Task attributes are endogenously determined elements (i.e., attributes whose values are determined via the execution of the task) as well as data provided as input to the task. For example, for a task that verifies a loan application, the loan amount would be a task attribute. We use a set of attributes D_T to denote process and task data in the usual sense, i.e., data provided as input to a process or task, data modified or impacted by a process or task and data generated as output by a process or task. Hence, a task t is represented by attribute-value pairs $v_t = (v_t^1, v_t^2 \ldots v_t^{D_T})$.

3.3   Context

Context is an important model element in our approach. Saidani et al. [22] define a meta-model of context for a business process. The meta-model comprises of context entity and context attributes. Context entities are connected to each other using context relationships. We leverage this meta-model and use context entities such as activity and resource, and their related contextual attributes. We refer to contextual attributes as contextual dimensions (as we further define attributes for a contextual dimension). While previous work has considered context for the overall process, we model context for tasks in the process. Contextual entities and dimensions captured in the model vary with the situation [22] - *"There is no context without context: the notion of context should be defined in terms of a purpose."*. Figure 1 illustrates the context model used for the purpose of task allocation recommendation. The contextual entities are task and resource. The generic contextual dimensions for task and resource are defined in the model. In addition, domain specific contextual dimensions would need to be defined and added. An example of a domain specific dimension for a resource would be a 'number of years in organization'. Task specific contextual dimensions such as time of the day of executing task, the duration of the task and time to finish are self explanatory. Generic contextual dimensions of resource that impact task allocation decisions are presented:

Workload can be either: number of tasks waiting at the start of execution of a task or the number of tasks that have been completed over a particular period [17]. It defines 'how busy' a resource is or has been when committing to a task. $WL(r, t) \rightarrow N$, where $WL(r, t)$ is the workload of a resource r at time t.

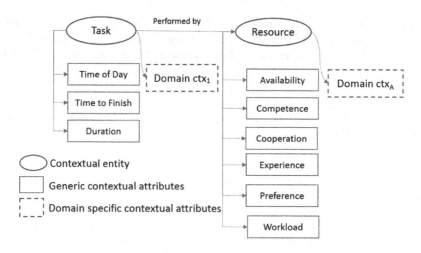

Fig. 1. Context model used for task recommendation

Availability indicates whether a resource is available to perform a task within a specific time limitation. Huang et al. [10] define resource availability measure, to predict if a resource is available at some time in the future. A simpler measure of availability of a resource r at time t is $Avail(r, t) \rightarrow \{true, false\}$, a boolean true or false where the $Avail(r, t) = false$ if $WL(r, t) \geq \tau$ where τ is defined for a specific task.

Competence is the ability to perform a certain type of task [10]. If a resource performs a certain type of task by using lower cost than the others, it means that the resource has a higher competence level than others to perform the task. The cost can be defined based on service system (e.g. completion time, quality). Competence measure as described in [10] is used.

Cooperation is the ability of working with other resources. Kumar et al. [13], define compatibility or cooperation as a measure of the degree to which resources cooperate with one another in a process. Cooperation between resources who perform tasks where there are hand offs, is measured as described in [13].

Experience is acquired and improved by performing tasks [11]. The number of times a task has been performed and the duration or time period for which the task is performed, is used to measure experience.

Preference is acquired knowledge or attitude to do a certain kind of task. For example, if a resource commits for a type of task frequently, the preference to the task is high. Preference $\rho(a, r)$ of a resource r on task type a is given as: $\rho(a, r) = Card(a, r)/Card(a)$, where $Card(a, r)$ is the number of tasks of task type a, resource r has completed and $Card(a)$ is the total number of tasks of type a completed by all resources.

Moreover, each contextual dimension c, can be defined by a set of q attributes $\{c_1, \ldots c_q\}$ having a hierarchical structure and capturing a particular type of context (e.g., experience of a resource). The values taken by attribute c_q define finer (more granular) levels, while c_1 values define coarser (less granular) levels of contextual knowledge. For example, Fig. 2 presents a two-level hierarchy for the contextual attribute c specifying experience of a resource to a task. While the root (coarsest level) of the hierarchy defines *experience* on an activity or task, the next level is defined by attribute $c_1 = \{experience\_case, experience\_customer\}$, which identifies the experience of a resource handling the specific case (other tasks related to the case) or handling a specific customer.

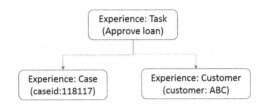

Fig. 2. Hierarchy structure of a contextual dimension

An important requirement for building and deploying a CARS is the availability of contextual information along with historical task executions. Our current approach infers contextual dimensions such as preference, workload, cooperation and competence from event logs. Figure 3 provides an example event log containing the details of the task, the resource owning the task, start time and completion time. Using the event data, for any new arriving task, the competence, preference is computed. The workload is derived by evaluating current active tasks of the resource. Similarly, other contextual measures can be computed.

Example log					Enriched Log						
Task Name	Resource	Start Time	Completion Time						Time on task (cost)	Preference for Task A	Workload	Competence for Task A
Task A	Joe	9/3/15 8:35	9/3/15 9:25		Task Name	Resource	Start Time	Completion Time				
Task A	Joe	9/3/15 9:10	9/3/15 11:00		Task A	Joe	9/3/15 8:35	9/3/15 9:25	50			
Task B	Carol	9/2/15 10:30	9/2/15 12:10		Task A	Joe	9/3/15 9:10	9/3/15 11:00	110			
Task B	Carol	9/2/15 12:30	9/2/15 13:50		Task B	Carol	9/2/15 10:30	9/2/15 12:10	100			
Task A	Sue	9/2/15 8:20	9/2/15 9:00		Task B	Carol	9/2/15 12:30	9/2/15 13:50	80			
Task B	Sue	9/2/15 13:10	9/2/15 14:40		Task A	Sue	9/2/15 8:20	9/2/15 9:00	40			
Task A	Carol	9/3/15 13:20	9/3/15 14:30		Task B	Sue	9/2/15 13:10	9/2/15 14:40	90			
Task A	Joe	9/3/15 10:20	9/3/15 11:10		Task A	Carol	9/3/15 13:20	9/3/15 14:30	70	0	0	0
					Task A	Joe	9/3/15 10:20	9/3/15 11:10	50	0.67	0	0.4

Prior event data is used to extract contextual attributes: preference, competence of Joe and Carol for Task A

Fig. 3. Extracting contextual attributes for a new task from past execution log

3.4 Rating

In CF, users provide ratings to as many items as possible. In this work, the outcome of past task executions is used to compute the rating of a resource to a task. Outcomes are typically performance indicators defined in the service system. Time to complete a task, quality level or percentage of tasks meeting a deadline are some examples of outcomes. Rating is an ordered set and needs to be on a common scale for all users. We use a sigmoid function to compute ratings. The computation of rating for a resource r_a, with completion time of task t as the outcome is given by a sigmoid function:

$$R(r_a, t) = \frac{1}{1 + e^{-k(\mu_t - \mu_{r_a, t})}} \tag{2}$$

where μ_t is the mean completion time of the task and $\mu_{r_a, t}$ is the mean completion time of the task t by the resource r_a. k is a parameter that can be varied to get the required rating interval. In particular, if the variance in outcome is high, k should be smaller to be more sensitive to these variances, similarly, if the variance is low, k should be higher. If there are multiple performance indicators, a rating can be arrived at by selecting from or combining different indicators. The ratings can be further scaled up to a suitable interval of [0,10].

3.5   Resource Similarity

Various similarity measures that calculate the similarity among resources or users, have been defined in the implementation of CF algorithms. Correlation-based similarity of two resources u and v is measured by computing $Pearson - r$ correlation $corr_{u,v}$. The correlation between two user's ratings on common tasks, is used to determine similarity. The correlation used from [23] is as follows:

$$s(u, v) = \frac{\sum_{i \in I_u \cap I_v} (r_{u,i} - \bar{r_u})(r_{v,i} - \bar{r_v})}{\sqrt{\sum_{i \in I_u \cap I_v} (r_{u,i} - \bar{r_u})^2} \sqrt{\sum_{i \in I_u \cap I_v} (r_{v,i} - \bar{r_v})^2}} \tag{3}$$

Where I_u are items or tasks executed by u and I_v are items or tasks executed by v. $r_{u,i}, r_{v,i}$ is the rating of item i by user u and v respectively. $\bar{r_u}, \bar{r_v}$ is the average rating of the user u, v respectively. Once the similarity is computed, k neighbors are selected and the prediction of a rating on task i for a resource u is arrived at by computing the sum of the ratings given by the neighbors users. Each rating is weighted by the corresponding similarity $s(u, v)$.

3.6   Context Aware Recommendation of Tasks to Resources

Information of the resource, task and context is used to predict the rating. Formally, with the multi-dimension data model, D_R and D_T are the dimensions of the resource and task respectively. The dimension D_R is a subset of Cartesian product of some attributes of the resource. For example, a resource dimension is defined as $Resource \subseteq Name \times Role \times Department$. Similarly, the task dimension is defined as $Task \subseteq Name \times Type$. Finally, the dimensions of context such as, $D_{workload}, D_{time}$ are included (and other relevant contextual dimensions). Given all the dimensions, the rating function F is defined as:

$F : D_R \times D_T \times D_{workload} \times D_{time} \rightarrow Rating$

There are multiple approaches to using contextual information in the recommendation process. We use contextual pre-filtering [1]. In this approach, contextual information drives data selection for that specific context. Information about the context is used for selecting relevant set of ratings of the resources to tasks. On the subset of the data selected, rating of a resource to a task is predicted using traditional collaborative filtering technique. Tasks with higher ratings are recommended to the resource.

4   Evaluation

In this section, we present the evaluation of our approach. First, we present the setup for evaluation. Then evaluations on two real-life event logs are detailed.

4.1   Evaluation Setup

In order to conduct our evaluation, we implement collaborative filtering based recommender using Apache Mahout library[1]. Figure 4 depicts the procedure for evaluating context-aware recommender system. We use real-world event logs. Based on the identified performance outcome (completion time, quality), ratings are computed for each resource, task pair. The event logs are enriched by computing additional information about context, using information of the task, resource executing the task, the task's start and end times. We use the data without contextual information and data with contextual information to carry out the validation using random sub-sampling validation. That is, we randomly pick 90 % of data to build a prediction model and use the remaining 10 % to test the model. Ten random splits were evaluated. In the approach without contextual data (marked as 1), rating of a task for a resource is predicted and compared with the actual rating. In the context enriched approach, additional contextual information is used to predict the rating of a task for a resource under that specific context. The predicted and actual ratings are compared and the mean absolute error (MAE), commonly used for evaluating CF is computed [9].

4.2   Incident Management Event Logs

To validate the effectiveness of using context in a real-life business process providing services, we use 2013 edition of the BPI challenge event log of Volvo IT services [4]. The log (Event log1) contains events of an incident management process. Each incident is a task that relates to a glitch in a product. An IT service personnel or resource works on the incident and restores service. The event log contains the information about the product associated to the incident, impact of the incident, resources who worked on the incident, time and status of the incident. Product related to the incident is used to categorize tasks or items. In the log, there is not much information about resource other than name of the

---

[1] http://mahout.apache.org/.

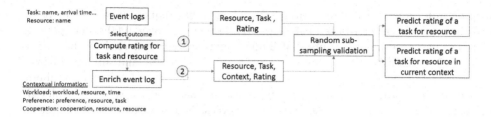

Fig. 4. Evaluation procedure

resource. We enrich the logs with additional contextual information: workload and preference of a resource. The workload of the resource at a specific time, is computed by evaluating the number of active incidents in the queue of the resource at that time. The preference for task (item) is the ratio of the number of tasks executed by the resource and associated to the product, to the total number of tasks associated to the product. Service levels attained for an item (outcome) is used to compute ratings. Hence, we use a sigmoid function by considering percentage of incidents that were completed within a target time. For predicting ratings, we consider only a subset of incidents where one single resource has worked on it. There are 110 resources, 41 tasks. k or number of neighbors for predicting rating is set to 10. Event logs involving multiple resources, do not provide clarity on the time spent by each resource on an incident and hence are not used. The mean absolute errors for completion time with and without context is shown in Fig. 5.

4.3 Financial Institute Event Logs

Our second study uses event logs of 2012 edition of BPI challenge (Event log 2), taken from a Dutch financial institute [2]. The event log represents an application

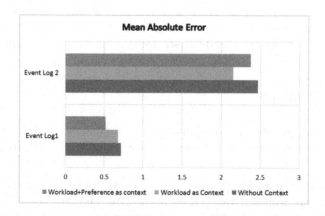

Fig. 5. Mean absolute error of predicted rating

process for a personal loan or overdraft. The amount requested by the customer is indicated as an attribute in the logs. While there are over 1000 events present in the log, we evaluate events that indicate manual effort exerted by the bank's staff. The manual effort is limited to 6 tasks. Task name and amount of loan requested are used as task attributes. There is no additional information about the resource. Resource who have executed at least 100 cases are considered. Hence, the we have 288 tasks and 43 resources. Number of neighbors is set to 10. Workload of a resource at a specific time and preference of a resource to a task is computed from the log. The rating is computed based on the completion times of task. We predict rating of a task for a resource with and without contextual information and compute MAE as indicated in Fig. 5.

4.4 Discussion

The results of evaluation indicate that the ratings of a task for a resource are influenced by context. As shown in Fig. 5, for event log 1, there is an improvement in prediction accuracy with additional contextual dimensions. However, in event log 2, addition of workload improves prediction accuracy while inclusion of workload and preference does not lower the mean absolute error. In this work, we have used a memory based collaborative filtering algorithm. A model based algorithm would help in identifying the influence of contextual dimensions on the performance outcome or rating. The event logs were collected for a time period of 3 months or less, and hence is limited as CARS requires sufficiently large data that captures ratings in varying situations. Hence, measuring and using additional contextual dimensions on a larger event log would be a useful activity. The models built for evaluation do not contain any domain specific contextual dimensions (due to lack of any additional information other than the log). It would be useful to build a model on a service system including domain specific contextual dimensions.

In real-world recommender systems, there could be a possibility that none of the resources are suitable for a task in their specific context. The task would be rated low for all resources. Such a situation could lead to a task not being picked up or completed on time. For handling such scenarios, additional alert mechanisms have to be built into the service system, to identify tasks that have rating below a specific threshold for all the active resources.

5   Related Work

Our work lies at the intersection of multiple research areas: contextual modeling in business process, resource behavior (used as context in our work), and task allocations.

Context Modeling in Business Processes: Modeling of context in business process has been proposed by Saidani et al. [21]. They introduce a taxonomy of contextual information for business processes consisting of four categories: (i) context related to location (ii) context related to time (iii) context related to resources and (iv) context related to organization. In their more recent work [22], a meta-model for context has been defined. The meta-model comprises of context entity and context attributes. Context entities are connected to each other using context relationships. We have leveraged this meta-model in our work, we use context entities such resource, task and their related contextual attributes or dimensions.

Ghattas et al. [6,7] use process context and process outcomes from execution histories to discover decisions taken in the past. In their work, the authors model the process context and outcomes. The definition of context is based on a Generic Process Model defined by the authors where, external events, that are out of the control of process execution are referred to as context. A decision tree is built to discover business decisions taken in the past. Our definition of context considers similar external factors.

In our earlier work [25], we use past execution histories and context information to further link with process outcomes and identify resource allocation decisions. However, decision rules are derived by considering all resources of a service system. Derived rules can guide centralized task allocations (push-based dispatch). In this work, the analysis of recommendations are for every resource. Context and outcomes of similar resources are considered for task allocation. Further, the notion of context has been identified for a task as compared to entire process. Hence, the task contains richer information of context specific to itself as well as the entire process.

Process context has also been defined by a different set of authors as "Minimum set of variables containing all relevant information that impact the design and execution of a business process."[19]. In our work, we consider a more specific definition of context and define some of the contextual characteristics that impact task allocation.

A large body of additional work exists in modeling and designing context-aware recommender systems for e-commerce and mobile systems, but space constraints preclude a detailed discussion of these.

Modeling Resource Behavior or Context: Resource behavior indicators [18], has been defined by Pika et al. In their work, the authors provide a framework for extracting resource behavior indicators from event logs and highlight the change in these indicators over time. Huang et al. [10] present resource behavior measures for competence, preference, availability and cooperation. These measures can be used to characterize resources further. Enriching resource model, to include additional resource characteristics, has also been described in [26]. In this work, we use the resource behavior model to define the contextual characteristics of a resource.

Resource Allocation Recommendation: There is a large body of work on resource allocation. While we present some of the work, the key distinction in our approach is the inherent support it has for pull-based dispatching, where the ownership of picking the task to work on, lies on the resource. In addition, our work provides the ability to consider multiple contextual characteristics that could potentially impact the outcome, when making recommendations.

Recent work by Vanderfeesten et al. [26] propose conceptual extensions to characterizing resource, tasks and process objectives or outcomes. The authors propose the need to extend the resource model with resource characteristics such as its capabilities, experience, preference and personal goals for better task allocation. In our work, we define contextual characteristics of a resource which have some of the resource characteristics and use the same for task allocation.

Cabanillas et al. [3] propose an approach to generate prioritized ranking of resources, based on preferences for task allocation. A preference model is defined and used to generate a prioritized list of resources for a task. The authors indicate the need for a preference model that prioritizes tasks for resources. In our work, we generate a ranking of tasks for each resource.

Much of the work has considered resource characteristics in isolation. Kumar et al. [13] propose cooperation among the team members involved in the process as a measure, and develop an allocation algorithm to maximize team cooperation. The authors, highlight the need for examining impact of cooperation on throughput and other process outcomes. Sonja et al. [12], define various measures of experience. The authors, further describe an experience breeding model [11], for maintaining experience levels of the resources. Detailed modeling of experience enables better evaluation of resource allocation decisions. In this work, experience has been defined as one of the contextual characteristics of a resource. In their work [17], Nakatumba et al. have analyzed the influence of workload on service times. The authors use event logs to extract service times and workload on a resource and build a regression model using workload as a single predictor of service time for every resource. Recommender system proposed in our work, learns from similar other resources, in the absence of sufficient information for a resource and uses multiple contextual characteristics in addition to workload.

Recommending the next action to take, based on a user's current execution history and specific goal, has been described in [24]. The approach evaluates past history of executions to mine recommendations. The work focuses on the control flow and the context is not considered. In one of the recent works [14], the authors present a general framework to derive and correlate process characteristics. The framework does not consider contextual characteristics of process, resources, and its influence on the process outcomes.

6   Conclusion and Future Work

This paper shows how history of past task executions and their associated contexts can be mined to provide guidance in recommending suitable tasks to resources. Research in the past has analyzed resource behavior or context, but in isolation. The work presented here, uses it in conjunction with outcomes and provides guidance by identifying outcomes of similar resources in similar context. This work further uses real-world event logs to derive resource context and discover influence of the context on performance outcome of tasks. In this work, we have used memory-based collaborative filtering. We would in future, evaluate model based collaborative filtering that creates a model by learning and finding hidden patterns and features in the data. Model based filtering is more robust to sparsity of data, that arises when using context as a pre-filter.

References

1. Adomavicius, G., Tuzhilin, A.: Context-aware recommender systems. In: Ricci, F., Rokach, L., Shapira, B., Kantor, P.B. (eds.) Recommender Systems Handbook, pp. 217–253. Springer, Boston (2011)
2. Bautista, A.D., Wangikar, L., Akbar, S.M.K.: Process mining-driven optimization of a consumer loan approvals process. In: Reichert, M., Reijers, H.A. (eds.) BPM 2015. LNBIP, vol. 256, pp. 219–220. Springer, Heidelberg (2013). doi:10.1007/978-3-642-36285-9_24
3. Cabanillas, C., García, J.M., Resinas, M., Ruiz, D., Mendling, J., Ruiz-Cortés, A.: Priority-based human resource allocation in business processes. In: Barros, A., Grigori, D., Narendra, N.C., Dam, H.K. (eds.) ICSOC 2015. LNCS, vol. 9435, pp. 374–388. Springer, Heidelberg (2013). doi:10.1007/978-3-642-45005-1_26
4. Dongen, B.F., Weber, B., Ferreira, D.R., Weerdt, J.: Report: business process intelligence challenge 2013. In: Reichert, M., Reijers, H.A. (eds.) BPM 2015. LNBIP, vol. 256, pp. 79–87. Springer, Heidelberg (2014). doi:10.1007/978-3-319-06257-0_7
5. Dourish, P.: What we talk about when we talk about context. Pers. Ubiquit. Comput. **8**(1), 19–30 (2004)
6. Ghattas, J., Soffer, P., Peleg, M.: A formal model for process context learning. In: Reichert, M., Reijers, H.A. (eds.) BPM 2015. LNBIP, vol. 256, pp. 140–157. Springer, Heidelberg (2010). doi:10.1007/978-3-642-12186-9_14
7. Ghattas, J., Soffer, P., Peleg, M.: Improving business process decision making based on past experience. Decis. Support Syst. **59**, 93–107 (2014)
8. Herlocker, J.L., Konstan, J.A., Borchers, A., Riedl, J.: An algorithmic framework for performing collaborative filtering. In: Proceedings of the 22nd ACM SIGIR Conference (SIGIR 1999), New York, pp. 230–237 (1999)
9. Herlocker, J.L., Konstan, J.A., Terveen, L.G., Riedl, J.: Evaluating collaborative filtering recommender systems. ACM Trans. Inf. Syst. **22**(1), 5–53 (2004)
10. Huang, Z., Lu, X., Duan, H.: Resource behavior measure and application in business process management. Expert Syst. Appl. **39**(7), 6458–6468 (2012)
11. Kabicher-Fuchs, S., Mangler, J., Rinderle-Ma, S.: Experience breeding in process-aware information systems. In: Nurcan, S., Soffer, P., Bajec, M., Eder, J. (eds.) CAiSE 2016. LNCS, vol. 9694, pp. 594–609. Springer, Heidelberg (2013). doi:10.1007/978-3-642-38709-8_38
12. Kabicher-Fuchs, S., Rinderle-Ma, S.: Work experience in PAIS - concepts, measurements and potentials. In: Proceedings of the Advanced Information Systems Engineering - 24th International Conference, CAiSE 2012, Gdansk, Poland, June 25–29, 2012, pp. 678–694 (2012)
13. Kumar, A., Dijkman, R., Song, M.: Optimal resource assignment in workflows for maximizing cooperation. In: Motahari-Nezhad, H.R., Recker, J., Weidlich, M. (eds.) BPM 2015. LNCS, vol. 9253, pp. 235–250. Springer, Heidelberg (2013). doi:10.1007/978-3-642-40176-3_20
14. Leoni, M., Aalst, W.M.P., Dees, M.: A general framework for correlating business process characteristics. In: Motahari-Nezhad, H.R., Recker, J., Weidlich, M. (eds.) BPM 2015. LNCS, vol. 9253, pp. 250–266. Springer, Heidelberg (2014). doi:10.1007/978-3-319-10172-9_16
15. Maglio, P.P., Vargo, S.L., Caswell, N., Spohrer, J.: The service system is the basic abstraction of service science. Inf. Syst. E-Bus. Manage. **7**(4), 395–406 (2009)
16. zur Muehlen, M.: Organizational management in workflow applications-issues and perspectives. Inf. Technol. Manage. **5**(3–4), 271–291 (2004)

17. Nakatumba, J., Aalst, W.M.P.: Analyzing resource behavior using process mining. In: Reichert, M., Reijers, H.A. (eds.) BPM 2015. LNBIP, vol. 256, pp. 69–80. Springer, Heidelberg (2010). doi:10.1007/978-3-642-12186-9_8

18. Pika, A., Wynn, M.T., Fidge, C.J., Hofstede, A.H.M., Leyer, M., Aalst, W.M.P.: An extensible framework for analysing resource behaviour using event logs. In: Nurcan, S., Soffer, P., Bajec, M., Eder, J. (eds.) CAiSE 2016. LNCS, vol. 9694, pp. 564–579. Springer, Heidelberg (2014). doi:10.1007/978-3-319-07881-6_38

19. Rosemann, M., Recker, J.: Context-aware process design exploring the extrinsic drivers for process flexibility. In: Proceedings of the CAISE*06 Workshop on Business Process Modelling, Development, and Support BPMDS 2006, 5–9 June 2006, Luxemburg (2006)

20. Russell, N., van der Aalst, W.M.P., ter Hofstede, A.H.M., Edmond, D.: Workflow resource patterns: identification, representation and tool support. In: Proceedings of the 17th International Conference, CAiSE 2005, Porto, Portugal, 13-17 June 2005, pp. 216–232, (2005). http://dblp.uni-trier.de/rec/bib/conf/caise/RussellAHE05

21. Saidani, O., Nurcan, S.: Context-awareness for adequate business process modelling. In: Proceedings of the Third IEEE International Conference on Research Challenges in Information Science, RCIS 2009, Fès, 22–24 April 2009, pp. 177–186 (2009)

22. Saidani, O., Rolland, C., Nurcan, S.: Towards a generic context model for BPM. In: 48th Hawaii International Conference on System Sciences, HICSS 2015, Kauai, Hawaii, USA, 5–8 January 2015, pp. 4120–4129 (2015)

23. Sarwar, B., Karypis, G., Konstan, J., Riedl, J.: Analysis of recommendation algorithms for e-commerce. In: Proceedings of the 2nd ACM Conference on Electronic Commerce, EC 2000, pp. 158–167. ACM, New York (2000)

24. Schonenberg, H., Weber, B., Dongen, B., Aalst, W.: Supporting flexible processes through recommendations based on history. In: Motahari-Nezhad, H.R., Recker, J., Weidlich, M. (eds.) BPM 2015. LNCS, vol. 9253, pp. 51–66. Springer, Heidelberg (2008). doi:10.1007/978-3-540-85758-7_7

25. Sindhgatta, R., Ghose, A., Dam, H.K.: Context-aware analysis of past process executions to aid resource allocation decisions. In: Nurcan, S., Soffer, P., Bajec, M., Eder, J. (eds.) CAiSE 2016. LNCS, vol. 9694, pp. 575–589. Springer, Heidelberg (2016). doi:10.1007/978-3-319-39696-5_35

26. Vanderfeesten, I., Grefen, P.: Advanced dynamic role resolution in business processes. In: Krogstie, J., Mouratidis, H., Su, J. (eds.) CAiSE 2016. LNBIP, vol. 249, pp. 87–93. Springer, Heidelberg (2015). doi:10.1007/978-3-319-19243-7_8

Semantic Pattern Mining Based Web Service Recommendation

Hafida Naïm[✉], Mustapha Aznag, Nicolas Durand, and Mohamed Quafafou

Aix-Marseille University, CNRS, LSIS UMR 7296, 13397 Marseille, France
hafida.naim@etu.univ-amu.fr,
{mustapha.aznag,nicolas.durand,mohamed.quafafou}@univ-amu.fr

Abstract. This paper deals with the problem of web service recommendation. We propose a new content-based recommendation system. Its originality comes from the combination of probabilistic topic models and pattern mining to capture the maximal common semantic of sets of services. We define the notion of semantic patterns which are maximal frequent itemsets of topics. In the off-line process, the computation of these patterns is performed by using frequent concept lattices in order to find also the sets of services associated to the semantic patterns. These sets of services are then used to recommend services in the on-line process. We compare the results of the proposed system in terms of precision and normalized discounted cumulative gain with Apache Lucene and SAWSDL-MX2 Matchmaker on real-world data. Our proposition outperforms these two systems.

Keywords: Web services · Recommendation · Topic models · Formal concept analysis · Concept lattice · Maximal frequent itemsets

1 Introduction

Web services[1] are defined as software systems designed to support interoperable machine-to-machine interaction over a network. They are "loosely coupled, reusable software components that semantically encapsulate discrete functionality and are distributed and programmatically accessible over standard Internet protocols". Web services are self contained, modular business applications that have open, internet-oriented and standards based interfaces. The explosion of web services with identical or similar functionalities over the internet has become a problem for the users. How can they find the best services that match their requirements from a large number of web services which have the requested functionality? Recommendation systems and selection techniques can be used to overcome this problem and assist users by recommending relevant web services from a large number of available web services [26].

---

[1] http://www.w3.org/standards/webofservices.

© Springer International Publishing Switzerland 2016
Q.Z. Sheng et al. (Eds.): ICSOC 2016, LNCS 9936, pp. 417–432, 2016.
DOI: 10.1007/978-3-319-46295-0_26

Recent research efforts on web service recommendation focus on two approaches: collaborative filtering and content-based recommendation. Collaborative filtering approaches [26,29] are used in almost all recommendation systems. They find relevant services for the current user by collecting information from other similar users. For example, a list of services that many users like, can be used as recommendations for other users that share a large overlap of services with this list. Content-based approaches [5,7] recommend web services on the basis of the similarity between the user request and the web service description (e.g., service functionalities). If the similarity between the user request and a service is high, this service is then recommended to the user.

In this paper, we propose a new content-based recommendation system. Its originality comes from the combination of probabilistic topic models and pattern mining to capture the maximal common semantic of sets of services. To the best of our knowledge, this is the first time that such approach combining the two domains is proposed. The core of the system is to identify the services which are very semantically linked. For this purpose, we defined the notion of semantic patterns. These latter correspond to maximal frequent itemsets of topics. Topics (or latent factors) correspond to a family of generative probabilistic models based on the assumption that documents (i.e., service descriptions) are generated by a mixture of topics where topics are probability distributions on words [23]. Topic models are used as efficient dimension reduction techniques which are able to capture semantic relationships between word-topic and topic-service [4]. The maximal frequent itemset discovery computes the maximal sets of items (i.e., topics), with respect to set inclusion, that appear together in at least a certain number of transactions (i.e., services) recorded in a database [12]. The semantic patterns allow to group together the services which are similar. Indeed, to each semantic pattern, the services containing this pattern can be associated. The services of a semantic pattern are very interesting: they are semantically linked and maximal. In order to compute semantic patterns and the corresponding sets of services, we used frequent concept lattices [27]. These sets of services are then stored in a special structure, called MFI-tree [11], in order to save space and perform quick searches by the recommendation engine. From a specified service, the recommendation engine uses this tree to find semantically similar services. The obtained services are then ranked and recommended to the user. For evaluation purposes, we conducted experiments on real-world data, and evaluated the quality of the recommended services. We also compared our system with two existing approaches: *Apache Lucene* and *SAWSDL-MX2 Matchmaker*.

The remainder of this paper is organized as follows. Section 2 provides an overview of related work. In Sect. 3 we describe in detail our service recommendation system. The experiments and the results are presented in Sect. 4. Finally, the conclusion and future work can be found in Sect. 5.

2   Related Work

Recommendation systems are assimilated to information filtering systems because the ideas and the methods are very close. We focus on two main types of filtering: content-based filtering and collaborative filtering. The interested reader can refer to [21] for further information about recommendation systems.

There is a lot of works on recommendation systems especially in the case of web navigation. So, we present some works in this context before considering the context of web services. Patterns are particularly used for collaborative filtering. These systems are based, for instance, on frequent itemsets, maximal frequent itemsets, clustering, formal concept analysis (i.e., concept lattices) or markov model [24]. The semantic aspects can be introduced in content-based approaches by using topic models or ontologies. In [20,25], the authors have computed topic models. The probabilistic topic model is Latent Dirichlet Allocation (LDA). They do not use patterns. Let us note that we do not use LDA but Correlated Topic Model (see Sect. 3.1). A notion of semantic patterns has been proposed in [14] but the definition does not correspond to ours. They do not consider topics. A semantic pattern is a path that connects a source type to a target type through pairs property-type. Our definition is: semantic patterns are maximal frequent itemsets of topics.

Let us consider the context of web services. Generally, every web service has a WSDL (Web Service Description Language) document that contains the description of the service. To enrich web service descriptions, several Semantic Web methods and tools are developed, for instance, the authors of [22] use an ontology to annotate the elements in web services. Nevertheless, the creation and maintenance of ontologies may be difficult and involve a huge amount of human effort [1]. The content-based approaches and/or the non-logic-based semantic approaches [7,13,17,18] aim to reduce the complexity of the discovery process by analysing the frequency of occurrence of some concepts and determine semantics which are implicit in service descriptions. These approaches generally use techniques such as information retrieval, data mining and linguistic analysis [17]. As the context of web navigation, the collaborative filtering approaches are widely used in web service recommendation systems [26,28,29]. In [29], the authors propose a collaborative filtering based approach for making personalized quality of service value prediction for the service users. In another context, Mehta et al. [16], propose an architecture for recommendation-based service mediation in which they take into account two more dimensions of service description: quality and usage pattern. The usage pattern permits to find applications with a similar usage pattern to the application making the request and then returns a recommendation list containing the services used by such applications.

As we can see, recommendation systems can use topic models or ontologies for considering semantics. Patterns are used especially for collaborative filtering and for capturing usages. The maximal frequent itemsets are not considered. We propose a content-based recommendation system leveraging probabilistic topic models and pattern mining (more precisely, maximal frequent itemset mining).

3 Web Service Recommendation System

In this section, we first give an overview of the proposed system. We then describe more in detail the different steps of our approach.

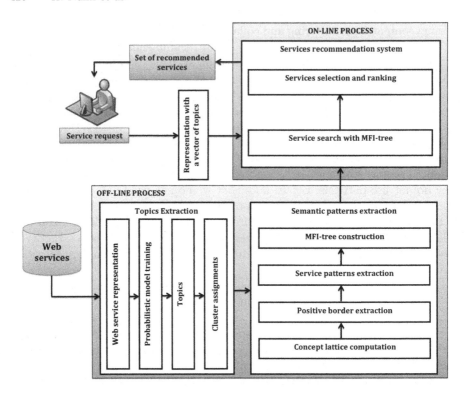

Fig. 1. Overview of the proposed recommendation system.

The proposed system relies on the notion of topics and semantic patterns. Topic models are used to capture semantic relationships between word-topic and topic-service. Semantic patterns capture the maximal common semantic of sets of services. The services corresponding to semantic patterns are used by the system. Let us note that this work extends our previous works on probabilistic web services clustering and discovery based on probabilistic topic models [2,4].

Figure 1 shows the overview of our system with the different steps involved. As shown in this figure, we can distinguish two kinds of process: online process and offline process. The different steps of the offline process are listed as follows: (1) Topics extraction, (2) Semantic patterns extraction. Once all these tasks are done, we can easily recommend web services from a service selected by the user in the list of services returned by a discovery system. We note that this is the only task of the online process.

3.1   Topics Extraction and Cluster Assignments

Topics (or latent factors) are a concept introduced by Probabilistic Topic Models [6]. They are a family of generative probabilistic models based on the assumption that documents are generated by a mixture of topics where topics are probability distributions on words. Topic models are used, in our context, as efficient dimension reduction techniques, which are able to capture semantic relationships between word-topic and topic-service interpreted in terms of probability distributions. In [2,4], we investigated the use of three probabilistic topic models PLSA, LDA and CTM [6] to extract topics from semantically enriched service descriptions and propose a probabilistic method for web services clustering and discovery. The results obtained from comparing the three methods based on PLSA, LDA and CTM showed that the CTM model provides a scalable and interoperable solution for automated service discovery and ranking in large service repositories. In this paper, we use the **Correlated Topic Model** (CTM) [6] to extract latent factors from web service descriptions.

After the CTM model is trained, the distribution of textual concepts for each topic is known and all the services in the dataset can be described as a distribution of topics (i.e. a vector $\overline{s} = \{z_1, z_2, ..., z_K\}$ where each dimension z_k reflects the probability of that service description being generated by sampling from topic k). Let $\theta^{(s)}$ refer to the multinomial distribution over topics in the service description s and $\phi^{(j)}$ refer to the multinomial distribution over concepts for the topic z_j. We create K clusters where K is the number of generated topics (i.e. a cluster for each topic). The distribution over topics $\theta^{(s)}$ for service s is used to determine which topic best describes the service s. More precisely, if a probability distribution $\theta^{(s)}$ over a specific z_j when given a web service s is high, then the service s can be affected to the cluster C_j. If a service s has more than one topic, the service will be assigned to each of the clusters corresponding to these topics [3]. To simplify, we use the *multiple topics assignment strategy* to assign a set of topics for each service by selecting a *topK* topics. Thus, a service could be assigned to multiple clusters (e.g., the three best fitting clusters). This will increase the scope of each search. Multiple cluster assignments achieve higher recommendation accuracy. However, it comes at the cost of increased number of comparisons and computations (see Sect. 4).

3.2   Semantic Pattern Extraction

In order to define the notion of semantic patterns, we need to introduce some definitions. A data mining context is denoted by $\mathcal{D} = (\mathcal{T}, \mathcal{I}, \mathcal{R})$ where $\mathcal{T}$ is a set of transactions (i.e., web services), $\mathcal{I}$ is a set of items (i.e., topics), and $\mathcal{R} \subseteq \mathcal{T} \times \mathcal{I}$ is a binary relation between transactions and items. Each couple $(t, i) \in \mathcal{R}$ denotes the fact that the transaction t is related to the item i (e.g., t contains i). A transactional database is a finite and nonempty multi-set of transactions. Table 1 provides an example of such database consisting of 6 transactions (each one identified by its "Id") and 8 items (denoted $A \ldots H$). In our context, services are transactions and topics are items. For each service, we assign the best topics (see Sect. 3.1). This assignment forms the binary relation $\mathcal{R}$.

An *itemset* is a subset of $\mathcal{I}$ (note that we use a string notation for sets, e.g., AB for $\{A, B\}$). An itemset is sorted in lexicographic order and is also called **pattern**. A transaction t supports an itemset X iff $\forall i \in X, (t, i) \in \mathcal{R}$. An itemset X is *frequent* if the number of transactions which support it, is greater than

Table 1. Example of transactional database.

Id	Items					
1	A		C	E		G
2		B	C	E		G
3	A		C	E			H
4	A			D	F		H
5		B	C		F		H
6		B	C	E	F		H

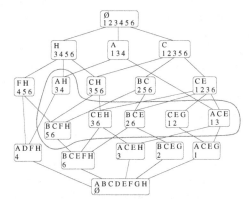

Fig. 2. Example of concept lattice (Bd^+ is encircled for $minsup = 2$).

(or is equal to) a minimum threshold value, noted $minsup$. The set of all-frequent itemsets is $S = \{X \subseteq \mathcal{I}, \ |\{t \in \mathcal{T}, \ \forall i \in X \ (t,i) \in \mathcal{R}\}| \ \geq minsup\}$. The set of all **maximal frequent itemsets** (MFI), w.r.t. set inclusion, in $\mathcal{D}$ is the **positive border** of S, noted $Bd^+(S)$, and is equal to $\{X \in S \mid \forall Y \supset X, Y \notin S\}$ [15]. Let us take the example of Table 1, if $minsup = 2$ then the itemset H is frequent because 4 transactions support it (3, 4, 5 and 6). BG is not frequent because only 2 supports it. CE is frequent but not maximal because CEH is also frequent. The set of MFIs is the positive border $Bd^+(S)$ and is equal to $\{AH, ACE, BCE, CEG, CEH, BCFH\}$.

A **semantic pattern** is a maximal frequent itemset of topics. To each semantic pattern, the transactions (i.e., services) containing this pattern can be associated. The services of a semantic pattern are very interesting: they are semantically linked and maximal. Thus, the proposed system uses these services. The minimum support threshold, $minsup$, allows to fix the minimum number of services for each semantic pattern. In order to extract the semantic patterns and their associated services, we compute the frequent concept lattice. Then, the set of services corresponding to each semantic pattern is selected and stored in a special structure called MFI-tree.

Concept Lattice Computation and Positive Border Extraction. Given $\mathcal{D}$, there is a unique ordered set which describes the inherent lattice structure defining natural groupings and relationships among the transactions and their related items. This structure is known as a concept lattice or Galois lattice [10]. Each element of the lattice is a couple (I, T) composed of a set of items (i.e., topics, the *intent*) and a set of transactions (i.e., services, the *extent*). Each couple (called **formal concept**) must be a complete couple with respect to $\mathcal{R}$, which means that the following mappings (noted f and g) hold. For $T \subseteq \mathcal{T}$ and $I \subseteq \mathcal{I}$, we have: (1) $f(T) = \{i \in \mathcal{I} | \forall t \in T, (t,i) \in \mathcal{R}\}$ and (2) $g(I) = \{t \in \mathcal{T} | \forall i \in$

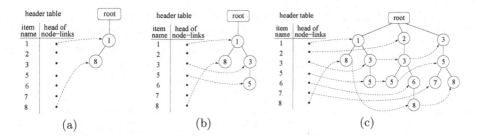

Fig. 3. MFI-tree construction.

$I, (t, i) \in \mathcal{R}\}$. $f(T)$ returns items common to all transactions $t \in T$, while $g(I)$ returns transactions that have at least all items $i \in I$. The idea of maximally extending the sets is formalized by the mathematical notion of *closure* in ordered sets. The operators $h_1 = f \circ g$ and $h_2 = g \circ f$ are the Galois closure operators. Let X be an itemset, if $h_1(X) = X$, then X is a *closed itemset*. A formal concept is composed of a closed itemset and of the set of transactions containing this closed itemset. The ***frequent concept lattice*** is formed using the formal concepts that have at least *minsup* transactions in their extent. The "bottom" concept (i.e., $(\mathcal{I}, \emptyset)$) is kept. Due to the fact that the intents of the frequent formal concepts form the set of all-frequent closed itemsets [19] and that the set of all-maximal frequent itemsets is a subset of frequent closed itemsets, we can easily find $Bd^+(S)$ (i.e., the set of semantic patterns) from the frequent concept lattice. The positive border corresponds to the frequent formal concepts just above the bottom. Figure 2 presents the concept lattice obtained using the example of Table 1. The bottom is $(A\ B\ C\ D\ E\ F\ G\ H, \emptyset)$. With $minsup = 2$, the frequent formal concepts are above the dashed line. The formal concepts corresponding to the $Bd^+(S)$ are encircled. So, the semantic patterns are $\{AH, \dots, BCFH\}$ and the corresponding sets of services are $\{\{3, 4\}\{1, 3\}\{1, 2\}\{2, 6\}\{3, 6\}\{5, 6\}\}$. Let us remark that the concepts of $Bd^+(S)$ can have more than $minsup$ transactions in their extent (see Sect. 4.3).

Service Pattern Extraction and MFI-tree Construction. The result of the previous step is the set of formal concepts corresponding to the $Bd^+(S)$ (i.e., the set of semantic patterns). The proposed system selects the extents of these formal concepts to form the sets of services which will be used by the online recommendation engine. These sets of services are considered as patterns. To facilitate the recommendation, we store these patterns of services in a variant of FP-tree (Frequent Pattern tree) called MFI-tree (Maximal Frequent Itemsets tree) [11]. This allows a space saving and a quick search of the patterns containing a given service by using indexes. Every branch of the tree represents a pattern. Compression is achieved by building the tree in such way that overlapping patterns share prefixes of the corresponding branch. The tree has a root labelled with "root". Children of the root are item prefix subtrees. Each node in the subtree has four fields: item-name, children-list, parent-link and node-link. All nodes with same item-name are linked together. The node-link points to the next node with same item-name. A header table is constructed for items in the MFI-tree. Each entry in the header table consists of two fields, item-name and head of a node-link. The node-link points to the first node with the same item-name in the MFI-tree. Let us take a new example (more complete than the first one) where we have extracted the semantic patterns and then found these patterns of services: $\{\{1,8\}\{1,3,5\}\{2,3,5\}\{3,5,7\}\{3,5,8\}\{2,3,6,8\}\}$. Figure 3 illustrates the construction of the tree. We get the first pattern $\{1,8\}$. It is inserted into the tree directly (see Fig. 3(a)). We then insert $\{1,3,5\}$ into the tree (see Fig. 3(b)). Figure 3(c) presents the complete tree.

3.3   Web Service Recommendation Task

From a service s, the proposed system find the services present with s in the patterns of services computed in the offline process. These services are ranked and recommended to the user. Algorithm 1 present the search of recommended services from a service s by using the MFI-tree constructed in the previous step. It returns the items (i.e., services) present in the patterns containing s. The idea of the algorithm is to use the header table of the tree to access directly to the different patterns containing the item s. For each node N corresponding to s (Step 2), we need to find the common prefix (PX) of the patterns (Steps 3 to 8). It corresponds to go up to the root node via the parent links. Then we find all the possible ends of the patterns (i.e., the suffixes SX) (Step 10). The items of the prefix and of the suffixes are merged (Steps 11 and 12) and will be returned at the end of the algorithm. Let us take an example: the service 5 and the tree of Fig. 3(c). For the first node corresponding to 5, $PX = \{1,3\}$ and $SX = \{\}$, we have $R = \{1,3\}$. For the second node, $PX = \{2,3\}$ and $SX = \{\}$, so we have $R = \{1,2,3\}$. For the last node, $PX = \{3\}$ and $SX = \{\{7\},\{8\}\}$. The services R to recommend are $\{1,2,3,7,8\}$. Let us note that it is possible to recommend services from a set of services S by intersecting the set of recommended services obtained for each service $s \in S$.

Once the recommended services are discovered using Algorithm 1, these services are ranked in order of their similarity score to the service request. Thus, we obtain automatically an efficient ranking of the recommended services. In our approach, we use the proximity measure called *Multidimentional Angle* (also known as *Cosine Similarity*); a measure which uses the cosine of the angle between two vectors. We calculate the similarity between the service request and each recommended web service by computing the Cosine Similarity between a vector containing the service request distribution over topics q and a vector containing the recommended service's distribution of topics p. The multidimensional angle between a vector p and a vector q can be calculated using Eq. 1 where t is the number of topics.

$$Cos(p,q) = \frac{p.q}{\parallel p \parallel \cdot \parallel q \parallel} = \frac{\sum_{i=1}^{t} p_i q_i}{\sqrt{\sum_{i=1}^{t} p_i^2 \sum_{i=1}^{t} q_i^2}}. \tag{1}$$

Algorithm 1. MFI-tree based web service recommendation algorithm

Require:
  - **s** : a service
  - **T** : the MFI-tree containing the patterns of services
Ensure: R: the set of recommended services
  1: N ← T.header-table[s]; // node N: head of node links for s
  2: **while** N != null **do**
  3:     Parent ← N.parent-link; // parent node of N
  4:     PX ← ∅; // common prefix
  5:     **while** Parent != null **do**
  6:         PX ← PX ∪ {Parent.item-name};
  7:         Parent ← Parent.parent-link;
  8:     **end while**
  9:     SX ← ∅; // set of patterns starting from N
 10:     findSuffixes(N, ∅, SX); // find patterns starting from N
 11:     merge(SX); // union of all the patterns contained in SX
 12:     R ← R ∪ PX ∪ SX; // add services to recommend
 13:     N ← N.node-link; // next node corresponding to s
 14: **end while**
 15: **return** R;

The multidimensional angle takes values in the interval [0, 1] where 0 indicates no similarity and 1 indicates identical vectors.

4 Evaluation

4.1 Web Services Corpus and Data Preprocessing

The experiments are performed out based on real-world web services obtained from the WSDL service retrieval test collection called *SAWSDL-TC3*[2]. The WSDL corpus consists of 1088 semantically annotated WSDL 1.0-based Web services which cover 9 different application domains. Each web service belongs to one out of nine service domains named as: Communication, Education, Economy, Food, Geography, Medical, Military, Travel and Simulation. The dataset contains 42 queries (i.e., requests). A service request is defined as a service that would perfectly match the request. Furthermore, a binary and graded relevance set for each query is provided which can be used in order to compute Information Retrieval (IR) metrics. The relevance sets for each query consists of a set of relevant services and each service s has a graded relevance value $relevance(s) \in \{1, 2, 3\}$ where "3" denotes *high relevance* to the query and "1" denotes a *low relevance*. Table 2 lists the number of services and requests from each domain.

To manage efficiently web service descriptions, we extract all features that describe a web service from the WSDL document. Before representing web services as a *TF-IDF* (Text Frequency and Inverse Document Frequency) vectors,

---

[2] http://www.semwebcentral.org/projects/sawsdl-tc.

Table 2. Number of services and queries for each domain.

Domain	Services	Queries	Domain	Services	Queries
Communication	58	2	Medical	73	1
Economy	358	12	Military	40	1
Education	285	6	Simulation	16	3
Food	34	1	Travel	164	6
Geography	60	10			

we need some preprocessing. The objective of this preprocessing is to identify the textual concepts of services, which describe the semantics of their functionalities. There are commonly several steps: *Features extraction, Tokenization, Tag and stop words removal, Word stemming* and *Service Transaction Matrix construction* (see [2] for more details). After identifying all the functional terms, we calculate the frequency of these terms for all web services. We use the Vector Space Model (VSM) technique to represent each web service as a vector of these terms. In fact, it converts service description to vector form in order to facilitate the computational analysis of data. In IR, VSM is identified as the most widely used representation for documents and is a very useful method for analyzing service descriptions. The TF-IDF algorithm is used to represent a dataset of WSDL documents and convert it to VSM form. We use this technique, to represent a services descriptions in the form of *Service Transaction Matrix*. In the service matrix, each row represents a WSDL service description, each column represents a word from the whole text corpus (vocabulary) and each entry represents the TF-IDF weight of a word appearing in a WSDL document. TF-IDF gives a weight w_{ij} to every term j in a service description i using the equation: $w_{ij} = tf_{ij}.\log(\frac{n}{n_j})$ where tf_{ij} is the frequency of term j in WSDL document i, n is the total number of WSDL documents in the dataset, and n_j is the number of services that contain term j. The observed textual concepts are represented in a Service Transaction Matrix (STM).

4.2 Protocol and Evaluation Metrics

To compute topics, we use the STM as training data for our implementation of the CTM model (based on the Blei's implementation[3], which is a C implementation of CTM using Variational EM for Parameter Estimation and Inference).

We analyse the impacts of the parameters *minsup* (i.e., the minimum support threshold) and *assign* (i.e., number of topic assignments) on the quality of the recommendations. For some *minsup* values and for some *assign* values, we adopted the following protocol: For the offline part: (1) Computation of the semantic patterns (by using CHARM-L [27] to generate the frequent concept lattice), (2) Extraction of the patterns of services, (3) Construction of the MFI-tree.

---

[3] http://www.cs.princeton.edu/~blei/ctm-c/index.html.

The steps to simulate the online part are: For each query present in the dataset: (4) Search the recommended services by using Algorithm 1, (5) Ranking of the list of recommended services, (6) Evaluation of the quality of the first n recommended services.

In order to compare our web service recommendation system (labelled *Topic-MFI*) to two existing systems, Step 4 is redone twice by replacing our system by a syntax-based approach powered by *Apache Lucene*[4] and a method from the *SAWSDL-MX2 Matchmaker*[5] hybrid semantic matchmaker for SAWSDL services, respectively.

In the test collection, we have the queries together with the correct/expected web services (see Sect. 4.1). Thus, we estimate how well is a recommendation method by discovering services corresponding to each query in the data. After that, we compare the returned list of services with the expected one. Finally, we evaluate the accuracy of the recommendation system by using standard measures used in IR. Generally, the top most relevant retrieved services are the main results which are selected and used by the user. Thus, we evaluated the quality of the first n recommended services by computing *Precision at n* (*Precision@n*) and *Normalized Discounted Cumulative Gain* (*NDCG_n*). These are standard evaluation techniques used in IR to measure the accuracy of a search and matchmaking mechanism.

In our context, *Precision@n* is a measure of the precision of the service discovery system taking into account the first n retrieved services. Therefore, *Precision@n* reflects the number of services which are relevant to the user query. The *Precision@n* for a list of retrieved services is given by Eq. 2 where the list of relevant services to a given query is defined in the collection.

$$Precision@n = \frac{|RelevantServices \cap RetrievedServices|}{|RetrievedServices|}. \tag{2}$$

$NDCG_n$ uses a graded relevance scale of each retrieved service from the result set to evaluate the gain, or usefulness, of a service based on its position in the result list. This measure is particularly useful in IR for evaluating ranking results. The $NDCG_n$ for n retrieved services is given by Eq. 3 where DCG_n is the Discounted Cumulative Gain and $IDCG_n$ is the Ideal Discounted Cumulative Gain.

$$NDCG_n = \frac{DCG_n}{IDCG_n}, \qquad DCG_n = \sum_{i=1}^{n} \frac{2^{relevance(i)} - 1}{log_2(1 + i)}. \tag{3}$$

The $IDCG_n$ is found by calculating the DCG_n of the first n returned services. n is the number of retrieved services and $relevance(s)$ is the graded relevance of the service in the ith position in the ranked list. The $NDCG_n$ values for all queries can be averaged to obtain a measure of the average performance of a ranking algorithm. $NDCG_n$ values vary from 0 to 1. $NDCG_n$ gives higher scores to systems which rank a search result list with higher relevance first and penalizes systems which return services with low relevance.

---

[4] http://lucene.apache.org/.

[5] http://projects.semwebcentral.org/projects/sawsdl-mx.

Table 3. Number and size of the patterns obtained for assign-4 (according to *minsup*).

minsup	# patterns of services	Avg. size of a pattern
1	307	3.54
2	205	5.01
3	159	6.37
4	137	7.21
5	111	8.71
6	101	9.71

In addition to these metrics, we also compute some statistics (the number of computed patterns and the average size of a pattern) and we measure the query response times. All experiments were performed on a personal computer with a Intel Core2Duo processor, 2.4 GHz, and 6 GB of RAM.

4.3 Results and Discussion

Figure 4 presents the comparaison of average Precision@n values over 42 queries obtained for our method with different values of *minsup* (1 to 6) and *assign* (2 to 10 topics assigned to each service). A low or a high value of *assign* does not give the best results. The worst precision is obtained with *assign* = 7. Our method gives the higher precision values with *assign* = 4 (for each *minsup* values). So, we investigated more precisely the system when the *assign* value is equal to 4.

Table 3 shows the number of service patterns obtained and the average number of services in a pattern, for *assign* = 4 and *minsup* varying from 1 to 6. As we can expected, the more the *minsup* value is low, the more the number of patterns is high. The average size of a pattern is more interesting. For instance, if *minsup* is equal to 1, a pattern can contain only one service. Nevertheless, we can observe that the average number of services is higher than the *minsup* value. The services are often correlated. Our system is able to find these correlations and is not restricted to the *minsup* value.

Figure 5 (left) and (right) present the average *Precision@n* and *NDCG@n* values, respectively. These measures are obtained over all 42 queries for our method *Topic-MFI*, *ApacheLucene* and *SAWSDL-MX2 Matchmaker*. In both cases, the results show that *Topic-MFI* gives a higher average *Precision@n* and $NDCG_n$ for all 42 queries. In fact, our method perform better than all methods. The results show that *ApacheLucene* and *SAWSDL-MX2* were unable to find some of the relevant web services that were not directly related to some of the requests through keywords or logic descriptions. This reflects that the retrieved services obtained by our method are specific to the user's query. *ApacheLucene* and *SAWSDL-MX2* have a low $NDCG_n$ because, as shown in the *Precision@n* results, both approaches are unable to find some of the highly relevant services. The results obtained for our method reflect the accuracy of our recommendation system.

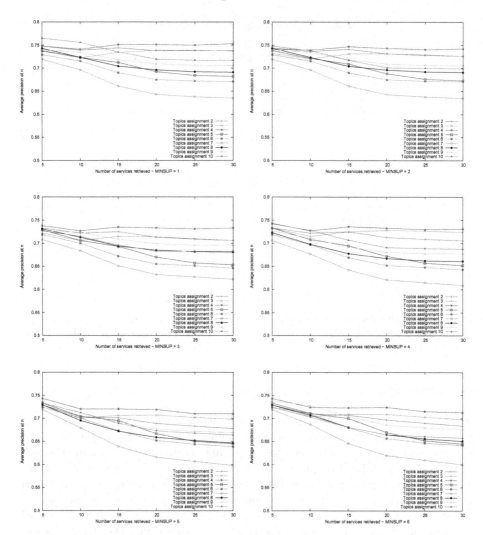

Fig. 4. Comparaison of average Precision@n values over 42 queries obtained for our method with different values of *minsup* and *assign* (# topics assigned to each service).

Table 4 presents the average query response times for *ApacheLucene*, *SAWSDL-MX2* and our method (*Topic-MFI*) for all 42 queries. As we can see, *Topic-MFI* gives a faster query response time than the other search methods. Our recommendation system is efficient and not time-consuming.

Table 4. Average query response times.

Method	Avg. query response time (ms)
Topic-MFI	68
ApacheLucene	1163
SAWSDL-MX2	3045

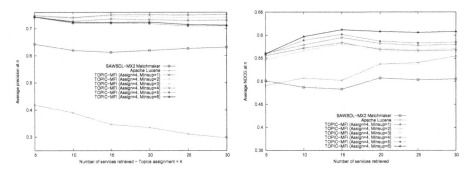

Fig. 5. (Left) Comparaison of average Precision@n values over 42 queries. (Right) Comparaison of average NDCGn values over 42 queries obtained for our method Topic-MFI and other baseline methods.

5   Conclusion

We have introduced a new content-based recommendation system leveraging probabilistic topic models and pattern mining. Its originality comes from the combination of the two domains for capturing the maximal common semantic of sets of services. For this purpose, we defined the notion of semantic patterns which are the maximal frequent itemsets of topics. To compute these patterns and the corresponding sets of services, we used frequent concept lattices. In order to save space and perform quick searches among the computed sets of services, the system stores them in a special structure, called MFI-tree. The recommendation engine uses this tree to find services from a specified service. The obtained services are ranked and recommended to the user. The experimental results obtained on real-world web services show that our system outperforms *ApacheLucene* and *SAWSDL-MX2 Matchmaker*. In future work, we will use the approximation of frequent itemset border [8,9] in order to extend our system and recommend supplementary services based on approximate semantic patterns.

References

1. Atkinson, C., Bostan, P., Hummel, O., Stoll, D.: A practical approach to web service discovery and retrieval. In: ICWS, pp. 241–248 (2007)
2. Aznag, M., Quafafou, M., Jarir, Z.: Correlated topic model for web services ranking. IJACSA **4**(6), 283–291 (2013)

3. Aznag, M., Quafafou, M., Jarir, Z.: Leveraging formal concept analysis with topic correlation for service clustering and discovery. In: ICWS (2014)

4. Aznag, M., Quafafou, M., Rochd, E.M., Jarir, Z.: Probabilistic topic models for web services clustering and discovery. In: Villari, M., Zimmermann, W., Lau, K.-K. (eds.) ESOCC 2014. LNCS, vol. 8745, pp. 19–33. Springer, Heidelberg (2013). doi:10.1007/978-3-642-40651-5_3

5. Blake, M.B., Nowlan, M.F.: A web service recommender system using enhancing syntactical matching. In: ICWS (2007)

6. Blei, D.M., Lafferty, J.D.: A correlated topic model of science. Ann. Appl. Stat. **1**, 17–35 (2007)

7. Cassar, G., Barnaghi, P., Moessner, K.: Probabilistic matchmaking methods for automated service discovery. TSC **7**(4), 654–666 (2013)

8. Durand, N., Quafafou, M.: Approximation of frequent itemset border by computing approximate minimal hypergraph transversals. In: Bellatreche, L., Mohania, M.K. (eds.) DaWaK 2014. LNCS, vol. 8646, pp. 357–368. Springer, Heidelberg (2014). doi:10.1007/978-3-319-10160-6_32

9. Durand, N., Quafafou, M.: Frequent itemset border approximation by dualization. In: Hameurlain, A., Küng, J., Wagner, R., Bellatreche, L., Mohania, M. (eds.) Transactions on Large-Scale Data- and Knowledge-Centered Systems XXVI. LNCS, vol. 9670, pp. 32–60. Springer, Heidelberg (2016)

10. Ganter, B., Wille, R.: Formal Concept Analysis: Mathematical foundations. Springer, Heidelberg (1999)

11. Grahne, G., Zhu, J.: Fast algorithms for frequent itemset mining using FP-Trees. TKDE **17**(10), 1347–1362 (2005)

12. Han, J., Cheng, H., Xin, D., Yan, X.: Frequent pattern mining: current status and future directions. Data Min. Knowl. Disc. **15**, 55–86 (2007)

13. Ma, J., Zhang, Y., He, J.: Efficiently finding web services using a clustering semantic approach. In: CSSSIA, pp. 1–8 (2008)

14. Maccatrozzo, V., Ceolin, D., Aroyo, L., Groth, P.: A semantic pattern-based recommender. In: Presutti, V. (ed.) ESWC 2014. CCIS, vol. 475, pp. 182–187. Springer, Cham (2014)

15. Mannila, H., Toivonen, H.: Levelwise search and borders of theories in knowledge discovery. Data Min. Knowl. Disc. **1**(3), 241–258 (1997)

16. Mehta, B., Niederée, C., Stewart, A., Muscogiuri, C., Neuhold, E.J.: An architecture for recommendation based service mediation. In: Bouzeghoub, M., Goble, C., Kashyap, V., Spaccapietra, S. (eds.) ICSNW 2004. LNCS, vol. 3226, pp. 250–262. Springer, Heidelberg (2004). doi:10.1007/978-3-540-30145-5_15

17. Mohebbi, K., Ibrahim, S., Khezrian, M., Munusamy, K., Tabatabaei, S.G.H.: A comparative evaluation of semantic web service discovery approaches. In: iiWAS, pp. 33–39 (2010)

18. Nayak, R., Lee, B.: Web service discovery with additional semantics and clustering. In: WI, pp. 555–558 (2007)

19. Pasquier, N., Bastide, Y., Taouil, R., Lakhal, L.: Efficient mining of association rules using closed itemset lattices. Inf. Syst. **24**(1), 25–46 (1999)

20. Mao, Q., Feng, B., Pan, S.: Modeling user interests using topic model. JATIT **48**(1), 600–606 (2013)

21. Ricci, F., Rokach, L., Shapira, B., Kantor, P.B.: Recommender Systems Handbook, 1st edn. Springer, New York (2011)

22. Sivashanmugam, K., Verma, A., Miller, J.: Adding semantics to web services standards. In: ICWS, pp. 395–401 (2003)

23. Steyvers, M., Griffiths, T.: Latent Semantic Analysis: A Road to Meaning, chap. Probabilistic topic models (2007)
24. Suguna, R., Sharmila, D.: An efficient web recommendation system using collaborative filtering and pattern discovery algorithms. IJCA **70**(3), 37–44 (2013)
25. Xu, G., Zhang, Y., Yi, X.: Modelling user behaviour for web recommendation using LDA model. In: WI-IAT, pp. 529–532 (2008)
26. Yao, L., Sheng, Q.Z., Ngu, A.H.H., Yu, J., Segev, A.: Unified collaborative and content-based web service recommendation. TSC **8**(3), 453–466 (2015)
27. Zaki, M., Hsiao, C.J.: Efficient algorithms for mining closed itemsets and their lattice structure. TKDE **17**(4), 462–478 (2005)
28. Zheng, Z., Ma, H., Lyu, M.R., King, I.: WSRec: a collaborative filtering based web service recommender system. In: ICWS, pp. 437–444 (2009)
29. Zheng, Z., Ma, H., Lyu, M.R., King, I.: QoS-aware web service recommendation by collaborative filtering. TSC **4**(2), 140–152 (2011)

Service UIs, APIs and Mashup

JSON Patch for Turning a Pull REST API into a Push

Hanyang Cao[1(✉)], Jean-Rémy Falleri[1], Xavier Blanc[1], and Li Zhang[2]

[1] University of Bordeaux, LaBRI, UMR 5800, 33400 Talence, France
{cao.hanyang,falleri,xblanc}@labri.fr
[2] Beihang University, Beijing, China
lily@buaa.edu.cn

Abstract. REST APIs together with JSON are commonly used by modern web applications to export their services. However, these services are usually reachable in a pull mode which is not suitable for accessing changing data. Turning a service from a pull to a push mode is therefore frequently asked by web developers that want to get notified of changes. Converting a pull API into a push one obviously requires to make periodical calls to the API but also to create a patch between each successive version of the data. The latter is the most difficult part and this is where existing solutions have some imperfections. To face this issue, we present a new patch algorithm supporting *move* and *copy* change operations. Our evaluation done with real industrial data shows that our algorithm creates small patches compared with other libraries, and creates them faster.

Keywords: REST · JSON · Diff · Patch · Web application

1 Introduction

Most of the web applications[1] provide an access to their services thanks to a REST API [9]. Their services are then directly reachable by HTTP requests, where the exchange of data is commonly done in JSON, the JavaScript Object Notation [7].

REST APIs have been however designed to be used in a pull mode request, which is inadequate for services that provide access to data that periodically change. For example, Twitter[2] provides a REST API with a service that returns a timeline of tweets. As any timeline changes quite frequently, the clients that use this API have actually to periodically call the service to refresh their views. Worst, if they just want to be aware of new tweets appearing in the timeline, they also have to create the patch describing the differences between the data they previously received and the new one just returned by the request, which can

---

[1] https://www.publicapis.com/.
[2] https://twitter.com.

© Springer International Publishing Switzerland 2016
Q.Z. Sheng et al. (Eds.): ICSOC 2016, LNCS 9936, pp. 435–449, 2016.
DOI: 10.1007/978-3-319-46295-0_27

be highly complex depending on the structure of the JSON documents contained in the response of the request.

In opposite to the pull mode, the push mode is more adequate for accessing changing data. Its principle is to send notification messages to the clients that have registered, and only when the data have changed. Further the messages contain the set of changes performed to the data rather than the new version of the data, letting the client react to them if needed.

Turning a service from a pull mode to a push mode is therefore frequently asked by web developers that want to access changing data and to get notified of performed changes. Some companies already supports this need. For example, our partner StreamData.io provides a proxy server that converts the pull mode API of an existing web application into push mode one.[3]

Converting a pull mode API into a push mode one obviously requires to make periodical calls to the API but also to create a patch between each successive received versions of the data. The latter is the most difficult part and this is where existing solutions have some imperfections. Indeed, creating a patch between two documents is a well-known very complex problem [4,15], which has not been studied yet for JSON documents. A JSON document is a labelled unordered tree that contains arrays (ordered sequences). Creating a patch between two JSON documents may therefore lead to a NP-hard problem depending both on the change operations that are considered (add, remove, move, copy), and on the quality of the created patch (in terms of size).

In this paper we propose a new patch algorithm that is tailored to JSON documents, and that drastically improves the conversion of pull mode APIs into push mode ones. Our algorithm returns a JSON Patch as specified by the JSON Patch RFC [3]. It therefore handles any changes that can be done on JSON documents, either on their basic properties or on their arrays, and supports simple changes (add, remove) as well as complex ones (move, copy), which allows clients to deeply understand changes that have been done.

We implemented our algorithm in JavaScript as it is the most commonly language used in web applications. We validate it by making a comparison with other JavaScript libraries that support the JSON patch RFC. This validation has been done by using real data provided by our partner StreamData.io.

As a main result, we provide:

- A new JSON patch algorithm that is fully complies with the JSON Patch RFC.
- A JavaScript implementation of our algorithm that performs better than the existing ones.

The structure of the paper is as follows. To start, the Sect. 2 gives a background about the JSON patch format as well as its computation, and further presents the existing approaches that support patch creation. The Sect. 3 presents our algorithm (named JDR). The Sect. 4 then presents the evaluation

---

[3] http://streamdata.io/.

of our JavaScript framework implementing our algorithm. The Sect. 5 finally presents our conclusion.

2 JSON Patch Background

2.1 JSON Document and JSON Patch

A JSON document is a very simple textual serialization of a JavaScript object. More precisely, it is a tree composed of three kinds of nodes (literal, array or object), where the root node cannot be a literal. A literal node can be either a boolean, a number or a string. An array node is a sequence of nodes. An object node has a set of child properties, each of them has a label[4] unique within the object, and a value that is a node. As an example, the Fig. 1 presents two simple JSON documents that contain literals, objects and arrays.

The JSON Patch RFC is an ongoing standard that specifies how to encode a patch that can be performed on a JSON document to transform it into a new one [3]. The RFC specifies that a patch is a sequence of change operations. It then specifies the five following change operations (a sixth operation is defined to perform tests):

- Add: this operation is performed to add a new node into the JSON document. The new node can be added within an array or as a new property of an object.
- Remove: this operation is performed to remove an existing node of the JSON document.
- Replace: this operation is performed to replace an existing node by another one.

```
{                                                 {
  "isOk": true,                                     "rank": 6,
  "rm": "2",                                        "isOk": false,
  "val": 3,                                         "va": 3,
  "mes1": {"who":"me", "exp":0},                    "mes1": {"who":"me", "exp":0},
  "res": [                                          "mes2": {"who":"me", "exp":0},
    "v1",                                           "res": [
    "v2",                                             "v6",
    "v3",                                             "v1",
    "v4",                                             "m2",
    "v5"                                              "v1",
  ],                                                  "v5",
  "inner" : {                                         "v3"
    "elts" : ["a","b"] ,                            ],
    "sum" : "test is ok"                            "inner" : {
  }                                                   "in": {
}                                                       "elts" : ["a","b","c"]
                                                      }
                                                    },
                                                    "sum" : "test is ok"
                                                  }
```

Fig. 1. A *source* (left) JSON document with several properties. A *target* (right) JSON document that has been transformed from the *source* JSON document.

---

[4] A string or a JavaScript name.

```
[
  { "op": "add",     "path": "/rank",  "value": 6 },
  { "op": "remove",  "path": "/rm"},
  { "op": "replace", "path": "/isOk",  "value": false},
  { "op": "move",    "path": "/va",    "from": "/val"},
  { "op": "copy",    "path": "/mes2",  "from": "/mes1"}
  { "op": "add",     "path": "/res/0", "value": "v6"},
  { "op": "replace", "path": "/res/2", "value": "m2"},
  { "op": "remove",  "path": "/res/4"},
  { "op": "copy",    "path": "/res/3", "from": "/result/1"},
  { "op": "move",    "path": "/res/5", "from": "/result/4"},
  { "op": "move",    "path": "/inner/in/elts",   "from": "/inner/elts"},
  { "op": "add",     "path": "/inner/in/elts/2", "value": "c"},
  { "op": "move",    "path": "/sum",   "from": "/inner/sum"}
]
```

Fig. 2. A RFC JSON Patch that, if applied to *source* JSON document of the Fig. 1, would get the *target* JSON document.

– Move: this operation is performed to move an existing node elsewhere in the JSON document.
– Copy: this operation is performed to copy an existing node elsewhere in the JSON document.

The RFC specifies a standard way to encode a patch into a JSON document. More precisely a patch is an array of change operations where each change operation is encoded by a single object with properties specifying the kind of operation, the source and target nodes, and the new value if needed. For instance, the Fig. 2 presents a patch that can be applied to *source* JSON document presented in the Fig. 1, and that contains change operations (adding a new literal node *rank*, removing a node of the array *res*, etc.). We use that example in the following sections.

Applying a patch to a JSON document is quite easy. It consists in applying all the editing operations of the patch in their defined order. Creating a patch that, given two versions of a JSON document, expresses how to transform the first version into the second one is however much more complex, especially when the goal is to create small patches and to create them as fast as possible.

2.2 Related Works

JSON documents are mainly labelled unordered trees (object nodes and their properties), where some nodes are arrays, hence ordered. The theory states that when just the *add*, *remove* and *replace* operations are considered, the problem of finding a minimal patch is $O(n^3)$ for ordered trees and NP-hard for unordered trees [2,10,14,16]. When the *move* operation is also considered, the problem is NP-hard for both kind of trees [2]. That is why several algorithms from the document engineering research field use practical heuristics. One of the most famous is the algorithm of Chawathe et al. [5] that computes patches (containing move actions) on trees representing LaTeX files. Several algorithms have also been designed specifically for XML documents [1,6]. One of them [13] is even capable of detecting copy operations.

Several existing approaches support the creation of JSON Patches.[5] By analyzing all of them, it appears that they all take one or two of these simplifications to make the problem tractable (see Table 1):

- They choose not to support the *move* and *copy* operations that are yet specified in the RFC, and therefore provide non-optimal patches. As an example in the Fig. 2, an optimal patch uses *move* operation to handle the property label renaming from *val* to *va*. Without such a *move* operation, the patch then uses a *remove* property *val* and a *add* property *va*. Moreover, an optimal patch uses a *copy* operation for the property *mes*2 and its value copied from *mes*1. The Table 1 shows that only one existing approach does support these operations.
- They choose not to support array node, or to support them poorly. In principle all the editing operations of the JSON RFC apply to array nodes as well as object nodes. A patch can then express changes done within an array. For instance in Fig. 2, an optimal patch uses the *move* operation to put *v*3 to the end of the array. Moreover, it uses the *copy* operation for copying the existing node *v*1. Regarding the support of array, the Table 1 shows that half of the approaches do not support array at all, and consider them as simple node (with nothing inside). The other half simply considers that an array is a stack, and therefore supports change operation that can apply to a stack (*push* and *pop*).

The Table 1 clearly shows that there is no approach that fully complies with the RFC in terms of change operation coverage. By compliance we mean that it can handle all editing operations that are defined by the RFC including the move and copy ones (the test one is not an editing operation). However there is no formal process that truly checks the RFC compliance. There is only JSON test[6] that just checks if the given patches can be applied. As we describe it in the next section, our algorithm goes beyond and does support all the changes

Table 1. Comparison of existing approaches

Category	Scenario	Libraries	
		move and *copy*	*Arraynode*
JavaScript	`jiff`	No	Stack
	`Fast-JSON-Patch`	No	No
	`JSON8 Patch`	No	No
	`rfc6902`	No	Stack
Python	`python-json-patch`	No	Stack
PHP	`json-patch-php`	No	No
Java	`json-patch`	Yes	No

---

[5] http://jsonpatch.com/.

[6] https://github.com/json-patch/json-patch-tests.

operations both on objects and on arrays, which is fully complies with JSON Patch RFC. However as there is no silver bullet, as a simplification it considers that changes made to JSON documents always target complete sub-trees rather than internal nodes, and therefore create patches that reflect this kind of change.

3   JDR: A JSON Patch Algorithm

By running several APIs we observed that changes performed to JSON documents commonly target a complete sub-tree, but never target several internal nodes. More precisely, a change either adds, removes, replaces, moves or copies a complete sub-trees but never changes the topology of a sub-tree by inserting, removing, or moving some nodes inside the sub-tree. The same is true for arrays, changes made to arrays always target one array but they never target two or more different arrays. These observations have then driven the design of our algorithm that aims to identify large sub-trees or arrays, which are targets of changes.

Based on this consideration, our algorithm inputs two versions of a JSON document (the *old* and the *new* versions) and proceeds the three following steps:

– First it builds a large common sub-tree that is shared between the *old* and the *new* versions. This sub-tree contains the root node of both the *old* and *new* versions, and all the object and literal nodes that both exist in the *old* and *new* versions, in the same locations, with the same labels (values can be different). The array nodes are considered in the following steps. The center part of the Fig. 3 presents the common sub-tree for our example. Once the common sub-tree has been created, for each of its label leaf node, if the value is not the same in the *old* and *new* version, a *replace* operation with the value of the *new* version is put into the patch. With our example, the *isOk* node corresponds to such a case.
– Second, for each object or literal node of the *old* version that does not belong to the common sub-tree but whose direct parent belongs to it, put a remove operation in the patch and mark the node as a removed one, unless there is a marked added node with the same value. In that case, put a move operation in the patch and mark the node as a moved one. The left part of the Fig. 3 presents these nodes. The *rm* node is a removed node. The *val* and *sum* nodes are moved nodes. Symmetrically, for each node of the *new* version that does not belong to the common sub-tree but whose direct parent belongs to it, put an add operation in the patch and mark the node as an added one, unless there is a marked removed node or a node in the common sub-tree with the same value. In case of a removed node, put a move operation in the patch and mark the node as a moved one. In case of a node in the common sub-tree, put a copy operation in the patch and mark the node as a copied node. The right part of the Fig. 3 presents these nodes for our example. The *rank* and *in* nodes are added nodes. The *val* and *sum* nodes are moved nodes. The *mes2* node is a copied node.

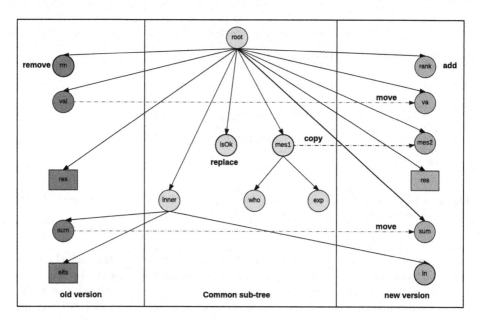

Fig. 3. The two versions of our example as a tree with object and label node presented with circles and array nodes with square. The central part represents the common sub-tree. The left part presents nodes direct children of the common tree and that belong to the *old* version. The right part presents nodes direct children of the common tree and that belong to the *new* version.

– Third, for each array node in the *old* version whose direct parent belongs to the common sub-tree, check if there is an array node in the *new* version, child of the same parent and with the same label. If so compare the two arrays (see the following array algorithm). If not, put a remove operation in the patch. For each array node in the *new* version whose direct parent belongs to the common sub-tree, put an add operation in the patch. The Fig. 3 presents these nodes. The *res* nodes are then compared. The *elts* node is removed.

As just described, our algorithm only creates a patch for two versions of a same array if and only if the array is in the exact same location in the two versions of the JSON document. Further as the change operations defined by the RFC can only target cells one by one (it is not possible to remove or move several cells with one operation), there is then no need to compute a LCS (Longest Common Subsequence [11]). Comparing pairs of cells is therefore sufficient for creating a patch.

The creation of the patch is then done by comparing the cells of the array with the intent to identify the common ones, the ones that have been removed and the ones that have been added. More precisely, our algorithm first sorts the cells of the two versions of the array by computing a similarity hash[7] of their

---

[7] https://github.com/darkskyapp/string-hash.

```
[
  { "op": "add",      "path": "/rank",  "value": 6 },
  { "op": "remove",   "path": "/rm"},
  { "op": "replace",  "path": "/isOk",  "value": false},
  { "op": "move",     "path": "/va",    "from": "/val"},
  { "op": "copy",     "path": "/mes2",  "from": "/mes1"}
  { "op": "add",      "path": "/res/0", "value": "v5"},
  { "op": "replace",  "path": "/res/2", "value": "m2"},
  { "op": "remove",   "path": "/res/4"},
  { "op": "copy",     "path": "/res/3", "from": "/result/1"},
  { "op": "move",     "path": "/res/5", "from": "/result/4"},
  { "op": "remove",   "path": "/inner/in/elts"},
  { "op": "add",      "path": "/inner/in", "value": {"elts":["a", "b", "c"]}},
  { "op": "move",     "path": "/sum",   "from": "/inner/sum"}
]
```

Fig. 4. A RFC JSON Patch generated by our approach that, if applied to *source* JSON document of the Fig. 1, would get the *target* JSON document.

value. Secondly, thanks to the similarity hash order, it iterates through the cells in the two versions of the array and creates a temporary array patch by applying the following rules. If an *old* cell has a corresponding *new* cell (with the same value), a move operation is put into a temporary patch. If an *old* cell has no corresponding *new* cell, a remove operation is put into the patch. If a *new* cell has no corresponding *old* cell, an add operation is put into the patch. Thirdly, it transforms the temporary array patch into a final patch by taking care of the indexes of the changed cells because the execution of a change operation may have an impact on the indexes of the following ones. This transforming index method is inspired by the classical Operational Transformation (OT) technology, which aims to solve concurrency control of collaborative editing in distributed systems [8,12]. To that extent, it sorts the operations of the temporary patch according to the indexes of the changed cells and to the type of change (*move* < *remove* < *add*), iterates through them and recompute the indexes. Further, if a *move* operation moves a cell to the same operation (the target index is equal to the source index), it is removed from the patch. This step is not so complex and this why we do not explain it in details. The whole pseudo code of our algorithm JDR is available on GitHub[8].

The Fig. 4 finally presents the patch created by our approach. The main difference with an optimal patch is that nodes that are not direct children of the common sub-tree are not target of any change. With our example, the sub-tree with the node *in* as a root is therefore fully created by the patch, and its child node *elts* is created from scratch whereas it should have been moved.

4   Efficiency Evaluation

Our patch algorithm has been developed in JavaScript and is available as an Open Source library.[9] We present in this section its efficiency evaluation in com-

---

[8] https://github.com/caohanyang/json_diff_rfc6902/blob/master/Algorithm.pdf.

[9] https://github.com/caohanyang/json_diff_rfc6902.

parison with all other existing JavaScript libraries that support the JSON Patch RFC (see Table 1).

Our evaluation consists in asking all the libraries to create JSON patches. We then compare them according to two quantitative factors: the time required to create the patch, and the size of the patch. Our claim is that a library is considered to be efficient if the patches it creates are small and if it creates them quickly.

Our evaluation is fully automated. It inputs a given REST service that provides access to a changing data, and periodically calls it 61 times to get 61 different versions of the changing data. Then, for each of the 60 consecutive versions it asks to all the existing libraries to generate the corresponding patch, and compares the time they take as well as the size of their returned patch. We repeat the generation of the patch 100 times to get an average value for both time and size. Our evaluation then returns 60 average values for both time and size for each library and for any given REST service. The evaluation has been executed on a desktop computer Intel Core i7-4770 CPU @3.40 GHz 8, 16 GB of RAM, and Ubuntu 14.04.2 LTS x86 64.

The choice of the called REST service has obviously an impact on the results obtained by our evaluation. We therefore choose to include into our dataset only real services provided by well-known web applications. Further, as the existing libraries mainly differ by their support of changes (see Table 1), we choose to include into our dataset three kinds of services: the one where changes are only made to objects' properties, the one where changes are only made to arrays, and the one where changes are made to both. Our industrial partner Streamdata.io then provides us one service for each such kinds. Our dataset, available on GitHub[10], includes the *Xignite* GetRealTimeRate, *Stackoverflow* Answers and *Twitter* Timeline services.

The Xignite GetRealTimeRate[11] service provides real-time currencies in the global financial market. The service returns a JSON document that contains one node object for each of the selected currencies (i.e. EURUSD, USDGBP). Changes between two successive versions are then only made to the properties of these objects. It should be note that a period of 15 s has been advised by our industrial partner between two consecutive versions.

The Stackoverflow Answers[12] service provides a list of Stackoverflow's answers. The service returns a JSON document that contains an array with the latest 20 answers. Changes between two successive versions are then only made to the array (new answers are added, last ones are deleted).

The Twitter Timeline[13] service provides the home timeline of a specific account with up-to-date Tweets. The service returns a collection of the most

---

[10] https://github.com/caohanyang/json_diff_rfc6902/tree/master/dataset.

[11] http://globalcurrencies.xignite.com/xGlobalCurrencies.json/GetRealTimeRate?
Symbol=EURUSD,USDGBP,EURJPY,CHFDKK&_token=[YOUR_TOKEN].

[12] https://api.stackexchange.com/2.2/answers?order=desc&sort=activity&site=
stackoverflow.

[13] https://api.twitter.com/1.1/statuses/home_timeline.json.

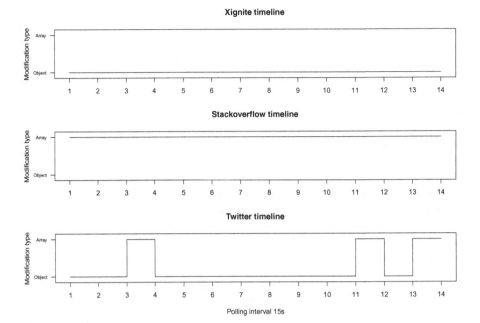

Fig. 5. Timeline modification type analysis for Xignite (top), Stackoverflow (middle) and Twitter (bottom), which represent *object server*, *array server* and *shift server* respectively.

recent 20 Tweets of the authenticated user. Changes between two successive versions can be made to the array or to the objects themselves when tweets' properties change.

The Fig. 5 shows an extract of successive versions that have been obtained by calling the services of our dataset. It clearly shows that changes performed to the data can be done either on objects' properties with the Xignite service, or on the array with Stackoverflow, or on both with Twitter.

The Figs. 6, 7, 8 then present the results of our evaluation for each service. Each figure presents one figure for the time and one figure for the size where the black dots present the 60 average values, and the bold red dot presents the median of these average values.

For the Xignite service, Fast-JSON-Patch, JDR and rfc6902 always generate small patches while jiff doesn't (see Fig. 6a). Curiously JSON8 chooses to simply replace the whole JSON document. Regarding time, Fast-JSON-Patch is the fastest followed by our library but the difference is no more than 0.5 ms (see Fig. 6b). rfc6902 takes much more time than the others.

For the Stackoverflow service it is interesting to see that Fast-JSON-Patch performs bad in term of size as it generates large patches (see Fig. 7a). JSON8 is again quite bad as it generated also large patches. JDR, jiff, rfc6902 behave quite well regarding size as they always yield small patches. Regarding time all the libraries behave quite well but rfc6902, which is slower (see Fig. 7b).

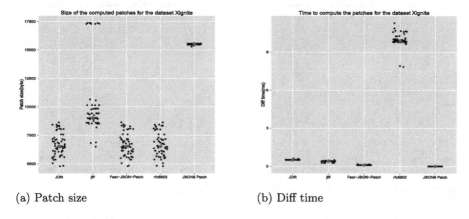

(a) Patch size   (b) Diff time

Fig. 6. Results for the Xignite dataset (Color figure online)

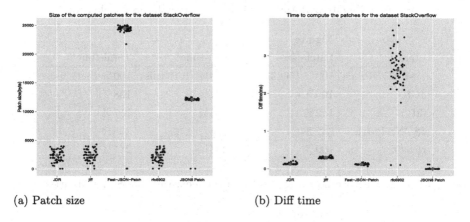

(a) Patch size   (b) Diff time

Fig. 7. Results for the StackOverflow dataset (Color figure online)

For the Twitter service, the Fig. 8a clearly shows that JDR always yields small patches in all situation. In some cases, Fast-JSON-Patch totally fails (see some black dots with high patch sizes). rfc6902 succeeds almost all the times but is sometimes not that fast. Regarding time, the Fig. 8b shows that JSON8 is definitively the fastest, then Fast-JSON-Patch. JDR and Jiff performs almost within the same time. Finally rfc6902 is slow.

The Figs. 6, 7, 8 are consistent with the analyse we provided in the Sect. 2, and clearly show the advantages and drawbacks of the existing libraries, depending on the support they provide to object or array. We then decided to combine the size and time factors considering that a patch has to be sent into the internet after it has been created (with a bandwidth of 10 Mbit/s) (See Tables 2, 3 and 4). The Table 2 shows that Fast-JSON-Patch is the best when the changes are only performed to the objects' properties but our library JDR is very close. Then, the Table 3 shows that our library JDR performs the best when the changes are only

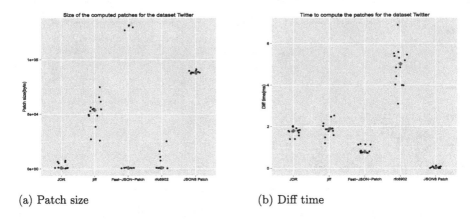

(a) Patch size   (b) Diff time

Fig. 8. Results for the Twitter dataset (Color figure online)

Table 2. Xignite performance of the 5 existing JavaScript libraries.

| Library | Xignite | | |
	Patch-size	Diff-time	Total-time
FastJSONPatch	100 % (6683Bytes)	100 % (0.103 ms)	100 % (5.45 ms)
JDR	100 %	502 %	108 %
jiff	152 %	385 %	157 %
JSON8 Patch	232 %	2 %	228 %
rfc6902	100 %	2531 %	281 %

Table 3. Stackoverflow performance of the 5 existing JavaScript libraries.

| Library | Stackoverflow | | |
	Patch-size	Diff-time	Total-time
JDR	100 % (2257 Bytes)	100 % (0.123 ms)	100 % (1.94 ms)
jiff	104 %	216 %	112 %
rfc6902	100.3 %	1880 %	228 %
JSON8 Patch	232 %	6 %	484 %
Fast-JSON-Patch	1045 %	88 %	995 %

performed to arrays. Finally, the Table 4 shows that our library JDR performs the best when the changes are performed to both objects' properties and arrays.

In conclusion, based on industrial real data, our JDR outperforms existing libraries regarding the size of created patches and the time needed to create them.

Table 4. Twitter performance of the 5 existing JavaScript libraries.

Library	Twitter		
	Patch-size	Diff-time	Total-time
JDR	100 % (2475 Bytes)	100 % (1.77 ms)	100 % (3.75 ms)
rfc6902	198 %	276 %	235 %
Fast-JSON-Patch	1525 %	50 %	827 %
jiff	2064 %	107 %	1140 %
JSON8 Patch	3575 %	3 %	1887 %

5   Conclusion

REST APIs together with JSON are commonly used by modern web applications to export their services. Such an architecture however makes the services reachable in a pull mode which is not suitable for accessing data that periodically changes (such as Twitter timeline, realtime currency, etc.). The push mode is on the contrary more adequate for accessing changing data, but very few web applications, if any, support it. Our partner StreamData.IO therefore provides a proxy server solution for turning a pull REST API into a push one. The proxy server makes periodical requests to the API and then generates patches that express the changes made to the new received versions of the data. Generating a patch for JSON document is obviously the difficult part and existing approaches handle it poorly. In this paper we then provide a new JSON patch algorithm towards this issue, with the objective to fully support the JSON patch RFC and to provide efficiency gain in comparison to existing libraries.

Our study first shows that the existing approaches are not optimal and that they take drastic simplifications. More precisely, we show that existing approaches do not support the *move* and *copy* change operations (except Java JSON-patch), and that few of them fully support changes performed to array.

We then propose our JSON patch algorithm that is compliant witht the JSON Patch RFC and that further supports all of the 5 change operations. Indeed, our algorithm succeeds to support *move* and *copy* operations for object nodes and for arrays. Its limitation is that it only considers changes that are performed on a whole sub-tree, and does not consider changes that modifies the structure of a sub-tree. Further, it only considers change to array that are localized in the same place in the two versions of a JSON document. Those limitations have however been driven by our observations performed on existing REST API, which showed that such changes almost never happen. Our approach only handles the transformation of pull mode services into push mode but not their updates. The future work is to study the subsequent API updates that may involve structural changes, which aims to better understand how far APIs are updated.

We evaluate the efficiency of the JavaScript implementation of our algorithm against existing JavaScript libraries that support the JSON Patch RFC.

The evaluation has been done by requesting real web applications with data suggested by our industrial partner. It clearly shows that our library outperforms the other libraries. It creates small patch quite fast, and can handle different situations (where the changes target objects' properties or arrays).

As a main conclusion, we provide an efficient algorithm to create a path between two versions of a JSON document. The patch created by our approach is fully complies with RFC. Even it is not optimal, it however expresses all change operations such as the *move* and *copy* ones, and the ones that target arrays. Our work is the most essential part for turning a pull REST API into a push one, which is frequently requested by the web developers to get notified of data changes. As an example we provide a prototype framework that can be used to convert a pull service into a push one (see the online demo[14]).

References

1. Al-Ekram, R., Adma, A., Baysal, O.: diffX: an algorithm to detect changes in multi version XML documents. In: Processing of the CASCON 2005, pp. 1–11 (2005)
2. Bille, P.: A survey on tree edit distance and related problems. Theor. Comput. Sci. **337**(1–3), 217–239 (2005)
3. Bryan, P., Nottingham, M.: JavaScript Object Notation (JSON) Patch. Technical report, RFC 6902, April 2013. http://www.hjp.at/doc/rfc/rfc6902.html
4. Buttler, D.: A short survey of document structure similarity algorithms. In: International Conference on Internet Computing, pp. 3–9 (2004)
5. Chawathe, S.S., Rajaraman, A., Garcia-Molina, H., Widom, J.: Change detection in hierarchically structured information. In: Jagadish, H.V., Mumick, I.S. (eds.) Proceedings of the 1996 ACM SIGMOD International Conference on Management of Data, Montreal, Quebec, Canada, 4–6 June 1996, pp. 493–504. ACM Press (1996)
6. Cobena, G., Abiteboul, S., Marian, A.: Detecting changes in XML documents. In: Agrawal, R., Dittrich, K.R. (eds.) Proceedings of the 18th International Conference on Data Engineering, San Jose, CA, USA, February 26–March 1 2002, pp. 41–52. IEEE Computer Society (2002)
7. Crockford, D.: RFC4627: JavaScript Object Notation (2006)
8. Ellis, C.A., Gibbs, S.J.: Concurrency control in groupware systems. In: ACM SIGMOD Record, vol. 18, pp. 399–407. ACM (1989)
9. Fielding, R.T., Taylor, R.N.: Principled design of the modern Web architecture. ACM Trans. Internet Technol. (TOIT) **2**(2), 115–150 (2002). http://dl.acm.org/citation.cfm?id=514185
10. Higuchi, S., Kan, T., Yamamoto, Y., Hirata, K.: An A* algorithm for computing edit distance between rooted labeled unordered trees. In: Okumura, M., Bekki, D., Satoh, K. (eds.) JSAI-isAI 2012. LNCS, vol. 7258, pp. 186–196. Springer, Heidelberg (2012)
11. Hirschberg, D.S.: Algorithms for the longest common subsequence problem. J. ACM (JACM) **24**(4), 664–675 (1977)
12. Lamport, L.: Time, clocks, and the ordering of events in a distributed system. Commun. ACM **21**(7), 558–565 (1978)

---

[14] http://diff-and-patch.pubstorm.site/.

13. Lindholm, T., Kangasharju, J., Tarkoma, S.: Fast and simple XML tree differencing by sequence alignment. In: Proceedings of the 2006 ACM Symposium on Document Engineering, DocEng 2006, pp. 75–84. ACM, New York (2006). http://doi.acm.org/10.1145/1166160.1166183

14. Pawlik, M., Augsten, N.: RTED: a robust algorithm for the tree edit distance. PVLDB **5**(4), 334–345 (2011)

15. Zhang, K., Shasha, D.: Simple fast algorithms for the editing distance between trees and related problems. SIAM J. Comput. **18**(6), 1245–1262 (1989). http://dx.doi.org/10.1137/0218082

16. Zhang, K., Statman, R., Shasha, D.: On the editing distance between unordered labeled trees. Inf. Process. Lett. **42**(3), 133–139 (1992)

User Interface Derivation
Based on Role-Enriched Business Process Model

Lei Han, Weiliang Zhao[✉], and Jian Yang

Macquarie University, North Ryde, NSW 2109, Australia
lei.han1@students.mq.edu.au, {weiliang.zhao,jian.yang}@mq.edu.au

Abstract. This work proposes an approach for User Interface (UI) derivation based on a role-enriched Business Process (BP) model with the capability to describe the details of the control flow and data operations in a BP. For each user role, data relationships are extracted according to the identified control flow patterns and data operation patterns. A set of mandatory and recommended UI derivation rules are specified as the cornerstones to derive the UI logic from a BP. The algorithm for UI derivation is provided. This UI derivation approach provides the basis for UI development and maintenance.

Keywords: User interface · Business process · Control flow pattern

1 Introduction

A business process is a collection of linked tasks that provides services. Each task is a unit of work performed by human users or applications. Users participate a BP through User Interfaces. Generally speaking the UI development for the BP needs a lot of hard coding efforts which normally constitute 70 % to 80 % of the manually written codes of a BP implementation (e.g. the interaction between BP and database/application systems/services). Because BPs and their UIs are tightly coupled, the existing UIs can not easily adapt to the BP changes without recoding. The realization and maintenance of UIs are often costly and effort-consuming, which impedes the quick adaptations of BP realization [3,6].

As a scenario example, Fig. 1(a) shows a recruitment process at the human resource department of a company. This process is represented with Business Process Model and Notation (BPMN) [9]. Three user roles as **personnel officer**, **applicant**, and **referee** are involved. In the recruitment process, there are tasks as: (1) the **personnel officer** announces a job vacancy; (2) an **applicant** lodges his application; (3) a **referee** writes a reference letter to support the application; (4) the **personnel officer** arranges an interview for the **applicant**; (5) the **applicant** confirms the interview; (6) the **personnel officer** reviews the reference letter; (7) the **personnel officer** conducts the interview; (8) the **personnel officer** makes the decision according to the evaluation of the reference letter and the interview report. Task 4, 5 are in parallel with task 6.

© Springer International Publishing Switzerland 2016
Q.Z. Sheng et al. (Eds.): ICSOC 2016, LNCS 9936, pp. 450–464, 2016.
DOI: 10.1007/978-3-319-46295-0_28

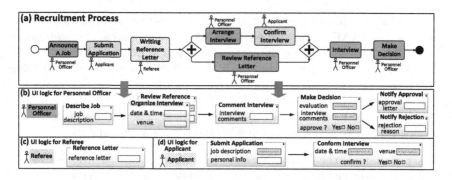

Fig. 1. Deriving UI logics from a business process

Users provide inputs to and retrieve information from a BP through UIs. The operation flow of input/output data for a specific user role in a BP is referred to as the UI logic of this user role. Input/output data will be grouped and put in different UI containers. For instance, Fig. 1(d) shows the UI logic for the user role `applicant`. There are two UI containers (`Submit Application` and `Confirm Interview`) and they will turn up in a sequential order. With `Submit Application`, an `applicant` can read the job information and provide the details of his application. With `Confirm Interview`), the `applicant` can check the interview date, time, location and confirm his attendance.

There are several works of UI derivation from BP models. The UI derivation approach provided in [5,6] is based on a BPMN process model, in which the detailed data operations inside tasks have not been covered. The derived UI logic cannot reflect UI requirements originated from detailed data operations in individual tasks of a BP. [14] proposes an artifact-centric BP model to derive the UI logic; PHILharmonicFlows [7,8] derives the UI logic based on an object-aware BP model. These BP models are lacking of the capability to describe the relations between a user role and the control flow of tasks in a BP. The derived UI logic by these approaches can not differentiate the UI logics of different user roles.

We believe the UI logic of a BP should have the following features: (1) each participating user role should have a UI logic; (2) each UI logic consists of a set of containers and the execution constraints of these containers; (3) each container includes a set of data items specified with access types (*read, write*). To support UI derivation, we propose a role-enriched business process model with the capability to specify complex control flow patterns and capture the details of data operations inside individual tasks. Based on this role-enrich BP model, the UI derivation steps are as follows:

1. The BP is abstracted and aggregated for each user role based on the role-enrich BP model. For each user role, the tasks related to this user role are reserved; the tasks not related to this user role are abstracted.

2. Data relationships are extracted from the abstracted and aggregated business process (AABP) for each user role. A set of elementary operations are developed according to the data operations inside individual tasks and the identified control flow patterns in the AABP. The extracted data relationships are the foundation to analyze and derive the UI logic.
3. The UI logic are derived from the extracted data relationships. A set of mandatory and recommended rules are specified. The UI logic is derived by using the UI derivation algorithm with these rules as cornerstones.

The remainder of the paper is organized as follows. Section 2 proposes an role-enriched BP model and identifies a set of control flow patterns and data operation patterns. Section 3 introduces BP abstraction and aggregation for each involved user role. Section 4 discusses how to extract data relationships. Section 5 presents a set of UI derivation rules and the algorithm for the UI derivation. Section 6 reviews existing works. Section 7 gives a conclusion.

2   Role-Enriched BP Model

Beyond existing works, the proposed BP model has the capability to specify: (1) how user roles are involved in tasks; (2) how data are operated in individual tasks; (3) how complex control flow patterns affect data relationships. This section provides the syntax of the proposed Role-enriched BP model. A set of control flow patterns and data operation patterns are specified with an extended Business Process Model and Notation.

2.1   Formal Syntax

We propose a role-enriched BP model to specify a BP with a set of tasks and control flow relations between these tasks. The participating user roles are labeled in individual tasks. The data operation flow in each task specifies a set of data items and the operation flow relations between these data items. Each data item has an access type as ((*read* or *write*)).

Definition 1: Data Operation Flow. A data operation flow is denoted as a tuple $df = (N_d, type_d, type_A, SF_d^{fix}, SF_d^{free})$, where:

- $N_d = \{e_d^s, e_d^e\} \cup G_d \cup A$ where e_d^s and e_d^e are the start event and end event respectively; $G_d = G_d^{in} \cup G_d^{out}$, G_d^{in} is a finite set of entry gateways and G_d^{out} is a finite set of exit gateways; A is a finite set of data items.
- $type_d$: $G_d \rightarrow \{Sequential, Parallel-A, Parallel-B, Conditional, Loop\}$ is a mapping function to give each gateway a type. These gateways are elements that control how the data flow diverges or converges.
- $type_A : A \rightarrow \{read, write\}$ is a mapping function to specify the access type of each data item $a \in A$. There are two kinds of access types as *read* and *write*.
- SF_d^{fix} and SF_d^{free} represent fixed-order sequence flow and free-order sequence flow respectively.

Note that fixed-order sequence flow means that the sequence of involved entities must be in a fixed order; free-order sequence flow means that the order in the sequence of involved entities is free.

Definition 2: Role-enriched Business Process Model. A role-enriched BP model is denoted as $rm = (N_t, type_t, SF_t^{fix}, SF_t^{free}, refine, R, \rho)$, where:

- $N_t = \{e_t^s, e_t^e\} \cup G_t \cup T$ where e_t^s and e_t^e are start event and end event respectively; $G_t = G_t^{in} \cup G_t^{out}$, G_t^{in} is a finite set of entry gateways and G_t^{out} is a finite set of exit gateways; T is a finite set of tasks.
- $type_t$: $G_t \rightarrow \{Sequential, Parallel-A, Parallel-B, Conditional, Loop\}$ is a mapping function to give each gateway a type. These gateways are elements that control how the task flow diverges or converges.
- SF_t^{fix} and SF_t^{free} represent fixed-order sequence flow and free-order sequence flow respectively.
- $refine : T \rightarrow DF$ is a refinement function on tasks. $DF = \{df_1, df_2, ..., df_n\}$ stands for a set of data operation flows. The refinement function links tasks and their corresponding data operation flows.
- R is a finite set of user roles.
- $\rho = T \times R$ specifies relationships between user roles and tasks.

2.2   Control Flow Patterns of Role-Enriched BP Model

This sub section describes the identified control flow patterns. These patterns are the basis of building up elementary operations for data relationship extraction later. The BPMN [9] is extended to specify: (1) relationships between tasks and user roles; and (2) complex control flow patterns and data operation patterns. Figure 2 shows the graphical notations with details as:

- A solid line with an arrow denotes the fixed-order sequence flow.
- A dashed line denotes the free-order sequence flow.
- The upper label of a task denotes its user roles.
- The upper label of a data item denotes its access type.
- A bar on the left/right side of a circle denotes an entrance/exit gateway.
- *Sequential, Parallel-A, Parallel− B, Conditional,* and *Loop* denote the gateway types.

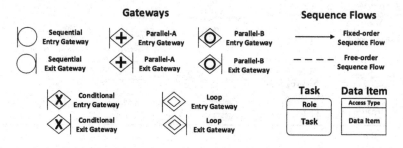

Fig. 2. Extended BPMN

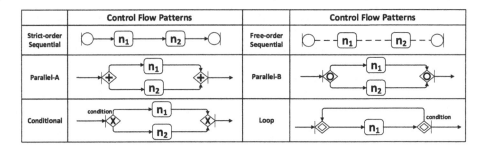

Fig. 3. Control flow patterns

Figure 3 shows the identified set of control flow patterns as:

- **Strict-order Sequential** specifies that nodes must be executed in a strict sequential order.
- **Free-order Sequential** specifies that nodes must be executed one after another but the order is free.
- **Parallel-A** specifies that all branches must be executed in parallel and the pattern completes when all branches have completed.
- **Parallel-B** specifies that all branches must be executed in parallel and the pattern completes when any branch has completed.
- **Conditional** specifies that the executed branch is decided according to the runtime condition.
- **Loop** specifies that nodes in the loop must be executed iteratively until the "jumping-out condition" is met.

In **Strict-order Sequential**, **Free-order Sequential**, **Conditional**, and **Loop**, each node n_i $(i = 1, 2)$ can be either a task or a data item inside a task. In **Parallel-A** and **Parallel-B**, each node n_i $(i = 1, 2)$ must be a task. When considering relationships between/among data items, each branch of the **Parallel-A** block must be completed by the same user role, and this user role

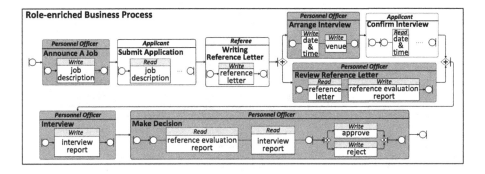

Fig. 4. Recruitment process specified with role-enriched BP model

must execute these branches one by one in a free order. One and only one branch of the **Parallel-B** block must be completed. When considering data operation patterns, **Parallel-A** equals to **Free-order Sequential**; **Parallel-B** equals to **Conditional**. **Parallel-A** or **Parallel-B** will never turn up in the data operation patterns.

Figure 4 illustrates how the role-enriched BP model specifies business process for the recruitment scenario example. Here, we only highlight details of data operation flows of the tasks participated by the user role `personnel officer`.

3   BP Abstraction and Aggregation

Different user roles have different UI logics. The role-enriched BP is abstracted and aggregated for each user role. The BP abstraction and aggregation are processed based on a set of identified control flow patterns. An abstracted and aggregated business process (AABP) for a particular user role contains tasks all related to this user role, abstracted nodes, as well as the control flow relations between the tasks and the abstracted nodes. Inside each task, the operated data items and their execution orders are specified. This part of work is relatively independent and its details will be provided in a separate paper.

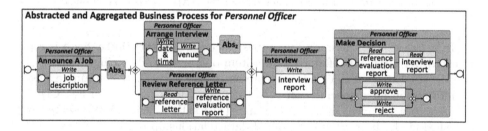

Fig. 5. AABP for personnel officer

Here we use the recruitment scenario example to show the result of BP abstraction and aggregation. Figure 5 shows the AABP for the user role `personnel officer`. The tasks for the `personnel officer` are all kept, and the tasks for the `applicant/referee` are abstracted (the tasks `Submit Application` and `Writing Reference Letter` are abstracted as Abs_1; the task `Confirm Interview` is abstracted as Abs_2).

4   Data Relationship Extraction

Data relationships are extracted and specified as a tree graph from an AABP. A series of elementary operations are specified on identified control flow patterns and data operation patterns of the AABP. The algorithm for data relationship extraction is built up on these elementary operations.

4.1   Data Relationships

After the AABP is generated for a user role, the data relationships, including operated data and data operation flow, are extracted from the AABP for this specific user role. A tree graph represents these extracted data relationships and it can be recorded with a JSON String. Figure 6 shows a tree graph representing the data relationships extracted from the AABP for `personnel officer`.

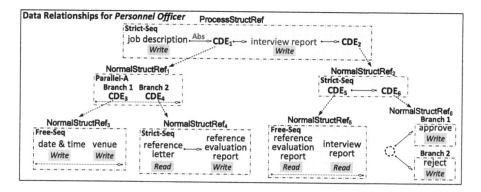

Fig. 6. Data relationships extracted from the AABP for personnel officer

In a tree graph, there are four types of nodes: (1) `Attribute Node` is represented by "Attr". It refers to a data item operated inside a single task of an AABP. (2) `Information Node` is represented by "INFO". It contains a piece of information for a specific user role. (3) `CDE Node` is represented by "CDE". It refers to a fragment of the tree graph. (4) `Virtual Node` is represented by a dashed circle. It starts a conditional data relationship pattern. For example, *approve* and *reject* in Fig. 6 are `Attribute Nodes` that follow a `Virtual Node`.

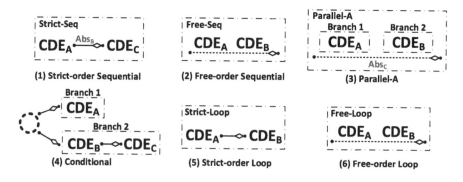

Fig. 7. Data relationship patterns

There are six data relationship patterns: **Strict-order Sequential**, **Free-order Sequential**, **Parallel-A**, **Conditional**, **Strict-Order Loop**, and **Free-Order Loop**. Figure 7 shows examples of these patterns with CDE Nodes. Except **Conditional**, a pattern is represented with a dot-dash rectangle, a pattern name, and node relationships. **Conditional** is represented with a Virtual Node and a set of branches with node relationships.

An Abs Label is used to represent control flow relations between tasks and abstracted nodes in the AABP. In a tree graph, an Abs Label only turns up above a solid edge (see Abs_B in (1) of Fig. 7) or under a dashed edge (see Abs_C in (3) of Fig. 7). The ProcessStructRef is the root of a tree graph. The NormalStructRef is the reference of a tree graph fragment.

4.2 From AABP to Data Relationhips

4.2.1 Elementary Operations

Figure 8 illustrates a series of elementary operations for data relationship extraction. Each elementary operation extracts data relationships from a particular control flow pattern of an AABP or a particular data operation pattern inside an individual task of an AABP. A control flow relation between/among tasks is represented by a set of CDE Nodes and edges in a tree graph. An abstracted node in an AABP is removed away totally or recorded by an Abs Label in a tree graph. A data operation relation between/among data items is represented by a set of Attribute Nodes and edges in a tree graph.

The **Conditional-Data-Deriv-1** in Fig. 8 shows how an elementary operation generates data relationships from a **Conditional** control flow pattern in an AABP. Each branch of the **Conditional** control flow pattern is inherited by the corresponding data relationship pattern. For a branch, there are rules: (1) If it is composed of only one abstracted node ($AbsNode_A$), an Information Node ($INFO_A$) is used to represent the execution status of this branch. (2) If a branch is composed of only tasks, CDE Nodes (CDE_B and CDE_C) are used to represent these tasks ($Task_B$ and $Task_C$). (3) If a branch is composed of both tasks and abstracted nodes, a CDE Node is used to represent a task; an Abs Label(Abs_E) is used to represent an abstracted node ($AbsNode_E$) between tasks; and an abstracted node ($AbsNode_G$) at one end of a branch is removed away.

4.2.2 Algorithm for Data Relationship Extraction

In order to extract the data relationships from an AABP, the control flow patterns of the AABP and the data operation patterns inside each individual task are identified and elementary operations are applied accordingly. A tree graph representing the extracted data relationships is built up by using **Algorithm** 1.

As an example, according to elementary operations **Sequential-Data-Deriv-1** and **Parallel-A-Data-Deriv-3** in Fig. 8, Abs_1 in Fig. 5 is inherited by label Abs in Fig. 6, and Abs_2 in Fig. 5 does not appear in Fig. 6.

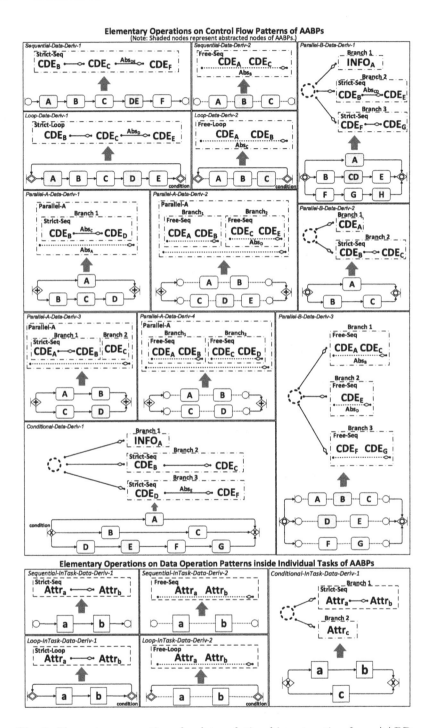

Fig. 8. Elementary operations for data relationship extraction from AABPs

---

Algorithm 1. Data Relationship Extraction

---

1 **Function** DeriveDataRelationships(AbsAggBusinessProcess *aabp*)
2   identify *cfPattern* and *cfElementSet* at coarsest granularity level of *aabp*;
3   *TreeGraph* = ∅;
4   **foreach** *cfElement* in *cfElementSet* **do**
5   **if** *cfElement* is Task **then**
6   get data operation flow *df_cfElement* from *cfElement*;
7   *result* = HandleDataOperationFlowInTask(*df_cfElement*);
8   add *result* to *TreeGraph*;
9   **else if** *cfElement* is ComplexStructure **then**
10   *cfElement* = DeriveDataRelationships(*cfElement*);

11   transform *cfElementSet* to *treeFragment* using elementary operation;
12   **if** *cfPattern* is on the coarsest granularity level **then**
13   assign ProcessStructRef to *treeFragment*;

14   **else**
15   assign NormalStructRef to *treeFragment*;

16   add *treeFragment* to *TreeGraph*;
17   **return** *TreeGraph*;

18 **Function** HandleDataOperationFlowInTask(DataOperationFlow *df*)
19   *TreeFragmentSet* = ∅;
20   identify *dfElementSet* at coarsest granularity level of *df*;
21   **foreach** *dfElement* in *dfElementSet* **do**
22   **if** *dfElement* is not DataItem **then**
23   *dfElement* = HandleDataOperationFlowInTask(*dfElement*);

24   transform *dfElementSet* to *treeFragment′* using elementary operation;
25   assign NormalStructRef to *treeFragment′*;
26   add *treeFragment′* to *TreeFragmentSet*;
27   **return** *TreeFragmentSet*;

---

5 User Interface Derivation

This section introduces the UI derivation from the extracted data relationships. The UI flow is derived for each user role involved in the BP. To derive the UI flow, a series of UI derivation rules are specified including constrains and recommendations. The algorithm for UI derivation is developed by utilizing these rules.

5.1 User Interface Flow

The UI flow has two granularity levels: the operation flow between UI containers, and data items included inside each UI container. Each data item needs to be specified with the **Access type** including *read* and *write*. A UI container holds the maximum amount of data items to be operated by a user role. The entire set of data items of the UI container will be shown to end users (see Fig. 10). The UI designers can divide this container into sub-containers. The UI containers can have operation flow relations as: **Strict-order Sequential**, **Free-order Sequential**, **Conditional**, **Strict-order Loop**, or **Free-order Loop**.

5.2   From Data Relationships to UIs

5.2.1   UI Derivation Rules

This sub section coins a set of rules for deriving the UI flow from the tree graph described previously. These UI derivation rules can be classified into two categories as **Constraints** and **Recommendations**. The **Constraints** include rules that must be followed by the UI designers. The **Recommendations** include rules that are recommended to be followed by the UI designers. Figure 9 describes these rules in a graphical view. The container flows are represented in the same way as data relationships. Note that all the "Node" labels in the following figures can represent either an `Attribute Node`, an `Information Node`, or a `CDE Node` in the tree graph. We have formalized each rule in Fig. 9. Due to space limitations, we only provide details of the rule **Sequential-Constraint-1** in Fig. 9 as an example.

Sequential-Constraint-1:

$\forall m$: "$TreeGraph[m]$"."$dataRelationshipPattern$" == "$Strict - Seq$",
iff $\forall i, j$: "$TreeGraph[m]$"."$graphNodes[i]$"."$postAbsOfNode$" ==
     "$TreeGraph[m]$"."$graphNodes[j]$"."$preAbsOfNode$",
then ("$TreeGraph[m]$"."$graphNodes[i]$" $\in con_i$) $\wedge$
     ("$TreeGraph[m]$"."$graphNodes[j]$" $\in con_j$) $\wedge$
     ((con_i, con_j) == "$Strict - Seq$").

Sequential-Constraint-1 specifies that in the **Strict-order Sequential** data relationship pattern, if there exists an `Abs Label` between two adjacent nodes, these two nodes must be separated into different containers.

All the UI generation rules are divided into two groups. *Group 1* includes rules about data relationships between inside data of a specific pattern, while *Group 2* includes rules about data relationships between inside data and outside data of a specific pattern. In Fig. 9, the rules in *Group 1* are not shaded; and the rules in *Group 2* are shaded.

5.2.2   Algorithm for UI Derivation

Here we provide **Algorithm 2** to derive the UI flow from an AABP. The tree graph is obtained by using **Algorithm 1** with the AABP as input. Then the UI flow is derived from the tree graph by applying UI derivation rules. The UI flow is represented by a set of containers and the operation flow of these containers.

Figure 10 shows the derived UI Flow for `Personnel Officer`. This UI flow contains seven containers with involved operation flow relations as **Strict-order Sequential**, **Free-order Sequential**, and **Conditional**. As an example of the details of the derivation process, data pointed by CDE_3 and CDE_4 in Fig. 6 are put into two containers `Organize Interview` and `Review Reference Letter`.

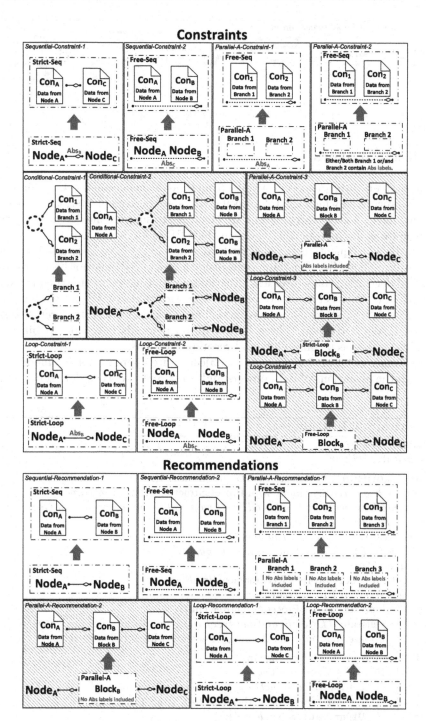

Fig. 9. UI derivation rules

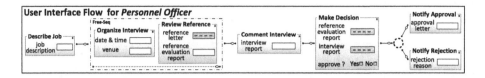

Fig. 10. UI flow for personnel officer

6 Related Work

J. Kolb et al. [5,6] propose a two-step method to generate the UI logic of a
BPMN process, in which the role-specific views are derived at first, then a series
of elementary and complex patterns are identified to support the derivation of the
UI logic from the role-specific views. In their BP model, only four basic control
flow patterns (sequential, parallel, exclusive, and loop) have been specified and
the execution flows between data items inside a task of BP have not been covered.
Their UI derivation rules cover less situations comparing to our rules described in
Sect. 5.2.1. K. Sousa et al. [11] develop an approach to derive UIs from a business
process with four steps as process modelling, task derivation, task refinement,
and UI model derivation. These UI derivation methods have no capability to
differentiate between constraints and recommendations.

V. Kunzle et al. in [7,8] propose an object-aware approach for BP modelling,
in which the evolutions of data objects and constraints between data objects are

---

Algorithm 2. UI Derivation

Input : *AABP*
Output: *UIFlow*

1 use **Algorithm 1** to extract *TreeGraph* from AABP;
2 retrieve *headTreeFragment* with ProcessStructRef from *TreeGraph*;
3 generate *UIFlowFrag* from *headTreeFragment* by applying rules in *Group 1*;
4 set *UIFlow* = *UIFlowFrag*;
5 UIDerivation(*headTreeFragment*);
6 process *UIFlow* by applying rules in *Group 2*;
7 **return** *UIFlow*;
8 **Function** UIDerivation(TreeFragment *treeFrag*)
9 | get *structRef* from *treeFrag*;
10 | **if** *structRef* is not ProcessStructRef **then**
11 | | generate *UIFlowFrag* from *treeFrag* by applying rules in *Group 1*;
12 | | update the *container* holding *structRef* with *UIFlowFrag*;
13 | **foreach** *node* of *treeFrag* **do**
14 | | **if** *node* is CDENode **then**
15 | | | get the value *structRef'* from *node*;
16 | | | retrieve *treeFrag'* with *structRef'* from *TreeGraph*;
17 | | | UIDerivation(*treeFrag'*);

specified. Their derived UI logic can only cover limited UI flow types due to that their BP model only includes the sequential and conditional data execution flow types.

Artifact-centric approach is another paradigm to model BPs. It focuses on the evolutions of artifacts and associated constraints [2,10]. A BP is specified with artifacts and data dependencies are explicitly described accordingly. S. Yongchareon et al. [14] develop a framework for UI derivation based on artifact techniques. An IBM team [1,4] develops the Siena and its successor Barcelona for supporting UI derivation from artifact-centric process models. These works cannot generate the UI flow types originated from BP control flow patterns such as **Free-order Sequential**, and **Parallel-B**.

N. Sukaviriya et al. [12,13] propose an approach to transform a process model into a human interaction perspective. This approach is very limited in providing details of UI layouts and UI flows based on the specified data elements, user roles, tasks.

7   Conclusion and Future Work

This paper proposes an approach of the UI derivation based on a BP model. It aims to support the analysing, developing, and updating of real UIs. The role-enriched BP model is proposed and how to abstract/aggregate a business process for each user role has been summarized. A tree graph representing the data relationships is extracted from an abstracted and aggregated BP for a specific user role. UI derivation rules are coined as a set of constraints and recommendations. By applying these rules, UI flows are derived from the tree graph. Our proposed approach has the capability to maintain the consistency between BPs and UIs. It provides an enable tool to derive UI logic from a BP. In the future work, the change management of BPs and UIs will be studied in a unified framework.

Acknowledgments. This work is supported by the Australian Research Council Linkage Project (LP120200231) and the China Scholarship Council.

References

1. Cohn, D., Dhoolia, P., Heath, F., Pinel, F., Vergo, J.: Siena: from powerpoint to web app in 5 minutes. In: Bouguettaya, A., Krueger, I., Margaria, T. (eds.) ICSOC 2008. LNCS, vol. 5364, pp. 722–723. Springer, Heidelberg (2008). doi:10. 1007/978-3-540-89652-4_63

2. Cohn, D., Hull, R.: Business artifacts: a data-centric approach to modeling business operations and processes. Bull. IEEE Comput. Soc. Tech. Committee Data Eng. **32**(3), 3–9 (2009)

3. Han, L., Zhao, W., Yang, J.: An approach towards user interface derivation from business process model. In: Cao, J., Liu, X., Ren, K. (eds.) PAS 2015. CCIS, vol. 602, pp. 19–28. Springer, Singapore (2015)

4. Heath, F.T., Boaz, D., Gupta, M., Vaculín, R., Sun, Y., Hull, R., Limonad, L.: Barcelona: a design and runtime environment for declarative artifact-centric BPM. In: Basu, S., Pautasso, C., Zhang, L., Fu, X. (eds.) ICSOC 2013. LNCS, vol. 8274, pp. 705–709. Springer, Heidelberg (2013). doi:10.1007/978-3-642-45005-1_65

5. Kolb, J., Hübner, P., Reichert, M.: Automatically generating and updating user interface components in process-aware information systems. In: Meersman, R., et al. (eds.) OTM 2012. LNCS, vol. 7565, pp. 444–454. Springer, Heidelberg (2012). doi:10.1007/978-3-642-33606-5_28

6. Kolb, J., Hübner, P., Reichert, M.: Model-driven user interface generation and adaptation in process-aware information systems. Open Access Repositorium der Universität Ulm (2012). http://dx.doi.org/10.18725/OPARU-2439

7. Künzle, V., Reichert, M.: A modeling paradigm for integrating processes and data at the micro level. In: Halpin, T., Nurcan, S., Krogstie, J., Soffer, P., Proper, E., Schmidt, R., Bider, I. (eds.) BPMDS/EMMSAD-2011. LNBIP, pp. 201–215. Springer, Heidelberg (2011). doi:10.1007/978-3-642-21759-3_15

8. Künzle, V., Reichert, M.: Philharmonicflows: towards a framework for object-aware process management. J. Softw. Maintenance Evol. Res. Pract. **23**(4), 205–244 (2011)

9. Model, B.P.: Notation (bpmn) version 2.0. OMG Specification, Object Management Group (2011)

10. Nigam, A., Caswell, N.S.: Business artifacts: an approach to operational specification. IBM Syst. J. **42**(3), 428–445 (2003)

11. Sousa, K., Mendonça, H., Vanderdonckt, J., Rogier, E., Vandermeulen, J.: User interface derivation from business processes: a model-driven approach for organizational engineering. In: Proceedings of the 2008 ACM Symposium on Applied Computing, pp. 553–560. ACM (2008)

12. Sukaviriya, N., Mani, S., Sinha, V.: Reflection of a year long model-driven business and UI modeling development project. In: Gross, T., Gulliksen, J., Kotzé, P., Oestreicher, L., Palanque, P., Prates, R.O., Winckler, M. (eds.) INTERACT 2009. LNCS, vol. 5727, pp. 749–762. Springer, Heidelberg (2009). doi:10.1007/978-3-642-03658-3_80

13. Sukaviriya, N., Sinha, V., Ramachandra, T., Mani, S., Stolze, M.: User-centered design and business process modeling: cross road in rapid prototyping tools. In: Baranauskas, C., Palanque, P., Abascal, J., Barbosa, S.D.J. (eds.) INTERACT 2007. LNCS, vol. 4662, pp. 165–178. Springer, Heidelberg (2007). doi:10.1007/978-3-540-74796-3_17

14. Yongchareon, S., Liu, C., Zhao, X., Xu, J.: An artifact-centric approach to generating web-based business process driven user interfaces. In: Chen, L., Triantafillou, P., Suel, T. (eds.) WISE 2010. LNCS, vol. 6488, pp. 419–427. Springer, Heidelberg (2010). doi:10.1007/978-3-642-17616-6_38

Service/Process Foundation

Deriving Consistent GSM Schemas
from DCR Graphs

Rik Eshuis[1], Søren Debois[2,3](✉), Tijs Slaats[2,4], and Thomas Hildebrandt[2]

[1] School of Industrial Engineering, Eindhoven University of Technology,
Eindhoven, The Netherlands
h.eshuis@tue.nl
[2] IT University of Copenhagen, Copenhagen, Denmark
{debois,tslaats,hilde}@itu.dk
[3] Exformatics A/S, Copenhagen, Denmark
debois@exformatics.com
[4] Department of Computer Science, University of Copenhagen,
Copenhagen, Denmark

Abstract. Case Management (CM) is a BPM technology for supporting flexible services orchestration. CM approaches like CMMN, an OMG standard, and GSM, one of CMMN's core influences, use Event-Condition-Action rules, which can be inconsistent due to cyclic interdependencies between the rules; repairing such an inconsistent case management schema is difficult. To avoid the problem of inconsistencies altogether, we provide a technique for automatically deriving consistent GSM case management schemas from higher-level business policies defined as DCR graphs, an alternative CM approach. Concretely, we define a behaviour-preserving mapping that (1) removes the burden from the modeller of GSM schemas to prove consistency and define the ordering of rules, (2) provides high-level patterns for modelling GSM schemas, and (3) gives a way to define a notion of progress (liveness) and acceptance for GSM instances. The mapping is illustrated by a running example of a mortgage loan application; and a prototype implementation available at http://dcr.itu.dk/icsoc16.

1   Introduction

The standard notations for business process modelling and service orchestration such as BPMN [4] and BPEL [3] are tailored to highly stable and repeatable business processes, for which it makes sense to pre-specify an explicit control flow in terms of classical imperative primitives for sequencing, looping and branching. However, recently Case Management has emerged as a response to the need for more flexibility when supporting knowledge workflows [23]. A knowledge workflow is characterised by having a more unpredictable sequencing of tasks and service executions, e.g. depending on the concrete case at hand and its context, individual tasks or service executions may need to be skipped or repeated, thereby deviating from the "happy path".

The OMG recently defined the standard Case Management Model and Notation (CMMN) [2], which takes a declarative approach and places a stronger focus

© Springer International Publishing Switzerland 2016
Q.Z. Sheng et al. (Eds.): ICSOC 2016, LNCS 9936, pp. 467–482, 2016.
DOI: 10.1007/978-3-319-46295-0_29

on describing the rules instead of the flow of a process. While CMMN is still only in its early stages and has no formal semantics yet, it has been highly influenced by the Guard Stage Milestone (GSM) model [16], which has both a formal semantics [5,10] and is supported by an open source implementation [14]. Activities, e.g. human tasks or service calls, in GSM are tied to *stages*. Conditions ("guards") referring to events and data, govern which stages are open, hence which activities/services are available, and which goals ("milestones") have been met. The constraint language used to specify guards in GSM is a variant on Event-Condition-Action (ECA) rules.

A particular challenge in the creation of GSM and CMMN Schemas is that the rules are *cascading*, i.e., the firing of one rule may require the firing of another in the same reaction step. To avoid race conditions and infinite cascading, rules are required to be *ordered* and *consistent*. The right ordering and consistency of rules can however be difficult in practice to obtain for the modeller: It is dangerously easy to accidentally specify two distinct rules where each trigger the condition of the other. Recent research has explored both syntactic [5,10] and semantic [13] approaches to *discovering* inconsistent rules. However, the question remains how modellers can repair discovered inconsistencies and how consistent GSM schemas can be modelled from high-level requirements and business policies.

In the present paper we address and answer this latter question by providing a mapping from Dynamic Condition Response (DCR) graphs [15] to GSM Schemas and prove that the resulting schema is always consistent. The DCR graph model is a formal, declarative case management notation which is implemented in and supported by an industrial modelling and simulation tool [12,17] and a commercial case management software product [6,8,21]. Compared to GSM and CMMN, the DCR graph model is centred around the high-level notion of *events*. An event can e.g. be the start or end of an activity/service invocation. Five basic relations between events allow to constraint their temporal ordering and define obligations before the process can end, e.g. that one event is a condition for another event to happen, or that an event is required as a response following another event.

The main technical contribution of the present paper is to provide a formal, semantics-preserving translation from DCR to GSM. This translation is notable for the following reasons.

1. It proves that *any* DCR graph has a semantically equivalent GSM schema (Theorem 1, Corollary 1).
2. It demonstrates how the notion of *acceptance* of DCR graphs can be recovered in GSM schemas *even though GSM does not have a corresponding primitive notion* (Subsect. 4.4).
3. It provides a method for deriving *consistent* GSM schemas from a given set of high-level rules, via formalisation of these rules in a DCR model (Lemma 1).
4. It relates the DCR notation via GSM to the emerging OMG CMMN standard [2,16].

In particular (3) shows that the present work embodies a potential solution to the thorny issue of consistency of GSM schemas: Using DCR rule-patterns as a high-level rule-specification mechanism, we can, using the translation, *generate automatically* a consistent GSM schema guaranteed to have the same semantics (1).

Related Work. Both GSM and DCR models are so-called "declarative notations", an approach introduced to the BPM community by the DECLARE [1] notation. Compared to DECLARE, GSM is strongly data-centric, whereas DCR combines a marking-based operational semantics with a smaller set of declarative constraints, yet yielding a higher degree of formal expressiveness.

Tentative steps to relating GSM and DCR were taken already at the inception of DCR graphs [18], but no full mapping has been developed prior to the present work. DCR models were formally proven to express exactly the union of regular and ω-regular languages in [7], via an encoding to Büchi automata. Otherwise, we are unaware of work relating DCR to other languages via formal translations.

GSM models were formalised as Data-Centric Dynamic Systems (DCDS) in [22], for the purposes of supporting automatic verification. The present work takes the inverse approach: We use DCR Graphs as a declarative policy language from which we can automatically derive consistent GSM models. Closer to the present work, [11] proposes a semi-automated approach to synthesise GSM models from UML activity diagrams, which specify the flow of multiple stateful objects between activities. However, whereas the UML language emphasises describing the life-cycles of objects in an imperative way, DCR emphasises describing in a declarative way compliance rules and policies that activity execution should adhere to. Finally, [19] provides a translation from Petri nets to GSM models to enable the use of process mining algorithms (which output Petri nets) for generating GSM models, while [20] maps GSM models to a public/subscribe abstraction. These papers do not address repair of inconsistencies.

Overview. In Sect. 2 resp. 3, we recall the formal definitions of DCR graphs and GSM schemas; we intertwine the formal definitions with a running example of a mortgage application process from [8]. In Sect. 4, we give the formal translation from DCR to GSM and prove it is semantics preserving. In Sect. 5, we conclude. Due to space limitations, proofs have been relegated to the technical report [9]. A prototype implementation of the translation is available in the DCR Workbench, available at http://dcr.itu.dk/icsoc16.

2   DCR Graphs

In this Section, we recall the theory of DCR graphs. We exemplify DCR graphs by giving a model of a mortgage application process based a real-world process [8]. The purpose of the process is to arrive at a point where a loan application can be assessed. This requires in turn:

1. Collecting appropriate documentation,
2. collecting a budget from the applicant, and
3. appraising the property.

The main actor in the process is the *caseworker*, who collects the documents, may perform a statistical appraisal of the property, and finally assesses the application. The budget needs to be submitted by the *customer*, then screened by an *intern*. The case worker only proceeds to assess the application once the intern has screened the budget.

If a statistical appraisal is unavailable or undesirable, a *mobile consultant* may instead perform an on-site appraisal, however, only one type of appraisal is required. In particular, if neighbourhood of the property will is marked as *irregular* by the IT system, an on-site appraisal is required. An on-site appraisal requires access to the property and therefore an appointment with the owner.

We shall shortly formalise this process as a DCR graph. First, let us define exactly what is such a graph:

Definition 1 (DCR Graph [15]). *A DCR graph is a tuple* (E, R, M) *where*

- E *is a finite set of (labelled) events, the nodes of the graph.*
- R *is the edges of the graph. Edges are partitioned into five kinds, named and drawn as follows: The* conditions (→•), *responses* (•→), *milestones* (→◇), *inclusions* (→+), *and* exclusions (→%).
- M *is the* marking *of the graph. This is a triple* (Ex, Re, In) *of sets of events, respectively the previously executed* (Ex), *the currently pending* (Re), *and the currently included* (In) *events.*

When G is a DCR graph, we write, e.g., E(G) *for the set of events of G, as well as, e.g.,* Ex(G) *for the executed events in the marking of G.*

The mortgage application process is formalised as a DCR graph in Fig. 1. The events of the process are nodes in the graph. Each event (node) has certain attributes, indicated graphically on the node: Assess loan application and Budget screening approve are initially pending, shown by the blue exclamation mark—they are the initial goals of the process. The label of the event provides both the role and name of the event. In the present paper all events have unique labels, so we will identify the event and its label.

Constraints between activities are represented as edges in the graph. DCR graphs have five kinds of constraints; we shall see all five in this example. First, *conditions*. To be screened, the budget must first have been submitted. This is require by the condition relation (→•) between Submit budget and Budget screening approve.

Second, *milestones*. As long as the budget is awaiting screening, the application cannot be assessed. The milestone relation (→◇) from Budget screening approve to Assess loan application ensures this.

Third, *response*. The customer may have an error in his submitted budget and submit a new one. Even if Assess loan application has already been executed, the blue *response* (•→) from Submit budget makes it a requirement to repeat that assessment. We call such a "required activity" *pending*.

Unlike the condition relation, an event constrained by a milestone can become blocked again, for example in our case, if a new budget is submitted then a new

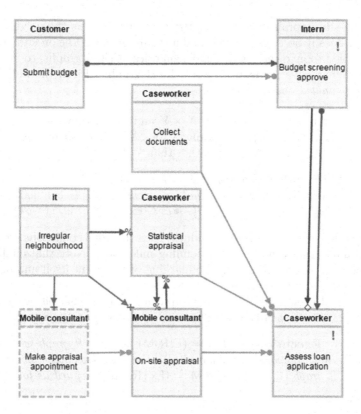

Fig. 1. Declarative DCR model of a mortgage application process (Color figure online)

screening is required, denoted by the response relation (•→) from Submit budget to Budget screening approve. If this occurs, the activity Budget screening approve becomes pending and the activity Assess loan application becomes blocked again. A new screening approval of the budget also requires a new assessment, denoted by the response relation between Budget screening approve and Assess loan application.

There are three more conditions for Assess loan application: Collect documents, Statistical appraisal and On-site appraisal. However, the two kinds of appraisals should be mutually exclusive. Hence, the third and fourth relations, *inclusions and exclusion*. The red *exclusions* (→%) between Statistical appraisal and On-site appraisal mean that when either activity is performed, the other is removed from the process.

Exclusions are dynamic and can be reverted: When the it system registers that the property is in an irregular neighbourhood Statistical appraisal is excluded, On-site appraisal is *included* by the green arrow (→+) (in case a statistical appraisal was already performed and removed it), as is Make appraisal appointment. Make appraisal appointment is a condition for On-site appraisal, but is initially excluded (denoted by the dashed border) and therefore does not block doing an on-site appraisal, only after the IT system marks the neighbourhood as irregular does it become included and a requirement for the on-site appraisal.

We proceed to give the operational semantics of DCR graphs; to answer the question: "What does it mean to *run* a DCR graph"? First, the notion of an event being *enabled*, ready to execute.

Notation. For a binary relation $\to \subseteq X \times Y$ and set Z, we write "$\to Z$" for the set $\{x \in X \mid \exists z \in Z.\ x \to z\}$, and similarly for "$X \to$". For singletons we usually omit the curly braces, writing $\to e$ rather than $\to \{e\}$.

Definition 2 (Enabled Events). *Let* $G = (\mathsf{E}, \mathsf{R}, \mathsf{M})$ *be a DCR graph, with marking* $\mathsf{M} = (\mathsf{Ex}, \mathsf{Re}, \mathsf{In})$. *We say that an event* $e \in \mathsf{E}$ *is* enabled *and write* $e \in \mathsf{enabled}(G)$ *iff (a)* $e \in \mathsf{In}$, *(b)* $\mathsf{In} \cap (\to\bullet e) \subseteq \mathsf{Ex}$, *and (c)* $\mathsf{In} \cap (\to\diamond e) \subseteq \mathsf{E}\backslash\mathsf{Re}$.

That is, enabled events (a) are included, (b) their included conditions are already executed, and (c) have no included pending milestones. Note that enabledness can be determined by considering the marking of the event itself and its immediate conditions and milestones.

The enabled events for the DCR Graph in Fig. 1 are: Submit budget, Collect documents, Statistical appraisal, On-site appraisal and Irregular neighbourhood.

Definition 3 (Execution). *Let* $G = (\mathsf{E}, \mathsf{R}, \mathsf{M})$ *be a DCR graph with marking* $\mathsf{M} = (\mathsf{Ex}, \mathsf{Re}, \mathsf{In})$. *Suppose* $e \in \mathsf{enabled}(G)$. *We may execute* e *obtaining the resulting DCR graph* $(\mathsf{E}, \mathsf{R}, \mathsf{M}')$ *with* $\mathsf{M}' = (\mathsf{Ex}', \mathsf{Re}', \mathsf{In}')$ *defined as follows.*

1. $\mathsf{Ex}' = \mathsf{Ex} \cup e$
2. $\mathsf{Re}' = (\mathsf{Re}\backslash e) \cup (e\bullet\to)$
3. $\mathsf{In}' = (\mathsf{In}\backslash(e\to\%)) \cup (e\to+)$

That is, to execute an event e one must: (1) add e to the set Ex of executed events; (2) update the currently required responses Re by first removing e, then adding any responses required by e; and (3) update the currently included events by first removing all those excluded by e, then adding all those included by e.

Definition 4 (Transitions, Runs, Traces). *Let* G *be a DCR graph. If* $e \in \mathsf{enabled}(G)$ *and executing* e *in* G *yields* H, *we say that* G *has* transition *on* e *to* H *and write* $G \longrightarrow_e H$. *A* run *of* G *is a (finite or infinite) sequence of DCR graphs* G_i *and events* e_i *such that* $G = G_0 \longrightarrow_{e_0} G_1 \longrightarrow_{e_1} \ldots$. *A* trace *of* G *is a sequence of labels of events* e_i *associated with a run of* G. *We write* $\mathsf{runs}(G)$ *and* $\mathsf{traces}(G)$ *for the set of runs and traces of* G, *respectively*

Not every run or trace represents an acceptable execution of the graph: We need also that every response requested is eventually fulfilled or excluded.

Definition 5 (Acceptance). *A run* $G_0 \longrightarrow_{e_0} G_1 \longrightarrow_{e_1} \ldots$ *is accepting iff for all* n *with* $e \in \mathsf{In}(G_n) \cap \mathsf{Re}(G_n)$ *there exists* $m \geq n$ *s.t. either* $e_m = e$, *or* $e \notin \mathsf{In}(G_m)$. *A trace is accepting iff it has an underlying run which is.*

Acceptance tells us which workflows a DCR graph accepts, its *language*.

Definition 6 (Language). *The* language *of a DCR graph G is the set of its accepting traces. We write* lang(*G*) *for the language of G.*

We exemplify the operational semantics of DCR graphs with a run of the model.

1. After executing the event Irregular neighbourhood in Fig. 1 this event is marked as executed, the event Make appraisal appointment becomes included and the event Statistical appraisal becomes excluded. Afterwards the event Make appraisal appointment will be enabled, but the events Statistical appraisal and On-site appraisal will no longer be enabled; the former because it is no longer included and the latter because a condition that was previously excluded is now included.
2. Executing the event Make appraisal appointment will mark it as executed, therefore satisfying the condition to On-site appraisal and making this event enabled again. Executing On-site appraisal will satisfy its condition to Assess loan application, but this event will not become included as there is still an unsatisfied included condition and blocking milestone.
3. Executing Collect documents will satisfy the remaining included condition (note that the condition from Statistical appraisal is no longer relevant as it was excluded).
4. Executing Submit budget will satisfy its condition to (and enable) Budget screening approve, it will also make this event a pending response (but since it already was a pending response this has no noticeable effect).
5. Executing Budget screening approve will remove it from the set of pending responses and thereby satisfy the milestone relation to Assess loan application, enabling it.
6. Finally, executing Assess loan application will remove the pending response on this event, meaning that there are no pending responses left and making the graph accepting. Note that it is not required to end the process at this point, it would for example be possible to execute Submit budget again, once more requiring Budget screening approve and thereafter Assess loan application.

3 GSM Schemas

In this Section, we recall the formal syntax and semantics of GSM [10]. Since we focus on GSM features that are similar to DCR graphs, we omit data attributes, hierarchy, and consider only external events that signify stage completions.

3.1 Syntax

A GSM schema defines the life cycles of artefacts. To simplify the presentation, we focus on the life cycle of a single artefact here.

Definition 7. *A GSM schema is a tuple $\Gamma = (Ev, Stg, Mst, R)$, where*

– *Ev is a set of events that can occur; each event is a stage completion event that refers to a stage in Stg or an internal change event;*

– *Stg is a set of stages;*
– *Mst is a set of milestones;*
– *R is a set of rules, defined in Definition 8;*

GSM schemas are governed by rules, also known as sentries. Rules can refer to events denoting that a stage or a milestone has changed value. If a is a stage or a milestone, then $+a$ (resp. $-a$) denotes that a becomes true (resp. false). Such changes are generated by the system in performing B-steps, whereas stage completion events are generated by the environment.

Definition 8. *A rule $r \in R$ has the form* **on** *e* **if** *cond* **then** $\odot a$, *where* $\odot \in \{+, -\}$. *The* **on** *part is optional. The event e is either a stage completion event or a change event $+a$ or $-a$ for some milestone or stage a. The condition cond is a boolean constraint that only refers to milestones and stages. We call e the trigger of φ and cond the condition of φ. The* **then** *part signifies the change: $+a$ means that a becomes true, while $-a$ means that a becomes false. For a rule $r =$* **on** *e* **if** *cond* **then** $\odot a$, *we let $trigger(r) = e$, $condition(r) = cond$, and $action(r) = \odot a$.*

A stage or milestone x is referenced *by a rule r if x occurs in the* **on** *or* **if** *parts. A stage or milestone x is* triggered *by a rule r if x occurs in the* **then** *part. Note that triggering may be negative, i.e., action $a = -x$.*

To illustrate these definitions, consider the partial GSM schema in Fig. 2 and the rules in Table 1. The rules define for each stage and each milestone a when the stage/milestone becomes true $+a$ (odd numbered rules) and false $-a$ (even numbered rules). Note the inter-dependencies between the rules. For instance, if rule R5 fires, it enables rule R3.
The GSM fragment expresses that:

– Submit budget is opened as soon as possible, but only once.
– If Submit budget completes, then the milestone Budget submitted is achieved, stage Submit budget is closed, and the stage Budget screening approve is opened.
– If Budget screening approved completes, then the milestone Budget screening approve is achieved, and the stage Budget screening approve is closed.

Note that this example GSM fragment is *more* restrictive than the DCR graph model, where both Submit budget and Budget screening approve can be executed repeatedly. A better GSM fragment can be derived from the DCR graph of the previous Section through the translation presented in the next.

Fig. 2. Part of GSM schema of mortgage application process

Table 1. Rules for GSM model in Fig. 2 (*not* equivalent to Fig. 1)

R1	if	true	then	+Submit budget
R2	on	+Budget submitted	then	−Submit budget
R3	if	Budget submitted	then	+Budget screening approve
R4	if	Budget screened	then	−Budget screening approve
R5	on	C:Submit budget	then	+Budget submitted
R6	on	+Submit budget	then	−Budget submitted
R7	on	C:Budget screening approve	then	+Budget screened
R8	on	+Budget screening approve	then	−Budget screened

3.2 Semantics

A snapshot Σ of a GSM schema is a tuple (S, M), where $S \subseteq Stg$ and $M \subseteq Mst$. A stage completion event e is applicable to Σ if e refers to a stage $s \in S$.

The semantics of a GSM schema is event-based: If a stage completion event occurs in a snapshot, the system takes a B-step in response, in which a set of "relevant rules" is fired.

Definition 9. (Relevant Rules). *Let e be a stage completion event. A rule in R is relevant for e if it may be fired in the subsequent B-step. The set of relevant rules R_e is defined inductively as follows*

– *each sentry of the form* **on** e **if** *condition is in R_e;*
– *if a sentry in R_e triggers a stage or milestone a, then each sentry that references a is in R_e.*

Each relevant rule that is fired results in a change of the stage or milestone that is triggered by the rule. To ensure that the rules have maximal effect, the rules are evaluated in a pre-specified order. A rule r_1 is evaluated before r_2, written $r_1 \prec r_2$ if r_1 triggers a stage or milestone that is referenced in r_2. For instance, if $r_1 = $ **on** e **then** $+m_1$ and $r_2 = $ **on** f **if** m_1 **then** $+S_2$, then $r_1 \prec r_2$ because of m_1 triggered by r_1 and referenced by r_2.

There are two healthiness constraints on GSM schema [10]. First, the induced $\prec$ ordering must be acyclic. This ensures that when an event e is processed, the set R_e of relevant rules can be evaluated and fired one by one according to the order specified by $\prec$, until eventually a snapshot is reached in which no rule is relevant and can be fired.

Second, the set of R_e of relevant rules should not specify contradictory effects, i.e. there are no two rules in R_e such that one rule has $+a$ and the other rule $-a$ as effect. If the set of rules is consistent, then each stage and milestone will change at most once during a response to an event (toggle-once property [5]). Toggle-once can also been ensured by defining a more liberal constraint that is, however, more intricate [10] and not needed for the purpose of this paper.

Definition 10. (Consistency). *A set R_e of relevant rules is consistent if the induced $\prec$ ordering is acyclic and the rules do not specify contradictory effects. A GSM schema Γ has consistent rules if for each event e its set of relevant rules R_e is consistent.*

Rules in B-steps are evaluated relative to snapshots Σ and a set I of input events. We write $(\Sigma, I) \models$ **on** e **if** $cond$ **then** $\odot a$, if $e \in I$ and $\Sigma \models cond$.

Let $(\Sigma, I) \models r$, where $r =$ **on** e **if** $cond$ **then** $\odot a$. The effect of rule r on Σ, denoted $apply(\Sigma, r)$, is $\Sigma' = (S', M')$ where:

- if $a \in S$ and $\odot = +$ then $S' = S \cup \{a\}$ and $M' = M$;
- if $a \in S$ and $\odot = -$ then $S' = S \backslash \{a\}$ and $M' = M$;
- if $a \in M$ and $\odot = +$ then $S' = S$ and $M' = M \cup \{a\}$;
- if $a \in M$ and $\odot = -$ then $S' = S$ and $M' = M \backslash \{a\}$.

We next define B-steps.

Definition 11 (B-step, Run [10]). *Let $\Gamma = (Ev, Stg, Mst, S, R)$ be a GSM schema, let Σ, Σ' snapshots of Γ, and e a stage completion event that is applicable to Σ, and let R_e be the set of relevant rules. The tuple (Σ, e, Σ') is a B-step of Γ if there is a sequence $\Sigma_0 = \Sigma, \Sigma_1, \Sigma_2, \ldots, \Sigma_n = \Sigma'$ of snapshots of Γ, such that $e \in Stg_\Sigma$ and each Σ_i is the result of applying a rule $r \in R_e$ to Σ_{i-1}, so $\Sigma_i = apply(\Sigma_{i-1}, r)$, for each $i \in [1..n]$ and the ordering of the applied rules is compatible with $\prec$.*

A GSM run is a sequence $\Sigma_0, \Sigma_1, .., \Sigma_n$ of snapshots interleaved with a sequence of events $e_0, e_1, .., e_n$ such that for each pair Σ_i, Σ_{i+1} of snapshots, where $i \geq 0$, $(\Sigma_i, e_i, \Sigma_{i+1})$.

4   Translating DCR to GSM

We define a translation from DCR graphs to GSM schemas. First, we define how GSM stages and milestones are derived from a DCR graph. Next, we define how GSM rules are derived from a DCR graph.

4.1   Defining GSM Stages and Milestones

We first need to interpret the DCR concept of an event in terms of GSM concepts. The obvious interpretation is to see a DCR event as being similar to a GSM event. However, each GSM event is either a stage completion event or an internal change event. Since a DCR event relates to an activity in DCR graphs, we interpret a DCR event as a GSM stage completion event. The corresponding stage is inferred from the label of the DCR event. For instance, the DCR event Submit budget in Fig. 1 translates into a GSM completion event C:Submit budget, which signals that stage Submit budget has completed.

So each DCR event e maps into a GSM stage s_e with stage completion event C:s_e. We shall arrange our encoding such that an *enabled* DCR event e has its corresponding stage s_e *active*. Execution of the DCR event will correspond to completion of the stage. We shall see below how a stage s_e is opened precisely when e becomes enabled.

Next, we define for a DCR event e, which corresponds to a GSM stage s_e, three different milestones. These milestones are needed to capture the different possible states of that event, according to DCR graphs.

1. An "executed" milestone m_e^{exec} is achieved when the stage s_e has completed for the first time. It stays true even after reopening of that stage.
2. A "response" milestone m_e^{res} is false when the stage s_e must be opened in the future. When the stage is subsequently opened, it becomes true, i.e., the response has been given.
3. An "inclusion" milestone m_e^{inc}, which is achieved when the corresponding stage is relevant. If the stage is not relevant, its execution is out of scope. Inclusion milestones represent varying scopes of the process, depending on the specific execution.

The use of these milestone is somewhat unconventional, compared to traditional GSM schemas. They are necessary to have the GSM schema reflect DCR notions of dynamic change of rules.

4.2 Defining GSM Rules

We first analyse the rules needed for opening and closing stages. A stage s_e should be open iff the underlying DCR event e is enabled. We derive the following three conditions, based on Definition 2.

First, an enabled DCR event e must be included. In the GSM translation, the milestone m_e^{inc} should be achieved. E.g., in Fig. 1 stage On-site appraisal can only open if milestone On-site appraisal^{inc} is achieved.

Second, for a DCR event e to become enabled, each predecessor event f of e that is a condition for e must have occurred, but only if f is included. In the translated GSM schemas, this means that stage s_e is only opened if for each DCR constraint $f \rightarrow\bullet e$, if the milestone m_f^{inc} has been achieved, then milestone m_f^{exec} has been achieved too. E.g., in Fig. 1 event Make appraisal appointment is a condition for On-site appraisal. Hence stage On-site appraisal can only open if milestone Make appraisal appointment^{inc} is not achieved (corresponding to event Make appraisal appointment not being included) or if milestone Make appraisal appointment^{inc} is achieved and Make appraisal appointment^{exec} is achieved too. Translating the DCR graph in Fig. 1 leads to stage On-site appraisal with guard:

On-site appraisal^{inc}

$\wedge$ (Make appraisal appointment^{inc} $\Rightarrow$ Make appraisal appointment^{exec}).

Third, for a DCR event e to become enabled, for each predecessor event f of e that is a DCR milestone for e, if f is included, then f must not be pending, i.e., f does not have to be executed in the future. In the translated GSM schemas,

Table 2. Definition of rule set R

Rule ID	Generated by	Rule definition
R1	$\forall e, f.\ e \rightarrow\!\!+ f$	**on** e **then** $+m_f^{\mathsf{inc}}$
R2	$\forall e, f.\ e \rightarrow\!\!\% f \wedge \neg e \rightarrow\!\!+ f$	**on** e **then** $-m_f^{\mathsf{inc}}$
R3	$\forall e.\ \neg\ (e \bullet\!\!\rightarrow e)$	**on** e **then** $+m_e^{\mathsf{res}}$
R4	$\forall e, f.\ e \bullet\!\!\rightarrow f \wedge e \neq f$	**on** e **then** $-m_f^{\mathsf{res}}$
R5	$\forall e$	**on** e **then** $+m_e^{\mathsf{exec}}$
R6	$\forall e$	**if** enabled(e) **then** $+s_e$
R7	$\forall e$	**if** $\neg$enabled(e) **then** $-s_e$

this means that stage s_e is only opened if for each DCR constraint $f \rightarrow\!\!\diamond e$, if the GSM milestone m_f^{inc} has been achieved, then GSM milestone m_f^{res} has been achieved too (recall that m_f^{res} signifies that stage s_f does not have to executed in the future). For instance, in Fig. 1 event Budget screening approve is a DCR milestone for Assess loan application. Therefore, stage Assess loan application can only open if either GSM milestone Budget screening approve^{inc} is not achieved or if GSM milestones Budget screening approve^{inc} and Budget screening approve^{res} are both achieved.

Altogether, these three conditions dictate, for a given DCR event e, when the corresponding stage s_e should be open. We capture these three conditions for a DCR event e in the predicate enabled(e), which states under what condition stage s_e opens:

$$\mathsf{enabled}(e) = m_e^{\mathsf{inc}} \wedge \bigwedge_{f \rightarrow\bullet e} (m_f^{\mathsf{inc}} \Rightarrow m_f^{\mathsf{exec}}) \wedge \bigwedge_{f \rightarrow\diamond e} (m_f^{\mathsf{inc}} \Rightarrow m_f^{\mathsf{res}})$$

If the predicate enabled(e) becomes true, stage s_e opens. If the predicate enabled(e) is no longer true, stage s_e needs to close.

Table 2 summarises the rules discussed so far. Rules R1-R5 define when the milestones m^{inc}, m^{res} and m^{exec} are achieved and invalidated, respectively. Rules R6 and R7 define when stages are opened and closed.

4.3   Formal Translation

Having discussed the ingredients of the translation, we present it in its entirety:

Definition 12. *Let $G = (\mathsf{E}, \mathsf{R}, \mathsf{M})$ be a DCR graph. We define the* corresponding *GSM schema $[\![G]\!] = (Ev, Stg, Mst, R)$ where*

- *$Ev = \mathsf{E}$;*
- *$Stg = \{s_e \mid e \in \mathsf{E}\}$;*
- *$Mst = \{m_e^{\mathsf{exec}} \mid e \in \mathsf{E}\} \cup \{m_e^{\mathsf{inc}} \mid e \in \mathsf{E}\} \cup \{m_e^{\mathsf{res}} \mid e \in \mathsf{E}\}$; and*
- *rules R are defined as indicated in Table 2.*

Assume the DCR marking is $M = (Ex, In, Re)$. *We define the* corresponding snapshot $\Sigma_{\llbracket G \rrbracket}$ *as follows.*

- $\Sigma_{\llbracket G \rrbracket} \models s_e \Leftrightarrow e \in \mathsf{enabled}(G)$;
- $\Sigma_{\llbracket G \rrbracket} \models m_e^{\mathsf{exec}} \Leftrightarrow e \in Ex$;
- $\Sigma_{\llbracket G \rrbracket} \models m_e^{\mathsf{inc}} \Leftrightarrow e \in In$;
- $\Sigma_{\llbracket G \rrbracket} \models m_e^{\mathsf{res}} \Leftrightarrow e \notin Re$.

In words: The events of $\llbracket G \rrbracket$ are simply the DCR events of G. Each such event has an associated stage s_e, which is open iff e is enabled in G. Moreover, e also has associated milestones $m_e^{\mathsf{exec}}, m_e^{\mathsf{inc}}$, and m_e^{res}, modelling the executed, included, and response states of e.

Note that the milestone for response is true iff e *does not* have a pending response. This is in accordance with GSM intuition where a milestone is true if we have achieved some goal; if e is pending, we have yet to achieve that goal.

We prove that the translation preserves DCR semantics. First, the next key Lemma states that consistency is guaranteed by the translation.

Lemma 1. *For any DCR graph G, the rules R of $\llbracket G \rrbracket$ are consistent.*

We next show that the encoding both preserves and reflects semantics, i.e., the GSM Schema $\llbracket G \rrbracket$ has exactly the same behaviour as the DCR graph G.

Lemma 2. *Let G be a DCR graph. Then for any event e of G we have*

1. *If $G \longrightarrow_e G'$ then $\Sigma_{\llbracket G \rrbracket} \longrightarrow_e \Sigma_{\llbracket G \rrbracket'}$; and*
2. *If $\Sigma_{\llbracket G \rrbracket} \longrightarrow_e \Sigma'$ then there exists exactly one G' such that $G \longrightarrow_e G'$ and $\llbracket G' \rrbracket = \Sigma_{\llbracket G' \rrbracket}$.*

It follows that trace semantics is preserved:

Theorem 1. *Let G be a DCR graph. G has a trace $\alpha = e_0, e_1, \ldots$ iff $\llbracket G \rrbracket$ has a trace $\bar{\alpha} = e_0, e_1, \ldots$.*

Proof. By induction on the length of the trace using Lemma 2.

4.4   Accepting Runs

Note that the notion of "accepting run" from DCR does not have a correspondent in the semantics of GSM, and so cannot be encoded into the GSM semantics: GSM does not make a distinction between "complete" and "incomplete" runs or workflows. It is, however, straightforward to transport the notion of acceptance from DCR to GSM as part of the translation: Simply stipulate that a run is accepting if whenever at step i a milestone m_e^{res} is not achieved yet m_e^{inc} is, then at some subsequent step $j > i$ either m_e^{res} is achieved or m_e^{inc} is not.

Corollary 1. *Let G be a DCR graph. G has an* accepting *trace α iff $\bar{\alpha}$ of Theorem 1 is accepting in the above sense.*

4.5 Prototype

The translation can be improved by removing unnecessary milestones, as explained in an accompanying technical report [9]. A prototype implementation of the translation is available at http://dcr.itu.dk/icsoc16. The prototype allows the user to input a DCR graph G (using existing mechanics of the DCR Workbench), and produces in response a CMMN 1.1 XML serialisation of the translated model $[\![G]\!]$. For readability, this output is generated in terms of the trimmed translation, suppressing semantically pointless milestones. As the non-finalised CMMN 1.1 standard does not support the full rule schemas of GSM, the output assumes certain extensions, e.g., that the expression language allows references to the achieved-state of milestones.

5 Conclusion

In this paper we introduced a formal mapping from DCR Graphs to GSM schemas. We showed that for any DCR Graph, a semantically equivalent GSM schema exists, and that the notion of acceptance of DCR graphs can be recovered in GSM schemas. This means that, when extended with the right acceptance criteria, GSM schemas are at least as expressive as DCR graphs[1]. An important practical application of the mapping is the possibility of deriving consistent GSM schemas from a given set of rules formalised in a DCR model, which provides a clear advantage over existing approaches where consistency of a GSM schema is typically checked after-the-fact by model checking. It also makes an important first step in relating the DCR notation to the CMMN standard, thereby increasing the industrial applicability of DCR Graphs.

In future work we intend to also develop the reverse mapping from GSM schemas to DCR Graphs. Because GSM schemas have a strong data-centric aspect to them, the addition of data concepts to the DCR notation is critical for obtaining a meaningful such mapping. While some initial work on adding data to DCR exists [18,21], many questions remain open. In addition the proposed technique for deriving consistent GSM schemas from a rule-based DCR model needs to be developed in more detail. Finally, to be able to relate DCR Graphs to the CMMN standard, a mapping from GSM to CMMN is required. While such a mapping may appear to be straightforward given the large influence GSM has had over the development of the standard, a lack of a formally defined semantics for CMMN presently hampers its development.

---

[1] with unique labels, see comments after Definition 1.

References

1. van der Aalst, W.M.P., Pesic, M.: DecSerFlow: towards a truly declarative service flow language. In: Bravetti, M., Núñez, M., Zavattaro, G. (eds.) WS-FM 2006. LNCS, vol. 4184, pp. 1–23. Springer, Heidelberg (2006)
2. BizAgi, et al.: Case Management Model and Notation (CMMN), v1, OMG Document Number formal/2014-05-05, Object Management Group, May 2014
3. Web Services Business Process Execution Language (BPEL), Version 2.0 (2007). http://docs.oasis-open.org/wsbpel/2.0/wsbpel-v2.0.html
4. Business Process Model and Notation (BPMN), Version 2.0 (2011). http://www.omg.org/spec/BPMN/2.0/PDF
5. Damaggio, E., Hull, R., Vaculín, R.: On the equivalence of incremental and fixpoint semantics for business artifacts with guard-stage-milestone lifecycles. Inf. Syst. **38**, 561–584 (2013)
6. Debois, S., Slaats, T.: The analysis of a real life declarative process. In: CIDM 2015, pp. 1374–1382 (2015)
7. Debois, S., Hildebrandt, T., Slaats, T.: Safety, liveness and run-time refinement for modular process-aware information systems with dynamic sub processes. In: Bjørner, N., Boer, F. (eds.) FM 2015. LNCS, vol. 9109, pp. 143–160. Springer, Heidelberg (2015)
8. Debois, S., Hildebrandt, T.T., Marquard, M., Slaats, T.: Hybrid process technologies in the financial sector. In: BPM 2015 (Industry track), pp. 107–119 (2015). http://ceur-ws.org/Vol-1439/paper9.pdf
9. Eshuis, R., Debois, S., Slaats, T., Hildebrandt, T.: Deriving consistent GSM schemas from DCR graphs (full version). IT University of Copenhagen (2016). http://itu.dk/people/debois/tr.pdf
10. Eshuis, R., Hull, R., Sun, Y., Vaculín, R.: Splitting GSM schemas: a framework for outsourcing of declarative artifact systems. Inf. Syst. **46**, 157–187 (2014)
11. Eshuis, R., Van Gorp, P.: Synthesizing data-centric models from business process models. Computing **98**(4), 345–373 (2016)
12. Exformatics: Dcrgraphs editor and simulator. http://DCRGraphs.net
13. Gonzalez, P., Griesmayer, A., Lomuscio, A.: Verifying GSM-based business artifacts. In: Proceedings of the 2012 IEEE 19th International Conference on Web Services (ICWS), pp. 25–32. IEEE Computer Society (2012)
14. Heath, F., Vaculín, R., Hull, R.: Barcelona: a design and runtime environment for modeling and execution of artifact-centric business processes. In: Proceedings of the 9th International Conference on Business Process Management, BPM (2011)
15. Hildebrandt, T.T., Mukkamala, R.R.: Declarative event-based workflow as distributed dynamic condition response graphs. In: PLACES, pp. 59–73 (2010)
16. Marin, M., Hull, R., Vaculín, R.: Data centric BPM and the emerging case management standard: a short survey. In: Rosa, M., Soffer, P. (eds.) BPM Workshops 2012. LNBIP, vol. 132, pp. 24–30. Springer, Heidelberg (2013)
17. Marquard, M., Shahzad, M., Slaats, T.: Web-based modelling and collaborative simulation of declarative processes. In: Motahari-Nezhad, H.R., Recker, J., Weidlich, M. (eds.) BPM. LNCS, vol. 9253, pp. 209–225. Springer, Heidelberg (2015)
18. Mukkamala, R.R.: A formal model for declarative workflows: dynamic condition response graphs. Ph.D. thesis, IT University of Copenhagen, June 2012
19. Popova, V., Fahland, D., Dumas, M.: Artifact lifecycle discovery. Int. J. Coop. Inf. Syst. **24**(1) (2015). http://dx.doi.org/10.1142/S021884301550001X

20. Sadoghi, M., Jergler, M., Jacobsen, H., Hull, R., Vaculín, R.: Safe distribution and parallel execution of data-centric workflows over the publish/subscribe abstraction. IEEE Trans. Knowl. Data Eng. **27**(10), 2824–2838 (2015)
21. Slaats, T., Mukkamala, R.R., Hildebrandt, T., Marquard, M.: Exformatics declarative case management workflows as DCR graphs. In: Daniel, F., Wang, J., Weber, B. (eds.) BPM 2013. LNCS, vol. 8094, pp. 339–354. Springer, Heidelberg (2013)
22. Solomakhin, D., Montali, M., Tessaris, S.: Formalizing guard-stage-milestone meta-models as data-centric dynamic systems. Technical report (2012)
23. Swenson, K.D.: Mastering the Unpredictable: How Adaptive Case Management will Revolutionize the Way that Knowledge Workers Get Things Done. Meghan-Kiffer, Tampa (2010)

A Formal Guidance Approach for Correct Process Configuration

Souha Boubaker[1(✉)], Amel Mammar[1], Mohamed Graiet[2], and Walid Gaaloul[1]

[1] SAMOVAR, Telecom SudParis, CNRS, Universite Paris-Saclay,
Évry, France
{souha.boubaker,amel.mammar,walid.gaaloul}@telecom-sudparis.eu
[2] ISIMM, Monastir University, Monastir, Tunisia
mohamed.graiet@imag.fr

Abstract. Configurable process models are recently gaining momentum as a basis for process *design by reuse*. Such models are designed in a generic manner to group common and variable parts of similar processes. Since these processes are usually large and complex, their configuration becomes manifestly a difficult task. This is why, an increasing attention is being paid to help achieving the process models configuration in a correct and domain-compliant manner. In this work, we propose an Event-B based formal approach that guides the process analyst to easily derive *correct* process variants while considering business domain constraints provided by *configuration guidelines*. To show the effectiveness of our approach, we conduct experiments on a case study.

Keywords: Business process management · Configurable process model · Process variants · Formal verification · Event-B

1 Introduction

Configurable process models are increasingly adopted by companies due to their capability of grouping the common and variable parts of similar processes. According to a specific business need, process models are configured and customized by selecting one design option for each configurable element. The obtained processes are called *variants*. Several approaches have been proposed for the aim of process variants configuration [10,14,20]. A number of them have attempted to help achieving this in a correct manner [2,3]. One of the most important correctness criterion for Business Process Management (BPM) is the soundness property [2]. Hence, the configurable process model should respect a set of structural constraints (e.g. no isolated activities or dead flows). Therefore, a design-time verification should be applied, since the initial configurable processes should be correct. In addition, the resulting derived variants should fulfill a set of behavioral constraints to avoid issues such as deadlock and lack of synchronization.

Furthermore, *configuration guidelines* describing business domain constraints have been introduced [19,20] in order to further limit the configuration decisions.

© Springer International Publishing Switzerland 2016
Q.Z. Sheng et al. (Eds.): ICSOC 2016, LNCS 9936, pp. 483–498, 2016.
DOI: 10.1007/978-3-319-46295-0_30

These guidelines denote the best practices in a given domain. While several approaches have attempted to provide guidance to analysts in selecting configuration choices according to a specific domain requirements [8, 17], these configuration choices are most often applied *manually* leaving the designer the full responsibility for applying correct ones. Thus, the correctness of resulting variants is most often difficult to preserve even if domain constraints are respected.

This work provides a systematic approach to guide the process analyst to easily configure process models while, not only preserving correctness, but also complying with domain requirements. The approach targets to answer two questions: (1) Is a configurable process model **correct**? (2) Which configuration choices analyst should take to obtain a **correct** variant **with respect to a specific domain constraints**? To do so, we define an Event-B based formal approach allowing first to analyze and check the correctness of a configurable process (*Objective 1*) and to produce correct variants (*Objective 2*). Configuration guidelines rules are also injected to our formal model to ensure that the obtained variants comply with their domain constraints (*Objective 3*). In essence, we formally define and verify constraints related to (i) structural and behavioral correctness properties; and (ii) domain-based configuration guidelines. Then, we use Event-B tools to perform an incremental verification by checking these constraints at each intermediate step of the configuration procedure.

The remainder of this paper is organized as follows. In Sect. 2, we motivate our approach using an example, used also to illustrate our contribution. We present the related work in Sect. 3. Then, we present basic concepts of Event-B method in Sect. 4. In Sect. 5, we give an overview of our approach. Section 6 illustrates our formalization of process configuration and its corresponding constraints using Event-B. The approach verification and validation using the RODIN tool are depicted in Sect. 7. In Sect. 8, our approach is evaluated using a case study. Finally, we conclude and provide insights for future work.

2 Motivation and Requirements

configurable business process integrates multiple process variants of a same business process in a given domain through variation points. These points are referred to as *configurable elements*. The configuration decision of a configurable element is made at design-time [20]. The non-configurable elements represent the commonalities in the configurable model.

Motivating Example. An example of a configurable process model for hotel reservation and car rental agency is captured by Fig. 1. This agency has many branches in different cities and countries. Each branch performs one variant of this process model which may differ in terms of its structure and behavior according to its specific needs. The customer first submits a request through a web form (*a1*). Next, five main functionalities are proposed: (1) the recommendation, i.e. the process fragment starting from *ops2* and ending with *a6*; (2) hotels and cars searching, i.e. the process fragment starting from *ops5* and

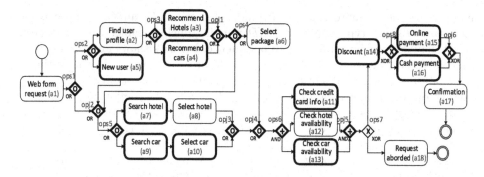

Fig. 1. A configurable hotel and car reservation process model

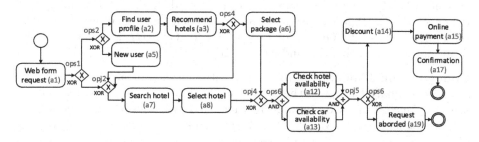

Fig. 2. A process variant derived from the configurable process in Fig. 1

ending with *opj3*; (3) checking phase, i.e. the process fragment starting from *ops6* and ending with *opj5*; (4) discount offer (*a14*); and, (5) payment, i.e. the process fragment starting from *ops8* and ending with *opj6*.

The process is modeled using the Configurable Business Process Model and Notation (C-BPMN) [7], a configurable extension to BPMN. We consider four main control flow elements: activity (represented with a rectangle), edge (control flow edges represented with arrows), event (represented with a circle) and connector (represented with a diamond). Three main connectors, OR ($\bigcirc$), exclusive OR ($\times$) and AND ($+$) are used to model the splits (e.g. *ops1*) and joins (e.g. *opj1*). C-BPMN includes two configurable elements: activities and connectors. This example presents 24 configurable elements (13 connectors and 11 activities) which are highlighted with a thicker border. For instance, activities *a1* and *a18* are non-configurable, so they should be included in every configured variant. Whereas, the activity *a11* and the connector *ops1* may vary from one process to another, as they are configurable.

A connector may be configurable to restrict its behavior by (i) changing its type (e.g. from OR to AND), or/and (ii) restricting its incoming or outgoing branches. A connector may change its type according to a set of configuration constraints [20] (see Table 1). Each row corresponds to the initial type that can be

Table 1. Constraints for the configuration of connectors [20]

FROM-TO	OR	XOR	AND	seq
OR	√	√	√	√
XOR		√		√
AND			√	

mapped to one or more types in columns. For example, an *OR* type can be configured to any type while an *AND* remains unchangeable. The connector *AND* should never be configured to a sequence. Figure 2 shows an example of a process variant derived from the configurable process of Fig. 1. In this variant, the analyst does not need neither the recommendation functionality for cars (*a4*) nor the option to rent a car (*a9* and *a10*). This refers to configuring *ops3* to a sequence starting from *a3* (i.e. the outgoing branch of *ops3* starting from *a4* is removed) and configuring *ops5* to a sequence starting with *a7* (i.e. the outgoing branch of *ops5* starting from *a9* is removed).

Also, a configurable activity may be needed in a process variant and not in another depending on specific requirements. Hence, these activities can be included (i.e. ON) or excluded (i.e. OFF) from the model [20]. In the process variant of Fig. 2, the analyst does not need the card checking functionality but does need the creation of a new user and the discount functionalities. This refers to configuring *a11* to OFF and *a5* and *a14* to ON: *a11* is removed in the resulting variant whereas *a5* and *a14* are kept.

Configuration Guidelines. To comply with specific domain business needs, the process analyst needs further guidelines to derive specific variants. *Configuration guidelines* provide recommendations and proposed best practices for a specific domain [8,20]. An example of such guidelines satisfied by the variant of Fig. 2 is: *"if the hotel recommendation functionality is included (i.e. a3) in the derived variant, then the hotel searching functionality (i.e. a7) should be also included."* These guidelines are expressed in the form of logical *If-Then*-rules where the if and then parts contain configurations of different configurable elements.

Correctness Checking. In Fig. 3a, *ops5* has been configured to a sequence starting from *a9* (the edge between *ops5* and *a7* disappears). Thus, the produced process is not sound, since activities *a7* and *a8* become unreachable from the initial event: they are dead as they can never be executed. In this paper, we aim at preventing these configurations by formally ensuring that every connector configuration involving outgoing or incoming branches restriction is implicitly followed by a transformation phase allowing to remove the isolated activities from the resulting process. Thereafter, an isolated node is either unreachable from the initial event, or are not on a sequence leading to a final event.

Besides checking structural correctness of the configurable process model, we aim to also ensure the behavioral correctness of the derived process variants [2]. Since processes may be complex with a large number of inter-dependencies between the different configuration alternatives, configuring a process model becomes a quite difficult task. Therefore, analysts may easily be mistaken in their choices which undermine the correctness of the resulting variant. In the following, we illustrate some soundness problems [22] that would happen during the process configuration resulting from mismatches between splits and joins.

– In Fig. 3b, the join operator *opj2* has been configured to an XOR while the connector *ops1* had been already configured to an AND-Split. The two outgoing branches from the AND-split will be activated, however, the XOR-join needs the completion of exactly one of its incoming branches. This leads to an improper termination of the process.

– In Fig. 3c, the connector *ops4* has been configured to an XOR-Split and the corresponding join *opj4* to an AND-join. This implies a deadlock, as only one branch is activated after the XOR-join, whereas the AND-join needs the completion of all its incoming branches.

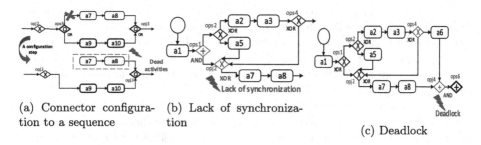

(a) Connector configuration to a sequence

(b) Lack of synchronization

(c) Deadlock

Fig. 3. Examples of configuration mistakes from the configurable process in Fig. 1

In view of these situations, the process configuration options should be evaluated with respect to all configuration soundness constraints as well as configuration guidelines to derive correct variants. Hence, our contribution consists not only in proving the correctness of the process configuration steps but also in guiding analyst choices with respect to these constraints using the ProB model checker.

3   Related Work

Several approaches have been proposed to model variability in configurable process models by restricting its behavior through configurable nodes [10,14,20]. A number of them tried to ensure the process configuration correctness [19]. Mainly, two criteria related to process variants correctness were defined: structural and behavioral correctness.

Table 2 provides a comparative overview of some configuration approaches in light of our evaluation criteria (inspired from [19]). We further decompose the *Correctness Support* column into three sub-criteria: (i) *structural* correctness, (ii) *soundness* and (iii) compliance with *domain*-specific configuration guidelines.

In [1,2,20], Petri net was used to formalize and verify correctness and soundness properties of Configurable EPC (C-EPC) processes. They highlight the soundness property and they derive propositional logic constraints that guarantee the behavioral correctness of the configured model. The approach in [3] used partner synthesis. Authors in [13] discuss ensuring soundness of variant models in the Provop framework which extends the process variants by *options*[14]. In [21], authors use CoSeNets (Configurable Service Nets) that allow to achieve correctness because of their no cycles syntactic restrictions. However, even if these proposals try to achieve configuration correctness, they nevertheless often lack the necessary guidance to become adaptable to a given domain and do not support the BPMN notation.

Existing approaches for assisting process analysts in selecting desirable configuration choices according to specific domain requirements are most often manual. The questionnaire-based approach in [17] offers guidance for configuring process models using a set of questions defined by domain experts and answered by designers. Authors in [16] introduce the use of configuration rules in order to configure a reference process template. In [6,11], authors propose a feature-oriented approach based on feature models to represent variability. Moreover, in [20], the notion of configuration guideline is introduced in order to meet specific domain requirements. Authors in [8] attempted to use configuration guidelines for assisting analysts in BPMN configuration. However, they do not consider any correctness criterion.

In our previous work [9], an Event-B based approach for deriving correct process variants was proposed. The current work strengthens this previous one by the integration of configuration guidelines, and conducting experiments with a group of users allowing to prove the approach usefulness. Thus, our approach intends to meet the defined criteria in Table 2. First, we consider three levels of verification: structural correctness, soundness and compliance with domain-specific configuration guidelines. These three issues were usually discussed individually. Then, we define a systematic formal approach for guiding analyst in deriving correct and domain-compliant BPMN variants using a step-based Event-B model animated by the ProB tool. Event-B is of special interest, since it supports incremental verification allowing to produce a correct specification by construction by proving the different constraints of the model at each step.

Table 2. Evaluation of related configuration approaches

Approaches	Criteria						
	Process modeling language	Correctness support			Guidance support	Incremental verification	Formal specification
		Structural	Soundness	Domain			
[1–3, 20]	C-EPC	+	+	+	−	−	+
[13]	Block-structured	+	+	−	−	−	±
[21]	CoSeNets	+	±	−	−	−	±
[16]	Block-structured	+	+	−	±	−	±
[6, 11]	Block-structured	+	+	−	±	−	+
[17]	C-EPC	±	−	+	+	−	+
[8]	C-BPMN	−	−	+	+	−	−
Our approach	C-BPMN	+	+	+	+	+	+

4   The Event-B Method

Event-B [4] is a state-based formal method for modeling and analyzing systems. It is based on classical logic and set theory. An Event-B model uses two types of components to describe a system: machines and contexts. A machine contains dynamic elements that describe the state of the system, which are variables v and events E to describe the behavior of a system. Variables are constrained by invariants $I(v)$, which are supposed to hold whenever the state of the system change. Whereas a context represents the static part of the model, consisting of sets, constants, and axioms that specifies their properties. Machines can be linked to each other by a *refinement* relation. To have access to its elements, a context is seen by a machine and its refinements. A context may be also extended by another to introduce more elements.

An event takes the form: evt $\triangleq$ **any** x **where** G **then** Act **end**; where x is the list of event parameters, G denotes a conjoined list of predicates defining the guard that are the necessary conditions for the event to occur. An action Act is a simple assignment to a state variable to describe the consequence of the event occurrence. In this paper, we restrict ourselves to the deterministic assignment, the becomes equal substitution, denoted by $(x := e)$.

To cope with the complexity of a system, Event-B defines several abstraction levels, using refinements, in order to gradually introduce the different elements of a system. A step wise refinement approach produces a *correct specification by construction* since we prove the different properties of the system at each step. Event-B is supported by the eclipse based RODIN platform [5] on which different external tools (provers, animators, model-checkers) can be plugged in order to animate/validate a formal development.

5   Approach Overview

This section gives an overview of our contribution detailed in the next sections. Figure 4 depicts the configuration procedure allowing to obtain correct process variants using Event-B as a formal method. Basically, we defined two abstraction levels: the first level introduces our model for process model configuration allowing to preserve correctness (machine M0, see Sect. 6.1). In this machine, configuration steps and their correctness are ensured by events and invariants (see Sect. 6.2). Next, configuration guidelines are formally integrated to our model in the second abstraction level as model refinement of the first level (machine M1, see Sect. 6.3). Event-B defines proof obligations to guarantee that the invariants are preserved by all events (see Sect. 7.1).

First of all, the correctness of the configurable process is verified with respect to the different invariants. The configuration can start only if all the invariants are verified. This allows to achieve our *objective 1* (defined in the Introduction). Then, the analyst uses ProB animator [18] to perform configuration steps involving each element configuration (see Sect. 7.2): firstly, the guards of each event are evaluated (step 1). These guards include both correctness and domain constraints. Then, only events whose guards are verified are enabled (step 2). Thus, the configuration step can be applied (step 3).

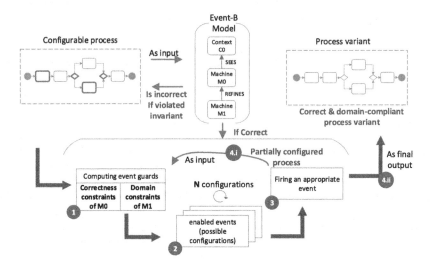

Fig. 4. Our approach overview

The set of potential configuration options is updated after each step. These steps are repeated (step 4.i) while there are configurable elements. As a result, the analyst derives a correct and domain-compliant process variant (step 4.ii), satisfying our *objectives 2* and *3*.

6 Event-B Formal Modeling of Process Configuration

In this section, we use the Event-B method to formally specify our configuration approach. Based on a correct Configurable process model (see Sect. 6.1), we define configuration steps (see Sect. 6.2) allowing to derive *correct* process variants with respect to a set of *configuration guidelines* (see Sect. 6.3). Thereafter, the analyst is able to generate correct variants thanks to this model. Due to lack of space, we outline in this paper the basic elements of our formalization[1].

6.1 Formalizing Configurable Process Models

We start by presenting the context *C0* which holds the following finite sets: (i) *BPS*, which defines the set of possible processes, (ii) *NODES*, which contains three values denoting types of nodes: activities (i.e. *ACTS*), split connectors (i.e. *CON_S*), and join connectors (i.e. *CON_J*), and (iii) *TYPES*, which defines three types of connectors: *OR*, *XOR* and *AND*.

---

[1] The complete Event-B model can be downloaded from our web page http://www-inf.it-sudparis. eu/SIMBAD/tools/GuideBPMEventB.

Then, we define the machine *M0* which sees the context *C0* described above. The variables of *M0* and their typing invariants are given in Listing 1. We define a variable *BP* to store the created processes. To map

Listing 1. M0's variables and typing invariants

```
MACHINE  M0   SEES  C0
VARIABLES   BP   BP_Nodes   Initial   Final   SEQ   CON_Type
INVARIANTS
Inv1 :  BP ⊆ BPS
Inv2 :  BP_Nodes ∈ BP ↔ NODES
Inv3 :  Initial ∈ BP → ACTS
Inv4 :  Final ∈ BP ↔ ACTS ∧ dom(Final) = BP
Inv5 :  CON_Type ∈ P_Nodes ▷ (CON_S ∪ CON_J) → TYPES
Inv6 :  SEQ ∈ BP → (NODES ↔ NODES)
Inv7 :  Configurable_Nodes ∈ BP_Nodes → BOOL
```

each process to its nodes, we introduce the relation *BP_Nodes* from *BP* to *NODES* (*Inv2*). We define the start and the end events as activities using respectively the total function *Initial* (*Inv3*) and the relation *Final* (*Inv4*); since we assume that a process has exactly one initial activity but may have several final ones. In BPMN, each connector, either a split or a join, has a type. This is modeled using the total function *CON_Type* (*Inv5*). The control flow perspective describes activities and their execution ordering through different constructors [15]. This execution order is modeled using the total function *SEQ* (*Inv6*). Finally, we define a total *Boolean* function *Configurable_Nodes* (*Inv7*) to state whether a given node is configurable or not in each process in which it appears.

Structural Constraints. To ensure consistent and structurally correct process control flow, we define a set of constraints to be respected. We illustrate some of them in Listing 2: (i) except the initial and the final nodes, each activity have exactly one outgoing (*Inv11*[2]); (ii) a split connector has at least two outgoings arcs (*Inv14*); and (iii) a join connector has exactly one outgoing arc (*Inv15*).

Listing 2. Structural constraints invariants

```
....
Inv11 :  ∀bp.(bp ∈ BP ⇒ (ACTS ◁ SEQ(bp)) ∈ ACTS ∩ BP_Nodes[{bp}] \ Final[{bp}]
                    → BP_Nodes[{bp}] \ Initial[{bp}]
...
Inv14 :  ∀bp, nd.(bp ∈ BP ∧ nd ∈ CON_S ∧ bp ↦ nd ∈ BP_Nodes ⇒ card(SEQ(bp)[{nd}]) ≥ 2)
Inv15 :  ∀bp.(bp ∈ BP ⇒ CON_J ◁ SEQ(bp) ∈ CON_J ∩ BP_Nodes[{bp}] → NODES) ...
```

A process is considered to be *sound* if it fulfills the following two conditions: (1) all nodes of the process can be activated, i.e. every node can be reached from the initial activity, as depicted by *Inv20* in Listing 3 where *cls*[3] is the transitive closure of a relation; and (2) for each activity in the process, there is at least one possible path leading from this activity to a final activity, i.e. the termination is always possible. This condition is captured by *Inv21* of Listing 3.

Listing 3. Soundness constraints invariants

```
Inv20 :  ∀bp, node.(bp ↦ node ∈ BP_Nodes ∧ node ≠ Initial(bp) ⇒ node ∈ (cls(SEQ(bp)))[{Initial(bp)}])
Inv21 :  ∀bp, node.(bp ↦ node ∈ BP_Nodes ∧ node ∉ Final[{bp}]⇒
         (cls(SEQ(bp)))[{node}] ∩ Final[{bp}] ≠ ∅)
```

---

[2] $A ◁ f$ denotes a domain restriction: $A ◁ f = \{x \mapsto y | x \mapsto y \in f \wedge x \in A\}$.

[3] $cls(r)$ denotes the closure of the relation r defined, for each relation ($r \in S \leftrightarrow S$), by: (1) $cls(r) = \bigcup_{i=1..\infty} r^i$; (2) $r^1 = r$; and (3) for each $n >= 2 r^n = (r; r^{n-1})$ The transitive closure formulations were expressed as machine theorems.

Behavioral Constraints. The configuration of a business process model may affect the soundness by two types of potential errors: *lack of synchronization* and *deadlocks* [22]. These situations result from a mismatch between splits and joins. To formally prevent these situa-

Listing 4. Synchronization invariant

```
1 Inv22: ∀bp, ops, n1, n2.(bp ↦ ops ∈ BP_Nodes ▷ CON_S
2   ∧ CON_Type(bp ↦ ops) = AND
3   ∧ n1 ∈ SEQ(bp)[{ops}]∧
4   n2 ∈ SEQ(bp)[{ops}] ∧ n1 ≠ n2
5 ⇒ (∀opj.opj ∈(∪t.t ∈ ((cls(SEQ(bp)))[{n1}] ∪ {n1})
6     ∩ ((cls(SEQ(bp)))[{n2}] ∪ {n2}) ∧
7     SEQ(bp) ∼ [{t}] ∩ (((cls(SEQ(bp)))[{n1}] ∪ {n1})
8     ∩ ((cls(SEQ(bp)))[{n2}] ∪ {n2})) = ∅ | {t})
9   ⇒ (CON_Type(bp ↦ opj) = AND ∨
10    (CON_Type(bp ↦ opj) = OR ∧
11    Configurable_Nodes(bp ↦ opj) = TRUE)) ))
```

tions during configuration procedure, we defined six invariants: three for the splits and three for the joins. These invariants should be preserved by all the events defined to capture configuration operations. For instance, the lack of synchronization could be captured by joining AND-split flows with XOR-join flows (see Fig. 3b). Thanks to *Inv22* (Listing 4[4]), this situation is not allowed in our model. Specifically, having a AND-split operator *ops* (line 2), for each couple of outgoing nodes *n1* and *n2* (lines 3 and 4), the first common node[5] *opj* (lines 4 to 7) should be an AND or a not yet configured OR connector that should be eventually configured as an AND (lines 9 and 10). Similar invariants are defined to ensure a deadlock-free control flow.

6.2 Formalizing Configuration Steps

In this section, we describe the formal modeling of the configurable elements: *activity*, and *connector*. In this formalization, each configuration step is performed by an appropriate event. In order to derive correct variants, we define a set of constraints using invariants and we prove that each event preserves them.

Activity Configuration. A configurable activity could be included or excluded in a process variant according to the analyst choice. To define this activity configuration, two invariants and two events are introduced.

With regard to events, activity configuration is performed through either: (i) *ConfigureACTON* event which keeps the activity; or (ii) *ConfigureACTOFF* event which excludes it. We present in Listing 5 the *ConfigureACTOFF* event. Based on a configurable process *bp1*, a configured process *bp2* is a result of excluding an activity *act*. As guard, *act* must be configurable (*grd3*). This event allows *bp2* to inherit from *bp1*: (i) its nodes whilst removing *act* (*act2*), (ii) its initial and final activities (*act3* and *act4*), (iii) all its nodes relations (i.e. SEQ(bp1)) while removing *act* dependencies and creating a new one connecting *act* successor and predecessor (*act5*), (iv) its configurable nodes (*act6*), and (iiv) types of its connectors. Finally, we define *bp2* as a configuration of *bp1* whilst excluding *act* (*act8*) [9]. Similarly, the event *ConfigureACTON* allows to maintain the same process by keeping the configurable activity[6].

---

[4] The inverse of a function f, (f^{-1}), is denoted in Event-B as $(f \sim)$.

[5] Having two nodes n1 and n2, the *first common node* is the first node which belongs to the transitive closure of both nodes n1 and n2.

[6] More details can be found in http://www-inf.it-sudparis.eu/SIMBAD/tools/GuideBPMEventB.

Listing 5. Excluding activity event

```
ConfigureACTOFF ≙    ANY    bp1    bp2    act
WHERE
grd1:  bp1 ∈ BP ∧ act ∈ ACTS ∧ bp1 ↦ act ∈ BP_Nodes ∧ bp2 ∈ BPS \ BP
grd2:  Configurable_Nodes(bp1 ↦ act) = TRUE
...
THEN
act1:  BP := BP ∪ {bp2}
act2:  BP_Nodes := BP_Nodes ∪ ({bp2} × (BP_Nodes[{bp1}] \ {act}))
act3:  Initial(bp2) := Initial(bp1)
act4:  Final := Final ∪ ({bp2} × (Final[{bp1}]))
act5:  SEQ(bp2) := (({act} ⩰ SEQ(bp1)) ⩰ {act}) ∪((SEQ(bp1)) ∼ [{act} × SEQ(bp1)[{act}])
act6:  Configurable_Nodes := Configurable_Nodes ∪ (⊔ node.node ∈ BP_Nodes[{bp1}] \ {act}
                | {bp2 ↦ node ↦ Configurable_Nodes(bp1 ↦ node)})
act7:  CON_Type := CON_Type ∪ (⊔ con.con ∈ BP_Nodes[{bp1}] ∩ (CON_S ∪ CON_J)
                | {bp2 ↦ con ↦ CON_Type(bp1 ↦ con)})
act8:  Is_Configuration_OFFAct := Is_Configuration_OFFAct ∪ {bp2 ↦ bp1}
```

Connector Configuration. A connector configuration has to consider the following requirements: (1) the configuration constraints for each type of connector, (2) only configurable nodes can be removed, and (3) the connectors types matching checking in order to prevent erroneous situations.

Concretely, in order to obtain a well-structured configured process, an invariant for each configuration choice should be respected. These configuration choices are insured by two events (either split or join) for each connector type. For instance, the event *ConfigureORSplit* allows configuring a configurable split connector from OR type to any type (according to Table 1) while preserving the number of branches greater than two. Recall that each branch can be removed only if all its nodes are configurable. Furthermore, all events should not lead to deadlock or lack of synchronization: for example, for every pair of outgoing branches if the corresponding join is an AND, then the split should be configured to an AND as well. More details about this event and other similar ones (e.g. *ConfigureORJoin*) are given in [9].

Finally, a connector can be configured to a sequence *Seq(N)* by keeping a single branch starting by the node *N*. This is modeled using the event *ConfigureCONSToSeq* for a split connector (resp. *ConfigureCONJToSeq* for a join).

6.3 Injecting Configuration Guidelines in the Model

Process providers may define specific business domain constraints for their process configurations. Thus, *configuration guidelines* are introduced to depict relevant inter-dependencies between the configuration decisions in order to be inline with domain constraints and best practices. Such guidelines are expressed via logical expressions of the form *If-Then*-rules. Both the *if* and *then* parts contain statements about binding configurable nodes to concrete values [20]. An example of such rules is: "*if* a9=OFF and ops5=*Seq*(a7) *then* a14=OFF", i.e. if the car searching and selection functionalities are excluded in a given variant, then the discount activity is excluded too. Note that the *if* part may contain many conditions and the *then* part contains only one statement.

In order to integrate these domain constraints in our model, we define a second abstraction level M1 that refines the first one, M0. We define for each type of *then* statement one invariant. For instance, the relation *ConfigurationG_ACT* (*inv1*, Listing 6) defines a guideline related to the configuration of an activity. Thus, the guideline may have five different conditions: an activity configuration (line 1), a split or join configuration to a type (line 2), and a split or join configuration to a sequence (line 3). Similarly, *ConfigurationG_CONS* defines the guideline for a split connector configuration.

Listing 6. Guidelines invariants

```
1  Inv1 : ConfigurationG_ACT ∈ P(ACTS x CONF) x
2      P(CON_S x TYPES×P1(NODES)) x P(CON_J x TYPES×P1(NODES)) x
3      P(CON_S x NODES) x P(CON_J x NODES) ↦ ACTS x CONF
4  Inv2 : ConfigurationG_CONS ∈ P(ACTS x CONF) x
5      P(CON_S x TYPES×P1(NODES)) x P(CON_J x TYPES×P1(NODES)) x
6      P(CON_S x NODES) x P(CON_J x NODES) ↦ CON_S x TYPES×P1(NODES)
   ...
```

As each configuration step must fulfill the configuration guidelines, we refined our abstract events by adding one guard for each guideline. For instance, considering the same example above, we have $\{a9 \mapsto OFF\} \mapsto \emptyset \mapsto \emptyset \mapsto \{ops5 \mapsto a7\} \mapsto \emptyset \mapsto (a14 \mapsto OFF) \in ConfigurationG\_ACT$. Thus, we have two conditions consisting of $\{a9 \mapsto OFF\}$ and $\{ops5 \mapsto a7\}$ that if satisfied, *a14* should be mapped to *OFF*. Hence, we added a guard in the event *ConfigureACTON* to ensure that in order to set an activity to *ON* at least one condition is not satisfied in a guideline leading to the configuration of this activity to *OFF*. In this particular case, *a14* can be set to *ON* if *a9* and *op5* have been both configured and *a9* has been set to *ON* or *ops5* has not been configured as a sequence of *a7*. Reciprocally, the configuration *a14* to *ON* is not allowed if at least one of *a9* and *op5* is not configured yet or both have been configured according to the guideline.

7   Verification and Validation

7.1   Verification Using Proof Obligations

In order to demonstrate that the formal specification of configurable process models is correct, a the number of generated proof obligations (POs) should be discharged. Using the Rodin tool [5], our model generated 358 proof obligations; most of them (272 POs $\simeq$ 76 %) were automatically discharged; more complex ones (86 POs $\simeq$ 24 %) required the interaction with the provers to help them find the right rules to apply but also to define additional rules that may lack in the rule base of the prover. These POs ensure that the invariants which model the different constraints on the configurable business processes and the derived variants, are always satisfied (i.e. they hold initially; and each event preserves them). For each event of the form (**WHEN** *G* **THEN** *Act*) with *G* and *Act* representing the guard and the action respectively, the following proof obligation is generated to verify that the execution of the action *Act* under the guard *G* permits to preserve the invariant [4]: $(Inv \wedge G) \Rightarrow [Act]Inv$.

An example of the proofs, we have established, concerns the event *ConfigureACTOFF* correctness with respect to the invariant *inv20*: we have to prove that even if an activity *act* is removed (set to OFF), it remains possible to reach each node from the initial one. This holds since we have added a control from linking the predecessor of *act* to its successor. To discharge this proof that refers to the closure of a relation, we have added the rule defining the closure of the union of two relation s and r:

$$r \in t \leftrightarrow t \wedge s \in t \leftrightarrow t \Rightarrow cls(r \cup s) = cls(r)((id(t) \cup cls(r)); s)+; (id(t) \cup cls(r))$$

7.2 Validation by Animation

Now, based on a correct model, we validate our Event-B specification by animation and model checking using the ProB plugin [18]. Concretely, we play and observe different scenarios and check the behavior of our model by showing at each step the values of each variable, which events are enabled or not.

For instance, we process the animation of the scenario captured by Fig. 3b as follows. After initializing the model using the process in Fig. 1, all invariants should be respected to ensure the correctness of the configurable process model. Next, we process our scenario by triggering enabled events, and at each configuration step, we observe that invariants are always re-established: (1) we trigger the *ConfigureORSplit* event to configure the split operator *ops1* from OR to an AND (*to = AND*) while maintaining the same branches, (2) *ops3* and *opj1* are configured (using *ConfigureToSeq* event) to a sequence starting from a3 (*a3* is set to *ON* as well), (3) the activity *a7* is set the to *ON* (using *ConfigureACTON*) since a3 in included in the previous step (the mapping of a7 to OFF is not allowed in accordance with the guideline defined in Sect. 2), (4) *ops5* and *opj3* are also configured to a sequence starting from *a7* (only this branch could be pre-
served, since the second branch nodes are configurable), next, (5) when configuring the join
operator *opj2*, the only allowed alternative is to
fire the event *ConfigureORJoin* with the connector type parameter AND (see Fig. 5). By
restricting configuration choices, we guaranteed
that the resulted variant have not improper termination caused by the lack of synchronization.

Fig. 5. The connector opj2 configuration restriction using ProB

8 Case Study

In order to evaluate the practical usefulness and identify the opportunities of using our approach, we conducted a case study with a group of business process experts and analysts. We examine its objectives, analyze and discuss its practical experience in conducting business process model configuration in the following.

Objective. The main goal of our work is to evaluate how our approach helps and guides analysts in generating correct and domain-compliant process configuration. Therefore, we define the following research question: How can our approach assist process analyst in applying correct configuration steps?

To answer this question, we formulate three hypotheses: our approach allows *(H1)* to save time and facilitate the identification of the configuration steps; *(H2)* to guarantee a correct process model at each configuration step; and *(H3)* to derive domain-compliant process variants based on the configuration guidelines.

Design, Data Collection and Execution. Our case study is a real configurable supervision process adopted by Orange, a French telecom industrial partner. Different variants of this process are used by Orange affiliates in different cities and countries according to their specific needs. Based on 28 variants, a set of configuration guidelines was generated by an automated approach and validated by a domain expert [8].

With a population of 9 participants that are familiar with process configuration, we targeted experiments to derive a set of different variants using the considered configurable process model. With this purpose, we divided the population into three groups of 3 people each. After a workshop organized to explain the basics needed in this study, the first group (G_1) is asked to manually derive a maximum of process variants without any guidance. Then, the second group (G_2) is also asked to manually derive process variants, but, while providing them with the generated configuration guidelines rules. Whereas, the third group (G_3) is provided with the complete Event-B model (installed under the RODIN tool) and asked to generate process variants with respect to the allowed configuration choices by the model checking. So, participants of latter group can apply only configuration steps that are allowed by our model. As mentioned in the previous sections, this model includes correctness and domain constraints. However, the first two groups take the burden of verifying the correctness of their choices.

The resulted process variants are then collected for comparison. In order to answer the identified research question and confirm its hypotheses, we evaluated the results according to two parameters: (1) the time needed to derive process variants for the different groups, (2) the number of errors for the identified correctness and domain constraints.

Results Analysis and Findings. Regarding the time needed to derive variants, the group G1 took in average 16 min and the group G2 took in average 14 min, whereas the group G3 took only 5 min. Table 3 shows the distribution of the time according to the correctness and the business criteria. Through this table, we notice that the more participants of G1 and G2 take time in deriving variants the less correctness errors are detected. This can explain that participants are making a special effort. Also, it is clear that the first two groups took much more time in deriving correct and domain-compliant variants than the group G3. It is worth noting that all derived variants by G3 contain neither structural nor behavioral correctness errors. No domain errors are detected as well. Moreover, the participants of group G3 affirmed that the ProB model checker is quite straightforward to use and it assisted them in defining appropriate configuration steps. They easily followed the enabled events to make their choices which helped them to be compliant not only to correctness constraints but also to domain recommendations. As a result, it can be concluded that our approach allows (1) to save time and to assist users in defining their configuration choices, which supports the hypothesis *H1*; and (2) to respect correctness and domain constraints, supporting *H2* and *H3*.

Table 3. The average time in minutes unit spent to derive variants either correct (C) or not (¬C), and either business-complaint (B) or not (¬B)

Group	Variant			
	C & B	C & ¬B	¬C & B	¬C & ¬B
G_1	23	17	15	8
G_2	17	×	11	×
G_3	5	×	×	×

Threats to Validity. First, the small number of the collected process variants, used to generate our configuration guidelines, can be considered as a threat of validity. However, in this study we have chosen 28 variants that are relevant and depict various business needs. Secondly, one case study has been only conducted by 9 participants. We believe that a larger group of participants with varied backgrounds need to be used to highlight the validity and reliability of the experiments results. We leave this to future work.

9 Conclusion

In this paper, we propose a formal Event-B based approach to derive correct variants from well-defined configurable processes. To do so, we introduce a step-based configuration approach to guide the analyst by providing at each step the potential configuration choices. We have succeeded to verify structural constraints of configurable process model (e.g. each node reachable from the initial activity, has always the option to complete). We have also reached our goal in preserving the variants soundness (no deadlocks and lack of synchronization situations). Finally, our approach respects domain requirements provided by *configuration guidelines* as well. As future work, we plan to extend the proposed approach by considering the required configurable cloud resource allocation [12] and adding a formal verification phase.

References

1. van der Aalst, W.M.P., Dumas, M., Gottschalk, F., ter Hofstede, A.H.M., La Rosa, M., Mendling, J.: Correctness-preserving configuration of business process models. In: Fiadeiro, J.L., Inverardi, P. (eds.) FASE 2008. LNCS, vol. 4961, pp. 46–61. Springer, Heidelberg (2008)

2. Aalst, W.V.D., et al.: Preserving correctness during business process model configuration. Formal Aspects Comput. **22**(3–4), 459–482 (2008)
3. Aalst, W.V.D., Lohmann, N., Rosa, M.L.: Ensuring correctness during process configuration via partner synthesis. Inf. Syst. **37**(6), 574–592 (2012)
4. Abrial, J.R.: Modeling in Event-B: System and Software Engineering, 1st edn. Cambridge University Press, New York (2010)
5. Abrial, J.R., et al.: Rodin: an open toolset for modelling and reasoning in Event-B. STTT **12**(6), 447–466 (2010)
6. Asadi, M., Mohabbati, B., Grner, G., Gasevic, D.: Development and validation of customized process models. J. Syst. Softw. **96**, 73–92 (2014)
7. Assy, N.: Automated support of the variability in configurable process models (2015)
8. Assy, N., Gaaloul, W.: Extracting configuration guidance models from business process repositories. In: Motahari-Nezhad, H.R., Recker, J., Weidlich, M. (eds.) BPM 2015. LNCS, vol. 9253, pp. 198–206. Springer, Heidelberg (2015)
9. Boubaker, S., Mammar, A., Graiet, M., Gaaloul, W.: An Event-B based approach for ensuring correct configurable business processes. In: The 23rd IEEE International Conference on Web Services, ICWS (2016)
10. Gottschalk, F., van der Aalst, W.M.P., Jansen-Vullers, M.H., La Rosa, M.: Configurable workflow models. Int. J. Coop. Inf. Syst. (IJCIS) **17**(2) (2008)
11. Groner, G., Boskovic, M., Silva Parreiras, F., Gasevic, D.: Modeling and validation of business process families. Inf. Syst. **38**(5), 709–726 (2013)
12. Hachicha, E., Assy, N., Gaaloul, W., Mendling, J.: A configurable resource allocation for multi-tenant process development in the cloud. In: Nurcan, S., Soffer, P., Bajec, M., Eder, J. (eds.) CAiSE 2016. LNCS, vol. 9694, pp. 558–574. Springer, Heidelberg (2016). doi:10.1007/978-3-319-39696-5_34
13. Hallerbach, A., Bauer, T., Reichert, M.: Guaranteeing soundness of configurable process variants in provop. In: IEEE Conference on Commerce and Enterprise Computing, CEC, pp. 98–105 (2009)
14. Hallerbach, A., Bauer, T., Reichert, M.: Capturing variability in business process models: the provop approach. J. Softw. Maintenance Evol. **22**(6–7), 519–546 (2010)
15. Kiepuszewski, B., Hofstede, A.T., Aalst, W.V.D.: Fundamentals of control flow in workflows. Acta Informatica **39**(3), 143–209 (2002)
16. Kumar, A., Yao, W.: Design and management of flexible process variants using templates and rules. Comput. Ind. **63**(2), 112–130 (2012)
17. La Rosa, M., Van Der Aalst, W., Dumas, M., ter Hofstede, A.: Questionnaire-based variability modeling for system configuration. Softw. Syst. Model. **8**(2), 251–274 (2008)
18. Leuschel, M., Butler, M.: ProB: an automated analysis toolset for the B method. Int. J. Softw. Tools Technol. Transf. **10**(2), 185–203 (2008)
19. Rosa, M.L., Aalst, W.V.D., Dumas, M., Milani, F.: Business process variability modeling: a survey (2013)
20. Rosemann, M., Aalst, W.V.D.: A configurable reference modelling language. Inf. Syst. **32**(1), 1–23 (2007)
21. Schunselaar, D.M.M., Verbeek, E., van der Aalst, W.M.P., Raijers, H.A.: Creating sound and reversible configurable process models using CoSeNets. In: Abramowicz, W., Kriksciuniene, D., Sakalauskas, V. (eds.) BIS 2012. LNBIP, vol. 117, pp. 24–35. Springer, Heidelberg (2012)
22. Van Dongen, B., Mendling, J., Aalst, W.V.D.: Structural patterns for soundness of business process models. In: Enterprise Distributed Object Computing Conference, pp. 116–128 (2006)

Social Services

iSim: An Efficient Integrated Similarity Based Collaborative Filtering Approach for Trust Prediction in Service-Oriented Social Networks

Mingding Liao[1], Xiao Liu[1], Xiaofeng Gao[1(✉)], Jiaofei Zhong[2], and Guihai Chen[1]

[1] Shanghai Key Laboratory of Data Science,
Department of Computer Science and Engineering,
Shanghai Jiao Tong University, Shanghai, China
liao.mingding@gmail.com, liuxiao.research@gmail.com,
{gao-xf,gchen}@cs.sjtu.edu.cn
[2] Department of Computer Science, California State University East Bay,
Hayward, USA
jiaofei.zhong@csueastbay.edu

Abstract. Service-oriented social networks gain increasing popularity among a huge user base in recent years. In social networks, trust prediction is significant for recommendations of high-quality service providers as well as in many other applications. In the literature, trust prediction problem can be solved by several strategies, such as matrix factorization, trust propagation, and K-NN search, etc. However, most of the existing works have not considered the possible complementarity among these mainstream strategies to optimize their effectiveness and efficiency. In this paper, we propose a novel trust prediction approach named iSim: an integrated similarity based collaborative filtering approach leveraging on user similarity, which integrates three kinds of factors to measure user similarity, including vector space similarity, matrix factorization, and propagated trust. This paper is the first work in the literature employing matrix factorization and propagated trust in the study of similarity. Additionally, we use several methods like adding inverted index to reduce the time complexity of iSim, and provide its theoretical time bound. Finally, the extensive experiments with real-world dataset show that iSim achieves great improvement for both efficiency and effectiveness over the state-of-the-art approaches.

Keywords: Trust prediction · Latent factor · Propagated trust · K-NN · Similarity · Service-oriented social network

This work has been supported in part by the China 973 project (2014CB340303), National Natural Science Foundation of China (Grant numbers 61133006, 61472252), the Opening Project of Key Lab of Information Network Security of Ministry of Public Security (The Third Research Institute of Ministry of Public Security) Grant number C15602, the Opening Project of Baidu (Grant number 181515P005267), the Open Project Program of Shanghai Key Laboratory of Data Science (Grant number 201609060001).

Q.Z. Sheng et al. (Eds.): ICSOC 2016, LNCS 9936, pp. 501–516, 2016.
DOI: 10.1007/978-3-319-46295-0_31

1   Introduction

The rapid development of online social network makes it an important platform for services, which leads to service-oriented social networks like Epinion.com. Users expect to obtain high-quality service through such platforms, and they usually make their choices according to the credits of service providers. Thus, trustworthiness has been considered as one of the most important factors for recommendations on high-quality service providers.

Some trust information might be gathered explicitly through targeted user survey feedback or implicitly through user behavioral analytics. However, a user can get in touch with only a few other users, so the trust information that can be collected is insufficient, which leads to a challenging problem of trust prediction to infer the unknown trust between any two users.

More specifically, in a service-oriented social network trust model, each user is represented by a node in a graph, while the trust relationship and the amount of trust is indicated by an weighted edge between two users. Since most of the pairwise trust ratings and reliability factors of the users are unknown, if we consider a sparse $n \times n$ trust rating matrix T for users, the objective of trust prediction problem is to predict the unknown values of matrix using some evidence derived from user behaviors or other metrics.

Trust prediction problem can be studied by several strategies, such as trust propagation [2,8,11,15–17], matrix factorization [23,27,28], and K-NN search [5,25], etc. However, the existing methods have many drawbacks: (1) Majority of them ignore the possible complementarity among mainstream strategies, yet it is helpful to solve trust prediction problem. (2) They suffer from low query efficiency in terms of time. Although some approaches speed up by preprocessing, they bear the consequences of high time cost in preprocessing. (3) Their prediction accuracy still have room for improvement.

To resolve the above drawbacks, we propose a novel efficient method named iSim: *an integrated similarity based collaborative filtering approach* for trust prediction with the help of user similarity. iSim integrates three similarity factors, say, vector space similarity, matrix factorization, and propagated trust, among which matrix factorization and propagated trust are first leveraged in the study of similarity. Next, we involve several methods like adding inverted index to reduce the time complexity of iSim, and compute its theoretical time bound precisely. Finally, we compare iSim with two state-of-the-art trust inference approaches: PROP [7] and SCMF [28] by extensive experiments with real-world dataset. Experiments show that iSim improves the predicting accuracy by 11.9 %–30.5 %, and its execution time is only 6.8 % of SCMF and 3.5 % of PROP.

In all, our contribution is summarized as follows: (1) We propose a novel integrating method based on collaborative filtering for trust prediction. (2) We define a hybrid similarity involving matrix factorization and propagated trust, which might be generalized to other related fields. (3) We have conducted extensive experiments on a trace dataset, which demonstrate that our approach achieves much higher accuracy and greatly faster speed than state-of-the-art approaches.

2   Related Works

Existing works for trust prediction in online social networks can be categorized into several classes: propagation based trust prediction, matrix factorization and matrix recovery trust, K-NN based methods, as well as other ad hoc methods.

Propagation Based Trust Prediction. Considering all paths from the source user to the target user, Hang et al. [8] predicted trust by calculating propagated trust through concatenation, aggregation, and selection operations. The multiplication propagating strategy has been exploited in [15,24], which predicts trust between two users based on the product of trust values on all links of a path. Moveover, Li et al. [15] discussed the feasibility of this strategy based on Baysian Inference. On the other hand, the average propagating strategy has been utilized in [17] for trust propagation, which predicts trustworthiness based on a weighted average of trust values on all links of a path between two users. Furthermore, min/max propagating strategy predicts trust between two users based on the minimal or maximal trust values on all links of a path, which is leveraged in [2,22], and [22] improves the efficiency of trust propagation by preprocessing. Instead of considering all possible paths, the trust prediction problem is transformed into the restricted k-optimal path problem [11,16,17], by establishing constraint on propagated trust path. Besides considering propagated trust on paths, path variance and path length are introduced to adjust the propagated trust [7].

Matrix Factorization and Matrix Recovery Trust. Matrix factorization can explain the trust ratings by featuring both trustors and trustees on several latent factors inferred from rating values. A trust prediction model was presented based on rating matrix factorization, which integrates both propagated trust and other related information to improve the result [23]. Another work proposed similarity regularization term to constrain matrix factorization [28]. Zheng et al. utilized matrix factorization in trust prediction in different context [27]. Huang et al. introduced joint factorization with the integration of user-item rating matrix and trust rating matrix [10]. Additionally, Matrix recovery was also exploited to predict unknown value in trust matrix [9].

K-NN Based Methods. According to the similarity of user ratings to films or commodities, the trustworthiness of a user to others can be represented by the weighted average of trust propensity of other K users who are the most similar to this user [5]. Another work integrated the authority similarity, interest similarity, and rating similarity to calculate the K-NN for trust prediction [25]. The main difference between iSim and the existing K-NN approaches is that iSim does not need additional information other than the trust ratings for trust prediction, while the others require much extra information.

Other Approaches. Trust sub-network extraction can improve the accuracy of trust prediction, and it has been studied with binary ant colony algorithm [26]. Trust balance theory can also be employed for trust prediction and adjustment [18]. The network flow from the source to the target can be transformed into the trust between them if we convert trust network to flow network [12]. Orman developed a Bayesian formulation, and a Bayesian Network analysis was employed to compute the unknown trust values [20].

3 Problem Statement

In most cases, trust rating value is defined as the belief one user has in the other. These values can be organized to a square matrix T with size n, which we call an n-user Trust Rating Matrix. We use $T_{i,j}$ to indicate the trust rating value a user i gives to user j. We call the user who gives trust ratings to others as *trustor*, and the user who receives trust ratings as *trustee*. To simplify our calculation, we assume that one user gives trust rating value to at least one other user. We denote our predicted trust rating value matrix as $\widetilde{T}$, whose value is generated by our prediction approach iSim. Definition 1 presents the basic problem statement.

Definition 1 (Trust Prediction Problem). *Given a trust rating matrix T, whose non-zero elements denote the trust rating values from the row users to the column users. Predict the most proper values for zero elements and fill T as $\widetilde{T}$.*

4 iSim: A Novel Trust Prediction Approach

Now we formally introduce our integrated similarity based trust prediction approach iSim, including its motivation, configuration, and detailed description.

Motivation: In a large-scale social network, some users may share, to some degree, similar kind of standards or preference when giving trust rating values. For example, as showed in Fig. 1, suppose there are 4 trusters i_1, i_2, i_3, i_4 and many trustees $j_k (k = 1, ..., n)$ in the network. Truster i_1, i_2 and i_3 have similar behaviors on putting trust ratings on trustee j_k while i_4 does not, that is, i_1, i_2, i_3 share high *behavior similarity* with each other and low with i_4. Different from i_3, i_2 and i_4 is given a trust rating directly by i_1, which suggests that i_1 is closely connected with i_2 and i_4. Comprehensively considering both factors of *behavior similarity* and *propagation*, we can finally speculate that i_1 and i_2 share higher *iSim similarity* when rating others, which will greatly assist the prediction of the unknown values from i_1 to j_2 in T.

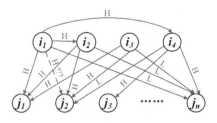

Fig. 1. An example scenario in social network

Work Flow: Figure 2 shows the flow path of iSim, which contains three main parts: iSim-VSS, iSim-LFS and iSim-PT. We first calculate the three parts independently based on the input trust rating matrix T, and then integrate them appropriately to get the similarity values between users. Finally, we generate an output predicted trust rating matrix $\widetilde{T}$ from these similarities based on K-NN collaborating filtering method.

In detail, for iSim-VSS, we use row vectors in T to describe a user's preference and find similarity between these preferences. Because this similarity is extracted directly from T, we call it explicit similarity. For iSim-LFS, we describe users' trust rating styles by the row vectors of specific matrix factorized from T, which reflect a promising similarity. Since this similarity is lurked in T, we call it implicit similarity. For iSim-PT, we depict the trust relationship between users via the weight-sums along the paths linking the two users in the social network generated by T. We then integrate the above three parts and adopt K-NN method to pick up top-K users who share the highest similarities with a particular user i. Finally, we will comprehensively consider the rating values these K users give to user j (if any) to predict the trust value user i will give to user j, which leads to our final predicted trust rating matrix $\widetilde{T}$.

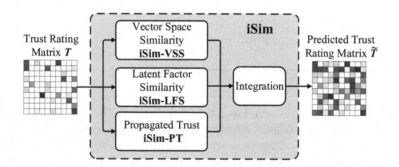

Fig. 2. The framework of iSim

iSim-VSS: The similarity between two users could be described by the rating values they give to their common trustees [16]. This kind of similarity, known as *vector space similarity* (VSS), shows how much the two users are in common on their rating preferences. Correspondingly, $VSS_{i,j}$, which is the VSS between user i and user j, can be defined as Eq. (1).

$$VSS_{i,j} = \frac{\sum\limits_{k \in From_i \cap From_j} T_{i,k} \cdot T_{j,k}}{\sqrt{\sum\limits_{k \in From_i \cap From_j} T_{i,k}^2} \cdot \sqrt{\sum\limits_{k \in From_i \cap From_j} T_{j,k}^2}} \qquad (1)$$

In Eq. (1), $From_i$ is the set of users that i trusts, and k is the user trusted by both i and j. Note that whenever we use terms like $VSS_{i,j}$ to represent the corresponding value related to users i and j, we will use VSS to represent a matrix storing such type of values by default. However, computing Eq. (1) is extremely time consuming, so we introduce inverted index to reduce the time complexity [14]. Algorithm 1 gives out the details. Here To_k is the set of users who give a trust rating value to user k, and we also call it the inverted index of i. Through inverted index, when calculating the similarity between user i and user j, we can avoid enumerating the users to whom user i or j does not give trust rating value, which can bring significant improvement on time efficiency.

Algorithm 1. iSim-VSS

Input: the training trust rating matrix T and the number of users n;
Output: the vector space similarity matrix VSS;
1 Initiate To_i by T, $\forall i \in \{1, 2, \ldots, n\}$;
2 Set $vsim_{i,j}, para1_{i,j}, para2_{i,j} \leftarrow 0, \forall i, j \in \{1, 2, \ldots, n\}$;
3 **foreach** $k \in \{1, 2, \ldots, n\}$ **do**   // optimize by inverted index
4   **foreach** $i, j \in To_k$ **do**   // update similarity related to k
5        $vsim_{i,j} \leftarrow vsim_{i,j} + T_{i,k} \cdot T_{j,k}$;
6        $para1_{i,j} \leftarrow para1_{i,j} + T_{i,k}^2$;
7        $para2_{i,j} \leftarrow para2_{i,j} + T_{j,k}^2$;

8 **foreach** $i, j \in \{1, 2, \ldots, n\}$ **do**
9     $VSS_{i,j} \longleftarrow vsim_{i,j}/(\sqrt{para1_{i,j}} \cdot \sqrt{para2_{i,j}})$;
10 **return** VSS

---

iSim-LFS: Sparsity problem has a fatal influence on the calculation of VSS. As a result, VSS alone cannot satisfy our demand when determining the similarity between two users. Therefore, we propose *latent factor similarity* (LFS) to overcome the sparsity problem, which describes a user's rating style. Actually, when users give trust rating values, they consider several factors. For example if i is familiar with j, it is possible that i puts a higher trust rating value on j. This is called *familiarity factor*. Another example is that some group may have a tendency to give out average higher trust values while other groups may not, which is named as *rating tendency factor*. Such factors are called "latent factors" and we denote ℓ as the number of latent factors. Thus, user i's rating style can be represented as a vector of size ℓ, named as trustor-specific vector $\boldsymbol{u_i}$, and these $\boldsymbol{u_i}$'s could form an $n \times \ell$ trustor-specific matrix U. Similar to iSim-VSS, we define *latent factor similarity* between users as the cosine value of their trust-specific vectors.

We can factorize our trust rating matrix T into trustor-specific matrix U and trustee-specific matrix V [28] according to matrix factorization method. To cooperate with $\boldsymbol{u_i}$, we denote the jth row vector in V as $\boldsymbol{v_j}$, which makes the inner product of $\boldsymbol{u_i}$ and $\boldsymbol{v_j}$ an approximation of trust rating value $T_{i,j}$. In order to get U and V, we need to minimize the sum-of-squared-error objective function with quadratic regularization terms [19]. In this case, we introduce an indicator matrix I to indicate whether there is a value in the corresponding position in T. Additionally, in order to avoid overfitting, two regularization terms from zero-mean spherical Gaussian priors are taken into consideration. Thus, we formulate our factorization function as Eq. (2):

$$\mathcal{L}(T,U,V) = \min_{U,V} \frac{1}{2} \sum_{i=1}^{n} \sum_{j=1}^{n} I_{i,j} \cdot ||T_{i,j} - \boldsymbol{u_i} \cdot \boldsymbol{v'_j}||_F^2 + \frac{\lambda_1}{2}||U||_F^2 + \frac{\lambda_2}{2}||V||_F^2 \quad (2)$$

where $||.||_F$ refers to *Frobenius norm* while λ_1 and λ_2 are coefficients controlling the extent of Gaussian priors. $I_{i,j}$ equals to 1 iff. $T_{i,j}$ exists, otherwise it is 0. We use gradient descent method to minimize the value of $\mathcal{L}(T,U,V)$ [19] by Eqs. (3) and (4). Algorithm 2 demonstrates the details to compute iSim-LFS.

$$\frac{\partial \mathcal{L}}{\partial U} = -\sum_{i=1}^{n} \sum_{j=1}^{n} I_{i,j} \cdot ||T_{i,j} - \boldsymbol{u_i} \cdot \boldsymbol{v'_j}||_F \cdot \boldsymbol{v_j} + \sum_{i=1}^{n} \lambda_1 \boldsymbol{u_i} \quad (3)$$

$$\frac{\partial \mathcal{L}}{\partial V} = -\sum_{i=1}^{n} \sum_{j=1}^{n} I_{i,j} \cdot ||T_{i,j} - \boldsymbol{u_i} \cdot \boldsymbol{v'_j}||_F \cdot \boldsymbol{u_i} + \sum_{j=1}^{n} \lambda_2 \boldsymbol{v_j} \quad (4)$$

Algorithm 2. iSim-LFS

Input: training trust rating matrix T, parameter λ_1, λ_2 and number of users n
Output: the latent factor similarity matrix LFS
1 Initiate U, V ;
2 Set appropriate step size β // β controls the convergence rate
3 **while** *not convergent* **do**   // update U, V by gradient descent method
4     $U \leftarrow U - \beta \cdot \frac{\partial \mathcal{L}}{\partial U}$;
5     $V \leftarrow V - \beta \cdot \frac{\partial \mathcal{L}}{\partial V}$;
6 **foreach** $i, j, \in \{1, 2, \ldots, n\}$ **do**
7     $LFS_{i,j} \leftarrow \frac{\boldsymbol{u_i} \cdot \boldsymbol{u_j}}{||\boldsymbol{u_i}|| \, ||\boldsymbol{u_j}||}$;   // cosine similarity
8 **return** LFS

---

iSim-PT: iSim-VSS and iSim-LFS are inspired by collaborative filtering. To make iSim specifically crafted for trust predicting problem, we consider trust propagation. It has been proved that in a real social network, users tend to trust a stranger if this person is a friend's friend [6], so propagated trust strategy predicts the unknown trust by calculating the propagated trust [2,11,22]. iSim-PT sets the base value of similarity of users based on propagated trust, because there is a correlation between preference similarity and trust [1,4].

Here, we use the min-max strategy [22] to calculate propagated trust matrix PT, which consists of propagated trust between any two users. Assume there are m paths from user i to user j. In one particular path, we pick up the maximal weight of all links in the path as the propagated trust of the path, and among these m paths, we pick up the path with minimal propagated trust, and that will be the value of $PT_{i,j}$.

However, there is a problem that only a few paths exist between two users in the directed graph. Thus, we transform the directed graph into an undirected one. For two users i and j, we set the weight of the undirected edge as the average of two weights of directed edge between them. It can be proved by the Cut Property [3] that $PT_{i,j}$ has the same value in the original undirected graph as that in the minimal spanning tree of the graph. Therefore, we reform Kruskal algorithm [13] in order to find out the matrix PT. Algorithm 3 gives out the detailed description of our method.

Algorithm 3. iSim-PT

Input: the training trust rating matrix T and the number of users n;

Output: the propagated trust matrix PT;

1   $T \longleftarrow (T + T')/2$;   `// get the undirect graph`

2   **Record** $\longleftarrow \{\{1\}, \{2\}, \ldots, \{n\}\}$;   `// initiate the Record by n sets`

3   Initialize the rating set $\{rate_k = (i_k, j_k, T_{i_k,j_k}) \mid T_{i_k,j_k} > 0\}$;

4   **foreach** $rate_k$ *in the ascending order of* T_{i_k,j_k} **do**   `// Kruskal Algorithm`

5   find the sets s_1, s_2 that $i_k \in s_1$ and $j_k \in s_2$, from **Record**;

6   **if** $s_1 \neq s_2$ **then**

7   **foreach** $i \in s_1$ **do**

8   **foreach** $j \in s_2$ **do**

9                  $PT_{i,j} \longleftarrow T_{i_k,j_k}$; `// the edge connecting` s_1 `and` s_2 `has the` `maximal weight in the path from` i `to` j

10   remove s_1, s_2 from **Record**, add $s_1 \cap s_2$ into **Record**

11 **return** PT

Trust Prediction: Comprehensively considering the effects of these factors, $VSS_{i,j}$ and $LFS_{i,j}$ respectively describes the explicit and implicit similarity between two users, while $PT_{i,j}$ pays attention to their trust relationship between them. Combing the three factors together, we define *hybrid similarity* for the first time by Eq. (5). Equation (5) multiplies the linear combination of explicit similarity and implicit similarity by similarity baseline derived from propagated trust. To measure similarity baseline, we explore the relationship among similarity, intimacy and trust. There is a linear relationship between similarity and intimacy among people [1], and the more intimate the relationship is, the harder people can strengthen trust by making the relationship more intimate (marginal effect) [4]. Therefore, trust can be treated as a logarithmic function on similarity, which leads to the similarity baseline in Eq. (5).

$$Sim_{i,j} = (\alpha_1 \cdot VSS_{i,j} + \alpha_2 \cdot LFS_{i,j}) \cdot e^{PT_{i,j}-1} \tag{5}$$

α_1 and α_2 are two coefficients used to balance the explicit similarity and implicit similarity, and $\alpha_1 + \alpha_2 = 1$.

So far, with the aforementioned definitions and concepts, we can predict the trust from the trustor to the trustee based on the set P generated by iSim. Let P_i be the set of K-NN of user i. Equation (6) is our formula of trust prediction.

$$\widetilde{T}_{i,j} = \left(\sum_{k \in P_i} Sim_{i,j} \cdot T_{k,j} \right) / \sum_{k \in P_i} Sim_{i,j} \tag{6}$$

5   Theoretical Analysis of iSim

In this section, we will analyze the time complexity of iSim. Our approach can be divided into two parts: the *pre-training process* and the *predicting process*. In the pre-training process, iSim calculates the similarities and finds the top-K similar users. In the predicting process, iSim predicts the trust rating values based on the similarity.

We first introduce three lemmas. Note that n is the number of users, t is the number of non-zero values in T, m is the number of iteration of matrix factorization, ℓ is the number of latent factors, K is the numbers of the similar users selected, and $\mathcal{A}^{-1}$ is the inverse of Ackermann's function [21].

Lemma 1. *The time complexity to compute matrix VSS is $\mathcal{O}(n^2 + \frac{t^2}{n})$.*

Proof. The time complexity is $\mathcal{O}(t)$ in Step 1, and it is $\mathcal{O}(n^2)$ in Step 2. iSim-VSS runs from Step 4 to Step 4 for k times, where $k = \sum_{i=1}^{n}(|To_i|)$. By the assumption that the data is randomly distributed, the time complexity is $\mathcal{O}(\frac{t^2}{n})$. Lastly, the time complexity from Step 8 to Step 8 is $\mathcal{O}(n^2)$. Thus, the total time complexity is $\mathcal{O}(n^2 + \frac{t^2}{n})$.   □

Lemma 2. *The time complexity to compute matrix LFS is $\mathcal{O}(n^2\ell + m\ell(n+t))$.*

Proof. The time complexity is $\mathcal{O}(n\ell)$ in Step 2, where ℓ is the number of latent factors. The algorithm runs from Step 3 to Step 3 with the complexity of $\mathcal{O}(m\ell(n+t))$, where m is the number of iterations. The complexity from Step 6 to Step 6 is $\mathcal{O}(n^2\ell)$. Thus, the total time complexity is $\mathcal{O}(\ell n^2 + m\ell(n+t))$.   □

Lemma 3. *The complexity to compute matrix PT is $\mathcal{O}(t\log t + t\mathcal{A}^{-1}(n,t) + n^2)$.*

Proof. The complexity is $\mathcal{O}(n^2)$ in Step 1, $\mathcal{O}(n)$ in Step 2, and $\mathcal{O}(t)$ in Step 3. Step 4 enumerates every record in ascending order. It determines the ascending order in $\mathcal{O}(t\log t)$, and enumerates t times. The operators in Step 5 and Step 10 can be executed by Disjoint Sets [21] in $\mathcal{O}(\mathcal{A}^{-1}(n,t))$, where $\mathcal{A}^{-1}$ is the inverse of Ackermann's function. It is hard to determine directly how many times the code in Step 9 would execute, but obviously every $PT_{i,j}$ is only calculated once. Thus, the time complexity from Step 4 to Step 4 is $\mathcal{O}(t\log t + t\mathcal{A}^{-1}(n,t) + n^2)$. Thus, the total time complexity is $\mathcal{O}(t\log t + t\mathcal{A}^{-1}(n,t) + t + n^2)$.   □

Theorem 1. *The time complexity of* $iSim$ *is* $\mathcal{O}(t \log t + t \mathcal{A}^{-1}(n,t) + n^2 \ell + m\ell(n+ t) + n^2 K)$.

Proof. Based on the the Lemmas 1, 2, and 3, the time complexity of pre-training process of $iSim$ is $\mathcal{O}(t \log t + t\mathcal{A}^{-1}(n,t) + \ell n^2 + m\ell(n+t))$. The time complexity to predict the trust between two users is $\mathcal{O}(K)$. Thus, the time complexity of $iSim$ to predict the trust of all pairs of users is $\mathcal{O}(t \log t + t\mathcal{A}^{-1}(n,t) + \ell n^2 + m\ell(n+t) + n^2 K)$.   □

6 Experimental Evaluation

In this section, we present the experimental results of $iSim$, and analyze the effectiveness and efficiency. All the experiments are based on a real-world dataset. All of the experiments are implemented using Matlab R2014b running on an PC with Intel Core i5, 2.6 GHz CPU, 4 GB RAM and Ubuntu 14.04 operating system.

6.1 Experiment Setup

Dataset Description. The dataset used in our experiment is *advotago*[1]. *advotago* is a trust-based social network for open source software development. To allow users to certify others, The social network provides 4 levels of trust ratings between users, which are "Observer", "Apprentice", "Journeyer", and "Master". The "Observer" is the lowest trust level, and the "Master" is the highest trust level. To quantify the dataset for calculation, we convert "Observer", "Apprentice", "Journeyer", and "Master" to 0.1, 0.4, 0.7, and 1.

We use the statistics that contains 7,425 users and 56,550 trust rating records. Each record contains the trust rating values that a user gives to another user. To support repeated experiments, we conduct random sampling for 50 times. In each sampling, 80 % of records are selected as training set, and 20 % are selected as testing set. $iSim$ may fail to predict trust values on rare occasions because of data sparsity of *advotago*. In that case, we use the average trust value of dataset as the default predicting value.

Metric Measures. In our experiments, Mean Absolute Error (MAE) and Root Mean Square Error (RMSE) are used to measure the predicting effectiveness, which are common metrics in the area of trust predicting [23,28]. The formulas of them are

$$MAE = \frac{\sum\limits_{i=1}^{n}\sum\limits_{j=1}^{n} I_{i,j}|T_{i,j}-\widetilde{T}_{i,j}|}{\sum\limits_{i=1}^{n}\sum\limits_{j=1}^{n} I_{i,j}}, \quad RMSE = \sqrt{\frac{\sum\limits_{i=1}^{n}\sum\limits_{j=1}^{n} I_{i,j}(T_{i,j}-\widetilde{T}_{i,j})^2}{\sum\limits_{i=1}^{n}\sum\limits_{j=1}^{n} I_{i,j}}}$$

In the formula, $T_{i,j}$ denotes the known trust rating from user i to user j, $\widetilde{T}_{i,j}$ denotes the predicted trust value from user i to user j. MAE is the average

---

[1] http://www.trustlet.org/datasets/advogato/.

value of each absolute error. RMSE is the variance of each absolute error. Compared with MAE, RMSE is sensitive to the large absolute error. The predicting accuracy is higher if MAE and RMSE is lower.

To measure the efficiency of iSim, we consider the execution time of the program. The unit of execution time is the second.

Competitive Methods. In order to evaluate the effectiveness and efficiency of iSim, we select two approaches (SCMF) [28] and (PROP) [7] for comparison. The SCMF is the most efficient trust predicting algorithm based on matrix factorization, which considers the trust rating value similarity and trust rating distribution similarity between users to constrain the process of matrix factorization and result in high predicting accuracy. The PROP predicts trust rating from user i to user j by finding a path with high propagated trust. The propagated trust consists of both mean and variance of trust of the edges on the path and the length of path.

6.2 Experiments for Parameter Settings

The selection of K in the K-NN query is very important. Figure 3(a) shows the influence of K in iSim. In this figure, we set $\alpha_1 = \alpha_2 = 0.5$, and try to set K from 10 to 50 in ascending order with the step of 5. The result shows MAE and RMSE are almost constant, so the accuracy of our approach is not sensitive to K. Thus, we set $K = 20$.

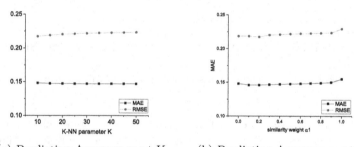

(a) Predicting Accuracy w.r.t K   (b) Predicting Accuracy w.r.t α_1

Fig. 3. Parameter setting experiments for iSim

The α_1 and α_2 determine the weight of two similarities, which influence the predicting accuracy. We try to test the influence of α_1 and α_2 for iSim, and the results are presented in Fig. 3(b). In this figure, $K = 20$, α_1 is set from 0 to 1 with the step of 0.1, and $\alpha_2 = 1 - \alpha_1$, respectively. It shows when α_1 increases from 0.2 to 1 or decreases from 0.2 to 0, the accuracy decreases. Thus, we select $\alpha_1 = 0.2$ and $\alpha_2 = 0.8$. Obviously, in the dataset, since the dataset is sparse, latent factor similarity is more important. However, it is hard to know the weight in the reality, so we also set $\alpha_1 = 0.5$ and $\alpha_2 = 0.5$ in the experiment.

The ℓ, λ_1 and λ_2 are the parameters in the matrix factorization. ℓ is the number of latent factors. A large ℓ can increase the accuracy of predicting but slow down the speed of prediction. λ_1 and λ_2 control the extent of Gaussian priors. We set the same values with SCMF: $\ell = 10$, $\lambda_1 = \lambda_2 = 0.01$. The parameter setting of SCMF and PROP are the same as the corresponding paper.

6.3 Evaluation Analysis

Effectiveness Analysis. We compare the predicting accuracy with SCMF and PROP. The results are shown in Fig. 4. In the figure, α_1 is set as 0.2. We can see that iSim outperforms other two approaches. Compared with PROP, the MAE decreases by 29.6 % and the RMSE decreases by 30.5 %. Compared with SCMF, the MAE decreases by 18.8 % and the RMSE deceases by 11.9 %. These results show that iSim achieves significant improvement, since SCMF is the state-of-art literature with excellent performance.

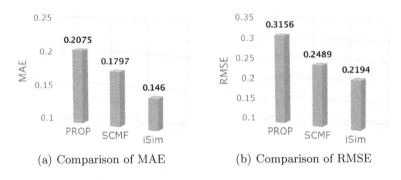

(a) Comparison of MAE   (b) Comparison of RMSE

Fig. 4. Accuracy comparisons of PROP, SCMF and iSim

Specially, we analyze the performance gain from different components. Table 1 shows the results of predicting accuracy of the approaches that adds iSim-VSS, iSim-PT, and iSim-LFS progressively. In the table, "VSS" only uses iSim-VSS, and "VSS+PT" uses iSim-VSS and iSim-PT, (set α_1 as 1). "VSS+PT+LFS" denotes iSim with $\alpha_1 = 0.2$. "norm VSS+PT+LFS" denotes iSim with $\alpha_1 = 0.5$. We compare all of them with SCMF, which is the best competitor.

Now we analyze the results in Table 1. Vector space similarity is a common metric of similarity, so we treat it as a basic form. In the result of the basic form, the accuracy is improved by 10.2 % in terms of MAE and improved by 5.4 % in terms of RMSE, if compared with the best competitor. If utilizing iSim-VSS and iSim-PT, the accuracy is improved by 13.8 % in terms of MAE and improved by 7.8 % in terms of RMSE. If utilizing iSim-VSS, iSim-PT, and iSim-LFS with $\alpha_1 = 0.5$, the accuracy is improved by 18.1 % in terms of MAE and improved by 11.3 % in terms of RMSE. If utilizing iSim-VSS, iSim-PT, and iSim-LFS with

Table 1. Accuracy gain analysis

Approach	MAE	RMSE
SCMF	0.1797	0.2489
VSS	0.1613	0.2355
VSS+PT	0.1549	0.2294
norm VSS+PT+LFS	0.1471	0.2208
VSS+PT+LFS	0.1460	0.2194

$\alpha_1 = 0.2$, the accuracy is improved by 18.8 % in terms of MAE and improved by 11.9 % in terms of RMSE. The results confirm that the three methods of measuring similarity are efficient.

Efficiency Analysis. In fact, some of the trust predicting approaches can be divided into pre-training process and predicting process, e.g., the SCMF. The pre-training process mines the information of datasets which can improve the effectiveness or efficiency of predicting, and then saves it in the small storage space. Thus, we compare the approaches in terms of the two process.

We first give the time complexity of the three approaches. In the pre-training process, the time complexity of iSim is $\mathcal{O}(t \log t + t\mathcal{A}^{-1}(n, t) + \ell n^2 + m\ell(n+t))$, while that of SCMF is $\mathcal{O}(mn^2\ell)$, which is higher than that of iSim. The PROP does not have pre-training process. In the predicting process, the time complexity of iSim to predict the trust of one pair of users is $\mathcal{O}(K)$, and that of SCMF is also p$\mathcal{O}(\ell)$. However, that of PROP is $\mathcal{O}((\frac{t}{n})^p)$, which is much higher. Note that p is the maximum length of paths from the two corresponding users. In all, combining the two process, iSim has the best time bound.

Now we consider the execution time of pre-training process. The PROP does not have pre-training process, so we compared the execution time between SCMF with our approach with different components. Figure 5(a) shows the comparisons of execution time. The labels in the figure are same as the previous subsection. Note that the setting of α_1 and α_2 does not affect the execution time. We can see that the pre-training time of iSim is only approximately 6.7 % of SCMF. If we do not use iSim-LFS, the execution time ratio of "VSS+PT" to SCMF is only approximately 2.8 %. If we do not consider iSim-PT neither, the ratio is only about 1.8 %. The pre-training executing efficiency is far superior to SCMF, because the constrain component of SCMF makes its time complexity much higher than simple matrix factorization.

Then we consider the execution time of predicting process. Note that the predicting execution time is the same regardless of the component of iSim. Figure 5(b) shows the comparison of execution time. in which log scale is used for the Y axis. We can see the predicting time of iSim is approximately same as that of SCMF, but it is merely about 0.012 % of that of PROP.

Moreover, we compare the total execution time of three approaches to predict the trust of the whole testing datasets. Figure 5(c) shows the results. We can

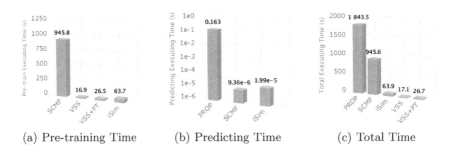

(a) Pre-training Time   (b) Predicting Time   (c) Total Time

Fig. 5. Comparison of execution time

see that the total execution time of iSim is only about 6.8 % of SCMF, and only about 3.5 % of PROP. Specially, if we only use VSS and PT to measure similarity, the total execution time of "VSS+PT" is merely about 2.8 % of SCMF and about 1.4 % of PROP. If we exclusively use iSim-VSS to measure similarity, the total execution time is merely 1.8 % of SCMF and 0.9 % of PROP. Obviously, iSim is superior to other two approaches in terms of execution time.

7   Conclusion

In this paper, we have proposed a trust predicting approach named iSim: *an integrated similarity based collaborative filtering approach* for trust prediction in service-oriented social networks. iSim measures the similarity from three respects: vector space similarity, latent factor similarity and propagated trust. It novelly integrates three strategies and makes use of their complementarity. We provide both theoretical analysis for time bound and numerical experiments with real-world dataset to validate the priority of iSim. Moreover, we innovatively leverage latent factor vector in the study of similarity, which might be an inspiration in other fields.

References

1. Brehm, S.S.: Intimate Relationships. Mcgraw-Hill Book Company, New York (1992)
2. Chen, K., Liu, G., Shen, H., Qi, F.: Sociallink: utilizing social network and transaction links for effective trust management in P2P file sharing systems. In: IEEE International Conference on Peer-to-Peer Computing (P2P), pp. 1–10 (2015)
3. Dasgupta, S., Papadimitriou, C., Vazirani, U.: Algorithms. McGraw-Hill, New York (2006)
4. Dimitrova-Grajzl, V., Grajzl, P., Guse, A.J.: Trust, perceptions of corruption, and demand for regulation: evidence from post-socialist countries. J. Socio-Econ. **41**(3), 292–303 (2012)
5. Ghodousi, E., Hamzeh, A.: A new approach for trust prediction by using collaborative filtering based of pareto dominance in social networks. Ciencia Natura **37**, 95–101 (2015)

6. Guha, R., Kumar, R., Raghavan, P., Tomkins, A.: Propagation of trust and distrust. In: International Conference on World Wide Web (WWW), pp. 403–412 (2004)
7. Hamdi, S., Bouzeghoub, A., Gancarski, A.L., Ben Yahia, S.: Trust inference computation for online social networks. In: IEEE International Conference on Trust, Security and Privacy in Computing and Communications (TrustCom), pp. 210–217 (2013)
8. Hang, C.W., Wang, Y., Singh, M.P.: Operators for propagating trust and theirevaluation in social networks. In: International Conference on Autonomous Agents and Multiagent Systems (AAMAS), vol. 2, pp. 1025–1032 (2009)
9. Huang, J., Nie, F., Huang, H., Lei, Y., Ding, C.H.: Social trust prediction using rank-k matrix recovery. In: International Joint Conference on Artificial Intelligence (IJCAI), pp. 2647–2653 (2013)
10. Huang, J., Nie, F., Huang, H., Tu, Y.C.: Trust prediction via aggregating heterogeneous social networks. In: ACM International Conference on Information and Knowledge Management (CIKM), pp. 1774–1778 (2012)
11. Jiang, W., Wang, G., Wu, J.: Generating trusted graphs for trust evaluation in online social networks. Future Gener. Comput. Syst. (FGCS) **31**, 48–58 (2014)
12. Jiang, W., Wu, J., Li, F., Wang, G., Zheng, H.: Trust evaluation in online social networks using generalized network flow. IEEE Trans. Comput. (TC) **65**, 952–963 (2016)
13. Kruskal, J.B.: On the shortest spanning subtree of a graph and the traveling salesman problem. Proc. Am. Math. Soc. **7**(1), 48–50 (1956)
14. Lee, D., Park, J., Shim, J., Lee, S.: An efficient similarity join algorithm with cosine similarity predicate. In: Bringas, P.G., Hameurlain, A., Quirchmayr, G. (eds.) DEXA 2010, Part II. LNCS, vol. 6262, pp. 422–436. Springer, Heidelberg (2010)
15. Li, L., Wang, Y., Lim, E.-P.: Trust-oriented composite service selection and discovery. In: Barros, A., Grigori, D., Narendra, N.C., Dam, H.K. (eds.) ICSOC 2015. LNCS, vol. 9435, pp. 50–67. Springer, Heidelberg (2009). doi:10.1007/978-3-642-10383-4_4
16. Liu, G., Liu, A., Wang, Y., Li, L.: An efficient multiple trust paths finding algorithm for trustworthy service provider selection in real-time online social network environments. In: IEEE International Conference on Web Services (ICWS), pp. 121–128 (2014)
17. Liu, G., Wang, Y., Orgun, M.A., Lim, E.P.: Finding the optimal social trust path for the selection of trustworthy service providers in complex social networks. IEEE Trans. Serv. Comput. (TSC) **6**(2), 152–167 (2013)
18. Ma, Y., Lu, H., Gan, Z., Ma, X.: Trust discounting and trust fusion in online social networks. In: Chen, L., Jia, Y., Sellis, T., Liu, G. (eds.) APWeb 2014. LNCS, vol. 8709, pp. 619–626. Springer, Heidelberg (2014)
19. Mnih, A., Salakhutdinov, R.R.: Probabilistic matrix factorization. In: Conference on Neural Information Processing Systems (NIPS), pp. 1257–1264 (2008)
20. Orman, L.V.: Bayesian inference in trust networks. ACM Trans. Manag. Inf. Syst. (TMIS) **4**, 48–68 (2013)
21. Tarjan, R.E., Van Leeuwen, J.: Worst-case analysis of set union algorithms. J. ACM (JACM) **31**(2), 245–281 (1984)
22. Xu, Y., Liu, J., Tang, M., Liu, X.: An efficient trust propagation scheme for predicting trustworthiness of service providers in service-oriented social networks. In: IEEE International Conference on Web Services (ICWS), pp. 467–474 (2013)

23. Yao, Y., Tong, H., Yan, X., Xu, F., Lu, J.: MATRI: a multi-aspect and transitive trust inference model. In: International Conference on World Wide Web (WWW), pp. 1467–1476 (2013)
24. Zhang, Y., Chen, H., Wu, Z.: A social network-based trust model for the semantic web. In: Calero, J.M.A., Yang, L.T., Mármol, F.G., García Villalba, L.J., Li, A.X., Wang, Y. (eds.) ATC 2011. LNCS, vol. 6906, pp. 183–192. Springer, Heidelberg (2006). doi:10.1007/11839569_18
25. Zhao, Q., Zuo, W., Tian, Z., Wang, X., Wang, Y.: Predicting trust relationships in social networks based on WKNN. J. Softw. 10(1), 71–81 (2015)
26. Zheng, X., Wang, Y., Orgun, M.A.: BiNet: trust sub-network extraction using binary ant colony algorithm in contextual social networks. In: International Conference on Web Services (ICWS), pp. 321–328 (2015)
27. Zheng, X., Wang, Y., Orgun, M.A., Liu, G., Zhang, H.: Social context-aware trust prediction in social networks. In: Barros, A., Grigori, D., Narendra, N.C., Dam, H.K. (eds.) ICSOC 2015. LNCS, vol. 9435, pp. 527–534. Springer, Heidelberg (2014). doi:10.1007/978-3-662-45391-9_45
28. Zheng, X., Wang, Y., Orgun, M.A., Zhong, Y., Liu, G.: Trust prediction with propagation and similarity regularization. In: AAAI Conference on Artificial Intelligence, pp. 237–243 (2014)

Expertise and Trust –Aware Social Web Service Recommendation

Ahlem Kalaï[1]([⊠]), Corinne Amel Zayani[1], Ikram Amous[1], and Florence Sedès[2]

[1] MIRACL Laboratory, Sfax University, Sfax, Tunisia
ahlem.kalai@gmail.com, {corinne.zayani,ikram.amous}@isecs.rnu.tn
[2] IRIT Laboratory, Paul Sabatier University, Toulouse, France
florence.sedes@irit.fr

Abstract. With the increasing number of Web services, the personalized recommendation of Web services has become more and more important. Fortunately, the social network popularity nowadays brings a good alternative for social recommendation to avoid the data sparsity problem that is not treated very well in the collaborative filtering approach. Since the social network provides a big data about the users, the trust concept has become necessary to filter this abundance and to foster the successful interactions between the users. In this paper, we firstly propose a trusted friend detection mechanism in a social network. The dynamic of the users' interactions over time and the similarity of their interests have been considered. Secondly, we propose a Web service social recommendation mechanism which considers the expertise of the trusted friends according to their past invocation histories and the active user's query. The experiments of each mechanism produced satisfactory results.

Keywords: Service recommendation · Expertise trust · Temporal factor · Social activities · Interest similarity

1 Introduction

The growing number of Web services makes it difficult for the user to discover the appropriate Web services by using the specialized search engines (e.g. Xmethods.net, WebServiceX.net, ProgrammableWeb.com) or public registries (e.g. UDDI, ebXml). The reason is that the latter ones suffer from low accuracy results [14] mainly because of their centralized structure and do not take into account the users' profiles (e.g. interests, preferences, behaviors). A successful approach to tackle information overload [22] is the Recommender System (RS) [20] which can help the users to provide a list of selected items (i.e. services, products) that they are likely to enjoy. Collaborative Filtering (CF) is one of the most successful approaches which utilizes the feedback of many users to find similar users and items that serve as a basis for the recommendations. However, this approach has some problems, such as the data sparsity and the cold start [23]. In the past few years, the advent of social media enables the user

© Springer International Publishing Switzerland 2016
Q.Z. Sheng et al. (Eds.): ICSOC 2016, LNCS 9936, pp. 517–533, 2016.
DOI: 10.1007/978-3-319-46295-0_32

to easily communicate and make relationships with other users. Frequently, the user spends more time to use his Egocentric (or personnel) Social Network (ESN) to find items which are liked by his friends in the past. Consequently, the CF approach has become unqualified to make more effective recommendation [23] because it always considers that the users one independent. In fact, the Social Recommendation (SR) approach appeared to provide the users with more personalized recommendation [23]. It takes into account the online users who are connected via various types of social relations (e.g. friendship, co-worker, family, business). Moreover, the SR takes advantage of research results from Social Network Analysis (SNA) in order to capture and analyze the social information.

At the first level, in our real life, the users would like to turn to his closest friends to solicit recommendations [13]. However, in SN, some noisy and malicious information, can be provided. This type of information may sneak into the inputs of RS [5]. For this reason, trust [8] is required to filter the big data about the users and to foster their successful interactions. In fact, how to detect trust relation between the users is another challenge. In general, trust is a complex relationship based on a wide range of factors [21] and may be affected by the users' interactions, their interests, etc. However, most of the trust– aware Web service recommendation studies neglect these users' social data and are based only on the measures which are related to the network structure, such as centrality degree [2], similarity of network structure [11] or users' proximity [12,15]. Other research studies [18,19] focused on users' interactions to compute the social trust but all of them have neglected the impact of the time. Contrariwise, [3,17] are considered the temporal factor. At the second level, the majority of SR approach use only the rating of similar or trusted users in the prediction step of service to be recommend but they neglect the user's expertise. Thus, in our real life, some users prefer the advice not only of their trusted friends but also of their expertise [12,27]. Some few works [15,27] have proposed to quantify the user's expertise, for example in terms of how many times the user has used the required Web service. For this reason, we envisage that the exploitation of the SN to capture the social trust from the collective users and their expertise are promising solutions to enhance Web service discovery process.

In this paper, we present an enhancement of our previous research on Web service decentralized discovery [11]. Our approach exploits the knowledge of users' social networks to provide higher quality recommendations than current CF approach. We propose, in the first step, a social trust detection mechanism between the users who are involved in ESN. The level of social trust is computed by aggregating two influential factors such as the degree of interaction over time between a couple of users and the similarity degree of their interests. In the second step, we propose to take into account the computed trust level to personalize the Web service recommendation of an active user according to the expertise of his trusted friends.

The rest of this paper is organized as follows. Section 2 presents briefly a background of the trust notion in social computing. Section 3 presents the enhanced architecture of our previous Web service decentralized discovery process.

Sections 4 and 5 detail respectively the social trust detection mechanism and the expertise– based web service social recommendation. Section 6 illustrates an example to explain better our idea. Section 7 exposes some experiments and discusses the obtained results for each proposed mechanism. Section 8 states some studies which related to Web service social recommendation. Finally, we conclude by outlining our future works.

2   Background

With the growing popularity of social media, Social Recommender System (SRS) [23] has attracted increasing attention. SRS is defined as any RS that recommends items with online social relations as an additional input. In addition, the main contributions of SRS are, firstly, significantly solve the problem of data sparsity [23] and, secondly, improve the recommendation quality since the connected users provide different types of information from similar users [10]. The success of social media, especially the SN, is largely due to their open and decentralized nature. However, these characteristics open an horizon for a wide range of perspectives and intentions. Indeed, trust is required to filter the big data about the users and to foster their successful interactions. In fact, how to detect trust [8] relation between the users is a another challenge. In literature, there is no universal definition of trust [21]. However, the majority of research studies agree that trust is a *subjective* notion which depends on the users' interactions and reflects their competences, etc. The value of trust was measured in several ways depending on some properties [21,28]. *Global* trust is defined as *a value representing the reputation of a user*. *Local* trust is defined as *a value assigned by a person to another according to his own knowledge of the latter*. *Direct* trust is the result of exclusive direct interactions between two persons. *Indirect* trust is the fact that the person can complete his knowledge about other persons only by the advice of his trusted friends. Trust is *asymmetric* [29] which means that is not necessarily identical in both directions. Trust is *dynamic* [29] in the way that it may decrease and increase, become less important or relevant, and decay with the time. A user trusting another is gradually built up and keeps changing over time. This change may be influenced by very important factors. In what follows, we enumerate some impact factors that we consider very important to deduct the trust level between a couple of users.

- *Social interactions.* The SN enables the users to communicate via various social activities (e.g. send message, share photo). These activities are considered a key indicator of the type and the quality of relation between two users. Some studies [19] used this factor to detect the trust relation in a SN.
- *Temporal factor.* Any interaction between two users occurs at a given time, in a given situation and in a particular place [21]. Thus, trust depends on the time. [3,17] is one of the few studies that considered the temporal dimension. [3] affirmed that the old feedback may not always be relevant in order to estimate global trust. Furthermore, in [17], old friends are considered more

trustworthy than new friends. From our point of view, this assumption is not necessarily correct because the social relations between friends change over time, and some friends who used to be very close may no longer be.

– *Users' similarity.* There is a strong correlation between trust and similarity [30]. The users prefer the suggestions that come from others with similar tastes and affinities. Likewise, they prefer in priority the recommendations that come from their closest friends [13]. That's why, the majority of the RS are mainly based on the similarity between users according to their rating to different items (e.g. movie, music, service). However, the recommendation quality is weak due to the data sparsity problem because the users' rating matrix is still sparse.

To synthesize, the richness of SN, such as the user's generated content and interaction [9], from our point of view, can be exploited to compute the level of trust between the users. Furthermore, the users' social networks are represented by their social profiles which describe their characteristics, interests, social activities, etc. Hence, the social information can be used as input to recommendation mechanism. In the next section, we will present our decentralized discovery approach.

3   Decentralized Web Service Discovery Process

Our current work is an evolution of our previous approach of decentralized web service discovery based on the user' social profile [11]. In this approach, we have inspired the idea of SOAF model [25] to integrate the users and their satisfactory Web services into the same structure network. We have proposed a SC-WSD system (for Social Context based Web Service Discovery) to analyze and filter the ESN for a given user. we have proposed a social relationship filtering step which is based on the network structure similarity in terms of mutual friends to keep only the user's closest friends. This step did not rely on the social trust on the one hand. On the other hand, we have not use the recommendation mechanism that is based on the friend's expertise. Hence, in this paper, we suggest extending our decentralized discovery approach by introducing the concept of social trust and the user's expertise. We think that if a user knows that the discovered services which are interacting by his trustworthy and expert friends, she will be more confident. As shown in Fig. 1, our novel version of our SC-WSD system is composed of three mechanisms.

1. **Social Trust Detection Mechanism (STDM).** This step consists, at the first level, in analyzing the user's social profile in order to extract the useful information. At the second level, computing the social trust level between a couple of users and keeping this level in Trust matrix $(U \times U)$. We choose to represent the personal and structural data by the semantics profiles with SOAF ontology [25]. Next, we represent the user's interactions with his friends by a vector which contains the type of each interaction (e.g. send a message, post a comment, share a photo), the date of interaction and the involved friends.

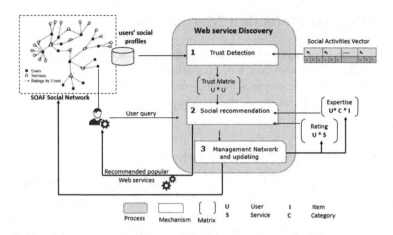

Fig. 1. A novel architecture of our SC-WSD [11]

2. **Social Recommendation Mechanism (SRM).** At first, we take into account the past invocation history of each trusted friends that is filtered by the user's query (i.e. is formulated by the items/keywords which are related to a specific domain/category). Secondarily, we compute the level of expertise for each friend by domain or extract it from the Expertise matrix $(U \times I \times C)$. Thereafter, we predict the score of each recommended Web service according to the Rating matrix $(U \times S)$. We aim to return for each active user a ranked list of the best Web services by descending order.

3. **Management Network and Updating Mechanism (MN and UM).** After each interaction between the user and the selected Web service (i.e. invoke and assign a score), SC-WSD system starts to implicitly update the SOAF user's social profile by the only successful Web services. This mechanism aims also at managing Web services (i.e. service advertisement and removal) in the global SN since this latter is characterized by its dynamic aspect. Thereafter, three possibles cases are presented in this mechanism. In the first case, if a web service and its properties (e.g. name, endpoint) have already existed in the user's profile, then we don't add it. Contrarily, we suggest adding this service and updating its assigned score in the Rating matrix $(U \times S)$. In the second case, if a service is removed from the SN by his provider, then it must be removed from the user's profile and his corresponding rating from matrix. In the last case, if a service is published and has never been used before by other friends, we suggest notifying them about this service by sending an E-mail.

In the two next sections, we will detail the STDM and SRM.

4   Social Trust Detection Mechanism

The STDM takes as input the social profile of an active user and his vector of social activities/interactions with his friends. This mechanism performs in two steps. The first step consists in analyzing the user's ESN. The second step consists in applying some measures to compute the social trust level between the users.

4.1   Egocentric Social Network Analysis

This step consists in analyzing the user's SN in order to extract useful information. In literature, two approaches of the SNA are distinguished [4]. The *socio-centric* approach (or complete network) focuses on all the actors and the links. The *ego-centric* approach (or personal network) focuses on the network surrounding one actor (ego) and his links. In this paper, we focus on an egocentric analysis to detect and calculate the social trust from the individual side. In our global SN, each user is described by his SOAF profile [11]. This profile contains various types of data about the user, like his permanent data (e.g. name, age, country), his dynamic data (e.g. interests, preferences, social activities, past invocation history with Web services). In order to detect and evaluate the social trust, we suggest two influential factors of trust. The first factor concerns the *time-aware interactions*. In fact, the SN sites enable the users to communicate via various social activities. These interactions can provide information of the relationship strength between a pair of users and can reflect how much they are close. The second factor concerns the *interest similarity*. Trusting someone does not necessarily mean sharing the same preferences or interests with him. Therefore, the similarity between users (in terms of interests, preferences, etc.) proves necessary.

4.2   Level of Trust Computing

In this step, we detect only trustworthy friends who have a direct connection with an ego user. On the one hand, we consider that (i) trust is asymmetric and non-transitive; (ii) a user can not trust strangers who do not have direct links with him; and (iii) trust is dynamic as it changes over time and may decay with time. On the other hand, We adopt a local metric of trust computing which varies from one user to another. Therefore, we compute the social trust level by aggregating the values of two factors (i.e. users' interests and their interactions). Compared to [18,19], our level of trust takes into account the temporal factor in order to compute the level of interaction between the users.

Time-Aware Interaction Degree. Based on the analysis step, we represent by a vector all the types of social interactions and we specify for each type of activity (e.g. comment, message) the date of interaction and the involved friends who have direct connection with the ego. Thereafter, we compute the degree of interaction between the users by taking into account the influence of the time factor. Firstly, we suggest calculating the number of interactions (NI_f) between the *ego* and his friend u_j in the period of time Δ_t (i.e. for each year) according to Eq. (1). Secondly, we calculate the total number of interactions (NI_{all}) of the ego, with all his friends in the same period Δ_t according to Eq. 2. Finally, the time-aware interaction degree measure $DoI(ego, u_j)$ is calculated according to Eq. 3.

$$NI_f(ego, u_j, \Delta_t) = \sum_{a_{ego,u_j}(\Delta_t) \in VA} k \tag{1}$$

$$NI_{all}(ego, \Delta_t) = \sum_{u_l \in F(ego)} NI_f(ego, u_l, \Delta_t) \tag{2}$$

$$DoI(ego, u_j)_{\Delta_t} = \frac{NI_f(ego, u_j, \Delta_t)}{NI_{all}(ego, \Delta_t)} \tag{3}$$

where Δ_t is the period between the date of the first interaction and the current date between ego and u_j.

Interests Similarity Degree. In the ESN, each user is usually characterized by his semantic social profile (i.e. RDF/FOAF ontology). By analyzing the SN, we compute the degree of similarity $DoS_{interest}$ between two users according, particularly, to their interests in order to find the closest friends of the ego-user. We adopted a Jaccard similarity coefficient as a measure of interest similarity which is based on the comparison of the common interests of *ego* and u_j. Therefore, we count the number of common interests and the total number of interests in both users. For each pair of nodes (ego, u_j), the degree of similarity $DoS_{interest}(ego, u_j)$ can thus be calculated as shown in Eq. 4.

$$DoS_{interest}(ego, u_j) = \frac{\|interests_{ego} \cap interests_{u_j}\|}{\|interests_{ego} \cup interests_{u_j}\|} \tag{4}$$

With $DoS_{interest}(ego, u_j)$ is in interval of [0,1]. If $DoS_{interest}(ego, u_j) = 1$, it indicates that the user u_j is similar to his friend ego while $DoS_{interest}(ego, u_j) = 0$ indicates that the user u_j completely different to his friend ego.

Level of Trust Metric. Based on the analysis of egocentric network, we propose that the trust degree between a user (ego) and his directed friends is a quantified value which is correlated with two main factors: time-aware interaction degree $DoI(ego, u_j)_{\Delta_t}$ and interest similarity $DoS_{interest}$. We proposed that the Level of social Trust $LoT(ego, u_j)$ denotes the trust value that user *ego* assigns implicitly to friend u_j. This level is in interval of [0, 1] and which is calculated by Eq. 5.

$$LoT(ego, u_j) = \alpha \times DoI(ego, u_j)_{\Delta_t} + \beta \times DoS_{interest}(ego, u_j) \tag{5}$$

where $DoI(ego, u_j)_{\Delta_t}$ is the interaction degree over time, and $DoS_{interest}$ (ego, u_j) is the interest similarity degree, with α and β are in the interval of [0, 1] and $\beta = 1 - \alpha$. If $LoT(ego, u_j) = 0$, it indicates that the user ego completely distrusts his friend u_j while $LoT(ego, u_j) = 1$ indicates that the user ego completely trusts his friend u_j.

Once the level of social trust applied to all the friends of the active user (ego), the obtained values of trust will be stored in a Trust matrix (U × U). In addition, the trust between two friends is dynamic because it depends on the change of their interaction frequency in time. In the recommendation purpose, the list of trusted friends differs from a user to another. In our STDM, we choose a dynamic trust threshold γ that adapts to each user instead of using the one static threshold that will be used for all the users in order to select their trusted friends like in [11]. In this case, the trust dynamicity is not detected. However, in our current research work, the best trusted friends of the user ego will be recommended where the level of social trust $LoT(ego, u_j) \geq \gamma$, and the dynamic trust threshold γ is calculated according to Eq. 6.

$$\gamma = \frac{\sum_{distinct(t_j) \in T_i} t_j}{j} \tag{6}$$

with T_i is the list of trust levels of u_i to all his friends and $distinct(t_j)$ is the list of distinct values in T_i.

In the next section, we will detail the steps of our Web service social recommendation mechanism which is based on the expertise concept.

5   Expertise– Based Social Recommendation Mechanism

Our social recommendation mechanism (SRM) enables to the user, on the basis of his query, to recommend a ranked list of the best services based on the trusted network which was generated in the previous step. We will present, in this section, the steps of our recommendation mechanism which is the enhancement of our previous discovery process [11]. This mechanism is performed in six steps as follows.

1. **Trustworthy friends extraction.** We consider the trustworthy friend who are all the users connected to the user ego via a particular type of relation, such as the trust. This relation is detected by the previous mechanism (STDM). The list of extracted friends constitutes the main input of our SRM.
2. **Level of expertise computing.** We consider that the friends who have frequently used the Web services in a specific domain are able to provide a recommendation with better quality. For this objective, we proposed a measure to compute the level of expertise LoE for each trusted friend U_i, who is extracted in the previous step, in a particular domain dom_j of the user's query. This level is calculated after each user's interaction with a recommended Web service in the past according to the next Eq. 7. The obtained

values recorded in the Expertise matrix $(U \times C \times I)$.

$$LoE(u_i, dom_j) = \frac{Nb_{invok}(u_i, dom_j)}{\sum_{dom_k \in C} Nb_{invok}(u_i, dom_k)} \qquad (7)$$

where $Nb_{invok}(u_i, dom_j)$ is the number of service invocation in the domain dom_j of the current user's query, and $\sum_{dom_k \in C} Nb_{invok}(u_i, dom_k)$ is the sum of the service invocation number in the list of domains C in our system.

3. **Past experience extraction.** We extract for each expert and trustworthy friend form his SOAF profile the information related to his Web services (e.g. name, description, operation, endpoint) which was invoked or published in the past. This extraction is performed by using the SPARQL[1] query. The result of this step is a list of Web services without redundancy.

4. **Web service filtering based on user query.** An active user formulates his needs in terms of Web services by selecting the domain (dom) of his query (e.g. travel, medical, food, education) and expressing a set of keywords (I). In this step, SRM filters according to the user's query the list of Web services which are extracted from the previous step. The purpose is to select only those that correspond the user's query.

5. **Rating prediction.** SRM predicts the score for each selected Web service in the previous step according to Eq. 8. This prediction is based, on the one hand, on the expertise of trusted friends who have invoked these Web services, and, on the other hand, on their attributed ratings to them which is recorded in the Rating matrix $(U \times S)$. Finally, the SRM selects only the best Web services that have a predicted scores above a threshold.

$$Rating_{pred}(ws_i, dom_k) = \frac{\sum_{u_j \in R} LoE(u_j, dom_k) \times Rating(u_j, ws_i)}{\sum_{u_j \in R} LoE(u_j, dom_k)} \qquad (8)$$

where $LoE(u_j, dom_k)$ is expertise level of the user u_j which is calculated in Eq. 7, and $Rating(u_j, ws_i)$ is the service's score attributed by the user u_j to the service ws_i.

6. **Web service ranking.** in this last step, SRM ranks the list of Web services will be recommended by descending order. This ranking is based on the predicted rating of each Web service which is calculated according to the Eq. 8.

In the next section, we will present an example that clarify more our motivation.

6   Illustrative Example

To better illustrate our service discovery proposition, let us consider a case study on a medical scenario. Suppose that *Bob*, a service requester, connected in his Facebook social network and he wants to look for a Web services related to

---

[1] http://www.w3.org/TR/rdf-sparql-query/.

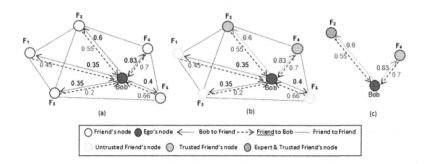

Fig. 2. (a)–Oriented and Weighted Sub-Graph from egocentric Social Network, (b)–Trusted Sub-Graph and (c)–Expertise and Trusted Sub-Graph

his query Q. Q is defined by a domain $dom = medical$ and a list of Keywords $nameDoctor, meetingpoint$. By exploring his ESN, *Bob* has five friends which are represented in the weighted sub-graph of his network as shown in Fig. 2–(a). The weights indicate the LoT which is deduced by our STDM (See Eq. 5) and recorded in the Trust matrix (See Fig. 1). Based on our STDM, the dynamic trust threshold $\gamma = (0.35 + 0.65 + 0.83 + 0.4)/4 = 0.545$ (See Eq. 6). Indeed, SRM filters in the first step the social relationships of Bob according to the LoT measure and the dynamic threshold γ. It selects only the friends F_2 and F_4 as trusted friends of *Bob* (See Fig. 2–(b)).

In the second step, SRM select only from the list trusted friends only who is an expert in the same domain of the Bob's query according to the Eq. 7 in order to provide a better recommendation quality. According to the Expertise matrix, suppose that the expertise in the different domains of $F_2 = \{$**medical = 0.6**, food = 0.37$\}$ and $F_4 = \{$medical = 0.45, **travel = 0.7**, food = 0.56$\}$. Based on these values, F_2 tends to use the Web services related to the medical domain (e.g. *FindDoctorService*, *ClinicInformationService*, *MeetingService*, etc.) and the food domain (e.g. *FindRestaurantService*, *getReceipeService*, etc.). Moreover, F_4 frequently used the services related to the medical domain (e.g. *FindDoctorService*, *ClinicInformationService*, *FindCommunityService*, etc.), the travel domain (e.g. *WSCountryHotel*, *WSCityHotel*, etc.) and the food domain (e.g. *FindRestaurantService*, *BookPizzaService*, etc.). Hence, F_2 is more expert in medical domain than F_4. Consequently, SRM selects F_2 as the most trusted and expert friend of *Bob*. In the next step, SRM extracts from the SOAF profile of F_2 the information (e.g. name, operation, endpoint) of his medical Web services and selects only those correspond to the Bob's query Q. SRM predicts the score for each selected Web services (*FindDoctorService* and *MeetingService*) according to the expertise of F_2 and their assigned ratings which is extracted from the Rating matrix (e.g. Rating(*FindDoctorService*) = 0.5 and Rating(*MeetingService* = 0.7). Finally, SRM recommends those services with predicted rating (See Eq. 8) in descending order. In the next section, we will detail the experiments and the obtained results for each mechanism.

7   Experimentation and Discussion

Our Web service decentralized discovery process is performed in two mecha-nisms:(i) the Social Trust Detection Mechanism (STDM) and (ii) the Expertise–based Social Recommendation Mechanism (SRM). In the fist section, we evalu-ate the first mechanism by evaluating the Level of Trust (LoT) measure that we proposed. In the second section, we focus on the second mechanism by evaluating the recommendation quality in terms of rating prediction.

7.1   First evaluation: STDM

Through the evaluation step, we propose to validate the following points: the importance of considering the time factor in the trust measure and the use of dynamic trust threshold rather than the static threshold. Furthermore, we choose the Facebook, a real-world social network, as an example just in order to evaluate our proposed trust metric. In addition, we have the opportunity to collect the social profile for each user. The Facebook social network contains 1326 nodes of users. We selected a sample of 20 users from this data where each user is represented by his RDF profiles. At the first level, we invited each user to connect into our SC-WSD system to select and save his Real trusted friends. At the second level, we conducted a comparison by using three popular metrics, such as the recall, the precision and the F-measure. The recall corresponds to the number of trustworthy friends who are returned by the system compared to the total number of real trustworthy friends who are identified by each user as shown in Eq. 9.

$$Recall = \frac{nb_{returendtrustedfriends}}{nb_{Realtrustedfriends}} \tag{9}$$

The precision is the number of real trustworthy friends who are returned by the system compared to the total number of returned friends as shown in Eq. 10.

$$Precision = \frac{nb_{returnedRealtrustedfriends}}{nb_{returnedfriends}} \tag{10}$$

The F-measure is a combination of the two previous metrics as shown in Eq. 11.

$$F - measure = \frac{2 \times Recall \times Precision}{Recall + Precision} \tag{11}$$

Impact of parameters α and β. Our proposed level of social trust (LoT) is based on the time-aware interaction degree (DoI) and the interest similarity degree (DoS) between the users (See Eq. 5). In Fig. 3 (a), we found that the best value of F-measure is the one with parameters: $\alpha = 0, 8$ and $\beta = 0, 2$. In addition, it seems that if parameter α is closer to 0 and parameter β is closer to 1, the level of social trust decrease over time. Consequently, the temporal factor of the users' interactions has an important influence on social trust.

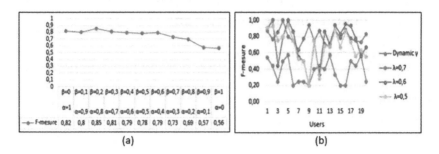

Fig. 3. (a)–Obtained results of F-measure with variation of α and β parameters, and (b)–Obtained results of F-measure with variation of static threshold ($\lambda = 0, 5, 0, 6$ and 0,7) compared to the dynamic threshold γ

Effect of Dynamic Trust Threshold γ. We suggest that the accuracy of the returned results depends highly on the chosen threshold. In our STDM, we used three static thresholds ($\lambda = 0, 5, 0, 6$ and 0,7) and the proposed dynamic threshold γ to filter the user's friends. In Fig. 3 (b), we observe that every time we increase λ (=0.6 or 0.7), the chance of selection of trusted friends (i.e. number of friends) is reduced. Otherwise, if we decrease λ (=0.5), some friends will be chosen and recommended to the ego user. According to these results, we observe that, for the majority of the users, the selection of trusted friends by γ is much better than by λ. In addition, we note that static threshold has better results for some users and less for others. Thus, we proved with this assessment the interest of using a dynamic threshold in order to select the trusted friends from a large number of users in the social network.

Comparison with other Trust metrics. We compared the obtained results of our level of social trust metric with two other metrics. The first, which is called Temporal Trust [17], is proposed to rank the user' friends according to the age of their relationship by considering the newest friends as the most trustworthy. The second measure, which is called Closest Friends [19], is based on social interactions between friends without considering the time factor. In general, the results obtained in terms of precision and recall show better results by taking into account the temporal factor on the users' interactions and the interest similarity. In Fig. 4 (c), we found that the precision of the obtained results by the Closest Friend metric is very low (precision average $= 25,85\%$) than our LoT metric ($=76,94\%$) and Temporal Trust metric ($=62,72\%$). This justifies our hypothesis that the non-consideration of the time factor may recommend to the user ego the friends who are considered trusted in the past and they are no longer. In addition, our metric gives better precision values than those obtained by the Temporal Trust with a difference of $14,22\%$ of the average precision. This first justifies that our measure detects and recommends for each user the real trusted friends who are identified by each user, and second, the time aware of the social interaction degree has a very strong impact than the age of relation (newest or oldest) which is taken into account in Temporal Trust metric. In Fig. 4 (d), we

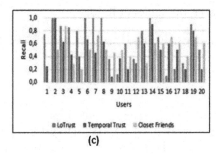 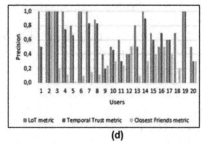

(c)   (d)

Fig. 4. Comparison of obtained results of our LoT metric with two metrics: temporal trust and closest friends in terms of recall (c) and precision (d)

found that the recall average of the obtained results by our metric is much better (=66,17 %) than the Closest Friend (=50.71 %) and Temporal Trust (=48.58 %). This justifies that our metric detects and recommends the trusted friends from the real trusted friends who are identified by each user. In the next section, we will evaluate the accuracy of our recommendation mechanism of web services.

7.2   Second Evaluation: Expertise–Based SRM

In this section, we aim to validate the recommendation accuracy by evaluating the metric of rating prediction according to the user's expertise (See Eq. 8). The majority of research works like [5] which interested to Web service recommendation have used the Epinions[2] dataset from which they have considered each item corresponds a Web service. In general, the Epinions dataset includes (i) a trust matrix which contains the trust values that are explicitly provided by the users, (ii) a rating matrix which is attributed to different products and (iii) a category matrix which contains the category of each item. In our context, we can not use this dataset to evaluate our STDM since it has no personal or social information provided for each user. However, we choose the trust values which are provided by Epinions and apply our SRM. We have used the popular metric to measure the error rate such as RMSE (Root Mean Squared Error). It calculates the difference between the predicted rate and the real rate as indicated by the following formula 12.

$$RMSE = \sqrt{\frac{\sum_{(u,s)|R_{u,s}}(r_{u,s} - \widehat{r}_{u,s})}{\mid (u,s)|R_{u,s}\mid}} \qquad (12)$$

with $R_{u,i}$ is a Boolean variable equal to 1 if the user u evaluates the item i,
$r_{u,i}$ the real rate which is attributed by the user u to an item i and
$\widehat{r}_{u,i}$ the predicted rate

---

[2] http://epinions.com.

Table 1. Comparison between the values of RMSE

RS	TidalTrust	MoleTrust	TrustWalker	SC-WSD
RMSE	1.216	1.430	1.192	**1.09**

Rating prediction based on the user's expertise Versus without expertise. We compared the prediction measure taht we used in our SC-WSD system with other RS like TidalTrust [8], MoleTrust [16] and TrustWalker [10]. The obtained results (See Table 1) showed that the gap between the real rate and the predicted rate in our proposed system is lower than in others. This result is explained by the importance of the consideration of the expertise which improves the recommendation quality.

8   Related Work

Web service recommendation approach has become a research directive for enhancing Web service discovery and help the users out of the service overload [22]. With the advent of social media, some SR approach [7,15,24], which are based on users' SNs, emerged to reduce the problems of FC approach such as the cold-start and data sparsity [22]. Moreover, with a prevalence of users' social networks, a great number of data were generated. Thus, the social trust [9] has been studied in different levels such as between (i) the web services (or applications) [7], (ii) the providers (e.g. Web sites, organizations, governments) [2,12], (iii) service consumers (e.g. organizations or individuals) [5,6,24], or (iv) recently between the Social Internet of Things [1]. [2] proposed a RS of composed Web services. This recommendation is based partly on the trust of service providers; and secondly, on the non-functional characteristics (e.g. response time, cost) of services. Trust between providers is global and implicit and measured on the basis of their position in the SN. To classify Web services, Bansal et al. suggested representing each Web service by its QoS which is calculated with the trust value of the service provider. [12] proposed a RS of Web services based on trust of the provider in a SN. The trust value is considered as local and transitive. It is implicitly calculated based on two measures, such as, the sociability of provider (i.e. position, social proximity and similarity). The second measure is the expertise of an agent (i.e. reliability, usability and quality score). The authors did not offer a specific formula to predict the service's rating, but, they proposed to classify these services according to the trust level of their providers. [5] proposed a RelevantTrustWalker RS in which the trust measure is local and non-transitive. This measure combines two values, the first value is an explicit trust provided by the user to another, the second value is the similarity between the users which is calculated by applying the cosine measure on the rating vectors which are assigned by two users. The rating prediction for web service is realized randomly by browsing the network in search for a trustworthy user who evaluated a service.

To summarize, the majority of the previous mentioned studies have used only the rating in the prediction step. Thus, in our real life, some users prefer the advice not only of their trusted friends but also of their expertise. In literature, some expertise -based recommendation [26] proposed to recommend a list of experts which combines the SNA and semantic concept to improve the effectiveness of personalized recommendation in the document retrieval context. In service computing, some RS have introduced the idea of expertise to make their service recommendation more accurate. For example, [27] proposed to quantify the user's expertise in terms of how many times the user has used the required web service. [15] computed the user's expertise in in particular area in the purpose of composition. [12] compute the trust in the expertise of providers in terms of QoS (e.g. usability, reliability). In fact, our work is different of other works in two levels. The first contribution is related to the temporal based- computing social trust that we have given an importance of the temporal factor to calculate the trust between users. The second contribution is related to the expertise based- SR from which the majority of research studies dont exploited the context of the user query and the expertise of trusted friends in the recommendation purpose.

9 Conclusion and Future Work

In this paper, we considered the social trust relation in the objective of Web service recommendation in order to enhance Web service discovery. We have proposed a new measure to compute the trust level between two users by taking into account semantic social information which are extracted from the egocentric network for a given user. Our proposed social trust is a local score which is computed from values of two measures: Time-aware interaction degree and Social interest similarity degree. According to the social trust level computation, the outcome of trust detection mechanism is a weighted directed graph of the user's egocentric network. With this relation, we were able to select trusted user's friends. The empirical results show that our proposed metric produces satisfactory results. In fact, the consideration of time has a positive influence on the detection of trusted friends. In addition, the use of a dynamic threshold to discriminate between the users' friends produces more results than the what of a static threshold. At the second level, we have integrate a social recommendation mechanism in our previous works. This mechanism exploits not only the social trust metric but also the expertise level of the trusted users' friends in the domain of the user's query. Our idea is to recommend to a given user a ranked web services which were used in the past by his experts and trusted friends. In our future work, we will be interested in reducing the cold start problem.

References

1. Abdelghani, W., Zayani, C.A., Amous, I., Sèdes, F.: Trust management in social internet of things: a survey. In: The 15th IFIP Conference on e-Business, e-Services and e-Society (I3E) (2016, To appear)

2. Bansal, S.K., Bansal, A.: Reputation-based web service selection for composition. In: World Congress on Services, SERVICES 2011, Washington, DC, USA, 4–9 July 2011, pp. 95–96 (2011)

3. Jsang, A., Ismail, R.: The beta reputation system. In: Proceedings of the 15th Bled Electronic Commerce Conference (2002)

4. D'Andrea, A., Ferri, F., Grifoni, P.: An overview of methods for virtual social networks analysis. In: Abraham, A., Hassanien, A.E., Sná, V. (eds.) Computational Social Network Analysis: Trends, Tools and Research Advances, pp. 3–25. Springer, London (2010)

5. Deng, S., Huang, L., Xu, G.: Social network-based service recommendation with trust enhancement. Expert Syst. Appl. **41**(18), 8075–8084 (2014)

6. Deng, S., Huang, L., Yinand, Y., Tang, W.: Trust-based service recommendation in social network. Appl. Math. Inf. Sci. **9**(3), 1567–1574 (2015)

7. Fallatah, H., Bentahar, J., Asl, E.K.: Social network-based framework for web services discovery. In: 2014 International Conference on Future Internet of Things and Cloud, FiCloud 2014, Barcelona, Spain, 27–29 August 2014, pp. 159–166 (2014)

8. Golbeck, J.: Trust on the world wide web: a survey. Found. Trends Web Sci. **1**(2), 131–197 (2006)

9. Golbeck, J. (ed.): Computing with Social Trust. Human-Computer Interaction Series. Springer, Berlin (2009)

10. Jamali, M., Ester, M.: Trustwalker: a random walk model for combining trust-based and item-based recommendation. In: Proceedings of the 15th ACM SIGKDD International Conference on Knowledge Discovery and Data Mining, Paris, France, 28 June–1 July 2009, pp. 397–406 (2009)

11. Kalai, A., Zayani, C.A., Amous, I.: User's social profile -based web services discovery. In: 8th IEEE International Conference on Service-Oriented Computing and Applications, SOCA, Rome, Italy, 19–21 October 2015, pp. 2–9 (2015)

12. Louati, A., Haddad, J.E., Pinson, S.: A distributed decision making and propagation approach for trust-based service discovery in social networks. In: Group Decision and Negotiation. A Process-Oriented View - Joint INFORMS-GDN and EWG-DSS International Conference, GDN 2014, Toulouse, France, 10–13 June 2014, pp. 262–269 (2014)

13. Ma, H., Zhou, D., Liu, C., Lyu, M.R., King, I.: Recommender systems with social regularization. In: Proceedings of the Fourth ACM International Conference on Web Search and Data Mining, WSDM'11, pp. 287–296 (2011)

14. Maamar, Z., Wives, L.K., Badr, Y., Elnaffar, S., Boukadi, K., Faci, N.: Linkedws: a novel web services discovery model based on the metaphor of "social networks". Simul. Model. Pract. Theory **19**(1), 121–132 (2011)

15. Maaradji, A., Hacid, H., Skraba, R., Lateef, A., Daigremont, J., Crespi, N.: Social-based web services discovery and composition for step-by-step mashup completion. In: IEEE International Conference on Web Services, ICWS 2011, Washington, DC, USA, 4–9 July 2011, pp. 700–701 (2011)

16. Massa, P., Avesani, P.: Trust-aware recommender systems. In: Proceedings of the 2007 ACM Conference on Recommender Systems, RecSys 2007, Minneapolis, MN, USA, 19–20 October 2007, pp. 17–24 (2007)

17. Moghaddam, M.G., Elahian, A.: A novel temporal trust-based recommender system. In: 2014 22nd Iranian Conference on Electrical Engineering (ICEE), pp. 1142–1146, May 2014

18. Nepal, S., Sherchan, W., Paris, C.: Strust: a trust model for social networks. In: IEEE 10th International Conference on Trust, Security and Privacy in Computing and Communications, TrustCom 2011, Changsha, China, 16–18 November 2011, pp. 841–846 (2011)
19. Podobnik, V., Striga, D., Jandras, A., Lovrek, I.: How to calculate trust between social network users? In: 20th International Conference on Software, Telecommunications and Computer Networks, SoftCOM 2012, Split, Croatia, 11–13 September 2012, pp. 1–6 (2012)
20. Resnick, P., Varian, H.R.: Recommender systems - introduction to the special section. Commun. ACM **40**(3), 56–58 (1997)
21. Sherchan, W., Nepal, S., Paris, C.: A survey of trust in social networks. ACM Comput. Surv. **45**(4), 47 (2013)
22. Su, X., Khoshgoftaar, T.M.: A survey of collaborative filtering techniques. Adv. Artif. Intell. **2009**, 421425:1–421425:19 (2009)
23. Tang, J., Hu, X., Liu, H.: Social recommendation: a review. Soc. Netw. Anal. Min. **3**(4), 1113–1133 (2013)
24. Tang, M., Xu, Y., Liu, J., Zheng, Z., Liu, X.F.: Trust-aware service recommendation via exploiting social networks. In: 2013 IEEE International Conference on Services Computing, Santa Clara, CA, USA, 28 June–3 July 2013, pp. 376–383 (2013)
25. Treiber, M., Truong, H.L., Dustdar, S.: SOAF - design and implementation of a service-enriched social network. In: 9th International Conference on Web Engineering, ICWE 2009, San Sebastián, pp. 379–393 (2009)
26. Xu, Y., Guo, X., Hao, J., Ma, J., Lau, R.Y.K., Xu, W.: Combining social network and semantic concept analysis for personalized academic researcher recommendation. Decis. Support Syst. **54**(1), 564–573 (2012)
27. Yuan, Z., Shuai, Z., Yan, W., Yanhong, C., Wenyu, Z., Xin, C.: A social network-based expertise-enhanced collaborative filtering method for e-government service recommendation. Adv. Inf. Sci. Serv. Sci. **5**(10), 724–735 (2013)
28. Zeng, J., Gao, M., Wen, J., Hirokawa, S.: A hybrid trust degree model in social network for recommender system. In: 2014 IIAI 3rd International Conference on Advanced Applied Informatics (IIAIAAI), pp. 37–41, August 2014
29. Zhou, X., Xu, Y., Li, Y., Jøsang, A., Cox, C.: The state-of-the-art in personalized recommender systems for social networking. Artif. Intell. Rev. **37**(2), 119–132 (2012)
30. Ziegler, C., Golbeck, J.: Investigating interactions of trust and interest similarity. Decis. Support Syst. **43**(2), 460–475 (2007)

Business Process Modeling (Short Papers)

A Novel Heuristic Method for Improving the Fitness of Mined Business Process Models

Yaguang Sun$^{(\boxtimes)}$ and Bernhard Bauer

Software Methodologies for Distributed Systems, University of Augsburg,
Augsburg, Germany
{yaguang.sun,bernhard.bauer}@informatik.uni-augsburg.de

Abstract. Business process model discovery (BPMD) is one of the most important research topics in the business process mining area. Many outstanding BPMD algorithms which perform well in most cases have been developed in the last years. As one of the most widely used BPMD algorithms, the Heuristics Miner meets great challenges while dealing with event logs that contain complex behaviours. As a result, process models with low fitness values might be obtained. In this paper, we propose a new technique that is able to locate the process behaviours recorded in an event log which cannot be expressed by the Heuristics Miner and then transform them into expressible behaviours so that a high-fitness model can be built.

Keywords: Business process mining · Business process model discovery · Model fitness improvement · Heuristics Miner

1 Introduction

The present BPMD techniques meet great challenges while mining models from real-life event logs. Such logs often contain complex trace behaviours which might be far beyond the expression ability of existing BPMD approaches [9]. Figure 1 shows an example event log L_1 and the model generated by carrying out the Heuristics Miner (HM) [3] on this log. The mined model for L_1 has a relatively low fitness (0.7752) due to the existence of inexpressible process behaviours for HM in L_1. Several pioneering approaches [6–9] have been put forward in academia for solving the problem mentioned above. These proposed methods are able to help mine high-fitness models expressed by Petri net [1]. However, few efforts have been made to help the HM (that expresses process model by Heuristics net) get better mining results. According to [10], the HM is one of the most important and widely utilised BPMD tools in the ProM framework [1] for dealing with real-life event logs. Developing an auxiliary method to help it mine high-fitness process models is far from trivial.

In this paper, we put forward a novel heuristic method named HIF which transforms the fitness improvement problem for the non-fitting models mined by HM into the problem of locating the inexpressible process behaviours of HM in

© Springer International Publishing Switzerland 2016
Q.Z. Sheng et al. (Eds.): ICSOC 2016, LNCS 9936, pp. 537–546, 2016.
DOI: 10.1007/978-3-319-46295-0_33

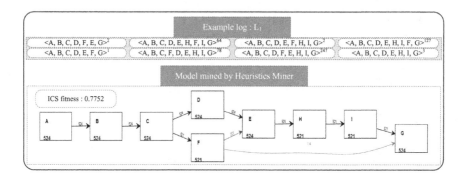

Fig. 1. The process model mined by executing Heuristics Miner on an example log L_1.

event logs and converting these found behaviours into expressible behaviours. As shown in Fig. 2, an element B_k in the process behaviour space (PBS) represents a kind of process behaviour extracted from a specific event log L. Afterwards, it is assessed whether B_k can be expressed by HM. If B_k cannot be expressed then all the process behaviours that pertain to B_k in L will be converted into expressible behaviours. Given an event log, how to build the PBS relevant to this log and how to locate the inexpressible behaviours in the PBS and then transform them into expressible behaviours for HM are the main problems that this paper is going to solve.

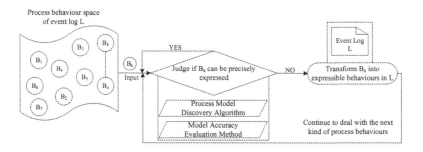

Fig. 2. The process for dealing with the inexpressible process behaviours in event logs.

2   Approach Design

In this section, some important basic notations and concepts are introduced in Subsect. 2.1. The details of the proposed method are elaborated in Subsects. 2.2, 2.3, 2.4 and 2.5.

2.1   Notation

Let L^+ be the set of event logs, $\Omega : L^+ \to M^+$ be a BPMD algorithm, where M^+ is the set of process models. $\Phi : (M^+, L^+) \to V^+$ represents a process model fitness evaluation mechanism which gets a process model together with its relevant event log as input and creates an assessed value from V^+ (the set of all possible values output by Φ) as output.

Definition 1 (Direct Activity Relation). Let SA_L be the set of activities from an event log L. Symbol $\succ_L$ represents a direct relation between two activities from SA_L. For two activities a and b from SA_L, $a \succ_L b = true$ if $|a \succ_L b| > 0$, where $|a \succ_L b|$ is the number of times that a is directly followed by b in L.

2.2   Build Process Behaviour Space (PBS)

How to effectively extract and organise process behaviours is the first challenge encountered by our approach. In this subsection, we present a method for collecting and structuring the process behaviours from event logs based on two concepts: *behaviour-related activity* and *behaviour-related sub-trace*.

Definition 2 (Behaviour-Related Activity). Let SA_L be the set of activities for event log L. Symbol $\Rightarrow_L$ represents a behaviour-based relation between any two activities from SA_L. For two activities $a, b \in SA_L$, $a \Rightarrow_L b = true$ if $a \succ_L b = true$ or $b \succ_L a = true$ and b is also called a behaviour-related activity (BRA) of a.

Definition 3 (Behaviour-Related Sub-trace). Let SA_L be the set of activities for event log L. Let t be a trace from L, $st \sqsubseteq t$ be a sub-trace of t and SA_{st} be the set of activities for st. Given an activity $a \in SA_{st}$, st is a behaviour-related sub-trace (BRST) of a if $\forall b \in SA_{st} \wedge b \neq a$ such that $a \Rightarrow_L b$ and $a \in SA_{st}$. And st is a maximal behaviour-related sub-trace (MRST) of a if $\nexists st'$ such that st' is a BRST of a and $st \sqsubset st'$.

Let's take event log L_1 depicted in Fig. 1 as an example. According to Definition 2, activity F has six BRAs which are activity D, E, H, I, G and C. Seven kinds of MRSTs for activity F can be discovered from L_1 (as shown in Fig. 3) according to Definition 3. It can be seen that every MRST of F contains activity F and all the other activities in the MRST are BRAs of F.

In our technique, the process behaviours recorded in an event log are divided into several groups where each group is relevant to a single activity from this log and the process behaviours for a group are stored in the MRSTs of its related activity. For instance, the PBS for log L_1 consists of nine sets of MRSTs where each set of MRSTs is relevant to a specific activity from L_1 (as shown in Fig. 3). Our technique is devised to detect each set of MRSTs stored in PBS iteratively for finding and converting inexpressible process behaviours for HM.

2.3   Activity Ranking

In this subsection, an activity ranking method is put forward in which the MRSTs related to the higher-ranked activities will be handled before the MRSTs

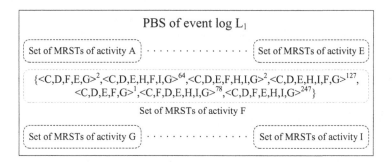

Fig. 3. The PBS built for the example event log L_1.

relevant to the lower-ranked activities. The proposed activity ranking method is based on two concepts: *behaviour-related activity weight* (BAW) and *activity ranking weight* (ARW). Given an activity a from event log L, the BAW of a is defined as:

$$BAW_a = |\bullet \succ_L a| + |a \succ_L \bullet|. \tag{1}$$

In Eq. 1, $|\bullet \succ_L a|$ represents the total number of activities from L that are directly followed by a at least once and $|a \succ_L \bullet|$ represents the total number of activities which directly follow a in L at least once.

Axiom 1.
The larger the BAW of an activity from an event log L is, the more possible this activity will be the main factor that leads to the inexpressible process behaviours in log L.

According to Axiom 1, the BAW is employed by our technique to quantify the complexity induced by an activity on its related process behaviours (i.e. the MRSTs of this activity) recorded in the relevant event log. However, Axiom 1 might not be applicable in all situations, e.g. an activity that only joins a concurrent behaviour may also have a large BAW but it will not cause any inexpressible process behaviour as long as the utilised BPMD algorithm can model concurrency. These additional situations are also considered in our approach proposed in the next subsection.

Let a be an activity from event log L, the ARW (activity ranking weight) of a is defined as:

$$ARW_a = \frac{BAW_a}{BAW_{max}} \times \frac{|a|}{OF_{max}}. \tag{2}$$

where BAW_{max} stands for the BAW of a particular activity from L which has the largest BAW, $|a|$ stands for the occurrence frequency of activity a in log L and OF_{max} represents the occurrence frequency of an activity from L which has the largest frequency of occurrence. According to Eq. 2, the ARW of an activity consists of two parts. The fist part is based on the BAW of this activity while the second part considers the influence level of activity on the fitness of the final mined model. In our method, the larger the ARW of an activity is, the higher ranking the activity will have.

2.4   Detection and Conversion of Inexpressible Process Behaviours

In this subsection, we first formalise a new concept called *environment item*. Then, a new method named DCIB is proposed.

Definition 4 (Environment Item). Let SA_L be the set of activities from event log L, activity a, b and c are three activities from SA_L, the tuple (b, c) is an environment item (EI) of activity a if $\exists t \in L$ such that $< b, < a \ldots >, c > \sqsubseteq t$, where t stands for a trace from L and $< a \ldots >$ represents a sub-trace that only consists of activity a (one or more).

According to Definition 4, the activity F in the example log L_1 has six EIs which are EI (D,E), (H,I), (E,H), (I,G), (E,G) and (C,D).

Axiom 2.
Converting an activity into a new activity under appropriate environment item will help reduce the complex process behaviours aroused by this activity.

Figure 4 shows an event log L_2 generated by converting activity F under environment (D,E) into a new activity F1 and converting F under environment (H,I) into a new activity F0 in log L_1. As illustrated in Fig. 4, the process model mined from the newly created log L_2 has a much higher fitness than the model mined from L_1. The main reason for such an improvement on fitness is that the conversion of activity F under environment (D,E) and (H,I) transforms the inexpressible (complex) process behaviours (related to F) for HM into expressible (simple) process behaviours.

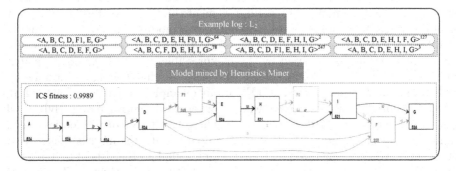

Fig. 4. The process model mined from newly generated log L_2.

The method DCIB (that will be) proposed in this subsection is able to assist in detecting the suitable EIs for a specific activity under which transforming the

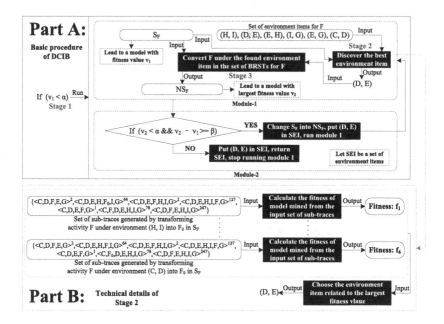

Fig. 5. The basic procedure for technique DCIB.

activity into new activities can help simplify the complex process behaviours led by this activity. The storage structure of process behaviours in PBS provides a basis for DCIB to fulfil such a function. Specifically speaking, for each time DCIB discovers the qualified EIs for a certain activity by detecting its MRSTs stored in the relevant PBS[1]. Let's take the activity F from log L_1 as an example to explain the primary procedure for DCIB. Let S_F stand for the set of MRSTs for activity F (the details of S_F are exhibited in Fig. 3), v_1 represent the fitness value of the process model mined from S_F, SEI be a set of EIs, α be a target fitness and β be a minimum fitness improvement threshold. As illustrated in part A of Fig. 5, DCIB contains three stages and two modules. In stage 1, it judges whether v_1 is less than the target fitness α. If it is not, DCIB stops because the negative influences aroused by the inexpressible process behaviours related to activity F is acceptable. In stage 2 and stage 3 (that belong to Module–1), DCIB searches for the best EI ((D,E) in our example) of activity F among all its EIs (mentioned above) under which converting F into a new activity will generate a new set of MRSTs NS_F for F where the fitness of the model mined from NS_F has the largest value (i.e. v_2) compared with the models mined from other set of MRSTs generated by transforming F under other EIs of F. Then the found EI (D,E) is removed from the original set of EIs for activity F. The part B of Fig. 5 shows the details for realising the stage 2 of DCIB. In Module–2, DCIB

---

[1] Detecting the qualified EIs in the MRSTs of an activity instead of in the whole process behaviours recorded in the event log will greatly reduce the detection time (i.e. the algorithm efficiency is improved).

judges if $v_2 < \alpha$ and $v_2 - v_1 \geq \beta$. If it is, put the found EI (D,E) in SEI, replace S_F by using NS_F and continue running Module–1. If $v_2 \geq \alpha$, DCIB stops because the EIs found so far are enough to help decrease the negative influence led by the complex process behaviours aroused by F to a certain extent (indicated by α). DCIB will also stop running if $v_2 - v_1 < \beta$. Because adding new activities will help improve the accuracy of the potential model but may also increase the complexity of the model at the same time. It is not worth to add new activities if the model fitness cannot be improved to a certain extent.

2.5   A Heuristic Method for Improving the Fitness of Mined Business Process Models (HIF)

In this subsection, we propose a heuristic method named HIF based on the discussions in the former subsections for improving the fitness of process models mined through HM. The details about HIF are shown in Algorithm 1.

Algorithm 1.   HIF

Input: an event log L, the set of activities SA_L of log L, a target fitness α, a model fitness improvement threshold β, a threshold μ for the number of newly added activities.

    Let x be a variable of type Integer.
    Let PBS_L be a set of sets of behaviour-related sub-traces.
    Let SEI be a set of environment items.
    Let LRA be a list of ranked activities.
    Let $CPBS$ be the PBS building method introduced in Subsection 2.2.
    Let AR be the activity ranking method introduced in Subsection 2.3.
1: $SEI \leftarrow null$, $x \leftarrow |SA_L|$ # x records the total number of activities in log L
2: $PBS_L \leftarrow CPBS(L, SA_L)$ # create the process behaviour space for event log L
3: $LRA \leftarrow AR(SA_L)$ # rank activities from SA_L
4: **repeat**
5:     get the activity a that has the highest ranking out of LRA
6:     $SEI \leftarrow DCIB(a, PBS_L, \alpha, \beta)$ # detect qualified environment items for activity a
7:     **repeat**
8:        get an environment item ei out of SEI
9:        convert activity a under ei into a new activity in log L
10:      put the newly generated activity for a in SA_L
11:    **until** $((|SA_L| - x) == (\mu \times x) \,||\, \Phi(\Omega(L), L) \geq \alpha \,||\, |SEI| == 0)$
12: **until** $((|SA_L| - x) == (\mu \times x) \,||\, \Phi(\Omega(L), L) \geq \alpha)$
Output: a business process model with higher accuracy $M = \Omega(L)$.

Firstly, the number of activities in the given log L is stored in variable x (step 1). Then, algorithm HIF creates the PBS for log L (step 2) and also a ranking list LRA for the activities in L (step 3) according to the method proposed in Subsect. 2.3. Next, HIF chooses an activity a which has the highest ranking in LRA and removes a from LRA (step 5). The inexpressible process behaviours aroused by a will be first handled which means that HIF always give priority to the main contradiction. Then, HIF searches for the qualified EIs for activity a through technique DCIB (introduced in Subsect. 2.4) and the found EIs are put in set SEI (step 6). Afterwards, for each environment item $ei \in SEI$, HIF changes the activity a into a new activity under environment ei in log L (this action will help improve the fitness of the model mined from L as demonstrated in the last subsection), removes ei from SEI and put the newly generated activity in the set of activities SA_L for log L (steps $7-11$). In HIF, a threshold μ is used to limit the number of the newly added activities because adding too many new activities might increase the complexity of the final model. If the number of the newly added activities is larger than $\mu \times x$ then HIF stops (step 11 and 12). The activity ranking procedure described in step 3 makes sure that the accuracy of the mined model could be improved as much as possible under the limitation given by μ. Furthermore, if the fitness of the model mined from L is larger than or equal to the given target fitness α then HIF also stops (step 11 and 12). Finally, a process model M with higher fitness value is output by HIF.

3   Evaluation

In our experiment, the ICS fitness [4] is used for evaluating the accuracy of mined models. The Extended Cardoso Metric (E-Cardoso) [5] and Place/Transition Connection Degree (PT-CD) [2] are employed for evaluating the impact of our method on the complexity of the mined models. We tested the effectiveness of HIF on four real-life event logs: the repair log (Repair) from [1], the log of the loan and overdraft approvals process (LOA) from Business Process Intelligence Challenge (BPIC) 2012, the log of Volvo IT incident and problem management (VIPM) from BPIC 2013 and log of CRM process (MCRM) from [2].

Table 1. Evaluation results for the proposed model fitness improvement method HIF.

Model	ICS-fitness	Precision	E-Cardoso	PT-CD	Event types	Time (s)
$M-Repair$	0.6768	0.426	31	2.3656	12	
$M-Repair_N$	**0.9989**	**0.7252**	**49**	**2.3611**	**16**	**6.39**
$M-LOA$	0.7878	0.6717	148	3.1478	36	
$M-LOA_N$	**0.9826**	**0.6511**	**178**	**2.9149**	**47**	**399.71**
$M-MCRM$	−0.1379	0.7454	64	2.4545	22	
$M-MCRM_N$	**0.8802**	**0.7641**	**79**	**2.3621**	**29**	**25.953**
$M-VIPM$	0.3594	0.86	54	2.8848	13	
$M-VIPM_N$	**0.8539**	**0.6**	**68**	**2.979**	**17**	**274.51**

In the experiment for HIF on the four logs, the target fitness α is set to 1, the model fitness improvement threshold β is set to 0.03 and the threshold for the number of newly added activities μ is set to 0.3. Table 1 shows the evaluation results. In Table 1, *M–Repair* represents the model generated by directly mining the original event log Repair and $M{-}Repair_N$ stands for the model output by HIF (the same applies to the other models). It can be seen that the technique HIF can improve the fitness of the mined models to a large extent, while for most of the models output by HIF their precision and complexity are kept within an acceptable range compared with their original models. The model $M{-}Repair_N$ only has four more activities than the model $M{-}Repair$ but the fitness for $M{-}Repair_N$ has been greatly improved (the same to the model $M{-}VIPM_N$). This benefits from the activity ranking method presented in Subsect. 2.3.

4   Conclusion

In this paper we proposed the technique HIF for helping improve the fitness of the models mined from event logs. The proposed technique is able to detect the inexpressible process behaviours recorded in event logs for HM and transform the found behaviours into expressible behaviours. As a result, more fitting process models can be generated. Through the evaluation results from Sect. 3 we demonstrated the effectiveness of HIF. Our future work will mainly be focused on adapting our method HIF to other BPMD techniques so as to help them mine better process models. In the meantime, we will also validate HIF on some other real-life cases.

References

1. van der Aalst, W.M.P.: Process Mining: Discovery, Conformance and Enhancement of Business Processes. Springer, Berlin (2011)
2. Weerdt, J.D., vanden Broucke, S., Vanthienen, J., Baesens, B.: Active trace clustering for improved process discovery. IEEE Trans. Knowl. Data Eng. **25**(12), 2708–2720 (2013)
3. Weijters, A., van der Aalst, W.M.P., Alves de Medeiros, A.K.: Process mining with the heuristics algorithm. In: BETA Working Paper Series 166, TU Eindhoven (2006)
4. de Medeiros, A.A.: Genetic process mining. Ph.D. thesis, Eindhoven University of Technology (2006)
5. Lassen, K.B., van der Aalst, W.M.P.: Complexity metrics for workflow nets. Inf. Softw. Technol. **51**, 610–626 (2009)
6. Bergenthum, R., Desel, J., Lorenz, R., Mauser, S.: Process mining based on regions of languages. In: Motahari-Nezhad, H.R., Recker, J., Weidlich, M. (eds.) BPM 2015. LNCS, vol. 4714, pp. 375–383. Springer, Heidelberg (2007). doi:10.1007/978-3-540-75183-0_27
7. van der Werf, J.M.E.M., van Dongen, B.F., Hurkens, C.A.J., Serebrenik, A.: Process discovery using integer linear programming. In: van Hee, K.M., Valk, R. (eds.) PETRI NETS 2008. LNCS, vol. 5062, pp. 368–387. Springer, Heidelberg (2008)

8. Leemans, S.J.J., Fahland, D., van der Aalst, W.M.P.: Discovering block-structured process models from event logs - a constructive approach. In: Colom, J.-M., Desel, J. (eds.) PETRI NETS 2013. LNCS, vol. 7927, pp. 311–329. Springer, Heidelberg (2013)

9. Fahland, D., Aalst, W.M.P.: Repairing process models to reflect reality. In: Motahari-Nezhad, H.R., Recker, J., Weidlich, M. (eds.) BPM 2015. LNCS, vol. 7481, pp. 229–245. Springer, Heidelberg (2012). doi:10.1007/978-3-642-32885-5_19

10. Claes, J., Poels, G.: Process mining and the ProM framework: an exploratory survey. In: Reichert, M., Reijers, H.A. (eds.) BPM 2015. LNBIP, vol. 132, pp. 187–198. Springer, Heidelberg (2013). doi:10.1007/978-3-642-36285-9_19

REST-Enabled Decision Making in Business Process Choreographies

Adriatik Nikaj$^{(\boxtimes)}$, Kimon Batoulis, and Mathias Weske

Hasso Plattner Institute at the University of Potsdam, Potsdam, Germany
{adriatik.nikaj,kimon.batoulis,mathias.weske}@hpi.de

Abstract. In the field of business process management, the interaction between business actors or services are modeled via business process choreographies. However, enforcing or implementing business process choreographies is a challenge particularly related to the choreography's exclusive gateways, which are used to model shared decisions among business actors. Since there is no central locus of control, participants may interpret the data relevant for decision making differently. To tackle this problem, this paper offers a solution by delegating the decision making to a decision service. This service is based on the recently published Decision Model and Notation standard and is provided to the choreography participants via a REST interface. The RESTful decision service assures a correct implementation of choreographies' exclusive gateways and provides a blueprint for RESTful services that offer decision-making solutions based on the DMN standard.

Keywords: Process choreographies · DMN · RESTful interactions

1 Introduction and Motivation

Business process choreography [1] is an intrinsic part of business process management (BPM) [2]. It is a modeling language for specifying interactions between business actors from a global perspective. It borrows, for a good part, a set of modeling components from business processes. While reusing modeling elements from business processes for choreographies is a good design approach, it does not come without drawbacks. Such a modeling element is the exclusive gateway.

Exclusive gateways are a key modeling construct in business processes. They are used to model alternative paths in the control flow based on the value of some data, e.g., if payment is completed send the shipment, otherwise send a reminder. They are also reused in choreographies to model alternative paths in the interaction between participants, e.g., the choice of the payment methods for a given service leads to different sequence of interactions between the client and the service. Nevertheless, in business process choreographies, differently from business processes, there is no central locus of control that is able to store and maintain the data used for the decision across participants.

Therefore, different constraints are introduced in BPMN 2.0 [1] for using exclusive gateways in choreographies. The data, once shared, does not change

© Springer International Publishing Switzerland 2016
Q.Z. Sheng et al. (Eds.): ICSOC 2016, LNCS 9936, pp. 547–554, 2016.
DOI: 10.1007/978-3-319-46295-0_34

until the point where the decision is taken. Thus, each participant takes its decision on the same data. However, it is assumed that the participants affected by the exclusive gateway have the same understanding of the data. We argue this strong assumption is a problem when it comes to the interaction of participants that represent companies or services which are different, e.g., in terms of area of expertise, domain, background and country.

In this paper we propose a solution to this problem by delegating the decision making to a decision service that uses the Decision Model and Notation (DMN) standard [3]. Using a standard, assures that the decision is taken properly by all the involved participants. Additionally, we introduce a generic RESTful API [4] for such a decision service that is responsible for executing the shared decision on behalf of the choreography's participants. After describing the decision service's generic RESTful API, we provide a procedure on how to embed the decision service into a RESTful choreography [5]—an extension of business process choreography with REST notation.

This way, we make sure that the choice made by each participant leads only to intended paths and introduces no deadlocks. Additionally, a higher degree of separation of concerns for decision and process logic is achieved, improving aspects such as the choreography's comprehensibility and maintainability [6].

This paper is structured as follows. Section 2 states the problem using a running example. Section 3 describes the proposed solution while Sect. 4 concludes the paper.

2   Problem Statement

Business process choreographies are introduced in the BPMN 2.0 specification [1]. They serve the purpose of modeling interactions between two or more business actors from a global perspective. More specifically, they abstract from internal business process activities and focus only on the messages exchanged between participants with the aim of reaching a common goal.

Figure 1 depicts an example of a choreography diagram that describes the interaction of a manufacturer with its suppliers. The manufacturer makes a request for tender to different suppliers for the product part it needs. The suppliers follow up by sending their offers. After receiving all offers, the manufacturer announces the score which represent the level of satisfaction for each supplier's offer. If there is at least a single score which passes a threshold then the supplier with the best score receives the payment from the manufacturer and sends the product part. On contrary, the tender is not successful and the suppliers are asked to send again their offers. This tender can be closed at anytime during this loop but it is not shown explicitly in the choreography model for simplification purposes.

In choreography diagrams exclusive gateways model alternative paths. However, choreographies' exclusive gateways are constrained in their usage compared to their respective counterparts in business processes. In order for the choreography to be enforceable the following constraints should hold: The data

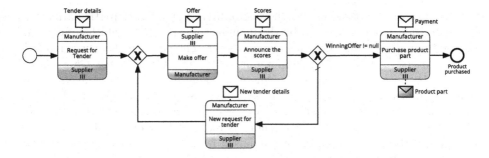

Fig. 1. A business process choreography for parts procurement by a manufacturer

used for the gateway conditions must have been in a message sent at some point in the choreography before the gateway. The message(s) containing the data is sent or received by all participants that are affected by the gateway and any change of the data must be visible to all these participants. And lastly, every participant must interpret the data in the same way.

However, there is a problem in implementing such constraints when it comes to the interaction of participants whose role can be filled by many possible business actors. The problem consists in that these different business actors can have different understandings of the data used for the decision making, leading the choreography to be out of sync. This is due to the fact that the business actors might be very diverse in terms of, e.g., domain and country. To ensure the enforceability of the choreography, we need to a go a level closer towards the implementation level. To this end, we use RESTful choreography—an extension of business process choreography with REST implementation information [5].

In order to make the decision clear for all participants we use DMN. Figure 2 shows an example decision model; *decisions* are rectangles, *input data* are ellipsis, *information requirement edges* are solid, and *knowledge sources* are rectangles with a wavy bottom. The decision element is associated with a FEEL (Friendly Enough Expression Language) expression displayed as an annotation next to it.

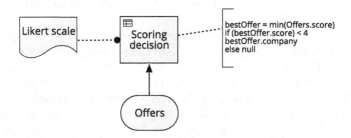

Fig. 2. Decision model used by the manufacturer to decide on a supplier (cf. right-most gateway in Fig. 1)

This example is based on the choreography in Fig. 1. More particularly, this is the decision model employed by the manufacturer to decide which supplier to choose from all the suppliers that made an offer. The decision element is labeled *Scoring decision* and takes as input data a list of *Offers*. These *Offers* have two attributes: *company* and *score*, where *company* is the name of the company which made the offer and *score* is the score that was assigned to that offer.

As one can see from Fig. 1, there are two possible outcomes: either there is no winning offer such that a new tender is requested, or one of the offers was chosen and the product parts are purchased from the respective supplier. The fact whether or not there is a winning offer depends on the scores, which can range from 1 to 5, according to the well known Likert scale. This scale says that the lower the score, the better. Therefore, the FEEL expression associated with the decision element first determines the offer with the minimum score. Then it checks if the score is less than four. If that is the case the respective company's name is returned. Otherwise, the decision yields a *null* value.

3   RESTful Decision Service

In this chapter we introduce the concept of RESTful decision service and how this service is used in conjunction with RESTful choreographies.

3.1   REST Interface Based on DMN

To solve the problem of the data misinterpretation we propose a RESTful decision service that is built on the DMN standard. The RESTful decision service provides a REST interface for creating, managing, and executing shared decisions. The decision owner is responsible for creating the decision logic and providing it to the decision service. Thus, we have a single decision making for all the participants to execute. The decision service is responsible for computing the decision each time it is called from the participants who are affected by the exclusive gateway. The output of the decision should comply to the conditions of the sequence flows originating from the exclusive gateway, hence, making it trivial for the other participants to relate the decision output with the correct path in the choreography.

For creating the RESTful API of the decision service, we map a REST interface to the main concepts of DMN. As explained in Sect. 2, these main concepts are the decision logic, inputs, outputs and execution. The REST interface is designed according to RESTful design rules [7] and design patterns [8]. A RESTful decision service provides the REST interface described in Table 1.

The creation of a new decision is the only action that is not included in the choreography diagram because it is performed just once by the decision owner. The decision owner is the participant of the choreography that is responsible for creating the decision logic like the manufacturer in Fig. 1. The choreography diagram models the interaction that the participants have with a particular decision logic, e.g., *Scoring decision* from Fig. 2. Hence, performing this action is a requirement for executing the choreography.

Table 1. The interface of a RESTful decision service

Decision action	REST request and response
Create a new decision (logic)	PUT /decisionName
	⇐ HTTP/1.1 200 OK
	{location: /decisionName}
Create a decision instance	⇒ POST /decisionName/
	⇐ HTTP/1.1 201 Created
	{Location: /decisionName/id
	Link: /decisionName/id/inputs
	Link: /decisionName/id/execute}
Insert the decision inputs	⇒ PUT /decisionName/id/inputs/inputName
	⇐ HTTP/1.1 200 OK
	{location: /decisionName/id/inputs/inputName}
Read the decision inputs	⇒ GET /decisionName/id/inputs/inputName
	⇐ HTTP/1.1 200 OK
	{location: /decisionName/id/inputs/inputName}
Execute the decision	PUT /decisionName/id/execute
	⇐ HTTP/1.1 200 OK
	{Link: /decisionName/id/output}

Anytime a new instance of the choreography gateway has to be executed, a new decision URI that corresponds to that gateway instance should be created by the decision owner, e.g., a new scoring decision id should be created for any tender that is requested and eventually decided at the gateway. It is important to distinguish between different decision instances because the participants should have access only to the decision instance that affects their behavior. For example, when $winningOffer = null$ a new tender is created and, therefore, a new decision instance has to be created. In this case the participants will distinguish the new tender from the old one from the new decision URL. The decision owner inserts the decision inputs after the decision instance is created. Providing the decision inputs completes all the requirements for the execution of the decision. This makes the decision service available for execution by any participant that knows the decision URL.

The participants can optionally read the inputs before executing the decision. However not every participant is allowed to change the input. This would lead to unintended paths in the choreography. The participants responsible for editing the input can be identified in the choreography diagram because the input data originates from them. For example, the choreography diagram in Fig. 1 shows that the manufacturer announces the scores and, hence, is responsible for the creating or editing the input data used in the decision. When a request is sent for the execution of the decision, the response provides the output of the decision. The output of the decision should be consistent with the conditional sequence flows that follow the exclusive gateway.

3.2   Decision Services in RESTful Choreographies

Having a REST interface for the decision service is not enough. The objective is to go from a business process choreography to a RESTful choreography that solves the exclusive gateway problem by incorporating the RESTful decision service. In this subsection, we provide a stepwise method for embedding the decision service into the RESTful choreography. We assume that the initial business process choreography is syntactically correct. Since RESTful choreography is an extension of business process choreography, we do not want to introduce errors that break the correctness of the choreography. To this purpose, we consider two main properties: *The activity sequencing property* [1] The initiator of each choreography task is either initiator or recipient in the direct preceding task. The very first choreography task is an exception since it does not have any preceding task; *Hyperlink completeness* [9] All REST-request links used in the RESTful choreography are provided to the initiator at some point upstream in the choreography. An exception is made for the first occurring REST-request.

The decision service can be an external participant i.e., an additional business actor who provides decision services or hosted by one of the participants. In terms of the REST interface, that is irrelevant because only the web domain would be different and the rest of the URI would not change. For the remainder of this paper, we assume the more complex and interesting case where the decision server is an external participant in the RESTful choreography.

The stepwise method for embedding the RESTful decision service in business process choreography is given below. As mentioned above, the only requirement to start this method is the creation of the decision by the decision owner. The method consists of the following five steps:

1. Locate the choreography task where the decision-relevant data is passed for the first time. Add before the located task a new RESTful task that creates a new decision instance. The response should contain the location of the instance, the URL of the decision input, and the URL of the decision execution. The initiator should be the decision owner.
2. Next to the newly added task, add a new RESTful task that inserts the decision inputs using the link passed from the previous task. Again, the initiator should be the decision owner.
3. Change the content of the initiating message of every choreography task that models the passing of the decision-relevant data. Replace the content with information that describes the location of the decision together with the inputs and execution links.
4. Locate the exclusive gateway. Add before the gateway as many RESTful task as participants (affected by the gateway) in parallel. Each participant sends a request for executing the decision to the decision service and receives the output of the decision service as a response. This step can be put into a sub-choreography to not overload the diagram when we have more than two participants.

Now we analyse whether the activity sequencing properties is preserved after each step: Step 1. The insertion of the new RESTful task does not break the property because the initiator remains the same; Step 2. The subsequent REST-ful task added has again the same initiator. This means that the property is preserved because the initiator is present in the direct preceding task; Step 3. In this step, there is no change in the participants of each choreography task. Only the message content has been changed; Step 4. The BPMN specification requires that the initiators of the choreography task following the gateway have to part of the choreography task that directly precedes the gateway. Adding parallel REST calls that execute the decision service does not introduce any breach of the property because the initiators involved in the call are those affected by the gateway. As a conclusion, the transition from a choreography diagram to a RESTful choreography diagram (hosting a decision service) does not break the activity sequencing property of the diagram.

Regarding the hyperlink completeness property, we show that it is preserved. The link used for the first time in step 1 is the first occurring link. The concrete decision link, inputs link and execution link are provided to the decision owner with the response from the REST call of step 1. Then, the decision owner enters a new input using the inputs link in step 2. In step 3, all links introduced before are provided to the participants. Eventually, the participants use these links to execute the decision in step 5. Concluding, all the links (except the very first) are provided to the participants before being used by them.

Figure 3 shows the output of our overall approach. It implements unambiguously the parts procurements decision (modeled in Fig. 2) so that all suppliers take the correct path following the exclusive split gateway.

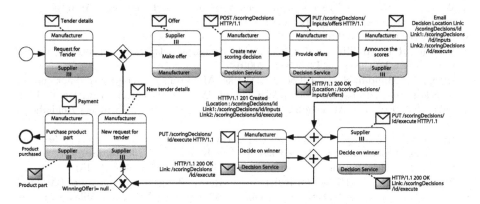

Fig. 3. A business process choreography for parts procurement by a manufacturer with the assist of a RESTful decision service

4 Conclusions

This paper tackles a problem related to the implementation of choreographies' exclusive gateways. We discuss the limitations of the BPMN specification regarding the implementation of choreography's exclusive gateways and state the problem induced by these limitations. Once the problem has been clearly stated, we suggest a solution by introducing the RESTful decision service—a service that is based on the Decision Model and Notation standard.

The RESTful decision service provides a REST interface to allow the proper interaction of the participants with the decision service. Additionally, we provide a stepwise method for embedding such a service in any choreography diagram. The result is a RESTful choreography diagram that describes the complete interaction. The RESTful decision service makes the decision-relevant data visible and consistent assuring that decision is always executed on the same input data. Using DMN standard mitigates the misinterpretation of the decision output. Moreover, using this standard we achieve an increasing degree of separation of concerns between decision and process logic, hence, improving the choreography's comprehensibility and maintainability.

Finally, we illustrated our approach with an example which represents the interaction of a single business actor with an undefined number of business partners. Future work will look at more complicated interaction patterns with more complex decisions, where we believe that the RESTful decision service will play even a bigger role for facilitating the implementation of decisions in choreographies.

References

1. OMG: Business Process Model and Notation (BPMN), Version 2.0, January 2011. http://www.omg.org/spec/BPMN/2.0/
2. Weske, M.: Business Process Management - Concepts, Languages, Architectures, 2nd edn. Springer, Heidelberg (2012)
3. OMG: Decision Model and Notation, Version 1.0, September 2015
4. Fielding, R.T.: Architectural styles and the design of network-based software architectures. Ph.D. thesis AAI9980887 (2000)
5. Nikaj, A., Mandal, S., Pautasso, C., Weske, M.: From choreography diagrams to RESTful interactions. In: Norta, A., Gaaloul, W., Gangadharan, G.R., Dam, H.K. (eds.) ICSOC 2015 Workshops. LNCS, vol. 9586, pp. 3–14. Springer, Heidelberg (2016)
6. Batoulis, K., Meyer, A., Bazhenova, E., Decker, G., Weske, M.: Extracting decision logic from process models. In: Zdravkovic, J., Kirikova, M., Johannesson, P. (eds.) CAiSE 2015. LNCS, vol. 9097, pp. 349–366. Springer, Heidelberg (2015)
7. Masse, M.: REST API Design Rulebook. O'Reilly Media Inc., Sebastopol (2011)
8. Palma, F., Gonzalez-Huerta, J., Moha, N., Guéhéneuc, Y.G., Tremblay, G.: Are RESTful APIs well-designed? Detection of their linguistic (anti)patterns. In: Barros, A., Grigori, D., Narendra, N.C., Dam, H.K. (eds.) ICSOC 2015. LNCS, vol. 9435, pp. 171–187. Springer, Heidelberg (2015)
9. Nikaj, A., Weske, M.: Formal specification of RESTful choreography properties. In: Bozzon, A., Cudré-Mauroux, P., Pautasso, C. (eds.) ICWE 2016. LNCS, vol. 9671, pp. 365–372. Springer, Heidelberg (2016). doi:10.1007/978-3-319-38791-8_21

Cloud and Internet of Services/Things
(Short Papers)

WiCare: A Synthesized Healthcare Service System Based on WiFi Signals

Hong Li, Wei Yang$^{(\boxtimes)}$, Yang Xu, Jianxin Wang, and Liusheng Huang

University of Science and Technology of China, Hefei 230027, China
qubit@ustc.edu.cn

Abstract. To help the independent-living elders or patients nursed in a single isolated ward, we propose a proof-of-concept prototype named WiCare, a non-intrusive and device-free healthcare service system based on ubiquitous WiFi signals. It extracts Channel State Information (CSI) from the physical layer and detects the unique variations of CSI values caused by human activities. We implement WiCare on two laptops equipped with the commercial 802.11n network interface cards. Two potential application scenarios are considered: a living room and a bedroom. The results demonstrate that the proposed scheme achieves overall recognition accuracies of 92.3 % in living room and 87.6 % in bedroom with low false positive rates. Moreover, WiCare can send alarm messages when the server recognizes the occurrences of emergency activities, which assist the users in getting help as quickly as possible.

Keywords: Daily activities recognition · Elder healthcare · Wireless · Device-free

1 Introduction

With the rapid increase of the older population, the need of special healthcare service for elders increases. Traditional healthcare service systems (HSS) utilize cameras, specialized hardware or wearable sensors to sense the human activities in a specific environment. However, these solutions have some unavoidable limits. Camera based techniques are sensitive to the light condition and violating personal privacy. Specialized hardware based techniques need specialized equipments, which probably leads to a high cost. Wearable sensors based techniques are inconvenient for users must wear different sensors.

There have been various WiFi-based human activities solutions which can be applied into HSS, such as WiSee [1], Wi-Gest [2], WiHear [3], etc. They are based on the insight that different human activities can introduce different amplitude distortions and phase shifts in WiFi signals. In this paper, we propose WiCare, a non-intrusive and device-free healthcare service system based on WiFi signals. We implement WiCare with two commercial off-the-shelf (COTS) WiFi devices, a sender (e.g., a wireless router) and a receiver (e.g., a laptop). The receiver is equipped with Intel 5300 network interface card (NIC), which is modified by the tools in [4], to obtain CSI measurements from the physical layer.

© Springer International Publishing Switzerland 2016
Q.Z. Sheng et al. (Eds.): ICSOC 2016, LNCS 9936, pp. 557–565, 2016.
DOI: 10.1007/978-3-319-46295-0_35

The main contributions of this paper are as follows:

(1) To the best of our knowledge, this is the first effort using WiFi signals to improve the welfare of target groups. We design WiCare, a synthesized healthcare service system, which exploits the reflections of WiFi signals to "sense" different human activities in a non-invasive and device-free manner.
(2) To evaluate the performances of our proposed system, we collect CSI values modulated by human activities in two potential indoor scenarios: a living room and a bedroom. The experiment results demonstrate that WiCare can correctly detect and recognize human activities with a high recognition accuracy and low false positive rate. Our system can be deployed to serve the independent-living elders or isolated patients.

The rest of this paper is organized as follows. Section 2 introduces the related work. Section 3 describes the specific design of WiCare, which is followed by the evaluation of the system in Sect. 4. We conclude this paper in Sect. 5.

2   Related Work

Existing solutions on device-free activity detection and recognition can be divided into three categories: RSSI based, specialized hardware based, CSI based.

RSSI based: Abdelnasser *et al.* presented WiGest which utilizes RSSI values of WiFi signals to sense hand gestures around the user's mobile device [2]. Sigg *et al.* proposed activity recognition schemes using RSSI values to recognize four human activities including crawling, lying down, standing up and walking [5,6]. However, RSSI values only provide coarse-grained information about channel changes and do not contain fine-grained information about small scale fading caused by micro-movements.

Specialized hardware based: Researchers have proposed solutions that employ software defined radio (SDR) platform and specialized hardware to recognize human activities. Pu *et al.* proposed WiSee [1] which uses SDR as a receiver to extract sophisticated WiFi signals to identify 9 human activities. Wang *et al.* proposed WiHear [3] which collects WiFi signals both from SDR platform and WiFi devices to hear people's talking. Kellogg *et al.* proposed AllSee [7], a self-designed hardware prototypes, which achieves classification accuracies as high as 97 % over a set of 8 gestures. Adib *et al.* built WiVi [8] and WiTrack [9]. WiVi employs specialized radar antennas to send wireless signals and traces positions of the object moving behind the wall. WiTrack utilizes USRP and other sophisticated hardwares to track the 3D motion of a user. The above solutions exhibit good performance in recognizing human gestures or movements, but they need specialized hardware such as USRP or self-made devices.

CSI based: CSI values obtained from COTS WiFi NICs (such as Intel 5300) have been employed recently to recognize human activities. Wang *et al.* presented E-eyes [10] that exploits CSI values for recognizing household activities. Ali *et al.* exhibited WiKey [11] which utilizes CSI values to identify keystrokes. Han *et al.* proposed WiFall [12] that uses CSI values as the indicator to sense people's fall. Liu *et al.* made WiSleep [13] which leverages WiFi signals collected in bedrooms to monitor a people's sleep. Although these CSI based activities recognition solutions achieved high time resolution using CSI, they still have some disadvantages. E-eyes and WiKey are relatively location-dependent and not resilient to environment changes, WiFall does not effectively denoise CSI values. WiSleep is tailored to identify a person's sleeping postures.

In this paper, we tend to utilize CSI values for both coarse-grained and fine-grained human activities detection and recognition in typical indoor environments, and further build a healthcare system to serve the independent-living elders or patients living in an isolated room.

3   System Design

In this section, we provide a specific design of our system including the Data Collection, Primitive Signal Processing, Segmentation and Activity Detection, Feature Extraction and Recognition and System Response.

3.1   Data Collection

WiCare runs on the 5 GHz band of IEEE 802.11n standard rather than 2.4 GHz band to maintain more stable communications between transmitter and receiver. It employs a W-point receive window to collect CSI values from the WiFi devices, W is related to the sampling rate and the durations of daily human activities. All data in the receive window are regarded as the minimum process unit. The process of data collection contains two phases: training phase and working phase.

During the training phase, each selected activity is done by the volunteer for several times to constitute the training set. WiCare uses the training set to train its parameters and the classifier. In the working phase, the pre-trained WiCare collects CSI in real time and periodically stores data for further processing.

3.2   Primitive Signal Processing

WiCare organizes the received CSI values into matrix $\mathbf{M}$ with dimensions $N \times W$, where N is the number of CSI streams and W represents receive window size. Since CSI values provided by commodity WiFi devices are inherently noisy due to the hardware imperfections (carrier frequency offsets (CFO), transmission power changes) and environment variations (path loss, shadowing and fading), the CSI streams must be sanitized before detecting and extracting motion information.

WiCare removes the DC component by subtracting the constant offset from each stream. The corresponding constant offset is calculated by a long-term averaging over the stream. Then, WiCare passes every row of the matrix $\mathbf{M}$ into the *Butterworth* filter to remove high frequency noise. We observe that the frequencies of the variations induced by human activities in CSI streams approximately lie between 1 Hz to 80 Hz. If the CSI sampling rate is $F = 2000$ Hz, the cut-off frequency w_c can be $(2\pi f)/F = (2\pi \times 80)/2000 \approx 0.25$ rad/s. Figure 1 illustrates the signal denoising process of the waveform of walk activity.

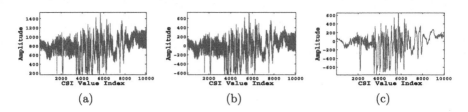

Fig. 1. Denoising process of a CSI stream. (a) Original CSI stream (b) CSI stream after reducing DC component (c) CSI stream through *Butterworth* low-pass filter

3.3 Segmentation and Activity Detection

Segmentation. WiCare divides the CSI matrix $\mathbf{M}$ into N_b bins along the row order, and each bin contains n CSI measurements, where n is set as $\frac{1}{4}F(=\frac{1}{4} \times 2000 = 500)$ and $n(N_b - 1) < W \leq nN_b$. Every bin can be reconstructed as a new matrix $\mathbf{H}_k(1 \leq k \leq N_b)$ with dimensions $N \times n$. Then, WiCare calculates the variance ν_k of each bin, and obtains a cumulative moving variance as $\Phi = \sum_{k=1}^{N_b} \nu_k$. WiCare sets a threshold σ_{var} to judge whether a human activity is happening. When $\Phi > \sigma_{var}$, it indicates the occurrence of a human activity and WiCare carries on the following operations. Otherwise WiCare keeps monitoring the WiFi devices and stays in low-power mode.

Activity Detection. After perceiving the existence of an activity, WiCare begins to detect the start and end points of the human activity. WiCare firstly calculates the correlation matrix $\mathbf{H}_k^T \times \mathbf{H}_k$ for each bin k and performs eigende-composition on the correlation matrix to get the eigenvectors. In terms of [14], the second eigenvector $\mathbf{q}_2$ and the second principal component $\mathbf{h}_2$ are related to the changes of CSI streams. When an activity occurs, the eigenvector $\mathbf{q}_2$ varies smoothly over neighboring subcarriers and the variance of $\mathbf{h}_2$ becomes larger, and vice versa. Therefore, WiCare calculates the variance $\sigma_{\mathbf{h}_2}^2$ of $\mathbf{h}_2$ and the mean $\mu_{\mathbf{q}_2}$ of the first difference of $\mathbf{q}_2$, where $\mu_{\mathbf{q}_2} = \frac{1}{N-1} \sum_{i=2}^{N} |\mathbf{q}_2(i) - \mathbf{q}_2(i-1)|$. Then, WiCare uses the ratio $\rho = \sigma_{\mathbf{h}_2}^2/\mu_{\mathbf{q}_2}$ as an indicator for efficiently detecting the start and end times of a human activity. We empirically choose the third quartile of the calculated set $\mathbf{P} = \{\rho_k | 1 \leq k \leq N_b\}$ as the threshold to automatically locate the profile of activities. WiCare picks top 5 CSI streams with the highest variances to aggregate an averaged stream as the final activity profile.

3.4 Feature Extraction and Recognition

Feature Extraction. Before extracting features, WiCare introduces weighted moving average [12] over each activity profile to eliminate some outliers and low-frequency noise. Because of the original profiles contain thousands of points as shown in Fig. 2. Hence, WiCare applys discrete wavelet transform to compress the activity profiles while preserving the time and frequency domain information.

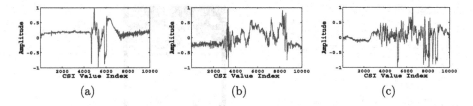

Fig. 2. CSI waveforms of different human activities. (a) *Fall* (b) *Help* (f) *Run*

From the Fig. 2 we observe that there are great differences among activities profiles in amplitude, duration, frequency of variation and so on. Thus, WiCare chooses the features of the activity profiles from both the time domain and the frequency domain to characterize different activities. The selected features can be referred in [15], and they are categorized and listed into two sets:

- Frequency-domain: (1) cumulative moving variances, (2) range, (3) period, (4) mean value, (5) median value, (6) first quartile, (7) third quartile, (8) variance.
- Time-domain: (1) spectral centroid, (2) spectral spread, (3) spectral skewness, (4) spectral kurtosis, (5) spectral roll-off, (6) spectral decrease, (7) spectral slope.

After compressing the activity profiles, WiCare can quickly calculate the above features for each extracted activity profile and combine all the features into a light-weighted feature vector for recognition.

Recognition. The process of recognition also contains the training phase and the working phase. As for the training phase, WiCare aggregates all the feature vectors extracted from different activities into a training set. Meanwhile, WiCare performs a 10-fold cross validation with the set on several different classifiers, such as Naive Bayes, Random Forest, Random Tree and C4.5, and compares the confusion matrices derived from different classifiers. WiCare empirically chooses C4.5 classifier because of it always produces the best recognition accuracy among the candidate classifiers. You can refer to [16] for specific description on C4.5 classifier. After that, WiCare turns to the working mode and employs the pretrained classifier to recognize the target activities in real time.

3.5 System Response

Since WiCare is designed as a healthcare service system, it must have the ability of alerting emergencies. Here, WiCare utilizes a server to dynamically monitor the recognition results, and synchronizes the data with our mobile application whose user interface is shown in Fig. 4. The target activities can be divided into two types, one is the normal activities such as running, walking, laying down, and the other is the emergency activities such as falling and calling for help. For the normal activities, WiCare just records their types and occurrence time.

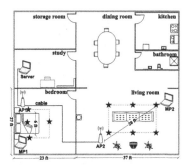

Fig. 3. Room settings of the apartment

Fig. 4. Mobile application interface of WiCare

However, when an emergency activity happens, WiCare will immediately set off the alarm and send the messages to the related people (families, doctors, security guards, etc.), which assists the user in getting help as quickly as possible.

4 Evaluation

4.1 Experimental Setting

Hardware Setting. We utilize three 3.3 GHz Intel(R) Core i5 CPU Thinkpad laptops which are equipped with Intel 5300 NICs. Two of them are deployed as the monitor points (MPs), and the left one is used as the server. Two TP-LINK TL-WDR4300 wireless routers are deployed as access points (APs) and operate at 5.745 GHz (channel 149 in IEEE 802.11n standard), which guarantees better recognition resolution owing to the shorter wavelength.

As shown in Fig. 3, MP1 and MP2 connect to the corresponding AP via different wireless links, respectively. Each MP has 3 omni-directional antennas and its firmware is modified as [4] to report the CSI values, and the APs are also installed with 3 antennas. The server connects to the APs via cables, and it has three significant functions: broadcasting continuous beacons to all MPs through APs, monitoring the recognition results and synchronizing the latest data with our mobile application. In the experiments, the sampling rate F can nearly reach 2000 packets/s on the MPs, and the size of receive window is set as 10000.

Experimental Scenarios. Figure 3 shows the experimental environment. Two typical indoor scenarios are considered: living room and bedroom. The size of the living room is 27 ft × 37 ft, and the bedroom is 27 ft × 23 ft. The rooms are separated by double cement concrete walls with a thickness of approximately 0.5 ft. The doors are made of wood and have a thickness of 0.16 ft. Two pairs of MPs and APs are deployed in the living room and bedroom, respectively. We place AP1 and MP1 on two bedside tables which lie at different sides of the bed,

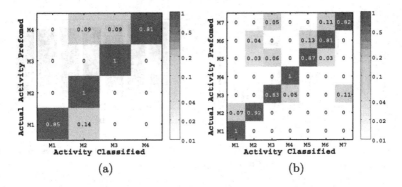

Fig. 5. Confusion matrix of human activities identification in different scenarios. (a) Living room (b) Bedroom

and their distance is about 6 ft. AP2 and MP2 are placed at the diagonal sections of the living room with a height of 2.7 ft, and they are around 20 ft between each other. In addition, there is a sofa lying between AP2 and MP2 which blocks the LOS path. We choose two sets of location-related human activities in these two scenarios which cover typical human daily activities:

- Living room: *Walk, Run, Fall* and *Help* (object waves hand).
- Bedroom: *Walk, Run, Fall, Help, Sleep, Lay down-get up* and *Sit down-stand up*.

4.2   Overall Performance

The volunteer performs activities at the positions marked with stars or along the dashed lines plotted in Fig. 3. During the training phase, we collect 30 samples for each activity in these two scenarios to generate the training set and mix the instances of the common activities (*walk, run, fall, help*) on a fifty-fifty basis to ensure the generality of the received data. We feed the initialized C4.5 classifier with the training set and finally obtain a well-trained WiCare. While in the working phase, WiCare works in real time and the volunteer randomly performs the typical daily activities.

We evaluate the overall performance of WiCare using two metrics: confusion matrices and false positive rate (FPR). Figure 5(a) and (b) show the confusion matrices of recognition results in living room and bedroom, respectively, where M1 - M7 separately refer to the activities of *walk, run, fall, help, sleep, lay down-get up* and *sit down-stand up*. The matrices demonstrate that the average classification accuracy is 92.3 % in living room and 87.6 % in bedroom. The average FPR in these two scenarios are around 2.6 % and 2.3 %, respectively.

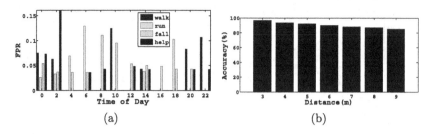

Fig. 6. Robustness evaluation of WiCare. (a) FPRs of different activities at different time (b) Average accuracies at different distances

4.3   Robustness Validation

Varying with Time. WiCare is based on the multipath propagation model, and the features derived from different target activities have distinct differences among each other. Except for the impact of dynamic multipath, WiFi signals are also influenced by temperature, humidity and atmospheric pressure, which are time-varying. It is necessary to evaluate the performances of WiCare at different time. Figure 6(a) plots the average FPRs of 4 different activities in the two scenarios every two hours during a day. The overall average FPRs of *walk*, *run*, *fall*, *help* are 4.13 %, 3.31 %, 5.05 % and 4.05 %, respectively. Therefore, WiCare is robust enough against time using the refined features.

Varying with Distance. We also investigate the relation between the recognition accuracy and the transceiver distance. The validation experiment is conducted in the living room. Every time we adjust the distance between AP2 and MP2, the volunteer is asked to do each activity of the set {*walk, run, fall, help*} for 20 times. Figure 6(b) illustrates the average recognition accuracy of WiCare when the distance between AP2 and MP2 changes. The result shows that the recognition accuracy declines with transceiver distance increasing. This is because closer distance leads to less path loss and higher Signal Noise Ratio. However, the recognition accuracies can still achieve more than 85 % in Fig. 6(b).

5   Conclusion

In this paper, we present WiCare, a synthesized healthcare service system, which is designed for independent-living elders or patients living in an isolated room. We implement WiCare using ordinary COTS WiFi devices and evaluate its performance in two typical indoor scenarios: living room and bedroom. 7 daily activities are selected to be the classification targets. With the trained C4.5 classifier, WiCare achieves overall recognition accuracies of 92.3 % in living room and 87.6 % in bedroom. WiCare can report the emergency circumstances when the emergency activities happen. Moreover, the factors of time and distance are also considered to further validate the robustness of WiCare. The results demonstrate that with the refined frequecny-domain and time-domain features, WiCare is robust to the time-varying environment and the transceiver distance.

Acknowledgement. This paper is supported by the National Natural Science Foundation of China (No. 61572456) and the Natural Science Foundation of Jiangsu Province of China (No. BK20151241).

References

1. Pu, Q., Gupta, S., Gollakota, S., Patel, S.: Whole-home gesture recognition using wireless signals. In: MobiCom, pp. 27–38. ACM (2013)
2. Abdelnasser, H., Youssef, M., Harras, K.A.: Wigest: a ubiquitous WiFi-based gesture recognition system. In: INFOCOM, pp. 1472–1480. IEEE (2015)
3. Wang, G., Zou, Y., Zhou, Z., Wu, K., Ni, L.M.: We can hear you with Wi-Fi! In: MobiCom, pp. 593–604. ACM (2014)
4. Halperin, D., Hu, W., Sheth, A., Wetherall, D.: Tool release: gathering 802.11n traces with channel state information. ACM SIGCOMM Comput. Commun. Rev. **41**(1), 53–53 (2011)
5. Sigg, S., Scholz, M., Shi, S., Ji, Y., Beigl, M.: RF-sensing of activities from noncooperative subjects in device-free recognition systems using ambient and local signals. IEEE Trans. Mob. Comput. **13**(4), 907–920 (2014)
6. Sigg, S., Shi, S., Buesching, F., Ji, Y., Wolf, L.: Leveraging RF-channel fluctuation for activity recognition: active and passive systems, continuous and RSSI-based signal features. In: Proceedings of International Conference on Advances in Mobile Computing and Multimedia, p. 43. ACM (2013)
7. Kellogg, B., Talla, V., Gollakota, S.: Bringing gesture recognition to all devices. In: 11th USENIX Symposium on Networked Systems Design and Implementation (NSDI 14), pp. 303–316 (2014)
8. Adib, F., Katabi, D.: See through walls with WiFi!, vol. 43. ACM (2013)
9. Adib, F., Kabelac, Z., Katabi, D., Miller, R.C.: 3D tracking via body radio reflections. In: 11th USENIX Symposium on Networked Systems Design and Implementation (NSDI 14), pp. 317–329 (2014)
10. Wang, Y., Liu, J., Chen, Y., Gruteser, M., Yang, J., Liu, H.: E-eyes: device-free location-oriented activity identification using fine-grained wifi signatures. In: MobiCom, pp. 617–628. ACM (2014)
11. Ali, K., Liu, A.X., Wang, W., Shahzad, M.: Keystroke recognition using wifi signals. In: MobiCom, pp. 90–102. ACM (2015)
12. Han, C., Wu, K., Wang, Y., Ni, L.M.: Wifall: Device-free fall detection by wireless networks. In: INFOCOM, pp. 271–279. IEEE (2014)
13. Liu, X., Cao, J., Tang, S., Wen, J.: Wi-sleep: contactless sleep monitoring via WiFi signals. In: RTSS, pp. 346–355. IEEE (2014)
14. Wang, W., Liu, A.X., Shahzad, M., Ling, K., Lu, S.: Understanding and modeling of WiFi signal based human activity recognition. In: MobiCom, pp. 65–76. ACM (2015)
15. Peeters, G.: A large set of audio features for sound description (similarity and classification) in the CUIDADO project (2004)
16. Quinlan, J.R.: C4. 5: programs for machine learning. Elsevier (2014)

Service Mining for Internet of Things

Bing Huang, Athman Bouguettaya, Hai Dong$^{(\boxtimes)}$, and Liang Chen

School of Science, RMIT University,
Melbourne, Australia
{bing.huang,athman.bouguettaya,hai.dong,liang.chen}@rmit.edu.au

Abstract. A service mining framework is proposed that enables discovering interesting relationships in Internet of Things services bottom-up. The service relationships are modeled based on spatial-temporal aspects, environment, people, and operation. An ontology-based service model is proposed to describe services. We present a set of metrics to evaluate the interestingness of discovered service relationships. Analytical and simulation results are presented to show the effectiveness of the proposed evaluation measures.

Keywords: Service mining · Service recognition · Service relationship · Interestingness · Service description

1 Introduction

The current Internet is evolving from interconnecting computers to interconnecting things [3]. The Internet of Things (IoT) refers to numerous connected things that rely on sensory, communication, networking, and information processing technologies [3]. Real-world things are heterogeneous in terms of features with little standard descriptions [3]. Service-Oriented Computing (SOC) paradigm provides a promising solution for exposing features of real-world things as services in a standard form.

As a result of the prevalence of IoT, an increasing number of real-world things will be connected to future Internet, leading to a proliferation in services. This proliferation of services will contribute to the increasing opportunities of service composition. Service composition aims at providing value-added services through aggregating component services. One the one hand, as more diverse services are available, the opportunities of composing services will surpass anyone's imagination. On the other hand, we may not sometimes know which group of services in IoT is related to each other and can cooperate to achieve a common goal. Therefore, the expected large number of services in IoT, coupled with the need for composing services, call for a service mining tool that can uncover the intrinsic correlations among services. We define *service mining as the process of proactively discovering interesting relationships among services.*

Service mining aims at discovering any interesting service relationships without specific search goals for defining the exact service functionality. A general

© Springer International Publishing Switzerland 2016
Q.Z. Sheng et al. (Eds.): ICSOC 2016, LNCS 9936, pp. 566–574, 2016.
DOI: 10.1007/978-3-319-46295-0_36

goal (i.e., smart home, which is a typical application domain in IoT) is provided at the beginning of service mining process to narrow down the mining scope. In the context of smart home, service mining may provide interesting correlations between different component services. For example, a TV service may hypothetically relate to a fridge service. There are three factors that provide the basis for the hypothetical relationship. The first factor is the collocation of both the TV set and the fridge [5]. The second factor is the temporal correlation (i.e., the fridge is sometimes accessed when the TV is on) [5]. The third factor is people (i.e., the TV and the fridge may be accessed by the same user) [6]. Another example is that an oven service may hypothetically relate to an air-conditioning service. An environment factor provides the basis for the hypothetical correlation [6]. When the oven is in use, temperature is rising. Then the air-conditioning is invoked to adjust room temperature. Thus, without any prior knowledge of specifying search goals, the service mining process has the potential of discovering interesting service relationships.

The key contribution is the service mining framework that aims at discovering service relationships in IoT. The paper is organized as follows: Sect. 2 proposes an ontology-based service description model. Section 3 elaborates the service mining framework. Section 4 shows experiment results. Section 5 concludes the paper and highlights some future work.

2   Ontology-Based Description of Services

Discovering service relationships requires the description of services so that service mining tools can understand services and form bonds among related services. We propose an ontology-based model for describing services (see Fig. 1). Unfilled nodes refer to ontology concepts that have been clearly defined in [4]. Gray nodes refer to extended ontology concepts. Numbers on edges denote the *has* relationship between ontology concepts. We formally define *service, environment, state, pre/postcondition,* and *people* as follows.

Definition 1: Service. A service S_i is defined by a tuple $\langle$ *name, des, Bind$_i$, Cat$_i$, Ope$_i$, Sta$_i$, Peo$_i$* $\rangle$ where:

- *name* and *des* are a name and a text summary about the service features, respectively.
- *Bind$_i$* is a set of binding protocols supported by S_i.
- *Cat$_i$* is a set of categories that S_i belongs to.
- *Ope$_i$* is a set of operations provided by S_i (cf. Definition 5).
- *Sta$_i$* is a set of states that S_i represents (cf. Definition 3).
- *Peo$_i$* is people who consume the service S_i (cf. Definition 6).

Definition 2: Environment. The environment Env_i is defined as a tuple $\langle$ *name, (val,uni,ts$_i$,loc$_i$)* $\rangle$, where:

- *name* is an environmental variable of Env_i.

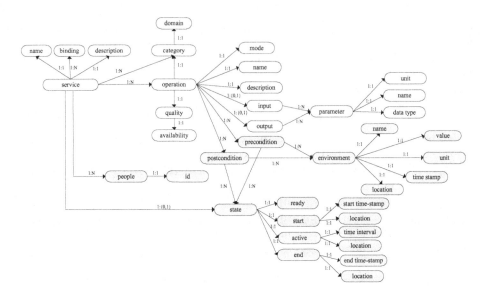

Fig. 1. Ontology-based description of services

- (val, uni, ts_i, loc_i) shows the recorded readings of the environmental variable. The readings include value val, unit uni, time-stamp ts_i and location loc_i. The location is uniformly defined as a GPS point with a user-defined spatial radius r. For simplicity, we use v_t to refer to the value of the environment variable at time point t.

Definition 3: State. The state Sta_i can only be an attribute in the tuple ⟨ *ready, start, active, end* ⟩ at a given time where:

- *ready*: the service is in the *ready* state if an invoking request has not been made.
- *start*: the *start* state means that the service execution has been initiated. The start state is defined by a tuple ⟨ st_i, loc_i ⟩ where st_i and loc_i are the start time stamp and the location of initiating the service, respectively.
- *active*: the service is in the *active* state if the service is executing. The active state is defined by a tuple ⟨ tin_i, loc_i ⟩ where tin_i and loc_i are the time interval and the location of the service execution, respectively, and $tin_i = et_i$-st_i.
- *end*: the service is in the *end* state if the service execution is terminated. The end state is defined by a tuple ⟨ et_i, loc_i ⟩ where et_i and loc_i are the end time stamp and the location of terminating the service, respectively.

Definition 4: Precondition and Postcondition. The precondition Pre_i is defined as a tuple ⟨ $(Sta_1, Sta_2 \cdots Sta_i)$, $(Env_1, Env_2 \cdots Env_i)$ ⟩ where:

- Sta_i is the required *state* before executing an operation (cf. Definition 3).
- Env_i is the required *environment* before executing an operation (cf. Definition 2).

The postcondition Pos_i is defined as a tuple $\langle$ $(Sta_1,\ Sta_2 \cdots Sta_i),\ (Env_1,$ $Env_2 \cdots Env_i)$ $\rangle$ where:

- Sta_i is the effect state after executing an operation (cf. Definition 3).
- Env_i is the effect environment after executing an operation(cf. Definition 2).

Definition 5: Operation. An operation Ope_i is defined by a tuple $\langle$ *name, des,* $Cat_i,\ Mod_i,\ Inp_i,\ Out_i,\ Qua_i,\ Pre_i,\ Pos_i$ $\rangle$ where:

- *name, des,* $Cat_i,\ Mod_i,\ Inp_i,\ Out_i,\ Qua_i$ refer to names, descriptions, categories, modes, input/output messages, and qualities, respectively [4].
- Pre_i gives the preconditions of an operation (cf. Definition 4).
- Pos_i gives the postconditions of an operation (cf. Definition 4).

Definition 6: People. Peo_i is defined as a tuple $\langle$ id $\rangle$ where

- *id* is the unique identifier of people.

3   Service Mining Framework

The service mining framework consists of three phases. The framework starts with the scope specification phase which consists of two steps. In the first step, the user specifies a list of domains termed as *mining context(MC)*. Domains are specified by a set of ontologies [2]. Hence, ontologies related to MC can be determined, which is denoted as $Ont(MC)$. In the second step, a list of services related to the mining context are identified, which are termed as *mining library(ML)*. Due to page limit, the detailed process of scope specification is omitted. The scope specification is followed by the automatic service recognition phase. In this phase, services will go through service recognition process for identifying related services which are represented as service composition leads. In the evaluation phase, evaluation methodologies are proposed to identify interesting service composition leads.

3.1   Service Recognition

We model service relationships from *states, environments, people,* and *operations* perspectives.

(1) Two services S_i and S_k have *state* relationship if they are spatial-temporal dependent. S_i and S_k have spatial dependency if $S_i.active.loc_i$ is located inside the spatial circle centred at $S_k.active.loc_k$ with a geographic radius r [1]. For example, the TV located in home A has a spatial dependency with the fridge located in home A. This TV has no spatial dependency with the fridge located in home B. We formalize the spatial dependency between S_i and S_k in Eq. (1).

$$distance(S_i, S_k) = 2arcsin\sqrt{sin^2\frac{a}{2} + cos(Lat_i) \times cos(Lat_k) \times sin^2\frac{b}{2}} \times r_e$$

$$(1)$$

where $a = Lat_i - Lat_k, b = Long_i - Long_k$, r_e is the radius of earth. Lat_i and $Long_i$ refer to the latitude and longitude of the location $S_i.active.loc_i$. $S_i.active.loc_i$ is GPS points of S_i. r is a user defined radius. If $distance(S_i, S_k) \leq r$, S_i and S_k are spatial dependent. S_i and S_k have temporal dependency if one of the following conditions is satisfied.

- S_i is invoked in the execution time interval of S_k. That is $S_i.start.st_i \geq S_k.start.st_k$ and $S_i.end.et_i \leq S_k.end.et_k$. For example, the fridge door is opened and closed during the time interval when TV is on.
- S_i is invoked before S_k. That is $S_i.end.et_i \leq S_k.start.st_k$. For example, the fridge door is closed and then TV is on.
- S_i is invoked before S_k and becomes the end state after S_k is invoked. That is $S_k.start.st_k < S_i.end.et_i < S_k.end.et_k$ and $S_i.start.st_i < S_k.start.st_k$. For example, the oven is in use for a while, then the air-conditioning is turned on. The air-conditioning keeps the active state for a time interval after the oven is turned off.

(2) Two services S_i and S_k have environment relationships if the following two conditions are satisfied. We use $\rightarrow$ to denote state changes.

- the value of environment variable Env_j is changed during the execution time interval t_{in} of S_i. That is $S_i.state = active$ and $Env_j.v_{st} \neq Env_j.v_{st+t_{in}}$.
- the state of S_k is transformed due to the environment changes. That is $S_k.ready \rightarrow S_k.start \rightarrow S_k.active$ or $S_k.active \rightarrow S_k.end \rightarrow S_k.ready$.

(3) Two services S_i and S_k are related through people if S_i and S_k are consumed by the same person in a time interval. That is $S_i.Peo_i = S_k.Peo_k$. For example, the TV and the fridge are used by the same people in a time interval.

(4) Two services S_i and S_k have operation relationships if the two operations $S_i.Ope_i$ and $S_k.Ope_k$ are syntactically compatible. The following two conditions must be satisfied.

- $S_i.Ope_i.Mod_i = $ notification and $S_k.Ope_k.Mod_k = $ one-way; or $S_i.Ope_i.Mod_i = $ one-way and $S_k.Ope_k.Mod_k = $ notification; or $S_i.Ope_i.Mod_i = $ solicit-response and $S_k.Ope_k.Mod_k = $ request-response; or $S_i.Ope_i.Mod_i = $ request-response and $S_k.Ope_k.Mod_k = $ solicit-response [4]. This condition implies that a one-way operation must be mapped to a notification operation and a solicit-response operation must be mapped to a request-response operation.
- $S_i.Ope_i.Out_i \supseteq S_k.Ope_k.Inp_k$.

3.2 Evaluation

Not all discovered service composition leads are necessarily interesting in the service recognition phase. An evaluation measure is needed to filter out uninteresting service composition leads. The evaluation phase consists of two steps.

The first step is *Correlation Degree (CD)* filtering which measures the relationship strength between two services. *Correlation Degree (CD)* is defined in Eq. (2).

$$CD(S_i, S_k) = \eta_1 \cdot State(S_i, S_k) + \eta_2 \cdot Env(S_i, S_k) + \eta_3 \cdot Peo(S_i, S_k) + \eta_4 \cdot Ope(S_i, S_k) \tag{2}$$

where $\eta_1 + \eta_2 + \eta_3 + \eta_4 = 1$, $State(S_i, S_k), Env(S_i, S_k), Peo(S_i, S_k), Ope(S_i, S_k)$ are binary values returned from the service recognition phase. We define a *correlation threshold* (ζ) which is the minimum value allowed for the CD. If $CD(S_i, S_k) \geq \zeta$, then leads of composed services S_i and S_k are selected for further evaluation. Otherwise S_i and S_k are filtered out.

The second step is *interestingness* evaluation. We first give the concept of *Availability (Ava)*, *Domain Correlation(DC)*, and *Diversity(Div)*, and then give the *interestingness* definition.

Availability. Ava is defined as a binary value (i.e., 1 for available, 0 for unavailable). The source of availability information can be a registry that keeps tack of the availability of services [2].

Domain Correlation. DC measures the relevance of two domains that services S_i and S_k belong to, respectively. The domain correlation of S_i and S_k is equivalent to the ontology correlation of $Ont(S_i)$ and $Ont(S_k)$. We formally define DC in Eq. (3).

$$DC(S_i, S_k) = e^{-\frac{1}{\lambda_0 \cdot \{sim(Ont(S_i), Ont(S_k)) + 1\}}} \tag{3}$$

Where

$$Sim(Ont(S_i), Ont(S_k)) =$$

$$w_1 \cdot \left(\frac{|N_{pre}(S_i)| \cap |N_{pre}(S_k)|}{|N_{pre}(S_i)| \cup |N_{pre}(S_k)|} \right) + w_2 \cdot \left(\frac{|N_{pos}(S_i)| \cap |N_{pos}(S_k)|}{|N_{pos}(S_i)| \cup |N_{pos}(S_k)|} \right)$$

$$+ w_3 \cdot \left(\frac{|N_{in}(S_i)| \cap |N_{in}(S_k)|}{|N_{in}(S_i)| \cup |N_{in}(S_k)|} \right) + w_4 \cdot \left(\frac{|N_{out}(S_i)| \cap |N_{out}(S_k)|}{|N_{out}(S_i)| \cup |N_{out}(S_k)|} \right)$$

where $S_i, S_k \in ML, w_i (i = 1, 2, 3, 4)$ is a weight such that $w_i \in [0, 1]$ and $\sum_1^4 w_i = 1$. $|N_{pre}(S_i)|$, $|N_{pos}(S_i)|$, $|N_{in}(S_i)|$, and $|N_{out}(S_i)|$ refer to the set of preconditions, postconditions, input parameters, and output parameters of concepts, respectively. Operators $\cap$ and $\cup$ are ontological overlap and union of two concepts. When $Sim(Ont(S_i), Ont(S_k)) = 0$, the correlation between two domains is assigned with an initial value $r_0 = e^{-\frac{1}{\lambda_0}}$. Equation (3) shows that $DC(S_i, S_k)$ approaches 1 as $Sim(Ont(S_i), Ont(S_k))$ increases. We define Div as the multiplicative inverse of the domain correlation. We bound the maximum value of Div to 1. The Div is formally defined as follows.

$$Div = \frac{r_0}{DC(S_i, S_k)} \tag{4}$$

The *interestingness* is defined as follows.

$$Interestingness = Ava \cdot w_1 + Div \cdot w_2 \tag{5}$$

where w_1, w_2 are weights for Availability and Diversity respectively, $w_i \in [0,1](i = 1,2)$, and $\sum_1^2 w_i = 1$. We define an interestingness threshold (ξ) which gives the minimum value allowed for interesting service composition leads. If the value of *interestingness* $\geq \xi$, then leads of composed services are considered interesting. Otherwise the service composition leads are considered uninteresting.

4 Experiment Results

We study the effect of variables listed in Table 1 on the total number of discovered service composition leads, the number of service composition leads after Correlation Degree filtering, and the number of interesting service composition leads. First, we model the ontology using a class whose domain attribute stands for the domain of the ontology. We can obtain services with different domain attributes through initializing the class by assigning different values to domains. The rules of generating values shown in Table 1. For example, we randomly generate its input/output parameters such that the number of these parameters uniformly falls in the range of 0 to 5. The data type of each parameter is integer. The bound of each parameter is 0 to 100. For simplicity, we only consider the exact input/output parameter data type match.

Figure 2 (line a) shows that the total number of service composition leads increases significantly as the number of services increases. This is an expected result because as more services are introduced to the mining process, a service has a higher chance of relating to other services. Figure 2 (line b) shows the effect of the *CD* on filtering out uninteresting service composition leads.

Table 1. Experiment settings

Variable	Value or Range
Number of input parameters per operation	0–5
Number of output parameters per operation	0–5
Number of pre/pos-condition per operation	0–3
Range of input/output per operation (integer)	0–100
Range of pre/pos-condition per operation (float)	0–1
Temporal range (time-stamp)	0–24
Availability	0/1
r	10
$\eta_1/\eta_2/\eta_3/\eta_4$	0.1/0.2/0.3/0.4
w_1/w_2	0.3/0.7
λ_0	0.1
ζ	0.3
ξ	0.6

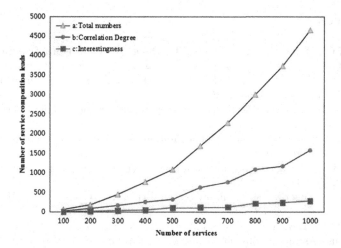

Fig. 2. Effects of key variables

With the number of services increasing, the *CD* can filter out uninteresting service composition leads to a large extent. Although the *CD* filtering technique reduces the number of service composition leads to a much smaller size, there are service composition leads that exhibit high *CD* values but are commonly known or useless. The interestingness measure (Fig. 2 (line c)) further filters out uninteresting service composition leads after the *CD* filtering. Compared with Fig. 2 (line b), interestingness measures can reduce uninteresting service composition leads significantly.

5 Conclusion

We propose a service mining framework that enables the proactive discovery of interesting service relationships. We propose an interestingness evaluation measure to sort out interesting service composition leads. We also proposes an ontology model for describing services. Future work includes developing a tool aiming at providing visual aids toward representing the discovered service composition leads. We also plan to improve the agility of our service mining framework to accommodate for the dynamic expansion of services.

Acknowledgements. This research was made possible by NPRP 7-481-1-088 grant from the Qatar National Research Fund (a member of The Qatar Foundation). The statements made herein are solely the responsibility of the authors.

References

1. Neiat, A.G., Bouguettaya, A., Sellis, T., Dong, H.: Failure-proof spatio-temporal composition of sensor cloud services. In: Barros, A., Grigori, D., Narendra, N.C., Dam, H.K. (eds.) ICSOC 2015. LNCS, vol. 9435, pp. 368–377. Springer, Heidelberg (2014). doi:10.1007/978-3-662-45391-9_26
2. Zheng, G., Bouguettaya, A.: Service mining on the web. IEEE Trans. Serv. Comput. **2**(1), 65–78 (2009)
3. Atzori, L., Iera, A., Morabito, G.: The internet of things: a survey. J. Comput. Netw. **54**(15), 2787–2805 (2010)
4. Medjahed, B., Bouguettaya, A.: Composing web services on the semantic web. J. VLDB **12**(4), 333–351 (2003)
5. Baldauf, M., Dustdar, S.: A survey on context-aware systems. J. Ad Hoc Ubiquit. Comput. **2**(4), 263–277 (2007)
6. Abowd, G.D., Dey, A.K., Brown, P.J., Davies, N., Smith, M., Steggles, P.: Towards a better understanding of context and context-awareness. In: Proceedings of International Symposium on Handheld and Ubiquitous Computing, pp. 304–307 (1999)

Service Analytics (Short Papers)

A Testing Approach for Hidden Concurrencies Based on Process Execution Logs

Kristof Böhmer[(⊠)] and Stefanie Rinderle-Ma

Faculty of Computer Science, University of Vienna, Vienna, Austria
{kristof.boehmer,stefanie.rinderle-ma}@univie.ac.at

Abstract. It is crucial to ensure correct process model executions. However, existing process testing approaches struggle with the verification of concurrent resource access patters that can lead to concurrency faults, such as, deadlocks or data corruption during runtime. Thus, we provide a concurrency verification approach that exploits recorded executions to verify the most frequently occurring concurrent resource access patterns with low test execution time. A prototypical implementation along with real life and artificial process execution logs is utilized for an evaluation.

Keywords: Process testing · Concurrency · Test case prioritization

1 Introduction

Ensuring fault free process executions is crucial [8]. However, this becomes challenging due to the increased complexity and interconnectivity of processes and their invoked services and applications [7] (i.e., shared resources). Moreover, organizations utilize a huge amount of process models [6], where each model likely spawns multiple *concurrently executed* process instances [13].

This can result in *Hidden Concurrencies* (HC). HCs are caused by concurrent activity executions which invoke the same *shared resources*. Figure 1 depicts an example HC. Two instances I1 and I2 are executed concurrently on two process models P1 and P2 (abstract notation inspired by Petri Nets). I1 and I2 both access the same *shared resources*, i.e., services S1 and S2, through activity execution. P2 also contains an obvious (modeled) concurrency based on a parallel split. The HC is caused by the concurrent access to service S2 by I1 and I2, i.e., activities in I1 and I2 invoke S2 within an overlapping time span.

The hidden concurrent access to S2 by I1 and I2 does not become evident at design time and might lead to a concurrency fault at runtime (i.e., a HC fault) *iff* S2 struggles when dealing with the access patterns caused by I1 and I2 (i.e., each HC fault is related to a HC, however, a HC can but does not necessarily lead to a HC fault). A *HC fault* occurs if multiple activities concurrently access the same shared resource in a way that creates inconsistencies/deadlocks [14]. Note, that developers do not always employ synchronization [2], paving the way for HC faults when a resource is concurrently accessed by multiple instances.

© Springer International Publishing Switzerland 2016
Q.Z. Sheng et al. (Eds.): ICSOC 2016, LNCS 9936, pp. 577–585, 2016.
DOI: 10.1007/978-3-319-46295-0_37

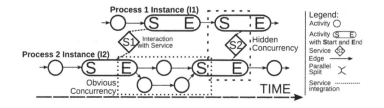

Fig. 1. *Hidden* and *obvious* (modeled) concurrent executions - example

Process instances are isolated from each other. However, their access on potentially faulty shared resources is *not* isolated which can result in HC faults. Moreover it is not obvious if/how multiple resources interact with each other. These interactions can lead to HC faults even if two "different" resources are accessed during concurrent executions. Moreover we found that current research on process verification, cf. [4], has neglected the detection of HCs so far.

Overall this paper addresses the following research questions:

RQ1. How can HCs in process instance executions be detected?
RQ2. How can the most likely HCs be verified with low testing efforts?
RQ3. How can the efficiency of the presented approaches be evaluated?

In order to address above research questions, an automatic verification heuristic for HCs is proposed. It exploits recorded process executions to determine the most frequently occurring HCs ↦ **RQ1**. Subsequently this information is utilized to select process test cases which verify the most frequently occurring concurrent resource access patterns ↦ **RQ2**. The conducted evaluation shows the efficiency and applicability of the presented approach ↦ **RQ3**.

This paper is organized as follows. Approaches to identify and prevent potential process model execution HC faults are discussed in Sect. 2. Evaluation, corresponding results, and their discussion are presented in Sect. 3. Section 4 discusses related work. Conclusions and future work is given in Sect. 5.

2   Preventing Hidden Concurrency Faults

Let $\mathcal{U}$ denote a *process repository* containing units u. Note that each unit $u \in \mathcal{U}$ is unique and represents a single activity. Assume further that *executions* of $u \in \mathcal{U}$ are logged. A unit's execution is reflected by an execution event $e := (u, t_s, t_e)$, where t_s and t_e denote time stamps which reflect the start and end of u's execution. Finally, let a bag O hold all execution events e for a given process repository $\mathcal{U}$. O can be interpreted as a simple execution log for process activities and instances, i.e., a collection of execution events over a process repository.

Let a test case, in short test, $t \in \mathcal{T}$, consist of a set of process model elements which are verified/covered by t [3]. Testing units $u \in \mathcal{U}$ is assumed sufficient, hence, $t :\subseteq \mathcal{U}$. Complete test definitions include additional information (e.g., expected variables values) which enable to detect concurrency faults.

Identifying Hidden Concurrencies. HCs are identified by analyzing the executions of each process unit. Those executions can be extracted from process execution logs which are generated by process execution engines. The presented approach identifies HCs based on *unit pairs*, (u, u'), $u, u' \in \mathcal{U}$, i.e., a pair of activities. Unit pairs are utilized because (a) a unit pair is the smallest entity that can provoke a HC; and is (b) concentrating on a minimal amount of interactions at once to simplify the interpretation of the findings; and (c) complex concurrency fault conditions can be represented by grouping units and unit pairs.

Basically, HCs can be observed in four flavors, cf. [1], depending on how the concurrent execution of two units $u, u' \in \mathcal{U}$ overlaps, cf. Definition 1:

Definition 1 (Overlapping Flavors). *Let $\mathcal{U}$ be a set of units and O be the bag of associated unit executions. Let further $e_1 = (u, t_{s_1}, t_{e_1})$, $e_2 = (u', t_{s_2}, t_{e_2}) \in O$ be two executions for a unit pair $u, u' \in \mathcal{U}$ and let $ov \in [0;1]$ be an overlapping factor. e_1, e_2 can be related under the following overlapping flavors:*

$OvlpF := O \times O \times [0;1] \mapsto \{start/end, complete, almost, no\}$
$OvlpF(e_1, e_2, ov) =$
$$:= \begin{cases} start/end & iff \ (t_{s_2} \leq t_{s_1} \wedge t_{e_2} \geq t_{s_1} \wedge t_{e_2} < t_{e_1}) \vee (t_{s_2} \geq t_{s_1} \wedge t_{s_2} \leq t_{e_1} \wedge t_{e_2} > t_{e_1}) \\ complete & iff \ (t_{s_1} \leq t_{s_2} \wedge t_{e_1} \geq t_{e_2}) \vee (t_{s_2} \leq t_{s_1} \wedge t_{e_2} \geq t_{e_1}) \\ almost & iff \ (t_{e_2} < t_{s_1} \vee t_{e_1} < t_{s_2}) \wedge (t'_{e_2} > t'_{s_1} \vee t'_{e_1} > t'_{s_2}) \\ no & otherwise \end{cases}$$

where

$d_1 := t_{e_1} - t_{s_1}, \ d_2 := t_{e_2} - t_{s_2},$
$t'_{s_1} := t_{s_1} - d_1 \cdot ov, t'_{e_1} := t_{e_1} + d_1 \cdot ov,$
$t'_{s_2} := t_{s_2} - d_2 \cdot ov, t'_{e_2} := t_{e_2} + d_2 \cdot ov$

Definition 1 is used to identify HCs for unit pairs in an execution log O. For this Eq. 1 compares the executions of all unit pairs $u, u' \in \mathcal{U}$ and determines the respective overlapping flavors and, hereby, the associated *HC risk*. The HC risk expresses how likely a HC can be observed for a given unit pair. Note, if a HC is observed frequently (high HC risk), then a related concurrency fault can have a high impact on process execution correctness, cf. [14].

$$Ovlp(O, ov) = \{(e.u, e', f) | e, e' \in O \wedge e.u \neq e'.u \wedge f := OvlpF(e, e', ov) \wedge f \neq no\} \tag{1}$$

Definition 2 calculates the HC risk of two units $u, u' \in \mathcal{U}$. Note, that the *min* function limits the concurrent execution likelihood of u and u' (i.e., the HC risk) to an interval of $[0, 1]$. Otherwise the HC risk could exceed > 1 if u' would be concurrently executed more than once for each execution of u.

Definition 2 (Concurrency Risk). *Let $\mathcal{U}$ be a set of units and O be the bag of associated unit executions. Let further $Ovlp(O, ov)$ be a set of overlapping units, cf. Eq. 1. Then the HC risk for two units $u, u' \in U$ is calculated as*

$$ConRisk(u, u') = min(\frac{co \cdot ct + seo \cdot set + ao \cdot at}{te}, 1)$$

where

- $te := |\{e \in O|e.u = u\}|;$
- $ovrlppngExectns := \{o := (u, e, f) \in Ovlp(O, ov)|o.u = u \wedge o.e.u = u'\};$
- $ce := |ovrlppngExectns|;$
- $co := |\{(u, e, f) \in ovrlppngExectns|f = complete\}|;$
- $ao := |\{(u, e, f) \in ovrlppngExectns|f = almost\}|;$
- $seo := |\{(u, e, f) \in ovrlppngExectns|f = start/end\}|;$
- $ct, set, at \in [0, 1]$ *weigh the different overlapping flavors (tuning variables)*

Definition 2 considers the number of executions of u (te), the number of executions of u that overlap with an execution of u' (ce), as well as the number of almost (ao), start/end (seo), and completely overlapping (co) executions of u with u'. Moreover, the executions can be weighed along the overlapping flavors using *tuning variables* (ct, set, at). This enables to model, for example, that an almost overlapping execution only represents a likely HC, i.e., it should not have the same impact on the calculated HC risk as, for example, a complete overlapping.

Equation 2 calculates the HC risk for all unit pairs $u, u' \in U \subseteq \mathcal{U}$:

$$OvlpRisk(U) = \{(u, u', r)|u, u' \in U \wedge u \neq u' \wedge r := \text{ConRisk}(u, u')\} \quad (2)$$

Calculating the HC risk for all unit pairs $u, u' \in U \subseteq \mathcal{U}$ enables the identification of units that frequently experience hidden concurrent executions. This is exploited to select a set of test cases which reaches a high amount of verified hidden concurrencies with a low amount of test cases and testing effort.

Test Group Selection. Groups of test cases are applied to identify HC faults. This is because the verification of HCs requires that multiple instances are executed concurrently. However, each test only spawns and verifies the execution of a single instance. Hence, for each unit u multiple test cases must be combined to a test group which verifies the HCs of u. So, it is necessary to identify which test cases should be selected from the existing set of test cases $\mathcal{T}$ and combined to test groups $tg :\subseteq \mathcal{T}$. As concurrent executions are the precondition for HC faults, the proposed approach relies on the HC risk during test group construction.

Intuitively, for unit u all units u' that have a non-zero HC risk with u, i.e., $\exists (u, u', risk) \in OvlpRisk(\mathcal{U})$, could be considered. However, this can result in large testing efforts or the non-verification of resource access patters which require the interaction of several units/instances. Algorithm 1 addresses these considerations by restricting the number of considered u' with $\exists (u, u', risk) \in OvlpRisk(\mathcal{U})$ to the top $gDist$ ones ($gDist \in \mathbb{N}$) with respect to HC risk. Definition 3 provides a function for determining units with maximum HC risk.

Definition 3 (Projection on Unit with Maximum Risk). *Let $OvlpRisk(\mathcal{U})$ be the set of overlapping units for the set of all units $\mathcal{U}$. For a given unit $u \in \mathcal{U}$, function maxRisk determines unit $u' \in \mathcal{U}$ which is the unit with the maximum HC risk in $OvlpRisk(\mathcal{U})$. Formally:*

$$maxRisk : \mathcal{U} \times 2^{OvlpRisk(\mathcal{U})} \longmapsto \mathcal{U}$$
$$maxRisk(u, OvlpRisk(\mathcal{U})) = u'$$
$$\text{with } \exists (u, u', r) \in OvlpRisk(\mathcal{U}) \land r = max\{r' \mid \exists o \in RelU \text{ with } o.r = r'\}$$
$$\text{where } RelU := \{o \in OvlpRisk(\mathcal{U}) \mid o.u = u)\}$$

Algorithm 1 creates an independent unit group for each unit $u \in \mathcal{U}$ considering its HC risk with concurrently executed $u' \in \mathcal{U}$ and the HC risks of transitively related units $u'' \in \mathcal{U}$, i.e., units that are executed concurrently with u'.

Algorithm DetUGrp(u, $OvlpRisk(U)$, $gDist$, $gLvl$)
    Data: $u \in U$, $OvlpRisk(U)$, $gDist$, $gLvl$
    Result: set $UGroup(u)$ for u
    $UGroup(u) := \{u\}$
    for $i=0; i < gDist \land gLvl \geq 0; i++$ **do**
        $maxR := maxRisk(u, OvlpRisk(U))$ acc. to Def. 3
        $OvlpRisk(U) := OvlpRisk(U) \setminus \{o \in OvlpRisk(U) \mid o.u = u, o.u' = maxR\}$
        $UGroup(u) := UGroup(u) \cup DetUGrp(maxR, OvlpRisk(U), gDist, gLvl - 1)$
    return $UGroup(u)$

Algorithm 1. Construct unit group for unit u based on the HC risk

---

We can illustrate a unit group, as determined by Algorithm 1, as a tree structure which uses u as its root note. Figure 2 depicts the construction of a unit group for unit S. By analyzing the HC risk of S it is detected that unit ① and ② have the highest risk to be executed concurrently with S. Hence, in a first step the unit group of S collects these two units ($gDist = 2$). Analogously, the search for related units with the highest HC risk is expanded to ①. The search stops at unit ③ and ④ as the maximum unit group level ($gLvl = 2$) is reached. Note, the same expansion is applied on unit ② (not depicted).

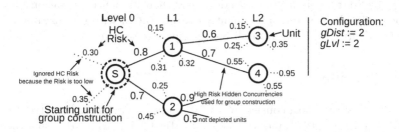

Fig. 2. Construction of a unit group, starting from unit S

Subsequently, each unit group $UGroup(u)$ is transformed into a new test group $TGroup(t)$. For each unit u in the analyzed unit group a test case $t \in \mathcal{T}$, were u is covered by t, is chosen and added to a test group, cf. Algorithm 2. This step is repeated until for each $u \in UGroup(u)$ a $t \in \mathcal{T}$ was added to $TGroup(t)$ that verifies the correctness of u. In Algorithm 2 $randSelect(u, \mathcal{T}) = t$ with t covers u.

```
Algorithm DetTestGroup(T, UGroup(u))
    Data: all tests T and a unit group UGroup(u)
    Result: a test group TGroup(t)
    TGroup(t):=∅
    foreach u ∈ UGroup(u) do
        test:=randSelect({ t ∈ T | u is covered by t})
        TGroup(t):=TGroup(t) ∪ {test}
    return TGroup(t)
```

Algorithm 2. Transforming a unit group into a test group

Test Group Prioritization. As an individual test group is created for each unit, executing each test group can take a substantial amount of time. Typically this problem is tackled by test case prioritization, cf. [9]. However, existing test case prioritization techniques are not applicable for the presented approach, cf. [4], because they (*a*) only rank single test cases (i.e., test case groups are not supported); and (*b*) are not specifically tailored for hidden concurrency testing.

Hence, this paper proposes a novel prioritization approach which uses seven metrics that focus on hidden concurrency fault detection. The **primary prioritization metrics** P are: test group execution time, test diversity, and HC risk. In addition, the **secondary prioritization metrics** S are: amount of test cases, covered back-end systems, additional coverage, and multi unit coverage. The $PrioValue(tg, P, S)$ of a test group tg is determined based on Eq. 3:

$$PrioValue(tg, P, S) := \sum_{i=0}^{|P|} \frac{1}{|P|} \cdot Prio_i^P(tg) + \sum_{j=0}^{|S|} \frac{1}{2 \cdot |S|} \cdot Prio_j^S(tg) \quad (3)$$

$Prio_i^P(tg)/Prio_i^S(tg)$, cf. Eq. 3, denote functions that determine the normalized primary/secondary metrics from P/S as described above. Note, that the division by 2 for secondary metrics decreases their influence. Equation 3 enables to repeatedly identify and subsequently execute the tg with the maximum identified $PrioValue(tg, P, S)$ until all test groups are executed.

3   Evaluation

The evaluation test data consists of *real life process execution logs* (BPIC) from the BPI Challenge 2015[1] and *artificial logs* (TeleClaim) which describe the handling of insurance claims in call centers (source: [12][2]).

The real life log data consists of 262,628 events, 5,649 process instance execution paths, and 398 activities – recorded from 2010 to 2015 and provided by five Dutch municipalities (BPIC15_1 to BPIC15_5). The artificial log data consists of 46,138 events, 3,512 process instance execution paths, and 11 unique activities. All evaluated logs contain the start and end time of each activity execution.

---

[1] http://www.win.tue.nl/bpi/2015/challenge—DOI:10.4121/uuid:
    31a308ef-c844-48da-948c-305d167a0ec1.

[2] http://www.processmining.org/event_logs_and_models_used_in_book.

Metrics and Evaluation. The evaluation was designed to assess if HCs occur during process model executions. Subsequently, it was checked if existing load testing approach are sufficient to test identified HCs. Finally, the efficiency of the proposed test prioritization approach is evaluated. For this multiple prioritization approaches are compared using the Average Percentage of Faults Detected (APFD) metric, cf. [9]. A high APFD ensures a high fault detection rate with a minimal amount of test group executions and test group execution time.

The APFD $\in [0,1]$ is calculated using Eq. 4. Hereby, n is the number of test groups TG, m is the number of known faults F to search for, and $Pos(tg, F_i)$ identifies the rank/position of the test group $tg \in TG$ that identifies fault $F_i \in F$.

$$APFD(n, m, TG, F) = 1 - \frac{\sum_{i=0}^{m} Pos(tg, F_i)}{n \cdot m} + \frac{1}{2 \cdot n} \qquad (4)$$

Note, the random aspects of the evaluation were evened out by executing it 100 times and taking the average result. The HC faults, which are "searched", in the following, were generated by randomly selecting pairs of activities that are executed concurrently, i.e., a HC. These randomly chosen activities are then marked as faulty and the analyzed testing approaches strive to construct test groups which cover those faulty HCs (11/3 HCs were marked as faulty for BPIC/ TeleClaim). Each recorded execution path is covered by at least one test.

Results. The results were generated by analyzing the BPIC and TeleClaim execution log files with a proof-of-concept implementation of the presented approach. The JAVA 7 source code/documentation of the implementation can be found on GitHub at https://github.com/KristofGit/Hidden_Concurrency.

The evaluation utilized an overlapping factor ov of 0.1 while the HC risk tuning variables were set to $at = 0.1$, $set = 0.8$, and $ct = 1$. The BPIC ($gDist = 5/gLvl = 3$) and TeleClaim ($gDist = 2/gLvl = 2$) data was analyzed with different values for $gDist/gLvl$ because the TeleClaim processes are simpler than the BPIC processes so that smaller test groups are sufficient.

We found that the analyzed execution logs contained tens of thousands HCs for each overlapping flavor. Hence, we checked if existing load testing based approaches are sufficient to test each HC in a reasonable amount of test execution time. Unfortunately, we found that load testing would require about 27 days test execution time to identify all HC faults in the TeleClaim processes. Note, the

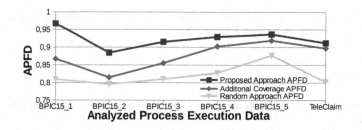

Fig. 3. Efficiency of the presented test group prioritization approach

BPIC processes are more complex and would require even more test execution time. Hence, test prioritization techniques are a necessity.

The evaluation shows (cf., Eq. 4 and Fig. 3) that the proposed approach creates the fastest test group ranking/execution order which identifies all artificial HC faults in the least amount of time. Note, that the proposed approach not only creates a better result than the baseline random approach but also as the additional coverage based approach which is a standard approach in existing work, cf. Fig. 3. When applying test group prioritization the amount of test group executions, required to identify all faults, is reduced to 127 (BPIC) and 2 (TeleClaim) because only minimal set of all available test groups must be executed to identify all faults. This significantly reduces the test group execution time, i.e., about 52 min would be required to identify all TeleClaim HC faults.

4   Related Work

Support for concurrency fault detection in the business process domain is limited, cf. [4]. For example, existing process testing approaches (cf. [5,10,11,15]) ignore concurrency or only consider a single process so that HCs will, most likely, not be identified. The last drawback applies to all the found work, cf. [4].

The most advanced approach, [5], reduces the concurrency testing workload by incorporating back-end services during test case selection by focusing on activities which could concurrently access the same back-end service. However, this work still ignores hidden concurrency faults generated by the concurrent execution of multiple processes and process instances (i.e., it only concentrates on a single process model and obvious modeled concurrent control flow paths).

5   Conclusions

The proposed test prioritization heuristic reduces the testing effort to process model execution scenarios and units which most likely trigger concurrency faults $\mapsto$ **RQ1** and **RQ2**. Moreover, the proposed algorithms were designed in a configurable fashion so that also very rarely occurring concurrency faults can be identified. The evaluation results show the efficiency/applicability of the presented approach for real life and artificial processes $\mapsto$ **RQ3**.

Acknowledgment. This work has been funded by the Vienna Science and Technology Fund (WWTF) through project ICT15-072.

References

1. Allen, J.F.: Maintaining knowledge about temporal intervals. ACM **26**, 832–843 (1983)
2. Alrifai, M., Dolog, P., Nejdl, W.: Transactions concurrency control in web service environment. In: Web Services, pp. 109–118. IEEE (2006)

3. Böhmer, K., Rinderle-Ma, S.: A genetic algorithm for automatic business process test case selection. In: Debruyne, C., Panetto, H., Meersman, R., Dillon, T., Weichhart, G., An, Y., Ardagna, C.A. (eds.) CoopIS, ODBASE, and C&TC 2015. LNCS, vol. 9415, pp. 166–184. Springer, Heidelberg (2015)
4. Böhmer, K., Rinderle-Ma, S.: A systematic literature review on process model testing: approaches, challenges, and research directions. arXiv (2015)
5. De Angelis, F., Fanì, D., Polini, A.: Partes: a test generation strategy for choreography participants. In: Automation of Software Test, pp. 26–32. IEEE (2013)
6. Dijkman, R.M., Rosa, M.L., Reijers, H.A.: Managing large collections of business process models - current techniques and challenges. Comput. Ind. **63**(2), 91–97 (2012)
7. Fdhila, W., Rinderle-Ma, S., Indiono, C.: Change propagation analysis and prediction in process choreographies. Coop. Inf. Syst. **24**, 47–62 (2015)
8. Leymann, F., Roller, D.: Production Workflow Concepts and Techniques. Prentice Hall PTR, Upper Saddle River (2000)
9. Malishevsky, A.G., Ruthruff, J.R., Rothermel, G., Elbaum, S.: Cost-cognizant test case prioritization. Technical report, University of Nebraska-Lincoln (2006)
10. Ruth, M.E.: Concurrency in a decentralized automatic regression test selection framework for web services. In: Mardi Gras Conference, pp. 7:1–7:8. ACM (2008)
11. Sriganesh, S., Ramanathan, C.: Externalizing business rules from business processes for model based testing. In: Industrial Technology, pp. 312–318. IEEE (2012)
12. Van Der Aalst, W.: Process Mining: Discovery, Conformance and Enhancement of Business Processes. Springer, Berlin (2011)
13. van der Aalst, W.M.P., Ter Hofstede, A.H., Weske, M.: Business process management: a survey. In: van der Aalst, W.M.P., Weske, M. (eds.) BPM 2003. LNCS, vol. 2678, pp. 1–12. Springer, Heidelberg (2003)
14. Wang, C., Said, M., Gupta, A.: Coverage guided systematic concurrency testing. In: Conference on Software Engineering, pp. 221–230. ACM (2011)
15. Yuan, Y., Li, Z.J., Sun, W.: A graph-search based approach to BPEL4WS test generation. In: Software Engineering Advances, p. 14. IEEE (2006)

autoCEP: Automatic Learning of Predictive Rules for Complex Event Processing

Raef Mousheimish[✉], Yehia Taher, and Karine Zeitouni

DAVID Laboratory, University of Versailles, 78000 Versailles, France
{raef.mousheimish,yehia.taher,karine.zeitouni}@uvsq.fr

Abstract. Complex Event Processing (CEP) is becoming more and more popular in service-oriented practices, especially to monitor the behaviour of continuous tasks within manual business processes, such as in logistics. The inference mechanisms of CEP engines are completely guided by rules, which are specified manually by domain experts. We argue that this user-based rule specification is a limiting factor that complicates the integration of CEP within the realm of Business Process Management (BPM) in a seamless way. Therefore, we present autoCEP as a two-phase data mining-based approach that automatically learns CEP rules from historical traces. In the first phase, complex temporal patterns are learned using early classification on time series techniques, then these patterns are algorithmically transformed into CEP rules in the second phase. Satisfactory results from evaluations on real data demonstrate the effectiveness of our framework.

Keywords: Complex event processing · Rule learning · Time series data mining · Violation prediction

1 Introduction

Manual processes are challenging to support as they usually contain continuous and dynamic tasks such as a Trucking activity in a logistics process. These tasks require an event-based processing with fine granularity, the thing that is beyond the reach of current activity-based BPMS. To cope with this challenge, researchers in the domain have found no solution better than exploiting CEP techniques to extend BPMS capabilities. Therefore this topic is storming the research in the area of BPM/CEP recently, and so many approaches [1–3,5,7] and a European project[1] are held on the subject.

Despite the noticeable amount of proposals, they have all disregarded the fact that the current standard way to define CEP rules is by writing them manually, and human users are in charge of this specification. Depending on the situation to detect (or predict) rules may become easily complicated, and this will add extra burden while managing business processes.

---

[1] http://getservice-project.eu/.

© Springer International Publishing Switzerland 2016
Q.Z. Sheng et al. (Eds.): ICSOC 2016, LNCS 9936, pp. 586–593, 2016.
DOI: 10.1007/978-3-319-46295-0_38

We deem the ultimate fact that experts are in charge of writing rules as a limiting factor for the prosperity and diffusion of CEP, especially that it holds the seamless integration within BPMS, and it restrains the jump towards the next phase of event-driven systems, i.e., proactive complex event processing. To turn around this limitation and instead of manually defining rules, we stress the need to step further, where rules could be extracted, learned from histories, and deployed into engines in an automatic manner with the minimum intervention of humans.

This paper proposes a novel two-phase framework that relies on data mining techniques, more specifically **early classification on time series**. The framework learns historical trends and patterns at the first phase, and then algorithmically transforms them into CEP rules at the second one. Thus addressing the problem of automatic rules generation. In general, the paper makes the following contributions: (1) It is the first approach to integrate time series data mining techniques within the domain of CEP. (2) Automatic learning of **predictive** CEP rules. (3) Any user can now employ an out-of-the-box configured CEP engine without the requirement of being a technical expert in the domain. (4) Since no expertise is required to use autoCEP, it could be seamlessly integrated within BPMS.

2   Background

Univariate Time Series: A univariate time series T is a sequence of real values for one attribute, $T = \{t_1, t_2, ..., t_N\}$. It is attributed a length and a class. The Euclidean distance is used to measure the similarity between two time series of the same length, denoted as $||T_1, T_2||$. In order to calculate the similarity between two time series of different lengths, e.g., s and T where $|s| = n < |T| = N$, one searches for the minimum distance between s and all subsequences q_i of T that has the same length as s, $|q_i| = |s|$. This distance is called the Best Matching Distance (BMD).

Shapelets: A shapelet is a new primitive for data mining that emerged recently [14], it is a temporal pattern that characterizes the time series of the same class. A shapelet is defined as a triple $\hat{s} = (s, \delta, c_s)$, where s is the subsequence that constitutes the shapelet $\hat{s}$, δ is the distance threshold that is going to be used for the run-time classification, c_s is the class of the shapelet. Taking this definition into account, new unclassified instances of time series T are labeled as early as possible with the same class as a specific shapelet $\hat{s}$, if the similarity between them $||\hat{s}, T||$ is less or equal to the distance threshold δ.

Complex Event Processing: CEP rules are defined using different CEP operators like windowing, selection, sequence, etc. These operators are considered the main enabler to define complex patterns. Regardless of the various concrete models, we will keep an abstract representation for rules that could be expressed in any description language. A CEP rule is divided into three blocks. First the timeframe (or window) of the rule, which is defined using the **within** construct.

Second the filter block, which contains the events that are relevant for the rule, they will be written between two curly brackets **{}**. Finally the conditions that need to be met on the captured sequence of events in order for the rule to be fired, this block is defined using the **where** construct. In general:

$$\textbf{within}[window] \ \{relevant \ events\} \ \textbf{where}[conditions] \qquad (1)$$

3   autoCEP: From History Records to CEP Rules

3.1   High-Level Framework

Figure 1 sheds some light on the proposed two-phase framework from a high-level perspective.

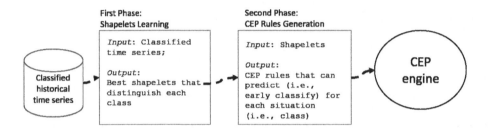

Fig. 1. Two phase high level framework

4   First Phase: Shapelets Learning

This stage contains our learning algorithm that can extract shapelets with the highest utility scores by learning them from historical time series. This algorithm is the outcome of surveying recent state-of-the-art approaches [4,6,12–14] regarding this kind of classification problems.

The algorithm that we have implemented to learn the shapelets is a brute force extraction algorithm [14] because it yields the most accurate results. In addition to the classified history, this algorithm requires two other input parameters, the minimum and the maximum length of the shapelets, i.e., to specify that the learned shapelets need to be between these two lengths. This is the place where domain expert knowledge could be exploited in order to guide the learning process, i.e., if experts have any prior knowledge about the lengths of the patterns to learn. However, autoCEP offers the capability for users without knowledge to fill these inputs with default values (the minimum and the maximum possible). In the evaluation section, we show the effect of these parameters on the performance of autoCEP.

5 Second Phase: CEP Rules Generation

At this point, the learned shapelets serve as inputs, where they will be automatically transformed into CEP rules to be used later for predictions.

The proposed algorithm in this phase extracts the three building blocks of the rule from the input shapelets and their parameters. For each shapelet a CEP rule is created, and thus we overcome the limitation of assuming just one rule for each composite event, which is the assumption that is made by other approaches [8].

Given a shapelet $\hat{s} = (s, \delta, c_s)$, the window parameter win for the **within** block is derived directly from the length of the shapelet, $win = |s|$. Then the relevant stream of events are of the same type as the elements that constitute the sequence s of the shapelet. Finally, the condition to be met in order to predict if a stream of incoming events correspond to c_s (the same class as the shapelet) is that $\hat{s}$ needs to cover the stream within the window win. This is listed in the following algorithm (Algorithm 1).

> **Input**: A set of shapelets $\hat{S}$
> **Output**: A set of CEP rules $rules$
> $rules \leftarrow \emptyset$;
> **for** *each shapelet $\hat{s}$ in $\hat{S}$* **do**
> $\quad$ /* create an empty cep rule cep $\qquad\qquad\qquad$ */
> $\quad win \leftarrow |\hat{s}.s|$;
> $\quad cep.setWindowBlock(win)$;
> $\quad E \leftarrow$ Extract event types from s;
> $\quad cep.setEventTypes(E)$;
> $\quad cep.setConditionBlock(\|\hat{s}, E\| \leq \delta)$;
> $\quad cep.setListener($ this stream is predicted to belong to the class $c_s)$;
> $\quad rules.add(cep)$;
> **end**
> **return** $rules$;

Algorithm 1. Transforming Shapelets into CEP Rules

6 Experiments

Interested readers are encouraged to download the programs that we have implemented from GitHub[2].

Two of the important factors that we are really interested in are the accuracy and the earliness of the predictions. To calculate the *Avg.f-score* (accuracy) we employed this formula (where C designates the set of classes):

$$\frac{1}{|C|} \sum_{cl \in C} \frac{2 \times precision(cl) \times recall(cl)}{precision(cl) + recall(cl)} \qquad (2)$$

with $precision(cl) = \frac{TP}{TP+FP}$ and $recall(cl) = \frac{TP}{TP+FN}$.

---

[2] https://github.com/rmgitting/autoCEP.

On the other hand, the earliness is computed from the average percentage of time points needed to make the predictions (i.e., how much in advance regarding the whole length of the tested time series). Given a dataset D, a time series T, and the shapelet $\hat{s}$ that was matched with T, we calculate the earliness percentage as (EMT is the point in time when $\hat{s}$ matched with T; how much data points was read from T):

$$\frac{1}{|D|} \sum_{T \in D} \frac{EMT(\hat{s}, T)}{|T|} \tag{3}$$

Artworks Transportation: In this kind of transport processes, the involved parties are interested in analyzing temperature readings and predict them in advance to prevent violations whenever possible (i.e., trespassing a minimum or a maximum threshold). These violations will eventually affect the qualities of the transported piece of arts. Table 1 presents information about the training and the evaluation data sets.

Table 1. Training and evaluation data sets (transport of artworks)

	Violated scenarios	Normal scenarios	Longest series	Shortest series
Train	16	17	451	51
Eval	17	17	460	39

The learning algorithm is implemented following a concurrent computing methodology, therefore the codes that build the shapelets and calculate their attributes are distributed over a pool of threads. From another point of view, the minimum and the maximum lengths of the shapelets that are provided as inputs for the algorithm may have some impacts on the performance of the framework as well. To this end, we ran different experiments to study the effects of the aforementioned factors.

The left side of Fig. 2 illustrates the learning time in minutes regarding two factors: the number of employed threads and the difference between the provided maximum and minimum lengths for the shapelets ($max - min$). On the other hand, the right side of Fig. 2 depicts the average f-score and the earliness of the framework when given larger spaces to build shapelets (different min and max).

6.1   Discussion

The tests done to predict temperature violations demonstrate that employing more threads can indeed improve the learning time. The graph in the left side of Fig. 2 also shows that this time is directly affected by the maximum and minimum lengths of the shapelets, because big differences between these lengths mean bigger spaces to search for patterns. The experience and the prior knowledge of domain experts should be used to calibrate these lengths and guide the

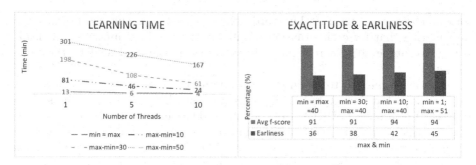

Fig. 2. The results of the experiments

learning phase. Although this is recommended but not required, and the software provides non domain experts the capability to set default values for the maximum and minimum lengths which comes on the expense of slower learning. A particular strength to note is the classification time (at run-time), which is as fast as the events in the window are received. This instantaneous run-time classification is the result of exploiting the processing speed of CEP engines instead of writing ad-hoc classification algorithms.

The experiments also show that the earliness and the accuracy are affected by the values of the maximum and minimum lengths (Fig. 2 right side), as giving the framework more space to search for patterns will eventually help it to detect more useful and smaller shapelets. The autoCEP framework proved to maintain high accuracies regardless of the shapelet lengths but with different earliness percentages.

7   Related Work

Little work exists on the learning of CEP rules, and to the best of our knowledge, only four related approaches [8–11] have suggested to take the path of integrating data mining to this end. However, none of them is capable of dealing with periodic and numeric readings of events or with trends recognition. In addition, all these approaches focus only on the detection of situations of interest, and not on the prediction. So as far as we can tell, this is the only work that is done on: first integrating trend mining techniques with CEP, and second automatically learning **predictive** CEP rules.

Authors in [8] proposed the iCEP framework for the automatic learning of CEP rules. The problem of learning CEP rules in this works is boiled down to the learning of the operators of these rules. Authors followed a flexible modular architecture, where they associated each operator with a module. Therefore in each module, ad-hoc algorithms could be used to learn one specific operator, and build one part of the rule. Although the followed methodology has its strong points regarding the rule expressiveness that it tries to achieve, but the most limiting factor is that it counts on the strict intersection theory that leads to one and only one rule. In other words, the proposals will only work under the assumption that for each situation of interest there is just **one** rule that leads to it. We argue that in real life different rules may indeed lead to the same situation.

Another approach to integrate data mining techniques is proposed in [11]. The authors have suggested an iterative framework (prediction-correction) to address the problem of CEP rules learning. The general idea is to first initiate the rule parameters with some arbitrary values, and then tune them after each iteration depending on human experts' feedback. To give more details, the domain of observed events is divided into time-based intervals. Then at the end of each interval, experts need to highlight the false positives and negatives, so the parameters of the rule could be tuned and used in the next interval. The tuning relies mainly on discrete Kalman filters. First, we noticed that the approach cannot learn the rules completely by itself, but experts need to create templates with placeholders for rules parameters, and then the framework will learn these parameters. Secondly, it is very user centric, and it requires the intervention of experts after each interval or window. Thirdly, the interval is not learned but it needs to be specified by experts, which is not an evident task. In a similar iterative fashion, the approach proposed in [10] helps experts to refine and tune the rules parameters, but it lacks the capability to learn rules completely.

In the work discussed in [9], authors proposed an extension for the hidden Markov models, called noise Hidden Markov Models or nHMM. These extended models could learn sequences of events but they could also discard the noise. More specifically, when a noisy event is received, the Markov model stays on the same state, and does not proceed to the next one. In general the work is more concerned with the exclusion of noisy events rather than learning a complete rule. In addition the approach is demonstrated to work just on sequence patterns, but it cannot take windowing constraints into account.

8   Conclusion and Future Work

The main goal of our work is twofold. First we targeted the problem of automatic CEP rules learning in certain fields, and so sparing domain experts from this tedious task. Second, we tackled the learning of predictive rules and thus adding proactivity to the domain of CEP. Therefore, autoCEP paves the way for non-expert users to easily exploit the predictive capabilities of CEP engines, and it allows for a seamless integration within BPMSs.

We introduced a novel two-phase framework that efficiently tackles the automatic learning of CEP rules. It is well suited to work in application fields where primitive events are observations made periodically over time. The framework exploits the latest advancements in the domain of early classification on time series to learn accurate and predictive rules. Shapelets, which constitute a new primitive in the data mining field are learned at the first phase, and effectively transformed into CEP rules at the second one.

In the near future, we project to adopt our algorithms to favor multivariate time series, and thus support the processing of simultaneous events and the prediction using multidimensional temporal patterns.

References

1. Baumgrass, A., Ciccio, D., Claudio, C., Dijkman, R., Hewelt, M., Mendling, J.J., Meyer, A.A., Pourmirza, S.S., Weske, M.M., Wong, T.: GET controller and UNI-CORN: event-driven process execution and monitoring in logistics. In: CEUR Workshop Proceedings (2015)
2. Cabanillas, C., Baumgrass, A., Mendling, J., Rogetzer, P., Bellovoda, B.: Towards the enhancement of business process monitoring for complex logistics chains. In: Lohmann, N., Song, M., Wohed, P. (eds.) BPM 2013 Workshops. LNBIP, vol. 171, pp. 305–317. Springer, Heidelberg (2014)
3. Cabanillas, C., Di Ciccio, C., Mendling, J., Baumgrass, A.: Predictive task monitoring for business processes. In: Sadiq, S., Soffer, P., Völzer, H. (eds.) BPM 2014. LNCS, vol. 8659, pp. 424–432. Springer, Heidelberg (2014)
4. Ghalwash, M.F., Obradovic, Z.: Early classification of multivariate temporal observations by extraction of interpretable shapelets. BMC Bioinf. **13**(1), 1 (2012)
5. Herzberg, N., Meyer, A.: Improving process monitoring and progress prediction with data state transition events. In: ZEUS, pp. 20–23 (2013)
6. Lin, Y.-F., Chen, H.-H., Tseng, V.S., Pei, J.: Reliable early classification on multivariate time series with numerical and categorical attributes. In: Cao, T., Lim, E.-P., Zhou, Z.-H., Ho, T.-B., Cheung, D., Motoda, H. (eds.) PAKDD 2015. LNCS, vol. 9077, pp. 199–211. Springer, Heidelberg (2015)
7. Maggi, F.M., Di Francescomarino, C., Dumas, M., Ghidini, C.: Predictive monitoring of business processes. In: Jarke, M., Mylopoulos, J., Quix, C., Rolland, C., Manolopoulos, Y., Mouratidis, H., Horkoff, J. (eds.) CAiSE 2014. LNCS, vol. 8484, pp. 457–472. Springer, Heidelberg (2014)
8. Margara, A., Cugola, G., Tamburrelli, G.: Learning from the past: automated rule generation for complex event processing. In: Proceedings of the 8th ACM International Conference on Distributed Event-Based Systems, pp. 47–58. ACM (2014)
9. Mutschler, C., Philippsen, M.: Learning event detection rules with noise hidden Markov models. In: 2012 NASA/ESA Conference on Adaptive Hardware and Systems (AHS), pp. 159–166. IEEE (2012)
10. Sen, S., Stojanovic, N., Stojanovic, L.: An approach for iterative event pattern recommendation. In: Proceedings of the Fourth ACM International Conference on Distributed Event-Based Systems, pp. 196–205. ACM (2010)
11. Turchin, Y., Gal, A., Wasserkrug, S.: Tuning complex event processing rules using the prediction-correction paradigm. In: Proceedings of the Third ACM International Conference on Distributed Event-Based Systems, p. 10. ACM (2009)
12. Xing, Z., Pei, J., Dong, G., Philip, S.Y.: Mining sequence classifiers for early prediction. In: SDM, pp. 644–655. SIAM (2008)
13. Xing, Z., Pei, J., Philip, S.Y., Wang, K.: Extracting interpretable features for early classification on time series. In: SDM, vol. 11, pp. 247–258. SIAM (2011)
14. Ye, L., Keogh, E.: Time series shapelets: a new primitive for data mining. In: Proceedings of the 15th ACM SIGKDD International Conference on Knowledge Discovery and Data Mining, pp. 947–956. ACM (2009)

Service Economy (Short Papers)

An Optimal and Iterative Pricing Model for Multiclass IaaS Cloud Services

Shuo Zhang[1], Li Pan[1(✉)], Shijun Liu[1(✉)], Lei Wu[1], Lizhen Cui[1], and Dong Yuan[2]

[1] School of Computer Science and Technology, Shandong University,
Jinan 250101, China
zs_sduzz@sina.com, {panli,lsj,i_lily,clz}@sdu.edu.cn
[2] School of Electrical and Information Engineering,
The University of Sydney, Sydney, Australia
dong.yuan@sydney.edu.au

Abstract. In this paper, we investigate optimal pricing models for profit maximization from the perspective of cloud providers in the presence of multiple classes of IaaS (Infrastructure as a Service) services. We propose an iterative model in which a cloud provider iteratively posts updated prices for the multiple classes of IaaS instances to users until reaching convergence that maximizes its profit. During this process, any interested user can determine the optimal class of IaaS instances and the optimal quantity to buy according to its own private utility function. In particular, we propose two algorithms to implement the iterative pricing process: a Genetic based near-optimal algorithm, and a hill climbing based cost-effective algorithm. The experimental results show that our iterative pricing algorithms can achieve advanced profitability in pricing multiclass IaaS instances in cloud environments.

Keywords: Pricing · IaaS · Cloud computing · Profit maximization

1 Introduction

Cloud computing delivers a new promising paradigm through which users can gain on-demand access to cloud services on a pay-per-use way [1]. Infrastructure as a Service (IaaS) is such a form of cloud computing service, by which cloud providers deliver computing resources in the form of Virtual Machines (VMs) over the Internet to end users. The cloud providers, who maintain pools of massive computing resources (e.g., computation, network, and storage), can gain profits from users' payment through economy of scale [2]. And generally a cloud provider supplies multiple classes of IaaS instances for fulfilling divergent users' requirements. In this situation, efficient pricing mechanisms become necessary for cloud providers to price their services optimally to obtain higher profit.

However, it is a challenging task for a cloud provider to price their multiple classes of services in an optimal way, which is mainly because of two reasons.

Q.Z. Sheng et al. (Eds.): ICSOC 2016, LNCS 9936, pp. 597–605, 2016.
DOI: 10.1007/978-3-319-46295-0_39

First, the users' preferences are unknown. In the perspective of a cloud provider, which class of IaaS instance and how many instances a user will choose to buy is unknown. The total profit a provider can gain is partially determined by users' choices. Second, the balance of demand and supply needs to be regulated by prices. Given the fixed total capacity of physical resources maintained by a cloud provider, the total requests from users may exceed the maximum capacity of the cloud if the price falls below a certain level. Conversely, if the price is too high, some resources will be idle. Thus, the price should be properly set.

In this paper, we propose two algorithms to solve the optimal pricing problem in cloud computing environments, where a cloud provider supplies multiple classes of instances with varying configurations. One of these two algorithms is an iterative algorithm based on the idea of Genetic Algorithm (GA). The pricing model based on this algorithm has superior profitability, but also has an obvious weakness, i.e., if the algorithm cannot converge very quickly, the cost of data communication will be high. Thus we propose another cost-effective pricing algorithm which is based on the idea of hill climbing. Although the profitability of this algorithm is a little lower than the Genetic based algorithm, the cost of data communication is nearly negligible. Based on the two proposed algorithms, a cloud provider can optimally pricing its multiple classes of IaaS instances according to current conditions in a public cloud service marketplace.

The rest of this paper is organized as follows. In Sect. 2 we discuss the related work. Section 3 gives an overview of the system model. Section 4 states the problem and its formulation. Section 5 presents our proposed two algorithms for the optimal IaaS pricing problem. Section 6 outlines the experimental results and Sect. 7 gives conclusion and future directions for this work.

2   Related Work

Pricing and bidding strategies about cloud services on Internet have been extensively investigated. Major research directions are as follows.

Profit-Optimization Pricing Strategy. There are pricing strategies studied in the perspective of profit or social welfare optimization [3]. Two solutions have been proposed to determine optimal policies for pricing cloud bandwidth reservations in public clouds [4], aiming at maximizing the total profit made by all the tenants and the cloud provider under the presence of demand uncertainty.

Cost-Saving Bidding and Auction. Auction-based resource trading is already adopted by cloud platforms such as Amazon EC2 [5]. But what prices should users bid is far from trivial. A nonlinear optimization problem is solved to minimize the cost of users in biding resources [6]. Besides, different pricing models may cause varying cost to users. Poola et al. [7] propose that users can reduce their costs by using spot instances rather than on-demand ones.

Compared with these works, the primary contribution of our work lies in that we address the optimal pricing problem from the perspective of cloud providers in the presence of multiple classes of IaaS instances, and our work can be used as a complementary mechanism to current pricing models used in public clouds.

3   The Cloud Platform

We consider a cloud computing platform with a pay-per-use model, in which there are a group of users who buy the IaaS cloud services in the form of VMs to run their jobs. As the same with other public cloud platforms such as Amazon EC2, there are multiple classes of VM instances with different physical resource configurations (e.g., c4.2xlarge, c4.4xlarge and c4.8xlarge). Generally, the price of a higher-performance VM instance is more expensive than a lower one. When purchasing IaaS instances from the cloud platform, an end user can choose an instance type (e.g., c4.2xlarge), platform (e.g., Unix or Windows) and so on.

Here we only consider the situation where each user is job-oriented, which means each user has a job that needs to be finished in time. We denote the number of users currently in the cloud platform as N and the number of types of VMs supported by the cloud platform as U. To keep the discussion simple, we assume that each user has a single job to run in the cloud platform.

A cloud provider usually owns a fixed number of physical machines on which it can host the IaaS instances required by users, and running these machines would incur cost. Since different classes of IaaS instances have divergent configurations and running cost, they may bring varying profitability. Thus, based on the up-to-date market situation, the provider needs to dynamically determine the prices of multiple classes of IaaS instances to maximize its own profit. From now on, in this paper we use the vector $\boldsymbol{p} = \{p_1, ..., p_U\}$ to denote a price setting for the U classes of IaaS instances supplied by the cloud provider.

4   Problem Statement

In this section, we first describe the user's model used in this paper, and then formulate the pricing problem of multiclass IaaS instances for a cloud provider.

4.1   User Model

As stated above, an end user can choose its favorite IaaS class to run its job. Here we assume each user is self-motivated and utility pursuing, thus it will choose an optimal class and quantity to maximize its own utility. The utility of a user can be calculated as the difference between the revenue obtained by completing a job and the cost for buying VMs to run the job. Currently we only consider batch type jobs, for which *response time*, i.e., job execution time, is a main QoS consideration. For a user i, its utility function is represented as:

$$f_i(T_u) - cost_u \tag{1}$$

Here T_u is the response time of the job submitted by user i if he chooses to use instance type u ($u \in \{1, 2, \cdots, U\}$), and $f_i(T_u)$ indicates user i's utility from using instance type u. As generally assumed, the function f_i is a differentiable and decreasing function of T. In fact many functions can satisfy this property and users can choose any utility functions which can represent their own preference. When the prices of U classes of instances are presented to users, the optimal VM class u^* for user i can be solved by:

$$u^* = \arg\max_{u \in U}(f_i(T_u) - cost_u) \tag{2}$$

where T_u can be estimated by sampling and prediction methods such as task-level benchmarking or regression [8], and $cost_u$ is the payoff to the provider.

4.2 The Pricing Problem

Apparently, a user's choice as well its final payment on buying IaaS instances is influenced by current price settings. From the perspective of the cloud provider, given a fixed group of users, the provider's profit for operating the cloud is the difference between the users' payment and the cost for running the cloud. A provider needs to find an optimal pricing setting properly to maximize its profit. While to calculate precisely its cost for running the cloud is a complicated problem, which is beyond the discussion of this paper, here we assume each type of VM instance has a fixed unit cost K_u. And this value can be estimated by cloud provider from the long-running history of operating the cloud. Given these concerns, the objective of a cloud provider to optimize its total profit can be formulated as:

Maximize

$$\sum_{u=1}^{U} p_u(t) \sum_{i=1}^{N} x_{iu} y_{iu} T_{iu} - \sum_{u=1}^{U} K_u \sum_{i=1}^{N} x_{iu} y_{iu} T_{iu} \tag{3}$$

Subject to

$$\forall y_{iu} \in \{0, 1\}.$$

Here, $p_u(t)$ denotes the price for the class of VM_u instances set by the cloud provider and the value of y_{iu} denotes whether the user i chooses the class of VM_u or not under current price settings. The term $y_{iu} = 1$ means user i chooses VM_u and x_{iu} is the quantity of VM_u it demands. The term T_{iu} denotes the time duration from the time type u instances are launched by user i until they are terminated, i.e., the execution time of its job.

But the main problem is that a cloud provider doesn't know the profit function of each user and thus it cannot obtain the optimal prices by this way. Since jobs are submitted online and the users' decisions are influenced by current price settings, in this paper we propose an iterative pricing model. In this model, the cloud provider periodically updates the price settings with the aim of improving its profit, according the feedbacks returned by the users in last pricing round, as shown in Fig. 1. The feedback from a user is in fact its choice of the class of VMs as well as the quantity it demands. A new pricing process can be started when the IaaS market conditions have changes, such as there are new job arrivals

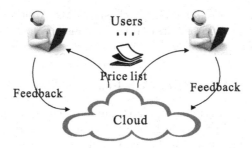

Fig. 1. The interactions between the cloud provider and end users

or more resources are becoming available. The price updating process continues until a convergence is reached. In next section we present two algorithms for implementing the iterative pricing process.

5   Iterative Pricing Algorithms

In this section, we present two algorithms for iteratively updating the prices of multiple classes of VMs to improve a cloud provider's profit.

5.1   Genetic Based Iterative Pricing Algorithm

In this subsection, we introduce a Genetic based algorithm (GAIP for short) which can obtain the near-optimal pricing strategies in acceptable iterations. The basic idea of our proposed Genetic based iterative pricing algorithm is to start an evolutionary process as a cloud provider begins to update its IaaS prices, use the best solution in current evolutionary generation as the pricing strategy in current pricing round, and evolve a new generation when the next pricing round begins, until a convergence is reached.

To apply the genetic evolution process, a specific setting of prices for all the U classes of VMs, i.e., $\boldsymbol{p} = \{p_1, ..., p_U\}$, is encoded into a chromosome. The length of a chromosome is equal to the number of VM classes and the uth gene represents the price for class VM_u. During each generation, we use the objective function (3) to calculate the fitness value of a chromosome. But a remaining question is, for a specific chromosome in current generation, without knowing each user's profit function, how a cloud provider can know the user's choices on that price settings encoded in a chromosome to calculate its fitness value. To deal with this problem, in our algorithm the cloud provider collects users' choices by sending the price settings in all the candidate chromosomes in current population to users, and then calculates each candidate chromosome's fitness value based on users' feedbacks, according to function (3).

The evolutionary process stops when the fitness value of the best solution so far is not changing any more for a number of generations. This means the optimal pricing strategy is reached and the price settings keeps stable at this point, as well as the user's choices in purchasing VMs. Another stopping criteria, which defines the maximum iteration rounds, is also used to prevent the pricing algorithm from running infinitely.

5.2 Hill Climbing Based Iterative Pricing Algorithm

Although the above Genetic based algorithm can achieve superior profitability, it has an obvious weakness, which is, if it cannot converge very quickly, the cost of data communication will be high. This is because in every generation a cloud provider needs to generate a population of prices and ask each user to give feedback on them. Thus we present another cost-effective algorithm which is based on the idea of hill climbing (HCIP for short).

Algorithm 1. Hill Climbing based Pricing Algorithm

Input:

Initial price of all types of instances $VM_u(u \in \{1, 2, \cdots, U\})$, P_u;

Initial step size, $step$; And the increase factor of iterative step, $basicStep$;

Output:

The approximate optimal price $Aopvalue_u$;

$oldFit \leftarrow Objective\ function\ value\ under\ P_u; newFit \leftarrow oldFit + 1$

while $newFit \geq oldFit$ **do**

    $P_u \leftarrow P_u + step$

    $newFit \leftarrow Objective\ function\ value\ under\ the\ all\ price\ P_u$

    if $newFit \geq oldFit$ **and** $newFit - oldFit \geq 1$ **then**

        $step \leftarrow step + basicStep * (newFit - oldFit)$

        $oldFit \leftarrow newFit$

    else

        $step \leftarrow step + basicStep$

    end if

end while

$basicFit \leftarrow Objective\ function\ value\ under\ the\ all\ price\ P_u$

for $i = 1 \rightarrow MaxIterativeTimes$ **do**

    $index \leftarrow i \mod u + 1$

    $TemP_{index} \leftarrow TemP_{index} + increaseFactor$

    $nowFit \leftarrow Objective\ function\ value\ under\ the\ all\ price\ TemP_u$

    if $nowFit \geq basicFit$ **then**

        $P_{index} \leftarrow TemP_u$

        $basicFit \leftarrow nowFit$

    end if

    if *The basicFit remain unchanged for successive U times of iterations* **then**

        break

    end if

end for

$Aopvalue_u \leftarrow p_u$

In HCIP, in every iteration, only one set of prices is generated and the objective value of this price setting is calculated according to (3), based on users' feedbacks. During the price updating process, at the beginning, for every class of VM instances, we use the half of the historical price upper bound as its initial price. Without loss of generality, the price of a VM class with a higher configuration, which has the a higher computing capability, is always higher than a VM class with a lower configuration. Thus we use different updating step sizes to raise their prices. And the iterative step size increases with the growing rate of objective function value proportionally.

When the fitness value stops increasing, a smaller adjustment will be adopted instead of using the previous iterative step. The iterative price updating process stops until the objective function value does not grow any more. That means the pricing updating process reaches convergence, and the price settings as well as users' choices on VM will remain stable. Algorithm 1 details the procedure of the hill climbing based iterative pricing process described above.

6   Experimental Results

In this section, the performance evaluation of the proposed two iterative pricing algorithms is presented. We have conducted extensive simulation experiments based on synthetic datasets to examine the performance of our algorithms. We use simulation approach because it enables us to perform repeatable experiments, and the cost incurred by performing experiments on real cloud infrastructure would be extremely high. We compare the profitability of different pricing models under the identical trading market conditions.

We take the number of vCPUs of different VMs as the main configuration parameter, referring to Amazon EC2. Without loss of generality, the proportion of computing capability between different classes of instances is not strictly equal to the ratio of VM configuration.

We consider each submitted job is a batch type job whose execution time on a standard VM follows a exponential distribution where λ (the parameter of exponential distribution) is 15 h. This value is generated according to the historical data from our real-world cloud computing platform. The number of users is 100. We have done simulations with different number of classes of VMs to evaluate the two algorithm's profitability. In order to avoid bias results due to randomness, we repeat these simulations many times.

From these simulations, we find that the average profit made by the HCIP is only less than the Genetic based algorithm by 6 %. As an example, Table 1 shows the comparison of profitability of these two proposed algorithms under two selected group of simulations: the first has four classes of instances, and the second has eight types of instances. Besides, the simulation results indicate that the difference of profitability between these two algorithms is still not enlarged with the expansion of the user's group scale. As we have discussed in Sect. 5.2, the Genetic based algorithm needs much more data communication than HCIP and the data communication cost for them is not in a same order of magnitude.

Table 1. Comparison between two proposed algorithms under different circumstances

Simulation no.	4 Types of instances (cents)		8 Types of instances (cents)	
	GAIP	HCIP	GAIP	HCIP
1	816.30	799.34	4596.14	4211.75
2	1545.08	1452.85	3409.20	3277.04
3	1242.99	1162.89	3741.77	3632.34

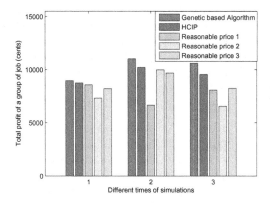

Fig. 2. The profit obtained by different pricing strategies

Thus we can conclude that the HCIP is more cost-effective, but not sacrificing too much profit compared with the Genetic based pricing algorithm.

Then, we compare the profitability of these two algorithms with other three fixed-pricing schemes, in which the prices of different VM classes are proportionally distributed to their hardware configurations. We obtain these prices based on the VM prices in real-world cloud platform such as Amazon EC2. Figure 2 shows the total profit of different pricing strategies, and the profitability of the two proposed algorithms is better than others. The average profit of our two algorithms is higher than the average of the other three by 21 % and 15 %, respectively.

7   Conclusions and Future Work

This paper proposes an iterative pricing model to solve the problem of pricing multiple classes of VMs optimally from the perspective of cloud providers. Due to lack of centralized controller and privacy conservation of users, cloud providers can only price their IaaS instances based on the feedback from users and iteratively update the price settings. In particular, we propose two algorithms to implement the iterative pricing process: one is Genetic based, which can achieve near-optimal pricing strategies, and the other one is based on the idea of hill climbing, which is more cost-effective. Through extensive experiments and simulations, we show that the proposed two pricing algorithms can achieve advanced profitability in pricing multiple classes of IaaS instances in cloud environments.

For the future, we plan to combine our pricing model with the Lyapunov stability theory to guarantee the stability of the cloud system and analyze how an optimal pricing strategy can be developed in that condition.

Acknowledgments. The authors would like to acknowledge the support provided by the National Natural Science Foundation of China (61402263, 91546203), the National High Technology Research and Development Program of China (2014AA01A302), the special funds of Taishan scholar construction project, the Independent Innovation Projects of Shandong Province (2014ZZCX08102, 2014ZZCX03409,2014CGZH1106), the Natural Science Foundation of Shandong Province (ZR2014FQ03), and the Science & Technology Development Projects of Shandong Province (2014GGX101028, 2014GGH201007).

References

1. Armbrust, M., Fox, A., Griffith, R., Joseph, A.D., Katz, R., Konwinski, A., Lee, G., Patterson, D., Rabkin, A., Stoica, I., Zaharia, M.: A view of cloud computing. Commun. ACM **53**, 50–58 (2010)
2. Buyya, R., Yeo, C.S., Venugopal, S.: Market-oriented cloud computing: vision, hype, and reality for delivering IT services as computing utilities. In: 10th IEEE International Conference on High Performance Computing and Communications, pp. 5–13. IEEE Press, Piscataway (2012)
3. Menache, I., Ozdaglar, A., Shimkin, N.: Socially optimal pricing of cloud computing resources. In: 5th International ICST Conference on Performance Evaluation Methodologies and Tools, pp. 322–331. ICST, United Kingdom (2011)
4. Niu, D., Feng, C., Li, B.: Pricing cloud bandwidth reservations under demand uncertainty. In: 12th Joint International Conference on Measurement and Modeling of Computer Systems, pp. 151–162. ACM Press, New York (2012)
5. Amazon Web Services. https://aws.amazon.com/
6. Zheng, L., Joe-Wong, C., Tan, C.W., Chiang, M., Wang, X.: How to bid the cloud. In: ACM Conference on Special Interest Group on Data Communication 2015, pp. 71–84. ACM Press, United States (2015)
7. Yi, S., Andrzejak, A., Kondo, D.: Monetary cost-aware checkpointing and migration on amazon cloud spot instances. IEEE Trans. Serv. Comput. **5**, 512–524 (2012)
8. Garg, S.K., Toosi, A.N., Gopalaiyengar, S.K., Buyya, R.: SLA-based virtual machine management for heterogeneous workloads in a cloud datacenter. J. Netw. Comput. Appl. **4**, 108–120 (2014)

A Study of the Energy Consumption of Databases and Cloud Patterns

Béchir Bani[✉], Foutse Khomh, and Yann-Gaël Guéhéneuc

SWAT Lab - Ptidej Team, Polytechnique Montréal, Montreal, QC, Canada
{bechir.bani,foutse.khomh,yann-gael.gueheneuc}@polymtl.ca

Abstract. Nowadays databases have become the backbone of cloud-based applications. Cloud-based applications are used in about every industry today. Despite their popularity and wide adoption, little is still known about the energy footprint of these applications and, in particular, of their databases. Yet, reducing the energy consumption of applications is a major objective for society and will continue to be so in the near to far future. In this paper, we study the energy consumption of three databases used by cloud-based applications: MySQL, PostgreSQL, and MongoDB, through a series of experiments with three cloud-based applications (a RESTful multi-threaded application, DVD Store, and JPetStore). We also study the impact of cloud patterns on the energy consumption because databases in cloud-based applications are often implemented in conjunction with patterns. We measure the energy consumption using the Power-API tool to keep track of the energy consumed at the process-level by the variants of the cloud-based applications. We report that the choice of the databases can reduce the energy consumption of a cloud-based application regardless of the cloud patterns that are implemented.

Keywords: Energy consumption · Relational databases · NoSQL databases · Performance · Sharding · Priority Message Queue

1 Introduction

With the continuous development of the Internet and cloud computing, companies use databases to store and perform analyses on large data-sets in cloud environments. These companies demand high performance databases when reading and writing data. In addition, they want to benefit from best practices encoded in the form of cloud patterns [6], which are general and reusable "good" solutions to recurring design problems for cloud-based applications. Design patterns have been applied to all fields of software engineering, including cloud computing. These patterns were refined to take into account the specificities and requirements of the cloud. To the best of our knowledge, none of previous works, that have benchmarked cloud applications [5], investigated the combined impact of databases and cloud patterns on the energy consumption of cloud-based applications. Consequently the benefits and trade-offs of different databases and combinations of cloud patterns are mostly intuitive and not validated. In this paper,

© Springer International Publishing Switzerland 2016
Q.Z. Sheng et al. (Eds.): ICSOC 2016, LNCS 9936, pp. 606–614, 2016.
DOI: 10.1007/978-3-319-46295-0_40

we evaluate the impact on energy consumption of three cloud patterns: Local Database Proxy, Local Sharding-Based Router, and Priority Message Queue, with three databases: two relational databases, PostgreSQL and MySQL, and one NoSQL database, MongoDB. To achieve this goal, we use three versions of three cloud-based applications (a RESTful multi-threaded application, DVD Store, and jPETStore) that use respectively MySQL, PostgreSQL, and MongoDB databases. We also implement the three studied patterns in each version of these applications. We choose these databases because they are the most popular relational databases in the last few years [2,4]. We measure energy consumption using the Power-API [3], which estimates the energy consumed by an application at the process-level. Our results show that MySQL database is the least energy consuming among the three databases and PostgreSQL is the most energy consuming among them. MongoDB consumes more energy than MySQL but less than PostgreSQL. We also show that various combinations of patterns impact energy consumption. The rest of the paper is structured as follows. Section 2 provides the most closely related works to our study. Section 3 presents the cloud-based applications used by our study and the design of our experiments. Section 4 discusses the results of our experiments. Section 5 discusses our results and possible threats to their validity. Section 6 concludes with some future works.

2   Related Work

The most closely related work to ours is by Abtahizadeh et al. [1]. They conducted an empirical study that aimed to compare the energy efficiency of the same three cloud patterns performed in our study. However, they only considered MySQL database in their work. Their results show that cloud patterns can reduce the energy consumption of a cloud-based application but only in some specific cases. In the same direction, Manotas et al. [7] conducted an empirical study in which they investigated the impact of four web servers on the energy consumption of a web application. They showed that the energy consumption of a web application depends on the web server used to handle requests, where each web server can increase or decrease the energy consumption of the web application, depending on the features for which it is executed. Sahin et al. [8] investigated the energy efficiency of 15 structural, behavioral and creational design patterns, implemented in an application. For each pattern, they examined the energy consumption of the versions of the application before and after applying design pattern. Their results show that design patterns have a significant impact on energy consumption, where certain design patterns like `Decorator` can increase the energy usage of an application by up to 700 %.

3   Study Design

In this section, we introduce our research questions, describe the objects and the design of our study, and analysis method. Our research questions are:

- **RQ1**: Does the choice of MySQL, PostgreSQL and MongoDB Databases affect the energy consumption of cloud applications (when no cloud patterns are implemented)?
- **RQ2**: Does the implementation of Local Database Proxy, Local Sharding Based Router or Priority Message Queue patterns affect the energy consumption of cloud applications using MySQL, PostgreSQL and MongoDB Databases?
- **RQ3**: Do the interactions between Local Database Proxy, Local Sharding Based Router and Priority Message Queue patterns affect the energy consumption of cloud applications using MySQL, PostgreSQL and MongoDB Databases?

3.1 Objects and Design

In our experiments, we use a combination of databases and cloud patterns encoded using a letter and a number. The Local Database Proxy pattern has three implementation strategies: Random Allocation (P1), Round-Robin (P2), and Custom Load Balancing (P3). The Local Sharding Based Router pattern also has three strategies: Modulo Algorithm (P4), Consistent Hashing (P5), and Lookup Algorithm (P6). The Priority Message Queue pattern is called P7. The databases are named: MySQL (D1), PostgreSQL (D2), and MongoDB (D3). We performed each experiment on three different systems, because one system could be intrinsically more complex to understand. We deployed them on 10 virtual machines (2 master nodes and 8 slaves nodes) in a private cloud. At first, for Experiment 1, we implement and deploy a multi-threaded distributed application that communicates through REST calls. The application interacts with one of the three chosen databases. *Sakila sample database* is used as it contains a large number of records, making it interesting for experiments. We adapted The schema of the *Sakila database* to PostgreSQL and MongoDB databases. For Experiment 2 and 3, we use DVDStore and JPetStore systems. DVDStore[1] is provided with the implementation of MySQL and PostgreSQL databases. We refactor the code of DVD Store to allow it to connect with a MongoDB database. Similarly, we also modified the code of JPetStore[2] to implement connections to MySQL, PostgreSQL and MongoDB databases. We perform our experiments using different numbers of clients, which are simulated using a multi-threaded architecture. The number of clients simulated varies from 100 to 1500 clients. Each execution is done using different databases and different cloud patterns.

3.2 Independent and Dependent Variables

MySQL, PostgreSQL and MongoDB databases are the independent variables of our study. Also, the three studied cloud patterns, as well as the strategies of these patterns are considered as independent variables. The application response time (measured in *milliseconds*) and the energy consumption measured by Power-API (measured in joules) are considered as dependent variables.

---

[1] http://linux.dell.com/dvdstore/.

[2] https://github.com/mybatis/jpetstore-6.

3.3   Hypotheses

To answer our research questions, we formulate the following null hypotheses, where P0 is the experiment consisting in comparing the energy consumption and response time of the three versions of each application using respectively MySQL, PostgreSQL, and MongoDB databases. Px ($x \in \{1 ... 6\}$), and P7 are the different patterns. In each experiment we compare two versions of a same application implementing two different databases Dy, Dz ($y, z \in \{1, 2, 3\}$ and $y \neq z$), with the same (combination) of patterns.

- H^1_{0yz}: There is no difference between the average amount of energy consumed by applications implementing databases D_y and D_z (without any cloud pattern).
- H^1_{xyz}: There is no difference between the average amount of energy consumed by applications implementing databases D_y and D_z in conjunction with patterns Px.
- H^1_{xyz7}: There is no difference between the average amount of energy consumed by applications implementing databases D_y and D_z in conjunction with the combination of patterns Px and P7.

To have more clear comprehension regarding the trade-offs between the energy consumption and the performance of a cloud-based application measured in terms of response time, we also formulate the following null hypotheses:

- H^2_{0yz}: There is no difference between the average response time of databases D_y and D_z by applying the design P0.
- H^2_{xyz}: There is no difference between the average response time of databases D_y and D_z by applying the design Px.
- H^2_{xyz7}: There is no difference between the average response time of databases D_y and D_z by applying the combination of designs Px and P7.

3.4   Analysis Method

To analyze our collected data (i.e., response time and energy consumption measurements), we performed the Mann-Whitney U test [9] to test the aforementioned hypotheses. Mann-Whitney U test is a non-parametric statistical test where its relevance is reflected in the assessment of two independent distributions. We also computed the Cliff's δ effect size because effect sizes are very important to understand the magnitude of the difference between 2 distributions.

4   Study Results

This section presents and discusses the results of our research questions.

4.1   Results and Answers to RQ1

Tables 1 and 2 summarizes the results of Mann-Whitney U test and Cliff's δ effect sizes for the energy consumption and the response time.

Table 1. Energy consumption p-value and Cliff's δ

Pattern	MySQL	PostgreSQL	p-value	Cliff's δ	MySQL	MongoDB	p-value	Cliff's δ	PostgreSQL	MongoDB	p-value	Cliff's δ
P0	262.5	568.2	0.01	medium	262.5	354.7	0.24	small	568.2	354.7	0.09	small
P1	490.2	1391.1	$< 10e-6$	large	490.2	890.0	$< 10e-6$	large	1391.1	890.0	0.09	small
P2	495.2	1529.9	$< 10e-6$	large	495.2	915.9	$< 10e-6$	large	1529.9	915.9	0.04	medium
P3	495.0	1476.5	$< 10e-6$	large	495.0	904.5	$< 10e-6$	large	1476.5	904.5	0.04	medium
P4	1331.9	6330.2	$< 10e-6$	large	1331.9	5826.4	$< 10e-6$	large	6330.2	5826.4	0.23	small
P5	611.6	4245.1	$< 10e-6$	large	611.6	3821.8	$< 10e-6$	large	4245.1	3821.8	0.23	small
P6	824.1	4929.4	$< 10e-6$	large	824.1	4194.4	$< 10e-6$	large	4929.4	4194.4	0.23	small
P1+P7	442.7	1379.8	$< 10e-6$	large	442.7	814.3	$< 10e-6$	large	1379.8	814.3	0.03	medium
P2+P7	468.8	1482.5	$< 10e-6$	large	468.8	891.9	$< 10e-6$	large	1482.5	891.9	0.03	medium
P3+P7	490.2	1391.1	$< 10e-6$	large	490.2	890.0	$< 10e-6$	large	1391.1	890.0	0.09	small
P4+P7	1255.5	5777.4	$< 10e-6$	large	1255.5	5622.9	$< 10e-6$	large	5777.4	5622.9	0.82	negligible
P5+P7	492.2	3884.5	$< 10e-6$	large	492.2	3386.6	$< 10e-6$	large	3884.5	3386.6	0.23	small
P6+P7	775.9	4526.8	$< 10e-6$	large	775.9	4127.4	$< 10e-6$	large	4526.8	4127.4	0.23	small

Table 2. Response time p-value and Cliff's δ

Pattern	MySQL	PostgreSQL	p-value	Cliff's δ	MySQL	MongoDB	p-value	Cliff's δ	PostgreSQL	MongoDB	p-value	Cliff's δ
P0	262.5	568.2	0.01	medium	262.5	354.7	0.24	small	568.2	354.7	0.09	small
P1	490.2	1391.1	$< 10e-6$	large	490.2	890.0	$< 10e-6$	large	1391.1	890.0	0.09	small
P2	495.2	1529.9	$< 10e-6$	large	495.2	915.9	$< 10e-6$	large	1529.9	915.9	0.04	medium
P3	495.0	1476.5	$< 10e-6$	large	495.0	904.5	$< 10e-6$	large	1476.5	904.5	0.04	medium
P4	1331.9	6330.2	$< 10e-6$	large	1331.9	5826.4	$< 10e-6$	large	6330.2	5826.4	0.23	small
P5	611.6	4245.1	$< 10e-6$	large	611.6	3821.8	$< 10e-6$	large	4245.1	3821.8	0.23	small
P6	824.1	4929.4	$< 10e-6$	large	824.1	4194.4	$< 10e-6$	large	4929.4	4194.4	0.23	small
P1+P7	442.7	1379.8	$< 10e-6$	large	442.7	814.3	$< 10e-6$	large	1379.8	814.3	0.03	medium
P2+P7	468.8	1482.5	$< 10e-6$	large	468.8	891.9	$< 10e-6$	large	1482.5	891.9	0.03	medium
P3+P7	490.2	1391.1	$< 10e-6$	large	490.2	890.0	$< 10e-6$	large	1391.1	890.0	0.09	small
P4+P7	1255.5	5777.4	$< 10e-6$	large	1255.5	5622.9	$< 10e-6$	large	5777.4	5622.9	0.82	negligible
P5+P7	492.2	3884.5	$< 10e-6$	large	492.2	3386.6	$< 10e-6$	large	3884.5	3386.6	0.23	small
P6+P7	775.9	4526.8	$< 10e-6$	large	775.9	4127.4	$< 10e-6$	large	4526.8	4127.4	0.23	small

Average Amount of Consumed Energy: Results presented in Table 1 show that, without using any pattern (in other words, by applying the design P0), there is a statistically significant difference between the average amount of energy consumed by application using MySQL and application using PostgreSQL. The effect size in this case is medium. Therefore, we reject H_{0yz}^{1} for D_y, D_z ($y = 1$, $z = 2$). However, there is not a statistically significant difference between the average amount of energy consumed by application using MySQL and application using MongoDB. Therefore, we cannot reject H_{0yz}^{1} for D_y, D_z ($y = 1$, $z = 3$). Similarly, there is not a statistically significant difference between the average amount of energy consumed by application using PostgreSQL database and application using MongoDB database. In these two cases the effect size is small. Therefore, we cannot reject H_{0yz}^{1} for D_y, D_z ($y = 2$, $z = 3$).

Average Response Time: Results presented in Table 1 show that, by applying the design P0, there is not a statistically significant difference between the average response time of application using MySQL database and application using PostgreSQL database. Therefore, we cannot reject H_{0yz}^{2} for D_y, D_z ($y = 1$, $z = 2$). However, there is a statistically significant difference between the average response time of application using MySQL database and application using MongoDB database. Similarly, there is a statistically significant difference between the average response time of application using PostgreSQL database and application using MongoDB database. Therefore, we cannot reject H^2_{0yz} for D_y, D_z ((y = 1, z = 3), (y = 2, z = 3)).

4.2 Results and Answers to RQ2

Average Amount of Consumed Energy: These results show that by apply-ing the Local Database Proxy pattern, there is a statistically significant difference between the average amount of energy consumed by application using MySQL database and application using PostgreSQL database. Similarly, also, between application using MySQL and application using MongoDB. Similarly also by application using PostgreSQL database and application using MongoDB data-base (where the effect size is large). But, except for the case where the proxy pattern is implemented using the random strategy, there is not a statistically significant difference between application using PostgreSQL database and appli-cation using MongoDB database. Therefore we reject H^1_{xyz} for P_x, D_y, D_z (x $\in$ {2, 3}, (y = 1, z = 2), (y = 1, z = 3)), but we cannot reject H^1_{xyz} for P_x, D_y, D_z (x = 1, y = 2, z = 3). By applying the Local Sharding Based Router, there is a statistically significant difference between the average amount of energy consumed by application using MySQL database and application using Post-greSQL database. Similarly also between application using MySQL and appli-cation using MongoDB (the effect size is large). But, there is not a significant difference between application using PostgreSQL database and application using MongoDB database. Therefore, we reject H^1_{xyz} for P_x, D_y, D_z (x $\in$ {4, 5, 6}, (y = 1, z = 2), (y = 1, z = 3)), but we cannot reject H^1_{xyz} for P_x, D_y, D_z (x $\in$ {4, 5, 6}, y = 2, z = 3).

Average Response Time: Results show that by applying the Local Database Proxy pattern, there is not a statistically significant difference between the aver-age response time of application using MySQL database and application using PostgreSQL database. Therefore, we cannot reject H^2_{xyz} for P_x, D_y, D_z (x $\in$ {1, 2, 3}, (y = 1, z = 2)). However, there is a statistically significant difference between the average response time of application using MySQL database and application using MongoDB database. Similarly, there is a statistically significant difference between the average response time of application using PostgreSQL database and application using MongoDB database. Therefore, we reject H^2_{xyz} for P_x, D_y, D_z (x $\in$ {1, 2, 3}, (y = 1, z = 3), (y = 2, z = 3)). Further results, by applying the Local Sharding Based Router, there is not a statistically significant difference between the average response time of application using MySQL database and application using PostgreSQL database. Therefore, we cannot reject H^2_{xyz} for P_x, D_y, D_z (x $\in$ {4, 5, 6}, (y = 1, z = 2)). However, there is a statistically significant differ-ence between the average response time of application using MySQL database and application using MongoDB database. Similarly, there is a statistically sig-nificant difference between the average response time of application using Post-greSQL database and application using MongoDB database. Therefore, we reject H^2_{xyz} for P_x, D_y, D_z (x $\in$ {4, 5, 6}, (y = 1, z = 3), (y = 2, z = 3)).

4.3   Results and Answers to RQ3

Average Amount of Consumed Energy: When we combine the Local Data-base Proxy pattern with the priority Message Queue pattern, results show that there is a statistically significant difference between the average amount of energy consumed by application using MySQL database and application using Post-greSQL database. Similarly also between application using MySQL and applica-tion using MongoDB (the effect size is large). The same is true for application using PostgreSQL database and application using MongoDB database (where the effect size is large). However, except applying the combination of the custom strat-egy with the Priority Message Queue pattern, there is not a statistically signifi-cant difference between application using PostgreSQL database and application using MongoDB database. Therefore, we reject H^1_{xyz7} for P_x, D_y, D_z (x $\in$ {1, 2, 3}, (y = 1, z = 2), (y = 1, z = 3)), but we cannot reject H^1_{xyz7} for P_x, D_y, D_z (x = 3, y = 2, z = 3). Also, when we combine the Local Sharding Based Router pattern with the priority Message Queue pattern, results show that there is a sta-tistically significant difference between the average amount of energy consumed by application using MySQL database and application using PostgreSQL data-base. Similarly also between application using MySQL and application using Mon-goDB (the effect size is large). However, there is no a significant difference between application using PostgreSQL database and application using MongoDB data-base. Therefore, we reject H^1_{xyz7} for P_x D_y, D_z (x $\in$ {4, 5, 6}, (y = 1, z = 2), (y = 1, z = 3)), but we cannot reject H^1_{xyz7} for P_x, D_y, D_z (x $\in$ {4, 5, 6}, y = 2, z = 3).

Average Response Time: By applying the Local Database Proxy pattern with the priority Message Queue pattern, there is not a statistically significant differ-ence between the average response time of application using MySQL database and application using PostgreSQL database. Therefore, we cannot reject H^2_{xyz7} for P_x, D_y, D_z (x $\in$ {1, 2, 3}, (y = 1, z = 2)). However, there is a statistically sig-nificant difference between the average response time of application using MySQL database and application using MongoDB database. Similarly, there is a statisti-cally significant difference between the average response time of application using PostgreSQL database and application using MongoDB database. Therefore, we reject H^2_{xyz7} for P_x, D_y, D_z (x $\in$ {1, 2, 3}, (y = 1, z = 3), (y = 2, z = 3)). Besides that, when we combine the Local Sharding Based Router pattern with the pri-ority Message Queue pattern, results show that there is not a statistically signif-icant difference between the average response time of application using MySQL database and application using PostgreSQL database. Therefore, we cannot reject H^2_{xyz7} for P_x, D_y, D_z (x $\in$ {4, 5, 6}, (y = 1, z = 2)). However, there is a statisti-cally significant difference between the average response time of application using MySQL database and application using MongoDB database. The combination of the Lookup strategy and the Priority Message Queue pattern there is not a significant difference. Similarly, there is a statistically significant difference between the average response time of application using PostgreSQL database and application using MongoDB database. The combination of the Lookup strategy and the Priority Message Queue pattern there is not a significant difference.

Therefore, we reject H^2_{xyz7} for P_x, D_y, D_z ($x \in \{4, 5\}$, ($y = 1, z = 3$), ($y = 2, z = 3$)), and we cannot reject H^2_{xyz7} for P_x, D_y, D_z ($x = 6$, ($y = 1, z = 3$), ($y = 2, z = 3$)).

5   Discussions and Threats to Validity

We showed that the implementation of the Local Database Proxy pattern does not impact the behavior of the databases but can significantly improve the energy efficiency of MySQL. Concerning the Local Sharding Based Router pattern, the Modulo strategy has a strong effect on the energy consumption of PostgreSQL and MongoDB databases but a small one for MySQL. Moreover, the Consistent strategy has a strong effect on the energy consumption of PostgreSQL but improves slightly the energy efficiency of MySQL and MongoDB. The Lookup strategy can significantly improve the energy efficiency of PostgreSQL and MongoDB. In addition, we showed that combining Local Database Proxy pattern with the Priority Message Queue pattern has no significant impact neither on the application response time nor on the energy consumed by the application, when it interacts with MySQL. This combination only has a small effect on the energy consumption of PostgreSQL and MongoDB. Interestingly, the implementation of the Local Sharding Based Router pattern with the Priority Message Queue pattern has a strong effect on the response time of the three Databases but without a significant impact on the energy consumption.

Our experiments, as any other experiment, are subject to threats to their validity. We now discuss these threats based on the guidelines provided by Wohlin et al. [10].

Construct validity threats concern the relation between theory and observations. In this study, they could be due to measurement errors. These measurements are subject to variation and perturbations depending of hardware and network. For this reason, we did several experiments, we conducted each experiment five times, and computed average values of these measurements.

Internal validity threats concern our selection of subject systems and analysis methods. Despite of using the three studied databases, the three cloud patterns and the two standard cloud applications, some of our findings may still be specific to our studied application which was designed specifically for the experiments. Future studies should consider using different RDBMS and NoSQL databases, and also other cloud applications implementing the cloud patterns.

External validity threats concern the possibility to generalize our findings. Further validation should be done on different cloud applications and with different relational and NoSQL databases and applying different cloud patterns to these databases can extend our understanding of the impact of databases on the energy consumption of cloud applications.

Reliability validity threats concern the possibility of replicating this study. We attempt to provide all the necessary details to replicate our study.

Finally, the *conclusion validity* threats refer to the relation between the treatment and the outcome. We mainly used non-parametric tests that do not require making assumptions about the distribution of the metrics.

6   Conclusion and Future Work

Nowadays, reducing energy consumption is a challenge for cloud-based applications. We contrasted the performance of various combinations of databases and cloud patterns in terms of energy consumption and response time of the cloud-based applications, with the aim to provide some guidance to software engineers about the usage of databases and cloud patterns for cloud-based applications. We carried on a series of experiments on different versions of a RESTful multi-threaded application implemented with three different databases and three different cloud patterns. We also used two standard cloud applications (DVD Store and JPetStore) because one system could be intrinsically more complex to understand. We showed that MySQL database is the least energy consuming but is the slowest among the three databases. PostgreSQL is the most energy consuming among the three databases, but is faster than MySQL but slower than MongoDB. MongoDB consumes more energy than MySQL but less than PostgreSQL and is the fastest among the three databases. As future work, we plan to examine how a match/mismatch between the selected database and the workload characteristic affects energy efficiency.

References

1. Abtahizadeh, S.A., Khomh, F., et al.: How green are cloud patterns?. In: 2015 IEEE 34th International Performance Computing and Communications Conference (IPCCC), pp. 1–8. IEEE (2015)
2. Aghi, R., Mehta, S., Chauhan, R., Chaudhary, S., Bohra, N.: A comprehensive comparison of SQL and MongoDB databases (2015)
3. Bourdon, A., Noureddine, A., Rouvoy, R., Seinturier, L.: PowerAPI: a software library to monitor the energy consumed at the process level. ERCIM News 2013(92) (2013)
4. Conrad, T.: PostgreSQL vs. MySQL vs. commercial databases: it's all about what you need (2006)
5. Cooper, B.F., Silberstein, A., Tam, E., Ramakrishnan, R., Sears, R.: Benchmarking cloud serving systems with YCSB. In: Proceedings of the 1st ACM symposium on Cloud computing, pp. 143–154. ACM (2010)
6. Fehling, C., Leymann, F., Retter, R., Schumm, D., Schupeck, W.: An architectural pattern language of cloud-based applications. In: Proceedings of the 18th Conference on Pattern Languages of Programs, p. 2. ACM (2011)
7. Manotas, I., Sahin, C., Clause, J., Pollock, L., Winbladh, K.: Investigating the impacts of web servers on web application energy usage. In: 2013 2nd International Workshop on Green and Sustainable Software (GREENS), pp. 16–23. IEEE (2013)
8. Sahin, C., Cayci, F., Gutiérrez, I.L.M., Clause, J., Kiamilev, F., Pollock, L., Winbladh, K.: Initial explorations on design pattern energy usage. In: 2012 First International Workshop on Green and Sustainable Software (GREENS), pp. 55–61. IEEE (2012)
9. Sheskin, D.J.: Handbook of Parametric and Nonparametric Statistical Procedures. CRC Press, Boca Raton (2003)
10. Wohlin, C., Runeson, P., Höst, M., Ohlsson, M.C., Regnell, B., Wesslén, A.: Experimentation in Software Engineering. Springer, Heidelberg (2012)

Service Management (Short Papers)

Data-Dependent QoS-Based Service Selection

Navati Jain[1], Chen Ding[1(✉)], and Xumin Liu[2]

[1] Department of Computer Science, Ryerson University, Toronto, ON, Canada
{navati.jain,cding}@ryerson.ca
[2] Department of Computer Science, Rochester Institute of Technology, Rochester, USA
xl@cs.rit.edu

Abstract. Data analytic applications and services are becoming increasingly important, especially in this age of Big Data. QoS properties such as latency, reliability, response time of such services can vary based on the attributes (e.g., size, number of dimensions, data types) of the dataset being processed. The existing QoS-based web service selection methods are not adequate for ranking this type of services because they do not consider these dataset attributes. In this paper, we have proposed a method to predict the QoS values for data analytic services based on the attributes of the dataset by incorporating a meta-learning approach. We could then rank these services according to the predicted QoS values. Our experiment results prove the effectiveness of this approach and the improvement in service ranking when compared with the traditional service selection approach.

Keywords: Quality of Service (QoS) · Service selection · QoS prediction · Data analytic service · Meta-learning

1 Introduction

Web service selection, especially Quality of Service (QoS) based service selection [1–3], has been an active research area in Service Computing community for over a decade. In this work, we consider a situation where a web service is used to process data, e.g., a data mining service [4]. As we advance into a Big Data era, data mining algorithms and predictive analytics [5] have become more applicable in many business sectors. Many cloud providers have started to offer analytic software as services to their users. In such situations, the traditional web service selection methods would not suffice because they often associate a QoS property of a service with a single value (either claimed by the service provider or averaged on monitored past invocations). However, for data mining or analytic services, values of some QoS properties might vary for different datasets. For instance, a common QoS property – latency, could be affected by the size (number of instances) of the dataset, and a larger dataset usually takes longer to process. Assume a service has been invoked 10 times in the past. The sizes of the datasets involved in the past invocations were around 10K–100K for 7 datasets and around 90M–100M for the other 3. Now there is a new dataset with the size 100M. If we use the average historical latency values of all 10 datasets to estimate the potential new latency, it will not be accurate. But if

© Springer International Publishing Switzerland 2016
Q.Z. Sheng et al. (Eds.): ICSOC 2016, LNCS 9936, pp. 617–625, 2016.
DOI: 10.1007/978-3-319-46295-0_41

we use the historical latency values of 3 bigger datasets which are similar to the current dataset in size to do the estimation, it will be more accurate.

Most of the existing service selection methods do not consider the impact of datasets on the QoS values of a service. Oftentimes, QoS values averaged on all the past invocations are used in the selection process, and QoS values are considered as per service, not per dataset. However, as we can see in the previous example, some QoS values of data analytic services can be highly data-dependent. To address this issue, we propose a QoS-based service selection method which considers the potential impact of the dataset attributes on QoS values to select a service most suitable for the given dataset. We further define two types of data-dependent QoS properties – per-dataset data-dependent QoS properties and per-service data-dependent QoS properties. Per-dataset data-dependent QoS properties such as latency, accuracy may have their values varied for each service on each dataset. Per-service data-dependent QoS properties such as reliability reflect the overall behavior of a service based on its performance on all the datasets.

Since the values of data-dependent QoS properties may vary for each dataset, a good selection approach should be able to estimate the QoS values of each service for the new input dataset. In this paper, we use a meta-learning model [6] to predict QoS values based on historical data observed on similar datasets. In our system, every time a service is invoked on a dataset, the information describing the dataset (its meta-attributes) as well as the QoS values for this dataset are collected through a monitoring system. The collected data, maintaining a log of QoS values that vary for different datasets, can be used as the data repository of our selection system. To rank services for a new dataset, we can first identify the most similar datasets from the existing data repository and then predict data-dependent QoS values. The estimated QoS values are in turn used as input to a QoS-based service selection algorithm for service ranking. This way, a service consumer can make a better decision without having to try all the services.

The rest of the paper is organized as follows. Section 2 describes the related work. Section 3 provides details of the proposed model. Section 4 discusses the experiment design and analyzes the results. Finally, Sect. 5 concludes the paper.

2   Related Work

There have been some research works on predicting QoS values of web services [7, 8]. Most of these works predict QoS values based on user or service similarity. Few of them see that QoS values of a same service could vary for different input data when the service is used to process data. The work in [8] considers the size of the input data, but not other attributes of the dataset, and not in a systematic way.

Algorithm selection in machine learning is a challenging task as it often relies on expensive trial-and-error techniques and specialized knowledge of the analyst. Meta-learning [6] offers a way to select machine learning algorithms by finding out the relationship between characteristics of the problem (e.g., meta-attributes of datasets) and performance of the algorithm. Most of the meta-learning models are proposed for classification algorithms [9], while only a few are for clustering algorithms [10]. The common meta-attributes considered include dataset size, dimension, data types, etc.

3 Data-Dependent QoS-Based Service Selection

In this paper, we take clustering services [11] as our example analytic services because the system [12] we used for the experiment mainly implemented clustering algorithms. With modifications, the selection model can also be applied to other types of services.

3.1 QoS Properties of Web Services

QoS properties usually include metrics such as response time, latency, reliability, availability, security, etc. As discussed previously, some QoS properties may be data-dependent while others may not be. We further categorize the data-dependent ones as per-dataset and per-service data-dependent properties. Among the common QoS properties, we consider accuracy, latency and response time as per-dataset data-dependent property, reliability as per-service data-dependent property, and availability, security as data-independent property. Although theoretically the model can include any QoS properties, in this work, we only include latency, accuracy and reliability in our model. The reason we choose these three is that they have been made available through the monitoring system we have used [12]. Below we give definitions of these 3 properties.

Latency is defined as the execution time of a service. For clustering services, we consider latency as the time to build the clustering model for a given dataset.

Accuracy is used to determine the quality of the clustering results. There are many possible evaluation metrics [10, 11]. Here we use a modified version of the Inaccuracy measure provided by Weka [13] as shown in Eq. 1.

$$Accuracy = 100 - \left(\frac{(N_w + N_u)}{N_I} \times 100 \right) \tag{1}$$

where N_w represents the number of instances incorrectly clustered, N_u is the number of instances not clustered, and N_I represents the total number of instances in a dataset.

Reliability is defined as the proportion of the number of datasets for which the service has successfully processed to the total number of datasets the service has processed as shown in Eq. 2. Here we have accommodated failures due to internal algorithm issues as well as web services being unable to process a certain type of datasets, e.g., a service not being able to handle numeric datasets or handling large dimensions.

$$Reliability = \left(\frac{M_V}{M_D} \times 100 \right) \tag{2}$$

where M_V is the number of datasets the service has successfully processed and M_D is the total number of datasets the service has processed in the past.

3.2   The Proposed Data-Dependent Service Selection Model

Since we assume that we only deal with clustering services, we can skip the functional matching part. To request a service, a user only needs to provide the dataset information and then the system will return a ranked list of services based on how good their predicted QoS values are for the given dataset. At first, a user provides the meta-attribute values $(A_{1s}, A_{2s}, \dots A_{ns})$ of the input dataset D_s (n is the number of meta-attributes). The system then consults the existing repository to identify datasets similar to D_s. The similarity calculation is based on the meta-attributes describing the datasets. The value of per-dataset data-dependent QoS property can be predicted for the candidate services with the help of the past QoS data of these services on the similar datasets. The value of per-service data-dependent QoS property can be computed as an overall value based on the service performance on all the datasets it has processed. Once the QoS values are estimated for all the candidate services for the input dataset, they can be used for ranking these services. The ranked list of services $(S_1, S_2, \dots, S_r)$ is then returned to the user. Suppose the user selects service S_t from this list. The selected service is then invoked. The invocation will be monitored through a monitoring system [12] and the QoS values will be recorded. For every service invocation, the system saves the meta-attribute values of the input dataset. It also saves the corresponding per-dataset data-dependent QoS values. The per-service data-dependent QoS values are updated based on all the datasets this service has processed.

Because we rely on the historical QoS values to make predictions, to make sure we don't have the cold-start problem, we run the system initially with synthetic datasets to record their QoS values. These initial datasets can vary on different meta-attributes (e.g., dataset size, number of dimensions, data type, etc.) so that we can have a diversified starting repository. This repository can be enhanced over time as more datasets are being used. The information recorded in the repository includes the dataset information (i.e., meta-attributes) and QoS values of the invoked services.

In the first step of the selection process, we calculate the similarity between datasets based on their meta-attributes. Since clustering algorithms may have different performance for different datasets, we identify the following meta-attributes for this work: (1) size (i.e., number of instances in a dataset); (2) number of dimensions (i.e., number of attributes); (3) data type (due to the constraints of the data generator used in the experiment, only two types considered here – numeric and nominal); (4) percentage of missing data; (5) data distribution pattern (only two considered here – random and grid). Although there are more meta-attributes defined in the literature [6, 9, 10], these five are the ones whose values are usually known (first three) or can be calculated (last two).

Based on the meta-attributes, we compute the similarity between the input dataset and each dataset available in the repository. From our preliminary results, we found that data distribution pattern and data type have the highest impact on prediction accuracy. Hence, we first compare if both datasets are of the same type i.e., if both are either numeric or nominal, and we also check if the patterns of the clusters are the same.

If the datasets match based on the aforementioned comparisons, we proceed to calculate the distance between each pair of numeric meta-attributes that can be quantified. In our list of meta-attributes, size, number of dimensions and percentage of missing data are the numeric meta-attributes. We use Manhattan distance to calculate the distance and then convert it to a similarity value. The overall similarity is calculated as the weighted sum of similarities on all the numeric meta-attributes as shown in Eq. 3.

$$Sim(D_{Inp}, D_{Rep}) = \sum_{i=1}^{N_A} w_i (1 - \frac{\left| V_{i.Inp} - V_{i.Rep} \right|}{MAX_i - MIN_i}) \tag{3}$$

where D_{Inp} and D_{Rep} represent the input and repository dataset respectively, $V_{i,Inp}$ and $V_{i,Rep}$ are the values of their ith meta-attribute, MAX_i and MIN_i are the maximum and minimum values for the ith meta-attribute among all the datasets, w_i is the weight of the ith meta-attribute, and N_A is the number of numeric meta-attributes. Equal weights are used in the experiment.

In the second step of our selection process, to estimate the per-dataset data-dependent QoS values, we use the QoS values on similar datasets to predict the QoS value on the new dataset. The predicted QoS value for the candidate service S_t on the input dataset D_{Inp} is calculated as shown in Eq. 4.

$$QoS_{S_t, D_{Inp}} = \frac{1}{\sum_{D_{Rep} \in D_Z} Sim(D_{Rep}, D_{Inp})} \sum_{D_{Rep} \in D_Z} Sim(D_{Rep}, D_{Inp}) \times QoS_{S_t, D_{Rep}} \tag{4}$$

where D_Z is the set of similar datasets to the input dataset D_{Inp}, and $QoS_{S_t, D_{Rep}}$ is the QoS value of service S_t on dataset D_{Rep}.

To identify the similar datasets, we define a threshold Th_Sim so that datasets with similarity values greater than this value are considered similar. Through our preliminary investigation, we implement an algorithm to automatically select the proper Th_Sim value. We first identify the highest similarity value from the most similar dataset. The Th_Sim value is then set to the biggest value that is a multiple of 0.05 (an interval value which can be adjusted) and is smaller than the highest similarity value. There is another parameter Th_Fail used in the prediction step, which can assist us in predicting if the service will fail for the input dataset. Failed service will not be ranked and returned to the user. Th_Fail is set to 50 % in the experiment.

After obtaining the predicted or updated QoS values, our final task is to rank the services to help the user select a service which is optimal for the given dataset. We use a utility-based approach to rank the services based on multiple QoS properties. The utility function considers both tendency of a QoS property and user preference on the property. If a QoS property (e.g., reliability) has a positive tendency, it means that a higher value indicates a better performance. If a QoS property (e.g., latency) has a negative tendency, it means that a lower value indicates a better performance. Users can additionally provide a priority value for each QoS property based on their preferences. For instance, a user may need a service that is time sensitive and thus give a higher priority to the latency. Another user may need services that could produce accurate results and thus give a higher preference to the accuracy. We use weights to represent user priorities. Equation 5 defines the utility function [2] for S_t.

$$U(S_t) = \sum_{i \in X} \frac{V_{it} - MIN_i}{MAX_i - MIN_i} * W_{ix} + \sum_{j \in Y} \frac{MAX_j - V_{jt}}{MAX_j - MIN_j} * W_{jy} \qquad (5)$$

where X is the set of positively monotonic QoS properties and Y is the set of negatively monotonic QoS properties, V_{it} (V_{jt}) is the value of the ith (or jth) QoS property for service S_t, W_{ix} (W_{jy}) represents its weight corresponding to the user-defined priority value (equal weights are used currently), and MAX_i and MIN_i (MAX_j and MIN_j) represent the maximum and minimum values for these QoS properties among all the services.

In this way, without actually invoking each candidate service on the input dataset, based on its meta-attribute values we can predict QoS values for each service. Using predicted values, we can calculate the utility score for each service and then rank all the services. As the system is used over time, more historical data would be available. Thus the prediction as well as the service ranking would become more accurate.

4 Experiment

4.1 Experiment Design

In the experiment, we mainly want to show that by considering meta-attributes of the dataset and data-dependent QoS properties, we could improve the selection accuracy for clustering services. To verify our proposed selection algorithm, we have generated 560 synthetic datasets using an artificial data generator provided by Weka [13], applied services that implement clustering algorithms on them, and collected their QoS values on all the datasets. The synthetic datasets vary on their five meta-attribute values. We have used the 10-fold cross-validation technique in the experiment.

As for the clustering services, we have used services created in [12] that wrap various clustering algorithms available through the Weka Toolkit API [13] as RESTful services. The clustering algorithms implemented in these services for our experiment include SimpleKMeans, FarthestFirst, XMeans, DBSCAN, EM, Hierarchical Clustering with Single or Complete or Average or Ward Link, CLOPE, and Cobweb. Most of the default settings in Weka are used for these services.

To evaluate the proposed algorithm, we consider two aspects: prediction accuracy and ranking accuracy. Prediction accuracy is only calculated for per-dataset data-dependent QoS properties and it is measured by the Mean Absolute Error (MAE).

$$MAE(Q) = \frac{1}{N_D \times N_S} \sum_{j=1}^{N_D} \sum_{i=1}^{N_S} \left| VA_{S_i,D_j}(Q) - VP_{S_i,D_j}(Q) \right| \qquad (6)$$

where $VA_{S_i,D_j}(Q)$ and $VP_{S_i,D_j}(Q)$ represent the actual and predicted QoS values of service S_i on dataset D_j, the number of datasets is represented by N_D and N_S is the number of services. A smaller MAE value (i.e. closer to 0) indicates a better prediction accuracy.

The ranking or selection accuracy is measured by Spearman's Rank Correlation (SRC) as shown in Eq. 7. To calculate SRC, the ranking generated based on predicted QoS values is compared with the ranking generated based on actual QoS values.

$$SRC(D) = 1 - \frac{6 \sum_{i=1}^{p} d_i^2}{p(p^2 - 1)} \tag{7}$$

where d_i is the difference between the ideal (based on actual QoS values) and predicted ranking position for the ith service, and p is the size of the ranking list. The SRC coefficient ranges from -1 to $+1$. A value close to 1 indicates two rankings are very similar.

We used Java for our system implementation. All the experiments were run on a computer with Intel Core i5 CPU, 8 GB RAM and Windows 7 operating system. The clustering services were hosted on a local Apache Server. We used MySQL as our database server. We used Weka API for dataset generation and clustering, and IBM CPLEX Optimization API for implementing the utility function.

4.2   Result Analyses

In the experiment, we have applied all the services on this set of 560 datasets. We get the overall MAE by computing the average MAE over all the services on all the datasets for accuracy and latency to assess our prediction accuracy. Since reliability is a per-service data-dependent QoS property and prediction is not involved, it does not have MAE values. The MAE value from our algorithm is compared with the case when we just use the average QoS values (averaged over all the datasets) in the selection process. The latter is considered the baseline algorithm. We get the overall SRC by computing the average SRC for all the datasets and this result is also compared with the baseline algorithm. Once we provide the ranked list of services to the user, he/she is likely to pick the service with the highest ranking for the input dataset unless the service is unavailable for some reason. To evaluate the capability of ranking the best service to the top position, we again compare our algorithm with the baseline. Here the accuracy is calculated as the percentage of the number of times the top-ranked service (based on the actual QoS values) is picked by the algorithm. All the results are shown in Table 1.

Table 1. Comparison between our algorithm and the baseline

	MAE - accuracy	MAE - latency	SRC	Accuracy on finding top service
Ours	0.058	0.192	0.960	74.11 %
Baseline	0.403	0.784	0.769	35.36 %

From the table, we can see that our MAE results for both latency and accuracy are much lower than the baseline, which indicates the importance of considering the data dependency for this type of QoS properties. Using the average value to approximate the possible QoS value of a service for a certain dataset could have a negative impact on the subsequent selection process. MAE on latency is higher than MAE on accuracy for baseline algorithm, which shows there is a bigger difference between the average latency value and the actual latency value, whereas such difference on accuracy is smaller. MAE on latency is also higher than MAE on accuracy for our algorithm, which shows the prediction accuracy on accuracy is better than that on latency. In terms of improvement of our algorithm over the baseline, it is 86 % on accuracy and 76 % on latency. By checking the individual latency and accuracy values, we observed that meta-attributes of the dataset, especially size and number of dimensions, have a bigger impact on latency than accuracy. There is also a higher variance among latency values and hence the prediction is less accurate.

In terms of SRC values, our result is also better than the baseline result, which shows the importance of using the predicted QoS values in the selection process. It generates a more accurate ranking order compared to the traditional selection algorithm in which the average QoS values are used. The high SRC value also indicates that our result is very close to the actual ranking result. Lastly, the accuracy on finding the top-ranked service is in a satisfactory level and it is more than twice as that of the baseline.

The experimental results show that incorporating a meta-learner for predicting QoS values and ranking is important. Relying on the traditional approaches with the average QoS values is certainly not sufficient and accurate for ranking data analytic services.

5   Conclusions

In this paper, we have addressed the problem of QoS-based service selection for data analytic services. We found that meta-attributes of the dataset could influence the QoS values of services, thereby affecting the service selection results. We have proposed an approach to predict QoS values of data analytic services according to the nature of the dataset and then rank them based on the predicted values. Our experimental results have shown that our prediction and ranking results are significantly better than the traditional approach which is to take average QoS values for the ranking purpose.

Acknowledgements. This work is partially sponsored by Natural Science and Engineering Research Council of Canada (grant 2015-05555).

References

1. Hang, C.W., Singh, M.P.: From quality to utility: adaptive service selection framework. In: 8th International Conference on Service Oriented Computing, pp. 456–470 (2010)
2. Kritikos, K., Plexousakis, D.: Mixed-integer programming for QoS-based web service matchmaking. IEEE Trans. Serv. Comput. 2(2), 122–139 (2009)
3. Qu, L., Wang, Y., Orgun, M.A., Liu, L., Liu, H., Bougeuttaya, A.: CCCloud: context-aware and credible cloud service selection based on subjective assessment and objective assessment. IEEE Trans. Serv. Comput. 8(3), 369–383 (2015)
4. Zorrilla, M., García-Saiz, D.: A service oriented architecture to provide data mining services for non-expert data miners. Decis. Support Syst. 55(1), 399–411 (2013)
5. Tsai, C.W., Lai, C.F., Chao, H.C., Vasilakos, A.V.: Big data analytics: a survey. J. Big Data 2, 21 (2015)
6. Lemke, C., Budka, M., Gabrys, B.: Metalearning: a survey of trends and technologies. Artif. Intell. Rev. 44(1), 117–130 (2015)

7. Yao, L., Sheng, Q.Z., Ngu, A.H.H., Yu, J., Segev, A.: Unified collaborative and content-based web service recommendation. IEEE Trans. Serv. Comput. **8**(3), 453–466 (2015)
8. Zhang, L., Zhang, B., Pahl, C., Xu, L., Zhu, Z.: Personalized quality prediction for dynamic service management based on invocation patterns. In: Basu, S., Pautasso, C., Zhang, L., Fu, X. (eds.) ICSOC 2013. LNCS, vol. 8274, pp. 84–98. Springer, Heidelberg (2013)
9. Brazdil, P.B., Soares, C., Da Costa, J.P.: Ranking learning algorithms: using IBL and meta-learning on accuracy and time results. Mach. Learn. **50**, 251–277 (2003)
10. Ferrari, D.G., de Castro, L.N.: Clustering algorithm recommendation: a meta-learning approach. In: Panigrahi, B.K., Das, S., Suganthan, P.N., Nanda, P.K. (eds.) SEMCCO 2012. LNCS, vol. 7677, pp. 143–150. Springer, Heidelberg (2012)
11. Jain, A.K., Murty, M.N., Flynn, P.J.: Data clustering: a review. ACM Comput. Surv. (CSUR) **31**(3), 264–323 (1999)
12. Rahman, M.S., Ding, C., Liu, X.M., Chi, C.H.: A testbed for collecting QoS data of cloud-based analytic services. In: 9th IEEE International Conference on Cloud Computing (2016)
13. Hall, M., Frank, E., Holmes, G., Pfahringer, B., Reutemann, P., Witten, I.H.: The WEKA data mining software: an update. ACM SIGKDD Explor. Newsl. **11**, 10–18 (2009)

A Mobile Service Engine Enabling Complex Data Collection Applications

Johannes Schobel[(✉)], Rüdiger Pryss, Wolfgang Wipp, Marc Schickler,
and Manfred Reichert

Institute of Databases and Information Systems, Ulm University, Ulm, Germany
{johannes.schobel,ruediger.pryss,wolfgang.wipp,marc.schickler,
manfred.reichert}@uni-ulm.de

Abstract. The widespread distribution of smart mobile devices offers
promising perspectives for the timely collection of huge amounts of data.
When realizing sophisticated mobile data collection applications, numerous technical issues arise. For example, as many real-world projects
require the support of different mobile operating systems, platform-
specific peculiarities must be properly handled. Existing approaches often
rely on specifically tailored mobile applications. As a drawback, changes
to the data collection procedure result in costly code adaptations. To
remedy this drawback, a model-driven approach is proposed, enabling
end-users (i.e., domain experts) to create mobile data collection applications themselves. This model relies on complex questionnaires called
instruments. An instrument not only contains all information about the
data to be collected, but additionally comprises information on how it
shall be processed on different mobile operating systems. For this purpose, we developed an advanced mobile (kernel) service being capable
of processing sophisticated instruments on various platforms. This paper
discusses fundamental kernel requirements and introduces the developed
architecture. Altogether, the mobile service allows for the effective use
of smart mobile devices in data collection application scenarios (e.g.,
clinical trials).

Keywords: Mobile process engine · Mobile data collection · Smart
mobile device · Mobile process · Mobile healthcare

1 Introduction

Smart mobile devices are increasingly used in everyday life. In line with this
trend, application domains for which huge amounts of data must be collected
(e.g., clinical trials) significantly benefit from using mobile applications. These
scenarios range from fitness trackers to applications monitoring vital parameters.
However, when realizing mobile data collection applications, profound knowledge
from real-world scenarios is essential.

In various large-scale mobile data collection applications we realized (cf.
Table 1), domain experts (e.g., medical doctors) were provided with specifically

© Springer International Publishing Switzerland 2016
Q.Z. Sheng et al. (Eds.): ICSOC 2016, LNCS 9936, pp. 626–633, 2016.
DOI: 10.1007/978-3-319-46295-0_42

Table 1. Realized mobile data collection applications

#	Data collection applications	Country	CN	Releases	Instances
1	Tinnitus research	World-Wide	○	3	≥20,000
2	Risk factors during pregnancy	Germany	○	5	≥1,000
3	Risk factors after pregnancy	Germany	○	1	≥100
4	PTSD in war regions	Burundi	●	5	≥2,200
5	PTSD in war regions	Uganda	○	1	≥200
6	Adverse childhood experiences	Germany	●	3	≥150
7	Learning deficits among medical students	Germany	●	3	≥200
8	Supporting parents after accidents of children	Switzerland	○	5	≥2,500
	Sum Σ			24	≥26,350

CN = Complex Navigation; PTSD = Posttraumatic Stress Disorder

tailored solutions. The questionnaires used in these scenarios (so-called *instruments*) not only provide questions, but also comprise sophisticated features for coordinating their processing (i.e., answering). For example, instruments require a proper navigation between questions based on already given answers. Recent approaches aim to realize such instruments as smart mobile applications to reduce the overall workload for domain experts by digitally transforming paper-based ways of data collection. For example, compared to traditional paper-based questionnaires, the data collected needs not to be digitized after completing an instrument, and, hence, mitigating transcription errors significantly.

To cope with these drawbacks, we propose a generic framework [9] that allows domain experts to create data collection instruments in a new way. According to this end-user programming approach, an instrument can be designed using a high-level modeling language (cf. Fig. 1, ①). The latter is then automatically transformed to an executable process model (cf. Fig. 1, ③), based on a well-defined mapping (cf. Fig. 1, ②). Finally, this process model can be deployed to mobile process engines running on smart mobile devices (cf. Fig. 1, ④).

Providing a process engine running as a *mobile service* on smart mobile devices, raises additional challenges. In particular, a modular architecture is indispensable. The following three major requirements must be particularly considered when developing such a mobile process engine:

R1 Provide offline execution. The mobile process engine shall allow for an offline execution of deployed process models as well as for storing the collected data on the smart mobile device. For example, in the Burundi project (cf. Table 1, #4), an international team of psychologists could not rely on robust Internet connection in rural areas.

R2 Enable process flexibility. The mobile process engine must support domain experts in changing (i.e., adapting) instruments during run time. For example, the order of questions often need to be flexibly changed in order to foster understandability of an instrument or to make it more convenient.

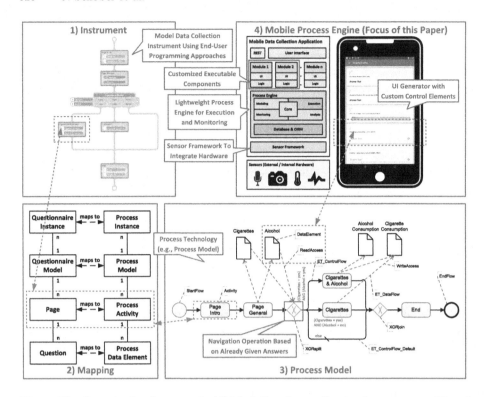

Fig. 1. The QuestionSys framework: (1) Modeling data collection instruments, (2) and (3) Mapping to process model, (4) Executing on smart mobile devices.

R3 Provide customizable user interfaces. The mobile process engine shall dynamically create the user interface of the respective instrument based on the model. For example, all information related to the structure and processing logic of the instrument as well as the meta-data of elements need to be taken into account by the rendering mechanism.

This paper presents a lightweight, modular mobile process engine, capable of executing sophisticated data collection instruments that takes multiple requirements into account. Moreover, a component for dynamically extending instruments is presented, which enables flexible adaptations of already deployed mobile applications during run time. Compared to hard-coded mobile data collection applications, therefore, changes of an instrument do not require its reimplementation and redeployment to multiple smart mobile devices. In addition, data from multiple releases must not be merged manually in order to avoid inconsistencies. Altogether, the approach enables flexibility regarding the design and execution of data collection instruments on smart mobile devices [8].

The remainder of the paper is structured as follows: Sect. 2 discusses fundamentals. Section 3 presents the architecture of the realized mobile engine, particularly its *Execution* component. Section 4 discusses related work and Sect. 5 concludes the paper.

2   Background: The QuestionSys Framework

This section introduces fundamentals of the QuestionSys framework, focusing on the mapping of a paper-based instrument to a mobile data collection application. Furthermore, the lifecycle phases for mobile data collection are introduced.

According to the QuestionSys approach, the structure of an instrument is directly mapped to an executable process model, which then can be enacted by a lightweight process engine running on smart mobile devices. Using this model-driven approach, a separation of the processing logic of an instrument from actual application code [7] of the data collection application becomes possible. Thereby, a process model acts as the schema for executing instrument instances. This model, in turn, consists of process steps (i.e., activities) and edges expressing the control and data flow between them. Additionally, gateways (e.g., AND and XOR-splits) provide functionality for describing complex control flow structures.

To properly support domain experts in creating a mobile data collection instrument, all phases of its lifecycle [9] shall be addressed. We introduce the lifecycle that consists of 5 different phases. The *Design & Modeling* phase enables domain experts to create sophisticated mobile data collection applications with complex logic themselves (i.e., end-user programming). The *Deployment* phase deploys the instrument on smart mobile devices. During the *Enactment & Execution* phase, multiple instances of the respective data collection instrument may be created and executed in a robust manner on the smart mobile devices. The *Monitoring & Analysis* phase provides functions enabling a real-time analysis of the data collected on the smart mobile device. Finally, the *Archiving & Versioning* phase enables release management for mobile data collection instruments.

The work presented in this paper focuses on the *Enactment & Execution* phase. In this context, a mobile service providing a lightweight process engine for executing data collection instruments has been developed.

3   QuestionSys Mobile Service

This section presents the architecture of the mobile process engine and provides in-depth information with respect to the *Execution* component.

The lightweight mobile process engine developed applies a service-driven approach. The engine comprises five components (cf. Fig. 2, left part): The most important one constitutes the core of the engine itself, which provides the data model, representing the process model, as well as operations to robustly interact with process instances (e.g., start or stop activities). Although, the process model relies on the ADEPT2 framework [6], other process meta-models (e.g., WS-BPEL) may be used as well. For this purpose, the core provides functions to import process models and map one model to another. The other components provide functions to support the different phases [10] of enacting process models locally on a smart mobile device. Note that these components only interact with the core itself and may be used as standalone functions as well (i.e., not all components are required). For example, the *Monitoring* component relies on

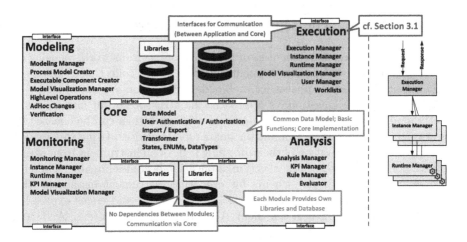

Fig. 2. Components of the mobile process engine

data from the *Execution* component in order to visualize the current state of the process instance or to provide information about upcoming process activities (e.g., insufficient data). This loose coupling of the components (e.g., no other dependencies between components exist) allows for a very customizable, but still lightweight mobile process engine.

As shown in Fig. 2, several components may provide similar functions. Consider, for example, the `ModelVisualizationManager` provided by the *Modeling*, *Execution* and *Monitoring* component. In general, these components require different functions of the respective managers (e.g., various notations) and, therefore, must be implemented several times. For example, the *Modeling* component needs to provide all elements of the process meta-model (e.g., process activities, data elements, control and data flow), whereas the *Execution* component may only provide information regarding the current and upcoming activities to be executed. The interface shared for this manager, however, is defined by the core of the mobile process engine. In addition, each component contains its own persistence layer. For example, the *Execution* component stores information about the current state of the enacted process instance (including user information, timestamps, data produced and consumed), whereas the *Analysis* component stores evaluation rules as well as the respective results for each process instance. These separated databases, in turn, foster the modular design of the process engine. Data between components, however, is shared through the core. Furthermore, each component may provide additional libraries to enhance functionality. For example, the *Analysis* component uses the Java Expression Language (JEXL) for evaluating data elements of process instances dynamically.

3.1   QuestionSys Mobile Execution Component

Recall that the mobile process engine runs as a service and may be embedded in another application based on its interfaces. The interaction between the mobile data collection application and the mobile process engine is shown in Fig. 3.

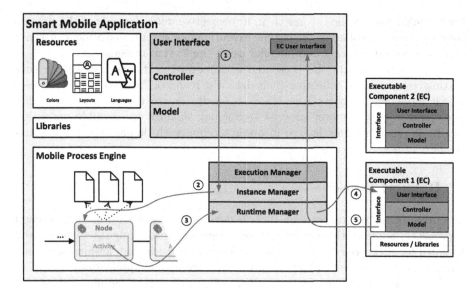

Fig. 3. Enacting executable components (ECs) during run time

First, the user, interacting with the smart mobile application, starts a new instance of an instrument. The mobile data collection application, in turn, directly interacts with the lightweight process engine, which provides access to the ExecutionManager ①. The latter offers functions allowing to control a particular process instance (i.e., move to the next page). *Second*, the InstanceManager validates whether the current node may be executed (e.g., the user has appropriate access rights) and all data elements needed are provided ②. The node is activated and handed over by a *third* step to the respective RuntimeManager, which is able to call the linked *executable component* (EC). The latter covers several aspects. The core functionality is to extract the main class file of the implementation of the EC as well as to create a list of all required *input* and *output variables* for the called component ③. *Fourth*, the RuntimeManager calls the EC by invoking its main method ④ and passing both input and output lists. As an EC can be seen as Micro Service [3], it may provide sophisticated logic as well as an user interface for interaction. Note that the EC may contain its own resource files as well as libraries. In a *fifth* step, the EC user interfaces are passed back to the ExecutionManager and the respective data collection application. This allows the latter to embed it as UI fragment inside the main user interface ⑤. Note that interactions with the UI of the EC (e.g., clicking a button) are handled by the EC itself and not by the *surrounding* mobile data collection application.

If the respective EC, which is executed as a mobile service, satisfies specific conditions (i.e., all mandatory fields are filled in), it produces the canBeFinished event. The latter indicates that the coordinating RuntimeManager may terminate the EC. Furthermore, all *output variables* of the EC are transferred back to the

`InstanceManager`, which stores them in respective *data elements* of the process instance. Log files collected during the execution of a specific instrument instance may be accessed by other components using the `ExecutionManager`.

In order to validate the presented architecture, a mobile application supporting researchers in collecting their data was realized. Altogether, the process-driven modeling supports researchers to easily create mobile data collection instruments. Furthermore, process technology enables the flexible execution locally on smart mobile devices in order to cope with domain-specific requirements.

4   Related Work

Executing business processes on mobile devices has been addressed by several approaches. Some of them provide proprietary execution languages specifically designed for respective scenarios, whereas others provide middlewares or frameworks enabling the development of process-aware mobile applications.

[1] presents extensions for WS-BPEL when integrating mobile devices into business processes. The authors discuss that in given scenarios the number of available mobile devices to coordinate is unknown. *Partner links*, bound to multiple endpoints, are introduced to cope with this issue.

In [5], an iPad application supporting medical staff during ward rounds is presented. Besides reviewing patient's health record or current diagnose, the staff is able to add further information during rounds. In order to execute a process, a lightweight process engine was implemented. Although the concept of automatically invoking processes based on user data is promising, the functionality of the respective engine is limited, as gateways are not supported, but only sequences of activities. Besides this limitation, only simple tasks may be executed.

[2,4] introduced a workflow engine being capable of running on PDAs. Both approaches use WS-BPEL to specify the business processes. Furthermore, they rely on Web Service standards (e.g., WSDL and SOAP) to specify activities to be called. Both use HTML for displaying user interfaces. In order to execute specific activities, one uses an own WS-BPEL extension, whereas the other ships with an Apache server to execute scripts. Both approaches provide core activities, like a browser, user forms, calendars and messaging services.

5   Summary and Outlook

Based on the insights we gained in several data collection scenarios, this paper advocates the need for sophisticated mobile services running on smart mobile devices. In order to mitigate the efforts between IT and domain experts, a sophisticated framework allowing domain experts to model data collection instruments themselves was proposed. In this context, a mobile service became necessary to process instruments directly on smart mobile devices. For this purpose, we present a flexible and modular architecture of a lightweight process engine. It allows extending the functionality of already installed mobile data collection applications during run time based on the concept of ECs. These components allow providing domain-specific logic as well as dynamically generated user interfaces for respective activities executed by the process engine.

To further validate the presented approach, a study for evaluating the user interface and user experience while working with the realized mobile data collection application is currently conducted. In particular, differences compared to paper-based questionnaires with respect to complex navigation features are evaluated. Moreover, the *Modeling*, *Analysis* and *Monitoring* components need to be implemented, leveraging the overall functionality of the proposed lightweight mobile process engine. In addition, ECs using sensors need to be realized allowing to collect additional data during enactment.

Altogether, the presented approach will significantly change the way instruments may be used in practice (e.g., clinical trials). Moreover, due to its flexibility, the proposed architecture may be suitable for other life domains relying on collecting and processing data in mobile scenarios as well.

References

1. Hackmann, G., Gill, C., Roman, G.C.: Extending BPEL for interoperable pervasive computing. In: IEEE International Conference on Pervasive Services, pp. 204–213. IEEE (2007)
2. Hackmann, G., Haitjema, M., Gill, C., Roman, G.-C.: Sliver: a BPEL workflow process execution engine for mobile devices. In: Dan, A., Lamersdorf, W. (eds.) ICSOC 2006. LNCS, vol. 4294, pp. 503–508. Springer, Heidelberg (2006). doi:10. 1007/11948148_47
3. Newman, S.: Building Microservices: Designing Fine-Grained Systems. O'Reilly Media, Inc., Sebastopol (2015)
4. Pajunen, L., Chande, S.: Developing workflow engine for mobile devices. In: 11th IEEE International Enterprise Distributed Object Computing Conference, EDOC 2007, pp. 279–279. IEEE (2007)
5. Pryss, R., Mundbrod, N., Langer, D., Reichert, M.: Supporting medical ward rounds through mobile task and process management. Inf. Syst. e-Bus. Manag. **13**(1), 107–146 (2015)
6. Reichert, M., Dadam, P.: Enabling adaptive process-aware information systems with ADEPT2. In: Cardoso, J., van der Aalst, W. (eds.) Handbook of Research on Business Process Modeling. Information Science Reference, Hershey (2009)
7. Reichert, M., Weber, B.: Enabling Flexibility in Process-Aware Information Systems: Challenges, Methods, Technologies. Springer, Heidelberg (2012)
8. Schobel, J., Pryss, R., Schickler, M., Reichert, M.: Towards flexible mobile data collection in healthcare. In: 29th IEEE International Symposium on Computer-Based Medical Systems. IEEE Computer Society Press, June 2016
9. Schobel, J., Pryss, R., Schickler, M., Reichert, M., Ruf-Leuschner, M., Elbert, T.: End-user programming of mobile services: empowering domain experts to implement mobile data collection applications. In: IEEE 5th International Conference on Mobile Services. IEEE Computer Society Press, June 2016
10. Weske, M.: Business Process Management: Concepts, Languages, Architectures. Springer Science & Business Media, Heidelberg (2012)

Service Recommendation (Short Papers)

Service Recommendation Based on Social Balance Theory and Collaborative Filtering

Lianyong Qi[1,2,3(✉)], Wanchun Dou[2], and Xuyun Zhang[2,4]

[1] State Key Laboratory of Software Engineering,
Wuhan University, Wuhan 430072, China
lianyongqi@gmail.com
[2] State Key Laboratory for Novel Software Technology,
Department of Computer Science and Technology,
Nanjing University, Nanjing 210023, China
douwc@nju.edu.cn, xuyun.zhang@auckland.ac.nz
[3] School of Information Science and Engineering, Qufu Normal University,
Rizhao 276826, China
[4] Department of Electrical and Computer Engineering, University of Auckland,
Auckland, New Zealand

Abstract. With the increasing popularity of web service technology, many users turn to look for appropriate web services to further build their complex business applications. As an effective manner for service discovery, service recommendation technique is gaining ever-increasing attention, e.g., Collaborative Filtering (i.e., CF) recommendation. Generally, the traditional CF recommendation (e.g., user-based CF, item-based CF or hybrid CF) can achieve good recommendation results. However, due to the inherent sparsity of user-service rating data, it is possible that the target user has no similar friends and the services preferred by target user own no similar services. In this exceptional situation, traditional CF recommendation approaches cannot deliver an accurate recommendation result. In view of this shortcoming, a novel Social Balance Theory (i.e., SBT)-based service recommendation approach, i.e., Rec_{SBT} is introduced in this paper, to help improve the recommendation performance. Finally, through a set of simulation experiments deployed on MovieLens-1M dataset, we further validate the feasibility of Rec_{SBT} in terms of recommendation accuracy and recall.

Keywords: Service recommendation · Target user · Friend user · Enemy user · Social balance theory · Collaborative filtering

1 Introduction

With the gradual popularity of SOA (Service Oriented Architecture), the available web service number in service communities is becoming increasingly larger. In this situation, many users are apt to find their interested web services through various recommendation techniques, e.g., well-known Collaborative Filtering (i.e., CF; e.g., user-based CF, item-based CF or hybrid CF) [1]. In CF recommendation, through analyzing known user-service rating data (only the subjective rating data is considered in this paper),

© Springer International Publishing Switzerland 2016
Q.Z. Sheng et al. (Eds.): ICSOC 2016, LNCS 9936, pp. 637–645, 2016.
DOI: 10.1007/978-3-319-46295-0_43

we can first determine the target user's similar friends or the target service (i.e., the service preferred by target user)'s similar services, and further recommend appropriate services to the target user.

While due to the inherent sparsity of user-service rating data [2], in certain situations, the target user does not have any similar friend and the target services do not own any similar service. In this situation, traditional CF recommendation approaches cannot deliver an accurate recommendation result, which brings a big challenge for recommendation effect. In view of this challenge, a novel Social Balance Theory [3] (i.e., SBT)-based service recommendation approach, i.e., Rec_{SBT} (Recommendation based on SBT) is put forward in this paper, to help improve the recommendation performance. Different from the traditional CF recommendation approaches, in Rec_{SBT}, we first look for the target user's "enemy" (i.e., antonym of "friend"), and further determine the target user's "possible friends" based on Social Balance Theory (e.g., "enemy's enemy is a friend" rule, "friend's enemy is an enemy" rule, "enemy's friend is an enemy" rule); finally, the services preferred by target user's "possible friends" are recommended to the target user.

The rest of paper is structured as below. In Sect. 2, we formalize the service recommendation problem and clarify the paper motivation. A novel service recommendation approach, i.e., Rec_{SBT} is brought forth in Sect. 3. In Sect. 4, we design a set of experiments to validate the feasibility of Rec_{SBT}. In Sect. 5, we introduce the related works and compare them with our approach. Finally, conclusions are presented in Sect. 6.

2 Formal Specification and Motivation

2.1 Formal Specification

Generally, the service recommendation problem could be formalized with following *Web_Ser_Rec (User_set, WS_set, Rating_set, user_{target})*, where

(1) *User_set* = {*user*$_1$, ..., *user*$_m$}: *user*$_i$ ($1 \leq i \leq m$) denotes a user in web service community and m is the number of users.
(2) *WS_set* = {*ws*$_1$, ..., *ws*$_n$}: *ws*$_j$ ($1 \leq j \leq n$) denotes a service in web service community and n is the number of web services.
(3) *Rating_set* = {r_{i-j} | $1 \leq i \leq m$, $1 \leq j \leq n$}: r_{i-j} denotes *user*$_i$'s rating over service *ws*$_j$. As our previous work [4] did, the popular $1* \sim 5*$ rating scores are adopted here to depict r_{i-j}.
(4) *user_{target}*: target user who requires service recommendation, and *user_{target}* $\in$ *User_set* holds here.

With the formal specification, we can clarify the service recommendation problem as below: according to the known user-service rating data (in *Rating_set*) between users (in *User_set*) and services (in *WS_set*), recommend appropriate services from *WS_set* to the target user *user_{target}*.

2.2   Motivation

Next, we demonstrate the motivation of our paper with the example presented in Fig. 1. In the example, user set $User\_set$ = {$John, Lily, Jack$} ($user_{target}$ is $John$) and service sets WS_set = {$ws_1, ..., ws_6$}. The user-service rating data (i.e., $Rating\_set$) is also shown in Fig. 1. As Fig. 1 shows, target user $John$ prefers services ws_1 and ws_2; therefore, ws_1 and ws_2 are called "target services" in the rest of paper.

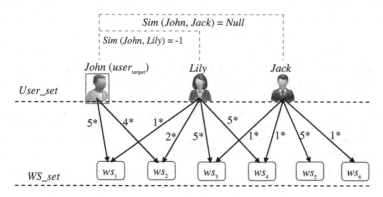

Fig. 1. Service recommendation scenario: an example

With the known data of $User\_set$, WS_set and $Rating\_set$, we can calculate the similarity between different users by the well-known Pearson Correlation Coefficient (i.e., PCC) [5]. Concretely, similarity Sim ($John, Lily$) = -0.27 and Sim ($John, Jack$) = $Null$ (as $John$ and $Jack$ have not invoked common web services). Likewise, we can also calculate the similarity between target services (i.e., ws_1 and ws_2) and other services (i.e., ws_3, ws_4, ws_5, ws_6). Concretely, Sim (ws_1, ws_3) = Sim (ws_1, ws_4) = Sim (ws_2, ws_3) = Sim (ws_2, ws_4) = -1, while Sim (ws_1, ws_5) = Sim (ws_1, ws_6) = Sim (ws_2, ws_5) = Sim (ws_2, ws_6) = $Null$.

With the above calculation, a conclusion could be drawn that the target user (i.e., $John$) has no similar friends and the target services (i.e., ws_1 and ws_2) own no similar services. In this situation, traditional CF recommendation approaches cannot deliver an accurate recommendation result. In view of this shortcoming, we introduce Social Balance Theory into service recommendation and bring forth a novel recommendation approach Rec_{SBT} in the next section.

3   SBT-Based Service Recommendation

3.1   Social Balance Theory

Social Balance Theory analyzes and formalizes the social relationships among involved three parties, and provides us a new perspective for friend recommendation in social network. Concretely, there are several intuitive rules in Social Balance Theory, e.g., "enemy's enemy is a friend", "enemy's friend is an enemy" and "friend's enemy is an enemy" (The details of SBT are omitted here due to page limit. Readers who are interested in SBT can turn to work [3] for reference).

3.2 Rec_{SBT}: A Service Recommendation Approach

Next, we introduce a novel service recommendation approach Rec_{SBT} by considering the rules in Social Balance Theory. Concretely, our proposal consists of the following three steps (see Fig. 2).

Step1: Determine "friend" or "enemy" relationship between different users. For different $user_i$ and $user_j (i \neq j)$, calculate their similarity $Sim(user_i, user_j)$ and further determine the "friend" or "enemy" relationship between them.

Step2: Determine "possible friends" of target user based on SBT. For target user $user_{target}$, determine his/her "possible friend" set $Possible\_friend\_set (user_{target})$ based on "enemy's enemy is a friend" rule, "enemy's friend is an enemy" rule and "friend's enemy is an enemy" rule in Social Balance Theory.

Step3: Service recommendation. For the "possible friends" in set $Possible\_friend\_set (user_{target})$, determine their preferred services and recommend them to $user_{target}$.

Fig. 2. Three steps of our proposed recommendation approach Rec_{SBT}

(1) Step1: Determine "friend" or "enemy" relationship between different users.

First, for two different users $user_i$ and $user_j$ ($user_i, user_j \in User\_set$ and $i \neq j$), we can calculate their similarity $Sim(user_i, user_j)$ based on PCC technique, whose formula is specified in (1). Here, set $Common\_ser\_set$ denotes the common service set that have been invoked and rated by $user_i$ and $user_j$; r_{i-k} and r_{j-k} denote web service ws_k's rating scores by $user_i$ and $user_j$ respectively; $\overline{r_i}$ and $\overline{r_j}$ represent $user_i$'s and $user_j$'s average rating scores over all his invoked services. Specially, if $user_i$ and $user_j$ have not invoked same services before (i.e., $Common\_ser\_set = Null$), then $Sim(user_i, user_j) = Null$ holds.

$$Sim(user_i, user_j) = \frac{\sum_{ws_k \in Common\_ser\_set} (r_{i-k} - \overline{r_i}) * (r_{j-k} - \overline{r_j})}{\sqrt{\sum_{ws_k \in Common\_ser\_set} (r_{i-k} - \overline{r_i})^2} * \sqrt{\sum_{ws_k \in Common\_ser\_set} (r_{j-k} - \overline{r_j})^2}}$$

$$(1)$$

Afterwards, according to the derived similarity $Sim(user_i, user_j)$ in (1), we can further determine the "friend" or "enemy" relationship between $user_i$ and $user_j$ by (2). In (2), Q ($0.5 \leq Q \leq 1$) is a pre-set similarity threshold for "friend" relationship; correspondingly, $-Q$ ($-1 \leq -Q \leq -0.5$) is a pre-set similarity threshold for "enemy" relationship. While $Friend\_set(user_i)$ and $Enemy\_set(user_i)$ denote friend set and enemy set of $user_i$, respectively.

$$user_j \begin{cases} \in Friend\_set(user_i) & \text{if } Sim(user_i, user_j) \geq Q \\ \in Enemy\_set(user_i) & \text{if } Sim(user_i, user_j) \leq -Q \end{cases} \tag{2}$$

(2) Step2: Determine "possible friends" of target user based on SBT.

As Fig. 1 shows, our paper only focuses on the service recommendation scenario where target user has no similar friends; so $Friend\_set(user_{target}) = Null$ holds based on (2). Namely, we can (but not definitely) only obtain the enemy set $Enemy\_set(user_{target})$ of target user. Next, we introduce how to get the "possible friends" of target user, based on the derived set $Enemy\_set(user_{target})$ (in Step1) and Social Balance Theory. Concretely, Step2 consists of the following two substeps (see Fig. 3).

Substep2.1: For each $user_x \in Enemy\_set(user_{target})$, determine his enemy $user_y$ (i.e., $user_y \in Enemy\_set(user_x)$) based on (1) and (2). Then according to "enemy's enemy is a friend" rule in SBT, we can conclude that $user_y$ is a candidate "possible friend" of $user_{target}$ and the credibility could be measured by $Friend\_probability$ $(user_{target}, user_y)$ in (3). Afterwards, $user_y$ is regarded as a qualified "possible friend" (denoted by set $Possible\_friend\_set$ $(user_{target})$) of $user_{target}$, if condition in (4) holds (here, Q denotes the pre-set user similarity threshold in (2)).

$$Friend\_probability(user_{target}, user_y) = Sim(user_{target}, user_x) * Sim(user_x, user_y) \tag{3}$$

$$Friend\_probability(user_{target}, user_y) \geq Q \tag{4}$$

Substep2.2: For each $user_x \in Enemy\_set(user_{target})$, determine his friend $user_z$ (i.e., $user_z \in Friend\_set(user_x)$) based on (1) and (2). Then according to "enemy's friend is an enemy" rule in SBT, we can also infer that $user_z$ is a candidate "enemy" of $user_{target}$ and the credibility could be calculated by $Enemy\_probability$ $(user_{target}, user_z)$ in (5). Afterwards, if condition in (6) holds, $user_z$ is considered as a qualified "enemy" of $user_{target}$ and put in set $Enemy\_set(user_{target})$. Similarly, for each $user_y \in Possible\_friend\_set$ $(user_{target})$, determine his enemy $user_k$ (i.e., $user_k \in Enemy\_set(user_y)$) based on (1)–(2). Then according to "friend's enemy is an enemy" rule in SBT, we can infer that $user_k$ is a candidate "enemy" of $user_{target}$ and the credibility could be calculated by $Enemy\_probability$ $(user_{target}, user_k)$ in (7). Afterwards, if condition (8) holds, $user_k$ is regarded as a qualified "enemy" of $user_{target}$ and put in $Enemy\_set$ $(user_{target})$.

$$Enemy\_probability(user_{target}, user_z) = Sim(user_{target}, user_x) * Sim(user_x, user_z) \tag{5}$$

$$Enemy\_probability(user_{target}, user_z) \leq -Q \tag{6}$$

$$Enemy\_probability(user_{target}, user_k) = Friend\_probability(user_{target}, user_y) \\ * Sim(user_y, user_k) \tag{7}$$

$$Enemy\_probability(user_{target}, user_k) \leq -Q \qquad (8)$$

Repeat Step1, Substep2.1 and Substep2.2 until the "possible friend" set of target user, i.e., *Possible_friend_set* $(user_{target})$ stays stable. Then we can obtain the target user's possible friends, i.e., $user_y \in$ *Possible_friend_set* $(user_{target})$.

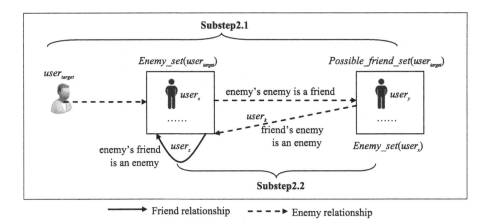

Fig. 3. Relationships of $user_{target}$, $user_x$, $user_y$, $user_z$ and $user_k$ in Step2

(3) **Step3: Service recommendation.**

After Step1 and Step2, we can obtain the target user's "possible friend" set *Possible_friend_set* $(user_{target})$. Next, for each $user_y \in$ *Possible_friend_set* $(user_{target})$, we select his/her preferred services (e.g., with 4* or 5* rating from $user_y$) and recommend them to the target user, so as to finish the whole service recommendation process.

4   Experiment Analyses

4.1   Experiment Dataset and Deployment

Our paper aims at the service recommendation problem with subjective user-service rating data. However, the available service rating data is really rare. Therefore, the popular MovieLens-1M [6] dataset is adopted here for simulation. MovieLens-1M contains 1000209 user-movie ratings from 6040 users over 3952 movies.

In our experiments, the service recommendation accuracy (i.e., *MAE*) and recall are tested respectively (due to the page limit, detailed calculation formula of accuracy and recall is omitted here). Besides, our proposed Rec_{SBT} approach is compared with another two ones, i.e., *WSRec* [7] and *SBT-SR* [4]. The experiments are deployed on a Lenovo PC (2.40 GHz CPU, 2.0 GB RAM), and the software configuration environment is: Windows 7 + JAVA 1.5.

4.2   Experiment Results

In our experiments, m is the number of users and Q denotes the user similarity threshold defined in Eq. (2). In the following two experiment profiles, m is varied from 200 to 1000 and $Q = 0.5$ holds.

(1) *Profile1*: Service recommendation accuracy

The *MAE* values of different approaches (i.e., *WSRec*, *SBT-SR* and *Rec_{SBT}*) are tested respectively, and their execution results are presented in Fig. 4. As shown in Fig. 4, *WSRec*'s recommendation accuracy is low (i.e., *MAE* is high), as only the average rating of the services invoked by target user is considered in *WSRec*. While Rec_{SBT} and *SBT-SR* achieve better accuracy than *WSRec*, which is because more social relationship information among different users are considered. Besides, the recommendation accuracy of Rec_{SBT} and *SBT-SR* are approximate, because the two approaches both consider the "enemy's enemy is a friend" rule in SBT.

(2) *Profile2*: Service recommendation recall

The recommendation recall values of three approaches are tested and presented in Fig. 5. It can be seen from Fig. 5 that *WSRec*'s recommendation recall is low, as the average idea is adopted in *WSRec*. Besides, the recommendation recall values of Rec_{SBT} and *SBT-SR* both increase with the growth of m, this is because more "possible friends" of target user could be found when the user number increases. Furthermore, our proposed Rec_{SBT} outperforms *SBT-SR* in terms of recommendation recall, which is due to the fact that *SBT-SR* considers "enemy's enemy is a friend" rule only, while our proposal considers "enemy's enemy is a friend" rule, "friend's enemy is an enemy" rule and "enemy's friend is an enemy" rule simultaneously.

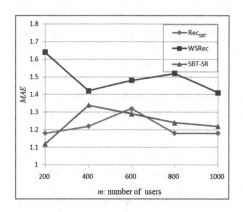

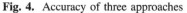

Fig. 4. Accuracy of three approaches

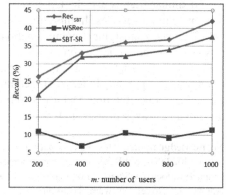

Fig. 5. Recall of three approaches

5   Related Works and Comparison Analyses

Collaborative Filtering (i.e., CF) has been proven a feasible resolution for service recommendation. Many researchers have investigated this recommendation problem and put forward various CF recommendation approaches, e.g., user-based CF [8], item-based CF [9] and hybrid CF [10], as well as their variants [11, 12].

However, the above works often assume that target user has similar friends or target service owns similar services, without considering the exceptional scenarios where neither similar friend (of target user) nor similar service (of target service) exists. In view of this shortcoming, *WSRec* approach is put forward in [7], where average rating of the services invoked by target user is recruited for service recommendation of target user. However, the recommendation accuracy of *WSRec* is often not high because of the adopted average idea. To improve the recommendation accuracy, *SBT-SR* approach is brought forth in our previous work [4], where "enemy's enemy is a friend" rule is employed for service recommendation. To further improve the recommendation performance, a novel recommendation approach named Rec_{SBT} is introduced in this paper, where more hidden social relationship information is taken into consideration, e.g., "enemy's enemy is a friend" rule, "friend's enemy is an enemy" rule and "enemy's friend is an enemy" rule. Through these social rules, more "possible friends" of target user could be found and correspondingly, more services that may be preferred by target user are recommended to the target user. At last, we validate the feasibility of our Rec_{SBT} approach through a set of simulation experiments deployed on well-known MovieLens-1M dataset.

6   Conclusions

Due to the inherent sparsity of user-service rating data, it is possible that the target user has no similar friends and the target service (i.e., the service preferred by target user) owns no similar services. In this situation, traditional CF recommendation approaches fail to deliver a satisfying recommendation result. In view of this shortcoming, we put forward a novel service recommendation approach Rec_{SBT} based on Social Balance Theory. Finally, a set of simulation experiments are deployed to validate the feasibility of our Rec_{SBT} approach in terms of recommendation accuracy and recall. In the future, we will introduce the time factor into service recommendation, so as to accommodate the dynamic waves of user preference.

Acknowledgements. This paper is partially supported by Natural Science Foundation of China (No. 61402258), Key Research and Development Project of Jiangsu Province (No. BE2015154), China Postdoctoral Science Foundation (No. 2015M571739), Open Project of State Key Laboratory for Novel Software Technology (No. KFKT2016B22), Open Project of State Key Laboratory of Software Engineering (No. SKLSE2014-10-03).

References

1. Wu, X., Cheng, B., Jun, L.C.: Collaborative filtering service recommendation based on a novel similarity computation method. IEEE Trans. Serv. Comput. doi:10.1109/TSC.2015.2479228

2. Xiang, Y.T., Jie, Z.: Dynamic personalized recommendation on sparse data. IEEE Trans. Knowl. Data Eng. **25**(12), 2895–2899 (2013)

3. Cartwright, D., Harary, F.: Structural balance: a generalization of Heider's theory. Psychol. Rev. **63**(5), 277 (1956)

4. Qi, L., Zhang, X., Wen, Y., Zhou, Y.: A social balance theory-based service recommendation approach. In: Yao, L., et al. (eds.) APSCC 2015. LNCS, vol. 9464, pp. 48–60. Springer, Heidelberg (2015). doi:10.1007/978-3-319-26979-5_4

5. Joseph, L.R., Alan, W.: Nicewander: thirteen ways to look at the correlation coefficient. Am. Stat. **42**(1), 59–66 (1988)

6. MovieLens-1M. http://www.grouplens.org/datasets/movielens/

7. Zi, B.Z., Hao, M., Michael, R.L., Irwin, K.: QoS-aware web service recommendation by collaborative filtering. IEEE Trans. Serv. Comput. **4**(2), 140–152 (2011)

8. Lin, S.Y., Lai, C.H., Wu, C.H., Lo, C.C.: A trustworthy QoS-based collaborative filtering approach for web service discovery. J. Syst. Softw. **93**, 217–228 (2014)

9. Li, D., Chen, C., Lv, Q., et al.: An algorithm for efficient privacy-preserving item-based collaborative filtering. Future Gener. Compt. Syst. **55**, 311–320 (2016)

10. Cao, J., Wu, Z., Wang, Y., et al.: Hybrid collaborative filtering algorithm for bidirectional web service recommendation. Knowl. Inf. Syst. **36**(3), 607–627 (2013)

11. Ming, D.T., Yu, X., Jian, X.L., Zi, B.Z., Frank, L.: Combining global and local trust for service recommendation. In: 21st IEEE International Conference on Web Services, pp. 305–312. IEEE Press, New York (2014)

12. Lian, Y.Q., Wan, C.D., Jin, J.C.: Weighted principal component analysis-based service selection method for multimedia services in cloud. Computing **98**, 195–214 (2016)

Personalized API Recommendation via Implicit Preference Modeling

Wei Gao[1]([⊠]), Liang Chen[2], Jian Wu[1], Hai Dong[2], and Athman Bouguettaya[2]

[1] College of Computer Science and Technology, Zhejiang University,
Hangzhou, China
{gw,wujian2000}@zju.edu.cn
[2] School of Computer Science and Information Technology,
RMIT, Melbourne, Australia
{liang.chen,Hai.dong,athman.bouguettaya}@rmit.edu.au

Abstract. With a huge amount of APIs on the Internet, understanding users' complex needs and preferences for APIs becomes an important task. In this paper, we aim to uncover users' implicit needs for APIs and recommend suitable APIs for users. Specifically, first different similarity scores between APIs are computed according to heterogeneous functional aspects of APIs. Next, users' preferences for APIs is combined with similarities of APIs measured with different functional aspects, and matrix factorization technique is used to learn the latent representation of users and APIs for each functional aspect. Then we use a personalized weight learning approach to combine the latent factors of different aspects to get the predicted preferences of users for APIs.

1 Introduction

With the development of Web 2.0 paradigm and mobile service computing, API (Application Programming Interface) as a form of REST-ful service has become prevalent in developing Web and mobile applications. Consumers can enjoy web or mobile service by simply invoking the APIs provided by service developers. As a result, the number of services has been experiencing a dramatic increase over the past few years. And platforms like ProgrammbleWeb[1], Mashape[2], APIStore[3] that collect, host and aggregate APIs on the Internet are emerged to help users find APIs that meet their requirements in an efficient manner. However, with the huge number of APIs on the web, it is quite challenging for a consumer to find APIs that are satisfactory to her. There is a need to understand users' implicit needs and preferences for APIs, predict what APIs they are likely to use and recommend a list of suitable APIs.

A lot of methods have been proposed for service recommendation, including collaborative-filtering based method [5, 10, 11], content-based method [2, 3, 6] and

---

[1] www.programmableweb.com.

[2] www.mashape.com.

[3] apistore.baidu.com.

© Springer International Publishing Switzerland 2016
Q.Z. Sheng et al. (Eds.): ICSOC 2016, LNCS 9936, pp. 646–653, 2016.
DOI: 10.1007/978-3-319-46295-0_44

a hybrid of both [7–9]. Our work can be regarded as a hybrid recommendation method that combines collaborative filtering and content-based method. In our API recommendation model, users and APIs are connected via the follow relations representing users historical preferences for APIs. Furthermore, APIs are linked with different aspects of functional information. For instance, each API is associated with its provider, category, tags, textual information or the mashups composing it. And different types of relations exist between APIs. For instance, the Facebook API and the Twitter API are linked to each other as they belong to the same Social category, and they are composed together by some mashup. As a result, there exist heterogeneous relations between APIs and these rich source of relations can be utilized in conjunction with user preference relations for hybrid API recommendation.

In this paper, we explore the multiple aspects of API functionalities and their effects on users' preferences, and propose a novel API recommendation approach. We identify several functional aspects of APIs that could impact the adoption of APIs for users, including APIs provider, category, developer, tag, textual description and mashups it composes. We propose to measure the similarities of APIs according to different functional aspects. Then we combine the users historical interaction data with different aspects of API similarities by propagating the user-API relations under different aspects of functionality. Matrix factorization technique is applied on the propagated user preference data and latent factor representation for users and APIs is calculated for each functional aspect of API accordingly. Then we combine these latent factors of different aspects with different weights personalized for each user. A weight learning method is proposed to learn a personalized recommendation model for each user. The final predicted scores of users' preferences for APIs are computed with the learned weights and top scoring APIs are used for recommendation. Our contributions in this work are summarized as follows.

1. We study the problem of discovering users' implicit preferences for APIs and make personalized recommendations by mining rich heterogeneous functional information of APIs with various aspects.
2. We combine matrix factorization based collaborative filtering as well as different types of functional aspects of APIs with personalized weights to perform API recommendation.
3. We conduct extensive experiments on the ProgrammableWeb dataset and the result demonstrate the effectiveness of our recommendation approach.

The remainder of this paper is organized as follows. In Sect. 2, we give an overview of the related work of service recommendation approaches. In Sect. 3, we present details of the proposed API recommendation approach. In Sect. 4, we present and analyze our experimental results. Section 5 concludes this paper.

2   Related Work

Service recommendation can be classified into three categories: functional-based service recommendation, non-functional service recommendation and a hybrid of both. Non-functional based service recommendation focus on predicting the non-functional features (i.e., Qos) of services and recommend services that gives the best Qos performance [5,10,11]. However, the Qos attributes of APIs are not always available due to expensive access cost to all APIs over the web. The functionality of services is usually analyzed by the functional description of services, such as structured WSDL files or free form textual descriptions. In [3], services with similar functionalities are clustered based on WSDL files and the result is used for service recommendation. [2] use LDA-based approach to model functionality of services using both WSDL files and tags. [6] propose a relational topic modeling (RTM) technique to model the functionality of mashups, services and their links. The hybrid service recommendation method combines both functionality and Qos attributes of services. Other available side information can also be utilized for recommendation. [7] use collaborative topic regression technique to integrate both users' preferences and functional features of services. [4] proposed to incorporate three heterogeneous factors to recommend APIs for mashup: the functionality of an API, the usage history of the API by mashups and the popularity of the API, and integrate different sources of information using Bayes' theorem. However, the heterogeneous functional aspects of APIs and whether it is informative to infer users' preferences is unexplored.

3   User Preference Modeling

In this section, we propose to model users' preferences for APIs in terms of different functional aspects of APIs and propose a novel personalized API recommendation model by combining heterogeneous functional information of APIs and collaborative information of other users. Specifically, with m users and n APIs, the user-API matrix $R \in \mathbb{R}^{m \times n}$ is constructed as follows: if a user u_i followed an API a_j, then the corresponding entry of R_{ij} is 1. Otherwise, it is 0. The goal is to predict preference score for unobserved user-API pairs by filling in the 0 entries. To this end, we propose the following recommendation method: First, six functional aspects of APIs, namely provider, category, developer, tag, textual descriptions and mashups, are extracted for each API and the similarities of APIs are evaluated under different aspects of API. Second, the user-API interaction matrix is constructed and is combined with API similarities measured with six aspects respectively. For each aspect of API, the user-API matrix is propagated. Then the six augmented matrices are factored into user latent factor matrices and API latent factor matrices respectively using matrix factorization technique. To predict users' preferences for APIs, the predicted score for each aspect is linearly combined with different weights for each user and a method is proposed to learn the weights from data. Finally, the predicted scores of users for APIs are calculated and APIs that receive the highest score for each user are recommended. The detailed explanation of the method is as follows:

First, we identify six aspects to model the functionalities of an API and their impact on users' preferences. We describe the similarity measuring method for each aspect as follows:

1. Provider. The provider of an API is usually a website that publishes APIs. If two APIs have the same developer, their similarity is 1, otherwise it is 0.
2. Category. Each API belongs to some categories curated by the ProgrammableWeb taxonomy. The similarity of APIs according to category is computed as the Jaccard similarity of the categories two APIs belongs to.
3. Developer. Developers are a group of people who contribute to the development process of APIs. The similarity of APIs with respect to developers is computed as the Jaccard similarity of the developers two APIs have.
4. Tag. Tagging is an effective method of annotating APIs with a list of keywords. The similarity of APIs with respect to tags is computed as the Jaccard similarity of the tags two APIs have.
5. Textual Description. Each API has a brief text describing its functions. We use Latent Dirichlet Allocation (LDA [1]) method, which is a probabilistic topic modeling technique that models the textual descriptions of APIs as a distribution on latent topics. The similarity is computed as the cosine similarity of two topic vectors of APIs.
6. Mashup. Besides functional similarity, different APIs may complement each other. Two APIs of different functionalities can be composed together to form a mashup. The complementarity of APIs is computed as the number of mashups that compose both APIs divided by the number of mashups that only compose one of them.

Next, we utilize heterogeneous aspects of APIs and incorporate them into the recommendation process. We construct an enhanced matrix $\widetilde{R}$ on the basis of R by adding functional aspects of APIs. To this end, we use the following equation to infer users' preferences for each aspect:

$$\widetilde{R}_{ij} = \frac{\sum_{k=1}^{n} R_{ik}\text{sim}(a_j, a_k)}{\sum_{k=1}^{n} \text{sim}(a_j, a_k)} \tag{1}$$

where $\text{sim}(a_j, a_k)$ measures the similarity of APIs under a particular aspect. From Eq. (2) we can see that the users' implicit preferences for unknown APIs are measured by two parts: (1) The observed user-API follow relations represented by R, and (2) the similarities between APIs for a certain aspect represented by $\text{sim}(\cdot)$ function. The predicted score of an unfollowed API is the aggregation of APIs followed by the user weighted by the similarity between them and the predicted API. In this way, the users' preferences are propagated from the original user-API follow matrix R by incorporating the functional aspect of APIs represented by their similarities.

Then, for each propagated user-API matrix, we use matrix factorization method to derive low rank matrices of users and APIs. Since the propagated matrix incorporates a specific type of similarity measurement of APIs, the latent representations of users and APIs are encoded with a certain aspect of API functionality. Specifically, for each propagated matrix $\widetilde{R}^{(l)}$, a pair of user-factor matrix $\widetilde{U}^{(l)}$ and item-factor matrix $\widetilde{V}^{(l)}$ is generatd. Each pair $(\widetilde{U}^{(l)}, \widetilde{V}^{(l)})$ represents users factors and APIs factors according to a certain aspect of APIs. The users' preferences for APIs under a specific aspect is then computed as

$\widetilde{R}^{(l)} = \widetilde{U}^{(l)}\widetilde{V}^{(l)T}$. The overall predicted user-API preference score is computed by combining different aspects of APIs together. As different users may have different preference on particular aspects of APIs, we assign a weight vector for each user to measure her personal preference on different aspects of APIs. The preference score prediction of user u_i to API a_j is defined as follows:

$$\widehat{R}(u_i, v_j) = \sum_{l=1}^{6} \theta_{il}\widetilde{U}_i^{(l)}\widetilde{V}_j^{(l)T} \tag{2}$$

where θ_{il} is the weight for user i on the lth aspect of API. The weight indicates how much impact the corresponding aspect of APIs has on the particular user.

Finally, we introduce how to learn the weight parameter θ for the personalized preference prediction model. The preference score of a user to a followed API should always be higher than the preference score of a user to a non-followed API. To be specific, for each user u_i, if API a_j is followed by user previously and API a_k has never been followed, then the predicted preference score of u_i to a_j should be higher than to a_k. That is, $\widehat{R}(u_i, a_j) > \widehat{R}(u_i, a_k)$ always holds. Assuming that the user-API follow relations are organized in the form of a series of triplets (u_i, a_j, a_k), which means u_i follows API a_j and did not follow a_k. Thus for each triplet, we can define the loss function as:

$$l(u_i, a_j, a_k) = \sigma(R(u_i, a_k) - R(u_i, a_j)) \tag{3}$$

where σ is the sigmoid function to constrain the value between 0 and 1. For all the triplets generated, the overall objective function is

$$L = \sum l(u_i, a_j, a_k) + \frac{\lambda}{2}\|\theta\|^2 \tag{4}$$

where λ is a regularization parameter. By minimizing L we can learn the parameter θ from the triplets. We employ stochastic gradient descent (SGD) method to estimate the parameter θ. The time complexity of the parameter learning process is $O(mn^2)$, which is infeasible for practical implementation. In reality, we only sample a small subset of triplets from data to make the learning process more efficient.

4   Experiments and Evaluation

We conduct a set of experiments to evaluate our proposed approach for API recommendation. We crawled all the APIs available on ProgrammableWeb up until March 2016 and their corresponding followers to construct user-API matrix. We also crawled each API's names, secondary categories, providers, textual descriptions, developers and mashup composition. In summary, our dataset contains 792 users and 9,650 APIs. And there are a total of 1,486 APIs used in 7,066 mashups. We split 80 % of the APIs each user followed into training set and the rest of the APIs as test set. We use precision, recall and F-score to evaluate the prediction accuracy when recommending top K APIs for each user and the metrics are averaged over all users to get the overall performance. We compare our method with the following baseline methods:

1. Neighborhood-based Collaborative Filtering (NBCF). It performs APIs recommendation based on users with similar preferences.
2. Matrix Factorization (MF). The user-API follow matrix R is directly factorized for learning and prediction.
3. Matrix Factorization + Single (MFS). We evaluate the recommendation performance of each of the six aspects one by one.
4. Matrix Factorization + Uniform Weight (MFU). Each aspect is aggregated with the same weight. That is, θ_l is a constant equals to $1/6$.
5. Matrix Factorization + Weight Learning (MFW). Different weights for each aspect of APIs are learned. However the weight vector of each user are all the same.
6. Matrix Factorization + Personalized Weight (MFPW). It is the personalized API recommendation method proposed in the paper with weights different for each user.

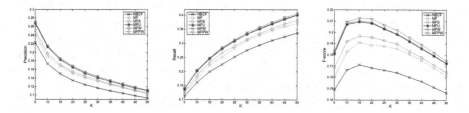

Fig. 1. Performance comparison of competitive methods

Figure 1 shows the recommendation accuracy of all the competitive methods as the number of recommended APIs K ranges from 5 to 50. For method MFS, we only plot the aspect that achieves the best performance to save space. We can see that MFPW consistently achieves the best recommendation performance among all the other methods, which demonstrates the effectiveness of our approach on API recommendation. For other baseline algorithms, Matrix factorization method outperforms neighborhood based method, which shows that latent factor model can capture user API preference relations more accurately. Furthermore, incorporating heterogeneous functional information of APIs can enhance the recommendation performance as MFS method outperforms MF method. And MFU achieves a better recommendation result than MFS, which proves that the idea of combining different aspects of APIs is more effective than only considering a single aspect. Still, MFU method can not yield a better result over MFW since the uniform combination method is too simple to model the difference of impact of API factors. MFPW learns a personalized weight for each user and model users' preferences at a finer granularity, as evidenced by the superior performance compared to MFW. In summary, the experimental results validate our theoretical analysis and show its efficacy in API preference modeling.

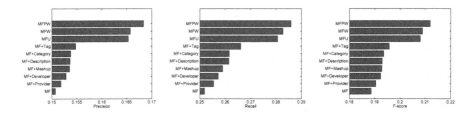

Fig. 2. Performance comparison of each aspect in MFS method

In particular, we plot the recommendation performance for each of the six aspects of APIs in the MFS method as well as other competitive methods. The result is shown in Fig. 2 with the number of recommended APIs K set to 20. Some observations can be drawn: First, compared to the basic MF method, the performance of incorporating each aspect of API all shows an increase with varying degrees. This shows that each aspect of API proposed is helpful for user preference modeling and API recommendation. In particular, different aspects of API has a different impact on users following pattern. The API tags reports the best performance among all the six aspects, which indicates tags are the most informative aspect for understanding users' preferences for APIs. And the API provider is the least informative information for characterizing users' preferences. Second, unifying each aspect of APIs together for recommendation (MFU, MFW, MFPW) performs better than only one single aspect is utilized for recommendation by a relatively large margin. This indicates that the idea of combining different aspects of APIs together is helpful in API recommendation.

5   Conclusion

In this paper, we propose a comprehensive approach for recommending APIs to users. We utilize the heterogeneous content information of APIs and explore the impact of different aspects of APIs on the preferences of users. We identify several aspects of APIs, including API's provider, category, developer, tag, textual descriptions and mashups composing them. Then users' preferences are propagated through different functional aspects of API and matrix factorization is employed for each propagated matrix to learn user and API latent factors under each aspect. To achieve personalized recommendation, latent factors of six functional aspects are combined with different weights for each user. The experimental results demonstrate that our approach outperforms other baseline approaches and proves its effectiveness for personalized API recommendation.

Acknowledgment. This research was partially supported by the Natural Science Foundation of China under grant of No. 61379119, National Science and Technology Supporting Program of China under grant of No. 2015BAH18F02, the Fundamental Research Funds for the Central Universities under grant of No. ZH2016007.

References

1. Blei, D.M., Ng, A.Y., Jordan, M.I.: Latent dirichlet allocation. J. Mach. Learn. Res. **3**, 993–1022 (2003)
2. Chen, L., Wang, Y., Yu, Q., Zheng, Z., Wu, J.: WT-LDA: user tagging augmented LDA for web service clustering. In: Basu, S., Pautasso, C., Zhang, L., Fu, X. (eds.) ICSOC 2013. LNCS, pp. 162–176. Springer, Heidelberg (2013). doi:10.1007/978-3-642-45005-1_12
3. Elgazzar, K., Hassan, A.E., Martin, P.: Clustering WSDL documents to bootstrap the discovery of web services. In: IEEE International Conference on Web Services, ICWS 2010, Miami, Florida, USA, 5–10 July 2010, pp. 147–154 (2010)
4. Jain, A., Liu, X., Yu, Q.: Aggregating functionality, use history, and popularity of APIs to recommend mashup creation. In: Barros, A., Grigori, D., Narendra, N.C., Dam, H.K. (eds.) ICSOC 2015. LNCS, vol. 9435, pp. 188–202. Springer, Heidelberg (2015). doi:10.1007/978-3-662-48616-0_12
5. Jiang, Y., Liu, J., Tang, M., Liu, X.F.: An effective web service recommendation method based on personalized collaborative filtering. In: IEEE International Conference on Web Services, ICWS 2011, Washington, DC, USA, 4–9 July 2011, pp. 211–218 (2011)
6. Li, C., Zhang, R., Huai, J., Sun, H.: A novel approach for API recommendation in mashup development. In: 2014 IEEE International Conference on Web Services, ICWS, 2014, Anchorage, AK, USA, 27 June–2 July 2014, pp. 289–296 (2014)
7. Liu, X., Fulia, I.: Incorporating user, topic, and service related latent factors into web service recommendation. In: 2015 IEEE International Conference on Web Services, ICWS 2015, New York, NY, USA, 27 June–2 July 2015, pp. 185–192 (2015)
8. Xu, W., Cao, J., Hu, L., Wang, J., Li, M.: A social-aware service recommendation approach for mashup creation. In: 2013 IEEE 20th International Conference on Web Services, Santa Clara, CA, USA, 28 June–3 July, 2013, pp. 107–114 (2013)
9. Yao, L., Sheng, Q.Z., Segev, A., Yu, J.: Recommending web services via combining collaborative filtering with content-based features. In: 2013 IEEE 20th International Conference on Web Services, Santa Clara, CA, USA, 28 June–3 July 2013, pp. 42–49 (2013)
10. Zheng, Z., Ma, H., Lyu, M.R., King, I.: Wsrec: a collaborative filtering based web service recommender system. In: IEEE International Conference on Web Services, ICWS 2009, Los Angeles, CA, USA, 6–10 July 2009, pp. 437–444 (2009)
11. Zheng, Z., Ma, H., Lyu, M.R., King, I.: Collaborative web service qos prediction via neighborhood integrated matrix factorization. IEEE Trans. Serv. Comput. **6**(3), 289–299 (2013)

Service Uis, APIs and Mashup (Short Papers)

Empirical Study on the Interface and Feature Evolutions of Mobile Apps

Youqiang Hao, Zhongjie Wang[✉], and Xiaofei Xu

Harbin Institute of Technology, Harbin 150001, Heilongjiang, China
{wind4869,rainy,xiaofei}@hit.edu.cn

Abstract. We make an empirical study on App evolution, especially on inter-App interface evolution and inner-App feature evolution, both from externally observable exhibitions of Apps. Interfaces are extracted from .apk files, and statistical methods are used to discover underlying patterns of interface evolution. Furthermore, potential trend on how interface evolutions of Apps result in the evolution of Global inter-App Network (GAN) is observed. Latent Dirichlet Allocation (LDA) is applied to extract updated features ("topics") from "What's New" of each version to explore the underlying patterns of feature evolution. A set of significant phenomena have been observed from the empirical study.

Keywords: Mobile Apps · Interface evolution · Feature evolution · Global inter-App Network

1 Introduction

Similar to the evolution of traditional web-based services, mobile Apps evolve frequently to eliminate bugs, add new functionalities, or optimize performance. App developers continuously update their Apps and publicize new versions to App stores. Changes between two neighboring versions of an App include changes on internal features and changes on external interfaces exposed to other Apps.

Evolution of Web services/APIs is a hot topic in service computing domain [1,4,10–12], such as exploring the characteristics of App evolution by the analysis of source codes of a series of versions [6,7]. Our work is focused on the "externally observable exhibitions" of App evolution, including the evolution of external interfaces and the evolution of internal features from the .apk files and update notes of App versions with the objective of discovering evolution patterns.

For the interface evolution, an Android App uses an *Intent* to trigger the execution of the functionality of its own or other Apps, and use *Intent-filters* to allow other Apps to invoke its own functionalities. Multiple Apps are connected together via *Intents* and *Intent-filters*, which are considered as the "interfaces" between Apps. From the perspective of one App, changes of its Intents and Intent-filters delineate the refactoring of the functionalities that it is required from and that it offers to other Apps, respectively. **RQ1** of this paper is

© Springer International Publishing Switzerland 2016
Q.Z. Sheng et al. (Eds.): ICSOC 2016, LNCS 9936, pp. 657–665, 2016.
DOI: 10.1007/978-3-319-46295-0_45

stated as follows: **Do interface evolutions of Apps follow any specific laws/patterns? If it is YES, what do such laws/patterns look like?**

Interface changes would take potential effects on the dependencies between related Apps, and further, on the structure of Global inter-App Network (GAN) which depicts the ecosystem of massive Apps. We conjecture that the evolution of GAN's structure would exhibit specific patterns. To discover such patterns would help App developers continuously update their Apps' interface design with the objective of upgrading their Apps' position and importance in GAN, and further, boosting competitiveness of Apps. This results in **RQ2: How does interface evolution of Apps affect the evolution of GAN structure and characteristics (e.g., scale and density)?**

A version upgrade brings changes on a variety of App features (functionalities, performance and so on), and such changes are usually explicitly recorded by "What's New", i.e., a text-based description of an App version. Similar to App interfaces, changes on these features may follow specific laws/patterns, i.e., **RQ3: How do the features of an App evolve over time, and are there any common patterns in the feature evolutions of massive Apps?**

In this paper, we conduct empirical study on the "externally observable exhibitions" of Apps to explore the characteristics of their evolutions, i.e., the exposed interfaces and the publicized "What's New", rather than their source code which is the main base of traditional evolution studies. We use a set of statistical metrics to measure the characteristics of interface evolution. To study the evolution of GAN, we construct a GAN every month in total 51 months and then measure changes of the scale and density of these GANs to explore GAN evolution characteristics. For the feature evolution, we employ the Latent Dirichlet Allocation (LDA) method to transform "What's New" into topic model which is then used to explore the underlying laws/patterns of feature evolution of one App.

Section 2 introduces two types of App evolutions, especially approaches on how to extract interfaces and features from externally observable exhibitions of App versions; Sect. 3 is the empirical study; Sect. 4 introduces related work; and Sect. 5 is the conclusion.

2   Mobile Apps and Two Types of Evolution

In Android Apps, there are two types of *Intents*: explicit and implicit ones. The former one specifically points out the exact App that will accept the Intent and be run next. The latter one does not specify the target App but includes enough information for the Intent-filters to be launched, and it is the Android system's responsibility to determine which installed App(s) is best to run for this Intent by "Intent resolution" (i.e., to map from a received Intent to a set of Intent-filters). This is called "Inter-Component Communication (ICC)". An explicit Intent results in a 1 : 1 relation between two Apps, while an implicit Intent results in a 1 : n relation which can be split into n number of 1 : 1 relations.

A Global inter-App Network (GAN) is a directed graph describing global inter-App relations. It is denoted as $GAN = (A, I, date)$, where A is a set of

Apps (nodes), I is a set of Intent-based relations (directed edges), and *date* is the moment when GAN is built. Each edge $icc_{ij} = (a_i, a_j, Intent_{ij}, \omega_{ij})$ indicates that a_i contains an $Intent_{ij}$ that matches with an Intent-filter of a_j, and ω_{ij} is used to clarify whether it is an explicit or implicit relation. Formal definition of GAN can be found in [3].

With the help of Android static analysis tools such as dex2jar, IntentAnalysis and APKParser, Intents and Intent-filters from .apk files are extracted and resolved for matching to identify possible explicit/implicit ICCs among Apps. There are two types of interface evolution: (1) *addition* and *removal*, i.e., new interfaces may be added into a new version, and an existing interface may be removed from a new version; (2) *amendment*, i.e., internal implementation of an interface may be modified along with possible renaming of the interface. Here we are focused on the former type of interface evolution but simply treat the interfaces that are amended in a new version as two different interfaces.

Interface evolution results in changes of dependencies among a group of related Apps and further lead to the evolution of GAN. To acquire the characteristics of GAN evolution, from January 2012 to March 2016, one GAN is constructed at the end of each month and total 51 GANs are obtained.

In most instances, developers of an App would like to write down such feature changes in details in "What's New" so that users would easily get to know their efforts for improving App quality. In our study, we use Latent Dirichlet Allocation (LDA) to extract the latent topics from "What's New", thus each natural language based App description is transformed into a calculable and numerical features called topic distribution vector (i.e., the probability that each latent topic is covered by each document). Underlying laws/patterns of feature evolution are then easily observed in terms of such topic models.

3 Empirical Study

3.1 Dataset

HiMarket[1] is selected as the data source of mobile Apps. It is a top-5 Android app store in China with millions of Apps in more than 15 categories as of March 2016. Compared with other App stores, it offers more comprehensive and detailed data of historical versions of Apps, which may well support our study.

Because the number of Apps is too large, it is difficult to consider all Apps for a limited time. We made a sampling on the complete set to get a representative subset Apps. Three principles are adopted for the sampling: (1) only those top-1000 Apps in the ranking of HiMarket are considered; (2) only those Apps that have at least 10 versions are considered; (3) In each App category, 3–5 most popular Apps are selected. Total 50 Apps are selected and all of their historical versions are crawled from the market. Both the length of lifecycle and the number of versions of these selected Apps show high diversities.

---

[1] http://apk.hiapk.com.

3.2   Interface Evolution

Evolution Patterns of Interface Coverage. We are firstly interested in the Time-to-Live (TTL) of each interface, or called the coverage degree of each interface relative to the lifecycle of an App. In other words, how many versions are covered by each interface and is such coverage continuous or interruptive? We identified four types of evolution patterns of interface coverage: (1) Entire Coverage (EC), i.e., an interface does exist in all the versions of an App; (2) Continuous Coverage (CC), i.e., an interface first appears in a specific version and exists until the latest version; (3) Interruptive Coverage (IC), i.e., an interface disappears in some versions but re-appears in a latter version; (4) Disappeared Coverage (DC), i.e., an interface disappears but never re-appears later.

Statistical studies on the four coverage patterns on 50 Apps are conducted. We calculate the ratios of interfaces belonging to each pattern. The ratios of interfaces (both Intents and Intent-filters) belonging to IC are generally low among all Apps (mostly in the range $[0, 0.2]$ for Intents and $[0, 0.1]$ for Intent-filters), indicating that developers seldom "turn back to crop the old grass". Another phenomenon is that the ratios of EC and CC of Intent-filters are higher than the ones of Intents (having mean values 0.70 and 0.57 and variance 0.11 and 0.18, respectively), indicating that Intent-filters are more stable than Intents (i.e., Apps prefer to expose stable functionalities to other Apps with less changes, but what they require from other Apps are less stable).

Interface Evolution Amplitude Between Neighboring Versions. In order to figure out the interface evolution amplitude between neighboring versions of an App, we use an interface coverage vector to delineate the absence or presence of all the interfaces in a specific version, then measure the Cosine similarity of two vectors of neighboring versions. If two neighboring versions cover quite different interfaces, the similarity would be low. For an App with total N versions, there are total $N - 1$ similarities.

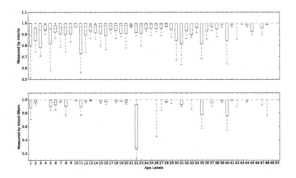

Fig. 1. Evolution amplitude in interfaces for each Apps

Boxplots in Fig. 1 show the distributions of these similarities on Intents and Intent-filters, respectively. We find that the similarities of Intent-filter coverage vectors are almost all distributed close to 1 within narrower ranges, indicating that Intent-filters have lower evolution amplitude (higher stability), and the ones of Intents are distributed within wider ranges, indicating that Intents tend to display more drastic changes in neighboring versions (lower stability).

If we compare among different Apps, their similarity distributions show quite diversified shapes, indicating different evolution strategies are adopted by their developers. For example, an App *Meituan* shows very wide similarity distribution of its Intent-filters; although it has only 13 versions, there are about 20 Intent-filters changed in each upgrade, implying significant evolutions on its interfaces. This might be driven by the fierce competition in China's O2O market.

3.3 GAN Evolution

Structure Evolution. Statistics on the scale and density of 51 GANs are shown in Fig. 2. The conclusions are straightforward: (1) the number of nodes is increasing over time, indicating more and more Apps join GAN and have dependencies with other Apps; (2) the growing tendencies of edges and density of GAN indicate that dependencies among Apps become richer and closer, i.e., the number of inter-App interfaces keep increasing. This would inspire App developers to design more interfaces so that their Apps could share more connections with others, and further, to gain better popularity in App ecosystem.

Evolution of Popularity of Core Interfaces. For details of GAN evolution, we study the evolution of 26 common Intents in these Apps. We make statistics on the number of Apps in which each Intent exists and the number of Apps that could match each Intent. Figure 3 shows changes of the two metrics over time. As shown in Fig. 3(a), almost half (12 out of 26) of these Intents are related to browsing webpages ("VIEW url"). Each of these Intents exists only in one or two Apps all the time, but has the largest and increasing number of matched Apps (proved by Fig. 3(b)), suggesting that web browsing becomes

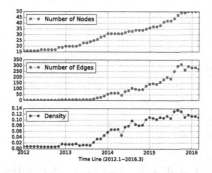

Fig. 2. Evolution of GAN's scale and density

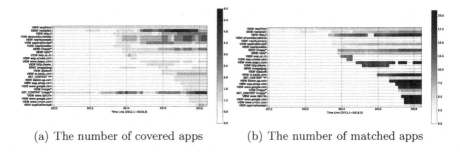

(a) The number of covered apps   (b) The number of matched apps

Fig. 3. Evolution of popularity of core interfaces

an increasingly common feature of Apps. Text sharing related Intent ("SEND text/plain"), image sharing related Intent ("SEND image/*") and image selection related Intent ("GET_CONTENT image/*") are most popular intents and have an increasing trend in the number of both covered and matched Apps, which indicates that a great mass of communications between Apps are to share contents like text, image and so on.

3.4 Feature Evolution

Evolution Pattern. We use the texts of "What's New" from 50 Apps to train a LDA model having 20 feature topics. Based on this topic model, "What's New" of each version of each App is transformed into a topic distribution vector describing the distribution probability of each latent topic with 20 dimensions. The 20-dimension probability vector of each version is demonstrated by a vertical bar composing of 20 squares which are filled by different shades of grey.

From the 50 Apps' topic evolutions we have found there are 3 types of evolution patterns for feature topics: (1) "Continuously Hot", i.e., those topics related to core features of an App are upgraded very frequently, thus they keep hot in the lifecycle of the App; (2) "Incontinuously Hot", i.e., those topics that are concerned not in every version upgrade but at set intervals; (3) "Only Once", representing those auxiliary features that do not need improvement many times.

Version Clustering. We conduct clustering on all versions of each App in terms of their topic distribution vectors. Versions with more similar topic distribution vectors address more similar feature upgrades. We found that the feature evolution of *WeChat* shows "temporal locality", implying that a group of neighboring versions prefer to upgrade similar features over a period of time, then developers switch to another group of similar features. Such "temporal locality" exists in the histories of all 50 Apps, which suggests that it tends to be a universal law of App evolutions.

Feature Evolution Amplitude Between Neighboring Versions. We use Cosine similarity of the topic distribution vectors to measure the similarity/difference on the upgraded features between two neighboring versions of an App. If an App has N versions, then there would be $N - 1$ feature evolution similarities. We find that almost all Apps have very wide distributions in the range $[0, 1]$, which suggests that most Apps have both fine tuning (small amplitude of feature evolution) and drastic changes (large amplitude) between neighboring versions. This is in accordance with traditional software evolution research, i.e., between two large-scale upgrades there are usually a set of small-scale ones.

However, some outliers do exist. For example, *PPlive*, being an App for online video playing, has a narrow distribution close to x-axis, indicating there are quite big differences between all pairs of its neighboring versions, probably because of its frequent and large-scale updates on the video contents. *When*, being a calendar App, is an opposite outlier whose distribution is narrow but quite close to 1, indicating its upgrades are usually small-scale, probably because of its simple functionalities.

3.5 Threats to Validity

We study App evolution based on externally observable exhibitions of Apps. Upgraded interfaces are accurately extracted from .apk file of each version via Android static analysis tools, and upgraded features are extracted from "What's New" of each version via topic-based LDA methods. Effectiveness of these tools and methods have been validated by related research, which ensures validity of data source of our empirical study.

We crawled Apps from HiMarket, one of the most popular App stores in China with millions of popular Apps. Especially, the most important consideration is that it offers all the historical versions of Apps, which brings great benefits to our study, i.e., to study the evolution in the full lifecycle of Apps. Although only 50 Apps are selected (the number is not so large), but the selection criterion we adopted ensure that they are representative enough in the perspectives like TTL, number of versions, categories they belong to, and so on.

4   Related Work

Concerning mobile App evolution, Minelli and Lanza [8] performed case studies on the evolution of source code, usage of third-party APIs and historical data of open source mobile Apps. Linares-Vásquez [6] detected four types of API changes in Android platform and third-party libraries, to help Android developers mitigate negative impact of API changes in App maintenance. McIlroy et al. [7] performed an empirical study on the mobile Apps updates, and besides update frequency, they also studied what is actually changing for frequent updates and the rationale. Palomba et al. [9] devised an approach named CRISTAL for tracing informative crowd reviews onto source code changes and for monitoring the extent to which developers accommodate crowd requests and follow-up user reactions as reflected in their ratings. Carreño et al. [2] used Information Extraction

(IE) techniques with topic modeling to automatically get constructive feedback from user comments to study the evolution of user requirements. Lin et al. [5] presented a novel framework for utilizing a semi-supervised variant of LDA that accounts for both text and metadata to characterize version features into a set of latent topics, and explored the effectiveness of using version features in App recommendation.

5   Conclusions

This paper makes an empirical study based on the "externally observable exhibitions" of Apps, i.e., a set of versions with installable files and human-readable update notes ("What's New") that are all publicized in App stores. Empirical study helps us draw valuable conclusions such as: (1) There are 4 types of interface evolution patterns, and Intent-filters look much more stable than Intents; (2) The scale and density of GAN become more higher over time, indicating that Apps tend to collaborate more tightly over time; (3) Feature evolution follows 3 types of patterns and shows significant "temporal locality".

Acknowledgments. Work in this paper is supported by the Natural Science Foundation of China (Nos. 61272187, 61472106).

References

1. Fokaefs, M., Mikhaiel, R., Tsantalis, N., Stroulia, E., Lau, A.: An empirical study on web service evolution. In: Proceedings of IEEE 18th International Conference on Web Services, pp. 49–56. IEEE (2011)
2. Galvis Carreño, L.V., Winbladh, K.: Analysis of user comments: an approach for software requirements evolution. In: Proceedings of International Conference on Software Engineering, pp. 582–591. IEEE (2013)
3. Hao, Y., Wang, Z., Xu, X.: Global and personal app networks: characterizing social relations among mobile apps. In: Proceedings of 13th International Conference on Services Computing, pp. 227–234. IEEE (2016)
4. Li, J., Xiong, Y., Liu, X., Zhang, L.: How does web service API evolution affect clients? In: Proceedings of IEEE 20th International Conference on Web Services, pp. 300–307. IEEE (2013)
5. Lin, J., Sugiyama, K., Kan, M.Y., Chua, T.S.: New and improved: modeling versions to improve app recommendation. In: Proceedings of 37th International ACM SIGIR Conference on Research & Development in Information Retrieval, pp. 647–656. ACM (2014)
6. Linares-Vásquez, M.: Supporting evolution and maintenance of android apps. In: Companion Proceedings of the 36th International Conference on Software Engineering, pp. 714–717. ACM (2014)
7. McIlroy, S., Ali, N., Hassan, A.E.: Fresh apps: an empirical study of frequently-updated mobile apps in the google play store. Empirical Softw. Eng. **21**(3), 1346–1370 (2016)
8. Minelli, R., Lanza, M.: Software analytics for mobile applications-insights & lessons learned. In: Proceedings of IEEE International Conference on Software Maintenance and Reengineering, pp. 144–153. IEEE (2013)

9. Palomba, F., Linares-Vásquez, M., Bavota, G., Oliveto, R., Di Penta, M., Poshy-vanyk, D., De Lucia, A.: User reviews matter! tracking crowdsourced reviews to support evolution of successful apps. In: Proceedings of IEEE International Conference on Software Maintenance and Evolution, pp. 291–300. IEEE (2015)
10. Romano, D., Pinzger, M.: Analyzing the evolution of web services using fine-grained changes. In: Proceedings of IEEE 19th International Conference on Web Services, pp. 392–399. IEEE (2012)
11. Sohan, S., Anslow, C., Maurer, F.: A case study of web API evolution. In: Proceedings of IEEE World Congress on Services, pp. 245–252. IEEE (2015)
12. Wang, S., Keivanloo, I., Zou, Y.: How do developers react to RESTful API evolution? In: Franch, X., Ghose, A.K., Lewis, G.A., Bhiri, S. (eds.) ICSOC 2014. LNCS, vol. 8831, pp. 245–259. Springer, Heidelberg (2014). doi:10.1007/978-3-662-45391-9_17

Service Package Recommendation for Mashup Development Based on a Multi-level Relational Network

Jian Cao[✉], Yijing Lu, and Nengjun Zhu

Department of Computer Science and Engineering, Shanghai Jiaotong University, Shanghai, People's Republic of China
{cao-jian,luyjcathy,zhu_nj}@sjtu.edu.cn

Abstract. With the number of services growing explosively, it has been a serious problem selecting appropriate services for mashup development. In this paper, we come up with a Multi-level Relational Network (MRN) based approach for service recommendation in mashup development, which captures deep relationships among services on top of latent topic, tag and service network. Specifically, by modeling the correlation among services, representing it as a Quadratic Knapsack Problem and solving it using Branch and Bound algorithm, we are able to recommend a package of services, which are complementary and possible to be used together in a mashup. Experiments on a realistic mashup data set have shown its effectiveness.

Keywords: Mashup creation · Multi-level relational network · Service package recommendation

1 Introduction

With the advent of Web 2.0, mashup, as a novel service composition implementation, is developing rapidly. There are some websites or communities providing supports for mashup, such as Yahoo Pipes[1], ProgrammableWeb[2], etc. Despite the convenience to create a mashup, there are still troubles finding suitable services to compose, because of the large amount of services available. As is often the case, users type down a few words describing the functionality of their mashups to be developed, and then get stuck on which service to choose. Therefore, recommending services in mashup development has been a vital problem. There is already some reasearch aiming to solve this. Information retrieval technology can be used to match the descriptions of mashup and APIs. It is intuitive but ignores the knowledge that can be captured from existing mashups. Another common approach is to discover frequent service composition sequences from historical mashups. In this case, when some services are chosen, other services can

---

[1] pipes.yahoo.com.

[2] www.programmableweb.com.

© Springer International Publishing Switzerland 2016
Q.Z. Sheng et al. (Eds.): ICSOC 2016, LNCS 9936, pp. 666–674, 2016.
DOI: 10.1007/978-3-319-46295-0_46

be recommended by searching relating frequent service composition sequences. However, in this case, the newly published services have no chance to be recommended. Moreover, these two approaches can only recommend optional services with similar function. Obviously, in mashup development, it is more useful to recommend a set of compatible services, rather than a list of similar services.

In this paper, we call the problem of recommending a set of compatible services for mashup development "service package recommendation". The problem we intend to solve is how to recommend a service package when a textual description for the mashup to be developed is given.

Our work is distinguished by three key contributions: (1) We propose a MRN model, which can capture the deep relationships among services and support service recommendation. (2) We formalize the service package recommendation as a Quadratic Knapsack Problem and solve it using Branch and Bound algorithm. (3) We carry out experiments on realistic data set which show that our approach is effective.

The remaining sections are organized as follows: Sect. 2 describes related work. In Sect. 3, we present our MRN model. In Sect. 4, we formalize the service package recommendation problem and describe in detail how it can be solved. The experiments on realistic dataset are presented in Sect. 5. Finally, we draw a conclusion of this paper in Sect. 6.

2   Related Work

One major service recommendation approach takes advantage of historical frequent service composition patterns for recommendation [1,2]. However, simply relying on frequent sequence fails in the situations where new patterns can be adopted, or when new services are published.

Since users are searching for some APIs to use, adopting traditional information retrieval technologies is also an intuitive method [3]. Furthermore, Chune Li et al. [4] adopted relational topic model in mashup development, which take into account the historical associations between mashup and API. Similar to topic model, tag as a user-driven way to feature mashup and APIs, is also capable of annotating frequent patterns [5]. These research gives us the inspiration that semantic approaches, though not working well singly, are helpful if properly used.

Some researchers are also investigating the possibility of applying recommender system and approaches in e-commerce into mashup domain [6–8] . But in our problem where only description is provided, these approaches cannot be applied directly.

Furthermore, there is some research trying to make use of more information to improve the recommendation. Among those approaches, the most widely used information is social relationship [9,10]. However, such social-aware methods rely too much on a complete social network. Once social information is incomplete or absent, they are not going to work well.

Our MRN model integrates topics, tags and services and their inherent relationships in a more comprehensive way. In addition, in the hope of recommending services with complementary functionality, we get inspiration from [11] which implemented bundle recommendation (similar to package recommendation) in e-commerce.

3 The Multi-level Relational Network Model

Our approach is based on the MRN model, which involves the relationships of topics, tags and services. In the rest of this section, we introduce each of the layers in detail.

3.1 Service Network

The bottom layer of the MRN is the service network. Once two services appear in the same mashup, we record them as a service pair (s_i, s_j). And thus, we can construct a service network, whose edge weight (i, j) indicates how many times (s_i, s_j) are connected based on historical mashup information.

To use service network, we assign a score between the given mashup and each of the candidate APIs upon service layer. The score is denoted as service utility. In the rating step, for mashup m_i and service s_j, the service utility is constructed as follows: we first obtain a list of services RS_{m_i} relevant to m_i through topic model, and then accumulate the edge weights between services on top of service network.

3.2 Tag Network

For a mashup m_i, the tags it has are denoted as $Tag_{m_i} = \{tag_{m_i,1}, tag_{m_i,2}, \cdots, tag_{m_i,j}, \cdots\}$. Services s_i also have their tags, denoted as $Tag_{s_i} = \{tag_{s_i,1}, tag_{s_i,2}, tag_{s_i,3}, \cdots, tag_{s_i,j}, \cdots\}$. We apply the association rule mining method described in [5] to discover the relationships between tags. For each mashup m_i, we consider Tag_{m_i} to be related to all the tags belonging to S_{m_i}. And also, since all the services in S_{m_i} are composed together, each pair of them is considered being associated in the tag network.

By identifying all the tag pairs in the mashup repository, we can get a network $Tag\_network$, in which the weight of each edge (i, j) represents how many times tag_i and tag_j are associated.

Given a mashup and a candidate set of APIs, we can assign a utility score between the mashup and each API from the viewpoint of tag network. In another word, we try to describe which API is closer to the mashup in a quantity way based on tag network. This can be done by taking out the tags of mashup and API, and accumulating the weight of the edge between each tag pair.

3.3   Topic Network

It is very useful to apply topic model in recommendation. LDA is used to model our resources. For each mashup and API, we collect their descriptions as corpus and extract a topic distribution. A topic distribution for mashup m_i is denoted as $Topic_{m_i} = \{topic_{m_i,1}, topic_{m_i,2}, topic_{m_i,3}, \cdots, topic_{m_i,\#TN}\}$, in which $\#TN$ is a number manually defined. Top K topics in the distribution are chosen to be relevant topics.

We use topic model as a part of our rating metrics, in the similar way we use tags. A topic pair $(topic_i, topic_j)$ is considered associated if they belong to a mashup and its API respectively, or to two APIs belonging to the same mashup. Finally, we can construct a topic network, the weight of each edge (i, j) represents how many times $topic_i$ and $topic_j$ are connected.

Moreover, like tag utility, we assign a score called topic utility to measure the cooperation degree between a mashup and API connection from the viewpoint of topic network, by cross-multiplying the relevant topics and adding their scores over topic network.

4   Service Package Recommendation

Package recommendation is sometimes called bundle recommendation, especially in e-commerce. Bundle originally refers to a set of items that customers consider or buy together [11]. When recommending a list of services to users, we want them to have the highest utilities, not only to the mashup, but also internally to each other. Thus, we can say that we are not recommending a list of services, but rather a package of services.

4.1   Model Construction

We propose our new model to calculate the total utilities. Given a mashup m_D and a set of services, we use a vector x to denote which service we pick into the final result. x_i is 0 if s_i is not chosen, and 1 if chosen. Then, the total utility can be denoted as:

$$U_{total}(m_D, x) = \sum_i U(m_D, s_i)x_i + \sum_{i<j} U(s_i, s_j)x_i x_j \qquad (1)$$

The goal of service package recommendation is to find a set of k items that maximize the total utility. Let:

$$r_i = U(m_D, s_i)$$

$$Q_{i,j} = \begin{cases} U(s_i, s_j) & \text{if } i \neq j \\ 0 & \text{if } i = j \end{cases}$$

The total utility can now be described as:

$$U_{total}(x) = r^T x + x^T Q x \qquad (2)$$

It is essentially a case of Quadratic Knapsack Problem [12].

$$\max_{x\in\{0,1\}^n,|x|=k} r^T x + x^T Q x \tag{3}$$

4.2 Solving QKP

Having $r = 0$, it is not hard to see that this problem reduces to a k-clique problem. Since k-clique problem is a NP-hard problem, it is supported by theorem that our problem is also a large-scale NP-hard problem. Luckily, we get the inspiration from [11] that solving the problem for all the items is equivalent to solving it for a carefully constructed candidate set.

As said by Zhu et al., it is observed in practice that only a few items have a high score, so it is intuitively understandable to construct a candidate set. As to our data set, we also observed such situation that to a given description of mashup, only a small set of services have relatively high utilities, while the majority have a low value. It is rigorously proved in [11] that items dominated by k or more items will not appear in an optimal selection, in which dominance is a relationship between items. Item α dominants item β if:

$$r_\alpha + Q_{\alpha\alpha} + \min_{A\subseteq U,|A|=k-1} \sum_{i\in A, i\neq\alpha} (Q_{\alpha i} + Q_{i\alpha}) >$$

$$r_\beta + Q_{\beta\beta} + \max_{B\subseteq U,|B|=k-1} \sum_{i\in B, i\neq\beta} (Q_{\beta i} + Q_{i\beta})$$

That implies we only need to find items dominated by no more than $k - 1$ items, which makes the candidate set size different for every item. Computations and empirical results show that the resultant candidate size is very small compared to the whole dataset. To decrease computational time and cost, it is acceptable to choose a fixed candidate set size m for every item, which is slightly larger than empirical data. So in our model, it is sufficient to solve the problem on top of a candidate set C_{set}.

We update our model as follows, where r_c and Q_c are the responding variables for C_{set}. With the size of potential candidates largely reduced, our problem is now tractable.

$$\max_{x\in\{0,1\}^n,|x|=k} r_c^T x + x^T Q_c x \tag{4}$$

We use Gurobi[3] as an assistance, which is a state-of-art mathematical programming solver.

5 Experiments

5.1 Dataset and Compareative Methods

The dataset we use comes from ProgrammableWeb.com, namely the largest mashup information sharing community. We crawled ProgrammableWeb and get

---

[3] http://www.gurobi.com/.

7674 valid mashups as well as 10240 services (called APIs in ProgrammableWeb). For each mashup and service, we got its full information especially service lists for mashup, description and annotating tags for both of them. There are totally 462 different tags involved. We selected information retrieval, recommendations based on single layer network and recommendation without considering package effect as our comparative methods.

5.2   Model Training

We use 90 % of the mashups to learn the model, and the rest 10 % to test. There are many parameters in our model. In this section, we show how they are selected and fitted.

The first parameter to deal with is the number of topics. We use the Stanford Topic Modeling Toolbox[4] to help train our topic model. We collect the descriptions of mashups and services together to train topic model with number of topics varying from 10 to 400. The best performance is reached when topic number equals 300, which is later chosen for our further experiments.

Another important arguments in our model is the weight of each network layer. It is hard to decide how much a layer should contribute to the final result theoretically. We can try different combination of values under some constraints, and get a best fit. To achieve this goal, we employ genetic algorithm to find the answer under a linear constraints. Finally we get the best fit of (α, β, γ) at $(0.4, 0.1, 0.5)$ respectively for topic network, tag network, and service network. This confirms the leading position of service layer in the recommendation process, but others can also help improve the results.

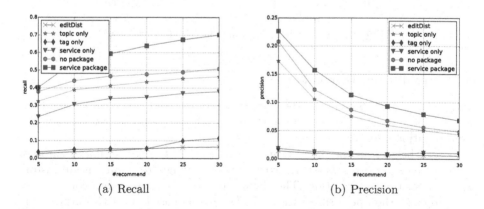

(a) Recall   (b) Precision

Fig. 1. Results of different approaches over various #recommendation

---

[4] http://www.nlp.stanford.edu/software/tmt/tmt-0.4/.

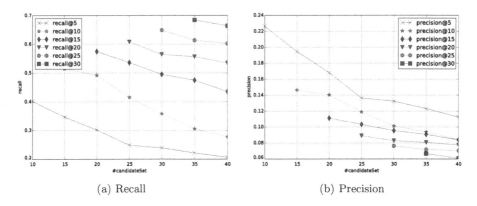

(a) Recall   (b) Precision

Fig. 2. Results of service package recommendation over various #candidateSet and #recommendation

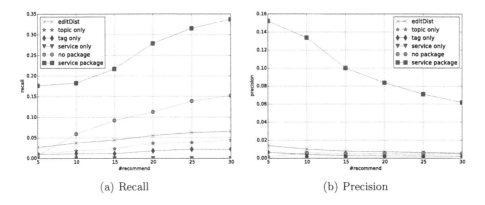

(a) Recall   (b) Precision

Fig. 3. Results when recommended services are new

5.3   Results and Discussion

Upon the selected best parameter values, we conducted experiments using each of the methods. Figure 1 shows the recall for all the methods over varying recommendation size.

It can be seen in the figure that, the methods of textual similarity through EditDistance performs worst, as expected, since it ignores many useful historical composition information. The three separate base approaches comes next, with topic method performing the best. The model based on MRN outperforms the comparative approaches to a great extent. Moreover, our service package recommendation approach further improves the performance.

The service package recommendation result in Fig. 1 is a part of our final experiments. We show the full results in Fig. 2, where various length of candidate set is considered, as well as the size of recommendation set. It is unexpected to see that given a recommendation number, the smaller candidate set size is, the better performance we get. This suggests that we need to choose a proper candidate set in practice.

It has been mentioned that our model is capable of recommending new services. We conduct an experiment to verify this. For each test case, we remove the effect of its services in the train set to make the services all new. The results are shown in Fig. 3. It can be seen from the figure that the integrated model can successfully recommend new services.

6 Conclusion and Future Work

In this paper, a multi-level relational network is applied to capture and model the comprehensive relationships between topics, tags, and services. Specifically, we propose the concept of service package recommendation, enabling to recommend a set of complementary services, rather than a list of similar ones. Experiments on realistic mashup data set have shown its effectiveness.

Acknowledgements. This work is partially supported by China NSF (Granted Number 61272438,61472253), Research Funds of Science and Technology Commission of Shanghai Municipality (Granted Number 15411952502).

References

1. Oliveira, F.T., Murta, L., Werner, C., Mattoso, M.: Using provenance to improve workflow design. In: Freire, J., Koop, D., Moreau, L. (eds.) IPAW 2008. LNCS, pp. 136–143. Springer, Heidelberg (2008). doi:10.1007/978-3-540-89965-5_15
2. Maaradji, A., Hacid, H., Skraba, R., Vakali, A.: Social web mashups full completion via frequent sequence mining. In: Proceedings - 2011 IEEE World Congress on Services, SERVICES 2011, pp. 9–16 (2011)
3. Platzer, C., Dustdar, S.: A vector space search engine for Web services. In: Third European Conference on Web Services (ECOWS 2005) (2005)
4. Li, C., Zhang, R., Huai, J., Sun, H.: A novel approach for API recommendation in mashup development. In: 2014 IEEE International Conference on Web Services (ICWS) (2014)
5. Goarany, K., Kulczycki, G., Blake, M.B.: Mining social tags to predict mashup patterns. In: Proceedings of the 2nd International Workshop on Search and Mining User-Generated Contents (SMUC 2010), pp. 71–78. ACM, New York (2010)
6. Cremonesi, P., Picozzi, M., Matera, M.: A comparison of recommender systems for mashup composition. In: Proceedings of 2012 3rd International Workshop on Recommendation Systems for Software Engineering, RSSE 2012, pp. 54–58 (2012)
7. Yao, L., Wang, X., Sheng, Q.Z., Ruan, W., Zhang, W.: Service recommendation for mashup composition with implicit correlation regularization. In: 2015 IEEE International Conference on Web Services (ICWS), pp. 217–224, June 2015
8. Zheng, Z., Lyu, M.R.: Component recommendation for cloud applications. In: Proceedings of RSSE, pp. 48–49 (2010)
9. Cao, B., Liu, J., Tang, M., Zheng, Z., Wang, G.: Mashup service recommendation based on user interest and social network. In: 2013 IEEE 20th International Conference on Web Services (ICWS), pp. 99–106 (2013)

10. Xu, W., Cao, J., Hu, L., Wang, J., Li, M.: A social-aware service recommendation approach for mashup creation. In: 2013 IEEE 20th International Conference on Web Services (ICWS), pp. 107–114 (2013)
11. Zhu, T., Harrington, P., Li, J., Tang, L.: Bundle recommendation in ecommerce. In: Proceedings of the 37th International ACM SIGIR Conference on Research and Development in Information Retrieval, SIGIR 2014, pp. 657–666 (2014)
12. Gallo, G., Hammer, P., Simeone, B.: Quadratic knapsack problems. In: Padberg, M.W. (ed.) Combinatorial Optimization, vol. 12, pp. 132–149. Springer, Heidelberg (1980)

Service/Process Foundation (Short Papers)

Integrating POMDP and SARSA(λ) for Service Composition with Incomplete Information

Hongbing Wang[1(✉)], Xingzhi Zhang[1], and Qi Yu[2]

[1] School of Computer Science and Engineering, Southeast University, Nanjing, China
hbw@seu.edu.cn, zhangxingzhi777@163.com
[2] College of Computing and Information Sciences, Rochester Institute of Technology,
Rochester, USA
qi.yu@rit.edu

Abstract. As a powerful computing paradigm for constructing complex distributed applications, service composition is usually addressed as a planning problem since the goal is to optimize a path for combining services to satisfy special requirements. Some planning methods assume that the state of running environment can be fully observed and monitored. However, the dynamic internet environment and opaque internal status, such as QoS attributes and invoking results, make the assumption too strict and not generally applicable. In this paper, we introduce a Partially Observable Markov Decision Process (POMDP) to model a service composition, which views the environment as partially observable and generates a policy with incomplete information. The partial observability relaxes the previous assumption and can handle the difficulties occurring in a dynamic and unpredictable environment. Based on this model, we propose a reinforcement learning algorithm to compute the optimal strategy. We conduct a series of experiments to verify the proposed algorithm, and compare it the comparison with other two algorithms. The results show the correctness and effectiveness of our algorithm.

1 Introduction

In a Service Oriented Computing (SOC) environment, services that are autonomous, loosely coupled and self-describing, are leveraged as fundamental components to develop interoperable distributed applications. Since a single web service may not satisfy the requirements of complex business requirements, service composition has attracted extensive attention in service computing [5].

In a service composition process, it mainly faces an uncertain and dynamic web environment. On the one hand, in most service-oriented systems, there exists uncertainty in services. For example, some behavior of a service may not be deterministic (which could depend on the input values) and hence the invocation result of the service may be uncertain. As another example, some QoS values of a service may not known in advance and others (e.g., response time and throughput) may change with the dynamic environment. These uncertain

© Springer International Publishing Switzerland 2016
Q.Z. Sheng et al. (Eds.): ICSOC 2016, LNCS 9936, pp. 677–684, 2016.
DOI: 10.1007/978-3-319-46295-0_47

factors can not be detected precisely and affect the process of a service composition. On the other hand, considering that the online services may evolve with the dynamic external environment, a service composition needs to be adaptive to these changes [13]. In summary, a viable solution to service composition should take both the incomplete information and a dynamic environment into consideration, and provide an effective mechanism to satisfy the uncertainty and adaptivity.

To address the challenges of dynamic implicit information in service composition, we propose a novel method that combines Partially Observable Markov Decision Process (POMDP) with reinforcement learning (RL) for service composition. The POMDP refers to a sequential decision-making problem under uncertainty [1,4]. This model does not assume that the environment is fully observable. Instead only some of the features are observed.

We use introduce the POMDP to model the service composition process. In the POMDP service composition framework, an agent does not need the exact state information, which is unavailable. It perceives the environment and gathers observations as computational basis at runtime. Then, the goal is adjusted to find a composition policy that maximizes the reward by the observations and past records. Inspired by the idea of RL, we present a learning algorithm combining eligibility trace (SARSA (λ)), to compose web services in the POMDP framework. Hence, our approach can handle the uncertainty issue in service composition while achieving the adaptivity and efficiency. The rest of this paper is organized as follows. An overview of related work is presented in Sect. 2. The problem formulation and key definitions are given in Sect. 3. The model and algorithm proposed in this paper are described in detail in Sect. 4. Experimental results are presented in Sect. 5 to verify the effectiveness of our approach. Finally, the conclusion is given in Sect. 6.

2   Related Work

In this section, we give an overview of existing approaches that have contributed to service composition, including Markov Decision Process (MDP), reinforcement learning (RL) and Partially Observable Markov Decision Process (POMDP).

Gao et al. [6] and Doshi et al. [3] proposed a web service composition approach based on MDPs. Given the QoS description, Gao et al. described some web service composition patterns, such as sequential, conditional and iterative, in an MDP framework. Doshi et al. developed a policy-based method to model workflow composition to address the issues in classical planning. In [14,16], the authors extended their previous studies to a multi-agent scenario. By combining reinforcement learning and multi-agent mechanism, their methods can improve the efficiency in service compostion.

In real-world applications, due to the dynamic network environments, uncertain performance of services and opaque QoS values, sometimes we can only obtain partial descriptions about the current state. The work in [10] described a

POMDP method to obtain better solutions for QoS-aware service composition, which utilizes the provenance data to assess POMDP distributions. In [15], the POMDP was applied to address the self-healing issue in service-oriented systems. The model works with belief states, which can help determine the best maintenance policy. In [8], the authors introduced the POMDP to model service composition as an uncertain planning problem. They also proposed a time-based learning method to balance the exploration and exploitation. These studies show the promising trend of using the POMDP in service composition.

3 Problem Formulation

In this section, we briefly present the problem description and some preliminaries, such as Web service composition and the Partially Observable Markov Decision Process (POMDP) for web service composition.

Definition 1 (Web Service). *A Web service can be modeled as a tuple $WS = <ID, Pr, E, QoS>$, where*

- *ID is a unique id of a Web service;*
- *Pr specifies the preconditions that need to be fulfilled to successfully invoke the Web service;*
- *E specifies the effect to the environment after executing the Web service (including both successful and unsuccessful executions);*
- *QoS is a n-tuple $< attr_1, \ldots, attr_n >$, where $attr_i(1 \leq i \leq n)$ represents a QoS attribute (e.g., Availability, Reliability, Throughput and Response time);*

Using MDP to model the service composition process has become popular, which reduces the computation cost based on the Markov property [3,6,14]. However, this model assumes that the environment information is fully observable and complete, which is too strict and not suitable for practical application scenarios. As a generalization of an MDP, a POMDP refers to a model for sequential stochastic decision problems that considers the information of system state as uncertain and partially observable [7]. This paper introduces the POMDP model into web service composition (WSC). The definition of POMDP in service composition is given as follows.

Definition 2 (WSC-Partially Observable Markov Decision Process). *A WSC-Partially Observable Markov Decision Process(WSC-POMDP) is formally described as a 6-tuple $< S, A, R, T, O, Z >$, where*

- *S denotes a finite set of states of an agent;*
- *A denotes the set of Web services that can be executed;*
- *R : $S \times A \to R$ denotes the reward function. When an agent invokes a service $ws \in A$, the world transits from s to s', and the agent receives an immediate reward r from the environment;*
- *T : $S \times A \times S \to [0,1]$ denotes the transition function. When an agent invokes a service $ws \in A$, the world transits from s to s' with a probability recorded as $T(s, a, s') = Pr(s'|s, a)$;*

– O denotes the observable information received by the agent;
– $Z : S \times A \times O \rightarrow [0,1]$ is the observation function indicating the probability distribution of observations. Formally, $Z(a, s', o) = Pr(o|s', a)$ means the probability of observation o after agents invoke a service a and change to state s';

An observation history h in a POMDP is defined as a sequence of actions executed and observations received that record the whole evolution of the process [2]. The goal of the agent is to learn a policy π, which maps the observation history h_t into an action a_t at time t to maximize the expected discounted cumulative reward $E[\sum_{t=0}^{T} \gamma^t r^t]$. However, such form of memory can grow indefinitely over time, making it impractical for long planning horizons. Fortunately, we can summarize the unbounded history $h_{1:t-1}$ into a sufficient statistic that compresses all the information of the past actions and observations. This compression pattern has been recognized by numerous studies, and the sufficient statistic is defined as a belief state [7,11], which is a probability distribution over the state space S. Therefore, a POMDP can be cast into a framework of a belief MDP, where the belief states comprise the continuous, but fully observable, MDP state space.

4   Adaptive Service Composition

In this section, we firstly introduce the belief MDP model for web service composition. Then, a RL algorithm is presented to compute the optimal policy in the composition model.

4.1   Belief MDP for Web Service Composition

Based on the above discussion, we convert a WSC-POMDP to a WSC-belief MDP by introducing the concept of belief state, which can be defined as follows:

Definition 3 (Web service composition belief MDP(WSC-belief MDP)). *A WSC-belief MDP is defined as a 5-tuple$< B, A, O, \Gamma, \rho >$, where*

– B is a set of belief states in the continuous space;
– A is a set of Web services;
– O is a set of possible observations;
– $\Gamma : B \times A \times O \rightarrow B$ is the belief transition function;
– $\rho : B \times A \rightarrow R$ is the reward function in the belief space, derived from the original reward function on world state, $\rho(b, a) = \sum_{s \in S} b(s)R(s, a)$;

When an agent executes a service a and perceives observation o, the belief state b will be updated to b' based on Bayes rule as follows:

$$b_o^a(s') = Pr(s'|b, a, o) = \eta Pr(o|s', a) \sum_{s \in S} Pr(s'|s, a)b(s) \tag{1}$$

where $\eta = 1/Pr(o|b,a)$ denotes a normalizing constant with $Pr(o|b,a) = \sum_{s'\in S} Pr(o|s',a) \sum_{s\in S} Pr(s'|s,a)b(s)$.

The policy is a function mapping belief state $b(b \in B)$ into service $a(a \in A)$, i.e., $\pi(b) \to a$. A policy $\pi(b_0)$ can be characterized by the value function $V^{\pi}(b_0)$ that is defined as the expected sum of discounted rewards received by following policy π starting at belief b_0:

$$V^{\pi}(b_0) = \sum_{t=0}^{h} \gamma^t \sum_{s\in S} b_t(s)R(s,\pi(b_t)) \tag{2}$$

where $\pi(b_t)$ represents the action specified by policy π at belief b_t. Based on above definition, it can be derived that an optimal policy π^* is a policy that can maximize its value function V^*(i.e., $V^*(b) \geq V^{\pi}(b) \ \forall(b)$). It prescribes the optimal action for each belief b to execute on time t and assumes that the agent will also act optimally in the future. The optimal value function V^* satisfies the *Bellman's equation*

$$V^*(b) = \max_a [\rho(b,a) + \gamma \sum_o Pr(o|b,a)V^*(b_o^a)] \tag{3}$$

where $Pr(o|b,a) = \sum_{s'\in S} Pr(o|s',a) \sum_{s\in S} Pr(s'|s,a)b(s)$, $\rho(b,a) = \sum_{s\in S} b(s)R(s,a)$ as defined above. b_o^a is the updated belief after performing action a and gathering observation o that is defined by Eq. (1).

4.2 SARSA(λ) Algorithm Based on Belief MDP

As a popular machine learning algorithm, RL assumes that an agent has no perfect knowledge of the environment. It demands the agent to interact with the dynamic environment and learn the optimal strategy with the reward value by the means of trial-and-error. There are many RL algorithms for MDP problems [14,17], such as Q-learning, SARSA, Monte Carlo and Temporal Difference(TD).

SARSA(λ) is a fast multi-step on-policy learning algorithm that introduces eligibility trace into SARSA(0) [9,12]. The basic concept of SARSA(λ) is to apply the TD(λ) prediction method to a state-action pair. It uses experience to learn estimates of an optimal Q-value function. Besides improving the learning efficiency, SARSA(λ) can make full use of past decisions and observations to optimize the current action and obtain the optimal strategy.

In the belief MDP problem, the available transition information at time step t is $< b(s_t), a_t, r_t, b(s_{t+1}) >$ and the Q-value in a belief MDP can be represented as $Q_t(b(s),a)$. Then, the Q-value update formula in SARSA(λ) with belief state is given by.

$$Q_{t+1}(b(s),a) \leftarrow Q_t(b(s),a) + \alpha * \delta_t * e_t(b(s),a) \tag{4}$$

where $0 \leq \alpha \leq 1$ denotes the learning rate, $\delta_t = r_t(b(s),a) + \gamma Q_t(b(s_{t+1}),a_{t+1}) - Q_t(b(s_t),a_t)$. r_t denotes the immediate reward received by an agent after invoking service a and making the environment transfer from state s_t to s_{t+1}. In addition, the eligibility traces are initialized to 0, and then are updated as follows:

$$e_t(b(s), a) = \begin{cases} \gamma \lambda e_{t-1}(b(s), a) & if \ b(s) \neq b(s_t) \\ 0 & if \ b(s) = b(s_t) \ and \ a \neq a_t \\ 1 & if \ (b(s), a) = (b(s_t), a_t) \end{cases} \quad (5)$$

where $\gamma(0 \leq \gamma \leq 1)$ denotes the discount factor and $\lambda(0 \leq \lambda \leq 1)$ denotes the decay factor.

5   Experiments and Analysis

In this section, we conduct a series of experiments to evaluate our service composition approach. To demonstrate the effectiveness of our approach, we also compare with other similar RL algorithms.

5.1   Experiment Setting

In the experiments, we assign each service node with random QoS values that follow the normal distribution. The algorithm proposed in this paper, i.e., SARSA(λ) for belief MDP, is referred to as b-SARSA(λ). We conduct comparative experiments with Time-based Learning method (referred to as TL) [8], and a multi-agent SARSA algorithm (referred to as multi-SARSA) [14]. A number of key parameters are set as follows. The learning rate α is set to 0.6 similar to the study in [14]. The discount factor γ is set to 0.9 and the ϵ-greedy exploration strategy value is set to 0.6. The experiments are conducted on an Intel i3-2120 3.30 GHz PC with 4 GB RAM.

5.2   Result Analysis

5.2.1   Validation of Effectiveness

In the first experiment, we mainly verify the effectiveness of b-SARSA(λ). The number of successful explorations of an algorithm is used as the standard to compare their convergency rate. The discount cumulative reward received by each algorithm is counted to represent the learning effect.

As shown in Fig. 1(a), b-SARSA(λ) has several superiority compared with other two algorithms. Compared to multi-SARSA, the b-SARSA(λ) algorithm has higher cumulative reward value. The multi-SARSA learns in the MDP model that judges the current state of environment without comprehensive understanding of the environment, while the POMDP computes and analyzes the environment based on belief states. Although multi-agent mechanism can accelerate the convergency rate in multi-SARSA, it obtains less reward value than b-SARSA(λ) in POMDP. On the other hand, in the same POMDP environment, b-SARSA(λ) has faster convergence rate than TL. The reason mainly lies in the introduction of eligibility traces in b-SARSA(λ), which can optimize current action with experience from past decisions to accelerate the learning rate.

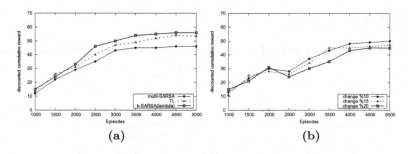

Fig. 1. (a) Validation of effectiveness (b) Validation of adaptability

5.2.2   Validation of Adaptability

Service QoS attributes may change in a dynamic web service environment. Therefore, this experiment mainly studies the adaptability of b-SARSA(λ). We allow 10 %, 15 % and 20 % of changes on the QoS values of a fixed number of candidate services during the learning process to simulate the dynamic environment. Also, we set QoS fluctuations between the 2000th episode and 2500th episode to enhance comparison. Figure 1(b) presents the experiment results. We can see that the b-SARSA(λ) algorithm converges finally in spite of the changes of the QoS, with just different convergence time. Even for huge QoS fluctuations, the reward values temporary decline, but the algorithm will relearn the current strategy and generate a new optimal strategy for the new environment. Therefore, the b-SARSA(λ) algorithm can handle the changes and find the optimal strategy adaptively.

6   Conclusions and Future Directions

In a dynamic service composition environment, the services' internal states and their QoS behaviors may be unpredictable and opaque. As a result, the available information for agents can be implicit. Therefore, this paper presents a reinforcement learning algorithm based on a POMDP model to address the non-observability issue in service composition, which utilizes the partially observed information to make decisions. By introducing the belief state, which presents the probability distributions over all states, the POMDP model can be converted into a belief MDP model. We also introduce the SARSA(λ) algorithm to run in a belief MDP, which combines the on-policy SARSA algorithm with the concept of multi-step prediction from eligibility traces. The algorithm can achieve better learning efficiency while enhancing the adaptability. The experiments validate the effectiveness and superiority of our approach in an incomplete information environment.

Acknowledgments. This work was partially supported by NSFC Projects (Nos. 61672152, 61232007, 61532013), Collaborative Innovation Centers of Novel Software Technology and Industrialization and Wireless Communications Technology.

References

1. Astrom, K.: Optimal control of Markov processes with incomplete state information. J. Math. Anal. Appl. **10**(1), 174–205 (1965)
2. Braziunas, D.: Pomdp solution methods. University of Toronto, Technical Report (2003)
3. Doshi, P., Goodwin, R., Akkiraju, R., Verma, K.: Dynamic workflow composition using Markov decision processes. In: Proceedings of the IEEE International Conference on Web Services, 2004, pp. 576–582. IEEE (2004)
4. Drake, A.W.: Observation of a Markov process through a noisy channel. Ph.D. thesis. Massachusetts Institute of Technology (1962)
5. Dustdar, S., Schreiner, W.: A survey on web services composition. Int. J. Web Grid Serv. **1**(1), 1–30 (2005)
6. Gao, A., Yang, D., Tang, S., Zhang, M.: Web service composition using Markov decision processes. In: Fan, W., Wu, Z., Yang, J. (eds.) WAIM 2005. LNCS, vol. 3739, pp. 308–319. Springer, Heidelberg (2005). doi:10.1007/11563952_28
7. Kaelbling, L.P., Littman, M.L., Cassandra, A.R.: Planning and acting in partially observable stochastic domains. Artif. Intell. **101**(1), 99–134 (1998)
8. Lei, Y., Jiantao, Z., Fengqi, W., Yongqiang, G., Bo, Y.: Web service composition based on reinforcement learning. In: 2015 IEEE International Conference on Web Services (ICWS), pp. 731–734. IEEE (2015)
9. Loch, J., Singh, S.P.: Using eligibility traces to find the best memoryless policy in partially observable Markov decision processes. In: ICML, pp. 323–331 (1998)
10. Naseri, M., Ludwig, S.: Automatic service composition using pomdp and provenance data. In: 2013 IEEE Symposium on Computational Intelligence and Data Mining (CIDM), pp. 246–253. IEEE (2013)
11. Smallwood, R.D., Sondik, E.J.: The optimal control of partially observable markov processes over a finite horizon. Oper. Res. **21**(5), 1071–1088 (1973)
12. Sutton, R.S., Barto, A.G.: Reinforcement Learning: An Introduction. MIT press, Cambridge (1998)
13. Trummer, I., Faltings, B.: Optimizing the tradeoff between discovery, composition, and execution cost in service composition. In: Proceedings of the IEEE International Conference on Web Services (ICWS), pp. 476–483. IEEE (2011)
14. Wang, H., Chen, X., Wu, Q., Yu, Q., Zheng, Z., Bouguettaya, A.: Integrating on-policy reinforcement learning with multi-agent techniques for adaptive service composition. In: Franch, X., Ghose, A.K., Lewis, G.A., Bhiri, S. (eds.) ICSOC 2014. LNCS, vol. 8831, pp. 154–168. Springer, Heidelberg (2014)
15. Wang, H., Wang, X., Yu, Q.: Optimal self-healing of service-oriented systems with incomplete information. In: 2013 IEEE International Congress on Big Data (BigData Congress), pp. 227–234. IEEE (2013)
16. Wang, H., Wang, X., Zhang, X., Yu, Q., Hu, X.: Effective service composition using multi-agent reinforcement learning. Knowl.-Based Syst. **92**, 151–168 (2016)
17. Wang, H., Wu, Q., Chen, X., Yu, Q.: Integrating gaussian process with reinforcement learning for adaptive service composition. In: Barros, A., Grigori, D., Narendra, N.C., Dam, H.K. (eds.) ICSOC 2015. LNCS, vol. 9435, pp. 203–217. Springer, Heidelberg (2015). doi:10.1007/978-3-662-48616-0_13

Formal Specification and Verification Framework for Multi-domain Ubiquitous Environment

Mohamed Hilia[1,2(✉)], Abdelghani Chibani[1], Karim Djouani[1], and Yacine Amirat[1]

[1] Signals, Images and Intelligent Systems Laboratory,
Paris-Est Créteil University (UPEC), Vity-sur-seine, France
mohamed.hilia@evidian.com, {chibani,djouani,amirat}@u-pec.fr
[2] Atos/Evidian, R&D, Les Clayes Sous Bois, France

Abstract. This paper deals with semantic composition of ubiquitous computing (Ubicomp) services in multi-domain heterogeneous environments. A new semantic framework enabling the specification of multi-domain composite services and proving their correctness is proposed. The proposed framework reduces the gap between safety critical systems including ubiquitous services and best effort engineering practices. It consists of an extensible Semantic Conceptual Model (SCM) for Ambient Intelligence systems and a composition formal system based on the Basic Constructive Description Logics $\mathcal{BCDL}_0$. The soundness property proof of the proposed formal system, as well as, the services composition correctness proofs are demonstrated along with the interactive theorem prover Isabelle/HOL.

Keywords: Ambient intelligence · Ontology specification and modeling · Theorem proving · Isabelle/HOL · Service composition

1 Introduction

Web/Internet of Things, Service Oriented Computing and Cloud Computing are considered as the main future enablers of both personal and professional applications. In this context, the composition of services, in particular those offered by heterogeneous connected things, is the suitable approach that allows creating more complex and ubiquitous services, which run an inter-organizational and heterogeneous environment called multi-domain [3]. In general, every domain has its own security and privacy policy and the configurations and interfaces description of the elementary services are completely heterogeneous from both data formatting and semantics point of views. Basically, composite services are specified by means of input, outputs, preconditions and post-conditions (i.e. effects) on elementary abstract services [5]. This context of heterogeneity makes that the correctness and soundness of the composite services at both operational and semantic levels are considered as the most complex issues in multi-domain environment with respect to robustness, safety and security [3]. Therefore, a

© Springer International Publishing Switzerland 2016
Q.Z. Sheng et al. (Eds.): ICSOC 2016, LNCS 9936, pp. 685–693, 2016.
DOI: 10.1007/978-3-319-46295-0_48

knowledge driven methodology and formal framework can help composite services designers to ensure the soundness and correctness of services compositions with respect to the heterogeneity of the domains and the applications requirements, which can be critical in scenarios where automation and robotic services are involved such as Manufacturing, Ambient Assisted Living (AAL) or eHealth [1,7]. The paper extends the proposed approach in [5] by implementing the complete framework with a sound formal system for multi-domain services composition specification. The proposed framework provides tools to verify the ability to compose services constructively by using Constructive Description Logics. The framework proposes also an extensible semantic model for multi-domain composition, with a set of software components enabling the automatic generation of $\mathcal{BCDL}_0$ statements, and the automatic generation of correctness proofs lemmas of the composite services that should be interactively proved. The paper is organized as follows. In Sect. 2 the architecture of the proposed framework is presented. Section 3 presents the formal system specification of service composition operators in Isabelle/HOL theorem prover and the proof of its soundness. Section 4 presents how the formal system is used to constructively assert the environment conceptual model, and its state. This formal system enables to specify a semantic model represented by an ontology, while the services composition model is presented in Sect. 5. This latter, details the formal specification of the services composition description model in Isabelle/HOL and the correctness proof. Section 6 discusses the related work, while, Sect. 7 concludes the paper and presents the ongoing work.

2   Semantic Framework for Multi-domain Ubiquitous Applications

The Fig. 1 depicts the relationship between the various components of the proposed framework. Figure 1 describes also the methodology used to build an ambient intelligence service-based systems.

The proposed *Formal System F_s* is based on $\mathcal{BCDL}_0$ [2]. This logic has several benefits such as providing computational capabilities and proof interpretation, and other mathematical properties such as soundness and completeness [4]. *(1) Semantic Conceptual Model* (SCM) consists of *AmI ontology*. It ensures, on the one hand, a common understanding of the shared concepts between the different heterogeneous entities in the environment such as sensors, actuators and agents, and formally represents the semantics of the multi-domain services. *(2) $\mathcal{BCDL}_0$-Based specification*, building the semantic conceptual model represents the first step of the proposed methodology. The conceptual model can be edited, maintained by using an ontology development tool such as Protégé[1]. The proposed framework includes an API to translate the designed ontology into $\mathcal{BCDL}_0$-based specification. Therefore, the resulting specification is used to specify the composite service according to the *Service Composition Model*. *(3) Service Composition*

---

[1] http://protege.stanford.edu/.

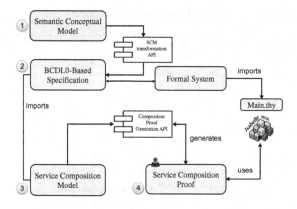

Fig. 1. Framework components

Model, this step enables the formal specification of the existing atomic and composite ubiquitous services in AmI environment and services behaviors. *(4) Service Composition Proof*, after constructing the composite service, the framework generates the lemmas of the applicability conditions to prove. The generated proofs statements are then proven interactively using Isabelle/HOL.

3 Formal Constructive Description Logics Based System

The formal system is described by the tuple $F_s = (L_\mathcal{N}, R)$, where, $L_\mathcal{N}$ represents the SCM description language and R the inference rules enabling the consequence logic computation within $L_\mathcal{N}$. F_s is specified within the assistant theorem prover Isabelle/HOL as a theory. *Isabelle/HOL* is a formal system based on higher order logic with a general natural deduction environment. It provides a sound meta-logic used for the specification of existing logics such as HOL or FOL and new formal systems. The main theory (Main.thy) is the elementary one that all theories are required to import.

3.1 Syntax Specification

F_s description language grammar (i.e. $L_\mathcal{N}$) is based on the basic description logic $\mathcal{ALC}$. It enables to describe a domain in terms of concepts (i.e. classes) NC, roles (i.e. properties, relationships) NR, individuals (i.e. instances) NI and VAR, set of *individual variables names*. $L_\mathcal{N}$ is defined as follows:

$$C, D := A \mid \neg\ C \mid C \sqcup D \mid C \sqcap D \mid \exists R.\ C \mid \forall R.\ C$$
$$K := \perp \mid t : C \mid A \sqsubseteq C \mid (s,\ t) : R$$

where C, $D \in$ NC, $R \in$ NR, and $s, t\ \in$ NI $\cup$ VAR. K represents the generated formulas. NR, NC, NI and the generated formulas are specified within Isabelle/HOL as datatype constructors see Table 1.

Table 1. Syntax specification

---

datatype 'nr role = AtomR 'nr
datatype ('nr,'nc) Concept = AtomC 'nc
datatype ('nr,'nc) Concept = AtomC 'nc
     | NotC " ('nr,'nc) Concept "
     | OrC " ('nr,'nc) Concept" "('nr,'nc) Concept "
     | AndC " ('nr,'nc) Concept" "('nr,'nc) Concept "
     | SomC " ('nr) role" "('nr,'nc) Concept "
     | AllC " ('nr) role" "('nr,'nc) Concept "
datatype ('nr, 'nc, 'ni) Kformulas = Bottom
     | RoleF " 'ni *'ni " " 'nr role "
     | ConceptF " 'ni" " ('nr,'nc) Concept "
     | AConceptF " 'nc" " ('nr,'nc) Concept "

3.2 Constructive Semantics Specification

Let's define $\mathcal{N}$ as a subset of NI ($\mathcal{N} \subseteq NI$), and $L_{\mathcal{N}}$ as the list of formulas generated by the finite subset $\mathcal{N}$. An *Interpretation (Model)* $\mathcal{M}$ for $\mathcal{L}_N$ consists of the pair $\left(\mathcal{D}^{\mathcal{M}}, \cdot^{\mathcal{M}}\right)$. $\mathcal{D}^{\mathcal{M}}$ defines the domain, corresponding to an not empty set, and $\cdot^{\mathcal{M}}$ is a valuation function which associates to every $c \in \mathcal{N}$, $c^{\mathcal{M}} \in \mathcal{D}^{\mathcal{M}}$, for every $A \in$ NC, $A^{\mathcal{M}} \subseteq \mathcal{D}^{\mathcal{M}}$, and for every $R \in$ NR, $R^{\mathcal{M}} \subseteq \mathcal{D}^{\mathcal{M}} \times \mathcal{D}^{\mathcal{M}}$. The specification of the classical interpretation and the validity notions are implemented in this work. However, the focus in this section is on the specification of the constructive interpretation and the proof of the soundness property of the proposed formal system. The constructive interpretation of $\mathcal{BCDL}_0$ is based on *information terms* semantics. Let's consider that $\mathcal{N} \subseteq NI$ and K *closed formula* of $\mathcal{L}_{\mathcal{N}}$. A *closed formula* is defined as a formula that does not contain individual variables names. Formally, an information term is the piece of information, called also a *type* of a given formula that gives a witness justifying the validity of this formula. The set of information terms $IT_{\mathcal{N}}(K)$ can be defined by induction on the structure of K. This algorithm is implemented by the function ITc (see Table 2).

Table 2. Information terms algorithm

---

fun ITc :: " 'ni set $\Rightarrow$ 'ni $\Rightarrow$ ('nr, 'nc) Concept $\Rightarrow$ 'ni It set " where
" ITc (N) c (AndC A B)   = (α,β) | α β. $\alpha \in$ ITc (N) c A $\wedge$ $\beta \in$ ITc (N) c B "
| " ITc (N) c (OrC A B)   = { (k, α) | k α. ((k = 1) $\wedge$ ($\alpha \in$ ITc (N) c A)) $\vee$
                                 ((k = 2) $\wedge$ ($\alpha \in$ ITc (N) c B)) } "
| " ITc (N) c (SomC R A) = {Ex (d,α)|α d.d $\in N \wedge$ $\alpha \in$ ITc (N) d A } "
| " ITc (N) c (AllC R A)   = $\cup$ ITc N d A | d. d $\in$ N " "
| " ITc (N) c (NotC A)   = tt "
| " ITc (N) c (AtomC A)   = tt "

The information terms represent a structured mathematical object that gives witnesses about the validity of these formulas in a classical model. When an information term η proves the validity of K formulas, this implies that the information term η realize the formula K. We write $M \triangleright \langle \eta \rangle K$. More information can be found in [2]. $\mathcal{BCDL}_0$ reasoning technique is compatible with the realisability relation of K formula by a given information term. The *realisability* relation is defined as follows: Let $\mathcal{M}$ be a Model for $\mathcal{L}_N$, K a closed formula and $\eta \in IT_{\mathcal{N}}(K)$. The *realisability* relation is defined as $M \triangleright \langle \eta \rangle K$ by induction on the structured of K. A part of the *realisability* relation specification is given in Table 3.

Table 3. Realisability relation specification

---
fun realizz :: "('nr,'nc,'ni) Interp $\Rightarrow$ 'ni It $\Rightarrow$ 'ni $\Rightarrow$ ('nr,'nc) Concept $\Rightarrow$ bool" where
"realizz (M) (et (α,β)) (c) (AndC A B) =
. . .

3.3 Inference Rules and Soundness Proof

The natural deduction calculus $\mathcal{ND}$ is the proof calculus for $\mathcal{BCDL}_0$, and gives the soundness theorem according to realisability relation and the natural deduction proofs of $\mathcal{ALC}$ formulas [2,4]. The formal system must be sound, i.e. it ensures that all computed inferences are valid. In the following, the soundness theorem is specified and proved in Isabelle/HOL using cases tactics on the different logical constructors of the constructive logics $\mathcal{BCDL}_0$.

Theorem (Soundness) Let $\mathcal{N}$ be a finit subset of NI and let $\pi::\Gamma \vdash K$ be a proof of $\mathcal{ND}$ over $\mathcal{L}_{\mathcal{N}}$ such that the formulas K in Γ are closed. Then, we have:

- $\Gamma \vDash K$, K is logical consequence of Γ
- For every model $\mathcal{M}$ and $\gamma \in IT(\Gamma)$, $\mathcal{M} \triangleright \langle \phi \rangle \Gamma$ implies $\mathcal{M} \triangleright \langle \phi_N^\pi(\gamma) \rangle K$

The Isabelle/HOL formalisation of the soundness theorem, and its proof is given in Table 4. The soundness property shows that when a formula K is proven by assuming a set of formulas Γ, the evidence of giving an information terms for the K formula based on the information terms extracted from Γ set is assumed. In such way the inference rules prove only formulas that are valid with respect to information terms semantics.

4 Semantic Conceptual Model

The *Semantic Conceptual Model* (SMC) consists of a set of concepts and relationships for representing the AmI ontology. The SCM is proposed to formalise the shared knowledge in multi-domain environment according to $\mathcal{BCDL}_0$-based specification.

Table 4. Soundness theorem proof

---

theorem soundness: assumes "$\Gamma \vDash$ K" shows
" realiz_setF (M) (γ) (Γ) $\longrightarrow$ realiz (M) $(\Phi\ (\gamma))$ (K)" using assms
proof induct
case (Bottom_elim Γ Bottom)then show ?case
apply auto
apply (rule realizz.induct)
. . .

Considering the knowledge base of an ambient intelligence environment where a companion robot assists people at home. The robot interacts with several services at home, and with services from other domains. The robot performs also different types of notifications, and can be located in one of the home's rooms. The formalization of this knowledge is formalized in Table 5.

Table 5. AmI ontology concepts specification

$TBox$	$ABox$
$(Ax1) : Notification \sqsubseteq \exists\ isPerformedBy.Robot$	$(ax1)\ :\ kompai : Robot$
$(Ax2) : Robot \sqsubseteq \exists\ isSituatedOn.Location$	$(ax2)\ :\ alert1 : Notification$
	$(ax3)\ :\ alert2 : Notification$
	$(ax4)\ :\ kitchen : Location$
	$(ax5)\ :\ room : Location$
	$(ax6)\ :\ (alert2, kompai) : isPerformedBy$
	$(ax7)\ :\ (kompai, room) : isSituatedOn$

Let us consider the formula which associates a robot to a location in the smart home, such as: $K = Robot \sqcap \exists isLocatedOn.Location$. Let's assume that NI is the set of all individuals in the knowledge base. The computation of the information terms interpretation of K is the following. Let N be the names of individuals in the model defined in Table 5. An example of an element $IT_N(Ax1)$ is a function ϕ which associates to each element c of N an element γ. Formally:

$$\gamma \in IT_N(c : Robot \sqcap \exists isLocatedOn.Location)$$
$$IT_N(K) = IT_N(c : Robot \sqcap \exists isLocatedOn.Location)$$
$$= (IT_N(c : (Robot)), IT_N(c : \exists isLocatedOn.Location)) = (tt, (d, tt))$$

Let's consider the definition of a new concept from the axioms that identifies a location of the robot by issuing a notification. In other words, the robot performs a notification action when it is in a specific location. The knowledge base of the Table 5 is considered and the following proof is constructed:

$\pi::\mathcal{T} \vdash (NotificationAction \sqsubseteq \exists isPerformedBy.(Robot \sqcap \exists isLocatedOn.Location))$

In the literature, several conceptual model (i.e. ontologies) have been designed for the AmI environment description purpose. For this reason, a transformation API to our formal system is added by the proposed framework (Fig. 1). The ontology specified is then used by the composition description model, which is detailed in the next section.

5   Composition Description Model

The composite service is constructed by using the atomic services and the composition rules (Table 7) as well as the applicability conditions (AC) associate to each rule. The correctness proof of the composite service requires the proof of the applicability conditions of the composite service.

5.1   Service Composition Specification

The service specification is an expression of the form $p(x) :: P \implies Q$ where: p is a label that identifies the service; x is the input parameter of the service (to be instantiated with an individual name from $\mathcal{N}$); P and Q are concepts over $\mathcal{L}_N$. P is called the service pre-condition, denoted by $Pre(s)$, and Q the service post-condition, denoted by $Post(s)$. The service implementation is modelled as a function $\Phi_s : \bigcup_{t \in \mathcal{N}} IT_N(t : P) \to \bigcup_{t \in \mathcal{N}} IT_N(t : Q)$. We denote by the pair $(p(x) :: P \implies Q, \Phi_s)$ (or with (p, Φ_p)) a service definition over $\mathcal{L}_\mathcal{N}$. The service's specification is formalised in Isabelle/HOL (Table 6).

Table 6. Service definition & implementation

datatype ('nr,'nc,'ni) ServiceSpec = SF "char " " " 'ni " "('nr,'nc)Concept" "('nr,'nc) Concept" (" _ _ :: _ ⇒ _")
definition Φ_s :: "('nr,'nc,'ni) ServiceSpec ⇒ 'ni set ⇒ (('ni It set) ⇒ 'ni It set)" where "Φ_s S N = (let A =∪ { IT N (ConceptF d (Pre_s S)) | d. d ∈ N } in (λ A. ∪ IT N (ConceptF d (Post_s S)) | d. d ∈ N)) "

5.2   Correctness Proof

The service specification provides the formal description of a service behaviour in terms of pre- and post- conditions. The function Φ_s represents a formal description of service implementation (i.e. of the input/output function). Essentially, a service definition corresponds to an effective Web service. The behaviour of the service depends on the environment where it is executed. Besides, the behaviour correctness of a service in such environment must be proved. This refers to the correctness property that is formalised by means of the following function $Unformaly\_solv$ (Table 8).

Table 7. Control flow rules and their applicability conditions

$$\frac{p(x)::A \Rightarrow B}{\begin{array}{l} p_1\,(x) :: A_1 \Rightarrow B_1 \\ p_2\,(x) :: A_2 \Rightarrow B_2 \\ \quad\vdots \\ p_n\,(x) :: A_n \Rightarrow B_n \end{array}}\ \textit{Composition Rule}$$

Composition rule	Applicability Conditions
Sequence	$AC = \begin{cases} T, x : A \mid_{\overline{\mathcal{BCDL}_0}} x : A_1 \\ T, x : B_{k-1} \mid_{\overline{\mathcal{BCDL}_0}} x : A_k, \text{for } k \in \{2,\ldots,n\} \\ T, x : B_n \mid_{\overline{\mathcal{BCDL}_0}} x : B \end{cases}$
Parallel Split	$AC = \begin{cases} T, x : A \mid_{\overline{\mathcal{BCDL}_0}} x : A_k, \text{for } k \in \{1,\ldots,n\} \\ T, x : B_1 \sqcap \ldots \sqcap B_n \mid_{\overline{\mathcal{BCDL}_0}} x : B \end{cases}$
Synchronization	$AC = \begin{cases} T, x : A_1 \sqcap \ldots \sqcap A_n \mid_{\overline{\mathcal{BCDL}_0}} x : B_k \\ \text{for } k \in \{1,\ldots,n\} \\ T, x : B_k \mid_{\overline{\mathcal{BCDL}_0}} x : B, \text{ for } k \in \{1,\ldots,n\} \end{cases}$

Table 8. Uniformaly solve

fun Unformaly_solv :: "('nr,'nc,'ni) Interp $\Rightarrow$ ('nr,'nc,'ni) ServiceDef $\Rightarrow$ bool" where
"Unformaly_solv (M) (S,Φ) = ($\forall$ N ::'ni set. $\forall$ t $\in$ (N). $\forall$ α $\in$ IT (N) (ConceptF t (Pre_s S)).
(realiz (M) (α)(ConceptF t (Pre_s S)) $\longrightarrow$ realiz (M) (Φ({ α }))(ConceptF t (Post_s S)))

6 Related Work

More recently, approaches combining ontologies and formal methods have been proposed specifically to describe the service composition flows. These approaches allow the description of the interaction of web services that represents an important condition for achieving dynamic composition of services. In this section, approaches based on theorem proving for service composition are investigated. These techniques apply deduction rules on a goal specified as a mathematical theorem in order to prove it. In general, theorem proving technique is a set of inference steps that can be used to simplify an objective proof to a list of simple sub-goals. These latter can be automatically proved by the primitive tactics of a proof assistant tool such as Coq, HOL4, Isabelle/HOL. These techniques have been little used in the field of service composition [8]. The majority of the proposed approaches are based on the web-semantic language (e.g. DAML-S or OWL-S) that offers no way to verify the correction. Therefore, other approaches have been used to transform these service descriptions into different formalism (e.g. π-calculus, Petri nets, Linear Logics) to enable the automatic reasoning, and therefore to prove several service composition properties [6,8]. Recently, research on alternative interpretations of classical formal representation of description logics has been conducted and the need to explore this area, which can improve the modeling techniques of the system, and we can also exploit its capabilities calculation [4]. Recall that the main problem with all these approaches composition and those proposed in the industrial part is checking the correction [9]. Moreover, a constructive description logic or intuitionistic called $\mathcal{BCDL}$ has been proposed [4]. Bozzato applied this logic for the composition of semantic Web services [2]. This approach deals with the composition of semantic web services, based on a subsystem of the basic logic of constructive description, called $\mathcal{BCDL}_0$. On the contrary of the proposed approaches, the proposed framework is based on sound and complete formal system. It benefits from the mathematical computation capabilities of the constructive description logic and correctness proof. In addition, the framework proposes also a reliable methodology to realise a proved correct application in multi-domain context.

7   Conclusion and Ongoing Work

The paper presents a semantic framework, and a formal methodology for developing multi-domain ambient intelligent applications. The framework is based on sound and complete formal system for sharing knowledge among multiple domains as Semantic Conceptual Model. The framework provides also a formal services composition model for the specification and the correction proof within Isabelle/HOL. In the future work, we study the dynamic aspects of changing the composite services and its impacts on the methodology. The framework's performances and development of AAL use cases will also be considered.

References

1. Benghazi, K., Hurtado, M.V., Hornos, M.J., Rodrguez, M.L., Rodrguez-Domnguez, C., Pelegrina, A.B., Rodrguez-Frtiz, M.J.: Enabling correct design and formal analysis of ambient assisted living systems. J. Syst. Softw. **85**(3), 498–510 (2012)
2. Bozzato, L., Ferrari, M.: A note on semantic web services specification and composition in constructive description logics. CoRR, abs/1007.2364 (2010)
3. Di Pietro, I., Pagliarecci, F., Spalazzi, L.: Model checking semantically annotated services. IEEE Trans. Softw. Eng. **38**(3), 592–608 (2012)
4. Ferrari, M., Fiorentini, C., Fiorino, G.: BCDL: basic constructive description logic. J. Autom. Reasoning **44**(4), 371–399 (2010)
5. Hilila, M., Chibani, A., Djouani, K., Amirat, Y.: Semantic service composition framework for multidomain ubiquitous computing applications. In: Liu, C., Ludwig, H., Toumani, F., Yu, Q. (eds.) Service Oriented Computing. LNCS, vol. 7636, pp. 450–467. Springer, Heidelberg (2012)
6. Papapanagiotou, P., Fleuriot, J.: A theorem proving framework for the formal verification of web services composition. In: Proceedings of the 7th International Workshop on Automated Specification and Verification of Web Systems, pp. 1–16 (2011)
7. Preuveneers, D., Novais, P.: A survey of software engineering best practices for the development of smart applications in ambient intelligence. J. Ambient Intell. Smart Environ. **4**(3), 149–162 (2012)
8. Rao, J., Küngas, P., Matskin, M.: Composition of semantic web services using linear logic theorem proving. Inf. Syst. **31**(4), 340–360 (2006)
9. Beek, M.H., Bucchiarone, A., Gnesi, S.: Formal methods for service composition. Ann. Math. Comput. Teleinformatics **1**(5), 1–10 (2007)

Social Services (Short Papers)

Studying Social Collaboration Features and Patterns in Service Crowdsourcing

Hao Yu, Zhongjie Wang$^{(\boxtimes)}$, Xu Chi, and Xiaofei Xu

Harbin Institute of Technology, Harbin 150001, Heilongjiang, China
{coderbdhao,rainy,chixu,xiaofei}@hit.edu.cn

Abstract. Service crowdsourcing follows typical social collaboration processes with stochastic and dynamic characteristics. In this paper, the "bug-fix" social collaboration on GitHub is used as a case scenario of crowdsourcing, and 53,475 issues in 10 OSS projects are collected to conduct an empirical study on features and patterns of service crowdsourcing. Seven collaboration features (CFs) are proposed to delineate social characteristics of crowdsourcing. In terms of these CFs, social collaboration processes are clustered and results show that these features have significant distinguishability. An extended Generalized Sequential Pattern (GSP) algorithm is put forward to identify two types of collaboration patterns called participant-oriented pattern (PP) and role-oriented pattern (RP), and the richness and individualized degree of collaboration patterns in different OSS projects are analyzed and compared.

Keywords: Service crowdsourcing · Social collaboration process · Collaboration pattern · Collaboration features · Open Source Software (OSS)

1 Introduction

Crowdsourcing [11] is an emerging Internet-based innovative service pattern that solve challenging problems by collective intelligence of the masses. Firstly challenge is publicized, and the masses participate into the collaborative problem-solving process in terms of their individual initiatives; each participant evaluates current state of the challenge and takes specific action on it in terms of his knowledge and skills; as a result, the state of the challenge is updated; such iteration continues, until the challenge is solved or is proved to be unsolvable. This is a typical social collaboration process.

Open Source Software (OSS) development is a representative service crowdsourcing [4]. Taking a "bug fix" in OSS development as an example, a bug reported by a user is a challenge, and distributed developers in the team reproduce the bug, analyze its root cause, locate the source code that might cause the bug, specify bug-fix solution, allocate a developer to fix it, then submit bug-fix code for evaluation and confirmation. Although all bug-fix process roughly follow above steps, there show diversified process structures for different bugs.

© Springer International Publishing Switzerland 2016
Q.Z. Sheng et al. (Eds.): ICSOC 2016, LNCS 9936, pp. 697–704, 2016.
DOI: 10.1007/978-3-319-46295-0_49

In traditional service choreography scenario [6], a collaboration process is defined as a set of correlated activities with pre-designed workflow and pre-specified responsibilities for each pre-specified role. However, in service crowd-sourcing, collaboration processes cannot be planned in advance. This is because different participants have different levels of knowledge/skills and different preferences/interests; therefore, their behaviors are determined by their own initiatives and the latest status of the challenge. To sum up, social collaboration processes of crowdsourcing show high degree of stochastic and dynamic nature.

Nevertheless, there should be some features used to delineate distinct characteristics of each crowdsourcing process. For example, number of steps in a social collaboration, total duration, number of participants, time intervals between neighboring steps, etc. With these features, we can summarize commonalities and diversities among collaboration processes of different crowdsourcing challenges, and get a deep understanding on the inherent laws of collective intelligence based problem solving.

In an OSS project, bugs keep constantly outpouring over time, and there is a core team that repeatedly participates into the bug-fix processes. We conjecture that, as time goes on, frequently-occurring social collaboration habits might gradually take shape, i.e., there might appear similar or repeated collaboration patterns. This leads to **RQ1: are there any frequent-occurring social collaboration patterns in service crowdsourcing?** For this RQ, we propose two types of social collaboration patterns (CP): Participant-oriented Pattern (PP), and Role-oriented Pattern (RP). An extended Generalized Sequential Pattern (GSP) algorithm is put forward to identify PPs and RPs. Statistical analysis is conducted on the characteristics of the identified patterns.

RQ2 of this paper is to validate **whether there are significant commonalities and diversities among different collaboration processes** in terms of social collaboration features and patterns. For this RQ, we cluster bug-fix processes *w.r.t* their CFs and summarize the commonality inside each cluster and the diversities among different clusters. We then measure the individualization degree of collaboration patterns in each long-standing crowdsourcing team (i.e., an OSS project). Results validate our conjecture and implicit commonalities and diversities are preliminarily identified.

This study is based on GitHub. We collect social collaboration related data for bug-fix ("issues") in 10 selected OSS projects and conduct an empirical study. To answer above RQs would help crowdsourcing coordinators get a clear understanding on the collaboration habits of their participants, thus facilitating better task allocation and collaboration predication. Besides, it extends traditional service choreography research on stable or fixed service processes into the concerning of stochastic and dynamic social collaboration processes which exist widely in more and more Internet-based service crowdsourcing scenarios.

2   Social Collaboration in Service Crowdsourcing

2.1   Challenges and "Actions" in Service Crowdsourcing

Problems to be solved in crowdsourcing is defined as *challenges*. For example, in OSS development each *to-be-fixed* bug is regarded as a challenge. In GitHub, it is called an *issue*. After an issue is reported, a social collaboration process is initialized to solve it.

An issue is described by attributes such as `Created time`, `Proposer`, `Closer`, `Labels/tags`, `Milestone`, `Assignee`, and `Status`. To solve an issue in the crowdsourcing way, GitHub offers a set of issue-related actions that can be taken by any participants with required permissions: `commit`, `createIssue`, `comment`, `closeIssue`, `reopen`, `addLabel`, `deleteLabel`, `addMilestone`, `deleteMilestone`, `reference`, and `assign`.

2.2   Collaboration Features (CF)

1. Collaboration Duration (CD): time interval from the date when an issue is reported to the date when it is closed (or current date if it is now still open);
2. Collaboration Steps (CS): total number of actions that participants take to fix the issue;
3. Max Interval (MaxI): the maximum time interval between two neighboring actions during the collaboration;
4. Min Interval (MinI): the minimum time interval between two neighboring actions during the collaboration;
5. Median Interval (MidI): the median time interval between two neighboring actions during the collaboration;
6. Number of distinct Participants (NP): how many participants are there in the collaboration to fix the issue;
7. Number of Comments (NC): how many comments are included in the actions of the collaboration.

2.3   Social Collaboration Patterns and GSP-Based Pattern Mining

We define two types of social collaboration patterns (CP) to describe the frequent-occurring collaboration habits in a long-standing crowdsourcing team who frequently collaborate for solving challenges. In GitHub, a team is a virtual group composed of developers from all over the world. A CP is composed of a set of sequential actions each of which is taken by a specific participant (such CP is called Participant-oriented Pattern, PP) or by an abstract role (such CP is called Role-oriented Pattern, RP). PP is to delineate the stable collaboration habits among concrete participants, while RP is focused solely on the sequence of actions but does not care about who takes each action, i.e., multiple participants can be abstracted into a role if they perform the same actions in multiple collaboration processes. Thus, a RP may be regarded as the abstraction of a set of PPs which own the same sequential actions but different groups of participants.

A PP is defined by $PP :: = < PS, AS, M >$ where PS is a set of participants each of which has a distinct identification; AS is a sequence of social actions each of which is defined by the action type, and M is the mapping between PS and AS, i.e., $\forall m \in M$, $m = p \to index(a)$ ($p \in PS, a \in AS$) indicates the action a is taken by the participant p, and $index(a)$ is the position where a is located in the sequence AS. The definition of RP is similar as the ones of PP: $RP :: = < RS, AS, M >$ where RS is a set of abstract roles; $\forall m \in M$, $m = r \to index(a)$ implies that the action a is taken by the role r.

In an issue fix process, all the actions occur sequentially in terms of their timestamps, so do CPs that are hidden in the process. Thus, traditional sequential pattern mining approaches can be employed to identify CPs from historical crowdsourcing processes. In our study, the Generalized Sequential Pattern (GSP) algorithm is adopted. As for PP, the GSP algorithm can be directly applied to the historical crowdsourcing processes. As for RP, extensions on GSP are required to deal with abstracting concrete participants into roles in terms of the responsibilities that each participant takes in these processes. Due to limited space, the pseudo-code is not given here.

3   Empirical Study

3.1   Dataset

To study social collaboration features (CFs) in crowdsourcing, we require a set of sample crowdsourcing processes; and to study social collaboration patterns (CPs), we requires there are a fair amount of crowdsourcing processes coming from the same long-standing crowdsourcing teams. By this criterion, from GitHub we select 10 OSS projects all having plenty of issues. They are diversified in a variety of perspectives, such as number of commits, team size, number of stars, and the programming languages.

We collect the issue-fix process data from GitHub Archive, an official data repository of GitHub. Data in GitHub Archive is organized by "events", i.e., every action taken by GitHub developers are recorded as an event. There are two types of events related to issues: *IssueCommentEvent* which logs a "comment" in an issue, and *IssuesEvent* which logs the rest of action types except "comment". Data is in the form of JSON. The time range of the collected data is between Year 2011 and 2016. In 10 projects, total 53,475 issues and 248,000 actions are collected. Social collaboration processes for these issues are recovered.

3.2   Analyzing Collaboration Features

Statistics of CFs. We calculate the values of 7 CFs for the collaboration processes of all issues, then make statistics on the distribution of each CF of issues that belong to the same project. The following phenomena are observed:

(1) Apart from few projects, all the 7 CFs have quite similar median and average among 10 projects, indicating that issue-fix processes have high degree of

similar characteristics on the whole, even these issues are from different projects. However, in terms of each CF, the distribution shapes in different projects look diversified (e.g., the distribution intervals, number of outliers, etc.).

(2) Distributions of the 7 CFs are all right-screwed, indicating that most of issues have relatively fewer participants, fewer collaboration steps, shorter time intervals between neighboring actions, and shorter durations. This further tells us that a majority of challenges in crowdsourcing do not require very complex social collaboration. However, the existence of outliers in the distribution of 7 CFs implies that a few challenges are to be solved by complex collaborations (i.e., longer duration, more participants and collaboration steps, etc.). This can be also proved by the fact that average values of these CFs are generally close to the upper quartile.

Clustering Issues of One Project *w.r.t* CFs. In order to check whether the proposed CFs have enough distinguishability, we make clustering analysis on the issues belonging to the same project. K-means clustering algorithm is adopted, and Xie-Beni index is used to evaluate the quality of clustering so that optimal number of clusters can be found. As different CFs have different distribution intervals, data normalization is made before clustering. For 10 projects, at least 2 and at most 9 clusters are obtained, and Fig. 1(a) and (b) demonstrates clustering results of the projects JQ and GO with 4 and 5 clusters, respectively. Spider diagram is employed to compare different clusters *w.r.t* CFs, in which the value on each dimension is the average of the corresponding CF of all the issues belonging to the same cluster.

Chi-square test is adopted to test the independence of four clusters *w.r.t* CF values, and the result shows that there are significant difference among them (p-value $= 0$). This proves that the proposed CFs have significant distinguishability.

Clustering Issues of Multiple Projects *w.r.t* CFs. Here we cluster issues of all the 10 projects together to identify whether there are commodities and difference between the social collaboration of different projects. By Xie-Beni index, the optimal number of clusters is 4, and the result is shown in Fig. 1(c).

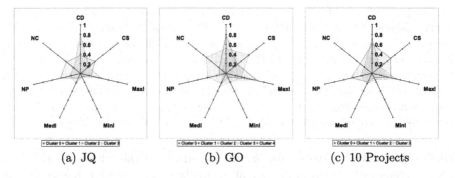

(a) JQ   (b) GO   (c) 10 Projects

Fig. 1. Issue clusters *w.r.t* 7 CFs

This result shows significant diversities among four clusters. Detailed analysis on such diversity is not presented here, but obviously the complexity of social collaborations becomes more and more lower from Cluster 0 to Cluster 3.

We make statistics on the percentages of issues belonging to each cluster in every project. The following phenomena are observed:

(1) Cluster 1 and Cluster 2 are dominating clusters because the proportions of these two clusters are about 30 %–40 % and 40 %–50 % in all projects, respectively. This indicates that there is a high degree of commonality among all projects. By observing CFs of the two clusters, we can describe such commonality by "the dominating social collaboration to solve crowdsourcing challenges is with medium complexity".

(2) The proportion of Cluster 0 in most of projects are comparatively low, indicating that there are not too many challenges that are to be solved in a very complicated way. However we also see there are some projects having higher proportion of Cluster 0 (such as FCC, GO and TJ), which proves that there are diversities among projects.

(3) The proportion of Cluster 3 in most of projects are more than 17 %. Collaboration processes of such challenges are in very low complexity and by small-scale teams, which is another commonality among projects.

(4) In terms of the proportions of four clusters, 10 projects are classified into three types: (a) FCC and GO which have comparatively higher proportion of Cluster 0 and lower proportion of Cluster 3; (2) ELE, DT, GOGS, JQ, TS and FS all of which have comparatively lower proportion of Cluster 0; (3) DK and TJ which have comparatively more balanced proportions of the four clusters.

3.3   Mining and Analyzing Social Collaboration Patterns (CP)

Comparison Between PP and RP. For CP mining from historical social collaboration processes, we use different *min_sup* for different projects because they have different number of issues. A *minimal support ratio* (r) is specified in the range $1\% - 5\%$, then *min_sup* for one project is set by multiplying r with the number of its issues.

First we make comparison on the numbers of the obtained PPs and RPs. The project JQ owning 2,094 issues is used as an example. Comparisons are shown in Fig. 2(a) under different r. It is seen that: (1) GSP-based algorithms can identify a large number of PPs and RPs, indicating that social collaboration patterns do exist in a long-standing crowdsourcing team; (2) With the increasing r, the difference between the numbers of PP and RP keeps decreasing, and when $r \geq 4\%$, the number of RP is larger than PP. This implies the fact that there do exist a type of collaboration processes which contain frequent-occurring sequential patterns, but these patterns are not always taken by the same group of participants, i.e., different participants tend to adopt the same collaboration styles.

Individualized Patterns. We are interested in whether there are *individualized* collaborations patterns, i.e., individualized collaboration habits among participants. A metric called Individualized Pattern Index (IPI) is proposed to

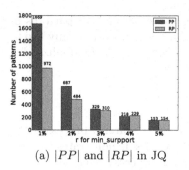
(a) $|PP|$ and $|RP|$ in JQ

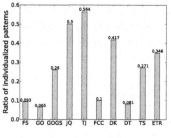
(b) Ratio of Individualized Patterns

Fig. 2. Comparison of RP/RP and comparison of individualized patterns

measure the individualized degree of a RP in a specific project. If a RP appears in many projects, it tends to be a common pattern; if it appears in only one or a few projects, it tends to be an individualized pattern. IPI is measured by $IPI(RP, i) = \frac{P(RP,i)}{\sum_{k=1}^{N} P(RP,k)/(N-1)}$ where N is number of projects (here $N = 10$), and $P(RP, i) = \frac{freq(RP,i)}{Num\_Issues_i}$ where $freq(RP, i)$ is times of occurrence of RP in the historical social collaboration of i-th project, and Num_Issues_i is total number of issues in i-th project.

This formula ensures that, if a pattern's occurrence frequency in one project is higher than in the other projects, it may be an individualized one of this project, so it has a greater IPI. A threshold for IPI is set to judge whether a pattern is individualized or not $w.r.t$ a project. In the study we set the threshold $= 3.0$.

Afterwards, we calculate the ratio of individualized patterns in each project, and result is shown in Fig. 2(b). This result further validates the fact that different crowdsourcing teams exhibit diversified social collaboration habits, although the individualized degree are not quite the same. Some projects such as JQ, TJ and DK demonstrate more individualized collaboration patterns, while projects such as FS, GO, and FCC tends to adopt more common collaboration patterns.

4 Related Work

Collaboration-based service crowdsourcing is essentially a set of incremental and iterative contributions on a set of artifacts. Participants observe state transitions of these artifacts and make decisions on what actions they would take [1]. This is what is called by Liptchinsky et al. [3] an "information-centric" approach to model social collaborations. Crowdsourcing occurs in web-based collaborative working environment and collaborative traces of participants are logged [2]. By mining these traces, social collaboration processes can be recovered by *process mining* [7], and mechanism of how collective intelligence comes into being were explored by Zhang et al.[10]. In terms of collaboration patterns, Smirnov et al. [8] made a multi-dimensional classification. Onoue et al. [5] used the percentages of a variety of social actions as the representation of behavior patterns in OSS. Xuan *et al.* [9] worked on a simple pattern which is composed of only two types of actions and a HMM model was employed to describe the individualized behavior patterns of OSS developers.

5   Conclusions

(1) We put forward 7 distinct CFs for service crowdsourcing processes. Result of clustering on bug-fix processes in terms of these CFs demonstrates that they can significantly distinguish different crowdsourcing processes, i.e., they have significant distinguishability. (2) Based on an extended GSP algorithm, two types of CPs (PP and RP) are mined and results have verified there indeed exist frequent collaboration patterns in long-standing crowdsourcing teams. (3) Besides significant commonalities, different OSS projects show discriminative CFs and CPs, too, especially on the ratio of individualized patterns and the ratio between numbers of RP and PP.

Acknowledgments. Work in this paper is supported by the Natural Science Foundation of China (No. 61272187, 61472106).

References

1. Dabbish, L., Stuart, C., Tsay, J., Herbsleb, J.: Social coding in GitHub: transparency and collaboration in an open software repository. In: Proceedings of ACM Conference on Computer Supported Cooperative Work, pp. 1277–1286 (2012)
2. Li, Q., Abel, M.H., Barthès, J.P.A.: Modeling and exploiting collaborative traces in web-based collaborative working environment. Comput. Hum. Behav. **30**, 396–408 (2014)
3. Liptchinsky, V., Khazankin, R., Schulte, S., Satzger, B., Truong, H.L., Dustdar, S.: On modeling context-aware social collaboration processes. Inf. Syst. **43**(C), 66–82 (2014)
4. Olson, D.L., Rosacker, K.: Crowdsourcing and open source software participation. Serv. Bus. **7**(4), 499–511 (2013)
5. Onoue, S., Hata, H., Matsumoto, K.: A study of the characteristics of developers' activities in GitHub. In: Proceedings of Asia-Pacific Software Engineering Conference, pp. 968–972 (2013)
6. Peltz, C.: Web services orchestration and choreography. IEEE Comput. **10**, 46–52 (2003)
7. Poncin, W., Serebrenik, A., van den Brand, M.: Process mining software repositories. In: Proceedings of 15th European Conference on Software Maintenance and Reengineering, pp. 5–14. IEEE (2011)
8. Smirnov, S., Weidlich, M., Mendling, J., Weske, M.: Action patterns in business process model repositories. Comput. Ind. **63**(2), 98–111 (2012)
9. Xuan, Q., Devanbu, P.T., Filkov, V.: Converging work-talk patterns in online task-oriented communities (2014). arXiv:1404.5708
10. Zhang, D., Guo, B., Yu, Z.: The emergence of social and community intelligence. IEEE Comput. **7**, 21–28 (2011)
11. Zhao, Y., Zhu, Q.: Evaluation on crowdsourcing research: current status and future direction. Inf. Syst. Front. **16**(3), 417–434 (2014)

Follow the Leader: A Social Network Approach for Service Communities

Hamza Labbaci[1], Brahim Medjahed[2(✉)], Youcef Aklouf[1], and Zaki Malik[3]

[1] USTHB University, Algiers, Algeria
{hlabbaci,yaklouf}@usthb.dz
[2] University of Michigan - Dearborn, Dearborn, USA
brahim@umich.edu
[3] Eastern Michigan University, Ypsilanti, USA
zaki.malik@emich.edu

Abstract. Web services partake in various types of interactions during their lifetime such as recommendation, substitution, and composition, hence giving rise to *social* behaviors. In this paper, we propose a social-aware approach for service communities. Communities are built around socially active services called *leaders*. The remaining services, called *followers*, use past interactions to elect their leaders and join communities. We introduce a clustering algorithm for multi-relation networks and define heuristics to identify community leaders and followers. We also define a new metric, called *interoperability degree*, to determine the degree to which members of a community are likely to socially interact. We conduct experiments to illustrate that leveraging social behaviors may help clump together services that are suited to interoperate.

1 Introduction

The number of existing Web services increased intensively during the last few years. Consequently, clients have to sift through a large service space to discover the services that meet their needs and requirements, hence exacerbating attempts to discover, select, and compose services. One solution to alleviate this problem is to organize services into *communities* [6–8]. In a nutshell, a community is a cluster of Web services that share the same features such as quality of service, domain of interest, and composability.

The issue of structuring services into communities has been subject of multiple research efforts [8,9]. However, most existing approaches look at Web services as isolated entities, while in reality services recommend/substitute each other and participate in compositions, hence leading to "social" behaviors [3,4]. The idea of using social network concepts for Web services was first introduced in [5,11]; the authors introduced five social networks for supervision, competition, substitution, collaboration, and recommendation to deal with issues related to trust in Web services. Besides, these five networks are used in silos, with no relationship between a social network and the others. What is still missing is

© Springer International Publishing Switzerland 2016
Q.Z. Sheng et al. (Eds.): ICSOC 2016, LNCS 9936, pp. 705–712, 2016.
DOI: 10.1007/978-3-319-46295-0_50

a holistic approach for defining communities that handles the different types of social interactions between Web services.

Service communities were introduced to enhance the discovery, selection, and composition of Web services [8]. [7] defines a community as a cluster of services with the same domain of interest according to a predefined ontology. [11] manages communities by gathering and analyzing interactions among services with the goal to assess Web services' social qualities like selfishness. However, most the existing techniques treat Web services as isolated entities and either ignore their interactions or handle those interactions independently from each other. We propose a holistic approach and provide a multidimensional perspective on social interactions by taking all interactions into consideration while building the communities.

The aim of this paper is to propose a social-aware approach for organizing services that are more likely to interoperate into communities based on a *multidimensional* analysis of their *social behavior*. By *social behavior*, we refer to the different interactions between services such as recommendation, composition, and substitution. By *multidimensional*, we mean that all social behaviors are considered simultaneously, in contrast to [5,11] that looks at each one separately. The proposed approach helps prune the large space of potential services needed during service composition or substitution and reduces human intervention during the discovery process. Our approach is based on the notions of *leaders* and *followers*. *Leaders* are the main nodes around which communities are built. *Followers* are dependent on the leader of the community they belong to and take advantage of their local neighbors' preferences to "pledge allegiance" to a leader more accurate. The resulting communities group together services that are suited to interoperate.

The rest of this paper is organized as follows. Section 2 describes the proposed social-aware approach for communities, Sect. 3 is devoted to experiments and performance analysis. We provide concluding remarks in Sect. 4.

2   Building Social-Aware Service Communities

Web services are the social entities that interact and make-up the nodes of our social network. The different interactions that occur between services constitute their relationships. As Web services have multiple types of relationships, we model a social network of Web services with a multiplex graph (also known as multi-relation graph) [2]. This is a particular kind of complex networks defined over a set of nodes from the same type linked by different types of relations. In our case, nodes denote Web services and edges represent relationships between them.

Definition 1. *A multi-relation social network of Web services is a directed graph* $G = (V, R_1, R_2, R_3)$ *where* V *is a set of given services, and* $R_k = (S_u, S_v) \in V * V$ *is the set of edges of the k-th relationship. Precisely,* R_1 *is the set of edges of the substitution relationship,* R_2 *is the set of edges of the composition relationship,* R_3 *is the set of edges of the recommendation relationship.*

For example an edge $(S_i, S_j) \in R_1$ indicates that there is a social relationship of type substitution between Web services S_i and S_j, precisely it indicates that S_j is a substitute of S_i and clients can invoke S_j for a substitution if S_i fails.

As mentioned above, the social network records the social relationship between services by gathering the different interactions (substitution, recommendation, and composition) among services and update the network (edges and weights).

As services interact with each other, we start distinguishing some services that may be more invoked and recommended, used more in substitutions, and participate more in compositions. We refer to those services as *leaders*. A leader constitutes the starting node around which a community is built. The remaining services that were not selected as leaders are considered as *followers*. Followers' "pledge allegiance" to a leader and join the community of that leader. They learn from their prior interactions in the social network whether it will be more interesting to join a given leader. They also take into account the interactions of their close neighbors in the social network.

2.1 Community Leaders

Leaders are Web services around which communities are built. They are those services that were subject to the most successful social interactions (recommendations, substitution, and composition). To identify such nodes, we propose two heuristics: *MaxRin* and *MaxWin*. *MaxRin* focuses on the number of incoming edges to a service (i.e., number of social interactions) while *MaxWin* looks at the weights of those edges (i.e., importance of those social interactions).

MaxRin: This heuristic assumes that leaders are Web services that were invoked the most to substitute their peers, participated the most in compositions, and also were the most recommended ones in the network. If a Web service was involved in the greatest number of social interactions, this leads as to believe that this service has one of the highest credibility levels in the social network. This heuristic is computed as follows where r represents a layer or relationship type (recommendation, substitution, composition) in the network:

$$\max_{\substack{S=1}}^{S=n} \left(\frac{\sum_{r=1}^{r=3} \alpha_r D_S^{r+}}{\sum_{r=1}^{r=3} \alpha_r} \right)$$

This heuristic sums-up the number of incoming relations of services in each of the layers of the social network and multiplies it by the coefficient α of each of the relationships. Then, it divides it by the sum of the relationships coefficients. D_S^{r+} is the number of the incoming edges of the service S in the layer r of the network. α is the coefficient of the layer r of the network.

MaxWin: This heuristic assumes that leaders are the services with the highest weights values for their incoming edges and computes the average value of those weights. The weight value of an edge increases as the target node has a successful interaction, and decreases otherwise. This heuristic is computed according to the following formula:

$$\max_{s=1}^{s=n} \left(\frac{\sum_{r=1}^{r=3} \alpha_r W_s^{r+}}{\sum_{r=1}^{r=3} \alpha_r} \right)$$

This heuristic sums-up the weight values of incoming relations of services in each of the layers of the social network and multiplies it by the coefficient value of each of the relationships. Then, it divides it by the sum of the relationships coefficients. W_s^{r+} is the sum of the weights of the incoming edges to the services in the layer r of the network. α is the coefficient of the relation r of the network.

2.2 Community Followers

Once leaders are detected, the community building process starts. The services that were not selected as leaders are considered as followers. Each follower F calculates a *leader preference vector* in which it ranks leaders according to the weights of the paths between F and the leaders. F belongs to the community built around the leader ranked at the top of F's leader preference vector. We adopt the definition of path on a multiplex network given in [10]. The function $path(u_\alpha \rightarrow v_\beta)$ returns an ordered sequence of nodes which starts from node u in layer α and ends in node v in layer β. We also define the functions $distance(path(u_\alpha \rightarrow v_\beta))$ and $weight(path(u_\alpha \rightarrow v_\beta))$ that return the number of edges and weight of the path, respectively. Each follower determines its leader by executing the following function *Follow*:

$$argmax(weight(argmin(distance(path(u_\alpha \rightarrow v_\beta)))))$$

where:

- $argmin(distance(path(u_\alpha \rightarrow v_\beta)))$ returns the path/paths with the minimum distance (in term of number of nodes) between services u and v.
- $argmax(weight(givenpaths))$ returns the path with the maximum weight value. This function is of particular importance especially when the $argmin$ function returns more than one path with the same number of nodes.

To illustrate our technique, we use the example in Fig. 1. The subgroup S_1, S_2, S_3 contains services identified as leaders. S_4 wants to compute its leader preference vector. First, it identifies the paths with the minimum distance that separate S_4 from the leaders. Then, we compute the weights of each of the precedent paths: The probability p_1 that S_4's request reaches the leader S_1 is the probability that S_4 uses S_5 for a substitution, and the probability that S_5 uses S_1 for a substitution. Hence, $p_1 = 0.8 * 0.72 = 0.576$.

Based on the results given above, S_4's leader preference vector contains S_1 as a leader with the highest weight, then S_3, and finally S_2. Consequently, S_4 selects S_1 as a leader and becomes member of its community.

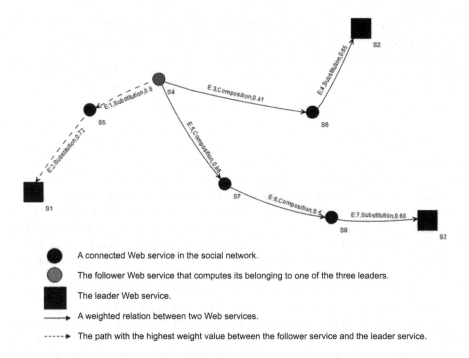

Fig. 1. Service leaders and followers: an example

2.3   Using Neighbors Preferences

Followers decide about their community membership by computing the probability of reaching the community leader. This probability depends on the follower's own social experience. We believe that the follower should rather seek the advice of like-minded peers, called *neighbors*. Such services may have more "social" experience (i.e., interactions), hence improving the accuracy of the community building process. In this paper, we adopt the multiplex neighborhood modularity introduced in [20]. In the following, $\Gamma^{mux}(u)$ represents the set of neighbors of the Web service u computed according to the multiplex neighborhood modularity:

$$\Gamma^{mux}(u) = \left\{ x \in \Gamma(u)^{tot} : \frac{\mid \Gamma(u)^{tot} \cap \Gamma(x)^{tot} \mid}{\mid \Gamma(u)^{tot} \cup \Gamma(x)^{tot} \mid} \geq \delta \right\} \delta \in [0, 1]$$

where:

- $\Gamma(u)^{tot}$ is the set of all services connected to service u.
- $\Gamma(x)^{tot}$ is the set of all Web services connected to service x.
- δ is a threshold that determines the minimum probability that the two services x and u should guarantee to be considered as neighbors.

   This formula returns the set of services considered as neighbors of a given service u in the network. Two services u and x are neighbors if and only if they share a certain number of services that connect to both of them. Once WS_f neighbors are identified, they elect the leaders using the Borda voting system by assigning points to each leader. For N leaders in the system, they attribute N points to their firstly ranked leader, N-1 to the next, and so on. The lastly ranked leader receives 1 point. The winner is the leader that obtains the greatest number of points by the voters.

2.4   Interoperability Degree

One of the key features of Web services is their ability to interoperate. As services engage into social interactions, they begin to knit creating groups of partners with highly dense relationships. Members of a community tend to interoperate more with each other. We estimate the ability of services to interoperate by calculating their connectivity within the obtained communities. We consider that if a dense connectivity exists among services within a community, this would definitely mean that this community groups interoperable services. By dense connectivity, we refer to the *clustering coefficient (CC)* of the nodes within the community. CC consists in the extent to which the nodes cluster. We define the average of the CC values of all members of a community as the *interoperability degree* (I-D). The I-D of a community is computed by averaging the I-D values of all services within that community. On the other hand, the I-D of the whole social network is calculated by averaging the I-Ds of all services within the social network.

To define the interoperability degree of a Web service S, we extend the clustering coefficient introduced in [1]:

$$I - D(S) = \frac{K}{N \times (N - 1)}$$

where N is the number of S's neighbors within the community and K is the number of connections among S's neighbors across the different layers. Suppose that service S has the following connections to its 5 neighbors ($N = 5$): substitution relationship to S_1 and S_2, composition relationship to S_3 and S_4, and recommendation relationship to S_1, S_3, and S_5. Suppose also that $S1$ and S_3 are connected to S_4 via composition and substitution relationships, respectively ($K = 2$). Then $I - D(S) = \frac{2}{5 \times 4} = 0.1$.

3   Experiments

The aim of our experiments is to illustrate that Web services are more interoperable within the obtained communities than with the rest of the social network. We developed a prototype in Java using the tool JUNG2 that offers the function *sparseMultiGraph()* to simulate a social network of Web services. The prototype takes as input the number of Web services in the social network and the types of interactions among services. It returns several states of the social network topology with different chaining scenarios among Web services and different weighting values.

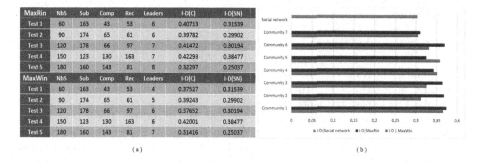

MaxRin	NbS	Sub	Comp	Rec	Leaders	I-D(C)	I-D(SN)
Test 1	60	163	43	53	6	0.40713	0.31539
Test 2	90	174	65	61	6	0.39782	0.29902
Test 3	120	178	66	97	7	0.41472	0.30194
Test 4	150	123	130	163	7	0.42293	0.38477
Test 5	180	160	143	81	8	0.32297	0.25037
MaxWin	NbS	Sub	Comp	Rec	Leaders	I-D(C)	I-D(SN)
Test 1	60	163	43	53	4	0.37527	0.31539
Test 2	90	174	65	61	5	0.39243	0.29902
Test 3	120	178	66	97	6	0.37652	0.30194
Test 4	150	123	130	163	6	0.42001	0.38477
Test 5	180	160	143	81	7	0.31416	0.25037

(a)   (b)

Fig. 2. Experiments

Figure 2a summarizes the different test runs performed in our experiments. We used the following notations in the table:

- MaxRin: Results obtained using the MaxRin heuristic.
- Nbs: Number of Web services populating the social network.
- Sub, Comp, Rec: Number of substitution, composition, and recommendation edges respectively.
- Leaders: Number of community leaders (i.e., communities).
- I-D(C): The highest I-D value obtained for a community.
- I-D(SN): The I-D value computed for the whole social network.

We implemented the proposed approach and conducted several experiments to detect communities over several states of the social network. We varied the leader heuristic between $maxRin$ and $maxWin$. Then, we computed the interoperability degree (I-D) of each generated community and compared it with the interoperability degree of the whole social network. The experiments were performed with δ equals 0.2. Figure 2b shows that the I-D of the obtained communities is greater than the I-D of the whole social network. This supports our claim that the proposed social-aware community approach groups together services that are best suited to interoperate. A client's request has a greater chance to be fulfilled inside one of the obtained community than across the social network.

4 Conclusion

In this paper, we proposed a social network-based approach for building communities that group together services that are most likely to interact though in substitutions, compositions, and recommendations. We adopted multiplex networks to model social networks of Web services. We defined heuristics to identify community leaders and help followers elect preferred leaders based on their past interactions in the social network. Followers leverage the selections made by more socially active neighbors to adjust their memberships. The generated communities are evaluated using a new metric, called interoperability degree, that measures the ability of services within the same community to interoperate. We validated our approach through experiments.

References

1. De Domenico, M., Solé, A., Gómez, S., Arenas, A.: Random walks on multiplex networks (2013). arXiv preprint arXiv:1306.0519
2. Hmimida, M., Kanawati, R.: Community detection in multiplex networks: a seed-centric approach. NHM **10**(1), 71–85 (2015). http://aimsciences.org/journals/displayArticlesnew.jsp?paperID=10840
3. Maamar, Z., Faci, N., Wives, L.K., Yahyaoui, H., Hacid, H.: Towards a method for engineering social web services. In: Proceedings of Engineering Methods in the Service-Oriented Context - 4th IFIP WG 8.1 Working Conference on Method Engineering, ME 2011, Paris, France, 20-22 April 2011, pp. 153–167 (2011). http://dx.doi.org/10.1007/978-3-642-19997-4_15
4. Maamar, Z., dos Santos, P.B., Wives, L.K., Badr, Y., Faci, N., de Oliveira, P.M.J.: Using social networks for web services discovery. IEEE Internet Comput. **15**(4), 48–54 (2011). http://dx.doi.org/10.1109/MIC.2011.27
5. Maamar, Z., Yahyaoui, H., Lim, E., Thiran, P.: Social engineering of communities of web services. In: Proceedings of 11th Annual International Symposium on Applications and the Internet, SAINT 2011, Munich, Germany, 18–21 July 2011, pp. 100–109 (2011). http://dx.doi.org/10.1109/SAINT.2011.23
6. Malik, Z., Bouguettaya, A.: Rateweb: Reputation assessment for trust establishment among web services. VLDB J. **18**(4), 885–911 (2009). http://dx.doi.org/10.1007/s00778-009-0138-1
7. Medjahed, B., Bouguettaya, A.: A dynamic foundational architecture for semantic web services. Distrib. Parallel Databases **17**(2), 179–206 (2005). http://www.springerlink.com/index/10.1007/s10619-004-0190-1
8. Mehdi, M., Bouguila, N., Bentahar, J.: Reputation in communities of agent-based web services through data mining. In: Agents and Data Mining Interaction - 10th International Workshop, ADMI 2014, Paris, France, 5–9 May 2014, Revised Selected Papers, pp. 79–92 (2014). http://dx.doi.org/10.1007/978-3-319-20230-3_7
9. Sellami, M., Bouchaala, O., Gaaloul, W., Tata, S.: Communities of web service registries: construction and management. J. Syst. Softw. **86**(3), 835–853 (2013). http://dx.doi.org/10.1016/j.jss.2012.11.019
10. Solé-Ribalta, A., Domenico, M.D., Gómez, S., Arenas, A.: Centrality rankings in multiplex networks. In: ACM Web Science Conference, WebSci 2014, Bloomington, IN, USA, 23–26 June 2014, pp. 149–155 (2014). http://doi.acm.org/10.1145/2615569.2615687
11. Yahyaoui, H., Maamar, Z., Lim, E., Thiran, P.: Towards a community-based, social network-driven framework for web services management. Future Gener. Comput. Syst. **29**(6), 1363–1377 (2013). http://dx.doi.org/10.1016/j.future.2013.02.003

Service Analytics (Industrial Papers)

A Data Services-Based Quality Analysis System for the Life Cycle of Tire Production

Yuliang Shi, Yu Chen, Shibin Sun, Lei Liu, and Lizhen Cui[✉]

School of Computer Science and Technology, Shandong University, Jinan, China
{shiyuliang,l.liu,clz}@sdu.edu.cn,
hitwhcy@gmail.com,sunshibin1013@163.com

Abstract. In the background of actual production demands, we develop data services to solve the problem of "information isolated island" in the tire production for achieving the unified management for data from diverse production systems. Based on the data services, the management system for tire production is designed. The system uses the decision tree algorithm with data fitting and data screening technologies to analyze the data from the whole production process and realize the forecast of product quality and defects analysis. The system has been applied to the production by Shandong Linglong Tire Co., Ltd. The practice has proved that our data services and system not only improve the tire pass rate and production efficiency, but also help enterprises to achieve the efficient management of production. In addition, we apply the service to the actual manufacturing industry, which plays a positive role in the promotion and improvement of service application.

Keywords: Data services · Data extraction · Quality analysis · Big data · Tire

1 Introduction

With the rapid development of society and the continuous innovation of information technology, the concepts of automated production and management have been well applied to the modern tire manufacturing enterprises. The automation not only means mechanization of production, but also means a programmable logic control system which seamlessly connects data generated from different stages of the production to realize the automated management of the whole process of production [1]. In the tire manufacturing industry, the tire production process includes many stages such as *rubber compound mixing*, *woven/steel cord preparation*, *building/curing* and *quality inspection* [2]. For some of tire manufacturing companies, although they have achieved the automated production of tires, the production workshops in different stages have separate management systems and data stores. Therefore, they can't achieve the efficient management of the whole tire production process. Figure 1 shows the four major stages of the tire production process, including *rubber mixing, semi-components, building/curing* and *external inspection*. Each stage has an independent management system. There are logic associations between those systems, but the data have different structures and storage modes, which leads to the information isolation and brings a lot of inconveniences to

© Springer International Publishing Switzerland 2016
Q.Z. Sheng et al. (Eds.): ICSOC 2016, LNCS 9936, pp. 715–729, 2016.
DOI: 10.1007/978-3-319-46295-0_51

the production of tires and quality inspection. The data generated in the tire manufacturing process are not uniformly collected, processed, analyzed and fully utilized, which causes the tire enterprises not to make accurate defects analysis and prediction of the product, and restricts the improvement of the production efficiency and the quality of the tire.

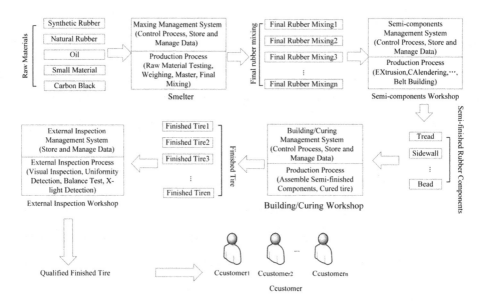

Fig. 1. Tire production process

In order to solve the above problems, Ruan et al. [3] designed a tire production process monitoring system realizing the data acquisition, processing, query and real-time monitoring. However, this system only monitors the tire production process and does not support the quality defects analysis of product. Abou-Ali et al. [4] proposed a comprehensive tire defects diagnosis expert system. By using an integrated diagnostic program, the system can diagnose the possible reasons of tire defects and realize the tire quality defects diagnosis. But it does not support the quality prediction. As the development of science and technology and social progress, service computing has been promoted and popularized in many fields of industrial production. Combining enterprise architecture with cloud computing services, Zimmermann et al. [5] proposed the service-oriented enterprise architecture. For the openness, dynamics and uncertainty of service oriented large-scale distributed computing environment, Li et al. [6] designed a reliable service computing platform for cross organizational workflow application. The platform has a significant impact on the integration of the modern enterprise management tactic, inter-organizational workflow services and heterogeneous systems. The risk assessment model of service oriented cloud computing system is established [7]. The model can realize the identification, prediction and evaluation of the security risk of cloud computing. Taking dynamic services into account, based on the event driven mechanism, Lv et al. [8] proposed a composite service adaptation method which can handle a variety of different types of dynamic services in real time, automatically check and update the composite services. Di Cosmo et al. [9] proposed a distributed software system based on complex services for automatic deployment and configuration of services. The software system not only meets the user requirements and related software dependencies, but also has the minimum the number of virtual machines. Ichikawa et al. [10] developed a data mining platform regarded as a service to open to the users. The platform can provide a variety of data mining algorithms for the users to deal with data in low-cost and simple way. Based on service agents, an approach to managing of autonomous and context aware resources is presented for cloud services [11]. Besides, a cloud service oriented management framework is proposed for service aggregation and service provision. Meanwhile, two kinds of support algorithms are designed to realize the service self-organization process. Service computing can not only solve the problem of technical platform and architecture, but also integrate and manage the business itself. In recent years, with the increasing maturity of service computing technology, it has become an indispensable technology in modern manufacturing enterprises.

In summary, a lot of methods of the management of tire production are mentioned above, but they can't completely solve the problems in Shandong Linglong Tire Co., Ltd. Services computing is a web oriented new paradigm. It uses a standardized, loosely coupled and transparent application integration approach to improve the interactive and agile ability of enterprise internal system, and to achieve fast, seamless integration and cooperation between application systems. Combining the advantages of service computing and the actual needs of the enterprises, we develop data services and design quality analysis system for tire production. This paper makes the following contributions: we develop data services to realize the unified management of data from different databases with multiple storage modes. The data services provide complete and standard data for other application systems through interfaces, which is convenient for design of the product management systems. Based on the data services, we realize the data correlation analysis of the whole production process to predict the product quality and track the reasons of the product defects. We apply services to industrial production, improving the quality of products and production efficiency, promoting the promotion and use of services.

The rest of the paper is organized as follows. Section 2 introduces data and fault management in SOC. Section 3 gives the design and implementation of data services. Section 4 describes the framework of the system and the model of quality and analysis. Section 5 presents the feasibility and usefulness of data services and the system. Section 6 ends the paper with the conclusions and for future work.

2   Data and Fault Management in SOC

Data quality is very important in SOC, and it not only affects the calculation results, but also relates to the calculation speed. How to effectively manage the data to ensure the authenticity of the data, integrity, correctness and unity, is one of the urgent problems we need to solve. At present, many methods have been put forward to manage and improve data. In order to solve the problems of multi data sources, Yu [12] built a service components pipeline model that is open with multi-source data extraction, service data packet mode and transparent access. Meanwhile, in order to avoid potential bottlenecks and conflicts (structural conflicts and data collision) in various service components of workflow, the model can adjust pipelining segment system from a single-stage workflow continuously and dynamically. Tao et al. [13] proposed an on-line point cloud data extraction algorithm for spatial scanning measurement of irregular surface in copying manufacture. Based on the algorithm, they presented a data extraction framework that can handle data points set of arbitrary size, density and shape. In addition, the framework can reduce the amount of the dense cloud data to ensure the accuracy of the data. Data standardization makes the value of data attributes drop in a certain range. Support vector machine is widely used in the kernel to transfer the data from the feature space in the input space to another feature space. On this basis, a linear algorithm is used to solve the classification problem. The standardization of the data will change the value of the data in the feature space [14]. Chatterjee et al. [15] introduced a standard data acquisition and analysis model. This model provides a method for checking the quality of standard data for achieving data extraction and standardization for multi-platform and multi-system, but it is not perfect for the big data with high requirements. Analyzing the time series, using exponential smoothing model and grey prediction model, Ma et al. [16] studied the quality of the gearbox shell in manufacturing process and forecasted the trend of the product quality. Zhao et al. [17] established a regression system based on phase. The system can make a quantitative evaluation for the online prediction results, which is helpful to improve the quality of the product. Using Apriori algorithm, the association prediction model of product quality forecasting data is constructed [18]. In addition, it uses k- means algorithm to achieve the link between the patterns. In order to meet the needs of quality analysis and processing quality problems, a causal relation analysis method is proposed in [19]. The model explores how to identify the causal relationship between production process variables and product quality variables. According to the causal relationship between process variables and product quality variables, a scheme to improve the quality of product is presented. A new intelligent product quality analysis and improvement system is proposed in [20]. It analyzes the problem to find out the cause of the problem by using decision tree and neural network and gives the method to improve the quality of the product. These methods of product quality analysis and prediction can predict the product with simple process. However, for tire production, its' process is more complex. For example, many parameters are used to evaluate the quality of the product. Therefore, these methods are not suitable for the analysis and prediction of the tire quality defects.

The above studies introduce some methods for data extraction, data standardization, product quality analysis and prediction. However, in the actual environment of tire production, these methods are not applicable. Therefore, considering the actual needs of the tire business and researching the existing technology, the paper designs a quality analysis system for the full life cycle of tire production based on data services.

3 Data Services

This section will introduce the design (Sect. 3.1) and implementation (Sect. 3.2) of data services.

3.1 Services Design

The data of tire production are stored in different databases. In order to keep the performance of original system when extracting data, we designed data services considering multiple storage sources and the dependence relationship for the data, as shown in Fig. 2. Data services contain six components that are extraction engine, data standardization, data cleaning, exception handling, automatic job scheduler and resource monitor-predictor.

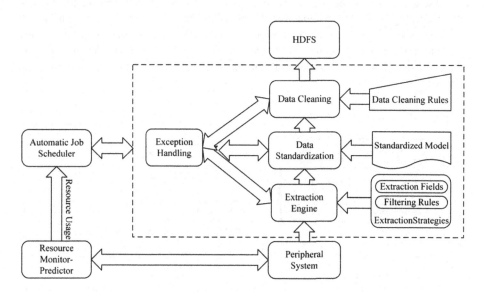

Fig. 2. A schematic diagram of data services architecture

According to the extraction strategies, the extraction engine extracts the data from the peripheral system. The extraction strategies contain the customizable extraction fields and the filtering rules. The customizable extraction fields allow the user to define the fields of the extraction so that the engine can only extract the useful data fields instead of the entire data records, which reduces the quantity of data transmission. Data in multiple systems are generated in order and they can be joined by "bar code". Therefore, according to existing standardized data sets and the filtering rules, the engine removes partly unrelated or dirty data to reduce the amount of data and the impact on the original system as much as possible. Due to the original data format is diverse and not uniform, the data can't be used directly. According to the standardized data model, based on Hadoop technology, standardized module uses multiple tasks in parallel to process the original data and achieve rapid data standardization. There may be dirty or incomplete data in the standardized data. Therefore, according to the rules of data cleaning, we clean the data. In order to quickly complete the cleaning work, we run the data cleaning tasks in parallel. Next, the data are classified into multiple data domains (e.g., sales data, production data, analysis data, environmental parameter, material information, etc.). Finally, these data are stored in a distributed file system (HDFS) to facilitate the application of the upper layer. When the extraction job, standardization job and cleaning job run, there may be errors caused by network, operating systems, procedures, or data resulting in the abnormal termination. Exception handling module captures the exception errors, which is convenient for users to view and process the errors. Resource monitor-predictor is responsible for monitoring all kinds of resources of peripheral system (IO, memory, CPU) to get the load capacity of database servers. It also informs the job scheduler of the servers' load capacity. The job scheduler will reasonably execute jobs according to the load capacity. When the database servers load seriously, job scheduler will delay the extraction jobs or divide them into a number of small extraction jobs to minimize the effects on the performance of original applications. When extraction job is finished, the job scheduler will automatically execute standardization and data cleaning job.

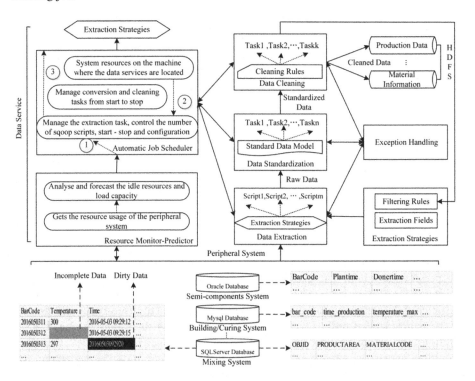

Fig. 3. Description of data services

3.2   Implementation Details

Data services realize four functions: data extraction, data standardization, data cleaning and job scheduling, as shown in Fig. 3.

In the peripheral system, diverse systems use different databases with different data storage formats. The *mixing* system uses the SQL Server database, the *semi-components* system uses the Oracle database, and the *building/curing* system uses the MySQL database. These databases have their own storage structures and naming rules. Meanwhile, for different workshop management systems, software designers are not necessary the same. Therefore, the attribute naming rules in database tables are diverse. As shown in Fig. 3, the SQL Server database uses the lower case letters and underline to name attributes, Oracle uses the first capital letters to name the attributes, and the MySQL database uses the full capitalization method to name attributes. The variety of attribute naming methods brings many difficulties to data processing. In each sub management system, there may be some useless data. For example, in the SQL Server database, the value of "time" in the third line is not standard. This kind of data calls dirty data. The "Temperature" value in the second line is empty. This kind of data is incomplete data. Through the intermediate database, the paper realizes the unity of the data formats and data structures. Meanwhile, the filtering rules help achieve the data cleaning and provide cleaned data for the upper applications.

Job scheduling algorithm

```
GenerateExtractJob:
     Get the database connection to extract;
     Get the extract fields;
     Get the filtering rules;
     Generate extract script;
     Generate the database connection for next extract;
JobScheduler:
     Obtain the load of the system by monitor;
     If system is idle
          Execute extraction job;
     Else
          Wait();
     If   system is not idle
        If extraction job is emergency;
          Split extraction job into k small jobs j₁,j₂…jₖ;
          Execute extraction job j₁,j₂..jₖ;
        End if
     Else
          Execute extraction job;
     End if
     Execute data conversion job;
     Execute data cleaning job;
     Generate filtering rules;
     Generate next extraction job;
```

The data services mainly include two stages: the extraction job and the job scheduling, as indicated below. First, the extraction engine uses *GenerateExtractJob* to read the extraction fields and the filter rules and generate extraction scripts. Then the extraction job is submitted to *JobScheduler*. *JobScheduler* analyzes the load of database servers. If the server is idle, the extraction job is performed. If the current system is busy and the job is urgent, the extraction job is divided into a number of small extraction jobs to decline the impact on the original system. If the job is not urgent, it is delayed until the system has enough resources. After extraction job, job scheduler calls data standardization and data cleaning job to achieve the unification of data formats and clean-up. Next, the data are stored in HDFS and the bar codes of the extracted data are stored in the filtering rules. Finally, *GenerateExtractJob* is called to produce the corresponding data extraction job of the next system.

4   Quality Analysis Management System

In the above, we have introduced the design and implementation of data services. This section will show the frame design of the system (Sect. 4.1) and quality analysis process (Sect. 4.2).

4.1   Framework of the System

The full life cycle quality analysis system of tire production mainly consists of five parts. From bottom to top, they are peripheral systems, data services, distributed storage platform, big data computing platform and graphical display, the framework of the system is shown as in Fig. 4.

The peripheral system is a general designation for all the sub management system of the tire production, such as MES-Manufacturing Execution System (*mixing, semicomponents, building/curing*), PDM-Product Data Management system, ERP-Enterprise Resource Planning system and Sale system. It stores all the original ecological data generated from the production to the sales, which provides data support for the system designed by this paper. Data services are responsible for obtaining data from a number of peripheral systems. Meanwhile, they standardize and clean the data in order to provide complete and effective data for system. The distributed storage platform is mainly used to store the basic data that are transferred from the data services and the result data generated by the upper applications. The storage system, which can provide high storage performance for mass data, is constructed based on Hadoop, Hive and Spark. The big data computing platform mainly makes the quality analysis calculation. The quality analysis calculation is used to predict the quality of tire and analyze the reasons of tire's quality defects. Graphical interface uses diverse and graphical visual interface display technology (e.g., echart, amchart, etc.) to more vividly and clearly show the results. Graphical display contains the functions that are the analysis of quality defects and unqualified reason analysis.

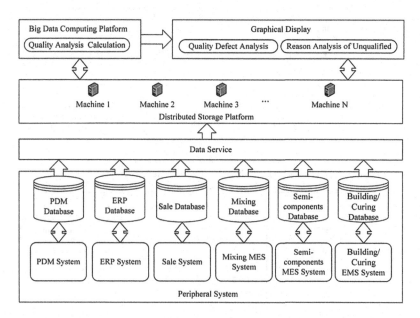

Fig. 4. A framework of the management system for the full life cycle of tire production

4.2 Quality Analysis Model

The process of tire quality analysis is shown in Fig. 5.

First, all the existing tire production data are regarded as a sample to train a decision tree. The paths of the decision tree are the rules of the qualified/unqualified product. Then the tire production data are matched with the path of the tree to judge whether the tire is qualified or not. If it is unqualified, the unqualified reasons can be found on the branches of the tree. The key steps in the tire quality analysis are the generation of rules and the analysis of data match. The following will introduce these two steps. In this paper, the decision tree algorithm is used to generate a variety of rules. First, the characteristics of the product are extracted as training sets from six aspects: man, machine, material, method, measure and environment. The characteristics contain operator, machine, material coding, steamer, temperature, pressures, formulation process, inspectors, inspection standards, and inspection machine. Then the decision tree is generated by ID3 algorithm, as shown in Fig. 6. Nodes' selection is an important step in the process of decision tree generation. First, an attribute is selected. According to this attribute, the training sets are divided into several sub sets. Next, the entropy of each subset is calculated. Based on entropy, the information gain is calculated. The information gains of other attributes are calculated in the same way. The attributes with the maximum information gain will be the root node of the decision tree. The other nodes are gotten in the same way. When the current attribute sets has only one attribute, the attribute is the leaf node. The tree may be too lush, which is not conducive to be understood or used. Therefore, the paper uses the post-pruning method to cut off the branches with small weight, which makes the tree more intuitive and easier to be used. The final decision tree is shown in Fig. 6.

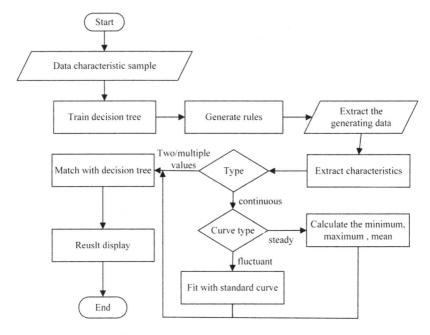

Fig. 5. Process of product quality analysis

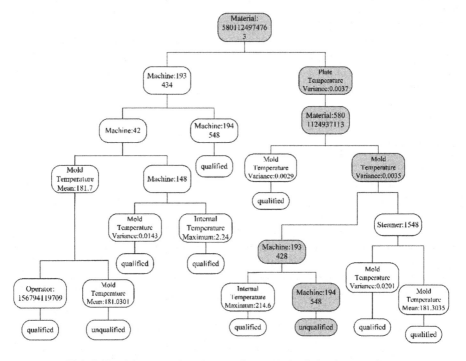

Fig. 6. Decision tree of product quality analysis (Color figure online)

Data matching analysis matches the characteristics information of product with the decision tree rules to decide whether the product is qualified or not. The characteristics information of the tire can be classified two categories: curve type and two or multiple value. For the characteristics information with two or multiple value, we can directly match them with the rules. The curve type information can be classified two categories: stable curve (e.g., mold temperature in vulcanization stage), and fluctuant curve (e.g., top bolt pressure in the mixing stage). For the stable curve, it needs to calculate the maximum, minimum and mean that are regarded as the judgment conditions in the decision tree. For the fluctuant curve, we firstly calculate a standard curve. The standard curve can be generated by the existing qualified product sample. The fluctuant curve is fitted with standard curve. The difference square sum (Q), regression error (S) and curve correlation ratio (R) are used to match the rules. Finally, we can know whether the product is qualified or not. For example, there is a product characteristic information (Material: 5801124983756, Plate Temperature Variance: 0.0038, Material: 5801124948215, Mold Temperature Variance: 0.0036, Machine: 196124). It matches the path with brown color in the decision tree shown in Fig. 6. From Fig. 6, we know that this product is not qualified and the path indicates the reason for the failure. Through practical applications, the accuracy rate of the decision tree model proposed in this paper is up to 90 %.

5   Feasibility and Usefulness

This section describes the feasibility of data services and system (Sect. 5.1), and discusses the application value in industry (Sect. 5.2).

5.1   Feasibility

As described above, the system proposed in this paper can analyze and display the reasons of the quality problems in each production stage of tire. These reasons can be used as the reference by skilled technicians. As shown in Fig. 7.

It shows the process of tire quality defects analysis in practical applications. The analysis results show the reasons for all kinds of unqualified product in the form of a tree. In the picture, the orange path indicates the reasons for unqualified. By fitting these rules, we can find the nonconforming product. In the bottom of Fig. 7, the list shows the process of product quality analysis. Figure 8 shows the analysis process of reasons for leading to off-specification product. The graphic display of the stage includes three parts: material properties, causality diagram and sample information. In the material properties section, the user can enter the material information to view. From the man, machine, material and other aspects, the causality diagram shows the cause of the failure of the product in the form of figures and tables. The sample information shows the information of substandard product in detail. The system can clearly show the process and results of the tire quality analysis, and it is feasible for the analysis and prediction of the tire quality defects.

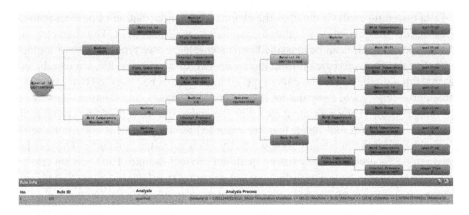

Fig. 7. Results of product analyzing quality defects

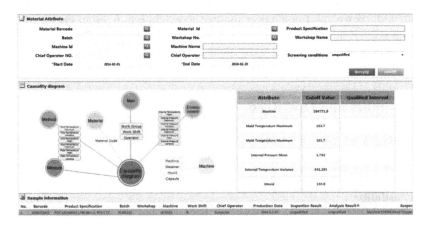

Fig. 8. Reasons for the failure of product

In the paper, the decision tree algorithm is used for the analysis of tire quality. Therefore, we give the performance evaluation for it, shown in Fig. 9. The horizontal axis is the training ratio. The training ratio is the ratio of the amount of the test data and the amount of the sample data for training decision tree. The vertical axis is the accuracy. The accuracy is the ratio of the number of records that the analysis results are consistent with the actual results and the total number of records. According to the definition of accuracy, we can measure the accuracy of the decision tree used to analyze whether the tire is standard or not. First, we choose a certain number of qualified/unqualified tires. The production data of those tires are used as the training sets to train our decision tree. Then we choose a certain number of tire production data measured, and with the help of the decision tree, we can know whether these tires are qualified or not. By comparing the results of the analysis with the results come from the tire quality inspection process, the accuracy of the decision tree can be got. From the Fig. 9, we can know that with the increase of training ratio, the accuracy of the decision tree algorithm increases first and then decreases. The ascending speed is relatively fast while the declining speed is relatively slow. We can also find that when the training ratio is 1.20, the accuracy of the decision tree reaches the maximum value. In the production, there are 200000 tires about millions data for each day. Therefore, there is enough sample data to train the decision tree to improve the accuracy of the decision tree.

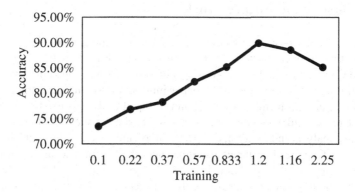

Fig. 9. Performance of decision tree for tire quality analysis

5.2 Usefulness

The data services and quality analysis system have been applied to Shandong Linglong Tire Co., Ltd. In actual production, we set every 10 min to start data services for extracting data. In 10 min, there are 10 thousand to 15 thousand records will be produced. According to the actual test, we know that the average time for the system to extract and process these data is 1.25 s. These are signs that data services can rapidly integrate the data from PDM, ERP and other systems without affecting the original application in these systems. They have a higher the efficiency and better in real time to provide a good data support for the real-time quality analysis and prediction of the tire. The process of tire production is complex and each process uses different materials. Therefore, there are a great number of factors leading to produce substandard products. It might be feasible for a small company to rely solely on manpower to analyze the reasons for each unqualified tire. However, Shandong Linglong Tire Co., Ltd. daily produces millions of tires. If for each unqualified tire, we analyze all the factors in each process, it will waste too much time. Hence, we extract the tire characteristic data to construct the decision tree and analyze the reason of the unqualified tires. In the practical application, the quality analysis can rapidly find the cause of the unqualified tire with high accuracy. Therefore, the staff can timely find wrong links and take remedial measures or recycle products that may not be qualified, which can improve the qualified rate of the tire and the credibility of enterprises. In practical applications, the accuracy of decision tree algorithm is about 90 %. The accuracy is related to the size of the training set and the extracted data characteristics. The data service and the system designed in this paper can not only solve the problems in the production of tire and help enterprises improve product quality, but also upgrade customers' satisfaction, enhance competitiveness and increase revenue. Moreover, they are not only applicable to tire industry, but also easily extended to other production areas and increase the reusability of IT assets. In this paper, the service computing is applied to the actual manufacturing industry, which plays a positive role in the promotion and improvement of service application.

6   Conclusion and Future Work

In order to solve the problem of information isolation among multiple heterogeneous systems in tire production, we develop data services. Based on the data services in conjunction with the big data analysis technology, the management system for tire production life cycle is designed. The paper introduces how to solve the problems of data scattered, non-uniform data format and tire quality defects existing in Shandong Linglong Tire Co., Ltd. From the aspects that are the data services implementation principle, quality analysis and forecast, this paper mines and analyzes the value of data using data service as the core. This paper also introduces the function design of the data services, and then describes the function design of the system based on the data services. At last, we give the implement processes of the data services, quality analysis and quality forecast. Practical results have proved that the data services and system developed in this paper is able to regulate the production process and improve production efficiency and product quality. In the future, we will develop monitoring services about the using of tire to help tire companies to produce tires that are suitable for a variety of geographical environments.

Acknowledgment.   The research work was supported by the National Natural Science Foundation of China under Grant No. 61572295, 61272241, the Innovation Methods Work Special Project No. 2015IM010200, the TaiShan Industrial Experts Programme of Shandong Province, the Natural Science Foundation of Shandong Province under Grant No. ZR2014FM031, ZR2013FQ014, the Shandong Province Science and Technology Major Special Project No. 2015ZDJQ01002, 2015ZDXX0201B03, 2015ZDXX0201A04, the Shandong Province Key Research and Development Plan No. 2015GGX101015, the Fundamental Research Funds of Shandong University No. 2015JC031.

References

1. Polymers Type Asia. http://w3.siemens.com/markets/global/en/tire/Documents/Polymers-Tire-Asia.pdf
2. How a Tire is Made. http://www.maxxis.com/other-automotive-information/how-a-tire-is-made
3. Ruan, J.F., Yu, W.J., Yang, Y., Hu, JB.: Design and realize of tire production process monitoring system based on cyber-physical systems. In: 2015 International Conference on Computer Science and Mechanical Automation, Hangzhou, pp. 175–179 (2015)
4. Abou-Ali, M.G., Khamis, M.: TIREDDX: an integrated intelligent defects diagnostic system for tire production and service. Expert Syst. Appl. **24**(3), 247–259 (2003)

5. Zimmermann, A., Pretz, M., Zimmermann, G., Firesmith, D.G., Petrov, L., El-Sheikh, E.: Towards service-oriented enterprise architectures for big data applications in the cloud. In: 2013 17th IEEE International Enterprise Distributed Object Computing Conference Workshops, pp. 130–135. IEEE, Vancouver (2013)
6. Li, S., Zhang, Q.Q., Chen, S.B., Tan, W.A., Tang, A.Q., Hu, X.M.: Reliable service computing platform architecture for cross-organizational workflows. In: 2014 IEEE International Conference on Systems, Man, and Cybernetics, pp. 3066–3701. IEEE, San Diego (2014)
7. Lin, F., Yang, L.Q., Zeng, W.H., Wang, Y.: Service oriented CSOMA model for risk evaluation of cloud computing system. Metall. Min. Ind. 7(9), 281–289 (2015)
8. Lv, C., Jiang, W., Hu, S.L.: Dynamic environment-oriented self-adaptation of service composition. Chin. J. Comput. 39(2), 305–322 (2016)
9. Di Cosmo, R., Eiche, A., Mauro, J., Zacchiroli, S., Zavattaro, G., Zwolakowski, J.: Automatic deployment of services in the cloud with aeolus blender. In: Barros, A., Grigori, D., Narendra, N.C., Dam, H.K. (eds.) ICSOC 2015. LNCS, vol. 9435, pp. 397–411. Springer, Heidelberg (2015). doi:10.1007/978-3-662-48616-0_28
10. Ichikawa, K., Yada, K., Washio, T.: Development of data mining platform MUSASHI towards service computing. In: 2010 IEEE International Conference on Granular Computing, pp. 235–240. IEEE, San Jose (2010)
11. Hou, F., Mao, X.J., Wu, W., Liu, L., Panneerselvam, J.: A cloud-oriented services self-management approach based on multi-agent system technique. In: 2014 IEEE/ACM 7th International Conference on Utility and Cloud Computing, pp. 261–268. IEEE/ACM, London (2015)
12. Yu, W.: A service components pipeline model based on multi-source data extraction. Signal Process. 124, 5–12 (2015)
13. Tao, Y., Li, Y., Wang, Y.Q., Ma, Y.Y.: On-line point cloud data extraction algorithm for spatial scanning measurement of irregular surface in copying manufacture. Int. J. Adv. Manuf. Technol. (2016). doi:10.1007/s00170-016-8592-6
14. Luor, D.C.: A comparative assessment of data standardization on support vector machine for classification problems. Intell. Data Anal. 19(3), 529–546 (2015)
15. Chatterjee, S., Kyasa, R.C., Gopidi, N.R., Rav,i P.P.: Data standardization and analysis model for enhanced global productivity. In: 14th Symposium on International Automotive Technology, Pune (2015)
16. Ma, Y.H., Kong, F.S., Liu, Z.H., Zhu, X.Y., Pan, Y.C.: Processing quality forecast and diagnosis for gear-box shell production line in manufacturing system. In: 2012 International Conference on Applied Mechanics and Manufacturing System, Guangzhou (2013)
17. Zhao, C.H.: A quality-relevant sequential phase partition approach for regression modeling and quality prediction analysis in manufacturing processes. IEEE Trans. Autom. Sci. Eng. 11(4), 983–991 (2013)
18. Ruhaizan, I., Zalinda, O., Azuraliza, A.B.: Associative prediction model and clustering for product forecast data. In: 2010 10th International Conference on Intelligent Systems Design and Applications, Cairo, pp. 1459–1464 (2010)
19. Du, S.: Improved product quality through causality analysis in product engineering. Int. J. Mater. Struct. Integrity 3(1), 47–65 (2009)
20. Wu, R.C., Chen, R.S.: The application of data mining technology for intelligent product quality analysis improvement system. WSEAS Trans. Inf. Sci. Appl. 4(4), 693–699 (2007)

Towards More Effective Solution Retrieval in IT Support Services Using Systems Log

Rongda Zhu[1], Yu Deng[2], Soumitra (Ronnie) Sarkar[2(✉)],
Kaoutar El Maghraoui[2], Harigovind V. Ramasamy[2], and Alan Bivens[2]

[1] Department of Computer Science, University of Illinois at Urbana Champaign,
Urbana, IL 61801, USA
rzhu4@illinois.edu

[2] IBM T.J. Watson Research Center, Yorktown Heights, NY 10598, USA
{dengy,sarkar,kelmaghr,hvramasa,jbivens}@us.ibm.com

Abstract. Technical support agents working in the IT support services field resolve IT problems. They are often faced with the daunting task of identifying the correct solution document through a search system from large corpora of IT support documents. Based on the observation that system logs may contain critical information for identifying the root cause of IT problems, we explore the idea of automatic query expansion by using system logs as a bridge to link queries with the most relevant documents. Given the original query from a user such as a technical support agent, an intermediate query is first formed by adding key terms extracted from system logs using domain-specific rules. Based on topic models, further key terms are selected from corpora of IT support documents, which are combined with the intermediate query to form the final query. Our experimental results show that expanding queries using system logs together with topic models yields better performance in retrieving relevant IT support documents than using topic models only.

Keywords: Log-aided query expansion · Topic model · Retrieval · IT support services

1 Introduction

In the IT support services field, technical support agents and system administrators shoulder the responsibility of troubleshooting and assisting customers with resolving IT problems. The initial information provided to an agent by a customer facing IT problems is often incomplete and may not even be particularly useful in resolving the problem other than to inform the agent that some problem has occurred. Faced with the pressure of resolving customer-reported problems as quickly as possible, technical support agents use a variety of methods to improve the problem determination process. In this work, we consider two methods: (1) the use of system logs to help understand the state of the system on which a problem has been reported, and (2) the use of search systems to retrieve the correct solution from large corpora of IT support documents, where

© Springer International Publishing Switzerland 2016
Q.Z. Sheng et al. (Eds.): ICSOC 2016, LNCS 9936, pp. 730–744, 2016.
DOI: 10.1007/978-3-319-46295-0_52

insights gathered from system logs are used to enhance end user search queries to improve the quality of search results.

There are many popular, publicly available search frameworks such as ElasticSearch [9], Sphinx [26], Lucene [19], Solr [25], Xapian [29], and Indri [13]. Over time, users of search systems become adept at effective query formulation. However, in search systems dealing with specialized domains, users often need to combine search skills with domain-specific knowledge for effective query formulation. For example, IT support services is a specialized domain with huge corpora of both public and proprietary information. While domain-specific knowledge can be acquired over time, it represents a barrier that must be lowered for two reasons: (1) high attrition rates for support agents and (2) the pressure to resolve IT problems in the quickest possible manner.

Various forms of user context have long been used in the field of information retrieval for improving information search efficacy. For example, user location, search history, and implicit user behavior have been used for search type-ahead and improved search engine ranking and accuracy. However, in specialized domains, we believe there is an opportunity to go even further. In particular, we consider *log-aided query expansion* for the domain of IT support services, i.e., the use of relevant *system (or application) logs* as a bridge to link queries with the most relevant IT support documents. We further enhance the expanded intermediate query with key terms selected from corpora of IT support documents through the use of topic models [4,5]. We present early experimental evidence demonstrating the promise of the approach in lowering the barrier for effective query formulation and raising the precision of search systems for IT support. We view this work as a first step towards IT remediation systems that can automatically leverage search to diagnose and resolve IT problems.

The rest of the paper is organized as follows: Sect. 2 presents an example which motivates the need for enhancing the search process for IT support. Section 3 describes the approach designed for log-aided query expansion. Experimental evaluation is discussed in Sect. 4. Section 5 discusses related work and compares them with our approach. The paper concludes with a summary and future work in Sect. 6.

2 Motivating Example

2.1 Example System Log Files

System logs are used to record events that occur at various layers of a computing system: *firmware, hypervisor, operating system, middleware,* and *applications.* These error log files are extremely valuable tools for diagnosing and managing systems. We present two real sample logs from IBM POWER systems [28] deployed at client sites, representing information that is used by IBM technical support representatives to diagnose system failures. The customer specific data in the logs have been altered for privacy reasons.

The first system log we show is an excerpt from the *iqyylog* file that is generated from an IBM Hardware Management Console (HMC) [28]. Mid-range and large IBM POWER servers need a HMC to create and manage logical partitions, dynamically reallocate resources, invoke Capacity on Demand, and facilitate hardware control. High-end servers with Bulk Power Controllers (BPC) require at least one HMC acting as a Dynamic Host Configuration Protocol (DHCP) server. Typically, more than one HMC is recommended for enhanced availability. When errors occur at the hardware level, the Flexible Service Processor (FSP) and/or BPC asynchronously notify the HMC that a platform error log or event log is available. The FSP is a firmware component that provides diagnostics, initialization, configuration, run-time error detection and correction functions. The FSP connects the managed system to the HMC. The HMC then reads the error log data from the FSP and BPC. Significant HMC events, including platform logs and problem analysis results, are recorded in the HMC *iqyylog*. The latter is a binary file and requires a decoder to view it. This log file among others is either submitted to IBM's technical support through an automated system called *Call Home*, or manually uploaded by the customer to one of IBM's FTP servers for further analysis by support representatives. Figure 1 contains sample content from a decoded *iqyylog* file with various events captured from an IBM POWER 7 system. Each entry in the log file shows a recorded platform event log (PEL_EVENT) along with its timestamp. Some of these events show reference codes and other error details that are key for problem determination. The entry also shows information related to the system that generated the event in the following format: TTTTMMM/NNNNNNN, where TTTT is the machine type, MMM is the model number, and NNNNNNN is the serial number. The example shows that problem analysis was triggered at 10:26 (tagged with PA_START). The results of the problem analysis shows the error code: *A7001152*. The error reported is a generic error that implies that the platform firmware detected a timeout condition which caused a reset of the service processor (FSP). For this particular customer problem, the support agent further examined the FSP dumps and determined that no action was needed, since the FSP was busy and slow to respond to the hypervisor, which in turn caused the timeout and hence a reset.

Another sample log file from an IBM POWER/AIX server is the *snap* file. The AIX *snap* command is used to gather a large amount of system configuration data and compress it into a *snap* core file. The file contains information such as the version of AIX the system is running, what hardware it is running on, what error messages were recorded, what processes were running when the system crashed, what is the firmware level, etc. The information gathered is used to identify and resolve system problems. The *snap* file can also be automatically uploaded to IBM's support repository or manually uploaded by a customer. Figure 2 shows an example error log entry captured from a POWER server. The log shows SCSI disk errors reported from hdisk2. Additional analysis of the diagnostics reported can be used to confirm that hisk2 is failing and needs to be replaced.

The examples discussed above illustrate that system log files contain valuable information that is often used by system administrators and technical support professionals to understand the root cause of a problem, and to gather enough data to effectively query existing knowledge sources in search of resolutions.

The key contribution of this paper is the insight that automatic expansion of support agent queries by analyzing system/application logs and extracting important search terms from those logs can lead to significant improvement in precision and recall. The initial agent query typically represents the customer view of the problem and focuses on the *symptom*, e.g., "my machine wont boot." Search results returned using such queries are not usually effective for problem resolution since the queries do not represent the *root cause*. System logs can complement the agent query in an effective manner, since they contain better indicators of the root cause, e.g., "SAS controller firmware update failure."

We propose an Automated Query Expansion (AQE) system which can identify a set of log file terms to complement the query terms submitted by an agent. In the above example, the AQE would automatically identify terms associated with the controller firmware update issue. That would improve the chances for problem resolution, especially if the machine boots from a remote SAS drive over a storage area network (SAN). While support services agents can perform this task manually, it takes years of experience and training to do it well; thus the value proposition of a systems log-aided AQE system that can perform the task automatically regardless of agent skill.

```
 1  [*] = default formatting; [r] = raw (hex dump)
 2
 3  [*][r]   6005 02-07-16 10:28:04:07 [ +1.0] +FSPDump_PWAD
 4  [*][r]   0B46 02-07-16 10:28:02:35 [ +1.0]  PA_DOM_PRM      domain=9179-MHD/052348T; primary=70
 5  [*][r]   E302 02-07-16 10:28:01:42 [ +1.0]  XUPD            E302F817 921138A9            00
 6  [*][r]   6005 02-07-16 10:27:57:34 [ +1.0] +FSPDump_FSPM
 7  [*][r]   E346 02-07-16 10:26:38:43 [ +1.0]  PA_END
 8  [*][r]   0B14 02-07-16 10:26:38:41 [ +1.0]  PA_Results      A7001152  null PN 57
 9  [*][r]   0B11 02-07-16 10:26:38:38 [ +1.0]  SHProbOpen      Problem 57
10  [*][r]   E346 02-07-16 10:26:38:26 [ +1.0]  End_PA_Queue
11  [*][r]   6010 02-07-16 10:26:36:60 [ +1.0]  PEL_Event       B1829543 9179-MHD/052348T
12  [*][r]   6010 02-07-16 10:26:35:24 [ +1.0]  PEL_Event       B1812638 9179-MHD/052348T
13  [*][r]   6010 02-07-16 10:26:35:21 [ +1.0]  PEL_Event       B1819522 9179-MHD/052348T
14  [*][r]   6010 02-07-16 10:26:35:15 [ +1.0]  PEL_Event       B1812A01 9179-MHD/052348T
15  [*][r]   6010 02-07-16 10:26:34:60 [ +1.0]  PEL_Event       B1812A01 9179-MHD/052348T
16  [*][r]   6010 02-07-16 10:26:34:56 [ +1.0]  PEL_Event       B1812A01 9179-MHD/052348T
17  [*][r]   6010 02-07-16 10:26:34:52 [ +1.0]  PEL_Event       B1812A01 9179-MHD/052348T
18  [*][r]   6010 02-07-16 10:26:34:48 [ +1.0]  PEL_Event       B1812A01 9179-MHD/052348T
19  [*][r]   6010 02-07-16 10:26:34:44 [ +1.0]  PEL_Event       B1812A01 9179-MHD/052348T
20  [*][r]   6010 02-07-16 10:26:33:97 [ +1.0]  PEL_Event       B1812A01 9179-MHD/052348T
21  [*][r]   6010 02-07-16 10:26:33:93 [ +1.0]  PEL_Event       B7006978 9179-MHD/052348T
22  [*][r]   6010 02-07-16 10:26:33:90 [ +1.0]  PEL_Event       B1819537 9179-MHD/052348T
23  [*][r]   6010 02-07-16 10:26:33:86 [ +1.0]  PEL_Event       B1812A01 9179-MHD/052348T
24  [*][r]   6010 02-07-16 10:26:33:80 [ +1.0]  PEL_Event       A7001152 9179-MHD/052348T
25  [*][r]   6010 02-07-16 10:26:33:77 [ +1.0]  PEL_Event       B7006979 9179-MHD/052348T
26  [*][r]   6010 02-07-16 10:26:33:25 [ +1.0]  PEL_Event       A7001151 9179-MHD/052348T
27  [*][r]   E346 02-07-16 10:26:33:24 [ +1.0]  PA_START
```

Fig. 1. A sample *iqyylog* events log

```
 1  LABEL:       SC_DISK_ERR4
 2  IDENTIFIER: DCB47997
 3
 4  Date/Time:        Wed Jan  10 09:57:34 2016
 5  Sequence Number: 2593
 6  Machine Id:       11B27B74411
 7  Node Id:          W4TSSLOG
 8  Class:            H
 9  Type:             TEMP
10  WPAR:             Global
11  Resource Name:    hdisk0
12  Resource Class:   disk
13  Resource Type:    vdisk
14  Location:         U9117.MMA.0626C64-V3-C2-T1-L8100000000000000
15
16
17  Description
18  DISK OPERATION ERROR
19
20  Probable Causes
21  MEDIA
22  DASD DEVICE
23
24  User Causes
25  MEDIA DEFECTIVE
26
27      Recommended Actions
28      FOR REMOVABLE MEDIA, CHANGE MEDIA AND RETRY
29      PERFORM PROBLEM DETERMINATION PROCEDURES
30
```

Fig. 2. A sample system error log file

2.2 Example System Log-Aided Query

We present a real-world example that illustrates the value added by log-aided query expansion. We consider a typical query used by support agents as part of their standard problem determination procedure. Error codes such as System Reference Codes (SRC) are often used to construct queries while troubleshooting hardware problems. An SRC code is a sequence of eight characters that identifies the name of the system component that detects the error and the underlying condition. The first 4 characters indicate the error type, while the last 4 characters provide additional information such as the underlying error condition.

Figure 3 shows search results returned when an IT support agent chose the SRC code *"10009028"* as the query term. What the agent did not know at the time of issuing the query was that this error code was being reported by a POWER7 system. The results obtained show documents that pertain to various versions of IBM POWER systems, with the relevant result appearing third from the top. Figure 4 shows the results from an expanded query formed based on the system's log data. The exact platform version (namely, POWER7) is extracted from the log data and the following expanded query is formed: *"10009028 POWER7"*. The top search result in this case is the correct document which describes how to resolve the error. The relevant document appearing ranked first versus third has the potential to cut down problem resolution time from hours to minutes, which in turn may significantly impact customer satisfaction.

Number	Document Title	Snippet	Confidence
1	10009028 (POWER6)	...-01.ibm.com/support/knowledgecenter/POWER6/area7/**10009028**.htm http://www-01.ibm.com/support/knowledgecenter/POWER6/area7/**10009028**.htm knowledgecenter POWER6 **10009028 10009028 10009028 10009028** Explanation SPCN Licensed Internal Code is not...	100%
2	10009028 (POWER8)	...-01.ibm.com/support/knowledgecenter/POWER8/p8eai/**10009028**.htm http://www-01.ibm.com/support/knowledgecenter/POWER8/p8eai/**10009028**.htm knowledgecenter **POWER8 10009028 10009028 10009028**...	97%
3	10009028 (POWER7)	...-01.ibm.com/support/knowledgecenter/POWER7/p7eail/**10009028**.htm http://www-01.ibm.com/support/knowledgecenter/POWER7/p7eail/**10009028**.htm knowledgecenter POWER7 **10009028 10009028** Subscribe to this information IBM PowerLinux information **10009028**...	96%
4	10009028 (POWER5 POWER6)	...-01.ibm.com/support/knowledgecenter/POWER5/area7/**10009028**.htm http://www-01.ibm.com/support/knowledgecenter/POWER5/area7/**10009028**.htm knowledgecenter POWER5 POWER6 **10009028 10009028 10009028 10009028** Explanation SPCN Licensed Internal Code is not...	95%
6	(1000) Reference codes (POWER5 POWER6)	...100091DD 10009023 100091DE 10009024 10009025 10007640 10007641 **10009028** 10009029 1000902D 10009031 10009032 10009033 10009034 10009035...10009022 10009023 10009023 10009024 10009024 10009025 10009025 **10009028 10009028** 10009029 10009029 1000902D 1000902D 10009031 10009031 10009032...	50%

Fig. 3. Search results from the support agent's original query

Number	Document Title	Snippet	Confidence
1	10009028 (POWER7)	http://www-01.ibm.com/support/knowledgecenter/**POWER7**/p7eai/**10009028**.htm knowledgecenter **POWER7 10009028 10009028** Subscribe to this information **POWER7** information **10009028** Explanation SPCN Licensed **Internal Code** is not valid. Response The Licensed **Internal Code** in the primary node is not valid. The code···	100%
2	(1000) Reference Codes (POWER7)	http://www-01.ibm.com/support/knowledgecenter/**POWER7**/p7eai/1000_info.htm knowledgecenter **POWER7** 10003125 10007602 10009109 10007603 10001500 10001501 10001502...100091DD 10009023 100091DE 10009024 10009025 10007640 10007641 **10009028** 10009029 1000902D 10009031 10009032 10009033 10009034 10009035...1000) Reference codes Subscribe to this information **POWER7** Information (1000) Reference codes 100000A0 100000AA 100000AC...	97%
3	10009028 (POWER6)	...-01.ibm.com/support/knowledgecenter/POWER6/area7/**10009028**.htm http://www-01.ibm.com/support/knowledgecenter/POWER6/area7/**10009028**.htm knowledgecenter POWER6 **10009028 10009028 10009028 10009028** Explanation SPCN Licensed Internal Code is not...	67%
4	10009028 (POWER8)	...-01.ibm.com/support/knowledgecenter/POWER8/p8eai/**10009028**.htm http://www-01.ibm.com/support/knowledgecenter/POWER8/p8eai/**10009028**.htm knowledgecenter **POWER8 10009028 10009028 10009028**...	66%

Fig. 4. Improved search results from the log-aided expanded query

3 Log Aided Search

Our approach is based on the observation that effective handling of an IT problem requires understanding the symptoms and causes of the problem and then identifying the relevant solution(s). In the IT support services context, information about symptom(s), cause(s) and solution(s) are usually obtained from diverse sources. Search queries submitted by end users experiencing IT problems (or by technical support agents on behalf of such users) often focus on the symptoms. System logs typically contain messages that are useful in understanding the underlying causes or the broader context of problems. Relevant solutions may be documented or described in corpora of knowledge sources.

The problem we are addressing is: how to guide the search engine in retrieving the most relevant IT support documents containing the solution(s) to the problem (as identified by its symptoms), taking into account the underlying cause(s) or broader context of the problem. Our solution consists of two functionally independent parts: (1) analysis of system logs and (2) topic modeling on the corpora of IT support documents. Implementation of the solution combines the two parts to help formulate more effective queries to the search system. Parsers are used to extract key information from log files, and topic modeling is used to discover hidden "themes" in the corpus. We expect each theme (topic) to be about three aspects of a single type of error, namely: symptom, cause and solution. After clustering corpus terms together into one topic, we expect to find terms related to solutions in the documents, using the symptom terms from the query and the causal terms from the system logs.

The system consists of two different modules, one offline and the other online. Two steps are performed in the offline module. First, documentation of the different types of logs for a domain of interest are analyzed, and parsers are built for each type of log files. The parsers take log files in raw text form as input and output critical information about the error messages in the log. This information can be about root causes, component names, or even possible solutions. Second, a topic model is built on the corpus. Our corpus consists of all the documents indexed in the search system. These documents represent different knowledge sources and cover most of the problems encountered by customers. Therefore, we expect to find words relevant to solutions in the topic model.

The online module is executed when a new query is submitted. It consists of three steps. When an agent submits a query, a case number is also provided to the system. The first step consists of fetching the log files for the case using the case number, and parsing the files to extract key information from each one. The log files may contain information about system profiles and events. We have implemented parsers to extract information from these log files. The extracted information is used to expand the original query, resulting in an intermediate query. The second step is to select terms from the corpus using a topic model-based generative process, forming an expanded query. In the third step, the terms in the expanded query are re-weighted to form the final query.

The five steps (two offline and three online steps) are outlined in an algorithm as follows. In this section, we use the domain of mid-range storage systems[1] to illustrate our solution.

Algorithm 1. System Log Aided AQE Algorithm

Parameter: Number of terms selected from topic model N, number of topics in topic model K, weight for expanded terms from system logs λ
Offline Steps:

- Log Analytics: select set of terms $\{w_1, w_2, \ldots, w_L\}$ from system logs
- Topic Modeling: get probability $p(w|t_i)$ for term w, where t_i is the ith topic

Online Steps:

- Form the intermediate query: expand the original query with terms from the logs
- Corpus term expansion: using the probability of a term given the intermediate query to select the terms from the corpus
- Term weighting and generating the final query

Output: Final query

The process is also illustrated in Fig. 5.

3.1 Offline Step 1: Log Analytics

In order to effectively analyze system logs, we have leveraged the expertise of our agents and incorporated their knowledge in the form of rules for extracting information from log files. Key pieces of information extracted include error messages, machine types, and names of components in abnormal states.

The agents documented 17 unique representative error types that appear in mid-range storage logs. These error types cover failures in five different components: *Controller, Enclosure, Drive, Logical Drive,* and *Arrays.* These components consist of many subcomponents which can fail. We have implemented a parser and analyzer to find evidence related to different types of subcomponent failures that appear in the log files. The common errors that the parser can identify in the log files include, but are not limited to, the following: *Controller Failure, Controller Reboot, Path Redundancy Loss, Impending Drive Failure, Cache Disabled, Insufficient Cache Backup Capacity, Bypassed Drive, Batteries Near Expiration, Batteries Not Available, ESM Failure, Power Fan Failure,* and *Individual Drive Degraded Path.*

The above error types can be very informative with regard to root cause analysis of a failure whose symptoms are observed by a customer. If this information can be incorporated into a query, the new (expanded) query will be more

---

[1] A mid-range storage system's performance and cost lies between expensive, high-end enterprise-class and cheap, low-performance storage systems.

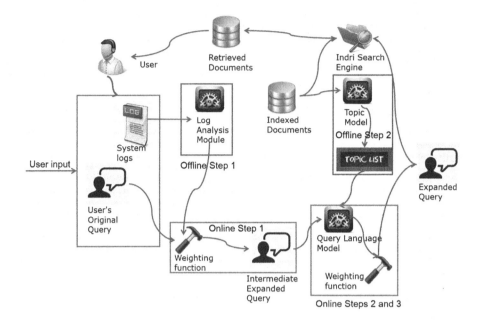

Fig. 5. Solution overview

powerful than the original in its ability to retrieve the most relevant documents which contain the solution to the problem that the customer is experiencing. For example, as we have shown in Sect. 2.2, adding the term "POWER7" from the log to the query "10009028" helps improve the search results.

3.2 Offline Step 2: Topic Modeling

In the first offline module, we incorporate the log terms which are mostly about errors or their root causes. In the second offline module, we further include select terms from the corpus of documents which describe solutions.

The goal of the second offline step is to help find information relevant to the case from the corpus to add to the query, so that the rank of relevant documents can be improved. As discussed above, topic modeling is expected to uncover solutions pertaining to specific types of errors given symptoms and root causes.

Specifically, we run the topic modeling algorithm Latent Dirichlet Allocation (LDA) [4] on all of the knowledge source documents in the corpus. The output is a set of topics, where each topic t is a probability distribution over all the terms in the vocabulary V. Using the topic model, we can get the probability $p(w|t)$, where $w \in V$.

3.3 Online Step 1: Intermediate Query

The online steps are performed each time a new query is processed. Inputs to this step include the text of the original query and system log files for the case.

The log files are fed to the log parser, the output of which identifies (log) terms to be added to the original query for forming an intermediate query. The terms identified from the log files are selected based on rules defined by experienced support agents. The intermediate query contains information from the original query as well as the log files. For example, for a case of mid-range storage systems, the key terms "path redundancy lost 1726" may be selected from the log files, where "1726" is the machine type and "path redundancy lost" is the error. The newly added terms from the logs are weighted, the procedure for which is described later in Sect. 3.5.

3.4 Online Step 2: Expanding Query with Corpus Terms

The goal of this step is to expand the intermediate query further by selecting terms from the corpus. Assume that the intermediate query is q. The approach is similar to that of query language models, i.e. we rank each of the corpus terms according to its probability of being generated by the intermediate query. Specifically, we use the following two-step generative process:

– Use the query q to generate a topic t
– Use the topic t to generate a word w

In this way, the probability of a word $w \in V$, given a specific query q can be computed as:

$$p(w|q) = \sum_i p(w|t_i)p(t_i|q)$$

where each t_i is a topic produced by running LDA on the corpus.

In this formula, the probability $p(w|t_i)$ can be computed directly from the output of LDA. Probability $p(t_i|q)$ is the topic mixture inferred by treating the query as a new short document, which can also be acquired directly by LDA inference using the corpus topic model. Therefore, all the probability terms in the right hand side are available from the topic model over the corpus. In this way, the words in vocabulary V can be ranked based on the above probability. Empirically, we choose to add only the top five words. For example, for the mid-range storage case mentioned in Sect. 3.3, the top terms "drive module array host" may be returned from the topic model.

3.5 Online Step 3: Term Weighting and Final Query

The procedure used to weight the terms is also very important. Since the terms from the original query are still the ones best characterizing the user's information need, they are each given a weight of 1. The terms added to form the intermediate query are from the system logs, which should also be directly and equally relevant to the information needed. Therefore, they are each assigned identical weights λ. The third part of the expanded query consists of terms from the documents, and they are ranked by the probability after the query is seen. Intuitively, they are not so directly relevant to the query, so we just use the ranking probability as the weight. Therefore, we compute the weight of the word w, μ_w as the following:

$$\mu_w = \begin{cases} 1 & \text{if } w \in q_o \\ \lambda & \text{if } w \text{ is from the log} \\ p(w|q) & \text{if } w \text{ is from the corpus} \end{cases}$$

Here q_o is the original query and q is the intermediate query.

4   Experiments

This section describes the verification of our approach using real world data. The data set used is a set of real query sessions by technical support agents using an IBM search system built on top of Indri [13]. A complete session consists of a piece of query text, a case number, a ranked list of returned documents, and the agent user's vote for the query. A vote, submitted by the user, is one of the returned documents that the user believes to be the most relevant to their case. These votes can be used as ground truth for the evaluation. The log files used to form the intermediate query are retrieved by the case number in the session from IBM's Enhanced Customer Data Repository (**ECuRep**[2]). Our first test data set consists of 18 such complete query sessions. The second test data set has 50 incomplete sessions where the log files are missing, but the query text, ranked list of results and votes are available. Note that these two data sets are completely separate from each other. We have used MALLET LDA package [20] in our implementation.

In the experiments, we measure the average rank of voted documents, and the percentage of the query sessions where the voted documents are ranked in the top five (GAIN@5) and the top ten (GAIN@10). For the first test set which has 18 complete sessions, we compare the above metrics using the original query, the expanded query with only the terms from the topic model, the expanded query with only log terms, and the final query expanded using both log terms and the terms from the topic model. For the second set which has 50 incomplete sessions, we only compare the performance of the original query with the expanded query using terms from the topic model.

In Table 1, we show the metrics of the first test set. The expanded queries, using either log terms or terms from the topic model or both, have better performance than the original queries for all three metrics. It also shows that using system logs in retrieving solution documents is critical in IT support services. In addition, it shows that expanding queries with both system logs and topic model can further boost the performance.

Table 2 shows the results for the second test set. The comparison here is between the original queries and the queries expanded with only terms from the

---

[2] http://www.ecurep.ibm.com.

Table 1. Retrieval performance on complete sessions

Metrics	Original query	AQE with topic model	AQE with system log	AQE with system log and topic model
Average rank	8.44	6.88	5.06	4.88
Gain@5	38.9 %	50.0 %	50.0 %	55.6 %
Gain@10	66.7 %	66.7 %	72.2 %	72.2 %

Table 2. Retrieval performance on incomplete sessions

Metrics	Original query	AQE with topic model
Average rank	8.26	6.36
Gain@5	48.0 %	56.0 %
Gain@10	72.0 %	82.0 %

topic model. In practice, the incomplete sessions represent situations where the log files are not sent by customers, or the log files are in an internal representation which is not easily parsable. As shown in the table, expanding queries using terms in the topic model has helped improve the performance consistently across all three metrics.

5 Related Work

Query expansion is the general process of reformulating a seed query to improve retrieval performance. A query is the primary statement of a user's information need. However, users don't always provide the most optimal queries due to limitations in their scope of knowledge, limited time for query formulation, intrinsic ambiguity of their information need, or the difference between the terms used by users and content providers. Therefore, an enhanced query can improve the performance of the retrieval system.

There have been many studies on the problem of automatic query expansion (AQE), which aims at expanding query terms automatically to better meet the user's information need. One of the most straightforward approaches is to perform linguistic analysis such as stemming [3,12,15], finding synonyms on thesauri such as WordNet [21] and applying other forms of semantic association [18,27]. However, such methods depend largely on the quality of the thesauri and can only utilize the semantic ties between the terms.

Other methods using corpus and query specific techniques utilize statistical features such as co-occurrence information, mutual information, or more complicated measurements of the corpus or query context [17,23,30]. A popular approach is the Relevance-based Model proposed by Lavrenko and Croft [17] along with its variants [6,10,16]. Lavrenko and Croft [17] present a method of estimating the probability of observing a word in the documents relevant to a query (relevance model) when no training data is available. The idea is to learn the parameters of a relevance model based on the fact that a query is a random sample from the model. The authors also investigate whether topics discovered in the corpus can be used for query expansion. The Relevance-based Model is followed by calculating a topic model based relevance model:

$$p(w|q) = \sum_i p(w|t_i)p(t_i|q)$$

Lavrenko and Croft show that $p(w|q)$ is a very good approximate measurement of the relevance of terms without training data. We borrow this idea in our work, with the key difference being that in our approach, an intermediate query is used in the above equation, which is an expansion of the original user query using terms from system logs. That expansion proves to be crucial for performance improvement in the IT support domain. Other approaches include utilizing information from various sources, such as tagging recommendations based on Wikipedia pages [22].

Another important category of methods is search log analysis, where the idea is to mine associations between different query sessions by a user. Different sessions can be associated chronologically, i.e. two adjacent queries will be associated, or semantically, i.e. two queries sharing terms or semantic overlap will be associated. After queries are associated, both the associated queries themselves [11,14,31] and the results retrieved based on the queries [1,2] can be used to enhance the original query. Previous work has also explored the use of clicked results of associated queries to extract search terms (e.g., [8,24]).

Though there has been extensive research on AQE, to the best of our knowledge, no previous work specifically targets the AQE problem in IT support services and utilizes system logs. A relatively close work is [7] on the use of LDA for web service clustering. However, there is no use of system logs as an important source of information for problem determination, which is a key focus of our work.

6 Conclusion

We have presented a novel systems log-aided method for the domain of IT support services for automatic query expansion, which can identify a set of terms from log files to complement the query terms submitted by an agent addressing a customer problem. Normally, this task is performed manually by support services agents, and they have to acquire years of experience and training to do it effectively. Our experimental results indicate that the systems log-aided method can improve retrieval performance significantly, and yield even better results when combined with topic modeling on the corpus.

In the future, we plan to explore techniques to perform key term selection from log files that are more flexible and domain independent. In addition, we plan to experiment with other topic modeling techniques and compare their performance with LDA.

References

1. Beeferman, D., Berger, A.: Agglomerative clustering of a search engine query log. In: Proceedings of the Sixth ACM SIGKDD International Conference on Knowledge Discovery and Data Mining, KDD 2000, pp. 407–416. ACM, New York, NY, USA (2000). http://doi.acm.org/10.1145/347090.347176
2. Billerbeck, B., Scholer, F., Williams, H.E., Zobel, J.: Query expansion using associated queries. In: Proceedings of the Twelfth International Conference on Information and Knowledge Management, CIKM 2003, pp. 2–9. ACM, New York, NY, USA (2003). http://doi.acm.org/10.1145/956863.956866
3. Bilotti, M.W., Katz, B., Lin, J.: What works better for question answering: stemming or morphological query expansion? In: Proceedings of the Information Retrieval for Question Answering (IR4QA) Workshop at SIGIR 2004 (2004)
4. Blei, D., Ng, A., Jordan, M.: Latent dirichlet allocation. J. Mach. Learn. Res. **3**, 993–1022 (2003). http://dl.acm.org/citation.cfm?id=944919.944937
5. Blei, D.M.: Probabilistic topic models. Commun. ACM **55**(4), 77–84 (2012). http://doi.acm.org/10.1145/2133806.2133826
6. Cartright, M.A., Allan, J., Lavrenko, V., McGregor, A.: Fast query expansion using approximations of relevance models. In: Proceedings of the 19th ACM International Conference on Information and Knowledge Management, CIKM 2010, pp. 1573–1576. ACM, New York, NY, USA (2010). http://doi.acm.org/10.1145/1871437.1871675
7. Chen, L., Wang, Y., Yu, Q., Zheng, Z., Wu, J.: WT-LDA: user tagging augmented LDA for web service clustering. In: Basu, S., Pautasso, C., Zhang, L., Fu, X. (eds.) ICSOC 2013. LNCS, vol. 8274, pp. 162–176. Springer, Heidelberg (2013)
8. Cui, H., Wen, J.R., Nie, J.Y., Ma, W.Y.: Query expansion by mining user logs. IEEE Trans. Knowl. Data Eng. **15**(4), 829–839 (2003). http://dx.doi.org/10.1109/TKDE.2003.1209002
9. ElasticSearch: https://www.elastic.co
10. Halpin, H., Lavrenko, V., St, C.: Relevance feedback between hypertext search and semantic search. In: Proceedings of the Semantic Search Workshop at the World Wide Web Conference (2009)
11. Huang, C.K., Chien, L.F., Oyang, Y.J.: Relevant term suggestion in interactive web search based on contextual information in query session logs. J. Am. Soc. Inf. Sci. Technol. **54**(7), 638–649 (2003). http://dx.doi.org/10.1002/asi.10256
12. Hull, D.A.: Stemming algorithms: a case study for detailed evaluation. J. Am. Soc. Inf. Sci. **47**(1), 70–84 (1996). http://dx.doi.org/10.1002/(SICI)1097--4571(199601)47:1⟨70:AID-ASI7⟩3.3.CO;2-Q
13. Indri: http://www.lemurproject.org/
14. Jones, R., Rey, B., Madani, O., Greiner, W.: Generating query substitutions. In: Proceedings of the 15th International Conference on World Wide Web, WWW 2006, pp. 387–396. ACM, New York, NY, USA (2006). http://doi.acm.org/10.1145/1135777.1135835
15. Krovetz, R.: Viewing morphology as an inference process. In: Proceedings of the 16th Annual International ACM SIGIR Conference on Research and Development in Information Retrieval, SIGIR 1993, pp. 191–202. ACM, New York, NY, USA (1993). http://doi.acm.org/10.1145/160688.160718
16. Lavrenko, V., Choquette, M., Croft, W.B.: Cross-lingual relevance models. In: Proceedings of the 25th Annual International ACM SIGIR Conference on Research and Development in Information Retrieval, SIGIR 2002, pp. 175–182. ACM, New York, NY, USA (2002). http://doi.acm.org/10.1145/564376.564408

17. Lavrenko, V., Croft, W.B.: Relevance based language models. In: Proceedings of the 24th Annual International ACM SIGIR Conference on Research and Development in Information Retrieval, SIGIR 2001, pp. 120–127. ACM, New York, NY, USA (2001). http://doi.acm.org/10.1145/383952.383972

18. Liu, Y., Li, C., Zhang, P., Xiong, Z.: A query expansion algorithm based on phrases semantic similarity. In: 2008 International Symposiums on Information Processing (ISIP), pp. 31–35, May 2008

19. Lucene: https://lucene.apache.org/

20. McCallum, A.K.: Mallet: a machine learning for language toolkit (2002). http://mallet.cs.umass.edu

21. Navigli, R., Velardi, P.: An analysis of ontology-based query expansion strategies. In: Workshop on Adaptive Text Extraction and Mining, Cavtat Dubrovnik, Croatia, 23 September 2003

22. Oliveira, V., Gomes, G., Belém, F., Brandão, W., Almeida, J., Ziviani, N., Gonçalves, M.: Automatic query expansion based on tag recommendation. In: Proceedings of the 21st ACM International Conference on Information and Knowledge Management, CIKM 2012, pp. 1985–1989. ACM, New York, NY, USA (2012). http://doi.acm.org/10.1145/2396761.2398557

23. Park, L.A.F.: Query expansion using a collection dependent probabilistic latent semantic thesaurus. In: Zhou, Z.-H., Li, H., Yang, Q. (eds.) PAKDD 2007. LNCS (LNAI), vol. 4426, pp. 224–235. Springer, Heidelberg (2007)

24. Riezler, S., Vasserman, A., Tsochantaridis, I., Mittal, V., Liu, Y.: Statistical machine translation for query expansion in answer retrieval. In: Proceedings of the 45th Annual Meeting of the Association for Computational Linguistics (ACL2007). Prague, Czech Republic (2007). http://www.stefanriezler.com/PAPERS/ACL07.pdf

25. Solr: http://lucene.apache.org/solr/

26. Sphinx: http://sphinxsearch.com/

27. Symonds, M., Zuccon, G., Koopman, B., Bruza, P., Sitbon, L.: Term associations in query expansion: a structural linguistic perspective. In: Proceedings of the 22nd ACM International Conference on Information and Knowledge Management, CIKM 2013, pp. 1189–1192. ACM, New York, NY, USA (2013). http://doi.acm.org/10.1145/2505515.2507852

28. Systems, I.P.: www.ibm.com/systems/power/

29. Xapian: http://xapian.org/

30. Xu, J., Croft, W.B.: Query expansion using local and global document analysis. In: Proceedings of the 19th Annual International ACM SIGIR Conference on Research and Development in Information Retrieval, SIGIR 1996, pp. 4–11. ACM, New York, NY, USA (1996). http://doi.acm.org/10.1145/243199.243202

31. Yin, Z., Shokouhi, M., Craswell, N.: Query expansion using external evidence. In: Boughanem, M., Berrut, C., Mothe, J., Soule-Dupuy, C. (eds.) ECIR 2009. LNCS, vol. 5478, pp. 362–374. Springer, Heidelberg (2009)

Top-Down Pricing of IT Services Deals with Recommendation for Missing Values of Historical and Market Data

Aly Megahed[1]([⊠]), Kugamoorthy Gajananan[2], Shubhi Asthana[1], Valeria Becker[1], Mark Smith[3], and Taiga Nakamura[1]

[1] IBM Research - Almaden, San Jose, CA, USA
{aly.megahed,sasthan,beckerv,taiga}@us.ibm.com
[2] IBM Research – Tokyo, Tokyo, Japan
gajan@jp.ibm.com
[3] IBM Global Technology Services, North Harbour, Portsmouth, Hampshire, UK
marksmith@uk.ibm.com

Abstract. In order for an Information Technology (IT) service provider to respond to a client's request for proposals of a complex IT services deal, they need to prepare a solution and enter a competitive bidding process. A critical factor in this solution is the pricing of various services in the deal. The traditional way of pricing such deals has been the so-called bottom-up approach, in which all services are priced from the lowest level up to the highest one. A previously proposed more efficient approach and its enhancement aimed at automating the pricing by data mining historical and market deals. However, when mining such deals, some of the services of the deal to be priced might not exist in them. In this paper, we propose a method that deals with this issue of incomplete data via modeling the problem as a machine learning recommender system. We embed our system in the previously developed method and statistically show that doing so could yield significantly more accurate results. In addition, using our method provides a complete set of historical data that can be used to provide various analytics and insights to the business.

Keywords: Service analytics · IT service deals · Predictive analytics · Pricing services · Estimating prices · Data mining · Machine learning · Recommender systems

1 Introduction

Clients requiring complex Information Technology (IT) services typically submit a request for proposals that can fulfil their demands. Service providers have to respond with a proposed solution and enter a competitive bidding process trying to win the contract [1]. One of the critical factors in this process is the pricing of various services included in the proposal, though it is not the only factor for winning the deals [1, 2].

© Springer International Publishing Switzerland 2016
Q.Z. Sheng et al. (Eds.): ICSOC 2016, LNCS 9936, pp. 745–760, 2016.
DOI: 10.1007/978-3-319-46295-0_53

Traditionally, solutioners responsible for preparing the solution proposal followed the "bottom-up" pricing approach. In this approach, they obtain a quote by determining costs and prices of each detailed service component included in the solution and then summing them up [3, 4], given the hierarchical nature of IT services [6]. This is often a time consuming and resource-intensive task; because, in a complex service proposal, there could be thousands of items at the lowest level to be priced. In our previous work [3, 4], we proposed a "top-down" pricing method for IT services and demonstrated how this approach could lead to efficient pricing with adequate accuracy. The method makes use of historical data of prior deals as well as market data to determine the price using a minimal input from the user. It works via mining those data at the highest level [3] or the second hierarchical level [4]. The algorithm works in two main steps; peer selection and cost calculation, where after selecting similar peer historical and market deals, it mines these deals to estimate the costs and later the prices.

Previous results showed that this approach enables efficient pricing and that using the second hierarchical level (referred to as level two below) can improve estimation accuracy. However, one challenge was that not all level two subservices in the deal being priced are always included in the chosen peer deals to be mined. Since every deal can have different IT services demands, it can happen that some of the demanded services were not included in the chosen peer deals. The difference could become more significant as they are computed at granular service levels. In our previous work [4], we described a simple way to treat this problem; that is we assumed that a missing service at level two in a peer deal has a cost equal to the average of the costs of that same service in all the chosen peer deals that have that service.

In this work, we do a more advanced way of addressing this problem. That is, we formulate it as a recommendation problem [5] to complement the missing data, then proceed with the rest of our pricing algorithm. Figure 1 gives the overview of all mentioned approaches. We statistically show that our new approach is significantly more accurate to use than our two previous approaches. In addition, doing the recommendation can be used in several other applications rather than deal pricing. One important such applications is performing all kinds of analytics and trend analysis on historical and market data. Obtaining these analytical insights could help the business revise and reassess their competitiveness.

Therefore, the contributions of this paper are three-folds. First, we provide a novel formulation of the problem of missing services data in historical and market deals as a machine learning recommender system. Second, we show how embedding the results of this system in our prior pricing algorithm significantly enhances our pricing accuracy, statistically speaking. Thirdly, our approach can be directly used to enable all kinds of data analytics on the historical deal data; an insight of high business value.

The rest of this paper is organized as follows: in Sect. 2, we provide a review of the literature in the area of our problem. In Sect. 3, we present our new approach and show how it can be embedded in the pricing algorithm. We then show our numerical results in Sect. 4 and end the paper with the conclusions and ideas for future work in Sect. 5.

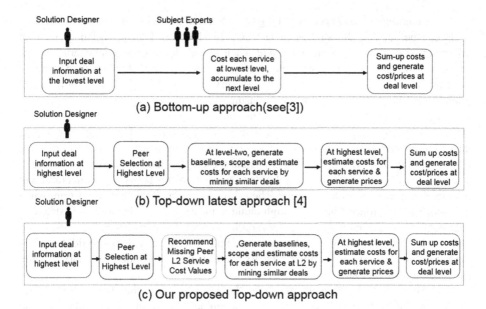

Fig. 1. Overview of the bottom-up approach for pricing IT service deals, top-down latest approach in [4], and our proposed one

2   Related Work

References [1, 2, 7–9] provide an overview of the area of IT services deals and how competitive bidding process works. For pricing these deals, we refer the reader to our previous works in [3, 4]. This paper is an extension to the latter two papers. In [3], we proposed a method for top-down pricing of IT service deals, in which high level data for the included services in these deals are used. A peer selection algorithm along with a calculation logic was presented. Numerical results showed the validity of the hypothesis in the paper that mining historical data can lead to more accurate pricing than the business-traditionally used approach of using market benchmark data. The algorithm was enhanced in [4], where the data mining was done at level two of the services although the input is still at level one and thus the concept of top down pricing is preserved. Results showed that doing the pricing at such lower level can yield more accurate results. Note that there is no justification of pricing at a lower level, or doing it at the nth level; since there is typically no known information at such lower levels when the deal is priced in the beginning of the reply to the request for proposal process. In addition, there are typically three, or at most four, levels of IT services in this type of business [3]. In this work, we extend the method in these latter two references and show the benefit of using a recommender system for augmenting missing data values.

Another related work in the literature is the work of Akkiraju et al. [9]. They presented a method for assessing the competitiveness of deals after being priced. That is, the deals need to be priced first in order for their method to work, rather than pricing the deals with minimal user input as the works in [3, 4] as well as the current one.

More literature about services pricing though not in the field of complex IT services deals can be seen in the studies in [10–20]. In [10], Li et al. provided a study of different pricing models for cloud storage. Their models focus on special characteristics of the cloud, e.g., storage types and configurations. Li et al. [11] studied queuing systems-based pricing models for other IT services. Ibrahim et al. [12] proposed a pricing framework for the pay-as-you-consume cloud computing service.

Basu et al. [13] developed optimal pricing strategies for cloud providers. Their method incorporates the utility of cloud users as a function of a set of parameters directly proportional to the utility and another set of parameters that have a negative effect on utility. In [14], Laatikainen and Ojala presented pricing models for software as a service (SaaS), in which they highlighted the relationship between architectural and pricing characteristics for this service. They showed that such relationship is tight when the value of firm proposition is at a high cloud maturity levels. Tawalbeh [15] stated an empirical study of a pricing method for mobile service providers driven by a cost based model. One of their main conclusions was that service providers should focus on market oriented pricing when their objectives are related to profitability, market share, and sales maximization.

For the sake of conciseness, we refer the reader to the other works for general services pricing [16–20]. In general, all these studies do not put in consideration the characteristics of IT services in complex deals as do our work and the prior two studies [3, 4] to it. Additionally, a literature survey for this class of these distantly related studies can be found in [21]. In the next section, we present our methodology in detail.

3   Methodology

In this section, we first present our notation in Sect. 3.1 followed by the formulation of our problem as a recommender system followed by the recommender algorithm that we used/applied to our real-world data in Sect. 3.2. We then show in Sect. 3.3 how we embed the results we can obtain from this modeling approach into our pricing algorithm.

3.1   Notation

We identify two categories of services that are included in any IT service deal in our context: regular services (referred to as services below) and common services. The regular services have baselines/units and their costs are independent of other services in a deal. Common services do not have baselines/units however their costs are dependent on different regular services included in the deal. Examples of regular services are databases and end user, and account management is a common service, for which the cost dependent on all regular services, which need some account management, in the deal.

We define any deal $d \in D$ by the tuple sets *(Meta Information, Services, Common Services), where D* is the set of deals (either historical or market benchmark), and Meta Information is the set of the meta-data of the deal, namely: *Meta Information = {Deal*

Outcome, Contract Year, Geography, Industry}. Deal Outcome is either won or lost (client did not pursue or provider withdraw from biding). *Contract year* is the calendar year at which delivery of the services will begin. *Geography* and *industry* refer to geographical location and industry of the client respectively.

We define the set of regular services as: *Services = {Service$_1$, ..., Service$_i$, ...,* *Service$_M$}*, where *M* is the cardinality of the set *Services*. Similarly, we specify the set of common services as: *Common Services = {Common Service$_1$, ..., Common Ser-* *vice$_j$, ..., Service$_N$}*, where *N* is the cardinality of the set *Common Services*.

Let us define (a) any regular service as *Service$_i$* ∈ *Services*, where $i = \{1, ..., M\}$, by the tuple *(Baseline, Cost, Price)*, and (b) any common service as *Common* *Serivce$_j$* ∈ *Common Services*, where $j = \{1, ..., N\}$, by the tuple *(Percentage of Total Cost, Cost, Price)*.

We further decompose each regular service *Service$_i$*, into a set of level two services: *L2Services = {L2Service$_1$, ..., L2Service$_a$, ..., L2Service$_P$}* where $a = \{1,..., P\}$, and *P* is the cardinality of the set *L2Services*. Similar to level one service *Service$_i$*, we define any *L2Service$_a$* with the tuple *(L2Baseline, L2Cost, L2Price)* where cardinality *P* may vary for different level one services.

Similarly, we break down each common service *Common Service$_j$* into a set of level two common services *L2 Common Services = {L2Common Service$_1$, ..., L2Common* *Service$_b$, ..., L2Service$_Q$}* where $b = \{1, ..., Q\}$, and *Q* is the cardinality of the set *L2Common Services*. Similar to level one service *Common Service$_j$*, we define any *L2Common Service$_b$* with the tuple *(L2Percentage of Total Cost, L2Cost, L2Price)* where cardinality *Q* may vary for different level-one common services.

Finally, we define any scenario *S* to be a new deal to be priced, by the tuple sets *{Meta Information, Service$_s$, Common Service$_s$}*. The following are the inputs for our approach: the elements of the set *Meta Information$_s$*, the values of *Baselines* for each *service$_k$* ∈ *Services$_s$* and the scope values for each *Common Service$_l$* ∈ *Common Services$_s$*. The output of our approach are: the estimated *Cost* and *Price* for each element of the sets *Services$_s$* and *Common Services$_s$*, and thus the total cost and price of *Scenario$_s$*. In the following section, we briefly describe the details of our approach.

3.2   Formulating Our Problem as a Recommendation System

In a typical recommendation system, there are "users" and "items". The "ratings" of some user-item pairs are known while the rest are unknown [22]. An example of this is the movie recommendation. In that problem, there are some users who have seen some movies and rated them, but not all users have seen all movies. The movies' provider would like to predict the rating of users for the movies that haven't seen so that he can recommend to them those movies that they would have rated highly had they seen them. Another example is in online retailers, where the "users" are buyers and the "items" are the products that they can purchase.

There are generally two main classes of recommender systems; content-based recommendations and collaborative recommendations [5]. In the former one, the user will be recommended items that are similar to the ones that he/she preferred in the past.

In the latter one, the user will be recommended items that were preferred in the past by people with similar tastes to him/her.

Now, we look into our problem. Considering the historical and market deals as users and the services at any level as items/movies, one can see the mapping between the two problems. Figure 2 shows this analogy.

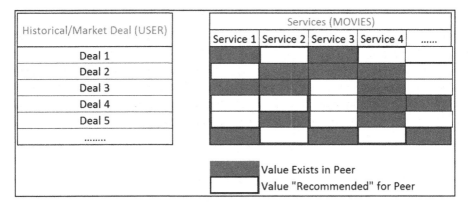

Fig. 2. Formulation of our problem as a recommender system

We note that the content-based recommendation is the one that better suits our application. This is because, in our pricing algorithm, we select peers at the highest level first and then perform cost mining for the preselected peers. Thus, the recommendation of missing data will be performed on the already filtered set of similar deals to our deal that we are trying to price. Thus, the collaborative recommendation is not applicable since we are already using a subset of "similar" deals. This observation was confirmed by a set of preliminary experiments that we did. Basically, we did a standard machine learning experiment, where we divided our data set into training and testing sets. Then, we trained several recommender systems on the training data set and applied them to the testing one. We found that the context based ones (also known as "item recommendation") give more accurate results on both sets. That is our method identified similar deals better than collaborative filtering; as it uses our expertise knowledge of problem structure. Thus, we decided to embed it in our approach.

We now provide an overview of the context-based recommender that we use. The basic idea is that we compute a similarity s between every item i that user u has no preference for yet and for every item j that he/she has a preference for. Then, u's preference for j, weighted by s is added to a running average. Lastly, the top items ranked by weighted average is returned. Note that, in our problem, that last step is not relevant; since we do not *recommend* the some services among the missing ones for each deal, but we are rather interested in only coming up with a score for item i (which would be that of j weighted by s. For a more detailed explanation of context-based recommendation, we refer the reader to [23]. In the next subsection, we show how/where we exactly embed this system in our pricing approach.

3.3   Embedding the Recommender System in Our Pricing Algorithm

Our previous studies [3, 4] extensively describe our top down pricing approach. In this paper, we provide a summary of the approach using similar definitions used in our previous work and in the above Subsect. 3.1.

Our approach contains the following steps: selecting peer deals, calculating scope and baselines for services at level two, recommending missing service cost values in peers at level two, and estimating costs/prices at level two and aggregating them to compute costs/prices at level one. In the following sub sections, we briefly describe each step.

Selecting Peer Deals. For each regular and common service of a scenario, our approach selects a set of historical and market benchmark deals as peers to draw the unit cost values of the service from them. Our approach compares the *Meta Information_s (Deal Outcome, Contract Year, Geography, and Industry)* of the scenario to that of all historical and market benchmark deals to select the matching ones. The reason behind the choice of suitable Meta Information are explained in detail in our previous work [3].

Once deals are selected based on the Meta information match, our approach sorts the deals based on two different criterias separately defined for regular and common services.

For each regular service $\forall$Service $k \in Services_s$, our approach adopts a criteria based on *baselines proximity*. We denote *Baseline Proximity$_{dsk}$* be the baseline proximity between deal $d \in D$ and scenario S for *Service $k \in Services_s$* and define it as:

$$Baseline\ Proximity_{dsk} = |Baseline\ for\ Service_i\ of\ deal\ d - Baseline\ for\ Service\ k\ of\ scenario\ S|$$

For each common service $\forall Common$ Service$l \in Common\ Services_s$, our approach sorts the selected deals based on a different proximity which is denoted as *Common Service Proximity$_{dsl}$* (the proximity between deal $d \in D$ and scenario S for *Common Service $l \in Common\ Services$*) and defined as follows:

$$Common\ Service\ Proximity_{dsl} = |Sum\ of\ Costs\ of\ regular\ services\ for\ deal\ d - Sum\ of\ costs\ of\ regular\ services\ for\ our\ scenario\ S|$$

We refer the readers to [3] for detailed explanation of the proximity criterias defined above.

Calculating Scope and Baselines for Services at Level Two. Note that our approach requires scope and baseline values for services at level one. Hence the approach estimates scope and baselines values for services at level two. Each $\forall$Service $k \in Services_s$ has many *L2Service$_{ka} \in L2Services_s$*. To decide which of them are in-scope, our approach rely on a set of predefined business rules. To calculate the baselines for *L2Service$_{ka} \in L2Services_s$*, the method uses the peer deal selected for the corresponding level one Service $k \in Services_s$ from market benchmark data. We denote

$p_m \in D$ as the market peer deal for a Service $k \in Services_s$ of a scenario S, $Baseline_{pma}$ as the baseline of the corresponding L2Serviceka of peer p_m, and $Baseline_{pmi}$ as the corresponding level one Servicei of peer p_m. Then the baselines for $L2Service_{ka} \in L2Services_s$ can be defined as:

$$L2Baseline_{ka} = \frac{L2BaseLine_{pma} * Baseline_k}{Baseline_{pmi}} \tag{1}$$

Recommending Missing Service Cost. We report on how our approach finds the recommended service cost values for selected peers for services of a scenario. For each service, Service $k \in Services_s$ of a scenario S, let us assume that there are selected peer deals $p_h \in D$ where $h = \{1, ..., H\}$, and H is the number of selected peers of that particular Service $k \in Services_s$. For each $L2Service_{ha} \in L2Services_h$, of the corresponding service from each peer, let us denote the cost as $L2Cost_{ha}$ which may be missing for some peers. For the peers that do not have the $L2Cost_{ha}$, our approach uses a recommender algorithm to estimate cost values from the pool of selected peers $p_h \in D$. Note that these selected peers of particular Service $k \in Services_s$ are similar to each other with respect to (a) their Meta information, and (b) baseline proximity for regular services. Note also that we implicitly assume, either here or in our overall methodology, that historical data is available. This is a quite realistic assumption practically speaking in this domain area.

Estimating Costs/Prices. We describe how our approach estimates the costs for each regular and common service for both the historical data and market benchmark views.

Cost Calculation for Regular Services of a Scenario. For each $L2Service_{ka}$ of Service $k \in Services_s$, our approach retrieves the unit costs of that level two service in each of its sorted peer deals and then compute the nth Percentile of these peer unit costs. For $L2Service_{ka}$, we denote the resulting unit cost as $L2Unit - Cost_{ka}$ and its cost is computed as follows:

$$L2Cost_{ka} = L2Unit{-}Cost_{ka} * L2Baseline_{ka} \tag{2}$$

Finally, our approach computes the cost of the Service $k \in Services_s$, as follows:

$$Cost_{ka} = \sum\nolimits_{a \in L2Services_k} L2Cost_{ka} \tag{3}$$

Cost Calculation for Common Services of a Scenario. For each $L2Common\ Service_{s,l,b}$ of *Common Servicel $\in$ Common Services_s*, our approach calculates the percentage of the cost for that level two service to the overall cost of the deal in each of its sorted peer deals. Then it use that percentage as is without any normalization and applies the lth Percentile to the set of percentages of these peer percentages values to get the percentage of that service to the total cost of our scenario S. For each $L2Common\ Service_{s,l,b}$, we denote the resulting percentage as $L2P_{s,l,b}$.

Let us describe how to calculate the cost values for each $L2Common\ Service_{s,l,b}$. Let us define the total cost of all services in our scenario S as

$$Sum_{s,all} = Sum_{s,com} + Sum_{s,reg} \qquad (4)$$

Where $SUM_{s,all}$ is the total cost of the scenario (sum of the costs for all services, both regular and common ones); $Sum_{s,reg}$ is the sum of the costs for the regular services-Service $k \in Services_s$; $SUM_{s,com}$ is the sum of the costs for the common services- $Common$ Service $l \in Common\ Services_s$ and computed as follows

$$Sum_{s,com} = \sum_{l \in Common\ Services_s} Cost_{s,l} \qquad (5)$$

Where $Cost_{s,l}$ refers to the cost of $Common\ Service\ l \in Common\ Services_s$. $Cost_{s,l}$ can be further defined using the level two cost values as follows:

$$Cost_{s,l} = \sum_{b \in L2Common\ Services_{s,l}} Cost_{s,l,b} \qquad (6)$$

Now we replace $Cost_{s,l}$ in Eq. (5) with the definition in Eq. (6) which lead to the following:

$$Sum_{s,com} = \sum_{l \in Common\ Services_s} \sum_{b \in L2Common\ Services_{s,l}} Cost_{s,l,b} \qquad (7)$$

Now we have that for each $L2Common\ Services_{s,l,b}$ in our scenario S:

$$Cost_{s,l,b} = Sum_{s,all} * L2P_{s,l,b} \qquad (8)$$

Finally we transform the above set of linear equations to a standard form as follows:

$$
\begin{aligned}
(L2P_{s,1,1} - 1) * Cost_{s,1,1} + L2P_{s,1,1} * Cost_{s,1,2} + \ldots + \\
L2P_{s,1,1} * Cost_{s,1,B_1} + L2P_{s,1,1} * Cost_{s,2,1} + \ldots + \\
L2P_{s,1,1} * Cost_{s,2,B_2} + \\
L2P_{s,1,1} * Cost_{s,L,B_L} = -L2P_{s,1,1} * Sum_{s,reg}
\end{aligned}
\qquad (10)
$$

$$
\begin{aligned}
L2P_{s,1,2} * Cost_{s,1,1} + (L2P_{s,1,2} - 1) * Cost_{s,1,2} + \ldots + \\
L2P_{s,1,2} * Cost_{s,1,B_1} + L2P_{s,1,2} * Cost_{s,2,1} + \ldots + \\
L2P_{s,1,1} * Cost_{s,2,B_2} + \\
L2P_{s,1,2} * Cost_{s,L,B_L} = -L2P_{s,1,2} * Sum_{s,reg}
\end{aligned}
\qquad (11)
$$

$$
\begin{aligned}
L2P_{s,l,b} * Cost_{s,1,1} + (L2P_{s,1,2} - 1) * Cost_{s,1,2} + \ldots + \\
L2P_{s,l,b} * Cost_{s,l,B_1} + L2P_{s,l,2} * Cost_{s,2,1} + \ldots + \\
L2P_{s,1,1} * Cost_{s,2,B_2} + \\
(L2P_{s,l,b} - 1) * Cost_{s,L,B_L} = -L2P_{s,L,B} * Sum_{s,reg}
\end{aligned}
\qquad (12)
$$

Where L refers to the cardinality of the set *Common Services$_s$*; $B_1, B_2, \ldots B_L$ are cardinalities of the sets *L2Common Sevices$_1$, ..., L2Common Services$_L$*. Our approach solves these equations straightforwardly as they fulfil the requirement for such set of linear equations (see, for instance, [24]). By solving above equations, the approach computes the cost of each common service at level-two ($Cost_{s,l,b}$) per year.

We refer the readers to [3] to understand the difference between the cost estimations for historical and market benchmark perspectives.

To aggregate the costs at deal level, our approach add the costs for services at level two to get the costs at level one. Then, it sums up all level one service costs to compute the cost at deal or scenario level. To estimate the price, our approach adds a chosen arbitrary gross profits to the estimated costs. Figure 3 shows the overall overview of our approach. We also note that market data follows the same structure as historical data, with the difference in its source; market data are from market rates rather than historical deals. Therefore, the exact same aforementioned method for calculating the historical price point applies for calculating the market price point.

Note that we can straightforwardly embed our outputted prices in a prediction model as the one in [2, 3] in order to assess the probability of winning the deal at

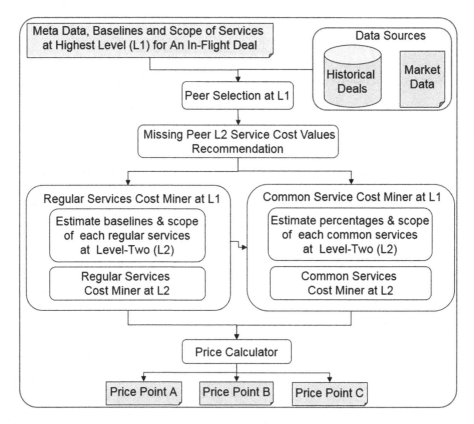

Fig. 3. Overall overview of our proposed pricing approach

different pricing points. We refer the reader to the details in these two references for the prediction model; since it is out of scope of the present work.

4 Evaluation

In this section, we first present our evaluation setup bed in Sect. 4.1 and then report some numerical results that show the usefulness of using our new approach.

4.1 Evaluation Setup

From an industrial data repository of an IT service provider, we retrieved 30 random historical deals with their complete cost structure (at level one and level two) information. For each of the deal, our test bed generated a corresponding scenario by using the deal's meta-data and baselines and scopes of level one services. The test bed further generated the cost estimation for the services of the scenarios by invoking the pricing approach described in Sect. 3. In addition, to compare with our previous approach, the test bed also generated the cost estimations for the services of the same scenarios, however by invoking the earlier version of top down pricing algorithm with recommending missing cost values of services of peer deals. The selected deals to create scenarios were excluded from being selected as peers when invoking the pricing algorithms. Figure 4 shows an overview of our test bed.

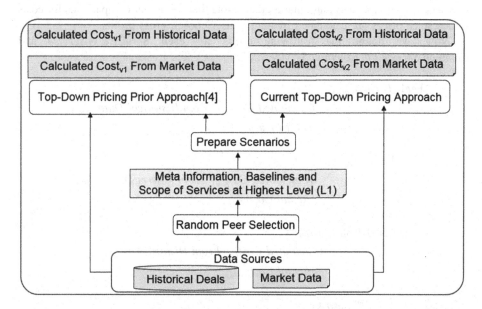

Fig. 4. Overview of our evaluation test bed

4.2   Numerical Results

For recommending missing values, we use the item-based recommender algorithm implementation in Apache Mahout [25]. More specifically, we use the Pearson Correlation based Item Similarity algorithm [26]. That is, similarity between any two services $u \in L2Services$ and $w \in L2Services$ is calculated from the below equation:

$$
\begin{aligned}
&Pearson's\ Similarity\ Correlation\ Coefficient\ (w, u) \\
&= \frac{\sum_{i \in L2Services} (c_i - c_{avg,w}) * (c_i - c_{avg,u})}{\sqrt{\sum_{i \in L2Services} (c_i - c_{avg,w})^2 * \sum_i (c_i - c_{avg,u})^2}}
\end{aligned} \tag{13}
$$

Where, c_i is the cost of service $i \in L2Services \setminus \{u, w\}$, while $c_{avg,w}$ is the average cost of service $w \in L2Service$ among all peer deals that have this service. $c_{avg,u}$ is the same but for service $u \in L2Service$. Note that if the denominator in Eq. (13) is zero, we set the corresponding coefficient to 1.

To use Mahout library, first our approach prepares the Mahout-compliant data. For that, the approach maps each peer deal's service data in the form: "dealID, serviceID, costValue", which is in the form of "userID, itemID, prefValue". Then, the approach invokes Mahout library's ItemSimilarity function to build the correlation map for the services from peer deals and GenericItemBasedRecommenderBuilder function to recommendations. Note that this all is done (the call to the Mahout library) in the appropriate step in our method, as explained in the previous section.

For each of our latest work in [4] and this work, we generated two cost points out of two perspectives; historical and market data. Note that we do our comparisons for costs values since prices are calculated by adding user chosen gross profits.

Now, we define the following errors for each $Service\ k \in Service$ and $Common\ Service\ l \in Common\ Services_s$:

$$
\begin{aligned}
Ver1\_Error_{historical\ data} \\
= |Calculated\ Cost_{i,v1}\ From\ Historical\ Data_{scenario_s} \\
- Actual\ Cost_{i,deal_s}|
\end{aligned}
$$

$$
\begin{aligned}
Ver1\_Error_{market\ data} = \\
|Calculated\ Cost_{i,v1}\ From\ Market\ Data_{scenario_s} \\
- Actual\ Cost_{i,deal_s}|
\end{aligned}
$$

$$
\begin{aligned}
Ver2\_Error_{historical\ data} = \\
|Calculated\ Cost_{i,v2}\ From\ Historical\ Data_{scenario_s} \\
- Actual\ Cost_{i,deal_s}|
\end{aligned}
$$

$$
\begin{aligned}
Ver2\_Error_{market\ data} = \\
|Calculated\ Cost_{i,v2}\ From\ Market\ Data_{scenario_s} \\
- Actual\ Cost_{i,deal_s}|
\end{aligned}
$$

Where $Veri\_Error_{historicaldata}$ is the absolute difference between the actual cost and that calculated using level i, where $i = 1$ (the previous work [4]) or $i = 2$ (this current work). Similarly, $Veri\_Error_{marketdata}$ shares the same definition but for market data.

Then, just like in [3, 4], we validate the same result for this work. That is; we obtain the results in Table 1 that show the confirming results that there is a significant increase in accuracy when historical data are mined to estimate costs compared to market ones. The paired t-test of hypothesis here (see [26, 27]) is as follows:

$$H_o : \mu_D = 0$$

$$H_1 : \mu_D < 0$$

Where,

$$\mu_D = \mu_{\{historical\,data\,error\}} - \mu_{\{market\,data\,error\}}$$

And, μ_D is the difference between the mean of the historical data errors ($Ver2\_Error_{historicaldata}$) and that of market data ($Ver2\_Error_{marketdata}$).

Next, we compare the costs obtained by our new pricing algorithm to that of the previous one in [4]. We use the difference between the errors of the two algorithms for historical data only. The reason for not performing this for market data is that typically, market data is complete and usually there is only one market deal for each geography setting. Thus, there is no need to apply our method for recommending missing values to that latter case.

Table 1. Hypothesis test result for difference between historical data and market data using the method in this paper

Service number	P-value	Reject Ho at significance level of 0.1
1	0.000	X
2	0.046	X
3	0.090	X
4	0.002	X
5	0.015	X
6	0.027	X

Table 2 shows the results of that comparison. One can see that our claim is justified; that is, statistically speaking, for almost all services in our study, performing calculations using the method presented in this paper is more accurate than the previous one in [4] (which was shown to outperform the previous results in [3]). The test of hypothesis in Table 2 is as follows:

$$H'_o : \mu'_D = 0$$

$$H'_1 : \mu'_D < 0$$

Where, $\mu'_D = \mu_{Ver_2} - \mu_{Ver_1}$

Here, μ'_D is the difference between the mean of the calculations for historical data errors of our current approach (e.g., $Ver1\_Error_{historical\ data}$) and that of our previous work (i.e., $Ver1\_Error_{historical\ data}$).

Table 2. Hypothesis test result for the difference between calculations using the method in this paper and those in [4] for historical data

Service number	P-value	Reject Ho at significance level of 0.1
1	0.007	X
2	0.084	X
3	0.095	X
4	0.073	X
5	0.16	
6	0.052	X

Lastly, note that using a paired t-test is justified using the same argument in [3, 4]. We also refer the reader to the texts in [26, 27] for more details on these tests. Also, note that the two-sided test is significant (H_o is rejected) for all the test shown above, and thus justifies doing the one sided tests whose results are shown in the three mentioned tables. Lastly, we note that we used a significance level of 0.1 and that at an 0.05 significance level, results will vary slightly as one can see in Table 2.

5   Conclusion and Future Work

In this paper, we presented an enhanced top-down pricing method for IT services deals. Our approach models the problem of missing values in the historical data, that is mined to estimate the costs for the deals to be priced, as an item-based recommender system. Using such system, we augment the missing values and embed the resulting complete set of data in the top-down pricing approach we proposed before. We showed that doing so could yield significant increase in the accuracy of services pricing, statistically speaking. Additionally, using the resulted complete set of data, one can perform more analytics to gain business insights and recommendations for the business. We also showed that our results still agree with the hypothesis we proposed in our previous works; that is, statistically speaking, using historical data could yield significantly more accurate results compared to the traditional business usage of market data.

There are multiple directions for future work. One direction is to further automate the user-input percentile step of our algorithm; as this could potentially improve the pricing accuracy. Another direction for future work is to apply some of the more sophisticated machine learning recommenders that use the context of both the users/items in the prediction. Lastly, applying this method to other general services that have a tinder process like ours, might be another direction for future research.

References

1. Greenia, B.D., Qiao, M., Akkiraju, R.: A win prediction model for IT outsourcing bids. In: Service Research and Innovation Institute Global Conference, pp. 39–42 (2014)
2. Megahed, A., Ren, G., Firth, M.: Modeling business insights into predictive analytics for the outcome of IT service contracts. In: Proceedings of the 12th IEEE International Conference on Services Computing (SCC), pp. 515–521 (2015)
3. Megahed, A., Gajananan, K., Abe, M., Jiang, S., Smith, M., Nakamura, T.: Pricing IT service deals: a more agile top-down approach. In: Barros, A., Grigori, D., Narendra, N.C., Dam, H.K. (eds.) Service-Oriented Computing. LNCS, vol. 9435, pp. 461–473. Springer, Heidelberg (2015)
4. Gajananan, K., Megahed, A., Nakamura, T., Abe, M., Smith, M.: A top-down pricing algorithm for IT service contracts using lower level service data. In: Proceedings of the 13th IEEE International Conference on Services Computing (2016, to appear)
5. Adomavicius, G., Tuzhilin, A.: Toward the next generation of recommender systems: a survey of the state-of-the-art and possible extensions. IEEE Trans. Knowl. Data Eng. 17(6), 734–749 (2005)
6. Gamma, N., Do Mar Rosa, M., Da Silva, M.: IT services reference catalog. In: IFIP/IEEE International Symposium on Integrated Network Management (IM), pp. 764–767 (2013)
7. Yin, P., Nezhad, H.R., Megahed, A., Nakamura, T.: A progress advisor for IT service engagements. In: Proceedings of the 12th IEEE International Conference on Services Computing, pp. 592–599 (2015)
8. Megahed, A., Yin, P., Nezhad, H.R.: An optimization approach to services sales forecasting in a multi-staged sales pipeline. In: Proceedings of the 13th IEEE International Conference on Services Computing (2016, to appear)
9. Akkiraju, R., Smith, M., Greenia, D., Jiang, S., Nakamura, T., Mukherjee, D., Pusapaty, S.: On pricing complex IT service solutions. In: Service Research and Innovation Institute Global Conference, pp. 55–64 (2014)
10. Li, N., Zhang, L., Xu, P., Wang, L., Zheng, J., Guo, Y.: Research on pricing model of cloud storage. In: Proceedings of the 9th IEEE World Congress on Services, pp. 412–419 (2013)
11. Li, Z., Li, M.: A hierarchical cloud pricing system. In: Proceedings the IEEE 9th World Congress on Services, pp. 403–411 (2013)
12. Ibrahim, S., He, B., Jin, H.: Towards pay-as-you-consume cloud computing. In: Proceedings of the 8th IEEE International Conference on Service Computing, pp. 370–377 (2011)
13. Basu, S., Chakraborty, S., Sharma, M.: Pricing cloud services—the impact of broadband quality. Omega 50, 96–114 (2015)
14. Laatikainen, G., Ojala, A.: SaaS architecture and pricing models. In: Proceedings of the 11th IEEE International Conference on Service Computing, pp. 597–604 (2014)
15. Tawalbeh, M.: The impact of marketing-oriented pricing on product mix pricing strategies – an empirical study on the mobile telecommunication providers in Jordan. Int. J. Econ. Commer. Manag. III(1), 1–18 (2015)
16. De Medeiros, R.W.A., Rosa, N.S., Pires, L.F.: Predicting service composition costs with complex cost behavior. In: Proceedings of the 12th IEEE International Conference on Service Computing, pp. 419–426 (2015)
17. Avlonitis, J.G., Indounas, A.K.: Pricing objective and pricing methods in the service sector. J. Serv. Mark. 19(1), 47–57 (2005)
18. Indounas, K., Avlonitis, G.J.: Pricing objectives and their antecedents in the services sector. J. Serv. Manag. 20(3), 342–374 (2009)

19. Xu, L., Jennings, B.: A cost-minimizing service composition selection algorithm supporting. In: Proceedings of the 7th IEEE International Conference on Service Computing, pp. 402–408 (2010)

20. Gaivoronski, A.A., Becker, D.: Differentiated service pricing on social networks using stochastic optimization. In: Proceedings of the 8th IEEE International Conference on Service Computing, pp. 386–393 (2011)

21. De Medeiros, R.W.A., Rosa, N.S., Campos, G.M.M., Pires, L.F.: A survey of cost accounting in service-oriented computing. In: Proceedings of the 10th IEEE World Congress on Services, pp. 77–83 (2014)

22. Pazzani, M.J., Billsus, D.: Content-based recommendation systems. In: Brusilovsky, P., Kobsa, A., Nejdl, W. (eds.) Adaptive Web 2007. LNCS, vol. 4321, pp. 325–341. Springer, Heidelberg (2007)

23. De Gemmis, M., Semeraro, G.: Content-based recommender systems: state of the art and trends. In: Ricci, F., Rokach, L., Shapira, B., Kantor, P.B. (eds.) Recommender Systems Handbook, pp. 73–105. Springer US, New York (2011)

24. Adhikari, M.R., Adhikari, A.: Text Book of Linear Algebra: Introduction to Modern Algebra. Allied Publisher Pvt Ltd., Hyderabad (2005)

25. Apache Mahout by Apache Software Foundation (2016). http://apache.org. Accessed 22 May 2016

26. Montgomery, D., Runger, G.: Applied Statistics and Probability for Engineers, 5th edn. Wiley, Hoboken (2010)

27. Walpole, R., Myers, R., Myers, S., Ye, K.: Probability and Statistics for Engineers and Scientists, 9th edn. Pearson, London (2011)

Service Design (Industrial Papers)

Context as a Service: Realizing Internet of Things-Aware Processes for the Independent Living of the Elderly

Lina Yao[1]([✉]), Boualem Benatallah[1], Xianzhi Wang[2], Nguyen Khoi Tran[2], and Qinghua Lu[3]

[1] School of Computer Science and Engineering, UNSW, Kensington 2052, Australia
{lina.yao,boualem.benatallah}@unsw.edu.au
[2] School of Computer Science,
The University of Adelaide, Adelaide, SA 5005, Australia
{xianzhi.wang,nguyen.tran}@adelaide.edu.au
[3] Department of Software Engineering, China University of Petroleum, Beijing, China
dr.qinghua.lu@gmail.com

Abstract. The Internet of Things (IoT) embodies the evolution from systems that link digital documents to systems that relate digital information with real-world physical items. It provides the infrastructure to transparently and seamlessly glue heterogeneous resources and services together by accessing sensors and actuators over the Internet. By connecting the physical world and the digital world, IoT creates numerous novel opportunities for many applications such as smart homes, smart cities, and industrial automation. However, on the other hand, IoT poses challenges to business process development, which unfortunately, have rarely been studied in the literature. In this paper, we present WITSCare, a research prototype of Web-based Internet of Things Smart home systems, with the aims of helping older people live in their own homes independently longer and safer. WITSCare exploits the heterogeneous contextual information (e.g., daily activities) captured and learned from IoT devices, then exposes the contexts as services to be integrated into personalized care management processes, and to support automatic and better decision making in an effective and user-friendly manner. The practical experiences gained from this project provide insights on developing real-world IoT applications.

Keywords: Internet of Things · Smart homes · Context · Service composition

1 Introduction

Worldwide, the population is aging. With recent developments in sensor and networking technologies, particularly the Internet of Things (IoT), has made it possible to develop a wide range of valuable applications such as the remote health monitoring and intervention. These applications offer the potential to

© Springer International Publishing Switzerland 2016
Q.Z. Sheng et al. (Eds.): ICSOC 2016, LNCS 9936, pp. 763–779, 2016.
DOI: 10.1007/978-3-319-46295-0_54

enhance the quality of life for the elderly, afford them a greater sense of security, and facilitate independent living [2,10,18]. As an example, in the following, we depict an assistant service, which tracks the completeness and consistency of daily routines performed by a person with dementia and determines when the resident needs assistance.

Scenario 1. *Thomas is a 77-year-old frail man living alone in an apartment. He is making a cup of tea and his kitchen knows it. Tiny sensors monitor his every move and track each tea-making step. If he pauses for too long, a nearby computer reminds him about what to do next. Later that day, Thomas's daughter accesses a secure website and scans a check-list, which was created from the computer in her father's apartment. She finds that her father took his medicine on schedule, ate normally, and continued to manage his daily activities on his own. This puts her mind at ease.*

There are much significant research efforts on building intelligent ambient environments like smart homes, such as House_n in MIT [5], CASAS [12], Adaptive House [11]. However, all these efforts focus on people's direct interaction with the technologies. Most of them either heavily rely on people's involvement such as wearing battery-powered sensors, or lacking a synthetic method of deploying ubiquitous available sensor data. To overcome these issues, on the one hand, we design an unobtrusive radio frequency-based smart home monitoring system, where we infer people's activities by analyzing received signal strength fluctuations of sensors [4,21]. On the other hand, we adopt the recently emerging Internet of Things (IoT) to make smart home interactivity a reality By providing the infrastructure for transparently and seamlessly gluing heterogeneous resources and services, IoT enables affordable smart homes that are accessible and interoperable from end user devices (e.g., smartphones and tablets) and cloud services based on the Web architecture.

In this paper, we present the design and development of a prototype system called WITSCare, to enable a smart home monitoring process built upon our previous work on Web-based management of the Internet of Things [20]. WITSCare can automatically learn the contexts in a smart home environment (such as the daily human activities and object usage) by analyzing the radio signal fluctuation caused by human mobility and interactions with objects, help the elderly residents be aware of their surroundings, and make better decisions. Sensing contexts are exposed as universal services (i.e., *context as a service*) for higher level process integration and customization via a dedicated real-time Web-based interface. The proposed system allows users to interact with IoT-enabled devices, objects, and contextual events (such as human activity and location) for creating personal rules and service customization through graphical icons and visual indicators as opposed to specifying them textually. With this first-hand exploration of smart home automation in the context of Internet of Things, the development of new IoT applications can benefit from the architecture and implementation of our system. In a nutshell, the main contributions are as the following:

- We develop a holistic view of smart home process management with Internet of Things support, consolidating the resource and service management all in one place. In particular, we present a layered monitoring architecture based on IoT and cloud, which provides the infrastructure to transparently access sensors, processors, and actuators using standardized protocols. Our architecture can achieve better interoperability, scalability, and flexibility in terms of resource management and personalized care management processes.
- We analyze and identify the IoT-enabled devices and contexts (e.g., resident activities, locations and their interactions with home appliances), which are abstracted and managed as *Context as a Service* under the Internet of Things architecture. We develop a series of machine learning approaches to acquire contexts by learning the signal fluctuation of deployed sensors in the IoT-enabled smart home environment. The obtained real-time contexts are automatically wrapped up and exposed as resources.
- We develop an easy-to-use Web interface for visual service customization, allowing end users to visually specify and manage complex rules with semantic information of these resources by manipulating the graphical icons of contexts as building blocks. Our system supports *drag-and-drop* with no programming efforts.

The remainder of this paper is organized as follows. Section 2 presents the layered architecture of the WITSCare system. Section 3 provides detailed processes and techniques on detecting main contextual information in WITSCare. Section 4 describes our design of visual process management in WITSCare. Section 5 reports the implementation and evaluations of WITSCare. Finally, Sect. 6 overviews some relevant literature and Sect. 7 offers some concluding remarks.

2   WITSCare Overview

In this section, we first overview the architecture of our system, followed by a brief description of the key components. WITSCare consists of hybrid pervasive sensor networks deployed in the house, and an intelligent in-home monitoring system running over the Internet of Things framework. It enables the seamless information access, exchange, and manipulation between the digital and physical worlds. WITSCare offers an integrated Web-based interface to manage (that is, connect, monitor, control, mashup, and visualize) things in an IoT environment, which helps people be aware of their surroundings and thereby make better decisions.

As depicted in Fig. 1, the system provides a layered architecture for managing and sharing the information produced by physical things. It is developed using the Microsoft .NET framework and SQL Server 2012. The bottom layer, *Data Access and the Sensor Hive*, takes care of: (i) managing sensors associated with the physical things, (ii) collecting and processing raw sensor data streams, and (iii) providing an API for internal or external programs to retrieve the status and abstraction. *Virtual Things*, *Localization* and *Activity Recognition* are on the same layer, which is responsible for generating and learning contextual events based on the collected sensor streams. The *Event Management* layer focuses on event processing that automatically extracts and aggregates localization, activity and object use events based on the data feeds from the virtual things layer in a pipelined fashion. Such contextual events can be directly used by high-level applications or further processed by other modules (e.g., event processing unit). We will give more technical details on context acquisition in Sect. 3. The *Service* layer provides flexible and full spectrum support for process management and customization, which can be harnessed to enable visual service composition (Sect. 4.1) for more Web-based enchanting applications via a user-friendly Web interface (Sect. 4.2.)

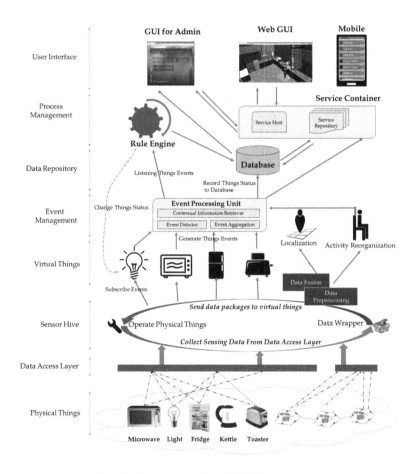

Fig. 1. Overview of the WITSCare system

3   Context Acquisition

In this section, we focus on contextual information recognition techniques that are important for the care management process in the WITSCare system, including activity recognition, localization and object use detection.

Figure 2 depicts a typical system setup in a room setting, where a sensor array (e.g., passive RFID tags in this work) is deployed on the wall, and sensor transmitter (e.g., a RFID reader) are placed on the other side, facing these tags.

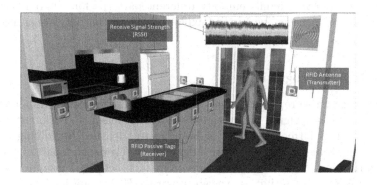

Fig. 2. Illustration of system setup

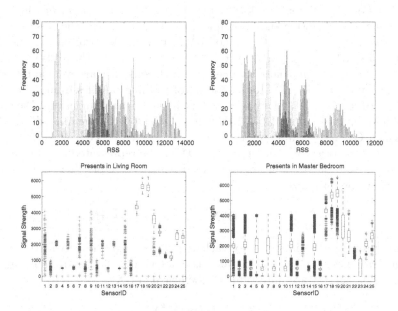

Fig. 3. (Top) Sensor signal strength distribution from different activities *Sitting leaning left* and *Sitting leaning right*, (bottom) sensor signal strength distribution from different rooms *Bedroom* and *Living room*

When a person performs different activities or presents in the room, the system collects signal strength variations, e.g., Received Signal Strength Indicator (RSSI), and discovers fluctuation patterns. The motivation of our work arises from the following observations. Although RSSI reflects the uncertainty and nonlinear distributed patterns, we discover that the variations of RSSI values allow us to distinguish among different activities and locations. Figure 3 (top) shows the distinctive changes of RSSI values of the tag array (e.g., passive RFID tags) according to different postures that a subject performs. Figure 3 (bottom) shows RSSI signal strength distribution in different rooms. From these observations, we believe that RSSI signals embody different patterns for different activities and locations, which can be further exploited for our activity recognition and localization.

3.1   Activity Recognition

We propose a sparse representation based approach to recognize human activities by investigating signal fluctuations. We learn one single dictionary for each activity, which is formed by a set of basis vectors learned by solving a sparse optimization problem. Each basis vector can effectively capture part of key structural information of given training data from each activity. Assuming we have predefined K types of activities, we can construct K dictionaries (one dictionary for each activity). A new signal strength vector is measured by using the coefficients of K dictionaries. We propose to compare the largest absolute value of coefficients of the different dictionary for given new signal, larger of which indicates that the new testing signal sample fits better to the specific corresponding dictionary than others. Let $\mathbf{O}^k = \{\mathbf{o}_1^k, \mathbf{o}_2^k, ..., \mathbf{o}_i^k\}$ be the training sample from activity class $\mathcal{C}^k$, to learn and encode the information of the testing samples belonging to a particular activity class, we first construct an overcomplete dictionary $\mathcal{D}^k$ for each class $\mathcal{C}^k$. Recall the set of training samples from k^{th} activity as $\mathbf{O}^k = \{\mathbf{o}_1^k, \mathbf{o}_2^k, ..., \mathbf{o}_N^k\}$, where $\mathbf{o}_i^k \in \mathbb{R}^m$, m is the feature dimensions. We intend to find a dictionary matrix $\mathbf{D}^k \in \mathbb{R}^{m \times K}$ having $K(K > m)$ vectors $\{\mathbf{d}_1^k, ..., \mathbf{d}_K^k\}$, over which $\mathbf{O}^k$ has a sparse representation $\mathbf{X}^k = \{\mathbf{x}_1^k, ..., \mathbf{x}_N^k\}$, where $\mathbf{x}_i^k \in \mathbb{R}^K$. In this case, the original training matrix $\mathbf{O}^k$ can be represented as a linear combination of no more than $\tau_0^k (\tau_0^k << K)$ dictionary vectors. The optimization problem can be formalized as:

$$\min_{\mathbf{D}^k, \mathbf{X}^k} ||\mathbf{O}^k - \mathbf{D}^k \mathbf{X}^k||_2^2, \text{ s.t. } ||\mathbf{x}_i^k||_0 \leq \tau_o^k \tag{1}$$

After profiling the dictionary for each activity, for a given query feature vector of signal samples $\mathbf{o}^*$, the activity label is associated with the training samples that have the largest absolute value of coefficients of $\mathbf{X}^k$:

$$l_{\mathbf{o}^*} = l(\max_i |\mathbf{X}|_i^k) \tag{2}$$

3.2   Presence Detection

Localization is critical to track and locate people in indoor environments. Monitoring the movements of an elderly person inside the home is especially important to spot abnormal behaviors, e.g., staying in the toilet over 30 min. Such contextual information is also important for the system to perform commonsense reasoning. For example, when an old person is detected lying down somewhere other than the bedroom, an alarm should be produced. Our system can provide coarse-grained location support, e.g., positioning which room a person presents.

We decompose the continuous signal stream collected from each room into 30-s segments. Since the common sampling rate is 0.5 s in this work, we get 60 time frames in each time interval. Therefore, each interval is formed as signal-vs-time $\mathbf{O}^k \in \mathbb{R}^{m^k \times t}$, where m^k is the dimension of features extracted from hybrid sensors in each room k, and t is the number of samples during each 30 s time window ($t = 60$). Each resulting feature matrix contains the signal values in 30 s. The coupling feature matrix is more informative and robust than one-dimensional feature vector. Since our objective is to identify whether a person presents in the room, our room-level localization problem can be formulated as: given N sample features $\{\mathbf{X}_i, y_i\}_{i=1}^N$ where $y_i \in \{-1, +1\}$ of the ith sample, indicating whether the person is in a room or not. Let $\mathbf{O} \in \mathbb{R}^{m \times n}$ be the coupling feature matrices every 30 s. To identify whether a person presents, we adopt the bilinear classifier, which can be formulated as:

$$\hat{y} = tr(\mathbf{W}_m^T \mathbf{O} \mathbf{W}_n) + b \tag{3}$$

where $\mathbf{W} \in \mathbb{R}^{m \times n} = \mathbf{W}_m \mathbf{W}_n^T$, $\mathbf{W}_m \in \mathbb{R}^{m \times d}$, $\mathbf{W}_n \in \mathbb{R}^{n \times d}$, and $d \leq \min m, n$. We can solve this problem under the maximum margin framework by measuring the margin of the bilinear classifier in Eq. 3 with matrix trace norm, e.g., sum of singular values for minimizing the matrix rank, resulting in the following optimization problem:

$$\min_{\mathbf{W}, b} \frac{1}{2} tr(\mathbf{W}^T \mathbf{W}) + C \sum_{i=1}^N \max \left(0, 1 - y_i \{tr(\mathbf{W}^T \mathbf{O}_i) + b\}\right) \tag{4}$$

3.3   Object Use Detection

Object usage is another important contextual information for our elderly care management process. For example, an interaction with a pill bottle may indicate that the older person takes her medication. We design two ways to detect usage events of things: a sensor-based approach for detecting state changes and an RFID-based approach for detecting mobility. In sensor-based detection, an object's usage is learned from changes of the attached sensors' status. For example, the status of a microwave oven moves from idle to busy when it's being used. In the RFID-based detection, an object's movement indicates that the object is being used. For example, if a coffee mug is moving, it's likely that the mug is being used. In this situation, we adopt a generic method that compares the descriptive statistics of signal variations in consecutive sliding windows. The statistics obtained from two consecutive windows are expected to differ significantly when an object is moved.

4   Context Recognition Services and Smart Home Processes

Based on the captured contexts, our WITSCare system can automatically wrap up the real-time contextual events and expose them as services in the form of RESTful APIs and further represent the APIs as graphical icons in the Visual Process Management interface (Fig. 5). In this section, we introduce how contexts work as services for building enchanting IoT-aware smart home business process through visual process management and real-time web presence.

4.1   Visual Smart Home Process Definition and Customization

The key challenges for advanced IoT applications (e.g., smart homes) is to create customizable services in an effective and user-friendly manner and to integrate an easy-to-use interface for information access, exchange, and manipulation with the applications. Service customization aims at integrating and adapting dynamic information to the contextual situations and personal needs via specifying business process patterns and rules.

Most current systems that specify customizable rules are either too difficult to use or only support simple patterns from limited context sources. In contrast, WITSCare provides a visual and intuitive interface for service customization and supports a higher level composition by aggregate the inferred contexts. In particular, complex rules can be specified and managed in a *drag-and-drop* fashion without any programming efforts. A rule engine works behind the visual interface and receives the string expressions of rules by analyzing and annotating the string statement based on a state machine. The string expression is then translated to a list of annotated objects. The rule parser is implemented based on the shunting-yard algorithm: it first compiles each part of the input sequence

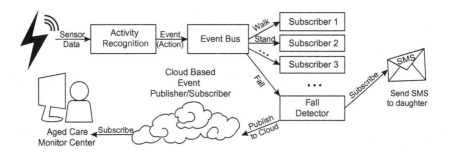

Fig. 4. An illustrative example of business process in fall detection

into a .NET Expression object, and then combines all such objects together into a complex Expression Tree, which is compiled into a Lambda expression. This Lambda expression object is stored in memory when the system is running. It can be invoked when a status changes or time elapses. If the Lambda expression returns true, a corresponding action will be called.

End users can access the smart home process via monitoring and remotely controlling Cloud Pub/Sub to publish events to subscribers. For example, the caregivers of older people can access the personal data like pulse, blood pressure, if the older people take medicine on time, and if they fall. It could be also subscribed from other public service providers, like a `WeatherForecast` service or a `TrafficCoordination` system. The whole *fall detection* process is illustrated in Fig. 4. Firstly, the activities learned from signal strength variation are wrapped up as events and then sent to the *Event Bus* at real-time. Once the abnormal event like fall is captured, an alarm (such as SMS) will be sent to Thomas's daughter and the caregiver via the cloud platform for medical assistance. This personalized care management process can be easily accomplished in WITSCare via its Web interface as shown in Fig. 5.

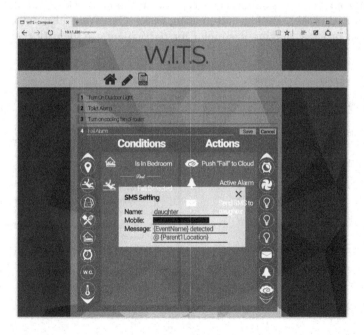

Fig. 5. Visual process management in WITSCare. For example, to edit a rule like sending an alarm when a person falls down, the user needs only to drag the person and fall icons to the *conditions subpanel*, the alarm icon to the *actions subpanel* and perform some simple adjustments (e.g., adjust the clock slider to set the time period).

4.2   Real-Time Web Presence

Our system offers two kinds of user-centric real-time Web presence. We further build up a *case wall* to simplify the integration of disparate services and to effectively build customized processes [14], in which a case in the context of in-home aged care consists of *Entities* and *Events and Tasks*. Entity describes who have the access to the case, especially the person who has the privilege to edit the case, activity recognition service and presence detection are also included. A case wall is to inform caseworkers about task progress to enable such participants to uniformly and collectively react, interact, and collaborate on the relevant case.

Cases can contain automated tasks, e.g., we can build an interactive case (Fig. 6) to list CaseWalls for medical assistance related to fall detection. The left side of the figure shows a set of entities involved in this case, like a caregiver, activity recognition service, and rule engine. The middle part shows a set of events that inform users the actions to take (if any). The right side shows the action sequence of interacting with external software such as a cloud publish/subscriber platform, or interacting between user to perform manual tasks (e.g., a caregiver decides whether to offer medical assistance after receiving a confirmation from Thomas's daughter) except the automatic task (e.g., fall detection is an automatic task). Besides automating tasks, CaseWalls also automates the notification process, making it simpler for participants to identify their tasks.

Entity	Events	Sequence	
Care Giver	AlarmReceived	[M]	Setup a rule
		[A]	Rule Activated
Cloud Platform	RegisterEventListener(from Care Giver)	[A]	Activity Monitor update activity change
	EventReceived(from Smart Home)	[A]	InDoor Position Monitor update position change
Activity Monitor	ActionChanged	[A]	A fall is detected in Bedroom
		[A]	A fall event has emitted
InDoor Position Monitor	PositionChanged	[A]	Alarm is send from Alarm
	RoomChanged	[A]	An SMS is send to daughter
		[M]	Daughter confirm cannot reach home in time
Rule Engine	FallDetected	[A]	An event pushed to Cloud Platform
		[A]	Care giver get notification from Cloud Platform
		[A]	Care giver confirm daughter not at home
Alarm	AlarmFired	[M]	Care giver starts medical assistance

Fig. 6. An illustration of real-time CaseWall with interactive behavior of medical assistance

We also develop a Web-based interface (Web UI) that offers a 3D scene in Web browsers. We particularly adopt the Web Graphics Library (WebGL) in HTML5 to enable 3D scene recreation. The 3D models are stored as Digital Asset Exchange (DAE) files, and imported and rendered by using three.js[1] with plugins. Things are visualized and managed by device plugins. Each visualized

---

[1] http://threejs.org.

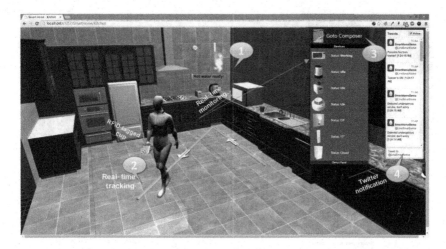

Fig. 7. 3D scene of the real-world on the Web browser. The microwave oven will be in a highlighted status (yellow) while it is being used; a steam is shown on the kettle icon when the real kettle in the kitchen is boiling water (circled 1), real-time location tracking (circled 2), visual service composition interface (circled 3) and social network notification in Twitter (circled 4). (Color figure online)

thing is considered as a device plugin, which contains one or more 3D model or animation settings. For instance, the kettle will show steam when it is boiling water. We use the ShaderParticleEngine plugin[2] for three.js to create the steam effect for the kettle (see Scenario 1 in Fig. 7). Each device plug-in also provides a serial of APIs (i.e., Web APIs), to communicate with the service layer for status changes of the corresponding things, and to reflect such changes on the Web browser. All the control and data flow can be manipulated through this lightweight Web interface, which provides an administrative portal for things management and activity reasoning (e.g., connecting and disconnecting things, and viewing event logs).

5   Evaluation

In this section, we report the main studies regarding the performance of several main modules of the WITSCare prototype, including activity recognition and human presence, to evaluate our approach.

We deployed our system using one Alien 9900+ RFID reader and four circular antenna (each antenna for each room) and multiple Squigg inlay passive RFID tags in the experiments. The tags were placed along the walls in a bathroom, a kitchen and several bedrooms, where each grid is roughly $0.8\,\mathrm{m} \times 0.8\,\mathrm{m}$. The antennas were arranged between $\approx 1.3\,\mathrm{m}{\sim}1.6\,\mathrm{m}$ height with angle $\approx 70°$. The hardware and setup are shown in Fig. 8.

---

[2] https://github.com/squarefeet/ShaderParticleEngine.

Fig. 8. Experimental setup: (a) kitchen setup and (b) bedroom setup

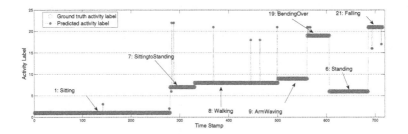

Fig. 9. An example of activity sequence

To evaluate the usability of our WITSCare system. we conducted a survey with 20 participants from diverse backgrounds and ask them to use the system and answer a questionnaire. Almost all participants reported that the system is fun and easy to use.

To test the consistency of performance, we continuously evaluated the system over 7 days. Figure 9 shows an example of the sequence of activities performed by subjects. The recognition accuracy is depicted in Fig. 10(b), where we observe the stable and consistent performance and only minor misclassification during the activity transitions of our method.

We also studied the performance of localization by detecting person's presence in a room. We collected the signal data in terms of empty status (no one is in a room) and the person showing up in a room, respectively. Then, followed by the person-independent strategy, we validated our presence detection approach. The results Fig. 10(a) show that bilinear classifier is most accurate than other methods since it models the streaming signal data as the confluence of a pair of signals and time interval, which better captures the dependency of data factors than the one-dimensional signal vector used by other classifiers. Figure 11 visualizes a subject traces of moving between four rooms, which shows bilinear performs good discriminative results in handling switching rooms.

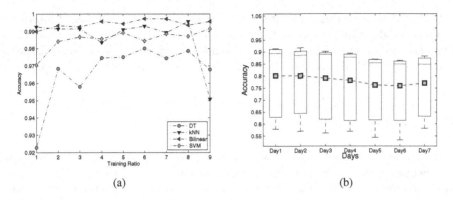

(a)   (b)

Fig. 10. (a) Accuracy of room-level person presence detection; (b) activity recognition performance consistency over 7 days evaluation

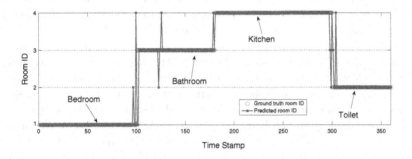

Fig. 11. Accuracy of room-level person presence detection

We conclude this section with some brief discussions on the latency handling in WITSCare. Fast detecting and notification are critical, particularly for aged care applications. For example, for the fall detection, we should send an alert to notify the caregivers as quickly as possible to offer medical assistance for the elderly people after a fall happens. Our system has $4 \sim 4.5$ s recognition latency, which results from three main reasons:

- Our system evaluates subject's postures every 0.5 s using the latest 2 s of signal stream. In other words, if the current system time is at timestamp t, our system will produce the predicted postures in the $[t-2, t-1]$ seconds, and $[t-1, t]$ seconds is used to backtrack check if the predicted label complies with predefined rules. For instance, assume that the label is estimated as: *lying in bed* at $[t-2, t-1]$ interval, if the predicted label in interval $[t-1, t]$ is *nobody*, our system will determine the predicted posture is still *lying in bed*.
- Signal collector is programmed with a timer to poll the signal variations with a predefined order of transmission, which takes around 1 s to complete a new measurement with no workarounds.

– It should be noted that we integrated our system into a Web-based interface, which sends AJAX requests to services for the latest results and then looks up the database to retrieve data for sending back to the Web interface with updating DOM (document object model) element. Completing such a querying process normally takes 300 ms to 500 ms.

6   Related Work

With billions of things interconnected and presented over the Web, there are significant challenges in developing IoT applications, due to their unique and inherent characteristics. The SENSEI project[3] proposes an architectural framework that focuses on addressing scalability issues in wireless sensor and actuator networks. The SemSorGrid4Env[4] develops a service-oriented architecture and a middleware that assists developers in building large-scale semantic-based sensor network applications. Both projects, however, deal with the connectivity issues IoT: how to compose heterogeneous things to the Web rather than how to describe and model things. The recent research and development activities at CSIRO [16] offer some interesting experience in applying IoT in a number of application domains such as smart farming. An ontology-enabled architecture has been developed where the sensor observations are published as linked data cube for long-term data analysis and sharing at the national scale. The system does not provide sufficiently suitable integrated abstractions for things.

The researchers from the University of Washington develop an IoT application, which unfortunately only focuses on managing the collected RFID data [19]. The work by Tranquillini et al. [17] focuses on wireless sensor networks (WSN) and proposes an extension for Business Process Modeling Notation (BPMN) and a compiler that transforms the extended BPMN models into WSN-specific code to distribute process execution over both a WSN and a standard business process engine. Paraimpu[5] provides a social platform for people to connect, compose, and share things. It is unclear on how this platform is realized. In Hyperpipe project[6], things are represented as Web services and connected using pipes so that users can easily compose. However, things are mostly resource-constrained and the traditional SOA standards like SOAP and BPEL may not be applicable. Many research projects are actively solving these challenges and one notable effort is IoT6 project[7], which focuses on the investigation of IPv6 and related standards (e.g., 6LoWPAN, CoAP) to overcome current fragmentation of the IoT. Compared to the existing work, our work provides a framework to seamlessly integrate IoT, specific context recognition techniques, and process management. We also present an intuitive visual environment that allows ordinary end users to easily and efficiently create personalized processes.

---

[3] http://www.sensei-project.eu/.

[4] http://www.semsorgrid4env.eu/.

[5] https://www.paraimpu.com/.

[6] http://geoweb.crs4.it/doku.php?id=hyperpipes.

[7] http://www.iot6.eu/.

The goal of activity recognition is to detect human physical activities from the data collected from various sensors. There are generally two main ways for activity recognition: (i) to instrument people, where sensors and RFID tags are attached to people, and (ii) to instrument the environment, where sensors are deployed inside the environment. Wearable sensors such as accelerometers and gyros are commonly used for recognizing activities. For example, the authors in [6] design a network of three-axis accelerometers distributed over a user's body. The user's activities can then be inferred by learning the data provided by these accelerometers about the orientation and movement of the corresponding body parts. However, such approaches have obvious disadvantages including discomfort of wires attached to the body as well as the irritability that comes from wearing sensors for a long duration. More work related to indoor location tracking and activity sensing include [1,7].

Recently, researchers are exploring smartphones equipped with accelerometers and gyroscopes to recognize activities and gesture patterns [9]. In a very recent work, Krishnan et al. propose an activity inference approach based on motion sensors installed in a home environment [8]. Apart from sensors, RFID has been increasingly explored in the area of human activity recognition. Some research efforts propose to realize human activity recognition by combining passive RFID tags with traditional sensors (e.g., accelerometers). Other efforts dedicate to exploit the potential of using "pure" RFID techniques for activity recognition [22]. There are also research on advanced Human-computer interaction. For example, both [3,13] focus on leveraging sensor techniques to assist better life for the elderly. The concept of smart home is proposed in [15] to theorize the domain of research.

However, such solutions either require people to carry RFID tags or even readers (e.g., wearing a bracelet) or only focus on localization and tracking. There are not much work on study fine-grain activity recognition. To our knowledge, the work by Hong and Ohtsuki [4] is the only such effort, which proposes a solution on device-free activity recognition by using a sensor array.

7   Conclusion

In this paper, we have proposed the design and development of a smart home system that leverages the emerging Internet of Things (IoT) for providing personalized, context-aware services that help older people stay at their homes safely. Our IoT-based system provides seamless integration of digital world and the physical world by managing things of interest and accessing their corresponding services over the Web. In particular, the system realizes care management processes for elderly people who live alone, in which both people's location and activities can be monitored by learning the signal strength fluctuations collected by passive RFID tags. We implemented the system and conducted extensive experiments to validate our system. The first hand practical experience from this system will be useful for building complex IoT applications.

References

1. Basu, C., Koehler, C., Das, K., Dey, A.K.: Perccs: person-count from carbon dioxide using sparse non-negative matrix factorization. In: UbiComp, pp. 987–998 (2015)
2. Blount, M., Ebling, M.R., Eklund, J.M., James, A.G., McGregor, C., Percival, N., Smith, K.P., Sow, D.: Real-time analysis for intensive care: development and deployment of the artemis analytic system. IEEE Eng. Med. Biol. Mag. **29**(2), 110–118 (2010)
3. Hoey, J., Boutilier, C., Poupart, P., Olivier, P., Monk, A., Mihailidis, A.: People, sensors, decisions: customizable and adaptive technologies for assistance in healthcare. TiiS **2**(4), 20 (2012)
4. Hong, J., Ohtsuki, T.: Ambient intelligence sensing using array sensor: device-free radio based approach. In: ACM Conference on Pervasive and Ubiquitous Computing Adjunct Publication (2013)
5. Intille, S.S., Larson, K., Tapia, E.M., Beaudin, J.S., Kaushik, P., Nawyn, J., Rockinson, R.: Using a live-in laboratory for ubiquitous computing research. In: Fishkin, K.P., Schiele, B., Nixon, P., Quigley, A. (eds.) PERVASIVE 2006. LNCS, vol. 3968, pp. 349–365. Springer, Heidelberg (2006)
6. Kern, N., Schiele, B., Junker, H., Lukowicz, P., Tröster, G.: Wearable sensing to annotate meeting recordings. Pers. Ubiquitous Comput. **7**(5), 263–274 (2003)
7. Koehler, C., Banovic, N., Oakley, I., Mankoff, J., Dey, A.K.: Indoor-ALPS: an adaptive indoor location prediction system. In: UbiComp, pp. 171–181 (2014)
8. Krishnan, N.C., Cook, D.J.: Activity recognition on streaming sensor data. Pervasive Mob. Comput. **10**, 138–154 (2014)
9. Kwapisz, J.R., Weiss, G.M., Moore, S.A.: Activity recognition using cell phone accelerometers. ACM SIGKDD Explor. Newsl. **12**(2), 74–82 (2011)
10. Mennicken, S., Vermeulen, J., Huang, E.M.: From today's augmented houses to tomorrow's smart homes: new directions for home automation research. In: UbiComp, pp. 105–115 (2014)
11. Mozer, M.: Lessons from an adaptive house. Ph.D. thesis, University of Colorado (2004)
12. Rashidi, P., Cook, D.J.: Activity knowledge transfer in smart environments. Pervasive Mob. Comput. **7**(3), 331–343 (2011)
13. Steele, R., Lo, A., Secombe, C., Wong, Y.K.: Elderly persons perception and acceptance of using wireless sensor networks to assist healthcare. Int. J. Med. Inf. **78**(12), 788–801 (2009)
14. Sun, Y.-J.J., Barukh, M.C., Benatallah, B., Beheshti, S.-M.-R.: Scalable SaaS-based process customization with casewalls. In: Ramanath, A., et al. (eds.) ICSOC 2015. LNCS, vol. 9435, pp. 218–233. Springer, Heidelberg (2015). doi:10.1007/978-3-662-48616-0_14
15. Suryadevara, N.K., Mukhopadhyay, S.C., Wang, R., Rayudu, R.: Forecasting the behavior of an elderly using wireless sensors data in a smart home. Eng. Appl. Artif. Intell. **26**(10), 2641–2652 (2013)
16. Taylor, K., et al.: Farming the Web of Things. IEEE Intell. Syst. **28**(6), 12–19 (2013)
17. Tranquillini, S., Spieß, P., Daniel, F., Karnouskos, S., Casati, F., Oertel, N., Mottola, L., Oppermann, F.J., Picco, G.P., Römer, K., Voigt, T.: Process-based design and integration of wireless sensor network applications. In: Barros, A., Gal, A., Kindler, E. (eds.) BPM 2012. LNCS, vol. 7481, pp. 134–149. Springer, Heidelberg (2012)

18. Tung, J., Snyder, H., Hoey, J., Mihailidis, A., Carrillo, M., Favela, J.: Everyday patient-care technologies for Alzheimer's disease. IEEE Pervasive Comput. **12**(4), 80–83 (2013)

19. Welbourne, E., Battle, L., Cole, G., Gould, K., Rector, K., Raymer, S., Balazinska, M., Borriello, G.: Building the Internet of Things using RFID: the RFID ecosystem experience. IEEE Internet Comput. **13**(3), 48–55 (2009)

20. Yao, L., Sheng, Q.Z., Dustdar, S.: Web-based management of the Internet of Things. IEEE Internet Comput. **19**(4), 60–67 (2015)

21. Yao, L., Sheng, Q.Z., Li, X., Wang, S., Gu, T., Ruan, W., Zou, W.: Freedom: online activity recognition via dictionary-based sparse representation of RFID sensing data. In: ICDM (2015)

22. Zhang, D., Zhou, J., Guo, M., Cao, J., Li, T.: TASA: tag-free activity sensing using RFID tag arrays. TPDS **22**(4), 558–570 (2011)

Enriching API Descriptions by Adding API Profiles Through Semantic Annotation

Meherun Nesa Lucky, Marco Cremaschi[(✉)], Barbara Lodigiani,
Antonio Menolascina, and Flavio De Paoli

University of Milan - Bicocca, Viale Sarca 336, Milan, Italy
{meherun.lucky,cremaschi,depaoli}@disco.unimib.it,
{b.lodigiani,a.menolascina}@campus.unimib.it

Abstract. In recent years several description tools and formats have been introduced for describing REST Web APIs both in human and machine readable formats. Although these descriptions provide functional information about the APIs (e.g. HTTP methods, URIs, model schema, etc.), the information that qualifies the properties of APIs (e.g. classification of input arguments and response data) is missing. We envisage that providing a complete set of information to the users will facilitate the composition of APIs to fulfil users' specific needs.

This paper analyses the current state of the art in Web API Descriptions and Semantic Annotations to show that although there are solutions with semantic capabilities, most of them fails to add semantic annotations automatically or semi-automatically. Moreover, advanced technical skills are needed to manage semantics and compose different Web APIs, which reduce the number of potential users of such solutions. The goal is to enhance actual API descriptions by creating a simple description format to annotate properties at semantic level to support semi-automatic composition. To achieve this goal, we propose an extension of the Open API Initiative (OAI) specification to create comprehensive descriptions. The approach focuses on the emerging concept of API Profiling to add descriptive information of data semantics by addressing Dublin Core Application Profile (DCAP) guidelines.

1 Introduction

As web-enabled software becomes the standard for business processes, the ways organisations, partners and customers interface with it have become a critical differentiator on the market. Therefore, the ability to provide appropriate and complete Web API descriptions to let users discover applications that satisfy a set of requirements and compose applications to fulfil more complex users' needs is critical for the success of any organisation. Although the process of implementing APIs has become common practice, meta-level API definition and implementation have yet to be settled to set widely-accepted standards. Today, description formats, such as Open API Initiative (OAI) specification[1], also known as

---

[1] http://openapis.org/specification.

© Springer International Publishing Switzerland 2016
Q.Z. Sheng et al. (Eds.): ICSOC 2016, LNCS 9936, pp. 780–794, 2016.
DOI: 10.1007/978-3-319-46295-0_55

Swagger[2], RAML, API Blueprint[3], are available to describe implementation details including resources, access points, status codes and input arguments [7]. These description formats are created by following the API-first approach[4] and using a meta-language based on XML, JSON or YAML. Moreover, a set of tools have been developed to create API descriptions interactively: such tools can auto-generate server-side code, testing options for different HTTP methods, or even fully functional API Clients (e.g. Swagger Codegen[5]). These formats and tools are mostly human-driven and lack supports for detailed information that qualifies the properties of an API (e.g. classification of input arguments and response data). Moreover, these formats may meet the requirements of developers to complete simple tasks, but they are inefficient in advanced API discovery or API composition due to the lack of machine processable semantics [19]. Moreover, such formats should be made easy to understand when the target users include high-level business experts or specific groups of people (e.g. the elderly, people with disabilities, etc.) who do not have specific programming expertise. We name these users as *"end-user developers"*. Several studies [1,8] show the need of interactive documentation that provides flexible navigation alternatives with a comprehensive set of information to support a wide range of users. As users background influences how they navigate the documentation, there are barriers for *end-user developers*, due to inconsistent and very technical terminology use. The final goal of our work is to develop descriptions that can be (semi) automatically composed by developers to support end-user composition of APIs, therefore we address the following questions:

- Are there widely adopted approaches, tools or standards for creating machine processable API descriptions with semantics?
- What are the missing features in current API Description formats to aid composition?
- How can existing approaches be improved by adding semantics to API Descriptions to facilitate (semi) automatic user-driven composition?

In this work, we consider the composition of REST Web APIs by adding machine readable semantic descriptions. The approach is to describe properties with semantic meaning by linking to concepts in shared vocabularies.

In the real world, if developers want to compose APIs, they may search directories such as Programmable Web[6], and understand the meaning of involved data, e.g. that *address* means *city* and *street*, or *latitude* and *longitude*, but a machine agent is unable to understand the meaning without a shared representation of property semantics. The use of links to concepts in shared vocabularies that allow a machine agent to compare and compose the actual data can address this issue. We propose to exploit API profiles to provide descriptive information

---

[2] https://www.swagger.io.

[3] http://raml.org/, https://apiblueprint.org/.

[4] http://www.api-first.com/.

[5] http://swagger.io/swagger-codegen/.

[6] http://www.programmableweb.com.

about the contents of the response according to the Application Profile[7] approach described as a set of metadata elements, policies, and guidelines defined for a particular application.

In this paper we evaluate the current approaches to create API descriptions and make a proposal to include additional qualifying information. Our goal is to enhance interoperability and composition by creating a standard description format that correlate properties at semantic level. To achieve this goal, we propose to include API profiles with the API descriptions created by following the OAI specification.

We adopt the Dublin Core Application Profile (DCAP) guidelines[8], to share data semantics in a specific representation format. We propose the use of a (semi) automatic method for adding annotation, TableMiner [24], which is a semantic table interpretation method to extract the most appropriate concepts from shared vocabularies in a (semi) automatic way by using context information. We will explain this technique elaborately in Sect. 2.

We conceived our approach to use existing vocabularies (about 558) indexed in the Linked Open Vocabularies search engine[9]. The statistics presented in [10] and [18] shows that the most used vocabularies are not domain dependent and as such they may cover different topical categories such as media, government, publications, life sciences, geographic, cross-domain, user-generated content, and social networking. However, the above vocabularies may not provide all needed terms thus, we can rely on additional domain specific vocabularies to get a practical solution covering a large set of areas. They will be integrated with existing vocabularies to ensure practicability.

The rest of the paper is organized as follows, Sect. 2 discusses the state of the art and motivation, Sects. 3 and 4 discusses our proposal, Sect. 5 describes how the system works and Sect. 6 drives some conclusions.

2   State of the Art and Motivation

Although there are many approaches proposed to enrich Semantic Web, each one claiming to be better than the others, strict methodologies to compare the existing description techniques and scientific evidences are missing [20]. In one hand, there are many works that have been proposed in Semantic Web Service community with concrete implementation, on the other hand they lack in facilitating automation in reality due to: (i) the manual work required to create descriptions and, (ii) the lack of standard that limits interoperability. To analyse the current state of the art aiming to facilitate user-driven API composition, we discuss existing approaches that facilitate the use of Web APIs by machine agents. We also analyse the existing approaches and tools considering API Descriptions, Semantic Correlation and Composition.

---

[7] http://dublincore.org/documents/2001/04/12/usageguide/glossary.shtml.

[8] http://dublincore.zsaorg/documents/profile-guidelines/.

[9] http://lov.okfn.org/dataset/lov/.

To accelerate the use of Web APIs by machine agents, Semantic-Web researchers proposed a number of solutions. Paper [20] emphasises on the need to provide self-descriptive descriptions that include metadata, that can be interpreted by machine agents in a bottom up way (i.e. information structure should be in pieces to whole). Paper [9] proposes a set of best practices to build self-descriptive RESTful services accessible by both humans and machines. Moreover, it defines a framework that extracts compliant descriptions from documents published on the Web, and makes them available to clients as resources. Paper [5] develops Hydra, a small vocabulary to describe Web APIs; this approach aims to introduce a new breed of interoperable Web APIs by breaking the descriptions down into small independent fragments. Paper [6] focuses on facilitating composition process by reasoning with tailored ontologies that capture user preferences.

To analyse current approaches regarding Descriptions, our discussion includes WSDL, WADL, hREST, RDFa, MicroWSMO, SA-REST, MSM, RESTdesc, SEREDASj following the discussions in [4,12,19,22]. Also metadata formats like Swagger, RAML, Hydra and API Blueprint have been discussed following papers [5,17]. WADL is specifically used for syntactic descriptions of RESTful services, instead of WSDL, which is used to describe Web Services in general. Both of them, however, do not support simple links and they appear to be too heavy to describe Web APIs. hREST and SA-REST are more approachable as they use microformats which are embedded in the Web page of the API documentations. Although these two approaches are more useful for the semantic correlation, they are not focusing enough on the description itself. RDFa follows the same consideration made for hREST and SA-REST about the specialisation in doing semantic-annotation, turning out to be even more complex to use [19].

For the purpose of this paper we place great emphasis on the analysis of previously listed approaches specific to Web APIs. MicroWSMO relies on hREST offering service property descriptors, but it also focuses on the semantic part of the descriptions. RESTdesc is a logic-based Web API description method that captures the functionality of Web APIs, describing an HTTP request and its preconditions and postconditions expressed in Notation3 (N3), which is a serialization form for the main Semantic Web language, RDF [22]. However, RESTDesc requires manual effort to produce the desired specifications [19] and also there are some complex use cases that cannot be covered, such as cases in smart environments where RDF or N3 are not providing proper solutions. SEREDASj provides a way to describe Web APIs with JSON-based method that is simpler to apply. However, it produces two different documents in order to provide a complete descriptions, proving to be difficult to maintain.

Although there exist API repositories like Programmable Web where users can search for APIs, well-structured API documentations enabling effective discovery are missing. Several frameworks have been introduced to create descriptions for REST APIs through *user-friendly* and *easy-to-use* description format editors [7]. Some REST metadata formats have been created to document REST APIs in a consistent way. These standards offer a way to represent an API by specifying entry point(s), resource paths, methods to access these resources, parameters to be supplied with these methods, formats of inbound/outbound representations, status codes, error messages and documentary information. Some of the most popular standards are the following: Swagger or Open API Initiative specification, which offers a large ecosystem of API tooling, has a very large community of active users and great support in almost every modern programming languages and allows developers to test the APIs immediately through easy deployment of server instances. API Blueprints, where an API description can be used in the Apiary[10] platform to create automated mock servers, validators etc. The Hydra specification, which is currently under heavy development, tries to enrich current web APIs with tools and techniques from the semantic web area. RAML is a well-structured and modern API modelling language. Swagger is obviously the dominant choice at the moment, though all specifications are promising [17]. We agree with this statement and choose to use Swagger instead of other formats because of its above mentioned promising features and also because it has the capability to provide human-readable API descriptions by using YAML, as well as JSON. Moreover, it defines a standard in the Web API description method, being partner of OAI specification as opposed to other specifications. We agree upon the objective of Open API Initiative, creating an open description format for API services that is vendor-neutral, portable and open to accelerating the vision of a truly connected world. Although API Description created by Swagger editor gives the opportunity to create descriptions easily, they lack detailed information qualifying the properties of an API (e.g. classification of input arguments and response data), which is relevant to address automatic discovery and composition performed by machines. To address these issues, we want to add additional information to the descriptions.

Extensive research has been conducted with the vision to create automatic integration of Web Services or APIs [11]. But in practice most of these approaches are having problems in communicating between candidate Web services or APIs due to the lack of semantic correlation of properties. To automate the interactions between Web APIs there is a need to describe the exchanged data with semantics. To achieve this there are two possibilities, one is by directly creating Web service descriptions following specifications defined in a logic based language, like the Web Ontology Language (OWL) and the second one is by linking existing descriptions to these ontologies (i.e. aligned descriptions to shared domain ontologies). As the first approach needs expertise in logic based languages, its adoption is curtailed. The latter is more approachable because it enriches the existing descriptions to be remain compliant with other semantic descriptions. Thus, this approach reduces the possibilities to lock out non-semantic descriptions.

To support automatic composition of Web Services, several approaches have been proposed focusing on semantic annotations, but many of them are either not validated or the validation lacks credibility [16]. Moreover, most of the existing tools are considering Web Services while we are focusing on Web APIs. For the

---

[10] https://apiary.io/.

purpose of this paper, we analyse two tools SWEET (Semantic Web sErvices Editing Tool)[11] and Karma[12], which emphasise on user-driven integration of Web APIs by enabling semantic annotations. SWEET is a tool that allows the development of mashup based on linked open data and services, by enabling the creation of semantic descriptions of Web APIs. The input is the HTML Web page describing a Web API and the result is a semantically annotated HTML page, or a RDF MicroWSMO description. Although SWEET allows the definition of semi-automatic annotations, the users have to make long effort because they need to find all the parameters to be annotated in Web APIs description pages. Karma [2,15] is another tool which allows users to integrate data from different data sources, including databases, spreadsheets, XML, JSON and Web APIs. The inputs to the process are an ontology, a data source and a database of semantic type that the system has learned to recognise, based on prior use of the tool. The system is based on a probabilistic model that is also capable of learning, with a model named conditional random field (CRF) [3], whenever users define a new mapping from data source in the ontology.

Both of these tools guide users in the process of composition of Web APIs and endeavour to suggest the correct annotations, based on the use of ontologies. The main difference between SWEET and Karma is that SWEET allows the addition of hREST tags in the HTML page, since it uses only HTML pages as inputs. Karma, instead, employs a table annotation technique creating a table where, once properties are input into the header row, API responses are populated in the columns. These properties are collected dynamically through different invocations of an API, by defining several different parameters to retrieve the most accurate representation. However, this tool does not consider the context outside tables. We therefore propose to use a different technique: TableMiner [24]. TableMiner is an innovative approach to classify table columns and disambiguate cell contents following different algorithms. This approach considers two types of contexts, one is defined as "in-table context", including column header, column content and row content, and another one is "out-table context", which could include semantic mark-up already inserted in a web page, the web-page title, paragraphs and table captions. The usage of this out-table context and the previously mentioned algorithms are taking TableMiner a step forward in the State-of-the-Art:

- first, it adopts a boostrapping, incremental approach to interpret columns with at least 51 % of non-empty rows and with mostly named entities;
- then, a forward-learning process uses an incremental inference with a stopping algorithm that makes a first semantic association with the contents of columns, followed by a process of disambiguation of the contents in the cells and the searching of the highest scoring entities which could represent the right concepts;
- at this point, a backward-update step kicks in to make an interpretation of the remaining data, guided by previously obtained results. This phase could

---

[11] http://sweet.kmi.open.ac.uk/index.html.

[12] http://usc-isi-i2.github.io/karma/.

modify the columns classification since there are new disambiguated entity content cells;
- finally, classifications and disambiguated entities are updated again with a mutually recursive pattern until they can be considered stabilised.

Another strong point in favour of TableMiner is the usage of predefined incremental inference with stopping algorithm, which does not require to analyse all the rows of a column, instead it stops when it feels confident, reducing considerably the computation time. Finally, TableMiner is adaptable to any knowledge bases.

```
info:
  title: Bike sharing API
host: api.bikesharing.com
produces:
  - application/json
paths:
  /bikes:
    get:
      description: |
        The Bikes endpoint returns information about
 available bikes at the nearest position.
      parameters:
        - name: lat
          in: query
          description: Latitude component of location.
          required: true
          type: number
          format: double
        - name: lng
          in: query
          description: Longitude component of location.
          required: true
          type: number
          format: double
      tags:
        - Bikes
      responses:
        200:
          description: An array of bikes
          schema:
            type: array
            items:
              $ref: '#/definitions/Bike'
```

```
info:
  title: Weather API
host: api.weather.com
produces:
  - application/json
paths:
  /weather:
    get:
    tags:
        - weather
      responses:
        200:
          description: An array of geographical area with
 weather indication
          schema:
            type: array
            items:
              $ref: '#/definitions/GeoArea'
```

Fig. 1. The APIs descriptions created following OAI specification

3 API Descriptions

To analyse how we can enrich the existing REST description formats, let's discuss OAI descriptions that follow the Swagger format by providing an example involving *end-user developers*. Assume that a couple of tourists, John and Mary just arrived at one of the airports near Milan to visit the city. To move around they have different alternatives: (i) public transports, or sharing services for (ii) cars or (iii) bikes. Mary and John want to choose one of them according to preferences and/or context (e.g. weather, time, location, accessibility, etc.). Unfortunately, they have to invoke different information services to collect data before making an informed decision. Moreover, data are often not easily comparable or complete: for example, in the descriptions of bike sharing and weather APIs (Fig. 1) spatial references are in different formats and with different meaning (e.g., longitude/latitude versus area by points). Furthermore, most of the

API descriptions are available only as HTML web pages, yet this is not adequate to support (semi) automatic comparison and composition of properties. We propose to extend OAI descriptions by mapping properties using DCAP to deliver API profiles, and defining a method for automatic extraction of concepts from shared vocabularies.

As for REST APIs, we should consider the use of HTTP OPTIONS method[13] to make REST APIs self-descriptive. Currently, the OPTIONS method is basically used to retrieve simple information about a resource, like the available HTTP methods that can be used in the communication with the specific API; however, since there is no standard response to an OPTIONS request, a full description could be returned in the response-body. With our approach API descriptions can be edited using the tool we developed, as explained in Sect. 5, and retrieved by invoking OPTIONS method. Other approaches that make the most of HTTP OPTIONS method are [13,21].

3.1   API Profiles

As defined in RFC6906[14] "a profile is not to alter the semantics of the resource representation itself, but to allow clients to learn about additional semantics (constraints, conventions, extensions) that are associated with the resource representation, in addition to those defined by the media type and possibly other mechanisms" [23]. Given this definition it can be stated that API profile documents can offer a view of what is supplied by an API, and how clients and servers can expose features in a machine-readable format. The Dublin Core Metadata Initiative[15] (DCMI) released the DCAP format to describe profile metadata defining the constraints on how the RDF vocabularies are used to create profiles by linking properties. DCAP has been developed following the concept of Metadata Profile[16] that supports additional descriptive information about the contents of the response (e.g. useful indexing properties of the document, terms of use, etc.). For example in Fig. 2, line 8 and 12 link spatial data to concepts of latitude (lat) and longitude (long) from shared vocabularies. The approach is to enrich existing descriptions (Fig. 1) with such explicit references to shared vocabularies (Fig. 2) to facilitate automatic composition.

4   Semantic Annotations in API Descriptions

As standard description formats are missing, we propose to add semantic annotations in API descriptions through API profiles by linking properties to concepts in shared vocabularies. To show how the proposed approach works, let's go back to our example: Mary and John may save time and effort if we can provide all information related to useful services (e.g. public transport in Milan) in an

---

[13] https://www.w3.org/Protocols/rfc2616/rfc2616-sec9.html.
[14] https://www.ietf.org/rfc/rfc6906.txt.
[15] http://dublincore.org/.
[16] https://www.w3.org/TR/html4/struct/global.html.

```
1. Description template: Bike id=bike
2.   minimum = 0; maximum = unlimited
3.   Statement template: model
4.      Property: http://dbpedia.org/property/name
5.      minimum = 0; maximum = 1
6.      Type of Value = "literal"
7.   Statement template: lat
8.      Property: http://www.w3.org/2003/01/geo/wgs84_pos#lat
9.      minimum = 1; maximum = 1
10.     Type of Value = "float"
11.  Statement template: lng
12.     Property: http://www.w3.org/2003/01/geo/wgs84_pos#long
13.     minimum = 1; maximum = 1
14.     Type of Value = "float"
15.     [..]
```

Fig. 2. An example DCAP profile

```
geo: http://www.w3.org/2003/01/geo/wgs84_pos#

1. definitions:                    OAI specification
2.   Bike:
3.      type: object              DCAP profile
4.      properties:
5.        bike_id:
6.           type: number
7.        description:
8.           type: string
9.        lat:
10.          type: number
11.          property: geo:lat
12.          type_of_value: float
13.        lng:
14.          type: number
15.          property: geo:lng
16.          type_of_value: float
```

Fig. 3. Adding API profile using DCAP specification in OAI specification

aggregated way by composing descriptions. For example, if they can compare weather forecast information with available mobility services, they can make informed decisions like using bike sharing service in case of a sunny day, or a car sharing service in case of rain. To improve the descriptions in Fig. 1, we propose to add API profile information by means of DCAP specifications, as shown in Fig. 3 that specifies a definition of a bike. The resulting description consists of a comprehensive set of information that facilitate composition of responses. For example, in order to identify the best solution for Mary and John, car and bike sharing API responses can be enriched with contextual information such as weather forecast, traffic congestion, accessibility for disabled or elders, etc. In Fig. 4, the position of a bike is uniquely identified by concepts *geo:lat* and *geo:lng*. Similarly, information about the weather have been linked to concept *schema.org/geo*. In this way, it is possible to compare the responses of the two APIs and find the weather conditions in the area in which the bike is located. Similarly, when the visitors want to use a car, they need to know if a parking place is available near their destination. They may use Google Places API by giving the value *parking* in the *types filter* for parking place searches. This API

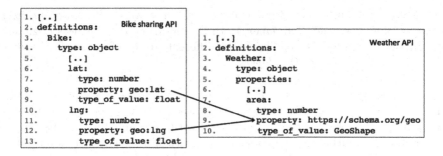

Fig. 4. Mapping of properties between responses of Bike sharing and Weather APIs

provides responses with the *address* property that shows geocoding results with a precise position. By correlating the semantics of properties of Weather API, *schema.org/geo*, and Google Places API, *schema.org/address*, the visitors can get required information to take a decision such as whether to book a open or closed parking place.

From the discussion in Sect. 2, we find an issue that developers often have to manually define the mappings between the information consumed and produced by Web APIs to shared vocabularies. In the following section we define the architecture of the tool that can address the discussed issues.

5   The Architecture - How the System Works

We have developed a system that target both *professional developers*, who have technical expertise in developing applications, and *end-user developers* that may not be familiar with the technologies discussed in the previous sections. Therefore, the aim is to create an abstraction layer to hide the technological complexity to the end-users and make the task of composing descriptions and services easier. The resulting system makes available a composition process through a REST API, which is provided by the *API Provider* component (Fig. 5).

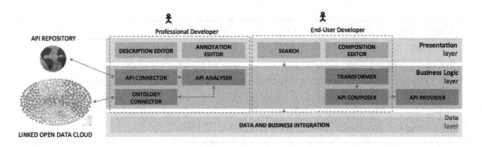

Fig. 5. The system architecture

The system architecture (Fig. 5) consists of three layers: *Presentation layer*, *Business logic layer* and *Data layer*. Both Presentation and Business Logic layers consist of components dedicated to different group of users: *Professional Developers* and *End-User Developers*.

The presentation layer dedicated to *professional developers* includes components that provide a user-friendly interface to enrich the descriptions of Web APIs, and manage semantic annotations. These tasks have been accomplished by extending the Swagger Editor, both for descriptions and annotations. In particular, the description process is semi-automatically managed by augmenting existing API descriptions, which can be retrieved from existing repositories (e.g. ProgrammableWeb), services registry, or by exploiting the HTTP OPTIONS method, as discussed in Sect. 3. Note that the OPTIONS method is also exploited by the system to support maintenance and evolution of descriptions already known by the system. If it is not possible to retrieve any initial description, the developer can insert a new API description manually using the Description Editor. These descriptions are represented in JSON or YAML format. For each resource, all relevant information such as available HTTP operations (e.g. GET, POST, PUT, DELETE, OPTIONS, HEAD, PATCH), the list of parameters for each operation, possible responses are collected. The process of creating a description is detailed in Algorithm 1.

The Business Logic Layer allows developers to semi-automatically add semantic annotations to inputs and outputs by following the approach discussed in [24,25]. The system automatically builds a table by putting properties in the header row, and filling up columns with API responses. These responses are collected dynamically by the *API Connector* component through multiple invocations of the involved APIs. The use of different input values allows the building of an accurate description of the APIs. In case of failure, the developer is asked to provide valid inputs to proceed. For the Bike sharing API example presented in Sects. 3, and 4, the header rows include input (e.g., "id_station") and output (e.g., "station name", "lat", "long", "free bikes", "total slots") properties, and the cell contents will be incrementally filled with data of each API invocation. So, the system is able to break up the response code (e.g. JSON, XML) in order to identify the output properties and their values.

Algorithm 1. Retrieve or create API description

Result: API description

1 **if** *description is available* **then**
2 | retrieve description from existing repositories, services registries or via OPTIONS method;
3 **else**
4 | create it manually using the Description Editor;

Algorithm 2. Create and add API profiles to API descriptions

Data: API description
Result: API description with API profile

1 Detect all resources' end-point;
2 **foreach** *end-point* **do**
   // collect data
3   **repeat**
4   generate input parameters following the API description;
5   **if** *input parameters cannot be generated* **then**
6   take input parameters from the user
7   invoke API with input parameters;
8   collect results;
9   **until** *at least N results are collected*   /* default N=10 */;
   // create tables
10   **foreach** *results* **do**
11   create a header row with API properties;
12   fill content-cells with values from inputs and responses;

   // add semantic annotations
13 **foreach** *tables* **do**
14   apply TableMiner technique;
15   show table to the user;
16   **if** *table annotation is not complete* **then**
17   show related vocabularies and/or alternatives to the user;
18   ask the user to manually add links;
19   **if** *the user wants to review the annotations* **then**
20   show related vocabularies to the user;
21   let the user confirm or modify the links;
22   insert API profile in API description;

In the Mary and John example, *lat*, *lng* and *area* are in the header row; values like "45.523", "9.219" and "[[45.524902, 9.216672], [45.526398, 9.218571], ...]", which is an array of spatial points, fill up the column cells.

Algorithm 2 defines the process, which extends the one proposed by Karma [14] with the use of TableMiner technique to analyse the semantic properties of the resulting table. The TableMiner annotation technique is applied by the *API Analyzer* component that follows the steps described in Sect. 2 to set the meaning of properties by automatically linking them to concepts in the shared vocabularies. However, if the semi-automatic process fails, the developer is able to provide semantic annotation manually using the editor. Moreover, the system can support the developers by showing shared domain vocabularies and annotation alternatives.

Finally, the *Data and Business Integration* component stores the data to support the analysis of the APIs, and the produced descriptions and semantic annotations, to support the creation of an *ecosystem* of services. This *ecosystem* is an open set of services that could be automatically retrieved and linked each others to be able to follow the evolving user needs. The descriptions are retrievable by the OPTIONS method, as already discussed, to support use and evolution. In the context of this paper, we consider Mary and John as information seekers who want to know some information to facilitate their mobility. They are representative of generic users who wants to know more information about specific services (e.g., mobility) and related services. They are provided with descriptions to select and compose APIs according to patterns that have been pre-defined by professional developers.

The *Composition Editor* component is devoted to create compositions of services. The first step is to search for Web APIs that are already stored in the system by using the *Search* component. All relevant results and their possible combinations are loaded and showed in the interface to let the user select the APIs that match a set of given requirements. The second step is to create compositions either by directly linking the outputs and inputs of selected APIs, or by including *transformation* services that transform and make outputs compatible to inputs according to the semantic relations hold in the annotations. The *Transformer* component has the task of managing the set of transformation rules that make properties compatible. Composition patterns are then stored and provided to users such as Mary and John that have the task to populate such patterns with the services of interests.

The Mary and John example can provide a general understanding of how these transformation rules work: after *lat* becomes *geo:lat*, and *lng* becomes *geo:lng* to build the augmented description (shown in Fig. 4), it is possible to identify which area includes the given pair of *geo:lat* and *geo:lng* values by applying the transformation rules. In such a way, it is possible to identify the weather conditions in the area in which a bike station is currently located. If the system cannot identify the appropriate rules to manage some annotated properties, the developer can insert new ones to enrich the system and ensure its evolution. In other words, the system provides end-users with synthetic information to accomplish a given task, anyway, if they are interested to see more details they can explore the process of transformation and composition. Moreover, if the user has the needed skills, he or she can contribute to the system evolution by adding transformation rules and/or composition patterns. One of the major advantage of the proposed system remains the separation of the annotation activities, which requires skills on semantic technologies, from the transformation and composition activities, which requires basic programming skills, or even no particular skills to just use the system as it is, like in the case of Mary and John.

6   Conclusion

Today, Web APIs are associated with textual descriptions that are not understandable by machines and cannot be composed (semi) automatically. There exist approaches, including WADL, WSMO Lite, Resource-Oriented Service

Model (ROSM) and RESTdesc, that provide rich semantic descriptions, but they are not widely adopted because of the required expertise in Semantic Web Languages (e.g. RDF, SPARQL, N3) as well as in-depth domain knowledge [19]. Although machine-readable descriptions (e.g. MicroWSMO, Minimal Service Model, SA-REST) have been introduced to support additional semantic information, tools for creating automatic or semi-automatic semantic annotations are missing. Such shortcomings motivate our work and our long term goal of defining an abstract layer on top of API descriptions and profiles to hide the intrinsic complexity to the end-users.

The current contribution is an extension to Open API Initiative (OAI) Specification following the Dublin Core Application Profile (DCAP) guidelines. Target users are technology experts and professional developers that can understand the involved concepts and drive the semi-automatic tool we developed. The next step is to introduce high-level concepts that target specific requirements (e.g. common needs and requirements of specific groups of users), and are understandable by generic users. Such concepts will be implemented in visual interfaces that can support actual user evaluation tests.

References

1. Danielsen, P.J., Jeffrey, A.: Validation and interactivity of web API documentation. In: 2013 IEEE 20th International Conference on Web Services (ICWS), pp. 523–530. IEEE (2013)
2. Gupta, S., Szekely, P., Knoblock, C.A., Goel, A., Taheriyan, M., Muslea, M.: Karma: a system for mapping structured sources into the semantic web. In: Simperl, E., Norton, B., Mladenic, D., Valle, E.D., Fundulaki, I., Passant, A., Troncy, R. (eds.) ESWC 2012. LNCS, vol. 7540, pp. 430–434. Springer, Heidelberg (2012)
3. Lafferty, J., McCallum, A., Pereira, F.C.: Conditional random fields: probabilistic models for segmenting and labeling sequence data, pp. 282–289 (2001)
4. Lanthaler, M., Gütl, C.: A semantic description language for restful data services to combat semaphobia. In: Digital Ecosystems and Technologies Conference (DEST), 2011 Proceedings of the 5th IEEE International Conference on Digital Ecosystems and Technologies, pp. 47–53. IEEE (2011)
5. Lanthaler, M., Gütl, C.: Hydra: a vocabulary for hypermedia-driven web APIs. In: LDOW 996 (2013)
6. Mayer, S., Inhelder, N., Verborgh, R., Van de Walle, R., Mattern, F.: Configuration of smart environments made simple: combining visual modeling with semantic metadata and reasoning. In: Internet of Things (IOT), 2014 International Conference on the Internet of Things, pp. 61–66. IEEE (2014)
7. Mitra, R.: Rapido: a sketching tool for web API designers. In: Proceedings of the 24th International Conference on World Wide Web Companion, pp. 1509–1514. International World Wide Web Conferences Steering Committee (2015)
8. Myers, B.A., Jeong, S.Y., Xie, Y., Beaton, J., Stylos, J., Ehret, R., Karstens, J., Efeoglu, A., Busse, D.K.: Studying the documentation of an API for enterprise service-oriented architecture. IGI Global (2012)

9. Panziera, L., De Paoli, F.: A framework for self-descriptive restful services. In: Proceedings of the 22nd International Conference on World Wide Web Companion, pp. 1407–1414. International World Wide Web Conferences Steering Committee (2013)

10. Schmachtenberg, M., Bizer, C., Paulheim, H.: Adoption of the linked data best practices in different topical domains. In: Mika, P., et al. (eds.) ISWC 2014, Part I. LNCS, vol. 8796, pp. 245–260. Springer, Heidelberg (2014)

11. Sheng, Q.Z., Qiao, X., Vasilakos, A.V., Szabo, C., Bourne, S., Xu, X.: Web services composition: a decades overview. Inf. Sci. **280**, 218–238 (2014)

12. Sheth, A.P., Gomadam, K., Lathem, J.: SA-REST: semantically interoperable and easier-to-use services and mashups. IEEE Internet Comput. **11**(6), 91 (2007)

13. Steiner, T., Algermissen, J.: Fulfilling the hypermedia constraint via HTTP OPTIONS, the HTTP vocabulary in RDF, and link headers. In: Proceedings of the Second International Workshop on RESTful Design, pp. 11–14. ACM (2011)

14. Taheriyan, M., Knoblock, C.A., Szekely, P., Ambite, J.L.: Rapidly integrating services into the linked data cloud. In: Cudré-Mauroux, P., et al. (eds.) ISWC 2012, Part I. LNCS, vol. 7649, pp. 559–574. Springer, Heidelberg (2012)

15. Taheriyan, M., Knoblock, C.A., Szekely, P., Ambite, J.L.: Semi-automatically modeling web APIs to create linked APIs. In: Proceedings of the ESWC 2012 Workshop on Linked APIs (2012)

16. Tosi, D., Morasca, S.: Supporting the semi-automatic semantic annotation of web services: a systematic literature review. Inf. Softw. Technol. **61**, 16–32 (2015)

17. Tsouroplis, R., Petychakis, M., Alvertis, I., Biliri, E., Lampathaki, F., Askounis, D.: Community-based API builder to manage APIs and their connections with cloud-based services. In: CAiSE Forum (2015)

18. Vandenbussche, P.Y., Atemezing, G.A., Poveda-Villalón, M., Vatant, B.: Linked open vocabularies (LOV): a gateway to reusable semantic vocabularies on the web. Semant. Web (Preprint) 1–16 (2015)

19. Verborgh, R., Harth, A., Maleshkova, M., Stadtmüller, S., Steiner, T., Taheriyan, M., Van de Walle, R.: Survey of semantic description of REST APIs. In: Pautasso, C., Wilde, E., Alarcon, R. (eds.) REST: Advanced Research Topics and Practical Applications, pp. 69–89. Springer, New York (2014)

20. Verborgh, R., Mannnens, E., Van de Walle, R.: Bottom-up web APIs with self-descriptive responses. In: Proceedings of the First Karlsruhe Service Summit Workshop-Advances in Service Research, p. 143. KIT Scientific Publishing (2015)

21. Verborgh, R., Steiner, T., Van Deursen, D., De Roo, J., Van de Walle, R., Vallés, J.G.: Description and interaction of restful services for automatic discovery and execution. In: 2011 FTRA International Workshop on Advanced Future Multimedia Services (AFMS 2011). FTRA (2011)

22. Verborgh, R., Steiner, T., Van Deursen, D., De Roo, J., Van de Walle, R., Vallés, J.G.: Capturing the functionality of web services with functional descriptions. Multimedia Tools Appl. **64**(2), 365–387 (2013)

23. Wilde, E.: The "profile" link relation type. https://www.ietf.org/rfc/rfc6906.txt. Accessed 24 May 2016

24. Zhang, Z.: Start small, build complete: effective and efficient semantic table interpretation using tableminer. Under Transpar. Rev.: Semant. Web J. (2014)

25. Zhang, Z.: Towards efficient and effective semantic table interpretation. In: Mika, P., et al. (eds.) ISWC 2014, Part I. LNCS, vol. 8796, pp. 487–502. Springer, Heidelberg (2014)

Service-Oriented Autonomic Pervasive Context

Colin Aygalinc(✉), Eva Gerbert-Gaillard, German Vega, and Philippe Lalanda

Grenoble Alpes University, Grenoble, France
{colin.aygalinc,eva.gerbert-gaillard,german.vega,
philippe.lalanda}@imag.fr

Abstract. Pervasive computing promotes environments where smart, communication-enabled devices cooperate to provide services to people. Due to their inherent complexity, many pervasive applications are built on top of service-oriented platforms, providing a set of facilities simplifying their development and execution. In this paper, we present such a platform, iCasa, extended with an autonomic, service-oriented context module. This module is programmed with a domain-specific service-oriented language built on top of iPOJO, the Apache service-oriented component model. It is validated on smart home applications developed with the Orange Labs.

Keywords: Pervasive computing · Context · Service-oriented components

1 Introduction

A growing number of smart, communication-enabled devices are integrated in our living environments. This is essentially due to major advances in hardware and networking technologies, which make sensors more powerful, cheaper and smaller in size. Such digitalized environments, said to be pervasive or smart, are increasingly accepted in all places where social or professional activities take place. They support the creation of new added-value services that are delivered anytime and in a non-obstructive way. This new form of computing is raising huge economical and societal expectations in domains like manufacturing, buildings and homes, energy, commerce, and even healthcare. Applications integrated in such smart, pervasive environments are context-aware by essence. They are able to adapt their behaviors and the provided services according to environmental conditions [1]. The notion of environment should be taken in its broad sense here. It includes any information that can be of interest for an application like, for instance, physical quantities, locations and expectations of human beings (implied or not in the functions provided by the application), the software itself, and even remote digital resources. Initially, context was essentially limited to location-awareness [2] and to information collection. Since then, it has evolved towards more elaborated models. As a consequence, developing and evolving context information for pervasive applications is still very challenging. This explains why research into context-awareness is a firmly grounded activity

© Springer International Publishing Switzerland 2016
Q.Z. Sheng et al. (Eds.): ICSOC 2016, LNCS 9936, pp. 795–809, 2016.
DOI: 10.1007/978-3-319-46295-0_56

in computer science and will continue to expand with the recent emergence of Internet of Things, IoT [3].

Context evolutions, in terms of models and supporting technologies, actually follow architectural evolutions of pervasive applications. Indeed, these applications are today very distributed from devices to cloud facilities, going through multiple gateways [4]. Contextual information is used at every level but with different requirements. For instance, at the cloud level, focus is on large scale and completeness whereas, at the fog level [4], concerns are more about reactivity and security. This leads to different ways to represent, query, build, and update contextual information. In our work, we focus on the fog level where contextual information is usually manipulated for two different purposes. First, it is used to implement local actions with stringent real-time requirements. Then, part or all of the gathered information is aggregated, synthesized and sent to the cloud level for longer-term analysis. In this paper, we propose a novel approach based on service-oriented and autonomic computing in order to better manage context at the fog level. Our solution relies on an architecture where context is a programming module, connected to the physical environment and publishing information as a dynamic set of services. Context is dynamic in order to reflect the changing nature of the execution environment but also to deal with applications evolving needs. Context also includes event-based facilities to make consumer applications aware of contextual evolutions. Finally, context is autonomic in the sense that it can self-adapt to those evolutions. Our solution is seamlessly integrated in a pervasive platform, called iCasa, used by our industrial partners (Orange and Schneider Electric). It heavily uses the facilities of the iPOJO service-oriented component model [5]. In order to ease context development, we have also developed a Domain-Specific service-oriented Language (DSL) allowing the straightforward definition of a context module and of its autonomic capabilities.

The structure of this paper is the following. The coming section provides background about our application domain and about the notion of context in pervasive computing. Section 3 presents the overall approach defended in this paper. Then, the following section gives details about the way it is implemented in iCasa. Section 5 is about the evaluation of the proposed approach. It has been experimented on smart home use cases, defined with the Orange Labs. Finally, related work is developed in Sect. 7, and Sect. 8 concludes this paper.

2   Background

Our research deals with pervasive applications in intelligent environments like smart homes, smart buildings or smart manufacturing (industry 4.0). These applications are now widely distributed, from the sensors up to cloud facilities. Some code is executed at the edge of the network, in an Internet gateway for instance, while other code is run in computing farms. More and more, code is also executed in intermediary machines in order to prune the volume of data to be transmitted in the cloud, and perform mediation operations. Depending

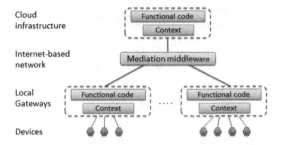

Fig. 1. Pervasive applications architecture.

on the code location, various forms of context are needed. They are based on different formalisms, different real-time constraints, and different interaction patterns between context providers and context consumers. Current architectures are illustrated here after by Fig. 1.

To make these various needs more concrete; let us focus on an actimetrics application that we have been investigating for years with the Orange Labs. Two major functions can be distinguished for actimetrics: the first one is about early diagnosis of degenerative diseases like Alzheimer whereas the second one is concerned with real-time supervision of people at home. The first function, concerned with identification of degenerative diseases, deals with long-term evolutions spanning several months. It requires complex time-series and event correlation analysis, and is based on a rich, slowly evolving context that is explicitly accessed and browsed by the analysis algorithms. The second function is about real-time supervision. It deals, for instance, with fall detections or automated alerting in case of unusual events like prolonged inactivity or irregular sleep hours. This second function may use the same environmental data as the first one, but it is has to deal with stringent real-time constraints: new information should be made available very rapidly to the application. This is made particularly difficult by the inherent dynamicity of pervasive environments.

Let us now define more precisely what we mean by context. Context is traditionally presented as a synchronized description of concepts and relationships between them pertaining to the execution environment. Precisely, contextual information comes from computing environment (memory, network, etc.), user environment (location, needs, preference, etc.) and physical environment (temperature, noise, etc.). It can be the description of a fact, a physical object, a physical value, or an event.

There are several architectural approaches to build context-aware applications. A popular solution is to separate context and applications into different programming modules (see Fig. 2). Context-specific tasks like information gathering (context acquisition), information processing through inferences or explicit code-based operations, information storing, and information presentation lie outside the application boundaries. This pattern where context and applications

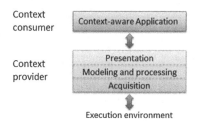

Fig. 2. Separation of context and applications.

are clearly separated improves code readability, debugging and evolution. It also allows context sharing between pervasive applications.

We subscribe to this architectural approach but we readily acknowledge that building a context module is complex. Multiple design trade-off decisions have to be made and implemented regarding data access, synchronization mechanisms, knowledge representation, reasoning, and presentation. A common solution to alleviate these difficulties is to use a context management framework. Its purpose is to deal with a number of generic features like information synchronization or publication. In our work, we concentrate on the fog level, where reactivity is essential. The supporting framework has to deal with dynamic environments, where resources can appear and disappear without notice, and dynamic applications that can be launched or de-activated anytime. Specifically, we have identified the following requirements:

– Coupling between applications and context middleware must be as loose as possible. Applications should not be aware of information sources. They have to be aware of the availability (or not) of the information and its quality.
– The context middleware must present the information in a format understandable by the application and in the expected quality (level of security or preciseness for instance) that can change overtime.
– The context middleware must be able to adapt dynamically in order to provide the best contextual information depending on the application needs without interruption of service.
– The context middleware must adapt autonomically since, in pervasive settings, no administrator is available or skilled enough to perform management operation. For instance, the middleware must be able to adjust synchronization frequencies depending on the application needs.
– The context middleware must be able to activate or deactivate the sources of information, in particular to save energy. Sensors that are not connected to the mains power source should be activated only when necessary.
– The context middleware must be able to alert running applications when contextual information of interest has changed since physical environment can change anytime without notice.

We believe that service-orientation coupled with autonomic features is well suited to meet these requirements. Our interest in services is twofold. We aim to present context as a service to pervasive applications. We also aim to implement the context module with service-oriented components to enhance self-adaptation of the context.

3 Overall Approach

We have integrated an autonomic, service-oriented context module in our pervasive platform, named iCasa [6,7]. This platform builds upon the Apache service-oriented component model, iPOJO. Context appears as a dynamic set of services. Depending on the sources availability and the platform needs, different services are published in and withdrawn from the platform service registry. They are then opportunistically used by the pervasive applications, coded in iPOJO. As illustrated, the context module receives goals from the platform that are used for context self-adaptation. The context module tracks any contextual modifications and sends an event to alert consumer applications. The overall approach is illustrated by Fig. 3. In our solution, services are made available in the iPOJO registry.

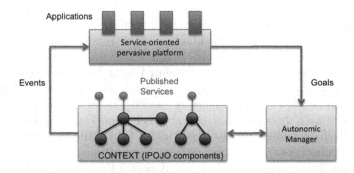

Fig. 3. Overall approach.

A major driver of our approach is not to go beyond what is necessary in order to achieve the applications expectations. This is the whole purpose of the autonomic management. It should only create and keep up to date the services of interest for the current applications, depending on the available sources. Our approach also enforces application development through dynamic composition of context services. An application specifies its required context services and, at run time, it is bounded to an appropriate service and kept informed of every evolution.

Regarding implementation, the context module is also based on the iPOJO service-oriented component model. Context is modeled as components representing concepts and relationships. Some of them can publish services. Others are used to compute information and are not proposed as external services. IPOJO containers include some autonomic features in the dynamic selection of services. Also, iPOJO includes touchpoints in the containers that can be used by more global autonomic manager. There are then several autonomic loops in the context module. It appears however that implementing the context and the associated autonomic manager is still rather complex, especially regarding the timing aspects. We have then developed a Domain Specific Language (DSL) to cope with identified context specific concerns.

4   Context Management Domain Specific Language

The purpose of the proposed DSL is to enforce the architectural pattern described in the previous section, and to help developers with the most common tasks found in context management. The DSL is an extension of the iPOJO Component Model.

4.1   Service Oriented Component

An iPOJO component is implemented as a plain Java class decorated with specific annotations to specify non-functional concerns. The set of Java annotations can be regarded as the concrete syntax of the DSL. The base iPOJO annotations support the dynamic service interaction pattern. To illustrate iPOJO core, the following code shows a simplified Light-follow-me using two context services: lights and presence.

An application component is implemented by a Java class decorated with the annotation @Component. Component dependencies are specified using the @Requires annotation. A dependency is specified in terms of a service specification defined by a Java interface (BinaryLight and PresenceService in the example). Each dependency is associated with a field of the class (binaryLights and presenceServices), which will be bound at runtime to the selected service. The field can then be used to transparently access the required service. Dependencies can specify filters to match the available service providers.

Java code for service-oriented components

```
@Component(name="LightFollowMeApplication")
@Instantiate
public class LightFollowMeApplication {

  @Requires(id="lights", optional = true,specification = BinaryLight.class,
     filter = "(!(locatedobject.object.zone=LOCATION_UNKNOWN))")
  private List<BinaryLight> binaryLights;

  @Requires(id="presence", optional = false,specification = PresenceService.class)
  private List<PresenceService> presenceServices; }
```

4.2   Context Service Description

Application development relies only on service descriptions to reduce coupling with the context. The example here after illustrates a simplified presence detection service. The service is specified as a Java interface, annotated with the

@ContextService marker. In this case, the interface proposes a single method (presenceInZone) to get the current detection status, in a zone associated with the context provider.

Java code for context service description

```
public @ContextService interface PresenceService {

  public @State static final String PRESENCE_SENSED = "presence.sensed";
  public @State static final String ATTACHED_ZONE = "zone.attached";

  public PresenceSensing presenceInZone();
  public enum PresenceSensing {YES,NO,NOT_MEASURED}}
```

As mentioned earlier, context management services also require event notifications. To do so, we have extended service specification with declaration of context service states. Changes in states are notified to consumers with events. In the example, we have declared (using the annotation @State) two states associated with the presence service: the presence status (PRESENCE_SENSED) and the detection zone (ATTACHED_ZONE). Note that the context service specification is a contract between the context provider and the requiring component. It is the responsibility of the context provider to generate appropriate events when state changes.

4.3   Context Service Usage

Applications use iPOJO facilities to react to context evolution. Two kinds of context events are of interest to applications: availability/unavailability of context providers, and changes in context service state. The following code example shows how the Light Follow Me application is programmed to react to changes in the context.

Java code for dynamic context service usage

```
@Component(name="LightFollowMeApplication")
public class LightFollowMeApplication {

  @Bind(id="presence")
  public void bindPresence(PresenceService presenceService){
    managelight(presenceService);}

  @Unbind(id="presence")
  public void unbindPresence(PresenceService presenceService){
    Set<BinaryLight> lightInZone = getLight-InZone(presenceService);
    lightInZone.stream().forEach((light) ->light.turnOff());
  }

  @Modified(id="presence")
  public void modifiedPresence(PresenceService presenceService){
    managelight(presenceService); }

  private void managelight(PresenceService presenceService){
    Set<BinaryLight> lightInZone = getLight-InZone(presenceService);
    if (presenceService.presenceInZone().equals(YES)){
      lightInZone.stream().forEach((light) ->light.turnOn());
```

```
}else {
  lightInZone.stream().forEach((light) ->light.turnOff());
}}}
```

Notification of providers availability is declared using the @Bind and @Unbind annotations. The annotated bind method is invoked each time a new matching provider is registered in the service registry (respectively, unbind methods are invoked when the provider is unregistered). In the simplified scenario for instance, when a new presence service provider is added to the context, the application simply turns on/off lights in the zone according to the current sensed presence status. Interest in changes of the state of the context service is declared using the @Modified annotation. The annotated method is invoked each time a state change event is triggered by the provider. The specified callback receives a reference to the source of the event and, optionally, the state that was modified.

Note again that the developer only declares interest in a given context event. All the code concerning callback registration and invocation is handled by the iCasa platform runtime. Notice also how, inside the event callbacks, the developer can directly use the injected dependency fields to transparently access the context services. The declarative nature of the DSL greatly reduces common errors and simplifies the programing model, as discussed in the evaluation section.

4.4   Context Entity

Developers implementing a context service must meet specific requirements. In general, they need to interact with physical devices; this interaction requires error-prone code for synchronization and event handling. We have developed specific DSL extensions to cope with this need. To illustrate this, the code of a component implementing the **BinaryLight** context service using the ZigBee protocol is presented. We assume that the code dealing with ZigBee is encapsulated a **ZigbeeDriver** component. As previously said, a context provider is implemented as an iPOJO component, using the @ContextEntity annotation to declare the provided context services (a single component may implement several context services). The component has to implement all methods and states declared in the context service declaration.

Java code for context entity implementation

```
@ContextEntity(services = {BinaryLight.class})
public class ZigbeeBinaryLight implements BinaryLight, ZigbeeDeviceTracker {

  @ContextEntity.State.Field(service = BinaryLight.class,
    state = BinaryLight.POWER_STATUS, value = "false")
  private boolean powerStatus;

  @Requires
  private ZigbeeDriver driver;

  @Override
  public boolean getPowerStatus() {return powerStatus;}

  @Override
  public void turnOn() {  powerStatus = true;}
```

```
@Override
public void turnOff() {  powerStatus = false;}

@ContextEntity.State.Apply(service = BinaryLight.class,state = POWER_STATUS)
Consumer<Boolean> setPowerStatus = newPowerStatus -> {
  if (newPowerStatus) {
    driver.setData(moduleAddress, "1");
  } else {
    driver.setData(moduleAddress, "0");
  }
};

public void deviceDataChanged(String address,Data oldData, Data newData) {
  if(address.compareTo(this.moduleAddress) == 0){
    pushPowerStatus(newData.getData());
  }
}

@ContextEntity.State.Push(service = BinaryLight.class,state = POWER_STATUS)
public boolean pushPowerStatus(String data){
  return data.compareTo("1")==0? true : false;
}

@ContextEntity.Relation.Field(owner = LocatedObject.class)
@Requires(id="zone", specification=Zone.class, optional=true)
private Zone zoneAttached;}
```

A common implementation pattern is to maintain within the component an in-memory representation of the current state of the environment, and keep this representation synchronized. Our DSL supports this pattern using state fields. In the code example, the component implementation class `ZigbeeBinaryLight` declares `powerStatus` to keep the current lamp state (on/off). State fields are marked with the `@ContextEntity.State.Field` annotation, but otherwise behave as normal Java fields. For instance, the service method `getPowerStatus` simply returns the current field value, and methods `turnOn` and `turnOff` directly modify it. Any modification to the in-memory field must be reflected on the environment, using the corresponding ZigBee actuator. The code performing synchronization is specified with the `@ContextEntity.State.Apply` annotation that provides a function which is invoked each time the associated field is modified. In the example, every time `powerStatus` is modified (using the `turnOn` and `turnOff` methods) the `setPowerStatus` function is invoked, which will in turn delegate to the ZigBee driver to do the actual action.

In general, environment synchronization is bi-directional. So, sensed changes in the environment must equally be reflected in the in-memory state representation. In our example, lights can be physically turned on/off using a mechanical button; this is detected by a ZigBee sensor associated with the lamp. Depending on the capabilities of the sensor and device protocol, environment information can be gathered synchronously or asynchronously.

The example shows an asynchronous update. Here, the protocol driver notifies the context entity (by invoking method `deviceDataChanged`) of changes in the status of the lamp, and from the raw data the component calculates the new state value by using the method `pushPowerStatus`. This method is declared using the annotation `@ContextEntity.State.Push` that associates it with a corresponding context state field. Each time the method is invoked, the return value is used to update the in-memory state representation. Synchronous updates declared with @ContextEntity.State.Pull are similar, except that the declaration specifies the periodicity used to calculate the new state value.

Using this declarative approach has two main advantages: it reduces the programming complexity and it allows autonomic adaptations at runtime. For instance, if a context entity is not used by any application at a given moment, the iCasa autonomic context manager can decide that updating the in-memory fields is not needed, avoiding unnecessary polling. A context entity can be related to other context entities. This is naturally supported in iPOJO as a service requirement. In the code example, the ZigbeeBinaryLight entity is related to a Zone context service, using the zoneAttached dependency field. This field is marked with @ContextEntity.Relation.Field to express that it can be handled by the context autonomic manager.

4.5 Context Service Provisioning

Context service provisioning is the process of deploying, instantiating, and relating context entities. This process is guided by external events: a device joining the network, a new application deployed in the platform, or an explicit demand by the platform administrator.

Part of this process can be automated using approaches like RoSE [8] and MUSIC [9] which provide a pattern to modularize and maintain the discovery of external events at runtime, but no specific support is provided for dynamic instantiation of context service providers. iPOJO runtime supports this behavior, but its establishment remains highly technical, tightly coupled to the iPOJO model and de facto become less feasible for developers.

Our middleware provides autonomic facilities regarding this issue, without cluttering the discovery code. As shown here after, discovery code emits now instantiation requests (previously it was direct instantiation) and the middleware choose to process or stock the requests according to the application contextual service requirements.

Java code for a context service dynamic provisionning

```
private @Creator.Field Creator.Entity<ZigbeeBinaryLight>
    binaryLightFactory;
public void zigbeeDiscoveryEvent(Map<Parameter> param){
  String id = ...;
...
  binaryLightFactory.create(id,param);
}
```

5 Runtime Support

In this work, we have extended the iPOJO runtime. Precisely, we implemented two additional handlers (see Fig. 4):

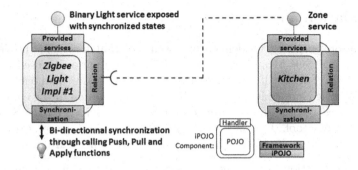

Fig. 4. Service-oriented component view of context model.

- A *Synchronization Handler* deals with state synchronization of entity components. It keeps the states up-to-date by managing the synchronization functions. Different strategies can be specified to do so. For example, the handler can periodically call pull functions or just wait for push callbacks to keep the state up-to-date. Additionally, the handler is in charge of publishing states as service properties. This publication has two main interests: it allows the processing of more advanced filters and state updates can be reported to the application without the burden of an Observer pattern, by relying on iPOJO notification mechanism.
- A *Relation Handler* is in charge of the dynamic service binding of relations.

To cope with changing runtime condition, we implemented autonomic behavior at two levels. First, local autonomic loops are executed in the component container. Their goal is to locally modify the topology of the context graph by using service substitutability and late binding. This behavior is interesting for abstract context entities. It can help to increase measurement relevance by correlating new low level context sources. The global autonomic loop is implemented in the context manager. Its goal is to dynamically adapt the global topology of the context graph and the configuration parameter exposed by our DSL in order to satisfy, in a best effort way, the application provisioning. To do so, we assume that applications are developed following the iPOJO model. It involves that applications specify their needs in terms of context service dependency. The context manager can adapt the running context graph to fit applications needs. Currently, it is possible to dynamically realize the following changes:

- Enable or disable context entity provisioning;
- Modify specific synchronization parameters;
- Replace context providers.

All of this adaption logic is hard coded in our context manager. We are currently investigating integration with dynamic deployment to provide finer grained context management.

6   Validation

For evaluation purposes, we defined two scenarios that have been implemented with traditional SOCM and with our DSL. The evaluation focused on design time activities. Specifically, we used the following metrics: number of lines of code, cyclomatic complexity, and technical debt (evaluation of the effort needed to fix all issues). These metrics are computed and provided by the SonarQube [10] management tool. The first scenario deals with the iCasa platform and its associated simulator. Precisely, the following functionalities are provided:

– A set of abstraction for devices, location, user, and their implementations;
– A web interface acting as a dashboard;
– A script language allowing to dynamically instantiate simulated device, location, and user.

In the reference development, contextual information was computed in an *ad hoc* way. It was coded without any specific strategy in a non-modular way (to be fair, we reused an existing implementation). It turned out to be difficult to extend and evolve. We then redesigned the code, using our DSL, and compared the two versions (see figure see Fig. 5).

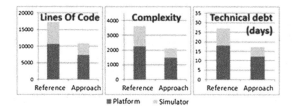

Fig. 5. Evaluation on iCasa platform and simulator.

Thanks to annotations, the number of lines of code decreased. By clearly identifying synchronization functions and limiting their number, cyclomatic complexity has been reduced too. We also noticed that the restructured implementation presents a high percentage of duplicated lines (approach 7 %, reference 3 %) due to iPOJO technical limitations: it doesn't support inheritance. The number of lines could therefore be reduced more. Our approach notably lightens the context layer development. It offers non-functional technical facilities. The context is modularized, extensible, and autonomic. The whole software is more consistent, testable, and maintainable.

The second evaluation compares two versions of the Light Follow Me application build upon the reference and the new platform (Fig. 6). This application is simple, yet it encompasses all requirements presented before. It is a typical home pervasive application that does not need complex reasoning algorithm but has to face the dynamism of the environment and directly influences the user environment. In the reference implementation, the application processes information

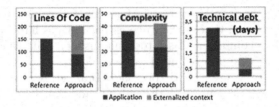

Fig. 6. Evaluation on Light Follow Me application. (Color figure online)

like the presence per zone by directly reasoning over the sensors and their location. In the new implementation, we decided to externalize this processing with a dedicated presence per zone context service (blue part on Fig. 6). This presence-per-zone service can be shared between applications and evolves independently of the business code of applications.

Modularizing the presence service brings an overhead in terms of lines of code and complexity. This is due to the fact that service provisioning must be implemented in our solution. However, this overhead can be shared between several applications. So, if we analyze only the application business code (orange part on Fig. 6), it is approximately divided by 2 and de facto becomes easy to test, maintain, and evolve.

As a conclusion, externalizing context requires an additional development task and the resulting architecture is more complicated, but this cost can be mutualized and shared among several applications. Moreover, new applications can be develop on top of more abstract services, which facilitates their implementation.

7   Related Work

Many surveys [1,3,11–13] about context middleware have been proposed. We compare our approach to those whose architecture can be adapted to a fog computing environment and its specific constraints.

The Context Toolkit [14] promotes code-reuse through the composition of distinct artifact called widgets to build the context. These widgets are used to hide the complexity of sensors and abstract context information. These reusable blocks are explicitly linked at design time, each block deciding which blocks to use. Our approach is similar in the sense that we divide the context in individual small pieces. However, we delegate composition at runtime with more variability expressed at design time. Moreover, Entity-Relation-like model offers more flexibility to design complex contexts.

COSMOS, COntext entitieS coMpositiOn and Sharing [15], is a component based context middleware. Each pieces of context is reified as a component called Context Node organized in a hierarchical structure. This approach provides separation of concerns by offering several built-in mechanisms like push/pull notifications. However, the strictly hierarchical approach of COSMOS context makes it difficult to model horizontal relations. Moreover, component specifications are strictly defined at design time, so runtime extensibility is hard to achieve.

DiaSuite [16] is a component based tool suite using a DSL, DiaSpec. DiaSuite, following the Sense/Compute/Control pattern, defines three primitive types of component: resource, context, and controller. DiaSpec is used to describe the structure of each component, and through an additional build time step, to generate the component skeleton. DiaSuite is similar to our approach in the sense that its main goal is to help developers. However, many things remain on developer side like programming of runtime component binding, and there is no support for synchronization. We believe that this behavior must be specified and not programmed in order to ease runtime reconfiguration. Also, java based annotations seem to be better accepted by developers.

ACoMS, Autonomic Context Management System [17] promotes a work dealing with fault-tolerance as regards to the dynamism of context provisioning by using autonomic behavior. Applications describe their needs in terms of context fact, and ACoMS can autonomously configure and reconfigure its context acquisition and pre-processing functionality. ACoMS promotes autonomous behavior, but context sources are at a sensor level and no clear guidelines are provided to construct more abstract concepts. Moreover, we think that by infusing autonomic touch points at a finer granularity, more advanced autonomic behavior can be brought to context management.

[18] work deals with proactive adaptation and context management based on a SOCM architecture. It underlines the fact that context interactivity is not just about providing the most powerful modeling and reasoning engine. Indeed, applications also can deal with context in a proactive manner, with the ability to change the context through actuators. Our approach, in this sense, is very similar. To do so, a specific query language is provided, with the issue of a steep learning curve.

8   Conclusion

In this paper, we have presented a service-based architecture to design context-aware applications. We have also described a Domain-Specific Language facilitating the development of a context module in iPOJO. These facilities are seamlessly integrated in the iCasa platform and tested on real-size applications with the Orange Labs.

We are now working in two complementary directions. First, we are trying to model more complex contextual entities. In particular, we believe it will be soon necessary to include IoT and other pervasive platforms in the context since these artifacts will be more and more present in smart environments. Second, we are seeking to better formalize the application possible adaptations as a function of the available contextual information and associated quality.

References

1. Baldauf, M., Dustdar, S., Rosenberg, F.: A survey on context-aware systems. IJAHUC **2**(4), 263–277 (2007)
2. Bauer, M., Becker, C., Rothermel, K.: Location models from the perspective of context-aware applications and mobile ad hoc networks. Pers. Ubiquit. Comput. **6**(5/6), 322–328 (2002)
3. Perera, C., Liu, C.H., Jayawardena, S., Chen, M.: A survey on internet of things from industrial market perspective. IEEE Access **2**, 1660–1679 (2014)
4. Bonomi, F., Milito, R.A., Zhu, J., Addepalli, S.: Fog computing and its role in the internet of things. In: Gerla, M., Huang, D. (eds.) Proceedings of the First Edition of the MCC Workshop on Mobile Cloud Computing, MCC@SIGCOMM, Helsinki, Finland, pp. 13–16. ACM, August 2012
5. Escoffier, C., Hall, R.S., Lalanda, P.: iPOJO: an extensible service-oriented component framework. In: 2007 IEEE International Conference on Services Computing, Salt Lake City, pp. 474–481. IEEE Computer Society (2007)
6. Escoffier, C., Chollet, S., Lalanda, P.: Lessons learned in building pervasive platforms. In: 11th IEEE Consumer Communications and Networking Conference, CCNC 2014, Las Vegas, pp. 7–12, January 2014
7. iCasa: platform and simulator releases
8. Bardin, J., Lalanda, P., Escoffier, C.: Towards an automatic integration of heterogeneous services and devices. In: 5th IEEE Asia-Pacific Services Computing Conference, APSCC 2010, Hangzhou, pp. 171–178, IEEE Computer Society (2010)
9. Rouvoy, R., Barone, P., Ding, Y., Eliassen, F., Hallsteinsen, S., Lorenzo, J., Mamelli, A., Scholz, U.: MUSIC: middleware support for self-adaptation in ubiquitous and service-oriented environments. In: Cheng, B.H.C., de Lemos, R., Giese, H., Inverardi, P., Magee, J. (eds.) Software Engineering for Self-adaptive Systems. LNCS, vol. 5525, pp. 164–182. Springer, Heidelberg (2009)
10. SonarQube: an open platform to manage code quality
11. Bettini, C., Brdiczka, O., Henricksen, K., Indulska, J., Nicklas, D., Ranganathan, A., Riboni, D.: A survey of context modelling and reasoning techniques. Pervasive Mob. Comput. **6**(2), 161–180 (2010)
12. Bellavista, P., Corradi, A., Fanelli, M., Foschini, L.: A survey of context data distribution for mobile ubiquitous systems. ACM Comput. Surv. **44**(4), 24 (2012)
13. Ibarra, U.A., Augusto, J.C., Clark, T.: Engineering context-aware systems and applications: a survey. J. Syst. Softw. **117**, 55–83 (2016)
14. Dey, A.K.: Understanding and using context. Pers. Ubiquit. Comput. **5**(1), 4–7 (2001)
15. Conan, D., Rouvoy, R., Seinturier, L.: Scalable processing of context information with COSMOS. In: Indulska, J., Raymond, K. (eds.) DAIS 2007. LNCS, vol. 4531, pp. 210–224. Springer, Heidelberg (2007)
16. Bertran, B., Bruneau, J., Cassou, D., Loriant, N., Balland, E., Consel, C.: Diasuite: a tool suite to develop sense/compute/control applications. Sci. Comput. Program. **79**, 39–51 (2014)
17. Hu, P., Indulska, J., Robinson, R.: An autonomic context management system for pervasive computing. In: Sixth Annual IEEE International Conference on Pervasive Computing and Communications (PerCom), pp. 213–223 (2008)
18. VanSyckel, S., Schiele, G., Becker, C.: Extending context management for proactive adaptation in pervasive. In: Han, Y.-H., Park, D.-S., Jia, W., Yeo, S.-S. (eds.) Ubiquitous Information Technologies and Applications. LNEE, vol. 214, pp. 823–831. Springer, Heidelberg (2013)

Service in Organization (Industrial Papers)

A Discrete Constraint-Based Method for Pipeline Build-Up Aware Services Sales Forecasting

Peifeng Yin[✉], Aly Megahed, Hamid Reza Motahari Nezhad,
and Taiga Nakamura

Cloud Services Analytics Group, IBM Almaden Research Center, San Jose, CA, USA
{peifengy,aly.megahed,motahari,taiga}@us.ibm.com

Abstract. Services organizations maintain a pipeline of sales opportunities with different maturity level (belonging to progressive sales stages), lifespan (time to close) and contract values at any time point. As time goes, some opportunities close (contract signed, or lost) and new opportunities are added to the pipeline. Accurate forecasting of contract signing by the end of a time period (e.g., quarterly) is highly desirable to make appropriate sales activity management with respect to the projected revenue. While the problem of sales forecasting has been investigated in general, two specific aspects of sales engagement for services organizations, which entail additional complexity, have not been thoroughly investigated: (i) capturing the growth trend of current pipeline, and (ii) incorporating current pipeline build-up in updating the prediction model. We formulate these two issues as a dynamic curve-fitting problem in which we build a sales forecasting model by balancing the effect of current pipeline data and the model trained based on historical data. There are two challenges in doing so, (i) how to mathematically define such a balance and (ii) how to dynamically update the balance as more new data become available. To address these two issues, we propose a novel *discrete-constraint method (DCM)*. It achieves the balance via fixing the value of certain model parameters and applying a *leave-one-out* algorithm to determine an optimal free parameter number. By conducting experiments on real business data, we demonstrate the superiority of DCM in sales pipeline forecasting.

1 Introduction

IT services organizations manage a pipeline of *sales opportunities*. Such sales opportunities/deals go through an elaborative process that may take three months to two years of negotiations and working until a contract is signed or the opportunity is lost. During this process, deals move from one sales stage (e.g. qualified) to another (e.g., conditional agreement). In order for an IT services organization to manage its sales effectively, they need to have the ability to forecast services sales revenue one quarter, two quarters, or sometimes up to a year in advance to harvest new opportunities or make sign/no-sign decisions on others.

© Springer International Publishing Switzerland 2016
Q.Z. Sheng et al. (Eds.): ICSOC 2016, LNCS 9936, pp. 813–828, 2016.
DOI: 10.1007/978-3-319-46295-0_57

Existing works for services sales forecasting (e.g., [10,17,24]) fit in one of two main categories. The first category includes those operating at the opportunity-level, i.e., predict the revenue by considering which opportunities currently present in the pipeline may turn as won. Then, projected win values are aggregated to get the estimated sales revenues. More technically, this can be described as learning/applying a sale conversion factors from historical data to compute the won value of the pipeline at the end of the target period. The next category operates at the aggregate pipeline level; i.e., the total value of opportunities at a given sales stage. They predict the sales revenue for the target quarter mainly by learning a model from historical aggregated values of pipeline. However, both categories are concerned only with the current pipeline information, and do not consider future opportunities that may still end up being won within the remaining time of the target period. In this context, an critical factor is predicting how much the pipeline may grow from that point in time, referred as "growth factor". This factor may be high in the beginning of the time period, where more opportunities are constantly added to the sales pipeline. From a given point of time, that varies depending to the type of business, the pipeline does not monotonically grow throughout the target period. Indeed, after some more time (e.g., after mid-period), this value may get smaller. This is because no new sales opportunities with a target closure date of that period are added anymore, and existing opportunities are identified as loss or their projected closure dates are transferred to a next target period. Therefore, it is important to consider the growth factor for a more accurate prediction.

In this paper, we focus on the problem of dynamic modeling of services sales forecasting in which both current pipeline build-up and the pipeline growth are considered in making sales forecast for a given target time period. As a modeling option for this problem, one may think of treating it as a time series problem [1,3,20,22]. However, the typical assumption of time series does not hold in this context. The classic time-series model, e.g., ARIMA, focuses on one single continuous timeline and the goal is to predict future value (e.g., $t + k$) based on historical data. In our problem, the sales forecasting data consists of multiple series of data with varying time lengths, in which sales opportunities get added with a target closing date at different points in time (e.g., few quarters in advance), each representing the change of pipeline value during the time period. These periods can not be simply concatenated to a single one because the life span of any two periods may overlap with each other. Also, compared to what a typical time series model expects, the number of data points in the series is extremely low. For example, in a typical real-world sales data set, it is not uncommon to have few data points. For instance, in our real-world data set used in the experiments of this paper, there are only 28 points per period. This sparse quantity makes it rather hard to apply models such as ARIMA that assumes large sets of data points in a time series.

Given the above context, we formulate the growth forecast as the process of a dynamic polynomial curve-fitting. With all historical records, we propose learning of a polynomial growth curve. It serves as a basis of the forecast.

The other issue with the curve-based methods is that the learned model is based on historical data. However, for any target period, as time goes, more estimated win contribution values will be available. In this case, the problem is then how to dynamically update the prediction accordingly. To solve this problem, we propose a *Discrete Constraint Method (DCM)*. The general idea is to enforce the similarity between the historical curve and the one that is fitted only on the current pipeline data. The key challenge lies in two-folds: (i) how to formulate such similarity degree and (ii) how to find an optimal similarity degree. Our model addresses the first one by limiting the number of free parameters, mainly according to their impact on objective function. With such design, the second issue is reduced to determining the optimal number of free parameters. To solve this latter problem, we apply a *leave-one-out algorithm*. This algorithm takes turns to mask one historical pipeline record as a pseudo target period. The optimal number is the one that achieves lowest prediction error in the validation.

Thus, in summary, the contributions of this work are as follows:

- We formulate the problem of services sales growth prediction as a dynamic curve-fitting problem, considering both the historical curve and current available pipeline data points.
- We solve the problem by designing models that control the degree of similarity between the historical curve and the one learned on current pipeline data. Particularly, we propose a Discrete Constraint Model which formulates the degree of similarity by fixing some of the model parameters to have the same value with the historical one, according to the absolute value of the gradient.
- We propose a leave-one-out algorithm that dynamically determines the constraint degree of similarity according to the amount of available data.
- We report the results of experiments on real business data to evaluate the performance of the model, which shows the superiority of the proposed method over existing works in terms of prediction accuracy.

The rest of the paper is organized as follows. Section 2 gives a literature review. Section 3 illustrates the curve-fitting problem. Sects. 4 and 5 give details of the solution and experiment results, respectively. Finally Sect. 6 concludes the whole work and describes potential future research.

2   Related Work

The related work can be studied in two broad categories: (i) the opportunity-level prediction and (ii) the time-series driven sales analysis. The former one relates to works that train different types of models according to information about each opportunity (or deals as mentioned in other works). The goal is to predict the outcome [6,10,23], the health status [18] or monitor the progress [24]. For further details on services in IT service contracts, we refer the reader to our previous works in [9,16].

From the first category, Greenia et al. [10] presented a quantitative-based approach for the prediction of deal outcomes and identified a number of key factors that are highly correlated to the deal's final outcome. The prediction approach is based on a Naïve Bayesian classifier that is trained on these factors (features). In [6], Carman et al. investigated the problem of comment-based opportunity outcome prediction. Nezhad et al. [18] presented an text analytics-based deal outcome prediction approach that integrates a concept clustering approach, and sentiment analysis, and a set of semantics-based features for deal outcome prediction. These new features are used to train classifiers to predict the outcome of each deal. In [23], Yan et al. apply the multi-dimension Hawkes process to model the probability of deal outcome. In that work, the deal information determines a base probability, which is then updated based on the history of interaction of sellers with the client. Such impact exponentially decays in terms of the time interval when those interactions happened. In our prior work [24], we applied multinomial and Dirichlet process to model the progress of a deal. Given the deal information and update records, the model is capable of predicting the next event type (new update, win or loss) as well as the time interval. These works provide methods and tools for sales manager on opportunity-level control. However, they focus on opportunities in the current pipeline and does not consider the future pipeline growth by the end of the target period.

There have been a few decades for research in time-series analysis. For a detailed review of this field, we refer readers to the survey by Gooijer and Hyndman [7]. As early as 1960, Winters [22] presented an exponential forecasting model for sales based on moving averages. ARIMA [4] (or its variant) is another popular method used in time-series sales prediction [2,5,13,21] and multiple works [8,19] have demonstrated its good performance in "mediate and short-term forecasts" [3]. Furthermore, artificial neural network (ANN) is a relative new method that is studied and compared with conventional ones [3,11,12,14]. Finally, a few works [1,3,15] propose to use hybrid methods of conventional ARIMA and ANN in time-series prediction. These methods work on a single long time-series data and requires a sufficiently large quantity of data points for training. In our problem, however, data consists of multiple overlapping time periods. These periods can not be concatenated to a single one because the life span of two periods may overlap with each other, and the target time period may not have the same time scale of the historical ones. Also, the length of each period is quite short compared to conventional time-series data. For example, in our experimental data set there are only 28 points for a given period. This small quantity makes it hard to apply complex model such as ARIMA. Finally, the number of periods is also relatively small as historical data from far back in the history may not be relevant to today's business due to the change of business strategy, business lines or products or services.

3   Problem Illustration

Services pipeline is building up as time passes and as new opportunities are arriving with an estimated closing date within the target time period. At any given point in time, there is a pipeline build up, and also future growth potential for the pipeline. Forecasting the period-end sales revenue needs to consider both current pipeline from the lens of historical model as well as the future growth in order to capture the full picture of pipeline sales by the end of the target period.

Formally, let $\mathbb{D}$ denote historical data and $\mathbf{Y}_n = \{y_1, \cdots, y_n\}$ represents the current data with only n available data points. Suppose T is the total number of time points for full period, the problem is then formulated as below. Given $\mathbb{D}$ and $\mathbf{Y}_n$, find a function $\mathbf{f} : |\mathbb{D}| \times n \to 1$ to make estimation $\hat{y}_T = \mathbf{f}(\mathbb{D}, \mathbf{Y}_n)$ such that $|\hat{y}_T - y_T|$ is minimized.

Although the goal is to predict the period-end pipeline value, we can model the change of the pipeline build up during the whole life cycle. At any given time point, there is a record of the pipeline. Connecting all these records models the growth of the pipeline as a curve and capturing the growth trend can thus be solved via curve fitting. Consider Fig. 1 as an illustration. In this figure, the blue line represents the curve fitted on historical data while the green crossing stands for the estimated win-contribution value of target period. The goal is to predict where the final green crossing will locate.

On one extreme, we may totally discard the current data and only rely on the historical curve, i.e., $\mathbf{f}(\mathbb{D}, \mathbf{Y}_n) \to \mathbf{f}'(\mathbb{D})$. Reflecting this method in Fig. 1, it is equivalent to use the end of blue line to estimate the value. This method is problematic. As can be seen, the green crosses does not lie closely to the curve, indicating that the target period growth may have a different pattern. Relying only on the history may suffer inaccuracy. On the other extreme, we may simply discard the historical model and fit a completely new curve based on the current data, i.e., $\mathbf{f}(\mathbb{D}, \mathbf{Y}_n) \to \mathbf{f}''(\mathbf{Y}_n)$. This method is illustrated in Fig. 2, which demonstrates a high possibility of overfit. Thus this method is also problematic.

We argue that a good strategy should combine both history and present, using current data to fit a new curve while at the mean time applying historical curve to avoid overfit. In another word, we need to find a balance point between

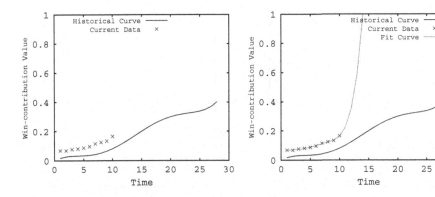

Fig. 1. Problem illustration   **Fig. 2.** Risk of overfit

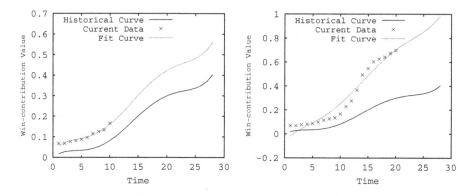

Fig. 3. A reasonable fit   **Fig. 4.** Dynamic update on curve

current data and historical model. Figure 3 shows an example of fitting considering these two factors. Finally, as time goes forward, more and more current data will be available. In this case, the balance point needs to be dynamically updated accordingly. Figure 4 displays an example of fitting when more data points are available. As can be seen, the curve is different from what it used to be in an earlier time as in Fig. 3.

As can be seen from the example above, there are two key challenges in the dynamic curve-fitting problem: (i) definition of balance point in combining current data and historical model and (ii) mechanism of dynamically updating such balance point as new data becomes available.

One intuitive method is to simply add the current data into historical one and fit a curve on this combined data. Figure 5 shows the result of this method. As can be seen, the first part of the fitted curve try to find a tradeoff between current and historical data. The latter part of the curve overlaps with the historical one.

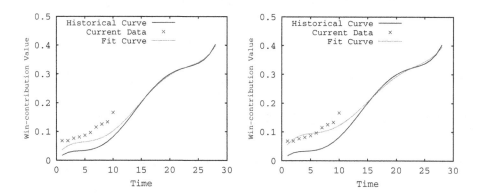

Fig. 5. Combine current data   **Fig. 6.** Replace history

Since we use the end of the curve as the prediction of period-end value, this method makes no difference with the one using history data only.

An alternative method is to replace part of historical data with current one and connect with other historical record. Then a curve can be fit on such hybrid data set, as shown in Fig. 6. It can be seen that the resulted curve tries fitting the current data and in later part goes closely to the historical data. Again the current data does not affect the final prediction in this method.

As can be seen from the two possible methods above, a straightforward way of combining historical and current data does not help much in forecast prediction. What is needed is a methodological approach to define the balancing mechanism in order to achieve a reasonable fit as shown in Fig. 3.

4   Pipeline Build-Up Aware Sales Forecasting

In this section we first introduces the curve-fitting approach. Then, we present the discrete constraint model. It formulates the problem as the determination of free and fixed parameters in the model. Also, we introduce a leave-one-out validation mechanism as a method to determine how many parameters should be fixed. For easy reference, we list all symbols and their meanings in Table 1.

Table 1. Summary of symbols

Symbol	Meaning
$\mathbf{w}$	Parameters of the curve
$\mathbf{w_0}$	Parameters of the curve learned on historical data
$\mathbf{Y}$	The current data
$\mathbf{C}$	The constraint matrix
l	The number of non-zero diagonal values in $\mathbf{C}$
M	The number of historical periods
$\mathbf{X_1} \cdots \mathbf{X_M}$	Historical data

4.1   Curve-Fitting Methodology

Curve-fitting is a special case of regression, one classic machine learning problem. Given a series of pair data, the goal is to fit a curve that can map the independent variable value to the dependent one. Particularly in this work we consider the polynomial curve-fitting where the independent variable is time and the dependent one is the corresponding sales win value in pipeline.

Formally, let $\mathbf{w}$ denote the vector of model parameter, which satisfies a zero-mean Gaussian distribution. Moreover, suppose the parameters are independent

of each other but shares the same standard deviation σ, we may construct the
objective function as in Eq. (1).

$$\mathfrak{L}(\mathbf{w}|\mathbf{Y}) = \mathfrak{R}(\mathbf{Y}, \mathbf{w}) + \log \mathcal{N}(\mathbf{w}; 0, \sigma^2)$$

$$= \mathfrak{R}(\mathbf{Y}, \mathbf{w}) + \log \left(\frac{1}{\sigma\sqrt{2\pi}} e^{-\frac{\mathbf{w}^T \mathbf{w}}{2\sigma^2}} \right) \propto \mathfrak{R}(\mathbf{Y}, \mathbf{w}) + \frac{\mathbf{w}^T \mathbf{w}}{2\sigma^2} \qquad (1)$$

where $\mathbf{w}^T$ is the transpose of a vector, $\mathbf{Y} = \{(t_1, y_1), \cdots, (t_n, y_n)\}$ represents
the current data and $\mathfrak{R}$ is an objective function evaluating the error of model
fitness with $\mathbf{w}$. Particularly in our problem scenario, this objective function is a
k-order polynomial curve-fitting where $\mathbf{w} = \{w_1, \cdots, w_k\}$, as shown in Eq. (2).

$$\mathfrak{R}(\mathbf{Y}, \mathbf{w}) = \sum_{i=1}^{n} (y_i - \sum_{j=0}^{k} t_i^j w_j)^2 \qquad (2)$$

The second part in Eq. (1) is the penalty of large difference between the
model and zero value. This term is widely used to avoid overfit, especially when
the polynomial order is bigger than the number of available data points.

4.2   Discrete Constraint Method

Given a model trained on historical data and partial data of target period, the
goal is to produce a new model that fits current data and at the same time keeps
consistent with historical model.

Recall that the use of curve for prediction is based on such assumption that
the shape of the pipeline growth is correlated with the final value. In the regression model, the shape of a polynomial curve is jointly controlled by the parameter
vector $\mathbf{w} = \{w_1, \cdots, w_k\}$. The change of its value affects the curve. However,
such impact is different among elements w_i. For instance, consider a parabola
represented as $y = w_1 + w_2 t + w_3 t^2$, the value change of w_1 will only move the
curve vertically and has no impact on the shape. On the other hand, the change
of w_2 and w_3 have different impacts, depending on the value of t. Specifically,
if $|t|$ is bigger than 1, w_3 has larger impact. Otherwise, w_2 changer curve more
than w_3. More generally, given an objective function $F(\mathbf{w})$, the impact of parameter on objective value is proportional to the absolute value its corresponding
gradient, i.e., $\frac{\partial F}{\partial \mathbf{w}}$.

In last section, the enforcement term in Eq. (1) prefers small parameter value,
i.e., close to zero unless there is strong evidence. Here we adopt a similar form.
Instead of a continuous parameter σ, we put a binary constraint on each parameter. Specifically, parameters that have big impact on the curve shape are forced
to be equal to historical model while those with small impact are free. The rationale behind is that historical data (or curve) determines the general shape of
growth curve, while the current partial data makes small modifications.

To formulate this principle mathematically, we first define a constraint
matrix, denoted as $\mathbf{C}$. It is a diagonal square matrix whose dimension is the

same with the order of polynomial curve. The element value has only two types, i.e., zero or positive infinity. Then given current data $\mathbf{Y}$ and historical curve $\mathbf{w}_0$, the objective function to combine the two can be written as below:

$$\mathcal{L}_{dc}(\mathbf{w}|\mathbf{Y}, \mathbf{w}_0, \mathbf{C}) = \mathfrak{R}(\mathbf{Y}, \mathbf{w}) + (\mathbf{w} - \mathbf{w}_0)^T \mathbf{C}(\mathbf{w} - \mathbf{w}_0)$$

$$= \mathfrak{R}(\mathbf{Y}, \mathbf{w}) + (\mathbf{w} - \mathbf{w}_0)^T \begin{pmatrix} c_1 \cdots 0 \\ \vdots \ddots \vdots \\ 0 \cdots c_k \end{pmatrix} (\mathbf{w} - \mathbf{w}_0) \tag{3}$$

$$= \mathfrak{R}(\mathbf{Y}, \mathbf{w}) + \sum_{i=1}^{k} c_i(w_i - w_{o_i})^2 \quad \text{where } c_i \in \{0, +\infty\}$$

As can be seen, when $c_i = 0$, the corresponding w_i goes with no constraint and is free for any value. On the other hand, when $c_i = +\infty$, there is such a strong constraint that w_i can only be equal to w_{0_i}.

The key challenge for this method is how to determine the value of c_i in constraint matrix $\mathbf{C}$. Firstly, without loss of generality, we assume elements of the parameter vector $\mathbf{w}$ are sorted in a non-descending order according to its impact on curve shape. Now the question is transformed to how to set the proper value for l. Heuristically if all data are available, then we do not need historical model ($l = 0$). On the other hand, if no data is available, we can only rely on the historical model ($l = |\mathbf{w}|$). However, it is unclear how the value to be set for a common case between these two scenarios. To solve this problem, we formulate it to an optimization task on historical data. Let $\mathbf{C}_l$ denote that the first l diagonal values are 0 while the other $k - l$ are set to $+\infty$. The objective function to determine the optimal l is defined as in Eq. (4).

$$\Gamma(l|\mathbf{X}_1, \cdots, \mathbf{X}_M) = \frac{1}{M} \sum_{m=1}^{M} \{\mathfrak{R}(\mathbf{X}_m, \mathbf{w}^*)\}$$

$$\text{where } \mathbf{w}^* = \arg \min_{\mathbf{w}} \mathcal{L}_{dc}(\mathbf{w}|\mathbf{X}_m^n, \mathbf{w}_0^{m-}, \mathbf{C}_l) \tag{4}$$

$$\text{where } \mathbf{w}_0^{m-} = \arg \min_{\mathbf{w}} \frac{1}{M-1} \sum_{j=1, j \neq m}^{M} \mathfrak{R}(\mathbf{X}_j, \mathbf{w})$$

Equation (4) defines a discrete search space for l and the space volume is equal to the number of parameters in the model. Specifically for polynomial curve fitting, it is an integer ranges from 1 to the polynomial order plus 1.

Algorithm 1 shows the specific steps. Given M historical data $\{\mathbf{X}_1, \cdots, \mathbf{X}_M\}$, number of available points n and polynomial order k, we take turns to remove one from the historical records and treat it as a pseudo "current data" with only n data points known (line 6). Then a historical model $\mathbf{w}_0$ is trained on the subset of historical data (line 7). After that, a new model $\mathbf{w}^*$ is obtained on partial data and $\mathbf{w}_0$ (line 8). Prediction error is evaluated on the full pseudo "current data" and is associated with corresponding parameter number (line 9).

Algorithm 1. Leave-one-out

1: **procedure** FINDL($\{\mathbf{X}_i | 1 \leq i \leq M\}, n, k$)
2:     $l^* \leftarrow 0, err^* \leftarrow +\infty$
3:     **for** $l \leftarrow 1$ to $k + 1$ **do**
4:         $err \leftarrow 0$
5:         **for** $i \leftarrow 1$ to M **do**
6:             $\mathbb{D} \leftarrow \{\mathbf{X}_j | 1 \leq j \leq M \wedge j \neq i\}$
7:             $\mathbf{w}_0 \leftarrow \arg\min_{\mathbf{w}} E_{\mathbf{X}_j \in \mathbb{D}}(\mathfrak{R}(\mathbf{X}_j, \mathbf{w}))$
8:             $\mathbf{w}^* \leftarrow \arg\min_{\mathbf{w}} \mathfrak{L}_{dc}(\mathbf{w} | \mathbf{X}_i^n, \mathbf{w}_0, \mathbf{C}_l)$
9:             $err \leftarrow err + \frac{\mathfrak{R}(\mathbf{X}_i, \mathbf{w}^*)}{M}$
10:         **end for**
11:         **if** $err^* > err$ **then**
12:             $l^* \leftarrow l, err^* \leftarrow err$
13:         **end if**
14:     **end for**
15:     **return** l^*
16: **end procedure**

Finally the proper l is the one with the minimum error of prediction (line 12). We name this method *leave-one-out algorithm*.

5   Evaluation

In this section, we present the results of some experiments that we performed on real-world business data set to evaluate the performance of our proposed method. The evaluation is done based on the effectiveness metric; that is, the prediction accuracy on the target-period's predicted revenue. We next describe our data set and experimental setup.

5.1   Data Set Description

The data set we use consists of 11 periods of real business pipeline data. The period here refers to a fiscal quarter. For each period, we are given aggregated deal records whose target closing date is the end of the particular quarter. Each period spans 13 weeks before the target quarter starts and goes forward until 2 weeks after the quarter ends, making the total of 28 weekly data for each period.

As mentioned earlier, a deal may go through several stages throughout its lifecycle in the pipeline. In the given data, each weekly record consists of total deal values for each stages (denoted as *current pipeline value*) as well as the value that turns out to be in won (denoted as *win contribution value*) by the end of the quarter. The prediction task is to predict, for any given week given this week's current pipeline value, the win stage's pipeline value of the final week.

5.2   Experimental Setup

From the 11 available quarters, we use the first 9 historical ones as training data and the remaining two as testing data. Testing is conducted for each weekly record, where only the current value of the pipeline is given. Note that the method we propose aims at predicting the growth curve of each week's win contribution value to the final win value. Thus, we apply two methods to estimate the win contribution value from the current pipeline value.

The first method we use is to compute the average rate of training data and then apply it to the testing data for prediction. Specifically, for a particular week, we check the training period data of the same week. For each stage, a conversion rate can be calculated via dividing the contribution value by the current pipeline value. Then the average rate is used to convert the testing period's pipeline current value to win contribution value. Finally, the DCM is applied to predict the period-end win value. The combination of this average ratio and our two models are denoted as *Avg-DCM*.

The second method, instead of computing the average, uses regression to predict the conversion rate. Specifically, to predict the conversion rate of a particular week, we fit a curve on the same week of all historical periods. Then, this curve is used to predict the next point, which is the conversion rate of the target period. This method combined with ours is denoted as *CF-DCM*.

Lastly, instead of using our models, we can purely apply curve-fitting in predicting the final win value. Firstly, we use curve fitting to predict the conversion rate as described above. Then, for each week, a growth rate can be calculated by dividing the final win value by that week's win contribution value. Now, applying the same curve-fitting technique, we can predict the growth rate of the target period. Finally, the sales win value is estimated by multiplying the current pipeline value by estimated conversion rates and growth rates. This method is denoted as *CurveFit*.

In evaluation, we use the relative error rate as our metric. Formally, let y denote the real value while y' denote the predicted value. The relative error is defined as $e_{rel} = \frac{|y-y'|}{y}$.

5.3   Results

In this section, we present the experiment results. Particularly, two sets of experiments are conducted and reported. In first one, we aim at evaluating the performance of the proposed models in a scenario where the actual win-contribution value (with 100 % accuracy) is provided. In second case, the goal is to evaluate the performance in a scenario where the win-contribution value is predicted by some other method. We next discuss the two scenarios in more detail.

Scenario I: Win Rate Is Given. As mentioned in Sect. 1, the pipeline value forecast consists of two steps: (i) win-contribution prediction (conversion prediction) and (ii) win-value growth prediction. Our model focuses on the second part.

In this experiment, we use the real win-contributions and testify its performance in growth prediction.

There are four baselines used for comparison. The first one uses only the historical data and completely ignores the current data, denoted as *History-only (HO)*. The second baseline, denoted as *History-combine (HC)*, simply adds the new data into the historical one, and fits a curve on this merged data set. The third one, denoted as *History-replace (HR)*, replaces the old data of the same time unit with the newly available ones. Thus, the combined life cycle consists of new data by current week and historical data for unknown weeks. Then a polynomial curve is fitted. Finally, we apply the curve-fitting method, denoted as *Ideal-CurveFit (ICF)*.

Table 2 shows the average error rate for different departments. Because of data confidentiality, we anonymize the real department name, and call departments *Dept X* instead, where X is a number. As can be seen, our DCM method outperforms all other methods in all departments except for Dept 3. In dept 3, all history-based methods achieve the top-3 performance. In this department, although the target period has a similar final win value, its early data points are different, which misleads the DCM and let it give a wrong prediction. Nevertheless, the difference is quite small. Apart from the department's impact, we next explore the impact of time in the prediction accuracy. Figure 7 shows the error rate of all evaluated methods with regards to different times. As can be seen, the error of DCM decreases as time proceeds. This scenario can be expected and justified for two reasons. Firstly, when the time is closer to the period end, there is less fluctuations in the data, and thus it is easier to predict. Secondly, as time moves forward, more data is available, and thus the prediction can be improved. Also, we observe that the curve-fitting has an error curve far above other methods, and the error fluctuates a lot. This scenario suggests the vulnerability of curve fitting to data noise. Another observation is that the three history-based methods (HO, HC, HR) display a stable performance that is independent of time. As shown earlier in Sect. 3, the latter part of the curve is based on history only and therefore the prediction does not change too much as time goes forward.

Scenario II: Win Rate Is Predicted. In this experiment, we aim at evaluating its performance in the real scenario, i.e., do the forecast with estimated win-contribution/conversion values. We apply two methods for estimating the win-contribution values. First, we compute the average rate of training data and then apply it to the test data for prediction. Specifically, for a particular week, we check the training period data of the same week. For each stage, a conversion rate can be calculated via dividing the contribution value by the current pipeline value. Then, the average rate is used to convert the testing period's pipeline current value to win contribution value. The second method applies the curve-fitting to estimate the current one. Particularly, we denote the first method as *Avg-DCM* and the second one as *CF-DCM*.

Table 2. Evaluation results in Win-Rate-Given Scenario

Department	Method				
	DCM	HO	HC	HR	ICF
Dept 1	**0.162**	0.292	0.292	0.293	0.241
Dept 2	**0.256**	0.423	0.423	0.422	1.120
Dept 3	0.421	**0.402**	0.403	0.408	0.835
Dept 4	**0.335**	0.384	0.384	0.387	0.804
Dept 5	**0.089**	0.227	0.227	0.226	0.132
Dept 6	**0.114**	0.200	0.200	0.201	0.313
Dept 7	**0.114**	0.143	0.143	0.142	0.487
Dept 8	**0.732**	1.094	1.094	1.100	0.837
Dept 9	**0.115**	0.240	0.240	0.239	0.395
Dept 10	**0.194**	0.416	0.416	0.416	0.231
Dept 11	**0.305**	0.689	0.690	0.692	0.305
Dept 12	**0.171**	0.284	0.284	0.285	0.396
Total	**0.251**	0.399	0.400	0.401	0.508

Table 3 displays the experimental results. For the sake of completeness, we also report the performance of DCM in Scenario I where the win rate is given (denoted as *WRG-DCM*) here. As can be observed, the CF-DCM method achieves the lowest error rate in all departments among all methods in the real scenario. The better performance of CF-DCM compared to Avg-DCM suggests the contribution of curve fitting in predicting conversion rates. Averaging over all departments, the Avg-DCM has a better performance than CurveFit, indicating the higher importance of growth prediction than conversion-rate estimates

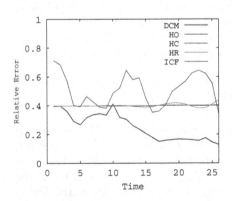

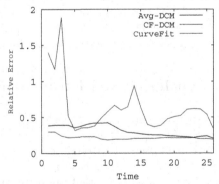

Fig. 7. Time impact in Win-Rate-Given Scenario

Fig. 8. Time impact in Win-Rate-Predicted Scenario

Table 3. Evaluation results in Win-Rate-Predicted Scenario

Department	Avg-DCM	CF-DCM	CurveFit	WRG-DCM
Dept 1	0.186	**0.105**	0.192	0.162
Dept 2	0.347	0.287	1.370	**0.256**
Dept 3	0.539	**0.315**	0.850	0.421
Dept 4	0.423	0.413	2.213	**0.335**
Dept 5	0.191	0.134	0.097	**0.088**
Dept 6	0.159	0.248	0.389	**0.114**
Dept 7	0.115	0.117	0.439	**0.114**
Dept 8	0.863	**0.352**	0.710	0.732
Dept 9	0.151	0.140	0.350	**0.115**
Dept 10	0.259	**0.150**	0.207	0.193
Dept 11	0.382	**0.224**	0.416	0.305
Dept 12	0.105	**0.101**	0.270	0.171
Total	0.310	**0.215**	0.625	0.251

in forecasting pipeline value. Another interesting observation is that the WRG-DCM outperforms the CF-DCM in half of our departments, and only achieves the second lowest error in all departments. A possible reason is the "noisy bump" in the data. In the records, the real win-contribution value may suddenly increase in some time and then decrease for the next time period. The can be attributed to either a data entry error or to the change of target closing date for some big opportunity/opportunities. In either case, such sudden jump misleads the ideal DCM, resulting in a higher prediction value and thus lets it end ends with a worse performance on average.

We also show the time impact on the forecasted performance in Fig. 8. Again, we can see the decreasing trend of all three methods with the proceeding of time. The CF-DCM shows the lowest error in the whole time line. We do observe that the CurveFit's relatively high error, especially at early stages. This demonstrates the robustness of our method in handling highly uncertain data.

6   Conclusion and Future Work

Services sales forecasting is different from traditional one as the pipeline is dynamic. At any given time point, some opportunities in the pipeline may reach an outcome (win or loss) and new ones may be identified and added. For more accurate prediction, a forecasting method should not only consider predicting the conversion/wining of current opportunities, but also need to predict the future pipeline growth. In this paper, we formulate the sales growth prediction as a dynamic curve fitting problem that combines historical data with the currently available data. The key challenge lies in how to combine the two aforementioned data sets to capture future pipeline growth. We introduced a discrete-constraint method (DCM) that enforces similarity of the new model to the historical one by keeping some parameters fixed during learning. As our experiments showed, the DCM achieved best performance among multiple methods.

The current method treats all historical pipeline data equally. For future work, we may add different importance factors to different records simulating the possible seasonality. Alternatively, it may be a good approach to collect more data about the context and use the contextual similarity to determine such importance factors.

References

1. Arunraj, N.S., Ahrens, D.: A hybrid seasonal autoregressive integrated moving average and quantile regression for daily food sales forecasting. IJPE **170**, 321–335 (2015)
2. Arunraj, N.S., Ahrens, D., Fernandes, M.: Application of SARIMAX model to forecast daily sales in food retail industry. IJORIS **7**(2), 1–21 (2016)
3. Aye, G.C., Balcilar, M., Gupta, R., Majumdar, A.: Forecasting aggregate retail sales: the case of South Africa. IJPE **160**, 66–79 (2015)
4. Box, G.E., Jenkins, G.M., Reinsel, G.C., Ljung, G.M.: Time Series Analysis: Forecasting and Control. Wiley, Hoboken (2015)
5. Bratina, D., Faganel, A.: Forecasting the primary demand for a beer brand using time series analysis. Organizacija **41**(3), 116–124 (2008)
6. Carman, S., Strong, R., Chandra, A., Oh, S., Spangler, S., Anderson, L., Bernard, J.J.: Predictive value of comments in the service engagement process. ASIST **49**, 1–6 (2012)
7. De Gooijer, J.G., Hyndman, R.J.: 25 years of time series forecasting. IJF **22**(3), 443–473 (2006)
8. Dugan, M.T., Shriver, K.A., Silhan, P.A.: How to forecast income statement items for auditing purposes. JBF **13**(2), 22 (1994)
9. Gajananan, K., Megahed, A., N.T., Abe, M., Smith, M.: A top-down pricing algorithm for IT service contracts using lower level service data. In: SCC. IEEE (2016, to appear)
10. Greenia, D.B., Qiao, M., Akkiraju, R.: A win prediction model for it outsourcing bids. In: SRII, pp. 39–42. IEEE (2014)
11. Hasin, M.A.A., Ghosh, S., Shareef, M.A.: An ANN approach to demand forecasting in retail trade in Bangladesh. IJTEF **2**(2), 154 (2011)
12. Kong, J., Martin, G.: A backpropagation neural network for sales forecasting. In: Neural Networks, vol. 2, pp. 1007–1011. IEEE (1995)
13. Lee, M.H., Hamzah, N.A.: Calendar variation model based on ARIMAX for forecasting sales data with Ramadhan effect. In: Proceedings of the RCSS, pp. 349–361 (2010)
14. Lee, W.I., Chen, C.W., Chen, K.H., Chen, T.H., Liu, C.C.: A comparative study on the forecast of fresh food sales using logistic regression, moving average and BPNN methods. JMST **20**(2), 142–152 (2012)
15. Luxhøj, J.T., Riis, J.O., Stensballe, B.: A hybrid econometric–neural network modeling approach for sales forecasting. IJPE **43**(2), 175–192 (1996)

16. Megahed, A., Gajananan, K., Abe, M., Jiang, S., Smith, M., Nakamura, T.: Pricing it services deals: a more agile top-down approach. In: Barros, A., Grigori, D., Narendra, N.C., Dam, H.K. (eds.) ICSOC 2015. LNCS, vol. 9435, pp. 461–473. Springer, Heidelberg (2015)
17. Megahed, A., Ren, G.J., Firth, M.: Modeling business insights into predictive analytics for the outcome of it service contracts. In: SCC, pp. 515–521. IEEE (2015)
18. Nezhad, H.R., Greenia, D.B., Nakamura, T., Akkiraju, R.: Health identification and outcome prediction for outsourcing services based on textual comments. In: SCC, pp. 155–162 (2014)
19. O'Donovan, T.M.: Short Term Forecasting: An Introduction to the Box-Jenkins Approach. Wiley, New York (1983)
20. Ramos, P., Santos, N., Rebelo, R.: Performance of state space and ARIMA models for consumer retail sales forecasting. RCIM **34**, 151–163 (2015)
21. Shukla, M., Jharkharia, S.: Applicability of ARIMA models in wholesale vegetable market: an investigation. IJISSCM **6**(3), 105–119 (2013)
22. Winters, P.R.: Forecasting sales by exponentially weighted moving averages. Manag. Sci. **6**(3), 324–342 (1960)
23. Yan, J., Zhang, C., Zha, H., Gong, M., Sun, C., Huang, J., Chu, S., Yang, X.: On machine learning towards predictive sales pipeline analytics. In: AAAI (2015)
24. Yin, P., Motahari Nezhad, H.R., Megahed, A., Nakamura, T.: A progress advisor for IT service engagements. In: SCC, pp. 592–599. IEEE (2015)

Clustering and Labeling IT Maintenance Tickets

Suman Roy[1(✉)], Durga Prasad Muni[1(✉)], John-John Yeung Tack Yan[1],
Navin Budhiraja[1], and Fabien Ceiler[2]

[1] Infosys Ltd., # 44 Electronics City, Hosur Road, Bangalore 560 100, India
{Suman_Roy,DurgaPrasad_Muni,Yeung_Chiang,Navin_Budhiraja}@infosys.com
[2] École Polytechnique, Route de Saclay, 91128 Palaiseau, France
fabien_cell@hotmail.com

Abstract. The goal of a Service System in an organization is to deliver
uninterrupted service towards achieving business success. Ticketing system is an example of a Service System which is responsible for handling
huge volumes of tickets generated by large enterprise IT (Information
Technology) infrastructure components and ensuring smooth operation.
Instead of manual screening one needs to extract information automatically from them to gain insights to improve operational efficiency. To
ensure better operation we propose a framework to cluster incident tickets based on their textual context that can eliminate manual classification of them, which is labor intensive and costly. Further we label each
of the clusters by generating meaningful keywords as logical itemsets,
extracting candidate labels from Wikipedia articles, and finally scoring
each of labels against each cluster. These labels can reflect an adequate
and concise specification of each cluster. Further we experiment our approach with industrial ticket data from three different domains and report
on the learned experience. We believe that our framework for clustering and labeling will enable enterprises to prioritize the issues in their
IT infrastructure and improve the reliability and availability of their
services.

Keywords: Services in organizations · Tickets · Fixed field · Free-form
field · Distance metric · Jaccard distance · Cosine distance · Clustering ·
Label · n-gram · Scoring function

1 Introduction

A Service System (SS) (or customer service system, CSS) is a configuration of
technology and organizational networks that is designed to deliver services satisfying the wants, or aspirations of customers (users) (quoted from Wikipedia).
Ticketing system is an example of a Service System in organizations which

---

This work was done when the Fabien Ceiler did his internship with Infosys during
June-Aug.'15.

© Springer International Publishing Switzerland 2016
Q.Z. Sheng et al. (Eds.): ICSOC 2016, LNCS 9936, pp. 829–845, 2016.
DOI: 10.1007/978-3-319-46295-0_58

uses tracking tools for overseeing troubleshooting and maintaining the network. Dozens of tickets are raised by users in an organization on the ticketing system for the purpose of resolving their problems while using local area network or, individual machines or, internet. A ticketing system tries to minimize the business impact of incidents by addressing the concerns of the raised tickets. Any prior knowledge which can be obtained by mining ticket data can help in quick redressal of the problem. The incident tickets record symptom description of issues, as well as details on the incident resolution using a range of structured fields such as date, resolver, affected servers and services and a couple of free-form entries outlining the description/summary of issues, note by users/administrators etc. If the occurred incident tickets in a specific IT environment are grouped into different clusters they can provide a better understanding on the types of issues present in the system. This can also enable the system to classify the alerts, incidents or requests. This can lead to efficient ticket management that would be capable of dealing with the most critical problems or the most pervasive incident types. Moreover, one may like to read off a concise specification of each cluster as its intended meaning which can be accomplished by generating meaningful labels and assigning them to it. Further the labels can be used to detect the most critical and frequent issues.

However, clustering of incident tickets and labeling of them can be quite challenging for various reasons. There would be a large number of tickets raised in the system (of the order of thousands in a year for a large IT environment), which makes their manual labeling practically impossible. The description of a ticket may contain a mixture of human and machine generated texts (from the monitoring system) with a very problem-specific vocabulary. Also the textual description of the tickets can differ from one IT environment to another IT environment as they are authored by different teams who use different monitoring systems and lingua. It may not be also immediate to recover a precise and short description of a cluster without some labels.

In this work we propose a framework for clustering and labeling tickets based on their customized description and textual contents. We consider a particular format of ticket data which is motivated by description of tickets maintained by different infrastructure and support teams of Infosys. The ticket data in spreadsheet format contains two kinds of fields: fixed and free-form. Fixed fields are customized (can be machine-supported) and record some particular information about the ticket: its identifier, its category and sub-category, its priority, time of closing the ticket, location where the ticket was raised, the user's name, the user's department, incident type, application name etc. We choose only some of these fields as other fields may not be useful for clustering purposes. We also deal with only one column entry of free field which contains a brief description about the incident/request concerning the ticket (written down by the user). It is possible to extract useful keywords from this description using shallow parsing techniques. We use this mixture of information from both free fields and fixed field for creating profiles for tickets. We define a new distance metric by taking a weighted combination of Jaccard distance for fixed fields and Cosine

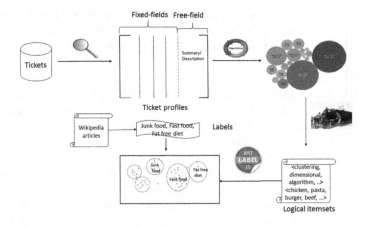

Fig. 1. A framework of clustering and labeling tickets

distance for free field and use this metric to compute distance between two tickets. Finally, we apply a suitable clustering algorithm to partition the tickets into different clusters. For labeling purposes of these clusters we extract semantically related keywords associated with each cluster by finding logical itemsets [11] for each cluster. The keywords appearing in a cluster may contain some noise as some of them may not occur frequently and as such they may not portray much meaningful information. Logical itemset helps in this regard by finding relevant semantic concepts in terms of frequently co-occurring keywords for each cluster. Next we generate labels by querying Wikipedia articles and selecting relevant Wikipedia titles as candidate labels. This is followed by computing an appropriate scoring function to measure the semantic similarity between a label and a logical itemset. Lastly we rank the labels using the scoring function and assign appropriate labels to each cluster. We also experiment our framework with data from different domains and report on the lessons we learn. A schematic diagram of this framework is shown in Fig. 1.

Related Work: Recently there have been some work on classification of incident tickets using unsupervised learning techniques like clustering. In [19] the authors have proposed a technique called TroubleMiner to mine trouble tickets and classify them using clustering. This technique holds promise to be applied to trouble tickets from the concerned network for finding out a pattern in network incidents and maintenance activities. An approach for classifying incident data based on clustering has been proposed in [16]. The authors employ two-stage clustering involving graph clustering and topic modeling, followed by hierarchical clustering or active learning. The method is evaluated in terms of manual labeling effort, prediction quality and efficiency on three real-world datasets. In another work [15] the authors propose a framework to cluster alerts and incidents on their textual content using unsupervised learning. Our work differs from the last two clustering efforts in the sense that our clustering technique takes into account both fixed field entries and free-form textual contents that appear in the incident tickets, and use a distance metric by combining both the Jaccard distance metric for the former and Cosine distance metric for the latter. However, none of above techniques do any labeling of the generated clusters.

Nonetheless there are several attempts to automatically label topic models. In [20], a probabilistic approach has been proposed to automatically label multinomial topic models. As an experiment the authors use this method to automatically label document clusters. They use k-medoied algorithm to cluster SIGMOD abstracts and use their topic labeling method to label the clusters by estimating a multinomial word distribution for each cluster based on maximum likelihood estimator. Our approach is different from these in the sense we represent each cluster by a collection of logical itemsets of keywords which provides a noise free and semantically meaningful representation of clusters. There are other methods of automatic topic labeling, *e.g.*, Lau *et al.*'s approach [13] for automatically labelling topics by generating candidate labels from the top-ranking topic terms using several measures such as point-wise mutual information, student t-test, Dice's co-efficient, Pearson's chi-square test, log likelihood ratio etc.; Basave *et al.*'s method [2] of automatic labeling of topics learned from Twitter as a summarisation problem; Aletras *et la.*'s unsupervised graph-based method [1] of textual labeling for topics and to name a few.

2   Mining IT Maintenance Tickets

Fig. 2. Different steps of NLP Processing

We collected tickets from the repository maintained by different business units. All these tickets have similar schema. These tickets usually consist of two fields [9,19], fixed and free formed. Fixed-fields are customized and inserted in a menu-driven fashion. Example of such items are the ticket's identifier, the time the ticket is raised or closed on the system or, if a ticket is of incident or request in nature. Various other information are captured through these fixed fields such as category of a ticket, employee number of the user raising the ticket etc., and also maintenance team performance parameters like response time, resolution time of the ticket etc. There is no standard value for free-form fields. The concern/issue for raising a ticket is captured as "call description" or "summary" as free-formed texts, - it can be a just a sentence that summarizes the problem reported in it, or it may contain a detailed description of the incident. By seeing freely generated part of tickets, administrators can get to know about unforeseen network incidents and can also obtain a much richer classification. In this section we describe ways to mine tickets that would help group the tickets into clusters [8,19]. We introduce a simple model of tickets based on vector of words. Let $\mathcal{T}$ be the set of n tickets, *i.e.*, $n = |\mathcal{T}|$. We shall select few features which can be extracted from the corresponding element $T \in \mathcal{T}$ and would best describe the ticket T.

2.1   Model of Tickets Based on Entries in Fixed Fields

Profile Selection for Fixed Fields: Each ticket in the repository contains a large amount of structured information in the form of fixed fields. For a fixed field entry we shall select an item as a feature in the profile. For some of the items we choose category representation, *i.e.*, we represent the element by the exact entry in the field in question; examples of which are category, sub-category, priority of the ticket. When some of the fields appear as Response Time (min), Time taken to Resolve (min) etc. we use *bucketed representation*. That is, we find out the range of values for them, use these ranges to define three buckets like, 'hi', 'med' and 'low' and put an appropriate entry in the proper bucket. For example, the range of Response time can vary from 0 min to 15960 mins. However most of tickets are responded within 100–1000 min. We choose three buckets as follows: low: 0–99, med: 100–1000, and hi: 1001–1600. We do not consider some of the fields like region (country name), location, Analyst, Customer name, Customer's project code, Analyst's name, Analyst's project etc. as they have very little to do with trouble tickets[1]. Similarly, customer's project code, customer's identification number etc. do not play any role with the nature of issues of trouble tickets. Finally, we consider only closed tickets having a value of 1 in the field Closed, and 0 in Open. We discard tickets from our consideration which have 1 in Open field and 0 in Closed field (we consider tickets which have been resolved fully and not left open), and 1 in both Open and Closed fields (this is ambiguous).

A Vector Representation: Finally a ticket can be modeled as a row vector of a fixed length which depend on the domain they are appearing. While some of the elements will contain categorical elements, the rest will have representation in the form of buckets.

2.2   Model of Tickets Based on Entries in Free-Form Fields

Keyword Selection for Profiling: Now we select features from the description of the free form field (listed as call description or summary) in tickets using keywords/keyphrases (more generally n-grams). We assume a free field to contain a succinct problem description associated with a ticket. We consider the collection of summary of tickets for keyword extraction purposes. Mainly we shall use NLP and Statistical Methods to automatically extract keywords [4,18,23] from these texts. In the beginning we perform lemmatization of the words in the summary of tickets. Then we use Stanford NLP tool [17] to parse the useful contents in the summary of the tickets and tag them as tokens. Then we use the tool to perform the PoS tagging of the tokens. One can recognize named entities by identifying the first upper-case letters. Next we divide the tokens by their POS tags and mark only nouns as potential keywords. Next we set up some rules for removing stopwords. Also we eliminate tokens with low frequency (when their

---

[1] The domain experts' comments play an important role in choosing the fixed fields.

occurrence is less than a threshold). Next, we compute the TF∗IDF[2] for these keyword candidates. We discard those words whose TF∗IDF score is less than $1/5^{th}$ of the maximum value of the same in the selected list. Further we shrink the list of keywords by studying metrics that reflect the degree of association between a keyword and some particular characteristic of the ticket, e.g., it may be application name or category or sub-category etc. (fxed fields). By this, we try to identify the keywords which are strongly correlated with ticket charac- teristics. To measure this we use ϕ-coefficient (ϕ), Cosine (IS), and Jaccard (ζ). They are computed as follows [25].

Let w_i be the ith keyword in the selected list so far after pre-processing and let c_j be j-th category (we consider this particular characteristic in our discussion) in the list of categories for the tickets. Let $P(w_i, c_j)$ denote the probability that the w_ith keyword appear in the free form field of a ticket which has a category c_j. Further, let $P(w_i|c_j)$ be the probability of choosing w_ith keyword in the free-form field of a ticket given that the ticket belongs to category c_j. Finally, $P(w_i)$ is the probability of choosing w_ith keyword and $P(c_j)$ is the probability of choosing a ticket of c_j category. Then an association metric $\alpha(w_i, c_j)$ are defined as follows in Table 1, where α can be ϕ, or IS or ζ. Moreover, we use the metric to rank the keywords in descending order. We pick a predefined number of top-ranking keywords (say 100), call this set $\mathcal{K}_1$. This will give us the unigram keywords. The selection of keywords are validated using entropy [12] as follows. Let η_j^k be the number of occurrences of the keyword w_j in the categry c_k, then the relative frequency of w_j in category c_k is $\nu_j^k = \frac{\eta_j^k}{\sum_k \eta_j^k}$. Correspondingly the entropy of the word w_j is given by $H(w_j) = -\sum_{k=1}^{r} \nu_j^k \lg \nu_j^k$. If the word w_j appears only in one category then the entropy $H_{\min}$ is minimal, that is, equal to 0. Conversely the entropy is maximal $H_{\max}$ if w_j appears in all the categories with the same frequency, that is w_j is a not a good feature to represent the ticket. Further we evaluate the following metric:

$$ECCD(w_j, c_k) = \{P(w_j|c_k) - P(w_j|\bar{c}_k)\} \times \frac{H_{\max} - H(w_j)}{H_{\max}}.$$

Recall $P(w_j|c_k)$ (respectively $P(w_j|\bar{c}_k)$) denote the probability of occurrence of keyword w_j in a ticket belonging to category c_k (respectively other categories) which can be computed as in [12]. Using this metric we can check whether our chosen keywords have low values for this metric.

In the next step we choose keyphrases consisting of bigrams and trigrams. Using the PoS tagging as before we collect adjacent nouns (in a sentence) having length at most three. Then we choose some of the heuristics [22] like All Words Heuristic, Any Word Heuristic to select the final set $\mathcal{K}_2$ of keyphrases. The final list of keywords and keyphrases is $\mathcal{K} = \mathcal{K}_1 \cup \mathcal{K}_2$.

---

[2] TF∗IDF is a popular metric in data mining literature [14].

Table 1. Different metrics capturing the degree of association between a word w_i and a category c_j

No	Measure	Formula
1	ϕ-co-efficient (ϕ)	$\dfrac{P(w_i,c_j)-P(w_i)P(c_j)}{\sqrt{P(w_i)P(c_j)(1-P(w_i))(1-P(c_j))}}$
2	Cosine (IS)	$\dfrac{P(w_i,c_j)}{\sqrt{P(w_i)P(c_j)}}$
3	Jaccard (ζ)	$\dfrac{P(w_i,c_j)}{P(w_i)+P(c_j)-P(w_i,c_j)}$

Vector of Keywords: We can model a trouble ticket as a vector T, where each element $T(k)$ represents the importance or the weight of a keyword, k with respect to the trouble ticket. One needs to choose a suitable weighing scheme to best describe these tickets. We shall use Document Frequency (DF) of a keyword (to be discussed) as its weight. Note the DF μ_{df} is the number of tickets containing the keyphrase [24].

Finally, we can combine the vector representation of a ticket both for entries in the fixed fields and n-grams (uni/bi/tri-grams) from free field to get a combined vector representation for a ticket.

3 Clustering Tickets

Given a vector representation of each ticket in the collection T, our mining algorithm will partition them using a suitable clustering algorithm. For this, we need to compute the distance between two tickets.

3.1 Distance Metric Between a Pair of Clusters

We consider a hybrid approach for computing the distance metric. When we profile tickets based on fixed fields we shall use Jaccard distance [7,14] to calculate the distance between two tickets. Consider the profiles of two tickets as $T = (x_1,\ldots,x_k,x_{k+1},\ldots,x_n)$ and $T' = (y_1,\ldots,y_k,y_{k+1},\ldots,y_n)$. Let the projection of tickets on fixed-fields be as follows: $T^{\text{fix}} = (x_1,\ldots,x_k)$ and $T'^{\text{fix}} = (y_1,\ldots,y_k)$, where elements $x_1,\ldots,x_k$ and $y_1,\ldots,y_k$ correspond to fixed-field entries in tickets T and T' respectively. We use the bag (multi-set) representation for these tickets as, $T_s^{\text{fix}} = \{x_1,\ldots,x_k\}$ and $T_s'^{\text{fix}} = \{y_1,\ldots,y_k\}$. Then we calculate Jaccard distance as $d_J(T^{\text{fix}},T'^{\text{fix}}) = 1 - \frac{|T_s^{\text{fix}} \cap T_s'^{\text{fix}}|}{|T_s^{\text{fix}} \cup T_s'^{\text{fix}}|}$.

For profiling tickets based on the free-form field we shall adopt a different weighing scheme. Given a set of n keyphrases we model a ticket T^{free} (projection of T on keyphrase elements chosen from the free-form field) as a row-vector having m elements, where each element represents the weight (importance) of a keyphrase wrt the ticket. As DF gives higher weights to keyphrases that appear in more tickets, the clustering algorithm will also provide higher emphasis to more frequent keyphrases. For this reason, we choose DF to be the weight of a keyphrase in our scheme. For a keyphrase w, if its DF is μ_{df} then $T(w) = \mu_{df}$. Given two ticket T^{free} and T'^{free} represented by row vectors $(x_1,\ldots,x_n)$ and $(y_1,\ldots,y_n)$, which are the weights corresponding to keyphrases extracted out of free form field, the Cosine distance [5,14] is given by $d_C(T^{\text{free}},T'^{\text{free}}) = \frac{\Sigma_i^n x_i y_i}{(\sqrt{\Sigma_i^n x_i^2})(\sqrt{\Sigma_i^n y_i^2})}$.

Now we create an aggregated profile of a ticket by combining profiles from both fixed field entries and keyphrases from free form fields. That is, if a ticket T has m elements coming from fixed fields and n elements arising out of n keyphrases chosen from free form field then T will be represented as a $(m + n)$-dimensional row vector. In such a case we combine both Jaccard distance and Cosine distance to define a distance metric on $T \times T$. If $(x_1, \ldots, x_l)$ and $(y_1, \ldots, y_k)$ are elements coming from weights corresponding to fixed fields and free form fields respectively for ticket T, and $(x'_1, \ldots, x'_l)$ and $(y'_1, \ldots, y'_k)$ for ticket T' then the combined distance from two tickets is given by

$$d(T, T') = \alpha * d_J(T(x_1, \ldots, x_l), T'(x'_1, \ldots, x'_l)) + (1 - \alpha)* $$
$$d_C(T(y_1, \ldots, y_k), T'(y'_1, \ldots, y'_k)),$$

where $\alpha \in (0, 1)$ is a weighing factor. Need to check $d(T, T')$ is indeed a distance metric for any two tickets T and T'. Clearly, $d(T, T') \geq 0$. Also, $d(T, T') = 0$ if and only if $T = T'$ given the fact that Jaccard and Cosine distances are distance metrics. Also easy to see that d is symmetric: $d(T, T') = d(T, T')$. We check the transitivity property for three tickets T, T' and T'', which we leave as an exercise. We can choose a suitable value of α. If there are k_{fix} elements corresponding to fixed field and k_{free} keyphrases chosen from free form texts then we set $\alpha' = \frac{k_{fix}}{k_{fix}+k_{free}}$. Now select $\alpha = \max\{0.1, \alpha'\}$. The parameter α provides appropriate weightage to fixed fields entires and keyphrases representing free field. If there are very few fixed field items we account for 10 % contribution from them for distance computation.

3.2 Grouping the Tickets

As k-means algorithm [14] works well when the data set are in Euclidean space we use a variant of K-means algorithm for clustering tickets in non-Euclidean domain. This is Partitioning Around Medoid (PAM or k-medoid) algorithm [10], which pre-supposes a distant metric on the objects (tickets in our case). In this approach, for finding k clusters, one maintains a representative object called medoid, for each cluster. A *medoid* of a cluster is the centrally most located object in the cluster. After the selection of k medoids, the rest of the objects are grouped with the medoid to which they are the closest. To be precise, let O_j be a non-selected object so far and O_m be a selected medoid. Then O_j is said to belong to the cluster represented by O_m if $d(O_j, O_m) = \min_{O_i} d(O_j, O_i)$, where minimum is taken over all the medoids O_i. PAM algorithm accepts the distance between each pair of objects. The goodness of clustering in PAM is measured by the average of distances between an object and the medoid of its cluster. In the classical PAM algorithm, one begins with arbitrarily selected k medoids. Then in each step a selected object O_m is swapped with a non-selected O_p, if it results in the improvement of the quality of clustering [21].

We deviate from this algorithm to suit our purpose in which the centroid update in K-means is replaced by a medoid update algorithm. Once we choose an initial set k of clusters with their representative medoids we look for a potentially better medoid for each cluster. Suppose O_m is the medoid in cluster $\mathcal{C}_m$. Fix a non-selected object O_p in the cluster and we seek to verify if O_m can be swapped with O_p. Let O_j be another non-selected object in $\mathcal{C}_m$. Also suppose O_k^j is the medoid of the cluster $\mathcal{C}_k$ that is closest to O_j without O_p and O_m. Now we compute the cost of swap between O_m and O_p. We consider two cases differently.

Case 1: Suppose that O_j is closer to O_k^j than O_p, i.e., $d(O_j, O_p) \geq d(O_j, O_k^j)$. Then the cost of swap is given by $\text{Cost}_{jmp} = d(O_j, O_k^j) - d(O_j, O_m)$.

Case 2: This time we assume O_j is closer to O_m than O_k^j, i.e., $d(O_j, O_p) < d(O_j, O_k^j)$. Then the cost of swap is $\text{Cost}_{jmp} = d(O_j, O_p) - d(O_j, O_m)$.

We now compute the total cost $\text{TCost}_{mp} = \sum_{O_j \neq O_p} \text{Cost}_{jmp}$ for all objects O_j other than O_p in the cluster $\mathcal{C}_m$ and find the minimum of them. If the minimum turns out to be negative for some p^*, that is $p^* = argmin_p \text{TCost}_{mp}$, we move the medoid of cluster $\mathcal{C}_m$ from O_m to O_{p^*}. Otherwise the medoid is unchanged. This is done for all the clusters. We can re-arrange the clusters with the new medoids and iterate this until a stopping criteria is reached in which case there is no improvement in the goodness of clusters or the latter has reached a pre-defined threshold value (which is a small negative value).

4   Logical Itemsets for Each Cluster

In this section we shall identify a set of keyphrases representing clusters in terms of loigcal itemsets. In [11] Kumar *et al.* proposed a framework called Logical Itemset Mining (LISM) that attempts to discover a logical itemset (latent customer intent/semantic concept) from a bag of items treated as mixture-of, projections-of, latent customer intent. LISM enjoys certain advantages over FIS (frequent itemset) in terms of discovery of high quality, noise-free and latent data set. Also we prefer LISM over traditional topic models such as LDA [3] because LDA is primarily computed based on term frequency of a term in the document, but clusters cannot be associated with such weights - a keyphrase is either present or is not present in a cluster and also LDA requires the user to specify apriori the number of concepts to be discovered which is hard in the text domain. We modify the original method of LISM proposed in [11] by associating a probability distribution of keyphrases with each logical itemset and generating a collection of logical itemsets for each cluster (analogous to bag of words in [11]).

Suppose $W = \{w_1, w_2, \ldots, w_n\}$ be the set of keyphrases. Let $\mathcal{C}_1, \ldots, \mathcal{C}_l$ be the collection of clusters formed out of ticket data. Each such cluster $\mathcal{C}_i$ contains keyphrases such as $\{w_1^i, \ldots, w_{l_i}^i\}$. LISM proceeds through stages as follows.

LISM Counting: In the beginning the co-occurrence counts between all pairs of keyphrases is computed in one pass. Recall the characteristic function: $\mathbf{1}_\mathcal{C}(w) = 1$, if $\mathcal{C}$ contains w; 0, otherwise. For a pair of keyphrases $u, v \in W$ the co-occurrence count between them is defined as $\psi(u, v) = \sum_{i=1}^l \mathbf{1}_{\mathcal{C}_i}(u).\mathbf{1}_{\mathcal{C}_i}(v)$. Note

$\psi(u,v) = \psi(v,u)$. Some of the pairs of keyphrases are removed using a threshold value of θ_{cooc}. The marginal count $\psi(u)$ for a keyphrase $u \in W$ is defined as the number of pairs in which the keyphrase u appeared with some other keyphrase in the data: $\psi(u) = \sum_{v \in W, u \neq v} \psi(u,v)$. The total count ψ_0 is defined as the the total number of pairs on which some keyphrase appears with some other keyphrase in the clusters: $\psi_0 = 1/2 \sum_{u \in W} \psi(u)$.

The co-occurrence and marginal probabilities can be computed from these three counts: $P(u,v) = \frac{\psi(u,v)}{\psi_0}$, $P(u) = \frac{\psi(u)}{\psi_0}$.

LISM-Consistency: In this stage the authors remove deceptive high co-occurrence arising out of noise due to mixture-intent, and preserve important low occurrences reflecting important logical connections between pairs of keyphrases. Towards that they work with a suit of metrics related to Co-occurrence Consistency indicating the degree of comparison of actual co-occurrence of a pair of keyphrases with random chance. We shall consider the metric Normalized Pointwise Mutual Information (NPMI) defined as $\phi_{nmi}(u,v) = \frac{\phi_{pmi}(u,v)}{-\log P(u,v)}$ which takes values between 0 and 1 where, $\phi_{pmi}(u,v) = \max\left\{0, \log\left(\frac{P(u,v)}{P(u)P(v)}\right)\right\}$. Some of the pairs of keyphrases are removed whose consistency metric NPMI is below a pre-defined threshold of θ_{consy}. The resulting co-occurrence consistency matrix is used to compute the logical itemset after it is subjected to further reduction of noise.

LISM-Denoise. To further remove noise this denoising algorithm uses co-occurrence consistencies obtained earlier to remove noisy co-occurrence counts and recompute the marginal and total probabilities until the convergence, that is, when the fraction of co-occurrence count becomes zero. The update equation for denoising is given in [11].

LISM-Discovery: At this stage it is assumed that intra logical itemset consistencies are high while inter logical itemset consistencies are low. One draws a co-occurrence consistency graph $\mathcal{G}$ by connecting two vertices u and v if their present co-occurrence consistency is higher than the threshold θ_{consy}. Given this graph a logical itemset is defined as a set of keyphrases $\mathcal{L} = \{w_1, \ldots, w_k\}$ such that each element in the set has a high co-occurrence consistency with all other items in the set. To find the largest logical itemset one seeks to find out the maximal clique in this graph. Although finding maximal clique is NP-hard an approximate polynomial time (in the number of vertices of the graph) algorithm is employed which finds out a maximal clique in all known example of graph. For finding the logical set for each cluster $\mathcal{C}_i$ we project the Co-occurrence Consistency graph $\mathcal{G}$ on the keyphrases appearing in $\mathcal{C}_i$, call this subgraph $\mathcal{G}_{\mathcal{C}_i}$. Then follow the above step for finding the collection of logical itemsets $\{\mathcal{L}_i\}_{h \in \mathbb{N}}$ on $\mathcal{G}_{\mathcal{C}_i}$ for each cluster $\mathcal{C}_i$.

Once a logical itemset $\mathcal{L} = \{w_1, \ldots, w_m\}$ is created we can assign a probability distribution of keyphrases $P(w_i|\mathcal{L})_{w_i \in W}$ such that $\sum_{w_i \in W} P(w_i|\mathcal{L}) = 1$. Set the total probability wrt $\mathcal{L}$ as $\psi_0^{\mathcal{L}} = \frac{1}{2} \sum_{u \in W, u \in \mathcal{L}} \sum_{v \in W, v \in \mathcal{L}} \psi(u,v)$. Given $w_i \in \mathcal{L}$ we have $\psi^{\mathcal{L}}(w_i) = \sum_{v \in W, v \in \mathcal{L}, w_i \neq v} \psi(w_i, v)$. Hence $P(w_i|\mathcal{L}) = \frac{\psi(w_i|\mathcal{L})}{2 \cdot \psi_0^{\mathcal{L}}}$.

5 Automatic Labeling of Clusters

Once a collection of logical itemsets is extracted from a cluster we try to generate semantic labels for each itemset in a manner similar to the approach for generating labels for topic models [20]. These kinds of labels may include words, phrases and sentences.

LISM Labeling. Given a logical itemset $\mathcal{L} = \{w_1, \ldots, w_m\}$ an *itemset label* l for this itemset $\mathcal{L}$ is a sequence of words which is semantically meaningful and cover the latent meaning of $\mathcal{L}$. However we only use phrases (ngrams) as itemset labels in our work. Also we define a *relevance score* of a label *wrt* a logical itemset, $\sigma(l, \mathcal{L})$ as the semantic similarity between the label and the itemset.

Given a logical itemset $\mathcal{L}$ corresponding to a cluster $\mathcal{C}$ the problem of itemset labeling is to identify (1) a set of candidate labels $\{l_1, \ldots, l_k\}$, (2) formulate a scoring function σ and (3) determine the most relevant lable l^* such that $l^* = argmax_{1 \leq i \leq k}\sigma(l_i, \mathcal{L})$.

We can generalize this notion to multiple itemset labels. Let $\Lambda = \{\mathcal{L}_1, \ldots, \mathcal{L}_n\}$ be a set of n logical itemsets corresponding to a cluster $\mathcal{C}$, and $\Gamma = \{l_1, l_2, \ldots, l_m\}$ be a set of candidate itemset labels. Then we wish to select a subset of labels $\Gamma_i \subseteq \Gamma$, where $\Gamma_i = \{l_{i,1}, \ldots, l_{i,m_i}\}$ corresponding to the cluster $\mathcal{C}$ and a ranking function $\rho(l_{i,j}, \mathcal{C})$ for each label $l_{i,j}$ using a relevance scoring function such that $\rho(l_{i,1}, \mathcal{C}) \geq \rho(l_{i,2}, \mathcal{C}) \geq \ldots \geq \rho(l_{i,n_i}, \mathcal{C})$ etc.

Candidate Label Generation. We assume that a vast majority of concepts are encapsulated in Wikipedia articles. Hence we use the titles of relevant Wikipedia articles as label candidates [13]. We choose the top 10 keyphrases (based on their marginal probabilities) from each logical itemset for each cluster. For each of the top 10 keywords, we do an open search on Wikipedia using the Wikipedia web service API. We restrict ourselves to 8 article titles returned from this Wikipedia search for each keyphrase. We consider these titles as primary candidate labels.

Next we extract noun chunks from the primary candidate labels and then for each noun chunk, we create n-grams ($n = \{1, 2, 3\}$). For these unigrams, bigrams and trigrams, we perform a Wikipedia open search to check if the n-gram is a title of a Wikipedia article or not. If it does not exist as an article then we remove the n-gram from the list. In this way, we obtain a set of n-grams as secondary candidate labels. Some of these n-grams are stopwords or are of little relevance to the ticket domain. So, we use RACO lexical association method given in [6] to remove those undesired secondary labels. In RACO (Related Article Conceptual Overlap), Wikipedia's link structure and category membership are considered to obtain the relatedness between the articles. For each primary and secondary label (for which Wikipedia article title is available), all outlinks that exist in the article are obtained. For each outlink, the set of Wikipedia categories are found. The union of the categories of all outlinks of an article is considered as the set of categories related to that article. The RACO similarity $sim_R(a, b)$ between the article a having a primary label and the article b having a secondary label is computed using categories of the articles by the similarity measure of two articles

(Eq. (2) in [6]). The average RACO similarity of a secondary label of an article with respect to all primary labels, that is, $sim_R(b) = \frac{\sum_a sim_R(a,b)}{\sum_a}$, is computed and if it is less than 0.1 then the secondary label is discarded. The remaining secondary labels and all primary labels, meant for a cluster, are considered as the candidate labels for that cluster.

Semantic Relevance Scoring. We adopt a scoring function called "First-order Relevance" [20] to score the generated labels with logical itemsets. If we assume that there is also a multinomial distribution $P(w|l)$ for a given l intuitively it is possible to check how good l a label for a logical itemset $\mathcal{L}$ is. Using the same approach we could define the relevance scoring function of label l wrt a logical itemset $\mathcal{L}$ using the Kullback-Leibler (KL) divergence. Moreover, the authors in [20] use a domain of context Δ as the domain of logical itemset modeling, which in our case will be Wikipedia. The scoring function is formulated as follows.

$$
\begin{aligned}
\sigma(l, \mathcal{L}) &= -\mathcal{D}(\mathcal{L}||l) = -\sum_w P(w|\mathcal{L}) \log \frac{P(w|\mathcal{L})}{P(w|l)} \\
&= \sum_w P(w|\mathcal{L}) \log \frac{P(w,l|\Delta)}{P(w|\Delta)P(l|\Delta)} - \mathcal{D}(\mathcal{L}||\Delta) \\
&\quad - \sum_w P(w|\mathcal{L}) \log \frac{P(w|l,\Delta)}{P(w|l)} \\
&= \sum_w P(w|\mathcal{L})\mathrm{PMI}(w,l|\Delta) - \mathcal{D}(\mathcal{L}||\Delta) + Bias(l,\Delta)
\end{aligned}
$$

The function is decomposed into three parts. As the candidate labels and the logical itemsets are generated from Wikipedia and the summary of tickets respectively, they are statistically independent. Hence $P(w|l, \Delta) = P(w)$ and $P(w|l) = P(w)$. Consequently the bias term evaluates to zero. Further the divergence is identical for all labels for a fixed domain of Wikipedia, hence it can be ignored in ranking labels. Noting that a logical itemset comes with the probability distribution of keyphrases $P(w|\mathcal{L})$ the rest of the entities in the first component can be computed as follows.

$$
P(w, l|\Delta) = \frac{\text{no of Wikipedia articles containing both } w \text{ and } l}{\text{total number of Wikipedia articles}}
$$

$$
P(w|\Delta) = \frac{\text{no of Wikipedia articles containing } w}{\text{total number of Wikipedia articles}}
$$

$$
P(l|\Delta) = \frac{\text{no of Wikipedia articles containing } l}{\text{total number of Wikipedia articles}}
$$

Ranking of a Label. It is possible that a cluster $\mathcal{C}$ is represented by multiple logical itemsets where each itemset can be associated with more than one candidate label. In such a scenario we want to determine the ranking of a candidate label with respect to cluster $\mathcal{C}$. We may pick up the first and the second ranked labels as the final labels of the cluster. Let $\rho(l, \mathcal{C})$ denote the rank of a label wrt the cluster $\mathcal{C}$, where we assume logical itemsets $\mathcal{L}_1, \ldots, \mathcal{L}_k$ correspond to cluster $\mathcal{C}$. Then we compute,

$$
\rho(l, \mathcal{C}) = \frac{\sigma(l, \mathcal{L}_1) + \cdots + \sigma(l, \mathcal{L}_k)}{k}.
$$

6   Experimental Results

Table 2. Statistics of open and closed tickets in the repository

Domain	Total tickets	Open	Closed	% of closed (considered)
Travel	3085	59	3026	98.09
AMD	4508	35	4473	99.22
LANM	65535	8629	56906 (10661 considered)	16.27

In this section we evaluate our clustering and labeling framework on IT maintenance tickets originating from 3 different domains over different periods of time. The domains are Travel request (Travel), Application Maintenance and Development (AMD) and Local Area Network Management (LANM). The tickets across these domains have the same format as described in Sect. 2. These tickets have fixed field entries,- closed and open, which will be marked as 0 or 1 with usual meaning. We decide to drop tickets from our discussion which were 'open' (that is, it contained 1 in the field of open), or which had 1 both in the fields of open and close. Table 2 shows the details of the fraction of tickets considered for further analysis. Given our computing framework we could consider only a maximum of 16.27 % tickets from LANM domain, which suggests we need to use a distributed framework for analyzing larger volume of ticket data. For the experiment we use Dell latitude e7440 machine having i5 dual core 2 GHz configuration with 4 GB RAM on Windows 32 bit system.

6.1   Clustering Tickets

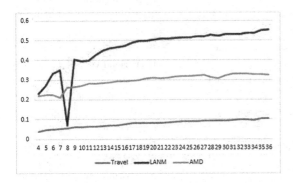

Fig. 3. Silhouette indices for clusters for different domains

While there were not much effort in building the profiles for fixed field entries for the tickets we used Statistical NLP technique for keyword selection. We use different number of elements to create a row vector for a ticket's profile based on fixed fields, 3 for Travel, 3 for AMD and 7 for LANM. Examples of some of these elements are category, sub-category, customer (user) dept, priority of the ticket, Response Time, Time taken to Resolve etc. Next we choose keywords from the free form entry in a ticket which is in the form of a description or summary of a ticket. Once we select the potential candidates for keywords after necessary tokenization and POS tagging as described in Sect. 2.2 we compute the TF*IDF for them. We further removed the words whose TF*IDF is less than 1/5 of the maximum value of the same among the words chosen earlier. Next we use a suitable measure of degree of association with an appropriate fixed field entry (as decided by domain expert) to prune the list of keywords. Finally on entropy validation we chose 100 keywords which is reasonable for the point of view of computation time and coverage *wrt* the tickets (that is each ticket has a representation in this chosen set of keywords). Further this set is augmented by bigrams and trigrams which are extracted as described earlier.

To measure the quality of the clustering for different domains we plot average Silhouette indices for different values of k for different domains as shown in Fig. 3. The average over all data of a cluster is a measure of how tightly grouped all the data in the cluster are. From the figure it could be seen that the tickets in Travel domain poorly grouped, the tickets in LANM is better grouped, and the tickets in AMD domain is moderately grouped. Probably the smaller number of tickets in Travel may have led to poor quality of grouping. We could have expected even a better quality of grouping if we were able to cluster all the tickets in LANM domain.

Table 3. A sample of keywords and cluster labels with ratings for different domains

Domains	Cluster no	5 keywords from clusters	Label candidates	Ratings
Travel	Cluster 1	Travel, claim, date, assignment, accommodation, insurance	Travel	1.524
			Accommodation	1.440
	Cluster 2	Approver, travel, approval, itravel, travel form, date	Approval	2.174
			Approval rating	0.880
	Cluster 3	Taxi, drop, travel, night, address	Taxi	1.650
			Taxicab	1.640
AMD	Cluster 1	Id, user, access, screen, item	User interface	1.700
			User friendly	1.066
	Cluster 2	Cost, lot, batch, product, bulk	Product	1.389
			Product lifecycle	0.804
	Cluster 3	Line, error, item, screen, user	Screen	0.718
			Screen shot	0.540
LANM	Cluster 1	Desktop, software, id, contact, email	Desktop	3.128
			Desktop environment	1.504
	Cluster 2	Machine, login, contact, email, user	Email	2.032
			Email address	1.705
	Cluster 3	Laptop, allocation, asset, approval, desktop	Desktop allocation	3.770
			Laptop allocation	3.116

6.2   Evaluation of Labeling

We collected ratings by different persons and computed the average of ratings for each labels in each domain. A sample of 5 keywords from logical item sets, corresponding label candidates and the average ratings are presented in Table 3.

We use two conventional measure to evaluate our labeling, this is related to **Top-1 average rating** and normalized discounted cumulative gain, **nDCG** computed for the top-1 (**nDCG-1**), top-3 (**nDCG-3**) and top-5 ranked system labels (**nDCG-5**). **Top-1 average rating** is the average human rating (between 0 and 3) assigned to the top-ranked label proposed by the system. This indicates the overall quality of the label as judged by the system to be the best one. Normalized discounted cumulative gain, **nDCG** is based on the difference between original order, and the order when the list is sorted by score. That is, items that are ranked optimally in a descending order of score, **nDCG-N** is equal to 1 at position n. Table 4 shows the results for evaluation of our labeling scheme for clusters for all domain for topmost 5 clusters in their decreasing size. The results indicate that the labeling shows similar patterns for the measures for AMD and LANM domains, and the measures for Travel ticket labels are more or less uniform.

Table 4. Evaluation of cluster labeling for different domains

Domains	Clusters of decreasing size	Top-1 average rating	nDCG-1	nDCG-3	nDCG-5
Travel	Cluster 1	3	1.00	0.90	0.98
	Cluster 2	3	1.00	0.50	0.75
	Cluster 3	2	1.00	0.76	0.95
	Cluster 4	2	1.00	0.70	0.81
	Cluster 5	3	1.00	0.82	0.82
AMD	Cluster 1	3	1.00	0.60	0.77
	Cluster 2	3	1.00	0.78	0.89
	Cluster 3	2	1.00	1.00	1.00
	Cluster 4	3	1.00	1.00	1.00
	Cluster 5	2	0.67	0.52	0.73
LANM	Cluster 1	3	1.00	0.53	0.79
	Cluster 2	2	1.00	0.57	0.75
	Cluster 3	3	1.00	1.00	1.00
	Cluster 4	1	0.50	0.55	0.81
	Cluster 5	1	0.33	0.86	0.97

7 Conclusion

In this paper we presented a framework of simultaneously clustering and labeling IT maintenance ticket data from the same domain. In future we would like to compare our labeling with other popular labeling techniques. Our ticketing solution can be operated as service. In a company an employer can create a ticket through its service tab, or create a new service ticket through the service desk module, or the clients can create a new service ticket through the email connector. These new tickets can be placed in the proper cluster for labeling using k nearest neighbor method. The IT department may have fixed certain guidelines for action items for different categories (labels) of tickets which may help taking redressal actions on the tickets. Thus correct labeling and grouping of tickets may accelerate the actions performed on those tickets.

References

1. Aletras, N., Stevenson, M.: Labelling topics using unsupervised graph-based methods. In: Proceedings of the 52nd Annual Meeting of the Association for Computational Linguistics, ACL 2014, pp. 631–636 (2014)
2. Basave, A.E.C., He, Y., Xu, R.: Automatic labelling of topic models learned from Twitter by summarisation. In: Proceedings of the 52nd Annual Meeting of the Association for Computational Linguistics, ACL 2014, pp. 618–624 (2014)
3. Blei, D.M., Ng, A.Y., Jordan, M.I.: Latent Dirichlet allocation. J. Mach. Learn. Res. **3**, 993–1022 (2003)
4. Dostál, M., Jezek, K.: Automatic keyphrase extraction based on NLP and statistical methods. In: Proceedings of the Dateso 2011: Annual International Workshop on DAtabases, TExts, Specifications and Objects, pp. 140–145 (2011)
5. Frakes, W., Baeza-Yates, R.: Information Retrieval: Data Structures and Algorithms. New Jersey Prentice Hall, Englewood Cliffs (1992)
6. Grieser, K., Baldwin, T., Bohnert, F., Sonenberg, L.: Using ontological and document similarity to estimate museum exhibit relatedness. JOCCH **3**(3), 10 (2011)
7. Hamming, R.: Error detecting and error correcting codes. Bell Syst. Tech. J. **9**, 147–160 (1950)
8. Hotho, A., Staab, S., Stumme, G.: Wordnet improves text document clustering. In: Proceedings of the SIGIR 2003 Semantic Web Workshop, pp. 541–544 (2003)
9. Johnson, D.: NOC internal integrated trouble ticket system functional specification wishlist. In: RFC 1297 (1992)
10. Kaufman, L., Rousseeuw, P.J.: Finding Groups in Data: An Introduction to Cluster Analysis. Wiley, Hoboken (1990)
11. Kumar, S., Chandrashekar, V., Jawahar, C.V.: Logical itemset mining. In: 12th IEEE International Conference on Data Mining Workshops, ICDM 2012, pp. 603–610 (2012)
12. Largeron, C., Moulin, C., Géry, M.: Entropy based feature selection for text categorization. In: Proceedings of the ACM Symposium on Applied Computing (SAC 2011), pp. 924–928 (2011)
13. Lau, J.H., Grieser, K., Newman, D., Baldwin, T.: Automatic labelling of topic models. In: The 49th Annual Meeting of the Association for Computational Linguistics: Human Language Technologies, Proceedings of the Conference, pp. 1536–1545 (2011). 19–24

14. Leskovec, J., Rajaraman, A., Ullman, J.: Mining of Massive Datasets, 2nd edn. Cambridge University Press, Cambridge (2014)
15. Lin, D., Raghu, R., Ramamurthy, V., Yu, J., Radhakrishnan, R., Fernandez, J.: Unveiling clusters of events for alert and incident management in large-scale enterprise it. In: The 20th ACM SIGKDD International Conference on Knowledge Discovery and Data Mining, KDD 2014, New York, NY, USA, 24–27 August 2014, pp. 1630–1639 (2014)
16. Maksai, A., Bogojeska, J., Wiesmann, D.: Hierarchical incident ticket classification with minimal supervision. In: IEEE International Conference on Data Mining, ICDM 2014, pp. 923–928 (2014)
17. de Marneffe, M.C., MacCartney, B., Manning, C.D.: Generating typed dependency parses from phrase structure parses. In: International Conference on Language Resources and Evaluation (LREC 2006), pp. 449–454 (2006)
18. Matsuo, Y., Ishizuka, M.: Keyword extraction from a single document using word co-occurrence statistical information. Int. J. Artif. Intell. Tools **13**(1), 157–169 (2004)
19. Medem, A., Akodjenou, M.I., Teixeira, R.: Troubleminer: mining network trouble tickets. In: Integrated Network Management-Workshops, IM 2009 (2009)
20. Mei, Q., Shen, X., Zhai, C.: Automatic labeling of multinomial topic models. In: Proceedings of the 13th ACM SIGKDD International Conference on Knowledge Discovery and Data Mining, pp. 490–499 (2007)
21. Ng, R.T., Han, J.: CLARANS: a method for clustering objects for spatial data mining. IEEE Trans. Knowl. Data Eng. **14**(5), 1003–1016 (2002)
22. Punuru, J., Chen, J.: Automatic acquisition of concepts from domain texts. In: IEEE International Conference on Granular Computing, GrC 2006, pp. 424–427 (2006)
23. Rose, S., Engel, D., Cramer, N., Cowley, W.: Automatic keyword extraction from individual documents. Text Min. 1–20, March 2010
24. Salton, G., Buckley, C.: Term weighing approaches in automatic text retrieval. Inf. Process. Manag. **24**(5), 513–523 (1988)
25. Tan, P., Kumar, V., Srivastava, J.: Selecting the right objective measure for association analysis. Inf. Syst. **29**(4), 293–313 (2004)

Author Index

Author Index

Printed in the United States
By Bookmasters